**The Council
of State
Governments**

THE BOOK OF
THE STATES

2020 EDITION · VOLUME 52

LEXINGTON, KENTUCKY
p 859.244.8000 | f 859.244.8001 | *www.csg.org*

Facebook: facebook.com/CSGovts · *Twitter:* twitter.com/CSGovts
LinkedIn: linkedin.com/company/council-of-state-governments
Issuu: issuu.com/csg.publications

The Council of State Governments

Headquarters

David Adkins, Executive Director/CEO
1776 Avenue of the States
Lexington, KY 40511
859.244.8000 • *www.csg.org*

Eastern

Wendell M. Hannaford, Director
22 Cortlandt Street, 22nd Floor
New York, NY 10007
212.482.2320 • *www.csg-erc.org*

Midwestern

Michael H. McCabe, Director
701 E. 22nd Street, Suite 110
Lombard, IL 60148
630.925.1922 • *www.csgmidwest.org*

Southern

Colleen Cousineau, Director
P.O. Box 98129
Atlanta, GA 30359
404.633.1866 • *www.slcatlanta.org*

Western

Edgar Ruiz, Director
1107 9th Street, Suite 730
Sacramento, CA 95814
916.553.4423 • *www.csgwest.org*

Washington, D.C.

444 N. Capitol Street, NW, Suite 401
Washington, D.C. 20001
202.624.5460 • *www.csgdc.org*

Foreword

Dear friends,

2020 is a year that will be remembered, even if those of us who lived through it would like to forget much of it. The events of the year – the largest public health crisis in a century and the greatest economic upheaval since the Great Depression – tested government institutions and provided vast opportunities for leadership in a crisis. These disrupters caused unspeakable pain, suffering and death while wreaking havoc on state government budgets.

Out of disruption often comes innovation. The research capacity of our universities helped advance our understanding of the coronavirus and how to best treat those infected or at risk of infection. State governments responded in novel ways, for example, by convening legislatures remotely for the first time and by deploying new ways to conduct elections and designing innovative alternatives to traditional classroom education. The pandemic forced hard choices on the states. Many governors met those hard choices with decisive leadership and emerged as national leaders relying on data, science, expertise, transparency and empathy to guide their communications and response strategies.

The pandemic also poignantly exposed the stark reality of inequality in the United States. With the death of George Floyd at the hands of police in Minneapolis, hundreds of thousands of protesters took to the streets to demand reforms in policing and the criminal justice system and to protest pervasive racism. The well-documented racial disparities in education, housing, wealth, employment, health care and criminal justice propelled the Black Lives Matter movement to the forefront of the news, catalyzing a call to action. Many suggest our nation is at a transformational moment as we confront the current realities, which are a legacy of our nation's original sin. An energized public emerged this year to bring renewed focus to the obligation we all share as citizens to carry out the purpose of our Constitution by working to create a more perfect union. Some states responded in real time passing legislation designed to create greater oversight on law enforcement and place limits on police conduct.

No aspect of our lives will remain untouched by the events of 2020. From these crises it is my hope that opportunity will emerge for meaningful and overdue change. The pandemic accelerated existing trends in our society. It will also accelerate the trend of innovation in the states. With crushing debt and political gridlock, the federal government's ability to lead on the most pressing issues is limited. States are the epicenter of innovation and many are boldly leading efforts to transform their economies, address climate change, enhance health and address infrastructure needs, including broadband access. As a result of the pandemic, states will also be innovating the way they conduct elections and how to prepare for and respond to public health needs.

With eight governors and 5,000 legislative seats up for election in 2020, it is likely that states will see many new faces when the 2021 legislative sessions begin. We look forward to partnering with them in our non-partisan, data-driven, consensus-based work and invite them to join their colleagues from other states to learn from each other and to find ways to innovate together through CSG.

The Council of State Governments was founded in 1933, the worst year of the Great Depression. What was true then remains true today: the states are stronger when they come together. CSG is proud of the role we have played in bringing state officials together during our nearly nine decades of service. We look forward to providing state leaders with the insights, information, assistance and intelligence they need to navigate the complexities of today's public policy challenges. We remain committed to providing exceptional convenings and unparalleled leadership development opportunities.

This edition of The Book of the States is dedicated to the many heroic state employees whose efforts during the pandemic inspired us and for which we are immensely grateful. The doctors, nurses, first responders, health care professionals, public health workers, researchers, scientists, National Guard members, educators, long-term care facility workers, corrections officers and the many other state employees who stepped up represent the best of state government. Their sacrifice, hard work, expertise, care and skill saved lives, lifted us up during dark days and gave us hope. They are the helpers, leaders and doers who made and continue to make a difference for all of us. We mourn the brave souls who made the ultimate sacrifice in service to their fellow citizens. Their legacy calls all of us to embrace our obligation to serve the greater good.

Do good. Be well.

David Adkins
Executive Director/CEO
The Council of State Governments

The Council of State Governments is our nation's only organization serving all three branches of state government. CSG is a region-based forum that fosters the exchange of insights and ideas to help state officials shape public policy. This offers unparalleled regional, national and international opportunities to network, develop leaders, collaborate and create problem-solving partnerships.

Staff Acknowledgements

The staff wishes to thank the hundreds of individuals in the states who responded to surveys conducted by The Council of State Governments; and national organizations of state officials, federal agencies and think tank organizations who made their most recent data and information available for this volume.

The Book of the States 2020

Managing Editor.......... Audrey S. Francis

Associate Editor........... Heather M. Perkins

Graphic Designers ...... Theresa Carroll
Stephanie Northern
Jessica Rusher

Disclaimer

Table of Contents

CONTENTS

CHAPTER FOUR
State Executive Branch

TABLES

CHAPTER FIVE
State Judicial Branch

TABLES

CHAPTER SIX
Elections

TABLES

CHAPTER SEVEN
State Finance

TABLES

CHAPTER EIGHT

State Management, Administration and Demographics

TABLES

CHAPTER NINE
Selected State Policies and Programs

TABLES

CONTENTS

CHAPTER TEN

State Pages

TABLES

CHAPTER ONE
STATE CONSTITUTIONS

TABLE 1.1
State Constitutional Changes: 2019

State	Legislative proposal		
	Number proposed	Number adopted	Percentage adopted
Delaware	(a)	1	(a)
Kansas	1	1	100.0
Louisiana	4	2	50.0
Maine	1	1	100.0
New Jersey	1	1	100.0
Pennsylvania	1	(b)	(b)
Texas	10	9	90.0
Washington	1	1	100.0
Totals	18 (c)	15 (c)	83.3 (c)

Source: John Dinan and The Council of State Governments.
Key:
(a)–Delaware is unique in not providing for submission of amendments to voters. The amendment adopted in 2019 was approved by the legislature in consecutive sessions.
(b)–Although a majority of Pennsylvania voters cast votes in favor of the lone amendment on the ballot, shortly before the election a state commonwealth court judge enjoined the votes from being counted, in a ruling upheld by the state supreme court the day before the election, on the ground that the measure, a Marsy's Law victims rights amendment, contained mutiple amendments and therefore violated the state constitutional requirement that multiple amendments be voted on separately.
(c)–Totals and percentage exclude the Delaware amendment that was not submitted to voters and the Pennsylvania amendment where counting of votes was enjoined.

TABLE 1.2

Themes and Patterns in State Constitutional Amendments Enacted in 2019

Rights

Victims' Rights: A majority of voters in Pennsylvania cast votes in favor of a Marsy's Law victims' rights amendment, but a week before the election, a state commonwealth court judge enjoined the counting of votes on the amendment, in a decision upheld by the state supreme court the day before the election. Therefore the amendment was not enacted.

Gender equality: The Delaware legislature gave the required second approval to an equal rights amendment, declaring: "Equality of rights under the law shall not be denied or abridged on account of sex." Because amendments in Delaware are not submitted to voters, the amendment took effect after this second legislative approval.

Policies

Tax limitations: A Texas amendment prohibits enactment of an individual income tax.

Governing institutions

Emergencies: A Washington amendment expands the situations that can be deemed emergencies, in which case the legislature is permitted to take steps "as may be necessary and proper for insuring the continuity of governmental operations." Prior to the amendment's passage, the legislature could take emergency action in case of an "enemy attack." The amendment permits emergency action in response to a "catastrophic incident" as well..

Source: John Dinan and The Council of State Governments.

TABLE 1.3
General Information on State Constitutions (As of January 1, 2020)

State or other jurisdiction	Number of constitutions*	Dates of adoption	Effective date of present constitution	Estimated length (number of words)**	Number of amendments Submitted to voters	Adopted
Alabama	6	1819, 1861, 1865, 1868, 1875, 1901	Nov. 28, 1901	402,852 (a)	1,280	946 (c)
Alaska	1	1956	Jan. 3, 1959	13,479	43	29
Arizona	1	1911	Feb. 14, 1912	47,306	280	156
Arkansas	5	1836, 1861, 1864, 1868, 1874	Oct. 30, 1874	59,120	208	108 (d)
California	2	1849, 1879	July 4, 1879	76,930	909	538
Colorado	1	1876	Aug. 1, 1876	84,239	355	164
Connecticut	2	1818 (f), 1965	Dec. 30, 1965	16,544	35	33
Delaware	4	1776, 1792, 1831, 1897	June 10, 1897	25,445	(e)	151
Florida	6	1839, 1861, 1865, 1868, 1886, 1968	Jan. 7, 1969	49,230	185	137
Georgia	10	1777, 1789, 1798, 1861, 1865, 1868, 1877, 1945, 1976, 1982	July 1,1983	41,684	107 (g)	83 (g)
Hawaii	1 (h)	1950	Aug. 21, 1959	21,498	140	114
Idaho	1	1889	July 3, 1890	24,626	214	126
Illinois	4	1818, 1848, 1870, 1970	July 1, 1971	16,401	22	15
Indiana	2	1816, 1851	Nov. 1, 1851	11,610	81	49
Iowa	2	1846, 1857	Sept. 3, 1857	11,089	59	54 (i)
Kansas	1	1859	Jan. 29, 1861	14,097	129	99 (i)
Kentucky	4	1792, 1799, 1850, 1891	Sept. 28, 1891	27,234	76	42
Louisiana	11	1812, 1845, 1852, 1861, 1864, 1868, 1879, 1898, 1913, 1921, 1974	Jan. 1, 1975	76,730	285	198
Maine	1	1819	March 15, 1820	16,313	207	174 (j)
Maryland	4	1776, 1851, 1864, 1867	Oct. 5, 1867	43,198	269	233 (k)
Massachusetts	1	1780	Oct. 25, 1780	45,283 (l)	148	120
Michigan	4	1835, 1850, 1908, 1963	Jan. 1, 1964	31,164	76	32
Minnesota	1	1857	May 11, 1858	12,016	218	121
Mississippi	4	1817, 1832, 1869, 1890	Nov. 1, 1890	26,229	164	126
Missouri	4	1820, 1865, 1875, 1945	March 30,1945	85,036	193	126
Montana	2	1889, 1972	July 1, 1973	12,790	58	32
Nebraska	2	1866, 1875	Oct. 12, 1875	34,934	354 (m)	230 (m)
Nevada	1	1864	Oct. 31, 1864	37,418	238	140
New Hampshire	2	1776, 1784	June 2, 1784	13,238	291 (n)	147
New Jersey	3	1776, 1844, 1947	Jan. 1, 1948	26,360	89	73
New Mexico	1	1911	Jan. 6, 1912	33,198	306 (y)	172 (x)
New York	4	1777, 1822, 1846, 1894	Jan. 1, 1895	49,360	305	229
North Carolina	3	1776, 1868, 1970	July 1, 1971	17,177	51	41
North Dakota	1	1889	Nov. 2, 1889	18,746	282	161 (o)
Ohio	2	1802, 1851	Sept. 1, 1851	63,140	294	177
Oklahoma	1	1907	Nov. 16, 1907	84,956	373 (p)	199 (p)
Oregon	1	1857	Feb. 14, 1859	49,430	505 (q)	258 (q)
Pennsylvania	5	1776, 1790, 1838, 1873, 1968 (r)	1968 (r)	26,078	40 (r) (z)	33 (r)
Rhode Island	2	1842 (f) 1986 (s)	Dec. 4, 1986	11,407	14 (s)	12 (s)
South Carolina	7	1776, 1778, 1790, 1861, 1865, 1868, 1895	Jan. 1, 1896	27,421	690 (t)	500 (t)
South Dakota	1	1889	Nov. 2, 1889	28,840	243	122
Tennessee	3	1796, 1835, 1870	Feb. 23, 1870	13,960	66	43
Texas	5 (u)	1845, 1861, 1866, 1869, 1876	Feb. 15, 1876	92,345	686 (v)	507
Utah	1	1895	Jan. 4, 1896	20,700	178	122
Vermont	3	1777, 1786, 1793	July 9, 1793	8,565	212	54
Virginia	6	1776, 1830, 1851, 1869, 1902, 1970	July 1, 1971	22,570	60	52
Washington	1	1889	Nov. 11, 1889	32,578	182	108
West Virginia	2	1863, 1872	April 9, 1872	33,324	126	75
Wisconsin	1	1848	May 29, 1848	15,102	197	147 (i)
Wyoming	1	1889	July 10, 1890	26,349	130	101
American Samoa	2	1960, 1967	July 1, 1967	6,000	15 (y)	7 (y)
CNMI***	1	1977	Jan. 9, 1978	13,700	60 (y)	56 (w) (y)
Puerto Rico	1	1952	July 25, 1952	9,400	8 (y)	6 (y)

See footnotes at end of table

TABLE 1.3
General Information on State Constitutions (As of January 1, 2020) (continued)

Source: John Dinan and The Council of State Governments, with research assistance from Wake Forest students Bradley Harper and Alec Papovich.

*The constitutions referred to in this table include those Civil War documents customarily listed by the individual states.

**In calculating word counts, supplemental information regarding dates of adoption and other material not formally a part of the constitution are generally excluded.

***Commonwealth of Northern Mariana Islands

(a) The Alabama constitution includes numerous local amendments that apply to only one county. An estimated 70 percent of all amendments are local. A 1982 amendment provides that after proposal by the legislature to which special procedures apply, only a local vote (with exceptions) is necessary to add them to the constitution.

(b) Computer word count.

(c) The total number of Alabama amendments includes one that is commonly overlooked.

(d) Eight of the approved amendments have been superseded and are not printed in the current edition of the constitution. The total adopted does not include five amendments proposed and adopted since statehood.

(e) Proposed amendments are not submitted to the voters in Delaware.

(f) Colonial charters with some alterations served as the first constitutions in Connecticut (1638, 1662) and in Rhode Island (1663).

(g) The Georgia constitution requires amendments to be of "general and uniform application throughout the state," thus eliminating local amendments that accounted for most of the amendments before 1982.

(h) As a kingdom and republic, Hawaii had five constitutions.

(i) The figure includes amendments approved by the voters and later nullified by the state supreme court in Iowa (three), Kansas (one), Nevada (six) and Wisconsin (two).

(j) The figure does not include one amendment approved by the voters in 1967 that is inoperative until implemented by legislation.

(k) Two sets of identical amendments were on the ballot and adopted in the 1992 Maryland election. The four amendments are counted as two in the table.

(l) The printed constitution includes many provisions that have been annulled.

(m) The 1998 and 2000 Nebraska ballots allowed the voters to vote separately on "parts" of propositions. In 1998, 10 of 18 separate propositions were adopted; in 2000, 6 of 9.

(n) The constitution of 1784 was extensively revised in 1792. Figure shows proposals and adoptions since the constitution was adopted in 1784.

(o) The figures do not include submission and approval of the constitution of 1889 itself and of Article XX; these are constitutional questions included in some counts of constitutional amendments and would add two to the figure in each column.

(p) The figures include six amendments submitted to and approved by the voters which were, by decisions of the Oklahoma or federal courts, rendered inoperative or ruled invalid, unconstitutional, or illegally submitted.

(q) One Oregon amendment on the 2000 ballot was not counted as approved because canvassing was enjoined by the courts.

(r) Certain sections of the constitution were revised by the limited convention of 1967-68. Amendments proposed and adopted are since 1968.

(s) Following approval of eight amendments and a "rewrite" of the Rhode Island Constitution in 1986, the constitution has been called the 1986 Constitution.

(t) In 1981 approximately two-thirds of the proposed and four-fifths of the adopted amendments were local. Since then the amendments have been statewide propositions.

(u) The Constitution of the Republic of Texas preceded five state constitutions.

(v) The number of proposed amendments to the Texas Constitution excludes three proposed by the legislature but not placed on the ballot.

(w) The total excludes one amendment ruled void by a federal district court.

(x) The total excludes one amendment approved by voters in November 2008 but later declared invalid on single subject grounds by the state supreme court.

(y) These totals for territorial constitutions are in some cases taken from 2011 data.

(z) Includes a 2019 amendment that was placed on the ballot but a court enjoined the votes from being counted.

Table 1.3 | State Constitutions

70%
of Alabama's constitution

is made up of local amendments that apply to only one county.

Constitution Length by Word Count

LONGEST		SHORTEST
Alabama • 402,852		Vermont • 8,565
Texas • 92,345		Iowa • 11,089
Missouri • 85,036		Rhode Island • 11,407
Oklahoma • 84,956		Indiana • 11,610
Colorado • 84,239		Minnesota • 12,016

Amendments Submitted

HIGHEST
#1 Alabama • 1,280
#2 California • 909
#3 South Carolina • 690
#4 Texas • 686
#5 Oregon • 505

LOWEST
#1 Rhode Island • 14
#2 Illinois • 22
#3 Connecticut • 35
#4 Pennsylvania • 40
#5 Alaska • 43

Amendments Adopted

HIGHEST
#1 Alabama • 946
#2 California • 538
#3 Texas • 507
#4 South Carolina • 500
#5 Oregon • 258

LOWEST
#1 Rhode Island • 12
#2 Illinois • 15
#3 Alaska • 29
#4 Michigan • 32
#5 Montana • 32

Amendments Adopted Per Year

HIGHEST
#1 Alabama • 8.0
#2 Louisiana • 4.5
#3 South Carolina • 4.1
#4 California • 3.8
#5 Texas • 3.5

LOWEST
#1 Vermont • 0.2
#2 Tennessee • 0.3
#3 Indiana • 0.3
#4 Illinois • 0.3
#5 Kentucky • 0.3

Highest Number of Constitutions

LOUISIANA • 11

GEORGIA • 10

SOUTH CAROLINA • 7

TABLE 1.4

Constitutional Amendment Procedure: By the Legislature, Constitutional Provisions

State or other jurisdiction	Legislative vote required for proposal (a)	Consideration by two sessions required	Vote required for ratification	Limitation on the number of amendments legislature can submit at one election
Alabama	3/5	No	Majority vote on amendment	None
Alaska	2/3	No	Majority vote on amendment	None
Arizona	Majority	No	Majority vote on amendment	None
Arkansas	Majority	No	Majority vote on amendment	3
California	2/3	No	Majority vote on amendment	None
Colorado	2/3	No	55% vote on amendment (y)	(b)
Connecticut	(c)	(c)	Majority vote on amendment	None
Delaware	2/3	Yes	Not required	No referendum
Florida	3/5	No	3/5 vote on amendment (d)	None
Georgia	2/3	No	Majority vote on amendment	None
Hawaii	(e)	(e)	(f)	None
Idaho	2/3	No	Majority vote on amendment	None
Illinois	3/5	No	(g)	3 articles
Indiana	Majority	Yes	Majority vote on amendment	None
Iowa	Majority	Yes	Majority vote on amendment	None
Kansas	2/3	No	Majority vote on amendment	5
Kentucky	3/5	No	Majority vote on amendment	4
Louisiana	2/3	No	Majority vote on amendment (h)	None
Maine	2/3	No	Majority vote on amendment	None
Maryland	3/5	No	Majority vote on amendment (h)	None
Massachusetts	Majority (j)	Yes	Majority vote on amendment	None
Michigan	2/3	No	Majority vote on amendment	None
Minnesota	Majority	No	Majority vote in election	None
Mississippi	2/3 (k)	No	Majority vote on amendment	None
Missouri	Majority	No	Majority vote on amendment	None
Montana	2/3 (i)	No	Majority vote on amendment	None
Nebraska	3/5 (w)	No	Majority vote on amendment (f)	None
Nevada	Majority	Yes	Majority vote on amendment	None
New Hampshire	3/5	No	2/3 vote on amendment	None
New Jersey	(l)	(l)	Majority vote on amendment	None (m)
New Mexico	Majority (n)	No	Majority vote on amendment (n)	None
New York	Majority	Yes	Majority vote on amendment	None
North Carolina	3/5	No	Majority vote on amendment	None
North Dakota	Majority	No	Majority vote on amendment	None
Ohio	3/5	No	Majority vote on amendment	None
Oklahoma	Majority (w)	No	Majority vote on amendment	None
Oregon	(o)	No	Majority vote on amendment (x)	None
Pennsylvania	Majority (p)	Yes (p)	Majority vote on amendment	None
Rhode Island	Majority	No	Majority vote on amendment	None
South Carolina	2/3 (q)	Yes (q)	Majority vote on amendment	None
South Dakota	Majority	No	Majority vote on amendment	None
Tennessee	(r)	Yes (r)	Majority vote in election (s)	None
Texas	2/3	No	Majority vote on amendment	None
Utah	2/3	No	Majority vote on amendment	None
Vermont	(t)	Yes	Majority vote on amendment	None
Virginia	Majority	Yes	Majority vote on amendment	None
Washington	2/3	No	Majority vote on amendment	None
West Virginia	2/3	No	Majority vote on amendment	None
Wisconsin	Majority	Yes	Majority vote on amendment	None
Wyoming	2/3	No	Majority vote in election	None
American Samoa	2/3	No	Majority vote on amendment (u)	None
CNMI*	3/4	No	Majority vote on amendment	None
Puerto Rico	2/3 (v)	No	Majority vote on amendment	3

See footnotes at end of table

TABLE 1.4

Constitutional Amendment Procedure: By the Legislature, Constitutional Provisions (continued)

Source: John Dinan and The Council of State Governments.

*Commonwealth of Northern Mariana Islands

Key:

(a) In all states not otherwise noted, the figure shown in the column refers to the proportion of elected members in each house required for approval of proposed constitutional amendments.

(b) Legislature may not propose amendments to more than six articles of the constitution in the same legislative session.

(c) Three-fourths vote in each house at one session, or majority vote in each house in two sessions between which an election has intervened.

(d) Three-fifths vote on amendment, except that an amendment for "new state tax or fee" not in effect on Nov. 7, 1994 requires two-thirds of voters in the election.

(e) Two-thirds vote in each house at one session, or majority vote in each house in two sessions.

(f) In Hawaii, the majority vote on amendment must be at least 50 percent of the total votes cast at the election; or, at a special election, a majority of the votes tallied which must be at least 30 percent of the total number of registered voters. In Nebraska the majority vote on amendment must be at least 35 percent of the total votes cast at the election.

(g) Majority voting in election or three-fifths voting on amendment.

(h) In Louisiana, if five or fewer political subdivisions of the state are affected, majority in state as a whole and also in each of affected subdivisions is required. In Maryland, if an amendent affects only the City of Baltimore or only one county, majority in state as a whole and also in affected subdivision is required.

(i) Two-thirds of all members of the legislature.

(j) Majority of members elected sitting in joint session.

(k) The two-thirds must include not less than a majority elected to each house.

(l) Three-fifths of all members of each house at one session, or majority of all members of each house for two successive sessions.

(m) If a proposed amendment is not approved at the election when submitted, neither the same amendment nor one which would make substantially the same change for the constitution may be again submitted to the people before the third general election thereafter.

(n) Amendments concerning certain elective franchise and education matters require three-fourths vote of members elected and approval by three-fourths of electors voting in state and two-thirds of those voting in each county.

(o) Majority vote to amend constitution, two-thirds to revise ("revise" includes all or a part of the constitution).

(p) Emergency amendments may be passed by two-thirds vote of each house, followed by ratification by majority vote of electors in election held at least one month after legislative approval.

(q) Two-thirds of members of each house, first passage; majority of members of each house after popular ratification.

(r) Majority of members elected to both houses, first passage; two-thirds of members elected to both houses, second passage.

(s) Majority of all citizens voting for governor.

(t) Two-thirds vote in the senate and majority vote in the house on first passage; majority in both houses on second passage. As of 1974, amendments may be submitted only every four years.

(u) Within 30 days after voter approval, governor must submit amendment(s) to U.S. Secretary of the Interior for approval.

(v) If approved by two-thirds of members of each house, amendment(s) submitted to voters at special referendum; if approved by not less than three-fourths of total members of each house, referendum may be held at next general election.

(w) The legislature may, by a four-fifths vote in Nebraska or a two-thirds vote in Oklahoma, call a special election for voters to consider amendments.

(x) There is an exception for an amendment containing a supermajority voting requirement, which must be ratified by an equal supermajority.

(y) An amendment repealing, in whole or in part, any constitutional provision only requires approval by a majority on the amendment.

TABLE 1.5

Constitutional Amendment Procedure: By Initiative, Constitutional Provisions

State or other jurisdiction	Number of signatures required on initiative petition	Distribution of signatures	Referendum vote
Arizona	15% of total votes cast for all candidates for governor at last election.	None specified.	Majority vote on amendment.
Arkansas	10% of voters for governor at last election.	Must include 5% of voters for governor in each of 15 counties.	Majority vote on amendment.
California	8% of total voters for all candidates for governor at last election.	None specified.	Majority vote on amendment.
Colorado	5% of total legal votes for all candidates for secretary of state at last general election.	2% of registered voters in each of the state senate districts	55% vote on amendment, except any amendment repealing a constitutional provision only requires a majority vote on amendment.
Florida	8% of total votes cast in the state in the last election for presidential electors.	8% of total votes cast in each of 1/2 of the congressional districts.	Three-fifths vote on amendment except any amendment for "new state tax or fee" not in effect Nov. 7, 1994 requires 2/3 of voters voting in election.
Illinois (a)	8% of total votes cast for candidates for governor at last election.	None specified.	Majority voting in election or 3/5 voting on amendment.
Massachusetts (b)	3% of total votes cast for governor at preceding biennial state election (not less than 25,000 qualified voters).	No more than 1/4 from any one county.	Majority vote on amendment which must be 30% of total ballots cast at election.
Michigan	10% of total voters for all candidates at last gubernatorial election.	No more than 15% from any one congressional district	Majority vote on amendment.
Mississippi (c)	12% of total votes for all candidates for governor in last election.	No more than 20% from any one congressional district.	Majority vote on amendment and not less than 40% of total vote cast at election.
Missouri	8% of legal voters for all candidates for governor at last election.	The 8% must be in each of 2/3 of the congressional districts in the state.	Majority vote on amendment.
Montana	10% of qualified electors, the number of qualified voters to be determined by number of votes cast for governor in preceding election in each county and in the state.	The 10% to include at least 10% of qualified voters in 2/5 of the legislative districts. (d)	Majority vote on amendment.
Nebraska	10% of registered voters.	The 10% must include 5% in each of 2/5 of the counties.	Majority vote on amendment which must be at least 35% of total vote at the election.
Nevada	10% of voters who voted in entire state in last general election.	10% of voters in each of the state's congressional districts	Majority vote on amendment in two consecutive general elections.
North Dakota	4% of population of the state.	None specified.	Majority vote on amendment.
Ohio	10% of total number of electors who voted for governor in last election.	At least 5% of qualified electors in each of 1/2 of counties in the state.	Majority vote on amendment.
Oklahoma	15% of votes cast at last general election for governor	None specified.	Majority vote on amendment.
Oregon	8% of total votes for all candidates for governor at last election at which governor was elected for four-year term.	None specified.	Majority vote on amendment except for supermajority equal to supermajority voting requirement contained in proposed amendment.
South Dakota	10% of total votes for governor in last election.	None specified.	Majority vote on amendment.
CNMI*	50% of qualified voters of commonwealth.	In addition, 25% of qualified voters in each senatorial district.	Majority vote on amendment if legislature approved it by majority vote; if not, at least 2/3 vote in each of two senatorial districts in addition to a majority vote.

Source: John Dinan and The Council of State Governments.
*Commonwealth of Northern Mariana Islands
Key:
(a) Initiatives can only be used to amend substantive or procedural aspects of Article IV, the Legislature Article, and cannot be used to amend any other articles.
(b) Before being submitted to the electorate for ratification, initiated measures must be approved at two sessions of a successively elected legislature by not less than one-fourth of all members elected, sitting in joint session.

(c) Before being submitted to the electorate, initiated measures are sent to the legislature, which has the option of submitting an amended or alternative measure alongside of the original measure.
(d) A 2002 amendment changed this geographic-distribution rule to require at least 10% of voters in 1/2 of the counties. After this amendment was held unconstitutional by a federal district court in a 2005 ruling, the state attorney general advised that the prior rule–2/5 of legislative districts–was in effect.

TABLE 1.6
Procedures for Calling Constitutional Conventions, Constitutional Provisions

State or other jurisdiction	Provision for convention	Procedure for calling a convention by initiative	Legislative vote for submission of convention question (a)	Popular vote to authorize convention	Periodic submission of convention question required (b)	Popular vote required for ratification of convention proposals
Alabama	Yes	No	Majority	ME	No	Not specified
Alaska	Yes	No	No provision (c)(d)	(c)	10 years; 2012 (c)	Not specified (c)
Arizona	Yes	No	Majority	(e)	No	MP
Arkansas	No	No	No			
California	Yes	No	2/3	MP	No	MP
Colorado	Yes	No	2/3	MP	No	ME
Connecticut	Yes	No	2/3	MP	20 years; 2008 (f)	MP
Delaware	Yes	No	2/3	MP	No	No provision
Florida	Yes	Yes (m)	(g)	MP	No	3/5 voting on proposal
Georgia	Yes	No	(d)	No	No	MP
Hawaii	Yes	No	Not specified	MP	10 years; 2018	MP (h)
Idaho	Yes	No	2/3	MP	No	Not specified
Illinois	Yes	No	3/5	(i)	20 years; 2008	MP
Indiana	No	No	No			
Iowa	Yes	No	Majority	MP	10 years; 2010	MP
Kansas	Yes	No	2/3	MP	No	MP
Kentucky	Yes	No	Majority (j)	MP (k)	No	No provision
Louisiana	Yes	No	(d)	No	No	MP
Maine	Yes	No	(d)	No	No	No provision
Maryland	Yes	No	Majority	ME	20 years; 2010	MP
Massachusetts	No	No	No			
Michigan	Yes	No	Majority	MP	16 years; 2010	MP
Minnesota	Yes	No	2/3	ME	No	3/5 voting on proposal
Mississippi	No	No	No			
Missouri	Yes	No	Majority	MP	20 years; 2002	Not specified (l)
Montana	Yes	Yes (m)	2/3	MP	20 years; 2010	MP
Nebraska	Yes	No	3/5	MP (o)	No	MP
Nevada	Yes	No	2/3	ME	No	No provision
New Hampshire	Yes	No	Majority	MP	10 years; 2012	2/3 voting on proposal
New Jersey	No	No	No			
New Mexico	Yes	No	2/3	MP	No	Not specified
New York	Yes	No	Majority	MP	20 years; 2017	MP
North Carolina	Yes	No	2/3	MP	No	MP
North Dakota	No	Yes (m)	No			
Ohio	Yes	No	2/3	MP	20 years; 2012	MP
Oklahoma	Yes	No	Majority	(e)	20 years; 1970	MP
Oregon	Yes	No	Majority	(e)	No	No provision
Pennsylvania	No	No	No			
Rhode Island	Yes	No	Majority	MP	10 years; 2014	MP
South Carolina	Yes	No	(d)	ME	No	No provision
South Dakota	Yes	Yes (m)	(d)	No	No	(p)
Tennessee	Yes (q)	No	Majority	MP	No	MP
Texas	No	No	No			
Utah	Yes	No	2/3	ME	No	ME
Vermont	No	No	No			
Virginia	Yes	No	(d)	No	No	MP
Washington	Yes	No	2/3	ME	No	Not specified
West Virginia	Yes	No	Majority	MP	No	Not specified
Wisconsin	Yes	No	Majority	MP	No	No provision
Wyoming	Yes	No	2/3	ME	No	Not specified
American Samoa	Yes	No	(r)	No	No	ME (s)
CNMI*	Yes	Yes (t)	Majority	2/3	10 years	MP and at least 2/3 in in each of 2 senatorial districts
Puerto Rico	Yes	No	2/3	MP	No	MP

See footnotes at end of table

TABLE 1.6

Procedures for Calling Constitutional Conventions, Constitutional Provisions (continued)

Source: John Dinan and The Council of State Governments.
*Commonwealth of Northern Mariana Islands
Key:
MP – Majority voting on the proposal.
ME – Majority voting in the election.
(a) In all states not otherwise noted, the entries in this column refer to the proportion of members elected to each house required to submit to the electorate the question of calling a constitutional convention.
(b) The number listed is the interval between required submissions on the question of calling a constitutional convention; where given, the date is that of the most recent submission of the mandatory convention referendum.
(c) Unless provided otherwise by law, convention calls are to conform as nearly as possible to the act calling the 1955 convention, which provided for a legislative vote of a majority of members elected to each house and ratification by a majority vote on the proposals. The legislature may call a constitutional convention at any time.
(d) In these states, the legislature may call a convention without submitting the question to the people. The legislative vote required is two-thirds of the members elected to each house in Georgia, Louisiana, South Carolina and Virginia; two-thirds concurrent vote of both branches in Maine; three-fourths of all members of each house in South Dakota; and not specified in Alaska, but bills require majority vote of membership in each house.
(e) The law calling a convention must be approved by the people.
(f) The legislature shall submit the question 20 years after the last convention, or 20 years after the last vote on the question of calling a convention, whichever date is last.
(g) The power to call a convention is reserved to the people by petition.
(h) The majority must be 50 percent of the total voted cast at a general election or at a special election, a majority of the votes tallied which must be at least 30 percent of the total number of registered voters.

(i) Majority voting in the election, or three-fifths voting on the question.
(j) Must be approved during two legislative sessions.
(k) Majority must equal one-fourth of qualified voters at last general election.
(l) Majority of those voting on the proposal is assumed. Vote must take place at a special election held no less than 60 days and no more than 6 months after convention.
(m) In Montana, North Dakota and South Dakota, conventions can be called by initiative petition in the same manner as provided for initiated amendments (see Table 1.3), and with approval by a majority of voters. In Florida, conventions can be called by filing an initiative petition with signatures equal to 15 percent of the votes cast in the preceding presidential election and also equal to 15 percent of signatures in half of the congressional districts in the state and then obtaining a majority of the voters at the ensuing election.
(n) Two-thirds of all members of the legislature.
(o) Majority must be 35 percent of total votes cast at the election.
(p) Convention proposals are submitted to the electorate at a special election in a manner to be determined by the convention. Ratification by a majority of votes cast.
(q) Conventions may not be held more often than once in six years.
(r) Five years after effective date of constitutions, governor shall call a constitutional convention to consider changes proposed by a constitutional committee appointed by the governor. Delegates to the convention are to be elected by their county councils. A convention was held in 1972.
(s) If proposed amendments are approved by the voters, they must be submitted to the U.S. Secretary of the Interior for approval.
(t) The petition must be signed by 25 percent of the qualified voters or at least 75 percent in a senatorial district.

CHAPTER TWO

FEDERALISM AND INTERGOVERNMENTAL RELATIONS

TABLE 2.1
Summary of State Intergovernmental Expenditures: 1944-2018 (In thousands of dollars)

Fiscal year	Total	To Federal government(a)	Total	For general local government support	Education	Public welfare	Highways	Health	Miscellaneous and combined
				To local governments — For specified purposes					
1944	$1,842,000	...	$1,842,000	$274,000	$861,000	$368,000	$298,000	...	$41,000
1946	2,092,000	...	2,092,000	357,000	953,000	376,000	339,000	...	67,000
1948	3,283,000	...	3,283,000	428,000	1,554,000	648,000	507,000	...	146,000
1950	4,217,000	...	4,217,000	482,000	2,054,000	792,000	610,000	...	279,000
1952	5,044,000	...	5,044,000	549,000	2,523,000	976,000	728,000	...	268,000
1953	5,384,000	...	5,384,000	592,000	2,737,000	981,000	803,000	...	271,000
1954	5,679,000	...	5,679,000	600,000	2,930,000	1,004,000	871,000	...	274,000
1955	5,986,000	...	5,986,000	591,000	3,150,000	1,046,000	911,000	...	288,000
1956	6,538,000	...	6,538,000	631,000	3,541,000	1,069,000	984,000	...	313,000
1957	7,440,000	...	7,440,000	668,000	4,212,000	1,136,000	1,082,000	...	342,000
1958	8,089,000	...	8,089,000	687,000	4,598,000	1,247,000	1,167,000	...	390,000
1959	8,689,000	...	8,689,000	725,000	4,957,000	1,409,000	1,207,000	...	391,000
1960	9,443,000	...	9,443,000	806,000	5,461,000	1,483,000	1,247,000	...	446,000
1962	10,906,000	...	10,906,000	839,000	6,474,000	1,777,000	1,327,000	...	489,000
1963	11,885,000	...	11,885,000	1,012,000	6,993,000	1,919,000	1,416,000	...	545,000
1964	12,968,000	...	12,968,000	1,053,000	7,664,000	2,108,000	1,524,000	...	619,000
1965	14,174,000	...	14,174,000	1,102,000	8,351,000	2,436,000	1,630,000	...	655,000
1966	16,928,000	...	16,928,000	1,361,000	10,177,000	2,882,000	1,725,000	...	783,000
1967	19,056,000	...	19,056,000	1,585,000	11,845,000	2,897,000	1,861,000	...	868,000
1968	21,950,000	...	21,950,000	1,993,000	13,321,000	3,527,000	2,029,000	...	1,080,000
1969	24,779,000	...	24,779,000	2,135,000	14,858,000	4,402,000	2,109,000	...	1,275,000
1970	28,892,000	...	28,892,000	2,958,000	17,085,000	5,003,000	2,439,000	...	1,407,000
1971	32,640,000	...	32,640,000	3,258,000	19,292,000	5,760,000	2,507,000	...	1,823,000
1972	36,759,246	...	36,759,246	3,752,327	21,195,345	6,943,634	2,633,417	...	2,234,523
1973	40,822,135	...	40,822,135	4,279,646	23,315,651	7,531,738	2,953,424	...	2,741,676
1974	45,941,111	$341,194	45,599,917	4,803,875	27,106,812	7,028,750	3,211,455	...	3,449,025
1975	51,978,324	974,780	51,003,544	5,129,333	31,110,237	7,136,104	3,224,861	...	4,403,009
1976	57,858,242	1,179,580	56,678,662	5,673,843	34,083,711	8,307,411	3,240,806	...	5,372,891
1977	62,459,903	1,386,237	61,073,666	6,372,543	36,964,306	8,756,717	3,631,108	...	5,348,992
1978	67,287,260	1,472,378	65,814,882	6,819,438	40,125,488	8,585,558	3,821,135	...	6,463,263
1979	75,962,980	1,493,215	74,469,765	8,224,338	46,195,698	8,675,473	4,148,573	...	7,225,683
1980	84,504,451	1,746,301	82,758,150	8,643,789	52,688,101	9,241,551	4,382,716	...	7,801,993
1981	93,179,549	1,872,980	91,306,569	9,570,248	57,257,373	11,025,445	4,751,449	...	8,702,054
1982	98,742,976	1,793,284	96,949,692	10,044,372	60,683,583	11,965,123	5,028,072	...	9,228,542
1983	100,886,902	1,764,821	99,122,081	10,364,144	63,118,351	10,919,847	5,277,447	...	9,442,292
1984	108,373,188	1,722,115	106,651,073	10,744,740	67,484,926	11,923,430	5,686,834	...	10,811,143
1985	121,571,151	1,963,468	119,607,683	12,319,623	74,936,970	12,673,123	6,019,069	...	13,658,898
1986	131,966,258	2,105,831	129,860,427	13,383,912	81,929,467	14,214,613	6,470,049	...	13,862,386
1987	141,278,672	2,455,362	138,823,310	14,245,089	88,253,298	14,753,727	6,784,699	...	14,786,497
1988	151,661,866	2,652,981	149,008,885	14,896,991	95,390,536	15,032,315	6,949,190	...	16,739,853
1989	165,415,415	2,929,622	162,485,793	15,749,681	104,601,291	16,697,915	7,376,173	...	18,060,733
1990	175,027,632	3,243,634	171,783,998	16,565,106	109,438,131	18,403,149	7,784,316	...	19,593,296
1991	186,398,234	3,464,364	182,933,870	16,977,032	116,179,860	20,903,400	8,126,477	...	20,747,101
1992	201,313,434	3,608,911	197,704,523	16,368,139	124,919,686	25,942,234	8,480,871	...	21,993,593
1993	214,094,882	3,625,051	210,469,831	17,690,986	131,179,517	31,339,777	9,298,624	...	20,960,927
1994	225,635,410	3,603,447	222,031,963	18,044,015	135,861,024	30,624,514	9,622,849	...	27,879,561
1995	240,978,128	3,616,831	237,361,297	18,996,435	148,160,436	30,772,525	10,481,616	...	28,926,886
1996	252,079,335	3,896,667	248,182,668	20,019,771	156,954,115	31,180,345	10,707,338	$10,790,396	18,530,703
1997	264,207,209	3,839,942	260,367,267	21,808,828	164,147,715	35,754,024	11,431,270	11,772,189	15,453,241
1998	278,853,409	3,515,734	275,337,675	22,693,158	176,250,998	32,327,325	11,648,853	12,379,498	20,037,843
1999	308,734,917	3,801,667	304,933,250	25,495,396	192,416,987	35,161,151	12,075,195	13,611,228	26,173,293
2000	327,069,829	4,021,471	323,048,358	27,475,363	208,135,537	40,206,513	12,473,052	15,067,156	19,690,737
2001	350,326,546	4,290,764	346,035,782	31,693,016	222,092,587	41,926,990	12,350,136	16,518,461	21,454,592
2002	364,789,480	4,370,330	360,419,150	28,927,053	227,336,087	47,112,496	12,949,850	20,816,777	23,276,887
2003	382,781,397	4,391,095	378,390,302	30,766,480	240,788,692	49,302,737	13,337,114	20,241,742	23,953,537
2004	388,559,152	4,627,356	383,931,796	29,718,225	249,256,844	42,636,305	14,008,581	19,959,396	28,352,445
2005	405,925,287	4,620,167	401,305,120	28,320,648	263,625,820	48,370,718	14,500,232	17,515,138	28,972,564
2006	432,265,206	6,502,059	425,763,147	30,486,739	280,090,982	48,409,237	15,495,306	18,144,795	33,136,088
2007	459,742,295	4,670,648	455,071,647	31,207,955	301,062,065	56,899,141	14,881,789	20,067,198	30,953,499
2008	478,530,574	4,765,734	473,764,840	32,035,268	315,424,647	57,730,369	16,549,366	20,342,928	31,682,262
2009	490,887,391	4,894,977	485,992,414	30,421,570	324,374,036	58,741,316	16,492,780	21,019,353	34,943,359
2010	485,557,187	4,339,166	481,218,021	27,821,681	317,389,500	58,858,443	18,043,061	18,274,329	40,831,007

See footnotes at end of table

TABLE 2.1

Summary of State Intergovernmental Expenditures: 1944-2018 (In thousands of dollars) (continued)

Fiscal year	Total	To Federal government(a)	Total	For general local government support	Education	Public welfare	Highways	Health	Miscellaneous and combined
				To local governments					
				For specified purposes					
2011	496,832,436	4,295,922	492,536,514	27,577,126	330,482,270	56,678,841	17,243,590	18,745,863	41,808,824
2012	481,883,230	4,157,695	477,725,535	27,289,870	317,839,562	55,913,067	17,787,581	19,350,451	39,545,004
2013	488,782,863	3,392,576	485,390,287	28,412,169	324,995,548	55,565,254	18,158,521	20,242,808	38,015,987
2014	498,710,149	3,389,399	495,320,750	30,459,571	330,140,870	54,781,687	20,992,876	19,979,130	38,966,616
2015	515,045,908	3,408,376	511,637,532	32,193,005	345,859,861	52,704,375	20,420,805	18,739,461	41,720,025
2016	532,665,290	3,388,085	529,277,205	31,189,834	360,117,773	57,049,413	19,675,932	19,529,120	41,715,133
2017	553,520,399	3,258,513	550,261,886	33,206,537	373,639,270	59,895,676	20,217,035	20,190,999	43,112,369
2018	562,587,857	3,280,506	559,307,351	34,196,679	382,855,837	58,184,136	20,512,463	20,828,546	42,729,690

Source: U.S. Census Bureau, Census of Governments: Finance (years ending in '2' and '7'), and Annual Survey of State Government Finances (remaining years).

Notes:

1. Data users who create their own estimates using these data should cite only the U.S. Census Bureau as the source of the original data. Data in this table are based on information from public records and contain no confidential data. Although the data in this table come from a census of governmental units and are not subject to sampling error, the census results may contain nonsampling error.

Additional information on nonsampling error, response rates, and definitions may be found within the survey methodology <https://www.census.gov/programs-surveys/state/technical-documentation/methodology.html>.

2. Detail may not add to total due to rounding.

Key:

N/A – Not available

(a) Represents primarily state reimbursements for the supplemental security income program.

TABLE 2.2
Summary of State Intergovernmental Expenditures, By State: 2009-2018 (In thousands of dollars)

State	2018	2017	2016	2015	2014	2013	2012	2011	2010	2009
United States	$562,587,857	$553,520,399	$532,665,290	$515,045,908	$498,710,149	$488,782,863	$481,883,230	$496,832,436	$485,557,187	$490,887,391
Alabama	7,006,778	6,931,626	6,672,049	6,612,535	6,474,302	6,476,073	6,563,313	6,800,787	6,604,013	6,535,634
Alaska	648,930	1,829,640	2,038,078	2,036,112	2,059,333	2,032,061	1,897,331	1,723,023	1,655,467	1,616,689
Arizona	10,268,171	10,030,152	10,904,370	7,832,147	7,448,459	8,209,708	8,023,697	8,668,387	9,179,514	9,618,970
Arkansas	5,489,804	5,426,820	5,882,840	5,214,039	5,199,089	4,937,560	5,047,345	5,151,981	5,057,598	4,698,889
California	108,218,508	107,877,299	103,512,395	97,968,328	91,869,167	95,069,461	85,425,616	91,501,553	90,530,131	94,909,240
Colorado	7,518,654	7,461,561	7,310,747	7,151,882	6,749,839	6,291,390	6,105,130	6,334,861	6,513,704	6,403,127
Connecticut	5,908,441	5,556,846	5,438,230	5,338,357	4,899,005	4,908,546	4,614,954	4,485,808	4,846,870	4,316,376
Delaware	1,611,413	1,605,571	1,511,805	1,454,859	1,390,686	1,271,359	1,161,381	1,293,106	1,235,608	1,205,247
Florida	18,958,978	18,243,072	20,407,866	19,173,628	18,707,624	17,809,542	17,340,127	19,725,217	18,478,449	17,677,928
Georgia	12,889,900	12,325,495	11,835,632	11,088,286	10,557,747	10,361,359	10,223,211	10,600,099	10,747,620	10,816,572
Hawaii	355,739	328,020	134,933	267,863	255,885	220,844	194,791	207,988	177,624	159,452
Idaho	2,570,844	2,408,796	2,277,298	2,156,220	2,015,071	1,981,659	1,956,717	2,036,312	2,022,896	2,077,028
Illinois	21,109,911	21,279,020	18,109,138	18,558,946	18,638,884	15,549,167	15,866,914	15,711,057	15,530,746	15,034,787
Indiana	10,328,805	9,989,433	9,711,681	9,548,136	9,314,957	9,292,344	9,313,044	9,265,386	9,705,254	8,214,991
Iowa	5,373,071	5,362,687	5,470,729	5,298,032	4,963,899	4,753,646	4,804,976	5,151,627	4,528,319	4,660,802
Kansas	5,030,280	4,860,130	4,799,630	4,849,983	4,108,481	4,057,504	3,953,778	4,208,664	4,176,958	4,314,940
Kentucky	4,890,345	4,871,480	4,780,430	4,709,948	4,649,395	4,802,691	5,029,106	5,069,137	5,078,845	4,769,871
Louisiana	6,380,598	6,415,070	5,766,006	5,726,498	6,053,019	6,241,308	6,387,767	6,580,164	6,658,397	6,505,389
Maine	1,347,094	1,306,593	1,288,779	1,254,898	1,285,064	1,238,618	1,286,233	1,301,692	1,346,639	1,325,723
Maryland	9,874,995	9,686,617	9,398,276	9,158,679	8,733,983	8,641,281	8,380,215	8,124,451	8,592,779	8,654,935
Massachusetts	9,434,585	9,167,867	9,080,507	9,379,933	9,811,813	9,401,248	9,291,231	8,826,190	9,107,483	8,890,500
Michigan	22,754,958	21,279,004	20,788,310	20,487,354	19,779,302	19,249,754	19,021,267	19,878,322	19,410,018	19,656,877
Minnesota	14,174,246	13,728,116	13,143,647	12,827,108	12,620,852	12,975,915	10,833,320	11,102,449	10,427,657	11,199,230
Mississippi	4,861,117	4,837,458	5,251,972	5,138,598	4,919,968	5,053,070	5,138,081	5,253,307	5,272,442	5,156,650
Missouri	6,336,401	6,343,380	6,172,736	5,987,018	5,785,229	5,771,802	5,877,847	5,948,493	6,227,955	5,936,688
Montana	1,113,197	1,141,773	1,094,338	1,395,263	1,382,045	1,373,069	1,316,548	1,352,917	1,334,478	1,276,112
Nebraska	2,668,741	2,457,060	2,417,506	2,303,467	2,202,196	2,170,630	2,170,016	2,306,692	2,192,338	2,064,173
Nevada	5,180,050	4,789,582	4,429,481	4,336,630	4,169,439	4,214,581	4,120,103	3,905,016	3,703,574	3,864,223
New Hampshire	1,764,616	1,739,302	460,460	573,048	1,268,583	1,300,770	1,226,012	1,191,097	1,261,454	1,278,589
New Jersey	15,250,952	15,050,010	11,672,318	12,470,093	12,104,168	11,102,269	11,789,109	11,167,301	11,877,592	11,135,809
New Mexico	5,176,572	4,903,764	4,986,006	4,871,707	4,604,669	4,500,634	4,450,387	4,325,766	4,322,463	4,766,207
New York	63,492,253	63,219,144	61,639,619	58,063,694	58,134,561	56,236,537	57,406,012	59,697,916	54,318,363	55,107,082
North Carolina	14,706,189	14,262,419	12,858,738	12,771,155	13,172,777	13,172,640	13,514,695	13,633,379	13,429,964	13,562,079
North Dakota	1,995,041	2,201,533	2,111,716	2,555,758	2,261,886	1,632,316	1,643,402	1,300,989	1,245,686	933,974
Ohio	18,933,185	18,584,950	18,552,156	17,872,592	16,647,880	16,517,064	17,932,406	18,488,325	18,348,743	18,963,232
Oklahoma	4,470,670	4,508,439	4,458,922	4,342,470	4,278,505	4,213,211	4,230,427	4,477,819	4,546,446	4,506,456
Oregon	6,320,421	5,668,831	5,551,653	6,209,293	6,007,393	5,495,337	5,657,912	5,774,682	5,864,882	5,703,775
Pennsylvania	22,327,616	22,499,190	20,050,597	19,407,646	18,835,531	18,834,325	18,526,116	19,944,576	18,871,434	19,144,305
Rhode Island	1,307,710	1,244,378	1,236,874	1,226,790	1,198,256	1,170,440	1,143,486	1,074,302	1,193,600	1,002,915
South Carolina	6,768,154	6,523,386	6,393,932	5,955,882	5,581,255	5,454,008	5,312,018	5,585,665	5,369,519	5,520,979
South Dakota	871,682	862,881	775,059	784,855	745,993	740,104	753,622	774,778	737,190	707,862
Tennessee	7,619,932	7,630,904	7,617,664	7,233,618	7,221,663	7,074,682	7,181,421	7,104,790	6,664,828	6,797,935
Texas	31,520,535	30,732,823	31,763,445	29,951,157	29,191,904	27,590,295	29,860,716	29,665,803	27,461,315	29,252,364
Utah	4,166,842	3,765,894	3,511,958	3,344,201	3,266,053	3,069,082	3,029,283	3,106,230	3,027,680	3,120,527
Vermont	1,839,019	1,800,749	1,771,590	1,725,060	1,695,983	1,501,657	1,636,024	1,552,853	1,518,129	1,532,766
Virginia	12,257,922	11,939,180	12,466,977	12,584,936	11,792,595	11,255,705	11,653,818	11,489,163	10,959,394	11,894,394
Washington	14,338,188	13,406,501	11,871,289	11,017,248	10,438,534	9,777,797	9,530,116	9,346,712	9,798,444	10,043,789
West Virginia	2,693,408	2,699,098	2,385,313	2,344,701	2,413,663	2,469,535	2,618,032	2,533,582	2,382,633	2,232,558
Wisconsin	11,108,614	11,250,257	9,031,939	10,387,801	9,890,474	9,637,247	9,741,343	10,428,954	10,253,124	10,199,520
Wyoming	1,353,782	1,486,589	1,867,516	2,097,456	1,913,090	1,681,018	1,702,814	1,653,068	1,760,946	1,919,231

Source: U.S. Census Bureau, Census of Governments: Finance (years ending in '2' and '7'), and Annual Survey of State Government Finances (remaining years).

Notes:

1. Data users who create their own estimates using these data should cite only the U.S. Census Bureau as the source of the original data. Data in this table are based on information from public records and contain no confidential data. Although the data in this table come from a census of governmental units and are not subject to sampling error, the census results may contain nonsampling error. Additional information on nonsampling error, response rates, and definitions may be found within the survey methodology *https://www.census.gov/programs-surveys/state/ technical-documentation/methodology.html.*

2. Includes payments to the federal government, primarily state reimbursements for the supplemental security income program. The statistics reflect state government fiscal years that end on June 30, except for four states with other ending dates: Alabama and Michigan (September 30), New York (March 31), and Texas (August 31).

3. Detail may not add to total due to rounding.

TABLE 2.3

State Intergovernmental Expenditures, By Function and By State: 2018 (In thousands of dollars)

State	Total	General local government support	Education	Public Welfare	Highways	Health	Miscellaneous and combined
				Specified functions			
United States	$555,581,079	$33,839,151	$377,514,927	$58,088,171	$20,498,107	$20,711,373	$44,929,350
Alabama	7,006,778	357,528	5,340,910	95,965	14,356	117,173	1,080,846
Alaska	648,930	55,616	0	155,732	15,128	78,439	344,015
Arizona	10,268,171	2,550,590	6,343,767	159,614	863,577	78,372	272,251
Arkansas	5,489,804	303,100	4,683,066	0	278,711	446	224,481
California	108,218,508	267,190	64,160,795	29,168,793	3,270,501	5,263,894	6,087,335
Colorado	7,518,654	162,415	5,174,826	930,240	558,345	119,686	573,142
Connecticut	5,908,441	528,374	3,517,509	1,079,910	166,917	139,022	476,709
Delaware	1,611,413	0	1,446,946	7,823	7,676	12,309	136,659
Florida	18,958,978	1,069,827	16,284,021	0	569,586	8,687	1,026,857
Georgia	12,889,900	0	11,279,515	524,634	240,928	252,072	592,751
Hawaii	355,739	263,428	319	1,560	2,871	33,420	54,141
Idaho	2,570,844	281,647	2,019,958	4,029	200,863	3,447	60,900
Illinois	21,109,911	5,014,819	10,635,814	2,619,094	610,739	134,215	2,095,230
Indiana	10,328,805	598,075	8,306,652	38,058	1,084,476	22,861	278,683
Iowa	5,373,071	171,651	3,922,690	132,081	692,263	133,021	321,365
Kansas	5,030,280	76,156	4,568,957	5,833	231,257	57,846	90,231
Kentucky	4,890,345	0	4,098,486	151,175	152,010	122,925	365,749
Louisiana	6,380,598	152,641	5,055,548	0	76,560	0	1,095,849
Maine	1,347,094	52,270	1,153,227	11,804	119,175	18	10,600
Maryland	9,874,995	138,825	7,034,493	2,974	184,265	1,148,404	1,366,034
Massachusetts	9,434,585	1,562,291	6,278,428	243,553	345,625	61,906	942,782
Michigan	22,754,958	1,318,669	14,757,127	3,208,601	1,751,151	513,690	1,205,720
Minnesota	14,174,246	1,745,965	9,752,165	683,550	1,080,646	148,002	763,918
Mississippi	4,861,117	967,437	3,015,457	320,057	121,383	125,227	311,556
Missouri	6,336,401	218,633	5,741,671	2,279	121,197	146	252,475
Montana	1,113,197	218,896	856,513	0	20,353	2,463	14,972
Nebraska	2,668,741	690,322	1,709,392	54,212	20,019	46,987	147,809
Nevada	5,180,050	1,478,308	3,388,943	115,583	94,131	25,366	77,719
New Hampshire	1,764,616	68,805	1,152,423	435,210	81,808	0	26,370
New Jersey	15,250,952	1,589,395	11,139,415	1,631,876	255,718	137,061	497,487
New Mexico	5,176,572	1,697,264	3,206,916	0	37,581	27,325	207,486
New York	63,492,253	1,218,203	34,010,940	8,093,527	1,091,788	6,747,105	12,330,690
North Carolina	14,706,189	641,880	10,931,936	1,288,759	245,935	643,441	954,238
North Dakota	1,995,041	425,580	1,166,767	86,106	126,453	5,787	184,348
Ohio	18,933,185	1,328,626	12,386,964	1,766,167	913,863	891,691	1,645,874
Oklahoma	4,470,670	194,417	3,551,287	42,757	400,635	125,410	156,164
Oregon	6,320,421	102,516	5,317,584	223,674	11,080	213,995	451,572
Pennsylvania	22,327,616	237,872	14,335,421	2,148,866	1,125,664	1,122,086	3,357,707
Rhode Island	1,307,710	92,855	1,115,151	88,325	0	0	11,379
South Carolina	6,768,154	1,994,054	4,344,542	317	84,360	9,389	335,492
South Dakota	871,682	32,392	725,215	2,591	61,896	11,957	37,631
Tennessee	7,619,932	347,081	5,741,299	698,082	178,679	98,527	556,264
Texas	31,520,535	318,770	28,073,828	837,025	65,336	325,231	1,900,313
Utah	4,166,842	0	3,961,409	18,492	95,975	26,959	64,007
Vermont	1,839,019	26,094	1,693,906	0	64,958	6	54,055
Virginia	12,257,922	677,521	7,728,779	697,089	1,265,673	591,152	1,297,708
Washington	14,338,188	155,868	11,653,165	20,144	717,509	825,119	966,383
West Virginia	2,693,408	156,251	2,267,198	28,260	5,761	63,326	172,612
Wisconsin	11,108,614	2,606,355	6,676,637	359,683	787,082	312,819	366,038
Wyoming	1,353,782	40,207	1,147,860	0	0	116	165,599

Source: U.S. Census Bureau, 2018 Annual Survey of State Government Finances.

Notes:

1. Data users who create their own estimates using these data should cite only the U.S. Census Bureau as the source of the original data. Data in this table are based on information from public records and contain no confidential data. Although the data in this table come from a census of governmental units and are not subject to sampling error, the census results may contain nonsampling error. Additional information on nonsampling error, response rates, and definitions may be found within the survey methodology *https://www.census.gov/programs-surveys/state/technical-documentation/methodology.html.*

2. Detail may not add to total due to rounding.

Table 2.3 | State Intergovernmental Expenditures

Total State Intergovernmental Expenditures *(in thousands of dollars)*

HIGHEST	LOWEST
California • $108,218,508	Hawaii • $355,739
New York • $63,492,253	Alaska • $648,930
Texas • $31,520,535	South Dakota • $871,682
Michigan • $22,754,958	Montana • $1,113,197
Pennsylvania • $22,327,616	Rhode Island • $1,307,710

Highest and Lowest Spending by Category *(in thousands of dollars)*

EDUCATION

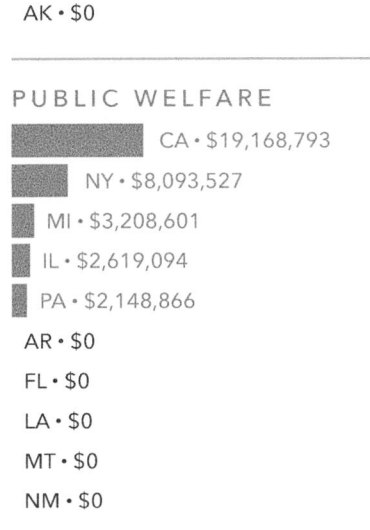

- CA • $64,160,795
- NY • $34,010,940
- TX • $28,073,828
- FL • $16,284,021
- MI • $14,757,127
- RI • $1,115,151
- MT • $856,513
- SD • $725,215
- HI • $319
- AK • $0

HEALTH

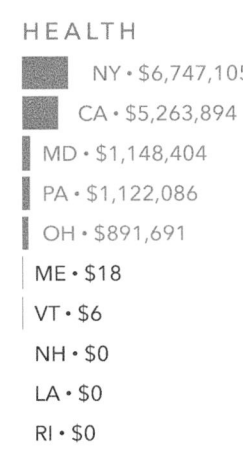

- NY • $6,747,105
- CA • $5,263,894
- MD • $1,148,404
- PA • $1,122,086
- OH • $891,691
- ME • $18
- VT • $6
- NH • $0
- LA • $0
- RI • $0

PUBLIC WELFARE

- CA • $19,168,793
- NY • $8,093,527
- MI • $3,208,601
- IL • $2,619,094
- PA • $2,148,866
- AR • $0
- FL • $0
- LA • $0
- MT • $0
- NM • $0
- VT • $0
- WY • $0

HIGHWAYS

- CA • $3,270,501
- MI • $1,751,151
- VA • $1,265,673
- PA • $1,125,664
- NY • $1,091,788
- DE • $7,676
- WV • $5,761
- HI • $2,871
- DE • $0
- AK • $0

TABLE 2.4

State Intergovernmental Expenditures, By Type of Receiving Government and By State: 2018
(In thousands of dollars)

State	Total intergovernmental expenditure	Federal	School districts	Other local governments
United States	$562,587,857	$3,280,506	$315,410,474	$243,896,877
Alabama	7,006,778	0	5,149,083	1,857,695
Alaska	648,930	0	0	648,930
Arizona	10,268,171	0	6,343,767	3,924,404
Arkansas	5,489,804	189	4,683,066	806,549
California	108,218,508	2,931,228	60,141,289	45,145,991
Colorado	7,518,654	1,987	4,624,594	2,892,073
Connecticut	5,908,441	0	281,401	5,627,040
Delaware	1,611,413	1,406	1,425,472	184,535
Florida	18,958,978	0	15,982,303	2,976,675
Georgia	12,889,900	0	11,279,451	1,610,449
Hawaii	355,739	382	0	355,357
Idaho	2,570,844	0	2,015,598	555,246
Illinois	21,109,911	15,375	10,635,814	10,458,722
Indiana	10,328,805	1,155	8,306,652	2,020,998
Iowa	5,373,071	0	3,920,591	1,452,480
Kansas	5,030,280	42	4,568,957	461,281
Kentucky	4,890,345	0	4,015,118	875,227
Louisiana	6,380,598	0	5,044,479	1,336,119
Maine	1,347,094	0	519,093	828,001
Maryland	9,874,995	0	0	9,874,995
Massachusetts	9,434,585	0	940,970	8,493,615
Michigan	22,754,958	1,615	14,745,940	8,007,403
Minnesota	14,174,246	1,766	9,749,593	4,422,887
Mississippi	4,861,117	0	3,015,457	1,845,660
Missouri	6,336,401	16,788	5,741,671	577,942
Montana	1,113,197	0	856,513	256,684
Nebraska	2,668,741	54,212	1,709,392	905,137
Nevada	5,180,050	3,790	3,388,943	1,787,317
New Hampshire	1,764,616	0	823,151	941,465
New Jersey	15,250,952	12,500	8,268,345	6,970,107
New Mexico	5,176,572	0	3,206,916	1,969,656
New York	63,492,253	0	17,353,223	46,139,030
North Carolina	14,706,189	0	0	14,706,189
North Dakota	1,995,041	0	1,164,813	830,228
Ohio	18,933,185	16,451	12,386,964	6,529,770
Oklahoma	4,470,670	44,907	3,539,872	885,891
Oregon	6,320,421	0	5,305,407	1,015,014
Pennsylvania	22,327,616	123,051	13,873,855	8,330,710
Rhode Island	1,307,710	19,907	55,758	1,232,045
South Carolina	6,768,154	0	4,344,038	2,424,116
South Dakota	871,682	0	725,215	146,467
Tennessee	7,619,932	0	172,233	7,447,699
Texas	31,520,535	0	28,045,603	3,474,932
Utah	4,166,842	0	3,961,409	205,433
Vermont	1,839,019	0	1,693,906	145,113
Virginia	12,257,922	135	0	12,257,787
Washington	14,338,188	0	11,619,579	2,718,609
West Virginia	2,693,408	0	2,258,519	434,889
Wisconsin	11,108,614	0	6,378,601	4,730,013
Wyoming	1,353,782	33,620	1,147,860	172,302

Source: U.S. Census Bureau, 2018 Annual Survey of State Government Finances.

Notes:

1. Data users who create their own estimates using these data should cite only the U.S. Census Bureau as the source of the original data. Data in this table are based on information from public records and contain no confidential data. Although the data in this table come from a census of governmental units and are not subject to sampling error, the census results may contain nonsampling error. Additional information on nonsampling error, response rates, and definitions may be found within the survey methodology <https://www.census.gov/programs-surveys/state/technical-documentation/methodology.html>.

2. Detail may not add to total due to rounding.

TABLE 2.5
State Intergovernmental Revenue from Federal and Local Governments: 2018
(In thousands of dollars)

State	Total intergovernmental revenue	From federal government				
		Total (a)	Education	Public welfare	Heath & hospitals	Highways
United States	$688,138,024	$670,548,803	$85,022,930	$454,338,760	$36,011,416	$43,175,723
Alabama	10,303,451	10,114,128	1,737,497	6,454,307	270,828	916,954
Alaska	3,457,365	3,448,655	328,576	1,708,064	86,979	595,085
Arizona	16,011,205	15,572,048	1,739,713	12,345,220	268,583	822,978
Arkansas	7,877,352	7,832,635	809,887	5,696,400	118,134	766,639
California	103,018,851	99,074,876	10,928,634	77,658,733	1,490,684	4,610,991
Colorado	9,402,733	9,338,266	1,476,255	5,920,161	353,927	769,477
Connecticut	7,440,296	7,206,925	689,080	4,885,763	273,319	562,418
Delaware	2,619,277	2,552,478	240,452	1,723,474	114,749	236,688
Florida	28,298,587	27,994,479	4,658,944	16,435,293	2,367,450	2,506,406
Georgia	15,295,883	15,229,931	3,036,722	7,976,250	1,821,380	1,436,257
Hawaii	3,013,717	3,005,181	552,587	1,920,633	10,630	141,044
Idaho	2,819,674	2,804,710	393,912	1,756,755	11	333,457
Illinois	22,429,882	22,042,413	3,126,295	15,651,466	499,367	1,305,810
Indiana	15,075,489	14,994,627	1,808,707	10,891,362	325,398	962,659
Iowa	6,075,843	6,030,784	971,090	3,814,530	124,700	541,576
Kansas	4,072,601	4,029,932	742,893	2,317,430	236,120	381,017
Kentucky	11,970,566	11,928,331	1,275,104	8,900,799	224,677	734,549
Louisiana	13,648,190	13,179,225	1,513,633	9,118,497	237,657	737,050
Maine	3,012,515	2,975,329	286,102	2,135,432	38,471	222,473
Maryland	13,023,465	12,747,119	1,724,646	7,197,671	2,018,341	687,917
Massachusetts	17,101,109	16,455,455	1,525,432	11,759,467	414,939	520,724
Michigan	21,365,685	21,207,961	3,439,545	13,891,328	1,282,810	701,534
Minnesota	11,742,550	11,548,779	1,353,673	8,631,863	264,468	680,802
Mississippi	8,271,815	8,152,399	942,795	5,805,019	202,346	529,167
Missouri	11,947,706	11,742,639	1,255,243	7,098,323	1,764,713	949,690
Montana	3,124,693	3,119,450	329,020	1,627,575	358,533	467,847
Nebraska	3,264,232	3,231,492	268,974	2,430,590	2,005	312,763
Nevada	5,454,068	5,258,544	654,442	3,323,741	151,341	380,546
New Hampshire	2,799,206	2,393,791	216,433	1,446,791	36,211	172,767
New Jersey	18,014,349	17,148,185	1,760,183	478,114	10,942,677	838,692
New Mexico	7,534,520	7,296,863	778,462	5,580,183	151,043	398,300
New York	64,587,716	63,271,908	4,657,710	50,597,809	872,555	1,707,540
North Carolina	18,704,775	18,532,821	2,744,131	12,994,203	346,589	1,183,350
North Dakota	1,742,138	1,694,899	273,475	878,215	95,152	261,404
Ohio	24,388,743	23,764,912	2,445,456	18,313,961	454,645	1,422,881
Oklahoma	7,100,962	6,945,621	1,075,315	3,462,952	1,218,298	649,873
Oregon	10,470,949	10,439,170	1,360,751	7,718,260	208,902	463,213
Pennsylvania	29,418,893	29,188,234	3,666,974	21,810,372	509,743	1,946,264
Rhode Island	2,868,687	2,788,520	226,330	1,754,229	304,842	221,193
South Carolina	9,916,827	9,633,306	1,405,021	6,130,392	337,230	988,315
South Dakota	1,499,310	1,466,916	273,591	658,840	88,741	282,404
Tennessee	11,826,420	11,718,391	1,426,306	7,219,927	870,113	904,713
Texas	47,201,933	43,967,109	7,106,878	27,153,974	1,992,415	3,986,435
Utah	4,724,208	4,721,316	1,023,229	2,722,839	239,213	415,410
Vermont	2,091,212	2,089,472	252,075	1,288,385	73,466	261,362
Virginia	10,957,750	10,173,474	1,965,315	6,075,804	550,592	1,009,555
Washington	14,446,364	14,098,406	2,427,227	9,038,353	969,099	852,842
West Virginia	4,846,089	4,753,828	525,661	3,351,111	99,376	388,160
Wisconsin	9,494,180	9,286,777	1,443,055	6,146,249	278,333	737,665
Wyoming	2,363,993	2,356,093	159,499	441,651	49,621	268,867

See footnotes at end of table

TABLE 2.5

State Intergovernmental Revenue from Federal and Local Governments: 2018
(In thousands of dollars) (continued)

State	Total (a)				
		From local governments			
		Education	Public welfare	Health & hospitals	Highways
United States	$17,589,221	$5,621,782	$4,735,791	$1,021,566	$2,205,545
Alabama	189,323	19,864	16,386	33,127	55,748
Alaska	8,710	7,360	0	0	0
Arizona	439,157	11,180	203,908	643	77,728
Arkansas	44,717	44,611	0	7	0
California	3,943,975	320,500	2,189,831	18,391	434,826
Colorado	64,467	24,942	249	17	25,463
Connecticut	233,371	301	0	0	0
Delaware	66,799	63,581	0	0	0
Florida	304,108	13,221	0	216,999	0
Georgia	65,952	11,626	0	0	32,141
Hawaii	8,536	0	0	0	0
Idaho	14,964	596	10,862	0	3,505
Illinois	387,469	27,732	243,997	0	92,042
Indiana	80,862	10,785	1,105	0	68,961
Iowa	45,059	191	0	3,247	31,134
Kansas	42,669	12,591	0	779	26,098
Kentucky	42,235	25,604	0	0	0
Louisiana	468,965	8,521	416,270	0	22,097
Maine	37,186	7,234	0	0	28,446
Maryland	276,346	22,059	0	99,927	40,663
Massachusetts	645,654	25,703	0	0	0
Michigan	157,724	9,452	72,520	23,145	15,618
Minnesota	193,771	13,187	107,256	11	57,350
Mississippi	119,416	3,184	0	0	63,716
Missouri	205,067	3,878	122,072	10,231	50,608
Montana	5,243	0	4,686	0	0
Nebraska	32,740	8,605	61	91	23,467
Nevada	195,524	1,846	148,814	26,982	192
New Hampshire	405,415	3,599	386,521	0	4,975
New Jersey	866,164	319,214	0	91,135	332,539
New Mexico	237,657	67,319	23,670	136,924	0
New York	1,315,808	364,982	203,689	0	23,889
North Carolina	171,954	9,071	110,176	6,249	24,765
North Dakota	47,239	1	268	4,175	30,156
Ohio	623,831	51,676	361,047	24,910	62,784
Oklahoma	155,341	871	439	6,416	33,211
Oregon	31,779	18,079	0	0	0
Pennsylvania	230,659	187,805	312	6,709	22,364
Rhode Island	80,167	21,961	0	0	0
South Carolina	283,521	107,942	12,428	6,888	86,265
South Dakota	32,394	18,407	4,380	962	6,237
Tennessee	108,029	21,120	36,993	3,398	32,865
Texas	3,234,824	3,059,154	5,629	166,940	0
Utah	2,892	2,626	0	186	0
Vermont	1,740	0	0	0	1,632
Virginia	784,276	440,461	0	70,023	255,383
Washington	347,958	216,944	0	28,513	43,223
West Virginia	92,261	2,971	0	0	0
Wisconsin	207,403	9,225	52,156	32,307	92,176
Wyoming	7,900	0	66	2,234	3,278

Source: U.S. Census Bureau, 2018 Annual Survey of State Government Finances.

Notes:

1. Data users who create their own estimates using these data should cite only the U.S. Census Bureau as the source of the original data. Data in this table are based on information from public records and contain no confidential data. Although the data in this table come from a census of governmental units and are not subject to sampling error, the census results may contain nonsampling error. Additional information on nonsampling error, response rates, and definitions may be found within the survey methodology *https://www.census.gov/programs-surveys/state/technical-documentation/methodology.html.*

2. Detail may not add to total due to rounding.

Key:

(a) Total includes other types of intergovernmental revenue not shown separately in this table.

Table 2.5 | State Intergovernmental Revenue

Total intergovernmental revenue *(in thousands of dollars)*

HIGHEST

California • $103,018,851	
New York • $64,587,716	
Texas • $47,201,933	
Pennsylvania • $29,418,893	
Florida • $28,298,587	

LOWEST

South Dakota • $1,499,310	
North Dakota • $1,742,138	
Vermont • $2,091,212	
Delaware • $2,363,993	
Rhode Island • $2,619,277	

Highest and Lowest Federal Spending by Category *(in thousands of dollars)*

EDUCATION

CA • $10,928,634
TX • $7,106,878
FL • $4,658,944
NY • $4,657,710
PA • $3,666,974
VT • $252,075
DE • $240,452
RI • $226,330
NH • $216,433
WY • $159,499

HEALTH & HOSPITALS

NJ • $10,942,677
FL • $2,367,450
MD • $2,018,341
TX • $1,992,415
GA • $1,821,380
ME • $38,471
NH • $36,211
HI • $10,630
NE • $2,005
ID • $11

PUBLIC WELFARE

CA • $77,658,733
NY • $50,597,809
TX • $27,153,974
PA • $21,810,372
OH • $18,313,961
VT • $1,288,385
ND • $878,215
SD • $658,840
NJ • $478,114
WY • $441,651

HIGHWAYS

CA • $4,610,991
TX • $3,986,435
FL • $2,506,406
PA • $1,946,264
NY • $1,707,540
DE • $236,688
ME • $222,473
RI • $221,193
NH • $172,767
HI • $141,044

CHAPTER THREE

STATE LEGISLATIVE BRANCH

TABLE 3.1
Names of State Legislative Bodies and Convening Places

State or other jurisdiction	Both bodies	Upper house	Lower house	Convening place
Alabama	Legislature	Senate	House of Representatives	State House
Alaska	Legislature	Senate	House of Representatives	State Capitol
Arizona	Legislature	Senate	House of Representatives	State Capitol
Arkansas	General Assembly	Senate	House of Representatives	State Capitol
California	Legislature	Senate	Assembly	State Capitol
Colorado	General Assembly	Senate	House of Representatives	State Capitol
Connecticut	General Assembly	Senate	House of Representatives	State Capitol
Delaware	General Assembly	Senate	House of Representatives	Legislative Hall
Florida	Legislature	Senate	House of Representatives	The Capitol
Georgia	General Assembly	Senate	House of Representatives	State Capitol
Hawaii	Legislature	Senate	House of Representatives	State Capitol
Idaho	Legislature	Senate	House of Representatives	State Capitol
Illinois	General Assembly	Senate	House of Representatives	State House
Indiana	General Assembly	Senate	House of Representatives	State House
Iowa	General Assembly	Senate	House of Representatives	State Capitol
Kansas	Legislature	Senate	House of Representatives	State Capitol
Kentucky	General Assembly	Senate	House of Representatives	State Capitol
Louisiana	Legislature	Senate	House of Representatives	State Capitol
Maine	Legislature	Senate	House of Representatives	State House
Maryland	General Assembly	Senate	House of Delegates	State House
Massachusetts	General Court	Senate	House of Representatives	State House
Michigan	Legislature	Senate	House of Representatives	State Capitol
Minnesota	Legislature	Senate	House of Representatives	State Capitol
Mississippi	Legislature	Senate	House of Representatives	State Capitol
Missouri	General Assembly	Senate	House of Representatives	State Capitol
Montana	Legislature	Senate	House of Representatives	State Capitol
Nebraska	Legislature	(a)		State Capitol
Nevada	Legislature	Senate	Assembly	Legislative Building
New Hampshire	General Court	Senate	House of Representatives	State House
New Jersey	Legislature	Senate	General Assembly	State House
New Mexico	Legislature	Senate	House of Representatives	State Capitol
New York	Legislature	Senate	Assembly	State Capitol
North Carolina	General Assembly	Senate	House of Representatives	State Legislative Building
North Dakota	Legislative Assembly	Senate	House of Representatives	State Capitol
Ohio	General Assembly	Senate	House of Representatives	State House
Oklahoma	Legislature	Senate	House of Representatives	State Capitol
Oregon	Legislative Assembly	Senate	House of Representatives	State Capitol
Pennsylvania	General Assembly	Senate	House of Representatives	Main Capitol Building
Rhode Island	General Assembly	Senate	House of Representatives	State House
South Carolina	General Assembly	Senate	House of Representatives	State House
South Dakota	Legislature	Senate	House of Representatives	State Capitol
Tennessee	General Assembly	Senate	House of Representatives	State Capitol
Texas	Legislature	Senate	House of Representatives	State Capitol
Utah	Legislature	Senate	House of Representatives	State Capitol
Vermont	General Assembly	Senate	House of Representatives	State House
Virginia	General Assembly	Senate	House of Delegates	State Capitol
Washington	Legislature	Senate	House of Representatives	State Capitol
West Virginia	Legislature	Senate	House of Delegates	State Capitol
Wisconsin	Legislature	Senate	Assembly (b)	State Capitol
Wyoming	Legislature	Senate	House of Representatives	State Capitol
Dist. of Columbia	"Council of the District of Columbia"	(a)		Council Chamber
American Samoa	Legislature	Senate	House of Representatives	Maota Fono
Guam	Legislature	(a)		Congress Building
CNMI*	Legislature	Senate	House of Representatives	Civic Center Building
Puerto Rico	Legislative Assembly	Senate	House of Representatives	The Capitol
U.S. Virgin Islands	Legislature	(a)		Capitol Building

Source: The Council of State Governments, *Directory I–Elective Officials 2018.*
*Commonwealth of Northern Mariana Islands

Key:
(a) Unicameral legislature. Except in the District of Columbia, members go by the title Senator.
(b) Members of the lower house go by the title Representative.

TABLE 3.2
Legislative Sessions: Legal Provisions

State or other jurisdiction	Regular sessions			
	Legislature convenes			Limitation on length of session (a)
	Year	Month	Day	
Alabama	Annual	Jan.; Mar.; Feb.	2nd Tues. (b); 1st Tues. (c); 1st Tues. (d)(e)	30 L in 105 C
Alaska	Annual	Jan.	3rd Tues. (g)	121 C; 90 Statutory (g)
Arizona	Annual	Jan.	2nd Mon.	(h)
Arkansas	Annual	Jan.	2nd Mon.; 2nd Mon.	60 C (i); 30C (i)
California	Biennium (k)	Jan.	1st Mon. (d)	None
Colorado	Annual	Jan.	No later than 2nd Wed.	120 C
Connecticut	Annual	Jan.(odd yrs.); Feb. (even-yrs.)	Wed. after 1st Mon.	(m)
Delaware	Biennium	Jan.	2nd Tues.	June 30
Florida	Annual	Mar.	1st Tues. after 1st Mon. (o)	60 C (i)
Georgia	Annual	Jan.	2nd Mon.	40 L
Hawaii	Annual	Jan.	3rd Wed.	60 L (i)
Idaho	Annual	Jan.	Mon. on or nearest 9th day	None
Illinois	Biennium	Jan.	2nd Wed.	None (q)
Indiana	Annual	Jan.	2nd Mon. (r)	odd-61 C or Apr. 29; even-30 C or Mar. 14
Iowa	Annual	Jan.	2nd Mon.	None (bbb)
Kansas	Annual	Jan.	2nd Mon.	odd-None; even-90 C (i)
Kentucky	Annual	Jan.	1st Tues. after 1st Mon.	even-60 L; odd-30 L (s)
Louisiana	Annual	Mar. (even-years); Apr. (odd-years)	second Mon. (even and odd-years)	even-60 L in 85 C; odd-45 L in 60 C
Maine	(t)	Dec.(even-years); January (subsequent even-year)	1st Wed. (quadrennial election year); Wed. after 1st Tues.	Calendar days set by statute (u)
Maryland	Annual	Jan.	2nd Wed.	90 C
Massachusetts	Biennium	Jan.	1st Wed.	(v)
Michigan	Annual	Jan.	2nd Wed.	None
Minnesota	Biennium	Jan. (odd years); agreed upon start in even years	1st Tues. after 1st Mon.	120 L
Mississippi	Annual	Jan.	Tues. after 1st Mon.	125 C (y); 90 C (y)
Missouri	Annual	Jan.	Wed. after 1st Mon.	May 30
Montana	Biennial-	Jan.	1st Mon. (w)	90 L
Nebraska	Biennium	Jan.	Wed. after 1st Mon.	odd-90 L; even-60 L
Nevada	Biennial-	Feb.	1st Mon.	120 C
New Hampshire	Annual	Jan.	Wed. after 1st Tues.	45 L
New Jersey	Biennium	Jan.	2nd Tues. of even year	None
New Mexico	Annual	Jan.	3rd Tues.	odd-60 C; even-30 C
New York	Annual	Jan. (dd)	Wed. after 1st Mon.	None
North Carolina	(ee)	Jan.	3rd Wed. after 2nd Mon. (odd-years)	None
North Dakota	Biennial-odd year	Jan.	First Tues. after the third day in Jan.	80 L in the biennium
Ohio	Biennium	Jan.	1st Mon. (gg)	None
Oklahoma	Annual	Feb.	1st Mon.	last Fri. in May
Oregon	Annual	Feb.	1st Mon.	(ff)
Pennsylvania	Biennium (hh)	Jan.	1st Tues.	None
Rhode Island	Annual	Jan.	1st Tues.	None
South Carolina	Biennium	Jan.	2nd Tues.	(ii)
South Dakota	Annual	Jan.	2nd Tues.	odd-40 L; even-40 L
Tennessee	Biennium (kk)	Jan.	2nd Tues.	90 L (ll)
Texas	Biennial-odd year	Jan.	2nd Tues.	140 C
Utah	Annual	Jan.	4th Mon.	45 C
Vermont	Annual (yy)	Jan.	Wed. after 1st Mon. (yy)	None
Virginia	Annual	Jan.	2nd Wed.	odd-30 C (i); even-60 C (i)
Washington	Annual	Jan.	2nd Mon.	odd-105 C; even-60 C
West Virginia	Annual	Jan	2nd Wed.	60 C (i)
Wisconsin	Biennium	Jan.	1st Mon.	None
Wyoming	Biennium	Jan.(odd yrs.); Feb. (even-yrs.)	2nd Tues. (odd-years); 2nd Mon. (even-years)	odd-40 L; even-20 L; biennium-60 L
Dist. of Columbia	(oo)		2nd day	None
American Samoa	Annual	Jan.; July	2nd Mon.; 3rd Mon.	45 L; 45 L
Guam	(pp)	Jan.	2nd Mon.	None (pp)
CNMI*	Annual	(rr)	(d)(rr)	90 L (qq)
Puerto Rico	Annual (rr)	Jan.; Aug.	2nd Mon.; 3rd Mon.	5 mo.; 4 mo.
U.S. Virgin Islands	Annual	Jan. (ss)	2nd Mon. (ss)	None

See footnotes at end of table

TABLE 3.2
Legislative Sessions: Legal Provisions (continued)

State or other jurisdiction	Special sessions		
	Legislature may call	Legislature may determine subject	Limitation on length of session
Alabama	No	Yes (f)	12 L in 30 C
Alaska	By petition, 2/3 members, each house	Yes	30 C
Arizona	By petition, 2/3 members, each house	Yes	None
Arkansas	No	No	None (j)
California	No	No	None
Colorado	By petition, 2/3 members, each house	Yes (l)	None
Connecticut	By petition, majority, each house (n)	Yes	None
Delaware	Joint call, presiding officers, both houses	Yes	None
Florida	Joint call, presiding officers, both houses or by petition	Yes	20 C (zz)
Georgia	By petition, 3/5 members, each house	No (p)	40 L
Hawaii	By petition, 2/3 members, each house (uu)	Yes	30 L (i)
Idaho	No	No	20 C
Illinois	Joint call, presiding officers, both houses; Governor also may call	Yes	None
Indiana	No	Yes	30 L or 40 C
Iowa	By petition, 2/3 members, each house	Yes	None
Kansas	Petition to governor of 2/3 members, each house	Yes	None
Kentucky	No	No	None
Louisiana	By petition, majority, each house	Yes	30 C
Maine	Joint call, presiding officers of both houses with the consent of a majority of the members of each political party	Yes	None
Maryland	By petition, majority, each house	Yes	30 C
Massachusetts	By petition (w)	Yes	None
Michigan	No	No	None
Minnesota	No (x)	Yes	None
Mississippi	No	No	None
Missouri	By petition, 3/4 members, each house	Yes (z)	30 C (z)
Montana	By petition, majority, each house (ww)	Yes	None
Nebraska	By petition, 2/3 members, each house	Yes	None
Nevada	By petition, 2/3 members, each house	Yes (aa)	20 C (aa)
New Hampshire	By petition, (xx)	Yes	15 L (bb)
New Jersey	By petition, majority, each house (cc)	Yes	None
New Mexico	By petition, 3/5 members, each house (l)	No (l)	30 C (l)
New York	By petition, 2/3 members, each house	Yes (l)	None
North Carolina	By petition, 3/5 members, each house	Yes	None
North Dakota	(ccc)	Yes	(ccc)
Ohio	Joint call, presiding officers, both houses	Yes	None
Oklahoma	By petition, 2/3 members, each house	Yes	None
Oregon	By petition, majority, each house	Yes	None
Pennsylvania	Governor may call	No	None
Rhode Island	Joint call, presiding officers, both houses	Yes	None
South Carolina	By vote, 2/3 members, each house	Yes	None
South Dakota	By petition, 2/3 members, each house	Yes (jj)	None
Tennessee	By petition, 2/3 members, each house	Yes	30 L (ll)
Texas	No	No	30 C
Utah	Yes (ddd)	Yes	30 C
Vermont	No (eee)	Yes	None
Virginia	(tt)	Yes	None (mm)
Washington	By vote, 2/3 members, each house	Yes	30 C
West Virginia	By petition, 3/5 members, each house	Yes (l)	None
Wisconsin	(nn)	No	None
Wyoming	By petition, majority members, each house. Joint call, presiding officers for purpose of resolving challenge or dispute of any kind in the determination of the presidential electors.	Yes	20 L (aaa)
Dist. of Columbia	...	...	...
American Samoa	No	No	None
Guam	Only the governor may call	No	None (pp)
CNMI*	Upon request of presiding officers, both houses	Yes (j)	10 C
Puerto Rico	No	No	20 C
U.S. Virgin Islands	No, governor calls	No	None

See footnotes at end of table

TABLE 3.2
Legislative Sessions: Legal Provisions (continued)

Source: The Council of State Governments' survey, December 2019 and state websites, February 2020.

* Commonwealth of Northern Mariana Islands

Key:

Annual–holds legislative sessions every year.

Biennial–odd year–holds legislative sessions every other year.

Biennium–holds legislative sessions in a two-year term of activity.

C–Calendar day

L–Legislative day (in some states called a session day or workday; definition may vary slightly, however, generally refers to any day on which either house of legislature is in session).

(a) Applies to each year unless otherwise indicated.

(b) General election year (quadrennial election year).

(c) In first year after quadrennial election.

(d) Legal provision for organizational session prior to stated convening date.

Alabama–in the year after quadrennial election, second Tuesday in January for 10 C.

California–in the even-numbered general election year, first Monday in December for an organizational session, recess until the first Monday in January of the odd-numbered year.

Commonwealth of Northern Mariana Islands–in year after general election, second Monday in January.

(e) In second and third years of quadrennium.

(f) By 2/3 vote each house.

(g) Convening date is statutory. Length of session is 121 calendar days, 90 by statute.

(h) No constitutional or statutory provision; however, by legislative rule regular sessions shall be adjourned sine die no later than Saturday of the week during which the 100th day from the beginning of each regular session falls. The Speaker/President may by declaration authorize the extension of the session for a period not to exceed seven additional days. Thereafter the session can be extended only by a majority vote of the House/Senate.

(i) Session may be extended by vote of members in both houses. Arkansas–2/3 vote to extend up to 75 days; 3/4 vote to go beyond 75 days. Even year fiscal session may be extended one-time only by a 3/4 vote, with the extention no more than 15 C days. Florida–3/5 vote, session may be extended by vote of members in each house. Hawaii–petition of 2/3 membership for maximum 15-day extension. Kansas–2/3 vote. Virginia–2/3 vote for 30 C extension. West Virginia–may be extended by the governor.

(j) After governor's business has been disposed of, members may remain in session up to 15C days by a 2/3 vote of both houses.

(k) Regular sessions begin after general election, in December of even-numbered year. In California, in the even-numbered general election year, first Monday in December for an organizational session, recess until the first Monday in January of the odd-numbered year.

(l) Only if legislature convenes itself. In New York, special sessions may also be called by the governor. Legislature may determine subject only if it has convened itself. In New Mexico, the constitution does not limit the subjects that may be considered in a special session that is called by the legislature. However, only those subjects specified by the governor may be considered in a specail session called by the governor. Special and extraordinary essions are limited to 30 days, but an extraordinary session may be extended if an impeachment trial is pending.

(m) Odd-numbered years–not later than Wednesday after first Monday in June; even-numbered years not later than Wednesday after first Monday in May.

(n) Adoption of a joint resolution by a majority of each house.

(o) A regular session of the legislature shall convene on the first Tuesday after the first Monday of each odd-numbered year, and on the first Tuesday after the first Monday in March, or such other date as may be fixed by law, of each even-numbered year.

(p) If three-fifths of the General Assembly certifies to governor that an emergency exists, governor must convene a special session for all purposes.

(q) Constitution encourages adjournment by May 31.

(r) Legislators may reconvene at any time after organizational meeting; however, second Monday in January is the final date by which regular session must be in process.

(s) During the odd-year session, members convene for four days, then break until February. Any legislation introduced but not enacted in the first part of the session carries over to the second part in February. No bills carry over after sine die of any session.

(t) Regular session begins after general election in even-numbered years. Session which begins in December of general election year runs into the following year (odd-numbered); second session begins in next even-numbered year. The second session is limited to budgetary matters; legislation in the governor's call; emergency legislation; legislation referred to committee for study.

(u) Statutory adjournment for the First Regular Session (beginning in December of even-numbered years and continuing into the following odd-numbered year) is the third Wednesday of June; statutory adjournment for the Second Regular Session (beginning in January of the subsequent even-numbered year) is the third Wednesday in April. The statutes provide for up to two extensions of up to five legislative days each for each session.

(v) Legislative rules say formal business must be concluded by Nov. 15th of the 1st session in the biennium, or by July 31st of the 2nd session for the biennium.

(w) Joint rules provide for the submission of a written statement requesting special session by a specified number of members of each chamber.

(x) Special session is called by the governor.

(y) 90 C sessions every year, except the first year of a gubernatorial administration during which the legislative session runs for 125 C.

(z) 30 C if called by legislature; 60 C if called by governor. On both the session called by governor or legislature, it must state specifically what is to be addressed.

TABLE 3.2
Legislative Sessions: Legal Provisions (continued)

(aa) Legislature may determine the subject if it calls itself into special session. Special sessions are limited to 20 calendar days except in cases of impeachment of state and judicial officers or expulsion of a member of the Legislature.

(bb) Limitation is on legislative pay and mileage.

(cc) Or by joint call, presiding officers, both houses.

(dd) Session officially begins on the first Wednesday following the first Monday of the new legislative term (commencing the first of the year), and lasts until the legislature completes its business and adjourns sine die. However, over the past several years, both houses have adopted the tactic of declaring a recess at the call of the leaders, in order to facilitate easy recall of the legislature to override vetoes, etc. Over time the custom has become to formally adjourn both houses just before the new session opens. This leads to the rather interesting convention that when the governor calls the legislature into session, it is considered "special" or "executive,"even though the regular session is ongoing.

(ee) Legal provision for session in odd-numbered year; however, legislature may divide, and in practice has divided, to meet in even-numbered years as well.

(ff) The Oregon Constitution establishes a maximum of 160 calendar days for an odd-year regular session and a maximum of 35 calendar days for an even-year regular session. Each regular session may be extended in five-day increments by the affirmative vote of two-thirds of the members of each house.

(gg) Unless Monday is a legal holiday; in second year, the General Assembly convenes on the same date.

(hh) Sessions are two years and begin on the 1st Tuesday of January of the odd-numbered year. Session ends on November 30 of the even-numbered year. Each calendar year receives its own legislative number.

(ii) The regular session ends the first Thursday in June; it can be extended with a two-thirds majority vote.

(jj) Legislators must address topic for which the special session was called.

(kk) Each General Assembly convenes for a First and Second Regular Session over a two-year period.

(ll) 90 legislative days over a two-year period. During special sessions members will be paid up to 30 legislative days; further days will be without pay or per diem.

(mm) No limitation, but the convening of the new General Assembly following an election would by operation end the special session.

(nn) The Legislature may call itself into Extraordinary Session on any subject by a majority vote of the organizing committees of each house, by joint resolution, or by a petition of a majority of each house. Only the governor may call a special session.

(oo) Each Council period begins on January 2 of each odd-numbered year and ends on January 1 of the following odd-numbered year.

(pp) Legislature meets on the first Monday of each month following its initial session in January. One legislative day or one special session day may become several calendar days. Special sessions may address only one subject.

(qq) 60 L before April 1 and 30 L after July 31.

(rr) Legislature meets twice a year. During general election years, the legislature only convenes on the January session.

(ss) The legislature convenes in January on the second Monday, March, June and September, the third Wednesday.

(tt) The Constitution provides that the governor must call a special session upon "application" of 2/3 of the members of each house.

(uu) Governor may call both houses of the legislature or the Senate alone into special session. Also, upon a 2/3 affirmative vote, the Senate may call itself into special session to consider judicial nominations.

(vv) If the first Monday falls on New Years Day, the Legislature convenes on the first Wednesday.

(ww) Majoirty of the total Legislature; i.e., 76 members of the combined 100-member House and 50-member Senate.

(xx) Petition filed with Secretary o State signed by not less than 50 members of House (not more than 10 from the same county) and not less than eight members of the Senate.

(yy) Wed. after 1st Monday for the biennial (odd numbered year) session. The adjourned session (even numbered year) is established legislatively in a resolution adopted at the conclusion of the biennial session. It is tradionally a date during the first two weeks of January.

(zz) Session may be extented by 3/5 vote Per s. 11.011, Florida Statutes, if 20 percent of the members of the Legislature certify in writing that conditions warrant convening a special session, the Department of State shall, within seven days
after receiving the required number of certificates, poll the members. Upon affirmative vote of 3/5 of the members of both houses, the Department of State shall fix the day and hour for convening the special session.

(aaa) Twenty legislative days if Legislature calls themseleves. Unlimited if governor calls special session.

(bbb) No formal limitation, but legislator per diems are limited by statute to 110 calander days during odd-year sessions and 100 calendar days during even-year sessions.

(ccc) Legislative management may call special session as long as the length of the special session is within 80 day limit. If special session is called by the Legislative Management, the 80 legislative day limit applies.

(ddd) Effective January 1, 2019, the Utah Constitution was amended to authorize the Legislature to convene into a limited session if two-thirds of the Utah Senate and House members agree that convening is necessary because of a fiscal crisis, war, natural disaster, or emergency in the affairs of the state. A session called under this new constitutional provision is limited to 10 calendar days. This type of session is in addition to the regular annual general session and any special sessions called by the governor. This new type of session allows the Legislature to determine the subject, while a special session called by the governor does not.

(eee) Governor may call. However, the General Assembly may adopt an adjournment resoultion that does not provide for a sine die adjournment and that grants the joint leadership the right to call back on an agreed upon or to be determined date.

TABLE 3.3
The Legislators: Numbers, Terms, and Party Affiliations: 2020

State or other jurisdiction	Senate						House/Assembly						Senate and House/Assembly totals
	Democrats	Republicans	Other	Vacancies	Total	Term	Democrats	Republicans	Other	Vacancies	Total	Term	
State and territory totals	899	1,089	10	7	2,072*	...	2,597	2,822	41	22	5,503	...	7,575*
State totals	859	1,058	1	5	1,972*	...	2,582	2,775	32	22	5,411	...	7,383*
Alabama	8	27	...	...	35	4	28	77	...	...	105	4	140
Alaska	7	13	...	...	20	4	14	22	3 (k)	1	40 (k)	2	60
Arizona	13	17	...	...	30	2	29	31	...	...	60	2	90
Arkansas	9	26	...	...	35	4	23	75	...	2	100	2	135
California	29	10	...	1	40	4	61	18	1 (b)	...	80	2	120
Colorado	19	16	...	..	35	4	41	24	...	...	65	2	100
Connecticut	22	14	...	...	36	2	91	60	...	...	151	2	187
Delaware	12	9	...	...	21	4 (g)	26	15	...	...	41	2	62
Florida	17	23	...	...	40	4	47	73	...	...	120	2	160
Georgia	20	35	...	1	56	2	75	105	...	...	180	2	236
Hawaii	24	1	...	...	25	4	46	5	...	...	51	2	76
Idaho	7	28	...	...	35	2	14	56	...	...	70	2	105
Illinois	40	19	...	...	59	(a)	74	44	...	...	118	2	177
Indiana	10	40	...	...	50	4	33	67	...	...	100	2	150
Iowa	18	32	...	...	50	4	47	53	...	...	100	2	150
Kansas	11	29	...	...	40	4	41	84	...	...	125	2	165
Kentucky	9	29	...	...	38	4	38	60	...	2	100	2	138
Louisiana	12	27	...	...	39	4	35	68	2 (b)	...	105	4	144
Maine	21	14	...	...	35	2	87	56	6 (c)	2	151	2	186
Maryland	32	15	...	...	47	4	98	42	...	1	141	4	188
Massachusetts	34	4	...	2	40	2	125	31	1 (q)	3	160	2	200
Michigan	16	22	...	...	38	4 (p)	52	58	...	...	110	2 (p)	148
Minnesota	32 (d)	35	...	...	67	4	75 (d)	59	...	...	134	2	201
Mississippi	16	36	...	...	52	4	45	75	2 (b)	...	122	4	174
Missouri	10	24	...	...	34	4	48	114	...	1	163	2	197
Montana	20	30	...	...	50	4	43	57	...	...	100	2	150
Nebraska	-------- Nonpartisan election --------			...	49	4	------------------------------ Unicameral ------------------------------						49
Nevada	13	8	...	...	21	4	28	13	...	1	42	2	63
New Hampshire	14	10	...	...	24	2	233	162	1 (s)	4	400	2	424
New Jersey	25	15	...	...	40	4 (f)	52	28	...	...	80	2	120
New Mexico	26	16	...	...	42	4	46	24	...	...	70	2	112
New York	40	23	...	...	63	2	103	43	1 (e)	3	150	2	213
North Carolina	21	29	...	...	50	2	55	65	...	...	120	2	170
North Dakota	10	37	...	...	47	4	15	79	...	...	94	4	141
Ohio	9	24	...	...	33	4	38	61	...	...	99	2	132
Oklahoma	9	38	...	1	48	4	23	77	...	1	101	2	149
Oregon	18	12	...	...	30	4	38	22	...	...	60	2	90
Pennsylvania	21	28	1	...	50	4	93	110	...	...	203	2	253
Rhode Island	33	5	...	...	38	2	65	8	1 (b)	1	75	2	113
South Carolina	19	27	...	...	46	4	44	80	...	...	124	2	170
South Dakota	5	30	...	...	35	2	11	59	...	...	70	2	105
Tennessee	5	28	...	...	33	4	26	73	...	...	99	2	132
Texas	12	19	...	...	31	4	67	83	...	...	150	2	181
Utah	6	23	...	...	29	4	16	59	...	...	75	2	104
Vermont	24 (r)	6	...	...	30	2	95	43	12 (r)	...	150	2	180
Virginia	21	19	...	...	40	4	55	45	...	...	100	2	140
Washington	29	20	...	...	49	4	57	41	...	...	98	2	147
West Virginia	14	20	...	...	34	4	41	58	1 (b)	...	100	2	134
Wisconsin	14	19	...	...	33 (h)	4	36	63	...	...	99 (h)	2	132
Wyoming	3	27	...	...	30	4	9	50	1 (b)	...	60	2	90
Dist. of Columbia (i)	10	0	2 (b)	1	13	4	------------------------------ Unicameral ------------------------------						13
American Samoa	----------------Nonpartisan election----------------			...	18 (j)	4	----------------Nonpartisan election----------------				21 (j)	2	38
Guam	10	5	...	...	15	2	------------------------------ Unicameral ------------------------------						15
CNMI**	...	6	3 (b)	...	9	4	...	13	7 (b)	...	20	2	29
Puerto Rico	7 (m)	20 (n)	2 (l)	1	30 (o)	4	15 (m)	34 (n)	2 (l)	...	51 (o)	4	78
U.S. Virgin Islands	13	...	2 (b)	...	15	2	------------------------------ Unicameral ------------------------------						15

See footnotes at end of table

TABLE 3.3

The Legislators: Numbers, Terms, and Party Affiliations: 2020 (continued)

Source: The Council of State Governments, February 2020.

* Note: Senate and combined body (Senate and House/Assembly) totals include Unicameral legislatures.

** Commonwealth of Northern Mariana Islands

Key:

… - Does not apply

(a) The entire Senate comes up for election in every year ending in "2" with districts based on the latest decennial Census. Senate districts are divided into three groups. One group elects senators for terms of four years, four years and two years; the second group for terms of four years, two years and four years; the third group for terms of two years, four years, and four years.

(b) Independent.

(c) Five Independent and Common Sense Independent.

(d) Democratic-Farmer-Labor.

(e) Independence Party.

(f) All 40 Senate terms are on a ten year cycle which is made up of a 2 year-term, followed by 2 consecutive four year terms, beginning after the decennial census.

(g) Some terms of 2 years occur during reapportionment.

(h) All House seats contested in even-numbered years; In the Senate 17 seats contested in gubernatorial years; 16 seats contested in presidential years.

(i) Council of the District of Columbia.

(j) Senate: senators are not elected by popular vote, but by county council chiefs. House: 21 seats; 20 are elected by popular vote and one appointed, non-voting delegate from Swains Island.

(k) One Non-affiliated, one Independent, one Undeclared.

(l) Senate: 1 Independent and I Puerto Rican Independence Party. House: I Puerto Rican Independence Party and 1 Independent.

(m) Popular Democratic Party.

(n) New Progressive Party.

(o) Constitutionally, the Senate consists of 27 seats and the House consists of 51 seats. However, extra at-large seats can be granted to the opposition to limit any party's control to 2/3.

(p) If a person is elected or appointed to fill a vacancy for more than one-half of a term, it shall be counted as one of the 2 times.

(q) Unenrolled.

(r) Senate: Of the 24 Democrats, three are listed as Democrat/Progressive and two as Progressive/Democrat. House: 5 Independent and 7 Progressive.

(s) Libertarian.

Table 3.3 | Legislative Partisan Control

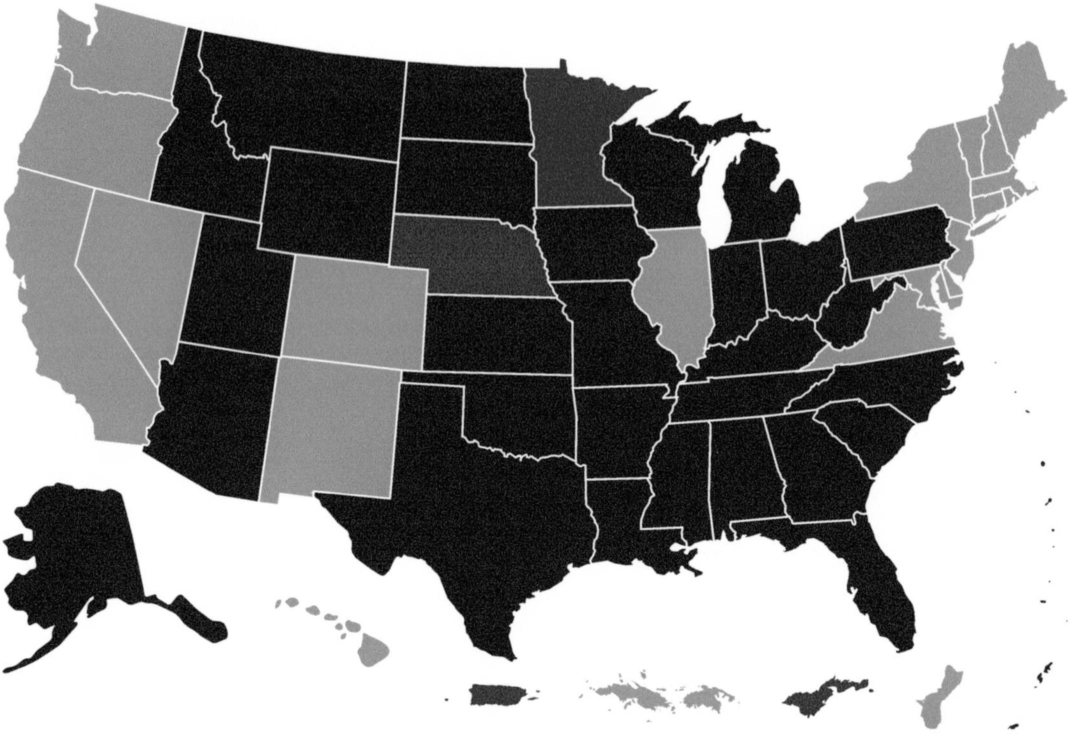

- Democrat (22, D.C. included)
- Republican (30)
- Split (1)
- Nonpartisan (2)
- New Progressive Party (1)

NEBRASKA IS THE ONLY STATE to have both a nonpartisan and unicameral legislature. It is also the smallest at 49 members.

Legislatures with highest percentage of Democrats

HI	RI	MA	CA	MD
92.1%	86.7%	79.5%	75.0%	69.1%

Legislatures with highest percentage of Republicans

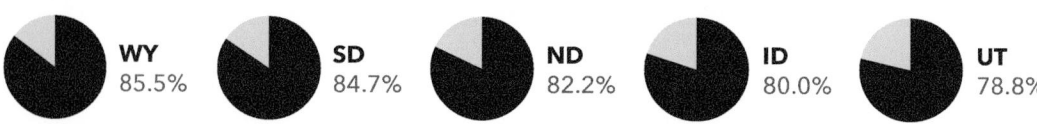

WY	SD	ND	ID	UT
85.5%	84.7%	82.2%	80.0%	78.8%

TABLE 3.4
Membership Turnover in the Legislatures: 2019

State or other jurisdiction	Senate			House/Assembly		
	Total number of members	Number of membership changes	Percentage change of total	Total number of members	Number of membership changes	Percentage change of total
Alabama	35	0	0	105	0	0
Alaska	20	1	5	40	0	0
Arizona	30	0	0	60	1	2
Arkansas	35	0	0	100	0	0
California	40	2	5	80	1	1
Colorado	35	1	3	65	3	5
Connecticut	36	2	6	151	7	5
Delaware	21	0	0	41	0	0
Florida	40	0	0	120	3	3
Georgia	56	0	0	180	4	2
Hawaii	25	0	0	51	0	0
Idaho	35	0	0	70	3	4
Illinois	59	4	7	118	5	4
Indiana	50	1	2	100	2	2
Iowa	50	1	2	100	1	1
Kansas	40	1	3	125	2	2
Kentucky	38	1	3	100	2	2
Louisiana	39	20	51	105	51	49
Maine	35	0	0	151	4	3
Maryland	47	2	4	141	7	5
Massachusetts	40	0	0	160	0	0
Michigan	38	0	0	110	0	0
Minnesota	67	1	1	134	3	2
Mississippi	52	14	27	122	28	23
Missouri	34	0	0	163	5	3
Montana	50	0	0	100	1	1
Nebraska	49	0	0	Unicameral		
Nevada	21	1	5	42	1	2
New Hampshire	24	0	0	400	0	0
New Jersey	40	1	3	80	7	9
New Mexico	42	2	5	70	2	3
New York	63	1	2	150	0	0
North Carolina	50	2	4	120	4	3
North Dakota	47	1	2	94	2	3
Ohio	33	4	12	99	8	8
Oklahoma	48	0	0	101	0	0
Oregon	30	2	7	60	3	5
Pennsylvania	50	4	8	203	3	1
Rhode Island	38	0	0	75	1	1
South Carolina	46	1	2	124	3	2
South Dakota	35	4	11	70	2	3
Tennessee	33	2	6	99	1	1
Texas	31	0	0	150	6	4
Utah	29	0	0	75	2	3
Vermont	30	0	0	150	3	2
Virginia	40	5	13	100	19	19
Washington	49	2	4	98	2	2
West Virginia	34	1	3	100	3	3
Wisconsin	33	0	0	99	1	1
Wyoming	30	0	0	60	0	0
Dist. of Columbia	13	0	0	Unicameral		
American Samoa	18	0	0	20	0	0
Guam	15	0	0	Unicameral		
CNMI*	9	0	0	18	0	0
Puerto Rico	30	0	0	51	0	0
U.S. Virgin Islands	15	0	0	Unicameral		

Source: The Council of State Governments, February 2020.
* Commonwealth of Northern Mariana Islands

TABLE 3.5
Legislators: Qualifications for Election

State or other jurisdiction	House/Assembly				
	Minimum age	U.S. citizen (years) (a)	State resident (years) (b)	District resident (years)	Qualified voter (years)
Alabama	21	...	3 (c)	1	★
Alaska	21	★	3	1	★
Arizona	25	★	3	1	...
Arkansas	21	★	2	1	★
California	18	3	3	1	★
Colorado	25	★	1	1	...
Connecticut	21	★	★	★	★
Delaware	24	★	3	1	...
Florida	21	...	2	...	★
Georgia	21	★	2 (c)	...	★
Hawaii	18	★	3	★	...
Idaho	21	★	1	1	1
Illinois	21	★	2	2 (d)	...
Indiana	21	★	2	1	...
Iowa	21	★	1	60 days	...
Kansas	18	★	★ (c)	★	★
Kentucky	24	★	2 (c)	1	...
Louisiana	18	★	2	1	...
Maine	21	5	1	3 mo.	...
Maryland	21	...	1 (c)	6 mo. (e)	★
Massachusetts	18	...	...	1	★
Michigan	21	★	★	(f)	...
Minnesota	21	...	1	6 mo.	★
Mississippi	21	...	4 (c)	2	★
Missouri	24	★	★	1	2
Montana	18	...	1	6 mo. (g)	...
Nebraska	U	U	U	U	U
Nevada	21	★	1 (c)	30 days (h)	★
New Hampshire	18	...	2 (c)	★	...
New Jersey	21	★	2 (c)	2	...
New Mexico	21	★	★	★	...
New York	18	★	5	1 (i)	★
North Carolina	21	...	...	1	★
North Dakota	18	...	1	30 days in precinct	★
Ohio	18	★	30 days	1 (o)	...
Oklahoma	21	★	★ (c)	★	★
Oregon	21	★	★	1	...
Pennsylvania	21	...	4 (c)	1	...
Rhode Island	18	★	30 days	...	★
South Carolina	21	...	...	★ (j)	...
South Dakota	21	★	2	...	★
Tennessee	21	★	(c)	1	★
Texas	21	★	2	1	...
Utah	25	★	3	6 mo.	★ (p)
Vermont	...	★	2	1	★
Virginia	21	★	★	1	★
Washington	18	★	...	...	★
West Virginia	18	1	1 (c)	...	...
Wisconsin	18	★	1	★ (k)	★ (k)
Wyoming	21	★	★ (c)	1	...
Dist. of Columbia	U	U	U	U	U
American Samoa	25	★ (l)	5	1	...
Guam	U	U	U	U	U
CNMI*	21	...	3	(f)	★
Puerto Rico	25	★	2	1 (n)	...
U.S. Virgin Islands	U	U	U	U	U

See footnotes at end of table

TABLE 3.5
Legislators: Qualifications for Election (continued)

State or other jurisdiction	Senate				
	Minimum age	U.S. citizen (years) (a)	State resident (years) (b)	District resident (years)	Qualified voter (years)
Alabama	25	...	3 (c)	1	★
Alaska	25	★	3	1	★
Arizona	25	★	3	1	...
Arkansas	25	★	2	1	★
California	18	3	3	1	★
Colorado	25	★	1	1	...
Connecticut	21	★	★	★	★
Delaware	27	★	3 (c)	1	...
Florida	21	...	2	...	★
Georgia	25	★	2 (c)	...	★
Hawaii	18	★	3	★	...
Idaho	21	★	1	1	★
Illinois	21	★	2	2 (d)	...
Indiana	25	2	2	1	...
Iowa	25	★	1	60 days	...
Kansas	18	★	★(c)	★	★
Kentucky	30	★	6 (c)	1	...
Louisiana	18	★	2	1	...
Maine	25	5	1	3 mo.	...
Maryland	25	...	1 (c)	6 mo. (e)	★
Massachusetts	18	...	5	(j)	★
Michigan	21	★	★	(f)	...
Minnesota	21	...	1	6 mo.	★
Mississippi	25	...	4 (c)	2	★
Missouri	30	★	★	1	3
Montana	18	...	1	6 mo. (g)	...
Nebraska	21	★	★(c)	1	...
Nevada	21	★	1 (c)	30 days (h)	★
New Hampshire	30	...	7 (c)	★	...
New Jersey	30	★	2 (c)	(j)	...
New Mexico	25	★	★	★	★
New York	18	★	5	1 (i)	★
North Carolina	25	...	2	1	★
North Dakota	18	...	1	30 days in precinct	★
Ohio	18	★	30 days	1 (o)	...
Oklahoma	25	★	★(c)	★	★
Oregon	21	★	★	1	...
Pennsylvania	25	...	4 (c)	1	...
Rhode Island	18	★	30 days	...	★
South Carolina	21	...	...	★ (j)	...
South Dakota	21	★	2	...	★
Tennessee	30	★	3	1	★
Texas	26	★	5	1	...
Utah	25	★	3	6 mo.	★(p)
Vermont	...	★	2	1	...
Virginia	21	★	★	1	★
Washington	18	★	...	...	★
West Virginia	25	5	5 (c)	...	...
Wisconsin	18	★	1	★(k)	★(k)
Wyoming	25	★	★(c)	1	...
Dist. of Columbia	18	...	1	★	★
American Samoa	30 (m)	★(l)	5	1	...
Guam	25	★	5	...	★
CNMI*	25	...	5	(f)	★
Puerto Rico	30	★	2	1 (n)	...
U.S. Virgin Islands	21	...	3 (c)	3	★

See footnotes at end of table

TABLE 3.5
Legislators: Qualifications for Election (continued)

Source: The Council of State Governments survey, December 2019 and state websites 2020

*Commonwealth of Northern Mariana Islands

Note: Many state constitutions have additional provisions disqualifying persons from holding office if they are convicted of a felony, bribery, perjury or other infamous crimes.

Key:

U – Unicameral legislature; members are called senators, except in District of Columbia.

★ – Formal provision; number of years not specified.

. . . – No formal provision.

(a) In some states candidate must be a U.S. citizen to be an elector, and must be an elector to run.

(b) In some states candidate must be a state resident to be an elector, and must be an elector to run.

(c) State citizenship requirement. In Tennessee- must be a citizen for three years.

(d) In the first election after a redistricting, a candidate may be elected from any district that contains a part of the district in which (s)he resided at the time of redistricting, and may be re-elected if a resident of the district (s)he represents for 18 months before re-election.

(e) If the district was established for less than six months, residency is length of establishment of district.

(f) Must be a qualified voter of the district; number of years not specified.

(g) Shall be a resident of the county if it contains one or more districts or if the district contains all or parts of more than one county.

(h) 30 days prior to close of filing for declaration of candidacy.

(i) After redistricting, candidate must have been a resident of the county in which the district is contained for one year immediately preceding election.

(j) At the time of filing.

(k) Ten consecutive days before any election.

(l) Or U.S. national.

(m) Must be registered matai.

(n) The district legislator must live in the municipality he/she represents.

(o) One year unless absent from the district on the public business of the United States or Ohio.

(p) In the district.

TABLE 3.6
Senate Leadership Positions: Methods of Selection

State or other jurisdiction	President	President pro tem	Majority leader	Assistant majority leader	Majority floor leader	Assistant majority floor leader	Majority whip	Majority caucus chair
Alabama (b)	(a)	ES	(b)	...	...	...	...	...
Alaska	ES	...	EC	...	...	...	EC	EC
Arizona	ES	AP	EC	...	...	...	EC	...
Arkansas	(a)	ES	EC	...	...	...	EC	...
California	(a)	ES	EC	...	...	...	EC	EC
Colorado	ES	ES	EC	EC	...	...	EC	EC
Connecticut	(a)	ES	EC	AT (nn)	...	...	...	...
Delaware	(a)	ES	EC	...	...	...	EC	...
Florida (ll)	EC/ES	ES	AP	AL	...	...	...	...
Georgia	(a)	ES	EC	...	...	...	EC	EC
Hawaii	ES	ES (e)	EC	...	EC	...	EC	EC (f)
Idaho	(a)	ES	EC	EC	...	...	...	EC
Illinois	ES	AP	AP	AP	...	...	AP	AP
Indiana	(a)	ES	...	...	AT	AT	AT	EC
Iowa	ES	ES	EC	EC	...	...	EC	...
Kansas	ES	ES (e)	EC	EC	...	...	EC	EC
Kentucky (i)	ES	ES	...	...	EC	...	EC	EC
Louisiana	ES	ES	...	...	...	...	...	...
Maine	ES	ES	EC	EC	...	...	...	...
Maryland	ES	ES	AP (n)	AP (n)	AP (n)	(n)	AP	AP
Massachusetts	EC	...	AP	AP	...	...	...	(p)
Michigan (q)	(a)	ES	EC	EC	EC	EC	EC	EC
Minnesota	ES	ES	EC	EC	...	...	AL	...
Mississippi	(a)	ES	...	...	...	...	...	...
Missouri (d)	(a)	ES	...	...	EC	EC	EC	EC
Montana	ES	ES	EC	...	EC (j)	...	EC	...
Nebraska (U)(g)	(a)	ES (r)	...	...	...	...	...	...
Nevada (s)	(a)	ES	...	...	EC	EC	EC (s)	...
New Hampshire	ES	AP	AP	...	...	...	...	...
New Jersey	ES	ES	MA	MA	MA	MA	MA	MA
New Mexico	(a)	ES	EC (t)	...	EC (t)	...	EC	EC
New York (u)	(a)	ES	(v)	AT (v)	AT (v)	...	AT	AT (v)
North Carolina	(a)	ES	EC	...	...	...	EC	EC
North Dakota	(a)	ES	EC	EC	...	...	...	EC
Ohio (w)(x)	ES (x)	ES	...	...	ES	...	ES	...
Oklahoma	(a)	ES	EC	EC	EC	EC	EC	EC
Oregon	ES	ES	EC	EC	...	...	EC	...
Pennsylvania	ES	ES	EC	EC	EC	EC	EC	EC
Rhode Island (y)	ES	ES	EC	AL	...	...	AL	...
South Carolina	(a)	ES	EC	...	...	...	...	...
South Dakota	(a)	ES	EC	EC	...	...	EC	...
Tennessee	ES	AP	EC	...	EC	EC	...	EC
Texas	(a)	ES	...	...	...	...	...	EC (k)
Utah (z)	ES	AL	EC	...	...	...	EC	...
Vermont	(a)	ES	EC	EC	EC (aa)	EC (aa)	EC (aa)	EC (aa)
Virginia	(a)	ES	EC (bb)	...	EC (bb)	...	...	EC
Washington (cc)	(a)	ES	EC	EC	EC	EC	EC	EC
West Virginia	ES	AP	AP	...	...	...	AP	...
Wisconsin	ES (dd)	ES	EC	EC	...	...	...	EC
Wyoming	ES	ES (e)	...	...	EC	...	...	...
Dist. of Columbia (U)	(ee)	(ff)	...	...	...	...	...	...
American Samoa	ES	ES	...	...	...	...	...	...
Guam (U)(gg)	ES (r)	ES (e)	EC	EC	EC	EC	EC	...
CNMI*	ES (hh)	...	(hh)	...	ES (ii)	...	...	...
Puerto Rico	ES (p)	EC	EC	...	EC (jj)	...	...	(kk)
U.S. Virgin Islands (U)	ES	...	ES	...	...	...	...	ES

See footnotes at end of table

TABLE 3.6

Senate Leadership Positions: Methods of Selection (continued)

State or other jurisdiction	Minority leader	Assistant minority leader	Minority floor leader	Assistant minority floor leader	Minority whip	Minority caucus chair
Alabama (b)	(b)	...	...	...	...	...
Alaska	EC	...	...	...	EC	EC
Arizona	EC	EC	...	...	EC	...
Arkansas	EC	...	...	...	EC	...
California	EC	...	...	...	EC	EC
Colorado	EC	EC	...	...	EC	EC
Connecticut	EC	AL(m)	...	...	AL(c)	...
Delaware	EC	...	...	...	EC	...
Florida (ll)	EC	EC	...	...	AL	AL
Georgia	EC	...	...	...	EC	EC
Hawaii	EC	...	EC	...	...	...
Idaho	EC	EC	...	...	...	EC
Illinois	EC	AL	...	...	AL	AL
Indiana	EC	...	EC	(h)	(h)	EC
Iowa	EC	EC	...	...	EC	...
Kansas	EC	EC	...	...	EC	EC
Kentucky (i)	...	...	EC	...	EC	...
Louisiana	...	...	...	...	...	...
Maine (ll)	EC	EC	...	...	...	...
Maryland	EC(o)	...	(o)	...	EC	...
Massachusetts	EC	...	...	...	...	(p)
Michigan (q)	EC	EC	EC	EC	EC	EC
Minnesota	EC	EC	...	...	EC	...
Mississippi	...	...	...	...	...	...
Missouri (d)	...	...	EC	EC	EC	EC
Montana	EC	...	EC(l)	...	EC	...
Nebraska (U)(g)	...	...	...	...	...	...
Nevada (s)	...	...	EC	EC	EC	(mm)
New Hampshire	EC	...	...	...	AL	...
New Jersey	MI	MI	MI	MI	MI	MI
New Mexico	EC(t)	...	EC(t)	...	EC	EC
New York (u)	EC(v)	AL(v)	AL(v)	AL(v)	AL(v)	AL(v)
North Carolina	EC	...	...	...	EC	EC
North Dakota	EC	EC	...	...	...	EC
Ohio (w)(x)	ES(x)	ES	...	...	ES	...
Oklahoma	EC	EC	EC	EC	EC	EC
Oregon	EC	EC	...	...	EC	...
Pennsylvania	EC	EC	EC	EC	EC	EC
Rhode Island (y)	EC	AL	...	...	AL	...
South Carolina	EC	...	...	...	...	...
South Dakota	EC	EC	...	...	EC	...
Tennessee	EC	...	EC	...	...	EC
Texas	...	...	...	...	...	EC(k)
Utah	EC	...	...	...	EC	...
Vermont	EC	EC	EC(aa)	EC(aa)	EC(aa)	EC(aa)
Virginia	EC	...	EC	...	...	EC
Washington (cc)	EC	EC	EC	EC	EC	EC
West Virginia	EC	...	...	...	AL	...
Wisconsin	EC	EC	...	...	...	EC
Wyoming	...	...	EC	...	EC	EC
Dist. of Columbia (U)	...	...	...	...	...	...
American Samoa	...	...	...	...	...	...
Guam (U)(gg)	EC	EC	EC	EC	EC	...
CNMI*	EC	...	...	...	...	...
Puerto Rico	EC(p)	...	EC(jj)	...	...	(p)
U.S. Virgin Islands (U)	ES	...	...	...	...	ES

See footnotes at end of table

TABLE 3.6
Senate Leadership Positions: Methods of Selection (continued)

Sources: The Council of State Governments' survey, December 2019 and state websites 2020.

*Commonwealth of Northern Mariana Islands

Note: In some states, the leadership positions in the Senate are not empowered by the law or by the rules of the chamber, but rather by the party members themselves.

Key:
ES–Elected or confirmed by all members of the Senate.
EC–Elected by party caucus.
AP–Appointed by president.
AT–Appointed by president pro tempore.
AL–Appointed by party leader.
MA–Elected by majority party.
MI–Elected by minority party.
(U)–Unicameral legislative body.
…–Position does not exist or is not selected on a regular basis.

(a) Lieutenant governor is president of the Senate by virtue of the office. Idaho–(Idaho Const. art.IV, § 13, Senate Rule 1.)

(b) Majority leader elected by the members of the majority party. Minority leader elected by members of the minority party. Additional leadership positions: deputy president pro tempore–appointed by Committee on Assignments and Dean of Senate–appointed by Committee on Assignments.

(c) Senate Republican caucus has three minority whips.

(d) Additional positions of minority caucus secretary (EC) and majority caucus secretary (EC)

(e) Official title is vice president. In Guam, vice speaker.

(f) Official title is majority caucus leader.

(g) Additional positions appointed by the majority leader: Senate Finance Committee chair, vice president pro tem, Majority Program Development Committee Chair, Majority Steering Committee chair, two assistant majority leaders, various deputies and assistants. Additional positions appoint by the minority leader: Senate Finance Committee ranking member, Minority Policy Committee chair, Minority Program Development chair, three additional minority leaders, various deputies and assistants.

(h) Appointed by minority leader.

(i) In each chamber, the membership elects chief clerk; assistant clerk; enrolling clerk; sergeant-at-arms; doorkeeper; janitor; cloakroom keeper; and pages.

(j) Same position as majority leader.

(k) Caucus chairs have no official role under Senate rules.

(l) Same position as minority leader.

(m) Senate Republican caucus has one minority leader pro tempore, one chief deputy minority leader, five deputy minority leaders, three assistant minority leaders, three minority whips.

(n) Majority leader also serves as majority floor leader; deputy majority leader is official title and serves as assistant majority floor leader. There is also an assistant deputy majority leader, a majority whip, deputy majority whip, and two assistant majority whips.

(o) Minority leader also serves as the minority floor leader.

(p) President and minority floor leader are also caucus chairs. In Puerto Rico, president and minority leader. In Oregon, majority leader and minority leader.

(q) Senate Rule 1.104 provides that the president pro tempore (ES), assistant president pro tempore (ES), and the associate president pro tempore (ES) are elected by a majority of the Senate.

(r) Official title is speaker. In Guam the Speaker is elected on the Floor by majority and minority members on Inauguration Day.

(s) Co-whips elected for 2017 session.

(t) Majority leader also serves as majority floor leader. Minority leader also serves as minority floor leader.

(u) Majority, appointed by president pro tem: Assistant majority leader on conference operations, Deputy majority whip, Assistant Senate majority whip, Deputy majority leader for policy, et al. Minority, appointed by minority leader: Assistant democratic conference leader for conference operations, Vice chair of democratic conference, Deputy democratic conference whip, Assistant democratic conference whip, et al.

(v) President pro tem is also majority leader. Assistant majority leader is called deputy majority leader for legislative operations. Majority floor leader is called assistant majority leader for house operations. Majority caucus chair called Senate majority caucus chair. Minority leader is called democratic conference leader, and independent democratic conference leader (i.e. two minority conferences); voting usually falls along conference lines. Assistant minority leader is called deputy democratic conference leader and deputy independent democratic conference leader. Minority floor leader is called assistant democratic leader for floor operations. Assistant minority floor leader is called deputy democratic conference floor leader. Minority whip is called democratic conference whip, and independent democratic conference whip. Minority caucus chair is called chair of democratic conference.

(w) While the entire membership actually votes on the election of leaders, selections generally have been made by the members of each party prior to the date of this formal election.

(x) In Ohio president acts as majority leader and caucus chair; minority leader also acts as minority caucus chair; the fourth ranking minority leadership position is assistant minority whip (ES).

(y) Additional positions include deputy president pro tempore.

(z) Majority assistant whip, minority assistant whip and minority caucus manager elected by party caucus.

(aa) Majority leader serves as majority floor leader, majority caucus chair and majority whip. Assistant majority leader serves as assistant majority floor leader. Minority leader serves as minority floor leader and minority caucus chair. Assistant minority leader serves as assistant minority floor leader and minority whip.

(bb) Majority party and Minority party in Senate elects caucus officers.

(cc) Washington Senate also has the leadership position of vice-president pro tem.

(dd) Caucus nominee elected by whole membership.

(ee) Chair of the Council, which is an elected position.

(ff) Appointed by the chair; official title is chair pro tem.

(gg) Additional positions include: Parliamentarian, elected by majority caucus and Senior Senator, elected by majority caucus.

(hh) Speaker also serves as majority leader.

(ii) Official title is floor leader.

(jj) Official title is alternate floor leader.

(kk) Official title is caucus chair.

TABLE 3.6
Senate Leadership Positions: Methods of Selection (continued)

(ll) All positions other than president, president pro tempore and
   majority leader are party caucus designations.
(mm) Co-Minority Caucus Coordinators elected by party caucus.
(nn) Senate Democratic caucus has one chief deputy president pro
   tempore, 13 deputy president pro tempore and one chief deputy
   majority leader and five deputy majority leaders.

TABLE 3.7
House/Assembly Leadership Positions: Methods of Selection

State or other jurisdiction	Speaker	Speaker pro tem	Majority leader	Assistant majority leader	Majority floor leader	Assistant majority floor leader	Majority whip	Majority caucus chair
Alabama	EH	EH	EC	...	...	...	...	...
Alaska	EH	...	EC	...	...	...	EC	EC
Arizona	EH	AS	EC	...	...	...	EC	...
Arkansas	EH	AS	EC	...	...	...	EC	...
California	EH	AS	...	...	AS	AS	AS	EC
Colorado (a)	EH	AS	...	EC	...	...	EC	EC
Connecticut	EH	AS (b)	EC	(b)	...	...	AS (b)	AS (b)
Delaware	EH	(hh)	EC	...	...	...	EC	...
Florida	EH	EH	AS	AS (ee)	...	...	AS (ee)	...
Georgia	EH	EH	EC	...	...	...	EC	EC
Hawaii (c)	EH	EH (d)	EC	EC	EC	EC	EC	...
Idaho	EH	...	EC	EC	...	...	...	EC
Illinois	EH	...	AS	AS (e)	...	...	...	AS (e)
Indiana	EH	AL	EC	AL	AL	AL	AL	AL
Iowa	EH	EH	EC	EC	...	...	EC	...
Kansas (f)	EH	EH	EC	EC	...	...	EC	EC
Kentucky (g)	EH	EH	...	...	EC	...	EC	EC
Louisiana	EH	EH	...	...	...	...	...	...
Maine	EH	AS (h)	EC	EC	...	...	...	...
Maryland (cc)	EH	EH (i)	AS (j)	AS (j)	(j)	AS	AS	(k)
Massachusetts	EC	...	AS	AS	...	...	...	...
Michigan (n)	EH	EH	...	...	EC	EC	EC	EC
Minnesota	EH	AS	EC	EC	...	...	EC	...
Mississippi	EH	EH	...	...	...	...	...	...
Missouri (ff)	EH	EH	...	...	EC	EC	EC	EC
Montana	EH	EH	...	...	...	...	EC	...
Nebraska	-- (o) --
Nevada (gg)	EH	EH	...	...	EC	EC	EC	...
New Hampshire	EH	AS (d)	AS	AS (dd)	AS	AS (dd)	...	...
New Jersey	EH	EH	MA	MA	MA	MA	MA	MA
New Mexico	EH	...	EC	...	EC (m)	...	EC	EC
New York (p)	EH	AS	AS	AS	(p)	...	AS	AS (q)
North Carolina	EH	EH	EC	...	...	...	EC	EC
North Dakota	EH	...	EC	EC	...	...	...	EC
Ohio (r)	EH (k)	EH	...	...	EH	EH	EH	...
Oklahoma	EH	EH	...	(bb)	AS	AS	AS	EC
Oregon	EH	EH	EC	EC	...	...	EC	...
Pennsylvania	EH	EH	EC	EC	EC	EC	EC	EC
Rhode Island	EH	EH	EC	AL	...	...	AL	...
South Carolina	EH	EH	EC	...	...	...	...	...
South Dakota	EH	EH	EC	EC	...	...	EC	...
Tennessee	EH	EH	EC	EC	EC	...	EC	EC
Texas	EH	AS	...	...	...	...	...	EC (ii)
Utah (s)	EH	AS	EC	...	...	...	EC	...
Vermont	EH	...	EC	EC	(t)	(t)	(t)	(t)
Virginia (u)	EH	...	EC (v)	...	EC (v)	...	EC	EC
Washington	EH	EH	EC	EC	EC	EC	EC	EC
West Virginia	EH	AS	AS	AS	...	...	AS	AS
Wisconsin	EH (x)	EH (x)	EC	EC	...	...	...	EC
Wyoming	EH	EH	...	...	EC	...	EC	...
Dist. of Columbia	-- (o) --
American Samoa	EH	EH (d)	...	...	...	...	...	...
Guam	-- (o) --
CNMI*	EH (y)	...	(y)	...	EH (z)	...	...	...
Puerto Rico	EH (k)	EH (d)	EC	...	EC (aa)	...	...	...
U.S. Virgin Islands	-- (o) --

See footnotes at end of table

TABLE 3.7

House/Assembly Leadership Positions: Methods of Selection (continued)

State or other jurisdiction	Minority leader	Assistant minority leader	Minority floor leader	Assistant minority floor leader	Minority whip	Minority caucus chair
Alabama	EC	...	...	...	...	...
Alaska	EC	...	...	...	EC	EC
Arizona	EC	EC	...	EC	EC	...
Arkansas	EC	...	...	...	EC	...
California	EC	...	EC	EC	EC	EC
Colorado (a)	EC	EC	...	...	EC	EC
Connecticut	EC	AL(b)	...	...	AL(b)	AL(b)
Delaware	EC	...	...	...	EC	...
Florida	EC	EC(ee)	AL	...	AL(ee)	AL(ee)
Georgia	EC	...	...	...	EC	EC
Hawaii (c)	EC	EC	EC	EC	EC	...
Idaho	EC	EC	...	...	...	EC
Illinois	EC	(e)	...	AL	...	AL(e)
Indiana	EC	AL	EC	AL	AL	AL
Iowa	EC	EC	...	...	...	...
Kansas (f)	EC	EC	...	...	EC	EC
Kentucky (g)	...	...	EC	...	EC	EC
Louisiana	...	...	...	...	...	...
Maine (bb)	EC	EC	...	...	...	...
Maryland (cc)	EC(l)	EC	EC(l)	EC(l)	EH	(k)
Massachusetts	EC	AL	...	...	...	...
Michigan (n)	EC	EC	EC	EC	EC	EC
Minnesota	EC	EC	...	...	EC	...
Mississippi	...	...	...	...	...	...
Missouri (ff)	...	...	EC	EC	EC	EC
Montana	EC	...	...	...	EC	...
Nebraska	--- (o) ---					
Nevada (gg)	...	...	EC	EC	EC	...
New Hampshire	AS	AL(dd)	AL	(dd)	...	...
New Jersey	MI	MI	MI	MI	MI	MI
New Mexico	EC	...	EC(m)	...	EC	EC
New York (p)	EH	AL	...	...	AL	AL(q)
North Carolina	EC	...	...	...	EC	EC
North Dakota	EC	EC	...	...	...	EC
Ohio (r)	EH(k)	EH	...	...	EH	...
Oklahoma	EC	...	AL	...	...	EC
Oregon	EC	EC	...	...	EC	...
Pennsylvania	EC	EC	EC	EC	EC	EC
Rhode Island	EC	AL	...	...	AL	...
South Carolina	EC	...	...	...	...	...
South Dakota	EC	EC	...	...	EC	...
Tennessee	EC	EC	EC	EC	EC	EC
Texas	...	...	...	...	...	EC(ii)
Utah	EC	...	...	...	EC	...
Vermont	EC	EC	(t)	(t)	(t)	(t)
Virginia (u)	EC(w)	...	EC(w)	...	AL	EC
Washington	EC	EC	EC	EC	EC	EC
West Virginia	EC	...	...	...	...	...
Wisconsin	EC	EC	...	...	...	EC
Wyoming	...	...	EC	...	EC	EC
Dist. of Columbia	--- (o) ---					
American Samoa	...	...	...	...	...	...
Guam	--- (o) ---					
CNMI*	EC	...	...	...	...	...
Puerto Rico	EC(k)	...	EC	...	...	(k)
U.S. Virgin Islands	--- (o) ---					

See footnotes at end of table

TABLE 3.7
House/Assembly Leadership Positions: Methods of Selection (continued)

Sources: The Council of State Governments' survey, December 2019 and state websites 2020.

*Commonwealth of Northern Mariana Islands

Note: In some states, the leadership positions in the House are not empowered by the law or by the rules of the chamber, but rather by the party members themselves.

Key:

EH–Elected or confirmed by all members of the House.

EC–Elected by party caucus.

AS–Appointed by speaker.

AL–Appointed by party leader.

MA–Elected by majority party.

MI–Elected by minority party.

…–Position does not exist or is not selected on a regular basis.

(a) Additional positions include deputy majority caucus chair (EC) and deputy majority whip (EC).

(b) Speaker pro tem–1 Deputy Speaker Pro Tempore, 8 Deputy Speakers and 4 Assistant Deputy Speakers. Assistant majority leader–Majority leader appoints 8 Deputy Majority Leaders; Speaker appoints 17 Assistant Minority Leaders (in consultation with Majority Leader). Majority Whip–1 Chief Majority Whip, 2 Majority Whip At-Large, 2 Deputy Majority Whips At-Large and 5 Assistant Majority Whips (in consultation with Majority Leader). Majority caucus chair–selected in consultation with Majority Leader. Assistant Minority Leader–1 Deputy Minority Leader, 4 Deputy Minority Leaders At-Large and 10 Assistant Minority Leaders. Minority Whip–1 Chief Minority Whip, 3 Senior Minority Whips and 6 Minority Whips. Minority Caucus Chair–1 Minority Caucus Chair and 2 Minority Policy Chairs.

(c) Other positions in Hawaii include speaker emeritus, majority policy leader (EC) and minority leader emeritus.

(d) In Hawaii, American Samoa and Puerto Rico, title is vice speaker. In New Hampshire, there is also a position of deputy speaker.

(e) The two deputy majority leaders appointed by the speaker are among eight assistant majority leaders; and the two deputy Republican (minority) leaders appointed by the Republican (minority) leader are among the eight assistant leaders. Majority and minority caucus chairs are selected by conference chairs.

(f) Additional positions include minority agenda chair (EC) and minority policy chair (EC).

(g) In each chamber, the membership elects chief clerk; assistant chief clerk; enrolling clerk; sergeant-at-arms; doorkeeper; janitor; cloakroom keeper; and pages.

(h) Speaker pro tem each occurrence.

(i) There is also a deputy speaker pro tem.

(j) Majority leader also serves as majority floor leader. Official title of assistant majority leader is deputy majority leader. There are also an assistant majority floor leader, majority whip, chief deputy majority whips, and deputy majority whips.

(k) Speaker and minority leader are also caucus chairs.

(l) Minority leader also serves as the minority floor leader. There are also a minority whip, assistant minority leader, a chief deputy minority whip, an assistant minority whip, and several deputy minority whips.

(m) Majority leader also serves as majority floor leader; minority leader also serves as minority floor leader.

(n) Other positions include: two associate speakers pro tempore (EH); majority caucus chair (EC); assistant majority whip (EC); assistant associate minority floor leader (EC); minority assistant caucus chair (EC); assistant minority whip (EC).

(o) Unicameral legislature; see entries in Table 3.6, "Senate Leadership Positions–Methods of Selection."

(p) Majority floor leader duties assumed by majority leader. Additional majority positions appointed by the speaker: deputy speaker, assistant speaker, deputy majority leader, deputy majority whip, assistant majority whip Steering Committee chair, various deputies and assistants. Minority leader voting along conference lines, the member with the second highest number of votes; minority floor leader duties are assumed by minority leader pro tem. Additional minority positions appointed by the minority leader: deputy minority leader, assistant minority leader, deputy minority whip, assistant minority whip, various deputies and assistants.

(q) Official titles: the majority caucus chair is majority conference chair; minority caucus chair is minority conference chair.

(r) While the entire membership actually votes on the election of leaders, selections generally have been made by the members of each party prior to the date of this formal election. Additional positions include assistant majority whip, the 6th ranking majority leadership position (EH) and assistant minority whip, the 4th ranking minority leadership position (EH).

(s) Majority assistant whip, minority assistant whip and minority caucus manager elected by party caucus.

(t) Majority leader also serves as majority floor leader; assistant majority leader also serves as assistant majority floor leader and majority whip; minority leader also serves as minority floor leader; assistant minority leader also serves as assistant minority floor leader and minority whip.

(u) The majority caucus also has a secretary, who is appointed by the speaker; the minority caucus has 2 vice-chairs, 1 vice-chair/treasurer and an interim sergeant-at-arms.

(v) The title of majority leader is not used in Virginia; the title is majority floor leader.

(w) The title of minority leader is not used in Virginia; the title is minority floor leader.

(x) Caucus nominee elected by whole membership.

(y) Speaker also serves as majority leader.

(z) Official title is floor leader.

(aa) Official title is alternate floor leader.

(bb) The Speaker appoints 3 deputy floor leaders and 2 deputy majority leaders.

(cc) There is a parliamentarian for the majority appointed by the Speaker and a minority parliamentarian elected by the minority party caucus.

(dd) Assistant majority leader official title is deputy majority leader. Assistant majority floor leader is deputy majority floor leader. Assistant minority leader official title is deputy Republican leader. Assistant minority floor leader is deputy Republican floor leader.

TABLE 3.7
House/Assembly Leadership Positions: Methods of Selection (continued)

(ee) The position of assistant majority leader is known as deputy majority leader. In addition to a majority whip, deputy whips are also appointed by the speaker. The position of assistant minority leader is known as minority leader pro tem. In addition to a minority whip, deputy whips are appointed by the party leader. There is no minority caucus chair–instead there is a policy chair.

(ff) Additional positions of minority and majority caucus secretaries (EC).

(gg) Co-assistant leaders, called deputy minority floor leaders, elected for 2019 session and two minority whips elected for the 2019 session; a chief deputy majority whip and 2 assistant majority whips elected for 2019 session.

(hh) The most Senior member of the Majority Party.

(ii) Caucus chairs have no official role under House rules.

TABLE 3.8
Method of Setting Legislative Compensation

State	Method
Alabama	Constitutional Amendment 57
Alaska	Compensation Commission; Alaska Stat. §24.10.100 , §24.10.101; §39.23.200 thru 39.23.260
Arizona	Compensation Commission Send to a Public Vote Arizona Revised Statutes 41-1103 and 41-1904
Arkansas	Amendment 70, Ark. Stat. Ann. §10-2-212 et seq.
California	State Constitution - Art. III, §8, which establishes a compensation commission.
Colorado	Colorado Stat. 2-2-307 (1)
Connecticut	Conn. Gen. Stat. Ann. §2-9a ; The General Assembly takes independent action pursuant to recommendations of a compensation commission.
Delaware	Del. Code Ann. Title 29, §710 et seq.; §§3301-3304; Are implemented automatically if not rejected by resolution.
Florida	Florida Statutes §11.13(1); statute provides members same percentage increase as state employees
Georgia	Ga. Code Ann. §45-7-4 and §28-1-8
Hawaii	Hawaii State Constitution Article XVI §3.5; Legislative Salary Commission recommendations take effect unless rejected by concurrent resolution
Idaho	Idaho Code 67-406a and 406b; Citizen's Committee on Legislative Compensation makes recommendations that the legislature can reduce or reject, but not increase
Illinois	25 ILCS 120-Compensation Review Act and 25 ILCS 115-General Assembly Compensation Act
Indiana	IC 2-3-1-1: An amount equal to 18% of the annual salary of a judge under IC 33-38-5-6, as adjusted under IC 33-38-5-8.1.
Iowa	Iowa Code Ann. §2.10; Iowa Code Ann. §2A.1 thru 2A.5
Kansas	Kan. Stat. Ann. §46-137a et seq.; §75-3212
Kentucky	Kentucky Rev. Stat. Ann. §6.226-229. The Kentucky committee has not met since 1995; the most recent pay raise was initiated and passed by the General Assembly.
Louisiana	La. Rev. Stat. 24:31 & 31.1
Maine	Maine Constitution Article IV, part third, §7 and 3 MRSA, §2 and 2-A. Increase in compensation is presented to the legislature as legislation; the legislature must enact and the governor must sign into law. Takes effect only for subsequent legislatures.
Maryland	Article III, §15. Commission meets before each four-year term of office and presents recommendations to the General Assembly for action. Recommendations may be reduced or rejected.
Massachusetts	Massachusetts Gen. Laws Ann. ch. 3, §§9, 10. In 1998, the voters passed a legislative referendum that, starting with the 2001 session, members will receive an automatic increase or decrease according to the median household income for the commonwealth for the following two-year period.
Michigan	Article IV §12. Compensation Commission recommends legislature by majority vote; must approve or reduce for change to be effective for the session immediately following the next general election.
Minnesota	Minn. Stat. Ann §3.099 et seq.; §15A.082; The Council submits salary recommendations to the presiding officers by May 1 in odd numbered years.
Mississippi	Miss. Code Ann. 5-1-41
Missouri	Art. III, §§16, 34; Mo. Ann. Stat. §21.140; Recommendations are adjusted by legislature or governor if necessary.
Montana	Mont. Laws 5-2-301; Tied to executive broadband pay plan.
Nebraska	Neb. Const. Art. III, §7; Neb. Rev. Stat. 50-123.01
Nevada	§218.210-§218.225
New Hampshire	Art. XV, part second
New Jersey	Article IV Sec. IV 7, 8; NJSA 52:10A-1; NJSA 52:14-15.111-114
New Mexico	Art. IV. §10 ; 2-1-8 NMSA
New York	Constitution - Art. 3, §6 ; Consolidated Laws of NY - Legislative Law, Section 5.
North Carolina	N.C.G.S. 120-3
North Dakota	NDCC 54-03-10 and 54-03-20
Ohio	Art. II, §31; Ohio Rev. Code Ann. title 1 ch. 101.27 thru 101.272
Oklahoma	Okla. Stat. Ann. title 74, §291 et seq.; Art V, §21; Title 74, §291.2 et seq.; Legislative Compensation Board
Oregon	Or. Rev. Stat. §171.072
Pennsylvania	Pa. Cons. Stat. Ann. 46 PS §5; 65 PS §366.1 et seq.; Legislators receive annual cost of living increase that is tied to the Consumer Price Index.
Rhode Island	Art. VI, §3
South Carolina	S.C. Code Ann. 2-3-20 and the annual General Appropriations Act
South Dakota	Art. III, §6 and Art. XXI, §2; S.D. Codified Laws Ann. §20402 et seq.
Tennessee	Art. II, §23; Tenn. Code Ann. §3-1-106 et seq.
Texas	Art. III, §24; In 1991, a constitutional amendment was approved by voters to allow Ethics Commission to recommend the salaries of members. Any recommendations must be approved by voters to be effective. The provision has yet to be used.
Utah	Art. VI, §9; Utah Code Ann. §36-2-2, et seq.
Vermont	Vt. Stat. Ann. title 32, §1051 and §1052
Virginia	Art. IV, §5; Va. Code Ann. §30-19.11 thru §30-19.14
Washington	Article II §§23 and 43.03.060, Washington Rev. Code Ann. §43.03.028. The salary commission sets salaries of the legislature and other state officials based on market study and input from citizens.
West Virginia	Art. 6, §33; W. Va. Code §4-2A-1 et seq.; Submits by resolution and must be concurred by at least four members of the commission. The Legislature must enact the resolution into law and may reduce, but shall not increase, any item established in such resolution.
Wisconsin	Wisconsin Statutes §§20.923 and 230.12, created by Chapter 90, Laws of 1973, and amended by 1983 Wisconsin Acts 27 and 33. Generally, compensation is determined as part of the state compensation plan for non-represented employees and is approved by vote of the joint committee on employment relations.
Wyoming	Wyo. Stat. §28-5-101 thru §28-5-105

Source: National Conference of State Legislatures 2016.

TABLE 3.9
Legislative Compensation and Living Expense Allowances During Sessions, 2020

State	Salaries			Mileage cents per mile	Session per diem rate
	Regular sessions				
	Per diem salary	Limit on days	Annual salary		
Alabama	...	...	$49,861	57.5/mile.	For overnight stays: $85/d. For two or more days with overnight stays: $100/d.
Alaska	...	...	$50,400	57.5/mile.	$287/d.
Arizona	...	...	$24,000	57.5/mile.	For legislators residing within Maricopa County: $35/d for the first 120 days of regular and special sessions and $10/d for all following days. For legislators residing outside of Maricopa County: $60/d for the first 120 days of regular and special sessions and $20/d for all following days. Set by statute.
Arkansas	...	...	$42,428	57.5/mile.	For legislators residing within 50 miles of the capitol: $55/d. For legislators residing more than 50 miles from the capitol: $151/d.
California	...	...	$114,877	53/mile.	$206/d.
Colorado	...	...	$40,242 for legislators whose terms commence in or after Jan. 2019; $30,000 for those whose terms began before Jan. 2019.	52/mile.	For legislators residing within 50 miles of the capitol: $45/d. For legislators living more than 50 miles from the capitol: $219/d. Set by the legislature (V).
Connecticut	...	...	$28,000	57.5/mile.	No per diem is paid.
Delaware	...	...	$47,291	40/mile.	No per diem is paid.
Florida	...	...	$29,697	44.5/mile.	$152/d for up to 50 days for senators and up to 60 days for representatives (V).
Georgia	...	...	$17,342	57.5/mile. Tied to federal rate.	$173/d (U). Set by the Legislative Services Committee.
Hawaii	...	...	$62,604	57.5/mile.	For legislators who do not reside on Oahu: $225/d. For legislators living on Oahu during the mandatory five-day recess only: $10/d.
Idaho	...	...	$18,415	57.5/mile.	For legislators residing within 50 miles of the capitol: $71/d. For legislators residing more than 50 miles from the capitol: $139/d.
Illinois	...	...	$69,464	57.5/mile.	$151/d.
Indiana	...	...	$27,204	57.5/mile. Tied to federal rate.	$184/d (U).
Iowa	...	...	$25,000	39/mile.	$169/d (U).
Kansas	$88.66/d (C)	...	...	57.5/mile. One round trip per week.	$151/d.
Kentucky	$188/d	...	...	57.5/mile. Tied to federal rate.	$166/d.
Louisiana	...	...	"$22,800 for senators; $16,800 for representatives."	57.5/mile. Tied to federal rate.	$161/d (U). Tied to federal rate.
Maine	...	...	$14,862 for the first regular session. $10,582 for the second regular session	44/mile.	$38/d lodging (or mileage and tolls up to $38/d in lieu of housing). $32/d meals. Set by statute.
Maryland	...	...	$50,330	57.5/mile. Legislators receive $750/y as taxable income for in-district travel, but they may decline the allowance.	$109/d for lodging. $56/d for meals.
Massachusetts	...	...	$66,256	No mileage reimbursement. Legislators residing within 50 miles of the statehouse receive an office expense stipend of $16,248 that can be used for travel expenses. Legislators residing more than 50 miles from the statehouse receive $21,664.	No per diem is paid. Legislators residing within 50 miles of the statehouse receive an office expense stipend of $16,248 that can be used for travel expenses. Legislators residing more than 50 miles from the statehouse receive $21,664.
Michigan	...	...	$71,685	57.5/mile.	No per diem is paid. Legislators receive an expense allowance of $10,800/y for session and interim (V). Set by the compensation commison.
Minnesota	...	...	$46,500	57.5/mile. One round trip per week. Tied to federal rate.	$86/d for senators; $66/d for representatives.
Mississippi	...	...	$23,500	57.5/mile.	$151/d (U). Tied to federal rate.
Missouri	...	...	$35,915	43/mile.	$121/d (U). Tied to federal rate.
Montana	$92.46 (L)	...	...	57.5/mile. Tied to federal rate.	$120.11/d

See footnotes at end of table

TABLE 3.9
Legislative Compensation and Living Expense Allowances During Sessions, 2020 (continued)

State	Salaries			Mileage cents per mile	Session per diem rate
	Regular sessions				
	Per diem salary	Limit on days	Annual salary		
Nebraska	...	...	$12,000	57.5/mile. Tied to federal rate.	For legislators residing within 50 miles of the capitol: $55/d. For legislators residing more than 50 miles from the capitol: $151/d.
Nevada	$164.69/d (C). Senators who are not up for reelection until 2022 receive $159.89/d (C).	Up to 60 days.	...	57.5/mile. Tied to federal rate.	$151/d.
New Hampshire	...		$100	57.5/mile. Tied to federal rate. Legislators can instead choose the state mileage reimbursement option, which is 38/mile for the first 45 miles, and 19/mile thereafter. With this alternative method, the reimbursement is taxed as income, and legislators do no need to drive their personal vehicle.	No per diem is paid.
New Jersey	...	...	$49,000	No mileage reimbursement.	No per diem is paid.
New Mexico	...	...	$0	57.5/mile. Tied to federal rate.	$192/d (V). Tied to federal rate.
New York	...	...	$110,000	57.5//mile. Tied to federal rate.	For non-overnight travel: $61/d. For overnight stays: $176/d.
North Carolina	...	...	$13,951	29/mile. One roundtrip per week.	$104/d (U). Set by statute.
North Dakota			$505/m until July 1, 2020. $515/m after July 1, 2020.	57.5/mile. Tied to federal rate.	$181/d until July 1, 2020. $186/d after July 1, 2020.
Ohio	...	...	$65,528	52/mile for legislators living outside Franklin County.	No per diem is paid.
Oklahoma	...	...	$35,021	57.5/mile. Tied to federal rate.	$166/d (U). Tied to federal rate.
Oregon	...	...	$31,200	57.5/mile	$151/d.
Pennsylvania	...	...	$90,335	57.5/mile.	$178/d.
Rhode Island	...	...	$15,959	57.5/mile.	No per diem is paid.
South Carolina	...	...	$10,400	58/mile. Tied to federal rate.	$140/d.
South Dakota			$11,892	One trip is paid at 5/mile, and the remaining are paid at 42/mile. One round trip per week.	$151/d (L) (U).
Tennessee	...	...	$24,316	47/mile.	For legislators residing within 50 miles of the capitol: $61/d. For legislators residing more than 50 miles from the capitol: $284/d (U). Tied to federal rate.
Texas	...	...	$7,200	50/mile. $1.21/mile for single, twin and turbo engine airplanes. Set by general appropriations bill.	$221/d (U). Set by ethics commission.
Utah	$393/d (C)	...	...	57/mile.	No per diem is paid. Legislators residing more than 100 miles from the capitol can receive expense reimbursement for meals and lodging.
Vermont	...	...	$742.92/w during session.	57.5/mile. Tied to federal rate.	$132/d lodging. $66/d for meals.
Virginia	...	...	$18,000 for senators; $17,640 for delegates.	57.5/mile.	$210/d.
Washington	...	...	$48,731	57.5/mile.	$120/d.
West Virginia	...	...	$20,000	48.5/mile.	$131/d (U). Set by compensation commission.
Wisconsin	...	...	$52,999	51/mile. One roundtrip per week.	"$115/d for senators. $162 (with overnight) for $81/d (no overnight) for representatives. Per diem can be claimed up to 90 days per year. "
Wyoming	$150/d	...	...	57.5/mile.	$109/d (V). Set by legislature.

Source: National Conference of State Legislatures, 2020.
Key:
C – Calendar day
L – Legislative day

(U) – Unvouchered
(V) – Vouchered
... – Not applicable

TABLE 3.10
Legislative Compensation: Other Payments and Benefits

State	Legislator's compensation for office supplies, district offices and staffing	Insurance benefits				
		Health	Dental	Vision	Disability insurance	Life insurance benefits
Alabama	None	S.A.	S.A.	S.A.	None	None
Alaska	$20,000/y Senators. $12,000/y Representatives for postage, stationery and other legislative expenses. Staffing allowance determined by rules and presiding officers, depending on time of year.	S.A.	S.A.	S.A.	S.A.	S.A.
Arizona	None	S.A., S.P.P.	S.A., O.P.	S.A., O.P.	S.P.P.	S.P.P.
Arkansas	Up to $3,600/y additional reimbursement for committee chairs, vice chairs and standing subcommittee chairs.	S.A.	S.A.	S.A.	S.A.	S.A.
California	Senate member expenses are paid directly and maintained by the Senate Rules Committee. Assembly member expenses are paid directly and maintained by the Assembly Rules Committee.	S.A., S.P.P.	(a)	(a)	Senators are covered by a long-term disability insurance policy; Assembly members do not have disability insurance coverage.	Senators are eligible for up to $250,000 term coverage: members pay 10% of the age-based premium plus the taxable value on coverage above $50,000. $250,000 term policy for the Assembly: members pay the taxable value on coverage above $50,000.
Colorado	None	S.A., S.P.P.– Amount differs according to plan selected	S.A., S.P.P.– Amount differs according to plan selected	(b)	None	S.A. State pays full amount for $50,000 policy. Additional is optional at legislator's expense.
Connecticut	$5,500 senators. $4,500 representatives.	S.P.P.	S.P.P.	Some health insurance plans include discounts on eyewear.	S.A., O.P.	S.A., O.P.
Delaware	None	S.A.	S.A.	S.A.	S.A.	S.A.
Florida	$44,452/y Senate district office expenses. $39,534/y House district office expenses.	S.A.	S.A.	S.A., O.P.	S.P.	S.A. State pays for $25,000 coverage.
Georgia	None	S.A.	S.A.	S.A.	S.A.	S.A.
Hawaii	Members receive $13,804/y for legislative related expenses, including office supplies, postage, official travel etc.	S.A. (e)	S.A. (c)	S.A. (c)	None	S.A., S.P.
Idaho	$2,500/y for unvouchered constituent expense.	S.A., S.P.P.	S.A., S.P.P.	S.A., S.P.P.	S.A., S.P.P.	S.A., S.P.P.
Illinois	$69,409/y for office expenses, including district offices and staffing.	S.A.	S.A.	S.A.	S.A.	S.A.
Indiana	None	S.A.	S.A.	S.A.	S.A.	S.A.
Iowa	$300/m district constituency postage, travel, telephone and other expenses.	S.A.	S.A.	S.A.	S.A.	S.A
Kansas	$7,083/y. Staffing allowances vary for leadership.	S.A.	S.A.	S.A.	S.A.	S.A.
Kentucky	$1,789/y district expenses during interim.	S.A.	S.A.	S.A.	None	S.A.
Louisiana	$2,000/m supplemental allowance for vouchered office expenses, rent and travel mileage in district. Newly elected members receive $2,000 for office furniture allowance and $500 upon each re-election. Staff allowance based on promotional grade, beginning at $27,300/y.	S.A., S.P.P.	S.A.–legislator pays 100%.	S.A.–legislator pays 100%.	O.P.–legislator pays 100%	O.P.–legislator pays 100%
Maine	None. However, supplies for staff offices are provided and paid for out of general legislative account.	S.A.–State pays up to 100% of legislator coverage and 50% of dependent coverage.	S.A., S.P.	O.P.	None	O.P.

See footnotes at end of table

TABLE 3.10
Legislative Compensation: Other Payments and Benefits (continued)

State	Legislator's compensation for office supplies, district offices and staffing	Insurance benefits				
		Health	Dental	Vision	Disability insurance	Life insurance benefits
Maryland	Senate–$45,165/y plus one institutionally compensated legislative aide. House–$54,732/y.	S.A.	S.A.	S.A.	S.A.	S.A.
Massachusetts	$16,248/y office stipend for legislators who live 50 miles or less from the statehouse; $21,664/y for members who live more than 50 miles from the statehouse.	S.A.	S.A.	S.A.	S.A.	S.A.
Michigan	Senate–No response House–$104,000/y office allowance per maj. member. $101,000/y office allowance per min. member.		No response		No response	No response
Minnesota	$2,112/y postage allotment. No allowance for district offices.	S.A.	S.A.	None	S.A.	S.A.
Mississippi	None		S.A.	O.P.	O.P.	O.P.	S.A., S.P.P.–State pays 50% and legislator pays 50%.
Missouri	$94,464/y for staff salaries. $24,100/y for mailings, travel, supplies and other office expenses.	S.A.	S.A.	S.A.	S.A.	S.A.
Montana	$1,500/y for constituent services.	S.A.	S.A.	S.A.	None	S.A.
Nebraska	None	O.P.	S.A., O.P.	S.A., O.P.	S.A., O.P.	S.A., O.P.
Nevada	None	S.A., O.P.	S.A., O.P.	S.A., O.P.	None	S.A., O.P.
New Hampshire	None	S.A., O.P.	S.A., O.P.	S.A., O.P.	None	
New Jersey	$135,000/y district office personnel. State provides stationery for each legislator and 10,000 postage stamps.	S.A. (d)	S.A. (d)	S.A. (d)	Permanent disability available if enrolled in pension plan.	Members enrolled in the pension plan–up to three times annual salary. Members enrolled in defined contribution plan–one and a half times annual salary. Members not covered by either plan–no death benefit.
New Mexico	None	S.A., O.P.	S.A., O.P.	S.A., O.P.	None	S.A., O.P.
New York	No response	No response	No response	No response	No response	No response
North Carolina	$2,275 per biennium for office expenses. No staffing allowance.	S.A.	S.A.	S.A.	S.A., O.P.	S.A.
North Dakota	None	S.A., S.P.	S.A.–premium paid by legislator.	S.A.–premium paid by legislator.	None	S.A. State pays for $7,000 term life policy.
Ohio	None	S.A.	S.A.	S.A.	S.A.	S.A.
Oklahoma	$2,000/y for office supplies and expense.	S.A.		S.A.		S.A.
Oregon	$65,939 per biennium for interim expenses. $56,008 session staffing. $4,880 for session services and supplies.	S.A., S.P.P.	S.A., S.P.P.	S.A., S.P.P.	S.A., O.P.	S.A., O.P.
Pennsylvania	$20,000 per fiscal year for office expenses. Staffing is determined by leadership.	(e)	(e)	(e)	None	S.A.
Rhode Island	None	S.A.	S.A.	S.A.	None	None
South Carolina	$1,000/m each member district expenses.	S.A.	S.A.	S.A.	S.A.	S.A.
South Dakota	None	None	None	None	S.P.–accidental death/ dismemberment ins. only.	None
Tennessee	$1,000/m expenses in district.	S.A.	S.A.	S.A.	None	S.A. State pays first $35,000 of the basic life insurance; remainder paid by legislator.
Texas	No response	No response	No response	No response	No response	No response
Utah	None	S.A., S.P.P.	S.A., S.P.P.	S.A.	S.A., S.P.	S.A., S.P.–State pays full premium for $25,000 basic term life coverage.
Vermont	No response	No response	No response	No response	No response	No response

See footnotes at end of table

TABLE 3.10

Legislative Compensation: Other Payments and Benefits (continued)

State	Legislator's compensation for office supplies, district offices and staffing	Insurance benefits				
		Health	Dental	Vision	Disability insurance	Life insurance benefits
Virginia	Leaders: $78,668/y staffing allowance. $1,750/m office expense allowance. Legislators: $57,783/y staffing allowance. $1,250/m office expense allowance.	S.A., S.P.P.	S.A.	S.A., O.P.	None	S.A., S.P.–The state pays for basic group life insurance. Optional Life Insurance (up to 4x salary) available at legislator's expense.
Washington	$9,000/y for legislative expenses, for which the legislator has not been other-wise entitled to reimbursement. No staffing allowance.	S.A.	S.A.	Included in health coverage.	S.A., S.P.P.	S.A., S.P.P.
West Virginia	None	O.P.	O.P.	O.P.	None	S.A., O.P.
Wisconsin	Senate: $223,650 per biennium staffing allowance. $55,955 per biennium office expenses. Assembly: $20,000 per biennium session office expenses.	S.A.	S.A.	S.A.	S.A.	S.A.
Wyoming	$750/quarter through constituent service allowance.	None	None	None	None	None

Source: National Conference of State Legislatures, 2019.
Key:
(U)–Unvouchered.
(V)–Vouchered.
d–day.
m–month.
w–week.
y–year.
O.P.–Optional at legislator's expense.
S.A.–Same as state employees.
S.P.–State pays full amount.
S.P.P.–State pays portion and legislator pays portion.

(a) California: State pays for basic plan; enhanced coverage is available at an additional cost to member.
(b) Colorado: Vision is part of health coverage without extra cost.
(c) Hawaii: Several plans are available with differing employee contribution rates and copayments.
(d) New Jersey: Members appointed or elected after 5/21/10 must pay full cost of coverage.
(e) Pennsylvania: Legislators pay 1% of salary toward medical/hospital, dental, vision and prescription benefits.

TABLE 3.11
Additional Compensation for Senate Leaders

State	Presiding officer	Majority leader	Minority leader	Other leaders and committee chairs
Alabama	Lt. gov. holds this position.	None	None	None
Alaska	$500/y	None	None	None
Arizona	(a)	(a)	(a)	None
Arkansas	Lt. gov. holds this position.	None	None	$5,600/y pres. pro tem.
California	Lt. gov. holds this position.	None	None	None
Colorado	(b)	(b)	(b)	(b)
Connecticut	Lt. gov. holds this position.	$8,835/y	$8,835/y	Leaders: $10,689/y pres. pro tem. $6,446/y each for dep. maj. ldrs, dep. min. ldrs. $4,241/y each for asst. maj. ldrs., asst. min. ldrs., maj. whips, min. whips. Committee chairs: $4,241/y.
Delaware	Lt. gov. holds this position.	$12,376/y	$12,376/y	Leaders: $19,983/y pres. pro tem. $7,794/y each for maj. whips, min. whips. Committee chairs: $11,459/y each for joint fin. Chair and vice chair. $4,578/y each for capital improvement chair and vice chair.
Florida	$11,484/year	None	None	None
Georgia	Lt. gov. holds this position.	$200/m	$200/m	Leaders: $400/m pres. pro tem. $100 floor leaders. Committee chairs: None.
Hawaii	$7,500/y	None	None	None
Idaho	$5,000/y	$2,000	$2,000	None
Illinois	$27,477/y	$20,649/y	$27,477/y	Leaders: $20,649/y each for asst. maj. ldrs., asst. min. ldrs., maj. caucus chairs, min. caucus chairs. Committee chairs: $10,327/y.
Indiana	Lt. gov. holds this position.	$5,500/y for maj. flr. leader	$6,000/y min. flr. leader	Leaders: $7,000/y pres. pro tem. $5,500/y maj. caucus chair. $4,000/y for majority whip. $2,000/y for minority whip. Committee Chairs: $1,000/y for each chair.
Iowa	$12,500/y	$12,500/y	$12,500/y	Leaders: $2,000/y pres. pro tem. Committee chairs: None.
Kansas	$14,039/y	$12,665/y	$12,665/y	Leaders: $7,165/y each for vice pres., asst. maj. ldrs, asst. min. ldrs. Committee chairs: $11,290/y w&m chair.
Kentucky	$47.35/d	$37.40/d	$37.40/d	Leaders: $28.66/d each for maj. caucus chairs, min. caucus chairs, maj. caucus whips, min. caucus whips. Committee chairs: $18.71/d.
Louisiana	$15,200/y	None	None	Leaders: $7,700/y pres. pro tem. Committee chairs: $15,200/y joint budget chair.
Maine	50% of base salary/y	25% of base salary/y	12.5% of base salary/y	None
Maryland	$15,041/y	None	None	None
Massachusetts	$86,656/y	$64,992/y	$64,992/y	Leaders: $54,160/y for pres. pro tem, $37,912/y for asst. maj. ldrs and asst. min. ldrs. Committee leaders: $70,408/y w&m chair. $32,496/y division chairs. $16,248/y for all other chairs. $5,633/y vice chairs.
Michigan	Lt. gov. holds this position.	$23,400/y	$19,800/y	Leaders: $10,800/y for maj. flr. ldr., $9,000/y for min. flr. ldr. Committee chairs: $6,300/y for app. cmte. chairs.
Minnesota	$3,600/y	$18,000/y	$18,000/y	Leaders: $3,600/y deputy ldrs. Committee chairs: $3,600/y fin. chair and tax chair.
Mississippi	$5,000/m	None	None	$1,250/m pres. pro tem
Missouri	Lt. gov. holds this position.	$1,500	$1,500	Leaders: $2,500 for pres. pro tem.
Montana	$5/d during session	None	None	None
Nebraska	Lt. gov. holds this position.	None	None	None
Nevada	Lt. gov. holds this position.	None	None	None
New Hampshire	$50/2-y term	None	None	None
New Jersey	$16,333	None	None	None
New Mexico	Lt. gov. holds this position.	None	None	None
New York	No Response	No Response	No Response	No Response
North Carolina	Lt. gov. holds this position.	$3,097/y	$3,097/y	Leaders: $24,200/year pres. pro tem. $7,788/year deputy pres. pro tem.
North Dakota	Lt. gov. holds this position.	$15/d during legislative sessions.	$15/d during legislative sessions.	Leaders: $10/d during session asst. ldrs. Committee chairs: $10/d all standing cmtes.

See footnotes at end of table

TABLE 3.11
Additional Compensation for Senate Leaders (continued)

State	Presiding officer	Majority leader	Minority leader	Other leaders and committee chairs
Ohio	$35,207/y	None	$26,605/y	Leaders: $26,605/y pres. pro tem. $21,403/y asst. pres. pro tem. $16,209 maj. whip. $18,808/y asst. min ldr. $11,013/y min whip. $2,909/y asst. min. whip. Committee chairs: $13,500/y fin. chair. $9,000/y each for fin. ranking min. member, fin. cmte standing subcmte chair, all other standing cmte chairs. $7,500/y fin. vice chair. $6,750/y each for ranking min. member fin. standing subcmte, vice chairs, ranking min. members, standing subcmte chairs. $3,250/y standing subcmte ranking min. members.
Oklahoma	No Response	No Response	No Response	No Response
Oregon	$2,600/month	None	None	None
Pennsylvania	Lt. gov. holds this position.	$39,745/year	$39,745/year	Leaders: $49,716/y pres. pro tem. $30,186/y maj. whips, min. whips. $12,430/y each for maj. caucus secretaries, min. caucus secretaries, maj. policy chairs, min. policy chairs, maj. caucus admin., min. caucus admin. Committee chairs: $30,186/y each for maj. app. chair, min. app. chair. $18,832/y each for maj. caucus chair, min. caucus chair.
Rhode Island	$15,959/y	None	None	None
South Carolina	Lt. gov. holds this position	None	None	Leaders: $11,000/y pres. pro tem. Committee Chairs: $600/y
South Dakota	Lt. gov. holds this position.	None	None	None
Tennessee	None	None	None	None
Texas	No Response	No Response	No Response	No Response
Utah	$5,000/y	$4,000/y	$4,000/y	Leaders: $3,000/y each for maj. whips, min. whips, asst. maj. whips, asst. min. whips. Committee leaders: $3,000/y app. chair.
Vermont	Lt. gov. holds this position.	None	None	Leaders: $482.50 bi-weekly pres. pro tem.
Virginia	None	None	None	None
Washington	Lt. gov. holds this position	$9,259/y	$4,629/y	None
West Virginia	$150/d during session.	$50/d during session	$50/d during session	Leaders: $150/d (up to 30 days) for a maximum of six add'l persons named by presiding officer. Committee chairs: $150.00/d (up to 30 days) fin. & judiciary chairs.
Wisconsin	None	None	None	None
Wyoming	$3/day	None	None	None

Source: National Conference of State Legislatures, 2019.
Key:
d–day
m–month
w–week
y–year

app.– Appropriations
w&m–Ways and means
Lt. gov.–lieutenant governor who is not a member of the Senate.
(a) Arizona. Generally approved for additional interim per diem.
(b) Colorado. All leaders receive $99/d salary during interim when in attendance at committee or leadership matters.

TABLE 3.12
Additional Compensation for House/Assembly Leaders

State	Presiding officer	Majority leader	Minority leader	Other leaders and committee chairs
Alabama	$18,000/y	None	None	None
Alaska	$500/y	None	None	None
Arizona	(a)	(a)	(a)	(a)
Arkansas	$5,883/y	None	None	None
California	$16,567/y	$8,284/y	$16,567/y	Leaders: $8.284/y second ranking min. ldr. Committee chairs: None.
Colorado	(b)	(b)	(b)	(b)
Connecticut	$10,689/y	$8,835/y	$8,835/y	Leaders: $6,446/y each for dep. spkr., dep. maj. ldrs., min. ldrs., asst. maj. ldrs., asst. min. ldrs. $4,241/y each for maj. whips, min. whips. Committee chairs: $4,241/y
Delaware	$19,893/y	$12,376/y	$12,376/y	Leaders: $7,794/y each for maj. whips, min. whips. Committee chairs: $11,459/y each for joint fin. Chair and vice chair. $4,578/y each for capital improvement chair and vice chair.
Florida	$11,484/y	None	None	None
Georgia	$6,811/m	$200/m	$200/m	Leaders: $400/m for spkr. pro tem. $100/m for gov.'s floor ldr. $100/m for asst. floor ldr. Committee chairs: None.
Hawaii	$7,500/y	None	None	None
Idaho	$5,000/y	$2,000	$2,000	None
Illinois	$27,477/y	$23,230/y	$27,277/y	Leaders: $19,791/y each for dep. maj. ldrs., dep. min. ldrs. $18,067/y each for asst. maj. ldrs., asst. min. ldrs and maj. conference chair. Committee chairs: $10,327/y each for chairs.
Indiana	No Response	No Response	No Response	No Response
Iowa	$12,500/y	$12,500/y	$12,500/y	Leaders: $2,000/y spkr. pro tem. Committee chairs: None.
Kansas	$14,039/y	$12,665/y	$12,665/y	Leaders: $7,165/y each for spkr. pro tem, asst. maj. ldrs., asst. min. ldrs. Committee chairs: $11,290/y app. chair.
Kentucky	$47.35/d	$37.40/d	$37.40/d	Leaders: $28.66/d each for maj. caucus chairs & whips, min. caucus chairs & whips. Committee chairs: $18.71/d.
Louisiana	$15,200/y	None	None	Leaders: $13,700/y spkr. pro tem.
Maine	50% of base salary	25% of base salary	12.5% of base salary	None
Maryland	$15,041/y	None	None	None
Massachusetts	$86,656/y	$64,992/y	$64,992/y	Leaders: $54,160/y for spkr. pro tem, $37,912/y for asst. maj. ldrs and asst. min. ldrs. Committee leaders: $70,408/y w&m chair. $32,496/y division chairs. $16,248/y for all other chairs. $5,633/y vice chairs.
Michigan	$24,300/y	None	$19,800/y	Leaders: $10,800/y for maj. floor ldr., $9,000/y for min. flr. ldr., $4,962/y for spkr. pro tem. Committee chairs: $6,300/y for app. cmte. chairs.
Minnesota	$18,000/y	$18,000/y	$18,000/y	None
Mississippi	No Response	No Response	No Response	No Response
Missouri	$2,500/y	$1,500/y	$1,500/y	None
Montana	$5/d during session	None	None	None
Nebraska	--N/A–Unicameral legislature--------------------------------------			
Nevada	$2/d during session	None	None	None.
New Hampshire	$50/2-y term.	None	None	None
New Jersey	$16,333	None	None	None
New Mexico	None	None	None	None
New York	No Response	No Response	No Response	No Response
North Carolina	$24,200/y	$3,097/y	$3,097/y	Leaders: $7,788/y spkr. pro tem.
North Dakota	$15/d during session	$15/d during session	$15/d during session	Leaders: $10/d for asst. ldrs. during session. Committee chairs: $10/d for all standing cmtes.
Ohio	$35,207/y	$21,403/y maj. flr. ldr.	$26,605/y	Leaders: $26,605/y spkr. pro tem. $16,209/y asst. maj. floor ldr. $11,013/y maj. whip. $5,815/y asst. maj. whip. $18,808/y asst. min. floor ldr. $11,013 min. whip. $2,909/y asst. min. whip. Committee chairs: $13,500/y fin. chair. $9,000/y each for fin. ranking min. member, fin. cmte standing subcmte chair, all other standing cmte chairs. $7,500/y fin. vice chair. $6,750/y each for ranking min. member fin. standing subcmte, vice chairs, ranking min. members, standing subcmte chairs. $3,250/y standing subcmte ranking min. members.
Oklahoma	$16,354/y	$11,276/y	$11,276/y	Committee chairs: $11,276/y each for app. chair, budget chair.
Oregon	$2,600/m	None	None	None
Pennsylvania	No Response	No Response	No Response	No Response
Rhode Island	$15,959/y	None	None	None
South Carolina	$11,000/y	None	None	Leaders: $3,600/y spkr. pro tem. Committee Chairs: $650/y
South Dakota	None	None	None	None

See footnotes at end of table

TABLE 3.12
Additional Compensation for House/Assembly Leaders (continued)

State	Presiding officer	Majority leader	Minority leader	Other leaders and committee chairs
Tennessee	$48,632/y	None	None	None
Texas	No Response	No Response	No Response	No Response
Utah	$5,000/y	$4,000/y	$4,000/y	Leaders: $3,000/y each for whips, asst. whips, minority caucus leaders and executive app. chair.
Vermont	$482.50 bi-weekly.	None	None	None
Virginia	$18,681/y	None	None	None
Washington	$9,259/y; $8,000/y eff. 7/1/2019.	None	$4,629/y; $4,000/y eff. 7/1/2019.	None
West Virginia	$150/d during session.	$50/d during session	$50/d during session	Leaders: $150/d (up to 30 days) for a maximum of six add'l persons named by presiding officer. Committee chairs: $150.00/d (up to 30 days) fin. & judiciary chairs.
Wisconsin	$25/m	None	None	None
Wyoming	$3/d	None	None	None

Source: National Conference of State Legislatures, 2019.
Key:
d–day.
m–month.
w–week.
y–year.

app.–Appropriations
w&m–Ways and means
(a) Arizona. Generally approved for additional interim per diem.
(b) Colorado. All leaders receive $99/d salary during interim when in attendance at committee or leadership matters.

TABLE 3.13
State Legislative Retirement Benefits

State	Participation	Requirements for regular retirement	Employee contribution rate	Benefit formula
Alabama	None available.			
Alaska	Optional	Four tiers. Varies depending upon tier. Detailed information set forth in Public Employees' Retirement System (PERS) plan comparison chart.	Four tiers. Varies depending upon tier. Detailed information set forth in Public Employees' Retirement System (PERS) plan comparison chart.	Four tiers. Varies depending upon tier. Detailed information set forth in Public Employees' Retirement System (PERS) plan comparison chart.
Arizona	Mandatory	No requirements, same as other federal qualified defined contribution plans.	Employee: 8%; Employer: 6%	2016 information: 4% x years of credited service x highest 3 yr. average in the past 10 years The benefit is capped at 80% of FAS. An elected official may purchase service credit in the plan for service earned in a non-elected position by buying it at an actuarially determined amount. AZ SB 1609 of 2011–For those elected to office after 1/1/2012: 3% x years of credited service x highest 5 yr. average in the past 10 years The benefit is capped at 75% of FAS.
Arkansas	Mandatory for those legislators first elected in 2003 or after. Optional for those elected before 2003.	Age 65 with 10 years of service; 55/12; any age with 28 years of service; any age if serving in the General Assembly on 7/1/79; any age if in elected office on 7/1/79 with 17½ years of service. As a regular employee, 65/5 or any age/28 years. Members of the contributory plan established in 2005 must have a minimum of 10 years legislative service if they have only legislative state employment.	Members pay 5%, state pays 15.32%	(Years of service) x (Final Average Compensation–high 3 years) x (Multiplier–2.00 for contributory members; 1.75 for service rendered prior to 7/1/07 and 1.72 for service after 7/1/07 for non-contributory members) = Retirement Annual Benefit
California	Legislators elected after 1990 are not eligible for retirement benefits for legislative service.			
Colorado	Mandatory	PERA: age 65 with 5 years of service; age 55 with 35 years of service; when age + service equals 85 or more (min. age of 55). State Defined Contribution Plan (DCP): no age requirement and immediate vesting.	Employee: 8% (inc. to 10% by 7/1/21)	PERA: 2.5% x FAS x years of service, capped at 100% of FAS. DCP benefit depends upon contributions and investment return.
Connecticut	Mandatory	Age 60 with 25 years credited service; age 62 with 10–25 years credited service; age 62 with 5 years actual state service. If elected after 2011–age 63 with 25 years of vesting service or age 65 with 10–25 years of vesting service. Reduced benefit available with earlier retirement ages.	Employee 2%	(1.33% x average annual salary) + (5% x average salary over "breakpoint") x credited service up to 35 years; 2003–$36,400; 2004–$38,600; 2005–$40,900; 2006–$43,400; 2007–$46,000; 2008–$48,800; 2009–$51,700. After 2009–increase breakpoint by 6% per year rounded to nearest $100.
Delaware	Mandatory. DE HB 81 of 2011–Mandatory for those elected after January 1, 2012.	Elected before 2012–Age 60 with 5 years of credited service; or 55 with 10 years of service. Elected after 2012–65 with 10 years of service; or 60 with 20 years of service. Vesting at 10 years.	Elected before 2012–3% of annual compensation in excess of $6,000. Elected after 2012–5% of annual compensation in excess of $6,000.	2% x FAS x years of service before 1997 + 1.85% times FAS times years of service from 1997 on. FAS = average of highest 3 years.
Florida	Optional.	DB Plan: Six to eight years to vest depending on the start date of service: Retirement at age 62 with at least 6 service years or 30 years of service regardless of age; or, Retirement at age 65 with at least 8 service years or 33 years of service regardless of age. DC Plan: One year to vest, retirement at any age.	Legislator contribution is 3%; employer contribution is 56.75%	DB plan–3% x years of creditable service x average final compensation (average of highest 5 years). DC plan–dependent upon investment experience.
Georgia	Optional.	Vested after 8 years. Age 62 with 8 years of service; age 60 with reduction for early retirement.	Employee: 3.75% + $7/m.	$36/month for each year of service.
Hawaii	Optional	Age 60 and 10 years service for normal retirement.	9.8% of monthly base salary.	3% x years of service x average final compensation.

See footnotes at end of table

TABLE 3.13
State Legislative Retirement Benefits (continued)

State	Participation	Requirements for regular retirement	Employee contribution rate	Benefit formula
Idaho	Mandatory; same plan as public employees (PERSI) except legislators are automatically vested.	Age 65 with 5 years of service; reduced benefit at age 55 with 5 years of service.	7.16% paid by member, 11.94% paid by employer.	Average monthly salary for highest 42 consecutive months x 2% x months of credited service.
Illinois	Optional; not the same as the State Employees' Retirement System. Only state senators, representatives and statewide elected officials have the option to participate.	Tier 1–age 55 with 8 years of service or age 62 with 4 years of service. Tier 2–age 67 with 8 years of service or age 62 with 8 years of service reduced ½ of 1% for each month.	11.5% of salary (includes contributions for retirement annuity and survivors annuity) or 9.5% of salary as contributions for just retirement annuity (no survivor annuity).	First 4 yrs x 3.0% = 12%; next 2 yrs x 3.5% = 7.0%; next 2 yrs x 4.0% = 8.0%; next 4 yrs x 4.5% = 18.0%; next 8 yrs x 5.0% = 40.0%
Indiana	Mandatory	Age 65 with 10 years of service; age 60 with at least 15 years of service or at least age 55 and years of service plus age equal at least 85. Reduced benefits available for those age 55 with at least 10 years of service.	5% paid by legislator, 7% paid by state contribution.	DB plan–monthly benefit: Lesser of (a) $40 x years of General Assembly service completed before 11/8/89; or (b) 1/12 of the average of the three highest consecutive years of General Assembly service salary. DC plan–numerous options for withdrawing accumulations in accord with IRS regulations. Loans are available. A participant in both plans may receive a benefit from both plans.
Iowa	Optional. Same as state employees plan (IPERS).	Age 65; age 62 with 20 years of service; Rule of 88; age 55 with reduced benefits.	6.29% paid by legislator, 9.44% paid by state.	2% x FAS. x years of service for first 30 years, + 1% x FAS x years in excess of 30 but no more than 5 in excess of 30. FAS is average of 3 highest years taken at June 2012, or average of 5 highest years.
Kansas	Legislators may elect to join the state retirement program unless they have already retired from state employment. Those individuals receive an 8% of income deposit by the state into a deferred compensation plan.	2016 info–Age 65; age 62 with 5 years of service, or when age plus years of service equals 85.	6% of the annualized salary.	2016 information–3 highest years x 1.75% x years of service ÷ 12= monthly benefit.
Kentucky	Optional. Those who opt out are covered by the state employees' plan. Legislators who were first elected prior to 1/1/2014 are eligible for the DB plan. Legislators first elected after 1/1/14 are eligible for the hybrid plan.	DB Plan: Vesting after 5 years of legislative service of 8 years of state governmental service. Age 65 for normal retirement benefits. Hybrid Plan: Age 65 with 5 years of active service credit or age 57 with 30 years of service.	DB Plan: Members electing to participate in the plan prior to 9/1/2008 contribute 5% of creditable compensation. Members electing to participate in the plan on or after 9/1/2008 contribute 6% of creditable compensation. Hybrid Plan: Members contribute 6% of creditable compensation, employer contributes 4%.	DB Plan: Final compensation x service credit rate x years of service. Final compensation is calculated as the average of the member's three highest years of legislative creditable compensation. Hybrid Plan: Multiple options available. Primary option is to receive monthly allowance payable for life by having accumulated account balance annuitized.
Louisiana	Not available			
Maine	Mandatory	Age 60 if 10 years of service on 7/1/93; age 62 if less than 10 years of service on 7/1/93. Reduced benefit available for earlier retirement.	7.65% legislators; employer contribution is actuarially determined.	2% of average final compensation (the average of the 3 high salary years) x years of service.
Maryland	Mandatory	Age 60 with 8 years; age 50 with 8+ years creditable service for early reduced retirement.	7% of annual salary.	2016 info: 3% of legislative salary for each year of service up to 22 years 3 months. Benefits are recalculated when legislative salaries are changed.
Massachusetts	Mandatory unless they are already receiving a pension from the Massachusetts State Employee Retirement System.	Vesting after 10 years. Eligible to retire at age 55 or 60 after 10 years of service depending on their hire date, eligible to retire at any age after 20 years of service.	9%, although some legislators are grandfathered at lower rates.	Age factor x years of creditable service x FAS. FAS is average of highest 60 or 36 months depending on when service began.
Michigan	Optional. Same as state employee retirement plan.	Age 55 with 5 years or when age plus years of service equal 70. Employee contributions are immediately vested. Employer contributions are vested as follows: Zero after one year; 50% after two years; 75% after three years; 100% after four years.	For legislators elected before 3/31/97–7–10% for (DB) plan. Elected after 3/31/97–(DC) plan, the state contributes 4% of salary. Members may contribute up to 3% of salary. The state will match the member's contribution in addition to the state 4% contribution.	Vesting for contributions to 401(k)– 2 years of service vested 50%; 3 years vested 75% and 4 years vested 100%.

See footnotes at end of table

TABLE 3.13
State Legislative Retirement Benefits (continued)

State	Participation	Requirements for regular retirement	Employee contribution rate	Benefit formula
Minnesota	Mandatory. Legislators elected since 1997 participate in a mandatory retirement plan called the Unclassified Plan; it is a defined contribution 401 (a) plan. Legislators elected prior to 1997 participate in the Legislators Plan which was closed to new members at that time; it is a defined benefit pension plan. All members may choose to participate in the Minnesota deferred compensation plan 457 (b).	Legislators Retirement Plan (LRP) before 7/1/97–62 years with 6 years of service and fully vested. LRP members do not have Social Security coverage. Defined Contribution Plan (DCP) since 1997–age 55 and immediate vesting. DCP members have Social Security coverage.	LRP–9%. DCP–5.75% (inc. to 6% 7/1/19) from member, 6% (inc. to 6.25% 7/1/19) from state.	LRP–2.5% x high 5 year average salary x years of service. DCP benefits depend upon contributions and investment return.
Mississippi	Mandatory	Age 60 with 4 or more years of service, or 25 years of service.	Regular–15.75% state, 9.00% member. Supplemental Legislative Retirement Plan–7.40% state, 3.00% member.	Legislators who qualify for regular state retirement benefits also automatically qualify for the legislators' supplemental benefits. Regular–2% x average compensation x years of service up to and including 25 years of service + 2.5% x average compensation x service in excess of 25 years. Average compensation is calculated using the highest 4 years of compensation. Supplement–1% x average compensation x years of legislative service through 25 years + 1.25% x average compensation x years of service in excess of 25.
Missouri	Mandatory. The retirement plan for Legislators is calculated differently from the plan for other state employees.	For those hired on or before 12/31/2010 –vesting at 6 years of service. Age 55; service in three full biennial assemblies (6 years) or Rule of 80. For those entering system after 1/1/2011 –vesting at 6 years of service. Age 62; service in three full biennial assemblies (6 years) or the Rule of 90 with a minimum age of 55.	For those hired on or before 12/31/2010–non-contributory. For those entering system after 1/1/2011–contribution of 4% of salary.	For those hired on or before 12/31/2010 –monthly pay divided by 24 x years of creditable service, capped at 100% of salary. Benefit is adjusted by the percentage increase in pay for an active legislator. For those entering system after 1/1/2011 –no change.
Montana	Optional. Same as state employees retirement plan.	Members hired before 7/1/11– Age 60 with at least 5 years service; age 65 regardless of years of service; or 30 years of service regardless of age. After 7/1/11–vesting at 5 years. Age 65 with 5 years service, or age 70 and in active service.	7.9% employee and 8.67% employer for DB and DC plan.	2016 info: DB plan–Membership Service Factor (see below) x years of Service Credit x HAC. More than 5 years and less than 10 years of membership service–1.5% Less than 30 years of membership service–1.7857% 30 years or more of membership service–2%
Nebraska	None available			
Nevada	Mandatory, but a legislator, within 30 days after he/she is first elected or appointed, may elect not to participate; a decision to terminate participation in the plan cannot be reversed. The legislators' retirement system is separate from the state employee retirement plan.	Must have at least 10 years of service, be age 60, and no longer be a legislator in order to retire without benefit reduction. A legislator who is no longer serving, has at least 10 years of service, but is under the age of 60 can elect to wait to receive his/her benefit until the age of 60 or begin receiving a reduced benefit prior to the age of 60.	15% of session salary.	Number of years (not to exceed 30) x $25 = monthly allowance.
New Hampshire	None available			
New Jersey	Mandatory	Age 60; no minimum service requirement.	7.5%	3% x FAS x years of service. FAS = higher of three highest years or three final years. Benefit is capped at 2/3 of FAS. Other formulas apply if a legislator also has other service covered by the Public Employee Retirement System.
New Mexico	Optional	Age 65 with 5 years of service or at any age with 10 years of legislative service.	$600 per year.	11% of the per diem rate in effect on the first day of the calendar year that the legislator retires x 60 and further multiplied by credited service as a legislator.

See footnotes at end of table

TABLE 3.13
State Legislative Retirement Benefits (continued)

State	Participation	Requirements for regular retirement	Employee contribution rate	Benefit formula
New York	Detailed information set forth in Your Retirement Plan: Legislative and Executive Plan, published by New York State Office of the State Comptroller.	Detailed information set forth in Your Retirement Plan: Legislative and Executive Plan, published by New York State Office of the State Comptroller.	Detailed information set forth in Your Retirement Plan: Legislative and Executive Plan, published by New York State Office of the State Comptroller.	Detailed information set forth in Your Retirement Plan: Legislative and Executive Plan, published by New York State Office of the State Comptroller.
North Carolina	Mandatory	Age 65 with 5 years of service; reduced benefit available at earlier ages.	7%.	Highest annual compensation x 4.02% x years of creditable service.
North Dakota	None available.			
Ohio	Optional. OPERS offers three plans for retirement–the traditional plan (a defined benefit plan); the member directed plan (a defined contribution plan); and the combined plan.	Varies depending upon plan. Detailed information set forth in Legislative Benefits, Privileges, and Restrictions of Office.	Varies depending upon plan. Detailed information set forth in Legislative Benefits, Privileges, and Restrictions of Office.	Varies depending upon plan. Detailed information set forth in Legislative Benefits, Privileges, and Restrictions of Office.
Oklahoma	Mandatory. Same as state employees retirement plan.	Vesting at 8 years. If member joined plan before 11/1/11: Age 62 with 6 years of service. If member joined plan after 11/1/11: Age 65 with 6 years of service. Early retirement with reduced benefits at age 55 or 60 with 10 years of service.	3.5% of total compensation.	2% FAS x total years of service. FAS = average of 3 or 5, depending on when member joined plan, highest years of last 10.
Oregon	Optional	OPSRP for general service members is age 65, or age 58 with 30 years of retirement credit. Tier 2–60 years or 30 years of retirement credit. Tier 1–58 or 30 years of retirement credit.	OPRSP DC component–employees contribute 6% of salary. DB component–non-contributory. 457 plans–members may contribute amounts to limits set by IRS.	OPRSP individual account component, or DC component–at retirement, employees may receive the IAP as a lump-sum payment or in equal installments over a 5, 10, 15 or 20-year period. DB component–benefit calculation is 1.5 percent x final average salary x years of service.
Pennsylvania	Optional. Same as state employee retirement plan.	Vesting at 10 years. Retirement age is 55 with 3 years of credited service or according to the Rule of 92 with a minimum of 35 years of service.	7.5% or 8.25% depending on plan.	Annual accrual rate x final average salary x credited years of service. FAS = average of 3 final years of service.
Rhode Island	None available.			
South Carolina	Optional (but not available to anyone first elected to the General Assembly after November 2012). Legislators elected after 2012 have the option of participating in the state employee retirement plan.	2016 information: Age 60 with 8 years of service. 30 years of service regardless of age. Act 278, Laws of 2012–SCRS: vesting at 8 years; retirement benefits at age 65 with 8 years of service or in accord with the Rule of 90. Reduced benefits are available at age 60 with 8 years of service. ORP: immediate vesting in employer contributions.	2016 information: 10% 11% as of January 1, 2013. Act 278, Laws of 2012–SCRS: 7% as of July 1, 2012, rising to 8% on July 1, 2014. ORP: 7% + 5% employer contribution, immediately vested.	2016 information: 4.82% x earnable compensation x years of service. "Earnable compensation" means 40 x the daily rate of remuneration, plus $12,000, of a member of the General Assembly, as from time to time in effect. Act 278, Laws of 2012–SCRS: 2.25% x years of service x final average compensation, which is the average of the member's 5 highest years of earned compensation. ORP: upon retirement a member may annuitize the balance in the account or take a lump sum or partial distribution. Federal provisions apply.
South Dakota	None available.			
Tennessee	Optional. Same as state employees retirement plan.	Hybrid plan–Vesting at 5 years, age 60 or any combination of age and service to equal 80. Legacy plan–Vesting at 4 years, age 55.	State contributes 4% toward defined benefit, 5% into 401K Member contributes 5% toward defined benefit, 2% into 401K. Legacy Plan–19.66% for original members.	Hybrid plan–$57.28 x years of service. Legacy plan–$89.72 x years of service.
Texas	Optional	Age 60 with 8 years of service; or age 50 with 12 years of service.	9.5%	2.3% x district judge's salary x length of service, with the monthly benefit capped at the level of a district judge's salary, and adjusted when such salaries are increased. Various annuity options are available. In September 2018, a district judge's salary was set at $140,000 a year.

See footnotes at end of table

TABLE 3.13
State Legislative Retirement Benefits (continued)

State	Participation	Requirements for regular retirement	Employee contribution rate	Benefit formula
Utah	Optional	Age 62 with 10 years and an actuarial reduction; age 65 with 4 years of service for full benefits.	Non-contributory. For the DC plan, employer will contribute 10% of compensation, which will vest after four years of service. Employees may, but are not required, to contribute.	$30.40/month (as of July 2018) x years of service; adjusted semi-annually according to consumer price index up to a maximum increase of 2%. An additional $3.50/month for each year of service is payable to elected and appointed legislators who were members of this plan before March 1, 2000.
Vermont	None available. Deferred compensation plan available.			
Virginia	Mandatory. Eligibility for various plans based on membership date. Same as state employees plan.	Plan 1–Age 50 with 30 years of service (unreduced); age 55 with 5 years of service; age 50 with 10 years (reduced). Plan 2–When age and service = 90; or normal Social Security retirement age with 5 years of service (unreduced); age 60 with 5 years of service (reduced). Hybrid plan–When age and service = 90; or normal Social Security retirement age with 5 years of service (unreduced); age 60 with 5 years of service (reduced).	Plan 1–members who qualify do not make an employee contribution. Plan 2–5% of creditable compensation. Hybrid plan–mandatory and voluntary contributions to defined benefit and defined contribution components.	Plan 1–1.7% of average final compensation x years of service (average over highest 36 consecutive months). Plan 2–1.65% of average final compensation x years of service (average over highest 60 consecutive months). Hybrid plan–1.65% of average final compensation x years of service (average over highest 60 consecutive months).
Washington	Optional. If before an election the legislator belonged to a state public retirement plan, he or she may continue in that plan by making contributions. Otherwise, new legislators may join PERS Plan 2 or Plan 3.	Plan 2–age 65 with 5 years of service credit. Plan 3–age 65 with 10 years of service credit for the DB side of the plan; immediate benefits (subject to federal restrictions) on the DC side of the plan. The member may choose various options for investment of contributions to the DC plan.	Plan 2–employee contribution of 7.41% for 2019. Plan 3–no required member contribution for the DB component. The member may contribute from 5% to 15% of salary to the DC component.	Plan 2–2% x years of service credit x average final compensation. Plan 3–DB is 1% x service credit years x average final compensation. DC benefit depends upon the value of accumulations.
West Virginia	Optional	Age 55, if years of service + age equal 80.	Before 10/1/87–7%. After 10/1/87–5%.	2% x final average salary x years of service. Final average salary is based on 3 highest years out of last 10 years.
Wisconsin	Mandatory. Same as state employees retirement plan.	Age 62 for members who began employment before 1/1/17; Age 65 for members who began employment on or after 1/1/17. Age 55 with reduced benefits.	2019 contribution rate is 6.6% of monthly gross salary to their state pension The employer matches this for a total contribution of 13.2%.	Final average monthly earnings x creditable service x formula multiplier x age reduction factor (if any) = monthly amount. Final average monthly earnings is calculated by adding the highest earnings for three calendar years and dividing this total by the creditable service earned during these years and then dividing by 12.
Wyoming	Optional–Deferred 457 Plan.		$20 minimum monthly contribution is required to participate.	

Source: National Conference of State Legislatures, 2019.
Key:
COLA–Cost of living adjustment.
CPI–Consumer price index.
DB–Defined Benefit.
DC–Defined Contribution.

FAS–Final average salary.
None available–No retirement benefit provided.
OPERS–Ohio Public Employee's Retirement System.
OPSRP–Oregon Public Employee's Retirement System.
PERA–Public Employee Retirement Association.
PERS–Public Employee's Retirement System.

TABLE 3.14
Bill Pre-Filing, Reference and Carryover

State or other jurisdiction	Pre-filing of bills allowed (b)	Bills referred to committee by:		Bill referral restricted by rule (a)		Bill carryover allowed (c)
		Senate	House/Assembly	Senate	House/Assembly	
Alabama	★(d)	(e)(f)	Speaker (f)	L, M	L, M	...
Alaska	★	President	Speaker	L, M	L, M	★
Arizona	★	President	Speaker	L	L	...
Arkansas	★	President (g)	Speaker	L	L	...
California	★(h)	Rules Cmte.	Rules Cmte.	L	L	★(h)
Colorado	★	President	Speaker	(i)	(i)	...
Connecticut	★	Pres. Pro Tempore	Speaker	M	M	...
Delaware	★	Pres. Pro Tempore	Speaker	L	L	★
Florida	★	President	Speaker	M	...	...
Georgia	★	President (f)	Speaker	...	...	★
Hawaii	(j)	(j)	Speaker	...	...	★
Idaho	...	President (e)	Speaker (e)	(qq)	(qq)	...
Illinois	★	Cmte. on Assignments	Rules Cmte.	(k)	(k)	★
Indiana	★(l)	Pres. Pro Tempore	Speaker	(m)	...	...
Iowa	★	President	Speaker	M	M	★
Kansas	★	President	Speaker	L(n)	L(n)	★
Kentucky	★	Cmte. on Cmtes.	Cmte. on Cmtes.	L, M	L, M	(oo)
Louisiana	★	President (o)	Speaker (o)	L	L	...
Maine	★	Secy. of Senate	Clerk of House	L	L	★(rr)
Maryland	★	President (q)	Speaker (q)	L	L	...
Massachusetts	★	Clerk	Clerk	M	M	★
Michigan	...	Majority Ldr.	Speaker	(uu)	(uu)	★
Minnesota	★(r)	President	Speaker	L, M	L, M	★(r)
Mississippi	★	President (e)	Speaker	L	L	...
Missouri	★	Pres. Pro Tempore	Speaker	L	L	...
Montana	★	President	Speaker	L(tt)	L(tt)	...
Nebraska	★	Reference Cmte. (s)	U	L	U	★(t)
Nevada	★	President (u)	Speaker (u)	L(v)	...	...
New Hampshire	★	President	Speaker	M	M	★(ss)
New Jersey	★	President	Speaker	L, M	L, M	★
New Mexico	★	(w)	Speaker	L	L, M	...
New York	★	President pro tem in consultation with Independent democratic conference leader	Speaker	L,M	L, M	★
North Carolina	...	Rules Chair	Speaker	M	M	★
North Dakota	★	Majority Leader	Speaker	L	L	...
Ohio	★(y)	Reference Cmte.	Rules & Reference Cmte.	L(z)	L, M (aa)	★(bb)
Oklahoma	★	Majority Leader	Speaker	L	L	★(cc)
Oregon	★	President	Speaker	(dd)	(ee)	...
Pennsylvania	(x)	President Pro Tempore	Chief Clerk	M	M	...
Rhode Island	★	President	Speaker	M	M	★
South Carolina	★	President	Speaker	M	M	★(ff)
South Dakota	★	President Pro Tempore	Speaker	L	L	...
Tennessee	★	Speaker	Speaker	L, M	L, M	★(gg)
Texas	★	President	Speaker	L	L	...
Utah	★	President (p)	Speaker (p)	L	L	...
Vermont	(hh)	President	Speaker	L, M	L, M	★
Virginia	★	Clerk	Clerk (ii)	L,M (jj)	(kk)	★(ll)
Washington	★	(mm)	Speaker	L	L	★
West Virginia (nn)	★	President	Speaker	L, M	L, M	...
Wisconsin	...	President	Speaker	L, M	L, M	...
Wyoming	★	President	Speaker	L(vv)	L(vv)	...
American Samoa	...	...	...	...	...	...
Guam	★	Committee on Calendar Chairs	U	L, M (pp)	U	★
CNMI*	★	President	Speaker	L	L	...
Puerto Rico	...	President	Secretary	M	M	...
U.S. Virgin Islands	...	Senate President in Pro-Forma meeting	U	L	U	★

See footnotes at end of table

TABLE 3.14
Bill Pre-Filing, Reference and Carryover (continued)

Source: The Council of State Governments' survey, December 2019 and update from state websites 2020.

*Commonwealth of Northern Mariana Islands

Key:

★ – Yes

. . . – No

L – Rules generally require all bills be referred to the appropriate committee of jurisdiction.

M – Rules require specific types of bills be referred to specific committees (e.g., appropriations, local bills).

U – Unicameral legislature.

(a) Legislative rules specify all or certain bills go to committees of jurisdiction.

(b) Unless otherwise indicated by footnote, bills may be introduced prior to convening each session of the legislature. In this column only: ★ –pre-filing is allowed in both chambers (or in the case of Nebraska, in the unicameral legislature); . . . – pre-filing is not allowed in either chamber.

(c) Bills carry over from the first year of the legislature to the second (does not apply in Alabama, Arkansas, Montana, Nevada, North Dakota, Oregon and Texas, where legislatures meet biennially). Bills generally do not carry over after an intervening legislative election.

(d) Except between the end of the last regular session of the legislature in any quadrennium and the organizational session following the general election and for special sessions.

(e) Lieutenant governor is the president of the Senate. Senate Rule 14. House Rule 10.

(f) Senate bills referred by president with concurrence of president pro tem. House bills referred by president pro tem with concurrence of president, if no concurrence, referred by majority leader for assignment.

(g) Senate chief counsel makes recommendations to the presiding officer.

(h) Bills may be drafted prior to session, but may not be introduced until the first day of session. Bills introduced in the first year of the regular session and passed by the house of origin on or before the January 31st constitutional deadline in the second year are carryover bills.

(i) In either house, state law requires any bill which affects the sentencing of criminal offenders and which would result in a net increase of imprisonment in state correctional facilities must be assigned to the appropriations committee of the house in which it was introduced. In the Senate, a bill must be referred to the Appropriations Committee if it contains an appropriation from the state treasury or the increase of any salary. Each bill which provides that any state revenue be devoted to any purpose other than that to which it is devoted under existing law must be referred to the Finance Committee.

(j) Prefiling allowed in the House by rule, seven calendar days before the commencement of the regular session, in even-numbered years. Senate allows prefiling of bills as determined on a year-to-year basis. Senate bills are referred to committee by the members of the majority leadership appointed by the President.

(k) In even-numbered years, the Committee on Assignments (Senate) or Rules Committee (House) is to refer to substantive committees only appropriation bills implementing the budget, and bills deemed by the Committee on Assignments (Senate) or Rules Committee (House) to be of an emergency nature or of substantial importance to the operation of government.

(l) Only in the Senate

(m) At the discretion of President Pro Tempore.

(n) Appropriation bills are the only "specific type" mentioned in the rules to be referred to either House Appropriation Cmte. or Senate Ways and Means.

(o) Subject to approval or disapproval. Louisiana–majority members present.

(p) Senate and House Rules Committees provide recommendations.

(q) The President and Speaker may refer bills to any of the standing committees or the Rules Committees, but usually bills are referred according to subject matter.

(r) Only in the House. Pre-filing of bills allowed prior to the convening of the 2nd year of the biennium. Bill carryover allowed if in second year of a two-year session.

(s) The Nebraska Legislature's Executive Board serves as the Reference Committee.

(t) Bills are carried over from the 90-day session beginning in the odd-numbered year to the 60-day session, which begins in even-numbered year. Bills that have not passed by the last day of the 60-day session are all indefinitely postponed by motion on the last day of the session. The odd-numbered year shall be carried forward to the even-numbered year.

(u) In the Senate any member may make a motion for referral, but committee referrals are under the control of the Majority Floor Leader. In the House any member may make a motion for referral, and a chart is used to guide bill referrals based on statutory authority of committee, but committee referrals are under the control of the Majority Floor Leader.

(v) Rules do not require specific types of bills be referred to specific committees.

(w) Sponsor subject to approval of the body.

(x) Only in the Senate.

(y) Senate Rule 33: Between the general election and the time for the next convening session, a holdover member or member-elect may file bills for introduction in the next session with the Clerk's office. Those bills shall be treated as if they were bills introduced on the first day of the session. House Rule 61(d): Bills introduced prior to the convening of the session shall be treated as if they were bills introduced on the first day of the session. Between the general election and the time for the next convening session, a member-elect may file bills for introduction in the next session with the Clerk's office. The Clerk shall number such bills consecutively, in the order in which they are filed, beginning with the number "1".

(z) Rule 35. (Bills, Second Consideration and Committee on Reference, Public Hearing.) On the second reading of a bill, the Committee on Reference shall, if no motion or order be made to the contrary, refer the bill to the proper standing committee in regular order. Further, no bill shall be reported for a third reading and passage unless the same shall have been considered at a

TABLE 3.14
Bill Pre-Filing, Reference and Carryover (continued)

meeting of the committee to which the same has been referred. All Senate bills and resolutions referred by the Committee on Reference on or before the first day of April in an even-numbered year shall be scheduled by the chairperson of the committee to which the same has been referred for a minimum of one public hearing.

(aa) House Rule 37: (a) All House bills and resolutions introduced on or before the fifteenth day of May in an even-numbered year, and in compliance with the rules of the House, shall be referred to a standing, select, or special committee or standing subcommittee, and shall be scheduled by the chairman of the committee for a minimum of one public hearing.
(b) The sponsor of a bill or resolution shall appear at least once before the committee that is considering the bill or resolution unless excused by the chairman of the committee or the Speaker. It is not in order for the committee to report the bill or resolution unless its sponsor has appeared or has been excused from appearing before the committee. Rule 65. (Bills carrying appropriations.) All bills carrying an appropriation shall be referred to the Finance Committee for consideration and report before being considered the third time.

(bb) Bills carry over between the first and second year of each regular annual session, but not to the next biennial 2-year General Assembly.
(cc) A legislature consists of two years. Bills from the first session can carry over to the second session only.
(dd) The President can refer bills to any standing or special committee and may also attach subsequent referrals to other committees following action by the first committee.
(ee) Rules specify bills shall be referred by the Speaker to any standing or special committee and may also attach subsequent referrals to other committees following action by the first committee.
(ff) Allowed during the first year of the two year session.
(gg) Bills and resolutions introduced in the First Regular Session may carry over to the Second Regular Session (odd-numbered year to even-numbered year) only.
(hh) Bills are drafted prior to session but released starting first day of session.
(ii) Under the direction of the speaker.
(jj) Jurisdiction of the committees by subject matter is listed in the Rules.
(kk) The House Rules establish jurisdictional committees. The Speaker refers legislation to those committees as he deems appropriate.

(ll) Even-numbered year session to odd-numbered year session.
(mm) By the floor leader.
(nn) Prefiling allowed only in the house in even-numbered years.
(oo) During the odd-year session, members convene for four days, then break until February. Any legislation introduced but not enacted in the first part of the session carries over to the second part in February. No bills carry over after sine die of any session.
(pp) Substantive resolutions referred to sponsor for public hearing.
(qq) Bills may be referred by the President to an appropriate standing committee (Senate Rule 14). In the House the " Speaker shall refer the instrument to a standing committee or shall order the instrument for a second reading."(House Rule 10).
(rr) Allowed between session in a biennium, not to subsequent legislatures.
(ss) Referred bills may be held in committee and acted on during second year session.
(tt) President and Speaker have broad discretion.
(uu) Senate Rule 3.203 a) The Senate Majority Leader shall refer all bills, joint resolutions and alternative measures to a standing committee no later than one (1) Senate legislative day after being submitted to the Secretary of the Senate. The presiding officer shall announce the reference of all bills, joint resolutions and alternative measures... c) The Senate Majority Leader may change the original referral of a bill, resolution or alternative measure by oral notice to the Senate or written communication submitted to the Secretary of the Senate before the end of session on the next Senate legislative day following the day of the original referral. Notices of the written communication shall be announced by the Secretary of the Senate during session and both oral and written notifications shall be printed in the Journal. House Rule 41: (4) The Speaker shall refer all bills and joint resolutions to a standing committee no later than one House legislative day after being submitted to the Clerk. (5) The Speaker may change the original referral of a bill or resolution by written communication submitted to the Clerk before the end of session on the next House legislative day following the day of the original referral. Notice of the referral shall be announced by the Clerk and printed in the Journal.
(vv) Bills containing an appropriation are rereferred to the Appropriations Committee.

TABLE 3.15
Time Limits on Bill Introduction

State or other jurisdiction	Time limit on introduction of bills	Procedures for granting exception to time limits
Alabama	House: no limit. Senate: 24th legislative day of regular session (a).	House: N.A. Senate: Unanimous vote to suspend rules
Alaska	35th C day of 2nd regular session.	Introduction by committee or by suspension of operation of limiting rule.
Arizona	House: 29th day of regular session; 10th day of special session. Senate: 22nd day of regular session; 10th day of special session.	House: Permission of rules committee. Senate: Permission of rules committee.
Arkansas	House: Appropriation bills shall be filed no later than the 50th day of the regular session nor after the 15th day of a fiscal session. Retirement and health care legislation affecting licensures shall be introduced during the first 15 days. Resolutions proposing constitutional amendments shall not be filed after the 35th day of the regular session. Senate: 55th day of regular session (50th day for appropriations bills). Retirement and health care legislation affecting licensures shall be introduced during the first 15 days.	2/3 vote of membership of each house for appropriations bills and all others except retirement and health care legislation affecting licensures which require 3/4 vote of the membership of each house.
California	Deadlines established by the Joint Rules Committee adpoted in each session.	Approval of Rules Committee and 3/4 vote of membership.
Colorado	House: 22nd C day of regular session. Senate: 17th C day of regular session.	Committees on delayed bills may extend deadline.
Connecticut	10 days into session in odd-numbered years, 3 days into session in even-numbered years (b).	2/3 vote of members present.
Delaware	House: no limit. Senate: no limit.	
Florida	House: noon of the first day of regular session (h). Senate: noon first day of regular session (h).	House: No exception as such; if needed, one would be granted by waiving the rule by 2/3 vote on the floor. Senate: Existence of an emergency reasonably compelling consideration notwithstanding the deadline.
Georgia	Only for specific types of bills	
Hawaii	Actual dates established during session.	Majority vote of membership.
Idaho	House: 20th day of session for personal bills; 36th day of session for all committees; beyond that only privileged cmtes. Senate: 12th day of session for personal bills; 36th day of session for all committees; beyond that only privileged cmtes.	House: speaker may designate any standing committee to serve as a privileged committee temporarily. House Rule 6. Senate: President may refer bill to privileged committee. Senate Rule 14.
Illinois	House: determined by speaker. Senate: determined by senate president.	House: the speaker may set deadlines for any action on any category of legislative measure, including deadlines for introduction of bills. Senate: At any time, the president may set alternative deadlines for any legislative action with written notice filed with the secretary.
Indiana	House: Mid-January. Senate: Date specific–set in Rules, different for long and short session. Mid-January	House: 2/3 vote. Senate: If date falls on weekend/Holiday–extended to next day. Sine die deadline set by statute, does not change.
Iowa	House: Drafting request received by Friday of 5th week of 1st regular session; or by Friday of 2nd week of 2nd regular session. Senate: Drafting request received by Friday of 5th week of 1st regular session; or by Friday of 2nd week of 2nd regular session.	House: Constitutional majority; Senate: Constitutional majority.
Kansas	Actual dates established in the Joint Rules of the House and Senate every two years when the joint rules are adopted.	Resolution adopted by majority of members of either house may make specific exceptions to deadlines.
Kentucky	House: No introductions after 14th L day of odd-year session, after 38th L day of even-year session. Senate: No introductions after 13th L day of odd-year session, after 40th L day of even-year session.	None.
Louisiana	House: 10th C day of odd year sessions and 23rd C day of even-year sessions. Senate: 10th C day of odd year sessions and 23rd C day of even-year sessions.	None.
Maine	House and Senate: Cloture dates established by the Legislative Council.	House and Senate: Bills filed after cloture date must be approved by a majority of the Legislative Council. Appeals heard by Legislative Council. Six votes required to allow introduction of legislation
Maryland	House: No introductions during the last 35 days of regular session, unless 2/3 of the elected members of a chamber vote yes. Additional limitations involve committee action. House bills introduced during the last 59 calendar days (after the 31st day) are referred to the House Rules Committee. The House Rules contain further provisions concerning the requirements for forcing legislation out of these committees. Senate: No introductions during the last 35 days of regular session, unless 2/3 of the elected members of a chamber vote yes. Additional limitations involve committee action. Senate bills introduced after the 27th calendar day must be referred to the Senate Rules Committee. Senate bills introduced on behalf of the Administration (Governor) after the 13th calendar day Senate bills introduced on behalf of other Executive Department agencies that are not prefiled, must be referred to the Senate Rules Committee upon introduction. The Senate Rules contain further provisions concerning the requirements for forcing legislation out of these committees.	House and Senate: 2/3 vote of elected members of each house.

See footnotes at end of table

TABLE 3.15
Time Limits on Bill Introduction (continued)

State or other jurisdiction	Time limit on introduction of bills	Procedures for granting exception to time limits
Massachusetts	1st Wednesday in December even-numbered years, 1st Wednesday in November odd-numbered years.	2/3 vote of members present and voting.
Michigan	No limit.	
Minnesota	No limit.	
Mississippi	14th C day in 90 day session; 49th C day in 125 day session (e).	2/3 vote of members present and voting.
Missouri	March 1.	Majority vote of elected members each house; governor's request for consideration of bill by special message.
Montana	Introduction of bills & resolutions: 10th L day if requested prior to convening or 2 days after receipt of finished bill draft after session convenes, whichever is earlier. Requests for general bills & resolutions: 12th L day; revenue bills: 17th L day; committee bills & resolutions: 36th L day; appropriations bills: 45th L day; interim study resolutions: 60th L day; committee revenue bills and bill proposing referenda: 62nd L day; committee bills implementing provision of a general appropriation act: 67th L day; resolutions confirm governor appointees or bill amending/repealing administrative rule: no deadline	2/3 vote of members.
Nebraska	10th L day of any session (f).	3/5 vote of elected membership
Nevada	Actual dates established at start of session.	Waiver granted by majority leader of the Senate and speaker of the Assembly acting jointly.
New Hampshire	Determined by rules.	2/3 vote of members present.
New Jersey	No limit.	
New Mexico	House: 15 days in short session/even years, 30 days in long session/odd years. Senate: 15 days in short session/even years, 30 days in long session/odd years.	None. Statutory limit for legislators; governor not limited and can send bill with message.
New York	Assembly: for unlimited introduction of bills, the final day is the last Tuesday in May of the 2nd year of the legislative term. Senate: Determined by the Majority Conference leaders, but no earlier than 1st Tuesday in March; except introduction by agencies is March 1, for all other program bills it is 1st Tuesday in April.	Assembly: By unanimous consent, by introduction by Rules Cmte., by message from the Senate, consent of the Speaker, or by members elected at special election who take office after the first Tuesday in May. Senate: Introduction by Rules Committee after 2nd Friday in June, or by message from the Assembly.
North Carolina	Actual dates established during session.	Senate: 2/3 vote of membership present and voting shall be required.
North Dakota	House: 8th L day. Senate: 13th L day (i).	2/3 vote of the floor or by approval of Delayed Bills Committee (i).
Ohio	No limit.	
Oklahoma	Time limit set in rules.	2/3 vote of membership.
Oregon	House: Set by House rules for odd-numbered year sessions. It was the 126th calendar day in 2019. All measures must be presession filed for even-year session. Senate: Set by Senate rules for odd-numbered year sessions. It was the 26th calendar day in 2019. All measures must be presession filed for even-year session.	House: Bills approved by the Rules Committee; appropriation or fiscal measures sponsored by the Cmte. on Ways and Means; other joint committee bills; member priority requests (limited to five measures for odd-year session, none for even-year session). Senate: Measures approved by the Senate President: appropriations or fiscal measures sponsored by the Cmte. On Ways and Means; other joint committee bills; caucus leaders are limited to two measure requests after the deadlines; member priority requests (limited to five measures for odd-year session, none for even-year session).
Pennsylvania	No limit.	
Rhode Island	Second week of February for Public Bills.	Sponsor must give one legislative day's notice.
South Carolina	House: Prior to April 15 of the 2nd yr. of a two-yr. legislative session; May 1 for bills first introduced in Senate. Rule 5.12. Senate: May 1 of regular session for bills originating in House. Rule 47	House and Senate: 2/3 vote of members present and voting.
South Dakota	Individual bills: 40-day session: 15th L day; 35-day session: 10th L day. Committee bills: 40-day session: 16th L day; 35-day session: 11th L day. If a session calendar is adopted for a period of 36 days to 39 days, the legislative deadlines for the 35-day session shall be increased by the number of days by which the length of the session calendar exceeds 35 days.	2/3 approval of members-elect.
Tennessee	General bills, 10th L day of regular session (g).	Unanimous approval by Delayed Bills Committee.
Texas	60th C day of regular session, except for local bills, emergency appropriations and all emergency maters submitted by the governor in special message to the legislature.	House: 4/5 vote of members present and voting. Senate: 4/5 vote of members.
Utah	12:00 p.m. on 11th day of session.	Floor motion for request must be approved by a constitutional majority vote.

See footnotes at end of table

TABLE 3.15
Time Limits on Bill Introduction (continued)

State or other jurisdiction	Time limit on introduction of bills	Procedures for granting exception to time limits
Vermont	House: 1st session–last day of February, individually introduced for standard form bills; 2nd session–For individually introduced standard form bills the Wednesday of the second week of the session. There are varying deadlines for short form and committee sposnored bills. Senate: 1st session–no limit; 2nd session–25 C days before start of session.	Approval by Rules Committee.
Virginia	Set by joint procedural resolution adopted at the beginning of the session (usually the second Friday of the session is the last day to introduce legislation that does not have any earlier deadline).	As provided in the joint procedural resolution (usually unanimous consent or at written request of the governor).
Washington	Until 10 days before the end of session unless 2/3 vote of elected members of each house.	2/3 vote of elected members of each house.
West Virginia	House: 35 C day. Senate: 41st C day.	2/3 vote of members present.
Wisconsin	No limit.	
Wyoming	House: 15th L day of session in odd numbered years. 5th L day in even numbered years. Senate: 12th L day of session in odd numbered years. 5th L day in even numbered years.	House: 2/3 vote of elected members. Senate: 2/3 vote of elected members. (During Budget Session need unanimous consent)
American Samoa	House: After the 25th L day of the fourth Regular Session. Senate: After the 15th L day.	
Guam	Public hearing on bill must be held no more than 120 days after date of bill introduction.	
CNMI*	No limit.	
Puerto Rico	1st session - within first 125 days; 2nd session - within first 60 days.	None.
U.S. Virgin Islands	No limit.	

Source: The Council of State Governments' survey, December 2019 and updates from state websites 2020.
*Commonwealth of Mariana Islands
Key:
C–Calendar
L–Legislative
(a) Not applicable to local bills, advertised or otherwise.
(b) Specific dates set in Joint Rules.
(c) Not applicable to appropriations bills.
(d) Not applicable to local bills and joint resolutions.
(e) Except Appropriation and Revenue bills (51st/86th C day) and Local & Private bills (83rd/118th C day).
(f) Except appropriations bills and bills introduced at the request of the governor, bills can be introduced during the first 10 legislative days of the session. Appropriation bills and bills introduced at the request of the governor can be introduced at any time during the session.

(g) Local bills have no cutoff.
(h) House: For Member-filed bills, noon of the first day of regular session. House Rule 5.2 sets a time limit for the introduction of bills, but this applies to Member-filed bills only. Proposed committee bills, local bills (dependent on completion of 30-day public notice period), and committee substitutes (treated by House Rules as new bills) are routinely filed after the first day of Session. Senate: Not applicable to appropriations bills, concurrent resolutions regarding certain subjects, local bills (which have no deadline), claim bills (deadline is August 1 of the year preceding consideration or within 62 days of a Senator's election), committee bills, trust fund bills, and public records exemptions linked to timely filed bills.
(i) Determination of introduction deadline generally is based upon second and third Mondays after convening of session.

TABLE 3.16
Enacting Legislation: Veto, Veto Override and Effective Date

State or other jurisdiction	Governor may item veto appropriation bills		Days allowed governor to consider bill (a)		
			During session	After session	
	Amount	Other (b)	Bill becomes law unless vetoed	Bill becomes law unless vetoed	Bill dies unless signed
Alabama	★ (e)	...	6 (f)	10A	
Alaska	★	...	15	20P	
Arizona	★	★	5	10A	
Arkansas	★	...	5	20A	
California	★(i)	...	12 (j)	30A	
Colorado	★	(l)	10P (ggg)	30A (m)	
Connecticut	★	...	5	15P	(o)
Delaware	★	...	10P	10P	30A
Florida	...	★	7 (ddd)	15P (m)	
Georgia	★	★	6	40A	
Hawaii (q)	★ (r)	...	10 (s)	45A (s)(p)	10P (p)
Idaho	★	★	5	10P	
Illinois	★	...	60 (m)	60P (m)	
Indiana	...	...	7	7P	
Iowa	★	★	3		30A
Kansas	★	★	10 (m)		10P
Kentucky	★	...	10	10A	
Louisiana (q)	★	★	10 (m)	20P (m)	
Maine	★	...	10		(v)
Maryland	★ (w)	★	6 (x)	30P (y)	(z)
Massachusetts	★	★	10	10P	10A
Michigan	★	★	14 (m)		14P (m)
Minnesota	★	(i)	3P	14A, 3P	3A, 14P
Mississippi	★	...	5	15P (dd)	
Missouri	★	...	15	45A	
Montana (q)	★	★	10 (m)	25A (m)	
Nebraska	★	...	5	5A, 5P	(ff)
Nevada	...	...	5 (gg)	10A (gg)	
New Hampshire	...	...	5	5P	
New Jersey	★	...	45		
New Mexico	★	★	3 (hh)		20A
New York	★	...	10 (ii)	(ii)	30A
North Carolina	...	...	10	30A	
North Dakota	★	★	3	15A	
Ohio	★	★	10	10P	10A
Oklahoma	★	...	5 (mm)		15A (mm)
Oregon	★	...	5	30A (s)	
Pennsylvania	★	★	10	30A	
Rhode Island	...	...	6	10P (oo)	(oo)
South Carolina	★	...	5	(qq)	
South Dakota	★	...	5 (rr)	15P (rr)	
Tennessee	★	...	10	(ss)	
Texas	★	...	10	20A	
Utah	★(iii)	...	10P	20A	
Vermont	...	...	5	5A	(fff)
Virginia	★	★(tt)	7 (m)	30A (uu)	
Washington	★	★	5	20A	
West Virginia	...	(i)	5	15A (xx)	
Wisconsin	★	★(eee)	6	6P	
Wyoming	★	★	3	15A	
American Samoa	★	...	10		30A
Guam	★	★	10	10P	30P (zz)
CNMI*	★	★	40 (m)(aaa)		
Puerto Rico	★	...	10		30P
U.S. Virgin Islands	★(ccc)	★(ccc)	10	10P	30A

See footnotes at end of table

TABLE 3.16
Enacting Legislation: Veto, Veto Override and Effective Date (continued)

State or other jurisdiction	Votes required in each house to pass bills or items over veto (c)	Effective date of enacted legislation (d)
Alabama	Majority of elected body	Date signed by governor, unless otherwise specified.
Alaska	2/3 elected (g)	90 days after enactment or the specified effective date.
Arizona	2/3 elected (h)	90 days after adjournment
Arkansas	Majority elected	91st day after adjournment
California	2/3 elected (hhh)	(k)
Colorado	2/3 elected	90 days after adjournment (n)
Connecticut	2/3 elected	Oct. 1, unless otherwise specified.
Delaware	3/5 elected	Immediately or enactment clause
Florida	2/3 members present in each house	60 days after adjournment since die or on specified date.
Georgia	2/3 elected	Unless other date specified, July 1 for generals, date signed by governor for locals.
Hawaii (q)	2/3 elected	Immediately or on the prospective date stated in the legislation.
Idaho	2/3 present	July 1
Illinois	3/5 elected (g)	Usually Jan. 1 of next year (t)
Indiana	Majority elected	(u)
Iowa	2/3 elected	July 1, unless otherwise specified. Effective date for bills which which become law on or after July 1, 45 days after approval, unless otherwise specified.
Kansas	2/3 membership	Upon publication or specified date after publication
Kentucky	Majority elected	90 days after adjournment sine die. Unless the bill contains an emergency clause or special effective date.
Louisiana (q)	2/3 elected	Aug. 1
Maine	2/3 elected	90 days after adjournment unless enacted as an emergency.
Maryland	3/5 elected (aa)	(bb)
Massachusetts	2/3 present	90 days after enactment
Michigan	2/3 elected and serving	Immediate effect if vote of 2/3 elected and serving. 90 days after adjournment, if immediate effect not given
Minnesota	2/3 elected- 90 House; 45 Senate	Aug. 1 unless other effective date given. (cc)
Mississippi	2/3 elected	July 1 unless specified otherwise.
Missouri	2/3 elected	Aug. 28 (ee)
Montana (q)	2/3 present	Oct. 1 (cc)
Nebraska	3/5 elected	90 days following adjournment sine die. Unless bill contains an emergency clause or a specific operative date.
Nevada	2/3 elected	Oct. 1, unless measure stipulates a different date.
New Hampshire	2/3 present	60 days after enactment, unless otherwise noted.
New Jersey	2/3 elected	Dates usually specified
New Mexico	2/3 present	90 days after adjournment unless other date specified. General appropriations acts or emergency clauses passed by 2/3 present take effect immediately.
New York	2/3 present	20 days after enactment unless otherwise prescribed in the bill.
North Carolina	3/5 elected	60 days after adjournment
North Dakota	2/3 elected	(jj)
Ohio	3/5 elected (kk)	91st day after filing with secretary of state. (ll)
Oklahoma	2/3 elected	90 days after adjournment unless specified in the bill.
Oregon	2/3 present	Jan. 1st of following year. (nn)
Pennsylvania	2/3 majority	60 days after signed by governor
Rhode Island	3/5 present	Immediately (pp)
South Carolina	2/3 vote of the members present and voting	Date of signature
South Dakota	2/3 elected	July 1
Tennessee	Constitutional majority	40 days after enactment unless otherwise specified
Texas	2/3 present	90 days after adjournment unless otherwise specified
Utah	2/3 elected	60 days after adjournment of the session at which it passed.
Vermont	2/3 present	July 1 unless otherwise specified.
Virginia	2/3 present (vv)	July 1 (ww)
Washington	2/3 present	90 days after adjournment
West Virginia	Majority elected	90 days after enactment
Wisconsin	2/3 present	Day after publication date unless otherwise specified
Wyoming	2/3 elected	Specified in act
American Samoa	2/3 elected	60 days after adjournment (yy)
Guam	10 votes to override	Immediately (bbb)
CNMI*	2/3 elected	Upon signing by the governor.
Puerto Rico	2/3 elected	Specified in act
U.S. Virgin Islands	2/3 elected	Immediately

See footnotes at end of table

TABLE 3.16
Enacting Legislation: Veto, Veto Override and Effective Date (continued)

Source: The Council of State Governments' survey, December 2019 and state websites 2020.

*Commonwealth of Northern Mariana Islands

Key:

★ – Yes

. . . – No

A – Days after adjournment of legislature.

P – Days after presentation to governor.

(a) Sundays excluded, unless otherwise indicated.

(b) Includes language in appropriations bill.

(c) Bill returned to house of origin with governor's objections.

(d) Effective date may be established by the law itself or may be otherwise changed by vote of the legislature. Special or emergency acts are usually effective immediately.

(e) The governor may line item distinct items or item veto amounts in appropriation bills, if returned prior to final adjournment.

(f) Except bills presented within five days of final adjournment, Sundays are included.

(g) Different number of votes required for revenue and appropriations bills. Alaska-3/4 elected. Illinois-Only the usual majority of members elected is required to restore a reduced item.

(h) Several specific requirements of 3/4 majority.

(i) Line item veto.

(j) For a bill to become law during session, if 12th day falls on a Saturday, Sunday, or holiday, the period is extended to the next day that is not a Saturday, Sunday, or holiday.

(k) For legislation enacted in regular sessions: January 1 of the following year. Urgency legislation: immediately upon chaptering by Secretary of State. Legislation enacted in special session: 91st day after adjournment of the special session at which the bill was passed.

(l) The governor may not line-item veto any portion of any bill (including appropriation clauses in bills) other than line items in the Long Appropriations Bill. The governor may line-item veto individual lines in the Long Appropriations Bill. In those instances, the governor must line-item veto the entire amount of any item; an item is an indivisible sum of money dedicated to a single purpose.

(m) Sundays included.

(n) An act takes effect on the date stated in the act, or if no date is stated in the act, then upon signature of the governor. If no safety clause on a bill, the bill takes effect 90 days after sine die if no referendum petition has been filed. The state constitution allows for a 90 day period following adjournment when petitions may be filed for bills that do not contain a safety clause.

(o) Bill enacted if not signed /vetoed within time frames.

(p) The governor must notify the legislature 10 days before the 45th day of his intent to veto a measure on that day. The legislature may convene at or before noon on the 45th day after adjournment to consider the vetoed measures. If the legislature fails to reconvene, the bill does not become law. If the legislature reconvenes, it may pass the measure over the governor's veto or it may amend the law to meet the governor's objections. If the law is amended, the governor must sign the bill within 10 days after it is presented to him in order for it to become law.

(q) Constitution withholds right to veto constitutional amendments proposed by the legislature.

(r) Governor can also reduce amounts in appropriations bills. In Hawaii, governor can reduce items in executive appropriations measures, but cannot reduce or item veto amounts appropriated for the judicial or legislative branches.

(s) Except Sundays and legal holidays. In Hawaii, except Saturdays, Sundays, holidays and any days in which the legislature is in recess prior to its adjournment. In Oregon, if the governor does not sign the bill within 30 days after adjournment, it becomes law without the governor's signature, Saturdays and Sundays are excluded.

(t) Effective date for bills which become law on or after July 1: A bill passed after May 31 cannot take effect before June 1 of the following year unless it states an earlier effective date and is approved by 3/5 of the members elected to each house.

(u) Varies with date of the veto.

(v) "If the bill or resolution shall not be returned by the governor within 10 days (Sundays excepted) after it shall have been presented to the Governor, it shall have the same force and effect as if the Governor had signed it unless the Legislature by their adjournment prevent its return, in which case it shall have such force and effect, unless returned within 3 days after the next meeting of the same Legislature which enacted the bill or resolution; if there is no such next meeting of the Legislature which enacted the bill or resolution, the bill or resolution shall not be a law." (excerpted from Article IV, Part Third, Section 2 of the Constitution of Maine).

(w) The Governor cannot veto the budget bill but may exercise a total veto or item veto on a supplementary appropriations bill. In practice, this means the Governor may strike items in the annual general capital budget bill. Occasionally, the Governor will also veto a bond bill or a portion of a bond bill.

(x) If a bill is presented to the governor in the first 83 days of session, the governor has only six days (not including Sunday) to act before the bill automatically becomes law.

(y) All bills passed at regular or special sessions must be presented to the governor no later than 20 days after adjournment. The governor has a limited time to sign or veto a bill after it is presented. If the governor does not act within that time, the bill becomes law automatically; there is no pocket veto. The time limit depends on when the presentment is made. Any bill presented in the last 7 days of the 90-day session or after adjournment must be acted on within 30 days after presentment. Bills vetoed after adjournment are returned to the legislature for reconsideration at the next meeting of the same General Assembly.

(z) The governor has a limited time to sign or veto a bill after it is presented. If the governor does not act within that time, the bill becomes law automatically; there is no pocket veto. The time limit depends on when the presentment is made.

(aa) Vetoed bills are returned to the house of origin immediately after that house has organized at the next regular or special session. When a new General Assembly is elected and sworn in, bills vetoed from the previous session are not returned. These vetoed bills are not subject to any further legislative action."

TABLE 3.16
Enacting Legislation: Veto, Veto Override and Effective Date (continued)

(bb) Unless otherwise provided, June 1 is the effective date for bond bills and July 1 is the effective date for budget, tax and revenue bills. By custom, October 1 is the usual effective date for other legislation. If the bill is an emergency measure, it may take effect immediately upon approval by the Governor or at a specified date prior to June 1. For vetoed legislation, 30 days after the veto is overridden or on the date specified in the bill, whichever is later. An emergency bill passed over the Governor's veto takes effect immediately.

(cc) Different date for fiscal legislation. Minnesota–July 1. Montana–Appropriations effective July 1 unless otherwise specified in bill; revenue bills effected July 1 unless otherwise specified in bill, often next Jan. 1.

(dd) Bills vetoed after adjournment are returned to the legislature for reconsideration. Mississippi–returned within three days after the beginning of the next session.

(ee) If bill has an emergency clause, it becomes effective upon governor's signature. If a bill is neither signed nor vetoed by a governor, it becomes law.

(ff) Nebraska allows a bill to become law without the signature of the governor. In addition, bills are carried over from the 90-day session beginning in the odd-numbered year to the 60-day session, which begins in even-numbered years. Bills that have not passed by the last day of the 60-day session are all indefinitely postponed by motion on the last day of the session.

(gg) The day of delivery and Sundays are not counted for purposes of calculating these periods.

(hh) For bills presented to governor before the last three days of session. If bills presented to the governor in the last three days of session, governor has 20 days from adjournment to sign; if not signed in this time period, bill is pocket vetoed.

(ii) If the legislature adjourns during the governor's consideration of a 10-day bill, the bill shall not become law without the governor's approval.

(jj) Postsession veto - 15 days, Saturdays and Sundays excluded. August 1 after filing with the secretary of state. Appropriations and tax bills July 1 after filing with secretary of state, or date set in legislation by Legislative Assembly, or by date established by emergency clause in a bill that passes each house by a vote of two-thirds of the members-elect of each house.

(kk) The exception covers such matters as emergency measures and court bills that originally required a 2/3 majority for passage. In those cases, the same extraordinary majority vote is required to override a veto.

(ll) Emergency, current appropriation, and tax legislation effective immediately. The General Assembly may also enact an uncodified section of law specifying a desired effective date that is after the constitutionally established effective date.

(mm) During session the governor has 5 days (except Sunday) to sign or veto a bill or it becomes law automatically. After Session a bill becomes a pocket veto if not signed 15 days after sine die.

(nn) Unless emergency declared or date specific in text of measure, which must be at least 90 days after adjournment sine die unless emergency is declared. Emergency cannot be declared in bills regulating taxation or exemption.

(oo) Bills become effective without signature if not signed or vetoed.

(pp) Date signed, date received by Secretary of State if effective without signature, date that veto is overridden, or other specified date.

(qq) Two days after the next meeting.

(rr) During a session, a bill becomes law if a governor signs it or does not act on it within five days, not including Saturdays, Sundays or holidays. If the legislature has adjourned or recessed or is within five days of a recess or an adjournment, the governor has 15 days to act on the bill. If he does not act, the bill becomes law.

(ss) Adjournment of the legislature is irrelevant; the governor has 10 days to act on a bill after it is presented to him or it becomes law without his signature.

(tt) If part of the item.

(uu) The governor has thirty days after adjournment of the legislature to act on any bills. The Constitution of Virginia provides that : "If the governor does not act on any bill, it shall become law without his signature."

(vv) Must include majority of elected members.

(ww) Unless a different date is stated in the bill. Special sessions–first day of fourth month after adjournment.

(xx) Five days for supplemental appropriation bills.

(yy) Laws required to be approved only by the governor. An act required to be approved by the U.S. Secretary of the Interior only after it is vetoed by the governor and so approved takes effect 40 days after it is returned to the governor by the secretary.

(zz) After Legislature adjourns sine die at end of two-year term.

(aaa) Twenty days for appropriations bills.

(bbb) U.S. Congress may annul.

(ccc) May item veto language or amounts in a bill that contains two or more appropriations.

(ddd) The governor has seven days, Sundays included, to act on presented bills while the Legislature is in session. If the Legislature adjourns sine die during the seven-day period or takes a recess of more than 30 days, the governor has 15 consecutive days from the date of presentation to act on the bill(s).

(eee) Governor may partially veto words or numbers in the case of appropriation bills.

(fff) In odd-numbered years 2 days prior to adjournment; in even numbered years 3 days subsequent to presentation following adjournment. However the actual practice is that bills are sent anytime prior the start of the next fiscal year (July 1). Governor has five business days (Sundays excepted) to sign.

(ggg) Ten calendar days after receipt of bill. When the Governor receives bills within the last 10 days of session, the Governor has 30 days to act on the bills.

(hhh) Per Joint Rule 58.5, the Legislature may consider a Governor's veto for only 60 legislative days or until adjournment sine die of the session in which the bill subject to the veto was passed by the Legislature, whichever period is shorter.

(iii) If a line item is vetoed, everything in the line item including all amounts and all language in that line item is vetoed.

TABLE 3.17
Legislative Appropriations Process: Budget Documents and Bills

State or other jurisdiction	Legal source of deadline		Budget document submission — Submission date relative to convening					Budget bill introduction		
	Constitutional	Statutory	Prior to session	Within one week	Within two weeks	Within one month	Over one month	Same time as budget document	Another time	Not until cmte. review of budget document
Alabama	★	★	(a)	★	...	...	...	★	...	...
Alaska	★	★	...	(a)	...	...	...	★	...	...
Arizona	...	★	★	...	...	...	...	...	...	★
Arkansas	...	★	★	...	...	...	...	...	...	★
California	★	...	...	...	...	(a)	...	★(b)	...	...
Colorado	...	★	★(a)	...	...	...	...	...	76th day by rule	...
Connecticut	...	★	...	...	...	(a)	...	★	...	...
Delaware	...	...	...	...	...	...	...	...	...	★
Florida	★	★	★	...	...	...	...	...	...	★
Georgia	★	...	...	(a)	...	...	...	★	...	★
Hawaii	...	★	30 days	...	...	...	...	...	★	...
Idaho	...	★	...	...	...	★(a)	...	...	...	★
Illinois	...	★	...	...	...	★(a)	...	...	★(c)	...
Indiana	...	★	...	...	...	...	...	...	★	...
Iowa	...	★	...	...	...	(a)	...	...	...	★(d)
Kansas	...	★	...	...	★(e)	...	...	...	★	...
Kentucky	★	...	...	...	...	(a)	...	★	...	...
Louisiana	...	★	(f)	(f)	...	...	...	(g)	...	...
Maine	...	★	...	(a)	...	...	...	★	...	...
Maryland	★	...	...	★(e)	...	...	...	★(h)	...	...
Massachusetts	...	★	...	...	...	★	...	★	...	...
Michigan	...	★	...	...	...	★	...	★	...	...
Minnesota	...	★	...	...	...	(a)	...	...	...	★
Mississippi	...	★	★	...	...	...	...	...	★	...
Missouri	★	...	...	...	...	★(a)	...	...	...	★
Montana	...	★	★	...	...	...	...	...	★	...
Nebraska	...	★	...	...	★(a)	★(a)	...	★(i)	...	...
Nevada	★	...	(a)	...	...	...	...	...	...	★
New Hampshire	...	★	...	...	...	(a)	...	...	★	...
New Jersey	...	★	...	...	...	...	...	...	...	★
New Mexico	...	★	★	...	...	(a)	...	...	★	...
New York	★	...	(a)	...	★(a)	...	...	...	★(j)	...
North Carolina	...	...	...	...	...	...	...	★	...	...
North Dakota	...	★	(k)	...	...	...	...	...	★(k)	...
Ohio	...	★	...	...	...	★(d)(e)	...	★(x)	...	...
Oklahoma	★	★	...	★	...	...	...	...	★	...
Oregon	...	★	★	...	...	...	★(l)	...	...	★(m)
Pennsylvania	★	...	...	...	...	...	...	★	...	★
Rhode Island	...	★	...	...	...	...	...	★	★	...
South Carolina	...	★	...	★	...	...	...	...	...	★
South Dakota	...	★	...	...	...	...	...	★(o)	★(p)	...
Tennessee	...	★	...	...	★(a)(e)	★(a)(e)	...	★	...	...
Texas	...	★	(n)	...	...	...	...	...	★(q)	...
Utah	...	★(t)	(a)	...	...	...	...	...	...	★
Vermont	...	★	(s)	...	...	...	...	...	...	★
Virginia	...	★	Dec. 20	...	...	...	...	★	...	...
Washington	★(t)	...	(u)	...	...	...	...	★	...	...
West Virginia	★	...	...	★	...	...	...	★	...	...
Wisconsin	...	★	...	...	...	★(v)	...	★	...	...
Wyoming	...	★	3rd Mon. in Nov.	...	...	...	...	...	...	★
American Samoa	...	★	★	...	...	...	...	★	...	...
Guam	...	★	...	...	...	★(w)	...	★	...	...
CNMI*	★	★	April 1	...	...	...	...	...	★	★
Puerto Rico	...	★	...	...	...	★	...	...	...	★
U.S. Virgin Islands	...	★	May 30	...	...	...	...	...	★	...

See footnotes at end of table

TABLE 3.17
Legislative Appropriations Process: Budget Documents and Bills (continued)

Sources: The Council of State Governments' survey, December 2019 and state websites, 2020.

*Commonwealth of Northern Mariana Islands

Key:

★ –Yes

…–No

(a) Specific time limitations:

Alabama–within first five days of session;

Alaska–December 15, 4th legislative day;

California–January 10;

Connecticut–not later than the first session day following the third day in February, in each odd numbered year;

Colorado–presented by November 1 to the Joint Budget Committee;

Georgia–first five days of session;

Idaho–September 1 (I.C. § 67-3502).

Illinois–Third Wednesday in February;

Iowa–no later than February 1;

Kentucky–On or before the 15th L day with a new governor, or on or before the 10th L day if not a new governor.

Maine–The Governor shall transmit the budget document to the Legislature not later than the Friday following the first Monday in January of the first regular legislative session…. A Governor-elect elected to a first term of office shall transmit the budget document to the Legislature not later than the Friday following the first Monday in February of the first regular legislative session (Maine Revised Statutes, Title 5, Chapter 149, Section 1666);

Minnesota–by the 4th Tuesday in January each odd-numbered year

Missouri: Missouri Constitution, Article III Section 24: The governor shall, within thirty days after it convenes in each regular session, submit to the general assembly a budget for the ensuing appropriation period, containing the estimated available revenues of the state and a complete and itemized plan of proposed expenditures of the state and all its agencies.

Nebraska–The budget bill is Nebraska's budget document and must be submitted to the governor by Jan. 15 of each odd-numbered year and by Feb. 1 when a governor is in their first year of office.

Nevada–No later than 14 days before commencement of regular session;

New Hampshire–Governor statutorily required to submit budget to legislature by February 15.

New Mexico–by January 10 in an odd year, January 5 in an even year. Legislative Finance Cmte. Must submit budget no later than first week of session.

New York–The legislative budget must be submitted to the governor no later than December 1. The executive budget must be submitted by the governor to the legislature by the 2nd Tuesday following the opening of session (or February 1 for the first session following a gubernatorial election);

Tennessee–on or before February 1 for sitting governor;

Utah–Must submit to the legislature by the calendared floor time on the first day of the annual session.

(b) Budget and Budget Bill are annual–to be submitted within the first 10 days of each calendar year.

(c) Deadlines for introducing bills in general are set by Senate president and House speaker.

(d) Executive budget bill is introduced and used as a working tool for committee.

(e) Later for first session of a new governor; Kansas–21 days; Maryland–10 days after; New Jersey–February 15; Ohio–by March 15; Tennessee–March 1;

(f) The governor shall submit his executive budget to the Joint Legislative Committee on the budget no later than 45 days prior to each regular session; except that in the first year of each term, the executive budget shall be submitted no later than 30 days prior to the regular session. Copies shall be made available to the entire legislature on the first day of each regular session.

(g) Bills appropriating monies for the general operating budget and ancillary appropriations, bills appropriating funds for the expenses of the legislature and the judiciary must be submitted to the legislature for introduction no later than 45 days prior to each regular session, except that in the first year of each term, such appropriation bills shall be submitted no later than 30 days prior to the regular session.

(h) Appropriations bill other than the budget bill (supplementary) may be introduced at any time. They must provide their own tax source and may not be enacted until the budget bill is enacted.

(i) Governor's budget bill is introduced and serves as a working document for the Appropriations Committee. The governor must submit the budget proposal by January 15 of each odd-numbered year. (Neb.Rev.Stat. sec.81-125). The statute extends this deadline to February 1 for a governor who is in his first year of office.

(j) Submission of the governor's budget bills to the legislature occurs with submission of the executive budget.

(k) Legislative Council's Budget Section hears the executive budget recommendations during legislature's December organizational session. Drafts of proposed general appropriations acts are required to be submitted seven days after adjournment of the organizational session. There is no requirement that the drafts be permitted to be introduced.

(l) Governor must propose budget by December of even-numbered year unless new governor is elected; if new governor is elected, then February 1 of odd-numbered year.

(m) Legislature introduces its own budget bills during legislative session that are not part of the governor's recommended budget.

(n) The Legislative Budget Board is required to submit a copy of the budget of estimated appropriations to the governor and members of the legislature not later than the fifth day after session convenes. The board is required to submit a copy of the general appropriations bill not later than the seventh day after session convenes.

(o) It is usually over a month. The budget must be delivered to the Legislature not later than the first Tuesday after the first Monday in December.

(p) It must be introduced no later than the 16th legislative day.

(q) State law does not specify a special deadline for filing the General Appropriations Act, but it is generally filed soon after the Legislative Budget Board submits the budget document.

(r) Legislative rules require budget bills to be introduced by the 43rd day of the session.

(s) Third Tuesday each year.

TABLE 3.17

Legislative Appropriations Process: Budget Documents and Bills (continued)

(t) And Rules.

(u) For fiscal period other than biennium, 20 days prior to first day of session.

(v) On or before the last Tuesday in January. A later submission date may be requested by the governor.

(w) Usually January before end of current fiscal year.

(x) Bill may actually be officially introduced a few days later; it is usually not immediately introduced upon the presentation of the governor's budget.

TABLE 3.18
Fiscal Notes: Content and Distribution

State or other jurisdiction	Content — Intent or purpose of bill	Content — Cost involved	Content — Projected future cost	Content — Proposed source of revenue	Content — Fiscal impact on local govt.	Content — Other	Distribution / Legislators — All	Distribution / Legislators — Available on request	Distribution / Legislators — Bill sponsor	Appropriations committee — Members	Appropriations committee — Chair only	Fiscal staff	Executive budget staff
Alabama	★	★	...	★	★	★ (a)	★	★	★	★	...	★	★
Alaska	...	★	★	★	...	...	★	★	★	...	...	★	★
Arizona	★	★	★	★	★	★	★	★	★	★	...	★	★
Arkansas (b)	...	★	★	...	★	★	★	...	...	...	...	...	...
California	★	★	★	★	★	...	★	...	...	...	...	★	★
Colorado	★	★	★	★	★	...	★	...	...	...	...	...	...
Connecticut	★	★	★	★	★	...	---------------------(c)---------------------						
Delaware	★	★	★	★	★ (m)	...	★	...	...	...	...	...	...
Florida	★	★	★	★	★	★	★	...	...	...	...	★	...
Georgia	...	★	★	...	★	...	★	★	...	...	...	...	...
Hawaii	...	...	...	...	...	★ (hh)	...	...	...	...	...	...	...
Idaho	★	★	★	★	★	(ll)	★	...	...	...	...	(e)	(e)
Illinois	...	★	★	★	★	...	★ (f)	★	★	...	...	...	...
Indiana	★	★	★	★	★	...	★	...	...	...	...	★	★
Iowa	★	★	★	★	★	...	---------------------(g)---------------------						
Kansas	★	★	★	★	★	...	★	★	★	...	★	★	★
Kentucky	★	★	★	★	★	...	...	★	★	★	...	★	★
Louisiana	...	★	★	...	★	...	★	★	...	...	★ (h)	...	...
Maine	...	★	★	★	★	...	...	★ (i)	★	...	...	★	★
Maryland	★	★	★	★	★	★ (j)	★ (k)	★ (k)	★ (k)	★ (k)	...	★ (k)	...
Massachusetts	...	★ (l)	★	...	...	★	★	...	...	...	★	...	...
Michigan	★	★	★	★	★	★ (m)	★ (n)	...	...	...	...	...	...
Minnesota	★	★	★	★	★	★ (ee)	...	...	★	...	★	★	★
Mississippi	...	★	★	★	...	...	...	...	★ (o)	...	...	...	...
Missouri	★	★	★	★	★	...	...	★	...	...	...	...	★
Montana	...	★	★	...	★	★ (p)	★	...	...	...	...	★	★
Nebraska	...	★	★	★	★	...	★	★	...	...	...	★	★
Nevada	...	★	★	★	★	...	★ (kk)	...	...	...	...	...	...
New Hampshire (ii)	★	★	...	★	★	...	...	★	...	★	...	★	★
New Jersey	...	★	...	★	★	...	★	...	...	...	...	★	★
New Mexico	★	★	★	...	★	...	★	...	...	★	...	(q)	(q)
New York	★	★	★	...	★	★ (r)	★	★	★	★	...	★	...
North Carolina	...	★	★	...	★	★	(s)	...	...	...	...	...	...
North Dakota	...	...	★	★	★	★ (t)	(u)	★	...	...	...	★	★
Ohio	★	★	★	★	★	...	(v)	★	...	...	...	★	...
Oklahoma	★	★	★	★	...	...	...	★	...	...	★	★	...
Oregon	★	★	★	★	★	...	★	...	...	...	...	★	...
Pennsylvania	...	★	★	★	...	...	...	...	...	★	...	★	...
Rhode Island	★	★	★	★	★	...	...	★	...	★	...	★	★
South Carolina	★	★	★	★	★	...	...	★	...	(w)	...	★	★
South Dakota	...	★	★	★	★	...	...	★	...	...	...	...	...
Tennessee	★	★	★	...	★	...	★	★	★	...	...	...	...
Texas	...	★	★	★	★	★ (x)	★	...	...	(jj)	...	...	...
Utah	...	★	★	★	★	★ (y)	★	★	★	...	...	★	★
Vermont	---------------(z)---------------						...	★	...	★	...	...	...
Virginia	★	★	★	★	★	★ (aa)	(bb)	...	★	...	★	★ (cc)	...
Washington	...	★	★	★	★	★ (dd)	★	★	★	★	★	★	...
West Virginia	...	★	★	★	★	...	...	...	...	★	...	...	...
Wisconsin	...	★	★	★	★	...	...	...	...	...	...	...	...
Wyoming	...	★	★	★	...	...	★	...	...	...	...	...	...
Guam	...	★	...	...	★	★ (ff)	★	...	...	★	★	★	...
CNMI*	★	★	★	★	★	★	...	...	...	...	★	★	★
Puerto Rico	---------------------------------(gg)---------------------------------												
U.S. Virgin Islands	★	★	...	★	...	...	★	...	...	...	...	...	...

See footnotes at end of table

TABLE 3.18
Fiscal Notes: Content and Distribution (continued)

Source: The Council of State Governments' survey, December 2019 and state websites 2020.

*Commonwealth of Northern Mariana Islands

Note: A fiscal note is a summary of the fiscal effects of a bill on government revenues, expenditures and liabilities.

Key:

★ –Yes

… –No

(a) Fiscal notes included on final passage calendar.

(b) Only retirement, corrections, revenue, tax and local government bills require fiscal notes. During the past session, fiscal notes were provided for education.

(c) The fiscal notes are printed with the bills favorably reported by the committees.

(d) Statement of purpose.

(e) Attached to bill, so available to both fiscal and executive budget staff. Joint Rule 18.

(f) A summary of each fiscal note is attached to the summary of its bill in the printed Legislative Synopsis and Digest, and on the General Assembly's Web site. Fiscal notes are prepared for the sponsor and attached to the bill on file with the House Clerk or Senate Secretary.

(g) Fiscal notes are available to everyone.

(h) Prepared by the Legislative Fiscal Office when a state agency is involved and prepared by Legislative Auditor's office when a local board or commission is involved; copies sent to House and Senate staff offices respectively.

(i) Distributed to members of the committee of reference; also available on the Legislature's Web site.

(j) A fiscal note is now known as a fiscal and policy note to better reflect the contents. Fiscal and policy notes also identify any mandate on local government and include analyses of the economic impact on small businesses.

(k) In practice fiscal and policy notes are prepared on all bills and resolutions prior to a public hearing on the bills/resolutions. After initial hard copy distribution to sponsor and committee, the note is released to member computer system and thereafter to the legislative Web site.

(l) Fiscal notes are prepared only if cost exceeds $100,000 or matter has not been acted upon by the Joint Committee on Ways and Means.

(m) In regards to Impact on Local Government, Fee Impact Statements are written.

(n) At present, fiscal information is part of the bill analysis on the legislative Web site.

(o) And committee to which bill referred.

(p) Mechanical defects in bill.

(q) Fiscal impact statements prepared by Legislative Finance Committee staff are available to anyone on request and on the legislature's Web site.

(r) Fiscal notes are required for retirement bills, bills enacting or amending tax expenditures, and all bills increasing or decreasing state revenues, or affecting appropriation or expenditure of state monies.

(s) Fiscal notes are posted on the Internet and available to all members.

(t) Notes required only if impact is $5,000 or more. Bills impacting workforce safety and insurance benefits or premiums have actuarial statements as do bills proposing changes in state and local retirement systems.

(u) Fiscal notes are available online to anyone from the legislative branch Web site.

(v) Fiscal notes are prepared for bills before being voted on in any standing committee or floor session. Fiscal notes for all introduced bills are posted on the Web. They are also distributed to the committees in which the bills are heard.

(w) Fiscal impact statements on proposed legislation are prepared by the Revenue and Fiscal Affairs Office and sent to the House or Senate standing committee that requested the impact. All fiscal impacts are posted on the Revenue and Fiscal Affairs website.

(x) Some bills may also require the preparation of one or more of the following: a dynamic economic impact statement, an actuarial impact statement, a criminal justice policy impact statement, an equalized education funding impact statement, a higher education impact statement, an open government impact statement, a tax equity note, or a water development policy impact statement.

(y) Fiscal notes are to include cost and revenue estimates on all bills that anticipate direct impact on state government, local government, residents, and businesses.

(z) Fiscal notes are not mandatory and their content will vary.

(aa) Technical amendments, if needed. Fiscal notes do not provide statements or interpretations of legislative intent for legal purposes. A summary of the stated objective, effect, and impact may be included.

(bb) Fiscal impact statements are widely available because they are also posted on the Internet shortly after they are distributed. The Joint Legislative Audit Review Commission (JLARC) also prepares a review of the fiscal impact statement if requested by a standing committee chair. The review statement is also available on the Internet.

(cc) Legislative budget directors.

(dd) Impact on private sector

(ee) Long-term costs.

(ff) Fiscal impact on local economy.

(gg) The Legislature of Puerto Rico does not prepare fiscal notes, but upon request the economics unit could prepare one. The Department of Treasury has the duty to analyze and prepare fiscal notes.

(hh) Hawaii does not require the submission of fiscal notes.

(ii) Whenever possible, fiscal notes appear at end of introduced version of bill.

(jj) A fiscal note must be distributed in committee before a bill is considered (house) or approved (senate) and must be attached to a committee report when distributed to the full membership. An updated fiscal note must be distributed to all the members before a conference committee report or a measure amended by the other chamber is acted on.

(kk) Fiscal notes are posted on the Legislature's website.

(ll) Joint Rule 18.

TABLE 3.19
Bill and Resolution Introductions and Enactments: 2019 Regular Sessions

State	Duration of session**	Introductions		Enactments/adoptions		Measures vetoed by governor (a)(b)	Length of session
		Bills	Resolutions*	Bills	Resolutions*		
Alabama	Mar. 5 - May 31, 2019	1,070	425	382	153	0	28L
Alaska	Jan. 15 - May 15, 2019	305	64	29	25	1 (a)	120C
Arizona	Jan. 14 - May 28, 2019	1,318	100	320	26	11	134C
Arkansas	Jan. 14 - Apr. 24, 2019	986	127	629	91	0	87C
California	Dec. 3, 2018 - Sep. 9, 2019	2,625	408	870	301	172 (a)	127L
Colorado	Jan. 4 - May 3, 2019	598	49	454	44	5	120C
Connecticut	Jan. 9 - Jun. 5, 2019	3,574	280	226	1 (e)	3	148C
Delaware	Jan. 8 - Jun. 30, 2019	455	170	219	147	0	46C
Florida	Mar. 5- May 4, 2019	1,027	68	184	0	6	60C
Georgia (k)	Jan. 14 - Apr. 2, 2019; Jan. 13 - Mar. 27, 2020	1,572	2,246	317	1,911	13	N/A
Hawaii	Jan. 16 - May 2, 2019	3,142	851	286	220	18	60L
Idaho	Jan. 7 - Apr. 11, 2019	522	67	329	37	2	95C
Illinois	Jan. 9 - Jun. 1, 2019	6,298	1,653	637	1,381	8 (a)(b)	71C
Indiana	Jan. 3 - Apr. 24, 2019	1,344	368	293	104	0	N/A
Iowa	Jan. 14 - Apr. 27, 2019	1,544	(g)	169	(g)	1 (a)	104C
Kansas	Jan. 14 - May 29, 2019	660	96	68	10	3 (a)	79C
Kentucky	Jan. 4 - Mar. 28, 2019	786	502	198	6	(a)(b)	30L
Louisiana	Apr. 8 - Jun. 6, 2019	844	866	454	826	6 (a)	45C
Maine (d)	Dec. 5, 2018 - Jun. 20, 2019	1,846	51	695	48	8	59L
Maryland	Jan. 9 - Apr. 8, 2019	2,481	16	772	2	92 (i)	90C
Massachusetts (k)	Jan. 2 - Dec. 31, 2019; Jan. 2 - Dec. 31, 2020	7,061	0	177	0	3	N/A
Michigan	Jan. 9 - Dec. 19, 2019	2,005	355	178	245	2 (a)	(f)
Minnesota	Jan. 8 - May 20, 2019	5,846	0	65	0	·	133C
Mississippi	Jan. 8 - Mar. 29, 2019	2,876	429	353	333	3	80C
Missouri	Jan. 9 - May 30, 2019	1,766	171	85	0	6	141C
Montana	Jan. 7 - Apr. 25, 2019	1,140	169	486	111	36	N/A
Nebraska (U)	Jan. 9 - May 31, 2019	739	278	257	122	4 (b)	60L
Nevada	Feb. 4 - Jun. 3, 2019	1,117	62	636	50	3	N/A
New Hampshire	Jan. 2 - Sep. 25, 2019	779	9	346	1	55 (b)	17L
New Jersey	Jan. 9, 2018 - Jan. 14, 2020	10,100	1,200	472	94	12 (a)	N/A
New Mexico	Jan. 15 - Mar. 16, 2019	1,483	37	309	5	36 (a)	60C
New York (k)	Jan. 9 - Jun. 21, 2019; Jan 8, 2020 - N/A	17,292	3,688	778	3,552	169	N/A
North Carolina (h)	Jan. 9, 2019 - (h)	1,679	54	251	36	14	(h)
North Dakota	Jan. 3 - Apr. 26, 2019	905	79	579	48	2 (a)(b)	76L
Ohio	Jan. 9 - Dec. 30, 2019 (j)	718	36	24	6	(a)	(j)
Oklahoma	Feb. 4 - May 23, 2019	2,855	91	510	40	16 (a)	N/A
Oregon	Jan. 21 - Jun. 30, 2019	2,768	(g)	701	59	(a)	160C
Pennsylvania	Jan. 1 - Dec. 18, 2019	3,071	899	89	N/A	3	N/A
Rhode Island	Jan. 1 - Jun. 30, 2019	1,788	520	440	450	3	N/A
South Carolina (k)	Jan. 8 - May 9, 2019; Jan. 14, 2020 - N/A	1,845	1,607	103	1,257	1	N/A
South Dakota	Jan. 8 - Mar. 29, 2019	464	32	218	1	2	N/A
Tennessee (k)	Jan. 8 - May 2, 2019; Jan. 14 - Apr. 22, 2020	5,833	2,436	1,106	1,821	0	N/A
Texas	Jan. 8 - May 27, 2019	7,324	3,553	1,429	3,152	58	140C
Utah	Jan. 28 - Mar. 14, 2019	763	79	511	63	1 (a)	45C
Vermont	Jan. 9 - May 29, 2019	729	258	83	230	2	80L

See footnotes at end of table

TABLE 3.19

Bill and Resolution Introductions and Enactments: 2019 Regular Sessions (continued)

State	Duration of session**	Introductions		Enactments/adoptions		Measures vetoed by governor (a)(b)	Length of session
		Bills	Resolutions*	Bills	Resolutions*		
Virginia	Jan. 9 - Feb. 23, 2019	1,999	1,126	849	1,015	34	45C
Washington (k)	Jan. 14 - Apr. 28, 2019; Jan. 13 - Mar. 12, 2020	3,662	229	468	9	2	N/A
West Virginia	Jan. 9 - Mar. 9, 2019	1,823	316	294	158	30 (b)	60C
Wisconsin (c)	Jan. 7, 2019 - Jan. 4, 2021	1,339	217	69	217	11 (a)	55L
Wyoming	Jan. 8 - Feb. 28, 2019	454	17	186	5	3 (a)(b)	36L

Source: The Council of State Governments' survey and legiscan. com, March 2020.

* Includes Joint and Concurrent resolutions.

**Actual adjournment dates are listed regardless of constitutional or statutory limitations. For more information on provisions, see Table 3.2, "Legislative Sessions: Legal Provisions."

Key:

C – Calendar day.

L – Legislative day (in some states, called a session or workday; definition may vary slightly; however, it generally refers to any day on which either chamber of the legislature is in session).

U – Unicameral legislature

N/A – Not available.

(a) Line item or partial vetoes: Alaska - 3; California - 1; Illinois - 1; Iowa - 1; Kansas - 1; Kentucky - 3; Louisiana - 9; Michigan - 16; New Mexico - 8; New Jersey - 69 (conditional and line item); North Dakota - 1; Ohio - 25 items in budget bill; Oklahoma - 1; Oregon - 2; Utah - 3; Wisconsin - 1; Wyoming - 4

(b) Number of vetoes overridden: Illinois - 1; Kentucky - 2; Nebraska - 4; New Hampshire - 1; North Dakota - 1; West Virginia - 2; Wyoming - 2

(c) Information for the 2019-2020 two-year session as of Jan. 8, 2020.

(d) The Maine Governor held 40 bills since the end of the 129th First Regular Session. At the beginning of the 129th Second Regular Session, some of these became law, some were vetoed, and some were recalled from the Governor's desk by the Legislature. Since these bills were enacted during the 1st Regular Session of the 129th Legislature, they are counted as enactments here. Vetoes of some of these bills, which occured during the 2nd Regular Session of the 129th are not counted here. The Resolutions

statistics do not include Constitutional Resolutions. Other than Constitutional Resolutions, there are two other types of Resolutions in Maine: ones that memorialize Congress and ones that recognize a person, day, week, or month such as Autism Awareness Month. These two types of Resolutions have different introduction and enactment procedures but are lumped together here.

(e) This number reflects the resolution proposing an amendment to the state constitution that passed both Senate and House, but does not reflect any executive or judicial nomination resolutions that passed both Senate and House.

(f) House held 115 session days, Senate 116 session days. There were 345 calendar days from convening to adjournment.

(g) Resolutions are included in bill numbers.

(h) Information as of 11/20/2019, for the 2019 session, which was set to continue on 1/14/20.

(i) Of the 92 measures vetoed by the governor, 13 were "policy vetoes" (governor had objections to the bills due to policy concerns), while the others were duplicative (the bill in the opposite chamber, which also passed, accomplished the same purpose, so the governor signed only one of the measures and vetoed the other).

(j) The House adjounred on Dec. 27, 2019 and the Senate on Dec. 30, 2019. The House of was in session for 140 calendar days and the Senate for 139 calendar days.

(k) Figures reflect the number of bills and resolutions introduced and enacted for the 2019-2020 two-year session as of March 3, 2020.

TABLE 3.20
Bill and Resolution Introductions and Enactments: 2019 Special Sessions

State	Duration of session**	Introductions Bills	Introductions Resolutions*	Enactments/adoptions Bills	Enactments/adoptions Resolutions*	Measures vetoed by governor	Length of session
Alabama	Mar. 6–12, 2019	10	16	3	0	0	5L
Alaska	May 16–Jun. 13, 2019	7;	1;	4;	0;	(a);	28C;
	Jul. 8–Aug. 6, 2019	6	1	2	0	(a)	29C
Arizona	No special session in 2019						
Arkansas	No special session in 2019						
California	No special session in 2019						
Colorado	No special session in 2019						
Connecticut	No special session in 2019						
Delaware	No special session in 2019						
Florida	No special session in 2019						
Georgia	No special session in 2019						
Hawaii (b)	Sep. 16–17, 2019;	0;	1;	0;	1;	0;	1L;
	Nov. 12–13, 2019	0	1	0	1	0	1L
Idaho	No special session in 2019						
Illinois	No special session in 2019						
Indiana	No special session in 2019						
Iowa	No special session in 2019						
Kansas	No special session in 2019						
Kentucky	Jul. 19–24, 2019	1	9	1	1	0	5L
Louisiana	No special session in 2019						
Maine (c)	Aug. 26, 2019	7	0	3	0	0	1L
Maryland	No special session in 2019						
Massachusetts	No special session in 2019						
Michigan	No special session in 2019						
Minnesota	May 24–25, 2019	31	0	13	0	0	1L
Mississippi	No special session in 2019						
Missouri	Sep. 9–16, 2019	35	2	1	0	0	6L
Montana	No special session in 2019						
Nebraska (U)	No special session in 2019						
Nevada	No special session in 2019						
New Hampshire	No special session in 2019						
New Jersey	No special session in 2019						
New Mexico	No special session in 2019						
New York	No special session in 2019						
North Carolina	No special session in 2019						
North Dakota	No special session in 2019						
Ohio	No special session in 2019						
Oklahoma	No special session in 2019						
Oregon	No special session in 2019						
Pennsylvania	No special session in 2019						
Rhode Island	No special session in 2019						
South Carolina	No special session in 2019						
South Dakota	No special session in 2019						
Tennessee	No special session in 2019						
Texas	No special session in 2019						
Utah	Sep. 16, 2019;	5;	1;	5;	1;	0;	1C;
	Dec. 12, 2019	2	0	2	0	0	1C
Vermont	No special session in 2019						
Virginia	Jul. 9–Nov. 18, 2019	72	85	0	75	0	N/A
Washington	No special session in 2019						
West Virginia	Mar. 10–Jul. 23, 2019;	16;	16;	47;	12;	0;	12L;
	Nov. 18, 2019	6	0	2	0	0	1C
Wisconsin	Nov. 7, 2019	0	0	0	0	0	1C
Wyoming	No special session in 2019						

See footnotes at end of table

TABLE 3.20

Bill and Resolution Introductions and Enactments: 2020 Special Sessions (continued)

Source: The Council of State Governments' survey and legiscan.com, Feb. 2020.

* Includes Joint and Concurrrent resolutions.

** Actual adjournment dates are listed regardless of constitutional or statutory limitations. For more information on provisions, see Table 3.2, "Legislative Sessions: Legal Provisions."

Key:

N/A – Not available

C–Calendar day.

L–Legislative day (in some states, called a session or workday; definition may vary slightly; however, it generally refers to any day on which either chamber of the legislature is in session).

U–Unicameral legislature.

(a) Two partial or line item vetoes.

(b) Two Senate special sessions were convened to confirm judicial nominations.

(c) The governor held one bill, which become law without her signature shortly after the convening of the 2nd Regular Session. Since it was enacted in the 2019 special session, it is included in the enactments statistic here.

TABLE 3.21
Staff for Individual Legislators

State or other jurisdiction	Senate Capitol Personal	Senate Capitol Shared	Senate District	House/Assembly Capitol Personal	House/Assembly Capitol Shared	House/Assembly District
Alabama	YR	YR/2	(a)	YR	YR/10	(a)
Alaska (b)	YR/SO	...	YR	YR/SO	...	YR
Arizona	YR (c)	...	...	...	YR (c)	...
Arkansas	...	YR	...	...	YR (d)	...
California	YR	...	YR	YR	...	YR
Colorado	SO (e)	YR (e)	...	YR (e)	YR (e)	...
Connecticut (f)	YR/1	...	...	...	YR/4	...
Delaware			(g)			
Florida	YR (h)	...	YR (h)	YR (h)	...	YR (h)
Georgia	...	YR/3, SO/68	...	...	YR/25, SO/113	...
Hawaii (nn)	YR/2	...	...	YR/1	...	...
Idaho	...	SO, YR (i)	...	...	SO, YR (i)	...
Illinois	YR (j)	YR (j)	YR (j)	YR (j)	YR (j)	YR (j)
Indiana	...	YR/2 (k)	...	...	YR	...
Iowa	SO/1 (oo)	...	(oo)	SO/1 (oo)	...	(oo)
Kansas	SO/1	...	...	(l)	SO/3	...
Kentucky	...	YR (m)	...	...	YR (m)	...
Louisiana	(n)	YR (o)	YR (n)	(n)	YR (o)	YR (n)
Maine	(p)	YR, SO (p)	...	...	YR/11 (q)	...
Maryland	(r)	...	YR (r)	YR (r)	SO (r)	YR (r)
Massachusetts	YR	...	...	YR	...	...
Michigan	YR (s)	...	...	YR/2 (s)	...	...
Minnesota	YR (t)	Varies	...	YR (t)	Varies	...
Mississippi	...	YR	...	...	YR	...
Missouri	YR/2	YR/1	...	YR/1	YR/1	...
Montana	...	SO	...	...	SO	...
Nebraska	YR/2	...	...	Unicameral		
Nevada	SO (u)	YR	...	SO (pp)	YR	...
New Hampshire	...	YR	...	...	YR	...
New Jersey	YR (h)	...	YR (h)	YR (h)	...	YR (h)
New Mexico	SO/1	...	...	...	SO/2	...
New York	YR (w)	...	YR (w)	YR (w)	...	YR (w)
North Carolina	YR (x)	YR	...	YR (x)	YR	...
North Dakota	...	SO (v)	...	...	SO (v)	...
Ohio	YR/2 (y)	...	(z)	YR/1 (aa)	...	(z)
Oklahoma	YR/1(bb)	YR (bb)	...	YR (bb)	YR/1 (bb)	...
Oregon	YR (cc)	YR	YR (dd)	YR (cc)	YR	YR (dd)
Pennsylvania	YR	...	YR	YR	...	YR
Rhode Island	...	YR (ee)	...	...	YR (ee)	...
South Carolina	...	YR/2	...	YR/4	...	...
South Dakota	(ff)	(ff)	...	(ff)	(ff)	...
Tennessee	YR/1	...	...	(gg)	YR/1	...
Texas	(hh)	...	(hh)	(hh)	...	(hh)
Utah	SO (ii)	YR /6-8(ii)	...	SO (ii)	YR/5-8(ii)	...
Vermont	YR/1 (jj)	...	...	YR/1 (jj)	...	...
Virginia	SO/1 (kk)	...	(kk)	SO (kk)	SO/2	(kk)
Washington	YR/1	...	IO/1	YR/1	...	YR/1
West Virginia	SO	...	...	...	SO/17	...
Wisconsin	(ll)	...	(ll)	(ll)	...	...
Wyoming	...	...	...	...	...	...
American Samoa	...	...	...	...	...	...
Guam	...	...	...	Unicameral		
CNMI*	YR (mm)	(mm)	...	YR (mm)	(mm)	(ll)
Puerto Rico	YR (mm)	...	...	YR (mm)	...	...
U.S. Virgin Islands	YR (mm)	...	...	Unicameral		

See footnotes at end of table

TABLE 3.21
Staff for Individual Legislators (continued)

Source: The Council of State Governments' survey, December 2019.
*Commonwealth of Northern Mariana Islands
Note: For entries under column heading "Shared," figures after
slash indicate approximate number of legislators per staff person,
where available.
Key:
…–Staff not provided for individual legislators.
YR–Year-round.
SO–Session only.
IO–Interim only.
(a) Six counties have local delegation offices with shared staff.
(b) The number of staff per legislator varies depending on their
position.
(c) Representatives share a secretary with another legislator; however,
House leadership and committee chairs usually have their own secretarial staff. All legislators share professional research staff.
(d) The legislators share eight member-services staff members; two
staff members per 25 legislators.
(e) Senate: Personal–Each Senator is granted 1,300 aide hours and
may employ up to two aides each fiscal year, with each aide working a maximum of 40 hours each week. Shared–The majority have
ten full time year round employees and two session-only positions. The minority have six full time year round employees and
two session-only positions. The Senate also employs nonpartisan
staff, including four full time year round employees and 13 session-only positions. There are also three session-only employees
in the bill room who are jointly managed by the Colorado Senate
and House. House: Personal–Each Representative is allowed to
hire up to 2 paid Legislative Aides who share a limit of 1,300
hours per fiscal year. Representatives may have an unlimited
number of unpaid interns and volunteers. Shared–The majority
have 10 full time year round employees and two session-only
positions. The minority employs 4 full time year round employees
and three session-only positions. The House also employs nonpartisan staff, including four full time year round employees and 20
session-only positions.
(f) The numbers are for staff assigned to specific legislators. There is
additional staff working in the leadership offices that also support
the rank and file members.
(g) Staffers are a combination of full time, part time, shared, personal, etc. and their assignments change throughout the year.
(h) Personal and district staff are the same. In Florida, district
employees may travel to the capitol for sessions (two district
employees in the Senate and one district employee in the House).
(i) The Senate has two full-time, year-round employees (chief of staff
to president pro tempore and secretary of the senate) and one
part-time, year-round employee (minority chief of staff). The Senate had 50 full-time employees during the 2019 legislative
session (January-April). The House has two full-time, year round
employees (chief of staff to the speaker and chief fiscal officer)
and one part-time, year-round employee (chief clerk of the hosue).
The House had 36 full-time employees during the 2019 legislative session (January-April).

(j) Each senator has one secretary and two House members share a
secretary. Partisan staffers also help legislators with many issues
as well as staffing committees. Most senators and representatives
have one or two district office employees, paid from a separate
allowance for that purpose.
(k) Leadership has one legislative assistant. During session, college
interns are hired to provide additional staff–one for every two
members. Leadership has one intern.
(l) One clerical staff person for three individual House members is
the norm. Chairpersons are provided their own individual clerical
staff person.
(m) The General Assembly is provided professional and clerical staff
services by a centralized, non-partisan staff, with the exception of
House and Senate leadership which employs partisan staff. No
district staff provided.
(n) Each legislator may hire as many assistants as desired, but pay
from public funds ranges from $2,000 to $3,000 per month per
legislator. Assistant(s) generally work in the district office but may
also work at the capitol during the session.
(o) The six caucuses are assigned one full-time position each (poten-
tially 24 legislators per one staff person).
(p) Presonal: No Senate positions are exclusive to any one member.
The President's Office does work for the Senate President, however
they also work in conjunction with the Majority Office caucus.
Shared: Year Round and Session Only. Secretary's Office: 10 YR, 5
SO; President's Office: 8 YR; Majority office: 8 YR; Minority office:
6 YR. This is difficult to quantify. It can fluctuate depending on the
office structure and total number of members for each caucus.
Currently, the Senate Democrats have 21 members and the Senate Republicans have 14. Number of legislators per staff person:
again, this is difficult to quantify. Legislative Aides are assigned to
multiple members, yet the Communications Director works for all
members of the caucus.
(q) This is an average as some have 12, 14 and one legislator has
seven. The 151 House members do not have individual staff.
Speaker's office: 8 year round. Clerk's office: 12 year round, 1 part-
time, 10 session-only.
(r) Senate: Funds are included to permit each senator to hire an
administrative aide that is a regular full-time, benefited employee.
The current salary range for these positions is $39,000 to
$71,190. Funds are included to permit each senator to hire a sec-
retary for the legislative session. This is generally a benefited
employee. For fiscal 2017, each position was budgeted at $8,118.
Each senator is provided with a District Office Allowance of
$18,965. Of this amount, $5,800 is restricted to staff assistance.
Nine leadership positions are each provided with $20,436, of
which $6,500 is restricted to staff assistance.Each senator is pro-
vided with a Supplemental Operating Fund in the amount of
$7,500. This amount is intended to supplement the District Office
Allowance and may be spent on operating expenses or for staff
assistance at the senator's option. House: Funds are included in
the House budget to provide for payment of salaries attributable
to specifically budgeted delegation staff positions. These are generally benefited positions that may work either a full-time or a
part-time schedule depending on workload. The applicable salary
for each budgeted delegation staff position is established based

TABLE 3.21
Staff for Individual Legislators (continued)

primarily on qualifications, experience, and anticipated workload. Funds are included to permit each delegate to hire a secretary for the legislative session. Each delegate's secretary was funded at $2,755 for fiscal 2017, which if combined with two other delegates, approximates the amount budgeted for each senator's secretary. Each delegate is provided with a District Office Allowance of $18,965. Of this amount, $5,800 is restricted to staff assistance. Twelve senior leadership positions are each provided with $20,436, of which $6,500 is restricted to staff assistance. Five delegation chair positions are each provided with $19,810, of which $5,800 is restricted to staff assistance. Each delegate is provided with a Supplemental Operating Fund in the amount of $3,546. This amount is intended to supplement the District Office Allowance and may be spent on operating expenses or for staff assistance at the delegate's option..

(s) Senate–majority, 2-6 staff per legislator; minority, 2-3 staff per legislator. House–2 staff per legislator.

(t) Senate: One to two staff persons per legislator. House: .5 to 1.5 staff persons per legislator

(u) Senate–Majority Leader, 3 staff; Minority Leader, 2 staff; Other Senators 1 staff per legislator. Secretarial staff. House–1 staff per legislator. Secretarial staff; Leadership positions are assigned additional staff.

(v) Secretarial staff; in North Dakota, leadership only.

(w) Varies depending upon allowance allocated to each member. Members have considerable independence in hiring personal and committee staffs. Legislative employees can be annual, session, or temporary.

(x) Part time during interim.

(y) Some leadership offices have more.

(z) Some legislators maintain district offices at their own expense.

(aa) Some offices have more.

(bb) Senate: Pro Tem–6 staff persons; Senate minority leader–1 staff person. House: year round one to eight, majority party only; minority party one staff person per legislator. Committee, fiscal and legal staffs are available to legislators on a year round.

(cc) Two staff persons per legislator during session.

(dd) Senate– Equivalent of one full-time staff. House–1 during interim.

(ee) The General Assembly has a total of 280 full time positions, 267 full-time shared staff and additional 13 full-time positions for the House.

(ff) The non-partisan Legislative Research Council serves all members of both houses year round. Committee secretaries and legislative interns and pages provide support during the sessions.

(gg) Several House members have year-round personal staff. It depends on seniority, duties (such as committee chairs), and committee assignments.

(hh) Staff numbers vary depending on the legislator. Each legislator is allotted and office budget and has independence in using that budget for hiring staff.

(ii) Most legislators are assigned one university student intern during session who is temporarily employed by the Office of Legislative Research and General Counsel. Some legislators provide their own personal intern (volunteer or financial arrangements are made between them). Senate: The Senate employs four full-time constituent services staff to take care of administrative matters and constituent inquiries year round. Three serve 23 majority members and one serves six minority members. House: The House Majority has seven full-time staffers that serve 59 majority house members. The House Minority has three full-time staffers who serve 16 minority house members. The Utah House of Representatives also employs three full-time non-partisan staff members.

(jj) No personal staff except one administrative assistant for the Speaker and one for the Senate Pro Tempore.

(kk) Senate–One administrative assistant (secretary) provided to the members during the session by the Clerk's offices. Members also receive a set dollar allowance to hire additional legislative assistants who may serve year round at the capitol and in the district. House–Members also receive a set dollar allowance to hire additional legislative assistants who may serve year round at the capitol and in the district.

(ll) Staffing levels vary according to majority/minority status and leadership or committee responsibilities. Members may assign staff to work in the district office.

(mm) Individual staffing and staff pool arrangements are at the discretion of the individual legislator.

(nn) Each senator has the authority to hire at least two full-time, year-round staff. Each representative has the authority to hire at least one full-time, year-round staff. Depending on leadership or committee chair assignment, additional staff positions may be authorized.

(oo) One clerk provided in capitol. District/Caucus–11 staff persons for Republicans and 9 staff persons for Democrats.

TABLE 3.22
Staff for Legislative Standing Committees

State or other jurisdiction	Committee staff assistance				Source of staff services**							
	Senate		House/Assembly		Joint central agency (a)		Chamber agency (b)		Caucus or leadership		Committee or committee chair	
	Prof.	Cler.	Prof.	Cler.	Prof.	Cler.	Prof.	Cler.	Prof.	Cler.	Prof.	Cler.
Alabama	•	★	•	★	B	...	...	B	H	S	...	...
Alaska	★	★	★	★	B	B	...	...	...	...	B	B
Arizona	★	★	★	★	B	B	B	B	B	B	B	B
Arkansas	★	★	★	★	B	B	B	B	...	...	...	...
California	★	★	★	★	B	B	B	B	B	B	B	B
Colorado	★	...	★	...	B	...	B	B	B	B (c)	...	...
Connecticut (m)	★	★	★	★	B	...	...	B	B	B	...	B
Delaware	...	★	...	★	B	...	B	...	B	...	...	B
Florida	★	★	★	★	B	B	B	B	B	B	B	B
Georgia	•	★	•	★	B	B	B	B	B	B	B	...
Hawaii	★	★	★	★	B	B	B	B	B	B	B	B
Idaho	...	★	...	★	B (d)	B (d)	B	B	...	B	...	...
Illinois	★	★	★	★	...	...	B	B	B	B	...	...
Indiana	★	...	...	...	...	...	S	...	S	...	...	...
Iowa	★	★	★	★	B	...	B (f)	B	B	...	...	B
Kansas	★	★	★	★	B	B (g)	B	B	B	B	B	B
Kentucky	★	★	★	★	B	B	B	B	B (h)	B (h)	...	...
Louisiana	★(i)	★	★(i)	★	B	B	B	B	B	B	B (j)	B (j)
Maine	★(k)	★(k)	★(k)	★(k)	B	B	B	B	B	B	...	B
Maryland	★(l)	★(l)	★(l)	★(l)	B	B	...	...	...	...	...	...
Massachusetts	★	★	★	★	...	...	...	...	...	...	...	...
Michigan	★	★	★	★	B	...	B	B	B	S	...	...
Minnesota	★	★	★	★	...	...	B	H	B	B	B	B
Mississippi	•	★	•	★	...	...	B	B	...	...	B	B
Missouri	★	...	★	...	B	...	B	...	S	S	B	...
Montana	★	★	★	★	B	...	B	...	...	...	...	...
Nebraska	★	★	U	U	...	...	...	...	...	...	S	S
Nevada	★	★	★	★	B	...	...	B	...	...	...	...
New Hampshire	★	★	★	★	B	B	B	B	...	S	...	S
New Jersey	★	★	★	★	B	B	B	B	...	...	...	...
New Mexico	★	★	★	★	...	...	B	B	...	...	...	...
New York	★	★	★	★	...	...	B	B	B	B	B	B
North Carolina	★	★(n)	★	★(n)	B	...	...	...	...	...	...	B (n)
North Dakota	...	★	...	★	B	B	...	...	...	B	...	...
Ohio	★	★	★	★	B	...	...	...	B	...	B	B
Oklahoma	★	★	★	★	...	...	B	B	S	...	B	B
Oregon	★	★	★	★	B	B	B	B	B	B	B	B
Pennsylvania	★	★	★	★	B	B	B	B	B	B	B	B
Rhode Island	•	★	•	★	B	B	...	B	...	...	B	...
South Carolina	★	★	★	★	B	B	B	B	B	B	B	B
South Dakota	★	★	★	★	B	...	...	(l)	...	(l)	...	(l)
Tennessee	★	★	★	★	B	...	B	B	...	...	...	B
Texas	★	★	★	★	B	B	B	B	...	...	B	B
Utah	★	★	★	★	B	B	...	...	...	...	...	...
Vermont	★	•	★	•	B	B	...	...	...	...	...	...
Virginia	★	★	★	★	B	...	B	B	...	...	(o)	(o)
Washington	★	★	★	★	...	...	B	B	B	B	B	B
West Virginia	★	★	★	★	B	B	B	B	B	B	B	B
Wisconsin	★	★	★	★	B	...	...	...	...	...	(p)	B
Wyoming	...	★	...	★	B	...	...	B	...	...	...	...
American Samoa	•	★	•	★	B	B	B	B	...	...	B	...
Guam	★	★	U	U	...	...	S	S	...	...	...	...
CNMI*	★	★	★	★	B (q)	B (q)	B (q)	B (q)	B (q)	B (q)	B (q)	B (q)
Puerto Rico	★	★	★	★	B (q)	B (q)	B (q)	B (q)	B (q)	B (q)	B (q)	B (q)
U.S. Virgin Islands	★	★	U	U	S (q)	S (q)	S (q)	S (q)	S (q)	S (q)	S (q)	S (q)

See footnotes at end of table

TABLE 3.22
Staff for Legislative Standing Committees (continued)

Source: The Council of State Governments' survey, December 2019.
*Commonwealth of Northern Mariana Islands
** – Multiple entries reflect a combination of organizations and location of services.
Key:
★ – All committees
• – Some committees
… – Services not provided
B – Both chambers
H – House
S – Senate
U – Unicameral

(a) Includes legislative council or service agency or central management agency.

(b) Includes chamber management agency, office of clerk or secretary and House or Senate research office.

(c) Senate - there is secretarial staff for both majority and minority offices for the Senate in the Capitol. Most of the clerical work is done by caucus staff. House - the clerical and secretarial staff for the House is more centralized and is supervised by the Clerk of the House.

(d) Professional staff and clerical support is provided via the Legislative Services Office, a non-partisan office serving all members of the House and Senate on a year-round basis. There are currently 65 employees working in the Legislative Services Office. Leadership in each party hire their respective support staff

(e) Leadership in each party hire their respective support staff.

(f) The Senate secretary and House clerk maintain supervision of committee clerks.

(g) Senators and House chairpersons select their secretaries and notify the central administrative services agency; all administrative employee matters handled by the agency.

(h) Leadership employs partisan staff to provide professional and clerical services. However, all members, including leadership are also served by the centralized, non-partisan staff.

(i) House Appropriations and Senate Finance Committees have Legislative Fiscal Office staff at their hearings.

(j) Staff are assigned to each committee but work under the direction of the chair.

(k) Standing committees are joint House and Senate committees.

(l) The clerical support comes from employees who are hired to work only during the legislative sessions. They are employees of either the House or the Senate, and are not part of the central agency.

(m) Committees are joint Senate and House. Professional nonpartisan staff serves committees, individual legislators and legislature as a whole, regardless of chamber or party.

(n) Member's personal secretary serves as a clerk to the committee or subcommittee that the member chairs.

(o) The House Appropriations Committee and the Senate Finance Committees have their own staff. The staff members work under the direction of the chair.

(p) Standing committees are staffed by subject specialists from the office of the Legislative Council staff.

(q) In general, the legislative service agency provides legal and staff assistance for legislative meetings and provides associated materials. Individual legislators hire personal or committee staff as their budgets provide and at their own discretion.

TABLE 3.23
Standing Committees: Appointment and Number

State or other jurisdiction	Committee members appointed by:		Committee chairpersons appointed by:		Number of standing committees during regular 2019 session		Number of joint committees during 2019 session
	Senate	House/Assembly	Senate	House/Assembly	Senate	House/Assembly	
Alabama	(v)	S	(v)	S	20	33	0
Alaska	CC	CC	CC	CC	10	10	3
Arizona	P	S	P	S	12	18	1
Arkansas	(a)	(b)	(a)	S (b)	9	10	7
California	CR	S	CR	S	22	32	8
Colorado	MjL	S	MjL	S	10	11	8
Connecticut	PT	S	PT	S	(c)	(c)	25 (c)
Delaware	PT	S	PT	S	17	23	4
Florida	P	S	P	S	18	9	4
Georgia	CC	S	CC	S	29	37	0
Hawaii	P	S	P	(d)	16	18	0
Idaho	PT (f)	S	PT	S	10	15	5
Illinois	P, MnL (w)	S, MnL (w)	P, MnL (w)	S, MnL (w)	26	35	0
Indiana	PT	S	PT	S	21	21	1
Iowa	MjL, MnL	S (x)	MjL	S	16	19	0
Kansas	(g)	(g)	P	S	15	28	12
Kentucky	CC	CC	CC	CC	15	19	0
Louisiana	P	S (h)	P	S	17	16	0
Maine	P	S	P	S	5	6	17
Maryland	P	S	P	S	6	7	19
Massachusetts	P	S	P	S	11	11	29
Michigan	MjL	S	MjL	S	19	21	3
Minnesota	CR	MjL	S	S	21	10	2
Mississippi	P	S	P	S	39	47	0
Missouri	PT (j)	S (j)	PT	S	22	28	13
Montana	CC	S	CC	S	17	16	0
Nebraska	CC	U	E	U	14	U	0
Nevada	MjL (e)	S	MjL	S	10	10	0
New Hampshire	P (k)	S (k)	P (k)	S (k)	12	24	0
New Jersey	CC	CC	CC	CC	14	25	7
New Mexico	CC	S	CC	S	9 (l)	14 (l)	0
New York	PT	S	PT	S	41	37	0
North Carolina	PT	S	PT	S	18	34	0
North Dakota	CC	CC	CC	CC	12	12	0
Ohio	P (m)	S (m)	P (m)	S (m)	16	27	5
Oklahoma	PT (e)	S	PT	S	14	22	0
Oregon	P	S	P	S	13	13	16
Pennsylvania	PT	S	PT	S	22	24	0
Rhode Island	P	S	P	S	10	13	2
South Carolina	(n)	S	(o)	E	15	13	4
South Dakota	PT	S	PT	S	14	14	2
Tennessee	S	S	S	S	9	14	4
Texas	P	S (p)	P	S	16	34	0
Utah	P	S	P	S	11	14	7
Vermont	CC	S	CC	S	11	14	16
Virginia	E	S	(q)	S	11	14	0
Washington	CC	CC	CC (r)	CC (s)	16	20	12
West Virginia	P	S	P	S	19	20	0
Wisconsin	MjL (y)	S (y)	MjL	S	19	47	10
Wyoming	P	S	P	S	...	...	12
Dist. of Columbia	(t)	U	(t)	U	13	U	0
American Samoa	P	S	E	S	N/A	N/A	N/A
Guam	(u)	U	(u)	U	11	U	0
CNMI*	P	S	P	S	7	11	0
Puerto Rico	P	S	P	S	25	35	8
U.S. Virgin Islands	E	U	E	U	11	U	0

See footnotes at end of table

TABLE 3.23
Standing Committees: Appointment and Number (continued)

Source: The Council of State Governments' survey, December 2019 and state websites 2020.

*Commonwealth of Northern Mariana Islands

Key:
CC–Committee on Committees
CR–Committee on Rules
E–Election
MjL–Majority Leader
MnL–Minority Leader
P–President
PT–President pro tempore
S–Speaker
U–Unicameral Legislature
…– None reported.
N/A–Not available

(a) Selection process based on seniority.

(b) For the 2019 session the Speaker appointed members and leadership of all committees. Beginning with the next General Assembly, committee selection process will be based on seniority for standing committees, House Budget Committee, Legislative Council, and Legislative Joint Auditing Committee. Committee composition balanced by geographical region. Speaker appoints members of select committees.

(c) Committees are joint Senate and House. There are 22 committees established under the Joint Rules and three committees established under statue.

(d) By resolution with members of majority party designating the chair, vice-chairs and majority party members of committees, and members of minority party designating minority party members.

(e) Minority Leader selects minority members.

(f) "The following standing committees shall be appointed by the leadership under the direction of the President Pro Tempore, by and with the advice and consent of the Senate … provided that the President Pro Tempore shall appoint a majority of each committee and the chairman of each committee from the membership of the political party having a majority in the Senate.…" (Senate Rule 19).

(g) Committee on Organization, Calendar and Rules.

(h) Speaker appoints only 12 of the 19 members of the Committee on Appropriations.

(i) There are currently 16 Joint Standing Committees, two Joint Select Committees, and a joint Government Oversight Committee.

(j) Senate minority committee members chosen by minority caucus, but appointed by president pro tempore. House minority members of committees appointed by the minority floor leader.

(k) Senate president and House speaker consult with minority leaders.

(l) Senate: includes eight substantive committees and one procedural committee. House: includes 12 substantive committees and two procedural committees.

(m) The minority leader may recommend for consideration minority party members for each committee.

(n) Appointment based on seniority (Senate Rule 19D).

(o) Appointed by seniority which is determined by tenure within the committee rather than tenure within the Senate. Also, chair is based on the majority party within the committee (Senate Rule 19E).

(p) For each standing substantive committee of the House, except for procedural committees, a maximum of one-half of the membership, exclusive of chair and vice-chair, is determined by seniority; the remaining membership of the committee is determined by the speaker.

(q) In the Virginia Senate, the chair is the committee member from the majority party who has the most seniority.

(r) Recommended by the Committee on Committees, approved by the president, then confirmed by the Senate.

(s) Recommended by the Committee on Committees, then confirmed by the House.

(t) Chair of the Council.

(u) Members are appointed by the Chairperson; Chairperson is elected during majority caucus prior to inauguration.

(v) Committee on Assignments.

(w) Senate: President and Minority Leader appoint committee members including chairperson and minority spokesperson. House: Speaker appoints chairperson and majority members; Minority Leader appoints minority members.

(x) Speaker confers with Minority Leader regarding minority member appointments.

(y) Minority party committee appointments are based on minority party leadership nominations.

TABLE 3.24
Rules Adoption and Standing Committees: Procedure

State or other jurisdiction	Constitution permits each legislative body to determine its own rules	Committee meetings open to public*		Specific, advance notice provisions for committee meetings or hearings	Voting/roll call provisions to report a bill to floor
		Senate	House/Assembly		
Alabama	★	★	★	Senate: Four hours, if possible. House: Twenty-four hours, except Rules & Local Legislations Committee. Exceptions after 27th legislative day and special sessions.	Senate: final vote on a bill, except a local bill, is recorded. House: recorded vote if requested by member of committee and sustained by one additional committee member.
Alaska	...	★	★	For meetings, by 4:00 p.m. on the preceding Thurs.; for first hearings on bills, 5 days.	Roll call vote on any measure taken upon request by any member of either house.
Arizona	★	★	★	Senate: Written agenda for each regular and special meeting containing all bills, memorials and resolutions to be considered shall be distributed to each member of the committee and to the Secretary of the Senate at least five days prior to the committee meeting. House: The committee chair shall prepare an agenda and distribute copies to committee members, the Information Desk and the Chief Clerk's Office by 4 p.m. each Wednesday for all standing committees meeting on Monday of the following week and 4 p.m. each Thursday for all standing committees meeting on any day except Monday of the following week.	Senate and House: roll call vote.
Arkansas	★	★	★	Senate: 2 days (anytime with 2/3s vote of the committee). House: 18 hours (2 hours with 2/3s vote of the committee)	Senate: roll call votes are recorded. House: report of committee recommendation signed by committee chair.
California	★	★	★	Senate: advance notice provisions exist and are published in the agendas of each house. House: public notice is published in the agendas of each house. For bill hearings, the first committee of reference has a four-day notice and the second committee of reference has a two-day notice. Informational hearings have a four-day notice. No public notice is required for resolutions or special session bills.	Senate and House: roll call.
Colorado	★	★	★	Senate: final action on a measure is prohibited unless notice is posted one calendar day prior to its consideration. The prohibition does not apply if the action receives a majority vote of the committee. House: Meeting publicly announced while the House is in actual session as much in advance as possible.	Senate and House: final action by recorded roll call vote.
Connecticut	★	★ (e)	★ (e)	Senate and House: one day notice for meetings, five days notice for hearings.	Senate and House: roll call required.
Delaware	★	★	★	Senate: agenda released one day before meetings. House: agenda for meetings released four days before meetings	Senate and House: results of all committee reports are recorded.
Florida	★	★	★	Senate: during session-3 weekdays for first 40 days, 4 hours thereafter. House: two days for first 45 days, 1 day thereafter.	Senate and House: vote on final passage is recorded.
Georgia	★	★	★	Senate: a list of committee meetings shall be posted by 10:00 a.m. the preceding Friday. House: none	Senate: bills can be voted out by voice vote or roll call.
Hawaii	★	★ (a)	★ (a)	Senate: 72 hours before 1st referral committee meetings, 48 hours before subsequent referral committee. House: 48 hours.	Senate and House A quorum of committee members must be present before voting.
Idaho	★	★ (a)	★ (a)	Senate: Yes, for committee meetings to be held in executive session. (Senate Rule 20). House: Yes, for committee meetings to be held in executive session. (House Rule 26). "The chair of each standing or select committee shall lay on the Clerk's desk, to be read previous to adjournment, notice of the time and place of meeting of such committee." (House Rule 55).	Senate: Bills can be voted out by voice vote or roll call. (Senate Rule 39). House: Bills can be voted out by voice vote or roll call. (House Rule 79).
Illinois	★	★ (b)	★ (b)	Senate and House: 6 days.	Senate and House: votes on all legislative measures acted upon are recorded.

See footnotes at end of table

TABLE 3.24
Rules Adoption and Standing Committees: Procedure (continued)

State or other jurisdiction	Constitution permits each legislative body to determine its own rules	Committee meetings open to public*		Specific, advance notice provisions for committee meetings or hearings	Voting/roll call provisions to report a bill to floor
		Senate	House/Assembly		
Indiana	★	★	★	Senate: 48 hours. House: prior to adjournment of the meeting day next preceding the meeting or announced during session	Senate: committee reports - do pass; do pass amended, Reported out without recommendation. House: majority of quorum; vote can be by roll call or consent.
Iowa	★	★	★	Senate and House: yes, but can be suspended.	Senate: final action by roll call. House: committee reports include roll call on final disposition.
Kansas	★	★	★	Senate and House: none.	Senate: vote recorded upon request of member. House: total for and against actions recorded.
Kentucky	★	★ (f)	★ (f)	Senate and House: none.	Senate and House: each member's vote recorded on each bill.
Louisiana	★	★ (a)	★ (a)	Senate: no later than 1:00 p.m. the preceding day. House: no later than 4:00 p.m. the preceding day	Senate and House: any motion to report an instrument is decided by a roll call vote.
Maine	★	★	★	Senate and House: must be advertised two weekends in advance.	Senate and House: recorded vote is required to report a bill out of committee.
Maryland	★	★	★	Senate and House: none . General directive in the Senate and House rules to the Department of Legislative Services to compile a list of the meetings and to arrange for distribution which in practice is done on a regular basis.	Senate and House: the final vote on any bill is recorded.
Massachusetts	★	★	★	Senate and House: 48 hours for public hearings.	Senate: voice vote or recorded roll call vote at the request of 2 committee members. House: recorded vote upon request by a member.
Michigan	★	★	★	Senate and House: Notice shall be published in the journal in advance of a hearing. Notice of a special meeting shall be posted at least 18 hours before a meeting. Special provisions for conference committees.	Senate: committee reports include the vote of each member on any bill. House: the daily journal reports the roll call on all motions to report bills.
Minnesota	★	★	★	Senate and House: 3 days.	Senate and House not needed.
Mississippi	★	★	★	Senate and House: none	Senate and House: bills are reported out by voice vote or recorded
Missouri	★	★	★	Senate and House: 24 hours	Senate and House: bills are reported out by a recorded roll call vote.
Montana	★	★	★	Senate and House: 3 legislative days or as circumstances require	Senate and House: every vote of each member is recorded and made public.
Nebraska	★	★	U	Seven calendar days notice before hearing a bill.	In executive session, majority of the committee must vote in favor of the motion made.
Nevada	★	★	★	Senate and House: by rule - "adequate notice" shall be provided. Senate: This rule may be suspended for emergencies by a two thirds vote of appointed committee members. House: This rule may be suspended for emergencies by a majority vote of appointed committee members. In the Assembly this rule does not apply to committee meetings held on the floor during recess or conference committee meetings.	Senate and House: recorded vote is taken upon final committee action on bills.
New Hampshire	★	★	★	Senate: 4 days. House: no less than 4 days.	Senate and House: committees report bills out by recorded roll call votes.
New Jersey	★	★	★	Senate and House: 5 days	Senate and House: the chair reports the vote of each member present on a motion to report a bill.
New Mexico	★	★	★	Senate and House: none	Senate and House: vote on the final report of the committee taken by yeas and nays. Roll call vote upon request.
New York	★	★ (a)	★ (a)	Senate: 1 week for meetings; Rules require that notice be given for public hearings, but the Rules are silent as to how long. House: 1 week for hearings, Thursday of prior week for meetings.	Senate and House: majority vote required
North Carolina	(c)	★	★	Senate and House: none. If public hearing, five calendar days.	Senate: majority vote required. House: roll call vote taken on any question when requested by member & sustained by one-fifth of members present.

See footnotes at end of table

TABLE 3.24
Rules Adoption and Standing Committees: Procedure (continued)

State or other jurisdiction	Constitution permits each legislative body to determine its own rules	Committee meetings open to public*		Specific, advance notice provisions for committee meetings or hearings	Voting/roll call provisions to report a bill to floor
		Senate	House/ Assembly		
North Dakota	★	★	★	Senate and House: Printed and online hearing schedules, electronic signage, floor announcements, rss feeds, handheld device application.	Senate and House: Recorded roll call vote of the committee members on each bill or resolution referred out of the committee and, in the case of divided reports, on each report.
Ohio	★	★	★	Senate: Rule 21 Each committee shall meet upon the call of its chairperson, and in case of the chairperson's absence, or refusal to call the committee together, a meeting may be called by a majority of the members of the committee. At least two days preceding the day bills or joint resolutions to propose a constitutional amendment are to be given a first hearing, bills and joint resolutions in each standing committee or subcommittee with the exception of the standing Committee on Rules. In a case of necessity, the notice of hearing may be given in a shorter period than two days by such reasonable method as shall be prescribed by the Committee on Rules. Where applicable, the rules of the Senate apply to the committee proceedings of the Senate. In addition, all Where applicable, the rules of the Senate apply to the committee proceedings of the Senate. In addition, all committee meetings shall be governed by section 101.15 of the Revised Code. On any occasion when a majority or more of the members of a standing committee, select committee, or subcommittee of a standing or select committee of the Senate meet together for a prearranged discussion of the public business of the committee or subcommittee, the meeting shall be open to the public unless closed in accordance with Ohio Constitution, Article II, Section 13. House: Rule 36(a) The chair of a standing committee, subcommittee, select committee, or joint committee shall give due notice of a meeting of the committee, subcommittee, select committee, or joint committee not later than twenty-four hours before the meeting, in accordance with section 101.15 of the Revised Code, and shall attempt to give that notice not later than five days before the meeting. The notice shall identify the committee; identify the chair; state the date, time, and place at which the meeting will be held; and set forth an agenda showing each bill, resolution, or other matter that will be considered at the meeting. (b) It is not in order for a committee to meet at a date, time, or place, or to consider any bill, resolution, or other matter at a meeting, other than as stated in the notice of the meeting, unless otherwise ordered by the House or the committee. If, however, an emergency requires consideration of a matter at a meeting, and the matter has not been stated in the notice of the meeting, the chair may revise or supplement the notice at any time before or during the meeting to include the matter and the matter may then be considered as the emergency requires."	Senate: Rule 24 The affirmative votes of a majority of all members of a committee shall be necessary to report or to postpone further consideration of bills or resolutions. Every member present shall vote, unless excused by the chair. At discretion of chair the roll call may be continued for a vote by any member who was present at the prior meeting, but no later than 10:00 a.m. of next calendar day. House: Rule 40 (b) The affirmative votes of a majority of all members constituting a committee shall be necessary to report a bill or resolution out of committee, and a record of every vote shall be kept by the necessary to agree to any motion to recommend for passage or to postpone indefinitely further consideration of bills or resolutions, and a record of such vote shall be kept by the committee. Every member present shall vote unless excused by the committee. Rule 41(a) No proxy vote shall be valid. Nor shall any member vote except while sitting in committee in actual session, unless the member shall have first been present and recorded as such immediately before or during actual session before the vote is taken, and by motion the roll call on a motion to recommend a bill or resolution for passage is continued for a vote by any member who is temporarily absent from the meeting until the adjournment thereof, which shall be not later than 12:00 o'clock noon one day following the committee meeting. It is not in order for a member to vote on an amendment unless the member is actually present when the amendment is voted upon. (b) Three consecutive absences from regular committee meetings shall operate to suspend a member from such committee, unless excused by the chair of said committee.
Oklahoma	★	★	★	Senate: 48 hours notice. House: 3 day notice.	Senate and House: roll call vote.
Oregon	★	★	★	Senate: At least 48 hrs. notice except at the end of session when President invokes 1 hr. notice when adjournment sine die is imminent. House: First public hearing on a measure must have at least 72 hours notice, all other meetings at least 48 hours notice except in case of emergency.	Senate and House: affirmative roll call vote of majority of members of committee and recorded in committee minutes.
Pennsylvania	★	★	★	Senate and House: written notice to members containing date, time, place and agenda	Senate and House: a majority vote of committee members.
Rhode Island	★	★	★	Senate and House: notice required.	Senate and House: majority vote of the members present.
South Carolina	★	★	★	Senate and House: 24 hours	Senate and House: favorable report out of committee (majority of committee members voting in favor).
South Dakota	★	★	★	Senate and House: at least one legislative day must intervene between the date of posting and the date of consideration in both houses.	Senate and House: a majority vote of the members-elect taken by roll call is needed for final disposition on a bill. This applies to both houses.

See footnotes at end of table

TABLE 3.24
Rules Adoption and Standing Committees: Procedure (continued)

State or other jurisdiction	Constitution permits each legislative body to determine its own rules	Committee meetings open to public*		Specific, advance notice provisions for committee meetings or hearings	Voting/roll call provisions to report a bill to floor
		Senate	House/ Assembly		
Tennessee	★	★	★	Senate: 6 days; House: 72 hours	Senate and House: majority referral to Calendar and Rules Committee, majority of Calendar and Rules Committee referral to floor.
Texas	★	★	★	Senate: 24 hours; House: Five calendar days notice during a regular session and 24 hours during a special session, with certain exceptions for formal meetings, but not public hearings, during session.	Senate and House: committee reports include the record vote by which the report was adopted, including the vote of each member.
Utah	★	★	★	Senate and House: Not less than 24 hours public notice.	Senate and House: All votes are recorded in the meeting minutes by legislator name. For a motion to pass, a quorum must be present and a majority of members present must vote in the affirmative.
Vermont	★	★	★	Senate and House: none	Senate and House: vote is recorded for each committee member for every bill considered.
Virginia	★	★ (a)	★ (a)	Senate and House:: none	Senate: recorded vote, except resolutions that do not have a specific vote requirement under the Rules. In these cases, a voice vote is sufficient. House: vote of each member is taken and recorded for each measure.
Washington	★	★	★	Senate and House: 5 days	Senate: bills reported from a committee carry a majority report which must be signed by a majority of the committee. House: every vote to report a bill out of committee is by yeas and nays; the names of the members voting are recorded in the report.
West Virginia	★	★	★	Senate and House:: none	Senate and House: majority of committee members voting.
Wisconsin	★	★	★	Senate and House: At least 24 hours prior to commencement of meetings unless impossible or impractical, then at least 2 hours.	Senate and House: number of ayes and noes recorded.
Wyoming	★	★	★	Senate and House: by 3:00 p.m. of previous day	Senate and House: bills are reported out by recorded roll call vote.
American Samoa	★	★ (d)	★ (d)	Senate and House: At least 3 calendar days in advance.	Senate and House: There are four methods of ascertaining the decision upon any matter: by raising of hands; by secret ballot, when authorized by law; by rising; and by call of the members and recorded by the Clerk of the vote of each.
Guam	★	★	U	Five days prior to public hearings.	Majority vote of committee members.
CNMI**	★	★	★	Senate: 3 days. House: 1 day.	Senate and House: majority.
Puerto Rico	★	★	★	Senate: Must be notified every Thurs., one week in advance. House: 24 hours advanced notice, no later than 4:00 p.m. previous day.	Senate: bills reported from a committee carry a majority vote. House: bills reported from a committee carry a majority vote by referendum or in an ordinary meeting.
U.S. Virgin Islands	★	★	U	Seven calendar days.	Bills must be reported to floor by Rules Committee.

Source: The Council of State Governments' survey, December 2019.
**Commonwealth of Northern Mariana Islands
Key:
* – Notice of committee meetings may also be subject to state open meetings laws; in some cases, listed times may be subject to suspension or enforceable only to the extent "feasible" or "whenever possible."
★ – Yes
U – Unicameral.
(a) "Each house when assembled shall … determine its own rules of proceeding. …" (Idaho Const. art. III, § 9). "The business of each house, and of the committee of the whole shall be transacted openly and not in secret session." (Idaho Const. art. III, § 12). "All meetings of any standing, special or select committee of either house of the legislature of the state of Idaho shall be open to the public at all times, except in extraordinary circumstances as provided specifically in the rules of procedure in either house, and

any person may attend any meeting of a standing, special or select committee, but may participate in the committee only with the approval of the committee itself." (I.C. § 74-207; see also House Rule 57 and Senate Rule 20).
(b) A session of a house or one of its committees can be closed to the public if two-thirds of the members elected to that house determine that the public interest so requires. A meeting of a joint committee or commission can be closed if two-thirds of the members of both houses so vote.
(c) Not referenced specifically, but each body publishes rules.
(d) Unless privileged information is being discussed with counsel or the security of the territory is involved.
(e) Committees are joint.
(f) All standing committee meetings are open to the public. Other committee meetings of either chamber are open at the discretion of the chamber, committee, or chair of the committee.

TABLE 3.25
Legislative Review of Administrative Regulations: Structures and Procedures

State or other jurisdiction	Type of reviewing committee	Rules reviewed	Time limits in review process
Alabama	Joint bipartisan, standing committee	P	If not approved or disapproved within 45 days of filing, rule is approved. If disapproved by committee, disapproval may be appealed to the lieutenant governor.
Alaska	Joint bipartisan, standing committee and Legislative Affairs Agency review of proposed regulations.	P, E	…
Arizona	Joint bipartisan	P, E	…
Arkansas	Joint bipartisan	P, E (f)	…
California	Standing committee	P, E	The Legislature may study and make recommendations regarding existing or proposed regulations. Comprehensive regulation review conducted by independent executive branch agency.
Colorado	Joint bipartisan	E	Rules continue unless the annual legislative Rule Reviews Bill discontinues a rule. The Rule Reviews Bill is effective upon the governor's signature, however, the Governor needs to sign the Rule Review Bill on or before midnight on May 15 or all of the rules and amendments to rules adopted during the year before will automatically expire pursuant to statute.
Connecticut	Joint bipartisan, standing committee	P	Initial submittal of proposed regulation shall be on the first Tuesday of month. After initial submittal, committee has 65 days thereafter. For a second/revised submittal, committee has 35 days thereafter to review /take action on revised regulation.
Delaware	Joint bipartisan, standing committee	P, E (e)	…
Florida	Joint bipartisan	P, E	…
Georgia	Standing committee	P	The agency notifies the Legislative Counsel 30 days prior to the effective dates of proposed rules.
Hawaii	Legislative agency	P	The legislative reference bureau may assist agencies in complying with a uniform style format. This does not affect the status of rules.
Idaho	Germane joint subcommittees	P, E	There is no set time limit for rules review other than by the end of session. Typically they review rules during the first 3-4 weeks of session. Proposed rules: Reviewed pursuant to I.C. § 67-454. Existing rules: "The legislature may review any administrative rule to ensure it is consistent with the legislative intent of the statute that the rule was written to interpret, prescribe, implement or enforce. After that review, the legislature may approve or reject, in whole or in part, any rule as provided by law." (Idaho Const. art. III, § 29).
Illinois	Joint bipartisan	P, E	An agency proposing non-emergency regulations must allow 45 days for public comment. At least five days after any public hearing on the proposal, the agency must give notice of the proposal to the Joint Committee on Administrative Rules, and allow it 45 days to approve or object to the proposed regulations.
Indiana		No formal rule review is performed by both legislative and executive branches.	
Iowa	Joint bipartisan	P, E	…
Kansas	Joint bipartisan	P	Agencies must give 60-day notice to the public and the Joint Committee of their intent to adopt or amend specific rules and regulations, a copy of which must be provided to the committee. Within the 60-day comment period, the Joint Committee must review and comment, if it feels necessary, on the proposals. Final rules and regulations which differ in subject matter or in any material respect from the rules and regulations originally proposed or which are not a logical outgrowth of the rules and regulations originally proposed must be resubmitted to the Joint Committee as part of new rulemaking.
Kentucky	Joint bipartisan statutory committee	P, E	The deadline for filing proposed regulations is the 15th of the month. Properly filed regulations are published in the Administrative Register on the first of the month following the deadline. Filing the regulation triggers a public comment period and a review by the Administrative Regulation Review Subcommittee (ARRS). The committee meets within 75 days of publication, unless the regulation receives comments, is deferred, or is withdrawn. The subject-matter committee, which has the option to review regulations after ARRS, may meet on a regulation within 90 days of referral of the regulation to the subject-matter committee.
Louisiana (a)	Standing committee	P	All proposed rules and fees are submitted to designated standing committees of the legislature. If a rule or fee is unacceptable, the committee sends a written report to the governor. The governor has 10 days to disapprove the committee report. If both Senate and House committees fail to find the rule unacceptable, or if the governor disapproves the action of a committee within 10 days, the agency may adopt the rule change. If the committees of both houses fail to find a fee unacceptable, it can be adopted. Committee action on proposed rules must be taken within 5 to 30 days after the agency reports to the committee on its public hearing (if any) and whether it is making changes on proposed rules.
Maine	Joint bipartisan, standing committee	P (d)	One legislative session.
Maryland	Joint bipartisan	P, E	All proposed regulations are submitted to the AELR Committee for review at least 15 days before they are submitted to the Maryland Register for publication. Often changes are negotiated between the committee and the unit before publication. The committee is not required to give its explicit approval in order for a proposed regulation to become effective. In the usual course, the unit may adopt a proposed regulation 45 days after the regulation was published in the Maryland Register. Thirty of the 45 days must be reserved as a public comment period. If the committee cannot complete its review of the proposed regulation within the 45-day period, it may delay, or "hold," the adoption of the regulation. During this time, the committee may suggest to the unit that certain changes be made. If no agreement is reached, the unit may subsequently notify the committee of its intent to adopt the regulation despite the committee's hold. The hold period ends on the later of the 30th day after the unit's notice to the committee or the 105th day after the initial publication of the regulation in the Maryland Register. At any time, the committee may formally vote to oppose the adoption of the regulation. In this case, notice of the opposition is sent to the governor and the unit, and further negotiations ensue. (continued on next page.)

See footnotes at end of table

TABLE 3.25

Legislative Review of Administrative Regulations: Structures and Procedures (continued)

State or other jurisdiction	Type of reviewing committee	Rules reviewed	Time limits in review process
Maryland (cont.)	Joint bipartisan	P, E	The governor may instruct the unit to withdraw or modify the regulation. However, once the committee has opposed the adoption of the regulation, it may not be adopted unless approved by the governor. Emergency regulations, which bypass the normal public notice and comment period, remain in effect for a limited period of time -not to exceed 180 days -to meet exigent circumstances. Although emergency regulations are not published in the Maryland Register before adoption, notice of the committee's receipt of the regulation is posted on the MGA website. In addition, the agency submitting the request for adoption of emergency status must post the text of the regulations on the agency website within three business days of submission to the AELR committee.If a member of the committee requests a public hearing on the emergency adoption of a regulation, the committee must hold the hearing. If no public hearing is requested, staff to the committee may poll on the emergency regulation as soon as 10 business days after receipt of the regulation. Approval by the committee is required for an emergency regulation to take effect.
Massachusetts (a)	Public hearing by agency	P	In Massachusetts, the General Court (Legislature) may by statute authorize an administrative agency to promulgate regulations. The promulgation of such regulations are then governed by Chapter 30A of the Massachusetts General Laws. Chapter 30A requires 21 day notice to the public of a public hearing on a proposed regulation. After public hearing the proposed regulation is filed with the state secretary who approves it if it is in conformity with Chapter 30A. The state secretary maintains a register entitled "Massachusetts Register" and the regulation does not become effective until published in the register. The agency may promulgate amendments to the regulations following the same process.
Michigan	Joint bipartisan	P	"Joint Committee on Administrative Rules (JCAR) has 15 session days in which to consider the rule. JCAR may waive the remaining session days, object to the rule, propose that the rule be changed, or decide to enact the subject of the rule into law. (1) If JCAR does not object or waives the remaining session days, the rule goes into effect. (2) If JCAR objects, a member of the JCAR shall introduce bills in both houses to rescind the rule, repeal the authorizing statute, or stay the effective date for up to one year. If the legislation does not pass within 15 session days, the agency may file the rule. (3) If the JCAR proposes the rule be changed, the agency has 30 days to change the rule and resubmit or decide to not change the rule. If the agency agrees to change the proposed rule, it withdraws the rule and resubmits it. If the agency does not agree to change the proposed rule, it notifies the JCAR which again has 15 session days to consider the rule. (4) If the JCAR decides to enact the subject of the rule into law, the JCAR chair or alternate chair shall introduce legislation in both houses to do so and the agency may not file the rule for 270 days after the introduction of the legislation. The JCAR can also meet between legislative sessions and suspend rules promulgated during the interim between sessions."
Minnesota	Joint bipartisan, standing committee	P, E	Minnesota Statute Sec. 3.842, subd. 4a
Mississippi	--No formal rule review is performed by both legislative and executive branches--		
Missouri	Joint bipartisan, statutory 536.037 RSMo.	P, E	The committee must disapprove a final order of rulemaking within 30 days upon receipt or the order of rulemaking is deemed approved.
Montana	Germane joint bipartisan committees	P	Prior to adoption.
Nebraska	Standing committee	P	If an agency proposes to repeal, adopt or amend a rule or regulation, it is required to provide the Executive Board Chair with the proposal at least 30 days prior to the public hearing, as required by law. The Executive Board Chair shall provide to the appropriate standing committee of the legislature, the agency proposal for comment
Nevada	Ongoing statutory committee (Legislative Commission)	P	Proposed regulations are either reviewed at the Legislative Commission's next regularly scheduled meeting (if the regulation is received more than 10 working days before the meeting), or they are referred to the Commission's Subcommittee to Review Regulations. If there is no objection to the regulation, then the Commission will "promptly" file the approved regulation with the Secretary of State. If the Commission or its subcommittee objects to a regulation, then the Commission will "promptly" return the regulation to the agency for revision. Within 60 days of receiving the written notice of objection to the regulation, the agency must revise the regulation and return it to the Legislative Counsel. If the Commission or its subcommittee objects to the revised regulation, the agency shall continue to revise and resubmit it to the Commission or subcommittee within 30 days after receiving the written notice of objection to the revised regulation.
New Hampshire	Joint bipartisan	P	Under APA, for regular rulemaking, the joint committee of administrative rules has 45 days to review a final proposed rule from an agency. Otherwise the rule is automatically approved. If JLCAR makes a preliminary or revised objection, the agency has 45 days to respond, and JLCAR has another 50 days to decide to vote to sponsor a joint resolution, which suspends the adoption process. JLCAR may also, or instead, make a final objection, which shifts the burden of proof in court to the agency. There is no time limit on making a final objection. If no JLCAR action in the 50 days to vote to sponsor a joint resolution, the agency may adopt the rule.
New Jersey	Joint bipartisan	...	...
New Mexico	----------------No formal review is performed by legislature. Periodic review and report to legislative finance committee is required of certain agencies.----------------		
New York	Joint bipartisan commission	P, E	...
North Carolina	Rules Review Commission; Public membership appointed by legislature	P, E	The Rules Review Commission must review a permanent rule submitted to it on or before the 20th of the month by the last day of the next month. The commission must review a permanent rule submitted to it after the 20th of the month by the last day of the second subsequent month.
North Dakota	Interim committee	E	The Administrative Rules Committee meets in each calendar quarter to consider rules filed in previous 90 days.
Ohio	Joint bipartisan	P, E (c)	The committee's jurisdiction is 65 days from date of original filing plus an additional 30 days from date of re-filing. Rules filed with no changes, pursuant to the five-year review, are under a 90 day jurisdiction.

See footnotes at end of table

TABLE 3.25
Legislative Review of Administrative Regulations: Structures and Procedures (continued)

State or other jurisdiction	Type of reviewing committee	Rules reviewed	Time limits in review process
Oklahoma	Standing committee (b)	P, E	The legislature has 30 legislative days to review proposed rules. The legislature reviews all agency rules submitted prior to April 1st. Any rules submitted after April 1st are to be reviewed the next legislative session.
Oregon	(g)	E	Agencies must copy Legislative Counsel within 10 days of rule adoption.
Pennsylvania	Joint bipartisan, standing committee	P	Time limits decided by the president pro tempore and speaker of the House.
Rhode Island			No formal rule review is performed by legislative and executive branches.
South Carolina	Standing committee. Submitted by General Assembly for approval.	P	General Assembly has 120 days to approve or disapprove. If not disapproved by joint resolution before 120 days, regulation is automatically approved. It can be approved during 120 day review period by joint resolution.
South Dakota	Joint bipartisan	P	Rules must be adopted within 75 days of the commencement of the public hearing; emergency rules must be adopted within 30 days of the date of the publication of the notice of intent. Many other deadlines exist; see SDCL 1-26-4 for further details.
Tennessee	Joint bipartisan	P	All permanent rules take effect 90 days after filing with the secretary of state. Emergency rules take effect upon filing with the secretary of state and may be effective for not longer than 180 days.
Texas	Standing committee	P	No time limit.
Utah	Created by statute (63G-3-501).	P, E	Unless a rule is explicitly mandated by a federal law or regulation or Utah's constitution grants specific constitutional authority, every agency rule that is in effect on February 28 of any calendar year expires May 1 of that year unless it has been reauthorized by the Legislature (Utah Code 63G-3-502)
Vermont	Joint bipartisan	P	The Joint Legislative Committee on Rules must review a proposed rule within 30 days of submission to the committee.
Virginia	Joint bipartisan, standing committee	P	Standing committees and the Joint Commission on Administrative Rules may object to a proposed or final adopted rule before it becomes effective. This delays the process for 21 days and the agency must respond to the objection. In addition or as an alternative, standing committees and the Commission may suspend the effective date of all or a part of a final regulation until the end of the next regular session, with the concurrence of the Governor.
Washington	Joint bipartisan	P, E	If the committee determines that a proposed rule does not comply with legislative intent, it notifies the agency, which must schedule a public hearing within 30 days of notification. The agency notifies the committee of its action within seven days after the hearing. If a hearing is not held or the agency does not amend the rule, the objection may be filed in the state register and referenced in the state code. The committee's powers, other than publication of its objections, are advisory.
West Virginia	Joint bipartisan	P, E	...
Wisconsin	Joint bipartisan	P, E	The standing committee in each house has 30 days to conduct its review for a proposed rule. If either objects the Joint Committee for the Review of Administrative Rules has 30 days to introduce legislation in each house overturning the rules. After 40 days the bills are placed on the calendar. If either bill passes, the rules are overturned. If they fail to pass, the rules go into effect. As an alternative, JCRAR may make an indefinite objection and the agency may not promulgate the rule unless a bill authorizing the promulgation is enacted.
Wyoming	Joint bipartisan	P, E	An agency shall submit copies of adopted, amended or repealed rules to the legislative service office for review within 10 days after the date of the agency's final action adopting, amending or repealing those rules. The legislature makes its recommendations to the governor who within 15 days after receiving any recommendation, shall either order that the rule be amended or rescinded in accordance with the recommendation or file in writing his objections to the recommendation.
American Samoa	Standing committee	E	...
Guam	Standing committee	P	45 calendar days
Puerto Rico	....		No formal rule review is performed by both legislative and executive branches. ....
U.S. Virgin Islands	....		No formal rule review is performed by both legislative and executive branches. ....

Source: The Council of State Governments' survey, December 2019.
Key:
P – Proposed rules
E – Existing rules
… – No formal time limits
(a) Review of rules is performed by both legislative and executive branches.
(b) House has a standing committee to which all rules are generally sent for review. In the Senate rules are sent to standing committee which deals with that specific agency.
(c) The Committee reviews proposed new, amended, and rescinded rules. The Committee participates in a five -year review of every existing rule.

(d) Major substantive Rules (as designated by the Legislature) are subject to legislative review and approval; Routine Technical Rules are not subject to any formal legislative review and approval process.
(e) The chair of a standing committee can call a hearing to review the rule during the interim. The Joint Legislative Oversight Committee can order a review of an agency's rules during regular session.
(f) Amendment 92 to the Arkansas Constitution, which passed in 2014, and laws enacted by Act 1258 of 2015 provided the General Assembly with the power of review and approval of all administrative rules and regulations.
(g) Appropriate substantive committee will review if the Legislative Counsel determines that rule exceeds intent or scope of enabling Act.

TABLE 3.26
Legislative Review of Administrative Rules/Regulations: Powers

State or other jurisdiction	Reviewing committee's powers			Legislative powers:
	Advisory powers only (a)	No objection constitutes approval of proposed rule	Committee may suspend rule	Method of legislative veto of rules
Alabama	...	★	★	If not approved or disapproved within 45 days of filing, rule is approved. If disapproved by committee, disapproval may be appealed to the lieutenant governor. If the lieutenant governor doesn't approve rule, it is disapproved. If lieutenant governor approves rule, rule is suspended until final adjournment, next regular session. Rule takes effect upon that final adjournment unless committee's disapproval is sustained by legislature. The committee may approve a rule.
Alaska	★	...	(b)	Constitution and Statute
Arizona	★	N.A.	N.A.	N.A.
Arkansas	(gg)	★	...	A motion may be made in the Legislative Council or its Administrative Rules and Regulations Subcommittee to not approve the rule. If such a motion is made, the legislator making the motion must state the basis for not approving the rule. The only two valid reasons for not approving the rule are that it is inconsistent with state or federal law or inconsistent with legislative intent.
California	★(cc)	...	...	Statute
Colorado	...	★(z)	...	Rules that the General Assembly has determined should not be continued are listed as exceptions to the continuation.
Connecticut	...	★	...	Statute CGS 4-170 (d) and 4-171; (c)
Delaware	★(ff)	...	...	N.A.
Florida	★(ee)	...	...	Statute
Georgia	...	★	...	Resolution (d)
Hawaii	★	...	...	...
Idaho	(ii)	★	(jj)	Concurrent resolution. All rules are terminated one year after adoption unless the legislature reauthorizes the rule.
Illinois	...	(e)	★(f)	(f)
Indiana	...	...	...	(g)
Iowa	...	...	(h)	By consitutional majority vote of each house, by joint resolution, with approval of governor not required.
Kansas	★	...	...	Statute
Kentucky	(x)	(y)	...	Enacting legislation to void the regulation or to amend the authorizing statute.
Louisiana	...	★	(i)	Concurrent resolution to suspend, amend or repeal adopted rules or fees. Proposed rules and emergency rules exist (i).
Maine	★(aa)	★(bb)	...	(j)
Maryland	★(k)	...	...	The Joint Committee on Administrative, Executive, and Legislative Review (AELR) is composed of 20 members -10 senators appointed by the President of the Senate and 10 delegates appointed by the Speaker of the House. There is a House chair and a Senate chair who alternate each calendar year as the presiding chair. The Department of Legislative Services (DLS) provides two counsel as the primary staff to AELR. In providing oversight of the regulatory activities of State agencies for the General Assembly, the primary function of AELR is to review any regulations that are proposed for adoption by a unit of the Executive Branch of State government to determine whether the regulations conform to the statutory authority of the unit and the legislative intent of the statute under which the regulations are proposed
Massachusetts	...	...	...	The legislature may pass a bill which would supersede a regulation if signed into law by the governor.
Michigan	...	...	(l)	Joint Committee on Administrative Rules (JCAR) has 15 session days in which to consider the rule. JCAR may waive the remaining session days, object to the rule, propose that the rule be changed, or decide to enact the subject of the rule into law. (1) If JCAR does not object or waives the remaining session days, the rule goes into effect. (2) If JCAR objects, a member of the JCAR shall introduce bills in both houses to recind the rule, repeal the authorizing statute, or stay the effective date for up to one year. If the legislation does not pass within 15 session days, the agency may file the rule. (3) If the JCAR proposes the rule be changed, the agency has 30 days to change the rule and resubmit or decide to not change the rule. If the agency agrees to change the proposed rule, it withdraws the rule and resubmits it. If the agency does not agree to change the proposed rule, it notifies the JCAR which again has 15 session days to consider the rule. (4) If the JCAR decides to enate the subject of the rule into law, the JCAR chair or alternate chair shall introduce legislation in both houses to do so and the agency may not file the rule for 270 days after the introduction of the legislation. The JCAR can also meet between legislative sessions and suspend rules promulgated during the interim between sessions.
Minnesota	★	...	...	(m)
Mississippi				(n)
Missouri	...	★	★	Concurrent resolution passed by both houses of the General Assembly.
Montana	...	...	★ (o)	Statute

See footnotes at end of table

TABLE 3.26
Legislative Review of Administrative Rules/Regulations: Powers (continued)

| State or other jurisdiction | Reviewing committee's powers | | | Legislative powers: |
	Advisory powers only (a)	No objection constitutes approval of proposed rule	Committee may suspend rule	Method of legislative veto of rules
Nebraska	★	★	...	...
Nevada	N.A.	★	★	Proposed regulations are either reviewed at the Legislative Commission's next regularly scheduled meeting (if the regulation is received more than 10 working days before the meeting), or they are referred to the Commission's Subcommittee to Review Regulations. If there is no objection to the regulation, then the Commission will "promptly" file the approved regulation with the Secretary of State. If the Commission or its subcommittee objects to a regulation, then the Commission will "promptly" return the regulation to the agency for revision. Within 60 days of receiving the written notice of objection to the regulation, the agency must revise the regulation and return it to the Legislative Counsel. If the Commission or its subcommittee objects to the revised regulation, the agency shall continue to revise and resubmit it to the Commission or subcommittee within 30 days after receiving the written notice of objection to the revised regulation.
New Hampshire	★	(q)	...	(r)
New Jersey	★	...	...	(s)
New Mexico	N.A.	N.A.	N.A.	No formal mechanism exists for legislative review of administrative rules.
New York	(hh)	...	...	There is no legislative veto of administrative rules outside of bill process in New York.
North Carolina	★	★	★	...
North Dakota	...	★(t)	...	
Ohio	★	...	...	Concurrent resolution. Committee recommends to the General Assembly that a rule be invalidated. The General Assembly invalidates a rule through adoption of concurrent resolution.
Oklahoma	★ (p)	★ (p)	★(p)	The legislature may disapprove (veto) proposed rules by concurrent or joint resolution. A concurrent resolution does not require the governor's signature. Existing rules may be disapproved by joint resolution. A committe may not disapprove; only the full legislature may do so. Failure of the legislature to disapprove constitutes approval. Pursuant to HB 2055 enacted in 2013, legislature shall adopt omnibus resolution approving all proposed permanent rules except those listed in resolution which are to be disapproved.
Oregon	★	★	(dd)	By passing statute that overrides terms of rule.
Pennsylvania	...	★	★	Upon vote of General Assembly
Rhode Island				(n)
South Carolina	...	★	...	...
South Dakota	...	★	★	The Interim Rules Review Committee may, by statute, suspend rules that have not become effective yet by an affirmative vote of the majority of the committee.
Tennessee	...	...	★	The Government Operations committee of either house may stay a permanent rule for up to 60 days, and may request an agency to repeal, amend or withdraw. In accordance with statutorily-imposed termination dates, all permanent rules filed in one calendar year expire on June 30 of the subsequent year unless the general assemble enacts legislation to extend the rules to a date certain or indefinitely.
Texas	★	...	...	Legislature may override agency rules only by bill.
Utah	★	...	...	All rules must be reauthorized by the legislature annually. This is done by omnibus legislation, which also provides for the sunsetting of specific rules listed in the bill.
Vermont		(u)		Statute
Virginia	...	...	(v)	The General Assembly must pass a bill enacted into law to directly negate the administrative rule.
Washington	★	★	★	N.A.
West Virginia	★	...	...	(w)
Wisconsin	...	★	★	The standing committee in each house has 30 days to conduct its review for a proposed rule. If either objects the Joint Committee for the Review of Administrative Rules has 30 days to introduce legislation in each house overturning the rules. After 40 days the bills are placed on the calendar. If either bill passes, the rules are overturned. If they fail to pass, the rules go into effect.
Wyoming	★	★	...	Action must be taken by legislative order adopted by both houses before the end of the next succeeding legislative session to nullify a rule.
American Samoa				The enacting clause of all bills shall be: Be it by the Legislature of American Samoa, and no law shall be except by bill. Bills may originate in either house, and may be amended or rejected by the other. The Governor may submit proposed legislation to the Legislature for consideration by it. He may designate any such proposed legislation as urgent, if he so considers it.
Guam	N.A	N.A	N.A	Legislation to disapprove rules and regulations.
CNMI*	★	★	★	
U.S. Virgin Islands				(n)

See footnotes at end of table

TABLE 3.26
Legislative Review of Administrative Rules/Regulations: Powers (continued)

Source: The Council of State Governments' survey, December 2019.
*Commonwealth of Northern Mariana Islands
Key:
★ –Yes
... –No
N.A.–Not applicable

(a) This column is defined by those legislatures or legislative committees that can only recommend changes to rules but have no power to enforce a change.

(b) Authorized, although constitutionally questionable.

(c) Disapproval of proposed regulations may be sustained, or reversed by action of the General Assembly in the ensuing session. The General Assembly may by resolution sustain or reverse a vote of disapproval.

(d) The reviewing committee must introduce a resolution to override a rule within the first 30 days of the next regular session of the General Assembly. If the resolution passes by less than a two-thirds majority of either house, the governor has final authority to affirm or veto the resolution.

(e) The Administrative Procedure Act is not clear on this point, but implies that the Joint Committee should either object or issue a statement of no objections.

(f) Joint Committee on Administrative Rules can send objections to issuing agency. If it does, the agency has 90 days from then to withdraw, change, or refuse to change the proposed regulations. If the Joint Committee determines that proposed regulations would seriously threaten the public good, it can block their adoption. Within 180 days the Joint Cmte., or both houses of the General Assembly, can "unblock" those regulations; if that does not happen, the regulations are dead.

(g) None–except by passing statute.

(h) Committee may delay or suspend object to rules, and has authority to approve emergency filed rules.

(i) If the committee determines that a proposed rule is unacceptable, it submits a report to the governor who then has 10 days to accept or reject the report. If the governor rejects the report, the rule change may be adopted by the agency. If the governor accepts the report, the agency may not adopt the rule. Emergency rules become effective upon adoption or up to 60 days after adoption as provided in the rule, but a standing committee or governor may void the rule by finding it unacceptable within 2 to 61 days after adoption and reporting such finding to agency within four days.

(j) No veto allowed. If Legislature wishes to stop a rule from being adopted, it must enact appropriate legislation prohibiting the agency from adopting the rule.

(k) Except for emergency regulations which require committee approval for adoption.

(l) Committee can suspend rules during interim.

(m) The Legislative Commission to Review Administrative Rules (LCRAR) ceased operating, effective July 1, 1996. The Legislative Coordinating Commission (LCC) may review a proposed or adopted rule. Contact the LCC for more information. See Minn. Stat. 3.842, subd. 4a.

(n) No formal mechanism for legislative review of administrative rules. In Virginia, legislative review is optional.

(o) A rule disapproved by the reviewing committee is reinstated at the end of the next session if a joint resolution in the legislature fails to sustain committee action.

(p) Pursuant to HB 2055 enacted in 2013, the legislature shall adopt omnibus resolution approving all proposed permanent rules except those listed in resolution which are to be disapproved. Full legislature may suspend rules.

(q) Failure to object or approve within 45 days of agency filing of final proposal constitutes approval.

(r) The legislature may permanently block rules through legislation. The vote to sponsor a joint resolution suspends the adoption of a proposed rule for a limited time so that the full legislature may act on the resolution, which would then be subject to governor's veto and override.

(s) Article V, Section IV, par. 6 of the NJ Constitution, as amended in 1992, says the legislature may review any rule or regulation to determine whether the rule or regulation is (s) Article V, Section IV, par. 6 of the NJ Constitution, as amended in 1992, says the legislature may review any rule or regulation to determine whether the rule or regulation is consistent with legislative intent. The legislature transmits its objections to existing or proposed rules or regulations to the governor and relevant agency via concurrent resolutions. The legislature may invalidate or prohibit an existing or proposed rule from taking effect by a majority vote of the authorized membership of each house, in compliance with constitutional provisions.

(t) Unless formal objections are made or the rule is declared void, rules are considered approved.

(u) JLCAR may recommend that an agency amend or withdraw a proposal. A vote opposing rule does not prohibit its adoption but assigns the burden of proof in any legal challenge to the agency.

(v) Standing committees and The Joint Commission on Administrative Rules may suspend the effective date of all or a part of a final regulation until the end of the next regular legislative session with the concurrence of the governor.

(w) State agencies have no power to promulgate rules without first submitting proposed rules to the legislature which must enact a statute authorizing the agency to promulgate the rule. If the legislature during a regular session disapproves all or part of any legislative rule, the agency may not issue the rule nor take action to implement all or part of the rule unless authorized to do so. However, the agency may resubmit the same or a similar proposed rule to the committee.

(x) The promulgating agency's proposed language may be amended upon agreement of the committee and the promulgating agency.

(y) The committee does not approve or disapprove regulations. The committee is charged with reviewing and commenting upon the regulations, may propose amendments for the agency to consider, make recommendations, request that the agency defer the regulation, or determine that a regulation should be found deficient. A finding of deficiency is nonbinding.

(z) The rule could still be objected to in future legislative sessions.

TABLE 3.26
Legislative Review of Administrative Rules/Regulations: Powers (continued)

(aa) Committee makes recommendations on Major Substantive Rules, but approval or disapproval is by the full Legislature (the instrument used is a resolve).

(bb) Under very specific circumstances the answer is yes with respect to Major Substantive Rules: if the rules are submitted in accordance with the timelines established by law, and the Legislature fails to act on them, the rules may be adopted as if the Legislature approved them.

(cc) Executive branch agency has more than advisory power.

(dd) Negative rule determinations are made public and remain on website until rule is modified to cmply with statutory authority, statute is modified to establish validity of rule or court case upholds validity of rule.

(ee) Joint Administrative Procedures Committee, with approval of the president and speaker, may seek judicial review of validity or invalidity of rules.

(ff) A standing committee can recommend a special session to consider committee's recommendations

(gg) Amendment 92 to the Arkansas Constitution, which passed in 2014, and laws enacted by Act 1258 of 2015 provided the General Assembly with the power of review and approval of all administrative rules and regulations.

(hh) Commission may hold hearings, subpoena witnesses, administer oaths, take testimony, and compel the production of books, papers, documents and other evidence.

(ii) Germane joint subcommittees can submit a report of objection to a rule to the germane standing committee and the Legislature. The Legislature as a whole has the final say in the rejection of rules when voting on the concurrent resolution of the rejection.

(jj) Final rules previously approved by the Legislature, can still be rejected in a subsequent session.

TABLE 3.27
Summary of Sunset Legislation

State or other jurisdiction	Scope	Preliminary evaluation conducted by	Other legislative review	Other oversight mechanisms in law	Phase-out period	Life of each agency (in years)	Other provisions
Alabama	C	Dept. of Examiners of Public Accounts	Standing Cmtes.	Perf. audit	No later than Oct. 1 of the year following the regular session or a time as may be specified in the Sunset bill.	(Usually 4)	Schedules of licensing boards and other enumerated agencies are repealed according to specified time tables.
Alaska	C	Budget & Audit Cmte.	...	...	1/y	...	...
Arizona	C	Legislative staff	Joint Cmte.	...	6/m	10	...
Arkansas	C (aa)	...	...	Interim legislative subcommittee given broad latitude in reviewing existing and proposed occupational licensing processes.	...	...	...
California	S	Jt. Legis. Sunset Review Cmte. (a)	...	Perf. eval.	...	Established by the Legislature	...
Colorado	R	Dept. of Regulatory Agencies	Legis. Cmtes. of Reference	Bills need adoption by the legislature.	1/y	Up to 15	State law provides certain criteria that are used to determine whether a public need exists for an entity or function to continue and that its regulation is the least restrictive regulation consistent with the public interest.
Connecticut	D (b)	Committee of cognizance of program/ entity being reviewed.	...	per CGS 2c-21: unless otherwise provided, a provision of law creating board/commission/ other body on or after Jan. 4, 1995, with primary purpose of issuing report, is deemed repealed 120 days after the date of required submission of such report	...	...	...
Delaware	C	Agencies under review submit reports to Joint Legislative Oversight and Sunset Cmte. based on criteria for review and set forth in statute. Cmte. staff conducts separate review.	...	Perf. audit	Dec. 31 of next succeeding calendar year	4	Yearly sunset review schedules must include at least four agencies.
Florida	S (f)	...	...	...	...	...	...
Georgia	R	Dept. of Audits	Standing Cmtes.	Perf. audit	...	...	A performance audit of each regulatory agency must be conducted upon the request of the Senate or House standing committee to which an agency has been assigned for oversight and review. (d)
Hawaii	R	Legis. Auditor	Standing Cmtes.	Perf. eval.	None	Established by the legislature	Schedules various professional and vocational licensing programs for repeal. Proposed new regulatory measures must be referred to the Auditor for sunrise analysis.
Idaho	S (e)	...	...	...	...	...	...
Illinois	R,S	Governor's Office of Mgmt. and Budget	Cmte. charged with re-enacting law	(g)	...	Usually 10	...
Indiana	...	...	...	...	...	...	...
Iowa	-------- No program --------						
Kansas	(h)	...	...	...	...	...	...

See footnotes at end of table

TABLE 3.27
Summary of Sunset Legislation (continued)

State or other jurisdiction	Scope	Preliminary evaluation conducted by	Other legislative review	Other oversight mechanisms in law	Phase-out period	Life of each agency (in years)	Other provisions
Kentucky	R (x)	...	(y)	Certification letters (z)	...	...	...
Louisiana	C	Standing cmtes. of the two houses with subject matter jurisdiction.	...	Perf. eval.	1/y	Up to 6	Act provides for termination of a department and all offices in a department. Also permits committees to select particular agencies or offices for more extensive evaluation. Provides for review by Jt. Legis. Cmte. on Budget of programs that were not funded during the prior fiscal year for possible repeal.
Maine	S (w)	Joint standing cmte. of jurisdiction.	Office of Program Evaluation & Government Accountability	...	...	Generally 10 years	...
Maryland	C, R	Office of Program Evaluation & Government Accountability	Office of Program Evaluation and Government Accountability; "committees of jurisdiction" (the committees of the General Assembly that routinely handle the policy issues and legislation related to a specific governmental activity or unit subject to review under the Program Evaluation Act).	Perf. eval.	...	Varies; had been 10 years in the past, but now evaluation will occur as directed by the Legislative Policy Committee, the Joint Audit and Evaluation Committee, the Executive Director of the Department of Legislative Services, the Director of Policy Analysis in the Deparmtment of Legislative Services, or the Director of the Office of Program Evaluation and Government Accountability	...
Massachusetts	No program						
Michigan	(e)	...	...	...	...	...	...
Minnesota	S (e)	...	...	...	...	...	...
Mississippi	(i)	...	...	...	...	...	...
Missouri	R	Oversight Division of Cmte. on Legislative Research	...	...	...	6, not to exceed total of 12	Can be extended. The provisions of this are located at 23.250 - 23.298 RSMo
Montana	(e)	...	...	...	...	...	...
Nebraska	D (e) (j)	...	...	...	...	...	...
Nevada	C (e) (c)	Sunset Subcommittee	Legislative Commission, Full Legislature	...	...	...	...
New Hampshire	(k)	...	...	...	...	...	...
New Jersey	(e)	...	...	...	...	...	...
New Mexico	S	Legis. Finance Cmte.	...	Public hearing before termination	1/y	Varies	...
New York	(e)	...	...	...	...	...	...
North Carolina	(l)	...	...	...	...	...	...
North Dakota	No program						
Ohio	C (m)	Sunset Review Cmte.	...	Perf. eval.	(n)	2-6	(bb)

See footnotes at end of table

TABLE 3.27
Summary of Sunset Legislation (continued)

State or other jurisdiction	Scope	Preliminary evaluation conducted by	Other legislative review	Other oversight mechanisms in law	Phase-out period	Life of each agency (in years)	Other provisions
Oklahoma	S, D	Stndng cmtes. with jurisdiction over sunset bills (Senate) Jt. Cmtes. With jurisdiction over sunset bills (House)	Appropriations and Budget Cmte.	...	1/y	6	...
Oregon	D (o)	...	(o)	(o)	...	...	...
Pennsylvania	R	Leadership Cmte.	...	...	...	Varies	...
Rhode Island	(p)	...	No	...	...	...	...
South Carolina	(q)	...	...	Perf. Eval.	1/y	...	...
South Dakota	(r)	...	...	...	...	...	...
Tennessee	C	Office of the Comptroller	Government Operations Committees	...	1/y	Up to 6 years	...
Texas	S	Sunset Advisory Commission staff	Legislature makes the final decisions on statutory changes to an agency, based on the commission's recommendations and public input.	...	1/y	May not exceed 12	...
Utah	S	Interim cmtes., then Legislative Mngmt. Cmte.	Standing cmtes. as amendments may be made to bill	...	(v)	(v)	...
Vermont	(s)	Legis. Council staff	Senate and House Government Operations Cmtes.	...	...	...	...
Virginia	S (e)	...	...	...	...	...	Sunset provisions vary in length. The only standard sunset required by law is on bills that create a new advisory board or commission in the executive branch of government. The legislation introduced for these boards and commisions must contain a sunset provision to expire the entity after three years.
Washington	D	...	...	Perf. Eval.	1/y	...	...
West Virginia	S	Jt. Cmte. on Govt. Operations	Performance Evaluation and Research Division	Perf. audit	1/y	6	Jt. Cmte. on Govt. Operations composed of five House members, five Senate members and five citizens appointed by governor. Agencies may be reviewed more frequently.
Wisconsin	S, D (e)	...	...	...	...	...	...
Wyoming	D (t)	Program evaluation staff who work for Management Audit Cmte.	...	Perf. eval. (u)	...	...	...
CNMI*			No	Perf. Eval.	1/y		

See footnotes at end of table

TABLE 3.27
Summary of Sunset Legislation (continued)

Source: The Council of State Governments' survey, December 2019.
*Commonwealth of Mariana Islands
Key:
C–Comprehensive–requires all statutory agencies to be subject to a
   sunset review once per review cycle.
R – Regulatory–review focus is on regulatory and licensing agencies
   and bureaus.
S–Selective–selective implementation and reviews are concentrated
   on entities such as occupational licensing and administrative agencies such as highway, health and education departments.
D–Discretionary–sunset review board has the ability to select which
   entities will face review.
d–day
m–month
y–year
…–No provision
(a) Jt. Legis. Sunset Review Cmte.–Review by the Jt. Legislative Sunset
   Review Cmte. of professional and vocational licensing boards, pursuant to Government Code 9147.7. Sunset clauses are included in
   other selected programs and legislation.
(b) No longer comprehensive–in 2016, funding for Legislative Program Review and Investigations Committee and staff eliminated; in
   2017, provisions of law requiring decennial review of certain pro-
   grams/entities repealed.
(c) The 2011 Nevada Legislature created the Sunset Subcommittee of
   the Legislative Commission with the enactment of Senate Bill 251
   (Chapter 480, Statutes of Nevada). The Subcommittee is to conduct
   reviews of all boards and commissions not provided for in the
   Nevada Constitution or created by Executive Order of the Governor,
   and is charged with determining whether those entities should be
   terminated, modified, consolidated, or continued. The Subcommittee must review each entity no less often than once every ten years.
   After making it's initial recommendations no later than June 30,
   2012, the Subcommittee must submit all subsequent recommendations to the Legislative Commission on or before June 30 of each
   even numbered year. The Legislative Commission may accept or
   reject the recommendations in whole or part and may then request
   that legislation be drafted for consideration by the full Legislature.
(d) The automatic sunsetting of an agency every six years was eliminated in 1992. The legislature must pass a bill in order to sunset a
   specific agency.
(e) While they have not enacted sunset legislation in the same sense
   as the other states with detailed information in this table, the legislatures in Idaho, Michigan, Minnesota, Montana, Nebraska, Nevada,
   New Jersey, New York, Virginia and Wisconsin have included sunset
   clauses in selected programs or legislation.
(f) Comprehensive agency sunset review and repeal was repealed in
   2011. Florida does have Open Government Sunset Review of public
   records and meetings exemptions with a 5-year review period
(g) Governor is to read GOMB report and make recommendations to
   the General Assembly every even-numbered year.
(h) Sunset legislation terminated July 1992. Legislative oversight of
   designated state agencies, consisting of audit, review and evaluation, continues.
(i) Sunset Act terminated December 31, 1984. House and Senate

Rules are available at *billstatus.ls.state.ms.us*. New Rules were
   adopted in January 2012.
(j) Sunset legislation is discretionary, meaning that senators are free
   to offer sunset legislation or attach termination dates to legislative
   proposals. There is no formal sunset commission. Nebraska. Revised
   Statutes section 50-1303 directs the Legislature's Government, Military and Veteran's Committee to conduct an evaluation of any board,
   commission, or similar state entity. The review must include, among
   other things, a recommendation as to whether the board, commission, or entity should be terminated, continued or modified.
(k) New Hampshire's Sunset Committee was repealed July 1, 1986.
(l) North Carolina's sunset law terminated on July 30, 1981. Successor
   vehicle, the Legislative Committee on Agency Review, operated until
   June 30, 1983.
(m) There are statutory exceptions.
(n) HB 471 of the 131st General Assembly
   revised and renewed the Sunset Review Committee to be convened
   each odd-numbered general assembly. Therefore, Sunset Review
   will operate on a recurring four-year cycle.
(o) Sunset legislation was repealed in 1993.No general law sunsetting rules or agencies. Oversight mechanisms, including auditing,
   reporting or performance measures, are discretionary but may be
   included in specific bills as determined by legislature.
(p) No standing sunset statutes or procedures at this time.
(q) Law repealed by 1998 Act 419, Part II, Sect. 35E.
(r) South Dakota suspended sunset legislation in 1979. A later law
   directing the Executive Board of the Legislative Research Council to
   establish one or more interim committees each year to review state
   agencies was repealed in 2012.
(s) Sunsets are at the legislature's discretion. Their structure will vary
   on an individual basis.
(t) Wyoming repealed sunset legislation in 1988.
(u) The program evaluation process evolved out of the sunset process,
   but Wyoming currently does not have a scheduled sunset of
   programs.
(v) Default is ten years, although years may be decreased by legislative decisions.
(w) Sometimes programs or agencies are subject to sunset provisions;
   this is entirely ad hoc as the Legislature determines appropriate.
   There is a general law, however, called State Government Evaluation
   Law that provides for regular reviews of agencies and boards by
   committee of jurisdiction; the committees can recommend termination (sunset) but, again, this is ad hoc.
(x) A regulation expires seven years after its last substantive review
   unless appropriate action is taken by agency.
(y) The certification process does not involve a specific review unless
   requested by a committee member.
(z) The agency is required to review its regulations for compliance
   with current law at least once every 7 years and file a certification letter stating whether the regulation will be amended or remain in
   effect without amendment. If the certification letter is not filed or
   the regulation is not repromulgated, the regulation will expire 7
   years after the last substantive committee review.
(aa) Act 600 of 2019 creates cyclical process for reviewing licensing
   entities.

TABLE 3.27
Summary of Sunset Legislation (continued)

(bb) Agency expiration schedule under the act: agencies will expire, unless renewed, according to the following schedule: (1) An agency in existence on January 1 in the year of the first regular session of an oddnumbered general assembly expires at the end of December 31 in the year of the second regular session of that general assembly; (2) An agency created during an even-numbered general assembly expires at the end of December 31 in the year of the second regular session of the next odd-numbered general assembly; and (3) An agency created during an odd-numbered general assembly expires at the end of December 31 in the year of the second regular session of the next odd-numbered general assembly.

CHAPTER FOUR

STATE EXECUTIVE BRANCH

TABLE 4.1
The Governors, 2020

State or other jurisdiction	Name and party	Length of regular term in years	Date of first service	Present term ends	Number of previous terms	Term limits	Joint election of governor & lieutenant governor(a)	Official who succeeds governor	Birthdate	Birthplace
Alabama	Kay Ivey (R)	4	4/2017 (c)	1/2023	(c)	2-4	No	LG	10/15/44	AL
Alaska	Mike Dunleavy (R)	4	12/2018	12/2022	...	2-4	Yes	LG	5/5/61	PA
Arizona	Doug Ducey (R)	4	1/2015	1/2023	1	2-4	(b)	SS	4/9/64	OH
Arkansas	Asa Hutchinson (R)	4	1/2015	1/2023	1	2A	No	LG	12/3/50	AR
California	Gavin Christopher Newsom (D)	4	1/2019	1/2023	...	2A	No	LG	10/10/67	CA
Colorado	Jared Schutz Polis (D)	4	1/2019	1/2023	...	2-4	Yes	LG	5/12/75	CO
Connecticut	Ned Lamont (D)	4	1/2019	1/2023	...	...	Yes	LG	1/3/54	DC
Delaware	John Carney Jr. (D)	4	1/2017	1/2021	...	2A	No	LG	5/20/56	DE
Florida	Ronald Dion DeSantis (R)	4	1/2019	1/2023	...	2-4	Yes	LG	9/14/78	FL
Georgia	Brian P. Kemp (R)	4	1/2019	1/2023	...	2-4	No	LG	11/2/63	GA
Hawaii	David Ige (D)	4	12/2014	12/2022	1	2-4	Yes	LG	6/26/38	NY
Idaho	Brad Little (R)	4	1/2019	1/2023	...	...	No	LG	2/15/54	ID
Illinois	J.B. Pritzker (D)	4	1/2019	1/2023	...	...	Yes	LG	1/19/65	CA
Indiana	Eric Holcomb (R)	4	1/2017	1/2021	...	2-12	Yes	LG	5/2/68	IN
Iowa	Kim Reynolds (R)	4	5/2017 (d)	1/2023	1 (d)	...	Yes	LG	8/4/59	IA
Kansas	Laura Kelly (D)	4	1/2019	1/2023	...	2-4	Yes	LG	1/24/50	NY
Kentucky	Andy Beshear (D)	4	12/2019	12/2023	...	2-4	Yes	LG	11/29/77	KY
Louisiana	John Bel Edwards (D)	4	1/2016	1/2024	1	2-4	No	LG	9/16/66	LA
Maine	Janet Trafton Mills (D)	4	1/2019	1/2023	...	2-4	(b)	PS	12/30/47	ME
Maryland	Larry Hogan (R)	4	1/2015	1/2023	1	2-4	Yes	LG	5/25/56	DC
Massachusetts	Charlie Baker (R)	4	1/2015	1/2023	1	...	Yes	LG	11/13/56	NY
Michigan	Gretchen Esther Whitmer (D)	4	1/2019	1/2023	...	2A	Yes	LG	8/23/71	MI
Minnesota	Timothy James Walz (DFL)	4	1/2019	1/2023	...	...	Yes	LG	4/6/64	NE
Mississippi	Tate Reeves (R)	4	1/2020	1/2024	...	2A	Yes	LG	6/5/74	MS
Missouri	Mark Parson (R)	4	6/2018 (e)	1/2021	...	2A	No	LG	9/17/55	MO
Montana	Steve Bullock (D)	4	1/2013	1/2021	1	2-16	Yes	LG	4/11/66	MT
Nebraska	Pete Ricketts (R)	4	1/2015	1/2023	1	2-4	Yes	LG	8/19/64	NE
Nevada	Steve Sisolak (D)	4	1/2019	1/2023	...	2A	No	LG	12/26/53	WI
New Hampshire	Chris Sununu (R)	2	1/2017	1/2021	1	...	(b)	PS	11/5/74	NH
New Jersey	Phil Murphy (D)	4	1/2018	1/2022	...	2-4	Yes	LG	8/16/57	MA
New Mexico	Michelle Lujan Grisham (D)	4	1/2019	1/2023	...	2-4	Yes	LG	10/24/59	NM
New York	Andrew Cuomo (D)	4	1/2011	1/2023	2	...	Yes	LG	12/6/57	NY
North Carolina	Roy Cooper (D)	4	1/2017	1/2021	...	2-4	No	LG	6/13/57	NC
North Dakota	Doug Burgum (R)	4	12/2016	12/2020	...	...	Yes	LG	8/1/56	ND
Ohio	Mike DeWine (R)	4	1/2019	1/2023	...	2-4	Yes	LG	1/5/47	OH
Oklahoma	Kevin Stitt (R)	4	1/2019	1/2023	...	2-A	No	LG	N/A	OK
Oregon	Kate Brown (D)	4	2/2015 (f)	1/2023	1 (f)	2-12	(b)	SS	3/5/47	WA
Pennsylvania	Tom Wolf (D)	4	1/2015	1/2023	1	2-4	Yes	LG	11/17/48	PA
Rhode Island	Gina Raimondo (D)	4	1/2015	1/2023	1	2-4	No	LG	5/17/71	RI
South Carolina	Henry McMaster (R)	4	1/2017 (g)	1/2023	1(g)	2-4	No	LG	5/27/47	SC
South Dakota	Kristi Noem (R)	4	1/2019	1/2023	...	2-4	Yes	LG	11/30/71	SD
Tennessee	Bill Lee (R)	4	1/2019	1/2023	...	2-4	No	SpS (h)	10/9/59	TN
Texas	Greg Abbott (R)	4	1/2015	1/2023	1	...	No	LG	11/13/57	TX
Utah	Gary Herbert (R)	4	8/2009 (i)	1/2021	3	...	Yes	LG	5/7/47	UT
Vermont	Phil Scott (R)	2	1/2017	1/2021	1	...	No	LG	8/4/58	VT
Virginia	Ralph Northam (D)	4	1/2018	1/2022	...	1-4	No	LG	9/13/59	VA
Washington	Jay Inslee (D)	4	1/2013	1/2021	1	...	No	LG	2/9/51	WA
West Virginia	Jim Justice (R) (j)	4	1/2017	1/2021	...	2-4	(b)	PS (h)	4/27/51	WV
Wisconsin	Anthony Steven Evers (D)	4	1/2019	1/2023	...	...	Yes	LG	11/5/51	WI
Wyoming	Mark Gordon (R)	4	1/2011	1/2019	1	2-16	(b)	SS	3/14/57	NY
American Samoa	Lolo Matalasi Moliga (I)	4	1/2013	1/2021	1	2-4	Yes	LG	1949	AS
Guam	Lourdes Leon Guerrero (D)	4	1/2019	1/2023	...	2-4	Yes	LG	11/8/50	Guam
CNMI*	Ralph Deleon Guerrero Torres (R)	4	12/2015 (k)	1/2023	1 (k)	2-4	Yes	LG	8/6/79	CNMI
Puerto Rico	Wanda Vázquez Garced (PNP) (I)	4	8/2019 (l)	1/2021(l)	...	...	(b)	SS (l)	7/9/60	PR
U.S. Virgin Islands	Albert Bryan (D)	4	1/2019	1/2023	...	2-4	Yes	LG	2/21/68	USVI

See footnotes at end of table

TABLE 4.1
The Governors, 2019 (continued)

Source: The Council of State Governments, March 2020.
Key:
*Commonwealth of the Northern Mariana Islands
C – Covenant
D – Democrat
DFL – Democratic-Farmer-Labor Party
I – Independent
PDP– Popular Democratic Party
PNP– New Progressive Party
R – Republican
LG – Lieutenant Governor
SS – Secretary of State
PS – President of the Senate
SpS – Speaker of the Senate
. . . – Not applicable
2A – Two terms, absolute.
2-4 – Two terms, re-eligible after four yrs.
2-12– Two terms, eligible for eight out of 12 yrs.
2-16 – Two terms, eligible for eight out of 16 yrs.
1-4 – One term, re-eligible after four years.
N/A – Not available
(a) The following also choose candidates for governor and lieutenant governor through a joint nomination process: Florida, Kansas, Maryland, Minnesota, Montana, North Dakota, Ohio, Utah, American Samoa, Guam, No. Mariana Islands and U.S. Virgin Islands.
(b) No lieutenant governor.
(c) Kay Ivey (R) took office on April 10, 2017, following the resignation of former governor Robert Bentley. Ivey then ran and was elected to a full term in the 2018 general election.

(d) Lt. Gov. Kim Reynolds was sworn in as governor on May 24, 2017 when Gov. Branstad accepted the U.S. Ambassadorship to China. She then ran and won a full term in office in the 2018 general election.
(e) Lt. Gov. Mark Parson was sworn in as governor in June 2018 after Eric Greitens resigned.
(f) Oregon Secretary of State Kate Brown became governor on February 18, 2015, following Gov. John Kitzhaber's resignation. Brown won a November 2016 special gubernatorial election to officially fill the position for the final two years of Gov. Kitzhaber's term. She was elected for a full term in the 2018 general election.
(g) Gov. McMaster was sworn in on January 24, 2017 after Gov. Nikki Haley resigned to become the United State ambassador to the United Nations. He was elected to a full term in the Nov. 2018 general election.
(h) Official bears the additional title of " lieutenant governor."
(i) Lt. Gov. Gary Herbert was sworn in as Governor on August 10, 2009 after Gov. Huntsman resigned to accept President Obama's appointment as ambassador to China. Utah law states that a replacement governor elevated in a term's first year will face a special election at the next regularly scheduled general election, November 2010, instead of serving the remainder of the term. Gov. Herbert was re-elected to serve full terms in Nov. 2012 and again in Nov. 2016.
(j) Gov. Jim Justice switched parties in August 2017.
(k) Torres became governor on Dec. 28, 2015 after Gov. Inos passed away. He was elected to a full term in November 2018.
(l) Justice Secretary Wanda Vázquez Garced took the oath of office on Aug. 7, 2019 becoming Puerto Rico's third governor within a week.

TABLE 4.2
The Governors: Qualifications for Office

State or other jurisdiction	Minimum age	State citizen (years)	U.S. citizen (years) (a)	State resident (years) (b)	Qualified voter (years)
Alabama	30	7	10	7	★
Alaska	30	★	7	7	★
Arizona	25	5	10	5	★
Arkansas	30	★	★	7	★
California	18	...	5	5	★
Colorado	30	...	★	2	...
Connecticut	30	6 months	★	★	★
Delaware	30	...	12	6	...
Florida	30	★	★	7	7
Georgia	30	...	15	6	...
Hawaii	30	...	5	5	★
Idaho	30	2	★	2	★
Illinois	25	★	★	3	★
Indiana	30	...	5	5	★
Iowa	30	2	★	2	★
Kansas	...	...	...	...	...
Kentucky	30	2	...	2	...
Louisiana	25	5	5	5	★
Maine	30	...	15	5	...
Maryland	30	...	(c)	5	5
Massachusetts	...	...	...	7	★
Michigan	30	...	★	★	4
Minnesota	25	...	★	1	★
Mississippi	30	★	20	5	★
Missouri	30	...	15	10	...
Montana	25	★	★	2	★
Nebraska	30	5	★	5	...
Nevada	25	2	...	2	★
New Hampshire	30	...	...	7	...
New Jersey	30	...	20	7	...
New Mexico	30	...	★	5	★
New York	30	...	★	5	...
North Carolina	30	...	5	2	★
North Dakota	30	...	★	5	★
Ohio	18	...	★	★	★
Oklahoma	31	...	10	10	(d)
Oregon	30	...	★	3	...
Pennsylvania	30	★	★	7	★
Rhode Island	18	30 days	30 days	30 days	30 days
South Carolina	30	5	★	5	...
South Dakota	21	★	★	2	★
Tennessee	30	7	★	...	...
Texas	30	...	★	5	...
Utah	30	5	3	5	★
Vermont	18	...	★	4	★
Virginia	30	★	★	5	1
Washington	18	...	★	★	★
West Virginia	30	5	★	★	★
Wisconsin	18	★	★	★	★
Wyoming	30	★	★	5	★
American Samoa	35	...	★	5	...
Guam	30	...	5	5	★
CNMI*	35	...	★	10	★
Puerto Rico	35	5	5	5	...
U.S. Virgin Islands	30	...	5	5	★

Source: The Council of State Governments survey of governors' offices, January 2020 and state websites.
*Commonwealth of the Northern Mariana Islands
Key:
★–Formal provision; number of years not specified.
... – No formal provision.
(a) In some states you must be a U.S. citizen to be an elector, and must be an elector to run.
(b) In some states you must be a state resident to be an elector, and must be an elector to run.

(c) Crosse v. Board of Supervisors of Elections 243 Md. 555, 221A.2d431 (1966) – opinion rendered indicated that U.S. citizenship was, by necessity, a requirement for office.
(d) In order to file as a candidate for nomination by a political party to any state or county office, a person must have been a registered voter of that party for the six-month period preceding the first day the filing perod (26 O.S.§. 5 - 105A - A).

TABLE 4.3
The Governors: Compensation, Staff, Travel and Residence

State or other jurisdiction	Salary	Governor's office staff (a)	Access to state transportation			Receives travel allowance	Reimbursed for travel expenses	Official residence
			Automobile	Airplane	Helicopter			
Alabama	127,833	38	★	★	★	...	★(b)	★
Alaska	145,000	82	★	★	...	...	★(b)	★
Arizona	95,000	29 (f)	★	★	...	...	★(b)	...
Arkansas	151,838	50	★	★	★	...	★	...
California	209,747	88	★	...	...	...	(d)	★
Colorado	92,700	50	★	★	...	★	★	★
Connecticut	150,000 (c)	27	★	...	...	...	...	(e)
Delaware	171,000	28	★	...	...	...	...	★
Florida	130, 273	276 (f)	★	★(j)	...	(b)	(b)	★
Georgia	175,000	56 (f)	★	★	★	...	...	★
Hawaii	165,048	51	★	...	...	★	★	★
Idaho	138,302	17	★	★	...	...	★	...(e)
Illinois	181,670 (c)	91	★	...	...	...	...	★
Indiana	121,331	35	★	...	★	★(b)	★(b)	★
Iowa	130,000	18	★	...	...	...	★	★
Kansas	110,707	24	★	★	★	...	★	★
Kentucky	152,181	45	★	★	★	...	★(b)	★
Louisiana	130,000	93 (f)	★	★	★	...	★	★
Maine	70,000	30	★	...	...	★	★	★
Maryland	170,000	85 (f)	★	★	★	(b)	(b)	★
Massachusetts	185,000	approx. 60	★	...	★	★(b)	★(b)	...(e)
Michigan	159,300	75	★	★	★	(b)	(b)	★
Minnesota	127,629	37	★	★	★	...	★	★
Mississippi	122,160	29	★	★(k)	...	...	★	★
Missouri	133,821	21	★	★	...	(b)	(d)	★
Montana	118,397	58 (f)	★	★	★	...	★	★
Nebraska	105,000	9	★	★	...	★	★	★
Nevada	149,573 (c)	19 (f)	★	★	...	★(b)	★(b)	★
New Hampshire	134,581	20	★	...	...	(b)	(d)	(e)
New Jersey	175,000	128	★	...	★	...	★(b)	★
New Mexico	110,000	33	★	★	★	...	★	★
New York	225,000	180	★	★	★	...	★	★
North Carolina	150,969	59	★	★	...	★	★	★
North Dakota	135,360 (c)	18	★	★	...	...	★	★
Ohio	159,182	58	★	★	★	(b)	(d)	(e)
Oklahoma	147,000	34	★	★	...	...(b)	★(b)	★
Oregon	98,600	65 (f)	★	...	...	★(b)	★(b)	★
Pennsylvania	201,729	68	★	★	...	...	★(b)	★
Rhode Island	145,755	39	★	...	★	...	★(b)	...
South Carolina	106,078	16	★	★	...	...	★	★
South Dakota	116,400	18.75	★	★	...	...	★	★
Tennessee	198,780	38	★	★	★	★(b)	(d)	★
Texas	153,750	277	★	★	★	...	★	★
Utah	160,746	23	★	★	★	...	★	★
Vermont	184,100	14	★	★	...	...	...	★
Virginia	175,000	36	★	★	★	...	★	★
Washington	182,179	36	★	★	...	(b)	(d)	★
West Virginia	150,000	56	★	★	★	(b)	...	★
Wisconsin	152,756	35	★	★	...	(b)	★(d)	★
Wyoming	105,000	18	★	★	...	...	★(b)	★
American Samoa	90,000	23	★	...	...	(b)	...	★
Guam	130,000	42	★	...	...	$218/day	...	★
CNMI*	70,000	16	★	...	...	(b)	...	★
Puerto Rico	70,000	28	★	(g)	(g)	...	★	★
U.S. Virgin Islands	150,000	84	★	...	...	...	★	★

See footnotes at end of table

TABLE 4.3
The Governors: Compensation, Staff, Travel and Residence (continued)

Sources: The Council of State Governments survey of governors' offices, June 2020 and state websites.

*Commonwealth of Northern Mariana Islands

Key:

★ – Yes

… –No

N.A.–Not available.

(a) Definitions of "governor's office staff" vary across the states–from general office support to staffing for various operations within the executive office.

(b) Travel expenses.

Alabama–According to state policy.

Alaska–$60/day per diem plus actual lodging expenses.

American Samoa–$105,000. Amount includes travel allowance for entire staff.

Arizona–Receives up to $64/day for meals based on location; receives per diem for lodging out of state; default $41/day for meals and $93/day lodging in state.

Florida–The Executive Office of the Governor allocates an annual budget for the governor's travel expenses. The Governor is not reimbursed for personally incurred travel expenses. The Executive Office of the Governor pays the governor's travel expenses directly (hotel accommodations, meals, etc.) out of funds allocated for travel.

Guam–The amount varies based on destination but averages $218/ per day.

Indiana–No statute provides for a separate travel allowance. Instead, travel allowance comes from the general appropriations made for the governor's office expenses. Travel expenses are approved in advance and are paid for; reimbursement is never necessary.

Kentucky–Mileage at same rate as other state officials.

Maryland–Travel allowance included in office budget.

Massachusetts–As necessary.

Michigan–The Governor is provided a $54,000 annual expense allowance, as determined by the State Officers Compensation Commission in 2010. "Expense allowance" is for normal, reimbursable personal expenses such as food, lodging, and travel costs incurred by an individual in carrying out the responsibilities of state office.

Missouri–Amount includes travel allowance for entire staff. Amount not available.

Nevada–Travel allowance inlcuded in office budget. Reimbursed for travel expenses per GSA/Conus rate.

New Hampshire–Travel allowance included in office budget.

New Jersey–Reimbursement may be provided for necessary expenses.

Northern Mariana Islands–Travel allowance included in office budget. Governor has a "contingency account" that can be used for travel expenses and expenses in other departments or other projects.

Ohio–Set administratively.

Oklahoma–Reimbursed for actual and necessary expenses.

Oregon–$1,000 a month for expenses, not specific to travel. Reimbursed for actual travel expenses.

Pennsylvania–Reimbursed for reasonable expenses.

Rhode Island–The majority of travel expenses are not reimbursed since the State has centralized direct pay agreements with the various airlines / hotels for approved travel for state employees. If necessary, the governor is subject to the same per diem allowance for personal meals as other state employees, which is a maximum of $35 per day.

Tennessee–Travel allowance included in office budget.

Washington–Travel allowance included in office budget.

West Virginia–Included in general expense account.

Wyoming–Actual lodging and transportation/federal M&IE rates.

(c) Governor's salary:

Connecticut–Governor Ned Lamont will forego his salary of $150,000.

Illinois–Governor Pritzker will not take his salary of $181,670.

Nevada–Gov. Sisolak pledged to donate his salary to K–12 schools. Salary amount, per NRS 223.050: "On the first Monday in January 2011 and on the first Monday of every fourth year thereafter, the salary of the Governor must be increased by an amount equal to the cumulative percentage increase in the salaries of the classified employees of this State during the immediately preceding term of the Governor."

North Dakota–Governor Doug Burgum has declined his salary of $135,360.

(d) Information not provided.

(e) Governor's residence: Many governors are choosing to live in their own residences even when an official residence is provided .

Connecticut–Provided by the Department of Administrative Services.

Idaho–A housing stipend of $54,608 annually is provided.

Massachusetts–Does not have an official governor's residence but allows a $65,000 housing alowance.

New Hampshire–The current governor does not occupy the official residence.

Ohio–The governor chooses not to live in the state provided housing.

(f) Governor's staff:

Arizona–There are 29 members of the governor's executive staff, not including administrative staff.

Florida–There are 276 full-time employees. Those are broken into the following areas: Executive Direction and Support Services–124 positions; Systems Development and Design–48 positions; Office of Policy and Budget–104 positions.

Georgia–Full-time employees–56 and 2 part-time employees.

Louisiana–Full-time employees–93, part-time (non-student)–21, students–25.

Maryland–Full-time employees–85 and 1 part-time employee.

Montana–Including 16 employees in the Office of Budget and Program Planning.

Nevada–Currently 19. Maximum permitted is 23.

Oregon–Of this total, 45 are true Governor's staff and 20 are on loan for agency staff.

Vermont–Voluntary 5 percent salary reduction.

(g) The Governor's office pays for access to an airplane or helicopter with a corporate credit card and requests a refund of those

TABLE 4.3
The Governors: Compensation, Staff, Travel and Residence (continued)

expenses with the corresponding documentation to the Dept. of Treasury.
(h) Provided for security reasons as determined by the state police.
(i) When not in use by other state agencies.
(j) Governor does not utilize a state-owned airplane, but instead uses his personal aircraft.
(k) Only for official business.

TABLE 4.4
The Governors: Powers

State or other jurisdiction	Budget making power		Item veto power				Legislative votes required to override governor's veto	Authorization for reorganization through executive order (a)
	Full responsibility	Shares responsibility	Governor has line item veto power	Governor has line item veto power on appropriations amounts	Governor has line item veto power on appropriations language	Governor has no item veto power		
Alabama	★(b)	...	★	★	★	...	Majority elected	...
Alaska	★	...	★	★	...	...	Three-fourths	★
Arizona	★(b)	...	★	...	...	...	Two-thirds elected	...
Arkansas	...	★	★	...	...	...	Majority elected	★
California	★(b)	...	★	★	★	...	Two-thirds elected	★(c)
Colorado	...	★	...	★	★	...	Two-thirds elected	★
Connecticut	...	★	★	★	...	...	Two-thirds elected	★(d)
Delaware	★(b)	...	★	...	...	...	Three-fifths elected	★
Florida	...	★	★	★	...	...	Two-thirds elected	★
Georgia	★	...	★	...	...	...	Two-thirds elected	★
Hawaii	...	★	★	★	...	...	Two-thirds elected	★
Idaho	...	★	★	★	★	...	Two-thirds elected	...
Illinois	...	★	★	★	...	...	Three-fifths elected	★
Indiana	★	...	...	...	...	★	Majority elected	★
Iowa	...	★	★	★	★	...	Two-thirds elected	★
Kansas	★	...	★	...	...	...	Two-thirds elected	★
Kentucky	★(b)	...	...	★	★	...	Majority elected	★
Louisiana	...	★	★	★	★	...	Two-thirds elected	★(e)
Maine	...	★	...	★	...	...	Majority elected	...
Maryland	★	...	★	★	...	...	Majority elected	★
Massachusetts	★	...	★	★	★	...	Two-thirds elected	★(c)
Michigan	★(f)	...	★	★	★	...	Two-thirds elected	★
Minnesota	...	★	★	★	★	...	Two-thirds elected	★(g)
Mississippi	...	★(h)	★	★	★	...	Two-thirds elected	★
Missouri	★(b)	...	★	★	★	...	Two-thirds elected	★
Montana	★	...	★	★	★	...	Two-thirds elected	★(i)
Nebraska	...	★	★	★	...	...	Three-fifths elected	...
Nevada	★(b)	...	...	...	...	★	Two-thirds elected	★(j)
New Hampshire	★(b)	...	...	...	...	★	Two-thirds elected	...
New Jersey	★(b)	...	...	★	★	...	Two-thirds elected	★(k)
New Mexico	★	...	★	★	...	...	Two-thirds elected	...
New York	...	★	★	★	★	...	Two-thirds elected	...
North Carolina	...	★	...	...	...	★	Three-fifths elected	★(l)
North Dakota	★	...	★	...	...	...	Two-thirds elected	★
Ohio	★	...	★	★	★	...	Three-fifths elected	...
Oklahoma	...	★	★	★	...	...	Two-thirds elected	★(m)
Oregon	...	★	★	★	...	...	Two-thirds elected	★
Pennsylvania	★	...	★	...	★	...	Two-thirds elected	...
Rhode Island	...	★	...	...	...	★	Three-fifths elected	★
South Carolina	...	★	★	★	...	...	Two-thirds elected	...
South Dakota	★	...	★	★	...	...	Two-thirds elected	★
Tennessee	...	★	★	★	...	...	Two-thirds elected	★
Texas	...	★	★	★	...	...	Two-thirds elected	...
Utah	...	★	★	...	...	...	Two-thirds elected	★
Vermont	★	...	...	...	...	★	Two-thirds elected	★
Virginia	★	...	★	...	...	...	Two-thirds elected	★(n)
Washington	★	...	★	★	★	...	Two-thirds elected	...
West Virginia	★	...	★	★	★	...	Majority elected	...
Wisconsin	★(b)	...	...	★(p)	★(p)	...	Two-thirds elected	...
Wyoming	...	★	★	★	★	...	Two-thirds elected	...
American Samoa	...	★	...	...	...	...	...	★
Guam	★	...	★	★	...	...	Two-thirds elected	★
CNMI*	...	★	★	★	★	...	Two-thirds elected	★
Puerto Rico	...	★	★	★	★	...	Two-thirds elected	★(o)
U.S. Virgin Islands	★	...	★	★	★	...	Two-thirds elected	★

See footnotes at end of table

TABLE 4.4
The Governors: Powers (continued)

Source: The Council of State Governments' survey of governors' offices, January 2020 and National Association of State Budget Officers.

*Commonwealth of the Northern Mariana Islands

Key:

★–Yes; provision for.

… – No provision.

(a) For additional information on executive orders, see Table 4.5.

(b) Full responsibility to propose; legislature adopts or revises and governor signs or vetoes.

(c) Authorization for reorganization provided for in state constitution.

(d) Governor cannot create a budgeted agency but may "direct such action by the several budgeted agencies as will, in his judgment, effect efficiency and economy in the conduct of the affairs of the state government."

(e) Only for agencies and offices within the Governor's Office.

(f) Governor has sole authority to propose annual budget. No money may be paid out of state treasury except in pursuance of appropriations made by law and passed by the legislature.

(g) Statute provides for reorganization by the Commissioner of Administration with the approval of the governor.

(h) Governor has the responsibility of presenting a balanced budget. The budget is based on revenue estimated by the Governor's office and the Legislative Budget Committee.

(i) The office of the governor shall continuously study and evaluate the organizational structure, management practices, and functions of the executive branch and of each agency. The governor shall, by executive order or other means within the authority granted to him, take action to improve the manageability of the executive branch.

(j) Only as to commissions, boards and councils.

(k) Executive reorganization plans can be disapproved by majority vote in both houses of the legislature.

(l) Executive Order must be approved by the legislature if changes affect existing law.

(m) The governor has the authority, through state statute , to enact executive orders that: create agencies, boards and commissions; and reassigns agencies, boards and commissions to different cabinet secretaries. However, in order for the continued operation of any agency created by executive order the state legislature must approve legislation that allows the agency to continue to operate, if not, the agency cannot continue operation beyond sine die adjournment of the legislature for the session.

(n) The governor submits a reorganization plan to the General Assembly which must approve the plan by a vote of a majority of the membership in each house.

(o) Only if it is not prohibited by law.

(p) In Wisconsin, the governor has "partial" veto over appropriation bills. The partial veto is broader than item veto.

TABLE 4.5
Gubernatorial Executive Orders: Authorization, Provisions, Procedures

State or other jurisdiction	Authorization for executive orders	Provisions								Procedures		
		Civil defense disasters, public emergencies	Energy emergencies and conservation	Other emergencies	Executive branch reorganization plans and agency creation	Create advisory, coordinating, study or investigative committees/commissions	Respond to federal programs and requirements	State personnel administration	Other administration	Filing and publication procedures	Subject to administrative procedure act	Subject to legislative review
Alabama	S, I, Case Law	★	★	★	...	★	...	...	...	★	...	...
Alaska	C	...	...	...	★	...	...	...	...	★	...	★
Arizona	I	★(a)	★(a)	★(a)	★(a)	★(a)	★(a)	★(a)	★(a)	★(b)	...	...
Arkansas	S, I, Common Law	★	★	★	★	★	★	★	...	...	...	...
California	I (c)	★	★	★	★	★	★	★	★	...	...	...
Colorado	C	★	★	★	★	★	★	★	★	★	★*	★
Connecticut	C, S	★	★	★	...	★	...	★	★	(b)	...	...
Delaware	C	★	★	★	★	★	★	★	...	★	...	...
Florida	C,S	★	★	★	★	★	★	★	...	...	★	...
Georgia	S, I (d)	★	★	★	★	★	★	★	...	★	...	...
Hawaii	C, S, Common Practice	★	★	★	★	★	★	★	...	★	★	★
Idaho	S	★	★	★	★	★	★	...	...	★	...	...
Illinois	C,S	★	★	★	★	★	★	...	★	★	★	★
Indiana	C,S, Case Law	★	★	...	★(limited)	★	★	★	...	...	...	...
Iowa	(e)	★	★	★	★	★	★	★	(f)	★	★	★
Kansas	C,S	★	★	★	★	★	...	★	...	...	...	(g)
Kentucky	C,S	★	★	★	★	★	★	★	★	★	...	...
Louisiana	C,S (l)	★	★	★	★	★	★	★	...	★	...	...
Maine	S,I	★	★	★	...	★	★	★	...	...	...	...
Maryland	C,S	★	★	★	★	★	★	★	★(m)	★	★	★(n)
Massachusetts	C, S	★	★	★	★	★	★	★	★	★	...	...
Michigan	C	★	★	★	...	★	★	...	★	★(o)	...	...
Minnesota	S	★	★	★	★	★	★	...	(p)(q)	★(b)	★	★(n)
Mississippi	C, S	★	★	★	★	★	★	...	...	(r)	(r)	...
Missouri	C, S, Common Law	★	...	★	★	★	★	★	★	★(n)	...	★(n)(s)
Montana	S, I, Common Law	★	★	★	★	★	★	★	★	★	...	...
Nebraska	C,S	★	★	★	...	★	★	...	...	★	...	...
Nevada	S,I	★	★	★	★	★	★	★	★	★(t)	...	...
New Hampshire	C,S	★	★(a)	★	★	★	★	★	★(j)	★	...	...
New Jersey	C,S,I	★	★	★	...	★	★	★	★(u)	★	...	...
New Mexico	C,S	★	★	★	★	★	★	★	★	★	...	...
New York	C,S	★	★	★	...	★	...	...	...	★	...	...
North Carolina	C,S	★	★	★	★	★	★	★	★	★	...	★(v)
North Dakota	S,I	★	★	★	...	...	...	...	(k)(p)(u)(w)(x)(y)	...	...	...
Ohio	C,S,I (z)	★	★	★	★	★	★	★	(aa)	★	...	...
Oklahoma	C	★	★	★	(bb)	★	★	★	...	★	...	...
Oregon	I	★	★	★	...	★	★	★	...	...	...	...
Pennsylvania	C,S	★	...	★(m)(cc)(dd)(ee)	...	★	★	...	★(dd)(ee)	★(b)(cc)	...	...
Rhode Island	S, I, Case Law	★	★	★	★	★	★	★	...	★(b)	...	...
South Carolina	S	★	★	★	...	★	★	...	★	★	...	...
South Dakota	C	★	★	★	★	★	★	★	★	★	...	...
Tennessee	C,S	★	★	★	★	★	★	★	★	★(b)	...	...
Texas	C,S,I	★	★	★	...	★	★	★	★	...	...	...
Utah	S, I	★	★	★	★	★	★	★	...	...	...	...
Vermont	S,I	★	★	...	★(ff)	★	★	...	...	...	...	★(gg)
Virginia	C,S	★	★	★	★	★	★	...	...	...	...	★(hh)
Washington	S	★	...	...	...	...	...	...	...	...	...	...
West Virginia	C,S	★	★	...	...	★	★	...	(ii)	...	...	...
Wisconsin	C,S	★	★	★	★	★	★	★	(jj)	★	...	...
Wyoming	(kk)	...	...	...	...	...	...	...	...	...	...	...
American Samoa	C,S	★	★	★	★	★	★	★	★	★(ll)	★(ll)	...
Guam	C	★	★	...	(h)	★	★	★	★	★	...	...
CNMI*	C	★	...	★	...	...	...	...	★	...	...	...
Puerto Rico	C, S, I, Case Law	★	★	★	★	★	★	★	★	(i)	...	...
U.S. Virgin Islands	S	★	★	★	★	★	★	★	★	★	...	...

See footnotes at end of table

TABLE 4.5
Gubernatorial Executive Orders: Authorization, Provisions, Procedures (continued)

Source: The Council of State Governments survey of governors' offices, January 2020 and state websites.

*Commonwealth of the Northern Mariana Islands

Key:

C – Constitutional

S – Statutory

I – Implied

★ – Formal provision.

… – No formal provision.

(a) Broad interpretation of gubernatorial authority. In Arizona, the governor is authorized to make executive orders in all of these areas and situations so long as there is not a conflicting statute in place.

(b) Executive orders must be filed with secretary of state or other designated officer.

(c) Authorization implied from constitution and statute as recognized by 63 ops. Cal. Atty. Gen. 583.

(d) Implied from Constitution.

(e) Constitution, statute, implied, case law, common law.

(f) Executive clemency.

(g) Only for EROs. When an ERO is submitted the legislature has 30 days to veto the ERO or it becomes law.

(h) Can reorganize, but not create.

(i) Executive Orders are filed in the Department of State.

(j) To impound or freeze certain state matching funds.

(k) To reduce state expenditures in revenue shortfall.

(l) Inherent.

(m) To control procedures for dealing with public.

(n) Reorganization plans and agency creation.

(o) Executive reorganizations not effective if rejected by both houses of legislature within 60 calendar days. Executive orders reducing appropriations not effective unless approved by appropriations committees of both houses of legislature.

(p) To assign duties to lieutenant governor, issue writ of special election.

(q) Filing.

(r) Governor is exempt from the Administrative Procedures Act and filing and administrative procedures Miss. Code Ann. § 25-43-102 (1972).

(s) Reorganization plans and agency creation and for meeting federal program requirements. To administer and govern the armed forces of the state.

(t) In addition to filing and publication procedures - Executive Orders are countersigned by and filed with the Secretary of State and published.

(u) To administer and govern the armed forces of the state.

(v) Must submit to the Secretary of State who must compile, index and publish Executive Orders. Copies must also be sent to President of the Senate, Speaker of House and Principal Clerk of each chamber

(w) To suspend certain officials and/or other civil actions.

(x) To designate game and wildlife areas or other public areas.

(y) Appointive powers.

(z) Executive authority implied by constitution except for emergencies which are established by statute.

(aa) General power to issue executive orders to execute the authority of the Governor as provided in the Constitution and state statute.

(bb) The governor has the authority, through state statute, to enact executive orders that: create agencies, boards and commissions; and reassigns agencies, boards and commissions to different cabinet secretaries. However, in order for the continued operation of any agency created by executive order the state legislature must approve legislation that allows the agency to continue to operate, if not, the agency cannot continue operation beyond sine die adjournment of the legislature for the session.

(dd) For fire emergencies.

(ee) To transfer funds in an emergency.

(ff) Subject to legislative approval when inconsistent with statute.

(gg) Only if reorganization order filed with the legislature.

(hh) Some statutes set forward requirements for executive orders, but few established procedures.

(ii) Expansion of governor's existing state of emergency power to now create a state of preparedness. The governor has the authority to issue an executive order for a state of preardness in advance of an anticipated event affecting public safety (as of March 8, 2014). During the first special session in 2016 the legislature gave the governor the power, in the event a budget bill has not been enacted by June 30 of any year, to, by executive order, direct scheduled payments of principal and interest due on bonds or notes of the state or its agencies, boards, or commissions.

(jj) The governor has power to direct the Department of Administration to conduct investigations of any executive or administrative agency in order to determine feasibility of consolidating, creating or rearranging agencies for the purpose of affecting the elimination of unnecessary state functions, avoiding duplication, reducing the cost of administration and increasing efficiency. Wis. Stat. 16.004(3)(a). The governor has power to coordinate services of personnel across state agencies. Wis. Stat. 14.03.

(kk) No specific authorization granted, general authority only.

(ll) If executive order fits definition of rule.

TABLE 4.6
State Cabinet Systems

State or other jurisdiction	Authorization for cabinet system				Criteria for membership			Number of members in cabinet (including governor)	Frequency of cabinet meetings	Open cabinet meetings
	State statute	State constitution	Governor created	Tradition in state	Appointed to specific office (a)	Elected to specified office (a)	Gubernatorial appointment regardless of office			
Alabama	★	★	★	★	★	...	...	22	Quarterly (p)	...
Alaska	★	★	...	...	★	...	★	17	Gov.'s discretion	★
Arizona	...	...	★	...	★	...	★	37	Quarterly	...
Arkansas	★	...	★	...	...	...	★	15	Quarterly	...
California	...	★	★	...	★	...	★	11	Every two weeks	...
Colorado	...	★	★	...	★	...	★	21	Bi-monthly	...
Connecticut	★(k)	...	...	...	...	...	★	29	Gov.'s discretion	...
Delaware	★	...	...	...	★	...	★	17	Gov.'s discretion	...
Florida	★	★	...	...	...	★	...	4	Appox. 1-2 per month	★
Georgia					------ (d) ------					
Hawaii	★	★	...	...	★	...	★	43	Bi-monthly	...
Idaho	★	★	...	...	...	...	★	39	Gov.'s discretion	...
Illinois (o)	★	...	★	...	...	...	★	65	Gov.'s discretion	(b)
Indiana	...	...	★	...	...	...	★	21	Gov.'s discretion	...
Iowa	★	★	★	★	★	...	...	30	Monthly	...
Kansas	...	★	...	...	...	...	★	15	Bi-weekly	...
Kentucky	★	★	★	...	...	...	★	13	Twice monthly	...
Louisiana	★	...	★	★	★	...	...	16	Monthly	...
Maine	...	...	...	★	...	...	★(q)	16	Monthly	...
Maryland	★	...	...	...	★	...	...	25	Every other week	...
Massachusetts	...	★	...	...	★	...	...	11	Weekly	...
Michigan	★	★	★	...	★	★	(e)	22	Gov.'s discretion	...
Minnesota	...	...	★	...	★	...	...	25	Quarterly	...
Mississippi					------ (d) ------					
Missouri	★	...	...	★	★	...	...	17	Gov.'s discretion	...
Montana	★	★	...	...	★	...	...	21	Monthly	★
Nebraska	...	...	★	★	★	...	★	31	Monthly	...
Nevada			------ (d) ------					21	At call of the governor	...
New Hampshire					------ (d) ------					
New Jersey	★	★	...	...	★	...	...	23	Gov.'s discretion	...
New Mexico	★	★	...	★	★	...	...	31	Gov.'s discretion	...
New York	...	...	...	★	...	...	★	75	Gov.'s discretion	...
North Carolina (f)	...	...	★	...	...	...	★	11	Weekly	(n)
North Dakota	...	...	★	...	...	...	★	17	Monthly	★
Ohio	...	...	...	★	★	...	...	27	Gov.'s discretion	...
Oklahoma	...	★	...	...	...	...	★	16 (h)	Monthly	...
Oregon					------ (d) ------					
Pennsylvania	★	★	★	...	★(i)	...	★	27	Gov.'s discretion	★
Rhode Island	...	...	★	★	...	...	★(l)	22	Gov.'s discretion	★(m)
South Carolina	★	★	...	...	★(i)	...	...	18	Monthly	★
South Dakota	★	★	...	...	★	...	...	20	Monthly	...
Tennessee	★	...	...	...	★	...	...	30	Monthly	...
Texas					------ (d) ------					
Utah	...	★	★	...	★	...	★	24	Monthly, weekly during legislative session	...
Vermont	★	★	...	...	★	...	...	12	Gov.'s discretion	...
Virginia	...	...	★	★(j)	★	...	★	16	Weekly	...
Washington	...	...	★	...	★	...	...	25	Monthly	...
West Virginia	...	...	★	★	★	...	...	17	Weekly	...
Wisconsin	★	★	...	...	★	...	...	17	Monthly	...
Wyoming	...	...	★	...	...	...	★	44	Quarterly	...
American Samoa	★	★	...	...	★	...	★	16	Gov.'s discretion	★
Guam	...	...	★	...	★	...	...	55	Bi-monthly	...
CNMI*	...	★	...	...	★	...	...	17	Gov.'s discretion	★
Puerto Rico	★	★	...	...	...	...	★	10 (c)	Every 6 weeks	...
U.S. Virgin Islands	★	...	...	...	★	...	...	21	Monthly	★

See footnotes at end of table

TABLE 4.6
State Cabinet Systems (continued)

Sources: The Council of State Governments survey of governors' offices, January 2020 and state websites.
*Commonwealth of the Northern Mariana Islands
Key:
★–Yes
. . .–No
N/A – Not available
(a) Individual is a member by virtue of election or appointment to a cabinet-level position.
(b) Certain cabinet meetings are open to the public and media.
(c) The Constitutional Cabinet has 10 members including the governor. There are other members of the Cabinet provided by statute.
(d) No formal cabinet system. In Nevada, the cabinet is comprised of directors, chairpersons and leaders of Nevada's top agencies, departments, institutions and the National Guard, in addition to the tt. governor.
(e) Membership determined by governor. Some officers formally designated as cabinet member by executive order.
(f) The Governor's cabinet consists of 10 department heads who have responsibility for the majority of the executive branch. They are appointed by the governor and report to the governor. The Council of State exists as a separate body and is composed independently elected statewide officials who oversee certain areas of the executive branch. While the Council of State is provided for in the Constitution and state statutes, the cabinet is created by the governor.
(g) Frequency of meetings may fluctuate with Governor's schedule.
(h) State statute allows for 15 cabinet members. With the Governor included there are 16 members.
(i) With the consent of the senate.
(j) While there is no specific state statute that establishes the cabinet system, the state code makes repeated references to cabinet secretaries and sets forth the duties of each secretary and the agencies assigned to the secretary.
(k) Governor's cabinet is specified in statute, but no longer in use. Governor directs department heads through commissioners' meetings and subject matter groups called clusters.
(l) At the discretion of the governor.
(m) Varies by meeting.
(n) Council of State, but not cabinet meetings, are open to the public.
(o) Agency directors are provided by statute. Governor may create and appoint other cabinet-level positions.
(p) Quarterly with weekly optional phone calls with the cabinet and governor.
(q) Consists of commmissioners who serve at the governor's pleasure.

TABLE 4.7
The Governors: Provisions and Procedures for Transition

State or other jurisdiction	Legislation pertaining to gubernatorial transition	Appropriation available to gov-elect	Provision for:					
			Gov-elect's participation in state budget for coming fiscal year	Gov-elect to hire staff to assist during transition	State personnel to be made available to assist gov-elect	Office space in buildings to be made available to gov-elect	Acquainting gov-elect staff with office procedures and routing office functions	Transfer of information (files, records, etc.)
Alabama	...	...	★	•	•	•	•	•
Alaska	•	•	...	•	•	•	•	★
Arizona	...	...	★	...	•	•	•	•
Arkansas	★	10,000	★	...	...	...	...	...
California	★	450,000	★	★	★	★	•	•
Colorado	★	10,000	★	★	★	★	•	★
Connecticut	★	★	★	★	★	★	★	★
Delaware	★	15,000	•	★	•	•	•	•
Florida	★	(b)	•	★	•	•	★	•
Georgia	★	50,000	•	★	★	★	•	★
Hawaii	★	50,000	★	★	•	★	•	•
Idaho	★	15,000	★	★	★	★	★	★
Illinois	★	...	...	•	...	★	★	★
Indiana	★	40,000	...	...	...	•	...	★
Iowa	•	100,000	★	•	•	•	•	★
Kansas	★	150,000 (c)	★	★	★	★	★	★
Kentucky	★	220,000	★	★	★	★	★	★
Louisiana	★	• 65,000	★	★	...	★	...	•
Maine	•	5,000	★	•	•	•	•	•
Maryland	★	•	...	★	•	★	★	★
Massachusetts	•	•	•	...	•	•	•	•
Michigan	•	$1.5 million • (v)	...	•	•	•	•	•
Minnesota	★	(e)	★	★	★	★	•	★
Mississippi	•	★(f)	★	★	★	★	★	★
Missouri	★	100,000	★	★	•	★	•	• (g)
Montana	★	★	★	★	★	★	★	•
Nebraska	★	85,288	★	...	★	★	★	★
Nevada	★	Reasonable amount	★	★	...	★	...	★
New Hampshire	★	75,000	★	★	★	★	★	...
New Jersey	★	★(j)	•	★	★	★	•	★
New Mexico	★	(k)	★	★	★	★	★	★
New York	...	...	...	...	★	★	★	★
North Carolina	★	★(l)	...	★	•	★	★	★
North Dakota	•	10,000	(m)	(n)	•	...	•	★
Ohio	★	Unspecified (o)	•	★	•	...	•	•
Oklahoma	•	•	★	•	•	★	•	•
Oregon	★	★	★	★	★	★	★	★
Pennsylvania	★	...	...	★	•	•	•	...
Rhode Island	★	(u)	•	★	★	★	•	•
South Carolina	...	•	•	•	•	•	•	•
South Dakota	★	...	...	...	...	...	...	...
Tennessee	★	★	•	★	★	★	•	• (u)
Texas	•	•	•	•	•	•	•	•
Utah	★	★(p)	★	★	★	★	★	★
Vermont	•	★(q)	★	...	★	...	...	...
Virginia	★	★(h)	★	★	★	★	★	★
Washington	★	★	•	★	•	★	•	•
West Virginia	...	•	...	•	...	•	•	•
Wisconsin	★	★	★	★	★	★	★	★
Wyoming	•	...	•	•	•	•	•	•
American Samoa	...	Unspecified	★(i)	★	•	•	★	•
Guam	★	(t)	...	...	★	★	★	...
CNMI*	★	Unspecified	...	★	★	★	★	★
Puerto Rico	★	...	★	★	★	★	★	★
U.S. Virgin Islands	★	100,000	...	★	★	★	★	★

See footnotes at end of table

TABLE 4.7

The Governors: Provisions and Procedures for Transition (continued)

Sources: The Council of State Governments survey of governors' offices, January 2020 and state websites.

* Commonwealth of the Northern Mariana Islands

Key:

… – No provisions or procedures.

★ – Formal provisions or procedures.

• – No formal provisions, occurs informally.

N.A. – Not applicable.

(a) Varies.

(b) Section 14.057, Florida Statute provides: Governor-elect; establishment of operating fund.– (1) There is established an operating fund for the use of the Governor-elect during the period dating from the certification of his or her election by the Elections Canvassing Commission to his or her inauguration as Governor. The Governor-elect during this period may allocate the fund to travel, expenses, his or her salary, and the salaries of the Governor-elect's staff as he or she determines. Such staff may include, but not be limited to, a chief administrative assistant, a legal adviser, a fiscal expert, and a public relations and information adviser. The salary of the Governor-elect and each member of the Governor-elect's staff during this period shall be determined by the Governor-elect, except that the total expenditures chargeable to the state under this section, including salaries, shall not exceed the amount appropriated to the operating fund. The Executive Office of the Governor shall supply to the Governor-elect suitable forms to provide for the expenditure of the fund and suitable forms to provide for the reporting of all expenditures therefrom. The Chief Financial Officer shall release moneys from this fund upon the request of the Governor-elect properly filed.

(c) Transition funds are used by both the incoming and outgoing administrations.

(d) Amount to be determined.

(e) 1.5% of amount appropriated for the fiscal year to the Governor's office.

(f) Miss. Code Ann.§ 7-1-101 provides as follows: the governor's office of general services shall provide a governor-elect with office space and office equipment for the period between the election and inauguration. A special appropriation to the governor's office of general services is hereby authorized to defray the expenses of providing necessary staff employees and for the operation of the office of governor-elect during the period between the election and inauguration. The department of finance and administration shall make available to a governor-elect and his designated representatives information on the following: (a) all information and reports used in the preparation of the budget report; and (b) all information and reports on projected income and revenue estimates for the state.

(g) Activity is traditional and routine, although there is no specific statutory provision.

(h) Determined every 4 years.

(i) Can submit reprogramming or supplemental appropriation measure for current fiscal year.

(j) $250,000 line item - necessary services and facilities.

(k) Legislature required to make appropriation; no dollar amount stated in legislation.

(l) Governor receives $80,000 and lieutenant governor receives $10,000.

(m) Responsible for submitting budget for coming biennium.

(n) Governor usually hires several incoming key staff during transition.

(o) Determined in budget.

(p) Appropriated by legislature at the time of transition.

(q) Governor-elect entitled to 70% of Governor's salary.

(t) Appropriations given upon the request of governor-elect.

(u) The governor's transition team was authorized $130,000 for transition costs during the 2014 - 2015 transition. Approximately $120,000 was spent.

(v) Typically the appropriation is included in the budget but may fluctuate in size.

(u) Subject to records retention and archival requirements

TABLE 4.8
Impeachment Provisions in the States

State or other jurisdiction	Governor and other state executive and judicial officers subject to impeachment	Legislative body which holds power of impeachment	Vote required for impeachment	Legislative body which conducts impeachment trial	Chief justice presides at impeachment trial (a)	Vote required for conviction	Official who serves as acting governor if governor impeached (b)	Legislature may call special session for impeachment
Alabama	★	H	maj. mbrs.	S	★	2/3 mbrs. present	LG	★
Alaska	★	S	2/3 mbrs.	H	(c)	2/3 mbrs.	LG	★
Arizona	★(d)	H	maj. mbrs.	S	★(e)	2/3 mbrs.	SS	★
Arkansas	★	H	maj. mbrs.	S	★	2/3 mbrs.	LG	...
California	★	H	...	S	...	2/3 mbrs.	LG	...
Colorado	★	H	maj. mbrs.	S	★	2/3 mbrs.	LG	...
Connecticut	★	H	maj. mbrs.	S	★(f)	2/3 mbrs. must be present	LG	★
Delaware	★	H	2/3 mbrs.	S	★	2/3 mbrs.	LG	...
Florida	★	H	2/3 mbrs.	S	★(g)	2/3 mbrs. present (h)	LG (i)	★
Georgia	★	H	...	S	★(e)	2/3 mbrs.	...	★(j)
Hawaii	★	H	2/3 mbrs.	S	...	2/3 mbrs.	LG	★
Idaho	★	H	2/3 mbrs.(k)	S	★	2/3 mbrs.	LG	...
Illinois	★	H	2/3 mbrs.	S	★	2/3 mbrs.	LG	★
Indiana	★(l)	H	2/3 mbrs.	S	★	2/3 mbrs.	LG	★
Iowa	★	H	maj. mbrs.	S	...	majority of elected mbrs.	LG	★
Kansas	★	H	(m)	S	...	2/3 mbrs.	LG	...
Kentucky	★	H	maj. mbrs.	S	★	2/3 mbrs. present	LG	...
Louisiana	★	H	(n)	S	...	(n)	LG	★
Maine	★	H	maj. mbrs.	S	...	2/3 mbrs. present	PS	★
Maryland	★	H	maj. mbrs.	S	...	2/3 mbrs.	LG	...
Massachusetts	★	H	maj. mbrs.	S	...	...	LG	★
Michigan	★	H	maj. mbrs.	S	★	2/3 mbrs.	LG	...
Minnesota	★	H	maj. mbrs.	S	...	2/3 mbrs. present	LG	...
Mississippi	★	H	maj. mbrs.	S	★(r)	2/3 mbrs. present (s)	LG	(u)
Missouri	★	H	...	(t)	(t)	(t)	LG	...
Montana	★	H	2/3 mbrs.	S	★	2/3 mbrs.	LG	★
Nebraska	★	S (v)	maj. mbrs.	(w)	(w)	(w)	LG	...
Nevada	★(d)	H	maj. mbrs.	S	★	2/3 mbrs.	LG	★
New Hampshire	★	H	...	S	★	...	PS	★
New Jersey	★	H	maj. mbrs.	S	★	2/3 mbrs.	LG	★(aa)
New Mexico	★	H	maj. mbrs.	S	★(p)	2/3 mbrs.	LG	★
New York	★	H	maj. mbrs.	S	★	2/3 mbrs. present	LG	★
North Carolina	★	H	2/3 mbrs.	S	★(x)	2/3 mbrs. present	LG	★
North Dakota	★(d)	H	maj. mbrs.	S	★	2/3 mbrs.	LG	...
Ohio	★	H	maj. mbrs.	S	...	2/3 mbrs. present	LG	★
Oklahoma	★	S	maj. mbrs.	H & S	★	2/3 mbrs. present	LG	★
Oregon					(y)			
Pennsylvania	★	H	...	S	...	2/3 maj. mbrs.	LG	★
Rhode Island	★	H	2/3 maj. mbrs.	S	★	2/3 maj. mbrs.	LG	★
South Carolina	★	H	2/3 mbrs.	S	★	2/3 mbrs.	LG	★
South Dakota	★	H	maj. mbrs.	S	★	2/3 mbrs.	LG	★
Tennessee	★	H	maj. mbrs.	S	★	2/3 mbrs. (z)	PS	★
Texas	★	H (o)	maj. mbrs.	S	...	2/3 mbrs. present	LG	...
Utah	★	H	2/3 mbrs.	S	★(f)	2/3 mbrs.	LG	★
Vermont	★	H	2/3 mbrs.	S	...	2/3 mbrs.	LG	...
Virginia	★	H	maj. mbrs. present	S	...	2/3 mbrs. present	LG	★(bb)
Washington	★(d)	H	maj. mbrs.	S	★	2/3 mbrs.	LG	...
West Virginia	★	H	maj. mbrs.	S	★	2/3 mbrs.	PS	★
Wisconsin	★	H	maj. mbrs.	S	...	2/3 mbrs.	LG	...
Wyoming	★	H	maj. mbrs.	S	★	2/3 mbrs.	SS	★
Dist. of Columbia					(p)			
American Samoa	(q)	H	2/3 mbrs.	S	★	2/3 mbrs.	...	...
Guam					(p)			
CNMI*	★	H	2/3 mbrs.	S	...	2/3 mbrs.	LG	...
Puerto Rico	★	H	2/3 mbrs.	S	★	3/4 mbrs.	SS	★
U.S. Virgin Islands					(p)			

See footnotes at end of table

TABLE 4.8
Impeachment Provisions in the States (continued)

Sources: The Council of State Governments survey of governors' offices, January 2020 and state websites.

* Commonwealth of the Northern Mariana Islands

Key:

★–Yes; provision for.

... - Not specified, or no provision for.

H - House or Assembly (lower chamber).

S - Senate.

LG - Lieutenant Governor

PS- President or Speaker of the Senate

SS - Secretary of state.

(a) Presiding justice of state court of last resort. In many states, provision indicates that chief justice presides only on occasion of impeachment of governor.

(b) For provisions on official next in line of succession if governor is convicted and removed from office, refer to Chapter 4, "The Governors."

(c) An appointed Supreme Court justice presides.

(d) With exception of certain judicial officers. In Arizona and Washington - justices of courts not of record. In Nevada - justices of the peace. In North Dakota - county judges, justices of the peace, and police magistrates.

(e) Should the Chief Justice be on trial, or otherwise disqualified, the Senate shall elect a judge of the Supreme Court to preside.

(f) Only if Governor is on trial.

(g) Except in a trial of the chief justice, in which case the governor shall preside.

(h) An officer impeached by the house of representatives shall be disqualified from performing any official duties until acquitted by the senate, and, unless impeached,
the governor may by appointment fill the office until completion of the trial.

(i) Governor may appoint someone to serve until the impeachment procedures are final.

(j) Special sessions of the General Assembly shall be limited to a period of 40 days unless extended by 3/5 vote of each house and approved by the Governor or unless at the expiration of such period an impeachment trial of some officer of state government is pending, in which event the House shall adjourn and the Senate shall remain in session until such trial is completed.

(k) No person shall be convicted without the concurrence of two-thirds of there senators elected. When the governor is impeached, the chief justice shall preside.

(l) Judicial officers technically not impeached, but there are removal provisions provided for in the state constitution.

(m) No statute, simple majority is the assumption.

(n) Concurrence of 2/3 of the elected senators.

(o) House votes on articles of impeachment; Senate presides over impeachment trial to remove official.

(p) Removal of elected officials by recall procedure only.

(q) Governor, lieutenant governor.

(r) When the governor is tried; if Chief Justice is unable to preside, the next longest serving justice shall preside.

(s) No person shall be convicted without concurrence of 2/3 of all senators present. Miss Const. 1890 Art. IV § 52.

(t) All impeachments are tried before the state Supreme Court, except that the governor or a member of the Supreme Court is tried by a special commission of seven eminent jurists to be elected by the Senate. A vote of 5/7 of the court of special commission is necessary to convict.

(u) It is implied but not addressed directly in Miss Const. 1890 Art. IV §§ 49-53.

(v) Unicameral legislature; members use the title "senator".

(w) Court of impeachment is composed of chief justice and supreme court. A vote of 2/3 present of the court is necessary to convict.

(x) Chief Justice presides if it is the Governor or Lieutenant Governor; otherwise , the President of the Senate presides.

(y) No provision for impeachment. Public officers may be tried for incompetence, corruption, malfeasance, or delinquency in office in same manner as criminal offenses.

(z) Vote of 2/3 of members sworn to try the officer impeached.

(aa) In the event of simultaneous vacancies in both the offices of governor and lieutenant governor resulting from any cause, the president of the Senate shall become governor until a new governor or lieutenant governor is elected and qualifies.

(bb) Two-thirds of both houses may call a special session for any purpose. The Senate may try impeachments in recess; the House may not impeach unless in session.

TABLE 4.9
Constitutional and Statutory Provisions for Number of Consecutive Terms of Elected State Officials
(All terms are four years unless otherwise noted)

State or other jurisdiction	Governor	Lt. Governor	Secretary of state	Attorney general	Treasurer	Auditor	Comptroller	Education	Agriculture	Labor	Insurance
Alabama	2 C	2 C	2 C	2 C	2 C	2 C	...	2 C	2 C	...	...
Alaska	2 C	2A	(a)	...	(b)	...	...	...	...	...	...
Arizona	2 C	(c)	2	2	2	...	...	2	...	...	...
Arkansas	2 T	2 T	2 T	2 T	2 T	2 T	...	...	...	...	...
California	2 T	2 T	2 T	2 T	2 T	...	2 T	2 T	...	...	2 T
Colorado	2 C	2 C	2 C	2 C	2 C	...	...	...	...	...	...
Connecticut	N	N	N	N	N	...	N	...	...	...	...
Delaware	2 T	2 T	...	N	N	N	...	...	...	...	N
Florida	2 C	2A	N	2 C	2 C (d)	...	2 C (d)	N	2 C	...	2 C (d)
Georgia	2 C	N	N	N	...	...	...	N	N	N	N
Hawaii	2 C	2 C	(a)	...	...	...	...	...	...	...	...
Idaho	N	N	N	N	N	...	N	N	...	...	...
Illinois	N	N	N	N	N	...	N	...	...	...	...
Indiana	2 (e)	N	2 (e)	...	2 (e)	2 (e)	(f)	...	...	...	...
Iowa	N	N	N	N	N	N	...	...	N	...	...
Kansas	2 C	2 C	N	N	N	...	...	...	...	...	N
Kentucky	2 C	2 C	2 C	2 C	2 C	2 C	...	...	2 C	2 C	...
Louisiana	2 C	N	N	N	N	...	...	N	N	...	N
Maine	2 C	(g)	...	...	...	...	...	...	...	...	...
Maryland	2 C	N	...	N	...	...	N	...	...	...	...
Massachusetts	N	N	N	N	N	N	...	...	...	...	...
Michigan	2 T	2 T	2 T	2 T	...	...	...	...	...	...	...
Minnesota	N	N	N	N	...	N	...	...	...	...	(h)
Mississippi	2 T	2 T	N	N	N	N	...	...	...	...	...
Missouri	2 T	N	N	N	2 T	N	...	...	...	...	...
Montana	2 (i)	2 (i)	2 (i)	2 (i)	...	2 (i)	...	2 (i)	...	...	...
Nebraska	2 C	2A	N	N	2 C	N	...	...	...	...	...
Nevada	2 T	2 T	2 T	2 T	2 T	...	2 T	...	...	...	...
New Hampshire	N (j)	...	...	...	...	...	...	...	...	...	...
New Jersey	2 C	N	...	...	...	...	...	...	...	...	...
New Mexico	2 C	2 C	2 C	2 C	2 C	2 C	...	...	...	...	...
New York	N	N	...	N	...	N (k)	N	...	...	...	...
North Carolina	2 C	2 C	N	N	N	N	...	N	N	N	N
North Dakota	N	N	N	N	N	N	...	N	N	N	N
Ohio	2 C	2 C	2 C	2 C	2 C	2 C	...	...	...	...	...
Oklahoma	2 (l)	2 T	...	N	N	N	...	N	...	N	N
Oregon	2 (e)	(m)	2 (e)	N	2 (e)	...	...	...	...	...	...
Pennsylvania	2 C	2 C	...	2 C	2 C (n)	2 C	...	...	...	...	...
Rhode Island	2 C	2 C	2 C	2 C	2 C	...	...	...	...	...	...
South Carolina	2 C	2 C	N	N	N	...	N	N	N	...	...
South Dakota	2 C	2 C	2 C	2 C	2 C	2 C	...	2 C	...	...	...
Tennessee	2 C	N	...	(o)	...	...	...	...	...	...	...
Texas	N	N	...	N	(k)	...	N	...	N	...	...
Utah	N	N	(a)	N	N	N	...	...	...	...	...
Vermont	N (j)	N (j)	N (j)	N (j)	N (j)	N (j)	...	...	...	...	...
Virginia	1 C	N	...	N	...	...	...	...	...	...	...
Washington	N	N	N	N	N	N	...	N	...	...	...
West Virginia	2 C	N (g)	N	N	N	...	N	...	N	...	...
Wisconsin	N	N	N	N	N	...	...	N	...	...	...
Wyoming	2 (i)	(m)	N	...	N	N	...	...	...	...	...
Dist. of Columbia	N (p)	...	...	...	...	...	...	...	...	...	...
American Samoa	2 C	2 C	(a)	...	...	...	(q)	...	...	...	...
Guam	2 C	2 C	(a)	2 C	...	2 C	(r)	...	...	...	...
CNMI*	2 T	2 T	...	...	...	2 T	(q)	...	...	...	(h)
Puerto Rico	N	(m)	...	...	...	...	...	...	...	...	...
U.S. Virgin Islands	2 C	2 C	(k)	...	(c)	...	(c)	...	...	...	(a)

See footnotes at end of table

TABLE 4.9

Constitutional and Statutory Provisions for Number of Consecutive Terms of Elected State Officials
(All terms are four years unless otherwise noted) (continued)

Source: The Council of State Governments, April 2020.

* Commonwealth of Northern Mariana Islands

Note: All terms last four years unless otherwise noted. Footnotes specify if a position's functions are performed by an official under a different title.

Key:

N – No provision specifying number of terms allowed.

C – Consecutive Terms

T – Total Terms

2A – After 2 consecutive terms must wait one term before being eligible again.

… – Position is appointed or elected by governmental entity (not chosen by the electorate).

(a) Lieutenant Governor performs this function.

(b) Deputy Commissioner of Department of Revenue performs function.

(c) Finance Administrator performs function.

(d) Chief Financial Officer performs this function as of January 2003.

(e) Eligible for eight years out of any period of 12 years.

(f) State auditor performs this function.

(g) President or speaker of the Senate is next in line of succession to the governorship. In Tennessee and West Virginia, speaker of the Senate has the statutory title " lieutenant governor."

(h) Commerce administrator performs this function.

(i) Eligible for eight out of 16 years.

(j) Two-year term.

(k) Comptroller performs this function.

(l) Limited to 8 years per office during a lifetime.

(m) Secretary of state is next in line to the governorship.

(n) Treasurer must wait four years before being eligible for the office of auditor general.

(o) Term is eight years; attorney general is appointed by the state Supreme Court.

(p) Mayor.

(q) State treasurer performs this function.

(r) General services administrator performs function.

TABLE 4.10
Selected State Administrative Officials: Methods of Selection

State or other jurisdiction	Governor	Lieutenant governor (a-1)	Secretary of state (a-2)	Attorney general (a-3)	Treasurer (a-4)	Adjutant general (a-5)	Admin. (a-6)	Agriculture (a-7)	Auditor (a-8)	Banking (a-9)
Alabama	CE	CE	CE	CE	CE	G	G	SE	CE	GS
Alaska	CE	CE	(a-1)	GB	AG	GB	GB	AG	L	AG
Arizona	CE	(a-2)	CE	CE	CE	GS	GS	GS	L	GS
Arkansas	CE	CE	CE	CE	CE	G	G	BG	CE	GS
California	CE	CE	CE	CE	CE	GS	N.O.	G	GB	GS
Colorado	CE	CE	CE	CE	CE	GS	GS	GS	L	A
Connecticut	CE	CE	CE	CE	CE	G	GE	GE	(b)	GE
Delaware	CE	CE	GS	CE	CE	GS	(c)	GS	CE	GS
Florida	CE	CE	GS	CE	CE	GS	GS	CE	L	CE
Georgia	CE	CE	CE	CE	B	G	G	CE	CL	G
Hawaii	CE	CE	N.O.	GS	GS	GS	(b)	GS	CL	AG
Idaho	CE	CE	CE	CE	CE	GS	GS	GS	L	(a-24)
Illinois	CE	CE	CE	CE	CE	GS	GS	GS	CL	GS
Indiana	CE	CE	CE	SE	CE	G	G	LG	CE	G
Iowa	CE	CE	CE	CE	CE	GS	GS	CE	CE	GS
Kansas	CE	CE	CE	CE	CE	GS	GS	GS	N.O.	GS
Kentucky	CE	CE	CE	CE	CE	G	N.O.	CE	CE	G
Louisiana	CE	CE	CE	CE	CE	GS	G	CE	GS	GS
Maine	CE	N.O.	CL	CL	CL	GLS	GLS	GLS	L	GLS
Maryland	CE	CE	GS	CE	CL	G	(a-16)	GS	N/A	AG
Massachusetts	CE	CE	CE	CE	CE	G	G	CG	CE	G
Michigan	CE	CE	CE	CE	GS	GS	GS	GS	CL	GS
Minnesota	CE	CE	CE	CE	(a-24)	GS	GS	GS	CE	A
Mississippi	CE	CE	CE	CE	CE	GE	GS	SE	CE	GS
Missouri	CE	CE	CE	CE	CE	GS	GS	GS	CE	GS
Montana	CE	CE	CE	CE	GS	GS	GS	GS	CE	A
Nebraska	CE	CE	CE	CE	CE	GS	GS	GS	CE	GS
Nevada	CE	CE	CE	CE	CE	G	G	BG	N.O.	A
New Hampshire	CE	(e)	CL	GC	CL	GC	GC	GC	...	GC
New Jersey	CE	CE	GS	GS	GS	GS	N.O.	BG	(g)	GS
New Mexico	CE	CE	CE	CE	CE	G	(a-26)	A	CE	N/A
New York	CE	CE	GS	CE	GS	G	G	GS	CE	GS
North Carolina	CE	CE	CE	CE	CE	A	G	CE	CE	G
North Dakota	CE	CE	CE	CE	CE	G	N.O.	CE	CE	GS
Ohio	CE	CE	CE	CE	CE	G	GS	GS	CE	A
Oklahoma	CE	CE	GS	CE	CE	GS	GS	GS	CE	GS
Oregon	CE	(a-2)	CE	SE	CE	G	GS	GS	SS	N.O.
Pennsylvania	CE	CE	GS	CE	CE	GS	G	GS	CE	GS
Rhode Island	SE	SE	CE	SE	SE	GS	GS	GS	LS	GS
South Carolina	CE	CE	CE	CE	CE	GS	GS	CE	B	A
South Dakota	CE	CE	CE	CE	CE	GS	GS	GS	CE	C
Tennessee	CE	CL(e)	CL	CT	CL	G	G	G	(a-14)	G
Texas	CE	CE	G	CE	(a-14)	G	A	SE	L	B
Utah	CE	CE	(a-1)	CE	CE	GS	GS	GS	CE	GS
Vermont	CE	CE	CE	SE	CE	SL	GS	GS	CE	GS
Virginia	CE	CE	GB	CE	GB	GB	GB	GB	SL	B
Washington	CE	CE	CE	CE	CE	G	GS	GS	CE	GS
West Virginia	CE	(e)	CE	CE	CE	GS	GS	CE	CE	GS
Wisconsin	CE	CE	CE	CE	CE	G	GS	GS	LS	GS
Wyoming	CE	(a-2)	CE	GS	CE	G	GS	GS	CE	AG
American Samoa	CE	CE	(a-1)	GB	GB	N/A	GB	GB	N/A	N/A
Guam	CE	CE	...	CE	CS	GS	GS	GS	CE	GS
CNMI*	CE	CE	...	GS	CS	...	G	...	GB	C
Puerto Rico	CE	...	GS	GS	GS	GS	...	GS	GS	GS
U.S. Virgin Islands	SE	SE	(a-1)	GS	GS	GS	GS	GS	GS	LG

See footnotes at end of table

TABLE 4.10
Selected State Administrative Officials: Methods of Selection (continued)

State or other jurisdiction	Budget (a-10)	Civil rights (a-11)	Commerce (a-12)	Community affairs (a-13)	Comptroller (a-14)	Consumer affairs (a-15)	Corrections (a-16)	Economic development (a-17)	Education (a-18)	Election admin. (a-19)
Alabama	CS	N.O.	G	G	CS	CS	G	(a-12)	B	CS
Alaska	G	GB	GB	(a-12)	AG	(a-12)	GB	(a-12)	BG	LG
Arizona	G	G	B	N/A	A	A	GS	B	CE	(a-2)
Arkansas	AG	N.O.	N.R.	N.O.	AG	N.O.	B	GS	BG	B
California	(a-24)	N.O.	N.O.	GS	CE	G	GS	N.O.	CE	G
Colorado	G	A	N.O.	A	A	AT	GS	G	AB	CS
Connecticut	CS	B	GE	GE	CE	GE	GE	GE	GE	CS
Delaware	GS	CG	(a-2)	N.O.	CG	AT	GS	(c)	GS	GS
Florida	G	A	N/A	A	CE	A	GS	GS	B	A
Georgia	G	G	B	B	N.O.	G	GD	GB	CE	SS
Hawaii	GS	B	GS	N.O.	GS	A	GS	GS	B	B
Idaho	GS	AB	GS	N.O.	CE	(a-3)	B	(a-12)	CE	(a-2)
Illinois	G	GS	GS	(a-12)	CE	(a-3)	GS	(a-12)	B	B
Indiana	G	G	G	G	(a-8)	AT	G	G	CE	N.R. (b)
Iowa	GS	GS	N.O.	A	N.O.	AT	GS	GS	GS	SS
Kansas	G	B	GS	N.O.	C	AT	GS	C	B	CE
Kentucky	G	B	G	G	CG	AT	G	GC	B	B
Louisiana	A	BG	GS	N.O.	G	A	GS	GS	B	AGS
Maine	A	B	(a-17)	(a-17)	A	GLS	GLS	GLS	GLS	SS
Maryland	GS	G	GS	N.O.	CE	A	GS	GS	B	B
Massachusetts	C	G	G	G	G	G	CG	G	B	CE
Michigan	GS	B	GS	N.O.	CS	N.O.	GS	GS	B	(b)
Minnesota	(a-24)	GS	GS	(a-17)	(a-24)	A	GS	GS	GS	(a-2)
Mississippi	(a-6)	N.O.	SE	A	(a-6)	A	GS	GS	BS	A
Missouri	AGS	B	GS	A	A	CE	GS	GS	B	SS
Montana	G	CP	GS	CP	CP	CP	GS	G	CE	SS
Nebraska	A	B	GS	A	A	CE	GS	GS	B	A
Nevada	(a-6)	G	G	N.O.	CE	A	G	G	G	(b)
New Hampshire	GC	CS	GC	N.O.	AGC	AGC	GC	AGC	B	CL
New Jersey	GS	A	(a-17)	GS	GS	A	GS	G	GS	A
New Mexico	G	N.O.	(a-17)	N.O.	N/A	AT	GS	GS	GS	CE
New York	G	GS	GS	GS	CE	GS	GS	GS	B	(b)
North Carolina	(a-24)	A	G	N.O.	G	N.O.	G	A	CE	G
North Dakota	A	G	G	N.O.	A	AT	G	(i)	CE	SS
Ohio	GS	B	GS	A	GS	A	GS	GS	B	CE
Oklahoma	A	N.O.	GS	N.O.	A	B	GS	N.O.	CE	L
Oregon	A	A	GS	G	N.O.	GS	GS	GS	SE	A
Pennsylvania	G	B	G	G	G	AT	GS	GS	GS	AG
Rhode Island	A	B	GS	N.O.	A	SE	GS	GS (j)	B	B
South Carolina	A	BG	GS	N.O.	CE	B	GS	GS	CE	B
South Dakota	C	N.O.	N.O.	N.O.	C	AT	GS	GS	GS	SS
Tennessee	A	G	G	G	SL	A	G	G	G	A
Texas	G	B	G	G	CE	(i)	B	G	B	(b)
Utah	G	A	GS	AB	AG	GS	GS	GS	B	LG
Vermont	CG	AT	GS	CG	CG	AT	CG	CG	GS	CE
Virginia	GB	AT	GB	GB	GB	A	GB	B	GB	GB
Washington	N.O.	I	GS	N.O.	G	N.O.	GS	N.O.	CE	N.O.
West Virginia	G	GS	GS	B	(a-8)	(a-3)	GS	(a-13)	B	(a-2)
Wisconsin	A	A	N.O.	N.O.	CS	A	GS	G	CE	BS
Wyoming	AG	(a-37)	GS	N.O.	(a-8)	SS	GS	(a-12)	CE	A
American Samoa	GB	N/A	GB	(a-12)	(a-4)	(a-3)	A	(a-12)	GB	G
Guam	GS	...	GS	...	CS	CS	GS	B	B	GS
CNMI*	G	A	GS	GS	C	GS	C	C	B	B
Puerto Rico	G	N/A	GS	N/A	GB	GS	GS	GS	GS	N/A
U.S. Virgin Islands	GS	GS	GS	GS	(a-24)	GS	GS	GS	GS	B

See footnotes at end of table

TABLE 4.10
Selected State Administrative Officials: Methods of Selection (continued)

State or other jurisdiction	Emergency management (a-20)	Employment services (a-21)	Energy (a-22)	Environmental protection (a-23)	Finance (a-24)	Fish & wildlife (a-25)	General services (a-26)	Health (a-27)	Higher education (a-28)	Highways (a-29)
Alabama	G	CS	CS	B	G	CS	CS	B	B	G
Alaska	AG	AG	(f)	GB	AG	GB	AG	GB	B	AG
Arizona	G	A	N/A	GS	(a-14)	B	A	GS	B	A
Arkansas	GS	G	G	BG/BS	G	B	GS	BG	BG	BS
California	GS	GS	G	GS	G	G	GS	GS (b)	B	(a-49)
Colorado	A	A	G	A	A	A	A	GS	GS	GS
Connecticut	GE	GE	GE	GE	GE	(b)	GE	GE	BG	GE
Delaware	CG	CG	CG	(a-35)	GS	CG	CG	CG	B	(a-49)
Florida	G	GS	A	GS	CE	B	GS	GS	B	GOC
Georgia	G	A	CE	BG	G	A	A	GD	B	A
Hawaii	A	CS	CS	CS	(b)	CS	GS	GS	B	CS
Idaho	A	(a-32)	GS	GS	GS	B	N.O.	B(b)	B	(a-49)
Illinois	GS	GS	(a-42)	GS	(a-10)	(a-35)	(a-6)	GS	B	(a-49)
Indiana	G	G	LG	G	G	A	(a-6)	G	G	(a-49)
Iowa	GS	GS	(a-17)	A	A	A	A	GS	N.O.	A
Kansas	(b)	GS	B	C	C	CS	GS	GS	B	GS
Kentucky	AG	AG	AG	G	G	G	N.O.	CG	B	CG
Louisiana	GS	GS	A	GS	G	GS	G	GS	BS	GS
Maine	A	(a-32)	(a-38)	GLS	(a-6)	GLS	A	GLS	N/A	(a-49)
Maryland	AG	A	G	GS	GS	GS	(a-6)	GS	G	AG
Massachusetts	G	CG	CG	CG	G	CG	G	CG	BC	G
Michigan	GS	CS	A	GS	(a-10)	(b)	N.O.	GS	N.O.	(a-49)
Minnesota	GS	N.O.	A	GS	GS	A	(a-6)	GS	B	GS
Mississippi	GS	GS	A	GS	(a-6)	GS	N.O.	BS	BS	B
Missouri	A	A	G	A	AGS	(b)	A	GS	B	B
Montana	CP	CP	CP	GS	CP	GS	CP	GS	CP	(a-49)
Nebraska	A	A	GS	GS	(b)	A	A	GS	B	GS
Nevada	A	A	G	A	(a-14)	GD	N.O.	(b)	B	(a-49)
New Hampshire	G	GC	G	GC	(a-6)	BGS	GC	AGC	B	(a-49)
New Jersey	(a-47)	A	A	GS	GS	B	(b)	GS	B	A
New Mexico	GS	(a-32)	GS	GS	GS	A	GS	GS	GS	A
New York	GS	GS	B	GS	CE	GS	G	GS	B	GS
North Carolina	G	G	A	G	G	G	G	G	B	A
North Dakota	A	G	G	A	A	G	G	G	B	(a-49)
Ohio	AG	GS	GS	GS	(b)	A	A	GS	B	GS
Oklahoma	GS	B	GS	B	GS	B	GS	GS	B	B
Oregon	AG	GS	G	B	(a-4)	B	(a-6)	A	B	A
Pennsylvania	G	AG	AG	GS	G	(b)	GS	GS	AG	AG
Rhode Island	G	GS	A	GS	GS	GS	GS	GS	B(b)	GS
South Carolina	A	GS	A	(b)	B	BS	A	(b)	B	GS
South Dakota	C	C	(a-42)	GS	GS	C	(a-6)	GS	BG	C
Tennessee	A	G	A	G	G	B	G	G	B	(a-49)
Texas	A	B	N.O.	B	(a-14)	B	B	BG	B	(a-49)
Utah	A	GS	G	GS	AG	(a-35)	(a-6)	GS	N.O.	(a-49)
Vermont	AG	GS	GS	CG	CG	CG	CG	CG	N.O.	CG
Virginia	GB	GB	A	GB	GB	B	GB	GB	B	GB
Washington	N.O.	GS	N.O.	GS	N.O.	GD	N.O.	G	N.O.	N.O.
West Virginia	GS	GS	GS	GS	CS	CS	CS	GS	B	GS
Wisconsin	A	A	A	A	A	A	GS	GS	B	(a-49)
Wyoming	G	GS	G	GS	G	GD	AG	GS	GB	GS
American Samoa	G	A	GB	GB	(a-4)	GB	G	GB	(a-18)	(a-49)
Guam	GS	GS	G	GS	GS	GS	CS	GS	B	GS
CNMI*	G	C	C	G	GS	C	GS	GS	B	C
Puerto Rico	N/A	GS	N/A	N/A	G	N/A	GS	GS	N/A	GS
U.S. Virgin Islands	GS	GS	GS	GS	GS	GS	GS	GS	GS	GS

See footnotes at end of table

TABLE 4.10
Selected State Administrative Officials: Methods of Selection (continued)

State or other jurisdiction	Information systems (a-30)	Insurance (a-31)	Labor (a-32)	Licensing (a-33)	Mental health & developmental disabilities (a-34)	Natural resources (a-35)	Parks & recreation (a-36)	Personnel (a-37)	Planning (a-38)	Post audit (a-39)
Alabama	CS	G	G	N.O.	G	G	CS	B	(a-12)	LS
Alaska	AG	AG	GB	AG	B	GB	AG	AG	N.O.	(a-8)
Arizona	A	GS	BS	N.O.	B	GS	GS	A	(a-10)	N.O.
Arkansas	GS	GS	G	G	A	G	G	AG	N.O.	L
California	G	CE	AG	G	(b)	GS	GS	GS	N.O.	N.O.
Colorado	G	BA	GS	A	A	GS	A	A	G	(a-8)
Connecticut	A	GE	GE	CS	(b)	CS	CS	GE	A	(a-8)
Delaware	GS	CE	GS	CG	(b)	GS	CG	GS	CG	(a-8)
Florida	GS	GOC	GS	A	N/A	GS	A	A	A	CE
Georgia	GD	CE	CE	SS	B	GB	A	A	(a-10)	(a-8)
Hawaii	GS	AG	GS	CS	G	GS	CS	GS	CS	CS
Idaho	GS	GS	GS	GS	A	B	B	GS	N.O.	(a-8)
Illinois	GS	GS	GS	(a-9)	(a-45)	GS	(a-35)	(a-6)	N.O.	(a-8)
Indiana	G	G	G	G	A	G	A	G	N.O.	G
Iowa	GS	GS	GS	A	A	GS	A	A	N.O.	N.O.
Kansas	G	SE	GS	B	C	GS	CS	C	N.O.	L
Kentucky	G	G	G	N.O.	CG	G	CG	G	G	CE
Louisiana	G	CE	GS	N.O.	GS	GS	LGS	B	A	CL
Maine	A	GLS	GLS	A	(a-45)	GLS	(a-35)	A	N/A	N/A
Maryland	A	GS	GS	A	(b)	GS	A	A	GS	A
Massachusetts	CG	G	C	G	(b)	CG	CG	CG	G	CE
Michigan	GS	(a-9)	GS	GS	CS	GS	CS	CS	N.O.	CL
Minnesota	GS	A	GS	A	GS	GS	A	(a-24)	N/A	(a-8)
Mississippi	BS	SE	N.O.	N.O.	B	GS	GS	B	A	CE
Missouri	A	GS	GS	A	BS	GS	A	G	AGS	CE
Montana	A	CE	GS	CP	CP	GS	CP	CP	G	L
Nebraska	GS	GS	GS	A	GS	GS	B	A	GS	CE
Nevada	G	A	A	N.O.	(b)	G	A	GS	N.O.	N.O.
New Hampshire	GC	GC	GC	GC	AGC	GC	AGC	AGC	...	(a-14)
New Jersey	A	GS	N.O.	N.O.	(b)	A	A	GS	A	N.O.
New Mexico	GS	G	GS	G	N.O.	GS	N/A	GD	N/A	(a-8)
New York	G	GS	GS	(b)	(b)	GS	GS	GS	GS	CE
North Carolina	G	CE	CE	N.O.	A	G	A	G	N/A	(a-8)
North Dakota	G	CE	G	N.O.	A	N.O.	G	A	N.O.	A
Ohio	G	GS	A	N.O.	(b)	GS	A	A	GS	CE
Oklahoma	A	CE	CE	N.O.	B	(a-48)	(a-48)	GS	N.O.	N.O.
Oregon	A	GS	SE	N.O.	A	N.O.	B	A	N.O.	SS
Pennsylvania	G	GS	GS	AG	G	GS	A	G	G	(a-8)
Rhode Island	A	GS	GS	(i)	GS	GS	GS	A	A	N.O.
South Carolina	A	GS	GS	GS	(b)	BS	GS	A	AB	B
South Dakota	GS	C	GS	N.O.	GS	(a-23)	C	GS	N.O.	(a-8)
Tennessee	A	G	G	A	G	G	A	G	N.O.	SL
Texas	B	G	B	B	B	B	B	N.O.	G	L
Utah	GS	GS	GS	(a-12)	(a-45)	GS	AB	GS	(a-10)	(a-8)
Vermont	GS	GS	GS	SS	CG	GS	CG	CG	N.O.	(a-8)
Virginia	B	B	GB	GB	GB	GB	GB	GB	(a-10)	(a-8)
Washington	GS	SE	GS	GS	N.O.	CE	I	N.O.	N.O.	N.O.
West Virginia	G	GS	GS	N.O.	(a-27)	(a-25)	(a-25)	C	(a-17)	LS
Wisconsin	A	GS	GS	GS	A	GS	A	A	N.O.	(a-8)
Wyoming	GS	GS	AG	CS	(b)	G	GS	AG	G	AG
American Samoa	(a-49)	G	N/A	N/A	(a-45)	AG	GB	A	(a-12)	G
Guam	GS	GS	GS	GS	GS	GS	GS	GS	GS	CE
CNMI*	C	CS	C	B	C	GS	C	GS	G	GS
Puerto Rico	N/A	N/A	GS	N/A	N/A	GS	GS	GS	GS	N/A
U.S. Virgin Islands	G	SE	GS	GS	GS	GS	GS	GS	G	L

See footnotes at end of table

TABLE 4.10
Selected State Administrative Officials: Methods of Selection (continued)

State or other jurisdiction	Pre-audit (a-40)	Public library development (a-41)	Public utility regulation (a-42)	Purchasing (a-43)	Revenue (a-44)	Social services (a-45)	Solid waste mgmt. (a-46)	State police (a-47)	Tourism (a-48)	Transportation (a-49)	Welfare (a-50)
Alabama	(a-14)	B	SE	CS	G	B	CS	G	G	(a-29)	(a-45)
Alaska	N.O.	AG	GB	AG	GB	GB	AG	GB	AG	GB	AG
Arizona	(a-14)	SS	B	A	GS	GS	A	GS	GS	GS	(a-45)
Arkansas	N/A	B	GS	AG	AG	G	BG/BS	BG	G	BS	G
California	(a-14)	N.O.	GS	(a-26)	BS	GS	G	GS	N.O.	GS	(a-45)
Colorado	(a-14)	BA	CS	CS	GS	GS	CS	A	CS	GS	GS
Connecticut	CE	B	GB	CS	GE	GE	CS	GE	A	GE	GE
Delaware	(a-8)	CG	CG	(a-26)	CG	(b)	B	CG	CG	GS	CG
Florida	CE	A	B	A	GOC	GS	A	GOC	N.O.	GS	A
Georgia	N.O.	N.O.	(a-12)	A	GS	GD	A	G	A	GB	A
Hawaii	CS	B	GS	GS	GS	GS	CS	N.O.	B	GS	CS
Idaho	(a-14)	B	GS	A	GS	GS	A	GS	(a-12)	B	A
Illinois	(a-14)	SS	GS	(a-6)	GS	GS	(a-23)	GS	(a-12)	GS	GS
Indiana	CE	G	G	A	G	G	A	G	LG	G	(a-45)
Iowa	A	B	GS	A	GS	GS	A	GS	A	GS	A
Kansas	CS	GS	B	C	GS	GS	C	GS	C	GS	N.O.
Kentucky	N.O.	G	G	G	G	G	AG	G	G	G	(a-45)
Louisiana	A	LGS	BS	A	GS	GS	GS	GS	LGS	GS	GS
Maine	(a-14)	B	G	CS	A	GLS	CS	A/GLS	(a-17)	GLS	(a-45)
Maryland	A	A	GS	A	A	GS	A	GS	A	GS	(a-45)
Massachusetts	CE	B	CG	CG	CG	CG	CG	CG	G	G	CG
Michigan	N.O.	N.O.	GS	CS	CS	GS	CS	GS	N.O.	GS	GS
Minnesota	(a-8)	N/A	(b)	A	GS	(a-34)	(a-23)	A	A	GS	(a-34)
Mississippi	CE	B	GS	A	GS	GS	A	GS	A	B	GS
Missouri	A	B	GS	A	GS	GS	A	GS	A	B	A
Montana	(a-39)	CP	CE	CP	GS	GS	GS	CP	CP	GS	GS
Nebraska	A	B	B	A	GS	GS	A	GS	B	GS	GS
Nevada	N.O.	(b)	G	A	G	G	(a-23)	G	GD	B	(b)
New Hampshire	(a-14)	AGC	GC	CS	GC	GC	AGC	AGC	AGC	GC	AGC
New Jersey	N.O.	N.O.	GS	GS	A	(b)	A	GS	A	GS	A
New Mexico	N/A	N/A	G	N/A	GS	N/A	N/A	GS	GS	GS	N/A
New York	CE	B	GS	G	GS	GS	GS	GS	GS	GS	GS
North Carolina	(a-8)	A	G	A	G	A	A	G	A	G	N.O.
North Dakota	N.O.	N.O.	CE	A	CE	G	A	G	G	G	G
Ohio	GS	B	BG	A	GS	(b)	A	GS	LG	GS	GS
Oklahoma	(a-14)	B	(b)	A	GS	GS	A	GS	GS	B	GS
Oregon	(a-10)	B	GS	A	GS	GS	N.O.	GS	N.O.	GS	(a-45)
Pennsylvania	(a-4)	G	GS	AG	GS	GS	AG	GS	A	GS	GS
Rhode Island	(a-14)	A	GS	A	GS	GS (b)	(h)	G	(a-17)	GS	GS
South Carolina	(a-14)	B	G	A	GS	GS	BS	GS	GS	BS	(a-45)
South Dakota	(a-8)	C	CE	C	GS	GS	N.O.	C	GS	GS	C
Tennessee	(a-14)	A	SE	A	G	G	A	G	G	G	G
Texas	(a-14)	A	B	A	(a-14)	(i)	N.O.	B	A	B	BG
Utah	(a-24)	A	A	(a-6)	A	GS	(a-23)	A	(a-17)	GS	(a-45)
Vermont	(a-24)	CG	BGS	CG	CG	GS	CG	GS	CG	GS	CG
Virginia	(a-14)	B	(b)	A	GB	GB	GB	GB	G	GB	GB
Washington	N.O.	N.O.	GS	N.O.	GS	GS	N.O.	GS	N.O.	GS	N.O.
West Virginia	(a-8)	B	GS	CS	GS	(a-27)	B	GS	GS	(a-29)	(a-27)
Wisconsin	(a-8)	A	GS	A	GS	GS	A	A	GS	GS	A
Wyoming	(a-8)	AG	G	CS	GS	(a-27)	AG	AG	AG	(a-29)	(a-45)
American Samoa	(a-4)	(a-18)	N/A	A	(a-4)	GB	GB	GB	(a-12)	(a-29)	N/A
Guam	GS	(i)	GS	GS	GS	GS	GS	GS	B	…	GS
CNMI*	G	B	B	C	C	C	A	GS	GB	CS	A
Puerto Rico	N/A	N/A	GS	GS	GS	N/A	N/A	GS	GS	GS	N/A
U.S. Virgin Islands	GS	GS	G	GS	GS	G	GS	GS	GS	GS	GS

See footnotes at end of table

TABLE 4.10
Selected State Administrative Officials: Methods of Selection (continued)

Source: The Council of State Governments' survey of state person-
nel agencies and state Web sites, June 2020.
*Commonwealth of Northern Mariana Islands
Key:
N/A–Not available
N.O.–No specific chief administrative official or agency in charge of
function
N.R.–Not reported
CE–Constitutional, elected by public
CL–Constitutional, elected by legislature
SE–Statutory, elected by public
SL–Statutory, elected by legislature
L–Selected by legislature or one of its organs
CT–Constitutional, elected by state court of last resort
CP–Competitive process
Appointed by: Approved by:
G–Governor
GS–Governor–Senate (in Nebraska, unicameral legislature)
GB–Governor–Both houses
GE–Governor–Either house
GC–Governor–Council
GD–Governor–Departmental board
GLS–Governor–Appropriate legislative committee & Senate
GOC–Governor & Council or cabinet
LG–Lieutenant Governor
LGS–Lieutenant Governor–Senate (in Nebraska, unicameral
legislature)
AT–Attorney General
ATS–Attorney General–Senate (in Nebraska, unicameral legislature)
SS–Secretary of State
C–Cabinet Secretary
CG–Cabinet Secretary–Governor
A–Agency head
AB–Agency head–Board
AG–Agency head–Governor
AGC–Agency head–Governor & Council
AGS Agency head–Senate (in Nebraska, unicameral legislature)
ALS–Agency head–Appropriate legislative committee
ASH–Agency head–Senate president & House speaker
B–Board or commission
BG–Board–Governor
BGS–Board–Governor & Senate
BS–Board or commission–Senate (in Nebraska, unicameral
legislature)
BA–Board or commission–Agency head
CS–Civil Service
LS–Legislative Committee–Senate (in Nebraska, unicameral
legislature)
(a) Chief administrative official or agency in charge of function:
(a-1) Lieutenant governor
(a-2) Secretary of state
(a-3) Attorney general
(a-4) Treasurer
(a-5) Adjutant general
(a-6) Administration

(a-7) Agriculture
(a-8) Auditor
(a-9) Banking
(a-10) Budget
(a-11) Civil rights
(a-12) Commerce
(a-13) Community affairs
(a-14) Comptroller
(a-15) Consumer affairs
(a-16) Corrections
(a-17) Economic development
(a-18) Education (chief state school officer)
(a-19) Election administration
(a-20) Emergency management
(a-21) Employment Services
(a-22) Energy
(a-23) Environmental protection
(a-24) Finance
(a-25) Fish and wildlife
(a-26) General services
(a-27) Health
(a-28) Higher education
(a-29) Highways
(a-30) Information systems
(a-31) Insurance
(a-32) Labor
(a-33) Licensing
(a-34) Mental Health & Developmental Disabilities
(a-35) Natural resources
(a-36) Parks and recreation
(a-37) Personnel
(a-38) Planning
(a-39) Post audit
(a-40) Pre-audit
(a-41) Public library development
(a-42) Public utility regulation
(a-43) Purchasing
(a-44) Revenue
(a-45) Social services
(a-46) Solid waste management
(a-47) State police
(a-48) Tourism
(a-49) Transportation
(a-50) Welfare
(b)
California–Health–Responsibilities shared between Director of
Health Care Services, Vacant, and Director of Public Health, Sonia
Angell, both (GS).
California–Mental Health and Developmental Disabilities - Responsibilities shared between Director of State Hospitals, Stephanie
Clendenin (GS) and Director of Developmental Services, Nancy A.
Bargmann, (GS).
Connecticut–Auditors–Responsibilities shared between Robert J.
Kane and John C. Geragosian. Positions are filled by the
legislature.

TABLE 4.10
Selected State Administrative Officials: Methods of Selection (continued)

Connecticut–Fish and Wildlife–Responsibilities shared between Chief of Wildlife, Richard Jacobson, (CS), Director of Inland and Marine Fisheries, Peter Aarrestad, (CS).

Connecticut–Mental Health and Developmental Disabilities–Responsibilities shared between Commissioner of Mental Health, Miriam Delphin–Rittmon, (GE) and Commissioner, Dept. of Developmental Services, Jordan Scheff, (GE).

Delaware–Mental Health and Developmental Disabilities–Responsibilities shared between Director, Division of Substance Abuse and Mental Health (CG); and Director, Division of Developmental Disabilities Services, same department (CG).

Delaware–Social Services–Responsibilities shared between Secretary of Health and Social Services (GS); and Secretary , Department of Services of Children, Youth and their Families (GS).

Hawaii–Administration–the functions are divided amongst the Director of Budget and Finance, Director of Human Resources Development, and the Comptroller.

Hawaii–Finance–Responsibilities shared between Director of Budget and Finance, Craig K. Hirai (GS) and the Comptroller, Curt Otaguro, (GS).

Idaho–Responsibilities are shared between seven (7) directors all chosen by (B). See Table 4.11 for names.

Indiana–Election Administration–Responsibilities shared between Co-Directors, Brad King and Angela Nussmeyer.

Kansas–Emergency management–Responsibilities shared between Adjutant General (GS) and Deputy Director (C)

Maryland–Mental Health and Developmental Disabilities–Responsibilities shared between Executive Director, Mental Hygiene Administration (A); and Secretary, Department of Disabilities (A).

Massachusetts–Mental Health and Developmental Disabilities–Responsibilities shared between Commissioner, Department of Developmental Disabilities (CG); and Commissioner, Department of Mental Health, Executive Office of Human Services (CG).

Michigan–Election Administration–Responsibilities shared between Secretary of State, (CE); and Director of Elections (CS).

Michigan–Fish and Wildlife–Responsibilities shared between Director, Chief of Fisheries, Jim Dexter, (CS) and Chief of Wildlife, Vacant, (CS).

Minnesota–Human/Social Services, Mental Health and Developmental Disabilities and Welfare are under the Commissioner of Human Services (GS).

Minnesota–Public Utility Regulation–Responsibilities shared between the five Public Utility Commissioners (G).

Missouri–Fish and Wildlife–Responsibilities shared between Administrator, Division of Fisheries, Department of Conservation; Administrator, Division of Wildlife, same department (AB).

Nebraska–Finance–Responsibilities shared between State Tax Commissioner, Department of Revenue (GS); Administrator, Budget Division (A) and the Auditor of Public Accounts (CE).

Nevada–Election Administration–Responsibilities shared between Secretary of State (CE), Deputy Secretary of State (SS), Chief Deputy, Secretary of State (A).

Nevada–Health–Responsibilities shared between Director of Health and Human Services (G) and Division Administrator, Health (AG).

Nevada–Mental Health and Developmental Disabilities–Responsi-

bilities shared between Director of Health and Human Services (G) and Division Administrator, MHDS (G).

Nevada–Public Library–Responsibilities shared between Director, Dept. of Tourism and Cultural Affairs (G) and Division Administrator of Library and Archives (A).

Nevada–Welfare–Responsibilities shared between Director of Health and Human Services (G) and Division Administrator, Welfare and Support Services (AG).

New Jersey–General Services–Responsibilities shared between Director, Division of Purchase and Property, Dept. of Treasury (GS), and Director, Division of Property Management and Construction, Dept. of the Treasury (A).

New Jersey–Mental Health and Developmental Disabilities–Responsibilities shared between Director, Division of Mental Health Services, Dept. of Human Services (A) and Assistant Commissioner, Division of Developmental Disabilities, Dept. of Human Services (A).

New Jersey–Social Services–Commissioner , Dept. of Human Services (GS) and Commissioner Dept. Of Children and Families (GS).

New York–Responsibilities shared between Board of Election members. Two co-chairs and two commissioners. (B)

New York–Licensing–Responsibilities shared between Secretary of State (GS) and Commissioner of State Education Department (B).

New York–Mental health & developmental disabilities–Responsibilities shared between Commissioner of Office for People with Developmental Disabilities (GS) and Commissioner of Office of Mental Health (GS.

Ohio–Finance–Responsibilities shared between Assistant Director, Office of Budget and Management (A) and Deputy Director same office (A).

Ohio–Mental Health and Developmental Disabilities–Responsibilities shared between Director, Dept. of Developmental Disabilities (GS) and Director, Department of Mental Health and Addiction Services. (GS).

Ohio–Social Services–Responsibilities shared between Director, OH Dept. of Job and Family Services (GS), Superintendent of Public Instruction, Dept. of Education (B), Executive Director of Opportunities for Ohioans with Disabilities (B), Director of Dept. of Aging (GS).

Oklahoma–Public Utility Regulation–Responsibilities shared between Director of Administration, Public Utility Division, Corporation Commission (B); and 3 Commissioners, Corporation Commission (SE).

Pennsylvania–Shared between Executive Director (Fish) (B) and Executive Director (Game) (B).

Rhode Island–Higher Education–This employee serves in a dual role as Commissioner of Higher Education and as the President of the Community College of Rhode Island.

Rhode Island–Social Services–This position is filled by two employees one, Stephen Costantino, is the Commissioner , Office of Health and Human Services; Sandra Powell serves as the Director of Human Services and reports to the Commissioner , Office of Health and Human Services.

South Carolina–Environmental Protection–Responsibilities shared between two Directors, both selected by (BS).

TABLE 4.10
Selected State Administrative Officials: Methods of Selection (continued)

South Carolina–Health–Responsibilities shared between Director of Health and Human Services (GS) and Director of Health & Environmental Control (BS).

South Carolina–Mental Health and Developmental Disabilities–Responsibilities shared between Director of Disabilities and Special Needs (B) and Director of Mental Health (B).

Texas–Election Administration–Responsibilities shared between Secretary of State (G); and Division Director of Elections, Elections Division, Secretary of State (A).

Virginia–Public Utility Regulation–No single position. Functions are shared between Energy Regulation and Utility and Railroad Safety, both (B).

Wyoming–Mental Health and Developmental Disabilities–Responsibilities shared between Director, State Hospital (AG) and Director, Life Resource Center, (AG).

(c) Department of Administration abolished July 1, 2005; responsibilities transferred to office of Management and Budget, General Services and Department of State. Economic Development Office was abolished in FY 2019; most responsibilities assigned to a new public-private partnership.

(d) Appointed by the House and approved by the Senate.

(e) In Maine, New Hampshire, Tennessee and West Virginia, the Presidents (or Speakers) of the Senate are next in line of succession to the Governorship. In Tennessee and West Virginia, the Speaker of the Senate bears the statutory title of Lieutenant Governor.

(f) The authority is a public corporation of the state and a body corporate and politic constituting a political subdivision within the Department of Commerce, Community, and Economic Development, but with separate and independent legal existence.

(g) The New Jersey State constitution states: "The State Auditor shall be appointed by the Senate and General Assembly in joint meeting for a term of five years and until his successor shall be appointed and qualify." So it is a Constitutional Officer, but is appointed, not elected by the legislature.

(h) Solid waste is managed by the Rhode Island Resource Recovery Corporation (RRIRRC). Although not a department of the state government, RRIRRC is a public corporation and a component of the State of Rhode Island for financial reporting purposes. To be financially self-sufficient, the agency earns revenue through the sale of recyclable products, methane gas royalties and fees for it services.

(i) Method not specified.

(j) The Rhode Island Economic Development Corporation is a quasi-public agency.

TABLE 4.11
Selected State Administrative Officials: Annual Salaries

State or other jurisdiction	Governor	Lieutenant governor (a-1)	Secretary of state (a-2)	Attorney general (a-3)	Treasurer (a-4)	Adjutant general (a-5)	Admin. (a-6)	Agriculture (a-7)	Auditor (a-8)	Banking (a-9)
Alabama	127,833	52,102	99,772	169,001	89,031	139,008	158,974	71,380	87,673	181,049
Alaska	145,000	115,000	(a-1)	141,156	163,770	141,156	141,156	110,304	169,332	122,988
Arizona	95,000	(a-2)	70,000	90,000	70,000	146,000	N/A	132,000	141,986	130,000
Arkansas	151,838	44,674	96,918	139,992	91,534	180,072	173,846	132,000	91,533	155,916
California	209,747	157,310	157,310	182,189	167,796	197,802	N.O.	217,292	217,292	197,798
Colorado	92,700	93,360	93,360	107,672	93,360	168,552	169,956	159,660	188,808	219,816
Connecticut	150,000 (d)	110,000	110,000	110,000	110,000	165,000	175,000	140,000	(c)	149,625
Delaware	171,000	82,239	132,011	149,893	117,582	126,156	(c)	123,333	112,667	115,595
Florida	130,273	124,851	141,000	128,972	(a-24)	170,352	141,000	128,972	140,004	(a-24)
Georgia	175,000	91,609	123,637	139,169	185,000	163,200	160,000	121,557	152,160	154,350
Hawaii	165,048	165,552	N.O.	162,552	162,552	245,838	(c)	154,812	154,812	125,400
Idaho	138,302	48,406	117,557	134,000	117,557	147,659	123,614	149,386	150,446	(a-24)
Illinois	181,670 (d)	139,200	160,800	160,800	139,200	135,600	168,000	157,200	170,400	159,600
Indiana	121,331	99,783	86,654	104,246	86,654	151,000	161,670	156,998	86,654	136,347
Iowa	130,000	103,212	103,212	123,669	103,212	223,393	154,300	103,212	103,212	128,890
Kansas	110,707	76,313	86,003	98,901	86,003	114,505	175,000	123,000	N/A	126,075
Kentucky	152,181	129,375	129,375	129,375	129,375	129,524	N.O.	129,375	129,375	128,553
Louisiana	130,000	115,003	115,000	110,740	110,740	200,262	237,500	110,740	132,620	145,000
Maine	70,000	(e)	104,104	105,914	79,518	139,734	139,734	139,734	111,134	115,274
Maryland	170,000	141,500	99,500	141,500	141,500	144,052 (b)	146,743 (b)	143,488 (b)	N.O.	101,463 (b)
Massachusetts	185,000	122,058	136,402	136,402	133,277	171,392	161,522	136,000	140,607	130,000
Michigan	159,300	111,510	112,410	112,410	178,500	185,859	(a-10)	170,000	180,169	170,000
Minnesota	127,629	82,959	95,722	121,248	(a-24)	190,300	144,991	144,991	108,485	130,918
Mississippi	122,160	60,000	90,000	108,960	90,000	141,105	150,000	90,000	90,000	156,900
Missouri	133,821	86,484	107,746	116,437	107,746	114,450	133,394	129,142	107,746	119,635
Montana	118,397	90,140	98,104	141,023	(a-6)	123,677	112,935	112,935	92,236	110,787
Nebraska	105,000	75,000	85,000	95,000	85,000	111,236	160,001	116,727	85,000	107,338
Nevada	149,573 (d)	63,648	102,898	141,086	102,898	118,200	128,998	118,200	N.O.	98,880
New Hampshire	134,581	(e)	105,930	128,260	105,930	105,930	117,913	100,171	N.O.	105,929
New Jersey	175,000	175,000	175,000	175,000	175,000	175,000	N.O.	175,000	151,952	175,000
New Mexico	110,000	85,000	85,000	95,000	85,000	203,950	156,000	82,980	85,000	90,000
New York	225,000	210,000	160,000	210,000	190,000	160,000	195,145	160,000	210,000	210,000
North Carolina	150,969	133,365	133,365	133,365	133,365	151,292	151,732	133,365	133,365	134,410
North Dakota	135,360 (d)	105,285	107,885	159,409	107,885	202,560	N.O.	116,836	107,885	142,404
Ohio	159,182	176,426	117,582	117,582	117,582	143,853	159,266	143,853	117,582	128,752
Oklahoma	147,000	114,713	140,000	132,825	114,713	190,289	11,150	126,508	114,713	196,721
Oregon	98,600	(a-2)	77,000	82,220	72,000	185,508	204,058	152,652	136,488	N.O.
Pennsylvania	201,729	169,451	145,244	167,838	167,838	176,760	161,390	145,244	167,838	145,244
Rhode Island (g)	145,755	122,740	122,740	132,521	122,740	141,259	136,510	(a-23)	159,248	135,000
South Carolina	106,078	46,545	92,007	92,007	92,007	163,257	217,643	92,007	165,872	126,615
South Dakota	116,400	56,375	93,046	116,277	93,046	124,140	107,244	126,075	93,046	113,391
Tennessee	198,780	72,948 (e)	209,520	193,488	209,520	161,904	209,520	161,904	(a-14)	161,904
Texas	153,750	7,200	197,415	153,750	(a-14)	178,196	N.O.	137,500	181,128	242,925
Utah	160,746	144,671	(a-1)	152,709	144,671	145,018	147,077	N/A	135,000	136,573
Vermont	184,100	78,145	$116,729	139,755	116,729	129,126	145,537	145,246	116,729	126,630
Virginia	175,000	36,321	176,730	150,000	177,172	143,453	176,730	176,730	178,950	175,100
Washington	182,179	111,180	130,560	167,381	149,103	190,289	173,856	173,856	128,120	137,808
West Virginia	150,000	20,000 (e)	95,000	95,000	95,000	125,000	95,000	95,000	95,000	75,000
Wisconsin	152,756	80,684	72,551	148,242	72,551	N/A	152,755	N/A	137,488	137,717
Wyoming	105,000	(a-2)	92,000	177,000	92,000	142,816	167,000	126,378	92,000	109,184
Guam	130,000	85,000	N.O.	105,286	52,492	68,152	88,915	60,850	100,000	88,915
CNMI*	70,000	65,000	N.O.	80,000	40,800 (b)	N.O.	54,000	40,800 (b)	80,000	40,800 (b)
Puerto Rico	70,000	N.O.	125,000	N/A	N/A	N/A	N/A	N/A	N/A	N/A
U.S. Virgin Islands	150,000	75,000	(a-1)	76,500	76,500	85,000	76,500	76,500	76,500	75,000

See footnotes at end of table

TABLE 4.11
Selected State Administrative Officials: Annual Salaries (continued)

State or other jurisdiction	Budget (a-10)	Civil rights (a-11)	Commerce (a-12)	Community affairs (a-13)	Comptroller (a-14)	Consumer affairs (a-15)	Corrections (a-16)	Economic development (a-17)	Education (a-18)	Election admin. (a-19)
Alabama	113,355	N.O.	177,891	170,553	147,580	(a-3)	165,183	(a-12)	268,797	(a-2)
Alaska	162,504	149,016	141,156	(a-12)	124,452	(a-12)	141,156	(a-12)	141,156	145,008
Arizona	130,000	145,000	250,000	N/A	140,000	133,729	185,000	(a-12)	85,000	142,518
Arkansas	120,543	N.O.	153,00	N.O.	149,594	N.O.	158,100	153,000	239,361	72,595
California	(a-24)	N.O.	N.O.	177,514	167,796	197,798	279,216	N.O.	182,189	154,464
Colorado	178,824	130,764	N.O.	159,648	152,100	158,712	175,104	159,648	283,416	143,436
Connecticut	167,590	141,039	15,000	(a-12)	110,000	147,798	167,500	(a-12)	192,500	120,616
Delaware	152,088	82,950	(a-2)	N.O	152,088	126,102	152,088	(c)	164,055	92,173
Florida	145,000	99,500	N/A	110,000	128,972	100,000	160,000	141,000	276,000	97,250
Georgia	225,000	105,202	135,000	163,200	N/A	134,227	163,200	188,700	123,270	106,793
Hawaii	162,552	113,616	154,812	N.O.	154,812	118,776	154,812	154,812	240,000	119,664
Idaho	144,186	88,317	139,069	N.O.	117,557	(a-3)	160,014	(a-12)	117,557	(a-2)
Illinois	166,770	135,600	168,000	(a-12)	139,200	(a-3)	176,400	(a-12)	249,600	156,000
Indiana	142,800	121,281	(a-17)	129,841	(a-8)	124,803	169,076	213,868	103,677	(c)
Iowa	154,300	97,460	N.O.	140,899	N.O	128,890	154,300	154,300	154,300	111,155
Kansas	120,750	86,423	123,000	N.O.	120,000	98,000	140,000	89,303	230,000	(a-2)
Kentucky	129,524	126,200	129,524	109,524	108,286	90,000	N/A	136,000	N/A	73,500
Louisiana	141,648	90,188	237,500	N.O.	(a-6)	140,670	136,719	237,500	275,000	113,695
Maine	104,645	95,098	(a-17)	(a-17)	118,934	130,811	139,734	139,734	139,734	110,219
Maryland	174,417 (b)	114,865 (b)	172,021 (b)	N.O	141,500	134,749 (b)	159,072 (b)	172,021 (b)	153,532 (b)	130,059 (b)
Massachusetts	134,589	137,382	161,522	145,000	176,624	145,000	150,000	161,522	161,522	136,402
Michigan	170,000	159,800	(a-32)	N.O.	153,428	N.O.	178,500	178,500	221,403	(c)
Minnesota	(a-24)	144,991	144,991	(a-17)	(a-24)	131,878	150,002	150,002	150,002	(a-2)
Mississippi	(a-6)	N.O.	90,000	130,000	(a-6)	108,960	132,000	183,000	300,000	82,500
Missouri	122,027	86,274	129,526	N/A	113,300	116,437	129,142	133,412	199,272	66,690
Montana	123,452	86,548	112,935	81,200	115,495	81,417	112,944	106,897	116,378	89,920
Nebraska	164,303	79,170	134,172	101,653	140,000	95,000	188,957	143,998	227,390	97,562
Nevada	(a-6)	88,651	128,998	N.O.	102,898	75,111	128,998	N/A	128,998	(c)
New Hampshire	105,930	80,971	114,554	N.O.	106,575	100,171	117,913	87,423	114,553	(a-2)
New Jersey	155,250	150,114	(a-17)	175,000	175,000	157,911	175,000	225,000	175,000	143,750
New Mexico	95,714	N.O.	156,000	N.O.	145,600	95,054	N/A	(a-12)	156,000	85,000
New York	209,684	120,000	160,000 (b)	160,000	210,000	210,000	210,000	(a-13)	210,000	(c)
North Carolina	(a-24)	109,533	159,903	N.O.	166,758	N.O.	183,888	128,125	133,365	143,500
North Dakota	(a-24)	(a-12)	162,396	N.O.	N.O.	149,784	165,804	142,400	122,810	55,080
Ohio	181,875	120,328	154,128	159,266	181,875	113,568	159,266	159,266	209,997	117,582
Oklahoma	110,600	N.O.	141,000	N.O.	120,000	132,833	185,000	N.O.	124,373	117,885
Oregon	157,884	112,428	168,276	156,773	N.O.	185,508	185,104	(a-13)	157,581	150,336
Pennsylvania	168,490	133,380	149,918	149,918	159,081	152,607	161,382	153,313	161,382	84,930
Rhode Island (g)	185,739	86,342	205,706	N/A	140,645	(a-3)	145,644	185,000 (j)	212,106	145,993
South Carolina	133,223	115,000	199,857	N.O.	92,007	125,243	199,857	(a-12)	92,007	111,649
South Dakota	96,111	N.O.	N.O.	N.O.	100028	70,000	129,150	144,013	135,300	77,203
Tennessee	168,144	116,964	(a-17)	(a-17)	209,520	100,116	161,904	169,392	200,004	151,128
Texas	205,000	123,769	N.O.	180,084	153,750	155,224	266,500	164,701	220,375	(c)
Utah	167,045	103,147	N/A	73,778	146,744	(a-12)	143,499	153,379	235,830	102,190
Vermont	135,283	114,982	145,537	113,588	135,283	114,982	129,126	120,265	145,537	116,729
Virginia	177,448	104,798	176,730	141,072	177,313	105,165	189,112	350,200	176,730	121,466
Washington	N.O.	120,044	173,856	N.O.	N.O.	(a-3)	186,888	(a-12)	145,860	(a-2)
West Virginia	93,000	55,000	95,000	81,548	(a-8)	(a-3)	90,504	(a-13)	230,000	(a-2)
Wisconsin	132,600	109,158	N.O.	N.O.	114,587	105,706	152,755	195,000	127,047	122,013
Wyoming	136,358	(a-37)	142,943	N.O.	(a-8)	136,260	150,628	(a-12)	92,000	100,134
Guam	88,915	N.O.	88,915	N.O.	83,400	55,341	67,150	82,025	82,025	61,939
CNMI*	54,000	49,000	52,000	52,000	40,800 (b)	52,000	40,800 (b)	45,000	80,000	53,000
Puerto Rico	N/A	N/A	N/A	N/A	N/A	N/A	N/A	N/A	N/A	N/A
U.S. Virgin Islands	76,500	60,000	76,500	(c)	76,500	76,500	76,500	85,000	76,500	135,000

See footnotes at end of table

TABLE 4.11
Selected State Administrative Officials: Annual Salaries (continued)

State or other jurisdiction	Emergency management (a-20)	Employment services (a-21)	Energy (a-22)	Environmental protection (a-23)	Finance (a-24)	Fish & wildlife (a-25)	General services (a-26)	Health (a-27)	Higher education (a-28)	Highways (a-29)
Alabama	151,496	176,855	(a-12)	172,967	N.R.	178,819	108,779	N.R.	242,025	(a-49)
Alaska	122,988	129,132	160,000	141,156	142,140	141,156	(a-43)	141,156	325,000	133,620
Arizona	112,500	135,000	N/A	175,000	(a-14)	160,000	120,000	205,505	120,000	145,000
Arkansas	112,477	162,872	139,800	139,800	(a-6)	135,383	142,252	225,306	173,847	229,944
California	217,292	199,056	164,123	217,292	217,292	195,709	197,798	(c)	337,380	(a-49)
Colorado	163,176	137,868	159,648	162,864	143,544	157,812	120,948	186,996	172,952	165,744
Connecticut	183,340	162,495	175,000	175,000	198,000	(c)	175,000	200,000	335,000	240,000
Delaware	94,583	100,014	100,108	(a-35)	152,088	102,525	117,355	175,040	117,150	(a-49)
Florida	141,000	141,000	91,960	150,000	128,972	140,737	141,000	N/A	200,000	150,000
Georgia	112,200	113,662	121,156	170,000	158,508	120,948	137,625	197,605	500,500	124,409
Hawaii	134,676	N/A	106,572 (b)	N/A	(c)	106,572 (b)	(a-14)	154,812	395,004	106,572 (b)
Idaho	143,853	(a-32)	102,336	134,867	144,997	148,054	N.O.	(c)	159,266	(a-49)
Illinois	152,400	168,000	(a-42)	157,200	(a-10)	(a-35)	(a-6)	176,400	214,800	(a-49)
Indiana	127,500	178,745	75,000	143,985	152,337	89,216	(a-6)	194,775	214,320	(a-49)
Iowa	112,070	154,300	(a-17)	131,955	140,005	137,613	142,542	151,008	N.O.	176,426
Kansas	(c)	123,000	96,175	118,721	120,000	85,075	99,935	179,375	250,000	(a-49)
Kentucky	84,349	65,000	129,524	105,000	136,000	140,000	N.O.	202,608	275,000	120,000
Louisiana	140,000	110,000	116,875	137,197	(a-6)	123,614	(a-6)	236,000	364,000	176,900
Maine	91,270	(a-32)	(a-38)	139,734	(a-6)	139,734	115,586	170,477	N/A	(a-49)
Maryland	150,000 (b)	161,975 (b)	138,631 (b)	104,235 (b)	174,417 (b)	116,185 (b)	(a-6)	170,997 (b)	157,558 (b)	160,742
Massachusetts	143,000	161,522	135,000	139,050	161,522	129,000	158,000	140,000	220,763	153,536
Michigan	(a-47)	N/A	115,000	170,000	(a-10)	(c)	N.O.	178,500	N.O.	(a-49)
Minnesota	154,992	N.O.	144,907	150,002	154,992	137,599	(a-6)	150,002	390,000	(a-49)
Mississippi	120,000	135,315	92,782	129,347	(a-6)	147,216	N.O.	215,000	300,000	172,700
Missouri	104,501	108,004	105,060	114,433	122,027	(c)	113,300	147,223	182,053	220,358
Montana	96,177	106,860	132,545	112,935	115,495	112,944	103,571	112,935	326,524	(a-49)
Nebraska	88,549	134,172	152,249	152,249	(c)	117,260	160,001	153,772	187,180	151,840
Nevada	118,200	128,998	107,973	125,021	(a-14)	118,200	N.O.	(c)	N/A	(a-49)
New Hampshire	105,930	105,930	80,971	114,554	(a-10)	100,171	(a-6)	100,171	79,664	(a-49)
New Jersey	(a-47)	155,250	123,625	175,000	155,250	134,847	(c)	175,000	175,000	146,050
New Mexico	114,400	156,000	156,000	156,000	114,400	156,000	156,000	156,000	156,000	(a-49)
New York	210,000	190,000	(c)	210,000	210,000	210,000	210,000	210,000	210,000	210,000
North Carolina	133,250	125,460	99,817	133,824	225,815	186,229	125,523	144,499	N/A	201,419
North Dakota	100,896	189,900	162,396	145,320	180,000	130,536	(a-24)	172,404	374,000	(a-49)
Ohio	121,909	174,678	159,266	156,187	(c)	117,520	119,018	236,330	195,229	159,266
Oklahoma	135,000	115,110	140,000	143,759	195,000	145,400	111,350	196,000	412,231	(a-49)
Oregon	129,936	168,276	145,476	152,652	(a-4)	152,652	(a-6)	185,508	186,084	184,724
Pennsylvania	148,011	145,742	151,316	161,382	168,490	(c)	153,313	161,382	153,879	154,974
Rhode Island (g)	136,489	135,000	140,513	135,000	(a-44)	(a-23)	(a-6)	134,975	265,000 (c)	(a-49)
South Carolina	104,198	188,700	115,881	(c)	106,670	134,458	146,592	(c)	204,111	160,056
South Dakota	93,258	79,359	(a-42)	124,140	140,375	95,422	(a-6)	133,395	338,250	113,887
Tennessee	134,400	161,904	165,000	168,708	209,520	168,708	161,904	176,880	200,004	161,904
Texas	198,164	182,500	N.O.	211,415	(a-14)	200,643	177,982	242,353	212,135	(a-49)
Utah	103,958	155,480	N/A	144,997	146,744	126,630	140,150	212,659	N.O.	(a-49)
Vermont	87,110	128,876	126,630	126,380	135,283	108,700	129,126	157,830	N.O.	126,110
Virginia	152,954	166,125	99,419	190,188	195,418	144,414	171,812	176,730	204,965	218,509
Washington	N.O.	177,132	N.O.	177,333	(a-14)	173,352	(a-6)	177,333	N.O.	N.O
West Virginia	80,000	75,000	82,404	95,000	75,902	75,000	82,668	150,000	289,388	120,000
Wisconsin	117,312	116,418	110,947	115,294	132,600	115,294	(a-7)	152,755	525,000	(a-49)
Wyoming	102,147	144,000	120,000	132,577	102,000	150,593	115,565	180,000	165,000	158,000
Guam	68,152	73,020	55,303	60,850	88,915	60,850	60,528	74,096	195,000	88,915
CNMI*	45,000	40,800 (b)	45,000	58,000	54,000	40,800 (b)	54,000	80,000	80,000	40,800 (b)
Puerto Rico	N/A	N/A	N/A	N/A	N/A	N/A	N/A	N/A	N/A	N/A
U.S. Virgin Islands	71,250	76,500	69,350	76,500	76,500	76,500	76,500	76,500	76,500	65,000

See footnotes at end of table

TABLE 4.11
Selected State Administrative Officials: Annual Salaries (continued)

State or other jurisdiction	Information systems (a-30)	Insurance (a-31)	Labor (a-32)	Licensing (a-33)	Mental health & developmental disabilities (a-34)	Natural resources (a-35)	Parks & recreation (a-36)	Personnel (a-37)	Planning (a-38)	Post audit (a-39)
Alabama	N.R.	176,314	(a-21)	N.O.	N.R.	(a-25)	(a-25)	213,740	(a-12)	241,695
Alaska	186,804	131,112	141,156	124,452	106,452	141,156	110,304	137,664	N.O.	(a-8)
Arizona	180,000	120,000	150,000	N.O.	120,058	175,000	175,000	130,000	(a-10)	N.O.
Arkansas	158,209	139,836	155,040	155,040	(c)	118,484	137,094	130,693	N.O.	191,793
California	197,798	167,796	217,292	186,389	(c)	217,292	186,389	204,955	N.O.	N.O.
Colorado	169,956	159,660	175,104	148,620	158,616	175,000	161,952	N/A	160,584	(a-8)
Connecticut	183,154	175,000	162,495	122,505	(c)	156,516	161,219	165,000	145,000	(a-8)
Delaware	165,055	112,667	123,333	113,399	(c)	132,011	102,525	132,011	99,093	(a-8)
Florida	130,000	134,158	141,000	71,400	N/A	150,000	114,000	111,000	100,000	(a-24)
Georgia	185,000	120,394	122,786	86,700	178,500	175,000	119,882	132,000	(a-10)	(a-8)
Hawaii	200,004	122,052	154,812	101,508 (b)	138,552	154,812	106,572 (b)	154,812	N/A	106,572 (b)
Idaho	122,013	123,490	(a-21)	94,494	124,010	139,069	110,282	133,890	N.O.	(a-8)
Illinois	176400	159,600	146,400	(a-9)	(a-45)	133,273	(a-35)	(a-6)	N.O.	(a-8)
Indiana	N/A	124,147	119,372	118,235	130,000	130,778	102,754	121,366	N.O.	130,096
Iowa	154,300	128,890	112,070	102,835	110,490	128,890	(a-25)	140,005	N.O.	N.O.
Kansas	175,000	86,003	123,000	87,125	N/A	123,000	123,000	102,305	N.O.	136,480
Kentucky	129,524	104,762	129,524	N.O.	116,500	100,000	104,762	129,524	136,000	(a-8)
Louisiana	150,000	110,740	137,000	N.O.	130,000	129,210	122,720	148,616	127,441	N.R.
Maine	130,811	115,274	139,734	139,734	(a-45)	139,734	(a-35)	118,934	N/A	N/A
Maryland	167,433 (b)	157,386 (b)	161,975 (b)	105,000 (b)	(b)(c)	159,312 (b)	116,053 (b)	141,365 (b)	135.048 (b)	73,361 (b)
Massachusetts	(a-44)	130,000	119,060	115,000	(c)	161,522	130,000	158,000	161,522	(a-8)
Michigan	161,099	(a-9)	175,000	170,000	294,977	170,000	138,625	185,566	N.O.	(a-8)
Minnesota	150,002	147,580	144,991	N.O.	154,992	154,992	137,599	(a-24)	N/A	(a-8)
Mississippi	173,209	90,000	N.O.	N.O.	170,180	129,347	147,216	145,000	93,500	(a-8)
Missouri	165,000	129,142	133,158	N/A	151,201	129,142	114,433	113,300	122,027	107,746
Montana	129,522	98,104	112,935	104,063	106,691	112,935	100,822	108,429	106,897	121,495
Nebraska	195,821	130,307	134,172	81,321	141,718	151,919	149,751	160,001	144,352	85,000
Nevada	118,200	118,200	98,880	N.O.	(c)	128,998	108,540	108,540	N.O.	N.O.
New Hampshire	117,913	105,930	105,930	105,930	105,930	114,554	91,965	88,933	N.O.	(a-14)
New Jersey	175,000	N/A	175,000	N.O.	(c)	143,750	136,755	175,000	142,640	N.O.
New Mexico	156,000	156,000	156,000	156,000	N.O.	156,000	109,200	156,000	80,830	85,000
New York	167,000	210,000	190,000	(c)	(c)	210,000	190,000	160,000 (b)	160,000 (b)	210,000
North Carolina	192,587	133,365	133,365	N.O.	N/A	151,733	133,548	164,572	N/A	(a-8)
North Dakota	214,700	107,885	102,000	N.O.	127,800	N.O.	120,000	144,000	N.O.	122,400
Ohio	150,072	154,710	131,123	(k)	(c)	174,678	120,640	122,949	159,266	(a-8)
Oklahoma	160,000	126,713	105,053	N.O.	173,318	141,000	141,000	111,350	N.O.	N.O.
Oregon	211,440	129,936	77,000	N.O.	136,488	N.O.	152,652	157,884	N.O.	(a-8)
Pennsylvania	156,050	145,244	161,382	N/A	154,456	153,313	147,209	156,558	156,011	(a-8)
Rhode Island (g)	205,706	(a-9)	(a-21)	(i)	135,000	(a-23)	(a-23)	146,994	102,860	N/A
South Carolina	176,868	160,917	143,560	143,560	(c)	134,458	149,008	133,223	N.O.	118,907
South Dakota	130,000	108,803	124,140	N.O.	124,140	(a-23)	96,111	127,000	N.O.	(a-8)
Tennessee	213,648	161,904	161,904	142,044	161,904	168,708	123,264	161,904	N.O.	(a-14)
Texas	184,792	202,383	182,500	179,375	227,000	211,415	200,643	N.O.	205,000	(a-8)
Utah	138,694	137,467	136,573	135,928	120,827	158,870	125,798	147,077	(a-10)	(a-8)
Vermont	145,537	126,630	128,876	95,700	129,126	145,246	112,507	128,876	N.O.	(a-8)
Virginia	194,468	170,000	143,487	136,818	241,463	176,730	155,745	N/A	177,448	(a-8)
Washington	187,536	133,250	177,333	173,856	(a-45)	145,860	160,944	(a-14)	(a-14)	N.O.
West Virginia	127,500	92,500	70,000	N.O.	(a-27)	(a-25)	(a-25)	70,000	(a-17)	105,664
Wisconsin	129,459	132,600	142,813	132,600	136,157	149,947	115,294	126,506	N.O.	(a-8)
Wyoming	153,300	124,904	103,200	71,527	(c)	125,257	128,433	126,000	175,000	102,000
Guam	88,915	88,915	73,020	88,915	75,208	60,850	60,850	88,915	88,915	100,000
CNMI*	45,000	40,800 (b)	45,000	45,360	40,800 (b)	52,000	40,800 (b)	60,000	45,000	80,000
Puerto Rico	N/A	N/A	N/A	N/A	N/A	N/A	N/A	N/A	N/A	N/A
U.S. Virgin Islands	71,250	75,000	76,500	76,500	70,000	76,500	76,500	76,500	76,500	55,000

See footnotes at end of table

TABLE 4.11
Selected State Administrative Officials: Annual Salaries (continued)

State or other jurisdiction	Pre-audit (a-40)	Public library development (a-41)	Public utility regulation (a-42)	Purchasing (a-43)	Revenue (a-44)	Social services (a-45)	Solid waste mgmt. (a-46)	State police (a-47)	Tourism (a-48)	Transportation (a-49)	Welfare (a-50)
Alabama	(a-14)	118,195	107,258	N.R.	N.R.	175,548	(a-23)	132,215	N.R.	(a-29)	(a-45)
Alaska	N.O.	137,664	137,664	N/A	141,156	(a-27)	114,420	141,156	122,988	141,156	142,140
Arizona	(a-14)	73,000	154,320	95,176	175,000	215,250	121,992	197,000	175,000	150,000	(a-45)
Arkansas	N.O.	116,442	139,836	130,693	134,406	287,042	139,800	155,916	137,094	(a-29)	(a-45)
California	(a-14)	N.O.	219,000	(a-26)	213,020	215,124	186,389	282,529	N.O.	200,000	N.O.
Colorado	(a-14)	149,868	116,112	124,884	161,952	N/A	154,500	97,776	130,512	175,104	176,952
Connecticut	(a-14)	53,827	150,000	154,653	197,064	205,000	149,062	183,340	N/A	240,000	205,000
Delaware	(a-8)	87,572	110,733	(a-26)	132,750	(c)	190,000	195,090	80,000	142,572	119,255
Florida	(a-24)	83,000	131,036	110,000	150,000	140,000	113,000	140,100	N.O.	141,000	N/A
Georgia	N.O.	N.O.	(a-22)	148,507	175,000	178,500	120,948	170,000	(a-17)	350,000	137,940
Hawaii	106,572 (b)	155,004	134,688	126,912	154,812	154,812	N/A	N.O.	283,500	154,812	101,508 (b)
Idaho	(a-14)	93,621	110,074	96,200	102,049	185,411	99,986	146,411	(a-12)	215,696	122,512
Illinois	(a-14)	118,800	132,000	(a-6)	168,000	176,908	(a-23)	156,000	(a-12)	176,400	168,000
Indiana	86,654	119,371	137,891	101,803	149,000	208,080	106,120	154,512	130,000	187,387	(a-45)
Iowa	114,941	150,717	128,890	146,536	154,300	154,300	(a-23)	128,890	69,763	154,300	143,333
Kansas	86,647	91,481	99,507	94,766	123,000	164,000	87,125	124,589	88,000	117,875	N.O.
Kentucky	N.O.	82,500	104,762	86,205	109,524	N/A	90,000	119,048	104,762	129,524	(a-45)
Louisiana	N/A	118,040	137,000	125,008	250,000	129,995	102,000	177,436	121,992	176,900	110,411
Maine	(a-14)	104,104	135,179	N/A	130,811	170,477	85,301	136,781	(a-17)	139,734	(a-45)
Maryland	114,752 (b)	123,236 (b)	165,565	(b)	132,569 (b)	167,488 (b)	140,489 (b)	167,661 (b)	113,763 (b)	174,419 (b)	(a-45)
Massachusetts	(a-8)	121,142	129,000	158,000	N/A	140,000	139,050	251,922	121,800	161,522	150,000
Michigan	N.O.	N.O.	142,800	153,428	138,779	178,500	136,000	170,000	N.O.	170,000	178,500
Minnesota	(a-8)	N/A	(c)	132,859	154,992	154,992	150,002	137,599	137,599	154,992	(a-34)
Mississippi	(a-8)	96,820	120,745	77,334	142,296	130,000	90,059	138,116	122,343	172,700	130,000
Missouri	113,300	88,392	113,142	113,300	133,412	147,723	81,230	144,240	N/A	220,358	111,607
Montana	(a-39)	108,557	111,179	92,931	112,935	(a-27)	94,534	111,753	96,731	112,935	(a-27)
Nebraska	140,000	109,051	137,025	120,001	163,781	220,001	100,630	152,249	104,449	151,840	220,001
Nevada	N.O.	(c)	125,021	98,880	128,998	128,998	(a-23)	128,998	118,200	128,998	(c)
New Hampshire	(a-14)	91,965	111,687	75,410	117,913	121,896	100,171	105,930	91,965	117,913	100,171
New Jersey	N.O.	N.O.	175,000	149,500	147,200	(c)	141,000	175,000	113,883	175,000	143,750
New Mexico	95,714	72,488	90,000	101,001	156,000	156,000	83,963	156,000	156,000	156,000	156,000
New York	210,000	210,000	190,000	210,000	190,000	210,000	210,000	210,000	160,000 (b)	210,000	210,000
North Carolina	(a-8)	116,786	149,451	118,142	151,732	155,800	118,815	151,292	81,549	227,899	N.O.
North Dakota	N.O.	N.O.	110,829	105,672	117,087	207,600	85,680	127,404	129,264	172,400	207,600
Ohio	(a-10)	113,589	159,994	119,018	159,266	(c)	100,922	159,266	110,885	159,266	174,678
Oklahoma	(a-14)	96,000	(c)	97,500	150,000	185,600	113,407	143,000	141,000	185,000	185,600
Oregon	(a-10)	138,504	160,285	123,828	168,276	185,508	N.O.	168,276	N.O.	185,103	(a-45)
Pennsylvania	(a-4)	153,879	155,813	147,209	153,313	161,382	151,316	153,313	147,209	161,382	161,382
Rhode Island (g)	(a-14)	113,146	117,412	125,874	130,100	(c)	(h)	148,937	(a-17)	135,000	(a-45)
South Carolina	(a-14)	110,371	178,619	127,268	196,311	181,689	181,689	160,056	149,008	251,232	(a-45)
South Dakota	(a-8)	87,666	108,514	65,243	124,140	140,075	N.O.	105,718	116,879	129,105	93,258
Tennessee	168,144	145,548	164,688	167,280	163,800	161,904	141,888	161,904	161,904	161,904	161,904
Texas	(a-14)	143,500	159,782	168,000	(a-14)	220,000	N.O.	232,969	164,701	299,812	275,000
Utah	(a-24)	123,469	111,904	(a-26)	88,296	142,646	126,006	130,811	130,187	171,683	(a-45)
Vermont	(a-24)	105,560	160,763	129,126	128,876	145,537	126,380	144,955	105,580	145,537	129,126
Virginia	(a-14)	157,809	(c)	141,750	169,179	214,748	195,418	189,784	183,890	218,509	214,748
Washington	(a-4)	(a-2)	149,028	N.O.	177,333	207,864	N.O.	207,864	N.O.	207,864	(a-45)
West Virginia	(a-8)	72,000	90,000	90,160	95,000	(a-27)	82,364	85,000	87,160	92,160	(a-27)
Wisconsin	(a-8)	128,544	135,013	114,046	147,907	137,717	115,294	118,123	132,600	147,930	121,410
Wyoming	(a-8)	107,600	121,692	83,936	128,994	(a-27)	117,620	126,152	141,000	(a-29)	(a-45)
Guam	88,915	55,303	1,200	88,915	88,915	74,096	88,915	74,096	88,591	N.O.	74,096
CNMI*	54,000	45,000	80,000	40,800 (b)	45,000	40,800 (b)	54,000	54,000	70,000	40,800 (b)	52,000
Puerto Rico	N/A	N/A	N/A	N/A	N/A	N/A	N/A	108,000	N/A	N/A	N/A
U.S. Virgin Islands	76,500	53,350	54,500	76,500	76,500	76,500	76,500	76,500	76,500	65,000	76,500

See footnotes at end of table

TABLE 4.11
Selected State Administrative Officials: Annual Salaries (continued)

Source: The Council of State Governments' survey of state personnel agencies and state Web sites, June 2020.

*Commonwealth of Northern Mariana Islands

Key:

N/A–Not available.

N.O.–No specific chief administrative official or agency in charge of
function.

(a) Chief administrative official or agency in charge of function:
(a-1) Lieutenant governor.
(a-2) Secretary of state.
(a-3) Attorney general.
(a-4) Treasurer.
(a-5) Adjutant general
(a-6) Administration.
(a-7) Agriculture
(a-8) Auditor
(a-9) Banking
(a-10) Budget.
(a-11) Civil rights
(a-12) Commerce.
(a-13) Community affairs.
(a-14) Comptroller.
(a-15) Consumer affairs.
(a-16) Corrections
(a-17) Economic development.
(a-18) Education (chief state school officer).
(a-19) Election administration
(a-20) Emergency administration
(a-21) Employment Services
(a-22) Energy.
(a-23) Environmental protection.
(a-24) Finance.
(a-25) Fish and wildlife
(a-26) General services.
(a-27) Health
(a-28) Higher education
(a-29) Highways.
(a-30) Information systems
(a-31) Insurance
(a-32) Labor.
(a-33) Licensing
(a-34) Mental Health
(a-35) Natural resources.
(a-36) Parks and recreation.
(a-37) Personnel.
(a-38) Planning
(a-39) Post audit.
(a-40) Pre-audit.
(a-41) Public library development
(a-42) Public utility regulation.
(a-43) Purchasing.
(a-44) Revenue.
(a-45) Social services.
(a-46) Solid waste management
(a-47) State police

(a-48) Tourism.
(a-49) Transportation.
(a-50) Welfare.
(b) Salary ranges, Lower figure appears in the table and top figure
in the range is listed below:
Hawaii: Energy, $177,408; Fish and Wildlife, $177,408; Highway,
$177,408; Licensing, $168,936; Parks and Recreation, $177,408;
Post-Audit, $177,408; Pre-Audit, $177,408; Welfare, $168,936.
Maryland: For these positions the salary in the chart is the actual
salary and the following are the salary ranges: Adjutant General,
$114,874-$153,532; Administration, $114,874-$153,532; Agriculture, $114,874-$153,532; Banking, $73,612-$118,197;
Budget, $133,069-$177,977; Civil Rights, $92,333-$123,236;
Commerce, $133,069-$177,977; Consumer Affairs, $83,836-
$134,749; Corrections, $133,069-$177,977; Economic
Development, $$133,069-$177,977; Elections Administration,
$99,275-$132,569; Emergency Management, $114,784-
$153,532; Workforce Development, $123,618-$165,281; Energy,
$99,275-$132,569; Environmental Protection, $123,618-
$165,281; Finance, $133,069-177,977; Fish and
Wildlife–$92,333-$123,236; Health, $133,069-$177,977;
Higher Education, $ 123,618-$165,281; Information Services,
$133,069-$177,977; Insurance, $133,069-$177,977; Labor,
$123,618-$165,281; Licensing, $92,333-$123,236; Mental
Health shared duties, $154,064-$254,576 (vacant at press time)
and $114,874-$153,532 (actual, $140,526); Natural Resources,
$123,618-$165,281; Parks and Recreation, $78,596-$126,186;
Personnel, $106,773-$142,646; Planning, $114,874-$153,532;
Post-Audit, $53,193-$85,401; Pre-Audit, $99,275-$132,569;
Public Library, $92,333-$123,236; Public Utility Regula-
tion–$153,027-$256,866, Purchasing $85,902-114,600 (vacant
at press time); Revenue, $99,275-$132,569; Social Services,
$133,069-$177,977; Solid Waste Management, $106,773-
$142,646; State Police, $133,069-$177,977; Tourism,
$106,773-$142,646; Transportation, $133,069-$177,977; Wel-
fare, $92,333-$123,236.
New York: Commerce, $180,000; Personnel, $180,000; Planning,
$180,000; Tourism, $180,000.
Northern Mariana Islands: $49,266 top of range applies to the fol-
lowing positions: Treasurer, Banking, Comptroller, Corrections, ,
Employment Services, Fish and Wildlife, Highways, Insurance,
Mental Health and Retardation, Parks and Recreation, Purchasing,
Social/Human Services, Transportation.
(c) Responsibilities shared between:
Arkansas–Mental Health and Developmental Disabilities, Responsi-
bilities shared between DHS DDS Commissioner Melissa Stone
$118,562 and State Hospital Chief Operating Officer James M.
Scoggins $134,406.
California–Health–Responsibilities shared between Director of
Health Care Services (Vacant), $215,124 and Director Sonia Angell
Department of Public Health $276,650.
California–Mental health & developmental disabilities–Responsi-
bilities shared between Director of State Hospitals, $215,119 and
Director Nancy A. Bargemann of Developmental Services,
$215,124.

TABLE 4.11
Selected State Administrative Officials: Annual Salaries (continued)

Connecticut–Auditor–Responsibilities shared between John C. Geragosian, $190,386 and Robert J. Kane, $160,188.

Connecticut–Fish And Wildlife–Responsibilities shared between Chief Richard Jacobson of Wildlife, $156,516 and Director Peter Aarrestad of Inland and Marine Fisheries, $133,476 .

Connecticut–Mental Health & Developmental Disabilities–Responsibilities shared between Commissioner Miriam Delphin-Rittmon Mental Health: $165,600 and Commissioner Jordan Scheff, Dept. of Developmental Services: $173,880.

Delaware–Administration The Dept. of Administration was abolished in 2005. Responsibilities are now shared between the Office of Management and Budget, General Services and Dept. of State.

Delaware–The Delaware Economic Development Office was abolished in FY 2019; most responsibilities assigned to a new public-private partnership.

Delaware–Mental Health–Responsibilities shared between Director, Division of Substance Abuse and Mental Health, Department of Health and Social Services, $148,376 and Director, Division of Developmental Disabilities Service, same department, $119,150.

Delaware–Social Services–Function split between two cabinet positions: Secretary, Dept. of Health and Social Services : $152,088 and Secretary, Dept. of Svcs. for Children, Youth and their Families, $137,240.

Hawaii–Administration–There is no single agency for Administration. The functions are divided amongst the Director of Budget and Finance, Director of Human Resources Development and the Comptroller.

Hawaii–Finance–Responsibilities shared between Director Craig K. Hirai of Budget and Finance, $162,552 and Comptroller Curt T. Otaguro, $154,812.

Idaho–Health–Responsibilities shared between 7 Directors–PHD1-$114,192, PHD2-$115,482, PHD3-$107,120, PD4-$146,869, PHD5-$102,294, PHD6-$115,190, PHD7-$107,370.

Indiana–Elections Administration–Responsibilities shared between Co-Directors Brad King, $105,050 and Angela Nussmeyer, $99,830.

Kansas–Emergency Management–Responsibilities shared between Adjutant General, $114,505 and deputy director, $93,684.

Maryland–Mental Health–Responsibilities shared between Executive Director of Mental Hygiene Administration, salary range $154,064-254,576 (position vacant at press time) and Secretary, Dept. of Disabilities ,$140,525, salary range $114,874-$153,532.

Massachusetts–Mental Health–Responsibilities shared between Commissioners Joan Mikula, $157,982 and Elin M. Howe, $153,511.

Michigan–Elections Administration–Responsibilities shared between Secretary of State, $112,410 and Director of Elections, $138,779.

Michigan–Fish and Wildlife–Responsibilities shared between Chief of Fisheries, Jim Dexter, $138,779 and Chief of Wildlife, Vacant.

Minnesota–Public Utility Regulation–Responsibilities shared between four commissioner's with salaries of $140,000 for each.

Missouri–Fish and Wildlife–Responsibilities shared between Administrator, Division of Fisheries, Department of Conservation,

position vacant; Administrator, Division of Wildlife, same department, $88,632.

Nebraska–Finance–Responsibilities shared between, Auditor of Public Accounts, Charlie Janssen–$85,000; Director of Administration, Gerry Oligmueller–$164,303 and State Tax Commissioner, Tony Fulton–$163,781.

Nevada–Elections Administration–Responsibilities shared between Secretary of State, $102,898; Deputy Secretary of State for Elections, $108,540 and Chief Deputy, Secretary of State, $118,200.

Nevada–Health–Responsibilities shared between Richard Whitley, Director, Health and Human Services, $128,998 and Cody Phinney, Division Administrator, DPBH, $125,021.

Nevada–Mental Health–Responsibilities shared between Director, Health and Human Services, $128,998 and Division Administrator, $125,021.

Nevada–Public Library Development–Responsibilities shared between Director, Department of Tourism and Cultural Affairs, $118,200 and Division Administrator, Library and Archives, $98,880.

Nevada–Welfare–Responsibilities shared between Richard Whitley, Director, Health and Human Services, $128,998 and Steve Fisher, Division Administrator, Welfare and Support Services, $118,200.

New Jersey–General Services–Responsibilities shared between Maurice Griffin, Director, Division of Purchase and Property, Dept. of the Treasury, $149,500 and Christopher Chianese, Director, Division of Property Management and Construction, Dept. of the Treasury, $149,500.

New Jersey–Mental Health–Responsibilities shared between Assistant Commissioner Valerie Mielke, Division of Mental Health Services, Dept. of Human Services, $147,200 and position of Assistant Commissioner Jonathan Seifried, Division of Developmental Disabilities, Dept. of Human Services, $143,750.

New Jersey–Social Services–Responsibilities shared between Carole Johnson, Commissioner, Department of Human Services, $175,000 and Christine Beyer, Commissioner, Department of Children and Families, $175,000.

New York–Elections Administration–Responsibilities shared between 2 co-chairs, $25,000 each and 2 commissioners, $25,000 each.

New York–Responsibilities shared between Chair–Richard Kauffman, $140,000 and President and CEO Alicia Barton, $160,000.

New York–Licensing–Responsibilities shared between Commissioner, State Education Department, $210,000; Secretary of State, Department of State, $160,000.

New York–Mental Health–Responsibilities shared between Commissioner of Office for People with Developmental Disabilities, $210,000 and Commissioner of Office of Mental Health, $210,000 .

Ohio–Finance–Responsibilities shared between, Assistant Director of Budget and Management,$157,227 and Deputy Director, Office of Budget and Management, $122,845.

Ohio–Mental Health–Responsibilities shared between Director of Dept. of Developmental Disabilities, $154,128 and Director, Dept. of Mental Health and Addiction Services, $165,006.

Ohio–Social Services–Responsibilities shared between Director,

TABLE 4.11
Selected State Administrative Officials: Annual Salaries (continued)

Dept. of Job and Family Services, $174,678; Superintendent of Public Instruction Dept. of Education, $209,997; Executive Director Opportunities for Ohioans with Disabilities, $133,578 and Director of Dept. of Aging, $133,578.

Oklahoma–Public Utility Regulation–Responsibilities shared between three Commissioners, Commissioner Bob Anthony, $114,713, Commissioner Dana Murphy, $114,713 and Commissioner Jimmie Hiett, $116,713 and Timothy Rhodes, Director of Administration Div., $142,000.

Pennsylvania–Fish and Wildlife–Responsibilities shared between Executive Director (Fish), $152,196 and Executive Director (Game), $142,436.

Rhode Island–Higher Education–Serves a dual role as Commissioner of Higher Education and as the President of the Community College of Rhode Island.

Rhode Island–Social Services–Responsibilities shared between Commissioner, Office of Health and Human Services,$141,828 and Director of the Dept. Human Service, $135,000, and reports to the Commissioner, Office of Health and Human Services.

South Carolina–Environmental protection–Responsibilities shared between Director Rick Toomey, $181,689 (BS) and Director Robert Boyles, Jr., $135,458 (B).

South Carolina–Health–Responsibilities shared between Director of Health and Human Services Joshua Baker, $181,689 and Director of Health and Environmental Control Rick Toomey, $181,689, See also Environmental Protection. .

South Carolina–Mental Health–Responsibilities shared between Interim Director for Disabilities and Special Needs, Mary Poole, $171,404 and Director of Mental Health,Mark W. Binkley $181,689.

Texas–Elections Administration–Responsibilities shared between Secretary of State, $197,415; and Division Director, $132,600.

U.S. Virgin Islands–Community Affairs–Responsibilities for St. Thomas, $74,400; St. Croix, $76,500; St. John, $74,400.

Virginia–Public Utility Regulation–Functions shared between Wil-liam F. "Bill" Stephens; Energy Regulation, $175,100; Utility and Railroad Safety, Massoud Tahamtani, $172,134.

Wyoming–Mental Health–Responsibilities shared between State Hospital, Heather Babbitt, $118,527 and Life Resource Center, William Rein, $150,000.

(d) These individuals have voluntarily taken no salary or a reduced salary:

Connecticut–Governor Ned Lamont will forego his salary of $150,000.

Illinois–Governor Pritzker will not take his salary of $181,670.

Nevada–Governor Sisolak pledged to donate his salary to K–12 schools all four years of his term.

North Dakota–Governor Doug Burgum has declined his salary of $135,360.

(e) In Maine, New Hampshire, Tennessee and West Virginia, the presidents (or speakers) of the Senate are next in line of succession to the governorship. In Tennessee and West Virginia, the speaker of the Senate bears the statutory title of lieutenant governor.

(g) A number of the employees receive a stipend for their length of service to the State (known as a longevity payment). This amount can vary significantly among employees and, depending on state turnover, can show dramatic changes in actual salaries from year-to-year.

(h) Solid waste is managed by the Rhode Island Resource Recovery Corporation (RRIRRC). Although not a department of the state government, RIRRC is a public corporation and a component of the State of Rhode Island for financial reporting purposes. To be financially self-sufficient, the agency earns revenue through the sale of recyclable products, methane gas royalties and fees for it services.

(i) Varies by department.

(j) The Rhode Island Economic Development Corporation is a quasi-public agency. The salary shown is for the previous director.

(k) Numerous licensing boards, too many to list.

TABLE 4.12
The Lieutenant Governors, 2020

State or other jurisdiction	Name and party	Method of selection	Length of regular term in years	Date of first service	Present term ends	Number of previous terms	Joint election of governor and lieutenant governor (a)
Alabama	Will Ainsworth (R)	CE	4	1/2019	1/2023	…	No
Alaska	Kevin Meyer (R)	CE	4	12/2018	12/2022	…	Yes
Arizona	....(b)..						
Arkansas	Tim Griffin (R)	CE	4	1/2015	1/2023	…	No
California	Eleni Kounalakis (D)	CE	4	1/2019	1/2023	…	No
Colorado	Dianne Primavera (D)	CE	4	1/2019	1/2023	…	Yes
Connecticut	Susan Bysiewicz (D)	CE	4	1/2019	1/2023	…	Yes
Delaware	Bethany Hall-Long (D)	CE	4	1/2017	1/2021	…	No
Florida	Jeanette Núñez (R)	CE	4	1/2019	1/2023	…	Yes
Georgia	Geoff Duncan (R)	CE	4	1/2019	1/2023	…	No
Hawaii	Joshua B. Green (D)	CE	4	1/2019	1/2023	…	Yes
Idaho	Janice McGeachin (R)	CE	4	1/2019	1/2023	…	No
Illinois	Juliana Stratton (D)	CE	4	1/2019	1/2023	…	Yes
Indiana	Suzanne Crouch (R)	CE	4	1/2017	1/2021	…	Yes
Iowa	Adam Gregg (R)	CE	4	5/2017 (c)	1/2023	…	Yes
Kansas	Lynn Rogers (D)	CE	4	1/2019	1/2023	…	Yes
Kentucky	Jacqueline Coleman (D)	CE	4	12/2019	12/2022	…	Yes
Louisiana	Billy Nungesser (R)	CE	4	1/2016	1/2024	1	No
Maine	....(b)..						
Maryland	Boyd Rutherford (R)	CE	4	1/2015	1/2023	1	Yes
Massachusetts	Karyn Polito (R)	CE	4	1/2015	1/2023	1	Yes
Michigan	Garlin Gilchrist II (D)	CE	4	1/2019	1/2023	…	Yes
Minnesota	Peggy Flanagan (DFL)	CE	4	1/2019	1/2023	…	Yes
Mississippi	Delbert Hosemann (R)	CE	4	1/2020	1/2024	…	No
Missouri	Mike Kehoe (R)	CE	4	(d)	(d) 1/2021	…	No
Montana	Mike Cooney (D)	CE	4	1/2016 (i)	1/2021	…	Yes
Nebraska	Mike Foley (R)	CE	4	1/2015	1/2023	1	Yes
Nevada	Kate Marshall (D)	CE	4	1/2019	1/2023	…	No
New Hampshire	....(b)..						
New Jersey	Sheila Oliver (D)	CE	4	1/2018	1/2022	1	Yes
New Mexico	Henry "Howie" C. Morales (D)	CE	4	1/2019	1/2023	…	Yes
New York	Kathy Hochul (D)	CE	4	1/2015	1/2023	1	Yes
North Carolina	Dan Forest (R)	CE	4	1/2013	1/2021	1	No
North Dakota	Brent Sanford (R)	CE	4	12/2017	12/2020	…	Yes
Ohio	John Husted (R)	SE	4	1/2019	1/2023	…	Yes
Oklahoma	Matt Pinnell (R)	CE	4	1/2019	1/2023	…	No
Oregon	....(b)..						
Pennsylvania	John Fetterman (D)	CE	4	1/2019	1/2023	…	Yes
Rhode Island	Dan McKee (D)	SE	4	1/2015	1/2023	1	No
South Carolina	Pamela Evette (R)	CE	4	1/2019	1/2023	…	No
South Dakota	Larry Rhoden (R)	CE	4	1/2019	1/2023	…	Yes
Tennessee	Randy McNally (R)	(f)	2	1/2019	1/2021	1	No
Texas	Dan Patrick (R)	CE	4	1/2015	1/2023	…	No
Utah	Spencer J. Cox (R)	CE	4	10/2013 (e)	1/2021	1	Yes
Vermont	David Zuckerman (D)	CE	2	1/2017	1/2021	1	No
Virginia	Justin Fairfax (D)	CE	4	1/2018	1/2022	…	No
Washington	Cyrus Habib (D)	CE	4	1/2017	1/2021	…	No
West Virginia	Mitch Carmichael (R)	(g)	2	1/2017	1/2021	1	No
Wisconsin	Mandela Barnes (D)	CE	4	1/2019	1/2023	…	Yes (h)
Wyoming	....(b)..						
American Samoa	Lemanu Peleti Mauga (D)	CE	4	1/2013	1/2021	…	Yes
Guam	Josh Tenorio (D)	CE	4	1/2019	1/2013	…	Yes
CNMI*	Arnold Palacios (R)	CE	4	1/2019	1/2023	…	Yes
Puerto Rico	....(b)..						
U.S. Virgin Islands	Tregenza Roach (I)	SE	SE	1/2019	1/2023	…	Yes

See footnotes at end of table

TABLE 4.12
The Lieutenant Governors, 2020 (continued)

Source: The Council of State Governments, April 2020.
*Commonwealth of Northern Mariana Islands
Key:
 …–No
 C–Covenant
 CE–Constitutional, elected by public
 D–Democrat
 DFL–Democratic-Farmer-Labor Party
 I–Independent
 LG–Lieutenant Governor
 PDP–Popular Democratic Party
 R–Republican
 SE–Statutorily elected
(a) The following also choose candidates for governor and
 lieutenant governor through a joint nomination process: Florida,
 Kansas, Maryland, Minnesota, Montana, North Dakota, Ohio, Utah,
 American Samoa, Guam, No. Mariana Islands, and U.S. Virgin
 Islands. For additional information see The National Lieutenant
 Governors Association website at *http://www.nlga.us.*
(b) No lieutenant governor.
(c) Gov. Kim Reynolds appointed Adam Gregg, the state's public
 defender, as lieutenant governor when she ascended to the office
 upon Terry Branstad's resignation. She and Gregg ran for and were
 elected to a full term in the 2018 general election.
(d) Mike Parson became Governor upon the resignation of Eric
 Greitens. There is no provision for filling this office. The President
 Pro Tem of the Missouri Senate is next in line to become governor,
 followed by Speaker of the House, and Secretary of State. On
 June 18, 2018, Governor Mike Parson appointed Mike Kehoe
 (R), as Lieutenant Governor. The appointment comes with legal

uncertainty, as the Constitution of Missouri states that
the governor can fill all vacancies "other than in the offices of
lieutenant governor, state senator or representative … ." However,
Parson stated that he believed that the Constitution gave him
authority to name Kehoe as lieutenant governor. The election for
lieutenant governor will be held in 2020.
(e) Spencer J. Cox was appointed to the office of lieutenant
 governor in Oct. 2013 after Lt. Gov. Greg Bell resigned to return to
 the private sector.
(f) In Tennessee, the president of the senate and the lieutenant
 governor are one in the same. The legislature provided in statute
 the title of lieutenant governor upon the senate president. The
 senate president serves two-year terms, elected by the Senate on
 the first day of the first session of each two year legislative term.
(g) In West Virginia, the president of the senate and the lieutenant
 governor are one in the same. The legislature provided in statute
 the title of lieutenant governor upon the senate president. The
 senate president serves two-year terms, elected by the Senate on
 the first day of the first session of each two year legislative term.
(h) The governor and lt. governor are elected on a joint ticket at the
 November general election. However, they run on separate party
 primary ballots in the August primary election.
(i) Governor Bullock appointed former Secretary of State Mike
 Cooney as his new lieutenant governor in December 2015, and
 he took the oath of office in January 2016 after Angela McLean
 resigned at the end of 2015. In a joint election in 2016 Gov.
 Bullock and Cooney won re-election on November 8, 2016.

TABLE 4.13
Lieutenant Governors: Qualifications and Terms

State or other jurisdiction	Minimum age	State citizen (years)	U.S. citizen (years)(a)	State resident (years)(b)	Qualified voter (years)	Length of term (years)	Maximum terms allowed
Alabama	30	7	10	7	...	4	2 C
Alaska	30	7	7	7	★	4	2 A
Arizona							
Arkansas	30	7	★	7	...	4	2 T
California	18	★	★	5	★	4	2 T
Colorado	30	...	★	2	...	4	2 C
Connecticut	30	★	★	★	★	4	...
Delaware	30	★	12	6	★	4	2 T
Florida	30	★	★	7	★	4	2 A
Georgia	30	10	★	15	★	4	...
Hawaii	30	5	★	5	★	4	2 C
Idaho	30	...	★	2	...	4	...
Illinois	25	...	★	3	...	4	...
Indiana	30	★	★	★	★	4	...
Iowa	30	...	2	2	...	4	...
Kansas	...	...	...	...	...	4	2 C
Kentucky	30	6	★	★	★	4	2 C
Louisiana	25	5	5	5	...	4	...
Maine							
Maryland	30	★	★	★	★	4	...
Massachusetts	...	★	★	★	★	4	...
Michigan	30	★	★	4	4	4	2 T(d)
Minnesota	25	...	★	1	...	4	...
Mississippi	30	...	20	5	★	4	2 A
Missouri	30	10	15	10	...	4	...
Montana	25	2	★	2	...	4	2 (e)
Nebraska	30	5	★	5	...	4	2 A
Nevada	25	2	★	2	★	4	2 T
New Hampshire							
New Jersey	30	...	20	7	...	4	...
New Mexico	30	★	★	5	★	4	2 C
New York	30	★	★	5	★	4	...
North Carolina	30	...	5	2	...	4	2 C
North Dakota	30	5	...	...	...	4	...
Ohio	18	...	★	★	★	4	2 C
Oklahoma	31	10	★	★	★	4	2 T
Oregon							
Pennsylvania	30	★	★	7	★	4	2 C
Rhode Island	18	★	★	★	★	4	2 C
South Carolina	30	5	5	5	★	4	2 C
South Dakota	21	2	★	2	★	4	2 C
Tennessee (f)	30	★	★	3	1	2	...
Texas	30	...	★	5	...	4	...
Utah	30	★	★	★	★	4	...
Vermont	18	4	★	4	★	2	...
Virginia	30	...	★	5	5	4	...
Washington	18	★	★	★	★	4	...
West Virginia (g)	25	5	...	5	★	2	...
Wisconsin	18	★	★	★	★	4	...
Wyoming							
American Samoa	35	(h)	★	5	★	4	2 C
Guam	30	...	5	5	★	4	2 C
CNMI*	35	★	★	★	★	4	2 T
Puerto Rico							
U.S. Virgin Islands	30	...	5	5	5	4	2 C

See footnotes at end of table

TABLE 4.13
Lieutenant Governors: Qualifications and Terms (continued)

Source: The Council of State Government's survey of state government websites, April 2020.

*Commonwealth of Northern Mariana Islands

Note: This table includes constitutional and statutory qualifications.

Key:

★ –Formal provision; number of years not specified

…–No formal provision

C–Consecutive terms

T–Total terms

2A–After 2 consecutive terms must wait one term before being eligible again.

(a) In some states you must be a U.S. citizen to be an elector, and must be an elector to run.

(b) In some states you must be a state resident to be an elector, and must be an elector to run.

(c) No lieutenant governor.

(d) In 1993 a constitutional limit of two lifetime terms in the office was enacted.

(e) Eligible for eight out of 16 years.

(f) In Tennessee, the speaker of the senate, elected from Senate membership, has statutory title of "lieutenant governor."

(g) In West Virginia, the president of the senate and the lieutenant governor are one in the same. The legislature provided in statute the title of lieutenant governor upon the senate president. The senate president serves two-year terms, elected by the Senate on the first day of the first session of each two year legislative term.

(h) Must be a U.S. national.

TABLE 4.14
Lieutenant Governors: Powers and Duties

State or other jurisdiction	Presides over Senate	Appoints committees	Breaks roll-call ties	Assigns bills	Authority for governor to assign duties	Member of governor's cabinet or advisory body	Serves as acting governor when governor out of state	Other duties (a)
Alabama	★	...	★	★	...	...	★(b)	(c)
Alaska	...	...	...	...	★	★	...	(c)
Arizona	-------------------------------(d)-------------------------------							
Arkansas	★	...	★	...	...	...	...	(c)
California	★(r)	...	★	...	★	...	★	(c)
Colorado	...	...	...	...	★	★	★	(c)
Connecticut	★	...	★	...	★	...	★	(c)
Delaware	★	...	★	...	...	...	...	(c)
Florida	...	...	...	...	★	...	...	...
Georgia	★	★	...	★	★	★	...	(c)
Hawaii	...	...	...	...	★	...	★	(c)
Idaho	★	...	★	...	★	...	★	...
Illinois	...	...	...	...	★	★	...	(c)
Indiana	★	...	★	...	...	...	...	(c)
Iowa	...	(e)	...	...	★	(f)	(g)	...
Kansas	...	...	...	...	...	★	...	...
Kentucky	...	...	...	...	★	...	(h)	(c)
Louisiana	...	...	...	...	★	★	★	(c)
Maine	-------------------------------(i)-------------------------------							
Maryland	...	...	...	...	★	★	...	...
Massachusetts	...	★	...	...	★	★	★	(c)
Michigan	★	...	★	...	★	★	★(j)	(c)
Minnesota	...	...	...	...	★	...	★	(c)
Mississippi	★	★	★	★	...	...	★	(c)
Missouri	★	...	★	...	★	...	★	(c)
Montana	...	...	...	...	★	★	(q)	...
Nebraska	★(k)	...	★	...	...	★	★	...
Nevada	★	...	★(l)	...	...	★	★	...
New Hampshire	-------------------------------(i)-------------------------------							
New Jersey	...	...	...	...	★	★	★	(c)
New Mexico	★	...	★	...	...	★	★	...
New York	★	...	★(m)	...	★	★	★	...
North Carolina	★	...	★	...	★	...	★	(c)
North Dakota	★	...	...	...	...	★	...	...
Ohio	...	...	...	...	★	★	...	...
Oklahoma	★(n)	...	★	...	...	...	★	(c)
Oregon	-------------------------------(d)-------------------------------							
Pennsylvania	★	...	★	...	...	...	...	(c)
Rhode Island	...	★	...	★	★	...	★	(c)
South Carolina	★	★	★	★	...	★	★	(c)
South Dakota	★	...	★	...	★	★	★	(c)
Tennessee	★	★	★	★	...	...	...	...
Texas	★	★	★	★	...	...	★	...
Utah	...	...	...	...	...	★	...	(c)
Vermont	★	★(o)	★	★(o)	...	★	★	...
Virginia	★	...	★	...	...	★	...	...
Washington	★	★	★	...	...	...	★	...
West Virginia	★	★	...	★	...	...	...	(c)
Wisconsin	...	...	...	...	★	...	★	...
Wyoming	-------------------------------(d)-------------------------------							
American Samoa	...	...	...	...	...	...	★	...
Guam	(k)	...	...	...	★	★	★	...
CNMI*	...	...	...	...	...	★	★	(c)
Puerto Rico	-------------------------------(d)-------------------------------							
U.S. Virgin Islands	...	...	...	...	★(f)	★	★	...

See footnotes at end of table

TABLE 4.14
Lieutenant Governors: Powers and Duties (continued)

Sources: The Council of State Governments' survey of state government websites, April 2020.
* Commonwealth of Northern Mariana Islands
Key:
★ – Provision for responsibility.
… – No provision for responsibility.
(a) Lieutenant governors may obtain duties through gubernatorial appointment, statute, the Constitution, direct democracy action, or personal initiative. Hence, an exhaustive list of duties is not maintained, but this chart provides examples which are not all inclusive.
(b) The lieutenant governor performs the duties of the governor in the event of the governor's death, impeachment, disability, or absence from the state for more than 20 days.
(c)
Alabama – Chairs the Alabama Job Creation & Military Stability Commission; member of the Alabama Historical Commission; a member of the Mental Health Board of Trustees and appoints more than 400 positions to approximately 167 boards and commissions
Alaska – The lieutenant governor is assigned the following: 1. Co-Chair of the Denali Commission per the Governor's designation; 2. Serves as Alaska Fisheries Advisor to the Governor; 3. Co-Chair of the Transboundary Waters Working Group per the Governor's Memo of Understanding with Canada; and 4. Co-Chair of the Criminal Justice Working Group
Arkansas – Lieutenant Governor Tim Griffin gets to appoint a member to two commissions: the Judicial Discipline and Disability Commission and the Ethics Commission.
California – Lieutenant governor is an ex-officio regent, University of California Board of Regents; ex-officio regent, California State University Board of Trustees; chair, California Commission for Economic Development; member and current chair, California State Lands Commission (chair rotates annually between Lt. Governor and State Controller); member, California Ocean Protection Council (membership rotates with chair of State Lands Commission); and ex-officio commissioner of the California Coastal Commission (membership rotates with chair of State Lands Commission);
Colorado – Additional responsibilities include: chair of the Colorado Commission of Indian Affairs (by statute); may be appointed by the governor to concurrently serve as the head of a department (by statute). Also serves as co-chair of the Colorado Space Coalition
Connecticut – The lieutenant governor is a member of the Finance Advisory Committee, the Commission on Intergovernmental Cooperation and the Corporation of Yale University.
Delaware – Serves as president of the Board of Pardons.
Georgia – The lieutenant governor, by statute, is responsible for board, commission and committee appointments. In addition the lieutenant governor appoints conference committees, rules on germaneness, and must sign all acts of the General Assembly. Also statutorily serves on the Georgia State Financing and Investment Commission, One Georgia Board and the Georgia Aviation Authority.

Hawaii – Also serves as Secretary of State.
Illinois – The lt. governor leads the Justice, Equity and Opportunity Initiative, and chairs the Illinois Council on Women and Girls, the Governor's Rural Affairs Council, the Military Economic Development Council and the Illinois River Coordinating Council.
Indiana – Serves as Secretary of Agriculture and Rural Development. Oversees six state agencies: Department of Agriculture, Office of Community and Rural Affairs, Office of Defense Development, Office of Tourism Development, Indianan Small Business Development Center and the Indiana Housing and Community Development Authority.
Kentucky – In addition to the duties set forth by the Kentucky Constitution, state law also gives the lieutenant governor the responsibility to act as chair, or serve as a member, on various boards and commissions. Some of these include: the State Property and Buildings Commission, Kentucky Turnpike Authority, Board of the Kentucky Housing Corporation, the Kentucky Council on Agriculture. The governor also has the power to give the lieutenant governor other specific job duties.
Louisiana – Serves as commissioner of the Department of Culture, Recreation & Tourism and appoints the members of the Board of Directors of the State Museum.
Massachusetts – The lieutenant governor is a member of, and presides over, the Governor's Council, an elected body of 8 members which approves all judicial nominations.
Michigan – The lieutenant governor serves as a member of the State Administrative Board; and represents the governor and the state at selected local, state, and national meetings. In addition the governor may delegate additional responsibilities.
Minnesota – Serves as the Chair of the Capitol Area Architectural and Planning Board Committee.
Mississippi – The lieutenant governor also appoints chairs of standing committees, appoints conferees to committees and is a member of the Legislative Budget Committee, chair of this committee every other year.
Missouri – The lieutenant governor is the only statewide elected official that is part of both the executive and legislative branches of state government. Under the constitution, the lieutenant governor is ex officio president of the Missouri Senate. The lieutenant governor is elected independently from the governor, and each can be members of different political parties. Upon the governor's death, conviction, impeachment, resignation, absence from the state or other disabilities, the lieutenant governor shall act as governor. By law, the lieutenant governor is a member of the Board of Public Buildings, Board of Fund Commissioners, Missouri Development Finance Board, Missouri Community Service Commission, Missouri State Capitol Commission, Missouri Housing Development Commission and the Tourism Commission. The lieutenant governor is an advisor to the Department of Elementary and Secondary Education on early childhood education and the Parents-as-Teachers program. The lieutenant governor is the state's official advocate for senior citizens, and serves on the Special Health, Psychological, and Social Needs of Minority Older Individuals Commission.

TABLE 4.14
Lieutenant Governors: Powers and Duties (continued)

New Jersey – The Lieutenant Governor will serve as the head of a principal department or other executive or administrative agency or delegate duties of the office of governor or both.

North Carolina – Serves as a voting member on the State Board of Education. Serves on the State Board of Economic Development. Serves on the State Community College Board. Serves as Chairman of the Energy Policy Council. Serves on the Military Affairs Commission. Serves as Chair of the eLearning Commission.

Oklahoma – Lieutenant Governor also serves on 10 boards and commissions: Tourism and Recreation Commission, Indian Cultural and Educational Authority, State Board of Equalization, School Land Commission, the Oklahoma Capitol Improvement Authority, the Oklahoma Archives and Records Commission, the Oklahoma Film and Music Advisory Commission, CompSource Oklahoma Board of Managers, the Commissioners of the Land Office, and the Oklahoma Linked Deposit Review Board.

Pennsylvania – Chairs the Board of Pardons (Constitutional); chairs the Pa. Emergency Management Council (appointed by Gov.); chairs the Pa. Military Community Enhancement Commission (member by statute, elected chair by members); chairs Local Government Advisory Commission (statute.)

Rhode Island – Serves as Chair of a number of advisory councils including issues related to emergency management, long term care and small business. Each year submits a legislative package to the General Assembly.

South Carolina – The lieutenant governor heads the State Office on Aging; appoints members and chairs the South Carolina Affordable Housing Commission.

South Dakota – The lieutenant governor also serves as the Chair of the Workers Compensation Advisory Commission and as a member of the Constitutional Revision Commission.

Utah – The lieutenant governor serves as chief election officer (statutory); chair of the Lieutenant Governor's Commission on Volunteers (statutory); chair of the Lieutenant Governor's Commission on Civic and Character Education (statutory); chair of the Utah Capitol Preservation Board (statutory);

West Virginia – The President of the Senate and the Lieutenant Governor are one in the same. The legislature provided in statute the title of Lieutenant Governor upon the Senate President. The West Virginia Constitution requires that, in case of the death, conviction or impeachment, failure to qualify, resignation, or other disability of the governor, the President of the Senate shall act as governor until the vacancy is filled, or the disability removed.

Northern Mariana Islands – The Lieutenant Governor is charged with overseeing administrative functions.

(d) No lieutenant governor; secretary of state is next in line of succession to governorship.

(e) Appoints all standing committees. Iowa – appoints some special committees.

(f) Presides over cabinet meetings in absence of governor.

(g) Only in emergency situations.

(h) The Kentucky Constitution specifically gives the lieutenant governor the power to act as governor, in the event the governor is unable to fulfill the duties of office.

(i) No lieutenant governor; senate president or speaker is next in line of succession to governorship.

(j) As defined in the state constitution, the lieutenant governor performs gubernatorial functions in the governor's absence. In the event of a vacancy in the office of governor, the lieutenant governor is first in line to succeed to the position.

(k) Unicameral legislative body. In Guam, that body elects own presiding officer.

(l) Except on final passage of bills and joint resolutions.

(m) With respect to procedural matters, not legislation.

(n) May preside over the Senate when desired.

(o) Appoints committees with the Pres. Pro Tem and one Senator on Committee on Committees. Committee on Committees assigns bills.

(p) In the event of a vacancy in the office of Governor resulting from the death, resignation or removal of a Governor in office, or the death of a Governor-elect, or from any other cause the Lieutenant Governor shall become Governor, until a new Governor is elected and qualifies.

(q) Only when asked or after 45 days of absence.

(r) Only upon invitation from the Senate.

Table 4.14 | Gubernatorial Succession

If Something Happens to the Governor, Who Fills the Office?

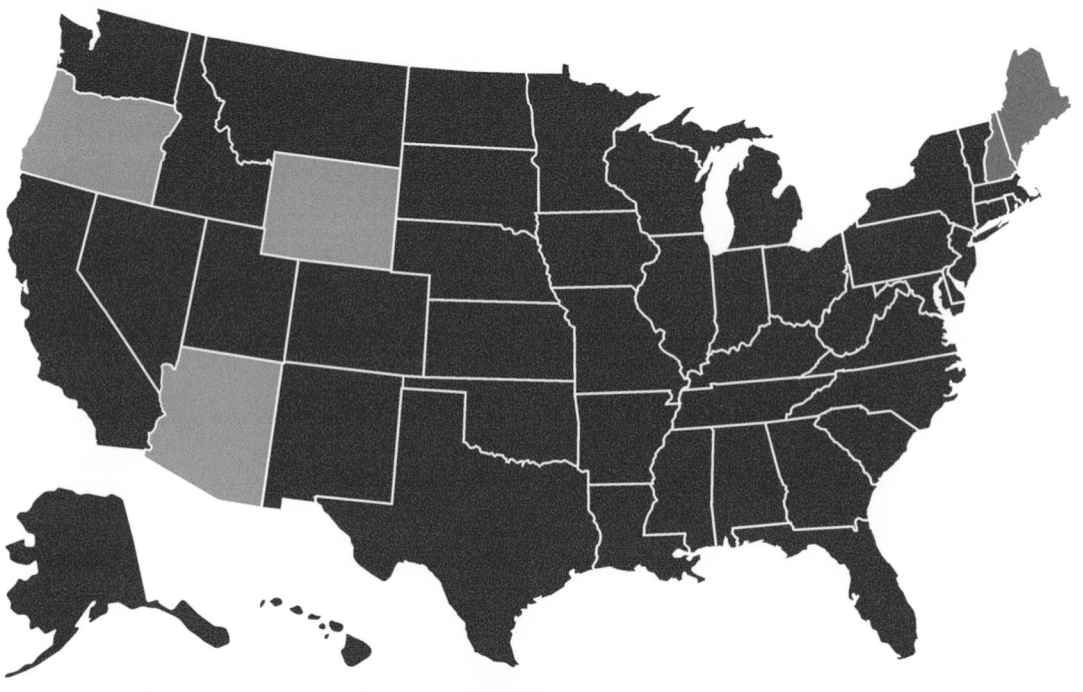

THE
Secretary of State
fills the office in 3 states.

Arizona
Oregon
Wyoming

These states have no lieutenant governor

THE
Lieutenant Governor
fills the office in 45 states.

Alabama	Kentucky	North Dakota
Alaska	Louisiana	Ohio
Arkansas	Maryland	Oklahoma
California	Massachusetts	Pennsylvania
Colorado	Michigan	Rhode Island
Connecticut	Minnesota	South Carolina
Delaware	Mississippi	South Dakota
Florida	Missouri	Tennessee
Georgia	Montana	Texas
Hawaii	Nebraska	Utah
Idaho	Nevada	Vermont
Illinois	New Jersey	Virginia
Indiana	New Mexico	Washington
Iowa	New York	West Virginia
Kansas	North Carolina	Wisconsin

THE
Senate President
fills the office in 2 states.

Maine
New Hampshire

These states have no lieutenant governor

TABLE 4.15
The Secretaries of State, 2020

State or other jurisdiction	Name and party	Method of selection	Length of regular term in years	Date of first service	Present term ends	Number of previous terms	Maximum consecutive terms allowed by constitution
Alabama	John Merrill (R)	E	4	1/2015	1/2023	1	2
Alaska	----------			---(a)---			
Arizona	Katie Hobbs (D)	E	4	1/2019	1/2023	0	2
Arkansas	John Thurston (R)	E	4	1/2019	1/2023	0	2
California	Alex Padilla (D)	E	4	1/2015	1/2023	1	2
Colorado	Jena Griswold (D)	E	4	1/2019	1/2023	0	2
Connecticut	Denise Merrill (D)	E	4	1/2011	1/2023	2	...
Delaware	Jeffrey Bullock (D)	A (b)	4	1/2009	...	0	...
Florida	Laurel Lee (R)	A	4	2/2019	...	0	2
Georgia	Brad Raffensperger (R)	E	4	1/2019	1/2023	0	...
Hawaii	----------			---(a)---			
Idaho	Lawerence Denney (R)	E	4	1/2015	1/2023	1	...
Illinois	Jesse White (D)	E	4	1/1999	1/2023	5	...
Indiana	Connie Lawson (R)	E	4	3/2012 (h)	1/2023	2	2
Iowa	Paul Pate (R)	E	4	12/2014	12/2022	1	...
Kansas	Scott Schwab (R)	E	4	1/2019	1/2023	0	...
Kentucky	Michael Adams (R)	E	4	12/2019	12/2023	0	2
Louisiana	Kyle Ardoin (R)	E	4	5/2018 (c)	1/2024	(c)	...
Maine	Matt Dunlap (D)	L	2	1/2005 (d)	1/2021	(d)	5 (e)
Maryland	John Wobensmith (R)	A	...	1/2015	...	0	...
Massachusetts	William Francis Galvin (D)	E	4	1/1995	1/2023	6	...
Michigan	Jocelyn Benson (D)	E	4	1/2019	1/2023	0	2
Minnesota	Steve Simon (DFL)	E	4	1/2015	1/2023	1	...
Mississippi	Michael Watson (R)	E	4	1/2020	1/2024	0	...
Missouri	Jay Ashcroft (R)	E	4	1/2017	1/2021	0	...
Montana	Corey Stapleton (R)	E	4	1/2017	1/2021	0	(f)
Nebraska	Robert Evnen (R)	E	4	1/2019	1/2023	0	...
Nevada	Barbara Cegavske (R)	E	4	1/2015	1/2023	1	2
New Hampshire	William Gardner (D)	L	2	12/1976	12/2020	21	...
New Jersey	Tahesha Way (D)	A	...	1/2018	...	0	...
New Mexico	Maggie Toulouse Oliver (D)	E	4	12/2016 (g)	12/2022	(g)	2
New York	Rossanna Rosado D)	A	...	6/2016	...	0	...
North Carolina	Elaine Marshall (D)	E	4	1/1997	1/2021	5	...
North Dakota	Alvin A. Jaeger (R)	E	4	1/1993	12/2022	6	...
Ohio	Frank LaRose (R)	E	4	1/2019	1/2023	0	2
Oklahoma	Michael Rogers (R)	A	4	1/2019	1/2023	0	...
Oregon	Bev Clarno (R)	E	4	4/2019 (k)	1/2021	0	2
Pennsylvania	Kathy Boockvar (D)	A	...	1/2019	...	0	...
Rhode Island	Nellie Gorbea (D)	E	4	1/2015	1/2023	1	2
South Carolina	Mark Hammond (R)	E	4	1/2003	1/2023	4	...
South Dakota	Steve Barnett (R)	E	4	1/2019	1/2023	0	2
Tennessee	Tre Hargett (R)	L	4	1/2009	1/2021	2	...
Texas	Ruth R. Hughs (R)	A	...	8/2019	...	0	...
Utah	----------			---(a)---			
Vermont	Jim Condos (D)	E	2	1/2011	1/2021	4	...
Virginia	Kelly Thomasson (D)	A	...	4/2016	...	0	...
Washington	Kim Wyman (R)	E	4	1/2013	1/2021	1	...
West Virginia	Andrew "Mac" Warner (R)	E	4	1/2017	1/2021	0	...
Wisconsin	Douglas LaFollette (D)	E	4	1/1974 (i)	1/2023	10 (i)	...
Wyoming	Ed Buchanan (R)	E	4	3/2018 (j)	1/2023	(j)	...
Dist. of Columbia	Kimberly Bassett (D)	A	...	12/2018	...	0	...
American Samoa	----------			---(a)---			
Guam	----------			---(a)---			
CNMI*	----------			---(a)---			
Puerto Rico	Elmer Roman (NPP)	A	...	12/2019	...	...	...
U.S. Virgin Islands	----------			---(a)---			

See footnotes at end of table

TABLE 4.15
The Secretaries of State, 2020 (continued)

Source: The Council of State Governments, June 2020.
* Commonwealth of Northern Mariana Islands
Key:
E - Elected by voters
A - Appointed by governor.
L - Elected by legislature.
. . . - No provision for.
(a) No secretary of state; lieutenant governor performs functions of this office.
(b) Appointed by the governor and confirmed by the Senate.
(c) Ardoin became acting secretary on May 2018, replacing Tom Schedler. He was elected to his first full term in November 2019.
(d) Secretary Matthew Dunlap previously served as secretary of state from 2005 to 2010. He was elected by the Legislature to serve again in January 2013 and re-elected in January 2015, 2017 and 2019.
(e) Statutory term limit of four consecutive two-year terms.
(f) Eligible for eight out of 16 years.
(g) Secretary Oliver was elected in November 2016 to fill the remaining two years of an unexpired term and was re-elected to her first full term in November 2018.
(h) Lawson was appointed in 2012 to serve out an unexpired term. She was then elected in 2014 and 2018.
(i) LaFollette was first elected in 1974 and served a four-year term. He was elected again in 1982 and has been re-elected since.
(j) Edward Buchanan was appointed March 5, 2018 to fill Ed Murray's term and was elected to his first full term in November 2018.
(k) Secretary Clarno was appointed in April 2019 by Gov. Kate Brown to fill the unexpired term of Dennis Richardson, who died in February 2019.

TABLE 4.16
Secretaries of State: Qualifications for Office

State or other jurisdiction	Minimum age	U.S. citizen (years) (a)	State resident (years) (b)	Qualified voter (years)	Method of selection to office
Alabama	25	7	5	★	E
Alaska			------(c)------		
Arizona	25	10	5	★	E
Arkansas	18	★	★	★	E
California	18	★	★	★	E
Colorado	25	★	2	...	E
Connecticut	18	★	★	★	E
Delaware	...	...	...	...	A
Florida			------(d)------		A
Georgia	25	10	4	★	E
Hawaii			------(c)------		
Idaho	25	★	2	★	E
Illinois	25	★	3	...	E
Indiana	...	★	★	★	E
Iowa	18	★	★	...	E
Kansas	...	...	...	...	E
Kentucky	30	★	2	★	E
Louisiana	25	5	5	★	E
Maine	...	...	...	...	(e)
Maryland	...	...	...	...	A
Massachusetts	18	★	5	★	E
Michigan	18	★	★	★	E
Minnesota	21	★	30 days	★	E
Mississippi	25	★	5	★	E
Missouri	...	★	1	...	E
Montana	25	★	2	★	E
Nebraska	★	★	★	★	E
Nevada	25	2	2	...	E
New Hampshire	18	...	...	...	(e)
New Jersey	18	★	★	★	A
New Mexico	30	★	5	★	E
New York	18	★	★	...	A
North Carolina	21	★	★	★	E
North Dakota	25	★	5	5	E
Ohio	18	★	★	★	E
Oklahoma	31	★	★	10	A
Oregon	18	★	★	★	E
Pennsylvania	...	...	...	...	A
Rhode Island	18	★	30 days	★	E
South Carolina	...	★	★	★	E
South Dakota	...	...	...	...	E
Tennessee	...	...	...	...	(e)
Texas	18	★	...	...	A
Utah			------(c)------		
Vermont	18	★	★	★	E
Virginia	...	...	...	...	A
Washington	18	★	★	★	E
West Virginia	...	★	5	★	E
Wisconsin	18	★	★	★	E
Wyoming	25	★	1	★	E
American Samoa			------(c)------		
Guam			------(c)------		
CNMI*			------(c)------		
Puerto Rico	...	5	5	...	A
U.S. Virgin Islands			------(c)------		

See footnotes at end of table

TABLE 4.16
Secretaries of State: Qualifications for Office (continued)

Source: The Council of State Governments survey of secretaries of state offices, 2020.

*Commonwealth of Northern Mariana Islands

Key:

★ –Formal provision; number of years not specified.

… –No formal provision.

A–Appointed by governor.

E–Elected by voters.

(a) In some states you must be a U.S. citizen to be an elector, and must be an elector to run.

(b) In some states you must be a state resident to be an elector, and must be an elector to run.

(c) No secretary of state.

(d) As of January 1, 2003, the office of Secretary of State shall be an appointed position (appointed by the governor). It will no longer be a cabinet position, but an agency head and the Department of State shall be an agency under the governor's office.

(e) Chosen by joint ballot of state senators and representatives. In Maine and New Hampshire, every two years. In Tennessee, every four years.

TABLE 4.17
Secretaries of State: Election and Registration Duties

State or other jurisdiction	Chief election officer	Determines ballot eligibility of political parties	Receives initiative and/or referendum petition	Files certificate of nomination or election	Supplies election ballots or materials to local officials	Files candidates' expense papers	Files other campaign reports	Conducts voter education programs	Registers charitable organizations	Registers corporations (a)	Processes and/or commissions notaries public	Registers securities	Registers trade names/marks
	Election								Registration				
Alabama	★	★	...	★	★	★	★	★	★	★	★	...	★
Alaska (b)	★	★	★	★	★	...	...	★	...	...	★	...	...
Arizona (aa)	★	★	...	★	...	★	★	★	★	...	★	...	★
Arkansas	★	★	★	★	...	★	★	★	...	★	★	...	★
California	★ (c)	★	...	★	★	★	★	★	(d)	★	★	...	★
Colorado	★	★	★	★	...	★	★	★	★	★	★	...	★
Connecticut	★	★	...	★	★	...	...	★	★	★	★	...	★
Delaware (g)	...	...	...	(e)	...	...	(f)	...	...	★	★	...	★
Florida (v)	★	★	★	★	...	★	★	...	...	★	★	...	★
Georgia	★	★	...	★	★	...	...	...	...	★	★	...	★ ★
Hawaii (b)	...	...	...	...	...	...	...	...	...	...	...	...	...
Idaho	★	★	★	★	★	★	★	★	★	★	★	...	★
Illinois	...	...	★	(h)	...	...	...	...	...	★	★	★	★
Indiana (i)	★	★	...	★	★	★	★	★	★	★	★	★	★
Iowa	★	★	...	★	...	...	...	★	★	★	★	...	★
Kansas	★	★	...	★	★	★	...	★	★	★	★	...	★
Kentucky	★	★	...	★	...	...	...	★	...	★	★	...	★
Louisiana	★	...	...	★	★	...	...	★	★	★	★	...	★
Maine	★	★	★	★	★	...	...	★	(y)	★	★	...	★
Maryland	...	★	★	★	...	...	...	...	★	...	★	...	★
Massachusetts	★	★	★	★	★	(f)	(f)	★	...	★	★	★	★
Michigan	★	★	★	★	...	★	★	★	...	★	★	...	...
Minnesota (z)	★	★	★	★	★	...	...	★	...	★	★	...	★
Mississippi	★	★	★	★	...	★	★	★	★	★	★	★	★
Missouri (bb)	★	★	★	★	...	...	...	★	★	★	★	★	★
Montana	★	★	★	★	...	...	...	★	★	★	★	...	★
Nebraska	★	★	★	★	★	...	...	★	★	★	★	...	★
Nevada (j)	★	★	★	★	★	★	★	★	★	★	★	★	★
New Hampshire	★	★	...	★	★	★	★	...	★	★	★	★	★
New Jersey	★	★	★	★	★	★	★	★	...	★	★	...	★
New Mexico	★	★	...	★	★	★	★	★	...	★	★	...	★
New York	...	...	...	...	...	...	...	...	★	★	★	...	★
North Carolina (k)	...	...	...	...	...	...	...	...	★	★	★	★	★
North Dakota	★	★	★	★	★	★	★	★	★	★	★	...	★
Ohio (l)	★	★	★	★(m)	★	★	★	★	...	★	★	★	★
Oklahoma	...	...	★	...	...	...	...	...	★	★ (n)	★	...	★
Oregon	★	★	★	★	★	★	★	★	★	★	★	...	★
Pennsylvania	★	★	...	★	...	...	★	★	★	★	★	...	★
Rhode Island (o)	★	★	...	★	★	...	...	★	...	★	★	...	★
South Carolina	...	...	...	...	...	...	...	...	★	★ (p)	★	...	★
South Dakota	★	★	★	★	...	★	★	★	...	★	★	...	★
Tennessee (q)	★	★	...	★	★	...	...	★	...	★	★	...	★
Texas	★	★	...	★	★	...	...	★	...	★	★	...	★
Utah (b)	★	★	★	★	★	★	★	★	...	...	...	...	...
Vermont (r)	★	...	...	★	★	★	...	★	...	★	★	...	★
Virginia (x)	...	...	...	...	...	...	...	...	★	★	...	...	...
Washington (w)	★	...	★	★	...	...	...	★	★	★	...	★	★
West Virginia	★	★	...	★	...	★	★	★	★	★	★	...	★
Wisconsin (s)	...	...	...	...	...	...	...	...	...	...	...	...	★
Wyoming	★	★	★	★	(t)	★	★	★	★	★	★	★	★
American Samoa (b)	...	...	...	★	...	★	★	★	★	★	★	...	...
Guam (b)	...	...	...	...	...	...	...	...	...	...	...	...	...
Puerto Rico	...	...	...	...	...	...	...	...	★	★	★	★	★
U.S. Virgin Islands (b)	...	...	...	...	...	...	...	...	★	★(u)	★	...	★

See footnotes at end of table

TABLE 4.17

Secretaries of State: Election and Registration Duties (continued)

Source: The Council of State Governments' survey of secretaries of state offices, 2020.

Key:

★ – Responsible for activity.

… – Not responsible for activity.

(a) Unless otherwise indicated, office registers domestic, foreign and non-profit corporations.

(b) No secretary of state. Duties indicated are performed by lieutenant governor. In Hawaii, election related responsibilities have been transferred to an independent Chief Election Officer. In U. S. Virgin Islands election duties are performed by Supervisor of Elections.

(c) Other election duties include: tallying votes from all 58 counties, testing and certifying voting systems for use by local elections officials, maintaining statewide voter registration database, publishing state Voter Information Guide/State Ballot Pamphlet and qualifying statewide ballot initiatives and referenda.

(d) This office does not register charitable trusts, but does register charitable organizations as nonprofit corporations; also limited partnerships, limited liability corporations, and domestic partners, Advanced Health care Directives, and administers the Safe at Home mail forwarding program.

(e) Files certificates of election for publication purposes only; does not file certificates of nomination.

(f) Federal candidates only.

(g) Registration duties include alternative business entities such as LLCs and partnerships.

(h) Office issues document, but does not receive it.

(i) Additional election duties include: statewide voter registration system administrator. Additional registration duties include securities enforcement and auto dealer registration and enforcement.

(j) Additional registration duties include: issues annual State Business License, registers domestic partnerships, registers advanced directives for health care, registers guardianship nominations. Charitable organizations soliciting tax deductible charitable contributions must file a charitable solicitation registration statements or claim of exemption before soliciting charitable contributions in Nevada.

(k) Other election duties: administers the Electoral College. Other registration duties: Maintains secure online registry of advance health care directives.

(l) Supplies poll worker training materials to county boards of elections: certifies official form of the ballot to county board of elections.

(m) Issues certificate of nomination or election to all statewide candidates and U.S. Representatives.

(n) Certifies U.S. Congressional election results to Washington D.C. Also registers limited partnerships, limited liability companies and limited liability partnerships.

(o) Additional registration duties include: Non-resident landlord appointment of agent for service and Uniform Commercial Code.

(p) Also registers the Cable Franchise Authority.

(q) Appoints the Coordinator of Elections who performs the election duties indicated above, and also prepares the elections manual and elections handbook for use by state officials. Also registers athlete agents, as well as individuals and entities seeking exemption from Tennessee's workers' compensation requirements.

(r) Additional registration duties include: registers temporary officiants for civil marriages.

(s) Additional registration duties include: Issues authentications and apostilles.

(t) Materials not ballots.

(u) Both domestic and foreign profit; but only domestic non-profit.

(v) Additional registration duties include: registers fictitious names and other types of business entities.

(w) Additional registration duties include: registers domestic partnerships and registers international student exchange programs.

(x) Additional registration duties include: registering organizations' mottos; registering logos and insignias; authentications.

(y) Registers nonprofit entities.

(z) Additional registration duties include: registers LLCs, limited partnerships.

(aa) Additional registration duties include partnerships, telephonic seller, advance directives and uniform commercial code.

(bb) Also administers the Safe at Home address confidentiality/mail forwarding program; issues authentications and apostilles.

TABLE 4.18
Secretaries of State: Custodial, Publication and Legislative Duties

State or other jurisdiction	Custodial				Publication					Legislative			
	Archives state records and regulations	Files state agency rules and regulations	Administers uniform commercial code provisions	Files other corporate documents	State manual or directory	Session laws	State constitution	Statutes	Administrative rules and regulations	Opens legislative sessions (a)	Enrolls or engrosses bills	Retains copies of bills	Registers lobbyists
Alabama	...	...	★	★	...	★	★	★	...	...	★	★	...
Alaska (b)	...	★	...	...	...	★	...	...	★	★	...	★	...
Arizona (w)	★	★	★	...	...	...	...	...	★	...	...	★	★
Arkansas (c)	★	★	★	★	...	★	...	...	★	...	...	★	★
California	★	★	★	★	★	...	...	...	...	...	(d)	...	★
Colorado	...	★	★	★	...	...	★	...	★	...	...	★	★
Connecticut	★(e)	★	★	★	★	...	...	...	★	S	...	★	...
Delaware (x)	★	★	★	★	...	...	...	...	...	...	...	★	★
Florida (u)	★	★	★	★	...	★	★	★	★	...	...	★	...
Georgia	★	★	...	...	...	★	...	...	...	...	...	★	...
Hawaii (b)	...	...	...	...	...	★	...	...	★	...	...	★	...
Idaho	...	...	★	★	...	...	★	★	...	...	...	★	★
Illinois	★	★	★	★	★	★	★	...	★	H	...	★	★
Indiana	(n)	...	★	★	...	...	...	...	...	H	...	(n)	...
Iowa (y)	★	...	★	★	...	★	★	...	...	...	★	★	...
Kansas (s)	...	★	★	★	★	★	...	(o)	★	★	...	★	★
Kentucky	★	...	★	★	...	★	...	...	...	...	★	★	...
Louisiana	★	...	★	★	★	...	...	★	★	...	★	★	(f)
Maine	★	★	★	★	...	...	★	...	★	...	★	★	...
Maryland	...	★	...	...	...	★	...	...	...	...	★	★	...
Massachusetts	★	★	★	★	★	★	★	★	★	...	★	★	★
Michigan	★	★	★	...	...	★	★	★	★	...	...	...	★
Minnesota	★	★	★	★	★	...	...	...	...	H	...	★	...
Mississippi	★	★	★	★	★	★	★	★	★	H	...	(p)	★
Missouri	★(h)	★	★	★	★	...	★	...	★	H	...	★	...
Montana	★	★	★	★	...	...	★	...	★	H	★	★	...
Nebraska	★	★	★	★	...	...	...	...	★	...	...	★	...
Nevada	★	★	★	★	...	...	...	...	★	...	...	★	...
New Hampshire	★	...	★	★	★	...	★	...	...	...	★	★	★
New Jersey	★	...	...	...	...	...	★	...	...	...	...	★	...
New Mexico (z)	...	...	★	★	...	★	★	★	...	H	...	★	★
New York	...	★	★	★	★	...	★	...	★	...	...	...	...
North Carolina (t)	★	★	★	...	★	...	★	...	...	...	★	★	★
North Dakota	...	...	★	★	...	...	...	...	...	...	...	★	★
Ohio (i)	★	★	★	★	★	★	★	...	...	...	...	★	...
Oklahoma (j)	...	★	...	★	...	...	★	...	★	...	...	★	...
Oregon	★	★	★	★	★	...	★	...	★	...	...	★	...
Pennsylvania	...	...	★	★	★	...	...	...	...	...	★	★	...
Rhode Island (k)	★	★	★	★	★	...	★	...	★	...	★	★	★
South Carolina	...	...	★	★	...	...	...	...	...	...	...	★	...
South Dakota	★	★	★	★	★	...	★	...	★	H	...	★	★
Tennessee	★(q)	★	★	★	★(l)	★	...	★	★	...	...	...	...
Texas	...	★	★	★	...	★	...	...	★	H	...	★	...
Utah (b)	...	...	...	...	...	...	...	...	...	...	...	★	★
Vermont (m)	★	★	★	★	★	★	★	...	★	H	...	★	★
Virginia (g)	...	...	...	...	★	...	...	...	...	...	...	...	...
Washington (v)	★	...	...	★	★	...	★	...	...	...	★	★	...
West Virginia	★	★	★	★	...	...	...	...	★	...	...	★	...
Wisconsin	★	...	...	...	...	...	...	...	...	...	...	...	...
Wyoming	★	★	★	★	★	...	★	...	★	H	...	★	★
American Samoa (b)	...	★	...	★	...	★	★	...	★	...	...	...	...
Guam (b)	...	...	...	...	...	...	...	★	...	...	...	...	...
Puerto Rico	...	★	★	★	...	★	★	★	★	...	...	...	...
U.S. Virgin Islands (b)	...	★	★	★	...	...	...	...	...	...	★	★	...

See footnotes at end of table

TABLE 4.18
Secretaries of State: Custodial, Publication and Legislative Duties (continued)

Sources: The Council of State Governments' survey of secretaries of state offices and websites, 2020.

Key:

★ – Responsible for activity.

… – Not responsible for activity.

(a) In this column only: ★–Both houses; H–House; S–Senate.

(b) No secretary of state. Duties indicated are performed by lieutenant governor.

(c) Additional custodial duties for the Arkansas Secretary of State include serving as the caretaker for the Arkansas State Capitol Building and Grounds, including all custodial duties, HVAC system, building maintenance, historic preservation and conducting tours.

(d) Office does not enroll or engross bills but does chapter bills that are signed into law and retains final chaptered copies.

(e) The secretary of state is keeper of public records, but the state archives is a department of the Connecticut State Library.

(f) Only registers political pollsters.

(g) Other custodial duties include: restoration of civil rights; liaison to Virginia Indians; gubernatorial appointments. Other publication duties include: state organization charts. Other registration duties include: Pardons; Service of Process

(h) Also responsible for the State Library.

(i) Additional publication duties include: elections statistics, official roster of federal, state, and county officers and official roster of township and municipal officers. Additional legislative duties include :Distributing laws to specified state and local government agencies.

(j) Other custodial duties include: Effective Financing Statements identifying farm products that are subject to a security interest, UCC and mortgage documents pertaining to transmitting utilities and also railroads and files open meeting notices.

(k) Additional duties include administering oaths of office to general officers and legislators.

(l) The Division of Publications of the Office of the Secretary of State also publishes the following: The Tennessee Blue Book, Board and Commission vacancies, and Executive Orders and Proclamations.

(m) Additional custodial duties include: records management, and certifying vital records.

(n) The Secretary of State's office receives and authenticates Bills and Enrolled Acts, but does not keep or maintain them. Post-session legislative materials are maintained by the Indiana Public Records Commission.

(o) Responsible for distribution only.

(p) Chapters and indexes all signed bill and chamber and concurrent resolutions.

(q) The Division of Records Management of the Office of the Secretary of State assists state agencies in the appropriate utilization, disposition, retention and destruction of state records.

(s) Additionally, the secretary of state publishes the Kansas Register and opens legislative reorganization meetings.

(t) Other publication duties include: Publishes state board and commission meeting notices online. Other legislative duties include: The Secretary of State is responsible for the certification of election results before legislators take the oath of office at the opening of each session of the General Assembly.

(u) Files other types of business entity and cable franchise documents, records federal tax liens and judgement liens and issues Apostilles

(v) Legislative duties also include: chapters bills.

(w) The secretary of state works hand-in-hand with the business community. The office is tasked with recording the partnerships of those who do business in Arizona and they register trademarks and issue certificates of registration. They also register telemarketers and veterans' charitable organizations. Improving the quality of life for Arizonans has been a priority of the office. The Arizona State Library, Archives and Public Records provides Arizonans access to information about their government, their state and their world. The information available from the State Library empowers citizens to become informed citizens. The Address Confidentiality Program allows victims of domestic violence, sexual abuse or stalking to keep their residential addresses confidential by giving them a substitute address.

(x) Other publication duties include constitutional amendments.

(y) Began administering a Safe at Home address confidentiality program for victims of domestic abuse, sexual assault and other violent crimes.
Approves voluntary non-urbanized annexations and files all annexations of territory by Iowa cities.

(z) Files Agency Code of Conduct; Administers Confidential Address Program Publish State Roster of Elected Officials; State Blue Book.

TABLE 4.19
The Attorneys General, 2020

State or other jurisdiction	Name and party	Method of selection	Length of regular term in years	Date of first service	Present term ends	Number of previous terms	Maximum consecutive terms allowed
Alabama	Steve Marshall (R)	E	4	2/2017 (h)	1/2023	1 (h)	2
Alaska	Kevin Clarkson (R)	A	...	1/2019	...	0	...
Arizona	Mark Brnovich (R)	E	4	1/2015	1/2023	1	2
Arkansas	Leslie Rutledge (R)	E	4	1/2015	1/2023	1	2
California	Xavier Becerra (D)	E	4	1/2017 (l)	1/2023	(l)	2
Colorado	Phil Weiser (D)	E	4	1/2019	1/2023	0	2
Connecticut	William Tong (D)	E	4	1/2019	1/2023	0	★
Delaware	Kathleen Jennings (D)	E	4	1/2019	1/2023	0	★
Florida	Ashley Moody (R)	E	4	1/2019	1/2023	0	2
Georgia	Christopher Carr (R)	E	4	10/2016 (j)	1/2023	(j)	★
Hawaii	Clare Connors (D)	A	4 (a)	1/2019	1/2023	0	...
Idaho	Lawrence Wasden (R)	E	4	1/2003	1/2023	4	★
Illinois	Kwame Raoul (D)	E	4	1/2019	1/2023	0	★
Indiana	Curtis Hill (R)	E	4	1/2017	1/2021	0	★
Iowa	Tom Miller (D)	E	4	1/1979 (b)	1/2023	9 (b)	★
Kansas	Derek Schmidt (R)	E	4	1/2011	1/2023	2	★
Kentucky	Daniel Cameron (R)	E	4	12/2019	12/2023	0	2
Louisiana	Jeff Landry (R)	E	4	1/2016	1/2024	1	★
Maine	Aaron Frey (D)	L (c)	2	1/2019	1/2021	0	4
Maryland	Brian Frosh (D)	E	4	1/2015	1/2023	1	★
Massachusetts	Maura Healey (D)	E	4	1/2015	1/2023	1	...
Michigan	Dana Nessel (D)	E	4	1/2019	1/2023	0	2
Minnesota	Keith Ellison (DFL)	E	4	1/2019	1/2023	0	★
Mississippi	Lynn Fitch (R)	E	4	1/2020	1/2024	0	★
Missouri	Eric Schmitt (R)	E	4	1/2019 (d)	1/2021	0	★
Montana	Tim Fox (R)	E	4	1/2013	1/2021	1	2
Nebraska	Doug Peterson (R)	E	4	1/2015	1/2023	1	★
Nevada	Aaron Ford (D)	E	4	1/2019	1/2023	0	2
New Hampshire	Gordon MacDonald (R)	A	4	4/2017	1/2021	0	...
New Jersey	Gubir Grewal (D)	A	4	1/2018	1/2022	0	...
New Mexico	Hector Balderas (D)	E	4	1/2015	1/2023	1	2 (f)
New York	Letitia James (D)	E	4	1/2019	1/2023	0	★
North Carolina	Josh Stein (D)	E	4	1/2017	1/2021	0	★
North Dakota	Wayne Stenehjem (R)	E	4 (g)	1/2001	12/2022	4 (g)	★
Ohio	David Yost (R)	E	4	1/2019	1/2023	0	2
Oklahoma	Mike Hunter (R)	E	4	2/2017 (e)	1/2023	(e)	★
Oregon	Ellen F. Rosenblum (D)	E	4	6/2012 (i)	1/2021	1 (i)	★
Pennsylvania	Josh Shapiro (D)	E	4	1/2017	1/2021	0	2
Rhode Island	Peter Neronha (D)	E	4	1/2019	1/2023	0	2
South Carolina	Alan Wilson (R)	E	4	1/2011	1/2023	2	★
South Dakota	Jason Ravnsborg (R)	E	4	1/2019	1/2023	0	2 (f)
Tennessee	Herbert Slatery (R)	(k)	8	10/2014	8/2022	0	...
Texas	Ken Paxton (R)	E	4	1/2015	1/2023	1	★
Utah	Sean Reyes (R)	E	4	12/2013	1/2021	1	★
Vermont	TJ Donovan	E	2	1/2017	1/2021	1	★
Virginia	Mark Herring (D)	E	4	1/2014	1/2022	1	(m)
Washington	Bob Ferguson (D)	E	4	1/2013	1/2021	1	★
West Virginia	Patrick Morrisey (R)	E	4	1/2013	1/2021	1	★
Wisconsin	Josh Kaul (D)	E	4	1/2019	1/2023	0	★
Wyoming	Bridget Hill (R)	A	...	1/2019	...	0	...
Dist. of Columbia	Karl Racine (D)	A	...	1/2015	1/2023	1	...
American Samoa	Mitzie Jessop Taase	A	4	2/2020	...	0	...
Guam	Leevin Camacho (I)	E	4	1/2019	1/2023	0	...
CNMI*	Edward Manibusan (I)	A	4	11/2015	...	0	...
Puerto Rico	Dennise Longo Quiñones	A	4	8/2019	...	0	...
U.S. Virgin Islands	Denise George-Counts	A	4	4/2019	...	0	...

See footnotes at end of table

TABLE 4.19
The Attorneys General, 2020 (continued)

Sources: The Council of State Governments, June 2020.
*Commonwealth of Northern Mariana Islands

Key:

★ – No provision specifying number of terms allowed.

... – No formal provision, position is appointed or elected by governmental entity (not chosen by the electorate).

A–Appointed by the governor.

E –Elected by the voters.

L–Elected by the legislature.

N.A.–Not available.

(a) Term runs concurrently with the governor.

(b) Attorney General Miller was elected in 1978, 1982, 1986, 1994, 1998, 2002, 2006, 2010, 2014 and 2018.

(c) Chosen biennially by joint ballot of state senators and representatives.

(d) Eric Schmitt was appointed in January 2019 to fill the unexpired term of Joshua Hawley, who was elected the U.S. Senate in November 2018.

(e) Mike Hunter was appointed in Feb. 2017 after Scott Pruitt left to serve as administrator of the U.S. Environmental Protection Agency. He was elected to his first full term in November 2018.

(f) After two consecutive terms, must wait four years and/or one full term before being eligible again.

(g) The term of the office of the elected official is four years, except that in 2004 the attorney general was elected for a term of two years.

(h) Steve Marshall was appointed on Feb. 10, 2017 to fill the unexpired term of Luther Strange. He was elected to his first full term in November 2018.

(i) Rosenblum was appointed by Gov. Kitzhaber on June 29, 2012 to fill the term left vacant when AG John Kroger resigned to become President of Reed College. She was elected in November 2012 to her first full term.

(j) Christopher Carr was appointed in October 2016 to fill the unexpired term of Sam Olens. He was elected to his first full term in November 2018.

(k) Appointed by judges of state Supreme Court.

(l) Attorney General Bercerra was appointed in January 2017 to fill the unexpired term of Kamala Harris and elected to his first full term in November 2018.

(m) Provision specifying individual may hold office for an unlimited number of terms.

(n) Must be confirmed by the Senate.

(o) Taase was appointed in 2020 to replace Talauega Eleasalo Ale who resigned to run for lieutenant governor in 2020.

TABLE 4.20
Attorneys General: Qualifications for Office

State or other jurisdiction	Minimum age	U.S. citizen (years)(a)	State resident (years)(b)	Qualified voter (years)	Licensed attorney (years)	Membership in the state bar (years)	Method of selection to office
Alabama	25	7	5	★	...	...	E
Alaska	18	★	...	...	★	★	A
Arizona	25	10	5	★	5	...	E
Arkansas	...	★	★	★	...	...	E
California	18	★	★	★	★	5	E
Colorado	27	★	2	★	★	...	E
Connecticut	18	★	★	★	10	10	E
Delaware	...	...	...	...	...	...	E
Florida	30	★	7	★	★	5	E
Georgia	25	10	4	★	7	7	E
Hawaii	...	1	1	...	★	(d)	A
Idaho	30	★	2	...	★	★	E
Illinois	25	★	3	★	★	★	E
Indiana	...	2	2	★	5	...	E
Iowa	18	★	★	...	...	...	E
Kansas	...	...	...	...	...	...	E
Kentucky	30	...	2 (e)	...	8	2	E
Louisiana	25	★	5	★	★	★	E
Maine	...	...	...	...	★	★	(f)
Maryland	...	★(g)	★	★	★	10	E
Massachusetts	18	...	5	★	...	★	E
Michigan	18	★	★	...	★	★	E
Minnesota	21	★	30 days	★	...	...	E
Mississippi	26	★	5	★	5	★	E
Missouri	...	★	1	...	...	...	E
Montana	25	★	2	...	5	★	E
Nebraska	...	...	★	...	...	...	E
Nevada	25	★	2	★	...	...	E
New Hampshire	...	★	★	...	★	★	A (h)
New Jersey	18	...	★	...	...	...	A
New Mexico	30	★	5	★	★	...	E
New York	30	★	5	...	(i)	...	E
North Carolina	21	★	★	★	★	(i)	E
North Dakota	25	★	5	★	★	★	E
Ohio	18	★	★	★	...	...	E
Oklahoma	31	★	★	10	...	...	E
Oregon	18	★	★	★	...	...	E
Pennsylvania	30	★	...	...	★	...	E
Rhode Island	18	...	...	...	★	★	E
South Carolina	...	★	30 days	★	...	...	E
South Dakota	18	★	★	★	(i)	(i)	E
Tennessee	...	...	...	...	...	...	(j)
Texas	...	★	1	...	(i)	(i)	E
Utah	25	★	5 (e)	★	★	★	E
Vermont	18	★	★	★	...	...	E
Virginia	30	★	1 (k)	★	...	5 (k)	E
Washington	18	★	★	★	★	★	E
West Virginia	25	...	5	★	...	...	E
Wisconsin	...	★	★	★	...	...	E
Wyoming	...	★	★	★	4	4	A (l)
Dist. of Columbia	...	...	★	...	★	★	A
American Samoa	...	...	(c)	...	(i)	(i)	A
Guam	...	...	...	...	...	...	A
CNMI*	...	...	3	...	5	...	A
Puerto Rico	...	★	...	...	★	★	A
U.S. Virgin Islands	...	...	★	★	★	★	A

See footnotes at end of table

TABLE 4.20
Attorneys General: Qualifications for Office (continued)

Sources: The Council of State Governments' survey of attorneys general, state constitutions and statutes, 2020.

* Commonwealth of Northern Mariana Islands

Key:

★ – Formal provision; number of years not specified.

… – No formal provision.

A – Appointed by governor.

E – Elected by voters.

(a) In some states you must be a U.S. citizen to be an elector, and must be an elector to run.

(b) In some states you must be a state resident to be an elector, and must be an elector to run.

(c) No statute specifically requires this, but the State Bar Act can be interpreted as making this a qualification.

(d) No period specified, all licensed attorneys are members of the state bar.

(e) State citizenship requirement.

(f) Chosen biennially by joint ballot of state senators and representatives.

(g) *Crosse v. Board of Supervisors of Elections* 243 Md. 555, 221A.2d431 (1966)–opinion rendered indicated that U.S. citizenship was, by necessity, a requirement for office.

(h) Appointed by the governor and confirmed by the governor and the executive council.

(i) Implied.

(j) Appointed by state supreme court.

(k) Same as qualifications of a judge of a court of record.

(l) Must be confirmed by the Senate.

TABLE 4.21
Attorneys General: Prosecutorial and Advisory Duties

State or other jurisdiction	Authority in local prosecutions: Authority to initiate local prosecutions	May intervene in local prosecutions	May assist local prosecutor	May supersede local prosecutor	Issues advisory opinions (a): To state executive officials	To legislators	To local prosecutors	On the constitutionality of bills or ordinances	Reviews legislation (b): Prior to passage	Before signing
Alabama	A	A,D	A,D	A	★	★	★	...	★	...
Alaska	(c)	(c)	(c)	(c)	★	★	...	★	★	★
Arizona	A,D,F	A,D	A,D,F	D,F	★	★	★	★(x)	(u)	(u)
Arkansas	D	...	D	...	★	★	★	★	...	...
California	A,B,C,D,E,F	A,B,C,D,E,F	A,B,C,D,E,F	A,B,C,D,E,F,G	★	★	★	★	(v)	(v)
Colorado	A, F	A	D,F	A	★	★	★	★	★	★
Connecticut	...	...	...	...	★	(d)	...	★	(e)	(e)
Delaware	A(f)	(f)	(f)	(f)	★	★	...	★	(g)	(g)
Florida	F	...	D	...	★	★	★	...	...	...
Georgia	B,D,F,G	...	A,D	...	★	★	★	...	...	...
Hawaii	A,B,C,D,E	A,B,C,D,E	A,B,C,D,E	A,B,C,D,E	★	★	...	★(h)	★	★
Idaho	B,D,F	D, F	D	...	★	★	★	...	★	★
Illinois	D,F	D,G	D	G	★	★	★	...	(i)	(i)
Indiana	F	...	D	...	★	★	★	★	...	...
Iowa	D,F	D,F	D,F	D,E,F	★	★	★	...	(j)	(j)
Kansas	B,C,D,F	B,C,D,F,G	D	B,C,D,F,G	★	★	★	...	...	...
Kentucky	D,F,G	B,D,G	D	B	★	★	★	★	...	...
Louisiana	D,E,G	D,E,G	D,E,G	E,G	★	★	★	...	★	★
Maine	A	A	A	A	★	★	...	...	...	...
Maryland	B,F	D	D	...	★	★	★	★	...	★
Massachusetts	A	A	A,D	A	★	★(k)	★	★	(l)	(l)
Michigan	A	A	A	A	★	★	★	★	...	...
Minnesota	B,D,F	B,D,G	A,B,D,G	B	★	★(k)	★	...	...	(l)
Mississippi	A,D,F	D,F	A,D,F	D,F	★	★	★	...	...	...
Missouri	B,F,G	F	B,F	G	★	★	★	...	(l)	(l)
Montana	D	E	D,E	E	★	★(m)	★	...	...	...
Nebraska	A,D	A,D	A,D,E,F	...	★	★	★	★	...	...
Nevada	A,B,D,E,F	A,B,D,E,F	A,B,D,E,F	A,B,D,E,F	★	...	★	★	...	...
New Hampshire	A,E (y)	A,E (y)	A,D,E	A,E	★	★	★	...	(n)	(n)
New Jersey	A,B,C,D	A,B,C,D	A,B,C,D	A,B,C,D	★	...	★	★	★	★
New Mexico	B,D,E,F	D,E,F	A,B,D,E,F	D,E,F,G	★	★	★	★	★	★
New York	B,F	B,D,F	D	B	★	★(k)	★	★	★	★
North Carolina	...	D	D	...	★	★	★	★	★	...
North Dakota	D,E,F,G	A,D,E,G	A,D,E,F,G	A,D,E,G	★	★	★	...	...	...
Ohio	D, F	D	D	F	★	(m)	★	...	...	...
Oklahoma	A,B,C,D,E,F,G	A,B,C,D,E,F,G	A,B,C,D,E,F,G	A,B,C,D,E,F,G	★	★	★	★	★	★
Oregon	B,D,F	B,D	B,D	B	★	★	★	...	...	★
Pennsylvania	A,D,F	D,F,G	D,F	G	★	...	...	...	...	...
Rhode Island	A	A	A	A	★	★	...	...	...	...
South Carolina	A,D,E,F	A,B,C,D,E,F	A,D,E	A,E	★	(q)	★	★	★(w)	★(w)
South Dakota	A,B,D,E,F (p)	D,G	A,B,D,E	D,F	★	★	★	...	★	...
Tennessee	D,F,G	D,G	D,F	F,G	★	★	★	★	...	...
Texas	F	...	D	...	(z)	(z)	(z)	(z)	...	...
Utah	A,B,D,E,F,G	E,G	D,E	E	★	★(q)	★	★	★(l)	★(l)
Vermont	A	A	A	G	★	★	★	★	★	★
Virginia	B,F	B,D,F	B,D,F	B	★	★	★	★	★	★
Washington	B,D,G	B,D,G	B,D,G	B,D,G	★	★	★	...	(o)	(o)
West Virginia	(r)	...	...	...	★	★	★	★	..	...
Wisconsin	B,C,D,F	B,C,D	D	B	★	★	★	★	(e)	(e)
Wyoming	B,D,F	B,D	B,D	G	★	★	★	★(h)	★	★
Dist. of Columbia	F	D	D	F	★	★	(s)	★	★	★
American Samoa	A(t)	(t)	(t)	(t)	★	...	(t)	(e)	(l)	(l)
Guam	A	A	A	A	★	★	★	★	(l)	B
CNMI*	A(t)	(t)	(t)	(t)	★	★	...	★	...	...
Puerto Rico	A	(t)	(t)	(t)	★	★	...	...	★	★
U.S. Virgin Islands	A(t)	(t)	(t)	(t)	★	...	...	★	★	★

See footnotes at end of table

TABLE 4.21
Attorneys General: Prosecutorial and Advisory Duties (continued)

Sources: The Council of State Governments' survey of attorneys general, state constitutions and statutes, 2020.

*Commonwealth of Northern Mariana Islands

Key:

A – On own initiative.
B – On request of governor.
C – On request of legislature.
D – On request of local prosecutor.
E – When in state's interest.
F – Under certain statutes for specific crimes.
G – On authorization of court or other body.
★ – Has authority in area.
. . . – Does not have authority in area.

(a) Also issues advisory opinions to: Alabama- Designated heads of state departments, agencies, boards, and commissions; local public officials; and political subdivisions. Hawaii- Judges/judiciary as requested. Kansas- to counsel for local units of government. Montana- county and city attorneys, city commissioners. Wisconsin-corporation counsel.

(b) Also reviews legislation: Alabama- when requested by the governor. Alaska- after passage. Arizona- at the request of the legislature. Kansas- upon request of Legislator, no formal authority.

(c) The attorney general functions as the local prosecutor.

(d) To legislative leadership.

(e) Informally reviews bills or does so upon request.

(f) The attorney general functions as the local prosecutor.

(g) Discretion to informally review upon request of legislative or executive branch, but reviews are not legal advice nor formal action.

(h) Bills, not ordinances.

(i) Review and track legislation that relates to the Office of Attorney General and the office mission.

(j) No requirements for review.

(k) To legislature as a whole not individual legislators.

(l) Only when requested by governor or legislature.

(m) To either the House of Representatives or the Senate, when so requested by resolution or passed by membership; To law directors of townships that have adopted limited self-government under R.C. Chapter 504.

(n) Provides information when requested by the Legislature. Testifies for or against bills on the Attorney General's own initiative.

(o) May review legislation at request of clients or legislature.

(p) Certain statutes provide for concurrent jurisdiction with local prosecutors.

(q) Only when requested by legislature.

(r) Can be involved in local at request of local prosecutors. If requested by local authority, can participate in criminal prosecutions.

(s) The office of attorney general prosecutes local crimes to an extent. The office's Legal Counsel Division may issue legal advice to the office's prosecutorial arm. Otherwise, the office does not usually advise the OUSA, the district's other local prosecutor.

(t) The attorney general functions as the local prosecutor.

(u) Reviews enacted legislation only when there is a compelling need.

(v) May review legislation at any time but does not have a de jure role in approval of bills as to form or constitutionality; California has a separate Legislative Counsel to advise the legislature on bills.

(w) Has concurrent jurisdiction with states' attorneys. Only when requested by governor or legislature.

(x) At the request of one or more members of the legislature, the attorney general shall investigate any ordinance, regulation, order or other official action adopted or taken by the governing body of a county, city or town that the member alleges violates state law or the Constitution of Arizona.

(y) Attorney general has statewide prosecutorial authority in any court. No request or order is required for the AG to initiate a prosecution. The Attorney General has authority to intervene, no request or order is required, but does not do so except in an extreme circumstance.

(z) The attorney general's office may issue an opinion on a question affecting the public interest or concerning the official duties of the requesting person. The opinion is a written interpretation of existing law. Authorized requestors are: the governor, head of a department of state government, the head or board or a penal institution, the head or board of an eleemosynary institution, the head of a state board, a regent or trustee of a state educational institution, a committee of a house of the Texas Legislature, a county auditor authorized by law, the chair of the governing board of a river authority and a district or county attorney.

Table 4.21 | Duties of Attorneys General

The length of a regular term for most attorneys general is **FOUR YEARS.**

In Vermont and Maine, the term is only two years. | In Tennessee, the length is eight years.

Iowa Attorney General Tom Miller is the longest continuously serving state attorney general.

He has been in office since 1995. He also served from 1979–1991.

The average time in office for the current group of attorneys general is

4.1 YEARS.

IN 6 STATES,
attorneys general are appointed rather than elected.

Alaska, Hawaii, New Hampshire, New Jersey, Tennessee and Wyoming

IN TENNESSEE, the Supreme Court is responsible for the appointment as opposed to the governor.

IN MAINE, the attorney general is elected by the Legislature.

Top 5 Salaries for Current Attorneys General

New York **$210,000**

Tennessee **$193,488**

California **$182,189**

Wyoming **$177,000**

New Jersey **$175,000**

Average **$187,535**

In seven states, you have to be at least 30 years old to serve as attorney general (Florida, Idaho, Kentucky, New Mexico, New York, Pennsylvania, Virginia). In Oklahoma, you must be at least 31.

23%
of attorneys general currently in office are women.

In 31 states and territories, the attorney general is required to be a licensed attorney.

TABLE 4.22
Attorneys General: Consumer Protection Activities, Subpoena Powers and Antitrust Duties

State or other jurisdiction	May commence civil proceedings	May commence criminal proceedings	Represents the state before regulatory agencies (a)	Administers consumer protection programs	Handles consumer complaints	Subpoena powers (b)	Antitrust duties
Alabama	★	★	★	★	★	•	A,B,C
Alaska	★	...	★	★	★	★	A,B,C,D
Arizona	★	★	...	★	★	★	A,B,C,D
Arkansas	★	...	★	★	★	•	A,B
California	★	★	★	★	★	★	A,B,C,D
Colorado	★	★	★	★	★	•	A,C,D
Connecticut	★	(d)	★	★	★	•	A,B,D
Delaware	★	★	★	★	★	★	A,B,D
Florida	★	...	...	★	★	★	A,B,D
Georgia	★	★	★	★	★	•	...
Hawaii	★	★	★	...	★	★	A,B,C,D
Idaho	★	...	★	★	★	★	A,B,D
Illinois	★	...	★	★	★	•	A,B,C
Indiana	★	...	★	★	★	★	A,B
Iowa	★	★	★	★	★	★	B,C
Kansas	★	★	...	★	★	★	A,B,D
Kentucky	★	★	★	★	★	★	A,B,C,D
Louisiana	★	...	★	★	★	(n)	A,B,D
Maine	★	★	★	★	★	★	A,B,C
Maryland	★	★(e)	★	★	★	★	B,C,D
Massachusetts	★	★	★	★	★	★	A,B,C,D
Michigan	★	★	★	★	★	★	A,B,C,D
Minnesota	★	...	★	★	★	★	A,B,C,D
Mississippi	★	★	...	★	★	★	A,B,C,D
Missouri	★	★	★	★	★	★	A,B,C,D
Montana	★	★	...	★	★	...	A,B
Nebraska	★	★	★	★	★	★	A,B,C,D
Nevada	★	★	★	★	★	•	A,B,C,D
New Hampshire	★	★	★	★	★	★	A,B,C
New Jersey	★	★	★	★	★	★	A,B,C,D
New Mexico	★	★	★	★	★	★	A,B,C (g)
New York	★	★	★	★	★	★	A,B,C,D
North Carolina	★	«(f)	★	★	★	★	A,B,C,D
North Dakota	★	...	...	★	...	★	A,B,C
Ohio (c)	★	...	★	★	★	★	A,B,C,D
Oklahoma	★	★	★	★	★	★	A,B,C,D
Oregon	★	★(f)	★	★	★	•	A,B,C,D
Pennsylvania	★	★	★	★	★	★	A,B
Rhode Island	★	★	...	★	★	★	A,B,C
South Carolina	«(a)	★(h)	★	...	(i)	•	A,B,C,D
South Dakota	★	★	★	★	★	★	A,B,C
Tennessee	★	(e)(f)	(f)	★	...	★	A,B,C,D
Texas	★	...	...	★	★	•	A,B,D
Utah	★(j)	★	★(j)	...	★(k)	•	A (l),B,C,D (l)
Vermont	★	★	★	★	★	★	A,B,C
Virginia	★	(f)	★	★(k)	★(k)	•	A,B,C,D
Washington	★	...	★	★	★	★	A,B,D
West Virginia	★	...	★	★	★	★	A,B,D
Wisconsin	★	★	★	★	★	★	A,B,C (g)
Wyoming	★	...	★	★	★	•	A,B
Dist. of Columbia	★	★(m)	★	★	★	★	A,B,C,D
American Samoa	★	★	★	★	★	...	...
Guam	★	★	★	★	★	•	A,B,C,D
CNMI*	★	★	★	★	★	★	A,B
Puerto Rico	★	★	...	...	...	★	A,B,C,D
U.S. Virgin Islands	★	★	★	★	★	•	A

See footnotes at end of table

TABLE 4.22
Attorneys General: Consumer Protection Activities, Subpoena Powers and Antitrust Duties (continued)

Sources: The Council of State Governments' survey of attorneys general, state constitutions and statutes, 2020.

*Commonwealth of Northern Mariana Islands

Key:

A–Has parens patriae authority to commence suits on behalf of consumers in state antitrust damage actions in state courts.

B–May initiate damage actions on behalf of state in state courts.

C–May commence criminal proceedings.

D–May represent cities, counties and other governmental entities in recovering civil damages under federal or state law.

★ –Has authority in area.

… –Does not have authority in area.

(a) May represent state on behalf of: the "people" of the state; an agency of the state; or the state before a federal regulatory agency.

(b) In this column only: ★ broad powers and ●limited powers.

(c) Also provides service to consumers through the Identity Theft Unit, administration of Ohio's Title Defect Rescission Fund, and the registration of non-charitable telephone solicitors.

(d) In certain cases only.

(e) May commence criminal proceedings with local district attorney.

(f) To a limited extent.

(g) May represent other governmental entities in recovering civil damages under federal or state law.

(h) When permitted to intervene.

(i) On a limited basis because the state has a separate consumer affairs department.

(j) Attorney general has exclusive authority.

(k) Attorney general handles legal matters only with no administrative handling of complaints.

(l) Opinion only, since there are no controlling precedents.

(m) In antitrust, not criminal proceedings.

(n) The office can issue Civil Investigative Demands, but would go to court in order to get a subpoena.

TABLE 4.23
Attorneys General: Duties to Administrative Agencies and Other Responsibilities

State or other jurisdiction	Serves as counsel for state	Appears for state in criminal appeals	Duties to administrative agencies							
			Issues official advice	Interprets statutes or regulations	Conducts litigation:		Prepares or reviews legal documents	Represents the public before the agency	Involved in rule-making	Reviews rules for legality
					On behalf of agency	Against agency				
Alabama	A,B,C (a)	★ (a)	★	★	★	★	(b)	(b)	★	★
Alaska	A,B,C	★	★	★	★	★	★	★	★	★
Arizona	A,B,C	★	★	★	★	...	★	...	★	★
Arkansas	A,B,C	★	★	★	★	★	★	★	...	...
California	A,B,C	★	★	★	★	...	★	...	★	★
Colorado	A,B,C	★	★	★	★	★	★	★	★	★
Connecticut	A,B,C	(b)	★	★	★	★	★	★	★	★
Delaware	A,B,C	★(d)	★	★	★	★	★	★	★	★
Florida	A,B,C	★	★	★	★	...	★	...	...	...
Georgia	A,B,C	★	★	★	★	...	★	...	...	★
Hawaii	A,B,C	★	★	★	★	★	★	★	★	★
Idaho	A,B,C	★	★	★	★	★	★	★	★	★
Illinois	A,B,C	★	...	★	★	...	★	...	...	...
Indiana	A,B,C	★	★	★	★	...	★	...	★	★
Iowa	A,B,C	★	★	★	★	★	★	★	★	★
Kansas	A,B,C	★	★	★	★	★	★	...	★	★
Kentucky	A,B,C	★	★	★	★	...	...	★	...	...
Louisiana	A,B,C	★ (m)	★	★	★	...	★	★	★	★
Maine	A,B,C	★	★	★	★	...	★	...	...	★
Maryland	A,B,C	★	★	★	★	(b)	★	★	★	★
Massachusetts	A,B,C	(b)(c)(d)	★	★	★	★	★	★	★	★
Michigan	A,B,C	★	★	★	★	★	★	★	★	★
Minnesota	A,B,C	(c)(d)	★	★	(a)	★	★	★	★	★
Mississippi	A,B,C	...	★	★	★	...	★	...	...	...
Missouri	A,B,C	★	★	★	★	...	★	...	★	...
Montana (f)	A,B,C	★	★	★	★	...	★	...	...	...
Nebraska	A,B,C	★	★	★	★	★	★	...	...	★
Nevada	A,B,C	★	★	★	★	...	★	...	★	★
New Hampshire	A,B,C	★	★	★	★	...	★	(l)	★	...
New Jersey	A,B,C	★	★	★	★	...	★	...	★	★
New Mexico	A,B,C	★	★	★	★	★	★	★	★	★
New York	A,B,C	(b)	...	★	★	(b)	★	(b)	...	...
North Carolina	A,B,C	★	...	★	★	★	★	(b)	★	★
North Dakota	A,B,C	★	★	★	★	★	★	...	★	★
Ohio	A,B,C	...	★	...	★	...	★	...	...	...
Oklahoma	A,B,C	★	★	★	★	★	★	★	★	★
Oregon	A,B	★	★	★	★	...	★	...	★	★
Pennsylvania	A,B	...	...	...	★	...	★	...	...	★
Rhode Island	A,B,C	★	★	★	★	★	★	...	...	...
South Carolina	A,B,C	★ (d)	(a)	★	★	(b)	★	...	★	★
South Dakota	A,B,C	★	★	★	★	★	★	...	...	...
Tennessee	A,B,C	★	★	★	★	...	★	(e)	(e)	★
Texas (g)	A,B	★ (k)	★	★	★	...	★	...	★	...
Utah	A,B,C	★ (a)	★	★	★	★	★	(b)	★	★
Vermont	A,B,C	★	★	★	★	★	★	★	★	★
Virginia	A,B,C	★	★	★	★	★	★	★	★	★
Washington	A,B,C	★ (i)	★	★	★	★	★	★	★	★
West Virginia	A,B,C	★	★	★	★	★	★	...	(j)	(j)
Wisconsin	A,B,C	★	★	★	★	(b)	(b)	(b)	(b)	(b)
Wyoming	A,B,C	★	★	★	★	★	★	...	★	★
Dist. of Columbia	A,B	★ (h)	★	★	★	...	★	...	★	★
American Samoa	A,B,C	★ (a)	★	★	★	...	★	...	★	★
Guam	A,B,C	★	★	★	(d)	★	★	(b)	★	★
CNMI*	A,B,C	★	★	★	★	★	★	...	★	★
Puerto Rico	A,B,C	★	★	★	★	...	★	...	★	★
U.S. Virgin Islands	A,B	★	★	★	★	★	★	★	...	★

See footnotes at end of table

TABLE 4.23

Attorneys General: Duties to Administrative Agencies and Other Responsibilities (continued)

Sources: The Council of State Governments' survey of attorneys general, state constitutions and statutes, 2020.

* Commonwealth of Northern Mariana Islands

Key:

A – Defend state law when challenged on federal constitutional grounds.

B – Conduct litigation on behalf of state in federal and other states' courts.

C – Prosecute actions against another state in U.S. Supreme Court.

★ – Has authority in area.

… – Does not have authority in area.

(a) Attorney general has exclusive jurisdiction.

(b) In certain cases only to prepare or review legal documents and represent the public before the agency.

(c) When assisting local prosecutor in the appeal.

(d) Can appear on own discretion.

(e) Consumer Advocate Division represents the public in utility rate making hearings and rule making proceedings.

(f) Most state agencies are represented by agency counsel who do not answer to the attorney general. The attorney general does provide representation for agencies in conflict situations and where the agency requires additional or specialized assistance.

(g) Other administrative duties include representing one state agency before another state agency.

(h) However, OUSA handles felony cases and most major misdemeanors.

(i) Limited to certain collateral challenges to state criminal convictions.

(j) On request of agency. Office acts as legal counsel to any state agency on request and that can include reviewing legislation and drafting rules and regulations.

(k) Regarding criminal appeals, the Office of Attorney General handles federal habeas corpus appeals only.

(l) The Attorney General serves as counsel for the public before 1 administrative body, but otherwise does not represent the public before agencies.

(m) May appear for the state in criminal appeals either as the actual prosecutor in the case or through the solicitor general if the state has a broader interest.

TABLE 4.24
The Treasurers and Other Chief Financial Officers: 2020

State or other jurisdiction	Name and party	Method of selection	Length of regular term in years	Date of first service	Present term ends	Maximum consecutive terms allowed by constitution
Alabama	John McMillan (R)	E	4	1/2019	1/2023	2
Alaska	Pamela Leary	A	Governor's Discretion	1/2014	…	…
Arizona	Kimberly Yee (R)	E	4	1/2019	1/2023	2
Arkansas	Dennis Milligan (R)	A	4	1/2015	1/2023	2
California	Fiona Ma (D)	E	4	1/2019	1/2023	2
Colorado	Dave Young (D)	E	4	1/2019	1/2023	2
Connecticut	Shawn Wooden (D)	E	4	1/2019	1/2023	★
Delaware	Colleen Davis (D)	E	4	1/2019	1/2023	★
Florida (a)	Jimmy Patronis (R) (b)	E	4	6/2017 (b)	1/2023	2
Georgia	Lynne Riley	A	Pleasure of the Board	5/2019	…	…
Hawaii (c)	Craig Hirai	A	Governor's Discretion	12/2019	…	…
Idaho	Julie Ellsworth (R)	E	4	1/2019	1/2023	★
Illinois	Mike Frerichs (D)	E	4	1/2015	1/2023	★
Indiana	Kelly Mitchell (R)	E	4	11/2014	1/2023	(d)
Iowa	Michael L. Fitzgerald (D)	E	4	1/1983	1/2023	★
Kansas	Jacob LaTurner (R)	E	4	4/2017	1/2023	★
Kentucky	Alison Ball (R)	E	4	1/2016	1/2024	2
Louisiana	John Michael Schroder Sr. (e)	E	4	11/2017 (e)	12/2023	★
Maine	Henry Beck	L	2	1/2019	1/2021	4
Maryland	Nancy K. Kopp (D)	L	4	2/2002	1/2023	★
Massachusetts	Deb Goldberg (D)	E	4	1/2015	1/2023	★
Michigan	Rachael Eubanks	A	Governor's Discretion	2019	…	…
Minnesota (f)	Myron Frans	A	Governor's Discretion	1/2015	…	…
Mississippi	David McRae (R)	E	4	1/2020	1/2024	★
Missouri	Scott Fitzpatrick (R) (i)	E	4	1/1/2019 (i)	1/2021	2
Montana	Gene Walborn	A	Governor's Discretion	5/2018	…	…
Nebraska	John Murante (R)	E	4	1/2019	1/2023	2
Nevada	Zach Conine (D)	E	4	1/2019	1/2023	2
New Hampshire	William Dwyer	L	2	12/2014	1/2021	★
New Jersey	Elizabeth Muoio	A	Governor's Discretion	1/2018	…	…
New Mexico	Tim Eichenberg (D)	E	4	1/2015	1/2023	2
New York	Christopher Curtis	A	Governor's Discretion	8/2016	…	…
North Carolina	Dale Folwell (R)	E	4	1/2017	1/2021	★
North Dakota	Kelly L. Schmidt (R)	E	4	1/2005	1/2021	★
Ohio	Robert Sprague (R)	E	4	1/2019	1/2023	2
Oklahoma	Randy McDaniel (R)	E	4	1/2019	1/2023	★
Oregon	Tobias Read (D)	E	4	1/2017	1/2021	2
Pennsylvania	Joseph Torsella (D)	E	4	1/2017	1/2021	2
Rhode Island	Seth Magaziner (D)	E	4	1/2015	1/2023	2
South Carolina	Curtis Loftis (R)	E	4	1/2011	1/2023	★
South Dakota	Josh Haeder (R)	E	4	1/2019	1/2023	2
Tennessee	David H. Lillard Jr.	L	2	1/2009	1/2021	…
Texas (g)	Glenn Hegar (R)	E	4	1/2015	1/2023	★
Utah	David Damschen (R) (h)	E	4	12/1/2015 (h)	12/2020	★
Vermont	Elizabeth Pearce (D)	E	2	1/2011	1/2021	★
Virginia	Manju Ganeriwala	A	Governor's Discretion	1/2009	…	…
Washington	Duane Davidson (R)	E	4	1/2017	1/2021	★
West Virginia	John D. Perdue (D)	E	4	1/1997	1/2021	★
Wisconsin	Sarah Godlewski (D)	E	4	1/2019	1/2023	★
Wyoming	Curt Meier (R)	E	4	1/2019	1/2023	★
American Samoa	Ueli Tonumaipea	A	4	N/A	…	…
Dist. of Columbia	Bruno Fernandes	A	Pleasure of CFO	8/2018	N/A	…
Guam	Rosita Fejeran	CS	…	N/A	…	…
CNMI*	Mark Rabauliman	A	4	N/A	N/A	…
Puerto Rico	Francisco Pares	A	4	7/2019	N/A	…
U.S. Virgin Islands	Kirk Callwood Sr.	A	4	1/2019	N/A	…

See footnotes at end of table

TABLE 4.24
The Treasurers and Other Chief Financial Officers: 2019 (continued)

Source: The Council of State Governments, January 2020.
* Commonwealth of Northern Mariana Islands
Key:
★–No provision specifying number of terms allowed.
…–No formal provision, position is appointed or elected by governmental entity (not chosen by the electorate).
A–Appointed by the governor. (In the District of Columbia, the Treasurer is appointed by the Chief Financial Officer. In Georgia, position is appointed by the State Depository Board.)
E–Elected by the voters.
L–Elected by the legislature.
CS–Civil Service
N/A–Not available
(a) The official title of the office of state treasurer is Chief Financial Officer.

(b) Gov. Rick Scott appointed Patronis after Jeff Atwater's resignation.
(c) The Director of Finance performs this function.
(d) Eligible for eight out of any period of twelve years.
(e) John Michael Schroder Sr. won the special election in 2017 to fill John Kennedy's term after he was elected to the U.S. Senate. He was elected to a full four-year term in 2019.
(f) The Commissioner of Management and Budget performs this function.
(g) The Comptroller of Public Accounts performs this function.
(h) Damschen was appointed in December 2015 to after Richard Ellis' resignation. He was elected to a full term in November 2016.
(i) Fitzpatrick was appointed in January 2019 after Treasurer Schmitt was appointed as attorney general.

TABLE 4.25
Treasurers: Qualifications for Office

State	Minimum age	U.S. citizen (years)	State resident (years)	Qualified voter (years)
Alabama	25	7	5	...
Alaska	...	...	...	...
Arizona	25	10	5	★
Arkansas	18	★	★	★
California	18	★	★	★
Colorado	25	★	2	★
Connecticut	18	★	★	★
Delaware	18	...	...	...
Florida	30	★	7	★
Georgia	...	...	...	...
Hawaii	...	★	1	...
Idaho	25	★	2	...
Illinois	25	★	3	...
Indiana	...	★	★	★
Iowa	18	...	★	★
Kansas	...	...	...	...
Kentucky	30	2	2	★
Louisiana	25	5	5	★
Maine	...	★	★	...
Maryland	...	...	...	...
Massachusetts	...	...	5	...
Michigan	...	...	...	...
Minnesota	...	...	...	...
Mississippi	25	★	5	...
Missouri	30	15	10	★
Montana	...	...	...	...
Nebraska	...	★	★	★
Nevada	25	2	2	★
New Hampshire	...	...	...	...
New Jersey	...	...	★	...
New Mexico	30	★	5	★
New York	30	★	5	...
North Carolina	21	★	1	★
North Dakota	25	★	5	★
Ohio	18	★	★	★
Oklahoma	31	★	10	10
Oregon	31	★	10	★
Pennsylvania	...	...	...	...
Rhode Island	18	★	30 days	★
South Carolina	18	★	★	★
South Dakota	...	...	...	...
Tennessee	...	...	...	...
Texas	18	★	★	...
Utah	25	★	5	★
Vermont	...	★	★	...
Virginia	...	...	...	...
Washington	18	★	...	★
West Virginia	18	★	5	★
Wisconsin	18	★	★	★
Wyoming	25	★	★	★
Dist. of Columbia	...	★	...	...

Source: The Council of State Governments' survey of state treasurers
offices, November 2019.
Key:
★ – Formal provision; number of years not specified.
... – No formal provision.
(a) Five years immediately preceding the date of qualification for
office.

TABLE 4.26
Responsibilities of the Treasurer's Office

State or other jurisdiction	Cash management	Banking services	Investment of retirement funds	Investment of trust funds	Deferred compensation	Management of bonded debt	Bond issuance	Debt service	Arbitrage	Unclaimed property	Archives for disbursement of documents	College savings	Collateral programs	Local government investment pool	Other
Alabama	★	★	...	★	...	★	...	★	...	★	...	★	★	...	...
Alaska	★	★	★	★	...	...	★	★	★	★	...	...	...	...	...
Arizona	★	★	...	★	...	...	...	...	...	...	...	...	...	★	...
Arkansas	★	★	★	...	...	...	...	...	...	...	...	★	...	★	...
California	★	★	...	★	...	★	★	★	★	...	...	★	★	★	...
Colorado	★	★	...	★	...	...	★	★	...	★	...	...	...	...	...
Connecticut	★	★	★	★	...	★	★	★	★	...	...	★	...	★	(a)
Delaware	★	★	...	★	★	★	...	★	...	...	...	★	...	...	(b)
Florida	★	★	...	★	★	...	...	...	...	★	...	...	★	...	(c)
Georgia	★	★	...	★	...	...	...	...	...	...	...	★	★	★	(d)
Hawaii	★	★	★	★	...	...	★	★	...	...	...	★	...	...	...
Idaho	★	★	...	...	...	★	...	...	...	★	...	★	...	★	...
Illinois	★	★	...	★	...	...	★	★	★	...	...	★	...	★	...
Indiana	★	★	★	★	...	★	...	...	...	...	★	★	...	★	(n)
Iowa	★	★	★	...	...	★	★	★	...	★	...	★	★	...	(d)
Kansas	★	★	...	...	...	...	...	...	...	★	...	★	...	...	(e)
Kentucky	★	★	...	...	...	...	...	...	...	★	★	...	...	...	(p)
Louisiana	★	★	...	★	...	★	★	★	★	...	...	★	★	★	(f)
Maine	★	★	★	...	...	★	★	★	★	...	...	★	...	...	(f)
Maryland	★	★	...	...	...	★	★	★	★	...	...	...	★	★	...
Massachusetts	★	★	★	★	★	★	★	★	★	...	★	...	...	★	...
Michigan	★	★	★	★	...	★	★	★	★	...	★	...	...	...	...
Minnesota	★	★	...	...	...	★	★	...	...	...	...	...	...	...	...
Mississippi	★	★	★	★	...	★	★	★	★	★	...	★	★	★	...
Missouri	★	★	...	★	...	...	...	★	★	...	...	★	...	...	(g)
Montana	★	★	...	...	...	★	★	★	★	...	...	...	★	...	(o)
Nebraska	★	★	...	...	...	...	...	...	...	★	...	★	...	...	(h)
Nevada	★	★	...	★	...	★	★	★	...	★	...	★	★	★	(m)
New Hampshire	★	★	...	★	...	★	★	★	★	★	...	★	...	...	...
New Jersey	★	★	★	★	★	★	★	★	★	★	...	...	...	★	...
New Mexico	★	★	...	...	...	★	...	★	...	...	★	...	...	★	...
New York	★	★	★	★	...	...	...	...	...	...	...	★	...	...	...
North Carolina	★	★	★	★	★	★	★	★	★	★	...	...	...	★	(q)
North Dakota	★	...	★	★	...	...	...	...	...	...	...	...	...	...	(i)
Ohio	★	★	...	★	...	★	★	★	★	...	...	...	★	★	...
Oklahoma	★	★	...	★	...	★	...	...	...	★	...	★	...	...	...
Oregon	★	★	★	★	★	★	★	★	...	...	...	★	★	★	...
Pennsylvania	★	★	...	...	...	★	★	★	★	★	...	★	...	★	...
Rhode Island	★	★	★	★	★	★	★	★	★	★	...	★	...	★	(l)
South Carolina	★	★	★	★	...	★	★	★	★	★	...	★	★	★	...
South Dakota	★	★	★	★	...	...	...	...	...	★	...	...	★	...	...
Tennessee	★	★	★	...	★	...	...	...	...	★	...	★	★	★	...
Texas	★	★	...	★	...	...	...	...	...	★	...	★	★	★	(j)
Utah	★	★	...	★	...	★	★	★	★	★	...	...	...	★	...
Vermont	★	★	★	★	★	★	★	★	★	★	...	...	...	...	...
Virginia	★	★	...	★	...	★	★	★	★	★	...	...	★	★	(k)
Washington	★	★	...	★	...	★	★	★	★	...	...	...	...	★	...
West Virginia	★	★	...	★	★	...	...	★	...	★	...	★	★	★	...
Wisconsin	...	...	...	...	...	...	...	...	...	★	...	...	...	★	...
Wyoming	★	★	...	★	...	★	★	★	★	★	...	...	...	★	(n)
Dist. of Columbia	★	★	★	★	★	★	★	★	★	★	...	★	★	...	...

See footnotes at end of table

TABLE 4.26
Responsibilities of the Treasurer's Office (continued)

Source: The Council of State Governments' survey of state treasurers offices, November 2019.

Key:

★–Responsible for activity.

...–Not responsible for activity.

(a) Second Injury Fund.

(b) Merchant services.

(c) State Accounting Disbursement, Fire Marshall, Insurance and Banking Consumer Services, Insurance Rehabilitation.

(d) Merchant card services and ABLE program.

(e) Municipal bond servicing.

(f) Municipal Revenue Sharing.

(g) Investment of all state funds; administers ABLE program.

(h) Nebraska Child Support Payment Center, Long-Term Care Savings Plan.

(i) Tax collection and distribution, investments, financial literacy. The treasurer serves on the State Investment Board, State Board of Equalization, State Historical Board, Teachers Fund for Retirement Board, Board of Trust Lands, State Canvassing Board.

(j) Tax administration, revenue collection, revenue estimating, state purchasing manager, various other legislatively designated programs.

(k) Risk Management.

(l) Crime Victims Compensation Program.

(m) Education Savings Accounts.

(n) The treasurer serves as the trustee of the Indiana State Police Pension Trust.

(o) Social Security Section 218 agreements; merchant card (Procard) services.

(p) STABLE KY (ABLE program) and the Kentucky Financial Empowerment Commission.

(q) The Treasurer serves on the State Banking Commission, the State Board of Education, the State Board of Community Colleges, the Teachers' and State Employees' Retirement System (TSERS) Board of Trustees, the Local Governmental Employees' Retirement System (LGERS) Board of Trustees, the Supplemental Retirement Plans (SRP) Board of Trustees, the State Health Plan for Teachers and State Employees (SHP) Board of Trustees, the Local Government Commission (LGC), the NC Capital Facilities Finance Agency (NCFFA), the Debt Affordability Advisory Committee and the NC Housing Partnership Board. Other responsibilities include: administration of TSERS, LGERS, SRP, SHP, LGC, and NCCFFA; local government debt approval; and monitoring fiscal health of local governments.

TABLE 4.27
State Auditors: 2020

State or other jurisdiction	State Agency	Agency head	Title	Legal basis for office	Method of selection	Term of office	U.S. citizen	State resident	Maximum consecutive terms allowed
Alabama	Department of Examiners of Public Accounts	Rachel Riddle	Chief Examiner	S	LC	7 yrs.	★	...	None
Alaska	Division of Legislative Audit	Kris Curtis	Legislative Auditor	C, S	L	(a)	...	...	None
Arizona	Office of the Auditor General	Lindsey Perry	Auditor General	S	LC	5 yrs.	...	...	None
Arkansas	Division of Legislative Audit	Roger A. Norman	Legislative Auditor	S	LC	Indefinite	★	★	None
California	Bureau of State Audits	Elaine M. Howle	State Auditor	S	G	4 yrs.	★	...	None
Colorado	Office of the State Auditor	Dianne E. Ray	State Auditor	C,S	LC	5 yrs.	...	...	None
Connecticut	Office of the Auditors of Public Accounts	John C. Geragosian and Robert Kane	State Auditors	S	L	4 yrs.	...	...	None
Delaware	Office of the Auditor of Accounts	Kathleen McGuiness	Auditor of Accounts	C, S	E	4 yrs.	★	★	None
Florida	Office of the Auditor General	Sherrill F. Norman	Auditor General	C, S	L	(a)	...	...	None
Georgia	Department of Audits and Accounts	Greg S. Griffin	State Auditor	S	L	Indefinite	...	...	None
Hawaii	Office of the Auditor	Les Kondo	State Auditor	C	L	8 yrs.	...	★	None
Idaho	Legislative Services Office - Legislative Audits	April J. Renfro	Division Manager	S	LC	(b)	...	...	None
Illinois	Office of the Auditor General	Frank Mautino	Auditor General	C, S	L	10 yrs.	...	...	None
Indiana	State Board of Accounts	Paul D. Joyce	State Examiner	S	GLC	4 yrs.	...	...	None
Iowa	Office of the Auditor of State	Rob Sand	Auditor of State	C, S	E	4 yrs.	★	★	None
Kansas	Legislative Division of Post Audit	Justin Stowe	Interim Legislative Post Auditor	S	LC	(b)	...	...	None
Kentucky	Office of the Auditor of Public Accounts	Mike Harmon	Auditor of Public Accounts	C, S	E	4 yrs.	★	★	2
Louisiana	Office of the Legislative Auditor	Daryl G. Purpera	Legislative Auditor	C, S	L	(a)	...	★	None
Maine	Department of Audit	Pola A. Buckley	State Auditor	S	L	4 yrs.	...	...	2
Maryland	Office of Legislative Audits	Gregory A. Hook	Legislative Auditor	S	ED	Indefinite	...	...	None
Massachusetts	Office of the Auditor of the Commonwealth	Suzanne M. Bump	Auditor of the Commonwealth	C, S	E	4 yrs.	★	★	None
Michigan	Office of the Auditor General	Doug Ringler	Auditor General	C	L	8 yrs.	...	★	None
Minnesota	Office of the Legislative Auditor	James R. Nobles	Legislative Auditor	S	LC	6 yrs. (a)	...	...	None
	Office of the State Auditor	Julie Blaha	State Auditor	C	E	4 yrs.	★	★	None
Mississippi	Office of the State Auditor	Shad White	State Auditor	C	E	4 yrs.	★	★	None
Missouri	Office of the State Auditor	Nicole Galloway	State Auditor	C, S	E	4 yrs.	★	★	None
Montana	Legislative Audit Division	Angus Maciver	Legislative Auditor	C, S	LC	2 yrs.	...	...	None
Nebraska	Office of the Auditor of Public Accounts	Charlie Janssen	Auditor of Public Accounts	C	E	4 yrs.	★	★	None
Nevada	Legislative Counsel Bureau, Audit Division	Daniel Crossman	Legislative Auditor	S	LC	Indefinite	...	...	None
New Hampshire	Office of the Legislative Budget Assistant	Michael W. Kane	Legislative Budget Assistant	S	LC	2 yrs. (b)	...	...	None
New Jersey	Office of the State Auditor	Stephen M. Eells	State Auditor	C, S	L	5 yr. term and until successor is appointed	★	★	None
	Office of the State Comptroller	Kevin Walsh	Acting State Comptroller	S	G	6 yrs.	...	★	2
New Mexico	Office of the State Auditor	Brian S. Colon	State Auditor	C, S	E	4 yrs.	★	★	2
New York	Office of the State Comptroller, State Audit Bureau	Thomas P. DiNapoli	State Comptroller	C, S	E	4 yrs.	★	★	None
North Carolina	Office of the State Auditor	Beth A. Wood	State Auditor	C	E	4 yrs.	★	★	None
North Dakota	Office of the State Auditor	Joshua Gallion	State Auditor	C, S	E	Indefinite	...	★	None
Ohio	Office of the Auditor of State	Keith Faber	Auditor of State	C, S	E	4 yrs.	...	...	2
Oklahoma	Office of the State Auditor and Inspector	Cindy Byrd	State Auditor and Inspector	C, S	E	4 yrs.	★	★	None
Oregon	Division of Audits	Kip Memmott	Director	C, S	SS	Indefinite	...	...	None
Pennsylvania	Department of the Auditor General	Eugene DePasquale	Auditor General	C, S	E	4 yrs.	...	...	2
Rhode Island	Office of the Auditor General	Dennis E. Hoyle	Auditor General	S	LC	(b)	...	...	None
South Carolina	Legislative Audit Council	Earle Powell	Director	S	LC	4 yrs.	...	...	None
	Office of the State Auditor	George Kennedy	State Auditor	S	SB	Indefinite (c)	...	...	None

See footnotes at end of table

TABLE 4.27
State Auditors: 2020 (continued)

State or other jurisdiction	State Agency	Agency head	Title	Legal basis for office	Method of selection	Term of office	U.S. citizen	State resident	Maximum consecutive terms allowed
South Dakota	Department of Legislative Audit	Martin L. Guindon	Auditor General	S	L	8 yrs. (a)	…	…	None
Tennessee	Comptroller of the Treasury, Dept. of Audit	Justin P. Wilson	Comptroller of the Treasury	C, S	L	2 yrs.	…	…	None
Texas	Office of the State Auditor	Lisa Collier	State Auditor	S	LC	(b)	…	…	None
Utah	Office of the State Auditor	John Dougall	State Auditor	C, S	E	4 yrs.	★	★	None
Vermont	Office of the State Auditor	Douglas R. Hoffer	State Auditor	C, S	E	2 yrs.	…	★	None
Virginia	Office of the Auditor of Public Accounts	Martha S. Mavredes	Auditor of Public Accounts	C, S	L	4 yrs.	…	…	None
Washington	Office of the State Auditor	Pat McCarthy	State Auditor	C, S	E	4 yrs.	★	★	None
West Virginia	Legislative Auditor's Office	Aaron Allred	Legislative Auditor	S	L	(a)	…	…	None
Wisconsin	Legislative Audit Bureau	Joe Chrisman	State Auditor	S	LC	Indefinite (b)	…	…	None
Wyoming	Department of Audit	Jeffrey C. Vogel	Director	S	GC	6 yrs.	…	★	None
Dist. Of Columbia	Office of the D.C. Auditor	Kathleen Patterson	District of Columbia Auditor						
American Samoa	AS Territorial Auditor Office	Liua Fatuesi	Territorial Auditor						
Guam	Office of the Public Auditor	Benjamin Cruz	Public Auditor	S	E	4 yrs.	★	★	None
CNMI*	Office of the Public Auditor	Michael Pai	Public Auditor	C,S,	GL	6 yrs.	N.A.	N.A.	2
Puerto Rico	Office of the Comptroller	Yesmin M. Valdivieso-Galib	Comptroller	C,S,	GL	10 yrs.	★	★	1
U.S. Virgin Islands	Office of the Inspector General	Steven van Beverhoudt	Inspector General						

Source: Auditing in the States: A Summary, 2019 edition, The National Association of State Auditors, Comptrollers and Treasurers.

* Commonwealth of Northern Mariana Islands

Key:
★–Provision for.
…–No provision for
E–Elected by the public.
L–Appointed by the legislature.
G–Appointed by the governor.
SS–Appointed by the secretary of state.
LC–selected by legislative committee, commission or council.
ED–appointed by the executive director of legislative services
GC–Appointed by governor, secretary of state and treasurer.
GL–Appointed by the governor and confirmed by both chambers of the legislature
GLC–Appointed by the governor and confirmed by legislative council
SB–Appointed by state budget and control board.
C–Constitutional
S–Statutory
N.A.– Not applicable.
(a) Serves at the pleasure of the legislature.
(b) Serves at the pleasure of a legislative committee.
(c) The term is indefinite, but the state auditor serves at the pleasure of the five-member board.

TABLE 4.28

State Auditors: Audit of Basic Financial Statements and Single Audit

State or other jurisdiction	Auditing of basic financial statements				Conducting the single audit			
	State audit agency conducts audit (100%)	State audit agency is primary auditor—% of total governmental, business type, fiduciary and component unit expenditures contracted to CPA firms	CPA firm(s) conducts audit (100%)	Selection of auditor if part/all of financial audit is contracted out	State audit agency conducts audit (100%)	State audit agency conducts part/CPA firm conducts part—% conducted by CPA firm	CPA firm(s) conducts audit (100%)	Selection of auditor if part/all of single audit is contracted out
Alabama	…	N/A	…	Individual departments/agencies	…	★ 0.4%	…	Individual departments/agencies
Alaska	…	★We summarize outside audit coverage by percent of assets and percent of revenue. Governmental activities: 89% assets/59% revenues; business type activities: 77% assets/66% revenues; aggregate discretely presented component units: 91% assets/92% revenues	…	Most of the outside audited entities are governmental corporations and the University. The outside entities select their own auditors. However, there are a few that require the legislative auditor approve the outside auditor.	…	★ 24.8%	…	State corporations select their own auditor.
Arizona	…	★ governmental (51.2%), business type activities (16.6%), blended component units - fiduciary funds (99.05%), discretely presented component units (55.49%)	…	The audited agency selects the auditor with help from the Auditor General's Office.	…	★ 85.33%	…	The audited agency selects the auditor with input from the Auditor General's Office.
Arkansas	…	★ 8.03%	…	State agency	…	★ 4.31%	…	The individual agency receiving a private audit selects the auditor.
California	★	…	…	…	…	…	★	The state auditor selects the contract auditor.
Colorado	…	★	…	…	…	★ 20%	…	State auditor
Connecticut	…	★ governmental (0%), business type activities (<1%), fiduciary (0%), component unit (100%)	…	…	★	…	…	…
Delaware	…	…	★	Office of Auditor of Accounts	★	…	…	Office of Auditor of Accounts
Florida	…	★ governmental (0%), business type activities (35.27%), fiduciary (1.88%), component unit (35%)	…	The agencies or entities being audited.	★	…	…	…
Georgia	…	★ governmental activities (3% of total assets, 7% of net position/fund balance, and 3% of total revenues/additions); business type activities (3% total assets and 6% of total net position/fund balance); aggregate discretely presented component units (86% of total assets, 79% of net position/fund balance, and 86% of total revenues/additions); governmental fund - general obligation bond fund projects (100% of total assets, 100% of net position/fund balance, and 100% of total revenues/additions); aggregate remaining fund information (87% of total assets, 48% of total revenues/additions)	…	The entity being audited selects the CPA firm through a bid process. The cost of audits performed by CPAs are paid by the audited entity.	★	★ 8% (92% audited by DOAA)	…	The state entities administering the major programs select the CPA firms.
Hawaii	…	…	★	Office of the Auditor	…	…	★	Office of the Auditor
Idaho	…	★ governmental (4.7%), business type activities (83.8%), fiduciary (100%), component unit (98%)	…	The entity going out for contract.	★	…	…	…
Illinois	★	…	…	…	…	…	★	Office of the Auditor General
Indiana	…	★ 2% (public employee's retirement system and component units are contracted to CPA firms)	…	The governing body of the component unit.	★	…	…	…
Iowa	…	…	★	Office of Auditor of State	★	…	…	…
Kansas	…	…	★	Contract Audit Committee	…	…	★	Contract Audit Committee

See footnotes at end of table

TABLE 4.28

State Auditors: Audit of Basic Financial Statements and Single Audit (continued)

State or other jurisdiction	Auditing of basic financial statements				Conducting the single audit			
	State audit agency conducts audit (100%)	State audit agency is primary auditor—% of total governmental, business type, fiduciary and component unit expenditures contracted to CPA firms	CPA firm(s) conducts audit (100%)	Selection of auditor if part/all of financial audit is contracted out	State audit agency conducts audit (100%)	State audit agency conducts part/ CPA firm conducts part—% conducted by CPA firm	CPA firm(s) conducts audit (100%)	Selection of auditor if part/all of single audit is contracted out
Kentucky	…	★ governmental activities (1.57%), business type activities (26.12%), component units (90.88%)	…	The Office of the Auditor of Public Accounts has the right of first refusal for all agencies and component units of the state. We decline some agencies/component units and allow the agency to contract with a CPA firm.	★	…	…	…
Louisiana	…	★ governmental (0%), business type activities (7.41%), fiduciary (61.96%), aggregate discretely component unit (15.9%) - Note: fiduciary funds are included in aggregate remaining funds	…	Legislative auditor	★	Single audits of some agencies are performed by CPA firms. The SEFA amounts in these stand-alone reports are not included in the SEFA in LA's Single Audit report.	…	…
Maine	★	…	…	…	★	…	…	…
Maryland	…	…	★	State Comptroller's Office	…	…	★	State Comptroller's Office
Massachusetts	…	…	★	Office of the State Comptroller	…	…	★	Office of the State Comptroller
Michigan	…	★ governmental (2% assets/2.6% revenues), business type (98.7% assets/80.8% revenues), fiduciary (6.4% assets/6.7% additions), component unit (95.2% assets/91.6% revenues)	…	14 component units (10 state universities and four others) and one enterprise fund select their own auditor. All other contract auditors are selected by the auditor general.	…	★ 6%	…	One component unit selects their own and the auditor general selects the rest.
Minnesota Legislative Auditor	…	★ business type activities (60%), component units (99%)	…	Each BTA and CU selects their own auditor	…	★ 7.1% (student financial assistance cluster)	…	Minnesota State (BTA) selects its own auditor.
State Auditor	…	Not involved in the state's financial audit	…	…	…	…	…	Not involved in state's single audit.
Mississippi	…	★ governmental (6-19%), business type activities (100%), fiduciary (100%), component units (100%)	…	Proposals are submitted to the Office of the State Auditor and are selected by representatives of the office with comments by the agencies being audited and Department of Finance and Administration (comptroller) considered.	…	★ 10%	…	The auditor is selected by the Office of the State Auditor with input from the state agencies and the Department of Finance and Administration.
Missouri	…	★ 32.2%	…	Generally, the entity being audited selects the auditor.	…	★ Single audits of public universities and other component units are performed by CPA firms. The federal award expenditures of these entities are not included in the state's SEFA.	…	The auditor is selected by the entity being audited.
Montana	★	…	…	…	★	…	…	…
Nebraska	★	…	…	…	★	…	…	…
Nevada	…	…	★	Audit Subcommittee of the Legislative Commission	…	…	★	Audit Subcommittee of the Legislative Commission
New Hampshire	…	★ 80%	…	Legislative budget assistant	…	…	★	Legislative budget assistant
New Jersey	…	Not involved in the state's financial audit	…	…	…	…	…	…
State Auditor	…	★ governmental activities (4%), business type activities (47%), fiduciary (99%), component units (100%)	…	Department of the Treasury, Judiciary, individual component units.	…	…	★	Department of the Treasury, Office of Management and Budget
State Comptroller	…	…	…	…	…	…	…	Not involved in state's single audit.

See footnotes at end of table

TABLE 4.28

State Auditors: Audit of Basic Financial Statements and Single Audit (continued)

State or other jurisdiction	Auditing of basic financial statements				Conducting the single audit			
	State audit agency conducts audit (100%)	State audit agency is primary auditor—% of total governmental, business type, fiduciary and component unit expenditures contracted to CPA firms	CPA firm(s) conducts audit (100%)	Selection of auditor if part/all of financial audit is contracted out	State audit agency conducts audit (100%)	State audit agency conducts part/CPA firm conducts part—% conducted by CPA firm	CPA firm(s) conducts audit (100%)	Selection of auditor if part/all of single audit is contracted out
New Mexico	...	★ Financial statement audits are prepared at a department level. The department level financial statements are used to compile the statewide CAFR. The Office of the State Auditor has a limited staff of auditors who conduct audits of agencies. Therefore, most of these engagements are performed by Independent Public Accountants.	...	Agencies that are contracting with Independent Public Accountants select an auditor from a list of audit firms approved on an annual basis by the Office of the State Auditor.	...	★ OSA has a limited staff of auditors who conduct audits of agencies. Therefore, most of these engagements are performed by Independent Public Accountants approved by the office.	...	Single audits are done at the department level, not statewide. Agencies that are contracting with Independent Public Accountants select an auditor from a list of audit firms approved on an annual basis by the Office of the State Auditor.
New York	...	...	★	Office of the State Comptroller	...	...	★	Office of the State Comptroller and Governor's Division of the Budget
North Carolina	★	...	...		★		...	
North Dakota	...	★ governmental (1.85%), business type (47%), fiduciary (99%), component unit (100%)	...	The state auditor selects the auditor.	...	★ Single audits of some agencies are performed by CPA firms. The SEFA amounts in these stand-alone reports are not included in the SEFA in ND's single audit report. 3% of major federal program expenditures were passed through to these agencies and audited by a CPA firm.	...	The Office of the State Auditor selects the auditor.
Ohio	...	★ Percentages are available in Ohio's 2018 CAFR, Independent Auditor's Report	...	Auditor of state makes selection with input from component units and other state officials.	★		...	
Oklahoma	...	★ governmental (4.03%), business type (83.31%), fiduciary (100%), component unit (100%);	...	It varies depending on statutory requirements.	...	★ outside audited major programs to total audited major programs (1.16%). Outside audited major programs to total SEFA expenditures (0.98%)	...	It varies depending on statutory requirements.
Oregon	...	★ fiduciary (95%), component unit (100%)	...	Division of Audits, via RFP process	★		...	
Pennsylvania	...	★ governmental (14%), business type (6%), fiduciary & component unit (100%)	...	Governor's Office of the Budget (audited entity)	...	★ 15% major program expenditure coverage	...	Governor's Office of the Budget
Rhode Island	N/A	N/A	N/A	N/A	N/A	N/A	N/A	N/A
South Carolina								
Legislative Audit Council	...	Our office does not have anything to do with financial audits in our state. The office of the state auditor is responsible for all financial audits, including contracting out.	...		...		...	Office of the State Auditor
State Auditor	...	★ governmental (60%), business type (80%), component units (100%)	...	Office of the State Auditor	...	★ single audit is a joint opinion issues by our office and a CPA firm	...	Office of the State Auditor
South Dakota	...	★ business type (10%), discretely presented component units (55%); remaining fund information (90%)	...	The audited entity with approval of Department of Legislative Audit	...	★ it depends of the year. A few grants are audited by CPA firms for agencies that have contracted audit services. Department of Legislative Audit audits the majority of grants.	...	Auditor is selected by the state agency, but the auditor and the final report must be approved by the Department of Legislative Audit.

See footnotes at end of table

TABLE 4.28
State Auditors: Audit of Basic Financial Statements and Single Audit (continued)

State or other jurisdiction	Auditing of basic financial statements				Conducting the single audit			
	State audit agency conducts audit (100%)	State audit agency is primary auditor—% of total governmental, business type, fiduciary and component unit expenditures contracted to CPA firms	Selection of auditor if part/all of financial audit is contracted out	CPA firm(s) conducts audit (100%)	State audit agency conducts audit (100%)	State audit agency conducts part/CPA firm conducts part—% conducted by CPA firm	CPA firm(s) conducts audit (100%)	Selection of auditor if part/all of single audit is contracted out
Tennessee	★	…		…	★		…	
Texas	…	★ 20.4%	The state entity receiving the audit	…	…	★ CPA firm is the primary auditor for the federal compliance portion of the single audit providing 66% coverage. Our office covers the remaining.	…	Texas State Auditor's Office
Utah	…	★ governmental (0.79%), business type (19.02%), fiduciary (19.32%), component unit (46.05%)	State auditor or contract officer	…	…	★ 15.75%	…	State auditor or contract officer
Vermont	…	…	Auditor of Accounts	★	…	…	★	Auditor of accounts
Virginia	…	★ We audit all of the primary government, except one business type entity that is a major fund and represents 60% of BTA total assets and deferred outflows and 38% of BTA net position. And we also do not audit one blended component unit that represents 2.4% of governmental activities assets/deferred outflows and 5% of governmental activities net position. We also do not audit some component units representing 29% of assets and deferred outflows, 24% of net position, and 8% of revenues of the aggregated discretely presented component unit opinion unit.	Most of the outsourced component units select their own auditor; however, we do handle the bidding process for a few of these entities. We also handle the bidding process for the BTA audit that is outsourced.	…	★	…		
Washington	…	★ 18%	We have allowed agencies to select their auditor.	…	★	…	…	
West Virginia Performance Evaluation Research Division	…	…						
Post Audit Division	…	…	The legislative auditor	★	…	…	★	The legislative auditor
Wisconsin	…	★ 16.4%	The auditee	…	★	…	…	
Wyoming	…	N/A	Department of Audit	★	…	…	★	Department of Audit
Guam	N/A	N/A	N/A	N/A	N/A	N/A	N/A	N/A
Puerto Rico	…	…	The CEO of each agency.	★	★	…	★	The CEO of each agency

Sources: Auditing in the States: A Summary, 2019 edition. The National Association of State Auditors, Comptrollers and Treasurers.

Key:
★—Provision for responsibility.   …—No provision for responsibility.   N/A—Did not respond.

TABLE 4.29
State Auditors: Audits of Local Governments

State or other jurisdiction	Audits local governments	Cities, towns & villages	Counties	Non-profit organizations/ for-profits receiving state/ federal awards	School districts
			Types of local governments audited		
Alabama	★	…	★(100%)	…	★(100% county school districts)
Alaska	…		…	…	
Arizona	★	…	★(67%)	…	…
Arkansas	★	★(92.4%)	★(100%)	…	★(81.7%)
California	★	★	★	★	★
Colorado	…	…	…	…	…
Connecticut	…	…		…	
Delaware	…	…		…	…
Florida	★	…	…	…	★(100%)
Georgia	★	…	…	…	★(approx. 84%)
Hawaii	…	…	…	…	…
Idaho	…	…	…	…	…
Illinois	★	…	…	…	…
Indiana	★	★(99%)	★(99%)	…	★(99%)
Iowa	★	★(10%)	★(40%)	…	★(1%)
Kansas	…	…	…	…	…
Kentucky	★	…	★(36%)	…	…
Louisiana	★	…	…	…	…
Maine	…	…	…	…	…
Maryland	…	…	…	…	…
Massachusetts	★	★	★	★	★
Michigan	…	…	…	…	…
Minnesota					
Legislative Auditor	…	…	…	…	…
State Auditor	★	★(0.4%)	★(47%)	…	…
Mississippi	★	…	★(30%)	…	…
Missouri	★	…	★(78%)	…	★
Montana	…	…	…	…	…
Nebraska	★	★(1%)	★(18%)	★(<1%)	★(<1%)
Nevada	…	…	…	…	…
New Hampshire	…	…	…	…	…
New Jersey					
State Auditor	★	…	…	…	★(<5% a year)
State Comptroller	★	★	★	★	★
New Mexico	★	…	…	…	…
New York	★	★(100%)	★(100%)	★(100%)	★(100%)
North Carolina	…	…	…	…	…
North Dakota	★	★(7%)	★(43%)	…	★(3%)
Ohio	★	★cities (33%); townships (62%); villages (62%)	★(78%)	…	★(65%)
Oklahoma	★	★(a)	★(100%)	★(a)	★(a)
Oregon	…	…	…	…	…
Pennsylvania	★	★	★	★	★(100%)
Rhode Island	N/A	N/A	N/A	N/A	N/A
South Carolina					
Legislative Audit Council	…	…	…	…	…
State Auditor	…	…	…	…	…
South Dakota	★	★a few, varies year to year	★(100%)	…	★a few, varies year to year
Tennessee	★	…	★(95%)	…	…
Texas	…	…	…	…	…
Utah	…	…	…	…	…
Vermont	…	…	…	…	…
Virginia	…	…	…	…	…
Washington	★	★(100%)	★(100%)	…	★(100%)
West Virginia					
Performance Evaluation					
Research Division	…	…	…	…	…
Post Audit Division	…	…	…	…	…
Wisconsin	…	…	…	…	…
Wyoming	★	★(2%)	…	…	★(20%)
Guam	N/A	N/A	N/A	N/A	N/A
Puerto Rico	★	★(100%)	…	…	★(100%)

See footnotes at end of table

TABLE 4.29
State Auditors: Audits of Local Governments (continued)

State or other jurisdiction	Types of local governments audited (con't.) Other	Audit standards used	GAAP required for local government financial statements
Alabama	...	GAAS, GAGAS	★
Alaska	...	...	...
Arizona	Community College Districts (92%)	GAAS, GAGAS, Federal Uniform Guidance	★
Arkansas	Prosecuting attorney judicial districts (100%)	GAAS, GAGAS; very small local governments may have a financial and compliance report in lieu of a full audit report.	No, regulatory basis per Arkansas Code.
California	Any publicly-created entity.	GAGAS	...
Colorado	...	...	...
Connecticut	...	GAGAS	★
Delaware	...	...	...
Florida	Cities, towns, etc., as directed by the Legislative Auditing Committee, through citizen petition, or the auditor general's discretion	GAAS, GAGAS	★
Georgia	...	GAGAS	★
Hawaii	...	...	...
Idaho	...	GAGAS	...
Illinois	As directed by the General Assembly	GAAS, GAGAS	By statute, GAAP is to be followed to the extent possible. Some smaller units of local government report on a cash basis.
Indiana	Public libraries, townships, special taxing districts, and state universities.	GAAS, GAGAS (c)	No, regulatory basis.
Iowa	Intergovernmental entities organized under Chapter 28E of the Code of Iowa, landfills, community colleges, area education agencies, merged area schools, hospitals	GAAS, GAGAS	GAAP is required for counties, schools, hospitals, community colleges, area education agencies and merged area schools; cash basis is used for cities, landfills and entities organized under Chapter 28E of the Code of Iowa.
Kansas	...	...	...
Kentucky	Clerk fee - 100%; sheriff fee - 100%; sheriff tax settlements - 100%	GAAS, GAGAS	No. Regulatory basis for 115/120 counties; 5 of 120 counties follow GAAP.
Louisiana	Almost all audit and other attest engagements of local governments are performed by CPA firms that are approved by the legislative auditor. However, the legislative auditor has the authority to perform local government audits in certain circumstances prescribe by the audit law. LLA's Financial Audit Services performed the audit of one local government (a retirement system) for the fiscal year ended 6/30/18.	GAGAS (d)	★ Louisiana local governments that may issue debt are required by LRS 24:514 to prepare their financial statements in accordance with GAAP.
Maine	...	GAAS, GAGAS	★
Maryland	...	GAAS	★
Massachusetts	Counties, cities, towns and school districts are audited by request. Nonprofit organizations are audited as vendors receiving state funds.	GAGAS	★
Michigan	...	...	...
Minnesota Legislative Auditor State Auditor	... Regional development commissions–10%	... GAGAS	... Most entities are required to prepare financial statements in accordance with GAAP. Very small entities report on a non-GAAP basis. Entities use both a cash basis and regulatory basis.
Mississippi	...	GAAS, GAGAS	Some counties prepare GAAP financial statements and some prepare OCBOA (cash/modified cash) financial statements.
Missouri	Other political subdivisions such as cities and special districts upon petition by a subdivision's voters. Also, performance audits of transportation development districts and community improvement districts under separate statutory authority.	GAGAS	No. Some local governments use cash basis.
Montana	...	GAAS, GAGAS	★
Nebraska	...	GAAS, GAGAS	No, cash basis
Nevada	...	...	...
New Hampshire	...	...	...
New Jersey State Auditor ⠀⠀⠀⠀⠀⠀⠀⠀⠀⠀⠀⠀⠀State Comptroller	There are 607 school districts in NJ. The office is statutorily required to audit any district with a negative fund balance. Also audits others based on a risk assessment. Actual school district audits - 3 to 4 per year. ...	GAGAS s GAGAS	School districts and public authorities follow GAAP; cities and counties follow OCBOA (modified cash basis) as required by Department of Community Affairs, Division of Local Government Services. ...

See footnotes at end of table

TABLE 4.29
State Auditors: Audits of Local Governments (continued)

State or other jurisdiction	Types of local governments audited (con't.) Other	Audit standards used	GAAP required for local government financial statements
New Mexico	The Office of the State Auditor has a limited staff of auditors who conduct audits of agencies, therefore, most of these engagements are performed by Independent Public Accountants.	GAAS, GAGAS	★Very small local governments may be eligible for an AUP engagement in lieu of a full audit. The determination is made based on cash basis annual revenue in accordance with the NM Audit Act. Use cash basis.
New York	...	GAGAS	★ The city of New York is required by law to prepare GAAP financial statements. School districts and Boards of Cooperative Education Services are required by the State Education Department to prepare GAAP financial statements. All other local governments are encouraged to do so, but are not required.
North Carolina	...	...	...
North Dakota	Parks, airports, soil conservation, water resource districts, health districts, and law enforcement centers - all types under 3% of total in ND.	GAAS, GAGAS, Uniform Guidance if single audit is required	No. Modified cash is used.
Ohio	Community schools - 33%	GAAS, GAGAS	★ Ohio Administrative Code 117-2-03 requires counties, cities and school districts, including educational service centers and community schools, and government insurance pools organized pursuant to section 9.833 or 2744.081 of the Ohio Revised Code to file annual financial reports prepared using GAAP. Other local governments follow OCBOA and regulatory basis.
Oklahoma	District attorneys - 100%; emergency medical service districts - 100%	GAAS, GAGAS (e)	No. Counties may chose GAAP or regulatory basis.
Oregon	...	GAAS, GAGAS	Cities and counties are required to follow GAAP, but other local government entities may not. They use cash/modified cash basis.
Pennsylvania	Audits of cities, towns, villages, and counties are only if part of the entity and not an audit of the complete entity. Examples are audits of pension plans that receive state funds and county offices that receive state funds or collect funds for the state with the audit limited to the state funds. All nonprofit volunteer firefighters' relief associations are audited, but other nonprofit or for-profit entities may receive state funds that we do not audit.	GAGAS (f)	No. Conducts primarily compliance audits related to state funding. Any financial audits are conducted by other auditors. For some engagements of counties and municipal government, conducts attestation examinations of statements prepared on a regulatory basis. Other audits of local governments are conducted as performance audits with the primary focus on compliance.
Rhode Island	N/A	N/A	N/A
South Carolina			
Legislative Audit Council	...	...	...
State Auditor	...	...	...
South Dakota	...	GAGAS	No. Not required of any local governments, but school districts all prepare GAAP statements. Local governments (other than school districts) generally use modified cash basis.
Tennessee	...	GAGAS	★
Texas	...	...	...
Utah	...	GAAS, GAGAS	★
Vermont	The office does not routinely audit municipalities, counties or school districts or nonprofits. However, statute gives us the authority to audit all three if state or federal money is involved.	(g)	No. Towns that do not use GAAP usually use cash basis.
Virginia	...	GAAS, GAGAS (h)	★
Washington	94%	GAAS, GAGAS	Local governments generally have a choice to report on either a regulatory cash basis of GAAP, although certain governments are required by regulatory or granting agencies to report GAAP. Also, school districts may report on regulatory modified-accrual basis, regulatory cash basis or GAAP.
West Virginia			
Performance Evaluation	...	...	...
Post Audit Division	...	...	...
Wisconsin	...	...	...
Wyoming	Audits not for financial purpose; schools done on about a 5-year cycle; town under 4,000 population done randomly approximately 2% per year.	GAGAS	★ Smaller entities can use cash basis.
Guam	N/A	N/A	N/A
Puerto Rico	...	GAAS (b)	★

See footnotes at end of table

AUDITORS AND COMPTROLLERS

TABLE 4.29
State Auditors: Audits of Local Governments (continued)

Sources: Auditing in the States: A Summary, 2019 edition. The National Association of State Auditors, Comptrollers and Treasurers and state constitutions and statutes.
Key:
★–Yes
…–No
N/A – Did not respond
GAAP – Generally Accepted Accounting Principles
GAAS – Generally Accepted Auditing Standards
GAGAS – Generally Accepted Government Auditing Standards
SAS – Statement on Auditing Standards
(a) Special investigative audits only.
(b) For audits started before June 30, 2016, the Office of the Comptroller had its own set of auditing standards. After July 1, 2016, all audits are performed under GAGAS.

(c) GAGAS is the standard for single audits only.
(d) Louisiana Revised Statute 24:513A. (5)(a)(i) requires CPAs to perform the audits and review engagements of local governments in accordance with GAGAS.
(e) Special investigative audits do not follow standards.
(f) Most, but not all, local government audits are conducted in accordance with GAGAS.
(g) Some towns have elected auditors and others hire external auditors (CPA firms). For those towns that hire external auditors, GAGAS is utilized.
(h) Localities are also required to follow the Auditor of Public Accounts Specifications for Audits, which include additional audit procedures specifically related to compliance with state laws and regulations.

TABLE 4.30
State Comptrollers, 2020

State	Agency or office	Name	Title	Legal basis for office	Method of selection	Approval or confirmation, if necessary	Length of term	Elected comptrollers maximum consecutive terms	Civil service or merit system employee
Alabama	Office of the State Comptroller	Kathleen Baxter	State Comptroller	S	(c)	AG	(b)	...	★
Alaska	Division of Finance	Hans Zigmund	Director, Department of Administration	S	(d)	AG	(a)	...	★
Arizona	General Accounting Office	Michael Smarick	Interim State Comptroller	S	(d)	AG	(b)	...	...
Arkansas	Dept. of Finance and Administration	Larry Walther	Chief Fiscal Officer, Director	S	G	...	(a)	...	...
	Office of the State Auditor	Andrea Lea	State Auditor						
California	Office of the State Controller	Betty Yee (D)	State Controller	C	E	...	4 yrs.	2 terms	...
	Department of Finance	Richard Gillihan	Chief Operating Officer						
Colorado	Department of Personnel and Administration	Bob Jaros	State Controller	S	(d)	AG	(o)	...	★
Connecticut	Office of the Comptroller	Kevin P. Lembo (D)	Comptroller	C	E	...	4 yrs.	unlimited	...
Delaware	Dept. of Finance	Jane Cole	Director, Division of Accounting	S	G	AL	(a)	...	...
Florida	Dept. of Financial Services	Jimmy Patronis	Chief Financial Officer	C,S	E	...	4 yrs.	2 terms	...
Georgia	State Accounting Office	Alan Skelton	State Accounting Officer	S	G	...	(a)	...	...
Hawaii	Dept. of Accounting and General Services	Curt Otaguro	State Comptroller	S	G	AS	4 yrs.	...	...
Idaho	Office of State Controller	Brandon Woolf	State Controller	C	E	...	4 yrs.	2 terms	...
Illinois	Office of the State Comptroller	Susana Mendoza (D)	State Comptroller	C	E	...	4 yrs.	unlimited	...
Indiana	Office of the Auditor of State	Tera Klutz	Auditor of State	C	E	...	4 yrs.	2 terms	...
Iowa	State Accounting Enterprise	Jay Cleveland	Chief Operating Officer	S	(d)	...	(i)	...	...
Kansas	Office of Accounts and Reports	Jocelyn Gunter	Director	S	(d)	...	(b)	...	...
Kentucky	Office of the Controller	Edgar C. Ross	Controller	S	(f)	AG	(i)	...	...
Louisiana	Office of Statewide Reporting and Accounting Policy	Afranie Adomako	Director, Division of Administration	S	G	...	(a)	...	...
Maine	Office of the State Controller	Douglas Cotnoir	State Controller	S	(f)	AG	(i)	...	...
Maryland	Office of the Comptroller of the Treasury	Peter Franchot (D)	State Comptroller	C	E	...	4 yrs.	unlimited	...
Massachusetts	Office of the Comptroller	Andrew Maylor	Comptroller	S	G	...	4 yrs	...	...
Michigan	Office of Financial Management	Heather Boyd	Director	S	SBD	SBD	(k)	...	★
Minnesota	Department of Finance	Myron Frans	Commissioner	S	G	AS	(a)	...	★
Mississippi	Department of Finance and Administration	Laura Jackson	Director, Office of Fiscal Management	C,S	G	...	(a)	...	...
Missouri	Division of Accounting	Stacy Neal	Director of Accounting	S	(d)	...	(i)	...	...
Montana	State Accounting Division	Cheryl Grey	Administrator	S	(m)	...	(b)	...	★
Nebraska	State Accounting Division	Philip Olsen	State Accounting Administrator	S	(d)	...	(b)	...	...
Nevada	Office of the State Controller	Catherine Byrne (D)	State Controller	C, S	E	...	4 yrs.	2 terms	...
New Hampshire	Department of Administration	Dana Call	State Comptroller	S	G	...	4 yrs.	...	...
New Jersey	Office of Management and Budget	David Ridolfino	State Comptroller	S	G	AS	(a)	...	...
New Mexico	Department of Finance and Administration, Financial Control Division	Donna Trujillo	State Controller	S	G	...	(a)	...	★
New York	Office of the State Comptroller	Thomas P. DiNapoli	State Comptroller	C,S	E	...	4 yrs.	unlimited	...
North Carolina	Office of the State Controller	Linda Combs	State Controller	S	G	GA	7 yrs.	...	...
North Dakota	Office of Management and Budget	Joe Morrisette	Director	S	G	...	(a)	unlimited	...
Ohio	Office of Budget and Management	Kim Murnieks	Director	S	G	...	(a)	...	...
Oklahoma	Office of State Finance	Lynne Bajema	State Comptroller	S	(g)	...	(h)	...	...
Oregon	Chief Financial Office	Robert Hamilton	Manager, Statewide Accounting and Reporting	S	(d)	...	(i)	...	...
Pennsylvania	Office of the Budget/ Comptroller Operations	Brian Lyman	Chief Accounting Officer	S	SBD	AG	(a)	...	...

See footnotes at end of table

TABLE 4.30
State Comptrollers, 2020 (continued)

State	Agency or office	Name	Title	Legal basis for office	Method of selection	Approval or confirmation, if necessary	Length of term	Elected comptrollers maximum consecutive terms	Civil service or merit system employee
Rhode Island	Office of Accounts and Control	Peter Keenan	State Controller	S	(d)	...	(b)	...	★
South Carolina	Office of the Comptroller General	Richard Eckstrom (R)	Comptroller General	C,S	E	...	4 yrs.	unlimited	...
South Dakota	Office of the State Auditor	Richard Sattgast (R)	State Auditor	C	E	...	4 yrs.	2 terms	...
	Bureau of Financial Management	Liza Clark	Commissioner	S	(n)	...	(a)		...
Tennessee	Division of Accounts	Mike Corricelli	Chief of Accounts	S	(f)	...	(b)	...	...
Texas	Office of the Comptroller of Public Accounts	Glenn Hegar (R)	Comptroller of Public Accounts	C,S	E	...	4 yrs.	unlimited	...
Utah	Division of Finance	John C. Reidhead	Director	S	(d)	AG	(i)	...	...
Vermont	Department of Finance and Management	Adam Greshen	Commissioner	S	(d)	AG,AS	(i)	...	...
Virginia	Department of Accounts	David A. Von Moll	State Comptroller	S	G	...	4 yrs.		...
Washington	Office of Financial Management	David Schumacher	Director	C	G	...		...	...
West Virginia	Office of the State Auditor	John McCuskey (R)	State Auditor	C	E	...	4 yrs.	unlimited	...
	Finance Division, Office of the State Comptroller	Dave Mullins	Acting Finance Director	S	(d)	AG	(a)(i)	...	...
Wisconsin	State Controller's Office	Carol Herwig	State Controller	S	CS	...	(b)	...	★
Wyoming	Office of the State Auditor	Kristi Racines (R)	State Auditor	C	E	...	4 yrs.	2 terms	...

Sources: Comptrollers: Technical Activities and Functions, 2018 edition, National Association of State Auditors, Comptrollers and Treasurers and The Council of State Governments, updated April 2020.

Key:
★ –Yes, provision for
... –No provision for
C–Constitutional
S–Statutory
N.A.–Not applicable
E– Elected by the public
G–Appointed by the Governor
CS–Civil Service
AG–Approved by the governor
AS–Approved/confirmed by the Senate
AL–Approved by the Legislature
SBD–Approved by State Budget Director
GA–Confirmed by the General Assembly
SDB–Confirmed by State Depository Board
(a) Serves at the pleasure of the governor. In South Dakota, also serves at the pleasure of the CFO.
(b) Indefinite.
(c) State merit system appointment; selected and recommended by state finance director.

(d) Appointed by the head of the department of administration or administrative services.
(e) Appointed by the head of finance. department or agency.
(f) Appointed by the head of financial and administrative services.
(g) Appointed by the director of management & enterprise services.
(h) Serves at the pleasure of the head of the director of management & enterprise services.
(i) Serves at the pleasure of the head of the financial and administrative services or administration.
(j) Appointed by the governor for a term coterminous with the governor.
(k) Two-year renewable contractual term; classified executive service.
(l) As of July 1, 2005, the responsibility for accounting and financial reporting in Georgia was transferred to the newly-created State Accounting Office.
(m) Hired through a selection process.
(n) Hired by the chief financial officer.
(o) One year contract similar to other division director.

TABLE 4.31
State Comptrollers: Qualifications for Office

State	Minimum age	U.S. citizen (years)	State resident (years)	Education years or degree	Professional experience and years	Professional certification and years	Other qualifications
Alabama	...	★	...	(n)	★, 10 yrs.	(a)	...
Alaska	...	...	...	...	...	...	...
Arizona	...	...	...	...	...	...	...
Arkansas	30	...	...	...	...	...	...
California	...	...	...	...	...	...	...
Colorado	...	...	...	...	...	...	...
Connecticut	...	...	...	...	...	...	...
Delaware	...	...	...	...	...	...	...
Florida	30	...	★, 7 yrs.	...	...	...	...
Georgia	...	...	...	...	...	...	...
Hawaii	...	...	30 days	...	...	...	...
Idaho	25	(b)	★, 2 yrs.	...	...	...	...
Illinois	25	★	★, 3 yrs.	...	...	...	...
Indiana	...	...	...	...	...	...	...
Iowa	...	...	...	...	...	...	...
Kansas	...	...	...	...	...	...	...
Kentucky	...	...	...	(c)	...	...	...
Louisiana	...	...	...	...	...	...	...
Maine	...	...	...	...	...	...	...
Maryland	...	...	...	...	...	...	...
Massachusetts	...	...	...	★(d)	...	...	...
Michigan	...	...	...	★, B.S.	★, 2 yrs.	...	...
Minnesota	...	...	...	...	...	...	...
Mississippi	...	...	...	...	...	...	(e)
Missouri	...	...	...	...	...	...	...
Montana	...	...	...	★(f)	★, 10 yrs.	★, CPA	...
Nebraska	...	...	...	★(g)	★, 3 yrs.	★, CPA	...
Nevada	25	★	★, 2 yrs.	...	...	...	...
New Hampshire	...	...	...	...	...	...	...
New Jersey	...	...	...	...	...	...	...
New Mexico	...	★	...	...	...	...	...
New York	30	★	★, (h)	...	...	...	...
North Carolina	...	...	...	★(i)	★	...	★(i)
North Dakota	...	...	...	...	...	...	...
Ohio	...	...	...	...	...	...	...
Oklahoma	...	★	...	...	...	...	...
Oregon	...	...	...	...	...	...	...
Pennsylvania	21	...	...	★, (j)	★, 10 yrs.	★, CPA	...
Rhode Island	...	★	...	★(k)	...	★, CPA	...
South Carolina	18	...	...	...	...	...	...
South Dakota	...	★	...	...	...	...	...
Tennessee	...	...	...	...	...	...	...
Texas	...	★(b)	...	...	...	...	...
Utah	...	★	...	★, (l)	★, 6 yrs.	★, CPA	...
Vermont	...	...	...	...	...	...	...
Virginia	...	...	...	...	...	...	...
Washington	...	★, Whole life	...	...	...	...	...
West Virginia- Office of State Auditor	25	★	...	...	...	...	...
Division of Finance, Office of State Comptroller	...	★	...	★, (m).	★, 4 yrs.	...	...
Wisconsin	...	...	...	★, (j)	...	★, CPA	...
Wyoming	25	★	...	...	...	...	...

See footnotes at end of table

TABLE 4.31
State Comptrollers: Qualifications for Office (continued)

Sources: Comptrollers: Technical Activities and Functions, 2018 edition, National Association of State Auditors, Comptrollers and Treasurers and The Council of State Governments, April 2020.

Key:

★ –Formal provision

… –No formal provision

N.A.–Not applicable

(a) One of the following CPA, CIA, CPM, CGFM or CGFO.

(b) Years not specified.

(c) In part the statute reads "the state controller shall be a person qualified by education and experience for the position and held in high esteem in the accounting community."

(d) Advanced degree in accounting, auditing, financial management, business administration or public administration (M.G.L.C. 7A, S.1)

(e) The executive director (a) shall be a certified public accountant ; or (b) shall possess a master's degree in business, public administration or a related field; or (c) shall have at least 10 yrs. experience in management in the private or public sector and a minimum of 5 yrs. experience in high level management with a documented record of management.

(f) Bachelor's degree in accounting.

(g) Four-year degree with a concentration in accounting.

(h) Five preceding elections.

(i) Qualified by education and experience for the office.

(j) Bachelor's degree

(k) Master's degree in accounting or business administration.

(l) Accounting or related college degree.

(m) College education with a major in business or public administration.

(n) Bachelor's degree with a major in accounting and a master's degree in accounting, business administration or public administration, both of which must be from an accredited college or university that is a member of one of the six regional accreditation associations in the United States.

TABLE 4.32
State Comptrollers: Duties, Responsibilities and Functions

State	Disbursements	Payroll	Tax reporting	Pre-audit	Post-audit	Operating the financial management system	Financial reporting	Debt management
Alabama	★	★	★	★	...	★	★	...
Alaska	★	★	★	...	...	★	★	...
Arizona	★	★	★	...	★	★	★	★
Arkansas	...	★	★	...	...	★	★	...
California	★	★	★	★	★	...	★	...
Colorado	★	★	★	★	...	★	★	...
Connecticut	★	★	★	★	★	★	★	...
Delaware	★	...	...	★	★	★	★	...
Florida	★	★	★	★	★	★	★	★
Georgia	...	...	...	...	...	★	★	...
Hawaii	★	★	...	★	★	★	★	...
Idaho	★	★	...	★	...	★	★	...
Illinois	★	★	★	★	★	★	★	...
Indiana	★	★	★	★	...	★	★	...
Iowa	★	★	★	★	★	★	★	...
Kansas	★	★	★	★	...	★	★	...
Kentucky	★	...	...	★	...	★	★	★
Louisiana	★	★	...	...	...	★	★	...
Maine	★	★	★	★	★	★	★	...
Maryland	★	★	★	★	★	★	★	...
Massachusetts	★	★	★	★	★	★	★	★
Michigan	...	★	★	...	...	★	...	...
Minnesota	★	★	...	...	...	★	★	★
Mississippi	★	★	...	★	★	★	★	...
Missouri	★	★	★	★	★	★	★	★
Montana	★	...	...	...	...	★	★	...
Nebraska	★	★	★	★	★	★	★	★
Nevada	★	...	★	...	...	★	★	...
New Hampshire	★	★	★	★	★	★	★	...
New Jersey	★	★	★	...	...	★	★	...
New Mexico	★	★	★	★	★	★	★	...
New York	★	★	★	★	★	★	★	★
North Carolina	★	★	...	...	...	★	★	...
North Dakota	★	★	★	...	...	★	★	...
Ohio	★	...	★	★	★	★	★	★
Oklahoma	★	★	★	★	★	★	★	...
Oregon	★	★	★	...	...	★	★	...
Pennsylvania	...	★	★	★	★	★	★	...
Rhode Island	★	★	...	★	★	★	★	...
South Carolina	★	★	...	★	...	★	★	...
South Dakota	★	★	★	★	...	...	...	...
Tennessee	★	★	...	★	★	...	★	...
Texas	★	★	★	★	★	★	★	...
Utah	★	★	...	...	★	★	★	★
Vermont	★	...	...	...	...	★	★	...
Virginia	★	★	...	★	★	★	★	...
Washington	...	...	...	...	...	...	★	...
West Virginia	★	★	★	★	★	...	★	...
Wisconsin	★	★	...	★	★	★	★	...
Wyoming	★	★	...	...	...	★	★	...

See footnotes at end of table

TABLE 4.32
State Comptrollers: Duties, Responsibilities and Functions (continued)

State	Investment management	Internal control oversight	Transparency	Quality assurance	Enterprise resource planning system responsibility	Data warehouse	Other
Alabama	...	CMIA	...	★	...	★	...
Alaska	...	...	...	★	...	★	(a)
Arizona	...	CMIA	★	★	...	★	...
Arkansas	...		...	★	...	★	...
California	...	★	★	★	...	...	(b)
Colorado	...	...	★	★	★	★	(c)
Connecticut	...	...	★	★	...	★	(d)
Delaware	...	...	★	★	★	...	(e)
Florida	★	★	...	★	...	★	(f)
Georgia	...	...	★	...	...	...	(g)
Hawaii	...	...	★	...	...	★	(h)
Idaho	...	...	...	★	...	★	(i)
Illinois	...	...	...	★	★	...	...
Indiana	...	...	...	★	...	★	(j)
Iowa	...	...	...	...	...	★	(k)
Kansas	...	...	★	★	...	...	(l)
Kentucky	★	★	★	★	...	★	(m)
Louisiana	...	...	...	★	...	★	(n)
Maine	...	...	★	★	★	★	(o)
Maryland	...	...	...	★	★	★	(p)
Massachusetts	...	...	★	★	★	★	(q)
Michigan	...	...	...	★	...	...	...
Minnesota	...	★	★	★	...	★	(r)
Mississippi	...	...	★	★	★	★	...
Missouri	...	...	★	★	...	...	(s)
Montana	...	★	...	...	...	...	(t)
Nebraska	...	...	★	★	★	...	(u)
Nevada	...	...	...	★	...	★	(v)
New Hampshire	...	...	...	★	...	...	(w)
New Jersey	...	★	...	...	...	...	(x)
New Mexico	...	★	★	...	★	...	(y)
New York	★	★	★	★	...	...	...
North Carolina	...	★	★	★	★	...	...
North Dakota	...	...	...	★	...	★	(z)
Ohio	...	...	★	★	★	...	(aa)
Oklahoma	...	...	...	★	★	...	(ab)
Oregon	...	...	...	★	★	★	(ac)
Pennsylvania	...	...	★	★	★	★(ad)	(ae)
Rhode Island	...	...	...	★	...	...	...
South Carolina	...	...	★	★	★	★	(af)
South Dakota	...	...	★	...	...	...	(ag)
Tennessee	...	...	...	★	★	...	(ah)
Texas	★	★	...	★	...	★	(ai)
Utah	...	...	★	★	★	★	(aj)
Vermont	...	...	★	...	...	...	(ak)
Virginia	...	...	★	★	★	...	...
Washington	...	...	...	...	...	...	(al)
West Virginia	...	...	...	...	...	...	(am)
Wisconsin	...	★	★	★	★	...	(an)
Wyoming	...	...	...	...	★(ao)	★(ao)	(ap)

See footnotes at end of table

TABLE 4.32
State Comptrollers: Duties, Responsibilities and Functions (continued)

Source: State Comptrollers: Technical Activities and Functions, 2018 edition, National Association of State Auditors, Comptrollers and Treasurers, April 2020.
Key:
★–Formal provision.
…–No formal provision.
CMIA–Cash Management Improvement Act of 1990
(a) Enterprise travel office and one-card program. Performs accounting for the Department of Revenue debt manager, but does not actually manage the debt program.
(b) Unclaimed property.
(c) Financial system operations; central collection services, purchasing and contracts.
(d) Also responsible for providing health insurance and other benefits to state employees and retirees; administer State Employee Retirement System and other retirement systems, and pays retiree pensions.
(e) Payroll compliance (not processing).
(f) State treasury–deposit security and funds management, risk management, and unclaimed property.
(g) Payroll shared services, state travel office and a/p shared services.
(h) Archives, records management, risk management, land survey, public works, office leasing, central services–repairs, custodial, district offices–school repairs and maintenance, motor pool and parking.
(i) Data center.
(j) Distributions to local governments. Administers the state's deferred compensation plan, Hoosier Start.
(k) Income offsets, CMIA and SWCAP, 1099 MISC and 1095 reporting.
(l) Municipals statewide, audit of agencies - new audit plan, internal control/systems monitoring. Tax reporting includes payroll tax withholding and remittance.
(m) State risk pools (fire and auto).
(n) Planning and budgeting, and facility planning and control (capital outlay).
(o) Risk management/self-insurance.
(p) Tax collection, tax compliance, field enforcement and revenue estimates.
(q) Risk management.
(r) Budget, human resources, cash management and management consulting.
(s) State Social Security administrator; general revenue cash flow monitoring/projections.
(t) Statewide procurement and contract services, local government audit and financial report review, and Social Security administration.
(u) Tax reporting limited to payroll and 1099; financial reporting includes SWCAP and single audit; P-card and federal letter of credit delayed draw administration.

(v) Tax reporting limited to 1099 reporting.
(w) Financial reporting includes SWCAP and single audit; financial management system is operated in conjunction with separate Division of Financial Data Management.
(x) Grant accounting and cash accounting.
(y) Systems functions are shared with the Department of Information Technology.
(z) Purchasing card program administration.
(aa) Budget, accounting and shared services, internal audit and 1099 reporting.
(ab) P-card administration (with state procurement) and state travel office.
(ac) Purchase card program administration. Statewide accounts receivable management.
(ad) The comptroller maintains reporting hierarchies for the CAFR in the data warehouse.
(ae) Employee travel planning and reimbursement, policy/planning, payable service center, contract review and internal audits.
(af) P-card administration (with state procurement) and state employee unemployment insurance program.
(ag) Bureau of Finance and Management also performs numerous comptroller functions.
(ah) Policy development, technical accounting training, CMIA and certain banking relationships.
(ai) The comptroller's office serves virtually every citizen in the state. As Texas' chief tax collector, accountant, revenue estimator, treasurer and purchasing managed, the agency is responsible for writing the check and keeping the books for the multi-billon dollar business of state government.
(aj) Loan servicing, debt collection, debt service, statewide accounting policies, CMIA, P-card administration, 1099 reporting. Shares system responsibilities with the Department of Technology Services.
(ak) Developing statewide budget, statewide accounting policies, SWCAP, SMIA, CAFR, single audit, train users in uses of statewide accounting system and 1099 reporting.
(al) Developing statewide budget, setting statewide admin. policies and procedures, HR policies/Labor Relations Office, and forecasting statewide population.
(am) Statewide accounting policies, SWCAP, Single Audit, and 1099 reporting.
(an) State treasury, SEFA report, Local Government Investment Pool, CAFR, Central Federal Draw, CMIA, 1099-Misc reporting, E-Payments.
(ao) Quality Assurance in the Office of State Auditor is for training on the state's uniform accounting system. Also, the data warehouse is for the state's uniform accounting system, which includes payroll data as well as financial data.
(ap) SEFA, TIN matching, 1099 reporting.

CHAPTER FIVE
STATE JUDICIAL BRANCH

TABLE 5.1
State Courts of Last Resort

State or other jurisdiction	Name of court	Justices chosen (a) At large	Justices chosen (a) By district	No. of judges (b)	Term (in years) (c)	Chief justice Method of selection	Term of office for chief justice
Alabama	S.C.	★		9	6	Partisan election	6 years
Alaska	S.C.	★		5	10	By court	3 years
Arizona	S.C.	★		7	6	Non-partisan popular election	5 years
Arkansas	S.C.	★		7	8	Non-partisan popular election	8 years
California	S.C.	★		7	12	Gubernatorial appointment with consent of Commission on Judicial Appointments	12 years
Colorado	S.C.	★		7	10	By court	10 years
Connecticut	S.C.	★		7	8	Gubernatorial appointment with consent of the legislature	8 years
Delaware	S.C.	★		5	12	Gubernatorial appointment from judicial nominating commission with consent of the legislature	12 years
Florida	S.C.	★(d)	★(d)	7	6	By court	2 years
Georgia	S.C.	★		9	6	By court	6 years
Hawaii	S.C.	★		5	10	Gubernatorial appointment from judicial nominating commission with consent of the senate	10 years
Idaho	S.C.	★		5	6	By court	4 years
Illinois	S.C.	★(e)	★(e)	7	10	By court	3 years
Indiana	S.C.	★		5	10	Judicial nominating commission	5 years
Iowa	S.C.	★		7	8	By court	8 years
Kansas	S.C.	★		7	6	By seniority of service	Duration of service
Kentucky	S.C.		★	7	8	By court	4 years
Louisiana	S.C.		★	7	10	By seniority of service	Duration of service
Maine	S.J.C.	★		7	7	Appointed by governor with consent of the legislature	7 years
Maryland	C.A.		★	7	10	Appointed by governor	To age 70
Massachusetts	S.J.C.	★		7	To age 70	Gubernatorial appointment with approval of elected executive council	To age 70
Michigan	S.C.	★		7	8	By court	2 years
Minnesota	S.C.	★		7	6	Non-partisan popular election	6 years
Mississippi	S.C.		★(g)	9	8	By seniority of service	Duration of service
Missouri	S.C.	★		7	12	By court	2 years
Montana	S.C.	★		7	8	Non-partisan popular election	8 years
Nebraska	S.C.	★(h)	★(h)	7	6	Gubernatorial appointment from judicial nominating commission	Duration of service
Nevada	S.C.	★		7	6	Rotation by seniority	(i)
New Hampshire	S.C.	★		5	To age 70	Gubernatorial appointment with approval of elected executive council	To age 70
New Jersey	S.C.	★		5	7/To age 70 (j)	Gubernatorial appointment with consent of the senate	7 years, plus tenure, to age 70
New Mexico	S.C.	★		5	8	By court	2 years
New York	C.A.	★		7	14	Gubernatorial appointment from judicial nominating commission with consent of the senate	14 years
North Carolina	S.C.	★		7	8	Partisan popular election	8 years
North Dakota	S.C.	★		5	10	By Supreme and District Court judges	5 years
Ohio	S.C.	★		7	6	Popular election (k)	6 years
Oklahoma	S.C.		★	9	6	By court	2 years
Oklahoma	S.C.	★		7	6	By court	6 years
Oregon	S.C.	★		7	10	Seniority	Duration of service
Pennsylvania	S.C.	★		5	Life	Gubernatorial appointment from judicial nominating commission with consent of the legislature	Hold office during good behavior
Rhode Island	S.C.	★		5	10	Legislative appointment	10 years
South Carolina	S.C.	★(l)	★(l)	5	8	By court	4 years
South Dakota	S.C.	★		5	8	By court	4 years / 2 years (m)
Tennessee	S.C.	★		9	6	Partisan election	6 years
Texas	S.C.	★		9	6	Partisan election	6 years
Texas	C.C.A.	★		9	6	Partisan election	6 years
Utah	S.C.	★		5	10	By court	4 years
Vermont	S.C.	★		5	6	Gubernatorial appointment from judicial nominating commission with consent of the legislature	6 years
Virginia	S.C.	★		7	12	By court	4 years
Washington	S.C.	★		9	6	By court	4 years
West Virginia	S.C.A.	★		5	12	By court	4 years
Wisconsin	S.C.	★		7	10	By court	2 years
Wyoming	S.C.	★		5	8	By court	4 years
Dist. of Columbia	C.A.	★		9	15	Judicial Nominating Commission appointment	4 years
Puerto Rico	S.C.	★		9	To age 70	Gubernatorial appointment with consent of the legislature	To age 70

See footnotes at end of table

TABLE 5.1
State Courts of Last Resort (continued)

Sources: National Center for State Courts, July 2020.
Key:
★ –Yes.
S.C. – Supreme Court
S.C.A. – Supreme Court of Appeals
S.J.C. – Supreme Judicial Court
C.A. – Court of Appeals
C.C.A. – Court of Criminal Appeals
(a) See Table 5.6, entitled, "Selection and Retention of Appellate Court Judges," for more detail.
(b) Number includes chief justice.
(c) The initial term may be shorter. See Table 5.6, entitled, "Selection and Retention of Appellate Court Judges," for more detail.
(d) Elected statewide, but each of five regional appellate districts entitled to at least one justice.
(e) Three justices chosen from First District (Cook County), rest from other Districts

(g) Three justices chosen from each of three districts
(h) Chief justice chosen statewide; associate judges chosen by district.
(i) The senior justice in commission is the chief justice, and in case the commissions of two or more of the justices bear the same date, the justices shall determine by lot who is the chief justice.
(j) All judges are subject to gubernatorial reappointment and consent by the Senate after an initial seven-year term; thereafter, they may serve until mandatory retirement at age 70.
(k) Party affiliation is not included on the ballot in the general election, but candidates are chosen through partisan primary nominations.
(l) Initially chosen by district; retention determined statewide.
(m) Four years for initial term; two years for additional terms.

Table 5.1 | State Courts of Last Resort

Number of Judges

9 JUDGES

 AL, GA, MS, OK, TX, WA, D.C., PR

7 JUDGES

 AZ, AR, CA, CO, CT, FL, IL, IA, KS, KY, LA, ME, MD, MA, MI, MN, MO, MT, NE, NV, NY, NC, OH, OR, PA, VA, WI

5 JUDGES

AK, DE, HI, ID, IN, NH, NJ, NM, ND, RI, SC, SD, TN, UT, VT, WV, WY

Term of Office for Judges

6 years · 15 states

7 years · 1 state

8 years · 12 states

10 years · 12 states

Life · 1 state

To age 70 · 3 states, 1 territory

15 years · 1 territory

14 years · 1 state

12 years · 5 states

Term of Office for Chief Justices

2 years · 6 states

3 years · 2 states

4 years 8 states/1 territory

5 years · 3 states

6 years · 7 states

Other · 4 states

To 70 · 3 states/1 territory

Duration of Service 5 states

14 years · 1 state

12 years · 2 states

10 years · 3 states

8 years · 5 states

7 years · 1 state

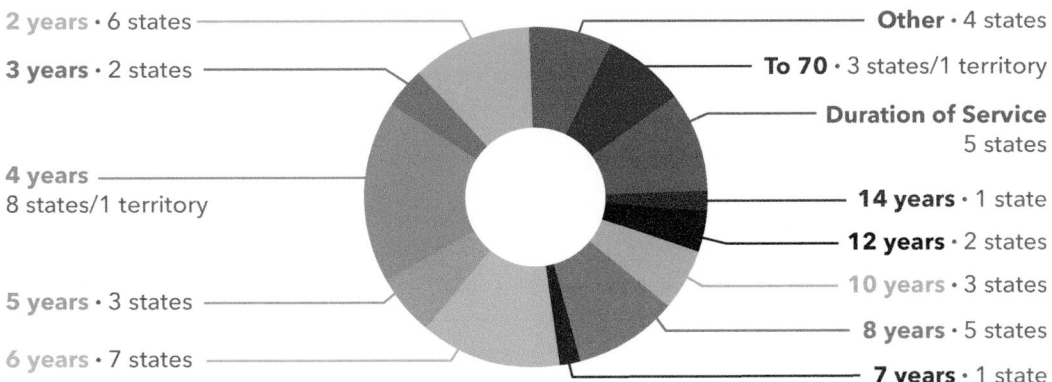

TABLE 5.2

State Intermediate Appellate Courts and General Trial Courts: Number of Judges and Terms

State or other jurisdiction	Intermediate appellate court			General trial court		
	Name of court	2020 No. of judges	Term (years)	Name of court	2020 No. of judges	Term (years)
Alabama	Court of Criminal Appeals	5	6	Circuit Court	144	6
	Court of Civil Appeals	5	6			
Alaska	Court of Appeals	3	8	Superior Court	42	6
Arizona	Court of Appeals	22	6	Superior Court	180	4
				Tax Court	1	4 (a)
Arkansas	Court of Appeals	12	8	Circuit Court	121	6
California	Courts of Appeal	99	12	Superior Court	1,680	6
Colorado	Court of Appeals	22	8	District Court	177 (b)	6
				Denver Juvenile Court	3	6
				Denver Probate Court	1	6
Connecticut	Appellate Court	9	8	Superior Court	163	8
Delaware	...	...	...	Superior Court	21	12
				Court of Chancery	5	12
Florida	District Courts of Appeals	64	6	Circuit Court	599	6
Georgia	Court of Appeals	15	6	Superior Court	213	4
Hawaii	Intermediate Court of Appeals	6	10	Circuit Court	30	10
Idaho	Court of Appeals	4	6	District Court	45	4
Illinois	Appellate Court	54	10	Circuit Court	934 (c)	6
Indiana	Court of Appeals	15	10	Superior Court, Probate Court and Circuit Court	317	6
	Tax Court	1	10			
Iowa	Court of Appeals	9	6	District Court	337 (d)	6
Kansas	Court of Appeals	14	4	District Court	245 (e)	4
Kentucky	Court of Appeals	14	8	Circuit Court	95	8
				Family Court	52	8
Louisiana	Courts of Appeal	53	10	District Court	218	6
				Juvenile & Family Court	18	6
Maine	...	...	...	Superior Court	17	7
				District Court	36	7
Maryland	Court of Special Appeals	15	10	Circuit Court	162	15
Massachusetts	Appeals Court	25	To age 70	Superior Court	77	To age 70
Michigan	Court of Appeals	27	6	Circuit Court	214	6
				Court of Claims	4	6
Minnesota	Court of Appeals	19	6	District Court	290	6
Mississippi	Court of Appeals	10	8	Circuit Court	57	4
Missouri	Court of Appeals	32	12	Circuit Court	346 (f)	6 (g)
Montana	...	...	...	District Court	46 (h)	6
				Water Court	5	4
				Workers' Compensation Court	1	6
Nebraska	Court of Appeals	6	6	District Court	55	6
Nevada	Court of Appeals	3	6	District Court	82	6
New Hampshire	...	...	...	Superior Court	22	To age 70
New Jersey	Appellate Division of Superior Court	33	7/To age 70 (i)	Superior Court	386	7/To age 70 (i)
New Mexico	Court of Appeals	10	8	District Court	94	6
New York	Appellate Division of Supreme Court	53	5 (j)	Supreme Court	269	14
	Appellate Terms of Supreme Court	11	Duration of term	County Court	122	10
North Carolina	Court of Appeals	15	8	Superior Court	104 (k)	8 (l)
North Dakota	Temporary Court of Appeals	3	1 (m)	District Court	51	6
Ohio	Courts of Appeals	69	6	Court of Common Pleas	449	6
Oklahoma	Court of Civil Appeals	12	6	District Court	241 (n)	4 (o)
Oregon	Court of Appeals	13	6	Circuit Court	172	6
				Tax Court	1	6
Pennsylvania	Superior Court	23	10	Court of Common Pleas	449 (p)	10
	Commonwealth Court	9	10			
Rhode Island	...	...	...	Superior Court	25 (q)	Life
South Carolina	Court of Appeals	9	6	Circuit Court	58	6
South Dakota	...	...	...	Circuit Court	43	8
Tennessee	Court of Appeals	12	8	Chancery Court	83	8
	Court of Criminal Appeals	12	8	Circuit Court	35	8
				Criminal Court	33	8
				Probate Court	2	8
Texas	Courts of Appeals	80	6	District Court	465	4
Utah	Court of Appeals	7	6	District Court	72	6
Vermont	...	...	...	Superior Court	34	6
Virginia	Court of Appeals	11	8	Circuit Court	157	8
Washington	Courts of Appeal	22	6	Superior Court	192	4

See footnotes at end of table

TABLE 5.2

State Intermediate Appellate Courts and General Trial Courts: Number of Judges and Terms (continued)

State or other jurisdiction	Intermediate appellate court			General trial court		
	Name of court	2020 No. of judges	Term (years)	Name of court	2020 No. of judges	Term (years)
West Virginia	…	…	…	Circuit Court	70	8
Wisconsin	Court of Appeals	16	6	Circuit Court	249	6
Wyoming	…	…	…	District Court	23	6
Dist. of Columbia	…	…	…	Superior Court	62	15
Puerto Rico	Court of Appeals	39	16	Court of First Instance	338 (r)	12 (s)

Source: National Center for State Courts, July 2020.
Key:
… – Court does not exist in jurisdiction or not applicable.
(a) Unless rotated to a different court by the presiding judge.
(b) Judges also serve Water Court.
(c) 514 circuit court judges and 378 associate judges.
(d) 146 of these are part-time judicial magistrates.
(e) Includes both district judges and district magistrate judges
(f) The number of Circuit Court judges includes associate judges.
(g) Associate circuit judges serve a term of four years.
(h) Three of those judges serve the Water Court.
(i) Followed by tenure. All judges are subject to gubernatorial reappointment and consent by the Senate after an initial seven-year term; thereafter, they may serve until mandatory retirement at age 70.
(j) Or duration.
(k) The number of Superior Court judges includes special judges.
(l) Special judges serve a term of four years.
(m) Assignments are for a specified time, not to exceed one year or the completion of one or more cases on the docket of the supreme court.
(n) The number of district court judges includes associate judges and special judges.
(o) District and associate judges serve four year terms; special judges serve at pleasure.
(p) Includes both active and senior judges.
(q) The number of judges includes magistrates.
(r) The number of Court of First Instance judges includes Municipal Division judges.
(s) Municipal judges serve a term of eight years.

TABLE 5.3
Qualifications of Judges of State Appellate Courts and General Trial Courts

State or other jurisdiction	Residency requirement				Minimum age		Legal Credentials	
	State		Local					
	A	T	A	T	A	T	A	T
Alabama	1 yr.	1 yr.	...	1 yr.	...	18	10 years state bar	5 years state bar
Alaska	5 yrs.	5 yrs.	...	...	...	...	8 years practice	5 years practice
Arizona	5/10 yrs. (a)	5 yrs.	(b)	1 yr.	30	30	(c)	(d)
Arkansas	...	...	★	...	...	...	8 years practice	6 years licensed in state
California	★	...	...	...	...	...	10 years state bar	10 years state bar
Colorado	★	★	...	★	...	...	5 years state bar	5 years state bar
Connecticut	★	★	...	...	...	...	Licensed attorney	Member of the bar
Delaware	★	★	...	★	...	...	"Learned in law"	"Learned in law"
Florida	★	★	★(f)	★(g)	...	...	10 years state bar	5 years state bar
Georgia	★	3 yrs.	...	must reside within court circuit	...	30	7 years state bar	7 years state bar
Hawaii	★	★	...	...	...	30	10 years state bar	10 years state bar
Idaho	2 yrs.	1 yr.	...	...	30	...	10 years state bar	10 years state bar
Illinois	★	★	★	★	...	...	Licensed attorney	Law degree
Indiana	★	1 yr.	...	...	...	...	10 years state bar (h)	Licensed attorney
Iowa	★	★	...	★	...	...	Licensed attorney	Admitted to state bar
Kansas	...	5 yrs.	...	...	30	30	10 years active and continuous practice (i)	5 years state bar
Kentucky	2 yrs.	2 yrs.	2 yrs.	2 yrs.	...	...	8 years state bar and licensed attorney	8 years state bar
Louisiana	1 yrs.	1 yrs.	1 yrs.	1 yrs.	...	...	10 years state bar	8 years state bar
Maine	...	...	...	...	...	...	"Learned in law"	1 year state bar
Maryland	5 yrs.	5 yrs.	6 mos.	6 mos.	30	30	State bar member	State bar member
Massachusetts	...	...	...	...	...	...	...	State bar member
Michigan	★	★	...	...	...	...	State bar member and 5 years practice	State bar member
Minnesota	30 days	30 days	...	30 days	...	...	Licensed attorney	Licensed attorney
Mississippi	5 yrs.	5 yrs.	★(j)	...	30	26	5 years state bar	5 years practice
Missouri	9 yrs. (k)	3 yrs. (k)	...	1 yr. (k)	30	30	State bar member	State bar member
Montana	2 yrs.	2 yrs.	...	...	...	...	5 years state bar	5 years state bar
Nebraska	3 yrs.	★	★	★	30	30	5 years practice	5 years practice
Nevada	2 yrs.	2 yrs.	...	...	25	25	State bar member (l)	2 years state bar member and 10 years practice
New Hampshire	...	...	...	...	...	...	10 years practice	State bar member
New Jersey	★	(m)	...	(m)	...	...	Admitted to practice in state for at least 10 years	10 years practice of law
New Mexico	3 yrs.	3 yrs.	...	★	35	35	10 years practice	6 years active practice
New York	★	★	...	...	...	18	10 years state bar	10 years state bar
North Carolina	...	★	...	(n)	...	...	State bar member	State bar member
North Dakota	★	★	...	★	...	...	License to practice law	State bar member
Ohio	★	★	...	★	...	...	6 years practice	6 years practice
Oklahoma	★	(o)	1 yr.	★	30	...	5 years state bar	(p)
Oregon	3 yrs.	3 yrs.	...	1 yr.	...	...	State bar member	State bar member
Pennsylvania	1 yr.	★	...	1 yr.	...	21	State bar member	State bar member
Rhode Island	...	...	...	...	21	...	License to practice law	State bar member
South Carolina	5 yrs.	5 yrs.	...	(q)	32	32	8 years state bar	8 years state bar
South Dakota	★	★	★	★	...	...	State bar member	State bar member
Tennessee	5 yrs.	5 yrs.	★(r)	1 yr.	35/30 (s)	30	License to practice law	License to practice law
Texas	★	...	...	2 yrs.	35	25	(t)	(u)
Utah	5 yrs.	3 yrs.	...	★	30	25	State bar member	State bar member
Vermont	...	...	...	...	...	...	5 years state bar	5 years state bar
Virginia	...	★	...	★	...	...	5 years state bar	5 years state bar
Washington	1 yr.	1 yr.	1 yr.	1 yr.	...	...	State bar member	State bar member
West Virginia	5 yrs.	★	...	★	30	30	10 years state bar	5 years state bar
Wisconsin	28 days	28 days	28 days	28 days	...	18	5 years state bar	5 years state bar
Wyoming	3 yrs.	2 yrs.	...	...	30	28	9 years practice	Law degree
Dist. of Columbia	N.A.	N.A.	90 days	90 days	...	...	5 years practice	5 years state bar (v)
Puerto Rico	5 yrs.	...	...	...	...	...	10 years practice	7 years state bar

See footnotes at end of table

TABLE 5.3
Qualifications of Judges of State Appellate Courts and General Trial Courts (continued)

Source: National Center for State Courts, July 2020.

Key:
A – Judges of courts of last resort and intermediate appellate courts.
T – Judges of general trial courts.
★ – Provision; length of time not specified.
... – No specific provision.
N.A.– Not applicable
(a) For court of appeals, five years.
(b) No local residency requirement stated for Supreme Court. Local residency of 3 years required for Court of Appeals.
(c) Supreme Court- 10 years state bar, Court of Appeals–five years state bar.
(d) Admitted to the practice of law in Arizona for five years.
(e) Court of Appeals minimum age is 30.
(f) The candidate must be a resident of the district at the time of the original appointment.
(g) Circuit court judge must reside within the territorial jurisdiction of the court.
(h) In the Supreme Court and the Court of Appeals, five years service as a general jurisdiction judge may be substituted.
(i) Relevant legal experience, such as being a member of a law faculty or sitting as a judge, may qualify under the 10 year requirement.
(j) Must reside within the district.
(k) At the appellate level must have been a state voter for nine years. At the general trial court level must have been a state voter for three years and resident of the circuit for one year.
(l) Minimum of two years state bar member and at least 15 years of legal practice.

(m) Restricted Superior court judgeships require residence within the particular county of assignment at time of appointment and reappointment.
(n) Resident judges of the Superior Court are required to have local residency, but special judges are not.
(o) District and associate judges must be state residents for six months if elected, and associate judges must be county residents.
(p) District Court: judges must be a state bar member for four years or a judge of court record. Associate judges must be a state bar member for two years or a judge of a court of record.
(q) Circuit judges must be county electors and residents of the circuit.
(r) Supreme Court: One justice from each of three divisions and two seats at large; no more than two may be from any grand division. Court of Appeals and Court of Criminal Appeals: Must reside in the grand division served.
(s) 35 for Supreme Court, 30 for Court of Appeals & Court of Criminal Appeals
(t) Ten years practicing law or a lawyer and judge of a court of record at least 10 years.
(u) District Court: judges must have been a practicing lawyer or a judge of a court in this state, or both combined, for four years.
(v) Superior Court: Judge must also be an active member of the unified District of Columbia bar and have been engaged, during the five years immediately preceding the judicial nomination, in the active practice of law as an attorney in the District, been on the faculty of a law school in the District, or been employed by either the by the United States or District of Columbia government.

TABLE 5.4
Compensation of Judges of Appellate Courts and General Trial Courts

State or other jurisdiction	Court of last resort	Appellate courts Chief Justice salaries	Associate Justice salaries	Intermediate appellate court	Judges salaries	General trial courts	Salary
Alabama	Supreme Court	$181,127	$172,716	Court of Criminal Appeals	$184,244	Circuit courts	$138,991
Alaska	Supreme Court	205,776	205,176	Court of Appeals	193,836	Superior courts	189,720
Arizona	Supreme Court	164,836	159,685	Court of Appeals	154,534	Superior courts	149,383
Arkansas	Supreme Court	183,600	174,925	Court of Appeals	169,672	Chancery courts	168,096
California	Supreme Court	256,059	253,189	Court of Appeals	237,365	Superior court	207,424
Colorado	Supreme Court	181,219	182,671	Court of Appeals	175,434	District courts	168,202
Connecticut	Supreme Court	200,599	185,610	Appellate Court	174,323	Superior courts	167,634
Delaware	Supreme Court	204,148	196,245	...	...	Superior courts	184,444
Florida	Supreme Court	178,420	220,600	District Court of Appeals	169,554	Circuit courts	160,688
Georgia	Supreme Court	175,600	175,600	Court of Appeals	174,500	Superior courts	173,714
Hawaii	Supreme Court	231,468	227,664	Intermediate Court	210,780	Circuit courts	205,080
Idaho	Supreme Court	149,700	151,400	Court of Appeals	141,400	District courts	135,400
Illinois	Supreme Court	229,345	234,391	Court of Appeals	220,605	Circuit courts	202,433
Indiana	Supreme Court	173,599	177,244	Court of Appeals	172,296	Circuit courts	147,164
Iowa	Supreme Court	183,001	174,808	Court of Appeals	158,420	District courts	147,494
Kansas	Supreme Court	142,793	142,089	Court of Appeals	137,502	District courts	125,499
Kentucky	Supreme Court	140,508	138,890	Court of Appeals	133,299	Circuit courts	127,733
Louisiana	Supreme Court	177,703	170,325	Court of Appeals	159,347	District courts	153,143
Maine	Supreme Judicial Court	154,981	138,070	...	...	Superior courts	129,397
Maryland	Court of Appeals	195,433	181,433	Court of Special Appeals	168,633	Circuit courts	159,433
Massachusetts	Supreme Judicial Court	199,989	200,984	Appellate Court	190,087	Superior courts	184,694
Michigan	Supreme Court	164,610	164,610	Court of Appeals	160,695	Circuit courts	146,721
Minnesota	Supreme Court	190,699	177,697	Court of Appeals	167,438	District courts	157,179
Mississippi	Supreme Court	159,000	152,250	Court of Appeals	144,827	Chancery courts	136,000
Missouri	Supreme Court	181,677	176,157	Court of Appeals	161,038	Circuit courts	151,840
Montana	Supreme Court	145,621	144,061	...	...	District courts	132,558
Nebraska	Supreme Court	173,694	176,299	Court of Appeals	167,484	District courts	163,077
Nevada	Supreme Court	170,000	170,000	Court of Appeals	165,000	District courts	160,000
New Hampshire	Supreme Court	167,271	175,837	...	...	Superior courts	164,911
New Jersey	Supreme Court	192,795	201,842	Appellate division of	191,534	Superior courts	181,000
New Mexico	Supreme Court	133,174	139,819	Court of Appeals	132,838	District courts	126,187
New York	Court of Appeals	222,500	230,200	Appellate divisions of	219,200	Supreme courts	208,000
North Carolina	Supreme Court	150,086	149,115	Court of Appeals	142,947	Superior courts	135,236
North Dakota	Supreme Court	161,517	157,009	...	...	District courts	143,869
Ohio	Supreme Court	174,700	172,200	Court of Appeals	160,500	Courts of common pleas	147,600
Oklahoma	Supreme Court	155,820	154,174	Court of Appeals	146,059	District courts	139,298
Oregon	Supreme Court	150,572	154,040	Court of Appeals	150,980	Circuit courts	142,136
Pennsylvania	Supreme Court	213,748	211,027	Superior Court	199,114	Courts of common pleas	183,184
Rhode Island	Supreme Court	193,458	183,872	...	...	Superior courts	165,545
South Carolina	Supreme Court	156,234	148,794	Court of Appeals	145,074	Circuit courts	141,354
South Dakota	Supreme Court	137,270	136,893	...	...	Circuit courts	127,862
Tennessee	Supreme Court	190,128	188,952	Court of Appeals	182,664	Chancery courts	176,364
Texas	Supreme Court	170,500	168,000	Court of Appeals	158,500	District courts	149,000
Utah	Supreme Court	180,500	182,950	Court of Appeals	174,600	District courts	166,300
Vermont	Supreme Court	166,130	163,757	...	...	Superior/District/Family	155,677
Virginia	Supreme Court	210,017	197,827	Court of Appeals	181,610	Circuit courts	171,120
Washington	Supreme Court	189,374	190,415	Court of Appeals	181,263	Superior courts	172,571
West Virginia	Supreme Court	136,000	136,000	...	...	Circuit courts	126,000
Wisconsin	Supreme Court	147,403	159,297	Court of Appeals	150,280	Circuit courts	141,773
Wyoming	Supreme Court	165,000	165,000	...	...	District courts	150,000

Source: National Center for State Courts, January 6, 2019.

Note: Compensation is shown rounded to the nearest thousand, and is reported according to most recent legislation, even though laws may not yet have taken effect. There are other non-salary forms of judicial compensation that can be a significant part of a judge's compensation package. It should be noted that many of these can be important to judges or attorneys who might be interested in becoming judges or justices. These include retirement, disability, and death benefits, expense accounts, vacation, holiday, and sick leave and various forms of insurance coverage.

TABLE 5.5
Selected Data on Court Administrative Offices

State or other jurisdiction	Title	Established	Appointed by (a)	Salary
Alabama	Administrative Director of Courts	1971	CJ	$126,408
Alaska	Administrative Director	1959	CJ (b)	203,176
Arizona	Administrative Director of Courts	1960	SC	158,250
Arkansas	Director, Administrative Office of the Courts	1965	CJ (c)	120,543
California	Administrative Director of the Courts	1960	JC	288,888
Colorado	State Court Administrator	1959	SC	174,226
Connecticut	Chief Court Administrator (d)	1965	CJ	192,763
Delaware	Director, Administrative Office of the Courts	1971	CJ	137,612
Florida	State Courts Administrator	1972	SC	137,000
Georgia	Director, Administrative Office of the Courts	1973	JC	147,084
Hawaii	Administrative Director of the Courts	1959	CJ (b)	151,776
Idaho	Administrative Director of the Courts	1967	SC	137,700
Illinois	Administrative Director of the Courts	1959	SC	215,856
Indiana	Executive Director, Division of State Court Administration	1975	CJ	144,279
Iowa	Court Administrator	1971	SC	154,000
Kansas	Judicial Administrator	1965	CJ	123,038
Kentucky	Administrative Director of the Courts	1976	CJ	127,122
Louisiana	Judicial Administrator	1954	SC	158,147
Maine	Court Administrator	1975	CJ	125,632
Maryland	State Court Administrator	1955	CJ	166,633
Massachusetts	Chief Justice for Administration & Management	1978	SC	189,378
Michigan	State Court Administrator	1952	SC	166,171
Minnesota	State Court Administrator	1963	SC	188,066
Mississippi	Court Administrator	1974	SC	107,000
Missouri	State Courts Administrator	1970	SC	126,966
Montana	State Court Administrator	1975	SC	112,694
Nebraska	State Court Administrator	1972	CJ	146,029
Nevada	Director, Office of Court Administration	1971	SC	131,347
New Hampshire	Director of the Administrative Office of the Court	1980	SC	111,560
New Jersey	Administrative Director of the Courts	1948	CJ	175,534
New Mexico	Director, Administrative Office of the Courts	1959	SC	131,165
New York	Chief Administrator of the Courts	1978	CJ	210,500
North Carolina	Director, Administrative Office of the Courts	1965	CJ	143,878
North Dakota	Court Administrator	1971	CJ	141,552
Ohio	Administrative Director of the Courts	1955	SC	146,494
Oklahoma	Administrative Director of the Courts	1967	SC	138,235
Oregon	Court Administrator	1971	SC	138,468
Pennsylvania	Court Administrator	1968	SC	195,978
Rhode Island	State Court Administrator	1969	CJ	150,797
South Carolina	Director of Court Administration	1973	CJ	136,591
South Dakota	State Court Administrator	1974	SC	115,515
Tennessee	Director	1963	SC	178,908
Texas	Administrative Director of the Courts	1977	SC	171,216
Utah	Court Administrator	1973	SC	162,250
Vermont	Court Administrator	1967	SC	150,738
Virginia	Executive Secretary to the Supreme Court	1952	SC	196,370
Washington	Administrator for the Courts	1957	SC	152,736
West Virginia	Administrative Director of the Supreme Court of Appeals	1975	SC	135,000
Wisconsin	Director of State Courts	1978	SC	139,059
Wyoming	Court Coordinator	1974	SC	125,000
Dist. of Columbia	Executive Officer, Courts of D.C.	1971	(d)	208,000
American Samoa	Administrator/Comptroller	N.A	N.A.	N.A.
Guam	Administrative Director of Superior Court	N.A.	CJ	N.A.
CNMI*	Director of Courts	N.A.	N.A.	N.A.
Puerto Rico	Administrative Director of the Courts	1952	CJ	N.A.
U.S. Virgin Islands	Court/Administrative Clerk	N.A.	N.A.	N.A.

See footnotes at end of table

TABLE 5.5
Selected Data on Court Administrative Offices (continued)

Source: National Center for State Courts, January 6, 2019.
Note: Compensation shown is rounded to the nearest thousand, and is reported according to most recent legislation, even though laws may not yet have taken effect. Other information from State Court Administrator web sites.
*Commonweatlh of Northern Mariana Islands
Key:
SC–State court of last resort.
CJ–Chief justice or chief judge of court of last resort.

JC–Judicial council.
N.A.–Not available.
(a) Term of office for all court administrators is at pleasure of appointing authority.
(b) With approval of Supreme Court.
(c) With approval of Judicial Council.
(d) Joint Committee on Judicial Administration.

TABLE 5.6
Selection and Retention of Appellate Court Judges

State or other jurisdiction	Name of court	Type of court	Method of selection		Method of retention	Geographic basis for selection
			Unexpired term	Full term		
Alabama	Supreme Court	SC	GU	PE	PE	SW
	Court of Civil Appeals	IA	GU	PE	PE	SW
	Court of Criminal Appeals	IA	GU	PE	PE	SW
Alaska	Supreme Court	SC	GN	GN	RE (a)	SW
	Court of Appeals	IA	GN	GN	RE (a)	SW
Arizona	Supreme Court	SC	GN	GN	RE	SW
	Court of Appeals	IA	GN	GN	RE	DS
Arkansas	Supreme Court	SC	GU	NP	NP	SW
	Court of Appeals	IA	GU	NP	NP	DS
California	Supreme Court	SC	GU	GU	RE	SW
	Courts of Appeal	IA	GU	GU	RE	DS
Colorado	Supreme Court	SC	GN	GN	RE	SW
	Court of Appeals	IA	GN	GN	RE	SW
Connecticut	Supreme Court	SC	GNL	GNL	GNL	SW
	Appellate Court	IA	GNL	GNL	GNL	SW
Delaware	Supreme Court	SC	GNL	GNL	GNL	SW
Florida	Supreme Court	SC	GN	GN	RE	DS and SW (b)
	District Courts of Appeal	IA	GN	GN	RE	DS
Georgia	Supreme Court	SC	GN	NP	NP	SW
	Court of Appeals	IA	GN	NP	NP	SW
Hawaii	Supreme Court	SC	GNL	GNL	JN	SW
	Intermediate Court of Appeals	IA	GNL	GNL	JN	SW
Idaho	Supreme Court	SC	GN	NP	NP	SW
	Court of Appeals	IA	GN	NP	NP	SW
Illinois	Supreme Court	SC	CS	PE	RE	DS
	Appellate Court	IA	SC	PE	RE	DS
Indiana	Supreme Court	SC	GN	GN	RE	SW
	Court of Appeals	IA	GN	GN	RE	DS
	Tax Court	IA	GN	GN	RE	SW
Iowa	Supreme Court	SC	GN	GN	RE	SW
	Court of Appeals	IA	GN	GN	RE	SW
Kansas	Supreme Court	SC	GN	GN	RE	SW
	Court of Appeals	IA	GL	GL	RE	SW
Kentucky	Supreme Court	SC	GN	NP	NP	DS
	Court of Appeals	IA	GN	NP	NP	DS
Louisiana	Supreme Court	SC	CS (c)	PE (d)	PE (d)	DS
	Courts of Appeal	IA	SC (c)	PE (d)	PE (d)	DS
Maine	Supreme Judicial Court	SC	GL	GL	GL	SW
Maryland	Court of Appeals	SC	GNL	GNL	RE	DS
	Court of Special Appeals	IA	GNL	GNL	RE	DS
Massachusetts	Supreme Judicial Court	SC	(e)	GNE (f)	(g)	SW
	Appeals Court	IA	(e)	GNE (f)	(g)	SW
Michigan	Supreme Court	SC	GU	PE (h)	PE (h)	SW
	Court of Appeals	IA	GU	PE (h)	PE (h)	DS
Minnesota	Supreme Court	SC	GU	NP	NP	SW
	Court of Appeals	IA	GU	NP	NP	SW
Mississippi	Supreme Court	SC	GU	NP	NP	DS
	Court of Appeals	IA	GU	NP	NP	DS
Missouri	Supreme Court	SC	GN	GN	RE	SW
	Court of Appeals	IA	GN	GN	RE	DS
Montana	Supreme Court	SC	GNL	NP	NP (i)	SW
Nebraska	Supreme Court	SC	GN	GN	RE	SW and DS (j)
	Court of Appeals	IA	GN	GN	RE	DS
Nevada	Supreme Court	SC	GN	NP	NP	SW
	Court of Appeals	IA	GN	NP	NP	SW
New Hampshire	Supreme Court	SC	GE	GE	(k)	SW
New Jersey	Supreme Court	SC	GL	GL	GL	SW
	Superior Court, Appellate Div.	IA	GL	GL (l)	GL (l)	SW
New Mexico	Supreme Court	SC	GN	PE	RE	SW
	Court of Appeals	IA	GN	PE	RE	SW
New York	Court of Appeals	SC	GNL	GNL	GNL	SW
	Supreme Ct., Appellate Div.	IA	GN	GN	GN	SW (m)
North Carolina	Supreme Court	SC	GU	PE	PE	SW
	Court of Appeals	IA	GU	PE	PE	SW
North Dakota	Supreme Court	SC	GN (n)	NP	NP	SW
	Temporary Court of Appeals	IA	(o)	SC (p)	(o)	SW

See footnotes at end of table

TABLE 5.6
Selection and Retention of Appellate Court Judges (continued)

State or other jurisdiction	Name of court	Type of court	Method of selection		Method of retention	Geographic basis for selection
			Unexpired term	Full term		
Ohio	Supreme Court	SC	GU	PE (q)	PE (q)	SW
	Courts of Appeals	IA	GU	PE (q)	PE (q)	DS
Oklahoma	Supreme Court	SC	GN	GN	RE	DS
	Court of Criminal Appeals	SC	GN	GN	RE	DS
	Court of Civil Appeals	IA	GN	GN	RE	DS
Oregon	Supreme Court	SC	GU	NP	NP	SW
	Court of Appeals	IA	GU	NP	NP	SW
Pennsylvania	Supreme Court	SC	GL	PE	RE	SW
	Superior Court	IA	GL	PE	RE	SW
	Commonwealth Court	IA	GL	PE	RE	SW
Rhode Island	Supreme Court	SC	GN	GN	(r)	SW
South Carolina	Supreme Court	SC	LA	LA	LA	SW
	Court of Appeals	IA	LA	LA	LA	SW
South Dakota	Supreme Court	SC	GN	GN	RE	DS and SW (s)
Tennessee	Supreme Court	SC	GL	GL	RE	SW
	Court of Appeals	SC	GL	GL	RE	SW
	Court of Criminal Appeals	IA	GL	GL	RE	SW
Texas	Supreme Court	SC	GU	PE	PE	SW
	Court of Criminal Appeals	SC	GU	PE	PE	SW
	Courts of Appeals	IA	GU	PE	PE	DS
Utah	Supreme Court	SC	GNL	GNL	RE	SW
	Court of Appeals	IA	GNL	GNL	RE	SW
Vermont	Supreme Court	SC	GNL	GNL	LA	SW
Virginia	Supreme Court	SC	GU (t)	LA	LA	SW
	Court of Appeals	IA	GU (t)	LA	LA	SW
Washington	Supreme Court	SC	GU	NP	NP	SW
	Courts of Appeals	IA	GU	NP	NP	DS
West Virginia	Supreme Court of Appeals	SC	GU (u)	NP	NP	SW
Wisconsin	Supreme Court	SC	GU	NP	NP	SW
	Court of Appeals	IA	GU	NP	NP	DS
Wyoming	Supreme Court	SC	GN	GN	RE	SW
Dist. of Columbia	Court of Appeals	SC	(v)	(t)	(t)	SW (w)
Puerto Rico	Supreme Court	SC	GL	GL	(x)	SW
	Court of Appeals	IA	GL	GL	GL	SW

See footnotes at end of table

TABLE 5.6
Selection and Retention of Appellate Court Judges (continued)

Source: National Center for State Courts, July 2020.
Key:
SC – Court of last resort
IA – Intermediate appellate court
N/S – Not stated
N.A.– Not applicable
AP – At pleasure
CS – Court selection
DS – District
DU – Duration of service
GE – Gubernatorial appointment with approval of elected executive council
GL – Gubernatorial appointment with consent of the legislature
GN – Gubernatorial appointment from judicial nominating commission
GNE – Gubernatorial appointment from judicial nominating commission with approval of elected executive council
GNL – Gubernatorial appointment from judicial nominating commission with consent of the legislature
GU – Gubernatorial appointment
ID – Indefinite
JN – Judicial nominating commission appoints
LA – Legislative appointment
NP – Non-partisan election
PE – Partisan election
RE – Retention election
SC – Court of last resort appoints
SCJ – Chief justice/judge of the court of last resort appoints
SN – Seniority
SW – Statewide
(a) A judge must run for a retention election at the next election, immediately following the third year from the time of initial appointment.
(b) Five justices are selected by region (based on the District Courts of Appeal) and two justices are selected statewide.
(c) The person selected by the Supreme Court is prohibited from running for that judgeship; an election is held within one year to serve the remainder of the term.
(d) Louisiana uses a blanket primary, in which all candidates appear with party labels on the primary ballot. The two top vote getters compete in the general election.
(e) There are no expired judicial terms. A judicial term expires upon the death, resignation, retirement, or removal of an incumbent.
(f) The Executive (Governor's) Council is made up of nine people elected by geographical area and presided over by the Lieutenant Governor.

(g) There is no retention process. Judges serve during good behavior to age 70.
(h) Candidates may be nominated by political parties and are elected on a nonpartisan ballot.
(i) If the justice/judge is unopposed, a retention election is held.
(j) Chief Justices are selected statewide while Associate Justices are selected by district.
(k) There is no retention process. Judges serve during good behavior to age 70.
(l) All Superior Court judges, including Appellate Division judges, are subject to gubernatorial reappointment and consent by the Senate after an initial seven-year term. Among all the judges, the Chief Justice designates the judges of the Appellate Division.
(m) The Presiding Judge of each Appellate Division must be a resident of the department.
(n) The Governor may appoint from a list of names or call a special election at his discretion.
(o) The supreme court may provide for the assignment of active or retired district court judges, retired justices of the supreme court, and lawyers, to serve on three-judge panels.
(p) There is neither a retention process nor unexpired terms. Assignments are for a specified time, not to exceed one year or the completion of one or more cases on the docket of the supreme court.
(q) Party affiliation is not included on the ballot in the general election, but candidates are chosen through partisan primary nominations.
(r) There is no retention process. Judges serve during good behavior for a life tenure.
(s) Initial selection is by district, but retention selection is statewide.
(t) Gubernatorial appointment is for interim appointments.
(u) Appointment is effective only until the next election year; the appointee may run for election to any remaining portion of the unexpired term.
(v) Initial appointment is made by the President of the United States and confirmed by the Senate. Six months prior to the expiration of the term of office, the judge's performance is reviewed by the tenure commission. Those found "well qualified" are automatically reappointed. If a judge is found to be "qualified"the President may nominate the judge for an additional term (subject to Senate confirmation). If the President does not wish to reappoint the judge, the District of Columbia Nomination Commission compiles a new list of candidates.
(w) The geographic basis of selection is the District of Columbia.
(x) There is no retention process. Judges serve during good behavior to age 70.

TABLE 5.7
Selection and Retention of Trial Court Judges

State or other jurisdiction	Name of court	Type of court	Method of selection		Method of retention	Geographic basis for selection
			Unexpired term	Full term		
Alabama	Circuit	GJ	GU (a)	PE	PE	Circuit
	District	LJ	GU (a)	PE	PE	County
	Municipal	LJ	MU	MU	RA	Municipality
	Probate	LJ	GU	PE	PE	County
Alaska	Superior	GJ	GN	GN	RE (b)	State (c)
	District	LJ	GN	GN	RE (d)	District
	Magistrate's Division	N.A.	PJ	PJ	PJ	District
Arizona	Superior	GJ	GN (e)	GN or NP (f)	NP or RE (f)	County
	Justice of the Peace	LJ	CO	PE	PE	Precinct
	Municipal	LJ	CC (g)	CC (g)	CC (g)	Municipality
Arkansas	Circuit	GJ	GU (h)	NP	NP	Circuit
	District	LJ	GU	NP	NP	District
	City	LJ	LD	LD	LD	City
California	Superior	GJ	GU	NP	NP (i)	County
Colorado	District	GJ	GN	GN	RE	District
	Denver Probate	GJ	GN	GN	RE	District
	Denver Juvenile	GJ	GN	GN	RE	District
	Water	GJ	SC (j)	SC (j)	RE	District
	County	LJ	GN	GN (k)	RE	County
	Municipal	LJ	MU	MU	RA	Municipality
Connecticut	Superior	GJ	GNL	GNL	GNL	State
	Probate	LJ	PE	PE	PE	District
Delaware	Superior	GJ	GNL	GNL	GNL	State
	Chancery	LJ	GNL	GNL	GNL	State
	Justice of the Peace	LJ	GNL (l)	GNL (l)	GU	County
	Family	LJ	GNL	GNL	GNL	County
	Common Pleas	LJ	GNL	GNL	GNL	County
	Alderman's	LJ	LD	CC	LD	Town
Florida	Circuit	GJ	GN	NP	NP	Circuit
	County	LJ	GN	NP	NP	County
Georgia	Superior	GJ	GN	NP	NP	Circuit
	Juvenile	LJ	CS (m)	CS (m)	CS (m)	County/Circuit
	Civil	LJ	GU	PE	PE	County
	State	LJ	GU	NP	NP	County
	Probate	LJ	GU	PE (n)	PE (n)	County
	Magistrate	LJ	LD	LD (o)	LD (o)	County
	Municipal/of Columbus	LJ	MA	Elected	Elected	Municipality
	County Recorder's	LJ	LD	LD	LD	County
	Municipal/City of Atlanta	LJ	MU	MU	LD	Municipality
Hawaii	Circuit	GJ	GNL	GNL	JN	State
	District	LJ	SCJ (p)	SCJ (p)	JN	Circuit
Idaho	District	GJ	GN	NP	NP	District
	Magistrate's Division	LJ	JN (q)	JN (q)	RE	County
Illinois	Circuit	GJ	SC	PE	RE	Circuit/County (r)
	Associate Division	N.A.	SC	PE	RE	Circuit/County (r)
Indiana	Superior	GJ	GU	PE (s)	PE (s)	County
	Circuit	GJ	GU	PE (t)	PE (t)	County
	Probate	GJ	GU	PE	PE	County
	County	LJ	GU	PE	PE	County
	City	LJ	GU	PE	PE	Municipality
	Town	LJ	GU	PE	PE	Municipality
	Small Claims/Marion County	LJ	GU	PE	PE	Township
Iowa	District	GJ	GN (u)	GN (u)	RE (u)	District
Kansas	District	GJ	GN and PE (v)	GN and PE (v)	RE and PE (v)	District
	Municipal	LJ	MU	MU	MU	City
Kentucky	Circuit	GJ	GN	NP	NP	Circuit
	District	LJ	GN	NP	NP	District
Louisiana	District	GJ	SC (w)	PE	PE	District
	Juvenile & Family	GJ	SC (w)	PE	PE	District
	Justice of the Peace	LJ	SC (w)	PE (x)	PE	Ward
	Mayor's	LJ	MA	LD	LD	City
	City & Parish	LJ	SC (w)	PE	PE	Ward
Maine	Superior	GJ	GL	GL	GL	State
	District	GJ	GL	GL	GL	State and District (y)
	Probate	LJ	GU	PE	PE	County
Maryland	Circuit	GJ	GNL	GNL	NP	County
	District	LJ	GNL	GNL	RA	District
	Orphan's	LJ	GU	PE (z)	PE (z)	County

See footnotes at end of table

TABLE 5.7
Selection and Retention of Trial Court Judges (continued)

State or other jurisdiction	Name of court	Type of court	Method of selection — Unexpired term	Method of selection — Full term	Method of retention	Geographic basis for selection
Massachusetts	Superior	GJ	(aa)	GNE (bb)	(cc)	State
	District	LJ	(aa)	GNE (bb)	(cc)	State
	Probate & Family	LJ	(aa)	GNE (bb)	(cc)	State
	Juvenile	LJ	(aa)	GNE (bb)	(cc)	State
	Housing	LJ	(aa)	GNE (bb)	(cc)	State
	Boston Municipal	LJ	(aa)	GNE (bb)	(cc)	State
	Land	LJ	(aa)	GNE (bb)	(cc)	State
Michigan	Circuit	GJ	GU	NP	NP	Circuit
	Claims	GJ	GU	NP	NP	Circuit
	District	LJ	GU	NP	NP	District
	Probate	LJ	GU	NP	NP	District and Circuit
	Municipal	LJ	LD	NP	NP	City
Minnesota	District	GJ	GN	NP	NP	District
Mississippi	Circuit	GJ	GU	NP	NP	District
	Chancery	LJ	GU	NP	NP	District
	County	LJ	GU	NP	NP	County
	Municipal	LJ	LD	LD	LD	Municipality
	Justice	LJ	LD	PE	PE	District in County
Missouri	Circuit	GJ	GU and GN (dd)	PE and GN (ee)	PE and RE (ff)	Circuit/County (gg)
	Municipal	LJ	LD	LD	LD	City
Montana	District	GJ	GN	NP	NP	District
	Workers' Compensation	GJ	GN	GN	RA	State
	Water	GJ	SCJ (hh)	SCJ (hh)	SCJ (ii)	State
	Justice of the Peace	LJ	CO	NP	NP	County
	Municipal	LJ	MU	NP	NP	City
	City	LJ	CC	NP	NP	City
Nebraska	District	GJ	GN	GN	RE	District
	Separate Juvenile	LJ	GN	GN	RE	District
	County	LJ	GN	GN	RE	District
	Workers' Compensation	LJ	GN	GN	RE	District
Nevada	District	GJ	GN	NP	NP	District
	Justice	LJ	CO	NP	NP	Township
	Municipal	LJ	CC	NP	NP	City
New Hampshire	Superior	GJ	GE	GE	(jj)	State
	District	LJ	GE	GE	(jj)	District
	Probate	LJ	GE	GE	(jj)	County
New Jersey	Superior	GJ	GL	GL	GL	County
	Tax	LJ	GL	GL	GL	State
	Municipal	LJ	MA or MU (kk)	MA or MU (kk)	MU	Municipality
New Mexico	District	GJ	GN	PE	RE	District
	Magistrate	LJ	GU	PE	PE	County
	Metropolitan/Bernalillo County	LJ	GN	PE	RE	County
	Municipal	LJ	MU	PE	PE	City
	Probate	LJ	CO	PE	PE	County
New York	Supreme	GJ	GL	PE	PE	District
	County	GJ	GL	PE	PE	County
	Claims	GJ	GNL	GNL	GU	State
	Surrogates'	LJ	GNL	PE	PE	County
	Family	LJ	GNL and MU (ll)	PE and MU (ll)	PE and MU (ll)	County and NYC
	District	LJ	(mm)	PE	PE	District
	City	LJ	Elected	Elected	LD	City
	NYC Civil	LJ	MA (nn)	PE	PE	City
	NYC Criminal	LJ	MA	MA	MA	City
	Town & Village Justice	LJ	LD	LD	LD	Town or Village
North Carolina	Superior	GJ	GU	PE	PE	District
	District	LJ	GU	PE	PE	District
North Dakota	District	GJ	GN	NP	NP	District
	Municipal	LJ	MA	NP	NP	City
Ohio	Common Pleas	GJ	GU	PE (oo)	PE (oo)	County
	Municipal	LJ	GU	PE (oo)	PE (oo)	County/City
	County	LJ	GU	PE (oo)	PE (oo)	County
	Claims	LJ	SCJ	SCJ	SCJ	N.A.
	Mayor's	LJ	Elected	PE	PE	City/Village
Oklahoma	District	GJ	GN (pp)	NP (pp)	NP (pp)	District
	Municipal Not of Record	LJ	MM	MM	MM	Municipality
	Municipal of Record	LJ	MU	MU	MU	Municipality
	Workers' Compensation	LJ	GN	GN	GN	State
	Tax Review	LJ	SCJ	SCJ	SCJ	District

See footnotes at end of table

TABLE 5.7
Selection and Retention of Trial Court Judges (continued)

State or other jurisdiction	Name of court	Type of court	Method of selection		Method of retention	Geographic basis for selection
			Unexpired term	Full term		
Oregon	Circuit	GJ	GU	NP	NP	District
	Tax	GJ	GU	NP	NP	State
	County	LJ	CO	NP	NP	County
	Justice	LJ	GU	NP	NP	County
	Municipal	LJ	CC	CC/Elected	CC/Elected	(qq)
Pennsylvania	Common Pleas	GJ	GL	PE	RE	District
	Philadelphia Municipal	LJ	GL	PE	RE	City/County
	Magisterial District Judges	LJ	GL	PE	PE	District
	Philadelphia Traffic	LJ	GL	PE	RE	City/County
Rhode Island	Superior	GJ	GN	GN	(rr)	State
	Workers' Compensation	LJ	GN	GN	(rr)	State
	District	LJ	GN	GN	(rr)	State
	Family	LJ	GN	GN	(rr)	State
	Probate	LJ	CC	CC or MA	RA	Town
	Municipal	LJ	CC	CC or MA	CC or MA	Town
	Traffic Tribunal	LJ	GN	GN	(rr)	State
South Carolina	Circuit	GJ	LA and GN (ss)(tt)	LA and GN (tt)	LA and GL (tt)	Circuit and State (tt)
	Family	LJ	LA	LA	LA	Circuit
	Magistrate	LJ	GL	GL	GL	County
	Probate	LJ	GU	PE	PE	County
	Municipal	LJ	CC	CC	CC	District
South Dakota	Circuit	GJ	GN	NP	NP	Circuit
	Magistrate	LJ	PJS	PJS	PJS	Circuit
Tennessee	Circuit	GJ	GU	PE (uu)	PE	District
	Chancery	GJ	GU	PE (uu)	PE	District
	Criminal	GJ	GU	PE (uu)	PE	District
	Probate	GJ	(v)	PE (uu)	PE	District
	Juvenile	LJ	(v)	PE (uu)	PE	County
	Municipal	LJ	LD	LD (uu)	LD	Municipality
	General Sessions	LJ	MU	PE (uu)	PE	County
Texas	District	GJ	GL	PE	PE	District
	Constitutional County	LJ	CO	PE	PE	County
	Probate	LJ	CO	PE	PE	County
	County at Law	LJ	CO	PE	PE	County
	Justice of the Peace	LJ	CO	PE	PE	Precinct
	Municipal	LJ	CC	LD	LD	Municipality
Utah	District	GJ	(ww)	GNL	RE	District
	Justice	LJ	MM (xx)	MM (xx)	RE and RA (yy)	County/Municipality
	Juvenile	LJ	(ww)	GNL	RE	District
Vermont	Superior (zz)	GJ	GNL	GNL	LA	State
	Judicial Bureau	LJ	PJ	PJ	AP	State
Virginia	Circuit	GJ	GU	LA	LA	Circuit
	District	LJ	CS (aaa)	LA	LA	District
Washington	Superior	GJ	GU	NP	NP	County
	District	LJ	CO	NP	NP	District
	Municipal	LJ	CC	MA/CC	MA/CC (bbb)	Municipality
West Virginia	Circuit	GJ	GU	NP	NP	Circuit
	Magistrate	LJ	PJ	NP	NP	County
	Municipal	LJ	LD	LD	LD	Municipality
	Family	LJ	GU	NP	NP	Circuit
Wisconsin	Circuit	GJ	GU	NP	NP	District
	Municipal	LJ	MU (ccc)	NP	NP	Municipality
Wyoming	District	GJ	GN	GN	RE	District
	Circuit	LJ	GN	GN	RE	Circuit
	Municipal	LJ	MA	MA	LD	Municipality
Dist. of Columbia	Superior	GJ	(ddd)	(ddd)	(ddd)	State (eee)
Puerto Rico	First Instance	GJ	GL	GL	GL	State

See footnotes at end of table

TABLE 5.7
Selection and Retention of Trial Court Judges (continued)

Sources: S. Strickland, R. Schauffler, R. LaFountain & K. Holt, eds. State Court Organization. Last updated 30 June 2017. National Center for State Courts. www.ncsc.org/sco. Table provided June 2020.

Key:
GJ–General jurisdiction court
LJ–Limited jurisdiction court
N/S–Not stated
N.A. –Not applicable
AP–At pleasure
CA–Court administrator appointment
CC–City or town council/commission appointment
CO–County board/commission appointment
CS–Court selection
DU–Duration of service
GE–Gubernatorial appointment with approval of elected executive council
GL–Gubernatorial appointment with consent of the legislature
GN–Gubernatorial appointment from judicial nominating commission
GNE–Gubernatorial appointment from judicial nominating commission with approval of elected executive council
GNL–Gubernatorial appointment from judicial nominating commission with consent of the legislature
GU–Gubernatorial appointment
JN–Judicial nominating commission appoints
LA–Legislative appointment
LD–Locally determined
MA–Mayoral appointment
MC–Mayoral appointment with consent of city council
MM–Mayoral appointment with consent of governing municipal body
MU–Governing municipal body appointment
NP–Non-partisan election
PE–Partisan election
PJ–Presiding judge of the general jurisdiction court appoints
PJS–Presiding judge of the general jurisdiction court appoints with approval of the court of last resort
RA–Reappointment
RE–Retention election
SC–Court of last resort appoints
SCJ–Chief justice/judge of the court of last resort appoints

(a) The counties of Baldwin, Jefferson, Lauderdale, Madison, Mobile, Shelby, Talladega, and Tuscaloosa use gubernatorial appointment from the recommendations of the Judicial Nominating Commission.
(b) A judge must run for retention at the next election immediately following the third year from the time of the initial appointment.
(c) Judges are selected on a statewide basis, but run for retention on a district-wide basis.
(d) Judges must run for retention at the first general election held more than one year after appointment.
(e) Maricopa, Pima and Pinal counties use the gubernatorial appointment from the Judicial Nominating Commission process.

The method for submitting names for the other counties varies.
(f) Maricopa, Pima and Pinal counties use the gubernatorial appointment from the Judicial Nominating Commission process. The other counties hold non-partisan elections.
(g) Municipal court judges are usually appointed by the city or town council except in Yuma, where judges are elected.
(h) The office can be held until December 31 following the next general election and then the judge must run in a non-partisan election for the remainder of the term.
(i) If unopposed for reelection, incumbent's name does not appear on the ballot unless a petition was filed not less than 83 days before the election date indicating that a write-in campaign will be conducted for the office. An unopposed incumbent is not declared elected until the election date. This is for the general election; different timing may apply for the primary election (see Elec. Code §8203).
(j) Judges are chosen by the Supreme Court from among district court judges.
(k) The mayor appoints Denver County Court judges.
(l) The Magistrate Screening Commission recommends candidates.
(m) Juvenile court judges are appointed by superior court judges in all but one county, in which juvenile judges are elected. Associate judges (formerly referees) must be a member of the state bar or law school graduates. They serve at the pleasure of the judge(s).
(n) Probate judges are selected in non-partisan elections in 66 of 159 counties.
(o) Magistrate judges are selected in nonpartisan elections in 41 of 159 counties.
(p) Selection occurs by means of chief justice appointment from the Judicial Nominating Commission with consent of the Senate.
(q) The Magistrate Commission consists of the administrative judge, three mayors and two electors appointed by the governor, and two attorneys (nominated by the district bar and appointed by the state bar). There is one commission in each district.
(r) There exists a unit less than county in Cook County.
(s) Non-partisan elections are used in the Superior Courts in Allen and Vanderburgh counties. Nominating commissions are used in St. Joseph County and in some courts in Lake County. In those courts that use the nominating commission process for selection; retention elections are used as the method of retention.
(t) Non-partisan elections are used in the circuit courts in Vanderburgh County.
(u) This applies to district judges only. Associate judges are selected by the district judges and retention is by a retention election. Magistrates are selected and retained by appointment from the County Judicial Magistrate Nominating Commission. The County Judicial Magistrate Nominating Commission consists of three members appointed by the county board and two elected by the county bar, presided over by a District Court judge.
(v) Seventeen districts use gubernatorial appointment from the Judicial Nominating Commission for selection and retention elections for retention. Fourteen districts use partisan elections for selection and retention.
(w) Depending on the amount of time remaining, selection may be by election following a Supreme Court appointment.

TABLE 5.7
Selection and Retention of Trial Court Judges (continued)

(x) Louisiana uses a blanket primary in which all candidates appear with party labels on the primary ballot. The top two vote getters compete in the general election.

(y) At least one judge who is a resident of the county in which the district lies must be appointed from each of the 13 districts.

(z) Two exceptions are Hartford and Montgomery counties where Circuit Court judges are assigned.

(aa) There are no expired judicial terms. A judicial term expires upon the death, resignation, retirement, or removal of an incumbent.

(bb) The Executive (Governor's) Council is made up of eight people elected by geographical area and presided over by the lieutenant governor.

(cc) There is no retention process. Judges serve during good behavior to age 70.

(dd) Gubernatorial appointment occurs in partisan circuits; gubernatorial appointment from Judicial Nominating Commission takes place in non-partisan circuits.

(ee) Partisan elections occur in some circuits; gubernatorial appointment from the Judicial Nominating Commission with a non-partisan election takes place in others.

(ff) Partisan elections take place in some circuits; retention elections occur in other circuits.

(gg) Associate circuit judges are selected on a county basis.

(hh) Selection occurs through Chief Justice appointment from Judicial Nominating Commission.

(ii) Other judges are designated by the District Court judges.

(jj) There is no retention process. Judges serve during good behavior to age 70.

(kk) In multi-municipality, joint, or countywide municipal courts, selection is by gubernatorial appointment with consent of the senate.

(ll) Mayoral appointment occurs in New York City.

(mm) The appointment is made by the County Chief Executive Officer with confirmation by District Board of Supervisors.

(nn) Housing judges are appointed by the Chief Administrator of the courts.

(oo) Party affiliation is not included on the ballot in the general election, but candidates are chosen through partisan primary nominations.

(pp) This applies to district and associate judges; special judges are selected by the district judges.

(qq) The geographic basis for selection is the municipality for those judges that are elected. Judges that are either appointed or are under contract may be from other cities.

(rr) There is no retention process. Judges serve during good behavior for a life tenure.

(ss) The governor may appoint a candidate if the unexpired term is less than one year.

(tt) In addition to Circuit Court judges, the Circuit Court has masters-in-equity whose jurisdiction is in matters referred to them in the Circuit Court. Masters-in-equity are selected by gubernatorial appointment from the Judicial Merit Selection Commission, retained by gubernatorial appointment with the consent of the senate, and the geographic basis for selection is the state.

(uu) Each county legislative body has the discretion to require elections to be non-partisan.

(vv) The selection method used to fill an unexpired term is established by a special legislative act.

(ww) There are no expired terms; each new judge begins a new term.

(xx) Appointment is by the local government executive with confirmation by the local government legislative body (may be either county or municipal government).

(yy) County judges are retained by retention election; municipal judges are reappointed by the city executive.

(zz) Effective 2011, the Family, District, Environmental and Probate Courts were combined into the Superior Court.

(aaa) Circuit Court judges appoint.

(bbb) Full-time municipal judges must stand for non-partisan election.

(ccc) A permanent vacancy in the office of municipal judge may be filled by temporary appointment of the municipal governing body or
jointly by the governing bodies of all municipalities served by the judge.

(ddd) The Judicial Nomination Commission nominates for Presidential appointment and Senate confirmation. Not less than six months prior to the expiration of the term of office, the judge's performance is reviewed by the Commission on Judicial Disabilities and Tenure. A judge found "well qualified" is automatically reappointed for a new term of 15 years; a judge found "qualified" may be renominated by the President (and subject to Senate confirmation). A judge found "unqualified" is ineligible for reappointment or if the President does not wish to reappoint a judge, the Nomination Commission compiles a new list of candidates.

(eee) The geographic basis for selection is the District of Columbia.

TABLE 5.8
Judicial Discipline: Investigating and Adjudicating Bodies

State or other jurisdiction	Investigating body	Adjudicating body	Appeals from adjudication are filed with:	Final disciplining body	Point at which reprimands are made public
Alabama	Judicial Inquiry Committee	Court of the Judiciary	Court of Last Resort	Court of the Judiciary	Filing of the complaint with the Court of the Judiciary
Alaska	Committee on Judicial Conduct	Supreme Court	Court of Last Resort	Supreme Court	Filing of recommendation with Supreme Court
Arizona	Commission on Judicial Conduct	Commission on Judicial Conduct	Court of Last Resort	Supreme Court	Within 15 days of formal charges being brought, unless a motion for reconsideration is filed
Arkansas	Judicial Discipline and Disability Committees	Commission	Court of Last Resort	Supreme Court	At disposition of case
California	Commission on Judicial Performance	Commission on Judicial Performance	Court of Last Resort	Commission on Judicial Performance	Upon commission determination (a)
Colorado	Commission on Judicial Discipline	Commission on Judicial Discipline	No appeal	Supreme Court	Adjudication
Connecticut	Judicial Review Council	Judicial Review Council; Supreme Court (b)	Court of Last Resort	Supreme Court	Public censure is issued at between 10 and 30 days after notice to the judge, provided that if the judge appeals there is an automatic stay of disclosure
Delaware	Preliminary Committee of the Court on the Judiciary	Court on the Judiciary	No appeal	Court on the Judiciary	Upon issuance of opinion and imposition of sanction
Florida	Judicial Qualifications Commission	Judicial Qualifications Commission (c)	No appeal	Supreme Court	Filing of formal charges by Committee with Supreme Court Clerk
Georgia	Judicial Qualifications Commission	Supreme Court	No appeal	Supreme Court	Formal Hearing
Hawaii	Commission on Judicial Conduct	Commission on Judicial Conduct	No appeal	Supreme Court	Imposition of public discipline by Supreme Court
Idaho	Judicial Council	Supreme Court	Court of Last Resort	Supreme Court	Filing with the Supreme Court
Illinois	Judicial Inquiry Board	Courts Commission	No appeal	Courts Commission	Filing of decision by Courts Commission
Indiana	Commission on Judicial Qualifications	Supreme Court	Court of Last Resort	Supreme Court	After disciplinary charges are filed and case is tried or agreed resolution is accepted by Supreme Court
Iowa	Judicial Qualifications Commission	Judicial Qualifications Commission	Court of Last Resort	Supreme Court	Referral by the commission to the Supreme Court recommending formal sanction
Kansas	Commission on Judicial Qualifications	Supreme Court	Court of Last Resort	Supreme Court	Reprimand is published if approved by Supreme Court
Kentucky	Judicial Conduct Commission	Judicial Conduct Commission	Court of Last Resort	Judicial Conduct Commission	Once the judge has responded to the formal charges
Louisiana	Judiciary Commission	Supreme Court	No appeal	Supreme Court	The lodging of the record of proceedings and a recommendation by the Judiciary Commission to the Supreme Court
Maine	Committee on Judicial Responsibility and Disability	Supreme Judicial Court	No appeal	Supreme Court	Filing of report to Supreme Judicial Court
Maryland	Commission on Judicial Disabilities	Commission on Judicial Disabilities	Court of Last Resort	Court of Appeals	Unless confidential, upon filing of a response (or expiration of the time for filing a response) with the Commission
Massachusetts	Commission on Judicial Conduct	Supreme Judicial Court	No appeal	Supreme Judicial Court	Supreme Judicial Court
Michigan	Judicial Tenure Commission	Supreme Court	Court of Last Resort	Supreme Court	Filing of formal complaint by commission with Supreme Court or upon filing in the Supreme Court a consent resolution to a matter

See footnotes at end of table

TABLE 5.8

Judicial Discipline: Investigating and Adjudicating Bodies (continued)

State or other jurisdiction	Investigating body	Adjudicating body	Appeals from adjudication are filed with:	Final disciplining body	Point at which reprimands are made public
Minnesota	Board on Judicial Standards	Supreme Court	No appeal	Supreme Court	Filing of formal charges by committee with Supreme Court
Mississippi	Commission on Judicial Performance	Supreme Court	No appeal	Supreme Court	Recommendation of Commission to Supreme Court
Missouri	Commission on Retirement, Removal and Discipline	Commission on Retirement, Removal and Discipline	Court of Last Resort	Supreme Court	Filing of recommendation by Committee to Supreme Court
Montana	Judicial Standards Commission	Supreme Court	No appeal	Supreme Court	Filing of record by Committee with Supreme Court
Nebraska	Commission on Judicial Qualification	Supreme Court	No appeal	Supreme Court	Commission may issue a public reprimand
Nevada	Commission on Judicial Discipline	Commission on Judicial Discipline	Court of Last Resort	Commission on Judicial Discipline	Discretion of the Commission, upon filing of report by Committee and service upon judge
New Hampshire	Supreme Court Committee on Judicial Conduct	Supreme Court	No appeal	Supreme Court	On issuance of reprimand
New Jersey	Advisory Committee on Judicial Conduct	Supreme Court	No appeal	Supreme Court	When reprimand is filed by Supreme Court
New Mexico	Judicial Standards Commission	Supreme Court	No appeal	Supreme Court	Upon recommendation of Commission to Supreme Court
New York	Commission on Judicial Conduct	Commission on Judicial Conduct	Court of Last Resort	Commission on Judicial Conduct and Court of Appeals	After a hearing at which a judge is admonished, censured, removed or retired, and after the judge is served
North Carolina	Judicial Standards Commission	Supreme Court	No appeal	Supreme Court	Public imposition of disciplinary action by the Supreme Court
North Dakota	Commission on Judicial Conduct	Supreme Court	No appeal	Supreme Court	At formal hearing
Ohio	Office of Disciplinary Counsel	Board of Commissioners on Grievance and Discipline	Court of Last Resort	Supreme Court	Adjudication
Oklahoma	Court on the Judiciary Trial Division Council	Court on the Judiciary Trial Division; Council on Judicial Complaints	Court on the Judiciary Division; no appeal from Council on Judicial Complaints	Court on the judiciary appellate division	Filing with clerk of the appellate court
Oregon	Commission on Judicial Fitness and Disability	Supreme Court	No appeal	Supreme Court	Allegations become public when the commission issues a notice of public hearing
Pennsylvania	Judicial Conduct Board	Court of Judicial Discipline	Court of Last Resort	Supreme Court	Once a final decision has been made
Rhode Island	Commission on Judicial Tenure and Discipline	Supreme Court	No appeal	Supreme Court	Unless private, after the commission files its recommendation with the Chief Justice
South Carolina	Commission on Judicial Conduct	Supreme Court	No appeal	Supreme Court	Adjudication
South Dakota	Judicial Qualifications Commission	Supreme Court	No appeal	Supreme Court	Filing with the Supreme Court
Tennessee	Board of Judicial Conduct	Board of Judicial Conduct	Court of Last Resort	General Assembly	Filing formal charges with Board of Judicial Conduct
Texas	State Commission on Judicial Conduct	State Commission on Judicial Conduct (d)	Court of Last Resort	Special Court of Review	When issued by the Commission
Utah	Judicial Conduct Commission	Judicial Conduct Commission (e)	Court of Last Resort	Supreme Court	10 days after filing appeal
Vermont	Judicial Conduct Board	Supreme Court	Court of Last Resort	Supreme Court	Supreme Court
Virginia	Judicial Inquiry and Review Commission	Supreme Court	Court of Last Resort	Supreme Court	Filing of formal complaint by Commission with Supreme Court
Washington	Commission on Judicial Conduct	Commission on Judicial Conduct	Supreme Court	Supreme Court	At termination of proceeding in CJC

See footnotes at end of table

TABLE 5.8
Judicial Discipline: Investigating and Adjudicating Bodies (continued)

State or other jurisdiction	Investigating body	Adjudicating body	Appeals from adjudication are filed with:	Final disciplining body	Point at which reprimands are made public
West Virginia	Judicial Investigation Commission	Judicial Hearing Board	Court of Last Resort	Supreme Court of Appeals	Upon decision by Supreme Court of Appeals
Wisconsin	Judicial Commission	Supreme Court	No appeal	Supreme Court	Filing of formal complaint with Supreme Court
Wyoming	Commission on Judicial Conduct and Ethics	Supreme Court	No appeal	Supreme Court or Special Supreme Court	Upon the recommendation of the Conduct and Ethics Commission and Order of the Supreme Court
Dist. of Columbia	Commission on Judicial Disabilities and Tenure	Commission on Judicial Disabilities and Tenure	Chief Justice of U.S. Supreme Court	Commission on Judicial Disabilities and Tenure	Public reprimands are issued with the judge's consent; orders of involuntary removal become public upon filing with the D.C. Court of Appeals
Puerto Rico	Judicial Discipline Commission	Supreme Court	No appeal	Supreme Court	Filing of formal complaint to the Judicial Discipline Commission

Sources: National Center for State Courts, July 2020.
Key:
N.A.–Not applicable
(a) Public admonishments or public censures are sent to the judge describing the improper conduct and stating the findings made by the commission; these notices are made available to the press and the general public.
(b) For suspensions in excess of one year or removal from office, the Judicial Review Council makes a recommendation and the Supreme Court makes the decision.

(c) The Judicial Qualifications Commission investigates and makes recommendations to the Supreme Court for discipline or removal.
(d) Decision by the conduct commission cannot be implemented until reviewed and approved by the Supreme Court
(e) Commission has the authority to issue sanctions, but recommendations of removal must be brought before the Supreme Court.

CHAPTER SIX
ELECTIONS

TABLE 6.1
State Executive Branch Officials to be Elected: 2020-2024

State or other jurisdiction	2020	2021	2022	2023	2024
Alabama	(a)	...	G,LG,AG,AR,A,SS,T (a)	...	(a)
Alaska		...	G,LG	...	
Arizona	(b)	...	G,AG,SS,SP,T (b)	...	(b)
Arkansas	...	...	G,LG,AG,A,SS,T (c)	...	...
California	...	...	G,LG,AG,C,CI,SS,SP,T (d)	...	...
Colorado	(e)	...	G,LG,AG,SS,T (e)	...	(e)
Connecticut	...	...	G,LG,AG,C,SS,T	...	...
Delaware	G,LG,CI	...	AG,A,T	...	G,LG,CI
Florida	...	...	G,LG,AG,AR,CFO	...	...
Georgia	(f)	...	G,LG,AG,AR,CI,SS,SP (f)	...	(f)
Hawaii	...	...	G,LG	...	...
Idaho	...	...	G,LG,AG,C,SS,SP,T	...	...
Illinois	...	...	G,LG,AG,C,SS,T	...	...
Indiana	G,LG,AG,SP	...	A,SS,T	...	G,LG,AG,SP
Iowa	...	...	G,LG,AG,AR,A,SS,T	...	...
Kansas	...	...	G,LG,AG,CI,SS,T	...	...
Kentucky	...	...	...	G,LG,AG,AR,A,SS,T	...
Louisiana	(g)	...	(g)	G,LG,AG,AR,CI,SS,T	(g)
Maine (h)	...	...	G	...	...
Maryland	...	...	G,LG,AG,C	...	...
Massachusetts	...	...	G,LG,AG,A,SS,T	...	...
Michigan	(i)	...	G,LG,AG,SS (i)	...	(i)
Minnesota	...	...	G,LG,AG,A,SS	...	...
Mississippi	...	...	...	G,LG,AG,AR,A,CI,SS,T	...
Missouri	G,LG,AG,SS,T	...	A	...	G,LG,AG,SS,T
Montana	G,LG,AG,A,SS,SP (j)	...	(j)	...	G,LG,AG,A,SS,SP (j)
Nebraska	(k)	...	G,LG,AG,A,SS,T (k)	...	(k)
Nevada	...	...	G,LG,AG,C,SS,T	...	...
New Hampshire	G	...	G	...	G
New Jersey	...	G, LG	...	...	...
New Mexico	(l)	...	G,LG,AG,A,SS,T (l)	...	(l)
New York	...	...	G,LG,AG,C	...	...
North Carolina	G,LG,AG,AR,A,CI,SS,SP,T (m)	...	...	...	G,LG,AG,AR,A,CI,SS,SP,T (m)
North Dakota	G,LG,A,CI,SP,T (n)	...	AG,AR,SS (n)	...	G,LG,A,CI,SP,T (n)
Ohio	...	...	G,LG,AG,A,SS,T	...	...
Oklahoma	(p)	...	G,LG,AG,A,CI,SP,T (p)	...	(p)
Oregon	AG,SS,T	...	G (r)	...	AG,SS,T
Pennsylvania	AG,A,T	...	G,LG	...	AG,A,T
Rhode Island	...	...	G,LG,AG,SS,T	...	...
South Carolina	...	...	G,LG,AG,AR,C,SS,SP,T (s)	...	...
South Dakota	(t)	...	G,LG,AG,A,SS,SP,T (t)	...	(t)
Tennessee	...	...	G	...	...
Texas	(u)	...	G,LG,AG,AR,C (u)	...	(u)
Utah	G,LG,AG,A,T	...	...	...	G,LG,AG,A,T
Vermont	G,LG,AG,A,SS,T	...	G,LG,AG,A,SS,T	...	G,LG,AG,A,SS,T
Virginia	...	G,LG,AG	...	...	...
Washington	G,LG,AG,A,CI,SS,SP,T (q)	...	...	...	G,LG,AG,A,CI,SS,SP,T (q)
West Virginia	G,AG,AR,A,SS,T	...	...	...	G,AG,AR,A,SS,T
Wisconsin	...	SP	G,LG,AG,SS,T	...	...
Wyoming	...	...	G,A,SS,SP,T	...	...
American Samoa	G,LG	...	...	...	G,LG
Guam	A	...	G,LG,AG	...	A
CNMI*	...	...	G,LG	...	...
Puerto Rico	G	...	...	...	G
U.S. Virgin Islands	...	...	G,LG	...	...

See footnotes at end of table

TABLE 6.1
State Executive Branch Officials to be Elected: 2020-2024 (continued)

State or other jurisdiction	2020	2021	2022	2023	2024
Totals for year					
Governor	13	2	39	3	13
Lieutenant Governor	10	2	33	3	10
Attorney General	10	1	31	3	10
Agriculture	2	0	7	3	2
Auditor	9	0	15	2	9
Chief Financial Officer	0	0	1	0	0
Comptroller	0	0	9	0	0
Comm. of Insurance	4	0	4	2	4
Secretary of State	7	0	26	3	7
Supt. of Public Inst. or Comm. of Education	5	1	8	0	5
Treasurer	9	0	24	3	9

Sources: The Council of State Governments' survey of state election office Web sites, March 2020.

* Commonwealth of Northern Mariana Islands

Note: This table shows the executive branch officials up for election in a given year. Footnotes indicate other offices (e.g., commissioners of labor, public service, etc.) also up for election in a given year. The data contained in this table reflect information available at press time.

Key:

…–No regularly scheduled elections of state executive officials.

G–Governor

LG–Lieutenant Governor

AG–Attorney General

AR–Agriculture

A–Auditor

C–Comptroller/Controller

CFO–Chief Financial Officer

CI–Commissioner of Insurance

SS–Secretary of State

SP–Superintendent of Public Instruction or Commissioner of Education

T–Treasurer

(a) Public Service Commissioner (3): 2022–2 seats (associate commissioners); 2024–1 seat (president).

(b) Corporation Commissioner (5)–4-year term: 2022–2 seats; 2024–3 seats. State Mine Inspector–4-year term, 2022.

(c) Commissioner of State Lands–4-year term.

(d) Four (4) Board of Equalization members are elected to serve 4-year concurrent terms. The State Controller is the 5th member of the Board.

(e) University of Colorado Board of Regents (9, one elected from each of the state's congressional districts and two at-large members)–6-year term: 2020–3 districts; 2022–1 statewide, 2 districts; 2024–1 statewide, 2 districts.

(f) Commissioner of Labor–4-year term, 2022; Public Service Commissioner (5)–6-year term, 2020–2, 2022–1, 2024–2.

(g) Public Service Commissioner (5)–6-year term, 2020–2, 2022–2, 2024–1.

(h) The Maine legislature elects constitutional officers (AG,SS,T) for 2-year terms; the auditor was elected by the legislature in 2016 and serves a 4-year term.

(i) Michigan State University trustees (8)–8-year term, 2020–2; 2022–2; 2024–2; University of Michigan regents (8)–8-year term, 2020–2, 2022–2; 2024–2.

Wayne State University governors (8)–8 year term, 2020–2, 2022–2, 2024–2. State Board of Education (8)–8 year term, 2020–2, 2022–2, 2024–2.

(j) Public Service Commissioner (5)–4-year term, 2020–3, 2022–2, 2024–3.

(k) Public Service Commissioner (5)–6-year term, 2020–1, 2022–2, 2024 -2.

(l) Commissioner of Public Lands–4-year term, 2022; Public Education Commission (10)–4-year terms, 2020–5; 2022–5; 2024–5. Public Regulation Commissioner (5)–4-year terms, 2020–2, 2022–1, 2024–2.

(m) Commissioner of Labor–4-year term.

(n) Tax Commissioner–4-year term, 2022; Public Service Commissioner (3)–6-year term, 2020–1, 2022–1, 2024–1.

(p) Commissioner of Labor–4-year term, 2022; Corporation Commissioner (3)–6-year term, 2020–1, 2022–1, 2024–1.

(q) Commissioner of Public Lands–4-year term.

(r) Commissioner of the Bureau of Labor and Industries, 4-year term.

(s) Adjutant General–4-year term.

(t) The title is Commissioner of Schools and Public Lands, 2022; Public Utility Commissioner (3)–6-year term, 2020–1, 2022–1, 2024–1.

(u) Commissioner of General Land Office–4-year term, 2022; Railroad Commissioner (3)–6-year term, 2020–1, 2022–1, 2024 -1.

TABLE 6.2
State Legislature Members to be Elected: 2020-2024

State or other jurisdiction	Total legislators		2020		2021		2022		2023		2024	
	Senate	House/Assembly	Senate	House/Assembly	Senate	House/Assembly	Senate	House/Assembly	Senate	House/Assembly	Senate	House/Assembly
Alabama	35	105	...	...	...	...	35	105	...	...	...	...
Alaska	20	40	10	40	...	...	10	40	...	...	10	40
Arizona	30	60	30	60	...	...	30	60	...	...	30	60
Arkansas	35	100	17	100	...	...	18	100	...	...	17	100
California	40	80	20 (a)	80	...	...	20 (b)	80	...	...	20 (a)	80
Colorado	35	65	18	65	...	...	17	65	...	...	18	65
Connecticut	36	151	36	151	...	...	36	151	...	...	36	151
Delaware	21	41	11	41	...	...	10	41	...	...	11	41
Florida	40	120	20 (a)	120	...	...	20 (b)	120	...	...	20 (a)	120
Georgia	56	180	56	180	...	...	56	180	...	...	56	180
Hawaii	25	51	13	51	...	...	12	51	...	...	13	51
Idaho	35	70	35	70	...	...	35	70	...	...	35	70
Illinois	59	118	20 (e)	118	...	...	39 (f)	118	...	...	20 (e)	118
Indiana	50	100	25	100	...	...	25	100	...	...	25	100
Iowa	50	100	25 (b)	100	...	...	25 (a)	100	...	...	25 (b)	100
Kansas	40	125	40	125	...	...	...	125	...	...	40	125
Kentucky	38	100	19 (a)	100	...	...	19 (b)	100	...	...	19 (a)	100
Louisiana	39	105	...	...	...	...	...	...	39	105	...	...
Maine	35	151 (f)	35	151	...	...	35	151	...	...	35	151
Maryland	47	141	...	...	...	...	47	141	...	...	...	...
Massachusetts	40	160	40	160	...	...	40	160	...	...	40	160
Michigan	38	110	...	110	...	...	38	110	...	...	...	110
Minnesota	67	134	67	134	...	...	...	134	...	...	67	134
Mississippi	52	122	...	...	...	...	...	...	52	122	...	...
Missouri	34	163	17 (a)	163	...	...	17 (b)	163	...	...	17 (a)	163
Montana	50	100	25	100	...	...	25	100	...	...	25	100
Nebraska	49	U	25 (a)	U	...	...	24 (b)	U	...	...	25 (a)	U
Nevada	21	42	10	42	...	...	11	42	...	...	10	42
New Hampshire	24	400	24	400	...	...	24	400	...	...	24	400
New Jersey	40	80	...	...	40	80	...	...	...	80	...	...
New Mexico	42	70	42	70	...	...	...	70	...	...	42	70
New York	63	150	63	150	...	...	63	150	...	...	63	150
North Carolina	50	120	50	120	...	...	50	120	...	...	50	120
North Dakota	47	94	23 (b)	46 (b)	...	...	24 (a)	48 (a)	...	...	23 (b)	46 (b)
Ohio	33	99	16 (b)	99	...	...	17 (a)	99	...	...	16 (b)	99
Oklahoma	48	101	24 (a)	101	...	...	24 (b)	101	...	...	24 (a)	101
Oregon	30	60	15	60	...	...	15	60	...	...	15	60
Pennsylvania	50	203	25 (a)	203	...	...	25 (b)	203	...	...	25 (a)	203
Rhode Island	38	75	38	75	...	...	38	75	...	...	38	75
South Carolina	46	124	46	124	...	...	...	124	...	...	46	124
South Dakota	35	70	35	70	...	...	35	70	...	...	35	70
Tennessee	33	99	16 (b)	99	...	...	17 (a)	99	...	...	16 (b)	99
Texas	31	150	16	150	...	...	15	150	...	...	16	150
Utah	29	75	15	75	...	...	14	75	...	...	15	75
Vermont	30	150	30	150	...	...	30	150	...	...	30	150
Virginia	40	100	...	...	...	100	...	...	40	100	...	...
Washington	49	98	25	98	...	...	24	98	...	...	25	98
West Virginia	34	100	17	100	...	...	17	100	...	...	17	100
Wisconsin	33	99	16 (b)	99	...	...	17 (a)	99	...	...	16 (b)	99
Wyoming	30	60	15 (b)	60	...	...	15 (a)	60	...	...	15 (b)	60
Dist. of Columbia	13	U	6	U	...	...	7	U	...	...	6	U
American Samoa	18 (c)	20 (c)	18 (c)	20 (c)	...	...	18 (c)	20 (c)	...	...	18 (c)	20 (c)
Guam	15	U	15	U	...	...	15	U	...	...	15	U
CNMI* (d)	9	20	3	20	...	...	6	20	...	...	3	20
Puerto Rico (e)	27	51	27	51	...	...	...	...	...	...	27	51
U.S. Virgin Islands	15	U	15	U	...	...	15	U	...	...	15	U
State Totals	1,972	5,411	1,165	4,710	40	180	1,108	4,958	131	407	1,165	4,710
Totals	2,069	5,502	1,249	4,801	40	180	1,169	4,998	131	407	1,249	4,801

See footnotes at end of table

TABLE 6.2
State Legislature Members to be Elected: 2020–2024 (continued)

Source: The Council of State Governments, March 2020.
* Commonwealth of Northern Mariana Islands
Note: This table shows the number of elections in a given year. The data presented in this table reflect information available at press time. See Chapter 3.3 table entitled, "The Legislators: Numbers, Terms, and Party Affiliations," for specific information on legislative terms.
Key:
…–No regularly scheduled elections
U–Unicameral legislature
(a) Odd-numbered Senate districts.

(b) Even-numbered Senate districts.
(c) In American Samoa, Senators are not elected by popular vote. They are selected by the county council of chiefs. House: 21 seats; 20 are elected by popular vote and one appointed, non-voting delegate from Swains Island.
(d) In 2009, voters approved a constitutional amendment (Senate Legislative Initiative 16-1) that changed future general elections from odd to even-numbered years.
(e) Constitutionally, the Senate consists of 27 seats and the House 51 seats. However, extra at-large seats can be granted to the opposition to limit any party's control to two thirds.

TABLE 6.3
Methods of Nominating Candidates for State Offices

State or other jurisdiction	Methods of nominating candidates
Alabama	Primary election; however, the state executive committee or other governing body of any political party may choose instead to hold a state convention for the purpose of nominating candidates. Submitting a petition to run as an independent or third-party candidate or an independent nominating procedure.
Alaska	Primary election. Petition for no-party candidates.
Arizona	Candidates who are members of a recognized party are nominated by an open primary election. Candidates who are not members of a recognized political party may file petitions to appear on the general election ballot. A write-in option is also available.
Arkansas	Primary election, convention and petition.
California	Primary election or independent nomination procedure.
Colorado	Primary election, convention or by petition.
Connecticut	Convention/primary election. Major political parties hold state conventions (convening not earlier than the 68th day and closing not later than the 50th day before the date of the primary) for the purpose of endorsing candidates. If no one challenges the endorsed candidate, no primary election is held. However, if anyone (who received at least 15 percent of the delegate vote on any roll call at the convention) challenges the endorsed candidate, a primary election is held to determine the party nominee for the general election.
Delaware	Primary election for Democrats and primary election and convention for Republicans..
Florida	Primary election. Minor parties may nominate their candidate in any manner they deem proper.
Georgia	Primary election.
Hawaii	Primary election.
Idaho	Primary election and convention. New political parties hold a convention to nominate candidates to be placed on a general election ballot.
Illinois	Primary election. The primary election nominates established party candidates. New political parties and independent candidates go directly to the general election file based on a petition process.
Indiana	Primary election, convention and petition. The governor is chosen by a primary. All other state officers are chosen at a state convention, unless the candidate is an independent. Any party that obtains between 2 percent and 8 percent of the vote for secretary of state may hold a convention to select a candidate.
Iowa	Primary election, convention and petition.
Kansas	Candidates for the two major parties are nominated by primary election. Candidates for minor parties are nominated for the general election at state party conventions. Independent candidates are nominated for the general election by petition.
Kentucky	Primary election. A slate of candidates for governor and lieutenant governor that receives the highest number of its party's votes but which number is less than 40 percent of the votes cast for all slates of candidates of that party, shall be required to participate in a runoff primary with the slate of candidates of the same party receiving the second highest number of votes.
Louisiana	Candidates may qualify for any office they wish, regardless of party affiliation, by completing the qualifying document and paying the appropriate qualifying fee; or a candidate may file a nominating petition.
Maine	Primary election or non-party petition.
Maryland	Primary election, convention and petition. Unaffiliated candidates or candidates affiliated with non-recognized political parties may run for elective office by collecting the requisite number of signatures on a petition. The required number equals 1 percent of the number of registered voters eligible to vote for office. Only recognized non-principal political parties may nominate its candidate by a convention in accordance with its by laws (at this time, Maryland has four non-principal parties: Libertarian, Green, Constitution and Populist.)
Massachusetts	Primary election.
Michigan	Governor, state house, state senate use primary election. Lieutenant governor runs as the running mate to gubernatorial candidate, not separately, and is selected through the convention process Secretary of state and attorney general candidates are chosen at convention. Nominees for State Board of Education, University of Michigan Regents, Michigan State University Trustees and Wayne State University Governors are nominated by convention. Minor parties nominate candidates to all partisan offices by convention.
Minnesota	Primary election. Candidates for minor parties or independent candidates are by petition. They must have the signatures of 2,000 people who will be eligible to vote in the next general election.
Mississippi	Primary election, petition (for independent candidates), independent nominating procedures (third-party candidate).
Missouri	Primary election.
Montana	Primary election and independent nominating procedure.
Nebraska	Primary election.
Nevada	Primary election. Independent candidates are nominated by petition for the general election. Minor parties nominated by petition or by party.
New Hampshire	Primary election. Minor parties by petition.
New Jersey	Primary election. Independent candidates are nominated by petition for the general election.
New Mexico	Statewide candidates petition to go to convention and are nominated in a primary election. District and legislative candidate petition for primary ballot access.
New York	Primary election/petition.
North Carolina	Primary election. Newly recognized parties just granted access submit their first nominees by convention. All established parties use primaries.
North Dakota	Convention/primary election. Political parties hold state conventions for the purpose of endorsing candidates. Endorsed candidates are automatically placed on the primary election ballot, but other candidates may also petition their name on the ballot.
Ohio	Primary election, petition and by declaration of intent to be a write-in candidate.
Oklahoma	Primary election.
Oregon	Primary election. Minor parties hold conventions.

See footnotes at end of table

TABLE 6.3
Methods of Nominating Candidates for State Offices (continued)

State or other jurisdiction	Methods of nominating candidates
Pennsylvania	Primary election, and petition. Nomination petitions filed by major party candidates to access primary ballot. Nomination papers filed by minor party and independent candidates to access November ballot.
Rhode Island	Primary election.
South Carolina	Primary election for Republicans and Democrats; party conventions held for minor parties. Candidates can have name on ballot via petition.
South Dakota	Convention, petition and independent nominating procedure.
Tennessee	Primary election/petition.
Texas	Primary election/convention. Minor parties without ballot access nominate candidates for the general election after qualifying for ballot access by petition.
Utah	Convention, primary election and petition.
Vermont	Primary election. Major parties by primary, minor parties by convention, independents by petition.
Virginia	Primary election, convention and petition.
Washington	Primary election.
West Virginia	Primary election, convention, petition and independent nominating procedure..
Wisconsin	Primary election/petition. Candidates must file nomination papers (petitions) containing the minimum number of signatures required by law. Candidates appear on the primary ballot for the party they represent. The candidate receiving the most votes in each party primary goes on to the November election.
Wyoming	Primary election.
Dist. of Columbia	Primary election. Independent and minor party candidates file by nominating petition.
American Samoa	Individual files petition for candidacy with the chief election officer. Petition must be signed by statutorily-mandated number of qualified voters.
Guam	Individual files petition for candidacy with the chief election officer. Petition must be signed by statutorily-mandated number of qualified voters.
CNMI*	Candidates are all nominated by petition. Candidates seeking the endorsement of recognized political parties must also include in their submitted petition submission a document signed by the recognized political parties' chairperson/president and secretary attesting to such nomination. Recognized political parties may, or may not, depending on their by-laws and party rules conduct primaries separate from any state election agency participation.
Puerto Rico	Primary election and convention.
U.S. Virgin Islands	Primary election.

Sources: The Council of State Governments' survey of state Web sites, March 2020.
Note: The nominating methods described here are for state offices; procedures may vary for local candidates. Also, independent candidates may have to petition for nomination.
* Commonwealth of Northern Mariana Islands

TABLE 6.4
Election Dates for National and State Elections (Formulas and Dates of State Elections)

State or other jurisdiction	National (a)		State (b)			Type of primary (c)
	Primary	General	Primary	Runoff	General	
Alabama	March, 1st T March 3, 2020	Nov., ★ Nov. 3, 2020	June, 1st T June 7, 2022	6th T AP July 19, 2022	Nov., ★ Nov. 8, 2022	Open
Alaska	(d) April 10, 2020	Nov., ★ Nov. 3, 2020	Aug., 3rd T Aug. 18, 2020	...	Nov., ★ Nov. 3, 2020	(e)
Arizona	T following March 15 March 17, 2020	Nov., ★ Nov. 3, 2020	10th T Prior Aug. 4, 2020	...	Nov., ★ Nov. 3, 2020	Partially Closed
Arkansas	T 3 wks. prior to runoff (bb) March 3, 2020	Nov., ★ Nov. 3, 2020	T 3 wks. prior to runoff March 3, 2020	June, 2nd T March 31, 2020	Nov., ★ Nov. 3, 2020	Open
California	March★ March 3, 2020	Nov., ★ Nov. 3, 2020	March ★ March 3, 2020	...	Nov., ★ Nov. 3, 2020	Top Two
Colorado	(d) (g) March 3, 2020	Nov., ★ Nov. 3, 2020	June, last T June 30, 2020	...	Nov., ★ Nov. 3, 2020	Partially Closed
Connecticut	April, Last T Aug. 11, 2020	Nov., ★ Nov. 3, 2020	Aug. 2nd T Aug. 11, 2020	...	Nov., ★ Nov. 3, 2020	Closed
Delaware	April, 4th T July 7, 2020	Nov., ★ Nov. 3, 2020	Sept., 2nd T after 1st M Sept. 15, 2020	...	Nov., ★ Nov. 3, 2020	Closed
Florida	March, 3rd T March 17, 2020	Nov., ★ Nov. 3, 2020	10th T prior to General Aug. 18, 2020	...	Nov., ★ Nov. 3, 2020	Closed
Georgia	(h) June 9, 2020	Nov., ★ Nov. 3, 2020	24th T prior to General June 9, 2020	9th T after Primary Aug. 11, 2020	Nov., ★ Nov. 3, 2020	Open
Hawaii	(d) Dem: May 22, 2020	Nov., ★ Nov. 3, 2020	Aug. 2nd S Aug. 8, 2020	...	Nov., ★ Nov. 3, 2020	Open
Idaho	(d) March 10, 2020	Nov., ★ Nov. 3, 2020	May, 3rd T May 19, 2020	...	Nov., ★ Nov. 3, 2020	Rep: Closed (i) Dem: Partially Closed
Illinois	March, 3rd T March 17, 2020	Nov., ★ Nov. 3, 2020	March, 3rd T March 17, 2020	...	Nov., ★ Nov. 3, 2020	Partially Open
Indiana	May, ★ June 2, 2020	Nov., ★ Nov. 3, 2020	May, ★ June 2, 2020	...	Nov., ★ Nov. 3, 2020	Partially Open
Iowa	(d) February 3, 2020	Nov., ★ Nov. 3, 2020	June, ★ June 2, 2020	...	Nov., ★ Nov. 3, 2020	Partially Open
Kansas	(d) (j) May 2, 2020	Nov., ★ Nov. 3, 2020	Aug. 1st T Aug. 4, 2020	...	Nov., ★ Nov. 3, 2020	Closed (k)
Kentucky	May, 1st T after 3rd M June 23, 2020	Nov., ★ Nov. 3, 2020	May, 1st T after 3rd M June 23, 2020	...	Nov., ★ Nov. 3, 2020	Closed
Louisiana	April, 1st S July 11, 2020	Nov., ★ Nov. 3, 2020	Oct., 2nd to last S (l) Oct. 21, 2023	...	Nov., 4th S AP (l) Nov. 18, 2023	Top Two
Maine	(d) March 3, 2020	Nov., ★ Nov. 3, 2020	June, 2nd T July 14, 2020	...	Nov., ★ Nov. 3, 2020	Closed (n)
Maryland	April, 4th T June 2, 2020	Nov., ★ Nov. 3, 2020	June, last T June 28, 2022	...	Nov., ★ Nov. 8, 2022	Closed (p)
Massachusetts	March, 1st T March 3, 2020	Nov., ★ Nov. 3, 2020	7th T Prior Sept. 15, 2020	...	Nov., ★ Nov. 3, 2020	Partially Closed
Michigan	March, 2nd T March 10, 2020	Nov., ★ Nov. 3, 2020	Aug., ★ Aug. 4, 2020	...	Nov., ★ Nov. 3, 2020	Open
Minnesota	(d) (r) March 3, 2020	Nov., ★ Nov. 3, 2020	Aug., 2nd T Aug. 11, 2020	...	Nov., ★ Nov. 3, 2020	Open
Mississippi	March, 2nd T March 10, 2020	Nov., ★ Nov. 3, 2020	Aug., ★ Aug. 8, 2023	3rd T AP Aug. 29, 2023	Nov., ★ Nov. 7, 2023	(s)
Missouri	March, 2nd T after 1st M March 10, 2020	Nov., ★ Nov. 3, 2020	Aug., ★ Aug. 4, 2020	...	Nov., ★ Nov. 3, 2020	Open
Montana	June, ★ June 2, 2020	Nov., ★ Nov. 3, 2020	June, ★ June 2, 2020	...	Nov., ★ Nov. 3, 2020	Open
Nebraska	May, 1st T After 2nd M May 12, 2020	Nov., ★ Nov. 3, 2020	May, 1st T After 2nd M May 12, 2020	...	Nov., ★ Nov. 3, 2020	Top Two
Nevada	(d) Feb. 22, 2020	Nov., ★ Nov. 3, 2020	June, 2nd T June 9, 2020	...	Nov., ★ Nov. 3, 2020	Closed
New Hampshire	(t) Feb. 11, 2020	Nov., ★ Nov. 3, 2020	Sept., 2nd T Sept. 8, 2020	...	Nov., ★ Nov. 3, 2020	Partially Closed (u)
New Jersey	June, ★ July 7, 2020	Nov., ★ Nov. 3, 2020	June, ★ June 8, 2021	...	Nov., ★ Nov. 2, 2021	Closed
New Mexico	June, ★ June 2, 2020	Nov., ★ Nov. 3, 2020	June, ★ June 2, 2020	...	Nov., ★ Nov. 3, 2020	Closed

See footnotes at end of table

TABLE 6.4
Election Dates for National and State Elections (Formulas and Dates of State Elections) (continued)

State or other jurisdiction	National (a)		State (b)			Type of primary (c)
	Primary	General	Primary	Runoff	General	
New York	Feb., 1st T (aa)	Nov., ★ Nov. 3, 2020	June, 4th T June 23, 2020	...	Nov., ★ Nov. 3, 2020	Closed
North Carolina	March, ★ March 3, 2020	Nov., ★ Nov. 3, 2020	March, ★ March 3, 2020	7 wks. AP June 23, 2020	Nov., ★ Nov. 3, 2020	Partially Closed
North Dakota	(d) March 10, 2020	Nov., ★ Nov. 3, 2020	June, 2nd T June 9, 2020	...	Nov., ★ Nov. 3, 2020	Open
Ohio	March, 2nd T after 1st M (v) April 28, 2020	Nov., ★ Nov. 3, 2020	May, ★(v) April 28, 2020	...	Nov., ★ Nov. 3, 2020	Partially Open
Oklahoma	March, 1st T March 3, 2020	Nov., ★ Nov. 3, 2020	June, last T June 30, 2020	Aug., 4th T Aug. 25, 2020	Nov., ★ Nov. 3, 2020	Dem: Partially Closed Rep: Closed (w)
Oregon	May, 3rd T May 19, 2020	Nov., ★ Nov. 3, 2020	May, 3rd T May 19, 2020	...	Nov., ★ Nov. 3, 2020	Closed
Pennsylvania	April, 4th T June 2, 2020	Nov., ★ Nov. 3, 2020	April, 4th T June 2, 2020	...	Nov., ★ Nov. 3, 2020	Closed
Rhode Island	April, 4th T June 2, 2020	Nov., ★ Nov. 3, 2020	Sept., 2nd T after 1st M Sept. 8, 2020	...	Nov., ★ Nov. 3, 2020	Partially Open
South Carolina	(d) Feb. 29, 2020	Nov., ★ Nov. 3, 2020	June, 2nd T June 9, 2020	2nd T AP June 23, 2020	Nov., ★ Nov. 3, 2020	Open
South Dakota	June, ★ June 2, 2020	Nov., ★ Nov. 3, 2020	June, ★ June 2, 2020	10th T AP (x) Aug. 11, 2020	Nov., ★ Nov. 3, 2020	Rep: Closed Dem: Partially Closed
Tennessee	March, 1st T March 3, 2020	Nov., ★ Nov. 3, 2020	Aug., 1st TH Aug. 6, 2020	...	Nov., ★ Nov. 3, 2020	Open
Texas	March, 1st T March 3, 2020	Nov., ★ Nov. 3, 2020	March, 1st T March 3, 2020	May, 4th T July 14, 2020	Nov., ★ Nov. 3, 2020	Open
Utah	(y) March 3, 2020	Nov., ★ Nov. 3, 2020	June, 4th T June 30, 2020	...	Nov., ★ Nov. 3, 2020	Rep: Closed (z) Dem: Open
Vermont	March, 1st T March 3, 2020	Nov., ★ Nov. 3, 2020	Aug., 2nd T Aug. 11, 2020	...	Nov., ★ Nov. 3, 2020	Open
Virginia	March, 1st T March 3, 2020	Nov., ★ Nov. 3, 2020	June, 2nd T June 8, 2021	...	Nov., ★ Nov. 2, 2021	Open
Washington	May, 4th T March 10, 2020	Nov., ★ Nov. 3, 2020	Aug., 1st T Aug. 4, 2020	...	Nov., ★ Nov. 3, 2020	Top Two
West Virginia	May, 2nd T June 9, 2020	Nov., ★ Nov. 3, 2020	May, 2nd T June 9, 2020	...	Nov., ★ Nov. 3, 2020	Partially Closed
Wisconsin	April, 1st T April 7, 2020	Nov., ★ Nov. 3, 2020	Aug., 2nd T Aug. 11, 2020	...	Nov., ★ Nov. 3, 2020	Open
Wyoming	(d) April 17, 2020	Nov., ★ Nov. 3, 2020	Aug., 1st T After 3rd M Aug. 18, 2020	...	Nov., ★ Nov. 3, 2020	Closed
Dist. of Columbia	June, 2nd T (q) June 2, 2020	Nov., ★ Nov. 3, 2020	June, 2nd T (q) June 2, 2020	...	Nov., ★ Nov. 3, 2020	Closed
American Samoa	(d) Dem: March 3, 2020 Rep: March 18, 2020	(m) ...	(o) ...	...	Nov., ★ Nov. 3, 2020	(o)
Guam	(d) Dem: delayed indefinitely Rep: March 14, 2020	(m) ...	Aug., last S Aug. 29, 2020	...	Nov., ★ Nov. 3, 2020	Open
CNMI*	(d) Dem: March 14, 2020 Rep: March 15, 2020	(m) ...	(o) ...	...	Nov., ★ Nov. 3, 2020	(o)
Puerto Rico	(f) Dem: July 12, 2020 Rep: June 7, 2020	(m) ...	N.A. July 12, 2020	...	Nov., ★ Nov. 3, 2020	Open
U.S. Virgin Islands	(d) Dem: June 6, 2020 Rep: TBD	(m) ...	Aug., 1st S Aug. 1, 2020	...	Nov., ★ Nov. 3, 2020	Closed

See footnotes at end of table

TABLE 6.4
Election Dates for National and State Elections (Formulas and Dates of State Elections) (continued)

Sources: The Council of State Governments, May 2020.
* Commonwealth of Northern Mariana Islands
Notes:

1. This table describes the basic formulas for determining when national and state elections will be held. For specific information on a particular state, the reader is advised to contact the state election administration office. All dates provided are based on the state election formula and dates are subject to change.
2. Due to the COVID-19 global pandemic, many states pushed back their primary and runoff election dates in the 2020 cycle.

Key:

★ – First Tuesday after first Monday.
. . . – No provision.
M –Monday.
T – Tuesday.
TH – Thursday.
S – Saturday.
SN – Sunday.
Prior – Prior to general election.
AP – After primary.

(a) National refers to presidential elections.
(b) State refers to election in which a state executive official or legislator is to be elected. See Table 6.1, State Executive Branch Officials to be Elected, and Table 6.2, State Legislature Members to be Elected.
(c)
Open: Voters can privately select which party's ballot to vote, regardless of party affiliation.
Closed: Voters must be a registered member of the party to vote its primary ballot.
Partially Open: Voters can choose in which primary to vote but that choice is not private. In certain states, a voter's primary ballot selection may be regarded as a form of registration with the corresponding party.
Partially Closed: Unaffiliated voters may participate in any party's primary. Members of a political party are not allowed to cross over and vote in a different political party's primary.
Top Two primaries: All voters in California and Washington receive one ballot with candidates from all parties listed together. The top two finishers face each other at the general election. Louisiana has a similar election type but its primary is held in October with a runoff election in November if no candidate garners 50 percent or more of the vote. Nebraska uses a single primary ballot to elect lawmakers to its nonpartisan legislature.
(d) The dates for presidential caucuses are set by the political parties.
(e) Alaska law allows a political party to select who may participate in their party's primary. Parties may expand or limit who may participate in their Primary Election by submitting a written notice with a copy of their pre cleared by-laws to the Director of Elections no later than September 1st of the year prior to the year in which a Primary Election is to be held.
(f) The primary law allows Puerto Rico parties affiliated with U.S. national parties to select a primary date any time between the first

Tuesday in March and June 15.
(g) The state parties have the option of choosing either the first Tuesday in March (March 3, 2020) date called for in the statute or moving up to the first Tuesday in February (Feb. 4, 2020).
(h) The Secretary of State has the authority to set the date of the presidential primary election. Scheduled for March, the presidential primary was held on June 9, 2020.
(i) In 2011, the Idaho Legislature passed HB 351, implementing a closed primary system. However, the law gives political parties the option of opening their primary elections to unaffiliated voters and members of other political parties. The party chairman must notify the Secretary of State 6 months prior to the primary if the party intends to open its primary election to those outside of the party. The Republican party currently allows only voters registered with its party to vote (closed), while the Democratic Party allows unaffiliated voters to vote in its primary (partially closed).
(j) In 2015, the Kansas legislature passed a bill (HB 2104) that repealed the statute calling for a presidential preference primary election. It replaces it with a requirement that each recognized political party select a presidential nominee in accordance with party procedures, for every presidential election beginning with the 2016 election.
(k) Unaffiliated voters may register with a party on primary day to vote in that party's primary.
(l) Louisiana has an open primary which requires all candidates, regardless of party affiliation, to appear on a single ballot. If a candidate receives over 50 percent of the vote in the primary, that candidate is elected to the office. If no candidate receives a majority vote, then a single election is held between the two candidates receiving the most votes. For national elections, the first vote is held on the first Saturday in October of even-numbered years with the general election held on the first Tuesday after the first Monday in November. For state elections, the election is held on the second to last Saturday in October with the runoff being held on the fourth Saturday after first election.
(m) Residents of U.S. territories may vote in presidential primaries, but the Electoral College system does not permit them to vote in presidential elections.
(n) Voters who have already registered but have not enrolled in a party may enroll in a party at the polls on Election Day. Any voter who wishes to change party enrollment must do so at least 15 days before the vote.
(o) American Samoa and the Northern Marianas Islands do not conduct primary elections. Instead, the law provides for a run off when none of the candidates receives more than 50% of the vote.
(p) Under Maryland law, parties may allow unaffiliated voters to cast ballots in their primaries by notifying the election board six months in advance. However, both major parties currently hold closed primaries.
(q) In 2014, the Council of the District of Columbia passed a bill (B20-0265) to move the presidential primary from the 1st Tuesday in April to the 2nd Tuesday in June.
(r) Parties must notify the Secretary of State's Office in writing prior to Dec. 1st the year preceding the date of the election of their

TABLE 6.4
Election Dates for National and State Elections (Formulas and Dates of State Elections) (continued)

intentions to hold a preference primary election. Unless the chairs of the two major political parties jointly propose a different date, the caucuses are held on the first Tuesday in February.

(s) Mississippi voters do not have to register with a party, but state law requires they must intend to support the party nominee if they vote in that party's primary election. Since voter intent is difficult to dispute in court, some characterize Mississippi's system an open partisan primary.

(t) The Secretary of State selects a date for the primary, which must be 7 days or more immediately preceding the date on which any other state holds a similar election.

(u) An unaffiliated voter may choose one party's ballot, which makes them a registered member of that party. However, temporary affiliation is possible, as voters can fill out a card at the polling place to return to undeclared status after the vote is cast.

(v) In 2015, Ohio lawmakers passed a bill (HB 153) that moves the date of the primary back one week to the second Tuesday after the first Monday in March. In non-presidential election years, the primary is held on the first Tuesday after the first Monday in May. The move to a later week allows Republicans to allocate delegates in a winner-take-all fashion.

(w) In November of each odd-numbered year, recognized political parties declare whether or not they will permit Independents to vote in their primary elections during the following two calendar years. For 2016 and 2017, the Democratic Party granted permission for Independents to vote in its primaries and runoff primaries. Independents cannot vote in Republican primaries.

(x) South Dakota only holds runoffs for the offices of U.S. Senator, U.S. Representative and governor.

(y) If funded, Utah can hold a primary on either the first Tuesday of February or in conjunction with the regular primary on the fourth Tuesday in June.

(z) In November, 2015, a federal judge ruled that the state cannot force political parties to open their primaries to unaffiliated voters, invalidating a provision in a 2014 law (SB 54). This decision allows the Utah Republican Party to continue to hold closed primaries.

(aa) In the past two election presidential primary cycles, New York has chosen to move their primary to April. The 2020 presidential primary was canceled due to the Coronavirus global pandemic.

(bb) In presidential election years, the primary is held on the first Tuesday in March.

Table 6.4 | 2020 State Election Calendar

State Primaries

MARCH

March 3, 2020 · Arkansas, California, North Carolina, Texas

March 17, 2020 · Illinois

APRIL

April 28, 2020 · Ohio

MAY

May 12, 2020 · Nebraska

May 19, 2020 · Idaho, Oregon

JUNE

June 2, 2020 · Indiana, Iowa, Montana, New Mexico, Pennsylvania, South Dakota

June 9, 2020 · Georgia, Nevada, North Dakota, South Carolina, West Virginia

June 23, 2020 · Kentucky, New York

June 30, 2020 · Colorado, Oklahoma, Utah

JULY

July 14, 2020 · Maine

AUGUST

August 4, 2020 · Arizona, Kansas, Michigan, Missouri, Washington

August 6, 2020 · Tennessee

August 8, 2020 · Hawaii

August 11, 2020 · Connecticut, Minnesota, Vermont, Wisconsin

August 18, 2020 · Alaska, Florida, Wyoming

SEPTEMBER

September 8, 2020 · New Hampshire, Rhode Island

September 15, 2020 · Delaware, Massachusetts

OTHER

American Samoa and CNMI* do not conduct primary elections. Instead, the law provides for a run off when none of the candidates receives more than 50% of the vote.

Runoff elections are held in 9 states.

March 31, 2020 · Arkansas

June 23, 2020 · North Carolina, South Carolina

July 14, 2020 · Texas

August 11, 2020 · Georgia, South Dakota

August 25, 2020 · Oklahoma

July 19, 2022 · Alabama

August 29, 2023 · Mississippi

The state general election in most states is Nov. 3, 2020

However, **6** states do not have state executive or legislative general elections in 2020.

Nov. 2, 2021 · New Jersey, Virginia

Nov. 8, 2022 · Alabama, Maryland

Nov. 7, 2023 · Louisiana, Mississippi

TABLE 6.5
Polling Hours: General Elections

State or other jurisdiction	Polls open	Polls close	Notes on hours (a)
Alabama	7 a.m.	7 p.m.	Polling places located in the Eastern Time Zone may be open from 7 a.m. to 7 p.m. ET.
Alaska	7 a.m.	8 p.m.	
Arizona	6 a.m.	7 p.m.	
Arkansas	7:30 a.m.	7:30 p.m.	
California	7 a.m.	8 p.m.	
Colorado	7 a.m.	7 p.m.	
Connecticut	6 a.m.	8 p.m.	
Delaware	7 a.m.	8 p.m.	
Florida	7 a.m.	7 p.m.	
Georgia	7 a.m.	7 p.m.	
Hawaii	7 a.m.	6 p.m.	
Idaho	8 a.m.	8 p.m.	Clerk has the option of opening all polls at 7 a.m. Idaho is in two time zones - MT and PT.
Illinois	6 a.m.	7 p.m.	
Indiana	6 a.m.	6 p.m.	For those counties on Central time, polling places will observe these times in Central time.
Iowa	7 a.m.	9 p.m.	
Kansas	7 a.m.	7 p.m.	Counties may open the polls earlier and close them later. Several western counties are in the Mountain Time Zone.
Kentucky	6 a.m.	6 p.m.	Counties may be either in Eastern or Central Time Zones.
Louisiana	6 a.m.	8 p.m.	
Maine	Between 6 and 10 a.m.	8 p.m.	Applicable opening time depends on variables related to the size of the precinct.
Maryland	7 a.m.	8 p.m.	
Massachusetts	7 a.m.	8 p.m.	Some municipalities may open their polls as early as 5:45 a.m.
Michigan	7 a.m.	8 p.m.	Eastern Time Zone and Central Time Zone
Minnesota	7 a.m.	8 p.m.	A few polling places in small townships located outside the 11-county metropolitan area may open as late as 10 a.m.
Mississippi	7 a.m.	7 p.m.	
Missouri	6 a.m.	7 p.m.	
Montana	7 a.m.	8 p.m.	A polling place having fewer than 400 registered electors must be open from at least noon to 8 p.m. or until all registered electors in any precinct have voted, at which time that precinct in the polling place must be closed immediately.
Nebraska	7 a.m. MT/8 a.m. CT	7 p.m. MT/8 p.m. CT	
Nevada	7 a.m.	7 p.m.	
New Hampshire	No later than 11 a.m.	No earlier than 7 p.m.	Polling hours vary from town to town.
New Jersey	6 a.m.	8 p.m.	
New Mexico	7 a.m.	7 p.m.	
New York	6 a.m.	9 p.m.	
North Carolina	6:30 a.m.	7:30 p.m.	
North Dakota	Between 7 and 9 a.m.	Between 7 and 9 p.m.	Polling locations cannot open earlier than 7 a.m. and must be open by 9 a.m., with the exception of those precincts in which fewer than 75 votes were cast in the last General Election, which must open no later than noon. All polling locations must remain open until 7 p.m. and close no later than 9 p.m.
Ohio	6:30 a.m.	7:30 p.m.	
Oklahoma	7 a.m.	7 p.m.	
Oregon	NA	NA	Oregon votes by mail. Official dropsites open eight hours or more and until 8 p.m. for depositing cast ballots. County Clerks office open 7 a.m. - 8 p.m. for issuing and depositing ballots
Pennsylvania	7 a.m.	8 p.m.	
Rhode Island	Between 7 and 9 a.m	8 p.m.	Polls open at 9 a.m. in special elections.
South Carolina	7 a.m.	7 p.m.	
South Dakota	7 a.m.	7 p.m.	

See footnotes at end of table

TABLE 6.5
Polling Hours: General Elections (continued)

State or other jurisdiction	Polls open	Polls close	Notes on hours (a)
Tennessee	8 a.m. (may be earlier)	7 p.m. CT/8 p.m. ET	Polling places must be open a minimum of ten continuous hours, but no more than 13 hours. In any county having a population of not less than 120,000, all polling places must open by 8 a.m., but nothing prevents an earlier opening time at the discretion of the county election commission.
Texas	7 a.m.	7 p.m.	
Utah	7 a.m.	8 p.m.	
Vermont	Between 5 and 10 a.m.	7 p.m.	The opening time for polls is set by local boards of civil authority.
Virginia	6 a.m.	7 p.m.	
Washington	NA	NA	Washington votes by mail. The ballot must be postmarked no later than Election Day; or returned to a designated ballot drop box by 8 p.m. on Election Day; or returned in person to the county elections department by 8 p.m. on Election Day.
West Virginia	6:30 a.m.	7:30 p.m.	
Wisconsin	7 a.m.	8 p.m.	
Wyoming	7 a.m.	7 p.m.	
Dist. of Columbia	7 a.m.	8 p.m.	
American Samoa	6 a.m	6 p.m.	
Guam	7 a.m.	8 p.m.	
CNMI*	7 a.m.	7 p.m.	
Puerto Rico	9 a.m.	5 p.m.	
U.S. Virgin Islands	7 a.m.	7 p.m.	

Sources: The Council of State Governments and state websites, March 2020.
*Commonwealth of Northern Mariana Islands
Note: Hours for primary, municipal and special elections may differ from those noted.

(a) In all states, voters standing in line when the polls close are allowed to vote; however, provisions for handling those voters vary across jurisdictions.

TABLE 6.6
Voter Registration Information

State or other jurisdiction	Closing date for registration before general election (Days)	Same-Day registration	Online registration	Automatic registration (a)	Residency requirements (b)	Registration in other places prohibited (c)	Provision regarding mental competency
Alabama	15	...	★		S	★	★
Alaska	30	(d)	★	★	S, D, 30	★	★
Arizona	29	...	★		S, C, 29	...	★
Arkansas	30	...	...		S, 30	★	★
California	15	★(e)	★	★	S	...	★
Colorado	22 days through voter registration drive, 8 online or by mail, Election Day in person	★	★	★	S, 22		...
Connecticut	14 by mail, 7 in person or online, Election Day	★	★	★	S, T	★	★
Delaware	24	...	★		S	★	★
Florida	29	...	★		S	...	★
Georgia	30 online, 29 in person, 28 by mail	...	★		S, C	...	★
Hawaii	29	★(g)	★		S	★	★
Idaho	25 or Election Day	★	★		S, C, 30	...	...
Illinois	28 (h)	★	★	★	S, P, 30	★	...
Indiana	29	...	★		S, P, 30	...	★
Iowa	15 by mail, 10 in person or online, Election Day	★	★		S	★	★
Kansas	21	...	★		S	★	...
Kentucky	29	...	★		S, P, 28	★	★
Louisiana	30	...	★		S, Parish, 30	★	★
Maine	21 by mail, up to Election Day in person	★	...		S, M	★	★
Maryland	21 by mail, early voting period in person	★(i)	★		S, 21	★	★
Massachusetts	20	...	★		S	...	★
Michigan	30 by mail, 21 in person	★	★(j)	★	S, M, 30	★	...
Minnesota	21 or Election Day	★	★		S, 20		★
Mississippi	30	...	(k)		S, T, 30	★	★
Missouri	28	...	★		S	...	★
Montana	30 by mail or up to Election Day in person	★	...		S, 30	★	★
Nebraska	18 by mail or online, 11 in person	...	★		S	★	★
Nevada	31 by mail, 21 in person or online	...	★		S, C, 30; P, 10	★	★
New Hampshire	10 or Election Day	★	...		S	★	...
New Jersey	21	...	...		S, C, 30	★	...
New Mexico	28	...	★		S	...	★
New York	25	...	★		S, P, 30	★	★
North Carolina	25 (l)	(l)	...		S, C, 30	★	...
North Dakota	(m)	(m)	(m)		S, P, 30	(m)	...
Ohio	30 (n)	(n)	★		S, 30	★	★
Oklahoma	25	...	★(f)		S	...	★
Oregon	21	...	★	★	S	★	★
Pennsylvania	30	...	★		S, D, 30	★	...
Rhode Island	30	★(d)	★	★	S, T	★	★
South Carolina	30	...	★		S,C,P	★	★
South Dakota	15	...	...		S	★	★
Tennessee	30	...	★		S	★	★
Texas	30	...	...		S, C	...	★
Utah	30 by mail, 7 in person or online (o)	...	★		S, 30	★	★
Vermont	Election Day	★(p)	★	★	S, T	...	...
Virginia	22	...	★		S	★	★
Washington	29 by mail or online, 8 in person	...	★		S, 30	★	★
West Virginia	21	...	★	★	S, T, 30	★	★
Wisconsin	20 by mail or Election Day	★	★		S, P, 28	...	★
Wyoming	14 by mail or Election Day	★	...		S, P	★	★
Dist. of Columbia	30 by mail, Election Day in person	★	★	★	D, 30	★	★
American Samoa	30	...	...		D	★	...
Guam	10	...	...		Territory	★	★
CNMI*	60	...	...		Territory, 120	★	★
Puerto Rico	50	...	...		Territory (q)	...	★
U.S. Virgin Islands	30	...	...		Territory, P, 90	★	★

See footnotes at end of table

TABLE 6.6
Voter Registration Information (continued)

Source: The Council of State Governments survey of state election web sites, May 2020.

Note: Many of these practices were amended/altered for the 2020 election cycle due to COVID-19. Most states allowed extended deadlines for registration and relaxed rules on absentee or vote-by-mail options.

*Commonwealth of Mariana Islands

Key:

★ –Provision exists

… –No state provision.

(a) Eligible citizens who interact with government agencies are automatically registered to vote unless they decline.

(b) Key for residency requirements: S – State, C – County, D – District, M – Municipality, P – Precinct, T – Town. Numbers represent the number of days before an election for which one must be a resident.

(c) State provision prohibiting registration or claiming the right to vote in another state or jurisdiction.

(d) Election-day registration is available in presidential election years, but voters who do so can vote only for the offices of President and Vice President, not in state or local races.

(e) California's same-day registration will take effect on January 1 of the year following the year in which the Secretary of State certifies that the state has a statewide voter registration database that complies with the requirements of the federal Help America Vote Act of 2002.

(f) Not yet implemented: Oklahoma, passed in 2015.

(g) In 2014 Hawaii lawmakers passed legislation (HB 2590) to allow voters to register at early voting sites beginning in 2016 or at their assigned polling places on Election Day starting in 2018.

(h) Registration closes 27 days before a general election. Illinois also has a "grace period" registration that extends registration from the normal close of registration up through the 3rd day before the election. Once registered, this voter may cast a ballot during this "Grace Period" at the election authority's office or at a location specifically designated for this purpose by the election

authority, or by mail, at the discretion of the election authority.

(i) A legislatively referred constitutional amendment to authorize the legislature to enact election day registration was approved by voters in November 2018.

(j) An online system allows voters to change their address for both their drivers license and voter registration at the same time. Michigan law requires that the same address be on record for both.

(k) In Mississippi, a registered voter can update an existing registration record online, but new applications must still be made on paper.

(l) In 2014, the North Carolina legislature eliminated voters' ability to register and vote on the same day at early voting locations. Registered voters may still update their name and address on their voter registration at an Early Voting site.

(m) No voter registration.

(n) In 2014, the Ohio Legislature passed a bill that eliminated the ability of voters to register during the six early voting days referred to as "Golden Week," when people could both register to vote and cast an in-person absentee ballot.

(o) Must be postmarked 30 days before an election. Voters can register in-person or online up to 7 days before the election.

However, these voters will not be eligible to participate in early voting, and must vote on election day.

(p) The Vermont Legislature passed a bill (SB 29) in 2015 to allow for same-day voter registration, effective January 1, 2017.

(q) Voters must have a permanent residence in Puerto Rico to be a qualified elector.

TABLE 6.6A
Voting Information

State or other jurisdiction	Vote by mail or online (a)	Early voting allowed (b)	Voter ID required (c)	Photo ID required	Absentee voting			Provisions for felons	
					Persons eligible for absentee voting (d)	Permanent absentee status available (e)	Absentee votes signed by witness or notary (f)	Voting rights revoked	Method/process or provision for restoration (g)
Alabama		No	Yes	Yes (h)	Excuse required	...	N or 2 W	★	B
Alaska	★ (i)	Yes	Yes (j)	No	No excuse required	...	N or 1 W	★	C
Arizona		Yes	Yes	No	No excuse required	★	...	★	B
Arkansas		Yes	Yes	Yes	Excuse required	...	...	★	C
California		Yes	No	No	No excuse required	★	...	★	C
Colorado	★ (l)	Yes	Yes	No	N.A.	N.A.	...	★	D
Connecticut		No	Yes	No	Excuse required	...	...	★	C
Delaware		No	Yes	No	Excuse required	...	...	★	B
Florida		Yes	Yes	Yes	No excuse required	...	...	★	B
Georgia		Yes	Yes	Yes	No excuse required	...	...	★	C
Hawaii		Yes	Yes	No	No excuse required	★	...	★	D
Idaho		Yes (m)	Yes	Yes (n)	No excuse required	...	...	★	C
Illinois		Yes	No	No	No excuse required	...	...	★	D
Indiana		Yes (m)	Yes	Yes	Excuse required	...	...	★	D
Iowa		Yes (m)	Yes	No	No excuse required	...	...	★	A
Kansas		Yes	Yes	Yes	No excuse required	...	...	★	C
Kentucky		No	Yes	Yes (k)	Excuse required	...	...	★	A
Louisiana		Yes	Yes	Yes	Excuse required	...	N or W	★	C
Maine		Yes (m)	No	No	No excuse required	...	...	...	N.A.
Maryland		Yes	No	No	No excuse required	...	...	★	D
Massachusetts		Yes (o)	No	No	Excuse required	...	...	★	D
Michigan		No	Yes	Yes	No excuse required	...	...	★	D
Minnesota		Yes (m)	No	No	No excuse required	★	N or W (p)	★	C
Mississippi		No	Yes	Yes	Excuse required	...	N (q)	★	B
Missouri		No	Yes	No	Excuse required	...	N (r)	★	C
Montana		Yes (m)	Yes	No	No excuse required	★	...	★	D
Nebraska		Yes	No	No	No excuse required	...	...	★	C
Nevada		Yes	No	No	No excuse required	★	...	★	D
New Hampshire		No	Yes	Yes	Excuse required	...	...	★	D
New Jersey		Yes (m)	No	No	No excuse required	★	...	★	C
New Mexico		Yes	No	No	No excuse required	...	...	★	C
New York		No	No	No	Excuse required	...	...	★	C
North Carolina		Yes	Yes	No (s)	No excuse required	...	N or 2 W	★	C
North Dakota		Yes	Yes	Yes	No excuse required	...	...	★	D
Ohio		Yes (m)	Yes	No	No excuse required	...	...	★	D
Oklahoma		Yes (m)	Yes	No (t)	No excuse required	...	N (u)	★	C
Oregon	★ (v)	N/A	No	No	N.A.	N.A.	...	★	D
Pennsylvania		No	No (w)	No (w)	No excuse required	...	...	★	D
Rhode Island		No	Yes	Yes	Excuse required	...	N or 2 W (x)	★	D
South Carolina		No	Yes	Yes (y)	Excuse required	...	W (z)	★	C
South Dakota		Yes (m)	Yes	Yes	No excuse required	...	(aa)	★	C
Tennessee		Yes	Yes	Yes	Excuse required	...	...	★	B
Texas		Yes	Yes	Yes	Excuse required	...	...	★	C
Utah	★ (l)	Yes	Yes	No	N.A.	N.A.	...	★	D
Vermont		Yes (m)	No	No	No excuse required	...	...	...	N.A.
Virginia		No	Yes	No	No excuse required	...	W	★	B (bb)
Washington	★ (cc)	N/A	No	No	N.A.	N.A.	...	★	C
West Virginia		Yes	Yes (dd)	No	Excuse required	...	...	★	C
Wisconsin		Yes (m)	Yes	Yes	No excuse required	...	W	★	C
Wyoming		Yes (m)	No	No	No excuse required	...	...	★	B
Dist. of Columbia		Yes	No	No	No excuse required	★	...	★	D
American Samoa		No	No	No	Excuse required	...	...	★	C
Guam		No	No	No	Excuse required	...	N	★	C
CNMI*		No	No	No	Excuse required	...	N	★	C
Puerto Rico		No	Yes	No	Excuse required	...	(ee)	...	N.A.
U.S. Virgin Islands		No	Yes	No	Excuse required	...	Affidavit	★	C

See footnotes at end of table

TABLE 6.6A
Voting Information (continued)

Sources: The Council of State Governments survey of state web sites, May 2020.

Note: Many of these practices were amended/altered for the 2020 election cycle due to COVID-19. Most states allowed extended deadlines for registration and relaxed rules on absentee or vote-by-mail options.

*Commonwealth of Northern Mariana Islands

Key:

★-Provision exists

…-No state provision.

N.A.-Not applicable

(a) Three states-Colorado, Oregon, and Washington-conduct elections by mail. All registered voters are automatically mailed a ballot in advance of Election Day. Alaska is the first state to allow all voters-not just those covered by the federal Uniformed and Overseas Citizens Absentee Voting Act (UOCAVA)-to submit an absentee ballot electronically. Civilian voters must apply for an electronic ballot beginning 15 days before the election.

(b) Early voting is usually done in person on the same equipment as that used on Election Day. An excuse is not required.

(c) Voter identification laws include both photo or non-photo identification requirements.

(d) Typical excuses include some or all of the following: absent on business; senior citizen; disabled persons; not absent, but prevented by employment from voting; out of state on Election Day; out of precinct on Election Day; absent for religious reasons; students; temporarily out of jurisdiction.

(e) State allows voters to be added to the permanent absentee voter list, in which an absentee ballot will be automatically sent for each election. No excuse is required. This does not include states that allow certain voters to be added to the list, including permanently disabled or ill voters, the elderly, uniformed service members and their families, or people who live outside the United States.

(f) Absentee votes must be signed by, N-Notary or W-Witness. Numbers indicated the number of signatures required.

(g) A-permanent disenfranchisement for all offenders; states that permanently disenfranchise all or some felons may allow felons to apply, on an individual basis, to the state for an exemption that will restore their voting rights.

B-restoration is dependent upon the type of conviction and/or the results of an individual petition to the state government.

C-voting rights restored after completion of sentence including prison, parole and probation.

D-voting rights restored after release from prison.

E-voting rights restored once released from prison and parole, probationers can vote.

(h) Photo identification is not required if two election officials can sign sworn statements saying they know the voter.

(i) Alaska is the first state to allow all voters-not just those covered by the federal Uniformed and Overseas Citizens Absentee Voting Act (UOCAVA)-to submit an absentee ballot electronically. Civilian voters must apply for an electronic ballot beginning 15 days before the election.

(j) An election officer may waive the identification requirement if

the election officials knows the identity of the voter.

(k) The Kentucky General Assembly passed a voter ID law in 2020 that will go into effect with the November 2020 general election.

(l) While all registered voters are automatically mailed a ballot prior to the election, the state also operates in-person voting sites.

(m) Functional early voting, as the state permits in-person absentee voting, in which voters, within a certain period of time before the election, can apply in person for an absentee ballot (no excuse required) and cast a ballot in the election office.

(n) A registered voter must either present a photo ID or sign a Personal Identification Affidavit. After signing the Affidavit, the voter will be issued a ballot to be tabulated with all other ballots.

(o) Beginning in 2016, Massachusetts will have early voting only during even-year November elections. There are no early voting periods for primaries or municipal elections.

(p) Unless the witness is a notary, the witness must also be a registered Minnesota voter.

(q) Disabled voters do not need to have an absentee ballot notarized, but it must be witnessed.

(r) All absentee ballots must be notarized with the exception of the following: Missouri residents outside the U.S., including military on active duty and their immediate family members; permanently disabled voters and those voting absentee due to illness or physical disability; and caregivers.

(s) Photo identification will be required starting in 2016. However, voters who are unable to obtain an acceptable photo ID due to a reasonable impediment may still vote a provisional ballot at the polls . Examples of a reasonable impediment include but are not limited to the lack of proper documents, family obligations, transportation problems, work schedule, illness or disability, among other reasonable impediments faced by the voter. Voters must also sign a declaration describing their impediment; and provide their date of birth and last four digits of their Social Security number, or present their current voter registration card or a copy of an acceptable document bearing their name and address. (Acceptable documents include a current utility bill, bank statement, government check, paycheck, or other government-issued document.) The provisional ballot will be counted when the information on the declaration is verified and all other eligibility requirements are met. On Dec. 31, 2019 a federal judge blocked the state from enforcing the voter ID law while a case challenging the law was being argued.

(t) A Voter Identification Card issued by the County Election Board is the only valid proof of identity that does not include a photograph.

(u) All absentee ballots must notarized with the following exceptions: Physically incapacitated voters and voters who care for physically incapacitated persons (ballot affidavit must be witnessed by two people); voters in a nursing home; overseas voters.

(v) State conducts election by mail. All registered voters are automatically mailed a ballot in advance of Election Day.

(w) In 2012, the legislature enacted a law requiring voters to show photo identification. However, in 2014 a state judge struck down

TABLE 6.6A
Voting Information (continued)

the law.

(x) All absentee ballots must be notarized or signed by two witnesses with the following exceptions: military and overseas voters.

(y) If a voter has a reasonable impediment to obtaining photo identification, he or she may vote a provisional ballot after showing a non-photo voter registration card. State law defines a reasonable impediment as any valid reason, beyond a person's control, that creates an obstacle to obtaining Photo ID. Some examples include: religious objection to being photographed; disability or illness; work schedule; lack of transportation; lack of birth certificate; family responsibilities; election within short time frame of implementation of photo ID law (January 1, 2013); and any other obstacle a person finds reasonable.

(z) All absentee ballots must be notarized or signed by one witness, with the exception of qualified voters under the Uniformed and Overseas Citizens Absentee Voters Act.

(aa) Absentee ballot applications (not absentee ballots) are required to be notarized unless a copy of the voter's photo identification is also submitted.

(bb) On Apr. 22, 2016, Virginia Gov. Terry McAuliffe signed an order restoring the vote to all felons in Virginia, regardless of their charge, who had completed their term of incarceration and their term of probation or parole. The governor's action will not apply to felons released in the future, but aides say the governor plans to issue similar orders on a monthly basis to cover people as they are released. The Virginia Supreme Court ruled that rights restoration must take place on an individual basis.

(cc) State conducts election by mail. All registered voters are automatically mailed a ballot in advance of Election Day. Only Pierce County offers in-person voting.

(dd) In 2016, the West Virginia Legislature approved a bill that will require voters to show some form of identification before casting a ballot. Approved forms of identification include any government-issued ID or permit, with or without a photo, including a voter registration card; any college or high school issued ID; a health insurance card; a utility bill; a bank card or bank statement; or verification of identification by another adult who has known the voter for at least 6 months, including a poll worker. It is effective January 1, 2018.

(ee) Absentee ballot applications (not absentee ballots) are required to be certified by various officials, depending on the reason for voting absentee, such as a college registrar, employer, or medical official.

TABLE 6.7
Voting Statistics for Gubernatorial Elections

State or other jurisdiction	Date of last election	Primary election				
		Republican	Democrat	3rd Party	Independent	Total votes
Alabama	2018	591,199	283,705	0	0	874,904
Alaska	2018	71,195	39,241 (a)	0	0	110,436
Arizona	2018	655,538	505,481	2,648	0	1,163,667
Arkansas	2018	206,405	105,919	0	0	312,324
California (b)	2018	2,519,136	4,350,513	91,481	0	6,961,130
Colorado	2018	503,205	637,002	0	0	1,140,207
Connecticut	2018	142,858	212,543	0	0	355,401
Delaware	2016	30,265	(c)	0	0	30,265
Florida	2018	1,622,124	1,519,492	0	0	3,141,616
Georgia	2018	607,441	555,089	0	0	1,162,530
Hawaii	2018	31,156	242,514	454	1,138	275,262
Idaho	2018	194,536	65,882	0	0	260,418
Illinois	2018	722,162	1,324,548	0	0	2,046,710
Indiana	2016	815,699 (c)	547,375 (c)	0	0	1,363,074
Iowa	2018	94,118 (c)	178,924	1,696	1,649	276,387
Kansas	2018	317,615	156,273	0	0	473,888
Kentucky	2019	259,866	394,513	0	0	654,379
Louisiana (f)	2019	696,434	636,963	0	10,966	1,344,363
Maine	2018	94,382	125,391	0	748	220,521
Maryland	2018	157,503 (c)	391,706	0	0	549,209
Massachusetts	2018	273,011	551,470	0	0	824,481
Michigan	2018	989,525	1,131,447	6975	0	2,127,947
Minnesota	2018	289,957	582,350	0	0	872,307
Mississippi	2019	383,080	302,390	0	0	685,470
Missouri	2016	684,251	325,413	3,515 (c)	0	1,013,179
Montana	2016	145,948	122,419	0	0	268,367
Nebraska	2018	169,860	91,942	0	0	261,802
Nevada	2018	142,184 (g)	145,420 (g)	0	0	287,604
New Hampshire	2018	92,583	122,966	1110	0	216,659
New Jersey	2017	258,880	527,332	0	0	786,212
New Mexico	2018	75,162 (c)	175,898	175	0	251,235
New York	2018	(c)	1,558,352	0	0	1,558,352
North Carolina	2016	1,072,655	1,034,432	0	0	2,107,087
North Dakota	2016	114,415	17,337 (c)	1,095	0	132,847
Ohio	2018	834,967	688,788	3,031	0	1,526,786
Oklahoma	2018	452,606	395,494	3558	0	399,052
Oregon	2016	304,892	480,852	0	23,332	809,076
Pennsylvania	2018	737,312	749,812 (c)	0	0	1,487,124
Rhode Island	2018	33,087	117,875	0	0	150,962
South Carolina	2018	367,983	240,468	0	0	608,451
South Dakota	2018	102,772	(c)	0	0	102,772
Tennessee	2018	792,888	373,390	0	0	1,166,278
Texas	2018	1,549,006	1,022,558	0	0	2,571,564
Utah	2016	229,656 (m)	(i)	0	0	229,656
Vermont	2018	35,811	57,248	0	4974	98,033
Virginia	2017	365,782	542,816	0	0	908,598
Washington	2016	596,092	756,759	18,989	22,582	1,394,422
West Virginia	2016	161,127 (c)	258,350	0	0	419,477
Wisconsin	2018	455,563	538,646	0	0	994,191
Wyoming	2018	116,786	18,076	0	0	134,862
American Samoa	2016	---------------------------------- (j) ----------------------------------				
Guam	2018	(c)	25,699	0	0	25,699
CNMI*	2018	(k)	(k)	(k)	(k)	(k)
Puerto Rico	2016	(c)	462,973	0	0	462,973
U.S. Virgin Islands	2018	N.A.	N.A.	N.A.	N.A.	N.A.

See footnotes at end of table

TABLE 6.7
Voting Statistics for Gubernatorial Elections (continued)

State or other jurisdiction	General election								
	Republican	Percent	Democrat	Percent	3rd Party	Percent	Independent and Write-In	Percent	Total votes
Alabama	1,019,558	59.5	691,671	40.4	0	0.0	2,614	0.2	1,713,843
Alaska	145,631	51.4	125,739	44.4	5,402	1.9	6,362	2.2	283,134
Arizona	1,330,863	56.0	994,341	41.8	50,962	4.8	275	0.0	2,376,441
Arkansas	582,406	65.3	283,218	31.8	25,885	3.1	0	0.0	891,509
California (d)	4,742,825	38.1	7,721,410	61.9	0	0.0	0	0.0	12,464,235
Colorado	1,080,801	42.8	1,348,888	53.4	95,373	4.7	0	0.0	2,525,062
Connecticut	650,138 (e)	48.2	694,510 (e)	50.7	62,081	0.0	74	0.0	1,406,803
Delaware	166,852	39.2	248,404	58.3	10,528	2.5	0	0.0	425,784
Florida	4,076,186	49.6	4,043,723	49.2	47,140	3.8	53,512	0.7	8,220,561
Georgia	1,978,408	50.2	1,923,685	48.8	37,235	2.4	432	0.0	3,939,328
Hawaii	131,719	33.7	244,934	62.7	10,123	13.5	4,067	1.0	390,843
Idaho	361,661	59.8	231,081	38.2	12,338	5.8	51	0.0	605,131
Illinois	1,765,751	38.8	2,479,746	54.5	302,045	3.3	115	0.0	4,547,657
Indiana	1,397,396	51.4	1,235,503	45.4	87,025	3.2	44	0.0	2,719,968
Iowa	667,275	50.3	630,986	47.5	28,889	3.6	488	0.0	1,327,638
Kansas	453,645	43.0	506,727	48.0	20,020	4.0	75,174	7.1	1,055,566
Kentucky	707,754	48.9	709,890	49.1	28,433	0.0	46	0.0	1,446,123
Louisiana (f)	734,286	48.7	774,498	51.3	0	0.0	0	0.0	1,508,784
Maine	272,311	43.2	320,962	50.9	37,268	8.4	126	0.0	630,667
Maryland	855,539	57.7	608,810	41.1	16,584	1.5	1,096	0.1	1,482,029
Massachusetts	885,770	33.1	1,781,341	66.6		3.3	7,504	0.3	2,674,615
Michigan	1,859,534	43.7	2,266,193	53.3	124,826	2.2	32	0.0	4,250,585
Minnesota	1,097,705	42.4	1,393,096	53.8	95,402	2.2	1,084	0.0	2,587,287
Mississippi	459,396	51.9	414,368	46.8	2,625	0.0	8,522	1.0	884,911
Missouri	1,424,730	51.3	1,261,110	45.4	61,503	2.2	30,511	1.1	2,777,854
Montana	236,115	46.4	255,933	50.2	17,312	3.4	0	0.0	509,360
Nebraska	411,812	59.0	286,169	41.0	0	3.5	0	0.0	697,981
Nevada	440,320	45.3	480,007	49.4	32,607	2.7	18,865 (g)	2.9	971,799
New Hampshire	302,764	52.8	262,359	45.7	8,197	1.4	282	0.0	573,602
New Jersey	899,583	41.9	1,203,110	56.0	44,722	2.1	0	0.0	2,147,415
New Mexico	298,091	42.8	398,368	57.2	0	0.0	0	0.0	696,459
New York	2,207,602 (h)	36.2	3,635,340 (h)	59.6	254,420	4.2	0	0.0	6,097,362
North Carolina	2,298,880	48.8	2,309,157	49.0	102,977	2.2	0	0.0	4,711,014
North Dakota	259,863	76.5	65,855	19.4	13,230	3.9	653	0.2	339,601
Ohio	2,231,917	50.4	2,067,847	46.7	129,460	3.3	358	0.0	4,429,582
Oklahoma	644,579	54.3	500,973	42.2	40,833	0.0	0	0.0	1,186,385
Oregon	684,321	43.8	796,006	51.0	46,446	3.0	35,046	2.2	1,561,819
Pennsylvania	2,039,882	40.7	2,895,652	57.8	77,021	0.0	0	0.0	5,012,555
Rhode Island	139,932	37.2	198,122	52.6	14,346	21.4	24,001	6.4	376,401
South Carolina	921,342	54.0	784,182	45.9	0	1.7	2,045	0.1	1,707,569
South Dakota	172,706	51.0	161,171	47.6	4,838	0.0	0	0.0	338,715
Tennessee	1,336,106	59.6	864,863	38.6	0	3.3	42,325	1.9	2,243,294
Texas	4,656,196	55.8	3,546,615	42.5	140,632	1.8	0	0.0	8,343,443
Utah	750,828	66.7	322,462	28.7	34,687	3.1	16,936	1.5	1,124,913
Vermont	151,261	55.2	110,335	40.3	3,694	1.3	8,797	3.2	274,087
Virginia	1,175,731	45.0	1,409,175	53.9	27,987	6.5	1,389	0.1	2,614,282
Washington	1,476,346	45.6	1,760,520	54.4	0	0.0	0	0.0	3,236,866
West Virginia	301,987	42.3	350,408	49.1	61,463	8.6	0	0.0	713,858
Wisconsin	1,295,080	48.5	1,324,307	49.6	31,312	0.0	21,643	0.8	2,672,342
Wyoming	136,412	67.1	55,965	27.5	9,761	2.4	1,100	0.5	203,238
American Samoa			-------------- (j) --------------						12,024
Guam	9,487	26.4	18,258	50.8	0	0.0	8,205	22.8	35,950
CNMI*	8922	62.2	0	0.0	0	0.0	5,420	37.8	14,342
Puerto Rico	614,190	38.9	660,510	41.8	39,159	4.4	266,325	16.9	1,580,184
U.S. Virgin Islands	0	0.0	9,711 (l)	39.2	0	0.0	15,811 (l)	60.8	25,522

See footnotes at end of table

TABLE 6.7
Voting Statistics for Gubernatorial Elections (continued)

Sources: The Council of State Governments' survey of state elections web sites, March 2020.

* Commonwealth of Northern Mariana Islands

Key:

N.A.–Not applicable

(a) In 2018, the Democratic Primary was known as the ADL ballot, which featured candidates from the Democratic, Libertarian and Independence Parties.

(b) California became an open primary state after passage of Proposition 14 in the June 2010 election. The top two vote-getters in primary races for congressional, state legislative and statewide offices, regardless of political party, will be in a face-off in the general election.

(c) Candidate ran unopposed.

(e) Republican vote total includes 25,388 votes from the Independent party. Democratic vote total includes 17,861 from the Working Families Party.

(f) Louisiana has an open primary which requires all candidates, regardless of party affiliation, to appear on a single ballot. If a candidate receives over 50 percent of the vote in the primary, he is elected to the office. If no candidate receives a majority vote, then a single election is held between the two candidates receiving the most votes.

(g) Nevada voters have the option to select "None of These Candidates." If the "None of These Candidates" option receives the most votes in an election, the actual candidate who receives the most votes wins the election. In the Democratic primary, the "None of These Candidates" option received 5,069 votes. In the Republican primary, 6,136 voters selected that option. The "None of These Candidates" option received 18,865 votes in the general election.

(h) Democratic vote includes 68,713 from the Independence Party, 27,733 from the Women's Equality Party, and 114,478 from the Working Families Party. The Republican vote includes 253,624 from the Conservative Party and 27,493 from the Reform Party.

(i) Candidate nominated by convention.

(j) There are no primaries. Instead, the law provides for a run off when none of the candidates receives more than 50% of the vote. All elections and candidates are nonpartisan, but candidates do identify with specific parties. The vote total in the general election was 12,024. Incumbent Lolo Matalasi Moliga won with 7,235 votes, Faoa Aitofele Sunia was next with 4,305 and Tuika Tuika received 484 votes.

(k) There are no primaries. Instead, the law provides for a run off when none of the candidates receives more than 50% of the vote.

(l) In the general election in the U.S. Virgin Islands, a runoff was held because no candidate received more than 50% of the vote. The vote total in the runoff election was 21,635, with the Democratic candidate Albert Bryan winnning with 54.5% of the vote.

(m) Incumbent Republican Governor of Utah, Gary Herbert, lost the GOP primary convention vote to challenger Jonathan Johnson. Under the "Count My Vote" law, Herbert was still guaranteed a spot on the ballot despite losing the convention vote (forcing an official primary).

Table 6.7 | Gubernatorial Elections

Republican
PERCENT–HIGHEST

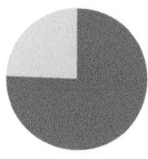 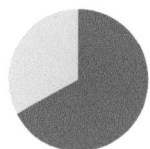 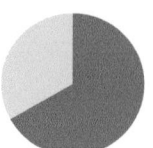 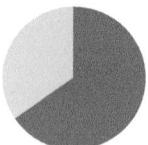 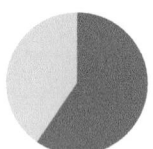

ND • 76.5%   WY • 67.1%   UT • 66.7%   AR • 65.3%   TN • 59.6%

Democrat
PERCENT–HIGHEST

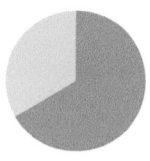 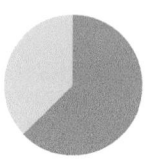   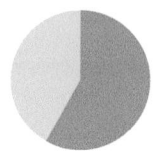

MA • 66.6%   HI • 62.7%   CA • 61.9%   NY • 59.6%   DE • 58.3%

Third Party
PERCENT–HIGHEST

 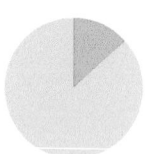  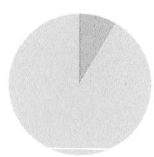 

RI • 21.4%   HI • 13.5%   WV • 8.6%   ME • 8.4%   VA • 6.5%

In a gubernatorial election, NEVADA voters have the option to select "None of These Candidates."

In the most recent general election, this option received 18,865 votes.

Of the states, **KANSAS** had the **highest total percentage** of independent and write-in votes.

7.1%

TABLE 6.8
Voter Turnout for Presidential Elections By Region: 2008, 2012 and 2016 (In thousands)

State or other jurisdiction	2016 Voting age population (a)	2016 Number registered	2016 Number voting (b)	2012 Voting age population (a)	2012 Number registered	2012 Number voting (b)	2008 Voting age population (a)	2008 Number registered	2008 Number voting (b)
U.S. Total	245,502	157,596	137,537	235,248	153,157	132,948	225,499	146,311	131,144
Alabama	3,717	2,526	2,095	3,594	2,556	2,154	3,497	2,438	2,126
Alaska	518	358	308	516	361	289	488	345	304
Arizona	5,196	3,145	2,769	4,863	2,812	2,412	4,688	2,874	2,497
Arkansas	2,216	1,456	1,241	2,198	1,376	1,124	2,108	1,317	1,092
California	29,894	16,096	14,416	28,357	15,356	13,462	26,993	14,885	13,828
Colorado	4,242	2,893	2,707	3,817	2,635	2,495	3,694	2,437	2,308
Connecticut	2,759	1,763	1,586	2,726	1,760	1,568	2,651	1,761	1,610
Delaware	729	487	417	693	470	431	648	447	408
Florida	16,202	9,604	8,578	15,034	9,102	8,107	14,069	8,774	7,951
Georgia	7,626	4,892	4,246	7,179	4,767	4,168	7,018	4,624	4,183
Hawaii	1,064	530	460	1,013	547	480	977	522	457
Idaho	1,224	790	714	1,129	745	679	1,095	723	644
Illinois	9,723	6,665	5,719	9,651	6,425	5,428	9,521	6,151	5,436
Indiana	4,988	3,298	2,795	4,852	3,270	2,801	4,686	3,105	2,758
Iowa	2,394	1,657	1,454	2,320	1,745	1,548	2,244	1,630	1,501
Kansas	2,142	1,438	1,243	2,120	1,467	1,249	2,037	1,343	1,219
Kentucky	3,348	2,253	1,850	3,291	2,303	1,895	3,179	2,259	1,952
Louisiana	3,463	2,446	2,067	3,321	2,498	2,148	3,161	2,393	2,149
Maine	1,058	830	754	1,042	787	700	1,020	801	716
Maryland	4,623	3,114	2,737	4,449	2,888	2,609	4,218	2,828	2,611
Massachusetts	5,374	3,660	3,315	5,170	3,759	3,382	4,962	3,293	3,044
Michigan	7,624	5,434	4,713	7,496	5,620	4,832	7,487	5,531	4,865
Minnesota	4,190	3,055	2,738	4,055	3,085	2,859	3,898	2,931	2,759
Mississippi	2,203	1,725	1,470	2,166	1,794	1,588	2,109	1,589	1,439
Missouri	4,626	3,333	2,906	4,521	3,384	2,818	4,430	3,224	2,846
Montana	798	581	521	768	553	495	731	516	473
Nebraska	1,407	1,008	893	1,371	901	798	1,308	939	844
Nevada	2,234	1,371	1,195	2,039	1,176	1,048	1,946	1,147	1,027
New Hampshire	1,044	763	698	1,028	752	688	1,015	756	708
New Jersey	6,862	4,165	3,665	6,730	4,326	3,670	6,489	4,022	3,637
New Mexico	1,547	916	765	1,553	978	878	1,473	937	846
New York	15,506	9,142	7,869	15,066	8,887	7,675	14,665	8,458	7,559
North Carolina	7,631	5,194	4,700	7,265	5,295	4,624	6,845	4,902	4,370
North Dakota	583	424	362	528	383	328	484	399	321
Ohio	8,811	6,128	5,408	8,750	6,076	5,395	8,499	6,108	5,483
Oklahoma	2,923	1,861	1,555	2,808	1,806	1,431	2,667	1,798	1,507
Oregon	3,185	2,147	1,942	2,998	2,086	1,897	2,904	1,961	1,818
Pennsylvania	9,980	6,909	6,008	9,847	6,795	5,824	9,449	6,451	5,747
Rhode Island	836	538	464	817	552	469	804	568	507
South Carolina	3,733	2,575	2,233	3,516	2,479	2,187	3,313	2,385	2,100
South Dakota	631	437	362	616	454	370	590	442	390
Tennessee	5,057	3,251	2,630	4,849	3,210	2,606	4,692	2,921	2,516
Texas	20,172	11,724	9,626	18,642	10,749	8,643	17,295	10,123	8,435
Utah	2,096	1,398	1,234	1,917	1,138	1,022	1,859	1,056	939
Vermont	500	351	305	496	357	308	487	345	308
Virginia	6,343	4,399	3,973	6,094	4,210	3,778	5,720	3,950	3,650
Washington	5,592	3,906	3,382	5,230	3,533	3,172	4,912	3,299	3,073
West Virginia	1,434	913	723	1,452	982	690	1,395	917	741
Wisconsin	4,465	3,323	3,068	4,352	3,318	3,127	4,212	3,095	2,887
Wyoming	436	304	277	427	268	247	397	270	250
Dist. of Columbia	553	420	380	517	385	350	469	324	306

Sources: U.S. Census Bureau, Table 4a: Reported Voting and Registration of the Citizen Voting-Age Population, for States: November 2016. U.S. Census Bureau, Table 4a: Reported Voting and Registration of the Citizen Voting-Age Population, for States: November 2012. U.S. Census Bureau, Table 4a: Reported Voting and Registration of the Citizen Voting-Age Population, for States: November 2008.

Key:
(a) Estimated population, 18 years old and over. Includes armed forces in each state, aliens, and institutional population.
(b) Number voting is number of ballots cast in presidential race.
(c) No statewide registration required.

TABLE 6.9
Statewide Initiative and Referendum

State or other jurisdiction	Changes to constitution			Changes to statutes			
	Initiative		Referendum	Initiative		Referendum	
	Direct (a)	Indirect (a)	Legislative (b)	Direct (c)	Indirect (c)	Legislative	Citizen petition (d)
Alabama	...	...	★	...	...	...	...
Alaska	...	...	★	...	★	...	★
Arizona	★	...	★	★	...	★	★
Arkansas	★	...	★	★	...	★	★
California	★	...	★	★	...	★	★
Colorado	★	...	★	★	...	★	★
Connecticut	...	...	★	...	...	...	...
Delaware	...	...	...	...	...	★	...
Florida	★	...	★	...	...	...	...
Georgia	...	...	★	...	...	...	...
Hawaii	...	...	★	...	...	...	...
Idaho	...	...	★	★	...	★	★
Illinois	★	...	★	...	...	★	...
Indiana	...	...	★	...	...	...	...
Iowa	...	...	★	...	...	...	...
Kansas	...	...	★	...	...	...	...
Kentucky	...	...	★	...	...	★	...
Louisiana	...	...	★	...	...	...	...
Maine	...	...	★	...	★	★	★
Maryland	...	...	★	...	...	★	★
Massachusetts	...	★	★	...	★	★	★
Michigan	★	...	★	...	★	★	★
Minnesota	...	...	★	...	...	...	...
Mississippi	...	★	★	...	...	...	...
Missouri	★	...	★	★	...	★	★
Montana	★	...	★	★	...	★	★
Nebraska	★	...	★	★	...	★	★
Nevada	★	...	★	...	★	★	★
New Hampshire	...	...	★	...	...	...	...
New Jersey	...	...	★	...	...	...	...
New Mexico	...	...	★	...	...	★	...
New York	...	...	★	...	...	...	...
North Carolina	...	...	★(e)	...	...	...	...
North Dakota	★	...	★	★	...	★	★
Ohio	★	...	★	...	★	★	★
Oklahoma	★	...	★	★	...	★	★
Oregon	★	...	★	★	...	★	★
Pennsylvania	...	...	★	...	...	...	...
Rhode Island	...	...	★	...	...	...	...
South Carolina	...	...	★	...	...	...	...
South Dakota	★	...	★	★	...	★	★
Tennessee	...	...	★	...	...	...	...
Texas	...	...	★	...	...	...	...
Utah	...	...	★	★	★	★	★
Vermont	...	...	★	...	...	...	...
Virginia	...	...	★	...	...	...	...
Washington	...	...	★	★	★	★	★
West Virginia	...	...	★	...	...	...	...
Wisconsin	...	...	★	...	...	...	...
Wyoming	...	...	★	...	★	...	★
American Samoa	...	...	★	...	...	...	...
CNMI*	★	★	★	★	★	★	★
Puerto Rico	...	...	★	...	...	★	...
U.S. Virgin Islands	★	...	★	...	...	★	...

See footnotes at end of table

TABLE 6.9
Statewide Initiative and Referendum (continued)

Sources: The Council of State Governments' survey of state election website, Initiative & Referendum Institute website and Ballotpedia websites, April 2020.

* Commonwealth of Northern Mariana Islands

Note: This table summarizes state provisions for initiatives and referendums. Initiatives may propose constitutional amendments or develop state legislation and may be formed either directly or indirectly. The direct initiative allows a proposed measure to be placed on the ballot after a specific number of signatures have been secured on a citizen petition. The indirect initiative must be submitted to the legislature for a decision after the required number of signatures has been secured on a petition and prior to placing the proposed measure on the ballot. Referendum refers to the process whereby a state law or constitutional amendment passed by the legislature may be referred to the voters before it goes into effect. Three forms of referendums exist: (1) citizen petition, whereby the people may petition for a referendum on legislation which has been considered by the legislature; (2) submission by the legislature (designated in table as "Legislative"), whereby the legislature may voluntarily submit laws to the voters for their approval; and (3) constitutional requirement, whereby the state constitution may require that certain questions be submitted to the voters.

Key:

★ –State Provision.

… –No state provision.

(a) See "Constitutional Amendment Procedure: By Initiative," for more detail.

(b) See "Constitutional Amendment Procedure: By the Legislature," for more detail.

(c) See tables on State Initiatives, for more detail.

(d) See tables on State Referendums, for more detail.

(e) Only the legislature can make statutory changes while in session. Proposed constitutional changes must be passed by the legislature and then are submitted to the citizens to be voted on.

TABLE 6.9A
State Ballot Questions in 2019

State or other jurisdiction	Title	Type	Date	Result	Vote totals		Subject	Short description
					Yes votes	No votes		
Alabama				----------- No Ballot measures in 2019 -----------				
Alaska				----------- No Ballot measures in 2019 -----------				
Arizona				----------- No Ballot measures in 2019 -----------				
Arkansas				----------- No Ballot measures in 2019 -----------				
California				----------- No Ballot measures in 2019 -----------				
Colorado	Proposition CC	LRSS	Nov. 5, 2019	Failed	46%	54%	Transportation and Education Revenue	Allows the state to retain excess revenue it is currently required to refund under the Taxpayer's Bill of Rights (TABOR); directs retained funds to be used for education and transportation purposes.
	Proposition DD	LRSS	Nov. 5, 2019	Passed	51%	49%	Gambling and Taxes	Authorize sports betting and authorizes the legislature to levy a tax of 10% on those conducting sports betting operations and use revenue to fund state water projects.
Connecticut				----------- No Ballot measures in 2019 -----------				
Delaware				----------- No Ballot measures in 2019 -----------				
Florida				----------- No Ballot measures in 2019 -----------				
Georgia				----------- No Ballot measures in 2019 -----------				
Hawaii				----------- No Ballot measures in 2019 -----------				
Idaho				----------- No Ballot measures in 2019 -----------				
Illinois				----------- No Ballot measures in 2019 -----------				
Indiana				----------- No Ballot measures in 2019 -----------				
Iowa				----------- No Ballot measures in 2019 -----------				
Kansas	Eliminate Revision of Census Population Amendment	LRCA	Nov. 5, 2019	Passed	60%	40%	Census	The measure would support ending the state's practice of adjusting the U.S. Census population regarding military personnel and students when redistricting the Kansas State Legislature.
Kentucky				----------- No Ballot measures in 2019 -----------				
Louisiana	Amendment 1	LRCA	Oct. 12, 2019	Failed	47%	53%	Property Tax	The amendment would extend an ad valorem tax exemption to property being stored in Louisiana but destined for the Outer Continental Shelf.
	Amendment 2	LRCA	Oct. 12, 2019	Passed	50.4%	49.6%	Education Funding	Approval allowed for appropriations from the Education Excellence Fund (EEF) to the Louisiana Educational Television Authority (LETA), Thrive Academy, and laboratory schools operated by public colleges.
	Amendment 3	LRCA	Oct. 12, 2019	Passed	58%	42%	Taxes	Approval allows the legislature through a two-thirds vote to give the Louisiana Board of Tax Appeals jurisdiction over the constitutionality of taxes, fees, and related matters. It also establishes authority for the board in the state constitution, subject to changes made by laws passed by a two-thirds vote in the legislature. States in the constitution that the Louisiana Board of Tax Appeals has jurisdiction over any disputes concerning state and local taxes, fees, or other claims against the state.
	Amendment 4	LRCA	Oct. 12, 2019	Failed	37%	63%	Taxes	Passage would have allowed New Orleans to exempt properties with no more than 15 residential units from taxes for the purpose of, according to the amendment, promoting and encouraging affordable housing.
Maine	Question 1	BI	Nov. 5, 2019	Passed	76%	24%	Bonds for Transportation Infrastructure	Approval supported the authorization of $105 million in general obligation bonds for transportation infrastructure projects.
	Question 2	LRCA	Nov. 5, 2019	Passed	76%	24%	Disabilities/ Initiative Petitions	This amendment authorizes legislation allowing for persons with physical disabilities that prevent them from signing their own names to use an alternative signature to sign petitions for citizen-initiated ballot measures.
Maryland				----------- No Ballot measures in 2019 -----------				
Massachusetts				----------- No Ballot measures in 2019 -----------				
Michigan				----------- No Ballot measures in 2019 -----------				
Minnesota				----------- No Ballot measures in 2019 -----------				
Mississippi				----------- No Ballot measures in 2019 -----------				

See footnotes at end of table

TABLE 6.9A
State Ballot Questions in 2019 (continued)

State or other jurisdiction	Title	Type	Date	Result	Vote totals Yes votes	No votes	Subject	Short description
Missouri					No Ballot measures in 2019			
Montana					No Ballot measures in 2019			
Nebraska					No Ballot measures in 2019			
Nevada					No Ballot measures in 2019			
New Hampshire					No Ballot measures in 2019			
New Jersey	Public Question 1	LRCA	Nov. 5, 2019	Passed	76%	24%	Property Taxes	Supports a constitutional amendment extend the $250 property tax deduction that veterans receive to continuing care retirement centers on behalf of the veterans living there and require the retirement centers to pass the value of the deduction on to veterans in the form of credits or payments.
New Mexico					No Ballot measures in 2019			
New York					No Ballot measures in 2019			
North Carolina					No Ballot measures in 2019			
North Dakota					No Ballot measures in 2019			
Ohio					No Ballot measures in 2019			
Oklahoma					No Ballot measures in 2019			
Oregon					No Ballot measures in 2019			
Pennsylvania	Marsy's Law Amendment	LRCA	Nov. 5, 2019	(a)	74%	26%	Marsy's Law	This measure would add specific rights of crime victims, together known as a Marsy's Law, to the Pennsylvania Constitution.
Rhode Island					No Ballot measures in 2019			
South Carolina					No Ballot measures in 2019			
South Dakota					No Ballot measures in 2019			
Tennessee					No Ballot measures in 2019			
Texas	Proposition 1	LRCA	Nov. 5, 2019	Failed	35%	65%	Municipal Judges	The amendment failed. It would have allowed persons to hold more than one office as an elected or appointed municipal judge in more than one municipality at the same time.
	Proposition 2	LRCA	Nov. 5, 2019	Passed	66%	34%	Bonds for Water/Sewer	This amendment allows the Texas Water Development Board to issue bonds on a continuing basis, but not exceeding $200 million.
	Proposition 3	LRCA	Nov. 5, 2019	Passed	85%	15%	Property Taxes	This amendment requires political subdivisions to provide temporary property tax exemptions in areas that the governor declared as disaster areas.
	Proposition 4	LRCA	Nov. 5, 2019	Passed	74%	26%	Income Taxes	This amendment prohibits the state from levying an income tax on individuals to the Texas Constitution, which requires a two-thirds legislative vote and a statewide referendum to amend.
	Proposition 5	LRCA	Nov. 5, 2019	Passed	88%	12%	Sales Taxes	This constitutional amendment dedicates revenue from the sales tax on sporting goods to the Texas Parks and Wildlife Department and the Texas Historical Commission.
	Proposition 6	LRCA	Nov. 5, 2019	Passed	64%	36%	Bonds for Research Institute	The amendment allows the legislature to increase the maximum amount of bonds for the Cancer Prevention and Research Institute of Texas from $3 billion to $6 billion.
	Proposition 7	LRCA	Nov. 5, 2019	Passed	74%	26%	State School Fund	Allows the General Land Office and State Board of Education to each transfer $600 million from the Permanent School Fund's lands and properties proceeds to the Available School Fund each year.
	Proposition 8	LRCA	Nov. 5, 2019	Passed	78%	22%	Flood Infrastructure Fund	Amendment creates the Flood Infrastructure Fund, which will be used to provide financing for flood drainage, mitigation and control projects.
	Proposition 9	LRCA	Nov. 5, 2019	Passed	51%	49%	Precious Metals Tax Exemptions	The amendment allows the legislature to exempt precious metals held in a precious metal depository from property taxation.
	Proposition 10	LRCA	Nov. 5, 2019	Passed	94%	6%	Law Enforcement Animals	The amendment allows for the transfer of a law enforcement animal to the animal's handler or another qualified caretaker if the transfer is in the animal's best interest.
Utah					No Ballot measures in 2019			

See footnotes at end of table

TABLE 6.9A
State Ballot Questions in 2019 (continued)

State or other jurisdiction	Title	Type	Date	Result	Vote totals Yes votes	Vote totals No votes	Subject	Short description
Vermont								No Ballot measures in 2019
Virginia								No Ballot measures in 2019
Washington	Referendum 88	VR	Nov. 5, 2019	Failed	49%	51%	Affirmative Action	The failed vote supported blocking I-1000 from going into effect, thereby continuing to restrict the state from implementing certain affirmative action policies in public employment, education, and contracting.
	Initiative 976	ITL	Nov. 5, 2019	(b)	53%	47%	Motor Vehicle Taxes	This initiative would limit annual license fees for vehicles weighing under 10,000 pounds at $30 except voter-approved charges; base vehicle taxes on the Kelley Blue Book value rather than 85% of the manufacturer's base suggested retail price; and repeal authorization for certain regional transit authorities, such as Sound Transit, to impose motor vehicle excise taxes.
	Senate Joint Resolution 8200	LRCA	Nov. 5, 2019	Passed	65%	35%	Legislature	The amendment authorizes the legislature to pass bills addressing the succession of powers and duties of public offices during periods of catastrophic incidents that are considered emergencies.
	Advisory Vote 20	AQ	Nov. 5, 2019	Failed	37%	63%	Health Care Taxes	The failed vote supported advising the legislature to repeal House Bill 1087, which was designed to levy 0.58% tax on wages to fund a program for long-term healthcare services.
	Advisory Vote 21	AQ	Nov. 5, 2019	Failed	41%	59%	Timber Taxes	The failed vote supported advising the legislature to repeal House Bill 1324, which was designed to extend a surcharge on timber products through July 2045 that was otherwise set to expire in June 2024.
	Advisory Vote 22	AQ	Nov. 5, 2019	Failed	38%	62%	Paint Tax	The failed vote supported advising the legislature to repeal House Bill 1652, which was designed to require producers of interior or exterior architectural paint sold in containers of 5 gallons or less to fund and take part in programs related to paint waste management.
	Advisory Vote 23	AQ	Nov. 5, 2019	Passed	67%	33%	Cigarette/ Vapor Taxes	The favorable vote supported advising the legislature to maintain House Bill 1873, which was designed to levy a tax on e-cigarettes and vapor products.
	Advisory Vote 24	AQ	Nov. 5, 2019	Failed	37%	63%	Business Activities Tax	The repeal vote supported advising the legislature to repeal House Bill 2158, which was designed to create the Workforce Education Investment Account to fund higher education programs through a tax on certain business activities.
	Advisory Vote 25	AQ	Nov. 5, 2019	Failed	45%	55%	Taxes	The repeal vote supported advising the legislature to repeal House Bill 2167, which was designed to impose an additional tax on certain financial institutions.
	Advisory Vote 26	AQ	Nov. 5, 2019	Failed	45%	55%	Sales Taxes	The failed vote supported advising the legislature to repeal Senate Bill 5581, which was designed to apply retail sales taxes on online retailers.
	Advisory Vote 27	AQ	Nov. 5, 2019	Failed	39%	61%	Petroleum Taxes	The failed vote supported advising the legislature to repeal Senate Bill 5993, which was designed to increase taxes on petroleum products.
	Advisory Vote 28	AQ	Nov. 5, 2019	Passed	55%	45%	Sales Taxes	The vote supported advising the legislature to maintain Senate Bill 5997, which was designed to limit the tax exemptions that residents from other U.S. states and Canada can receive while in Washington.
	Advisory Vote 29	AQ	Nov. 5, 2019	Failed	35%	65%	Excise Taxes	The failed vote supported advising the legislature to repeal Senate Bill 5998, which was designed to increase the excise tax on real property.
	Advisory Vote 30	AQ	Nov. 5, 2019	Failed	44%	56%	Business Taxes	The failed vote supported advising the legislature to repeal Senate Bill 6004, which was designed to increase the business and occupation tax on specified tour operators and travel agents.
	Advisory Vote 31	AQ	Nov. 5, 2019	Passed	57%	43%	Business Taxes	The vote supported advising the legislature to maintain Senate Bill 6016, which was designed to increase the business and occupation tax on specified international investment management services.
West Virginia								No Ballot measures in 2019
Wisconsin								No Ballot measures in 2019

See footnotes at end of table

TABLE 6.9A
State Ballot Questions in 2019 (continued)

State or other jurisdiction	Title	Type	Date	Result	Vote totals Yes votes	No votes	Subject	Short description
Wyoming	No Ballot measures in 2019							
American Samoa	No Ballot measures in 2019							
Guam	No Ballot measures in 2019							
CNMI*	No Ballot measures in 2019							
Puerto Rico	No Ballot measures in 2019							
U.S. Virgin Islands	No Ballot measures in 2019							

Sources: The Council of State Governments' survey of state election sites, Initiative & Referendum Institute website an Ballotpedia websites, April 2020.

Key:
AQ–Advisory Question
BI–Bond Initiative
CI–Citizen Initiative/Referendum
CICA–Citizen Initiated Constitutional Amendment
CISS–Citizen Initiative State Statute
CR–Commission referred
ConCon–Constitution Convention
IndISS–Indirect Initiated State Statute
ITL–Initiatives to the Legislature
LR–Legislatively Referred
LRCA–Legislatively Referred Constitutional Amendment
LRSS–Legislatively Referred State Statute
VR–Veto Referendum

(a) The amendment was blocked. The League of Women Voters of Pennsylvania and Lorraine Haw filed a lawsuit that challenged the proposed Marsy's Law as violating the separate vote requirement for constitutional amendments. A judge issued a preliminary injunction on October 30, 2019, and enjoined the secretary of state from counting and certifying votes on the ballot measure, pending a final ruling; It was appealed to the Pennsylvania Supreme Court, which upheld the lower court's injunction on November 4.

(b) This initiative was approved by voters, however has yet to go into effect due to pending litigation. disputing the ballot language as "misleading to voters." A King County Superior Court judge issued a temporary injunction in November 2019 and the case is pending further action from the Washington Supreme Court.

TABLE 6.10
State Initiatives: Requesting Permission to Circulate a Petition

State or other jurisdiction	Applied to (a)		Signatures required to request a petition (b)		Request submitted to	Request form furnished by (c)	Restricted subject matter (d)	Individual responsible for petition		Financial contributions reported (e)	Deposits required (f)
	Const. amdt.	Statute	Const. amdt.	Statute				Title	Summary		
Alabama	...	...	...	...	...	...	...	...	...	...	...
Alaska	...	I	...	100	LG	(p)	Y	LG	LG	Y	$100
Arizona	D	D	...	...	SS	SS	N	P, SP	P, SP	Y	N
Arkansas	D	D	...	...	AG	SP	N	AG	AG	Y	N
California	D	D	25 (g)	25 (g)	AG	...	Y	AG	AG	Y	$200
Colorado	D	D	...	...	SS	SS	N	(i)	(i)	Y	N
Connecticut	...	...	...	...	...	...	...	...	...	...	...
Delaware	...	...	...	...	...	...	...	...	...	...	...
Florida	D	...	...	...	SS	SP	N	SP	SP	Y	N (q)
Georgia	...	...	...	...	...	...	...	...	...	...	...
Hawaii	...	...	...	...	...	...	...	...	...	...	...
Idaho	...	D	...	20	SS	SP	N	AG	AG	Y	N
Illinois	D	...	...	...	...	...	Y	...	...	Y	N
Indiana	...	...	...	...	...	...	...	...	...	...	...
Iowa	...	...	...	...	...	...	...	...	...	...	...
Kansas	...	...	...	...	...	...	...	...	...	...	...
Kentucky	...	...	...	...	...	...	...	...	...	...	...
Louisiana	...	...	...	...	...	...	...	...	...	...	...
Maine	...	I	...	6 (j)	SS	SS	Y	P	SS	Y	N
Maryland	...	...	...	(k)	SS (l)	SBE	Y	...	...	Y	N
Massachusetts	I	I	10	10	AG	SS	Y	AG	AG	Y	N
Michigan	D	I	...	...	SS	...	Y	SP	SP	Y	N
Minnesota	...	...	...	...	...	...	...	...	...	...	...
Mississippi	D	...	...	...	SS	...	Y	AG	AG	Y	$500
Missouri	D	D	...	...	SS	SP	Y	SS,AG	SS,AG	Y	N
Montana	D	D	...	...	SS (o)	SP	Y	AG	AG	Y	N
Nebraska	D	D	...	...	SS	SP	Y	SP	SP	Y	N
Nevada	D	I	...	...	SS	SS	Y	P, SP	P, SP	Y	N
New Hampshire	...	...	...	...	...	...	...	...	...	...	...
New Jersey	...	...	...	...	...	...	...	...	...	...	...
New Mexico	...	...	...	...	...	...	...	...	...	...	...
New York	...	...	...	...	...	...	...	...	...	...	...
North Carolina	...	...	...	...	...	...	...	...	...	...	...
North Dakota	D	D	25	25	SS	SP	N	SS,AG	SS	Y (e)	N
Ohio	D	I	1,000	1,000	AG	(m)	Y	(m)	(m)	Y	N
Oklahoma	D	D	...	...	SS, AG	O	N	P	P	Y	N
Oregon	D	D	1,000	1,000	SS	SS	N	AG	AG	Y	N
Pennsylvania	...	...	...	...	...	...	...	...	...	...	...
Rhode Island	...	...	...	...	...	...	...	...	...	...	...
South Carolina	...	...	...	...	...	...	...	...	...	...	...
South Dakota	D	D	...	...	SS	SS	Y	AG	AG	Y	N
Tennessee	...	...	...	...	...	...	...	...	...	...	...
Texas	...	...	...	...	...	...	...	...	...	...	...
Utah	...	D, I	...	5 SP	LG	LG	N	SP	SP	Y	N
Vermont	...	...	...	...	...	...	...	...	...	...	...
Virginia	...	...	...	...	...	...	...	...	...	...	...
Washington	...	D, I	...	...	SS	SP	N	AG	AG	Y	$5
West Virginia	...	...	...	...	...	...	...	...	...	...	...
Wisconsin	...	...	...	...	...	...	...	...	...	...	...
Wyoming	...	I	...	100	SS	SS	Y	SS	SS	Y	$500
American Samoa	...	...	...	...	...	...	...	...	...	...	...
CNMI*	D	I	...	...	AG	AG	Y	SP	SP	Y	N
Puerto Rico	...	D	...	...	SBE	(n)	N	(n)	(n)	Y	$500
U.S. Virgin Islands	D	...	...	...	SBE	SBE	Y	SBE	SBE	Y	N

See footnotes at end of table

TABLE 6.10
State Initiatives: Requesting Permission to Circulate a Petition (continued)

Sources: The Council of State Governments' survey of state election website, Initiative & Referendum Institute website and Ballotpedia website, April 2020.

*Commonwealth of Northern Mariana Islands

Key:

…–No provision
AG–Attorney General
D–Direct initiative
O–Other
I–Indirect initiative
P–Proponent
EV–Eligible voters
ST–State
LG–Lieutenant Governor
SP–Sponsor
SS–Secretary of State
Y–Yes
SBE–State Board of Elections
N–No

(a) An initiative may provide a constitutional amendment or develop a new statute, and may be formed either directly or indirectly. The direct initiative allows a proposed measure to be placed on the ballot after a specific number of signatures have been secured on a petition. The indirect initiative must first be submitted to the legislature for decision after the required number of signatures have been secured on a petition, prior to placing the proposed measure on the ballot.

(b) Prior to circulating a statewide petition, a request for permission to do so must first be submitted to a specified state officer.

(c) The form on which the request for petition is submitted may be the responsibility of the sponsor or may be furnished by the state.

(d) Restrictions may exist regarding the subject matter to which an initiative may be applied. The majority of these restrictions pertain to the dedication of state revenues and appropriations, and laws that maintain the preservation of public peace, safety, and health. In Illinois, amendments are restricted to "structural and procedural subjects contained in" the legislative article.

(e) In some states, a list of financial contributors and the amount of their contributions must be submitted to the specified state officer with whom the petition is filed. In North Dakota, must report any contributions and/or expenditures in excess of $100. Must also report the gross total of all contributions received and gross totals of all expenditures made. Must give total cash on hand in the filer's account at the start and close of a reporting period.

(f) A deposit may be required after permission to circulate a petition has been granted. This amount is refunded when the completed petition has been filed correctly.

(g) Signatures required to seek assistance of Office of Legislative Counsel in drafting measure before filing with the Attorney General's office.

(h) The secretary of state charges a 10 cent fee per signature that must be verified for ballot consideration.

(i) Title Setting Board–secretary of state, attorney general, director of legislative legal services.

(j) The signature of six voters.

(k) Three percent of the total qualified voters from the last gubernatorial election.

(l) Secretary of state accepts and turns over to State Board of Elections.

(m) Petitioners must prepare the summary and submit it to the Ohio Attorney General, who then must certify whether the summary fully and accurately describes the proposal.

(n) Office of the Supervisor of Elections Titling Board.

(o) After submitted, the secretary of state transfers it over to the Legislative Services Division.

(p) Division of Elections.

TABLE 6.11
State Initiatives: Circulating the Petition

State or other jurisdiction	Basis for signatures (see key below)		Maximum time period allowed for petition circulation (a)	Can signatures be removed from petition (b)	Completed petition filed with	Days prior to election	
	Const. amdt.	Statute				Const. amdt.	Statute
Alabama	...	...	...	...	...	...	...
Alaska	...	10% TV from 3/4 SLD (c)	1 yr.	Y	LG	...	...
Arizona	15% VG	10% VG	2 yr.	Y	SS	4 mos.	4 mos.
Arkansas	10% VG (d)	8% VG (d)		N	SS	120 days	
California	8% VG	5% VG	150 days	Y	(e)	131 days	131 days
Colorado	5% VSS	5% VSS	6 mos. (3 mos prior to election)	Y	SS	90 days	90 days
Connecticut	...	...	...	...	...	...	...
Delaware	...	...	...	...	...	...	...
Florida	8% VEP, 8% from 1/2 CD	...	2 yr.	N	SS	Feb. 1 (f)	...
Georgia	...	...	...	...	...	...	...
Hawaii	...	...	...	...	...	...	...
Idaho	...	6% EV (cc)	(g)	Y	SS	...	4 mos.
Illinois	8% VG	...	18 mos. prior to election	Y	SBE	6 mos.	...
Indiana	...	...	...	...	...	...	...
Iowa	...	...	...	...	...	...	...
Kansas	...	...	...	...	...	...	...
Kentucky	...	...	...	...	...	...	...
Louisiana	...	...	...	...	...	...	...
Maine	...	10% VG	1 yr.	...	SS	...	(h)
Maryland	...	...	...	...	...	...	...
Massachusetts	3% VG, no more than 25% from 1 county	3% VG, no more than 25% from 1 county (i) 8% VG	From 3rd Wed. in Sept. to 1st Wed. in Dec. (k)	Y (j)	SS (k)	(i)	(l)
Michigan	10% VG no more than 15% from each CD	8% VG, no more than 15% from each CD	180 days	N (m)	SS	120 days	160 days
Minnesota	...	...	...	...	(e)	...	...
Mississippi	12% VG (n)	...	1 yr.	Y	SS (e)	90 days prior to LS	...
Missouri	8% VG, 8% each from 2/3 CD	5% VG, 5% each from 2/3 CD	Approx. 18 mos.	Y	SS	6 mos.	6 mos.
Montana	10% VG and 10% in 40 of the SLD	5% VG and 5% in 34 of the SLD	(o)	Y	SS	(o)	(o)
Nebraska	10% EV	7% EV	...	Y	SS	4 mos.	4 mos.
Nevada	10% TV (p)	10% TV (p)	(q)	Y	SS	90 days	30 days prior to LS
New Hampshire	...	...	...	...	...	...	...
New Jersey	...	...	...	...	...	...	...
New Mexico	...	...	...	...	...	...	...
New York	...	...	...	...	...	...	...
North Carolina	...	...	...	...	...	...	...
North Dakota	4% resident population (r)	2% resident population (r)	1 yr.	N	SS	120 days	120 days
Ohio	10% VG, 5% each from 1/2 counties	3% VG, 1.5% each from 1/2 counties	...	Y	SS	90 days	(s)
Oklahoma	15% VG (t)	8% VG (t)	90 days	Y	SS	60 days	60 days
Oregon	8% VG	6% VG	...	Y (u)	SS	4 mos.	4 mos.
Pennsylvania	...	...	...	...	...	...	...
Rhode Island	...	...	...	...	...	...	...
South Carolina	...	...	...	...	...	...	...
South Dakota	10% VG	5% VG	(v)	N	SS	...	...
Tennessee	...	...	...	...	...	...	...
Texas	...	...	...	...	...	...	...
Utah	...	10% VEP, 10% each from 26 of 29 senate districts (w)	316 days	Y	LG	...	June 1
Vermont	...	...	...	...	...	...	...
Virginia	...	...	...	...	...	...	...
Washington	...	8% VG	6 to 9 mos. (x)	N	SS	...	(y)
West Virginia	...	...	...	...	...	...	...
Wisconsin	...	...	...	...	...	...	...
Wyoming	...	15% TV, from 2/3 counties	18 mos.	Y	SS	...	120 days
American Samoa	...	...	...	...	...	...	...
CNMI*	50% (z)	20%	(aa)	Y	...	...	...
Puerto Rico	...	(bb)	...	...	...	...	...
U.S. Virgin Islands	...	10 % ED	180 days	Y	SS	...	6 mos.

See footnotes at end of table

TABLE 6.11
State Initiatives: Circulating the Petition (continued)

Sources: The Council of State Governments' survey of state election website, Initiative & Referendum Institute website and Ballotpedia website, April 2020.

*Commonwealth of the Northern Mariana Islands

Key:

…–No provision

VG–Total votes cast for the position of governor in the last election.

EV–Eligible voters.

VH–Total votes cast for the office receiving the highest number of votes in last general election.

TV–Total voters in last election.

VSS–Total votes cast for all candidates for the office of secretary of state at the previous general election.

VEP–Total votes cast in the state as a whole on the last presidential election.

ED–Election district.

CD–Congressional district.

SBE – State Board of Elections.

SLD–State legislative district for house.

LG–Lieutenant Governor

SS–Secretary of State

LS–Legislative session

Y–Yes

N–No

T– Tuesday

(a) The petition circulation period begins when petition forms have been approved and provided to sponsors. Sponsors are those individuals granted permission to circulate a petition, and are therefore responsible for the validity of each signature on a given petition.

(b) Should an individual wish to remove his/her name from a petition, a request to do so must be submitted in writing to the state officer with whom the petition is filed.

(c) Signed by qualified voters who are equal in number to at least ten per cent of those who voted in the preceding general election, who are resident in at least three-fourths of the house districts of the State, and who, in each of those house districts, are equal in number to at least seven percent of those who voted in the preceding general election in the house district.

(d) Distributed across at least 15 counties.

(e) County elections officials.

(f) February 1 of the general election year.

(g) Eighteen months from receipt of ballot title or April 30 of year of election on initiative, whichever occurs first.

(h) To be placed on November ballot, petitions must be submitted to SS by 5:00 p.m. on 50th day after convening of Legislature in 1st regular session, or by 5:00 p.m. on 25th day in 2nd regular session.

(i) First Wednesday in December.

(j) Should an individual wish to remove his/her name from a petition, a request to do so must be submitted in writing to the local election official before the petition is submitted for certification of signatures.

(k) Petitions first must be submitted to local municipal clerks for signature certification.

(l) After legislative inaction, petitions must be filed no later than the 1st Wednesday in July, signed by not less than 1/2 of 1 percent of the last vote cast for governor.

(m) Not after petition has been filed.

(n) the signatures must be distributed among the state's Congressional districts. If less than the minimum in any one district, the entire petition will be ruled invalid.

(o) There is a maximum of one year to circulate petitions and receive certification from county election officials. The county officials must submit each verified petition to the secretary of state by the final filing deadline, which is the third Friday of the fourth month prior to the election. Proponents must submit their petitions to county officials no sooner than nine months and no later than four weeks prior to the final filing deadline.

(p) In each "petition district" (per SB 212, effective 2009) which are set the same as Congressional districts.

(q) Each have different deadlines and circulation periods. Amendments: Initial filing cannot be made before Sept. 1 of the year preceding the election year and the petition must be filed with the county officials by the third Tuesday in June of an even-numbered year. Statues: Initial filing cannot be made before Jan. 1 of the year preceding the next regular legislative session and the petition must be filed with county officials by the second Tuesday in November of an even-numbered year.

(r) Percentage of resident population of the state at the last federal decennial census.

(s) Ten days prior to commencement of General Assembly session for initial filing; second petition must be filed within 90 days after General Assembly takes no action, fails to enact or passes amended form; the petition is filed with the secretary of state.

(t) In 2012, voters approved a constitutional amendment placed on the ballot by the legislature that changed the signature requirement from percentage of votes cast for the office receiving the highest number of votes in last general election to percentage of votes cast for position of governor in the last election.

(u) Only by the chief petitioners before submitting signatures for verification. Signatures many not be removed once the signatures have been submitted to the Secretary of State

(v) No more than 24 months preceding the election date specified on the petition, however petition is submitted 12 months before the election.

(w) Five percent in both categories for indirect.

(x) Six months for direct initiative and nine months for indirect initiative. Signatures for direct initiatives are due at least four month prior to the general election. Signatures for indirect initiatives are due at least 10 days prior to the beginning of the session.

(y) Initiatives to the legislature must be turned in 10 days before the legislature convenes. If the legislature does not act, the initiative goes to the next General Election ballot.

(z) At least 25 percent in each senate district.

(aa) Until 120 days before the date of the election.

(bb) Ten percent district and 41 percent territorial.

(cc) Geographic distribution shall be as follows: 6% of the qualified electors at the time of the last general election in each of at least 18 legislative districts; provided however, the total number of signatures shall be equal to or greater than 6% of the qualified electors in the state at the time of the last general election.

TABLE 6.12
State Initiatives: Preparing the Initiative to be Placed on the Ballot

State or other jurisdiction	Signatures verified by: (a)	Within how many days after filing	Number of days to amend/appeal a petition that is: Incomplete (b)	Not Accepted (c)	Penalty for falsifying petition (denotes fine, jail term)	Petition certified by: (d)
Alabama	...	...	...	...	...	...
Alaska	Division of Elections	60 days	...	...	Class B misdemeanor	LG
Arizona	County recorder	(e)	...	...	Class 1 misdemeanor	SS
Arkansas	SS	30 days	30 days	30 days	Class A misdemeanor	SS
California	County clerk	30 days	...	...	Felony or misdemeanor (depending on severity)	SS
Colorado	SS	30 days	10 days	...	(f)	SS
Connecticut	...	...	...	...	...	...
Delaware	...	...	...	...	...	...
Florida	Supervisor of elections	N.A.	N.A.	N.A.	First degree misdemeanor	SS
Georgia	...	...	...	...	...	...
Hawaii	...	...	...	...	...	...
Idaho	County clerk	60 days	...	10 days	$5,000, 2 yrs.	SS
Illinois	SBE (g)	...	(h)	(h)	Class 3 felony	SBE
Indiana	...	...	...	...	...	...
Iowa	...	...	...	...	...	...
Kansas	...	...	...	...	...	...
Kentucky	...	...	...	...	...	...
Louisiana	...	...	...	...	...	...
Maine	Registrar of voters	...	...	...	...	SS
Maryland	...	...	...	...	...	...
Massachusetts	Local board of registrar	2 weeks	...	...	$1,000, 1 yr.	SS
Michigan	SS	Approx. 60 days	...	...	$500, 90 days	BSC
Minnesota	...	...	...	...	...	...
Mississippi	Circuit clerk	...	10 days	10 days	$1,000, 1 yr.	CC
Missouri	County clerk	63 days	...	10 days	Class A misdemeanor	SS
Montana	County election administrators	4 weeks	10 days	10 days	$500, 6 mos.	SS
Nebraska	County clerk	40 days	...	...	...	SS
Nevada	County clerk	(i)	5 days (j)	...	...	SS
New Hampshire	...	...	...	...	...	...
New Jersey	...	...	...	...	...	...
New Mexico	...	...	...	...	...	...
New York	...	...	...	...	...	...
North Carolina	...	...	...	...	...	...
North Dakota	SS	35 days	...	...	(k)	SS
Ohio	County board of elections	10 days	10 days	...	5th degree felony	SS
Oklahoma	SS	...	10 days	...	$1,000, 1 yr.	SS
Oregon	County clerk	30 days	(l)	...	(m)	SS
Pennsylvania	...	...	...	...	...	...
Rhode Island	...	...	...	...	...	...
South Carolina	...	...	...	...	...	...
South Dakota	SS	...	...	...	Class 1 misdemeanor	SBE
Tennessee	...	...	...	...	...	...
Texas	...	...	...	...	...	...
Utah	County clerk	30 days	...	14 days	Class A misdemeanor	LG
Vermont	...	...	...	...	...	...
Virginia	...	...	...	...	...	...
Washington	SS	...	5 days	5	Fine or imprisonment	SS
West Virginia	...	...	...	...	...	...
Wisconsin	...	...	...	...	...	...
Wyoming	SS	60 days	30 days	30 days	$1,000, 1 yr.	SS
American Samoa	...	...	...	...	...	...
CNMI*	Election Commission	(n)	30 days (o)	119 days	(p)	AG
Puerto Rico	Office of the Supervisor of Elections	15 days	3 days	...	...	SBE
U.S. Virgin Islands	Office of the Supervisor of Elections	15 days	7 days	...	...	Office of the Supervisor of Elections

See footnotes at end of table

TABLE 6.12
State Initiatives: Preparing the Initiative to be Placed on the Ballot (continued)

Sources: The Council of State Governments' survey of state election website, Initiative & Referendum Institute website and Ballotpedia website, April 2020.

*Commonwealth of the Northern Mariana Islands

Key:

…–No provision.

CC–Circuit Clerk.

SS–Secretary of State.

LG–Lieutenant Governor.

BSC–Board of State Canvassers.

SBE–State Board of Elections.

(a) The validity of the signatures, as well as the correct number of required signatures must be verified before the initiative is allowed on the ballot.

(b) If an insufficient number of signatures is submitted, sponsors may amend the original petition by filing additional signatures within a given number of days after filing. If the necessary number of signatures has not been submitted by this date, the petition is declared void.

(c) In some cases, the state officer will not accept a valid petition. In such a case, sponsors may appeal this decision to the Supreme Court, where the sufficiency of the petition will be determined. If the petition is determined to be sufficient, the initiative is required to be placed on the ballot.

(d) A petition is certified for the ballot when the required number of signatures has been submitted by the filing deadline, and are determined to be valid.

(e) Removal of petition and ineligible signatures by Secretary of State's office 20 days, certification by County Recorder 15 days after receipt from secretary of State's office.

(f) Secretary conducts hearing, then turns over to the attorney general for investigation/possible criminal prosecution.

(g) State Board of Elections and County Clerks or Municipal Boards of Election Commissioners. Individual petition sheets must be from a single jurisdiction. The SBE verifies that all signatures are from a single jurisdiction and the County Clerks or Municipal Boards verify the signatures against their registration files.

(h) Amendments are not permitted. Judicial review must be sought within ten days after determination be State Board of Elections.

(i) 1. Within four days county clerk totals the number of signatures and forwards to the secretary of state. 2. The secretary of state immediately notifies county clerks if they are to proceed or not proceed with the signature verification. 3. If ordered by the secretary of state, the county clerks verify signatures within nine days (excluding weekends and holidays).

(j) In Nevada, appeal must be within 5 working days after SS determines the petition is not sufficient.

(k) Any violations discovered will be reported to the attorney general for investigation and prosecution.

(l) Additional signatures may be submitted if signatures were turned in prior to deadline for submitting signatures.

(m) Whether a penalty is assessed would be based upon what information on the petition was falsified.

(n) Within 90 days before the date of election.

(o) 30 days if submitted 150 days before the date of the election. No amendment/appeal if submitted 120 days before the date of election.

(p) Subject to statute governing fraud and perjury.

TABLE 6.13
State Initiatives: Voting on the Initiative

State or other jurisdiction	Ballot (a)		Election where initiative voted on	Effective date of approved initiative (b)		Days to contest election results (c)	Can an approved initiative be:			Can a defeated initiative be refiled?
	Title by:	Summary by:		Const. amdt.	Statute		Amended?	Vetoed?	Repealed?	
Alabama	...	...	...	...	...	...	...	...	...	...
Alaska	LG	LG	GE,PR or SP	...	90 days (d)	10	Y	N	Y (e)	N
Arizona	SS, AG	SS, AG	GE	...	IM(f)	5	(g)	N	N	Y
Arkansas	AG	AG	GE	30 days	30 days	20	Y	N	Y	Y
California	AG	AG	GE	1 day (h)	1 day (h)	5 (d)	Y(i)	N	Y(i)	Y
Colorado	TB (j)	TB (j)	GE, Odd year	30 days	30 days	10	N (k)	N (k)	N (k)	...
Connecticut	...	...	...	...	...	...	...	...	...	...
Delaware	...	...	...	...	...	...	...	...	...	...
Florida	SP	SP	GE	(m)	...	10	Y(n)	N	Y(n)	Y
Georgia	...	...	...	...	...	...	...	...	...	...
Hawaii	...	...	...	...	...	...	...	...	...	...
Idaho	AG	AG	GE	...	IM	20	Y	N	Y	Y
Illinois	...	SS (o)	GE	...	...	30	(p)	...	...	Y
Indiana	...	...	...	...	...	...	...	...	...	...
Iowa	...	...	...	...	...	...	...	...	...	...
Kansas	...	...	...	...	...	...	...	...	...	...
Kentucky	...	...	...	...	...	...	...	...	...	...
Louisiana	...	...	...	...	...	...	...	...	...	...
Maine	Sponsor, SS	SS	REG or SP	...	30 days (f)	5	Y	N	Y	...
Maryland	...	...	...	...	...	...	...	...	...	...
Massachusetts	AG	AG	GE	30 days	30 days	10	Y	Y	Y	after 2 biennial elections
Michigan	BSC	BSC	GE	45 days	10 days	2 (r)	Y	N	Y	Y
Minnesota	...	...	...	...	...	...	...	...	...	...
Mississippi	AG	AG	GE	30 days	...	...	Y (s)	Y (s)	N	after 2 yrs.
Missouri	SS,AG	SS,AG	GE	30 days	IM	30 (r)	Y	N	Y	Y
Montana	AG	AG	GE	Jul. 1	Oct. 1	1 yr.	Y	N	Y	Y
Nebraska	AG	AG	GE	10 days	10 days	40	Y	N	Y	N (t)
Nevada	SS,AG	SS,AG	GE	(u)	(u)	14	(v)	(v)	(v)	Y
New Hampshire	...	...	...	...	...	...	...	...	...	...
New Jersey	...	...	...	...	...	...	...	...	...	...
New Mexico	...	...	...	...	...	...	...	...	...	...
New York	...	...	...	...	...	...	...	...	...	...
North Carolina	...	...	...	...	...	...	...	...	...	...
North Dakota	SS,AG	SS	PR or GE	30 days	30 days (w)	14	(x)	N	(x)	Y
Ohio	Ohio Ballot Board	(y)	GE	30 days	30 days	15	(z)	N	N	Y
Oklahoma	AG	P	GE or SP	IM	IM	...	Y	Y	Y	after 3 yrs. (aa)
Oregon	AG	AG	GE	30 days	30 days	40	Y	Y	Y	Y
Pennsylvania	...	...	...	...	...	...	...	...	...	...
Rhode Island	...	...	...	...	...	...	...	...	...	...
South Carolina	...	...	...	...	...	...	...	...	...	...
South Dakota	AG	AG	GE	(bb)	(bb)	...	Y	N	N	Y
Tennessee	...	...	...	...	...	...	...	...	...	...
Texas	...	...	...	...	...	...	...	...	...	...
Utah	LLS	LLS	GE	...	5 days (cc)	40	Y	N	N	after 2 yrs.
Vermont	...	...	...	...	...	...	...	...	...	...
Virginia	...	...	...	...	...	...	...	...	...	...
Washington	AG	AG	GE	...	30 days	10 days	Y(l)	...	Y(l)	Y
West Virginia	...	...	...	...	...	...	...	...	...	...
Wisconsin	...	...	...	...	...	...	...	...	...	...
Wyoming	SS	SS,AG	GE 120 days after LS	...	90 days	15 after Canvass	Y	N	after 2 yrs.	after 5 yrs.
American Samoa	...	...	...	...	...	...	...	...	...	...
CNMI*	AG	AG	GE	(q)	(q)	30	...	...	...	Y
Puerto Rico	LC	AG, LLS	GE	...	IM	...	Y	...	...	Y
U.S. Virgin Islands	Office of Supervisor of Elections	Office of Supervisor of Elections	Any election	IM	IM	7	(v)	...	(v)	Y

See footnotes at end of table

TABLE 6.13
State Initiatives: Voting on the Initiative (continued)

Sources: The Council of State Governments' survey of state election website, Initiative & Referendum Institute website and Ballotpedia website, April 2020.

*Commonwealth of Northern Mariana Islands

Key:
PR–Primary election
…–No provision
GE–General election
LG–Lieutenant Governor
REG–Regular election
SS–Secretary of State
SP–Special election
AG–Attorney General
IM–Immediately
P–Proponent
LS–Legislative session
LC–Legislative Council
TB–Title Board
LLS–Legislative Legal Services
Y–Yes
BSC–Board of State Canvassers
N–No
SBE–State Board of Elections
w/i–Within

(a) In some states, the ballot title and summary will differ from that on the petition.

(b) A majority of the popular vote is required to enact a measure. In Massachusetts and Nebraska, apart from satisfying the requisite majority vote, the measure must receive, respectively, 30% and 35% of the total votes cast in favor. An initiative approved by the voters may be put into effect immediately after the approving votes have been canvassed. In California and Nebraska, the measure may specify an enacting date. In Colorado, measures take effect from the date of proclamation by governor, but no later than 30 days after votes have been canvassed and certified by secretary of state. In Nebraska, 10 days after completion of canvass by the State Board of Canvassers.

(c) Individuals may contest the results of a vote on an initiative within a certain number of days after the election including the measure proposed.

(d) After certification of election.

(e) May not be repealed within 2 years of its effective date.

(f) Upon governor's proclamation.

(g) Initiative can be amended by three-fourths of the members of each house of the legislature (AZ Constitution Article 4, Part 1, Section 14.

(h) Unless the measure requires otherwise.

(i) Changes must be submitted to voters unless the measure provided for legislative amendment or repeal.

(j) Ballot title: Drafted by Legislative Council of the General Assembly, then finalized by three board members called the Title Board. Summary by: Legislative Council of the General Assembly.

(k) If it is statutory it can be changed by the legislature.

(l) No initiated statute can be amended or repealed within 2 years without a 2/3s super majority in both chambers. Any initiated law so amended is not subject to veto referendum.

(m) It is effective the first Tuesday after the first Monday in January following election unless specified in the amendment.

(n) Amendments or repeal must be voted on by the voters.

(o) Subject to approval of the Attorney General.

(p) Changing a constitutional amendment would require another constitutional amendment.

(q) Effective upon approval by voters and certification of election result by Election Commission: usually 15 days after date of election or later if there is an election contest.

(r) After election is certified.

(s) The approved initiative to amend the Constitution can be adopted, amended or rejected by the legislature or no action can be taken. In all cases, the initiative and alternative adopted are placed on the next statewide general election ballot.

(t) Not on next ballot.

(u) Constitutional amendment–after passed twice by the voters it becomes effective upon the completion of the canvass of votes by the Supreme Court on the fourth Tuesday of November following the election. Statute–effective on the date approved by the governor or the canvass of the vote by the Supreme Court.

(v) It cannot be amended or repealed within three years from the date it takes effect.

(w) An initiative to repeal a statute is effective immediately following the election.

(x) A measure approved by the electors may not be amended or repealed by the legislative assembly for seven years from its effective date, except by a two-thirds vote of the members elected to each house; majority vote thereafter.

(y) No summary, but the Ohio Ballot Board prescribes the ballot language. Also explanations and arguments for and against the proposal may be prepared by the petitioner and the person(s) appointed by the governor or, if appropriate, the General Assembly. The Ohio Ballot Board must prepare any missing explanation or argument.appointed by the governor or, if appropriate, the General Assembly. The Ohio Ballot Board must prepare any missing explanation or argument.

(z) Initiated constitutional amendment proposed by petition cannot be vetoed; cannot be amended or repealed except by another constitutional amendment. Initiated statute cannot be vetoed by the governor, but may be amended or repealed after its effective date via legislation or another initiative.

(aa) Three year waiting period unless proponents can gather signatures equal to 25 percent of total vote cast in last governor's election.

(bb) Upon completion of official canvass of votes.

(cc) If an indirect initiative is adopted by the legislature, it takes effect 60 days after the adjournment of the legislative session in which it is passed. Unless otherwise specified in the measure, direct initiatives take effect five days after the governor proclaims the official election results.

TABLE 6.14
State Referendums: Requesting Permission to Circulate a Citizen Petition

State or other jurisdiction	Citizen petition (a)	Signatures required to request a petition (b)	Request submitted to:	Request forms furnished by: (c)	Restricted subject matter (d)	Individual responsible for petition		Financial contributions reported (e)	Deposit required (f)
						Title	Summary		
Alabama	...	...	...	...	...	...	...	...	...
Alaska	Y	100	LG	DV	Y	LG	LG	Y	$100
Arizona	Y	5% VG	SS	SS	Y	P	P	Y	N
Arkansas	Y	8% VG initiative; 6% referendum VG	AG	SP	N	AG	AG	Y	N
California	Y	25	AG	LC	Y	AG	AG	N	$200
Colorado	Y	At least 2 people representing issue	LS, SS	LS	Y	SP	LS	Y	N
Connecticut	...	...	...	...	...	...	...	...	...
Delaware	...	...	...	...	...	...	...	...	...
Florida	Y	8% of vote in last presidential election & 1/2 of congressional districts	SS	SS	N (g)	SP	SP	Y	N (h)
Georgia	...	...	...	...	...	...	...	...	...
Hawaii	...	...	...	...	...	...	...	...	...
Idaho	Y	20	SS	SP	N	AG	AG	Y	N
Illinois	Y	...	...	...	Y	P	...	Y, for $3,000 or more	...
Indiana	(i)	Varies	SS	SS	Y	Varies	...	...	...
Iowa	...	...	...	...	...	...	...	...	...
Kansas	...	...	...	...	...	...	...	...	...
Kentucky	...	...	...	.....	...	...	...	...	...
Louisiana	...	...	...	...	...	...	...	...	...
Maine	Y	5	SS	SS	Y	SP, SS	SS (j)	Y	...
Maryland	Y	(k)	SS	SBE	Y	SP	AG	Y	N
Massachusetts	Y	10	AG	SS	Y	AG	AG	Y	N
Michigan	Y	8% VG, initiative; 5% VG, referendum VG	SS	SS	Y	Board of State Canvassers	Board of State Canvassers	Y	N
Minnesota	...	...	...	...	...	...	...	...	...
Mississippi	Y	Any "qualified elector" may file	SS	SS	Y	AG	AG	Y	$500
Missouri	Y	...	SS	DV	Y	SS, AG	SS, AG	Y	N
Montana	Y	(l)	LS, SS, AG	SP	Y	AG	AG	Y	N
Nebraska	Y	...	SS	...	Y	SP	SP	Y	N
Nevada	Y	(r)	SS	SS	Y	P, SP	P, SP	Y	N
New Hampshire	...	...	...	...	...	...	...	...	...
New Jersey	...	...	...	...	...	...	...	...	...
New Mexico	...	...	...	...	...	...	...	...	...
New York	...	...	...	...	...	...	...	...	...
North Carolina	...	...	...	...	...	...	...	...	...
North Dakota	Y	25 "qualified voters"	SS	SP	N	SS, AG	SS	Y	N
Ohio	Y	1,000 "qualified electors"	SS, AG	PE	Y	PE	PE (m)	Y	$25
Oklahoma	Y	(n)	SS	SS	N	P	P	Y	N
Oregon	Y	4% of VG	LC, SS (o)	SS	Y	AG	AG	Y	N
Pennsylvania	...	...	...	...	...	...	...	...	...
Rhode Island	...	...	...	...	...	...	...	...	...
South Carolina	...	...	...	...	...	...	...	...	...
South Dakota	Y	5% of VG	LS	SP	Y	AG	AG	Y	N
Tennessee	...	...	...	...	...	...	...	...	...
Texas	...	...	...	...	...	...	...	...	...
Utah	Y	5 SP	LG	LG	Y (p)	SP	SP	Y	...
Vermont	...	...	...	...	...	...	...	...	...
Virginia	...	...	...	...	...	...	...	...	...
Washington	Y	8% VG, initiative; 4% VG, referendum VG	SS	SS	Y (q)	AG	AG	Y	$5
West Virginia	...	...	...	...	...	...	...	...	...
Wisconsin	...	...	...	...	...	...	...	...	...
Wyoming	Y	100	SS	SS	Y	SS	SS	Y	$500
American Samoa	...	...	...	...	...	...	...	...	...
CNMI*	Y	...	...	...	Y	SP	AG	Y	N
Puerto Rico	Y	10% district/41% territorial	Other	SBE	N	SP	Other	Y	N
U.S. Virgin Islands	...	...	L	L	N	L	L	N	N

See footnotes at end of table

TABLE 6.14
State Referendums: Requesting Permission to Circulate a Citizen Petition (continued)

Sources: The Council of State Governments' survey of state election websites, Initiative & Referendum Institute website and Ballotpedia website, April 2020.

*Commonwealth of Northern Mariana Islands

Key:
…–No provision for
EV–Eligible voters
AG–Attorney General
VG–Total votes cast for the position of governor in the last election
P–Proponent
PE–Petitioner
LG–Lieutenant Governor
ST–State
LS–Legislative services
SP–Sponsor
L–Legislature
Y–Yes
SS–Secretary of State
N–No
SBE–State Board of Elections
LC–Office of Legislative Counsel
DV–Division of Elections

(a) Three forms of referenda exist: citizen petition, submission by the legislature, and constitutional requirement. This table outlines the steps necessary to enact a citizen's petition.

(b) Prior to circulating a statewide petition, a request for permission to do so must first be submitted to a specified state officer. Some states require such signatures to only be those of eligible voters.

(c) The form on which the request for petition is submitted may be the responsibility of the sponsor or may be furnished by the state.

(d) Restrictions may exist regarding the subject matter to which a referendum may be applied. The majority of these restrictions pertain to the dedication of state revenues and appropriations, and laws that maintain the preservation of public peace, safety and health. In Kentucky, referenda are only permitted for the establishment of soil and water and watershed conservation districts.

(e) In some states, a list of individuals who contribute financially to the referendum campaign must be submitted to the specified state officer with whom the petition is filed.

(f) A deposit may be required after permission to circulate a petition has been granted. This amount is refunded when the completed petition has been filed correctly.

(g) New fees/taxes requires 2/3 majority vote

(h) The secretary of state charges a 10 cent fee per signature that must be verified for ballot consideration.

(i) A referendum can only be placed on the ballot if authorized by a state law. As a result, a county or town election board cannot print any referendum on the ballot unless the legislature has already passed a law to permit the referendum. Therefore, each statute is different.

(j) Petition sponsor may submit proposed petition summary for approval to State Administrator of Elections but a formal request to circulate a petition is not required.

(k) No specific requirement to request a petition. Legislative Services receives the request and reviews it, and then the sponsor submits it to the Secretary of State and Attorney General for petition format review and legal and constitutional sufficiency review.

(l) State auditor writes the fiscal note.

(m) Petitioners must prepare the summary, and submit it to the Ohio Attorney General, who then must certify whether the summary fully and accurately describes the proposal.

(n) Five percent of legal voters based upon the total number of votes cast at the last general election for the state office receiving the highest number of votes

(o) LC must also reasonably expect the measure to be put to a vote w/ verified # of signatures (4% for referendum of VG, statutory/const amdts different)

(p) May not challenge laws passed by two-thirds of each house of the legislature; any measure prohibiting/limiting wildlife hunting/management takes two-thirds vote in support.

(q) No bills with an emergency clause.

(r) The information required to be provided includes the name and signature of the person filing the petition, the names of up to three individuals who are authorized to withdraw or amend the petition, and the name of the Political Action Committee (PAC) formed to advocate for the passage of the petition.

TABLE 6.15
State Referendums: Circulating the Citizen Petition

State or other jurisdiction	Basis for signatures	Maximum time period allowed for petition circulation (a)	Can signatures be removed from petition (b)	Completed petition filed:	
				With	Days after legislative session
Alabama	...	...	...	...	...
Alaska	10% TV, from 3/4 ED	w/i 90 days of LS	Y	LG	90 days
Arizona	5% VG	24 months prior to GE	Y	SS	90 days
Arkansas	8% for initiated act; 6% for referenda VG	...	N	SS	90 days
California	5% VG	90 days; 131 days for initiatives prior to GE	Y	(c)	...
Colorado	5% of votes cast for prior SS election	6 months	Y	SS	...
Connecticut	...	...	...	...	...
Delaware	...	...	...	...	...
Florida	8% of TV in prior Presidential election	Up to 2 years (d)	.....	CES	...
Georgia	...	...	...	...	...
Hawaii	...	...	...	...	...
Idaho	6% EV	w/i 60 days after LS	Y	SS	60 days
Illinois	8% VG (e)	24 months prior to GE	Y	SBE	...
Indiana	...	...	...	...	...
Iowa	...	...	...	...	...
Kansas	...	...	...	...	...
Kentucky		...	...	...	...
Louisiana		...	...	...	...
Maine	10% VG	18 months	...	SS	50 days for 1st session; 25 days for 2nd session
Maryland	3 % VG	(f)	Y	SS	...
Massachusetts	1.5% VG for emergency; 2% or immediate suspension	First state election 60 or more days after filing certified petition	Y (g)	SS	90 days after signed by governor
Michigan	5% VG	90 days after LS	N	SS	90 days after enactment
Minnesota	...	...	...	...	...
Mississippi	...	...	...	...	...
Missouri	5% VG, from 2/3 ED	w/i 90 days after LS	Y	SS	90 days
Montana	5% EV and 5% from 34 of 100 ED	(h)	Y	SS	6 mos.
Nebraska	5% EV	...	Y	SS	90 days
Nevada	10% EV last GE	(i)	Y	CC, SS	120 prior to next GE
New Hampshire	...	...	...	...	...
New Jersey	...	...	...	...	...
New Mexico	...	...	...	...	...
New York	...	...	...	...	...
North Carolina	...	...	...	...	...
North Dakota	2% total population	90 days	N	SS	(j)
Ohio	6% VG, 3% each from 1/2 counties	90 days	Y	SS	90 days
Oklahoma	5% VH	w/i 90 days of LS	Y	SS	90 days
Oregon	4% VG	w/i 90 days of LS	Y (k)	SS	90 days
Pennsylvania	...	...	...	...	...
Rhode Island	...	...	...	...	...
South Carolina	...	...	...	...	...
South Dakota	5% VG	24 months prior to GE	N	SS	90 days
Tennessee	...	...	...	...	...
Texas	...	...	...	...	...
Utah	10% VG	40 days after LS	Y	CC	40 days
Vermont	...	...	...	...	...
Virginia	...	...	...	...	...
Washington	4% VG	Approx. 90 days	N	SS	90 days
West Virginia	...	...	...	...	...
Wisconsin	...	...	...	...	...
Wyoming	15% TV, from 2/3 county	18 months	N	SS	90 days
American Samoa	...	...	...	...	...
CNMI*	...	Up to 120 days before election	Y	AG	...
Puerto Rico	...	...	...	...	...
U.S. Virgin Islands	No. of registered voters	180 days	...	...	...

See footnotes at end of table

TABLE 6.15
State Referendums: Circulating the Citizen Petition (continued)

Sources: The Council of State Governments' survey of state election website, Initiative & Referendum Institute website and Ballotpedia website, April 2020.

*Commonwealth of Northern Mariana Islands

Key:

…–No provision for.

VG–Total votes cast for the position of governor in the last election.

EV–Eligible voters.

TV–Total voters in the last general election.

VH–Total votes cast for the office receiving the highest number of votes in last general election.

VSS–Total votes cast for all candidates for the office of secretary of state at the previous general election.

ED–Election district.

GE–General election.

LS–Legislative session.

LG–Lieutenant governor.

SBE–State Board of Elections.

SS–Secretary of state.

AG–Attorney General.

CC–County clerk.

CES–County election supervisor.

Y–Yes

N–No

w/i–Within

(a) The petition circulation period begins when petition forms have been approved and provided to or by the sponsors. Sponsors are those individuals granted permission to circulate a petition, and are therefore responsible for the validity of each signature on a given petition.

(b) Should an individual wish to remove his/her name from a petition, a request to do so must first be submitted in writing to the state officer with whom the petition is filed.

(c) County elections office.

(d) Signatures must be verified by Feb 1 in year of election.

(e) Referenda are advisory only.

(f) No signature may be collected until the final action of the General Assembly. Session ends the second Monday in April. One third of the signatures must be submitted not later than May 31. The remaining signatures are due no later than June 30th.

(g) Should an individual wish to remove his/her name from a petition, a request to do so must first be submitted in writing to the local election official prior to the petition being submitted for certification of signatures.

(h) No specific beginning date for circulation of petitions, so there is no maximum time period. There is an ending deadline of 6 months after legislative session.

(i) Not later than the third Tuesday in May of even-numbered years.

(j) Within 90 days after the legislation is filed in the Secretary of State's office.

(k) Only by the chief petitioners before submitting signatures before verification. Signatures may not be removed once the signatures have been submitted to the secretary of state for verification.

TABLE 6.16
State Referendums: Preparing the Citizen Petition Referendum

State or other jurisdiction	Signatures verified by: (a)	Within how many days after filing	No. of days to amend/appeal petition that is: Incomplete (b)	Not accepted (c)	Penalty for falsifying petition (denotes fine, jail term)	Petition certified by: (d)
Alabama	...	...	...	...	...	...
Alaska	Division of elections	60	10	10	Class B misdemeanor	LG
Arizona	County recorder	(e)	...	...	Class 1 misdemeanor	SS
Arkansas	SS	30	...	30	Class D felony	SS
California	County clerk	8 (f)	...	...	Felony or misdemeanor (depending on severity)	SS
Colorado	SS	(g)	15	3 months and 3 weeks before election	Fines up to $1,000 and forgery is a Class 5 felony	SS
Connecticut	...	...	...	...	...	...
Delaware	...	...	...	...	...	...
Florida	Supervisor of Elections	30	...	...	1st degree misdemeanor	SS
Georgia	...	...	...	...	...	...
Hawaii	...	...	...	...	...	...
Idaho	County clerk	...	...	...	$5,000, 2 yrs.	SS
Illinois	State Board of Elections	varies	...	...	Class 3 felony	SBE
Indiana	County clerk	...	...	...	...	...
Iowa	...	...	...	...	...	...
Kansas	...	...	...	...	...	...
Kentucky	...	...	...	...	...	...
Louisiana	...	...	...	...	...	...
Maine	Registrars of voters	30	...	...	Class E crime	SS
Maryland	Local Board of Elections	20	...	...	Misdemeanor (h)	SS, SBE
Massachusetts	Local boards of registrars	14	...	...	$1,000, 1 year	SS
Michigan	SS	Approx. 60	...	...	$500, 90 days	BSC
Minnesota	...	...	...	...	...	...
Mississippi	...	...	...	...	...	...
Missouri	County clerk	(i)	...,	10	Class A misdemeanor	SS
Montana	County election administrators	28	10	10	$500, 6 mos.	SS
Nebraska	County clerk	40	...	...	Penalty up to $1,000 and 1 year in prison	SS
Nevada	County clerk	(j)	5	...	...	SS
New Hampshire	...	...	...	...	...	...
New Jersey	...	...	...	...	...	...
New Mexico	...	...	...	...	...	...
New York	...	...	...	...	...	...
North Carolina	...	...	...	...	...	...
North Dakota	SS	35	...	20	(k)	SS
Ohio	SS	no later than 105 days before election	10	...	5th degree felony	SS
Oklahoma	SS	...	10	...	$1,000, 1 year	SS, State Supreme Court
Oregon	SS, county clerk	30	...	...	(l)	SS
Pennsylvania	...	...	...	...	...	...
Rhode Island	...	...	...	...	...	...
South Carolina	...	...	...	...	...	...
South Dakota	SS	...	...	...	Class 2 misdemeanor	SS
Tennessee	...	...	...	...	...	...
Texas	...	...	...	...	...	...
Utah	County clerks	55 (m)	...	10	Class A misdemeanor	LG
Vermont	...	...	...	...	...	...
Virginia	...	...	...	...	...	...
Washington	SS	(n)	...	10	Class C felony (possible)	SS
West Virginia	...	...	...	...	...	...
Wisconsin	...	...	...	...	...	...
Wyoming	SS	60	60	60	$1,000, 1 yr.	SS
American Samoa	...	...	...	...	...	...
CNMI*	AG	...	(o)	(o)	(p)	AG
Puerto Rico	...	...	...	...	...	...
U.S. Virgin Islands	Supervisor of Elections	15	...	...	...	Supervisor of Elections

See footnotes at end of table

TABLE 6.16
State Referendums: Preparing the Citizen Petition Referendum (continued)

Sources: The Council of State Governments' survey of state election website, Initiative & Referendum Institute website and Ballotpedia website, April 2020.

*Commonwealth of Northern Mariana Islands

Key:

…–Not applicable.

SS–Secretary of State.

LG–Lieutenant Governor.

BSC–Board of State Canvassers.

SBE–State Board of Elections.

(a) The validity of the signatures, as well as the correct number of required signatures must be verified before the referendum is allowed on the ballot.

(b) If an insufficient number of signatures are submitted, sponsors may amend the original petition by filing additional signatures within a given number of days after filing. If the necessary number of signatures have not been submitted by this date, the petition is declared void.

(c) In some cases, the state officer will not accept a valid petition. In such cases, sponsors may appeal this decision to the Supreme Court, where the sufficiency of the petition will be determined. If the petition is determined to be sufficient, the referendum is required to be placed on the ballot.

(d) A petition is certified for the ballot when the required number of signatures have been submitted by the filing deadline, and are determined to be valid.

(e) In Arizona, the secretary of state has 20 days to count signatures and to complete random sample; the county recorder then has 15 days to verify signatures.

(f) Clerk has 8 days to report raw totals of signatures and 30 days for random sampling to verify signatures

(g) At least 30 days for internal review process to conduct random sampling; must verify at least 90% are valid

(h) Misdemeanor, punishable by a $10-$250 fine or 30 days-six months in jail, or both.

(i) In Missouri, must be certified as sufficient or insufficient by the 13th Tuesday prior to the general election.

(j) 1. Within four days county clerks count total number of signatures and forward to the secretary of state. 2. The secretary of state immediately notifies county clerks if they are to proceed or not proceed with the signature verification. 3. If ordered by the secretary of state, the county clerks verify signatures within nine days (excluding weekends and holidays).

(k) Any violations discovered will be reported to the attorney general for investigation and prosecution.

(l) Whether a penalty is assessed would be based upon what information on the petition was falsified.

(m) After the end of the legislative session.

(n) Not later than the third Tuesday following the primary election.

(o) Incomplete: 30 or more days if submitted 150 days before date of the election; none if submitted 120 days before date of election. Not accepted: If submitted 119 days or less before the election.

(p) Subject to statute governing fraud or perjury.

TABLE 6.17
State Referendums: Voting on the Citizen Petition Referendum

State or other jurisdiction	Ballot (a) Title by:	Summary by:	Election where referendum voted on	Effective date of approved referendum (b)	Days to contest election results (c)
Alabama	...	...	...	...	...
Alaska	LG	LG	1st statewide election 180 days after LS	30 days	10
Arizona	SS, AG	LC	GE	(d)	10
Arkansas	AG	...	GE	...	20
California	AG	AG	GE or PR	1 day	5 (e)
Colorado	...	...	...	...	...
Connecticut	...	...	...	...	...
Delaware	...	...	...	...	...
Florida	...	...	...	...	...
Georgia	...	...	...	...	...
Hawaii	...	...	...	...	...
Idaho	AG	AG	GE	30 days	20 (e)
Illinois	...	...	GE	Advisory only	30
Indiana	...	...	...	...	...
Iowa	...	...	...	...	...
Kansas	...	...	...	...	...
Kentucky	...	...	GE or SP	IM	...
Louisiana	...	...	...	...	...
Maine	...	...	GE or statewide election more than 60 days after filing	30 days	5
Maryland	SS	LSS	GE	(f)	...
Massachusetts	SS, AG	AG	GE more than 60 days after filing	30 days	10
Michigan	BSC	BSC	GE	10 days	2 (e)
Minnesota	...	...	...	...	...
Mississippi	...	...	...	...	...
Missouri	SS, AG	SS	GE	IM	30
Montana	AG	AG	GE	(g)	1 yr.
Nebraska	AG	AG	GE	...	...
Nevada	SS, AG	SS, AG	GE	Nov., 4th Tues.	14
New Hampshire	...	...	...	...	...
New Jersey	...	...	...	...	...
New Mexico	...	...	...	...	...
New York	...	...	...	...	...
North Carolina	...	...	...	...	...
North Dakota	SS, AG	SS	PR	30 days	14 (e)
Ohio	...	...	GE more than 60 days after filing.	IM	15 (h)
Oklahoma	LLS, AG	LLS	GE or SP	...	...
Oregon	AG	AG	GE (i)	30 days	40
Pennsylvania	...	...	...	...	...
Rhode Island	...	...	...	...	...
South Carolina	...	...	...	...	...
South Dakota	AG	AG	GE	July 1	...
Tennessee	...	...	...	...	...
Texas	...	...	...	...	...
Utah	LLS	LLS	GE	5 days	40
Vermont	...	...	...	...	...
Virginia	...	...	...	...	...
Washington	AG	AG	GE	30 days	10
West Virginia	...	...	...	...	...
Wisconsin	...	...	...	...	...
Wyoming	SS	SS, AG	GE more than 120 days after LS	90 days	15
American Samoa	...	...	...	...	...
CNMI*	AG	AG	GE or special election if specified	(j)	30 days
Puerto Rico	...	...	...	...	...
U.S. Virgin Islands	...	...	...	...	...

See footnotes at end of table

TABLE 6.17
State Referendums: Voting on the Citizen Petition Referendum (continued)

Sources: The Council of State Governments' survey of state election website, Initiative & Referendum Institute website and Ballotpedia website, April 2020.

*Commonwealth of Northern Mariana Islands

Key:

…–No provision
LG–Lieutenant Governor
GE–General election
AG–Attorney General
PR–Primary election
SS–Secretary of State
REG–Regular election
BSC–Board of State Canvassers
SP–Special election
LC–Legislative Counsel
IM–Immediately
LSS–Legislative Legal Services
LS–Legislative session
SBE–State Board of Elections

(a) In some states, the ballot title and summary will differ from that on the petition.

(b) A majority of the popular vote is required to enact a measure in every state. In Arizona, a referendum approved by the voters becomes effective upon the governor's proclamation. In Nebraska, a referendum may be put into effect immediately after the approving votes have been canvassed by the Board of State Canvassers and upon the governor's proclamation. In Massachusetts the measure must also receive at lease 30 percent of the total ballots cast in the last election. In Oklahoma, put into effect upon certification of election results by state election board. In Utah, after proclamation by governor and date specified in petition.

(c) Individuals may contest the results of a vote on a referendum within a certain number of days after the election including this matter. In Alaska, five days to request recount with appeal to the court within five days after recount.

(d) Upon proclamation of the governor after the canvas. (AZ Const. Article 4, Part 1, Section 13).

(e) After election is certified.

(f) After the certification of election results. Depends on date Board of State Canvassers meets. They must meet within 35 days after General Election.

(g) Unless specifically provided by the legislature in an act referred by it to the people or until suspended by a petition signed by at least 15% of the qualified electors in a majority of the legislative representative districts, an act referred to the people is in effect as provided by law until it is approved or rejected at the election. An act that is rejected is repealed effective the date the result of the canvass is filed by the secretary of state under 13-27-503. An act referred to the people that was in effect at the time of the election and is approved by the people remains in effect. An act that was suspended by a petition and is approved by the people is effective the date the result of the canvass is filed by the secretary of state under 13-27-503. An act referred by the legislature that contains an effective date following the election becomes effective on that date if approved by the people. An act that provides no effective date and whose substantive provisions were delayed by the legislature pending approval at an election and that is approved is effective October 1 following the election.

(h) After election is certified or if recount conducted, 10 days after recount.

(i) Special election can be held at the request of the Legislative Assembly.

(j) Upon approval by voters and certification of election results by Election Commission, usually 15 days after date of election if no contest.

TABLE 6.18
State Recall Provisions

State or other jurisdiction	Provision for recall	Officials subject to recall	Constitutional and statutory citations for recall of state officials	Constitutional or statutory language
Alabama	No			
Alaska	Yes	All (a)	Const. Art., 11 § 8; AS § 15.45.510-710, 15.60.010, 29.26.250-350	All elected public officials in the State, except judicial officers, are subject to recall by the voters of the State or political subdivision from which elected.
Arizona	Yes	All	Const. Art. 8, § 1-6; ARS § 19-201 - 19-234	Every public officer in the state of Arizona, holding an elective office, either by election or appointment, is subject to recall from such office by the qualified electors of the electoral district from which candidates are elected to such office.
Arkansas	No			
California	Yes	All	Const. Art. 2, § 13-19; CA Election Code § 11000-11386	Recall is the power of the electors to remove an elective officer. Recall of a state officer is initiated by delivering to the Secretary of State a petition alleging reason for recall. Sufficiency of reason is not reviewable.
Colorado	Yes	All	Const. Art. 21, § 1; CRS § 1-12-101 - 1-12-122, 23-17-120.5, 31-4-501-505	Every elective public officer of the state of Colorado may be recalled from office at any time by the registered electors entitled to vote for a successor of such incumbent through the procedure and in the manner herein provided for, which procedure shall be known as the recall, and shall be in addition to and without excluding any other method of removal by law.
Connecticut	No			
Delaware	No			
Florida	No			
Georgia	Yes	All	Const. Art. 2, § 2.4; GA Code § 21-4-1 et seq.	The General Assembly is hereby authorized to provide by general law for the recall of public officials who hold elective office. The procedures, grounds, and all other matters relative to such recall shall be provided for in such law.
Hawaii	No			
Idaho	Yes	All (a)	Const. Art 6, § 6; ID Code § 34-1701 - 34-1715	Every public officer in the state of Idaho, excepting the judicial officers, is subject to recall by the legal voters of the state or of the electoral district from which he is elected. The legislature shall pass the necessary laws to carry this provision into effect.
Illinois (b)	Yes	(b)	Const. Art 3, § 7	"The recall of the Governor may be proposed by a petition signed by a number of electors equal in number to at least 15% of the total votes cast for Governor in the preceding gubernatorial election, with at least 100 signatures from each of at least 25 separate counties. A petition shall have been signed by the petitioning electors not more than 150 days after an affidavit has been filed with the State Board of Elections providing notice of intent to circulate a petition to recall the Governor. The affidavit may be filed no sooner than 6 months after the beginning of the Governor's term of office. The affidavit shall have been signed by the proponent of the recall petition, at least 20 members of the House of Representatives, and at least 10 members of the Senate, with no more than half of the signatures of members of each chamber from the same established political party."
Indiana	No			
Iowa	No			
Kansas	Yes	All (a)	Const. Art. 4, § 3; KSA § 25-4301 - 25-4331	All elected public officials in the State, except judicial officers, shall be subject to recall by voters of the state or political subdivision from which elected. Procedures and grounds for recall shall be prescribed by law.
Kentucky	No			
Louisiana	Yes	All (a)	Const. Art. 10, § 26; LRS § 18:1300.1 - 18:1300.17	The legislature shall provide by general law for the recall by election of any state, district, parochial, ward, or municipal officer except judges of the courts of record. The sole issue at a recall election shall be whether the official shall be recalled. However, no recall petition may be submitted for certification to or accepted for certification by the registrar of voters or any other official if less than six months remain in the term of office.
Maine	No			
Maryland	No			
Massachusetts	No			
Michigan	Yes	All (a)	Const. Art. 2, §8; MCL § 168.951 - 168.975	Laws shall be enacted to provide for the recall of all elective officers except judges of courts of record upon petition of electors equal in number to 25 percent of the number of persons voting in the last preceding election for the office of governor in the electoral district of the officer sought to be recalled. The sufficiency of any statement of reasons or grounds procedurally required shall be a political rather than a judicial question.
Minnesota	Yes	(c)	Const. Art. 8, § 6; MS § 211C.01 et. seq.	A state officer other than a judge may be subject to recall for serious malfeasance or nonfeasance during the term of office in the performance of the duties of the office or conviction during the term of office for a serious crime.
Mississippi	No			
Missouri	No			
Montana	Yes	All	Mont. Code § 2-16-601 - 2-16-635	Every person holding a public office of the state or any of its political subdivisions, either by election or appointment, is subject to recall from such office.

See footnotes at end of table

TABLE 6.18
State Recall Provisions (continued)

State or other jurisdiction	Provision for recall	Officials subject to recall	Constitutional and statutory citations for recall of state officials	Constitutional or statutory language
Nebraska	No			
Nevada	Yes	All	Const. Art. 2, § 9; NRS § 294A.006, Chapter 306	Every public officer in the State of Nevada is subject, as herein provided, to recall from office by the registered voters of the state, or of the county, district, or municipality which he represents.
New Hampshire	No			
New Jersey	Yes	All	Const. Art. 1, § 2; NJRS § 19:27A-1 - 19:27A-18	The people reserve unto themselves the power to recall, after at least one year of service, any elected official in this State or representing this State in the United States Congress.
New Mexico	No			
New York	No			
North Carolina	No			
North Dakota	No			
Ohio	Yes	All (d)	Const. Art. 3, § 1 and 10; ND Century Code § 16.1-01-09.1	Any elected official of the state, of any county or of any legislative or county commissioner district shall be subject to recall by petition of electors equal in number to twenty-five percent of those who voted at the preceding general election for the office of governor in the state, county, or district in which the official is to be recalled.
Oklahoma	No			
Oregon	No			
Pennsylvania	Yes	All (d)	Const. Art. 2, § 18; ORS § 249.865 - 249.880	Every public official in Oregon is subject, as herein provided, to recall by the electors of the state or of the electoral district from which the public official is elected.
Rhode Island	No			
South Carolina	Yes	(e)	Const. Art. 4, § 1	Recall is authorized in the case of a general officer who has been indicted or informed against for a felony, convicted of a misdemeanor, or against whom a finding of probable cause of violation of the code of ethics has been made by the ethics commission.
South Dakota	No			
Tennessee	No			
Texas	No			
Utah	No			
Vermont	No			
Virginia	No			
Washington	No (f)			
West Virginia	Yes	All (a)	Const. Art. 1, Sec. 33-34; WRC §29.82.010 - 29.82.220	Every elective public officer of the state of Washington except judges of courts of record is subject to recall and discharge by the legal voters of the state, or of the political subdivision of the state, from which he was elected whenever a petition demanding his recall, . . . is filed with the officer with whom a petition for nomination, or certificate for nomination, to such office must be filed under the laws of this state, and the same officer shall call a special election as provided by the general election laws of this state. and the result determined as therein provided.
Wisconsin	No			
Wyoming	Yes	All	Const. Art. 13, §12; Wisc. Stat. §9.10	The qualified electors of the state, of any congressional, judicial or legislative district or of any county may petition for the recall of any incumbent elective officer after the first year of the term for which the incumbent was elected, by filing a petition with the filing officer with whom the nomination petition is filed, demanding the recall of the incumbent.
CNMI*	No			
Puerto Rico	Yes	All	Const. Art. 9, § 3; 2 CMC §6502	Elected public officials are subject to recall by the voters of the Commonwealth or of the island, islands or district from which elected.
U.S.V.I.	No			
	Yes	All	U.S.C., Title 48, Ch. 12, Subchapter IV, § 1593	An elected public official of the Virgin Islands may be removed from office by a recall election carried out under this subsection. The grounds for recall are any of the following: lack of fitness, incompetence, neglect of duty, or corruption.

Sources: The Council of State Governments, state constitutions and statutes, April 2020.
*Commonwealth of the Northern Mariana Islands
Note: This table refers only to officials elected to statewide office. Many local governments allow recall of elected officials.
N.A. Not available
(a) Except judicial.
(b) Illinois allows for recall of the governor.
(c) State executive officers, legislators, and judicial officers.
(d) Except for U.S. Congress.
(e) Governor, Lieutenant Governor, Secretary of State, Treasurer, and Attorney General.
(f) Virginia permits a recall trial not a recall election. See Virginia Code §24.2-233.

TABLE 6.19
State Recall Provisions: Applicability to State Officials and Petition Circulation

State or other jurisdiction	Officers to whom recall is applicable (a)	No. of times recall can be attempted	Recall may be initiated after official has been in office	Recall may not be initiated with days remaining in term	Basis for signatures (b) (see key below)		Maximum time allowed for petition circulation (c)
					Statewide officers	Others	
Alabama	...	...	...	...	...	...	...
Alaska	All but judicial officers	...	120 days	180	25% VO	25% VO	...
Arizona	All elected officials	1 (d)	6 mos./5 days legislators	...	25% VO (e)	25% VO (e)	120 days
Arkansas	...	...	...	...	...	...	...
California	All elected officials	(f)	90 days	6 mos.	12% VO, 1% from 5 counties	20% VO	160 days
Colorado	All elected officials	(g)	6 mos	6 mos.	25% VO	25% VO	60 days
Connecticut	...	...	...	...	...	...	...
Delaware	...	...	...	...	...	...	...
Florida	...	...	...	...	...	...	...
Georgia	All state level officials, county and city elected officials	...	180 days	180	15% EV (h), 1/15 from each congressional district	30% EV (h)	(i)
Hawaii	...	...	...	...	...	...	...
Idaho	All but judicial officers	(d)	90 days	...	20% EVg	50%VO	60 days
Illinois	Governor	...	...	...	15% VO from 25 counties	20 state Rep. and 10 state Sen.	150 days
Indiana	...	...	...	...	...	...	...
Iowa	...	...	...	...	...	...	...
Kansas	All but judicial officers	1	120 days	180	40% VO	40% VO	90 days
Kentucky	...	...	...	...	...	...	...
Louisiana	All but judicial officers	(j)	1 day	6 mos.	33 1/3% EV (k)	40% EV (k)	180 days
Maine	...	...	...	...	...	...	...
Maryland	...	...	...	...	...	...	...
Massachusetts	...	...	...	...	...	...	...
Michigan	All but judicial officers	No limit	1 year	1 year	25% VG in district	25% VG in district	60 days
Minnesota	All state level officials	No limit	...	6 mos.	25% VO	25% VO	90 days
Mississippi	...	...	...	...	...	...	...
Missouri	...	...	...	...	...	...	...
Montana	All state level officers & elected officials	(l)	2 mos.	...	10% EV	(m)	3 mos.
Nebraska	...	...	...	...	...	...	...
Nevada	All but judicial officers	(d)	6 mos. (n)	...	25% VO in given	25% VO in given	90 days
New Hampshire	...	...	...	...	...	...	...
New Jersey	All elected officials	(o)	(p)	(q)	25% EV in given jurisdiction	25% EV in given jurisdiction	(r)
New Mexico	...	...	...	...	...	...	...
New York	...	...	...	...	...	...	...
North Carolina	...	...	...	...	...	...	...
North Dakota	All elected state officials	1	...	190	25% Evg	25% Evg	...
Ohio	...	...	...	...	...	...	...
Oklahoma	...	...	...	...	...	...	...
Oregon	All elected state officials	No limit	180 days (s)	...	15% (t)	15% (t)	90 days
Pennsylvania	...	...	...	...	...	...	...
Rhode Island	Gov., lt. gov., atty. gen., sec. of state, treasurer	...	6 mos.	...	15% VO	...	90 days
South Carolina	...	...	...	...	...	...	...
South Dakota	...	...	...	...	...	...	...
Tennessee	...	...	...	...	...	...	...
Texas	...	...	...	...	...	...	...
Utah	...	...	...	...	...	...	...
Vermont	...	...	...	...	...	...	...
Virginia	...	...	...	...	...	...	...
Washington	All but judges of courts of record	...	IM	180	25% VO	35% VO	(u)
West Virginia	...	...	...	...	...	...	...
Wisconsin	All elected officials	1	1 yr.	...	25% VG (v)	25% VG (v)	60 days
Wyoming	...	...	...	...	...	...	...
CNMI*	All elected officials	(w)	180 days	...	40% EV (x)	...	(y)
Puerto Rico	...	...	...	...	...	...	...
U.S. Virgin Islands	All elected officials	Unlimited	1 year	365	...	Registered electors	180 days

See footnotes at end of table

TABLE 6.19
State Recall Provisions: Applicability to State Officials and Petition Circulation (continued)

Source: The Council of State Governments, state election websites, April 2020.

*Commonwealth of the Northern Mariana Islands

Key:

. . . – No provision.

All – All elective officials.

VO – Number of votes cast in the last election for the office or official being recalled.

EVg – Number of eligible voters in the last general election for governor.

EV – Eligible voters.

VG – Total votes cast for the position of governor in the last election.

VP – Total votes cast for position of president in last presidential election.

IM – Immediately.

(a) An elective official may be recalled by qualified voters entitled to vote for the recalled official's successor. An appointed official may be recalled by qualified voters entitled to vote for the successor(s) of the elective officer(s) authorized to appoint an individual to the position.

(b) Signature requirements for recall of those other than state elective officials are based on votes in the jurisdiction to which the said official has been elected.

(c) The petition circulation period begins when petition forms have been approved and provided to sponsors. Sponsors are those individuals granted permission to circulate a petition, and are therefore responsible for the validity of each signature on a given petition.

(d) Additional recall attempts can be made provided that the state treasury is reimbursed the cost of the previous recall attempt(s). The specific reason for recalling on one petition cannot be the basis for a second recall petition during the current term of office.

(e) 25% of the number of votes cast at the preceding general election for all candidates for the office held by the officer, even if the officer was not elected at that election, divided by the number of offices that were being filled at that election. (A.R.S.§ 19-201.

(f) Open ended.

(g) One attempt unless a second petition is circulated and valid signatures gathered are at least 50% of votes cast for all candidates in last election.

(h) Eligible voters for office at last general election to fill office.

(i) For any statewide office, 90 days. Any officer holding an office other than statewide office and for whom no less than 5,000 signatures are required for the recall petition, 45 days. Any officer is first reimbursed for all expenses of the preceding election.

(j) Unlimited. Once every 18 months.

(k) Basis for signatures 33 1/3 percent if over 1,000 eligible voters; 40 percent if under 1,000 eligible voters.

(l) No recall petition may be filed against an officer for whom a recall election has been held for a period of 2 years during his term of office unless the state or political subdivisions financing such recall election is first reimbursed for all expenses of the preceding election.

(m) 15 percent of eligible for district offices.

(n) For legislators, anytime after 10 days from the beginning of the first legislative session after their election.

(o) An elected official sought to be recalled who is not recalled as the result of a recall election shall not again be subject to recall until after having served one year of a term calculated from the date of the recall election.

(p) The recall drive may not commence before the 50th day preceding the completion of the elected official's first year of the current term.

(q) No election to recall an elected official shall be held after the date occurring six months prior to the general election or regular election for that office, as appropriate, in the final year of the officials term.

(r) The maximum time allowed for petition circulation is 320 days for a governor or U.S. Senator or 160 days for other elected officials.

(s) Unless it is a state senator or representative and then it is anytime after fifth day form the beginning of legislative session or after election of legislator.

(t) 15 percent of the total number of votes cast in the public officer's electoral district for all candidates for governor at the last election at which a candidate for governor was elected to a full term.

(u) Statewide officials 270 days; others 180 days.

(v) At least 25 percent of the vote cast for the office of governor at the last election within the same district or territory as that of the officeholder being recalled.

(w) Not more than once a year or not during the first six months in office.

(x) Grounds for recall must be stated and must be signed by 40% of voters represented by the elected official.

(y) Until 120 days before the election.

TABLE 6.20
State Recall Provisions: Petition Review, Appeal and Election

State or other jurisdiction	Signatures verified (a) by:	Days to amend/appeal a petition that is:		Penalty for falsifying petition (denotes fines, jail time)	Days allowed for petition to be certified (d)	Days to step down after certification (e)	Voting on the recall (f)		Days to contest election results (g)
		Incomplete (b)	Not accepted (c)				Election held	Election type	
Alabama	...	...	...	...	...	...	...	...	...
Alaska	Division of Elections	20	20	Class B misdemeanor	30	1	60-90 days after cert.	GE,PR,SP	10
Arizona	County recorder	...	...	Class 1 misdemeanor	70	5	(h)	(i)	5
Arkansas	...	...	...	...	...	...	...	...	...
California	County clerk/ registrar of voters	10	10	...	10	(j)	60-80 days after cert.	GE	5
Colorado	SS	...	15 (k)	...	10	5	45-75 days after cert.	SP or GE	10
Connecticut	...	...	...	...	...	...	...	...	...
Delaware	...	...	...	...	...	...	...	...	...
Florida	...	...	...	...	...	...	...	...	...
Georgia	Registrar of voters	...	...	Misdemeanor	30-45	...	30-45 days after cert.	SP	5
Hawaii	...	...	...	...	...	...	...	...	...
Idaho	County clerk	30	...	$5,000, 2 yrs.	10	5	45+ days after cert. (l)	SP , PR, GE (l)	20 (m)
Illinois	SBE	...	...	...	...	...	100 days after cert.	SP	...
Indiana	...	...	...	...	...	...	...	...	...
Iowa	...	...	...	...	...	...	...	...	...
Kansas	County clerk	...	...	Class B misdemeanor; up to $1,000, up to one year or both.	30	Next day	60-90 days after cert.	SP	5 (m)
Kentucky	...	...	...	...	...	...	...	...	...
Louisiana	Registrar of voters	(n)	(n)	...	15-20 days	(o)	(p)	SP	(q)
Maine	...	...	...	...	...	...	...	...	...
Maryland	...	...	...	...	...	...	...	...	...
Massachusetts	...	...	...	...	...	...	...	...	...
Michigan	SS, local election officials (r)	...	...	$500, 90 days	35	...	(s)	SP	2 (m)
Minnesota	SS	90	...	Felony	10	...	(t)	GE	7
Mississippi	...	...	...	...	...	...	...	...	...
Missouri	...	...	...	...	...	...	...	...	...
Montana	County election administrators	10	10	$500 or six months in county jail, or both.	(u)	5	(v)	SP or GE (dd) (v)	12 mos.
Nebraska	...	...	...	...	...	...	...	...	...
Nevada	County clerk, registrar of voters	5	...	Misdemeanor	(w)	5	(x)	SP	(y)
New Hampshire	...	...	...	...	...	...	...	...	...
New Jersey	Recall elections official	...	...	Crime of the 4th degree	10	5	(z)	SP or GE	(aa)
New Mexico	...	...	...	...	...	...	...	...	...
New York	...	...	...	...	...	...	...	...	...
North Carolina	...	...	...	...	...	...	...	...	...
North Dakota	SS	...	...	...	30	10	50-60	SP	14 (bb)
Ohio	...	...	...	...	...	...	...	...	...
Oklahoma	...	...	...	...	...	...	...	...	...
Oregon	County clerk	(cc)	...	(dd)	10	5	w/i 35 days after resignation period	SP	40
Pennsylvania	...	...	...	...	...	...	...	...	...
Rhode Island	SBE	w/i 90 days	...	Misdemeanor and/ or felony	90	...	...	SP	...
South Carolina	...	...	...	...	...	...	...	...	...
South Dakota	...	...	...	...	...	...	...	...	...
Tennessee	...	...	...	...	...	...	...	...	...
Texas	...	...	...	...	...	...	...	...	...
Utah	...	...	...	...	...	...	...	...	...
Vermont	...	...	...	...	...	...	...	...	...

See footnotes at end of table

TABLE 6.20
State Recall Provisions: Petition Review, Appeal and Election (continued)

State or other jurisdiction	Signatures verified (a) by:	Days to amend/appeal a petition that is:		Penalty for falsifying petition (denotes fines, jail time)	Days allowed for petition to be certified (d)	Days to step down after certification (e)	Voting on the recall (f)		Days to contest election results (g)
		Incomplete (b)	Not accepted (c)				Election held	Election type	
Virginia	...	...	...	...	...	...	...	...	...
Washington	SS	30	...	Class B felony or misdemeanor	not specified	...	45-60 days after cert. (ee)	SP	3
West Virginia	...	...	...	...	...	...	...	...	...
Wisconsin	SBE	...	...	Class 1 felony - $10,000, 3 yrs. prison or both.	31	10	6 weeks after cert.	GE or PR	3 (ff)
Wyoming	...	...	...	...	...	...	...	...	...
CNMI*	AG	150 days	...	Statute governs fraud or perjury.	15 days	...	(gg)	GE, SP	30
Puerto Rico	...	...	...	...	...	...	...	...	...
U.S. Virgin Islands	Office of the Supervisor of Elections	...	...	...	10	IM	...	GE	5

Sources: The Council of State Governments, state election websites, April 2020. .
*Commonwealth of the Northern Mariana Islands
Key:
... – Not applicable.
SBE - State Board of Elections.
SS – Secretary of State.
SP – Special election.
GE – General election.
PR – Primary election.
IM – Immediate and automatic removal from office.
w/i – Within
N.A. – Information not available.
(a) The validity of the signatures, as well as the correct number of required signatures must be verified before the recall is allowed on the ballot.
(b) If an insufficient number of signatures are submitted, sponsors may amend the original petition by filing additional signatures within a given number of days. If the necessary number of signatures have not been submitted by this date, the petition is declared void.
(c) In some cases, the state officer will not accept a valid petition. In such a case, sponsors may appeal this decision to the Supreme Court, where the sufficiency of the petition will be determined. When this is declared, the recall is required to be placed on the ballot.
(d) A petition is certified for the ballot when the required number of signatures has been submitted by the filing deadline, and are determined to be valid.
(e) The official to whom a recall is proposed has a certain number of days to step down from his position before a recall election is initiated, if he desires to do so.
(f) A majority of the popular vote is required to recall an official in each state.
(g) Individuals may contest the results of a vote on a recall within a certain number of days after the results are certified. In Alaska, an appeal to courts must be filed within five days of the recount.
(h) The election order is issued within 15 days if the officer does not resign within five days after certification.
(i) To be held on the next consolidated election date pursuant to §

16-204 that is 90 days or more after the order calling the election (A.R.S. § 19-209(A)).
(j) Prior to election being called.
(k) After determination of sufficiency.
(l) In Idaho, the dates on which elections may be conducted are the first Tuesday in February, the fourth Tuesday in May, the first Tuesday in August, or the Tuesday following the first Monday in November. In addition, an emergency election may be called upon motion of the governing board of a political subdivision. Recall elections conducted by any political subdivision shall be held on the nearest of these dates which falls more than 45 days after the clerk of the political subdivision orders that the recall election shall be held.
(m) After election is certified. In Michigan, if a petition is filed against a local officer, a recount can be requested up to 6 days after certification of recall election.
(n) The Registrar of Voters shall honor the written request of any voter who either desires to have his handwritten signature stricken from or added to the petition at any time prior to certification of the petition, or within five days after receipt of such signed petition, whichever is earlier.
(o) (y) Election returns are certified on the fifth day after the election, and the office is immediately vacant.
(p) The local registrar of voters sends the original certified recall petition to the governor, who issues, within 15 days, a proclamation calling a special election, placing the special election on the next regularly scheduled election date.
(q) Not later than 4:30 p.m. of the 30th day after the official promulgation of the results of the election. Promulgation is on or before the 12th day after the election.
(r) Secretary of state if filed on the state level; county or local clerks if filed on county level.
(s) Under Michigan's consolidated elections, the recall election is held on the next fixed election date that falls at least 95 days after the recall petition is filed.
(t) An election will not be held in the last 6 mos. of a term after certification.
(u) County election administrators have 30 days; sponsor has three mos. to submit the petition from the date of certification.
(v) A special election is called unless the filing is within 90 days of a

TABLE 6.20
State Recall Provisions: Petition Review, Appeal and Election (continued)

general election.

(w) Within four days, county clerks count signature totals and forward to the Secretary of State. The Secretary of State immediately notifies the clerks if they are to proceed with signature verification.

(x) In Nevada, a recall election is held 10-20 days after the Secretary of State completes notification of the petition sufficiency unless a complaint is filed, the clerk shall issue a call for the election which is to be held within 30 days after the issuance of the call.

(y) Five days after recount is completed or 14 days after the election if no recount is demanded.

(z) New Jersey Permanent Statutes, 19:27A-13, In the case of an office which is ordinarily filled at the general election, a recall election shall be held at the next general election occurring at least 55 days following the fifth business day after service of certification, unless it was indicated in the notice of intention to recall that the recall election shall be held at a special election in

which case the recall election official shall order and fix the date for holding the recall election to be the next Tuesday occurring during the period beginning with the 55th day and ending on the 61st day following the fifth business day after service of the certification of the petition.

(aa) New Jersey Permanent Statutes, 19:27A-16.

(bb) Fourteen days after the canvas board has certified the results.

(cc) Chief petitioners may submit additional signatures if the deadline for submitting signatures has not passed.

(dd) Whether a penalty is assessed would depend on what information on the petition was falsified.

(ee) If possible to be held on a regularly scheduled election; cannot be held between the primary and general.

(ff) Business days.

(gg) The election is held at the next regular general election or at a special election set forth in the recall petition.

CHAPTER SEVEN
STATE FINANCE

TABLE 7.1
Fiscal 2018 General Fund, Actual (In millions of dollars)

State	Beginning balance	Revenues	Adjustments	Total resources	Expenditures	Adjustments	Ending balance	Rainy day fund balance
Total	$36,863	$842,737		$898,087	$823,178		$49,426	$67,983
Alabama	150	8,750	0	8,900	8,307	0	593	784
Alaska (a)	0	2,414	745	3,158	4,489	820	(2,151)	2,533
Arizona (a)	151	10,033	74	10,258	9,808	0	450	458
Arkansas (a)	0	5,495	0	5,495	5,495	0	0	127
California (a)	5,702	131,116	(1,050)	135,767	124,756	(408)	11,419	20,842
Colorado* (a)	614	11,724	99	12,437	11,215	(145)	1,366	1,366
Connecticut (a)	0	18,199	0	18,199	18,685	(3)	(483)	1,185
Delaware* (a)	475	4,393	0	4,868	4,118	0	750	232
Florida	1,515	31,962	0	33,476	31,830	0	1,646	1,417
Georgia* (a)	2,399	24,320	143	26,863	24,134	0	2,729	2,557
Hawaii	894	7,660	0	8,554	7,804	0	750	376
Idaho (a)	101	3,732	12	3,845	3,466	140	239	354
Illinois* (a)	1,368	36,943	4,313	42,624	35,409	7,090	125	4
Indiana (a)	303	15,837	150	16,289	15,736	186	366	1,419
Iowa (a)	0	7,384	0	7,384	7,224	33	127	620
Kansas (a)	109	7,299	4	7,411	6,649	0	762	0
Kentucky (a)	116	10,941	470	11,527	11,330	168	29	94
Louisiana (a)	123	9,903	26	10,051	9,605	138	308	321
Maine (a)	57	3,506	33	3,595	3,515	6	75	288
Maryland (a)	259	17,373	35	17,666	17,287	(211)	590	857
Massachusetts* (a)	1,448	32,442	12,594	46,484	31,503	12,594	2,387	2,001
Michigan (a)	623	10,570	(57)	11,136	10,082	265	788	1,006
Minnesota* (a)	3,333	22,297	0	25,630	22,347	0	3,283	2,092
Mississippi (a)	4	5,694	0	5,699	5,576	118	5	295
Missouri (a)	168	9,469	125	9,762	9,267	0	495	616
Montana (a)	48	2,406	2	2,455	2,287	(19)	187	0
Nebraska (a)	248	4,567	(11)	4,803	4,350	0	454	340
Nevada (a)	434	4,019	102	4,554	4,018	112	425	180
New Hampshire (a)	0	1,596	0	1,596	1,504	17	74	110
New Jersey (a)	718	35,520	485	36,723	35,733	0	991	0
New Mexico* (a)	496	6,881	52	7,430	6,191	55	1,185	527
New York*	7,749	71,420	0	79,169	69,724	0	9,445	1,798
North Carolina (a)	472	23,565	0	24,037	22,746	295	995	1,849
North Dakota (a)	65	1,972	377	2,414	2,160	0	253	113
Ohio (a)	557	32,471	0	33,028	31,807	0	1,221	2,034
Oklahoma (a)	84	6,606	(274)	6,416	6,034	382	0	452
Oregon (a)	1,000	10,281	(37)	11,245	9,773	0	1,471	940
Pennsylvania (a)	(1,539)	34,567	(1,035)	31,993	31,949	22	22	0
Rhode Island (a)	62	3,908	(109)	3,861	3,799	10	53	199
South Carolina* (a)	1,076	8,124	21	9,221	7,895	139	1,187	509
South Dakota (a)	8	1,593	15	1,616	1,591	8	17	160
Tennessee (a)	1,647	14,855	(458)	16,044	13,828	1,077	1,140	800
Texas (a)	883	57,155	928	58,966	56,050	2,768	148	11,043
Utah (a)	85	7,038	41	7,164	6,739	107	317	578
Vermont (a)	0	1,635	5	1,641	1,564	77	0	133
Virginia	783	19,879	0	20,662	20,450	0	212	440
Washington (a)	1,101	21,712	(349)	22,464	20,448	0	2,016	1,369
West Virginia (a)	398	4,245	4	4,648	4,232	38	378	710
Wisconsin (a)	579	16,144	608	17,332	17,139	(396)	589	320
Wyoming (a)	0	1,126	404	1,530	1,530	0	0	1,538

See footnotes at end of table

TABLE 7.1
Fiscal 2018 General Fund, Actual (In millions of dollars) (continued)

Source: National Association of State Budget Officers, Fall 2019.

Note: For all states, unless otherwise noted, transfers into budget stabilization funds are counted as expenditures, and transfers from budget stabilization funds are counted as revenues.

Key:

*–The ending balance includes the balance in the rainy day fund.

(a)

Alaska–Revenues: Spring 2019 Revenue Sources Book (Total Revenue) Revenue Adjustments: SLA2018 Enacted Fiscal Summary (Lines 3–7) Expenditures: SLA2018 Enacted Fiscal Summary (Line 48) Expenditure Adjustments: SLA2018 Enacted Fiscal Summary (Line 49 and 52) Rainy Day Balance: State of Alaska Fiscal Summary FY18 and FY19 (Part 2) Number listed is EoY Balance. Rainy day balance includes any anticipated draws. Ending balance includes multi-year appropriations. Started reporting shared taxes as expenditures instead of Revenues

Arizona–Adjustments come from other fund transfers to the General Fund.

Arkansas–Total available revenue amounts are reported as net of refunds and special dedications/payments.

California–Revenue and expenditure adjustments to the beginning fund balance consist primarily of adjustments made to major taxes and K-12 spending. Total revenues reflect revenues after transfers to the rainy day fund. The ending balance includes the Special Fund for Economic Uncertainties (SFEU) but excludes the BSA (a rainy day reserve held in a separate fund). The excluded amount is $10,807.4 million at the end of FY 2018. Adding these amounts to the FY 2018 ending balance, the projected total balance is $22,226.5 million in FY 2018. The rainy day balance is made up of the SFEU and the BSA, however, withdrawals of mandatory deposits from the BSA are subject to provisions of Proposition 2, 2014. Ending balance Includes a reserve for encumbrances of $1,384.5 million representing amounts which will be expended in the future for state obligations for which goods and services have been ordered/contracted, but have not been received by the end of the fiscal year. These amounts are shown as a reserve to the fund balance instead of a hit to the fund balance.of a hit to the fund balance.

Colorado–Revenue adjustments include transfers to the General Fund. Expenditure adjustments include reversions and accounting adjustments. Colorado's rainy day fund is included within the General Fund.

Connecticut–The state of CT has a volatility cap that applies to the Estimates and Finals component of the Personal Income Tax and the state's Pass-through Entity Tax. The cap was $3,196.8 million in FY 2019 which resulted in a deposit of $949.6 million. The cap is $3,294.2 million in FY 2020 estimated to deposit $318.3 million. These amounts are deposited to the Rainy Day Fund in addition to the operating surplus at the end of each fiscal year. Net Rainy Day Fund deposit of $972.4 million includes $1,471.3 million transfer to the Rainy Day Fund due to volatility cap less $482.9 million deficit and $16.1 million transfer to retired teachers' health service fund. $3.4 million in miscellaneous adjustments per Office of State Comptroller's Report

Delaware–Fiscal year ending balance includes encumbered appropriations and those appropriations legislatively continued into the ensuing fiscal year.

Georgia–FY 18 beginning balance reflects final fund balances as of June 30, 2017 for Revenue Shortfall Reserve as reported on the FY 17 Combined Balance Sheet of the Budgetary Compliance Report. Adjustments to Revenues include FY17 agency surplus returned and early remittance of FY 18 surplus from state agencies.

Idaho–Revenue adjustments: $5.9 m for reappropriation; $2.6 m for prior-year reversion; $.1 m misc. adjustments; and $3.6 m from the Immunization Fund. Expenditure adjustments: $34.5 million to the Budget Stabilization Fund (statutory transfer); $2 million to the Opportunity Fund; $45.3 million to the Permanent Building Fund; $.4 million to the Wolf Control Fund; $2.5 million to the Workforce Development Training Fund; $20 million to the Fire Suppression Fund; $27.7 to the Idaho Transportation Department (prior year surplus eliminator); $1 million to the Water Management Fund; $.2 million for deficiency warrants; $.8 misc.; and $5.9 million for reappropriation.

Illinois–Total revenues include $4,032M in base federal revenues (excludes the $1,206M referenced below). Estimated revenue adjustments include $802M in interfund borrowing and fund reallocations from other state funds, $2,500M in proceeds from the issuance of backlog borrowing bonds, and $1,206M in federal match from the paydown of prior year Medicaid liabilities. Estimated expenditures include $3,777M in Transfer Out, $28M in prior year adjustments, $3,721 in vouchers payable adjustments, and $128M in transfers to repay interfund borrowing.

Indiana–Revenue adjustments include a transfer to the General Fund to assist with the Integrated Tax System, a transfer from the State Tuition Reserve Account, and a transfer from the Rainy Day Fund. Expenditure adjustments include reversions from distributions, capital, and reconciliations; state agency and university line item capital projects; the cost of a 13th check for pension recipients; and transfers to the Rainy Day Fund.mbly to support infrastructure projects. Total revenues include forecasted General Fund revenues as well as unforecasted revenues such as HAF, QAF, dedicated fund SWCAP, and outside acts.

Iowa–Revenue adjustments include an estimated $18.2 million of residual funds transferred to the General Fund after the Reserve Funds are filled to their statutorily set maximum amounts. The ending balance of the General Fund is transferred in the current fiscal year to the Reserve Funds in the subsequent fiscal year. After the Reserve Funds are at their statutorily set maximum amounts, the remainder of the funds are transferred back to the General Fund in that subsequent fiscal year. Also included in revenue adjustments is $131.1 million transferred from the Cash Reserve Fund as authorized by the Legislature under SF 516 and $13.0 million transferred from the Economic Emergency Fund as authorized by Governor Reynolds with the issuance of an Official Proclamation to bring the General Fund into balance.

Kansas–$3.6 million in Prior year released encumbrances shows as revenue.

TABLE 7.1
Fiscal 2018 General Fund, Actual (In millions of dollars) (continued)

Kentucky–Revenue includes $102.6 million in Tobacco Settlement funds. Adjustments for Revenues includes $201.5 million that represents appropriation balances carried over from the prior fiscal year, and $268.9 million from fund transfers into the General Fund. Adjustment to Expenditures represents appropriation balances forwarded to the next fiscal year and budget balances to be expended in the next fiscal year. The FY 2018 $13.3 million ending balance was budgeted for use in FY 2019.

Louisiana–Revenues adjustments - Includes $19.1 in carryforwards, $6.5 in fund transfer. Expenditure adjustments - Includes $11.1 in transfers to the Coastal Protection and Restoration Fund, $63.0 Appropriated in FY19, $63.7 in general Fund Direct Carryforwards to FY19, and various funds transfers.

Maine –Revenue and Expenditure adjustments reflect Legislatively authorized transfers. The total balance reported for FY18 includes up to $55 million earmarked for repayment of disallowed costs from the Centers for Medicare and Medicaid Services.

Maryland –Revenue adjustments include $21.8 million in transfers from tax credit reserves and $9.0 million in transfers from other funds. Expenditure adjustments represent $144.2 million in reversions to the unappropriated General Fund balance and $66.5 million in legislative reductions and executive branch agency midyear reductions.

Massachusetts–General Fund is defined as all budgeted operating funds, adjusted for expenditures funded by federal reimbursements. This is to better align with spending reported in the State Expenditure Report and be more comparable to most other states, which book federally reimbursed expenditures in a separate federal fund; adjustments also account for certain transfers between budgeted funds. Ending balance includes $371.5 million in reserved balances projected to be spent in the next fiscal year.

Michigan–Revenue totals are net of payments to local governments. Adjustments to Revenue: Restatement of beginning balance. Offsetting adjustments made to School Aid Fund beginning balance. Adjustments (Expenditures): $265 million transfer to Budget Stabilization Fund/Rainy Day Fund.

Minnesota–Rainy Day Fund balance includes cash flow account of $350 million and a budget reserve of $1.698 billion. Includes stadium reserve of $44.171 million.

Mississippi–Adjustments to expenditures reflect transfers to the state's Rainy Day and Capital Expense Funds. Designated portion of ending balance: Reappropriation from FY2018 to FY2019, 4.8M

Missouri–Revenue adjustments include transfers from other funds into the general revenue fund.

Montana–Revenue adjustments reflect prior year revenue activity and expenditure adjustments reflect prior year expenditure activity and adjustments to fund balance as a result of the annual CAFR reconciliation.

Nebraska–Revenue adjustments are transfers between the General Fund and other funds. Among others, this includes a $221 million transfer from the General Fund to the Property Tax Credit Cash Fund. Also included are transfers totaling $225 million from the Cash Reserve Fund to the General Fund for budget stabilization.

Nevada–Revenue adjustments are restricted revenue, reversion, Rainy Day Fund transfers in and reserve transfers in. Expenditure adjustments are restricted transfers out.

New Hampshire–Expenditure Adjustments: As the result of standalone legislation in FY 2018, $10 million was authorized to be deposited in the revenue stabilization reserve account (Rainy Day Fund). Additionally, $6.6 million of general funds was authorized to be deposited in the Public School Infrastructure Fund at year end.

New Jersey–Adjustments include Lapses; transfers to other funds; reservation of fund balance

New Mexico– FY17 reflects actual amounts received from solvency legislation per LFC/DFA sweeps tracking - includes Laws 2016, Chapter 12 (HB311, $75 million fund sweeps); Laws 2016, Second Special Session, Chapter 4 (SB2, $93 million general fund sweeps and transfers), Chapter 5 (SB8, $103.2 million capital outlay sweeps), and Chapter 6 (SB9, $27.9 million PED appropriation reductions); Laws 2017, Chapter 1 (HB4, $89 million adjusted reversion date for fire protection fund and law enforcement protection fund), Chapter 2 (SB113, $55.2 million general fund sweeps), and Chapter 3 (SB114, $40.8 million school cash balances); Laws 2017, First Special Session, Chapter 1 (SB1, $82.1 million public school capital outlay swap and general fund sweeps).

North Carolina–Expenditure adjustments include funds for the R&R Reserve, $64.8M, the Capital Project Reserve $155.2, and the Medicaid Transformation Reserve, $75M.

North Dakota–Revenue adjustments are transfers of $183.0 million from the tax relief fund, $124.0 million from the strategic investment and improvements fund and $70.0 million from other special fund sources, to the general fund.

Ohio–FY 2018 expenditures include expenditures against prior year encumbrances as well as $80.0 million in transfers out of the GRF. The fiscal 2018 ending balance included funds to support $371.2 million in open encumbrances. In addition, the ending balance supported $687.5 million in surplus transfers which occurred in fiscal 2019. Federal reimbursements for Medicaid expenditures funded from the General Revenue Fund (GRF) are deposited into the GRF. Federal reimbursements for Medicaid expenditures from non-GRF sources are deposited into the appropriate federal fund. Expenditures of federal funds are contained in the General Fund number to be consistent with Ohio accounting practices and with other portrayals of Ohio's general fund. This will tend to make Ohio's GRF revenue and expenditures look higher relative to most other states that don't follow this practice.

Oklahoma–Revenue adjustment for FY-2017 is the net cash flow reserve amount available for the fiscal year. FY-2017 ending balance expended in the FY-2018 budget. These numbers include collections and estimates for the two largest appropriated funds (the General Revenue Fund and the OK Education Reform Revolving Fund) which constitute the majority of the state appropriated budget.

Oregon–Revenue adjustments include: a revenue adjustment for a statutory transfer to local governments for local property tax relief.

Pennsylvania– Revenue adjustments include refunds, lapses and adjustments to beginning balances. Expenditure adjustments include transfers to the Budget Stabilization Reserve Fund (rainy day).

TABLE 7.1
Fiscal 2018 General Fund, Actual (In millions of dollars) (continued)

Rhode Island–Adjustments to revenues reflects $119.1 million to the Budget Reserve (Rainy Day) Fund, offset by reappropriation of $10.3 million from FY 2017. Expenditure adjustments reflect reappropriations to the following fiscal year (FY 2019). Designated portion of ending balance–Reappropriations authorized by the Governor totaling $10.1 million

South Carolina–Revenue Adjustments: Litigation Recovery Account ($16.2M) & South Carolina Farm Aid Fund ($4.5M). Expenditure Adjustments: Prior Yr. 2% Capital Reserve ($139.2M) transferred to state agencies. Designated portion of ending balance: Capital Reserve Fund–$145.1M; Appropriations Carried Forward $484.5M

South Dakota–The beginning balance of $7.9 million and adjustment to expenditures reflects the prior year's ending balance that is transferred to the rainy day fund. Adjustments to revenue of $14.6 million is from one-time receipts. The ending balance of $16.9 million is cash that is obligated to the Budget Reserve fund the following fiscal year. This $16.9 million is not included in the total rainy day fund balance of $159.5 million.

Tennessee–Adjustments (Revenues): $55.5 million transfer from debt service fund unexpended appropriations. -$132.0 million transfer to Rainy Day Fund. -$85.0 million transfer to Highway Fund. -$296.1 million transfer to dedicated revenue reserves. Adjustments (Expenditures): $630.9 million transfer to capital outlay projects fund. $156.9 million transfer to state office buildings and support facilities fund. $3.6 million transfer to debt service fund. $1.0 million transfer to reserves for dedicated revenue appropriations. $284.3 million transfer to reserves for unexpended appropriations. Ending Balance: $529.8 million reserve for appropriations 2018-2019. $610.1 million unappropriated budget surplus at June 30, 2018.

Texas–$928.2 reflected in adjustments to revenue was realized from dedicated account balances now available. $2,768.2 is a transfer of revenue to the ESF and State Highway to be allocated equally.

Utah–Expenditure adjustments include $107.2 million of surplus revenue collections automatically transferred to rainy day funds and other funds at the end of FY 2018 based on statutory formulas. Revenue adjustments include transfers to the General Fund and Education fund, the amount set aside for economic development cash incentives, and other revenue adjustments. $159.1 million of the $316.9 million FY 2018 ending balance was designated by the Legislature to be appropriated for one-time items in FY 2019.

Vermont–$5.2M in adjusted revenues reflect the use of Rainy Day reserve funds to partly address a $28.8M general fund revenue downgrade forecasted as of July 2017. Subsequent to the general fund revenue downgrade forecasted as of July 2017, and relative to enacted rescissions as a result of the downgrade, actual receipts exceeded forecasted expectations. As a result, $76.9M of expenditure adjustments reflect a combination of $26.19M in net contributions to reserve accounts (inclusive of $5.2M transferred from the Rainy Day reserve to the General Fund), as well as $50.71M in net transfers to other funds. Specifically, $76.9M of general fund expenditure adjustments included a $20.4M transfer to the Education Fund that was carried forward for uses in fiscal year 2019, a $26.23M transfer to the Vermont Teachers' Retirement Fund in excess of the fiscal year 2018 ADEC, and a $9.8M transfer to the Education Fund budget stabilization reserve to meet statutory reserve requirements.

Washington–Revenue adjustments reflect the net of transfers in and out of the General Fund, as well as prior biennium recoveries and similar resource adjustments.

West Virginia–Fiscal Year 2018 Beginning balance includes $285.1 million of Reappropriations, Unappropriated Surplus Balance of $76.2 million, $1.0 million of cash balance adjustments, and FY 2017 13th month expenditures of $35.8 million. Total Revenues show the FY 2018 actual general revenue collections of $4,254.2 million. Adjustments (Revenue) are prior year redeposits of $2.6 million and special revenue expirations of $1.6 million. Total Expenditures include current year general revenue appropriated expenditures of $4,040.1 million, surplus appropriation expenditures of $30.5 million, reappropriation expenditures of $125.7 million, $-0.3 million of cash adjustments, and $35.9 million of 31 day prior year expenditures. Adjustment (Expenditures) represent $38.0 million which was the amount transferred to the Rainy Day Fund from 1/2 of the FY 2017 surplus. The Ending Balance is mostly the historically carried forward reappropriation from previous fiscal years (estimated amounts that will remain and be reappropriated to the next fiscal year), the estimated 13th month expenditures applicable to the current fiscal year & any unappropriated surplus balance (estimated) from the current fiscal year.

Wisconsin–Revenue adjustments include Tribal Gaming, $27.7m; Prior Year Designated Balance, $52.1m; and Other Revenue, $528.6m. Expenditure adjustments include Transfers, $73.3m; Lapses, -$469.3m; and Compensation Reserves, $0.3m

Wyoming– The State of Wyoming budgets on a biennial basis, to arrive at annual figures certain assumptions and estimates were required.

Table 7.1 | Fiscal 2018 General Fund

2018 Beginning Balances (In millions)

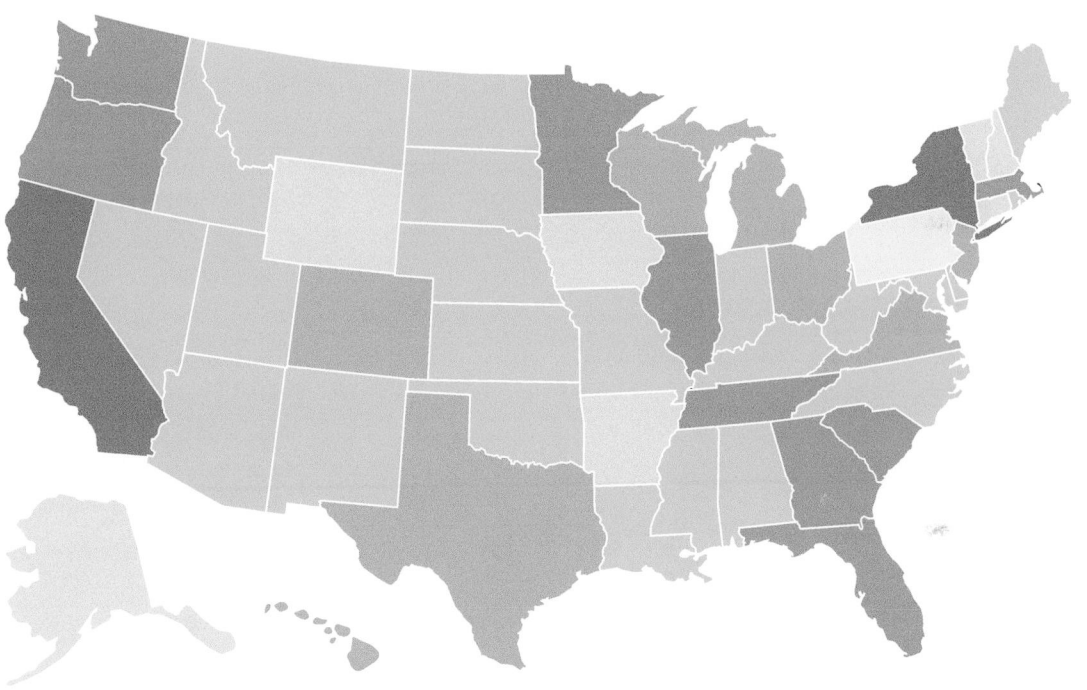

- Less than 0
- 0
- 1 to 499
- 500 to 999
- 1000 to 5000
- More than 5000

Highest Rainy Day Fund Balance Fiscal 2018 (in millions)

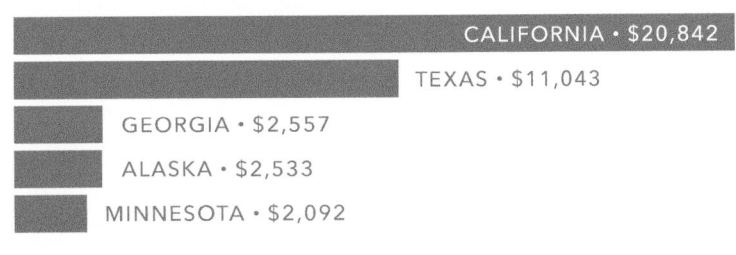

CALIFORNIA · $20,842

TEXAS · $11,043

GEORGIA · $2,557

ALASKA · $2,533

MINNESOTA · $2,092

California's Fiscal 2018 general fund ending balance was **NEARLY 50% HIGHER** than its beginning balance.

In Fiscal 2018, 38 states had higher revenues than expenditures.

Table 7.1 | Fiscal 2018 General Fund *(cont.)*

2018 Ending Balances (In millions)

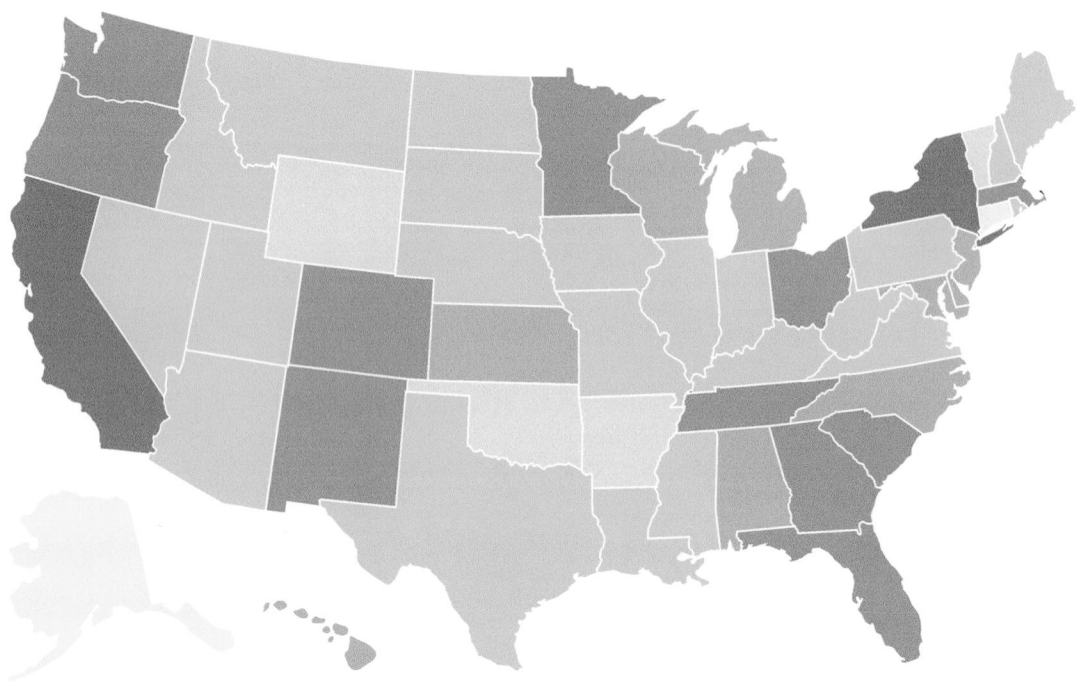

Less than 0
0
1 to 499
500 to 999
1000 to 5000
More than 5000

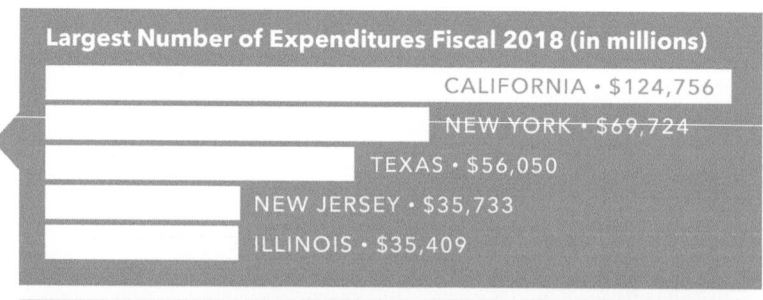

Largest Number of Expenditures Fiscal 2018 (in millions)

CALIFORNIA • $124,756
NEW YORK • $69,724
TEXAS • $56,050
NEW JERSEY • $35,733
ILLINOIS • $35,409

Smallest Number of Expenditures Fiscal 2018 (in millions)

NEW HAMPSHIRE • $1,504
WYOMING • $1,530
VERMONT • $1,564
SOUTH DAKOTA • $1,591
NORTH DAKOTA • $2,160

TABLE 7.2
Fiscal 2019 General Fund, Preliminary Actual (In millions of dollars)

State	Beginning balance	Revenues	Adjustments	Total resources	Expenditures	Adjustments	Ending Balance	Rainy day fund balance
Total	$53,569	$880,859		$953,526	$871,019		$57,637	$72,345
Alabama (a)	593	9,317	0	9,910	8,775	337	798	848
Alaska (a)	0	2,683	2,785	5,468	4,889	1,052	(472)	2,288
Arizona (a)	450	11,131	100	11,681	10,414	271	996	713
Arkansas (a)	0	5,921	0	5,921	5,626	0	295	153
California (a)	11,419	138,046	0	149,465	142,693	0	6,772	20,646
Colorado* (a)	1,366	12,584	17	13,967	12,828	0	1,140	1,140
Connecticut (a)	0	19,650	0	19,650	19,279	0	371	2,506
Delaware* (a)	750	4,592	0	5,342	4,394	0	947	240
Florida	1,646	34,052	0	35,698	33,494	0	2,204	1,483
Georgia (a)	2,729	25,571	76	28,376	25,404	0	2,972	N/A
Hawaii	750	7,917	0	8,667	7,915	0	752	378
Idaho (a)	118	3,735	64	3,917	3,691	124	102	373
Illinois* (a)	125	39,195	1,000	40,320	36,335	3,519	466	4
Indiana (a)	366	16,693	56	17,116	16,280	1	835	1,436
Iowa (a)	0	7,859	71	7,930	7,528	113	289	762
Kansas (a)	762	7,368	7	8,137	7,033	0	1,104	0
Kentucky (a)	29	11,510	475	12,014	11,661	223	130	129
Louisiana (a)	308	9,554	211	10,073	9,765	308	0	405
Maine (a)	75	3,834	27	3,936	3,708	89	139	309
Maryland (a)	590	18,199	19	18,807	17,912	(79)	974	877
Massachusetts* (a)	2,387	34,947	13,011	50,345	33,495	13,011	3,839	2,832
Michigan (a)	788	10,389	0	11,177	10,432	100	645	1,149
Minnesota* (a)	3,283	22,941	0	26,224	23,144	0	3,080	2,474
Mississippi (a)	5	5,781	0	5,786	5,544	238	5	348
Missouri (a)	495	9,567	132	10,195	9,541	0	654	651
Montana (a)	187	2,574	(1)	2,760	2,415	(14)	358	61
Nebraska (a)	454	4,896	(247)	5,103	4,367	0	737	334
Nevada (a)	425	4,288	158	4,870	4,426	108	336	332
New Hampshire (a)	74	1,621	0	1,696	1,505	(1)	192	115
New Jersey* (a)	991	37,981	390	39,361	37,721	0	1,640	401
New Mexico* (a)	1,185	7,824	299	9,308	7,565	35	1,707	1,868
New York* (a)	9,445	70,544	0	79,989	72,783	0	7,206	2,048
North Carolina (a)	995	24,827	0	25,822	23,666	447	1,709	1,254
North Dakota (a)	253	1,916	649	2,818	2,206	547	65	659
Ohio (a)	1,221	33,768	0	34,989	33,451	0	1,538	2,692
Oklahoma (a)	0	7,691	(12)	7,679	7,015	355	310	806
Oregon (a)	1,471	11,516	(93)	12,895	10,172	190	2,532	1,288
Pennsylvania (a)	22	34,858	(1,162)	33,718	33,401	317	0	23
Rhode Island (a)	53	4,021	(112)	3,961	3,922	10	29	204
South Carolina* (a)	1,187	8,805	4	9,996	8,142	145	1,709	531
South Dakota (a)	17	1,641	16	1,674	1,638	17	19	170
Tennessee (a)	1,140	14,997	(50)	16,087	14,939	282	866	875
Texas (a)	1,905	57,868	559	60,332	52,281	3,330	4,721	10,089
Utah (a)	317	7,543	42	7,902	7,578	34	291	697
Vermont (a)	0	1,692	2	1,693	1,596	97	0	224
Virginia	212	21,462	0	21,674	21,445	0	230	792
Washington (a)	2,016	22,188	(495)	23,709	22,908	0	801	1,671
West Virginia (a)	378	4,756	5	5,139	4,604	18	518	753
Wisconsin (a)	589	17,341	769	18,699	17,964	(352)	1,087	649
Wyoming (a)	0	1,205	325	1,530	1,530	0	0	1,667

See footnotes at end of table

TABLE 7.2
Fiscal 2019 General Fund, Preliminary Actual (In millions of dollars) (continued)

Source: National Association of State Budget Officers, Fall 2019.
Note: For all states, unless otherwise noted, transfers into budget stabilization funds are counted as expenditures, and transfers from budget stabilization funds are counted as revenues.
Key:
* – The ending balance includes the balance in the rainy day fund.
N/A – Not available
(a)

Alabama –Expenditure Adjustments include transferring $64.2 million to the Budget Stabilization Fund and $272.3 million to the Advancement and Technology Fund.

Alaska –Revenues: Spring 2019 Revenue Sources Book ,Revenue Adjustments: Fiscal Year 2020 Enacted Fiscal Summary Expenditures: Fiscal Year 2020 Enacted Fiscal Summary Expenditure Adjustments: State of Alaska Fiscal Summary - FY19 and FY20 (Part 1) Rainy Day Balance: State of Alaska Fiscal Summary FY19 and FY20 (Part 2) Number listed is EoY Balance. Rainy day balance includes any anticipated draws. Ending balance includes multi-year appropriations. Started reporting shared taxes as expenditures instead of Revenues

Arizona – Adjustments come from other fund transfers to the General Fund.

Arkansas – Total available revenue amounts are reported as net of refunds and special dedications/payments. 16.3% of the ending balance was transferred to create a restricted reserve fund for FY19, 58.7% was transferred to the General Revenue Allotment Reserve Fund, and the remaining 25% was transferred to the Arkansas Highway Transfer Fund.

California – Total revenues reflect revenues after transfers to the rainy day fund. The ending balance includes the SFEU but excludes the BSA and the Safety Net Reserve Fund. The excluded amount is $14,358.4 million for the BSA and $900 million for the Safety Net Reserve Fund at the end of FY 2019. Adding these amounts to the FY 2019 ending balance, the projected total balance is $22,030.6 million in FY 2018. The rainy day balance is made up of the SFEU, BSA, and the Safety Net Reserve Fund, however, withdrawals of mandatory deposits from the BSA are subject to provisions of Proposition 2, 2014. Ending balance Includes a reserve for encumbrances of $1,384.5 million representing amounts which will be expended in the future for state obligations for which goods and services have been ordered/contracted, but have not been received by the end of the fiscal year. These amounts are shown as a reserve to the fund balance instead of a hit to the fund balance.

Colorado – Revenue adjustments include transfers to the General Fund. Colorado's rainy day fund is included within the General Fund.

Connecticut – BRF balance includes: $212.9 million balance from prior year, $1,471.3 million due to volatility cap, $-482.9 transfer out to extinguish FY 2018 deficit, and $-16.1 million transfer out to the Retired Teachers Health Service Fund. The volatility cap which automatically transfers a portion of income tax collections above a certain threshold. Expenditures Adjustments: Miscellaneous adjustments, 3.4.

Delaware – Fiscal year ending balance includes encumbered appropriations and those appropriations legislatively continued into the ensuing fiscal year.

Georgia – FY 2019 adjustments to revenues include FY18 agency surplus returned and early remittance of FY19 surplus from state agencies. Ending balance reflects preliminary Revenue Shortfall Reserve prior to final FY19 agency surplus and appropriation of the 1% midterm adjustment for FY 2020.

Idaho – Beginning fund balance different due to statutory transfer to budget stabilization and strategic initiatives fund. Revenue Adjustments: $2.8M for reappropriation, $6.1M for prior-year reversion, $13.1 million from the Group Insurance Account, $40.4M for Budget Stabilization Fund (statute expired -), $1.3M misc. Expenditure Adjustments: $2 million to the STEM Education Fund; $.4 million to the Wolf Control Fund; $44.1 million to the Permanent Building Fund; $22 million to the Technology Stabilization Fund; $2.4 million to the Water Resources Revolving Development Fund, $32M to Public Education Stabilization Fund, $21M to Water Mgmt. Fund, $.17M for deficiency warrants.

Illinois – Total revenue increases are attributed to growth in income and sales tax receipts. Total revenues include $33,560M in state sources, $3,600M federal, and $2,196M transfers in. Revenue adjustments include $750M in Treasurer investment borrowing and $250M in interfund borrowing. Estimated expenditure adjustments include $3,609M in statutory transfers out.

Indiana – Revenue adjustments include a transfer to the General Fund to assist with the Integrated Tax System and a one-time deposit of gaming license transfer fees. transfer from the Rainy Day Fund. Expenditure adjustments include reversions from distributions, capital, and reconciliations; reversions from prior year Medicaid appropriations; state agency and university line item capital projects; the cost of a 13th check for pension recipients; a one-time appropriation for the Indiana Biosciences Research Institute; and a one-time transfer to teachers retirement fund pensions.

Iowa – Total Revenues are as actual, also included in revenue adjustments is $71.0 million of residual funds transferred to the General Fund after the Reserve Funds are filled to their statutory maximum amounts. Total Expenditures actual appropriations including $168.6 million of supplemental appropriations for FY2019. Included in expenditure adjustments is a transfer from the General Fund to the State's Cash Reserve Fund of $113.1 million. The ending balance of the General Fund is transferred in the current year to the Reserve funds in the subsequent fiscal year. After the Reserve Funds are at their statutorily set maximum amounts, the remainder of the funds are transferred back to the General Fund in that subsequent fiscal year.

Kansas – $6.8 million in Prior year released encumbrances shows as revenue.

Kentucky – Revenue includes $117.6 million in Tobacco Settlement funds. Adjustments for Revenues includes $168.0 million that represents appropriation balances carried over from the prior fiscal year, and $307.0 million from fund transfers into the General Fund. Adjustment to Expenditures represents appropriation balances forwarded to the next fiscal year and budget balances to be expended in the next fiscal year. The FY 2019 surplus of $130.1 million was appropriated in FY 2020: $70 million to Teachers' Retirement Medical Insurance Fund, and $60.1 million to the Kentucky state employees' non-hazardous retirement's unfunded liability.

Louisiana – Revenues adjustments - Includes $63.7 in carryforwards, $63.0 in use of prior year undesignated fund balance, $53.3 transfer of funds and $30.8 in prior year undesignated fund balance. Expenditure adjustments - includes transfers of $77.0 to the Budget Stabilization Fund, $30.8 to the UAL Retirement systems, $10.7 in Funds transfers and $100.8 in supplemental funding. FY19 numbers are budgeted and not actuals.

Maine – Revenue and Expenditure adjustments reflect Legislatively

TABLE 7.2
Fiscal 2019 General Fund, Preliminary Actual (In millions of dollars) (continued)

authorized transfers. The total balance reported for FY19 includes up to $60.3 million earmarked for repayment of disallowed costs from the Centers for Medicare and Medicaid Services.

Maryland – Revenue adjustment includes $23.3 million in transfers from tax credit reserves and -$4.6 million in revenue under attainment from transfers. Expenditure adjustments represent $79.0 million in reversions.

Massachusetts – Data as of 7/31/19. General Fund is defined as all budgeted operating funds, adjusted for expenditures funded by federal reimbursements. This is to better align with spending reported in the State Expenditure Report and be more comparable to most other states, which book federally reimbursed expenditures in a separate federal fund; adjustments also account for certain transfers between budgeted funds. Ending balance includes $322.2 million in reserved balances projected to be spent in the next fiscal year. Fiscal 2019 Preliminary Actual ending balance additionally includes significant undesignated balances due to the FY19 tax surplus; on September 6, 2019, the Governor filed a bill recommending spending, transfers to off-budget funds, and continuing spending authorization to address undesignated year-end balances.

Michigan – Revenue totals are net of payments to local governments. Adjustments (Expenditures): $100 million transfer to Budget Stabilization Fund/Rainy Day Fund. Expenditure total reflects a large GF supplemental from higher than anticipated one-time revenues. Michigan's fiscal year is October 1 through September 30; final fiscal year 2019 revenue and expenditure totals will be published in the State of Michigan Comprehensive Annual Financial Report, due March 2020

Minnesota – Rainy Day Fund balance includes cash flow account of $350 million and a budget reserve of $2.075 billion. Includes stadium reserve of $49.595 million.

Mississippi – Ending balance includes reappropriation from FY2018 to FY2019.

Missouri – Revenue adjustments include transfers from other funds into the general revenue fund.

Montana –Revenue adjustments reflect prior year revenue activity and expenditure adjustments reflect prior year expenditure activity and adjustments to fund balance as a result of the annual CAFR reconciliation.

Nebraska – Revenue adjustments are transfers between the General Fund and other funds. Among others, this includes a $221 million transfer from the General Fund to the Property Tax Credit Cash Fund, as well as a $62 million Transfer to the Cash Reserve for Revenues in excess of the Certified Forecast for FY 2018. Also included are transfers totaling $48 million from the Cash Reserve Fund to the General Fund for budget stabilization.

Nevada – Revenue adjustments are restricted revenue, reversion, Rainy Day Fund transfers in and reserve transfers in. Expenditure adjustments are restricted transfers out.

New Hampshire – Expenditure Adjustments: The make-up of this adjustment total for FY 2019 includes a positive pick up of $9.4 million through a GAAP adjustment, a movement of $ 5.3 million to the Rainy Day Fund, and the movement of $3.5 million to the Public School Infrastructure Fund at year end. The entire amount of the General Fund undesignated fund balance of $ 191.6 million from FY 2019 is obligated in FY 2020.

New Jersey – Adjustments include estimated Lapses; transfers to other funds; reservation of fund balance.

New Mexico –Adjustments are net of reversions and transfers from other funds.

New York –The Rainy Day Reserve increased by $250 million. This was the result of a transfer from the State Purposes Account to the Rainy Day Reserve Fund. These funds are components of New York State's General Fund.

North Carolina – Expenditure adjustments includes funds transferred to Budget Stabilization Reserve (Savings Reserve), $221.5 million, Medicaid Transformation Reserve, $135 million, and funds to the Department of Transportation from the General Fund of $90 million. Budget Stabilization Reserve (Rainy Day) balance was reduced in the middle of FY 2019 to aid in the Hurricane Florence recovery efforts. The funds were placed in restricted statewide reserve similar to the Rainy Day Fund and transferred to the operating budget as needed to cover FEMA federal match and state supported programs for Hurricane Florence Recovery efforts. Ending Balance is higher than normal due to North Carolina not having a comprehensive budget at the time of this survey due to the Governor's veto of the General Assembly's budget. Normally, some of the year-end credit balance is directed by an approved budget to areas like capital, repair and renovation, and the Rainy Day Fund.

North Dakota –Revenue adjustments are transfers of $124.0 million from the strategic investment and improvements fund, $455.3 million transfer from the legacy fund and $70.0 million from other special fund sources, to the general fund. Expenditure adjustments include a $545.9 million transfer to the budget stabilization fund and $899,000 in misc. transfers. The negative general fund revenue variance from FY 2018 to FY 2019 is due to the majority of the state's share of $400 million in oil and gas tax revenues being collected in FY 2018.

Ohio – FY 2019 expenditures include expenditures against prior year encumbrances and $773.0 million in transfers out of the GRF. The fiscal 2019 ending balance included cash to support $391.6 million in open encumbrances and $312.4 million in surplus transfers which occurred in fiscal 2020. Federal reimbursements for Medicaid expenditures funded from the General Revenue Fund (GRF) are deposited into the GRF. Federal reimbursements for Medicaid expenditures from non-GRF sources are deposited into the appropriate federal fund. Expenditures of federal funds are contained in the General Fund number to be consistent with Ohio accounting practices and with other portrayals of Ohio's general fund. This will tend to make Ohio's GRF revenue and expenditures look higher relative to most other states that don't follow this practice.

Oklahoma – FY19 revenue adjustments were -$15.7 million net cash flow reserve difference and the addition of $3.7 million returned to the General Revenue Fund from legislative action which re-captured that amount from the GRF appropriation to the State Department of Health during the 2019 fiscal year. The expenditure adjustment reflects the end-of-year deposit into the Constitutional Reserve Fund (Rainy Day Fund).

Oregon –Revenue adjustments include: a revenue adjustment for a statutory transfer to local governments for local property tax relief. Expenditure adjustment includes: the cost of Tax Anticipation Notes, as well as the required deposit into the Rainy Day Fund. Because General Fund revenues for the 2017-19 biennium are anticipated to exceed projections by more than two percent, there will be a refund of personal income taxes ""Kicker"". This refund, which is projected at roughly $1,569.5 million will be returned to taxpayers as a credit on their 2019 income tax return (which will be filed in 2020).

TABLE 7.2
Fiscal 2019 General Fund, Preliminary Actual (In millions of dollars) (continued)

Pennsylvania –Revenue adjustments include refunds, lapses and adjustments to beginning balances. Expenditure adjustments include transfers to the Budget Stabilization Reserve Fund (rainy day).

Rhode Island –Adjustments to revenues reflects $122.2 million to the Budget Reserve (Rainy Day) Fund, offset by reappropriation of $10.1 million from FY 2018. Expenditure adjustments reflect reappropriations to the following fiscal year (FY 2020). Designated portion of ending balance - Reappropriations authorized by the Governor totaling $10.3 million"

South Carolina –Revenue Adjustments: Litigation Recovery Account ($4.1M). Expenditure Adjustments: Prior Yr. 2% Capital Reserve ($145.1M) transferred to state agencies. Designated portion of ending balance: Capital Reserve Fund - $151.6M; Appropriations Carried Forward $432.0M

South Dakota – The beginning balance of $16.9 million and adjustment to expenditures reflects the prior year's ending balance that is transferred to the rainy day fund. Adjustments to revenue of $15.8 million is from one-time receipts. The ending balance of $19.3 million is cash that is obligated to the Budget Reserve fund the following fiscal year. This $19.3 million is not included in the total rainy day fund balance of $169.8 million.

Tennessee – Adjustments (Revenues): $45.2 million transfer from debt service fund unexpended appropriations. -$20.5 million transfer to Highway Fund. -$75.0 million transfer to Rainy Day Fund. Adjustments (Expenditures): $261.1 million transfer to capital outlay projects fund. $16.3 million transfer to state office buildings and support facilities fund. $3.7 million transfer to debt service fund. $1.0 million transfer to reserves for dedicated revenue appropriations. Ending Balance: $865.5 million unappropriated budget surplus at June 30, 2019

Texas –$128.0 reflected in adjustments to revenue was realized from dedicated account balances now available. As well as $58 and $372.9 of fund balances from the available school fund and the state technology and instructional materials fund were made available. End of year adjustments made by the Comptroller account for the difference between the ending balance of FY 2018 to the beginning balance of FY 2019. $3,330 is a transfer of revenue to the ESF and State Highway to be allocated equally. Total general fund revenue was impacted due to a constitutional dedication of a portion of sales tax collected by the state to be reallocated from the general fund to the State Highway Fund to address infrastructure needs.

Utah –Expenditure adjustments include $33.5 million of surplus revenue collections automatically transferred to rainy day funds at the end of FY 2019 based on statutory formulas. Revenue adjustments include transfers to the General Fund and Education fund, the amount set aside for economic development cash incentives, and other revenue adjustments. $206.2 million of the $290.8 ending FY 2019 ending balance was designated by the Legislature to be appropriated for one-time items in FY 2020.

Vermont – Preliminary fiscal year 2019 actual results include revenue adjustments comprised of $1.6M in reversions of General Fund appropriations. Expenditure adjustments include the allocation of $96.9M in operating surplus as transfers and reserves as follows: $73.9M in net transfers to other funds most notably comprised of paying-in-full a $22.2M interfund loan from the General Fund to the Retired Teachers' Health and Medical Benefits fund (OPEB), a one-time transfer of $9.4M for use during FY 2020 for general fund appropriations, a $25.6M transfer to the Vermont State Employees' Postemployment Benefits Trust fund, as well as making an additional

contribution of $13.3M above the Actuarily Determined Employer Contribution to the Vermont Teachers' Retirement Fund; $23.0M in reserves inclusive of meeting the Budget Stabilization reserve requirement while making a $19.1M contribution to the "Rainy Day" reserve fund. Additionally, there was a $78.1M transfer from an Agency of Human Service's special fund to the General Fund's designated Human Services Caseload reserve (net-neutral transfer on a statewide basis).

Washington –Revenue adjustments reflect the net of transfers in and out of the General Fund, as well as prior biennium recoveries and similar resource adjustments. A portion of the FY 2019 ending balance is programmed to be spent in FY 2020.

West Virginia –Fiscal Year 2019 Beginning balance includes $297.3 million of Reappropriations, Unappropriated Surplus Balance of $36.1 million, $1.3 million of cash balance adjustments, and FY 2018 13th month expenditures of $42.9 million. Total Revenues show the FY 2019 actual general revenue collections of $4,756.3 million. Adjustments (Revenue) are prior year redeposits of $744,230 and special revenue expirations of $4.7 million. Total Expenditures include general revenue appropriated expenditures of $4,748.1 million, surplus appropriation expenditures of $10.7 million, reappropriation expenditures of $81.7 million, $-0.3 million of cash adjustments, and $42.9 million of 31 day prior year expenditures. Adjustment (Expenditures) represent $18.0 million which was the amount transferred to the Rainy Day Fund from 1/2 of the FY 2018 surplus. The Ending Balance is mostly the historically carried forward reappropriation from previous fiscal years (estimated amounts that will remain and be reappropriated to the next fiscal year), the estimated 13th month expenditures applicable to the current fiscal year & any unappropriated surplus balance (estimated) from the current fiscal year.

Wisconsin –Revenue adjustments include Tribal Gaming, $29.1m; Prior Year Designated Balance, $238.5m; and Other Revenue, $501.7m. Expenditure adjustments include Transfers, $363.3m; Lapses, -$755.8m; and Compensation Reserves, $40.5m.

Wyoming – The State of Wyoming budgets on a biennial basis, to arrive at annual figures certain assumptions and estimates are required.

TABLE 7.3
Fiscal 2020 General Fund, Enacted (In millions of dollars)

State	Beginning balance	Revenues	Adjustments	Total resources	Expenditures	Adjustments	Ending balance	Rainy day fund balance
Total (a)	$55,342	$903,568	0	$975,768	$913,164		$39,255	$72,390
Alabama (a)	798	9,259	0	10,057	9,318	532	207	945
Alaska (a)	0	2,304	3,106	5,409	4,337	1,183	(111)	2,279
Arizona (a)	764	11,083	71	11,918	11,583	271	65	1,019
Arkansas (a)	0	5,737	0	5,737	5,737	0	0	153
California (a)	6,772	143,805	0	150,577	147,781	0	2,796	19,204
Colorado * (a)	1,140	13,096	71	14,307	13,261	0	1,046	1,046
Connecticut (a)	0	19,460	0	19,460	19,319	0	141	2,965
Delaware * (a)	947	4,617	(126)	5,438	4,668	0	771	252
Florida	2,204	33,126	0	35,330	34,150	0	1,180	1,574
Georgia (a)	2,972	26,143	0	29,115	26,143	0	2,972	N/A
Hawaii	752	8,202	0	8,954	8,306	0	648	396
Idaho (a)	101	4,025	13	4,139	3,910	62	166	373
Illinois * (a)	466	40,188	100	40,754	37,486	2,650	618	4
Indiana (a)	835	16,924	5	17,764	16,831	95	838	1,446
Iowa (a)	0	7,966	188	8,154	7,634	0	520	784
Kansas (a)	1,104	7,432	0	8,536	7,750	110	676	0
Kentucky (a)	130	11,580	368	12,078	11,849	229	(0)	304
Louisiana	0	9,725	0	9,725	9,725	0	0	430
Maine (a)	139	3,904	10	4,053	3,923	21	110	306
Maryland (a)	718	18,566	196	19,479	19,419	(35)	95	1,198
Massachusetts * (a)	3,839	35,208	13,106	52,154	34,972	13,106	4,075	3,308
Michigan * (a)	N/A	N/A	N/A	N/A	N/A	N/A	N/A	N/A
Minnesota * (a)	3,080	23,518	0	26,598	23,950	0	2,648	2,487
Mississippi (a)	5	5,858	0	5,863	5,747	0	116	465
Missouri (a)	654	9,822	143	10,619	10,326	0	293	654
Montana	358	2,512	0	2,870	2,566	0	304	118
Nebraska (a)	737	4,929	(463)	5,202	4,625	288	290	510
Nevada (a)	336	4,446	62	4,844	4,431	72	341	394
New Hampshire (a)	192	1,590	0	1,781	1,563	231	(13)	115
New Jersey * (a)	1,640	38,199	(169)	39,670	38,403	0	1,267	401
New Mexico * (a)	1,707	7,780	334	9,821	7,516	36	2,270	2,015
New York* (a)	7,206	77,117	0	84,323	77,857	0	6,466	2,476
North Carolina (a)	N/A	N/A	N/A	N/A	N/A	N/A	N/A	N/A
North Dakota (a)	65	2,062	461	2,588	2,422	0	166	727
Ohio (a)	1,538	34,163	0	35,701	35,045	0	656	2,692
Oklahoma (a)	310	7,844	0	8,153	7,491	0	662	N/A
Oregon (a)	2,532	10,043	(22)	12,553	10,981	0	1,572	1,487
Pennsylvania (a)	0	35,497	(1,143)	34,354	33,998	178	178	340
Rhode Island (a)	25	4,179	(126)	4,078	4,078	0	0	210
South Carolina* (a)	1,709	8,717	30	10,455	8,575	537	1,344	569
South Dakota (a)	19	1,701	0	1,721	1,701	19	1	189
Tennessee (a)	866	15,536	(232)	16,170	15,714	439	18	1,100
Texas (a)	4,721	60,778	194	65,693	60,775	3,179	1,740	7,830
Utah (a)	291	7,801	10	8,101	7,959	0	142	791
Vermont (a)	0	1,647	0	1,647	1,645	3	0	226
Virginia (a)	230	22,529	0	22,759	22,751	0	8	1,375
Washington (a)	801	24,316	(216)	24,901	24,360	0	541	1,948
West Virginia (a)	518	4,710	0	5,228	4,791	18	418	810
Wisconsin (a)	1,087	17,304	564	18,955	18,387	(364)	931	N/A
Wyoming (a)	0	1,205	325	1,530	1,530	0	0	1,667

See footnotes at end of table

TABLE 7.3
Fiscal 2020 General Fund, Enacted (In millions of dollars) (continued)

Source: National Association of State Budget Officers, Fall 2019.
Note: For all states, unless otherwise noted, transfers into budget stabilization funds are counted as expenditures, and transfers from budget stabilization funds are counted as revenues.
Key:
N/A–Not available
*–The ending balance includes the balance in the rainy day fund.
(a)
Totals–Michigan and North Carolina had not yet finalized their fiscal 2020 budgets at the time of publication. Totals include the fiscal 2020 general fund amounts for Michigan and North Carolina reported in NASBO's Spring 2019 Fiscal Survey of States, based on the governor's recommended budget. This information is being used as placeholders in order to calculate 50-state total figures that are comparable to prior fiscal years for the purposes of this report.
Alabama–Expenditure Adjustments include transferring $66.5 million to the Budget Stabilization Fund and $465.0 million to the Advancement and Technology Fund. We anticipate spending $110.7m of a carryover balance in 2020.
Alaska–Revenues: Spring 2019 Revenue Sources Book (Total Revenue); Revenue Adjustments: Fiscal Year 2020 Enacted Fiscal Summary; Expenditures: Fiscal Year 2020 Enacted Fiscal Summary; Expenditure Adjustments: State of Alaska Fiscal Summary–FY19 and FY20 (Part 1); Rainy Day Balance: State of Alaska Fiscal Summary FY19 and FY20 (Part 2) Number listed is EoY Balance. Rainy day balance includes any anticipated draws. Ending balance includes multi-year appropriations. Started reporting shared taxes as expenditures instead of Revenues
Arizona–Adjustments come from other fund transfers to the General Fund.
Arkansas–Total available revenue amounts are reported as net of refunds and special dedications/payments.
California–Total revenues reflect revenues after transfers to the rainy day fund. The ending balance includes the SFEU, but excludes the BSA, the Safety Net Reserve Fund, and the Public School System Stabilization Account (PSSSA) (a rainy day reserve for schools). The excluded amount is $16,516.4 million for the BSA, $900 million for the Safety Net Reserve Fund, and $376.5 million for the PSSSA at the end of FY 2020. Adding these amounts to the FY 2020 ending balance, the projected total balance is $20,589 million in FY 2020. The rainy day balance is made up of the SFEU, BSA, the Safety Net Reserve Fund, and PSSSA, however, withdrawals of mandatory deposits from the BSA are subject to provisions of Proposition 2, 2014. ; Ending balance Includes a reserve for encumbrances of $1,384.5 million representing amounts which will be expended in the future for state obligations for which goods and services have been ordered/contracted, but have not been received by the end of the fiscal year. These amounts are shown as a reserve to the fund balance instead of a hit to the fund balance.
Colorado–Revenue adjustments include transfers to the General Fund. Colorado's rainy day fund is included within the General Fund.

Connecticut–FY 2020 projected Rainy Day Fund balance also includes projected $318.3 million transfer due to the volatility cap.
Delaware–Effective July 1, 2019 and per 82 Del Law c 64 (HB 225, § 77) $126.3 million was allocated to the Budget Stabilization Fund, a special fund holding account. Funds in the account require an act of the General Assembly to enable appropriation and spending authority. Fiscal year ending balance includes encumbered appropriations and those appropriations legislatively continued into the ensuing fiscal year.
Georgia–FY 20 beginning balance reflects general fund balances as of June 30, 2019 for Revenue Shortfall Reserve (Preliminary) as reported on the FY 19 State Funds and Funds Available from Beginning Fund Balance Sheet of the Report of Georgia Revenues and Reserves. Georgia is required by its constitution to maintain a balanced report. The fund balances for FY 19 and 20 reflect the Governor's balanced budget. Georgia does not project future Rainy Day fund balances but expects the reserve to continue to grow in future years.
Idaho–Revenue Adjustment: $12.8M for corporate income tax conformity. Expenditure Adjustments: $1M to STEM Education Fund; $20M to Fire Suppression Deficiency Fund; $1M to POST Fund; $21.5 to Permanent Building Fund; $.2M to Wolf Control Fund; $8.6M to Public Education Stabilization Fund; $8.1M to Technology Infrastructure Stabilization Fund; $2M to Disaster Emergency Fund. Includes updated General Fund revenue forecast not yet adopted by legislature
Illinois–Total revenue increases include growth in income and sales tax receipts. Total revenues include $34,295M in state sources, $3,697M federal, and $2,196M transfers in. Revenue adjustments include $100M in interfund borrowing. Estimated expenditure adjustments include $364M in statutory transfers out, $2,201 in debt service, and $85M in interfund borrowing repayment.
Indiana–Revenue adjustments include a transfer to the General Fund to assist with the Integrated Tax System and a casino relocation fee. Expenditure adjustments include reversions from distributions, capital, and reconciliations; reversions from prior year Medicaid appropriations; state agency and university line item capital projects; the cost of a 13th check for pension recipients; and minimal one-time expenditures.
Iowa–Total Revenues are as estimated by the October 2019 REC, also included in revenue adjustments is $187.6 million of estimated residual funds transferred to the General Fund after the Reserve Funds are filled to their statutory maximum amounts. Total Expenditures are adjusted for final standing appropriations estimates for FY2020. The ending balance of the General Fund is transferred in the current year to the Reserve funds in the subsequent fiscal year. After the Reserve Funds are at their statutorily set maximum amounts, the remainder of the funds are transferred back to the General Fund in that subsequent fiscal year.
Kansas–Expenditure Adjustments equal the amount of FY 2019 underspending that reappropriated for FY 2020 expenditure.

TABLE 7.3
Fiscal 2020 General Fund, Enacted (In millions of dollars) (continued)

Kentucky–Revenue includes $118.1 million in Tobacco Settlement funds. Adjustments for Revenues includes $52.3 million that represents appropriation balances carried over from the prior fiscal year, and $315.9 million from fund transfers into the General Fund. Adjustment to Expenditures represents appropriation balances forwarded to the next fiscal year and budget balances to be expended in the next fiscal year.

Maine–Revenue and Expenditure adjustments reflect Legislatively authorized transfers. The total balance reported for FY20 includes up to $56.8 million earmarked for repayment of disallowed costs from the Centers for Medicare and Medicaid Services.

Maryland–Revenue adjustments include $37.5 million in transfers from tax credit reserves and a $158 million transfer from the Revenue Stabilization Account (Rainy Day). Expenditure adjustments represent $35 million in reversions. The FY 2020 Enacted starting balance does not match the FY 2019 Actual ending balance because the FY 2020 Enacted budget did not incorporate updated revenue and expenditure figures from FY 2019.

Massachusetts–Data as of 7/31/19. General Fund is defined as all budgeted operating funds, adjusted for expenditures funded by federal reimbursements. This is to better align with spending reported in the State Expenditure Report and be more comparable to most other states, which book federally reimbursed expenditures in a separate federal fund; adjustments also account for certain transfers between budgeted funds. Ending balance includes $81.5 million in reserved balances projected to be spent in the next fiscal year. Other - Caps on Full-Time Equivalent employees are in effect for executive department agencies

Michigan–Information on Michigan's fiscal 2020 enacted budget was not available at the time of publication. Initial appropriations have been enacted, but Michigan's fiscal year 2020 budget is not yet finished.

Minnesota–Rainy Day Fund balance includes cash flow account of $350 million and a budget reserve of $2.075 billion. Includes stadium reserve of $62.297 million.

Mississippi–Adjustments to expenditures reflect transfers to the state's Rainy Day and Capital Expense Funds

Missouri–Revenue adjustments include transfers from other funds into the general revenue fund.

Nebraska–Revenue adjustments are transfers between the General Fund and other funds. Among others, this includes a $221 million transfer, Plus an additional $51 million transfer from the General Fund to the Property Tax Credit Cash Fund, bringing the total transfer amount to $272 million. There are also $48.5 million in usual and customary transfers into the General Fund from Other Cash Funds. There was also a $176 million Transfer to the Cash Reserve Fund for Revenues in excess of the Certified Forecast for FY 2019, and an $11 million transfer to the Water Sustainability Fund. Expenditure adjustments include $317.8 million reserved for unexpended FY 2019 carryover obligations, an estimated lapse of $35 million in carryover obligations, and $5 million reserved for potential deficit appropriations.

Nevada–Revenue adjustments are restricted revenue, reversion, Rainy Day Fund transfers in and reserve transfers in. Expenditure adjustments are restricted transfers out.

New Hampshire–Expenditure Adjustments: The enacted budget bills for the FY 2020-2021 Biennium anticipated one time appropriations of $162.9 million for a number of initiatives, with an additional $68.1 million being transferred to the Education Trust Fund. The choice to appropriate funds for these one-time expenditures was predicated on the anticipated FY 2019 unexpended available general fund surplus which is estimated preliminarily to be $191.6 million. Special Note: It is not a requirement of New Hampshire law that the first year of the biennial budget have revenues and unexpended general surplus be in balance with anticipated expenditures.

New Jersey–Adjustments include transfers to other funds; reservation of fund balance

New Mexico–Adjustments are net of reversions and transfers from other funds.

New York–The Rainy Day Reserve is expected to increase by an additional $428 million in FY 2020 after a planned transfer from the State Purposes Account to the Rainy Day Reserve Fund, fiscal conditions permitting. These funds are components of New York State's General Fund.

North Carolina–North Carolina was not able to report fiscal 2020 enacted budget figures, as the state's fiscal 2020-2021 budget was not finalized in time for publication.

North Dakota–Revenue adjustments are transfers of $8.6 million from the tax relief fund, $382.2.0 million from the strategic investment and improvements fund and $70.0 million from other special fund sources, to the general fund.

Ohio–FY 2020 expenditures include expenditures against prior year encumbrances and $683.7 million in estimated transfers out of the GRF. Federal reimbursements for Medicaid expenditures funded from the General Revenue Fund (GRF) are deposited into the GRF. Federal reimbursements for Medicaid expenditures from non-GRF sources are deposited into the appropriate federal fund. Expenditures of federal funds are contained in the General Fund number to be consistent with Ohio accounting practices and with other portrayals of Ohio's general fund. This will tend to make Ohio's GRF revenue and expenditures look higher relative to most other states that don't follow this practice.

Oklahoma–At this time adjustments to revenues (net cash flow or other possible adjustments) cannot be calculated, nor can any adjustments to expenditures be projected, such as a possible deposit into the Rainy Day Fund. Ending balance cannot be reasonably calculated at this time.

Oregon–Revenue adjustments include: a revenue adjustment for a statutory transfer to local governments for local property tax relief. It is important to note that General Fund revenues for the 2019-21 biennium were reduced by approximately $423 million as a result of HB 3427. This bill reduced personal income tax rates while also establishing a Corporate Activities Tax. The revenue generated through the Corporate Activities Tax for the 2019-21 biennium is estimated at $1,598 million and will Other Funds revenue dedicated to the Fund for Student Success.

TABLE 7.3
Fiscal 2020 General Fund, Enacted (In millions of dollars) (continued)

Pennsylvania–Revenue adjustments include refunds, lapses and adjustments to beginning balances. Expenditure adjustments include transfers to the Budget Stabilization Reserve Fund (rainy day).

Rhode Island–Adjustments to revenues reflect a transfer of $126.1 million to the Budget Reserve (Rainy Day) Fund.

South Carolina–Revenue Adjustments: Litigation Recovery Account ($9.6M); Transfer of Non-Recurring Revenue to Recurring Revenue ($20.4M) Expenditure Adjustments: Prior Yr. 2% Capital Reserve ($151.6M) transferred to state agencies; Taxpayer Rebate Fund ($61.4M); FY19 Non-Recurring Supplemental Appropriations ($323.8M). Designated portion of ending balance: Capital Reserve Fund - $162.5M; Appropriations Carried Forward $432.0M (estimated)

South Dakota–The beginning balance of $19.3 million and adjustment to expenditures reflects the prior year's ending balance which is transferred to the rainy day fund.

Tennessee–Adjustments (Revenues): -$225.0 million transfer to Rainy Day Fund. -$6.1 million transfer to Highway Fund. -$0.4 million other adjustments. Adjustments (Expenditures): $396.5 million transfer to capital outlay projects fund. $38.1 million transfer to state office buildings and support facilities fund. $3.7 million transfer to debt service fund. $1.0 million transfer to reserves for dedicated revenue appropriations. Ending Balance: $17.5 million undesignated balance. $15 million of the ending balance is reserved for future tax relief.

Texas–$193.79 reflected in adjustments to revenue was realized from dedicated account balances now available. $3,178.8 is a transfer of revenue to the ESF and State Highway to be allocated equally. The annual expenditure change for Enacted Fiscal 2020 excluding property tax relief expenditures of $2,340.0 is 11.8%.

Utah–Revenue adjustments include transfers to the General Fund and Education fund, the amount set aside for economic development cash incentives, and other revenue adjustments.

Vermont–$2.6M in expenditure adjustments includes a $1.6M contribution to the General Fund Budget Stabilization reserve, and $1.0M in transfers to other funds.

Washington–Revenue adjustments reflect the net of transfers in and out of the General Fund, as well as prior biennium recoveries and similar resource adjustments. It is currently projected that a portion of the FY 2020 ending balance will be programmed to be spent in FY 2021.

West Virginia–Total Revenue is the official estimate for FY 2020 Total General Revenue collections. Total Expenditures are FY 2020 General Revenue appropriations of $4,693.6 million, FY 2020 surplus appropriations of $18.4 million, and estimated 13th month expenditures of $42.8 million. Adjustment (Expenditures) represents the $18.4 million transferred in August 2019 to the Rainy Day Fund from 1/2 of the FY 2019 surplus. The Ending Balance is mostly the historically carried forward reappropriation amounts that will remain and be reappropriated to the next fiscal year, the 13th month expenditures from the previous fiscal year & any unappropriated surplus balance.

Wisconsin–Revenue adjustments include Tribal Gaming, $23.8m; and Other Revenue, $540.5m. Expenditure adjustments include Transfers, $43.3m; Lapses, -$420.2m; and Compensation Reserves, $13.3m. There is no official estimate for the rainy day fund (Budget Stabilization Fund).

Wyoming–The State of Wyoming budgets on a biennial basis, to arrive at annual figures certain assumptions and estimates are required.

TABLE 7.4
Fiscal 2019 General Fund Revenue Collections Compared With Projections Used in Adopting Fiscal 2019 Budgets (In millions)

State	Sales Tax		Personal Income Tax		Corporate Income Tax		Gaming/Lottery Revenue		All Other Revenue	
	Original Estimate	Preliminary Actual	Original Estimate	Preliminary Actual	Original Estimate	Preliminary Actual	Original Estimate	Preliminary Actual	Original Estimate	Preliminary Actual
Total	$264,090	$267,360	$392,846	$401,771	$51,633	$59,516	$9,064	$9,320	$138,609	$143,950
Alabama	2,455	2,649	3,756	4,070	401	428	N/A	N/A	2,028	2,170
Alaska	N/A	N/A	N/A	N/A	145	120	11	12	2,103	2,552
Arizona	4,946	5,097	4,593	5,009	324	514	90	83	468	273
Arkansas (a)	2,488	2,465	3,429	3,520	482	570	68	72	476	517
California	26,674	26,100	95,011	98,304	12,259	13,774	5	5	(617)	(136)
Colorado	3,359	3,592	7,782	8,247	780	920	N/A	N/A	478	504
Connecticut	4,154	4,338	9,108	9,640	1,520	1,061	556	619	3,671	3,991
Delaware	N/A	N/A	1,486	1,528	93	148	210	216	2,579	2,701
Florida	25,070	25,385	N/A	N/A	2,376	3,140	404	270	4,407	4,619
Georgia	6,209	6,250	12,304	12,177	1,078	1,271	N/A	N/A	5,731	5,873
Hawaii	3,562	3,542	2,537	2,568	105	164	N/A	N/A	1,646	1,643
Idaho	1,545	1,598	1,759	1,661	199	283	N/A	N/A	166	193
Illinois	8,181	8,409	18,095	19,236	2,068	2,389	999	1,000	8,077	8,161
Indiana	7,886	7,915	5,997	6,057	975	948	392	431	932	1,055
Iowa	3,039	3,046	4,985	4,944	649	706	86	90	(1,119)	(927)
Kansas	2,752	2,767	3,575	3,756	445	437	N/A	N/A	459	408
Kentucky	3,908	3,938	4,531	4,545	573	556	249	264	1,937	2,091
Louisiana	3,919	3,828	3,413	3,445	300	400	402	409	1,409	1,472
Maine	1,528	1,563	1,619	1,701	204	253	57	63	259	269
Maryland (a)	4,751	4,812	9,874	10,272	926	1,033	527	552	1,686	1,729
Massachusetts	4,796	4,852	16,632	17,109	2,339	2,927	1,195	1,301	8,344	8,758
Michigan	1,912	2,039	7,040	7,119	273	514	N/A	N/A	1,187	1,181
Minnesota	5,745	5,739	12,436	12,415	1,343	1,603	67	64	3,439	3,572
Mississippi	2,375	2,464	1,853	1,898	531	644	140	143	757	818
Missouri	2,204	2,198	6,588	6,664	331	348	N/A	N/A	295	358
Montana	59	65	1,341	1,429	145	187	73	75	815	818
Nebraska	1,685	1,658	2,471	2,546	308	424	N/A	N/A	267	269
Nevada	1,262	1,285	N/A	N/A	N/A	N/A	797	758	2,018	2,244
New Hampshire	N/A	N/A	N/A	N/A	400	475	N/A	N/A	1,131	1,146
New Jersey	11,026	10,853	15,978	15,912	3,257	4,364	N/A	N/A	6,866	6,852
New Mexico	2,652	2,750	1,557	1,643	116	124	62	65	2,893	3,242
New York	14,114	14,165	50,410	48,088	5,626	5,501	15	15	2,495	2,775
North Carolina	7,625	7,751	12,705	13,166	710	830	N/A	N/A	2,891	3,079
North Dakota	883	957	358	414	48	148	11	15	507	382
Ohio (a)	10,338	10,573	8,748	8,910	1,582	1,630	N/A	N/A	13,041	12,655
Oklahoma	2,764	2,779	2,542	2,713	166	293	158	155	1,667	1,751
Oregon	N/A	N/A	8,901	9,790	521	927	N/A	N/A	729	491
Pennsylvania	10,753	11,100	14,174	14,096	2,926	3,397	154	132	5,968	6,133
Rhode Island	1,101	1,126	1,386	1,394	178	155	392	398	942	948
South Carolina	3,146	3,186	3,862	4,161	314	449	N/A	N/A	914	1,009
South Dakota	1,029	1,025	N/A	N/A	N/A	N/A	123	126	489	490
Tennessee	8,227	8,532	143	102	2,131	2,328	346	390	2,691	3,646
Texas	29,506	29,839	N/A	N/A	N/A	N/A	1,402	1,523	26,081	26,506
Utah	2,102	2,116	4,116	4,320	411	521	N/A	N/A	574	586
Vermont	N/A	N/A	847	875	90	134	N/A	N/A	365	684
Virginia	3,547	3,580	14,184	15,227	912	943	N/A	N/A	1,531	1,557
Washington	11,418	11,867	N/A	N/A	N/A	N/A	N/A	N/A	10,120	9,826
West Virginia	1,316	1,370	2,004	2,109	142	198	75	74	903	1,017
Wisconsin	5,635	5,696	8,715	8,994	932	1,338	N/A	N/A	1,349	1,314
Wyoming	444	499	N/A	N/A	N/A	N/A	N/A	N/A	566	690

Source: National Association of State Budget Officers, Fall 2019.
Note: Unless otherwise noted, original estimates reflect the figures used when the fiscal 2019 budget was adopted.
Key:
N/A–N/A indicates data are not available because, in most cases, these states do not have that type of tax, or it is not part of the general fund.
(a) Arkansas–Revenue amounts here are reported as "gross" (before refunds and special dedications/payments.
Maryland–Legislative action in 2018 diverted $200M from individual income tax revenues to the Commission on Innovation and

Excellence in Education Fund. This creates a $200M discrepancy between the revenues reported in Table 7.2 versus total actual revenues reported in this table for fiscal 2019.
Ohio–Corporate Income Tax: Ohio doesn't have a corporate income tax and instead has a commercial activities tax (CAT). All Other General Revenue Fund Revenue: Federal reimbursements for Medicaid expenditures make up the majority of revenue in this category. The reduction between original fiscal year 2019 revenue estimates and actuals are the result of federal expenditures coming in below estimate.

TABLE 7.5

Comparison of General Fund Revenue Collections in Fiscal 2018, Fiscal 2019, and Enacted Fiscal 2020
(in millions of dollars)

State	Sales Tax			Personal Income Tax			Corporate Income Tax		
	Fiscal 2018	Fiscal 2019	Fiscal 2020	Fiscal 2018	Fiscal 2019	Fiscal 2020	Fiscal 2018	Fiscal 2019	Fiscal 2020
Total (a)	$255,512	$265,321	$277,241	$380,679	$394,653	$405,438	$49,252	$59,002	$55,355
Alabama	2,471	2,649	2,696	3,822	4,070	4,017	386	428	420
Alaska	N/A	N/A	N/A	N/A	N/A	N/A	120	120	135
Arizona	4,788	5,097	5,347	4,544	5,009	4,961	373	514	435
Arkansas (a)	2,418	2,465	2,572	3,360	3,520	3,579	407	570	405
California	24,974	26,100	27,241	93,776	98,304	102,413	12,313	13,774	13,133
Colorado (a)	3,404	3,592	3,530	7,577	8,247	8,303	782	920	766
Connecticut	4,202	4,338	4,444	10,770	9,640	9,673	921	1,061	1,100
Delaware	N/A	N/A	N/A	1,428	1,528	1,803	90	148	111
Florida	24,139	25,385	26,137	N/A	N/A	N/A	2,413	3,140	2,730
Georgia	5,946	6,250	6,525	11,644	12,177	12,754	1,004	1,271	1,260
Hawaii	3,396	3,542	3,643	2,430	2,568	2,659	131	164	128
Idaho	1,490	1,598	1,666	1,828	1,661	1,910	239	283	269
Illinois	7,810	8,409	8,543	17,725	19,236	19,703	2,017	2,389	2,444
Indiana	7,663	7,915	8,076	5,816	6,057	6,174	660	948	851
Iowa	2,942	3,046	3,316	4,747	4,944	4,831	565	706	653
Kansas	2,748	2,767	2,785	3,374	3,756	3,750	392	437	450
Kentucky	3,606	3,938	4,056	4,604	4,545	4,661	511	556	557
Louisiana	4,317	3,828	3,861	3,269	3,445	3,513	478	400	400
Maine	1,483	1,563	1,630	1,595	1,701	1,770	186	253	205
Maryland (a)	4,646	4,812	5,026	9,508	10,272	10,377	820	1,033	962
Massachusetts (a)	4,598	4,852	5,177	16,240	17,109	17,386	2,392	2,927	2,525
Michigan (a)	2,063	2,039	N/A	7,130	7,119	N/A	372	514	N/A
Minnesota	5,453	5,739	5,890	11,784	12,415	12,796	1,315	1,603	1,293
Mississippi	2,340	2,464	2,481	1,827	1,898	1,900	572	644	555
Missouri	2,174	2,198	2,313	6,600	6,664	6,840	300	348	315
Montana	60	65	58	1,298	1,429	1,411	167	187	166
Nebraska	1,603	1,658	1,750	2,361	2,546	2,625	314	424	325
Nevada	1,189	1,285	1,364	N/A	N/A	N/A	N/A	N/A	N/A
New Hampshire	N/A	N/A	N/A	N/A	N/A	N/A	481	475	434
New Jersey	10,459	10,853	11,152	15,038	15,912	16,493	2,484	4,364	3,607
New Mexico	2,437	2,750	3,008	1,519	1,643	1,585	107	124	86
New York	13,553	14,165	15,136	51,501	48,088	52,150	4,916	5,501	6,104
North Carolina	7,337	7,751	8,156	12,518	13,166	12,892	739	830	687
North Dakota	829	957	928	364	414	397	92	148	65
Ohio (a)	10,148	10,573	11,014	8,411	8,910	8,726	1,523	1,630	1,639
Oklahoma	2,665	2,779	2,919	2,424	2,713	3,110	234	293	237
Oregon	N/A	N/A	N/A	8,872	9,790	8,512	739	927	479
Pennsylvania	10,381	11,100	11,454	13,399	14,096	14,570	2,879	3,397	3,558
Rhode Island	1,057	1,126	1,180	1,345	1,394	1,427	128	155	164
South Carolina	3,034	3,186	3,294	3,856	4,161	4,096	334	449	353
South Dakota	989	1,025	1,075	N/A	N/A	N/A	N/A	N/A	N/A
Tennessee (a)	8,294	8,532	8,914	165	102	69	2,317	2,328	2,394
Texas (a)	30,889	29,839	32,779	N/A	N/A	N/A	N/A	N/A	N/A
Utah	2,019	2,116	2,247	3,999	4,320	4,410	448	521	527
Vermont (a)	259	N/A	N/A	832	875	853	98	134	98
Virginia	3,462	3,580	3,730	14,106	15,227	15,263	862	943	1,031
Washington	10,925	11,867	12,352	N/A	N/A	N/A	N/A	N/A	N/A
West Virginia	1,247	1,370	1,390	1,926	2,109	2,155	110	198	137
Wisconsin	5,448	5,696	5,877	8,479	8,994	8,923	894	1,338	1,166
Wyoming	480	499	508	N/A	N/A	N/A	N/A	N/A	N/A

See footnotes at end of table

TABLE 7.5

Comparison of General Fund Revenue Collections in Fiscal 2018, Fiscal 2019, and Enacted Fiscal 2020
(In millions of dollars) (continued)

State	Gaming/Lottery Revenue			All Other Revenue		
	Fiscal 2018	Fiscal 2019	Fiscal 2020	Fiscal 2018	Fiscal 2019	Fiscal 2020
Total (a)	$8,933	$9,320	$9,093	$138,300	$142,770	$145,180
Alabama	N/A	N/A	N/A	2,070	2,170	2,125
Alaska	11	12	13	2,283	2,552	2,156
Arizona	68	83	96	334	273	317
Arkansas (a)	67	72	33	476	517	467
California	32	5	5	21	(136)	1,012
Colorado (a)	N/A	N/A	N/A	578	504	507
Connecticut	612	619	594	1,693	3,991	3,649
Delaware	212	216	210	2,663	2,701	2,493
Florida	357	270	22	4,309	4,619	4,054
Georgia	N/A	N/A	N/A	5,726	5,873	5,605
Hawaii	N/A	N/A	N/A	1,703	1,643	1,715
Idaho	N/A	N/A	N/A	175	193	180
Illinois	991	1,000	1,003	8,400	8,161	8,495
Indiana	432	431	418	1,000	1,055	1,033
Iowa	85	90	92	(954)	(927)	(1,052)
Kansas	N/A	N/A	N/A	784	408	447
Kentucky	253	264	256	1,865	2,091	1,932
Louisiana	414	409	416	1,410	1,472	1,535
Maine	62	63	57	261	269	155
Maryland (a)	535	552	548	1,864	1,729	1,652
Massachusetts (a)	1,155	1,301	1,355	8,057	8,758	8,766
Michigan (a)	N/A	N/A	N/A	1,452	1,181	N/A
Minnesota	66	64	65	3,679	3,572	3,567
Mississippi	136	143	142	816	818	781
Missouri	N/A	N/A	N/A	395	358	353
Montana	71	75	72	810	818	806
Nebraska	N/A	N/A	N/A	290	269	229
Nevada	711	758	811	2,118	2,244	2,271
New Hampshire	N/A	N/A	N/A	1,115	1,146	1,132
New Jersey	N/A	N/A	N/A	7,539	6,852	6,947
New Mexico	62	65	67	2,756	3,242	3,035
New York	15	15	15	1,435	2,775	3,712
North Carolina	N/A	N/A	N/A	2,971	3,079	3,096
North Dakota	11	15	10	676	382	662
Ohio (a)	N/A	N/A	N/A	12,389	12,655	12,781
Oklahoma	162	155	176	1,121	1,751	1,402
Oregon	N/A	N/A	N/A	633	491	1,029
Pennsylvania	123	132	181	7,785	6,133	5,734
Rhode Island	366	398	414	1,012	948	994
South Carolina	N/A	N/A	N/A	898	1,009	974
South Dakota	119	126	129	485	490	498
Tennessee (a)	343	390	388	3,736	3,646	3,771
Texas (a)	1,385	1,523	1,431	24,881	26,506	26,568
Utah	N/A	N/A	N/A	572	586	617
Vermont (a)	N/A	N/A	N/A	451	684	697
Virginia	N/A	N/A	N/A	1,451	1,557	1,534
Washington	N/A	N/A	N/A	10,438	9,826	11,748
West Virginia	75	74	75	894	1,017	953
Wisconsin	N/A	N/A	N/A	1,323	1,314	1,338
Wyoming	N/A	N/A	N/A	913	690	710

See footnotes at end of table

TABLE 7.5

Comparison of General Fund Revenue Collections in Fiscal 2018, Fiscal 2019, and Enacted Fiscal 2020 (in millions of dollars) (continued)

Source: National Association of State Budget Officers, Fall 2019.

Note: Unless otherwise noted, fiscal 2018 figures reflect actual collections, fiscal 2019 figures reflect preliminary actual collections, and fiscal 2020 figures reflect the estimates based on states' enacted budgets.

Key:

N/A.–Indicates data are not available because, in most cases, these states do not have that type of tax, or it is not part of the general fund.

(a)

Total–include state collections by revenue type where amounts were provided/applicable for all three years; Michigan's fiscal 2018 and fiscal 2019 figures are excluded from the totals for all revenue types, as the state was not able to provide amounts for fiscal 2020.

Arkansas–Revenue amounts here are reported as "gross" (before refunds and special dedications/payments).

Maryland–Legislative action in 2018 diverted $200M from individual income tax revenues to the Commission on Innovation and Excellence in Education Fund. This creates a $200M discrepancy between the revenues reported in Table 7.2 versus total revenues reported in this table for fiscal 2019.

Massachusetts–Figures for FY18-FY20 are re-stated to better align with the State Expenditure Report and be more comparable to most other states, which book federally reimbursed expenditures in a separate federal fund.

Michigan–Michigan's fiscal 2018 and fiscal 2019 figures are excluded from the totals for all revenue types, as the state was not able to provide amounts for fiscal 2020.

Ohio–Corporate Income Tax: Ohio doesn't have a corporate income tax and instead has a commercial activities tax (CAT). All Other General Revenue Fund Revenue: Federal reimbursements for Medicaid expenditures make up the majority of revenue in this category. The reduction between original fiscal year 2019 revenue estimates and actuals are the result of federal expenditures com-

ing in below estimate.

Tennessee–Sales tax, personal income tax, and corporate income tax are shared with local governments. Corporate income tax includes franchise tax.

Texas–Included increased forecast for General Fund spending do to passage of House Bill 1525 and Comptroller's issuance of new guidance. As a result of the Legislature's restructuring of the Education Fund's revenue sources in the As Passed FY 2019 budget, there was a decrease of -$301.2M in the annual transfer of General Funds to the Education Fund. In lieu of the annual transfer of General Funds to the Education Fund, 100% of Sales and Use and 25% of Meals and Rooms taxes will be deposited directly into the Education Fund, which were revenues previously attributed to the General Fund. As part of the fiscal year 2019 Budget Adjustment bill, $272.4M of the State Health Care Resources Fund ongoing revenue sources will be recognized as General Fund Revenue, and this shift in recognition of revenue sources accounts for the upward change in fiscal year 2019 General Fund revenue as compared to what was reported in the Fall 2018 survey.

Vermont–As a result of the Legislature's restructuring of the Education Fund's revenue sources in the As Passed FY 2019 budget, there was a decrease of -$301.2M in the annual transfer of General Funds to the Education Fund. In lieu of the annual transfer of General Funds to the Education Fund, 100% of Sales and Use and 25% of Meals and Rooms taxes will be deposited directly into the Education Fund, which were revenues previously attributed to the General Fund. As part of the fiscal year 2019 Budget Adjustment bill, $272.4M of the State Health Care Resources Fund ongoing revenue sources will be recognized as General Fund Revenue, and this shift in recognition of revenue sources accounts for the upward change in fiscal year 2019 General Fund revenue as compared to what was reported in the Fall 2018 survey.

TABLE 7.6
Total State Expenditures: Capital Inclusive (In millions of dollars)

State	General fund	Federal funds	Other state funds	Bonds	Total
			Actual fiscal 2017		
Total	$791,583	$600,152	$509,397	$36,306	$1,937,438
Alabama (a)	8,296	9,865	8,039	460	26,660
Alaska	4,486	3,763	1,483	0	9,732
Arizona	9,608	15,016	10,440	485	35,549
Arkansas (a)	5,261	7,857	11,988	58	25,164
California (a)	119,291	95,337	44,249	2,340	261,217
Colorado	10,512	9,367	16,931	0	36,810
Connecticut	17,763	6,253	5,405	2,954	32,375
Delaware	4,106	2,171	4,000	398	10,675
Florida	30,267	26,317	18,129	1,667	76,380
Georgia	22,455	14,266	11,836	952	49,509
Hawaii	7,486	2,571	3,927	682	14,666
Idaho	3,255	2,682	1,559	0	7,496
Illinois	29,424	14,833	22,387	1,359	68,003
Indiana	15,971	12,421	3,536	0	31,928
Iowa	7,258	6,389	9,034	6	22,687
Kansas	6,371	3,749	5,048	393	15,561
Kentucky	11,075	12,258	10,230	0	33,563
Louisiana	9,118	11,159	7,841	304	28,422
Maine	3,346	2,601	2,186	114	8,247
Maryland (a)	17,153	12,018	13,015	1,136	43,322
Massachusetts (a)	26,436	13,903	12,285	2,704	55,328
Michigan	9,882	20,290	24,137	72	54,381
Minnesota	21,103	10,406	5,318	641	37,468
Mississippi	5,645	7,819	5,786	1,124	20,374
Missouri	9,153	8,186	8,047	164	25,550
Montana	2,333	2,810	1,814	0	6,957
Nebraska	4,329	3,030	4,508	0	11,867
Nevada	3,990	4,393	5,308	223	13,914
New Hampshire	1,512	2,221	2,097	104	5,934
New Jersey	33,827	15,172	8,116	2,166	59,281
New Mexico	6,065	8,128	4,842	662	19,697
New York	68,080	52,985	31,519	4,431	157,015
North Carolina	22,143	14,778	10,707	538	48,166
North Dakota	2,600	1,616	2,574	2	6,792
Ohio (a)	34,502	12,596	18,584	2,591	68,273
Oklahoma	5,044	7,186	10,703	329	23,262
Oregon	8,955	10,189	20,759	138	40,041
Pennsylvania	33,036	29,001	18,868	2,223	83,128
Rhode Island	3,672	2,977	2,109	128	8,886
South Carolina	7,804	8,184	8,565	617	25,170
South Dakota	1,548	1,420	1,239	20	4,227
Tennessee (a)	14,162	12,261	6,417	0	32,840
Texas (a)	54,292	35,174	16,537	1,717	107,720
Utah (a)	6,411	3,809	4,002	0	14,222
Vermont	1,498	1,914	2,096	49	5,557
Virginia	20,227	10,308	18,805	962	50,302
Washington	19,357	12,270	11,741	1,316	44,684
West Virginia	4,231	4,314	8,397	77	17,019
Wisconsin	15,858	10,993	20,141	0	46,992
Wyoming (a)	1,386	926	2,113	0	4,425
Dist. Of Columbia	7,179	3,442	1,063	874	12,558

See footnotes at end of table

TABLE 7.6

Total State Expenditures: Capital Inclusive (In millions of dollars) (continued)

State	General fund	Federal funds	Actual fiscal 2018 Other state funds	Bonds	Total
Total	$820,047	$621,269	$528,622	$34,281	$2,004,219
Alabama (a)	8,259	9,958	8,456	589	27,262
Alaska	4,504	3,614	2,184	0	10,302
Arizona	9,815	15,999	11,307	373	37,494
Arkansas (a)	5,374	7,920	12,299	44	25,637
California (a)	124,756	92,352	49,655	2,905	269,668
Colorado	11,308	9,928	18,578	0	39,814
Connecticut	18,611	6,141	5,487	2,913	33,152
Delaware	4,118	2,492	3,990	247	10,847
Florida	31,658	27,401	17,902	1,562	78,523
Georgia	23,517	14,446	12,265	1,166	51,394
Hawaii	7,804	2,628	3,636	1,131	15,199
Idaho	3,465	2,684	1,814	0	7,963
Illinois	35,409	16,940	19,900	534	72,783
Indiana	15,846	13,578	4,197	0	33,621
Iowa	7,254	6,260	9,860	8	23,382
Kansas	6,649	3,773	5,113	399	15,934
Kentucky	11,221	12,441	10,390	0	34,052
Louisiana	9,548	12,085	9,328	292	31,253
Maine	3,415	2,698	2,192	106	8,411
Maryland (a)	17,169	12,147	13,025	1,455	43,796
Massachusetts (a)	27,196	14,432	12,803	2,694	57,125
Michigan	10,148	20,733	25,586	147	56,614
Minnesota	22,347	11,353	5,711	408	39,819
Mississippi	5,575	7,787	5,624	667	19,653
Missouri	9,263	8,360	8,226	189	26,038
Montana	2,242	2,863	1,847	0	6,952
Nebraska	4,350	3,101	4,690	0	12,141
Nevada	4,018	4,624	5,339	282	14,263
New Hampshire	1,504	2,297	2,257	73	6,131
New Jersey	35,124	15,628	7,883	2,140	60,775
New Mexico	6,102	8,496	5,355	507	20,460
New York	69,724	56,808	32,502	4,710	163,744
North Carolina	22,746	15,296	11,542	248	49,832
North Dakota	2,103	1,472	2,289	25	5,889
Ohio (a)	31,727	15,113	19,975	2,868	69,683
Oklahoma	5,854	7,522	8,915	378	22,669
Oregon	10,180	10,476	19,801	162	40,619
Pennsylvania	34,915	29,145	20,222	627	84,909
Rhode Island	3,799	2,996	2,237	230	9,262
South Carolina	8,056	8,593	8,433	175	25,257
South Dakota	1,591	1,407	1,439	20	4,457
Tennessee (a)	14,907	12,618	6,662	3	34,190
Texas (a)	55,643	39,376	18,537	1,652	115,208
Utah (a)	6,739	3,924	3,794	332	14,789
Vermont	1,587	1,926	2,098	64	5,675
Virginia	20,884	10,163	20,070	959	52,076
Washington	20,535	12,293	12,219	974	46,021
West Virginia	3,638	4,481	8,715	23	16,857
Wisconsin	16,464	11,575	20,160	0	48,199
Wyoming (a)	1,386	926	2,113	0	4,425
Dist. Of Columbia	7,715	3,351	1,163	1,083	13,312

See footnotes at end of table

TABLE 7.6
Total State Expenditures: Capital Inclusive (In millions of dollars) (continued)

| State | Estimated fiscal 2019 | | | | |
	General fund	Federal funds	Other state funds	Bonds	Total
Total	**$864,177**	**$650,435**	**$563,741**	**$40,756**	**$2,119,109**
Alabama (a)	8,481	10,165	7,774	277	26,697
Alaska	5,943	3,973	1,788	0	11,704
Arizona	10,389	15,544	11,740	333	38,006
Arkansas (a)	5,504	7,829	12,384	54	25,771
California (a)	142,693	100,007	61,226	7,399	311,325
Colorado	12,533	9,781	19,324	0	41,638
Connecticut	19,244	6,318	5,672	2,827	34,061
Delaware	4,394	2,403	4,231	297	11,325
Florida	32,849	29,809	25,004	1,652	89,314
Georgia	25,401	14,426	12,526	1,184	53,537
Hawaii	7,915	2,528	4,155	1,021	15,619
Idaho	3,702	3,260	2,329	0	9,291
Illinois	35,678	17,055	18,909	576	72,218
Indiana	16,208	13,777	4,294	0	34,279
Iowa	7,644	6,513	9,399	7	23,563
Kansas	7,123	4,166	5,487	429	17,205
Kentucky	11,556	12,667	10,614	0	34,837
Louisiana	9,898	14,263	10,553	167	34,881
Maine	3,658	2,797	2,209	148	8,812
Maryland (a)	17,911	13,166	13,812	1,346	46,235
Massachusetts (a)	29,136	14,494	13,508	2,694	59,832
Michigan	10,571	22,849	23,553	198	57,171
Minnesota	23,144	12,050	6,363	610	42,167
Mississippi	5,548	9,372	6,206	898	22,024
Missouri	9,536	8,490	8,287	89	26,402
Montana	2,304	2,983	1,886	0	7,173
Nebraska	4,367	2,791	4,951	0	12,109
Nevada	4,404	4,888	5,285	181	14,758
New Hampshire	1,505	2,313	2,318	98	6,234
New Jersey	37,349	16,695	8,717	2,050	64,811
New Mexico	6,364	8,474	5,409	287	20,534
New York	72,783	60,416	31,138	6,538	170,875
North Carolina	23,666	14,438	13,009	400	51,513
North Dakota	2,159	1,639	2,746	47	6,591
Ohio (a)	32,678	15,417	20,106	2,803	71,004
Oklahoma	6,180	8,153	9,203	297	23,833
Oregon	9,613	10,835	21,869	324	42,641
Pennsylvania	35,522	30,640	22,755	596	89,513
Rhode Island	3,934	3,334	2,478	357	10,103
South Carolina	8,294	8,058	9,159	147	25,658
South Dakota	1,638	1,449	1,372	32	4,491
Tennessee (a)	15,693	14,164	6,963	89	36,909
Texas (a)	52,054	38,331	19,912	1,459	111,756
Utah (a)	7,493	4,664	4,521	150	16,828
Vermont	1,650	1,887	2,212	87	5,836
Virginia	21,774	11,447	20,734	1,309	55,264
Washington	23,643	12,111	12,502	1,274	49,530
West Virginia	3,792	4,975	9,488	25	18,280
Wisconsin	17,152	11,787	21,304	0	50,243
Wyoming (a)	1,507	844	2,357	0	4,708
Dist. Of Columbia	N/A	N/A	N/A	N/A	N/A

See footnotes at end of table

TABLE 7.6
Total State Expenditures: Capital Inclusive (In millions of dollars) (continued)

Source: National Association of State Budget Officers, 2019 State Expenditure Report.

Notes: Small dollar amounts, when rounded, cause an aberration in the percentage increase. In these instances, the actual dollar amounts should be consulted to determine the exact percentage increase. "State funds" refers to general funds plus other state fund spending. State spending from bonds is excluded. "Total funds" refers to funding from all sources -- general fund, federal funds, other state funds and bonds. For all states, Medicaid reflects provider taxes, fees, assessments, donations, and local funds in Other State Funds.

Key:

N/A – Not available

(a)

Alabama: Amounts shown in fiscal years 2017 and 2018 are based on actual expenditures during these years, regardless of the year appropriated. Fiscal 2019 amounts shown are equal to actual expenditures through 9 months (June 30, 2019) and then annualized for the year.

Arkansas: Fiscal 2018 Amounts were modified to reflect actual final funding and were previously based on estimates.

California: The fiscal 2019 spending increase for the General Fund is primarily due to supplemental pension payments, local assistance for healthcare programs, fire protection resources for CalFIRE, planning and progress grants to address homelessness, and transfers to the State Project Infrastructure Fund to support capital outlay projects. The fiscal 2019 spending increase for Other State Funds is generally due to various department program expenditure changes including carryovers and reappropriations.

Maryland: FY 2017 Federal Fund Revenues were restated due to clerical error.

Massachusetts: Fiscal 2019 estimated general fund expenditures are as of July 31, 2019.

Ohio: Federal reimbursements for Medicaid expenditures funded from the General Revenue Fund (GRF) are deposited into the GRF. Federal reimbursements for Medicaid expenditures from non-GRF sources are deposited into the appropriate federal fund. Expenditures of federal funds are contained in the General Fund number to be consistent with Ohio accounting practices and with other portrayals of Ohio's general fund. This amounts to $9,757.9 million in fiscal 2019. This will tend to make Ohio's GRF expenditures look higher and conversely make Ohio's federal expenditures look lower relative to most other states that don't follow this practice. Also, inherent in Ohio's budgetary accounting environment are significant overstatements of total state spending due to two phenomena. First, fiduciary fund expenditures represent the distribution of funds collected by the state on behalf of other entities. These are not operating, program, or subsidy expenditures of the state. Examples of this would be the collection and distribution of county and local permissive sales taxes or motor vehicle registration taxes. Fiduciary fund group expenditures totaled $7,848.6 million in fiscal 2019. Second, "double counting" of revenue and expenditures related to intrastate transactions overstates overall state expenditure activity. Intrastate transactions totaled $755.4 million in fiscal 2019. These accounting practices will tend to make Ohio's "All-Other" expenditures look higher, on a dollar and percentage basis, and conversely make Ohio's other categories look lower, on a percentage basis, relative to other states that don't follow similar practices.

Tennessee: Collects personal income tax on income from dividends on stocks and interest on certain bonds. Tax revenue estimates do not include federal funds and other departmental revenues. However, federal funds and other departmental revenues are included in the budget as funding sources for the general fund, along with state tax revenues.

Texas: The decrease in spending for fiscal 2019 is due to its biennial budget process, with the first year of the biennium being front loaded and the subsequent fiscal year not carrying those funding levels forward. The levels vary across individual programs for a large swath of state agencies. The funding from the prior year is often able to be carried forward within the biennium should the agency not expend the funds during the previous fiscal year.

Utah: When funds are transferred from General Funds to restricted accounts, Utah was previously reporting the final expenditures under Other State Funds. For this survey and future surveys, Utah is now reporting the expenditures under the original funding source, General Funds.

Wyoming: Part of Wyoming's yearly variation in expenditure totals is due to the fact that the state budgets on a two-year cycle.

Table 7.6 | Total State Expenditures (In millions of dollars)

2017 Actual | 2018 Actual | 2019 Estimated *(in millions of dollars)*

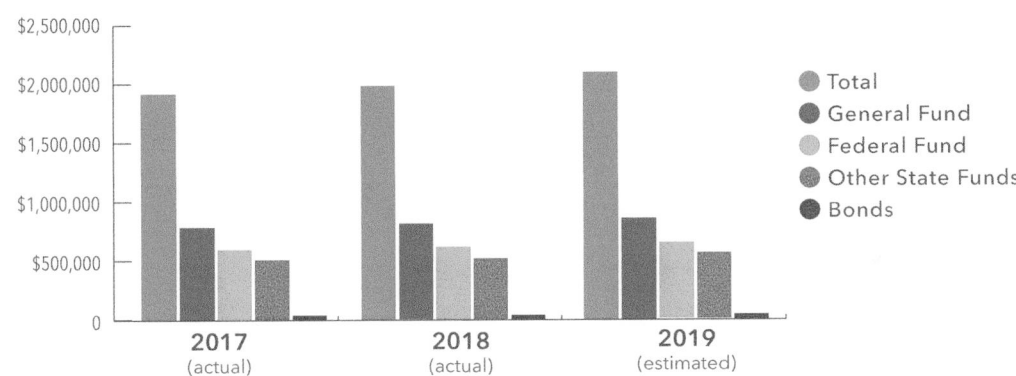

- ● Total
- ● General Fund
- ● Federal Fund
- ● Other State Funds
- ● Bonds

Highest and Lowest Spending by Category FY 2018 *(in millions of dollars)*

GENERAL FUND

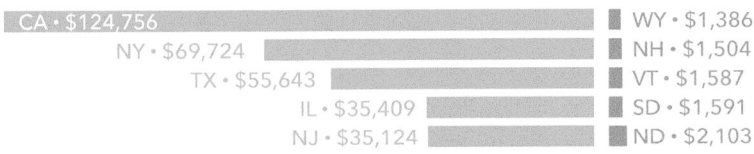

CA • $124,756	WY • $1,386
NY • $69,724	NH • $1,504
TX • $55,643	VT • $1,587
IL • $35,409	SD • $1,591
NJ • $35,124	ND • $2,103

FEDERAL FUND

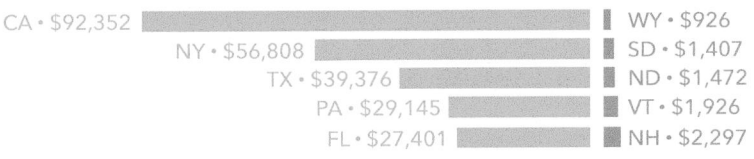

CA • $92,352	WY • $926
NY • $56,808	SD • $1,407
TX • $39,376	ND • $1,472
PA • $29,145	VT • $1,926
FL • $27,401	NH • $2,297

OTHER STATE FUNDS

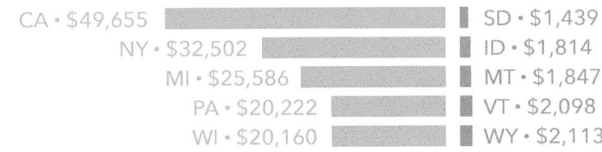

CA • $49,655	SD • $1,439
NY • $32,502	ID • $1,814
MI • $25,586	MT • $1,847
PA • $20,222	VT • $2,098
WI • $20,160	WY • $2,113

BONDS

NY • $4,710	ID • $0
CT • $2,913	MT • $0
CA • $2,905	WY • $0
OH • $2,868	AK • $0
MA • $2,694	IN • $0

CALIFORNIA HAD THE HIGHEST TOTAL SPENDING FY 2018

$269,668

WYOMING HAD THE LOWEST TOTAL SPENDING FY 2018

$4,425

TABLE 7.7
Elementary and Secondary Education Expenditures (In millions of dollars)

State	General fund	Federal funds	Actual fiscal 2017 Other state funds	Bonds	Total
Total	$282,750	$52,878	$43,086	$2,157	$380,871
Alabama (a)	4,373	1,010	203	60	5,646
Alaska	1,379	226	63	0	1,668
Arizona	4,321	1,173	245	0	5,739
Arkansas	2,241	548	767	0	3,556
California	46,231	6,694	57	150	53,132
Colorado (a)	3,768	602	4,703	0	9,073
Connecticut	3,248	528	5	278	4,059
Delaware	1,415	195	795	133	2,538
Florida	10,939	1,722	1,319	0	13,980
Georgia	9,083	2,319	388	252	12,042
Hawaii	1,709	256	55	0	2,020
Idaho	1,612	282	82	0	1,976
Illinois	7,477	2,255	61	60	9,853
Indiana	8,039	1,042	157	0	9,238
Iowa	3,223	460	91	0	3,774
Kansas	3,112	479	1,027	0	4,618
Kentucky	4,974	879	38	0	5,891
Louisiana	3,575	1,163	491	0	5,229
Maine	1,193	213	29	0	1,435
Maryland (a)	5,998	1,052	498	337	7,885
Massachusetts	5,535	1,231	825	23	7,614
Michigan	220	1,698	12,093	0	14,011
Minnesota	8,901	775	45	2	9,723
Mississippi	2,227	691	327	5	3,250
Missouri	3,297	1,013	1,505	1	5,816
Montana	819	175	47	0	1,041
Nebraska	1,268	324	54	0	1,646
Nevada	1,471	267	360	0	2,098
New Hampshire	87	190	967	12	1,256
New Jersey	13,312	920	17	0	14,249
New Mexico	2,671	414	6	244	3,335
New York	23,204	3,763	3,460	50	30,477
North Carolina	8,623	1,507	758	0	10,888
North Dakota	888	145	154	0	1,187
Ohio (a)	8,253	1,970	1,183	237	11,643
Oklahoma	1,725	674	1,041	0	3,440
Oregon	3,737	610	444	0	4,791
Pennsylvania	11,432	2,482	622	0	14,536
Rhode Island	1,113	194	32	3	1,342
South Carolina	2,978	976	907	0	4,861
South Dakota	522	168	6	0	696
Tennessee	4,715	1,124	159	0	5,998
Texas (a)	20,627	4,915	3,321	0	28,863
Utah	3,168	446	110	0	3,724
Vermont	417	129	1,269	1	1,816
Virginia	5,745	1,040	809	0	7,594
Washington	9,234	783	228	286	10,531
West Virginia	1,907	347	91	23	2,368
Wisconsin	6,744	809	276	0	7,829
Wyoming	0	0	896	0	896
Dist. of Columbia	1,909	248	19	410	2,586

See footnotes at end of table

TABLE 7.7

Elementary and Secondary Education Expenditures (In millions of dollars) (continued)

State	Actual fiscal 2018				
	General fund	Federal funds	Other state funds	Bonds	Total
Total	$294,145	$53,000	$44,922	$2,965	$395,032
Alabama (a)	4,418	1,051	244	27	5,740
Alaska	1,401	230	38	0	1,669
Arizona	4,544	1,181	266	0	5,991
Arkansas	2,259	543	833	0	3,635
California	48,762	6,721	50	603	56,136
Colorado (a)	4,080	595	4,804	0	9,479
Connecticut	3,084	537	5	518	4,144
Delaware	1,435	196	785	129	2,545
Florida	11,445	1,853	1,291	0	14,589
Georgia	9,605	2,310	383	252	12,550
Hawaii	1,777	226	93	0	2,096
Idaho	1,713	283	96	0	2,092
Illinois	8,219	2,212	61	2	10,494
Indiana	8,221	1,056	186	0	9,463
Iowa	3,254	474	91	0	3,819
Kansas	3,405	475	1,082	0	4,962
Kentucky	4,937	854	35	0	5,826
Louisiana	3,618	1,134	517	0	5,269
Maine	1,230	220	30	0	1,480
Maryland (a)	6,068	1,092	501	362	8,023
Massachusetts	5,714	1,246	858	33	7,851
Michigan	121	1,687	12,643	0	14,451
Minnesota	9,233	772	46	0	10,051
Mississippi	2,215	701	325	5	3,246
Missouri	3,351	990	1,518	3	5,862
Montana	780	183	49	0	1,012
Nebraska	1,249	380	59	0	1,688
Nevada	1,492	297	371	0	2,160
New Hampshire	84	183	962	12	1,241
New Jersey	13,306	907	18	0	14,231
New Mexico	2,684	414	29	239	3,366
New York	24,148	3,394	3,580	111	31,233
North Carolina	8,893	1,510	731	0	11,134
North Dakota	728	139	304	0	1,171
Ohio (a)	8,402	1,848	1,204	422	11,876
Oklahoma	1,739	661	1,092	0	3,492
Oregon	4,253	639	426	0	5,318
Pennsylvania	11,858	2,517	516	0	14,891
Rhode Island	1,161	184	34	0	1,379
South Carolina	3,071	957	936	0	4,964
South Dakota	557	167	7	0	731
Tennessee	4,961	1,160	155	3	6,279
Texas (a)	21,840	5,167	4,025	0	31,032
Utah	3,373	493	147	0	4,013
Vermont	461	128	1,277	0	1,866
Virginia	6,021	1,034	791	0	7,846
Washington	10,263	848	258	221	11,590
West Virginia	1,908	348	8	23	2,287
Wisconsin	6,804	803	266	0	7,873
Wyoming	0	0	896	0	896
Dist. of Columbia	2,092	280	28	368	2,768

See footnotes at end of table

TABLE 7.7
Elementary and Secondary Education Expenditures (In millions of dollars) (continued)

State	General fund	Federal funds	Estimated fiscal 2019 Other state funds	Bonds	Total
Total	$307,705	$56,234	$47,161	$2,679	$413,779
Alabama (a)	4,565	1,414	201	13	6,193
Alaska	1,422	259	42	0	1,723
Arizona	6,212	1,088	305	0	7,605
Arkansas	2,263	540	748	0	3,551
California	52,791	7,396	48	704	60,939
Colorado (a)	4,117	616	5,202	0	9,935
Connecticut	3,250	554	4	228	4,036
Delaware	1,515	202	809	199	2,725
Florida	11,892	1,892	1,432	0	15,216
Georgia	10,183	2,490	395	305	13,373
Hawaii	1,837	251	93	0	2,181
Idaho	1,815	289	101	0	2,205
Illinois	8,391	2,279	66	6	10,742
Indiana	8,354	1,056	188	0	9,598
Iowa	3,288	501	96	0	3,885
Kansas	3,514	503	1,079	0	5,096
Kentucky	5,032	920	36	0	5,988
Louisiana	3,637	1,226	650	0	5,513
Maine	1,322	210	27	0	1,559
Maryland (a)	6,180	1,235	586	421	8,422
Massachusetts	5,999	1,261	905	32	8,197
Michigan	133	1,857	13,028	0	15,018
Minnesota	9,599	832	50	2	10,483
Mississippi	2,219	837	377	0	3,433
Missouri	3,464	969	1,536	0	5,969
Montana	805	187	55	0	1,047
Nebraska	1,251	349	53	0	1,653
Nevada	1,453	280	382	0	2,115
New Hampshire	96	184	962	15	1,257
New Jersey	14,280	918	14	0	15,212
New Mexico	2,790	443	17	84	3,334
New York	25,118	4,068	3,474	133	32,793
North Carolina	9,399	1,527	812	0	11,738
North Dakota	729	136	306	0	1,171
Ohio (a)	8,585	1,887	1,209	174	11,855
Oklahoma	2,136	766	1,130	0	4,032
Oregon	4,125	667	665	0	5,457
Pennsylvania	12,323	2,671	421	0	15,415
Rhode Island	1,187	219	47	7	1,460
South Carolina	3,179	954	911	0	5,044
South Dakota	558	171	4	0	733
Tennessee	5,156	1,139	153	0	6,448
Texas (a)	19,744	5,333	4,552	0	29,629
Utah	3,570	520	171	0	4,261
Vermont	137	110	1,664	2	1,913
Virginia	6,318	1,074	748	0	8,140
Washington	12,615	770	248	331	13,964
West Virginia	1,980	371	8	23	2,382
Wisconsin	7,177	813	272	0	8,262
Wyoming	0	0	879	0	879
Dist. of Columbia	N/A	N/A	N/A	N/A	N/A

See footnotes at end of table

TABLE 7.7
Elementary and Secondary Education Expenditures (In millions of dollars) (continued)

Source: National Association of State Budget Officers, *2019 State Expenditure Report.*

Notes: Small dollar amounts, when rounded, cause an aberration in the percentage determine the exact percentage increase.

Key:

N/A–Not available

(a)

Alabama: Federal Funds received directly by local school systems are not reported at state budget level. Totals include capital expenditures.

Colorado: School personnel are paid at the school district level -- state costs for employer contributions to employee pensions and health benefits only reflect Colorado Dept. of Education personnel. Funds library-related programs across the state. Regarding capital expenditures, some funding for school facilities certificates of participation are included.

Maryland: The $112 million increase in Elementary and Secondary Education General Funds from FY 2018 to FY 2019 is largely driven by education local aid formulas. The $85 million increase

in Elementary and Secondary Education Other State Funds from FY 2018 to FY 2019 is mostly due to increased Education Trust Fund revenues, generated by casino proceeds.

Ohio: Employer contributions to current employees' pensions are not directly appropriated, or fully funded, by the state; however, some of the unrestricted support provided to localities for elementary and secondary education is used to help cover these costs. There are no direct appropriations for employer contributions to health benefits, though it can be assumed that some of the unrestricted support provided for elementary and secondary education is used for these costs.

Texas: Texas' decrease in spending for fiscal 2019 is due to its biennial budget process, with the first year of the biennium being front loaded and the subsequent fiscal year not carrying those funding levels forward. The levels vary across individual programs for a large swath of state agencies. The funding from the prior year is often able to be carried forward within the biennium should the agency not expend the funds during the previous fiscal year.

TABLE 7.8
Medicaid Expenditures (In millions of dollars)

State	Actual Fiscal 2017				Actual Fiscal 2018			
	General fund	Federal funds	Other state funds	Total	General fund	Federal funds	Other state funds	Total
Total	$157,216	$345,736	$57,030	$559,982	$164,151	$359,659	$61,475	$585,285
Alabama (a)	732	4,534	1,224	6,490	665	4,615	1,300	6,580
Alaska	633	1,386	4	2,023	643	1,411	4	2,058
Arizona	1,640	9,212	1,261	12,113	1,690	9,485	1,249	12,424
Arkansas	1,057	5,509	600	7,166	1,088	5,481	534	7,103
California	21,860	56,309	7,157	85,326	22,974	53,373	8,801	85,148
Colorado (a)	2,518	4,817	1,020	8,355	2,782	5,378	1,247	9,407
Connecticut (a)	3,783	3,617	0	7,400	4,519	3,561	0	8,080
Delaware	740	1,251	64	2,055	750	1,462	62	2,274
Florida	6,279	14,748	4,256	25,283	6,059	14,672	4,674	25,405
Georgia	2,673	7,009	573	10,255	2,717	7,450	662	10,829
Hawaii	765	1,422	33	2,220	626	1,448	66	2,140
Idaho	471	1,245	250	1,966	502	1,343	302	2,147
Illinois	2,282	9,934	3,728	15,944	5,256	13,044	4,327	22,627
Indiana	2,097	8,701	762	11,560	2,229	8,088	953	11,270
Iowa	1,320	2,641	815	4,776	1,300	3,137	936	5,373
Kansas	1,187	1,829	256	3,272	1,215	1,850	307	3,372
Kentucky	1,708	7,695	491	9,894	1,881	7,947	501	10,329
Louisiana	1,821	7,226	1,211	10,258	1,835	8,053	1,253	11,141
Maine (a)	751	1,638	266	2,655	763	1,749	312	2,824
Maryland	3,492	6,795	1,015	11,302	3,638	6,888	975	11,501
Massachusetts (a)	6,967	7,447	1,057	15,471	6,988	8,054	1,647	16,689
Michigan	2,718	12,126	2,116	16,960	2,710	12,147	2,393	17,250
Minnesota	4,350	6,381	306	11,037	4,977	7,226	471	12,674
Mississippi	678	3,820	657	5,155	705	3,823	553	5,081
Missouri	2,109	5,175	2,414	9,698	2,173	5,371	2,617	10,161
Montana	309	1,340	109	1,758	315	1,420	99	1,834
Nebraska	982	1,052	37	2,071	998	1,116	36	2,150
Nevada	593	2,719	242	3,554	669	2,883	218	3,770
New Hampshire	628	1,300	242	2,170	667	1,267	244	2,178
New Jersey	4,098	9,257	1,160	14,515	4,205	9,351	1,239	14,795
New Mexico	910	4,430	268	5,608	909	4,429	275	5,613
New York	12,453	33,672	7,799	53,924	13,708	36,787	7,836	58,331
North Carolina	3,515	9,022	1,634	14,171	3,654	9,265	1,029	13,948
North Dakota	417	689	6	1,112	460	754	6	1,220
Ohio (a)	17,437	5,943	2,284	25,664	14,483	8,621	3,357	26,461
Oklahoma	664	2,983	1,680	5,327	884	2,992	1,656	5,532
Oregon	710	7,065	1,463	9,238	1,315	6,503	989	8,807
Pennsylvania	8,501	16,686	3,177	28,364	9,297	17,949	3,388	30,634
Rhode Island	1,112	1,532	11	2,655	1,118	1,583	11	2,712
South Carolina	1,103	4,615	838	6,556	1,155	4,664	785	6,604
South Dakota	373	500	4	877	369	522	4	895
Tennessee (a)	3,533	6,701	840	11,074	3,576	6,979	698	11,253
Texas (a)	12,452	20,112	301	32,865	12,106	21,484	266	33,856
Utah	435	1,735	493	2,663	479	1,819	494	2,792
Vermont (a)	318	919	362	1,599	307	914	381	1,602
Virginia	4,768	4,610	3	9,381	5,027	4,831	3	9,861
Washington	3,709	7,804	500	12,013	3,918	7,836	555	12,309
West Virginia	525	3,114	438	4,077	533	2,968	326	3,827
Wisconsin	2,773	5,165	1,573	9,511	3,053	5,347	1,402	9,802
Wyoming	267	304	30	601	261	319	32	612
Dist. of Columbia	739	2,159	81	2,979	732	2,169	85	2,986

See footnotes at end of table

TABLE 7.8
Medicaid Expenditures (In millions of dollars) (continued)

| State | Estimated Fiscal 2019 | | | |
	General fund	Federal funds	Other state funds	Total
Total	$170,374	$378,623	$64,098	$613,095
Alabama (a)	756	5,024	1,280	7,060
Alaska	647	1,636	8	2,291
Arizona	1,717	10,451	1,266	13,434
Arkansas	1,250	5,619	552	7,421
California	23,243	56,670	11,506	91,419
Colorado (a)	2,940	5,574	1,437	9,951
Connecticut (a)	4,367	3,733	0	8,100
Delaware	711	1,423	47	2,181
Florida	6,833	16,460	5,016	28,309
Georgia	2,974	7,055	625	10,654
Hawaii	739	1,522	66	2,327
Idaho	580	1,495	210	2,285
Illinois	4,493	12,469	3,990	20,952
Indiana	2,536	8,717	1,229	12,482
Iowa	1,505	3,252	778	5,535
Kansas	1,348	2,114	298	3,760
Kentucky	1,825	7,849	507	10,181
Louisiana	1,843	8,690	1,032	11,565
Maine (a)	806	1,863	306	2,975
Maryland	3,791	7,052	995	11,838
Massachusetts (a)	7,839	8,005	1,324	17,168
Michigan	2,716	12,640	2,703	18,059
Minnesota	4,922	7,034	496	12,452
Mississippi	659	4,223	521	5,403
Missouri	2,153	5,499	2,616	10,268
Montana	309	1,395	101	1,805
Nebraska	1,034	1,149	35	2,218
Nevada	682	3,037	252	3,971
New Hampshire	655	1,256	281	2,192
New Jersey	4,398	9,692	1,255	15,345
New Mexico	923	4,433	264	5,620
New York	15,597	39,094	5,683	60,374
North Carolina	3,759	9,484	1,044	14,287
North Dakota	467	726	6	1,199
Ohio (a)	15,053	8,635	3,284	26,972
Oklahoma	974	3,320	1,498	5,792
Oregon	946	6,902	1,522	9,370
Pennsylvania	9,146	18,636	4,512	32,294
Rhode Island	1,136	1,627	9	2,772
South Carolina	1,182	4,751	837	6,770
South Dakota	364	549	4	917
Tennessee (a)	3,826	7,587	742	12,155
Texas (a)	12,413	23,804	276	36,493
Utah	517	2,300	597	3,414
Vermont (a)	595	968	110	1,673
Virginia	5,254	5,840	207	11,301
Washington	4,028	7,968	572	12,568
West Virginia	526	3,415	404	4,345
Wisconsin	3,139	5,653	1,759	10,551
Wyoming	258	333	36	627
Dist. of Columbia	N/A	N/A	N/A	N/A

See footnotes at end of table

TABLE 7.8
Medicaid Expenditures (In millions of dollars) (continued)

Source: National Association of State Budget Officers, *2019 State Expenditure Report.*

Notes: States were asked to report Medicaid expenditures as follows: General funds: all general funds appropriated to the Medicaid agency and any other agency which are used for direct Medicaid matching purposes under Title XIX. Other state funds: other funds and revenue sources used as Medicaid match, such as local funds and provider taxes, fees, donations, assessments (as defined by the Centers for Medicare and Medicaid Services). Federal Funds: all federal matching funds provided pursuant to Title XIX.

(1) The states were asked to separately detail the amount of provider taxes, fees, donations, assessments and local funds reported as Other State Funds.

(2) Small dollar amounts, when rounded, cause an aberration in the percentage increase. In these instances, the actual dollar amounts should be consulted to determine the exact percentage increase.

(3) "State funds" refers to general funds plus other state fund spending. State spending from bonds is excluded.

(4) "Total funds" refers to funding from all sources -- general fund, federal funds, other state funds and bonds.

(5) For all states, Medicaid reflects provider taxes, fees, assessments, donations, and local funds in Other State Funds.

Key:

N/A - Not available

(a)

Alabama: Other State Funds includes Medicaid provider taxes in the amounts of: $377M for FY17; $374M for FY18; and $397M for Estimated FY19.

Connecticut: The Medicaid appropriation in the Department of Social Services (DSS) is "net funded" while other Medicaid expenditures remain gross funded, with federal funds deposited directly to the State Treasury (Funding for the Hospital Supplemental Payments account in DSS was net funded in FY 17 but is gross funded beginning in FY 18). With the exception of enhanced FMAP available for certain populations and services, CT's FMAP is 50%. Includes Medicaid expenditures for administrative services organizations and fiscal intermediaries in DSS. Excludes state portion of Medicare Savings Program and School Based Child Health as those expenditures are netted out of federal Medicaid reimbursement. Also excludes provider taxes, which are deposited directly to the State Treasury.

Colorado: CHIP expenditures are excluded from the Medicaid category and added to the All Other category to adhere more closely to the survey directions. In previous surveys, CHIP expenditures were included in Medicaid.

Maine: In last year's State Expenditure Report, Medicaid, Other State Funds, 2017 Actual was reported as $274 and should have been $266; 2018 Actual was reported as $274 and should have been $312.

Massachusetts: Figures for fiscal 2017 and fiscal 2018 are re-stated to better differentiate federal spending on Medicaid.

New York: Medicaid spending includes all agencies with reported Medicaid spending consistent with State's Financial Plan. Medicaid spending reported in prior surveys excluded spending from agencies other than the Department of Health.

Ohio: Federal reimbursements for Medicaid expenditures funded from the General Revenue Fund (GRF) are deposited into the GRF. Federal reimbursements for Medicaid expenditures from non-GRF sources are deposited into the appropriate federal fund. Expenditures of federal funds are contained in the General Fund number to be consistent with Ohio accounting practices and with other portrayals of Ohio's general fund. This amounts to $9,757.9 million in fiscal 2019. This will tend to make Ohio's GRF expenditures look higher and conversely make Ohio's federal expenditures look lower relative to most other states that don't follow this practice.

Tennessee: Premium revenue: fiscal 2017 totals $323 million, fiscal 2018 totals $323 million, and fiscal 2019 totals $323 million. Certified Public Expenditures – Local fund from Hospitals: fiscal 2017 totals $200 million, fiscal 2018 totals $204 million, and fiscal 2019 totals $150 million. Nursing Home Tax: fiscal 2017 totals $121 million, fiscal 2018 totals $121 million, and fiscal 2019 totals $130 million. ICF/MR 6 percent Gross Receipts Tax: fiscal 2017 totals $11 million, fiscal 2018 totals $11 million, and fiscal 2019 totals $11 million. Intergovernmental Transfers: fiscal 2017 totals $100 million, fiscal 2018 totals $100 million, and fiscal 2019 totals $100 million.

Texas: Medicaid figures in this survey submission reflect only programs which the non-federal share is state General Revenue. Medicaid supplemental payments (i.e. uncompensated care, delivery system reform incentive program), funded primarily through local intergovernmental transfers, are excluded from this survey.

Vermont: The breakdown of local funds, etc. included in Other State Funds is as follows for fiscal 2017 (in millions): provider tax $159; employee assessment $19; local match provided by schools $23; tobacco litigation settlement funds $30; other $131. The breakdown is as follows for fiscal 2018: provider tax $164; employee assessment $20; local match provided by schools $27; tobacco litigation settlement funds $21; other $149. The breakdown is as follows for estimated fiscal 2019: provider tax N/A; employee assessment N/A; local match provided by schools $28; tobacco litigation settlement funds $20; other $61.

TABLE 7.9
Higher Education Expenditures–Capital Inclusive (In millions of dollars)

State	Actual fiscal 2017					Actual fiscal 2018					Estimated fiscal 2019				
	General fund	Federal funds	Other state funds	Bonds	Total	General fund	Federal funds	Other state funds	Bonds	Total	General fund	Federal funds	Other state funds	Bonds	Total
Total	$78,468	$20,290	$97,357	$5,231	$201,346	$79,733	$20,906	$101,387	$4,494	$206,520	$82,940	$21,580	$104,080	$5,060	$213,660
Alabama (a)	1,566	1,183	2,821	0	5,570	1,597	1,085	3,012	0	5,694	1,655	1,054	3,029	5	5,743
Alaska	330	126	318	0	774	322	119	332	0	773	332	146	380	0	858
Arizona	698	818	4,280	83	5,879	705	912	4,678	83	6,378	726	985	4,941	83	6,735
Arkansas	776	9	2,882	0	3,667	785	7	3,129	0	3,921	806	7	3,056	0	3,869
California	13,694	5,001	36	320	19,051	14,446	5,220	208	337	20,211	15,799	5,416	149	418	21,782
Colorado (a)	1,000	346	3,966	0	5,312	947	281	4,671	0	5,899	1,051	270	4,287	0	5,608
Connecticut	713	216	2,351	337	3,617	640	225	2,341	56	3,262	654	252	2,408	28	3,342
Delaware	241	47	115	16	419	238	51	113	5	407	249	50	112	9	420
Florida	4,022	98	3,324	45	7,489	4,557	95	3,215	104	7,971	4,591	109	3,390	96	8,186
Georgia	2,607	59	6,267	340	9,273	2,803	61	6,493	410	9,767	2,978	158	6,875	490	10,501
Hawaii	471	12	565	120	1,168	485	11	682	163	1,341	506	9	557	124	1,196
Idaho	427	5	280	0	712	445	5	287	0	737	469	16	471	0	956
Illinois	2,035	224	115	44	2,418	1,705	195	115	58	2,073	1,758	143	119	39	2,059
Indiana	1,936	0	10	0	1,946	1,806	250	14	0	2,070	1,970	0	16	0	1,986
Iowa	843	472	4,727	0	6,042	817	466	4,902	0	6,185	829	493	4,965	0	6,287
Kansas (a)	759	343	1,628	74	2,804	762	338	1,648	81	2,829	799	331	1,769	84	2,983
Kentucky	1,141	925	6,142	0	8,208	1,147	835	6,201	0	8,183	1,132	871	6,228	0	8,231
Louisiana	912	59	1,566	67	2,604	1,014	55	1,667	45	2,781	1,029	83	1,740	50	2,902
Maine	297	0	8	6	311	302	0	7	6	315	310	0	9	2	321
Maryland (a)	1,958	369	3,373	420	6,120	1,977	396	3,521	392	6,286	2,062	405	3,711	348	6,526
Massachusetts	1,167	9	16	238	1,430	1,173	8	10	148	1,339	1,267	6	15	118	1,406
Michigan	1,534	113	498	40	2,185	1,434	119	637	84	2,274	1,216	139	908	135	2,398
Minnesota	1,556	3	49	108	1,716	1,651	3	53	74	1,781	1,639	4	58	131	1,832
Mississippi	841	142	2,839	97	3,919	794	152	2,861	85	3,892	788	164	2,961	72	3,985
Missouri	901	1	240	83	1,225	853	1	237	76	1,167	858	0	250	8	1,116
Montana	233	42	409	0	684	224	31	414	0	669	227	11	422	0	660
Nebraska	756	336	1,782	0	2,874	652	544	1,670	0	2,866	746	554	1,653	0	2,953
Nevada	554	3	331	9	897	605	3	347	15	970	619	3	340	6	968
New Hampshire	128	1	0	9	138	131	0	0	8	139	132	0	0	6	138
New Jersey	2,431	15	2,574	0	5,020	2,364	10	2,942	0	5,316	2,523	13	3,107	0	5,643
New Mexico	786	667	1,657	106	3,216	779	612	1,586	86	3,063	804	584	1,628	93	3,109
New York (a)	2,876	318	6,745	632	10,571	2,834	347	6,999	645	10,825	2,981	357	7,006	645	10,989
North Carolina	3,957	51	2,293	41	6,342	4,060	51	2,365	99	6,575	4,283	133	2,183	205	6,804
North Dakota	443	112	651	2	1,208	380	119	635	25	1,159	376	219	980	47	1,622
Ohio (a)	2,540	22	38	280	2,880	2,554	21	26	296	2,897	2,588	20	28	260	2,896
Oklahoma	653	998	3,997	23	5,671	651	954	3,930	11	5,546	658	931	3,877	11	5,477
Oregon	863	41	544	29	1,477	1,022	40	214	69	1,345	927	41	197	197	1,362
Pennsylvania	1,659	0	121	190	1,970	1,675	0	127	189	1,991	1,717	0	131	163	2,011
Rhode Island	198	14	877	53	1,142	221	14	938	63	1,236	234	8	970	82	1,294
South Carolina	690	120	4,089	595	5,494	670	126	3,986	133	4,915	710	145	4,396	130	5,381
South Dakota	235	70	450	19	774	240	70	613	14	937	242	73	506	4	825
Tennessee	2,014	73	2,570	0	4,657	2,278	69	2,754	0	5,101	2,169	63	2,671	0	4,903
Texas	7,842	3,976	5,640	0	17,458	7,783	4,214	5,713	0	17,710	7,883	4,468	5,787	0	18,138
Utah	1,110	9	816	0	1,935	1,102	9	877	0	1,988	1,321	8	859	0	2,188
Vermont	85	0	6	4	95	88	0	6	7	101	88	0	6	4	98
Virginia	1,963	1,164	3,838	445	7,410	1,862	859	4,184	528	7,433	1,993	914	4,276	796	7,979
Washington	1,536	5	4,595	302	6,438	1,578	4	4,455	99	6,136	1,645	4	4,792	169	6,610
West Virginia	383	20	1,473	54	1,930	453	246	2,018	0	2,717	472	254	2,018	2	2,746
Wisconsin	1,700	1,652	3,411	0	6,763	1,713	1,672	3,520	0	6,905	1,789	1,665	3,748	0	7,202
Wyoming	408	1	34	0	443	409	1	34	0	444	340	1	95	0	436
Dist. of Columbia	78	21	45	10	154	80	20	62	12	174	N/A	N/A	N/A	N/A	N/A

See footnotes at end of table

TABLE 7.9
Higher Education Expenditures–Capital Inclusive (In millions of dollars) (continued)

Source: National Association of State Budget Officers, 2019 State Expenditure Report.

Notes:

1. Small dollar amounts, when rounded, cause an aberration in the percentage increase. In these instances, the actual dollar amounts should be consulted to determine the exact percentage increase.
2. "State funds" refers to general funds plus other state fund spending. State spending from bonds is excluded.
3. "Total funds" refers to funding from all sources–general fund, federal funds, other state funds, and bonds.

Key:

N/A – Not available

(a)

Alabama: Capital expenditures are not captured/available at state budget level. Reported Bond Funds for Higher Ed represent bond proceeds paid directly to vendors by the State's Debt Management division.

Colorado: HED colleges and universities pay pension and health benefits out of their allotments, which include but are not limited to, state general fund appropriations (as well as tuition and other sources). Tuition and fee are paid straight to institutions by the student, or on behalf of the student, and show up as cash funds to the institutions in the state budget; however not all fees charges by institutions are included, only mandatory fees charged to most students are included. Only a small part of research in E&G is funded by the state; for all practical purposes it is funded by outside grants. The College Opportunity Fund (COF) provides some (stipend) funds to students who attend private colleges and universities. However, this sum is very small relative to the total expenditure; as such, it is categorized as excluded for purposes of this survey.

Kansas: Employer contributions to employee health benefits excludes the contributions of USDs for their employee health benefits; includes contributions for KSDE employees.

Maryland: FY 2017 Actual for bond funds was updated to include an additional $248,000 in bond funds from Baltimore City Community College that were inadvertently omitted. Prior years submission excluded Academic Revenue Bonds from the the Total Bond Funds. Total Bond Funds includes these bonds in this submission.

New York: Spending for 2018 Other State Funds has been adjusted from the prior year survey to include $4 million in Higher Education Facilities Corporation spending.

Ohio: Employer contributions to current employees' pensions and employer contributions to employee health benefits are not direct expenditures of the state; however, some of the unrestricted support provided to higher education institutions can be assumed to have been used to help cover these costs. The majority of career-technical education/vocational education is funded through appropriations made to the Ohio Department of Education for career-technical/vocational education for students starting as early as the 7th grade. Ohio provides assistance to private colleges and universities through financial aid to students with the greatest need through the Ohio College Opportunity Grant (OCOG). Students attending private colleges and universities are eligible to receive OCOG.

TABLE 7.10
Total Public Assistance Expenditures (In millions of dollars)

State	Actual Fiscal 2017				Actual Fiscal 2018				Estimated Fiscal 2019			
	General fund	Federal funds	Other state funds	Total	General fund	Federal funds	Other state funds	Total	General fund	Federal funds	Other state funds	Total
Total	$8,334	$14,906	$2,318	$25,558	$7,956	$14,383	$2,415	$24,754	$7,813	$15,847	$2,563	$26,223
Alabama	0	25	0	25	0	24	0	24	0	25	0	25
Alaska	83	20	15	118	82	20	14	116	81	22	18	121
Arizona	0	222	0	222	0	217	0	217	0	223	0	223
Arizona	159	297	30	486	162	300	14	476	151	300	28	479
California	3,825	4,801	2,029	10,655	3,590	4,623	2,150	10,363	3,572	4,799	2,278	10,649
Colorado	0	1,434	0	1,434	0	1,423	0	1,423	0	1,434	0	1,434
Connecticut	386	0	0	386	384	0	0	384	385	0	0	385
Delaware	21	3	2	26	20	2	2	24	19	1	2	22
Florida	137	56	0	193	125	26	0	151	128	58	0	186
Georgia	0	340	0	340	0	326	0	326	0	328	0	328
Hawaii	45	25	0	70	48	10	0	58	45	10	0	55
Idaho	16	1	0	17	16	1	0	17	15	2	0	17
Illinois	93	0	0	93	98	0	0	98	99	0	0	99
Indiana	27	189	0	216	21	222	0	243	21	211	0	232
Iowa	46	30	9	85	53	20	6	79	50	33	9	92
Kansas	0	15	0	15	0	13	0	13	0	12	0	12
Kentucky	64	99	1	164	56	105	0	161	55	101	0	156
Louisiana	0	141	0	141	0	140	0	140	0	140	0	140
Maine	43	42	93	178	41	60	92	193	32	66	92	190
Maryland	64	1,100	12	1,176	55	1,029	10	1,094	45	1,102	10	1,157
Massachusetts	510	2	0	512	499	3	0	502	514	2	0	516
Michigan	137	118	16	271	120	135	15	270	105	142	15	262
Minnesota	175	216	0	391	173	188	0	361	169	191	0	360
Mississippi	27	842	5	874	24	801	4	829	25	1,043	5	1,073
Missouri	39	68	32	139	36	60	31	127	35	70	31	136
Montana	12	27	0	39	11	31	0	42	12	20	0	32
Nebraska	18	34	0	52	17	33	0	50	12	28	0	40
Nevada	25	17	0	42	25	17	0	42	25	19	0	44
New Hampshire	49	22	0	71	49	42	0	91	56	47	0	103
New Jersey	159	58	0	217	143	51	0	194	145	44	0	189
New Mexico	1	128	0	129	1	127	0	128	1	132	0	133
New York (a)	1,130	2,300	0	3,430	1,137	2,161	0	3,298	1,038	3,088	0	4,126
North Carolina	58	44	58	160	58	44	58	160	58	44	58	160
North Dakota	0	2	2	4	1	0	3	4	0	2	1	3
Ohio	162	710	0	872	150	685	0	835	149	663	0	812
Oklahoma	87	106	0	193	78	64	0	142	78	64	0	142
Oregon	57	63	0	120	43	89	2	134	45	93	0	138
Pennsylvania	305	649	2	956	290	656	2	948	285	606	2	893
Rhode Island	30	76	0	106	31	73	0	104	30	91	0	121
South Carolina	19	62	1	82	15	58	1	74	35	42	1	78
South Dakota	9	11	0	20	9	11	0	20	9	10	0	19
Tennessee	14	43	0	57	12	37	0	49	14	99	0	113
Texas	50	8	0	58	50	4	0	54	50	8	0	58
Utah	21	82	0	103	21	77	0	98	21	56	0	77
Vermont	26	69	2	97	25	65	2	92	22	66	4	92
Virginia	40	91	0	131	39	95	0	134	43	85	0	128
Washington	51	132	0	183	47	121	0	168	48	129	0	177
West Virginia	30	85	0	115	28	93	0	121	28	93	0	121
Wisconsin	84	1	9	94	73	1	9	83	63	3	9	75
Wyoming	0	0	0	0	0	0	0	0	0	0	0	0
Dist. of Columbia	58	119	1	178	67	68	1	136	N/A	N/A	N/A	N/A

See footnotes at end of table

TABLE 7.10
Total Public Assistance Expenditures (In millions of dollars) (continued)

Source: National Association of State Budget Officers, *2019 State Expenditure Report*

Notes:

1. This table reflects TANF and other cash assistance expenditures.
2. Small dollar amounts, when rounded, cause an aberration in the percentage increase. In these instances, the actual dollar amounts should be consulted to determine the exact percentage increase.
3. "State funds" refers to general funds plus other state fund spending. State spending from bonds is excluded.
4. "Total funds" refers to funding from all sources–general fund, federal funds, other state funds, and bonds.

Key:

N/A–Not available

(a) New York: The increase in fiscal 2019 federal TANF spending is due to payment timing. Several programs within TANF that underspent in fiscal years 2017 and 2018 disbursed in fiscal 2019 causing the significant year over year change.

TABLE 7.11
Corrections Expenditures–Capital Inclusive (In millions of dollars)

State	Actual Fiscal 2017					Actual Fiscal 2018					Estimated Fiscal 2019				
	General fund	Federal funds	Other state funds	Bonds	Total	General fund	Federal funds	Other state funds	Bonds	Total	General fund	Federal funds	Other state funds	Bonds	Total
Total	$52,951	$508	$4,968	$896	$59,323	$54,649	$512	$5,018	$760	$60,939	$56,726	$607	$5,425	$694	$63,452
Alabama	497	26	92	0	615	533	25	101	0	659	610	26	115	0	751
Alaska	323	8	36	0	367	340	8	7	0	355	379	10	8	0	397
Arizona	1,071	9	66	0	1,146	1,087	8	68	0	1,163	1,122	9	72	0	1,203
Arkansas	434	0	80	0	514	456	0	62	0	518	462	0	63	0	525
California	10,772	93	2,635	0	13,500	11,596	62	2,709	0	14,367	12,553	100	2,851	0	15,504
Colorado (a)	764	6	91	0	861	788	5	115	0	908	836	5	101	0	942
Connecticut	608	3	25	21	657	604	3	23	7	637	632	4	24	61	721
Delaware	305	0	5	4	314	320	0	5	6	331	352	1	5	4	362
Florida	2,622	59	115	0	2,796	2,791	61	104	0	2,956	2,836	106	157	0	3,099
Georgia	1,678	12	86	67	1,843	1,720	12	75	89	1,896	1,735	8	14	10	1,767
Hawaii	255	1	15	0	271	259	1	13	0	273	278	1	14	0	293
Idaho	252	3	42	0	297	265	3	40	0	308	285	5	51	0	341
Illinois	1,333	0	53	12	1,398	1,996	0	63	22	2,081	1,623	0	48	23	1,694
Indiana	744	3	59	0	806	755	3	53	0	811	778	3	55	0	836
Iowa	379	1	65	0	445	374	0	56	0	430	381	1	60	0	442
Kansas	347	5	20	5	377	349	3	19	5	376	377	4	22	5	408
Kentucky	626	11	45	0	682	640	20	59	0	719	703	10	35	0	748
Louisiana	738	1	87	1	827	765	1	97	5	868	815	3	113	3	934
Maine	182	2	3	0	187	179	1	3	0	183	188	1	2	0	191
Maryland	1,443	33	79	26	1,581	1,394	34	73	9	1,510	1,424	34	84	13	1,555
Massachusetts	1,362	27	6	55	1,450	1,428	26	5	57	1,516	1,493	34	5	48	1,580
Michigan	2,114	40	48	0	2,202	2,100	41	52	1	2,194	2,153	49	56	3	2,261
Minnesota	567	3	96	4	670	571	4	108	4	687	600	6	117	18	741
Mississippi	315	0	22	0	337	310	0	25	0	335	307	0	35	0	342
Missouri	654	2	30	2	688	664	2	28	9	703	660	2	62	2	726
Montana	200	1	13	0	214	199	10	16	0	225	200	15	16	0	231
Nebraska	319	1	28	0	348	318	1	33	0	352	327	1	56	0	384
Nevada	266	2	36	13	317	290	2	43	20	355	304	3	21	24	352
New Hampshire	109	0	5	28	142	115	0	5	14	134	125	0	6	2	133
New Jersey	1,535	11	48	0	1,594	1,140	10	40	0	1,190	1,172	9	38	0	1,219
New Mexico	294	0	33	9	336	298	0	34	6	338	306	0	34	6	346
New York (a)	2,646	23	33	271	2,973	2,635	28	9	348	3,020	2,605	4	120	251	2,980
North Carolina	1,469	2	30	2	1,503	1,529	1	28	3	1,561	1,576	3	25	3	1,607
North Dakota	102	4	12	0	118	101	5	12	0	118	107	4	9	0	120
Ohio (a)	1,880	7	61	77	2,025	1,940	11	60	83	2,094	2,007	10	70	110	2,197
Oklahoma	425	1	150	0	576	487	1	95	0	583	520	1	85	0	606
Oregon	956	15	23	38	1,032	1,024	15	21	11	1,071	1,038	19	24	22	1,103
Pennsylvania	2,677	17	119	145	2,958	2,544	17	131	29	2,721	2,713	24	145	32	2,914
Rhode Island	212	1	4	0	217	232	1	4	0	237	236	2	10	0	248
South Carolina	544	6	82	0	632	580	6	85	0	671	605	5	83	0	693
South Dakota	98	4	4	0	106	100	4	3	0	107	109	3	3	0	115
Tennessee	904	1	36	0	941	953	0	58	0	1,011	1,015	1	20	0	1,036
Texas	3,654	18	130	1	3,803	3,505	20	126	0	3,651	3,487	20	109	0	3,616
Utah	384	4	8	0	396	394	2	9	0	405	529	6	18	0	553
Vermont	148	1	7	0	156	147	1	8	0	156	150	1	7	0	158
Virginia	1,295	37	72	24	1,428	1,345	51	66	26	1,488	1,370	49	70	27	1,516
Washington	1,033	3	6	91	1,133	1,071	3	55	6	1,135	1,125	3	52	27	1,207
West Virginia (a)	191	0	11	0	202	157	0	9	0	166	252	0	111	0	363
Wisconsin	1,086	1	109	0	1,196	1,122	0	98	0	1,220	1,132	2	116	0	1,250
Wyoming	139	0	7	0	146	139	0	7	0	146	134	0	8	0	142
Dist. of Columbia	225	0	21	2	248	226	0	25	3	254	N/A	N/A	N/A	N/A	N/A

See footnotes at end of table

TABLE 7.11
Corrections Expenditures–Capital Inclusive (In millions of dollars) (continued)

Source: National Association of State Budget Officers, *2019 Expenditure Report*

Note: Small dollar amounts, when rounded, cause an aberration in the percentage increase. In these instances, the actual dollar amounts should be consulted to determine the exact percentage increase.

Key:

N/A–Not available

(a)

Colorado: Juvenile delinquent counseling programs are funded in the Colorado Department of Human Services, Division of Youth Corrections (DYC). Funding for the Youthful Offender System (youths convicted as adults) is in the Colorado Dept. of Corrections. Regarding institutions for the criminally insane, San Carlos services significantly mentally ill inmates, but note that the Colorado Dept of Human Services Forensics Institute serves mentally ill people including those found not guilty by reason of insanity.

New York: Prior years surveys included spending from the Division of Criminal Justice Services (DCJS). Based upon the provided definition of Corrections expenditures, we have determined these costs should be excluded, as such, this year's survey no longer includes DCJS spending in the reported 2017, 2018 and 2019 totals for Corrections expenditures.

Ohio: While employer contributions to current employees' pensions and employer contributions to employee health benefits are included in the expenditure totals, agencies do not receive specific appropriations for these purposes. As of fiscal year 2016, drug recovery services within Department of Rehabilitation and Correction (DRC) institutions are provided by the Department of Mental Health and Addiction Services. However, DRC continues to fund drug abuse rehabilitation programs in community settings through per-bed or per-diem payments to Halfway Houses and Community Based Correctional Facilities.

West Virginia: In fiscal 2019, West Virginia enacted a code change that combined the Division of Corrections, Regional Jail Authority, and Juvenile Services into one division. It is now the Division of Corrections and Rehabilitation.

TABLE 7.12
Transportation Expenditures–Capital Inclusive (In millions of dollars)

State	Actual fiscal 2017					Actual fiscal 2018					Estimated fiscal 2019				
	General fund	Federal funds	Other state funds	Bonds	Total	General fund	Federal funds	Other state funds	Bonds	Total	General fund	Federal funds	Other state funds	Bonds	Total
Total	$6,275	$44,196	$91,210	$13,350	$155,031	$7,640	$43,284	$96,328	$10,564	$157,816	$8,204	$46,252	$104,989	$12,466	$171,911
Alabama	0	834	650	314	1,798	0	948	747	395	2,090	0	746	559	223	1,528
Alaska	275	1,216	262	0	1,753	243	1,079	293	0	1,615	253	911	274	0	1,438
Arizona	0	645	2,207	402	3,254	2	693	2,278	290	3,263	2	734	2,346	250	3,332
Arkansas	1	650	1,079	0	1,730	1	734	942	0	1,677	1	506	913	0	1,420
California	203	4,816	7,953	427	13,399	213	4,517	9,576	264	14,570	227	6,113	13,399	1,042	20,781
Colorado (a)	0	731	1,242	0	1,973	0	702	1,026	0	1,728	0	392	1,214	0	1,606
Connecticut	0	779	1,447	1,273	3,499	0	743	1,519	897	3,159	0	703	1,638	1,224	3,565
Delaware	5	217	567	129	918	5	347	584	3	939	4	292	686	12	994
Florida	3	2,281	6,418	398	9,100	0	2,581	6,219	275	9,075	0	2,288	8,200	349	10,837
Georgia	1,635	1,438	454	115	3,642	1,644	1,477	387	110	3,618	1,999	1,600	98	112	3,809
Hawaii (a)	0	137	1,152	42	1,331	0	174	1,209	329	1,712	0	285	1,561	346	2,192
Idaho	0	195	347	0	542	0	266	429	0	695	0	544	674	0	1,218
Illinois	0	90	4,679	770	5,539	4	74	4,538	289	4,905	5	82	4,317	298	4,702
Indiana	571	931	776	0	2,278	47	1,009	1,244	0	2,300	48	1,031	1,324	0	2,403
Iowa	0	676	1,340	0	2,016	0	575	1,554	0	2,129	0	565	1,228	0	1,793
Kansas	10	479	413	195	1,097	10	401	269	197	877	0	415	476	210	1,101
Kentucky	13	900	1,502	0	2,415	13	802	1,533	0	2,348	10	898	1,602	0	2,510
Louisiana	3	745	621	129	1,498	14	741	603	93	1,451	6	801	570	60	1,437
Maine (a)	0	224	475	92	791	0	233	451	69	753	0	203	411	124	738
Maryland	0	953	3,619	0	4,572	0	981	3,993	0	4,974	0	1,148	4,067	0	5,215
Massachusetts (a)	140	650	2,307	1,286	4,383	167	634	2,188	1,273	4,262	127	639	2,164	1,248	4,178
Michigan	9	1,256	2,429	7	3,701	205	1,090	2,676	1	3,972	357	1,318	2,929	4	4,608
Minnesota	140	265	3,144	263	3,812	158	286	3,322	134	3,900	210	749	3,534	219	4,712
Mississippi	0	566	739	122	1,427	0	586	697	91	1,374	0	599	730	127	1,456
Missouri	20	89	1,916	0	2,025	12	79	1,961	0	2,052	18	78	1,935	0	2,031
Montana	10	382	279	0	671	7	395	284	0	686	39	471	363	0	873
Nebraska	0	340	552	0	892	0	329	661	0	990	0	345	501	0	846
Nevada	0	369	406	180	955	0	381	395	220	996	0	368	548	112	1,028
New Hampshire	1	247	269	14	531	1	248	311	8	568	1	243	277	10	531
New Jersey	1,529	1,571	1,101	1,735	5,936	1,567	1,586	1,048	1,756	5,957	1,774	1,682	1,518	2,050	7,024
New Mexico	0	748	460	11	1,219	0	788	694	30	1,512	25	807	713	23	1,568
New York	107	2,095	6,748	1,559	10,509	118	1,688	6,899	1,340	10,045	607	1,706	5,136	2,403	9,852
North Carolina	0	1,330	3,574	431	5,335	0	1,494	4,409	110	6,013	0	1,506	5,266	82	6,854
North Dakota	46	303	620	0	969	18	255	406	0	679	7	318	320	0	645
Ohio (a)	11	1,465	1,534	338	3,348	15	1,382	1,408	391	3,196	14	1,456	1,431	513	3,414
Oklahoma	0	698	740	119	1,557	0	673	737	90	1,500	0	635	692	85	1,412
Oregon	11	46	2,103	20	2,180	13	39	1,708	13	1,773	11	42	1,769	8	1,830
Pennsylvania	962	2,109	5,800	1,243	10,114	2,920	1,924	6,313	196	11,353	2,261	2,279	6,740	203	11,483
Rhode Island	0	240	176	36	452	0	242	212	125	579	0	325	301	183	809
South Carolina	120	855	1,179	9	2,163	60	988	1,138	15	2,201	15	727	1,461	0	2,203
South Dakota	1	332	263	0	596	1	280	309	0	590	1	282	322	0	605
Tennessee (a)	0	874	854	0	1,728	0	913	998	0	1,911	0	1,084	1,158	0	2,242
Texas	276	4,498	5,519	1,170	11,463	2	3,820	6,388	863	11,073	2	4,431	7,557	447	12,437
Utah	3	406	964	0	1,373	1	402	865	332	1,600	4	382	1,275	150	1,811
Vermont	0	272	266	0	538	0	311	259	0	570	0	269	264	1	534
Virginia	40	1,252	4,892	123	6,307	40	1,096	5,680	68	6,884	41	1,209	5,621	118	6,989
Washington	1	577	2,104	398	3,080	2	525	1,875	297	2,699	2	468	2,016	230	2,716
West Virginia	12	563	1,083	0	1,658	7	525	1,053	0	1,585	7	500	752	0	1,259
Wisconsin	107	752	1,909	0	2,768	120	1,139	1,963	0	3,222	126	1,051	2,033	0	3,210
Wyoming	10	109	77	0	196	10	109	77	0	196	0	26	106	0	132
Dist. of Columbia	317	210	250	196	973	369	245	236	316	1,166	N/A	N/A	N/A	N/A	N/A

See footnotes at end of table

TABLE 7.12
Transportation Expenditures–Capital Inclusive (In millions of dollars) (continued)

Source: National Association of State Budget Officers, 2019 Expenditure Report.

Notes:

1. Small dollar amounts, when rounded, cause an aberration in the percentage increase. In these instances, the actual dollar amounts should be consulted to determine the exact percentage increase.
2. "State funds" refers to general funds plus other state fund spending. State spending from bonds is excluded.
3. "Total funds" refers to funding from all sources—general fund, federal funds, other state funds, and bonds.

Key:

N/A – Not available

(a)

Colorado: Port authority operations, gasoline tax and fee collections, and motor vehicle licensing are at Dept. of Revenue. State police/highway patrol is funded at the Dept. of Public Safety. SB18-001 transferred $2.5 million to the SW Chief/Front Range Passenger Rail Fund to fund planning efforts for a Front Range Passenger Rail line in FY 2018-19.

Hawaii: Transportation expenditures are expenditures from Airports, Harbors, Highways, and Administration.

Maine: In last year's State Expenditure Report, Transportation, Other State Funds, 2017 Actual was reported as $440 and should have been $475; 2018 Actual was reported as $415 and should have been $451. Motor Vehicle licensing expenditures were not included in this category in previous surveys.

Massachusetts: Totals do not include certain transportation spending, such as non-state bond cap investments at the Massachusetts Bay Transportation Authority (MBTA).

Ohio: While employer contributions to current employees' pensions and employer contributions to employee health benefits are included in the expenditure totals, agencies do not receive specific appropriations for these purposes. The Ohio Department of Public Safety and the Ohio Public Utilities Commission are responsible for truck enforcement/regulatory programs. A portion of spending by the Ohio Public Works Commission to retire debt for local road and bridge projects is not included in road assistance subsidy programs for local government.

Tennessee: Bond estimates represent bond authorizations, while actual bonds represent bond proceeds utilized.

TABLE 7.13
All Other Expenditures–Capital Inclusive (In millions of dollars)

State	Actual fiscal 2017					Actual fiscal 2018				
	General fund	Federal funds	Other state funds	Bonds	Total	General fund	Federal funds	Other state funds	Bonds	Total
Total	$205,590	$121,637	$213,429	$14,664	$555,320	$211,775	$129,528	$217,076	$15,497	$573,876
Alabama (a)	1,128	2,253	3,049	86	6,516	1,046	2,210	3,052	167	6,475
Alaska	1,463	782	786	0	3,031	1,474	748	1,496	0	3,718
Arizona	1,878	2,937	2,381	0	7,196	1,787	3,503	2,768	0	8,058
Arkansas	594	843	6,550	58	8,045	623	856	6,785	44	8,308
California	22,706	17,623	24,382	1,443	66,154	23,175	17,836	26,161	1,701	68,873
Colorado (a)	2,463	1,431	5,910	0	9,804	2,711	1,545	6,716	0	10,972
Connecticut	9,025	1,110	1,577	1,045	12,757	9,380	1,072	1,598	1,435	13,485
Delaware	1,379	458	2,452	109	4,398	1,350	434	2,439	103	4,326
Florida	6,265	7,353	2,697	1,224	17,539	6,681	8,113	2,399	1,183	18,376
Georgia	4,779	3,089	4,068	178	12,114	5,028	2,810	4,265	305	12,408
Hawaii	4,241	718	2,107	520	7,586	4,609	758	1,573	639	7,579
Idaho	477	951	558	0	1,986	524	783	660	0	1,967
Illinois	16,204	2,330	13,751	473	32,758	18,130	1,415	10,795	163	30,503
Indiana	2,557	1,555	1,772	0	5,884	2,767	2,950	1,747	0	7,464
Iowa	1,447	2,109	1,987	6	5,549	1,456	1,588	2,315	8	5,367
Kansas	957	599	1,705	119	3,380	908	692	1,789	116	3,505
Kentucky	2,549	1,748	2,011	0	6,308	2,547	1,879	2,061	0	6,487
Louisiana	2,069	1,823	3,864	107	7,863	2,301	1,961	5,191	149	9,602
Maine	880	482	1,312	16	2,690	900	435	1,297	31	2,663
Maryland	4,198	1,716	4,419	353	10,686	4,037	1,727	3,952	692	10,408
Massachusetts	10,755	4,537	8,074	1,102	24,468	11,227	4,461	8,095	1,183	24,966
Michigan	3,150	4,939	6,937	25	15,051	3,458	5,514	7,171	61	16,204
Minnesota	5,414	2,762	1,678	264	10,118	5,584	2,874	1,711	196	10,365
Mississippi	1,558	1,758	1,197	900	5,413	1,527	1,724	1,158	486	4,895
Missouri	2,133	1,838	1,910	78	5,959	2,174	1,857	1,834	101	5,966
Montana	750	843	957	0	2,550	706	793	985	0	2,484
Nebraska	986	943	2,055	0	3,984	1,116	698	2,231	0	4,045
Nevada	1,081	1,016	3,933	21	6,051	937	1,041	3,965	26	5,969
New Hampshire	510	461	614	41	1,626	457	557	735	31	1,780
New Jersey	10,763	3,340	3,216	431	17,750	12,399	3,713	2,596	384	19,092
New Mexico	1,403	1,741	2,418	292	5,854	1,431	2,126	2,737	146	6,440
New York	25,664	10,814	6,734	1,919	45,131	25,144	12,403	7,179	2,266	46,992
North Carolina	4,521	2,822	2,360	64	9,767	4,552	2,931	2,921	36	10,440
North Dakota	704	361	1,129	0	2,194	415	200	923	0	1,538
Ohio (a)	4,218	2,480	13,484	1,659	21,841	4,183	2,545	13,920	1,677	22,325
Oklahoma	1,490	1,726	3,095	187	6,498	2,015	2,177	1,405	277	5,874
Oregon	2,620	2,349	16,182	51	21,202	2,510	3,150	16,441	70	22,171
Pennsylvania	7,500	7,058	9,027	645	24,230	6,331	6,082	9,745	213	22,371
Rhode Island	1,007	920	1,009	36	2,972	1,036	899	1,038	42	3,015
South Carolina	2,350	1,550	1,469	13	5,382	2,505	1,794	1,502	27	5,828
South Dakota	310	335	512	1	1,158	315	353	503	6	1,177
Tennessee	2,982	3,445	1,958	0	8,385	3,127	3,460	1,999	0	8,586
Texas (a)	9,391	1,647	1,626	546	13,210	10,357	4,667	2,019	789	17,832
Utah	1,290	1,127	1,611	0	4,028	1,369	1,122	1,402	0	3,893
Vermont	504	524	184	44	1,256	559	507	165	57	1,288
Virginia	6,376	2,115	9,191	369	18,051	6,552	2,197	9,346	336	18,431
Washington	3,793	2,966	4,308	239	11,306	3,656	2,956	5,021	351	11,984
West Virginia	1,183	185	5,301	0	6,669	552	301	5,301	0	6,154
Wisconsin	3,363	2,613	12,853	0	18,829	3,580	2,614	12,902	0	19,096
Wyoming	562	512	1,069	0	2,143	567	497	1,067	0	2,131
Dist. of Columbia	3,853	685	646	256	5,440	4,149	569	726	384	5,828

See footnotes at end of table

TABLE 7.13
All Other Expenditures–Capital Inclusive (In millions of dollars) (continued)

State	General fund	Federal funds	Other state funds	Bonds	Total
			Estimated fiscal 2019		
Total	$230,415	$131,288	$235,427	$19,853	$616,983
Alabama (a)	895	1,876	2,590	36	5,397
Alaska	2,829	988	1,059	0	4,876
Arizona	610	2,054	2,810	0	5,474
Arkansas	571	857	7,024	54	8,506
California	34,508	19,513	30,995	5,235	90,251
Colorado (a)	3,590	1,491	7,082	0	12,163
Connecticut	$9,955	$1,072	$1,598	$1,286	$13,911
Delaware	1,544	434	2,570	72	4,620
Florida	6,569	8,896	6,809	1,207	23,481
Georgia	5,532	2,787	4,519	267	13,105
Hawaii	4,510	450	1,864	551	7,375
Idaho	538	909	822	0	2,269
Illinois	19,309	2,081	10,369	210	31,969
Indiana	2,501	2,759	1,482	0	6,742
Iowa	1,591	1,668	2,263	7	5,529
Kansas	1,085	787	1,844	130	3,846
Kentucky	2,799	2,018	2,206	0	7,023
Louisiana	2,568	3,320	6,448	54	12,390
Maine	1,000	454	1,362	22	2,838
Maryland	4,409	2,190	4,359	564	11,522
Massachusetts	11,897	4,547	9,095	1,248	26,787
Michigan	3,891	6,704	3,914	56	14,565
Minnesota	6,005	3,234	2,108	240	11,587
Mississippi	1,551	2,505	1,577	699	6,332
Missouri	2,348	1,872	1,857	79	6,156
Montana	712	883	929	0	2,524
Nebraska	997	365	2,653	0	4,015
Nevada	1,321	1,178	3,742	38	6,279
New Hampshire	440	583	792	65	1,880
New Jersey	13,057	4,337	2,785	0	20,179
New Mexico	1,515	2,075	2,753	81	6,424
New York	24,837	12,099	9,719	3,106	49,761
North Carolina	4,591	1,741	3,621	110	10,063
North Dakota	473	234	1,124	0	1,831
Ohio (a)	4,282	2,745	14,084	1,745	22,856
Oklahoma	1,814	2,436	1,921	201	6,372
Oregon	2,521	3,071	17,691	97	23,380
Pennsylvania	7,077	6,424	10,804	198	24,503
Rhode Island	1,111	1,062	1,141	85	3,399
South Carolina	2,568	1,434	1,470	17	5,489
South Dakota	355	361	533	28	1,277
Tennessee	3,513	4,191	2,219	89	10,012
Texas (a)	8,475	267	1,631	1,012	11,385
Utah	1,531	1,392	1,601	0	4,524
Vermont	658	473	157	80	1,368
Virginia	6,755	2,276	9,812	367	19,210
Washington	4,180	2,769	4,822	517	12,288
West Virginia	527	342	6,195	0	7,064
Wisconsin	3,725	2,600	13,369	0	19,694
Wyoming	775	484	1,233	0	2,492
Dist. of Columbia	N/A	N/A	N/A	N/A	N/A

See footnotes at end of table

TABLE 7.13
All Other Expenditures–Capital Inclusive (In millions of dollars) (continued)

Source: National Association of State Budget Officers, *2019 Expenditure Report*

Notes:

1. Small dollar amounts, when rounded, cause an aberration in the percentage increase. In these instances, the actual dollar amounts should be consulted to determine the exact percentage increase.
2. "State funds" refers to general funds plus other state fund spending. State spending from bonds is excluded.
3. "Total funds" refers to funding from all sources–general fund, federal funds, other state funds, and bonds.

Key:

N/A – Not available

(a)

Alabama: Capital expenditures from Federal and Other State Funds are not reported separately; combined amounts are included in the Other State Funds.

Colorado: CHIP expenditures are excluded from the Medicaid category and added to the All Other category to adhere more closely to the survey directions. In previous surveys, CHIP expenditures were included in Medicaid.

Ohio: While employer contributions to current employees' pensions and employer contributions to employee health benefits are included in the expenditure totals, agencies do not receive specific appropriations for these purposes. Some expenditures in community and institutional care for the developmentally disabled are included in the Medicaid totals. Most of the expenditures of the Ohio Housing Finance Agency occur outside of the state financial system and are excluded from the housing totals.

Texas: Regarding the All Other Federal Funds category, figures for 2017 and 2018 are actuals and estimated expenditures respectively. However, for 2019 the most concrete numbers available are what was appropriated by the legislature in the previous budget setting session. The figure will likely increase after the fiscal year ends on August 31st and the agencies report the actual expenditures. For example, Hurricane Harvey expenditures were not originally budgeted, but the CDBG expenditures will be accounted for following end of year reporting.

TABLE 7.14
State Tax Amnesty Programs, 1982–2019

State or other jurisdiction	Amnesty period	Legislative authorization	Major taxes covered	Accounts receivable included	Collections ($ millions) (a)	Installment arrangements permitted (b)
Alabama	1/20/84 – 4/1/84	No (c)	All	No	3.2	No
	2/1/09 – 5/15/09	Yes	Ind. Income, Corp. Income, Business, Sales & Use	N/A	8.1	N/A
	6/30/16 – 8/30/16	Yes	All	No	N/A	No
	7/1/18 – 9/30/18	Yes	All (aa)	No	N/A	No
Arizona	11/22/82 – 1/20/83	No (c)	All	No	6.0	Yes
	1/1/02 – 2/28/02	Yes	Individual Income	No	N/A	No
	9/1/03 – 10/31/03	Yes	All (t)	N/A	73.0	Yes
	5/1/09 – 6/1/09	N/A	All	N/A	32.0	N/A
	9/1/15 – 10/31/15	Yes	All	Yes	55.5	No
	9/1/16 – 10/31/16	Yes	All	Yes	N/A	Yes
Arkansas	9/1/87 – 11/30/87	Yes	All	No	1.7	Yes
	7/1/04 – 12/31/04	Yes	All	N/A	N/A	No
California	12/10/84 – 3/15/85	Yes	Individual Income	Yes	154.0	Yes
		Yes	Sales	No	43.0	Yes
	2/1/05 – 3/31/05	Yes	Income, Franchise, Sales	N/A	N/A	Yes
Colorado	9/16/85 – 11/15/85	Yes	All	No	6.4	Yes
	6/1/03 – 6/30/03	N/A	All	N/A	18.4	Yes
	10/1/11 – 11/15/11	Yes	All	No	N/A	No
Connecticut	9/1/90 – 11/30/90	Yes	All	Yes	54.0	Yes
	9/1/95 – 11/30/95	Yes	All	Yes	46.2	Yes
	9/1/02 – 12/2/02	N/A	All	N/A	109.0	N/A
	5/1/09 – 6/25/09	Yes	All	No	40.0	No
	9/16/13 – 11/15/13	Yes	All	Yes	193.5	No
	10/31/17 – 11/30/18	No	All	No	N/A	No
Delaware	9/1/09 – 10/30/09	Yes	All	Yes	N/A	Yes
Florida	1/1/87 – 6/30/87	Yes	Intangibles	No	13.0	No
	1/1/88 – 6/30/88	Yes (d)	All	No	8.4 (d)	No
	7/1/03 – 10/31/03	Yes	All	N/A	80.0	N/A
	7/1/10 – 9/30/10	Yes	All	Yes	N/A	Yes
Georgia	10/1/92 – 12/5/92	Yes	All	Yes	51.3	No
Hawaii	5/27/09 – 6/26/09	N/A	All	No	14.0	No
Idaho	5/20/83 – 8/30/83	No (c)	Individual Income	No	0.3	No
Illinois	10/1/84 – 11/30/84	Yes	All (u)	Yes	160.5	No
	10/1/03 – 11/17/03	Yes	All	N/A	532.0	N/A
	10/1/10 – 11/8/10	Yes	All	Yes	314 (y)	No
Indiana	9/15/05 – 11/15/05	Yes	All	Yes	244.0	Yes
Iowa	9/2/86 – 0/31/86	Yes	All	Yes	35.1	N/A
	9/4/07 – 10/31/07	Yes	All	Yes	N/A	N/A
Kansas	7/1/84 – 9/30/84	Yes	All	No	0.6	No
	10/1/03 – 11/30/03	Yes	All	Yes	53.7	N/A
	9/1/10 – 10/15/10	Yes	All	Yes	N/A	No
	9/1/15 – 10/15/15	Yes	All	Yes	N/A	No
Kentucky	9/15/88 – 9/30/88	Yes (c)	All	No	100.0	No
	8/1/02 – 9/30/02	Yes (c)	All	No	100.0	No
	10/1/12 – 11/30/12	Yes	All	Yes	N/A	N/A

See footnotes at end of table

TABLE 7.14
State Tax Amnesty Programs, 1982–2019 (continued)

State or other jurisdiction	Amnesty period	Legislative authorization	Major taxes covered	Accounts receivable included	Collections ($ millions) (a)	Installment arrangements permitted (b)
Louisiana	10/1/85 – 12/31/85	Yes	All	No	1.2	Yes (f)
	10/1/87 – 12/15/87	Yes	All	No	0.3	Yes (f)
	10/1/98 – 12/31/98	Yes	All	No (q)	1.3	No
	9/1/01 – 10/30/01	Yes	All	Yes	192.9	No
	9/1/09 – 10/31/09	Yes	All	N/A	303.7	N/A
	9/23/13 – 11/22/13	Yes	All	Yes	435.0	No
	10/15/14 – 11/14/14	Yes	All	Yes	N/A	Yes
	11/16/15 – 12/15/15	Yes	All	Yes		Yes
Maine	11/1/90 – 12/31/90	Yes	All	Yes	29.0	Yes
	9/1/03 – 11/30/03	Yes	All	N/A	37.6	N/A
	9/1/09 – 11/30/09	Yes	All	Yes	16.2	No
Maryland	9/1/87 – 11/2/87	Yes	All	Yes	34.6 (g)	No
	9/1/01 – 10/31/01	Yes	All	Yes	39.2	No
	9/1/09 – 10/31/09	Yes	Income, Withholding, Sales & Use	Yes	9.6	Yes
	9/1/15 – 10/30/15	Yes	All	Yes		Yes
Massachusetts	10/17/83 – 1/17/84	Yes	All	Yes	86.5	Yes (h)
	10/1/02 – 11/30/02	Yes	All	Yes	96.1	Yes
	1/1/03 – 2/28/03	Yes	All	Yes	11.2	N/A
	4/1/10 – 6/1/10	Yes	All	Yes	32.6	No
	9/2/14 – 10/31/14	Yes	All	Yes	N/A	No
	3/16/15 – 5/15/15	Yes	Corporate	Yes	18.6	No
	4/1/16 – 5/31/16	Yes	All	No	N/A	No
Michigan	5/12/86 – 6/30/86	Yes	All	Yes	109.8	No
	5/15/02 – 6/30/02	Yes	All	Yes	N/A	N/A
	5/15/11 – 6/30/11	Yes	All	Yes	76.0	No
Minnesota	8/1/84 – 10/31/84	Yes	All	Yes	12.1	No
Mississippi	9/1/86 – 11/30/86	Yes	All	No	1.0	No
	9/1/04 – 12/31/04	Yes	All	No	7.9	No
Missouri	9/1/83 – 10/31/83	No (c)	All	No	0.9	No
	8/1/02 – 10/31/02	Yes	All	Yes	76.4	N/A
	8/1/03 – 10/31/03	Yes	All	Yes	20.0	N/A
	9/1/15 – 11/30/15	Yes	All	Yes		No
Nebraska	8/1/04 – 10/31/04	Yes	All	No	7.5	No
Nevada	2/1/02 – 6/30/02	N/A	All	N/A	7.3	N/A
	7/1/08 – 10/28/08	No	Sales, Business, License	Yes	N/A	No
	7/1/10 – 10/1/10	Yes	All	Yes	N/A	No
New Hampshire	12/1/97 – 2/17/98	Yes	All	Yes	13.5	No
	12/1/01 – 2/15/02	Yes	All	Yes	13.5	N/A
	12/1/15 – 2/15/16	Yes	All	Yes	18.9	No
New Jersey	9/10/87 – 12/8/87	Yes	All	Yes	186.5	Yes
	3/15/96 – 6/1/96	Yes	All	Yes	359.0	No
	4/15/02 – 6/10/02	Yes	All	Yes	276.9	N/A
	5/4/09 – 6/15/09	Yes	All	N/A	725.0	N/A
	10/1/14 – 11/17/14	N/A	All	Yes	N/A	No
	11/15/2018 – 1/15/2019	N/A	All	N/A	N/A	N/A
New Mexico	8/15/85 – 11/13/85	Yes	All (i)	No	13.6	Yes
	8/16/99 – 11/12/99	Yes	All	Yes	45.0	Yes
	6/7/10 – 9/30/10	Yes	All	No	N/A	Yes
	11/8/2018 – 12/31/18	N/A	N/A	N/A	N/A	N/A

See footnotes at end of table

TABLE 7.14
State Tax Amnesty Programs, 1982–2019 (continued)

State or other jurisdiction	Amnesty period	Legislative authorization	Major taxes covered	Accounts receivable included	Collections ($ millions) (a)	Installment arrangements permitted (b)
New York	11/1/85 – 1/31/86	Yes	All (j)	Yes	401.3	Yes
	11/1/96 – 1/31/97	Yes	All	Yes	253.4	Yes (o)
	11/18/02 – 1/31/03	Yes	All	Yes	582.7	Yes (s)
	10/1/05 – 3/1/06	N/A	Income, Corporate	N/A	349.0	N/A
	1/15/10 – 3/15/10	Yes	All	Yes	56.5	No
New York City	10/20/03 – 1/23/04	Yes	All (v)	Yes (w)	N/A	No
North Carolina	9/1/89 – 12/1/89	Yes	All (k)	Yes	37.6	No
North Dakota	9/1/83 – 11/30/83	No (c)	All	No	0.2	Yes
	10/1/03 – 1/31/04	Yes	N/A	N/A	6.9	N/A
Ohio	10/15/01 – 1/15/02	Yes	All	No	48.5	No
	1/1/06 – 2/15/06	Yes	All	No	63.0	No
	1/1/18 – 2/15/18	Yes	All	Yes	N/A	No
Oklahoma	7/1/84 – 12/31/84	Yes	Income, Sales	Yes	13.9	No (l)
	8/15/02 – 11/15/02	N/A	All (r)	Yes	N/A	N/A
	9/15/08 – 11/14/08	Yes	All	Yes	81.0	Yes
	9/14/15 – 11/13/15	Yes	All	Yes	N/A	Yes
Oregon	10/1/09 – 11/19/09	Yes	Personal, Corporate, Inheritance	No	N/A	No
Pennsylvania	10/13/95 – 1/10/96	Yes	All	Yes	N/A	No
	4/26/10 – 6/18/10	Yes	All	Yes	261.0	No
	4/21/17 – 6/19/17	Yes	All	Yes	N/A	No
Rhode Island	10/15/86 – 1/12/87	Yes	All	No	0.7	Yes
	4/15/96 – 6/28/96	Yes	All	Yes	7.9	Yes
	7/15/06 – 9/30/06	N/A	All	Yes	6.5	Yes
	9/2/12 – 11/15/12	Yes	All	Yes	22.3	Yes
	12/1/17 – 2/15/18	Yes	All	Yes	N/A	Yes
South Carolina	9/1/85 – 11/30/85	Yes	All	Yes	7.1	Yes
	10/15/02 – 12/2/02	Yes	All	Yes	66.2	N/A
South Dakota	4/1/99 – 5/15/99	Yes	All	Yes	0.5	N/A
Texas	2/1/84 – 2/29/84	No (c)	All (m)	No	0.5	No
	3/11/04 – 3/31/04	No (c)	All (m)	No	N/A	No
	6/15/07 – 8/15/07	No (c)	All (m)	No	100	No
	6/12/12 – 8/17/12	No (c)	All (m)	No	100	No
	5/1/18 – 6/29/18	Yes	All (bb)	No	N/A	No
Vermont	5/15/90 – 6/25/90	Yes	All	Yes	1 (e)	No
	7/20/09 – 8/31/09	Yes	All	N/A	2.2	N/A
Virginia	2/1/90 – 3/31/90	Yes	All	Yes	32.2	No
	9/2/03 – 11/3/03	Yes	All	Yes	98.3	N/A
	10/7/09 – 12/5/09	Yes	All	Yes	102.1	No
Washington	2/1/11 – 4/30/11	Yes	All	Yes	346.0	No
West Virginia	10/1/86 – 12/31/86	Yes	All	Yes	15.9	Yes
	9/1/04 – 10/31/04	Yes	All	N/A	10.4	Yes
Wisconsin	9/15/85 – 11/22/85	Yes	All	Yes (n)	27.3	Yes
	6/15/98 – 8/14/98	Yes	All	Yes	30.9	N/A
Dist. of Columbia	7/1/87 – 9/30/87	Yes	All	Yes	24.3	Yes
	7/10/95 – 8/31/95	Yes	All (p)	Yes	19.5	Yes (p)
	8/2/10 – 9/30/10	Yes	All (p)	Yes	N/A	No
CNMI*	9/30/05 – 3/30/06	Yes	All	N/A	N/A	N/A

See footnotes at end of table

TABLE 7.14
State Tax Amnesty Programs, 1982–2019 (continued)

Source: The Federation of Tax Administrators, January 2019.
*Commonwealth of Northern Mariana Islands
Key:
N/A–Not available.
(a) Where applicable, figure includes local portions of certain taxes collected under the state tax amnesty program.
(b) "No" indicates requirement of full payment by the expiration of the amnesty period. "Yes" indicates allowance of full payment after the expiration of the amnesty period.
(c) Authority for amnesty derived from pre-existing statutory powers permitting the waiver of tax penalties.
(d) Does not include intangibles tax and drug taxes. Gross collections totaled $22.1 million, with $13.7 million in penalties withdrawn.
(e) Preliminary figure.
(f) Amnesty taxpayers were billed for the interest owed, with payment due within 30 days of notification.
(g) Figure includes $1.1 million for the separate program conducted by the Department of Natural Resources for the boat excise tax.
(h) The amnesty statute was construed to extend the amnesty to those who applied to the department before the end of the amnesty period, and permitted them to file overdue returns and pay back taxes and interest at a later date.
(i) The severance taxes, including the six oil and gas severance taxes, the resources excise tax, the corporate franchise tax, and the special fuels tax were not subject to amnesty.
(j) Availability of amnesty for the corporation tax, the oil company taxes, the transportation and transmissions companies tax, the gross receipts oil tax and the unincorporated business tax restricted to entities with 500 or fewer employees in the United States on the date of application. In addition, a taxpayer principally engaged in aviation, or a utility subject to the supervision of the State Department of Public Service was also ineligible.
(k) Local taxes and real property taxes were not included.
(l) Full payment of tax liability required before the end of the amnesty period to avoid civil penalties.

(m) Texas does not impose a corporate or individual income tax. In practical effect, the amnesty was limited to the sales tax and other excises.
(n) Waiver terms varied depending upon the date of tax liability was accessed.
(o) Installment arrangements were permitted if applicant demonstrated that payment would present a severe financial hardship.
(p) Does not include real property taxes. For the 1995 amnesty, all interest was waived on tax payments made before July 31, 1995. After this date, only 50% of the interest was waived.
(q) Exception for individuals who owed $500 or less.
(r) Except for property and motor fuel taxes.
(s) Multiple payments can be made so long as the required balance is paid in full no later than March 15, 2003.
(t) All taxes except property, estate and unclaimed property.
(u) Does not include the motor fuel use tax.
(v) All NYC taxes administered by the NYC Dept. of Finance are covered except for Real Estate Tax. NYC Sales & Use Tax & NYC Resident Personal Income Tax also are not covered because they are administered by the NY State Dept. of Taxation & Finance.
(w) Taxpayers under audit as of 3/10/03 are ineligible; Taxpayers with an existing installment agreement are ineligible; Taxpayers under criminal investigation are ineligible; Taxpayers party to an administrative or court proceeding must withdraw as a condition of.
(x) The Massachusetts Department of Revenue is required to hold an amnesty to end before June 30, 2010.
(y) In Illinois, the 2010 Amnesty collected a total of $717 million, $314 million for the state General Fund and the rest for local governments.
(z) In Rhode Island, the full amount must be paid by December 14, 2012.
(aa) All taxes except motor fuel, motor vehicle and property taxes.
(bb) Does not apply to local motor vehicle tax, IFTA taxes, PUC gross receipts assessments or unclaimed property payments.

TABLE 7.15A
State Tobacco Product and Vaping Excise Tax Rates (As of January 2020)

State or other jurisdiction	General sales and gross receipts tax (percent)	Cigarettes (cents per pack)	Cigarette excise tax rank in nation	Other tobacco products tax (n)	Taxation of E-Cigarettes/Vaping Products Tax Rate/Base (j)
Alabama	4.0	67.5 (c)	41	Cigars 3¢-40.5¢/10 cigars; Tobacco/Snuff 2¢-8¢/oz. (o)	…
Alaska	(a)	200	17	75% WP	…
Arizona	5.6	200	17	Cigars 22.01¢-$2.18/10 cigars; Tobacco/Snuff 22.3¢/oz.	…
Arkansas	6.5	115	35	68% MP	…
California	7.25 (b)	287	11	59.27% WP (p)	59.27% WP (m) (u)
Colorado	2.9	84	39	40% MP	…
Connecticut	6.35	435	2	50% WP (p)(q)	10% open , or .40¢/ml - closed container
Delaware	(a)	210	15	30% WP (p)(q)	5¢/ml
Florida	6.0	133.9 (d)	31	Tobacco/Snuff 85% WP (r)	…
Georgia	4.0	37	49	Little Cigars 2.5¢/cigars; Other cigars 23% WP; Tobacco 10% WP	…
Hawaii	4.0	320	6	Large Cigars - 50% WP; Tobacco/Snuff 70% WP (s)	…
Idaho	6.0	57	45	40% WP	…
Illinois	6.25	198 (c)	10	36% WP (p)(q)	15% WP (k)
Indiana	7.0	99.5	38	24% WP	…
Iowa	6.0	136	30	50% WP (s)	…
Kansas	6.5	129	33	10% WP (p)	5¢/ml
Kentucky	6.0	110	36	15% WP (q)	…
Louisiana	4.45	108	37	Cigars 8%-20% MP; Snuff/Smoking Tobacco 20%-33% MP (p)	5¢/ml
Maine	5.5	200	17	Chewing Tob./Snuff $2.02/oz.; Smoking Tob./Cigars (7) 43% WP	43% WP *e-cigarette products subject to Other Tobacco Tax (m)
Maryland	6.0	200	17	Tobacco/Snuff 30% WP; Cigars 70% WP	…
Massachusetts	6.25	351	5	40% WP (p)	75% WP (l)
Michigan	6.0	200	17	32% WP	…
Minnesota	6.875	304 (e)	8	95% WP (p)	95% WP (m) (u)
Mississippi	7.0	68	40	15% MP	…
Missouri	4.225	17 (c)	51	10% MP	…
Montana	(a)	170	25	50% WP (q)	…
Nebraska	5.5	64	42	20% WP (q)	…
Nevada	6.85	180	23	30% WP (p)	30% WP (m) (u)
New Hampshire	(a)	178	24	65.03% WP (p)	30¢/ml - closed container 8% WP - open
New Jersey	6.625	270	12	30% WP (p)(q)	10% Open , or 10 ¢/ml- closed container
New Mexico	5.125	166	17	25% WP Product value (p)	12.5% Open , or 50¢/cartridge-closed
New York	4.0	435 (c)	2	75% WP (p)(q)	20% Retail Price
North Carolina	4.75	45	47	12.8% WP (p)	5¢/ml
North Dakota	5.0	44	48	Cigars & Tobacco 28% WP; Chew Tobacco/Snuff 16¢-60¢ /oz.	…
Ohio	5.75	160	27	17% WP (p)	10¢/ml
Oklahoma	4.5	203	16	Cigars- Little/Large $1.20/ 10 cigars; Tobacco/Snuff 60%-80% Factory list price	…
Oregon	(a)	133	32	65% WP (q)	…
Pennsylvania	6.0	260	13	55¢/oz.- tobacco (p)(s)	40% WP
Rhode Island	7.0	425	4	80% WP	…
South Carolina	6.0	57	45	5% MP	…
South Dakota	4.5	153	28	35% WP	…
Tennessee	7.0	62 (c)(f)	43	6.6% WP	…
Texas	6.25	141	29	Cigar 1¢-15¢/10 cigars; Tobacco/Snuff -$1.22 /oz.	…
Utah	6.1 (i)	170	25	86% MP (q)(s)	…
Vermont	6.0	308	7	92% WP - Cigar $20-$40/10 cigars; Tobacco/Snuff $2.57/ oz. (p) (q)	92% WP (m) (u)
Virginia	5.3 (h)	30 (c)	50	10% MP (q)	…
Washington	6.5	302.5	9	95% WP (p)(q)(s)	9 /ml - open 27¢/cartridge closed
West Virginia	6.0	120	34	12% WP (p)	7.5¢/ml
Wisconsin	5.0	252	14	71% MP (p)(q)	5¢/ml
Wyoming	4.0	60	44	20% WP (q)	…
Dist. of Columbia	6.0	450 (g)	1	91% WP (p)(t)	96% WP (m) (u)

See footnotes at end of table

TABLE 7.15A
State Tobacco Product and Vaping Excise Tax Rates (As of January 2020) (continued)

Source: Compiled by The Federation of Tax Administrators from various sources, January 2020.

Key:

… – No

N.A. – Not applicable

MP – Manufacturer's Price

WP – Wholesale Price

(a) These states do not have a general sales and gross receipts tax.

(b) The tax rate may be adjusted annually according to a formula based on balances in the unappropriated general fund and the school foundation fund.

(c) Counties and cities may impose an additional tax on a pack of cigarettes: in Alabama, 1¢ to 25¢; Illinois, 10¢ to $4.18; Missouri, 4¢ to 7¢; New York City, $1.50; Tennessee, 1¢; and Virginia, 2¢ to 15¢.

(d) Florida's rate includes a surcharge of $1 per pack.

(e) In addition, Minnesota imposes an in lieu cigarette sales tax determined annually by the Department. The current rate is 61.0¢ through December 31, 2020.

(f) Dealers pay an additional enforcement and administrative fee of 0.05¢ in Tennessee.

(g) In addition, District of Columbia imposes an in lieu cigarette sales tax calculated every March 31. The current rate is 48¢.

(h) Includes statewide 1.0% tax levied by local governments in Virginia.

(i) Includes a statewide 1.25% tax levied by local governments in Utah.

(j) The volume-based tax rates were converted to cents per milliliter of solution. Some states charge different rates for closed cartridges versus volume liquid vaping solution.

(k) Cook County imposed an additional 20 cent/ml tax.

(l) Massachusetts imposed an excise tax on electronic nicotine delivery systems effective June 1, 2020.

(m) These state subject e-cigarette products to the Other Tobacco Tax.

(n) The volume-based tax rates were converted to cents per 10 cigars or per ounce for consistency.

(o) Alabama's cigar tax rate rises with the retail price; the rate on smoking tobacco and snuff depends on package weight.

(p) Twenty-one states (and Massachusetts effective June 1, 2020) impose an excise tax on e-cigarettes or vaping products. See www.taxadmin.org/e-cigarettes for current rates.

(q) Tax rate on Snuff per ounce is $3.00 in CT, 92¢ in DE, 30¢ in IL, 4.75¢ in KY, 95% in MN, 85¢ in MT, 44¢ in NE, 75¢ in NJ, $2.00 in NY, $1.78 in OR, $1.83 in UT, 18¢ in VA, $2.57 in VT, $2.105 in WA, 100% in WI and 60¢ in WY.

(r) Florida's rate includes a 60% surtax.

(s) Little cigars are taxed as cigarettes.

(t) The Dist. of Columbia adjusts the tax rate annually, effective October 1st each year.

(u) E-cigarette products subject to other tobacco tax.

TABLE 7.15B
State Motor Fuel Tax Rates (As of January 1, 2020)

State or other jurisdiction	Gasoline			Diesel fuel			Gasohol		
	Excise	Fee/Tax	Total	Excise	Fee/Tax	Total	Excise	Fee/Tax	Total
Federal (j)	18.3	0.1	18.4	24.3	0.1	24.4	18.3	0.1	18.4
Alabama (a)(i)	24.0		24.0	25.0		25.0	24.0		24.0
Alaska (k)	8.0	0.95	8.95	8.0	0.95	8.95	8.0	0.95	8.95
Arizona (h)(j)	18.0	1.0	19.0	26.0	1.0	27.0	18.0	1.0	19.0
Arkansas (k)	21.5	3.3	24.8	22.5	6.3	28.8	21.5	3.3	24.8
California (g)(k)	47.3	6.0	53.3	36.0	32.0	68.0	47.3	6.0	53.3
Colorado	22.0		22.0	20.5		20.5	22.0		22.0
Connecticut (k)	25.0		25.0	46.5		46.5	25.0		25.0
Delaware (k)	23.0		23.0	22.0		22.0	23.0		23.0
Florida (b)(k)	18.3	16.096	34.396	19.3	13.9	33.2	18.3	16.096	34.396
Georgia (e)(k)	27.9		27.9	31.3		31.3	27.9		27.9
Hawaii (a)(k)	16.0		16.0	16.0		16.0	16.0		16.0
Idaho (k)	32.0	1.0	33.0	32.0	1.0	33.0	32.0	1.0	33.0
Illinois (a)(c)(e)(j)(k)	38.0	1.1	39.1	45.5	1.1	46.6	38.0	1.1	39.1
Indiana (e)(j)	30.0		30.0	49.0		49.0	30.0		30.0
Iowa	30.5		30.5	32.5		32.5	29.0		29.0
Kansas (k)	24.0	0.03	24.03	26.0	0.03	26.03	24.0	0.03	24.03
Kentucky (c)(d)(k)	24.6	1.4	26.0	21.6	1.4	23.0	24.6	1.4	26.0
Louisiana (k)	20.0	0.001	20.001	20.0	0.001	20.001	20.0	0.001	20.001
Maine	30.0		30.0	31.2		31.2	30.0		30.0
Maryland (e)	36.7		36.7	37.45		37.45	36.7		36.7
Massachusetts	24.0		24.0	24.0		24.0	24.0		24.0
Michigan (k)	26.3		26.3	26.3		26.3	26.3		26.3
Minnesota (k)	28.5	0.1	28.6	28.5	0.1	28.6	28.5	0.1	28.6
Mississippi (k)	18.0	0.4	18.4	18.0	0.4	18.4	18.0	0.4	18.4
Missouri (k)	17.0	0.42	17.4	17.0	0.42	17.4	17.0	0.3	17.3
Montana	32.0		32.0	29.45		29.45	32.0		32.0
Nebraska (e)(k)	29.3	0.9	30.2	29.3	0.3	29.6	29.3	0.9	30.2
Nevada (a)(k)	23.0	0.805	23.805	27.0	0.75	27.75	23.0	0.805	23.805
New Hampshire (k)	22.2	1.625	23.825	22.2	1.625	23.825	22.2	1.625	23.825
New Jersey (k)	10.5	30.9	41.4	13.5	35.0	48.5	10.5	30.9	41.40
New Mexico (k)	17.0	1.875	18.875	21.0	1.875	22.875	17.0	1.875	18.875
New York (k)	8.05	17.4	25.45	8.0	15.65	23.65	8.05	17.4	25.5
North Carolina (e)(k)	36.1	0.25	36.35	36.1	0.25	36.35	36.1	0.25	36.35
North Dakota	23.0		23.0	23.0		23.0	23.0		23.0
Ohio	38.5		38.5	47.0		47.0	38.5		38.5
Oklahoma (k)	19.0	1.0	20.0	19.0	1.0	20.0	19.0	1.0	20.0
Oregon (a)	36.0		36.0	36.0		36.0	36.0		36.0
Pennsylvania (e)(k)	57.6		57.6	74.1		74.1	57.6		57.6
Rhode Island (e)(j)	34.0	1.0	35.0	34.0	1.0	35.0	34.0	1.0	35.0
South Carolina (i)(j)(k)	22.0	0.75	22.75	22.0	0.75	22.75	22.0	0.75	22.75
South Dakota (a)(k)	28.0	2.0	30.0	28.0	2.0	30.0	26.6	2.0	28.6
Tennessee (a)(k)	26.0	1.4	27.4	27.0	1.4	28.4	26.0	1.4	27.4
Texas	20.0		20.0	20.0		20.0	20.0		20.0
Utah (d)	31.1		31.1	31.1		31.1	31.1		31.1
Vermont (e)(k)	12.1	18.71	30.81	28.0	4.0	32.0	12.1	18.71	30.81
Virginia (a)(f)	16.2		16.2	20.2		20.2	16.2		16.2
Washington (k)	49.4		49.4	49.4		49.4	49.4		49.4
West Virginia (k)	20.5	15.2	35.7	20.5	15.2	35.7	20.5	15.2	35.7
Wisconsin (k)	30.9	2.0	32.9	30.9	2.0	32.9	30.9	2.0	32.9
Wyoming (k)	23.0	1.0	24.0	23.0	1.0	24.0	23.0	1.0	24.0
Dist. of Columbia	23.5		23.5	23.5		23.5	23.5		23.5

See footnotes at end of table

TABLE 7.15B
State Motor Fuel Tax Rates (As of January 1, 2019) (continued)

Source: Compiled by FTA from various sources. Fee/Taxes column is for comparison purposes and does not include all taxes/fees levied. January 2020.

Note: The tax rates listed are fuel excise taxes collected by distributor/supplier/retailers in each state. Additional taxes may apply to motor carriers. Carrier taxes are coordinated by the International Fuel Tax Association.

Key:

(a) Tax rates do not include local option taxes. In AL, 1 - 3 cents; HI, 8.8 to 18.0 cent; IL, 5 cents in Chicago and 6 cents in Cook county (gasoline only); NV, 4.0 to 9.0 cents; OR, 1 to 5 cents; SD and TN, one cent; and VA 2.1%.

(b) Local taxes for gasoline and gasohol vary from 0 cents to 6.0 cents. Includes Inspection Fee, SCETS, & Statewide Local Tax.

(c) Carriers pay an additional surcharge equal to IL-14.9 cents, KY-2% (g) 4.7% (d).

(d) Tax rate is based on the average wholesale price and is adjusted annually The actual rates are: KY, 9%; and UT, 16.5%.

(e) Portion of the rate is adjustable based on maintenance costs, sales volume, cost of fuel to state government, or inflation.

(f) Large trucks pay an additional (d) 3.5 cents (g) 12.6 cents. Actual rates (g) 5.1%, (d) 6%.

(g) Califonia Gasoline subject to 2.25% sales tax. Diesel subject to a 13% sales tax.

(h) Diesel rate specified is the fuel use tax rate on large trucks. Small vehicles are subject to 18 cent tax rate.

(i) On July 1, 2020, SC tax will increate to 24 cents. On October 1, 2020, AL tax will increase to 26 cents (g) and 27 cents (d).

(j) LUST tax or fee

(k)

Alaska – Refining surcharge
Arkansas – Environmental fee, W. Sales Tax
California – Includes prepaid sales tax

Connecticut – Plus a 8.1% Petroleum tax (gas)
Delaware – Plus 0.9% GRT
Florida – Sales tax added to excise
Georgia – Local sales tax additional
Hawaii – Sales tax additional
Idaho – Clean water fee
Illinois – Sales tax add & environmental fee
Indiana – Sales tax additional
Kansas – Inspection fees
Kentucky – Environmental fee
Louisiana – Inspection fee
Michigan – Sales tax additional
Minnesota – Inspection fee
Mississippi – Environmental fee
Missouri – Inspection & Load fees
Nebraska – Petroleum fee
Nevada – Inspection & cleanup fee
New Hampshire – Oil discharge cleanup fee
New Jersey – Petroleum fee
New Mexico – Petroleum loading fee
New York – Petroleum Tax, Sales tax aditional
North Carolina – Inspection tax
Oklahoma – Environmental fee
Pennsylvania – Oil franchise tax only
South Carolina – Inspection fee
South Dakota – Inspection fee (gasohol E10)
Tennessee – Petroleum Tax & Envir. Fee
Vermont – Cleanup Fee & Trans. Fee
Washington – 0.5% privilege tax
West Virginia – Sales tax added to excise
Wisconsin – Petroleum inspection fee
Wyoming – License tax

TABLE 7.15C
State Alcoholic Beverage Excise Taxes (As of January 2020)

State or other jurisdiction	Distilled spirits			Wine			Beer		
	Excise tax rate ($ per gallon)	General sales tax applies	Other taxes	Excise tax rate ($ per gallon)	General sales tax applies	Other taxes	Excise tax rate ($ per gallon)	General sales tax applies	Other taxes
Alabama	(a)	Yes		$1.70	Yes	$0.26/gallon local; over 16.5% – $9.16/gallon.	$0.53	Yes	$0.52/gallon local tax statewide.
Alaska	12.8	N.A.	under 21% – $2.50/gallon.	2.50	N.A.		1.07	N.A	
Arizona	3	Yes		0.84	Yes	over 24% – $4.00/gallon.	0.16	Yes	
Arkansas	2.5	Yes	under 5% – $0.50/gallon, under 21% – $1.00/gallon; $0.20/case; 3% off- 14% on-premise retail taxes.	0.75	Yes	under 5% – $0.25/gallon; $0.05/case; 3% off- and 10% on-premise.	0.23	Yes	3% off- 10% on-premise tax.
California	3.3	Yes	over 50% – 6.6./gallon.	0.20	Yes	sparkling wine – $0.30/gallon	0.20	Yes	
Colorado	2.28	Yes		0.28	Yes		0.08	Yes	
Connecticut	5.4	Yes	under 7% – $2.46/gallon.	0.79	Yes	over 21% – $1.98/gallon; sparkling – $1.94/gallon.	0.24	Yes	
Delaware	4.5	N.A.	25% or less – $3.00/gallon.	1.63	N.A.		0.26	N.A	
Florida	6.5	Yes	under 17.259% – $2.25/gallon; over 55.780% – $9.53/gallon.	2.25	Yes	over 17.259% – $3.00/gallon; sparkling wine $3.50/gallon.	0.48	Yes	
Georgia	3.79	Yes	$0.83/gallon local tax.	1.51	Yes	over 14% – $2.54/gallon; $0.83/gallon local tax.	0.32	Yes	$0.53/gallon local tax.
Hawaii	5.98	Yes		1.38	Yes	sparkling wine – $2.12/gallon, wine coolers – $0.85/gallon.	0.93	Yes	$0.54/gallon draft beer.
Idaho	(a)	Yes		0.45	Yes		0.15	Yes	over 4% – $0.45/gallon.
Illinois	8.55	Yes	under 20% – $1.39/gallon; $2.68/gallon in Chicago and $2.50/gallon in Cook County.	1.39	Yes	over 20% – $8.55/gallon; ($0.36 - $0.89/gallon in Chicago; ($0.24 - $0.45)/gallon in Cook County.	0.231	Yes	$0.29/gallon in Chicago and $0.09/gallon in Cook County.
Indiana	2.68	Yes	under 15% – $0.47/gallon.	0.47	Yes	over 21% – $2.68/gallon.	0.115	Yes	
Iowa	(a)	Yes		1.75	Yes	under 5% - $0.19/gallon.	0.19	Yes	
Kansas	2.5	N.A.	8% off- and 10% on-premise retail tax.	0.30	...	over 14% – $0.75/gallon; 8% off- and 11% on-premise.	0.18	...	8% off- and 10% on-premise.
Kentucky	1.92	Yes	under 6% – $0.25/gallon; $0.05/case and 11% wholesale tax.	0.50	Yes	10.0% wholesale.	0.08	Yes	10.0% wholesale tax.
Louisiana	3.03	Yes		0.76	Yes	14% to 24% – $1.32/gallon; over 24% and sparkling wine – $2.08/gallon.	0.40	Yes	$0.048/gallon local tax.
Maine	(a)	Yes		0.60	Yes	over 15.5% – sold through state stores, sparkling wine – $1.25/gallon; 7% on-premise sales tax	0.35	Yes	7% on-premise sales tax.
Maryland	1.5	Yes	9% sales tax	0.40	...	9% sales tax	0.09	...	9% sales tax.
Massachusetts	4.05	N.A.	under 15% – $1.10/gallon, over 50% alcohol – $4.05/proof gallon; 0.57% on private club sales.	0.55	...	sparkling wine – $0.70/gallon;	0.11	...	0.57% on private club sales.
Michigan	(a)	Yes		0.51	Yes	over 16% – $0.76/gallon	0.20	Yes	
Minnesota	5.03	N.A.	$0.01/bottle (except miniatures) and 9% sales tax.	0.30	...	14% to 21% – $0.95/gallon; under 24% and sparkling wine – $1.82/gallon; over 24% – $3.52/gallon;	0.148	...	under 3.2% – $0.077/gallon, 9% sales tax.
Mississippi	(a)	Yes		0.35	Yes	sparkling wine and champagne – $1.00/gallon.	0.427	Yes	
Missouri	2	Yes		0.42	Yes	includes additional charges.	0.06	Yes	
Montana	(a)	N.A.		1.02	N.A.	over 16% – sold through state stores.	0.14	N.A	
Nebraska	3.75	Yes		0.95	Yes	over 14% – $1.35/gallon.	0.31	Yes	
Nevada	3.6	Yes	5% to 14% – $0.70/gallon, 15% to 22% – $1.30/gallon.	0.70	Yes	14% to 22% – $1.30/gallon; over 22% – $3.60/gallon.	0.16	Yes	
New Hampshire	(a)	N.A.		0.30	N.A.		0.30	N.A	
New Jersey	5.5	Yes		0.875	Yes		0.12	Yes	
New Mexico	6.06	Yes		1.70	Yes		0.41	Yes	
New York	6.44	Yes	under 24% – $2.54/gal.; additional $1.00/gal. in New York City.	0.30	Yes		0.14	Yes	additional $0.12/gallon in New York City.

See footnotes at end of table

TABLE 7.15C
State Alcoholic Beverage Excise Taxes (As of January 2020) (continued)

State or other jurisdiction	Distilled spirits			Wine			Beer		
	Excise tax rate ($ per gallon)	General sales tax applies	Other taxes	Excise tax rate ($ per gallon)	General sales tax applies	Other taxes	Excise tax rate ($ per gallon)	General sales tax applies	Other taxes
North Carolina	(a)	Yes (b)		1.00	Yes	over 17% – $1.11/gallon.	0.617	Yes	
North Dakota	2.5	N.A.	7% state sales tax.	0.50	...	over 17% – $0.60/gallon; 7% sales tax.	0.16	...	7% state sales tax, bulk beer $0.08/gal.
Ohio	(a)	Yes		0.30	Yes	over 14% to 21% – $0.98/gal., vermouth – $1.08/gal., sparkling wine – $1.48/gal.	0.18	Yes	
Oklahoma	5.56	Yes	13.5% on-premise.	0.72	Yes	sparkling wine – $2.08/gallon; 13.5% on-premise.	0.40	Yes	under 3.2% – $0.36/gallon; 13.5% on-premise.
Oregon	(a)	N.A.		0.67	N.A.	over 14% – $0.77/gallon.	0.08	N.A	
Pennsylvania	(a)	Yes		(c)	Yes		0.08	Yes	
Rhode Island	5.40	Yes		1.40	Yes	sparkling wine – $0.75/gallon.	0.11	Yes	$0.04/case wholesale tax.
South Carolina	2.72	Yes	$5.36/case and 9% surtax; additional 5% on-premise tax.	0.90	Yes	$0.18/gallon additional tax.	0.77	Yes	
South Dakota	3.93	Yes	under 14% – $0.93/gallon; 2% wholesale tax.	0.93	Yes	14% to 20% – $1.45/gallon; over 21% and sparkling wine – $2.07/gallon; 2% wholesale tax.	0.27	Yes	
Tennessee	4.4	Yes	15% on-premise; under 7% – $1.10/gallon.	1.21	Yes	15% on-premise.	1.29	Yes	Excise Barrelage Tax and Wholesale Tax
Texas	2.4	Yes	14.95% on-premise and $0.05/drink on airline sales.	0.204	Yes	over 14% – $0.408/gallon and sparkling wine – $0.516/gallon; 6.7% on-premise and $0.05/drink on airline sales.	0.194	Yes	14.95% on-premise and $0.05/drink on airline sales.
Utah	(a)	Yes		(c)	Yes		0.423	Yes	over 3.2% – sold through state store.
Vermont	(a)	No	10% on-premise sales tax.	0.55	Yes	over 16% – sold through state store; 10% on-premise sales tax.	0.265	Yes	more than 6% alcohol – $0.55; 10% on-premise sales tax.
Virginia	(a)	Yes		1.51	Yes	under 4% – $0.2565/gallon and over 14% – sold through state stores.	0.256	Yes	
Washington	14.27 (d)	N.A.	$9.24/gal. on-premise, 20.5% retail sales tax, 13.7% sales tax to on-premise.	0.87	Yes	over 14% – $1.75/gallon.	0.26	Yes	
West Virginia	(a)	Yes		1.00	Yes	5% local tax.	0.18	Yes	
Wisconsin	3.25	Yes	$0.03/gallon administrative fee.	0.25	Yes	over 14% – $0.45/gallon.	0.06	Yes	
Wyoming	(a)	Yes		(c)	Yes		0.02	Yes	
Dist. of Columbia	1.5	N.A.	9% off- and on-premise sales tax.	0.30	...	9% off- and on-premise sales tax; over 14% – $0.40/gal.; Sparkling – $0.45/gal.	0.09	Yes	9% off- and on-premise sales tax.

Source: Compiled by FTA from state sources.
Key:
N.A. – not applicable.
... – none.
(a) In 17 states, the government directly controls the sales of distilled spirits. Revenue in these states is generated from various taxes, fees, price mark-ups, and net liquor profits.

(b) General sales tax applies to on-premise sales only.
(c) All wine sales are through state stores. Revenue in these states is generated from various taxes, fees, price mark-ups, and net profits.
(d) Washington privatized liquor sales effective June 1, 2012.

TABLE 7.15D
State Cannabis Taxes and Legal Status: July 2020

State or other jurisdiction	Cannabis legality				Other (notes, taxes, agencies, revenues and upcoming ballot initiatives)
	Medical	Recreational	CBD *	Hemp cultivation*	
Alabama	No	No	Restrictions	Yes	The State Attorney General has held that only CBD is legal. Statewide, cannabis that contains more than 0.3-percent THC remains illegal. In March 2020, the AL Senate approved SB 165, that would allow medical marijuana. The legislative session was cut short by the COVID-19 closures and did not receive a House vote.
Alaska	Yes	Yes	Yes	Yes	Legalization was approved with Ballot Measure 2 in 2014. The first cultivation license was granted in July 2016, with retail sales beginning in October 2016 **Taxes:** Excise tax of $50/ounce for flowers Excise tax of $15/ounce for stems and leaves Excise tax of $25/ounce for immature flowers/buds (added 10/2018) **Revenue information:** FY 2017 Revenues $1.7 million. **Agencies Administering:** Licensing and Tracking: Marijuana Control Board: https://www.commerce.alaska.gov/web/AMCO Tax Administration: Alaska Dept. of Revenue: http://tax.alaska.gov/
Arizona	Yes	No	Yes	Yes	**Upcoming 2020 Ballot Initiatives:** 1. Arizona Cannabis Legalization Initiative (2020) 2. Arizona Changes to Medical Marijuana Laws Measure (2020) 3. Arizona Marijuana Legalization, Ban on Taxes, and Automatic Pardons Initiative (2020) 4. Arizona Marijuana Legalization Initiative (2020) 5. Arizona Medical Marijuana Program Rules Amendment (2020)
Arkansas	Yes	No	Yes	Yes	**Upcoming 2022 Ballot Initiative:** Arkansas Recreational Marijuana Initiative (2022) Arkansas Recreational Marijuana Initiative (2022)
California	Yes	Yes	Yes	Yes	Legalization was approved with Proposition 64 in 2016. Personal use and growth were legal beginning in November 2016. Retail sales began January 2018 **Taxes:** Cultivation Tax of $9.25/ounce for flowers [$9.65 after 1/1/20] $2.75/ounce for leaves [$2.87 after 1/1/20] Fresh plant material $1.29/ounce [$1.35 after 1/1/20] Excise tax of 15% of Retail Sales State retail sales tax applies (7.25% plus local taxes) *notes, medical marijuana was exempted from the state sales tax on November 2016 by Prop. 64. **Revenue Information:** FY 2018 Revenues (two quarters) $134 million. **Agencies Administering:** Tracking and Licensing: CalCannabis Cultivations Licensing (CA Dept. of Food & Agriculture); http://calcannabis.cdfa.ca.gov/ Tax Administration: California Dept. of Tax and Fee Administration: https://www.cdtfa.ca.gov/
Colorado	Yes	Yes	Yes	Yes	Legalization began when voters approved Constitutional Amendment 64 in 2012. Colorado became the first state to begin legal sales when retail stores opened in January 2014. **Taxes:** Excise Tax of 15% of Average Market Rate, sales to retail stores Retail Tax of 15% (10% before July 2017) – local government receive 10% of this tax. (2.9% retail sales tax before July 2017) Local Option Retail Tax up to 8% **Revenue Information:** FY 2018 State Revenues $251 million.
Connecticut	Yes	No	Yes	Yes	Medical marijuana is legal.
Delaware	Yes	No	Yes	Yes	Medical marijuana is legal.
Florida	Yes	No	Yes	Yes	**Upcoming Ballot Initiatives:** Florida Marijuana Legalization Initiative (2022) Florida Marijuana Legalization and Medical Marijuana Treatment Center Sales Initiative (2022) Florida Medical Marijuana Plants Initiative (2022) Florida Medical Marijuana for Mental Health Disorders Initiative (2022)
Georgia	No	No	Restrictions	Yes	Medical cannabis oil with up to 5% THC is legal.
Hawaii	Yes	No	Yes	No	Medical marijuana is legal.
Idaho	No	No	Restrictions	No	The Idaho Attorney General delivered the 2015 opinion that CBD containing 0% THC is permissible as long as it is derived from one of the five identified (non-flower) parts of the cannabis plant.
Illinois	Yes	Yes	Yes	Yes	Bipartisan bill H.B. 1438, which the General Assembly passed May 31, will allow adults 21 and older to buy marijuana from licensed dispensaries starting January 1, 2020. Pritzker signed the bill June 25. 7% Tax on Sales to Dispensaries **Retail Excise Taxes** 10% on marijuana with THC level of 35% or less 20% on cannabis-infused products 25% for marijuana with THC level above 35% Local option tax up to 3% [7/1/2020]
Indiana	No	No	Restrictions	Yes	CBD oil containing no more than 0.3 percent THC is legal.
Iowa	No	No	Restrictions	Yes	Medical cannabis oil is legal. Effective July 1, 2020, the law allows products with a total of 4.5 grams of THC every 90 days, with some exceptions where a greater quantity is needed.
Kansas	No	No	Restrictions	Yes	

See footnotes at end of table

TABLE 7.15D
State Cannabis Taxes and Legal Status: July 2020 (continued)

State or other jurisdiction	Cannabis legality				Other (notes, taxes, agencies, revenues and upcoming ballot initiatives)
	Medical	Recreational	CBD *	Hemp cultivation*	
Kentucky	No	No	Restrictions	Yes	Medical cannabis oil is legal. In February 2020, the Kentucky House passed a medical cannabis bill, HB 136. Due to the COVID-19 pandemic, the Senate chose not to focus on the issue before their April 2020 adjournment.
Louisiana	Yes	No	Yes	Yes	Medical marijuana is legal.
Maine	Yes	Yes	Yes	Yes	Voters approved marijuana legalization with the Ballot Question 1 in 2016. This allowed possession and individuals to grow marijuana beginning on January 30, 2017. On May 2, 2018, the Legislature overrode the Governor's veto of LD 1719, An Act to Implement a Regulatory Structure for Adult Use Marijuana. **Taxes:** Excise tax of $335 per pound – flower Excise tax of $94 per pound – trim Excise tax of $0.35 per seed Retail sales tax of 10%
Maryland	Yes	No	Yes	Yes	Medical marijuana is legal.
Massachusetts	Yes	Yes	Yes	Yes	Legalization was approved with Ballot Question 4 in 2016. While the ballot question set January 2018 as the date for retail sales to begin, legislation H 3818 delayed first sales until after July 1, 2018 and set various tax rates. It also created a Cannabis Control Commission with 5 appointed members. The first cultivation license was issued on June 21, 2018, and the first retail store opened on November 20, 2018. **Taxes:** 10.75% Excise Tax on Retail sales (initially 3.75% on ballot) 6.25% Retail Sales Tax applies Local Option Excise Tax of up to 3% is permitted (initially 2% on ballot) **Agencies Administering: Tracking and Licensing: Massachusetts Cannabis Control Commission** *https://mass-cannabis-control.com/* Taxes: Massachusetts Dept. of Revenue *https://www.mass.gov/marijuana-retail-taxes* *https://www.mass.gov/marijuana-retail-taxes*
Michigan	Yes	Yes	Yes	Yes	Voters recently approved Ballot Proposal 1 in the 2018 election authorizing the cultivation, distribution and retail sales of recreational Marijuana. State policymakers now need to approve legislation to implement the proposal. Details on taxes and regulation will be spelled out in future legislation. Legal retail sales began on December 6, 2019. **Taxes:** 10% Retail Excise Tax 6% State Sales Tax (effective February 6, 2020) **Agencies Administering:** Tracking and Licensing: Michigan Dept. of Licensing and Regulatory Affairs *https://www.michigan.gov/lara/0,4601,7-154-89334_79571_90056---,00.html* **Taxes: To Be Administered by the Michigan Department of Treasury** *https://www.michigan.gov/treasury* The Department has recently released Bulletin 2019-17 discussing collections of retail excise tax.
Minnesota	Yes	No	Yes	Yes	Medical marijuana is legal.
Mississippi	No	No	Restrictions	No	**Upcoming Ballot Initiatives:** Mississippi Initiative 65 and Alternative 65A, Medical Marijuana Amendment (2020) 1. Mississippi Marijuana Legalization, Criminal Record Expungement, and Firearm Possession for Non-Violent Felons Amendment (2022) 2. Mississippi Marijuana Legalization Amendment (2022)
Missouri	Yes	No	Yes	Yes	Medical marijuana is legal.
Montana	Yes	No	Yes	Yes	Medical marijuana is legal. **Upcoming Ballot Initiatives:** 1. Montana CI-118, Allow for a Legal Age for Marijuana Amendment (2020 2. Montana I-190, Marijuana Legalization and Tax Initiative (2020)
Nebraska	No	No	No	Yes	**Upcoming Ballot Initiatives:** 1. Nebraska Cannabis Legalization Initiative (2020) 2. Nebraska Medical Marijuana Initiative (2020) 3. Nebraska Cannabis Legalization Initiative (2020)
Nevada	Yes	Yes	Yes	Yes	Legal sales of Marijuana were approved by the voters with Ballot Question 2 in 2016. While the Ballot Question setup January 1, 2017 as the start date for retail sales, the Dept. of Taxation approved regulations allowing sales to begin on July 1, 2017. Due to supply conditions, the Department temporarily permitted medical facilities to sell recreational marijuana. **Taxes:** Wholesale Excise Tax 15% [Fair Market Value determined by DOT], also applied to medical marijuana Retail Tax 10% Sales tax imposed 6.85% (plus local) **Agencies Administering:** Tracking, Licensing and Taxes: Nevada Dept. of Taxation *http://marijuana.nv.gov/*
New Hampshire	Yes	No	Yes	No	Medical marijuana is legal.
New Jersey	Yes	No	Yes	Yes	Medical marijuana is legal. **Upcoming Ballot Initiatives:** New Jersey Marijuana Legalization Amendment (2020)

See footnotes at end of table

TABLE 7.15D
State Cannabis Taxes and Legal Status: July 2020 (continued)

| State or other jurisdiction | Cannabis legality | | | | Other (notes, taxes, agencies, revenues and upcoming ballot initiatives) |
	Medical	Recreational	CBD *	Hemp cultivation*	
New Mexico	Yes	No	Yes	Yes	Medical marijuana is legal.
New York	Yes	No	Yes	Yes	Medical marijuana is legal.
North Carolina	No	No	Restrictions	Yes	
North Dakota	Yes	No	Yes	Yes	**Upcoming Ballot Initiatives:** 1. North Dakota Legalize Marijuana and Allow Home Growth Amendment (2020) 2. North Dakota Marijuana Legalization Statutory Initiative (2020)
Ohio	Yes	No	Yes	No	**Upcoming Ballot Initiatives:** 1. Ohio Marijuana Legalization Initiative (2020) 2. Ohio Right to Marijuana Use Initiative (2020)
Oklahoma	Yes	No	Yes	Yes	**Upcoming Ballot Initiatives:** 1. Oklahoma State Question 808, Constitutional Right to Cannabis Consumption Initiative (2020) 2. Oklahoma State Question 812, Marijuana Decriminalization Initiative (2020) 3. Oklahoma State Question 813, Marijuana Legalization Initiative (2020)
Oregon	Yes	Yes	Yes	Yes	Voters approved Initiative Measure 91 in 2014 that legalized recreational marijuana allowing possession of up to 8 ounces and four plants. It also required the Liquor Control Commission to regulate sales. Legislation was approved in the 2015 session that allowed retail sales to begin on October 1, 2015, initially through medical dispensaries on a temporary basis. Recreational marijuana retail licenses were granted beginning October 1, 2016. **Taxes:** 17% Retail Sales Tax a temporary 25% tax was imposed on Medical Dispensary sales January–December 2016. Local Option sales tax up to 3% **Agencies Administering:** Tracking and Licensing: Oregon Liquor Control Commission *https://www.oregon.gov/olcc/Pages/index.aspx* Taxes: Oregon Dept. of Revenue *https://www.oregon.gov/DOR/Pages/index.aspx* **Upcoming Ballot Initiatives:** Oregon Amend Recreational and Medical Cannabis Laws Initiative (2020)
Pennsylvania	Yes	No	Yes	Yes	Medical marijuana is legal.
Rhode Island	Yes	No	Yes	Yes	Medical marijuana is legal.
South Carolina	No	No	Restrictions	Yes	
South Dakota	No	No	No	Yes	Upcoming Ballot Initiatives 1.South Dakota Constitutional Amendment A, Marijuana Legalization Initiative (2020) 2. South Dakota Initiated Measure 26, Medical Marijuana Initiative (2020)
Tennessee	No	No	Restrictions	Yes	
Texas	No	No	Restrictions	Yes	Medical cannabis oil is legal.
Utah	Yes	No		Yes	Medical marijuana is legal.
Vermont	Yes	Yes	Yes	Yes	In January 2018, the governor signed H. 511 permitting the possession of 1 ounce of marijuana and two plants. It did NOT allow the retail sales of marijuana but created a Marijuana Advisory Commission which would submit recommendations to the legislature on future retail sales. **Agencies Administering:** Vermont Marijuana Advisory Commission *https://marijuanacommission.vermont.gov/*
Virginia	No	No	Restrictions	Yes	Medical cannabis oil is legal.
Washington	Yes	Yes	Yes	Yes	Voters approved Measure Initiative 502 in 2012 which legalized the possession, distribution and sales of marijuana. It required the State Liquor Control Board to regulate and tax the retail sale of marijuana. Legislation in 2015 (H 2136) changed the tax rate (from 25% wholesale and retail tax) to the current 37% rate and changed the name to the Washington State Liquor and Cannabis Board. Retail sales began July 2014, with Washington became the second state to permit retail sales of recreational marijuana. Note, medical dispensaries were required to obtain a retail license after June 2016. **Taxes:** 37% Tax on Retail Sales 6.5% Retail Sales Tax (plus local tax) [medical is exempt from sales taxes after June 2016] **Agencies Administering:** Tracking, Licensing and Taxes: Washington State Liquor and Cannabis Board *https://lcb.wa.gov/* **Upcoming Ballot initiatives:** Washington Prohibit Marijuana Cultivation and Sales in Residential Zones Initiative (2020)
West Virginia	Yes	No	Yes	Yes	Medical marijuana is legal.
Wisconsin	No	No	Restrictions	Yes	
Wyoming	No	No	Restrictions	Yes	CBD products that contain less than 0.3% THC by weight are legal to use and possess.
Dist. of Columbia	Yes	Yes	Yes	No	Medical and recreational marijuana are legal. Voters approved Ballot Initiative 71 in 2014 that allowed possession of less than two ounces of marijuana. However, Federal law does NOT permit the cultivation, distribution and retail sales of Marijuana.
Guam	Yes	Yes	Restrictions	Yes	Legal for medical purposes since 2015 and legal for recreational purposes since April 2019. Passing via a ballot referendum in 2014.
CNMI*	Yes	Yes	Yes	Yes	On September 21, 2018 Gov. Ralph Torres legalized recreational cannabis consumption for adults (over age 21), and medical use of cannabis.

See footnotes at end of table

TABLE 7.15D
State Cannabis Taxes and Legal Status: July 2020 (continued)

Source: The Federation of Tax Administrators and The Council of State Governments' survey of state web sites, July 2020.

* Commonwealth of Northern Mariana Islands

Notes:

1. Hemp-derived CBD products are legal under Federal Law in the United States; however, individual state laws vary widely. The states may enact their own laws governing hemp-derived CBD.

2. The 2018 Farm Bill re-classified hemp as an agricultural commodity and made its cultivation federally legal. This created a legal distinction between hemp and marijuana. Hemp is defined as cannabis with less than 0.3% THC, and marijuana refers to cannabis with more than 0.3% THC. This distinction under federal law legalized CBD derived from cannabis with less than 0.3% THC, as long as it has been cultivated following federal and state regulations. Under federal legal criteria, CBD oil must contain no more than 0.3 percent THC. The 2018 Farm Bill legislation does not legalize CBD throughout the United States. The Food and Drug Administration (FDA) has the authority to regulate CBD product labeling, therapeutic claims and the use of CBD as a food additive. The FDA has declared that hemp-derived CBD may not be added to food and beverages, or marketed as a dietary supplement. The agency prohibits labeling that could be interpreted as medical claims about CBD. The Farm Bill, in addition to regulating CBD also gave states the option to regulate and prohibit the cultivation and commerce of CBD. States may still regulate CBD in food, beverages, dietary supplements, and cosmetic products independently, even before the FDA finalizes its policies. There are currently no laws in the CNMI stating that CBD cannot be used as an additive in food.

TABLE 7.16A
State Sales Tax Rates and Food and Drug Exemptions (As of January 1, 2020)

State or other jurisdiction	Tax rate (percentage)	Exemptions		
		Food (a)	Prescription drugs	Nonprescription drugs
Alabama	4.0	...	★	...
Alaska	none	none	none	none
Arizona	5.6	★	★	...
Arkansas	6.5	1.5% (c)	★	...
California (b)	7.25	★	★	...
Colorado	2.9	★	★	...
Connecticut	6.35	★	★	...
Delaware	none	none	none	none
Florida	6.0	★	★	★
Georgia	4.0	★ (c)	★	...
Hawaii	4.0	...	★	...
Idaho	6.0	...	★	...
Illinois	6.25	1%	1%	1%
Indiana	7.0	★	★	...
Iowa	6.0	★	★	...
Kansas	6.5	...	★	...
Kentucky	6.0	★	★	...
Louisiana	4.45	★ (c)	★	...
Maine	5.5	★	★	...
Maryland	6.0	★	★	★
Massachusetts	6.25	★	★	...
Michigan	6.0	★	★	...
Minnesota	6.875	★	★	★
Mississippi	7.0	...	★	...
Missouri	4.225	1.225%	★	...
Montana	none	none	none	none
Nebraska	5.5	★	★	...
Nevada	6.85	★	★	...
New Hampshire	none	none	none	none
New Jersey	6.625	★	★	★
New Mexico	5.125	★	★	...
New York	4.0	★	★	★
North Carolina	4.75	★ (c)	★	...
North Dakota	5.0	★	★	...
Ohio	5.75	★	★	...
Oklahoma	4.5	...	★	...
Oregon	none	none	none	none
Pennsylvania	6.0	★	★	★
Rhode Island	7.0	★	★	...
South Carolina	6.0	★	★	...
South Dakota	4.5	...	★	...
Tennessee	7.0	4% (c)	★	...
Texas	6.25	★	★	★
Utah	6.1 (d)	3.0% (d)	★	...
Vermont	6.0	★	★	★
Virginia	5.3 (e)	2.5% (e)	★	★
Washington	6.5	★	★	...
West Virginia	6.0	★	★	...
Wisconsin	5.0	★	★	...
Wyoming	4.0	★	★	...
Dist. of Columbia	6.0	★	★	★

Source: Compiled by FTA from various sources, January 2020.
Key:
★ –Indicates exempt from tax.
... –Indicates subject to general sales tax rate.
(a) Some states tax food, but allow a rebate or income tax credit to compensate poor households. They are: HI, ID, KS, OK, and SD.
(b) Tax rate may be adjusted annually according to a formula based on balances in the unappropriated general fund and the school foundation fund.
(c) Food sales subject to local taxes.
(d) Includes a statewide 1.25% tax levied by local governments in Utah.
(e) Includes statewide 1.0% tax levied by local governments in Virginia.

TABLE 7.16B
State Sales Tax Rates and Vendor Discounts (As of January 1, 2020)

State or other jurisdiction	State sales tax rate (percent)	Rank	Vendor discount (percent)	Max/Min
Alabama	4.0%	41	5.0%-2.0% (a)	$400/month (max)
Alaska		N/A		
Arizona	5.6	28	1 (b)	$10,000/year (max)
Arkansas	6.5	9	2.0	$1,000/month (max)
California	7.25	1	None	
Colorado	2.9	46	4.0 (c)	
Connecticut	6.35	12	None	
Delaware		N/A		
Florida	6.0	16	2.5	$30/report (max)
Georgia	4.0	41	3.0-0.5 (a)	
Hawaii	4.0	41	None	
Idaho	6.0	16	None (d)	
Illinois	6.25	13	1.75	$5/year (min)
Indiana (e)	7.0	2	0.73 (e)	
Iowa	6.0	16	None	
Kansas	6.5	9	None	
Kentucky	6.0	16	1.75-1.5 (a)	$50/month (max)
Louisiana	4.5	36	0.84%	$1,500/month (max)
Maine	5.5	29	None (d)	
Maryland	6.0	16	1.2-0.90 (a)	$500/return (max)
Massachusetts	6.25	13	None	
Michigan	6.0	16	0.5 (f)	$6/month (min), $15,000/month (max)
Minnesota	6.875	6	None	
Mississippi	7.0	2	2.0	$50/month (max)
Missouri	4.225	39	2.0	
Montana		N/A		
Nebraska	5.5	29	2.5	$75/month (max)
Nevada	6.85	6	0.25	
New Hampshire (g)		N/A		
New Jersey	6.625	8	None	
New Mexico	5.125	31	None	
New York	4.0	41	5.0	$200/quarter (max)
North Carolina	4.75	35	None	
North Dakota	5.0	32	1.5	$110/month (max)
Ohio	5.75	27	0.75	
Oklahoma	4.5	36	None	
Oregon		N/A		
Pennsylvania	6.0	16	1.0	$25/month (min)
Rhode island	7.0	2	None	
South Carolina	6.0	16	3.0-2.0 (a)	$10,000/year (max)
South Dakota	4.5	36	1.5	$70/month (max)
Tennessee	7.0	2	None	
Texas	6.25	13	0.5 (h)	
Utah (i)	4.7	34	1.31	
Vermont	6.0	16	None	
Virginia (i)	4.3	39	1.6-0.8 (j)	
Washington	6.5	9	None	
West Virginia	6.0	16	None	
Wisconsin	5.0	32	0.5	$10/period (min), $1,000 (max)
Wyoming	4.0	41	1.95-1.0 (a)	$500/month (max)
Dist. of Columbia	6.00	16	None	
U. S. Median	6.00		27 states allow vendor discounts	

See footnotes at end of table

TABLE 7.16B

State Sales Tax Rates and Vendor Discounts (As of January 1, 2020) (continued)

Source: Compiled by FTA from various sources. January 2020.
Key:

(a) In some states, the vendors' discount varies by the amount paid. In AL and SC, the larger discounts apply to the first $100. In GA, the larger discount applies to the first $3,000. In KY, the larger discounts apply to the first $1,000, while MD applies the larger discount to annual collections of $6,000. In WY, the larger discount applies to the first $6,250. The lower discounts apply to the remaining collections above these amounts.

(b) In Arizona, vendor discount rate is 1.2% for electronic filers with a $12,000 annual maximum.

(c) Local option sales tax discount varies from 0% to 3.33%.

(d) Vendors are allowed to keep any excess collections prescribed under the bracket system.

(e) Utilities are not permitted to take discount. Collection allowances are 0.73% if total sales tax collected is less than $60,000; 0.53% if total taxes are between $60,000 and $600,000; 0.26% if total sales tax collected is more than $600,000.

(f) Vendor discount only applies to the first 4.0% of the tax. A 0.75% discount if paid by the 12th of the month.

(g) New Hampshire imposes a 9% tax on meals and rooms, with a vendor discount of 3%.

(h) An additional discount of 1.25% applies for early payment.

(i) Rate does not include a statewide local rate of 1.0% in VA and 1.25% in UT. In UT, a discount of 1% is applicable to local taxes.

(j) Discount varies; 1.1% (1.6% for food) of the first $62,500, 0.84% (1.2%) of the amount to $208,000, and 0.56% (0.8%) of the remainder. Applies to the state tax only. No discount allowed on electronically filed returns.

TABLE 7.17
State Individual Income Taxes (Tax rates for the tax year 2020 – as of January 1, 2020)

State or other jurisdiction	Tax rate range (in percents) Low	High	Number of brackets	Income brackets Lowest	Highest	Personal exemptions Single	Married	Dependents	Standard deduction Single	Married	Federal income tax deductible
Alabama	2.0	5.0	3	500 (b)	3,001 (b)	1,500	3,000	500 (e)	2,500 (y)	7,500 (y)	★
Alaska					(No state income tax)						...
Arizona (a)	2.59	4.5	5	26,500 (b)	159,000 (b)	...	...	100 (c)	12,400 (d)	24,800 (d)	...
Arkansas (a)	2.0	6.6 (f)	6	4,600	80,801	26 (c)	52 (c)	26 (c)	2,200	4,400	...
California (a)	1.0	12.3 (g)	9	8,809 (b)	590,742 (b)	122 (c)	244 (c)	378 (c)	4,537 (a)	9,074 (a)	...
Colorado	4.63		1	Flat rate		(d)	(d)	(d)	12,400 (d)	24,800 (d)	...
Connecticut	3.0	6.99	7	10,000 (b)	500,000 (b)	15,000 (h)	24,000 (h)	0	(h)	(h)	...
Delaware	0.0	6.6	7	2,000	60,001	110 (c)	220 (c)	110 (c)	3,250	6,500	...
Florida					(No state income tax)						★
Georgia	1.0	5.75	6	750 (i)	7,001 (i)	2,700	7,400	3,000	4,600	6,000	...
Hawaii	1.4	11.0	12	2,400 (b)	200,000 (b)	1,144	2,288	1,144	2,200	4,400	...
Idaho (a)	1.125	6.925	7	1,541 (b)	11,554 (b)	(d)	(d)	(d)	12,400 (d)	24,800 (d)	...
Illinois (a)	4.95		1	Flat rate		2,275	4,550	2,275	...	...	...
Indiana	3.23		1	Flat rate		1,000	2,000	2,500 (j)	...	...	...
Iowa (a)	0.33	8.53	9	15,666	74,970	40 (c)	80 (c)	40 (c)	2,110 (a)	5,210 (a)	★
Kansas	3.1	5.7	3	15,000 (b)	30,000 (b)	2,250	4,500	2,250	3,000	7,500	...
Kentucky	5.0		1	Flat rate		None			2,590	2,650	...
Louisiana	2.0	6.0	3	12,500 (b)	50,001 (b)	4,500 (k)	9,000 (k)	1,000	(k)	(k)	★
Maine (a)	5.8	7.15	3	22,200 (l)	52,600 (l)	4,300	8,600	4,300	12,400 (d)	24,800 (d)	...
Maryland	2.0	5.75	8	1,000 (m)	250,000 (m)	3,200	6,400	3,200	2,250 (z)	4,500 (z)	...
Massachusetts	5.0		1	Flat rate		4,400	8,800	1,000	...	...	...
Michigan (a)	4.25		1	Flat rate		4,400	8,800	4,400	...	...	...
Minnesota (a)	5.35	9.85	4	26,960 (n)	164,401 (n)	(d)	(d)	4,250	12,400 (d)	24,800 (d)	...
Mississippi	3.0	5.0	3	5,000	10,001	6,000	12,000	1,500	2,300	4,600	...
Missouri (a)	1.5	5.4	9	1,053	8,424	(d)	(d)	(d)	12,400 (d)	24,800 (d)	★(o)
Montana (a)	1.0	6.9	7	3,100	18,400	2,510	5,020	2,510	4,710 (z)	9,420 (z)	★(o)
Nebraska (a)	2.46	6.84	4	3,290 (b)	31,750 (b)	140 (c)	280 (c)	140 (c)	7,000	14,000	...
Nevada					(No state income tax)						...
New Hampshire				(State income tax of 5% on dividends and interest income only.)							...
New Jersey	1.4	10.75	6	20,000 (p)	5,000,000 (p)	1,000	2,000	1,500	...	...	...
New Mexico	1.7	4.9	4	5,500 (q)	16,001 (q)	(d)	(d)	(d)	12,400 (d)	24,800 (d)	...
New York (a)(aa)	4.0	8.82	8	8,500 (b)	1,077,550 (b)	0	0	1,000	8,000	16,000	...
North Carolina	5.25		1	Flat rate		None			10,750	21,500	...
North Dakota (a)	1.1	2.9	5	40,125 (r)	440,600 (r)	(d)	(d)	(d)	12,400 (d)	24,800 (d)	...
Ohio (a)	0.0	4.797	6	21,750	217,400	2,350 (s)	4,700 (s)	2,350 (s)	...	...	...
Oklahoma	0.5	5.0	6	1,000 (t)	7,200 (t)	1,000	2,000	1,000	6,350	12,700	...
Oregon (a)	4.75	9.9	4	3,600 (b)	125,000 (b)	210 (c)	420 (c)	210 (c)	2,315	4,630	★(o)
Pennsylvania	3.07		1	Flat rate		None			...	...	...
Rhode Island (a)	3.75	5.99	3	65,250	148,350	4,100	8,200	4,100	8,900 (y)	17,800 (y)	...
South Carolina (a)	0.0	7.0	6	3,070	15,400	(d)	(d)	(d)	12,400 (d)	24,800 (d)	...
South Dakota					(No state income tax)						...
Tennessee	(State income tax of 1% on dividends and interest income only (x).)					1,250	2,500	0	...	...	...
Texas					(No state income tax)						...
Utah	4.95		1	Flat rate		...	...	...	(u)	(u)	...
Vermont (a)	3.55	8.75	4	40,350 (v)	204,000 (v)	4,250	83,500	4,250	6,150	12,300	...
Virginia	2.0	5.75	4	3,000	17,001	930	1,860	930	4,500	9,000	...
Washington					(No state income tax)						...
West Virginia	3.0	6.5	5	10,000	60,000	2,000	4,000	2,000	...	...	...
Wisconsin (a)	4.0	7.65	4	11,970 (w)	263,480 (w)	700	1,400	700	11,050 (y)	22,999 (y)	...
Wyoming					(No state income tax)						...
Dist. of Columbia	4.0	8.95	6	10,000	1,000,000	(d)	(d)	(d)	12,400 (d)	24,800 (d)	...

See footnotes at end of table

TABLE 7.17
State Individual Income Taxes (Tax rates for the tax year 2020 – as of January 1, 2020) (continued)

Source: The Federation of Tax Administrators from various sources, February 2020.

Key:

★ – Provision for

… – No provision

(a) 19 states have statutory provision for automatically adjusting to the rate of inflation the dollar values of the income tax brackets, standard deductions, and/or personal exemptions. Michigan indexes the personal exemption only. Oregon does not index the income brackets for $125,000 and over.

(b) For joint returns, taxes are twice the tax on half the couple's income.

(c) The personal exemption takes the form of a tax credit instead of a deduction

(d) These states use the personal exemption/standard deduction amounts provided in the federal Internal Revenue Code.

(e) In Alabama, the per-dependent exemption is $1,000 for taxpayers with state AGI of $20,000 or less, $500 with AGI from $20,001 to $100,000, and $300 with AGI over $100,000.

(f) Arkansas has separate brackets for taxpayers with income under $75,000 and $21,000.

(g) California imposes an additional 1% tax on taxable income over $1 million, making the maximum rate 13.3% over $1 million.

(h) Connecticut's personal exemption incorporates a standard deduction. An additional tax credit is allowed ranging from 75% to 0% based on state adjusted gross income. Exemption amounts are phased out for higher income taxpayers until they are eliminated for households earning over $71,000.

(i) The Georgia income brackets reported are for single individuals. For married couples filing jointly, the same tax rates apply to income brackets ranging from $1,000, to $10,000.

(j) In Indiana, includes an additional exemption of $1,500 for each dependent child.

(k) The amounts reported for Louisiana are a combined personal exemption-standard deduction.

(l) The income bracket reported for Maine are for single individuals. For married couples filing jointly, the same tax rates apply to income brackets ranging from $44,450 to $105,200.

(m) The income brackets reported for Maryland are for single individuals. For married couples filing jointly, the same tax rates apply to income brackets ranging from $1,000, to $300,000.

(n) The income brackets reported for Minnesota are for single individuals. For married couples filing jointly, the same tax rates apply to income brackets ranging from $39,410 to $273,470.

(o) The deduction for federal income tax is limited to $5,000 for individuals and $10,000 for joint returns in Missouri and Montana, and to $6,500 for all filers in Oregon.

(p) The New Jersey rates reported are for single individuals. For married couples filing jointly, the tax rates also range from 1.4% to 10.75%, with 8 brackets and the same high and low income ranges.

(q) The income brackets reported for New Mexico are for single individuals. For married couples filing jointly, the same tax rates apply to income brackets ranging from $8,000 to $24,000.

(r) The income brackets reported for North Dakota are for single individuals. For married couples filing jointly, the same tax rates apply to income brackets ranging from $67,050 to $440,600.

(s) Ohio provides an additional tax credit of $20 per exemption. Exemption amounts reduced for higher income taxpayers.

(t) The income brackets reported for Oklahoma are for single persons. For married persons filing jointly, the same tax rates apply to income brackets ranging from $2,000, to $12,200.

(u) Utah provides a tax credit equal to 6% of the federal personal exemption amounts (and applicable standard deduction).

(v) Vermont's income brackets reported are for single individuals. For married taxpayers filing jointly, the same tax rates apply to income brackets ranging from $67,450 to $248,350.

(w) The Wisconsin income brackets reported are for single individuals. For married taxpayers filing jointly, the same tax rates apply income brackets ranging from $15,960, to $351,310.

(x) Tennessee Hall Tax Rate on Dividends and Interest is being phased out, 1% reduction each year

(y) Alabama standard deduction is phased out for incomes over $23,000. Rhode Island exemptions & standard deductions phased out for incomes over $203,850; Wisconsin standard deduciton phases out for income over $15,939.

(z) Maryland standard deduction limited to 15% of AGI; Montana, 20% of AGI.

TABLE 7.18
State Personal Income Taxes: Federal Starting Points (As of January 1, 2020)

State or other jurisdiction	Relation to Internal Revenue Code	Federal tax base used as starting point to calculate state taxable income
Alabama	. . .	. . .
Alaska	⸺ No state income tax ⸺	
Arizona	1/1/19	Adjusted gross income
Arkansas	. . .	. . .
California	1/1/15	Adjusted gross income
Colorado	Current	Taxable income
Connecticut	Current	Adjusted gross income
Delaware	Current	Adjusted gross income
Florida	⸺ No state income tax ⸺	
Georgia	1/1/19	Adjusted gross income
Hawaii	12/31/18	Adjusted gross income
Idaho	1/1/19	Taxable income
Illinois	Current	Adjusted gross income
Indiana	1/1/19	Adjusted gross income
Iowa	Current	Adjusted gross income
Kansas	Current	Adjusted gross income
Kentucky	12/31/18	Adjusted gross income
Louisiana	Current	Adjusted gross income
Maine	12/31/18	Adjusted gross income
Maryland	Current	Adjusted gross income
Massachusetts	1/1/05	Adjusted gross income
Michigan	Current (a)	Adjusted gross income
Minnesota	12/31/18	Adjusted gross income
Mississippi	. . .	. . .
Missouri	Current	Adjusted gross income
Montana	Current	Adjusted gross income
Nebraska	Current	Adjusted gross income
Nevada	⸺ No state income tax ⸺	
New Hampshire	⸺ On interest and dividends only ⸺	
New Jersey	. . .	. . .
New Mexico	Current	Adjusted gross income
New York	Current	Adjusted gross income
North Carolina	1/1/19	Adjusted gross income
North Dakota	Current	Taxable income
Ohio	3/30/18	Adjusted gross income
Oklahoma	Current	Adjusted gross income
Oregon	12/31/18	Taxable income
Pennsylvania	. . .	. . .
Rhode Island	Current	Adjusted gross income
South Carolina	12/31/18	Taxable income
South Dakota	⸺ No state income tax ⸺	
Tennessee	⸺ On interest and dividends only ⸺	
Texas	⸺ No state income tax ⸺	
Utah	Current	Adjusted gross income
Vermont	12/31/18	Adjusted gross income
Virginia	12/31/18	Adjusted gross income
Washington	⸺ No state income tax ⸺	
West Virginia	12/31/18	Adjusted gross income
Wisconsin	12/31/17	Adjusted gross income
Wyoming	⸺ No state income tax ⸺	
Dist. of Columbia	Current	Adjusted gross income

Source: Compiled by the Federation of Tax Administrators from various sources. January 2020.
Note: Includes all legislation enacted through January 1, 2019. The TCJA was signed into law on December 22, 2017, and the Bipartisan Budget Act revising many expired tax breaks was signed on February 9, 2018. A conformity date before these dates would not incorporate those changes.
Key:
. . . – State does not employ a federal starting point.
Current – Indicates state has adopted the Internal Revenue Code as currently in effect.

Dates indicate state has adopted IRC as amended to that date.
(a) Michigan's taxpayers can choose to use either current or 1/1/2018 federal law.

TABLE 7.19
Range of State Corporate Income Tax Rates (For Tax Year 2020 – as of January 1, 2020)

State or other jurisdiction	Tax rate (percent)	Tax brackets		Number of brackets	Financial institution tax rates (percent)(a)	Federal income tax deductible
		Lowest	Highest			
Alabama	6.5	Flat Rate		1	6.5	★
Alaska	0 - 9.4	25,000	222,000	10	0 - 9.4	...
Arizona	4.9 (b)	Flat Rate		1	4.9 (b)	...
Arkansas	1.0 - 6.5	3,000	100,001	6	1.0 - 6.5	...
California	8.84 (b)	Flat Rate		1	10.84 (b)	...
Colorado	4.63	Flat Rate		1	4.63	...
Connecticut	7.5 (c)	Flat Rate		1	7.5 (c)	...
Delaware	8.7	Flat Rate		1	8.7 - 1.7 (d)	...
Florida	4.458 (e)	Flat Rate		1	4.458 (e)	...
Georgia	5.75	Flat Rate		1	5.75	...
Hawaii	4.4 - 6.4 (f)	25,000	100,001	3	7.92 (f)	...
Idaho	6.925 (g)	Flat Rate		1	6.925 (g)	...
Illinois	9.5 (h)	Flat Rate		1	9.5 (h)	...
Indiana	5.5 (i)	Flat Rate		1	6.0	...
Iowa	6.0 - 12.0	25,000	250,001	4	5.0	★ (j)
Kansas	4.0 (k)	Flat Rate		1	2.25 (k)	...
Kentucky	5.0	Flat Rate		1	(a)	...
Louisiana	4.0 - 8.0	25,000	200,001	5	4.0 - 8.0	★
Maine	3.5 - 8.93	350,000	3,500,000	4	1.0 (l)	...
Maryland	8.25	Flat Rate		1	8.25	...
Massachusetts	8.0 (m)	Flat Rate		1	9.0 (m)	...
Michigan	6.0	Flat Rate		1	(a)	...
Minnesota	9.8 (n)	Flat Rate		1	9.8 (n)	...
Mississippi	0 - 5.0	2,000	10,001	4	0 - 5.0	...
Missouri	4.0	Flat Rate		1	7.0	★ (j)
Montana	6.75 (o)	Flat Rate		1	6.75 (o)	...
Nebraska	5.58 - 7.81	100,000		2	(a)	...
Nevada		No corporate income tax				...
New Hampshire	7.7 (p)	Flat Rate		1	7.7 (p)	...
New Jersey	9.0 (q)	Flat Rate		1	9.0 (q)	...
New Mexico	4.8 - 5.9	500,000		2	4.8 - 5.9	...
New York	6.5 (r)	Flat Rate		1	6.5 (r)	...
North Carolina	2.5	Flat Rate		1	2.5	...
North Dakota	1.41 - 4.31 (s)	25,000	50,001	3	1.41 - 4.31 (s)	...
Ohio		(t)			(t)	...
Oklahoma	6.0	Flat Rate		1	6.0	...
Oregon	6.6 - 7.6 (u)	1 million		2	6.6 - 7.6 (u)	...
Pennsylvania	9.99	Flat Rate		1	(a)	...
Rhode Island	7.0 (b)	Flat Rate		1	9.0 (b)	...
South Carolina	5.0	Flat Rate		1	4.5 (v)	...
South Dakota		No corporate income tax			6.0 - 0.25 (b)	...
Tennessee	6.5	Flat Rate		1	6.5	...
Texas	(w)				(w)	...
Utah	4.95 (b)	Flat Rate		1	4.95 (b)	...
Vermont	6.0 - 8.5 (b)	10,000	25,000	3	(a)	...
Virginia	6.0	Flat Rate		1	6.0	...
Washington		No corporate income tax				...
West Virginia	6.5	Flat Rate		1	6.5	...
Wisconsin	7.9	Flat Rate		1	7.9	...
Wyoming		No corporate income tax				...
Dist. of Columbia	8.25 (b)	Flat Rate		1	8.25 (b)	...

See footnotes at end of table

TABLE 7.19
Range of State Corporate Income Tax Rates (For tax year 2019–as of January 1, 2019) (continued)

Source: Compiled by the Federation of Tax Administrators from various sources January 2020.

Key:

★ – Yes

… – No

(a) Rates listed are the corporate income tax rate applied to financial institutions or excise taxes based on income. Some states have other taxes based upon the value of deposits or shares.

(b) Minimum tax is $800 in California, $250 in District of Columbia, $50 in Arizona and North Dakota (banks), $400 ($100 banks) in Rhode Island, $200 per location in South Dakota (banks), $100 in Utah, $300 in Vermont.

(c) Connecticut's tax is the greater of the 7.5% tax on net income, a 0.31% tax on capital stock and surplus (maximum tax of $1 million), or $250 (the minimum tax). A 10% surcharge is imposed for tax year 2020.

(d) The Delaware Bank marginal rate decreases over 4 brackets ranging from $20 to $650 million in taxable income. Building and loan associations are taxed at a flat 8.7%.

(e) The Florida tax rate may be adjusted downward if certain revenue targets are met.

(f) Hawaii taxes capital gains at 4%. Financial institutions pay a franchise tax of 7.92% of taxable income (in lieu of the corporate income tax and general excise taxes).

(g) Idaho's minimum tax on a corporation is $20. The $10 Permanent Building Fund Tax must be paid by each corporation in a unitary group filing a combined return. Taxpayers with gross sales in Idaho under $100,000, and with no property or payroll in Idaho, may elect to pay 1% on such sales (instead of the tax on net income).

(h) The Illinois rate of 9.5% is the sum of a corporate income tax rate of 7.0% plus a replacement tax of 2.5%.

(i) The Indiana Corporate tax rate is scheduled to decrease to 5.25% on July 1, 2020. Bank tax rate is scheduled to decrease to 5.5% on 1/1/21.

(j) 50% of the federal income tax is deductible.

(k) In addition to the flat 4% corporate income tax, Kansas levies a 3.0% surtax on taxable income over $50,000. Banks pay a privilege tax of 2.25% of net income, plus a surtax of 2.125% (2.25% for savings and loans, trust companies, and federally chartered savings banks) on net income in excess of $25,000.

(l) The state franchise tax on financial institutions is either (1) the sum of 1% of the Maine net income of the financial institution for the taxable year, plus 8¢ per $1,000 of the institution's Maine assets as of the end of its taxable year, or (2) 39¢ per $1,000 of the institution's Maine assets as of the end of its taxable year.

(m) Business and manufacturing corporations pay an additional tax of $2.60 per $1,000 on either taxable Massachusetts tangible property or taxable net worth allocable to the state (for intangible property corporations). The minimum tax for both corporations and financial institutions is $456.

(n) In addition, Minnesota levies a 5.8% tentative minimum tax on Alternative Minimum Taxable Income. Minnesota also imposes a surtax ranging up to $10,380.

(o) Montana levies a 7% tax on taxpayers using water's edge combination. The minimum tax per corporation is $50; the $50 minimum applies to each corporation included on a combined tax return. Taxpayers with gross sales in Montana of $100,000 or less may pay an alternative tax of 0.5% on such sales, instead of the net income tax.

(p) New Hampshire's 7.7% Business Profits Tax is imposed on both corporations and unincorporated associations with gross income over $50,000. In addition, New Hampshire levies a Business Enterprise Tax of 0.675% on the enterprise base (total compensation, interest and dividends paid) for businesses with gross receipts over $208,000 or enterprise base over $104,000, adjusted every biennium for CPI. The Business Profits Tax is scheduled to decrease to 7.5% for tax year 2021.

(q) New Jersey also imposes a 1.5% surtax on taxpayers with income over $1 million in tax year 2020. Small businesses with annual entire net income under $100,000 pay a tax rate of 7.5%; businesses with income under $50,000 pay 6.5%. The minimum Corporation Business Tax is based on New Jersey gross receipts. It ranges from $500 for a corporation with gross receipts less than $100,000, to $2,000 for a corporation with gross receipts of $1 million or more.

(r) New York's General business corporate rate shown. Corporations may also be subject to a capital stocks tax, which is being phased out through 2021. A minimum tax ranges from $25 to $200,000, depending on receipts ($250 minimum for banks). Certain qualified New York manufacturers pay 0%.

(s) North Dakota imposes a 3.5% surtax for filers electing to use the water's edge method to apportion income.

(t) Ohio no longer levies a tax based on income (except for a particular subset of corporations), but instead imposes a Commercial Activity Tax (CAT) equal to $150 for gross receipts sitused to Ohio of between $150,000 and $1 million, plus 0.26% of gross receipts over $1 million. Banks continue to pay a franchise tax of 1.3% of net worth. For those few corporations for whom the franchise tax on net worth or net income still applies, a litter tax also applies.

(u) Oregon's minimum tax for C corporations depends on the Oregon sales of the filing group. The minimum tax ranges from $150 for corporations with sales under $500,000, up to $100,000 for companies with sales of $100 million or above.

(v) South Carolina taxes savings and loans at a 6% rate.

(w) Texas imposes a Franchise Tax, otherwise known as margin tax, imposed on entities with more than $1,130,000 total revenues at rate of 0.75%, or 0.375% for entities primarily engaged in retail or wholesale trade, on lesser of 70% of total revenues or 100% of gross receipts after deductions for either compensation or cost of goods sold.

TABLE 7.20
State Severance Taxes: 2020

State	Title and application of tax (a)	Rate
Alabama	Iron Ore Mining Tax (c)	$.03/ton
	Forest Products Severance Tax	Varies by species and ultimate use.
	Oil and Gas Conservation & Regulation of Production Tax	1% of production from wells permitted from July 1, 1996 thru June 30, 2002 for five years from first production; 1.66% of gross proceeds from offshore production from depths greater than 8,000 feet below mean sea level; 2% of all other production.
	Oil and Gas Privilege Tax on Production	8% of gross value at point of production; 4% of gross value at point of incremental production resulting from a qualified enhanced recovery project; 4% if wells produce 25 bbl. or less oil per day or 200,000 cu. ft. or less gas per day; 6% of gross value at point of production for certain on-shore and off-shore wells. A 50% rate reduction for wells permitted by the oil and gas board on or after July 1, 1996 and before July 1, 2002 for 5 years from initial production, except for replacement wells for which the initial permit was dated before July 1, 1996; 3.65% gross proceeds from offshore production greater than 8,000 ft. below sea level;
	Coal Severance Tax	$0.335/ton (a $0.135/ton tax rate and $0.20/ton tax rate). Effective Aug. 1, 2017, the additional tax rates for coal are $0.025 per ton on underground mining and $0.05 per ton on surface mining. The additional tax will expire two years after its effective date.
	Local Solid Minerals Tax	Varies by county for sand, clay, gravel, granite, shale, and other products.
	Uniform Natural Minerals Tax	$.10/ton.
Alaska	Common Property Fisheries Assessment (b)	$0.10/lb; determined annually by the department of revenue.
	Dive Fishery Management Assessment (b)	Elective; currently 5% or 7% of value for select dive fishery species in select management regions.
	Fisheries Business Tax	Tax based on unprocessed value of fishery resources processed in or exported from the state. 1% of value for shore-based processing in developing fisheries; 3% of value for floating processing in developing fisheries or shore-based processing in established fisheries; 4.5% of value for salmon cannery processing in established fisheries; 5% of value for floating processing in established fisheries.
	Fishery Resource Landing Tax	Tax based on unprocessed value of fishery resources processed outside and first landed in the state. 1% of value for developing fisheries; 3% of value for established fisheries.
	Mining License Tax	Up to 7% of net income and royalties received in connection with mining properties and activities in Alaska. Quarry rock, sand and gravel, and marketable earth mining operations are exempt from the mining license tax. New mining operations exempt for 3-1/2 years after production begins.
	Alaska Oil Production Tax	Alaska will impose a base rate of 35 percent on oil companies' net profits in the state.
	Salmon Enhancement Tax (b)	Elective; 2% or 3% of value for salmon sold in or exported from select aquaculture regions.
	Seafood Development Tax (b)	Elective; currently 1% of value for select commercial fish species in select seafood development regions.
	Seafood Marketing Assessment (b)	Elective; currently 0.5% of value for all commercial fish species exported from, landed or processed in-state.
Arizona	Severance Tax	.025% for metalliferous mining; 0.0313% for nonmetal mining. Additional severance taxes on these and other products are levied at the city or county level. For timber, $2.13 per thousand for board fee (Ponderosa) and $1.50 per thousand board feet (other).
Arkansas	Timber Severance Tax	$0.17/ton (pine), all other $0.125/ton.
	Natural Gas Severance Tax	1.25%, 1.5%, and 5% depending on well classification
	Oil Severance Tax	Crude oil 4% to 5% depending on production levels; additional taxes of 5 mils and $0.02 per barrel of oil produced in the state
	Other Severance Taxes	Separate Rate for each Substance.
	Oil and Gas Conservation Assessment	Maximum 43 mills/bbl. of oil and 9 mills per MCF produced of gas.
	Brine Severance Tax	Tax rate equals $2.75 per 1,000 barrels or $0.00275 per barrel.
California	Oil and Gas Production Assessment	Rate determined annually by Department of Conservation to fund agency operations; no state severance tax. The assessment rate for fiscal year 2019/20 is $0.565336900.
	Lumber Products Assessment	1% on purchases of lumber products and engineered wood products for use in California, based on the selling price of the products.
Colorado	Severance Tax	$0.803 for amount of coal produced above 300,000 tons, rate updated monthly by the department of revenue. 2.25% for metallic minerals above $19 million in gross producer income. $0.05/ton of molybdenum above 625,000 tons. Oil and gas rate varies from 2% to 5% depending on gross income brackets; up to 15 barrels per day of oil 90,000 cubic feet of gas per producing day are exempt. Oil shale is taxed based on years of operation, where 1 year = 1%, 2 years, = 2%, etc. up to 4% of the gross proceeds above the threshold and after the first 180 days of production.
	Oil and Gas Conservation Levy (d)	0.07% charge on all oil, natural gas, and CO2 produced

See footnotes at end of table

TABLE 7.20
State Severance Taxes: 2020 (continued)

State	Title and application of tax (a)	Rate
Florida	Oil Production Tax	5% of gross value for small well oil, and 8% of gross value for ordinary oil production, and 12.5% for escaped oil; tiered formula for tertiary oil.
	Gas and Sulfur Production Tax	The gas base rate ($0.171) times the gas base adjustment rate each fiscal year for gas (Rate as of July 1, 2019 is $0.225 per MCF); and the sulfur base rate ($2.43) times the sulfur base rate adjustment each fiscal year for sulfur (Rate as of July 1, 2019 is $5.79 per ton).
	Solid Minerals Tax (e)	8% of the value of the minerals severed; heavy minerals (rate computed annually at $1.34/ton plus times the base rate adjustment currently at 2.83490). Year 2020 Tax Rate $3.80 per ton; phosphate rock (rate computed annually at a base rate of $1.80/ton)
Idaho	Mine License Tax	1% of net value of ores mined or extracted and royalties received from mining.
	Oil and Gas Production Tax	2.5% of the gross income earned for the sale of oil and gas.
Illinois	Oil and Gas Production Tax	For first 24 months, rate for oil and gas is 3% of the value. Thereafter, rate will be 6% of the value of gas and rate on oil will be based on each well's average daily production (ADP). ADP less than 25 barrels, rate is 3%; ADP of at least 25 and less than 50 barrels, rate is 4%; ADP of at least 50 and less than 100 barrels, rate is 5%; at least 100 barrels, rate is 6%.
	Timber Fee	4% of purchase price (g)
Indiana	Petroleum Severance Tax (h)	1% of value of petroleum; $0.24 per barrel for oil; and $0.03 per 1000 cu. ft. of natural gas
Kansas	Mineral Tax (i)	8% of gross value of oil and gas, less property tax credit of 3.67% for oil and gas; and $1/ton of coal.
	Oil Inspection Fee/Barrel (i)	$0.015/barrel
	Oil and Gas Conservation Tax	91.00 mills/bbl. crude oil or petroleum marketed or used each month; 12.9 mills/1,000 cu. ft. of gas sold or marketed each month.
	Mined-Land Conservation & Reclamation Tax	"The first-time fee for a mining license is $300. Licenses must be renewed annually. The annual renewal fee varies between $25 and $150 depending upon the amount of material sold or consumed in the previous year. Plus per ton fee of $.03"
Kentucky	Oil Production Tax	4.5% of market value
	Coal Severance Tax	4.5% of gross value, less transportation expenses; $0.50/ton minimum for extraction and processing
	Natural Resource Severance Tax	4.5% of gross value, less transportation expenses
Louisiana	Natural Gas Severance Tax (j)	The natural gas severance tax rate effective July 1, 2019 through June 30, 2020 has been set at 12.5 cents per thousand cubic feet (MCF) measured at a base pressure of 15.025 pounds per square inch absolute and at the temperature base of 60 degrees Fahrenheit.
	Oil/Condensate Severance Tax (j)	Value on a per barrel basis (42 gallons) the rates are: full-rate, 12.5%; incapable oil rate, 6.25%; strip-per oil rate, 3.125%; reclaimed oil, 3.125%; produced water full-rate, 10%; produced water incapable oil rate, 5.0%; produced water stripper oil rate, 2.5%
	Timber Severance Tax (j)	Trees and timber: 2.25% of current stumpage value. Pulpwood: 5% of current stumpage value.
	Mineral Severance Tax (j)	Sulphur, $1.03 per long ton of 2,240 lbs; salt, $0.06 per ton of 2,000 lbs; marble, $0.20 per ton; stone, $0.03 per ton; sand, $0.06 per ton; lignite, $0.12 per ton; salt content in brine, when used in the manufacture of other products and not marketed as salt: $0.005 per ton.
	Oil Field Site Restoration Fee	$.015 per barrel of oil and condensate; $.003 for every thousand cubic feet of gas
	Freshwater Mussel Tax	5% of revenues from the sale of whole freshwater mussels, at the point of first sale.
Maine	Mining Excise Tax	The greater of a tax on facilities and equipment or a tax on gross proceeds.
Maryland	Mine Reclamation Surcharge	$.15/ton of coal removed by open-pit, strip or deep mine methods. Of the $.15 , $.06 is remitted to the county from which the coal was removed.
Michigan	Gas and Oil Severance Tax	5% (gas), 6.6% (oil) and 4% (oil from stripper wells and marginal properties) of gross cash market value of the total production. Maximum additional fee of 1% of gross cash market value on all oil and gas (2020 fee).
Minnesota	Taconite and Iron Sulfides (Production Tax)	$2.811 per taxable ton of concentrates or pellets (rate indexed to inflation by law - 2019 rate is reflected)
	Direct Reduced Iron (k)	$2.811 per taxable ton of concentrates plus an additional $.03 per ton for each 1% that the iron content exceeds 72%
Mississippi	Natural Gas Severance Tax	6% of value at point of gas production; 1.3% for gas produced from a horizontally drilled well for the first 30 months from the first sale of production or until payout of the well cost is achieved, whichever comes first.
	Oil Severance Tax	6% of value at point of oil production; 3% reduced rate for wells using the enhanced oil recovery method; 1.3% for oil produced from a horizontally drilled well for the first 30 months from the first sale of production or until payout of the well cost is achieved, whichever comes first.
	Timber Severance Tax	Varies depending on type of wood and ultimate use.
	Salt Severance Tax	3% of value of entire production in state.

See footnotes at end of table

TABLE 7.20
State Severance Taxes: 2020 (continued)

State	Title and application of tax (a)	Rate
Montana	Coal Severance Tax	Varies from 3% to 15% depending on quality of coal and type of mine.
	Metal Mines License Tax (I)	Progressive rate, taxed on amounts in excess of $250,000. For concentrate shipped to smelter, mill or reduction work, 1.81%. Gold, silver or any platinum group metal shipped to refinery, 1.6%.
	Oil and Natural Gas Production Tax	Varies from 0.8% to 15.1% according to the type of well and type of production.
	Micaceous Mineral Mines License Tax	$.05/ton of concentrates mined, extracted, or produced.
	Cement and Gypsum License Tax	$.22/ton of cement, $.05/ton of gypsum or gypsum products.
	Resource Indemnity Trust & Ground Water Assessment Tax	$25 plus 0.5% of gross value greater than $5,000. For talc, $25 plus 4% of gross value greater than $625. For coal, $25 plus 0.40% of gross value greater than $6,250. For vermiculite, $25 plus 2% of gross value greater than $1,250. For limestone, $25 plus 10% of gross value greater than $250. For industrial garnets, $25 plus 1% of gross value greater than $2,500
	Electrical Energy Producers License Tax	$.0002/kilowatt-hour of electrical energy generated, manufactured or produced.
	Bentonite Production Tax	First 20,000 wet tons per year, $0.00 per ton; 20,001-100,000 wet tons per year, $1.82 per ton; 100,001–250,000 wet tons per year, $1.75 per ton; 250,001-500,000 wet tons per year, $1.63 per ton; 500,001–1,000,000 wet tons per year, $1.46 per ton; over 1,000,000 wet tons per year, $1.17 per ton.
Nebraska	Oil and Gas Severance Tax	3% of value of nonstripper oil and natural gas; 2% of value of stripper oil
	Oil and Gas Conservation Tax	0.3%
	Uranium Tax	2% of gross value over $5 million. The value of the uranium severed subject to tax is the gross value less transportation and processing costs.
Nevada	Minerals Extraction Tax	Between 2% and 5% of net proceeds of each geographically separate extractive operation, based on ratio of net proceeds to gross proceeds of whole operation.
	Oil and Gas Conservation Fee	Up to $0.20 per 50,000 cubic feet of natural gas or barrel of oil.
New Hampshire	Refined Petroleum Products Tax	0.1% of fair market value
	Excavation Tax	$.02 per cubic yard of earth excavated.
	Timber Tax	10% of stumpage value at the time of cutting. Not assessed under the general property tax but rather is taxed by municipalities.
New Mexico	Resources Excise Tax	Severance: potash .5%, molybdenum .125%, all others .75% of value. Processing: timber .375%. Potash .125%. Molybdenum .125%. All others .75%
	Severance Tax	Copper .5%, Timber .125% of value. Pumice, gypsum, sand, gravel, clay, fluorspar and other non-metallic minerals, .125% of value. Gold, silver .20%; Lead, zinc, thorium, molybdenum, manganese, rare earth and other .125% of value. Coal is $.57 per short ton for surface coal and $.55 per short ton for underground coal.
	Oil and Gas Severance Tax	Rate varies according to type of well and production.
	Oil and Gas Emergency School Tax	3.15% of value of oil, other liquid hydrocarbons and carbon dioxide. 4% of value of natural gas.
	Natural Gas Processor's Tax	$0.116/Mmbtu tax on volume.
	Oil and Gas Ad Valorem Production Tax	Varies, based on property tax in district of production.
	Oil and Gas Conservation Tax (m)	0.19% of value.
North Carolina	Primary Forest Product Assessment Tax	$.50/1,000 board ft. for softwood sawtimber, $.40/1,000 board ft. for hardwood sawtimber, $.20/cord for softwood pulpwood, $.12/cord hardwood pulpwood.
	Extracted Energy Minerals Tax	Oil and condensates: 2% of gross price paid. Gas: 0.9% of the market value as determined in as determined in N.C. Gen. Stat. § 105-187.78.
North Dakota	Oil Gross Production Tax	5% of gross value at well.
	Gas Gross Production Tax	$0.712/MCF rate through June 30, 2020 (n)
	Coal Severance Tax	$.375/ton plus $.02/ton. (o)
	Oil Extraction Tax	5%, adjusted between 5% and 6% whenever the average price is above or below the "trigger price" per bbl for 3 consecutive months. The "trigger price" is set by the tax commissioner each year and is $93.28 for 2020.
Ohio	Resource Severance Tax	$.10/bbl. of oil; $.025/1,000 cu. ft. of natural gas; $.04/ton of salt; $.02/ton of sand, gravel, limestone and dolomite; $.10/ton of coal; and $0.01/ton of clay, sandstone or conglomerate, shale, gypsum or quartzite.
Oklahoma	Oil, Gas and Mineral Gross Production Tax	0.75% levied on asphalt and metals. 7% on gross production of oil and gas after the first three years of production. During the first 3 years of production, rate of 5% of gross production. Oil Gross Production Tax is now a variable rate tax, beginning with January 1999 production, at the following rates based on the average price of Oklahoma oil: a) If the average price equals or exceeds $17/bbl, the tax shall be 7%; b) If the average price is less than $17/bbl, but is equal to or exceeds $14/bbl, the tax shall be 4%; c) If the average price is less than $14/bbl, the tax shall be 1%.
	Petroleum Excise Tax	Oil and Natural gas .095%

See footnotes at end of table

TABLE 7.20
State Severance Taxes: 2020 (continued)

State	Title and application of tax (a)	Rate
Oregon	Forest Products Harvest Tax	$4.1322/1000 board ft. harvested from public and private land. –through Dec. 31, 2020. The first 25,000 board feet of timber harvested by an owner each year is exempt.
	Oil and Gas Production Tax	6% of gross value at well.
	STF Severance Tax - Eastern Oregon Forestland Option	$4.78/1000 board ft. harvested from land under the Small Tract Forestland Option.–through Dec. 31, 2020
	STF Severance Tax - Western Oregon Forestland Option	$6.15/1000 board ft. harvested from land under the Small Tract Forestland Option.–through Dec. 31, 2020
Pennsylvania	Natural Gas Impact Fee	The state issues an annual fee based on the average price of gas for that year along with the number on a schedule that considers a wells years in production. Local fees and taxes determined by county.
South Carolina	Forest Renewal Tax	Softwood products: 50 cents per 1,000 board feet or 20 cents per cord. Hardwood products: 25 cents per 1,000 board feet or 7 cents per cord.
South Dakota	Precious Metals Severance Tax	$4 per ounce of gold severed plus additional tax depending on price of gold; 10% on net profits or royalties from sale of precious metals, and 8% of royalty value.
	Energy Minerals Severance Tax (p)	4.5% of taxable value of any energy minerals.
	Conservation Tax	2.4 mills of taxable value of any energy minerals.
Tennessee	Oil and Gas Severance Tax	3% of sales price.
	Coal Severance Tax (q)	$1.00/ton (effective 7/17/13)
	Mineral Tax	Up to $0.15 per ton, rate set by county legislative body. (f)
Texas	Natural Gas Production Tax	7.5% of market value of gas. Condensate Production Tax: 4.6% of market value of gas.
	Crude Oil Production Tax	4.6% of market value or $.046/bbl.
	Cement Production Tax	$0.55 per ton or $.0275/100 lbs. or fraction of 100 pounds of taxable cement.
	Oil-Field Cleanup Regulatory Fees	5/8 of $.01/barrel; 1/15 of $.01/1000 cubic feet of gas.
	Oyster Sales Fee	$1 per 300 lb. barrel of oysters taken from Texas waters.
Utah	Mining Severance Tax	2.6% of taxable value for metals or metalliferous minerals sold or otherwise disposed of.
	Oil and Gas Severance Tax	3% of value for the first $13 per barrel of oil, 5% from $13.01 and above; 3% of value for first $1.50/ mcf natural gas, 5% from $1.51 and above; and 4% of taxable value of natural gas liquids.
	Oil and Gas Conservation Fee	.002% of market value at wellhead.
Virginia	Forest Products Tax	$1.15 per 1000 feet B.M. of pine lumber and 1000 board feet of pine logs. $0.475 collected per cord of pine pulpwood.
	Coal Surface Mining Reclamation Tax	Varies depending on balance of Coal Surface Mining Reclamation Fund and the type of mine.
Washington	Enhanced Food Fish Tax	0.09% to 5.62% of value (depending on species) at point of landing.
	Timber Excise Tax	5% of stumpage value for harvests on public and private lands.
West Virginia	Coal Severance Tax	Coal: State rate is greater of 5% or $.75 per ton Special state rates for coal from new low seam mines. For seams between 37" and 45" the rate is greater of 2% or $.75/ton (1.65% for state purposes and .35% for distribution to local governments). For seams less than 37" the rate is greater of 1% or $.75/ton (.65% for state purposes and .35% for distribution to local governments). For coal from gob, refuse piles, or other sources of waste coal, the rate is 2.5% (distributed to local governments). Additional tax for workers' compensation debt reduction is $.56/ton. Special reclamation taxes at $.02/clean ton.
	Natural Resource Severance Taxes	5% for sand, gravel, oil, natural gas, coalbed methane, limestone, sandstone, or other natural gas liquids
	Timber Severance Tax	1.50%
Wisconsin	Mining Net Proceeds Tax	Progressive net proceeds tax ranging from 0% to 15% is imposed on the net proceeds from mining metalliferous minerals. The tax brackets are annually adjusted for inflation based on the change in the GNP deflator.
	Oil and Gas Severance Tax	7% of market value of oil or gas at the mouth of the well.
	Forest Crop Law Severance Tax	$2.52 per acre, rate effective through 2022
	Managed Forest Law Tax	Land entered after 2004 (2005 and later): Open land $2.04/acre; close land $10.20/acre. Land entered before 2005 (1997-2004): Open land $0.74/acre; close land $1.75. Rates effective through 2022.
Wyoming	Severance Taxes	Severance Tax is defined as an excise tax imposed on the present and continuing privilege of removing, extracting, severing or producing any mineral in this state. Except as otherwise provided by W.S. 39-14-205. The total Severance Tax on crude oil, lease condensate or natural gas shall be six percent (6%). Stripper oil is taxed at four percent (4%). Surface coal is taxed at seven percent (7%). Underground coal is taxed at three and three-fourths percent (3.75%). Trona is taxed at four percent (4%). Bentonite, sand and gravel, and all other minerals are taxed at two percent (2%). Natural Gas (6%) Uranium (4%)

See footnotes at end of table

TABLE 7.20
State Severance Taxes: 2020 (continued)

Sources: The Council of State Governments, May 2020.
Note: Severance tax collection totals may be found in the Chapter Seven table entitled "State Government Revenue, By Type of Tax."
Key:
(a) Application of tax is same as that of title unless otherwise indicated by a footnote.
(b) Tax rates and applicability for these severance taxes determined by a vote of the appropriate association within the seafood industry, by the Alaska Seafood Marketing Institute, or by the Department of Revenue. Proceeds from these elective assessments are customarily appropriated for benefit of the seafood industry.
(c) The iron ore tax was suspended as of Oct. 1, 2014 by administrative rule due to the cost of administering the collection of the tax exceeded the total amount of the tax collected
(d) As of July 1, 2007, set at .0007 mill/$1.
(e) Clay, gravel, phosphate rock, lime, shells, stone, sand, heavy minerals and rare earths.
(f) Counties and municipalities also authorized to levy severance taxes on sand, gravel, sandstone, chert and limestone at a rate up to $.15/ton.
(g) Buyer deducts amount from payment to grower; amount forwarded to Department of Natural Resources.
(h) Petroleum, oil, gas and other hydrocarbons. Oil inspection fee rate based Department of Revenue factsheet.

(i) Coal, oil and gas, based on Department of Revenue information.
(j) Oil inspection fee rate based Department of Revenue factsheet.
(k) Coal, oil and gas, based on Department of Revenue information.
(l) The metal mines license tax is based on the gross value of the product and is applied to the payment the mining company receives from metal traders, smelters, roasters, or refineries. The metal mines license tax only applies to gross values over $250,000. Gross values under $250,000 are subject to the Resource Indemnity and Ground Water Assessment Tax (RIT).
(m) Natural resources except oil, natural gas, liquid hydrocarbons or carbon dioxide.
(n) Oil, coal, gas, liquid hydrocarbons, geothermal energy, carbon dioxide and uranium.
(o) Rate reduced by 50 percent if burned in cogeneration facility using renewable resources as fuel to generate at least 10 percent of its energy output. Coal shipped out of state is subject to the $.02/ton tax and 30% of the $.375/ton tax. The coal may be subject to up to the $.375/ton tax at the option of the county in which the coal is mined.
(p) Asphalt and ores bearing lead, zinc, jack, gold, silver, copper or petroleum or other crude oil or other mineral oil, natural gas or casinghead gas and uranium ore.
(q) Any mineral fuel used in the production of energy, including coal, lignite, petroleum, oil, natural gas, uranium and thorium.

TABLE 7.21
State Government Tax Revenue, By State and Selected Types of Tax: 2018 (In thousands of dollars)

State	Total taxes	Corporations Net Income Taxes	Death and Gift Taxes	Documentary and Stock Transfer Taxes	Individual Income Taxes	License Taxes	Property taxes	Sales and Gross Receipts Taxes	Severance Taxes	Taxes, NEC
United States	$1,027,084,678	$47,705,854	$5,036,401	$9,693,648	$390,188,478	$57,158,841	$17,461,386	$484,307,927	$12,628,238	$2,903,905
Alabama	11,055,577	577,516	0	46,014	3,912,800	521,990	406,288	5,534,807	56,162	0
Alaska	1,656,352	196,321	0	0	0	153,636	122,341	252,970	931,084	0
Arizona	16,293,917	373,076	0	18,263	4,545,242	495,034	1,047,254	9,708,694	24,562	81,792
Arkansas	9,819,284	390,756	0	44,892	2,866,175	409,856	1,188,905	4,834,983	54,655	29,062
California	178,437,038	12,488,304	577	0	95,152,230	10,504,521	2,837,386	57,345,108	108,912	0
Colorado	14,924,842	782,679	0	0	7,510,366	816,832	0	5,712,243	102,722	0
Connecticut	18,934,012	778,232	224,126	169,695	9,733,258	431,196	0	7,596,995	0	510
Delaware	4,219,706	254,802	4,425	146,774	1,652,335	1,574,576	0	585,645	0	1,149
Florida	45,961,204	2,426,900	1,927	2,916,100		2,123,462	0	38,456,615	36,200	0
Georgia	23,602,510	1,004,298	0	0	11,643,781	719,422	927,590	9,132,965	0	174,454
Hawaii	7,714,451	146,831	29,351	100,605	2,430,032	275,600	0	4,732,032	0	0
Idaho	4,848,359	240,809	0	0	1,835,864	367,178	0	2,396,117	5,463	2,928
Illinois	39,857,069	2,587,141	382,081	80,309	15,296,693	2,751,479	59,589	18,699,777	0	0
Indiana	19,397,879	698,725	409	0	5,816,072	749,114	12,927	12,119,558	1,074	0
Iowa	10,088,480	443,187	82,600	22,210	3,897,236	954,503	1,671	4,687,073	0	0
Kansas	9,546,790	437,967	0	0	3,413,677	433,229	714,895	4,494,809	52,213	0
Kentucky	12,059,970	511,353	48,248	3,480	4,499,086	499,502	660,902	5,714,427	122,972	0
Louisiana	11,357,686	358,208	0	0	3,246,226	393,129	60,172	6,864,723	435,228	0
Maine	4,410,632	185,737	13,801	35,242	1,605,096	281,155	39,308	2,250,293	0	0
Maryland	22,427,037	1,033,175	214,378	241,668	9,507,776	850,913	808,763	9,567,244	0	203,120
Massachusetts	29,654,803	2,408,947	472,956	308,291	16,280,331	1,154,719	7,197	9,022,362	0	0
Michigan	30,046,808	971,032	16	350,280	10,166,720	1,945,619	2,182,188	14,398,369	32,548	36
Minnesota	26,697,469	1,357,004	214,698	234,141	11,882,330	1,476,228	818,513	10,614,808	49,623	50,124
Mississippi	7,890,571	437,407	0	0	1,852,937	492,415	29,540	5,030,854	47,418	0
Missouri	13,025,070	333,724	54	12,331	6,510,224	596,167	33,267	5,539,227	2	74
Montana	3,003,980	175,954	0	0	1,304,315	379,198	300,258	655,034	185,397	3,824
Nebraska	5,393,093	313,690	0	17,207	2,360,596	196,215	129	2,502,020	3,236	0
Nevada	9,157,036	0	0	111,422	0	661,240	317,136	7,329,456	155,938	581,844
New Hampshire	2,920,888	790,011	0	154,903	105,759	435,544	408,769	1,025,902	0	0
New Jersey	35,365,046	2,235,653	605,845	513,967	15,037,845	1,542,213	5,016	15,424,507	0	0
New Mexico	5,539,329	111,297	0	0	1,071,125	322,473	84,224	2,874,807	1,042,547	32,856
New York	88,541,099	3,617,910	1,203,725	1,269,623	52,738,515	1,771,629	0	26,399,319	0	1,540,378
North Carolina	27,855,861	742,512	10,735	79,982	12,609,608	2,197,653	0	12,213,458	1,913	0
North Dakota	4,205,184	107,277	0	0	367,635	214,463	4,549	1,395,503	2,115,757	0
Ohio	29,068,270	9,046	213	0	8,698,901	2,237,002	0	18,056,988	66,120	0
Oklahoma	9,429,242	234,817	0	21,112	3,260,447	1,018,657	0	4,194,272	699,937	0
Oregon	12,640,306	804,453	176,453	1,772	8,879,552	1,087,449	20,116	1,654,829	15,682	0
Pennsylvania	40,709,545	2,486,379	982,470	625,056	12,800,890	2,721,979	34,399	21,034,252	0	24,120
Rhode Island	3,491,697	118,118	133,103	115,800	1,329,152	110,799	2,704	1,682,021	0	0
South Carolina	10,530,212	404,164	0	126,174	4,432,104	582,294	37,298	4,948,178	0	0
South Dakota	1,917,548	32,376	0	187	0	291,896	0	1,585,089	8,000	0
Tennessee	14,269,061	1,644,159	0	251,574	246,508	1,763,747	0	10,343,084	1,025	18,964
Texas	60,328,843	0	0	0	0	3,635,024	0	51,462,209	5,231,610	0
Utah	9,414,073	460,657	0	0	4,661,910	347,888	0	3,901,286	42,015	317
Vermont	3,284,231	110,819	22,935	38,366	819,330	126,404	1,065,767	1,095,321	0	5,289
Virginia	23,484,945	861,897	932	386,598	14,105,766	878,751	31,890	7,082,742	2,695	133,674
Washington	26,579,324	0	208,610	1,161,436	0	2,070,931	2,769,520	20,327,520	41,307	0
West Virginia	5,442,628	110,068	0	12,036	1,950,571	219,003	7,316	2,731,739	411,895	0
Wisconsin	18,748,320	910,466	1,733	76,138	8,151,462	1,187,392	163,446	8,232,896	10,667	14,120
Wyoming	1,837,401	0	0	0	0	187,522	250,153	862,797	531,659	5,270

Source: U.S. Census Bureau, 2018 Annual Survey of State Government Tax Collections

Notes:

1. Data users who create their own estimates using these data should cite only the U.S. Census Bureau as the source of the original data. Data in this table are based on information from public records and contain no confidential data. Although the data in this table come from a census of governmental units and are not subject to sampling error, the census results may contain nonsampling error. Additional information on nonsampling error, response rates, and definitions may be found within the survey methodology *https://www.census.gov/programs-surveys/state/technical-documentation/methodology.html.*

2. Detail may not add to total due to rounding.

TABLE 7.22
State Government Sales and Gross Receipts Tax Revenue: 2018 (In thousands of dollars)

State	Total	General sales or gross receipts	Total	Alcoholic Beverages Sales Tax	Amusements Sales Tax	Insurance Premiums Sales Tax	Motor Fuels Sales Tax	Other Selective Sales and Gross Receipts Taxes	Pari-mutuels Sales Tax	Public Utilities Sales Tax	Tobacco Products Sales Tax
						Selective sales taxes					
United States	$484,307,927	$319,702,418	$164,605,509	$6,782,834	$8,169,039	$22,392,810	$48,324,660	$47,077,698	$127,379	$12,356,797	$19,374,292
Alabama	5,534,807	2,786,833	2,747,974	214,615	0	376,766	648,639	579,222	1,146	747,657	179,929
Alaska	252,970	0	252,970	39,217	11,002	62,429	47,149	32,854	0	4,819	55,500
Arizona	9,708,694	7,687,992	2,020,702	76,378	3,621	550,438	869,183	186,286	183	21,805	312,808
Arkansas	4,834,983	3,498,073	1,336,910	58,036	64,580	223,362	492,945	268,924	2,335	0	226,728
California	57,345,108	39,682,734	17,662,374	381,670	0	2,569,271	6,351,756	5,227,196	15,871	688,489	2,428,121
Colorado	5,712,243	3,211,909	2,500,334	46,989	124,714	262,411	675,962	1,195,852	525	0	193,881
Connecticut	7,596,995	4,400,808	3,196,187	63,211	300,740	209,026	487,327	1,492,283	5,602	261,184	376,814
Delaware	585,645	0	585,645	26,556	0	110,292	131,864	140,612	67	53,228	123,026
Florida	38,456,615	29,562,900	8,893,715	293,098	207,460	1,084,872	2,799,610	939,931	8,352	2,387,900	1,172,492
Georgia	9,132,965	5,938,448	3,194,517	195,696	0	505,054	1,801,798	467,059	0	0	224,910
Hawaii	4,732,032	3,529,065	1,202,967	51,383	0	165,602	88,377	659,578	0	117,641	120,386
Idaho	2,396,117	1,790,830	605,287	9,710	0	97,359	362,234	81,367	884	2,592	51,141
Illinois	18,699,777	11,336,866	7,362,911	296,162	888,260	456,406	1,367,939	2,143,567	6,387	1,439,894	764,296
Indiana	12,119,558	7,795,091	4,324,467	51,578	602,410	236,175	1,420,135	1,391,450	1,760	202,149	418,810
Iowa	4,687,073	3,279,789	1,407,284	22,183	303,374	114,363	671,937	40,101	3,818	39,039	212,469
Kansas	4,494,809	3,304,091	1,190,718	142,126	304	408,321	461,075	48,272	0	373	130,247
Kentucky	5,714,427	3,600,598	2,113,829	145,648	196	165,161	702,651	802,594	7,704	61,126	228,749
Louisiana	6,864,723	4,252,693	2,612,030	75,774	708,462	870,872	631,641	146,971	5,191	9,349	163,770
Maine	2,250,293	1,529,113	721,180	19,647	56,264	99,654	250,468	139,189	1,435	21,573	132,950
Maryland	9,567,244	4,716,179	4,851,065	31,682	1,022,368	541,758	1,084,195	1,651,726	1,175	145,437	372,724
Massachusetts	9,022,362	6,490,305	2,532,057	85,843	70,467	406,251	769,144	605,292	887	0	594,173
Michigan	14,398,369	9,595,949	4,802,420	165,758	115,424	393,367	1,473,002	1,694,284	2,855	36,823	920,907
Minnesota	10,614,808	5,830,256	4,784,552	91,745	75,597	519,547	936,893	2,566,114	1,192	54	593,410
Mississippi	5,030,854	3,557,752	1,473,102	40,883	129,880	338,576	436,245	386,289	0	1,496	139,733
Missouri	5,539,227	3,686,274	1,852,953	38,932	369,410	464,418	717,894	164,891	0	0	97,408
Montana	655,034	0	655,034	36,502	60,336	107,646	258,958	66,339	226	44,497	80,530
Nebraska	2,502,020	1,900,037	601,983	31,230	5,815	62,662	373,889	26,184	138	44,942	57,123
Nevada	7,329,456	5,095,689	2,233,767	45,340	915,531	395,701	343,386	310,345	3	46,300	177,161
New Hampshire	1,025,902	0	1,025,902	12,828	530	111,972	183,366	454,982	539	48,987	212,698
New Jersey	15,424,507	10,459,419	4,965,088	142,459	217,736	591,243	458,892	1,915,627	0	978,816	660,315
New Mexico	2,874,807	2,073,118	801,689	23,811	63,138	213,597	230,303	159,883	842	31,747	78,368
New York	26,399,319	14,820,163	11,579,156	258,327	2,848	1,623,191	1,636,749	6,007,581	21,310	877,997	1,151,660
North Carolina	12,213,458	8,009,850	4,203,608	411,971	76	589,037	1,974,782	935,277	0	322	292,143
North Dakota	1,395,503	912,532	482,971	8,819	3,139	63,274	196,649	131,928	1,498	49,663	28,001
Ohio	18,056,988	12,148,485	5,908,503	104,977	270,480	582,794	1,912,191	1,193,768	5,185	898,003	941,105
Oklahoma	4,194,272	2,855,176	1,339,096	122,247	26,429	328,756	485,276	16,834	1,085	45,058	313,411
Oregon	1,654,829	0	1,654,829	19,216	0	70,903	533,976	756,241	1,876	8,757	263,860
Pennsylvania	21,034,252	10,920,832	10,113,420	397,092	1,429,632	836,186	3,375,429	1,537,195	10,182	1,155,009	1,372,695
Rhode Island	1,682,021	1,048,957	633,064	19,918	0	81,519	79,858	244,353	1,074	59,651	146,691
South Carolina	4,948,178	3,303,220	1,644,958	179,115	39,774	239,215	646,581	484,071	0	29,003	27,199
South Dakota	1,585,089	1,103,624	481,465	18,939	9,135	92,488	187,424	110,634	177	3,510	59,158
Tennessee	10,343,084	7,469,547	2,873,537	201,713	0	970,831	1,086,693	357,107	0	8,520	248,673
Texas	51,462,209	36,129,876	15,332,333	1,321,516	30,023	2,445,005	3,710,307	5,748,579	6,510	630,057	1,440,336
Utah	3,901,286	2,784,489	1,116,797	51,420	0	147,452	557,490	197,908	0	45,800	116,727
Vermont	1,095,321	397,691	697,630	26,892	0	59,370	82,953	448,459	0	8,878	71,078
Virginia	7,082,742	4,076,636	3,006,106	231,250	84	516,743	1,031,034	954,481	0	112,131	160,383
Washington	20,327,520	15,643,017	4,684,503	370,738	4,434	630,657	1,713,782	1,040,201	1,724	500,703	422,264
West Virginia	2,731,739	1,311,930	1,419,809	17,576	35,152	169,607	419,528	477,666	2,704	119,736	177,840
Wisconsin	8,232,896	5,484,375	2,748,521	62,498	214	207,729	1,051,479	447,251	239	361,696	617,415
Wyoming	862,797	689,207	173,590	1,920	0	23,481	113,622	2,900	4,698	4,893	22,076

Source: U.S. Census Bureau, 2018 Annual Survey of State Government Tax Collections

Notes:

1. Data users who create their own estimates using these data should cite only the U.S. Census Bureau as the source of the original data. Data in this table are based on information from public records and contain no confidential data. Although the data in this table come from a census of governmental units and are not subject to sampling error, the census results may contain nonsampling error. Additional information on nonsampling error, response rates, and definitions may be found within the survey methodology *https://www.census.gov/programs-surveys/state/technical-documentation/methodology.html.*

2. Detail may not add to total due to rounding.

TABLE 7.23
State Government License Tax Revenue: 2018 (In thousands of dollars)

State	Total license revenue	Alcoholic beverages license	Amusements license	Corporations license	Hunting and fishing license
United States	57,158,841	714,092	758,924	5,981,237	1,622,063
Alabama	521,990	4,032	0	152,538	21,451
Alaska	153,636	1,433	0	0	35,608
Arizona	495,034	8,592	0	14,493	37,005
Arkansas	409,856	6,128	488	29,673	26,672
California	10,504,521	60,519	20,583	80,029	112,138
Colorado	816,832	9,102	728	21,265	76,251
Connecticut	431,196	13,968	230	30,705	5,754
Delaware	1,574,576	1,816	321	1,378,003	3,759
Florida	2,123,462	6,418	16,000	263,623	16,629
Georgia	719,422	4,103	0	59,608	35,418
Hawaii	275,600	0	0	1,818	665
Idaho	367,178	1,721	258	2,962	46,428
Illinois	2,751,479	18,160	15,918	342,729	39,534
Indiana	749,114	12,726	5,792	8,582	19,495
Iowa	954,503	16,456	30,314	34,590	28,200
Kansas	433,229	3,647	6,993	28,187	32,780
Kentucky	499,502	6,801	279	115,618	30,531
Louisiana	393,129	0	0	148,116	31,994
Maine	281,155	6,237	536	11,095	16,578
Maryland	850,913	1,524	1,953	119,084	17,207
Massachusetts	1,154,719	3,702	15,767	25,701	5,637
Michigan	1,945,619	18,764	0	26,675	60,404
Minnesota	1,476,228	2,765	1,144	9,045	66,634
Mississippi	492,415	1,252	26,515	137,989	2,703
Missouri	596,167	5,478	28	2,200	33,692
Montana	379,198	2,275	4,714	4,920	64,067
Nebraska	196,215	707	710	16,086	15,906
Nevada	661,240	0	82,640	78,782	12,144
New Hampshire	435,544	17,991	365	67,236	11,899
New Jersey	1,542,213	4,199	50,100	248,405	14,685
New Mexico	322,473	0	6,365	32,175	31,802
New York	1,771,629	66,675	0	2,746	41,964
North Carolina	2,197,653	26,757	222	757,312	33,282
North Dakota	214,463	395	1,088	0	15,286
Ohio	2,237,002	43,804	34,850	297,490	36,260
Oklahoma	1,018,657	1,037	168,006	58,897	20,494
Oregon	1,087,449	4,868	2,799	40,017	57,598
Pennsylvania	2,721,979	51,644	215,406	5,717	76,245
Rhode Island	110,799	92	202	4,910	1,844
South Carolina	582,294	12,600	6,389	110,199	18,898
South Dakota	291,896	1,222	6,353	5,984	28,690
Tennessee	1,763,747	1,862	283	920,053	36,730
Texas	3,635,024	78,742	16,387	152,899	110,770
Utah	347,888	10,791	0	497	31,299
Vermont	126,404	469	23	3,686	7,294
Virginia	878,751	14,591	107	64,102	29,393
Washington	2,070,931	152,625	13,914	41,834	42,450
West Virginia	219,003	3,444	3,672	737	12,325
Wisconsin	1,187,392	1,958	482	22,225	67,571
Wyoming	187,522	0	0	14,205	37,187

See footnotes at end of table

TABLE 7.23
State Government License Tax Revenue: 2018 (In thousands of dollars) (continued)

State	Motor vehicle license	Motor vehicle operators license	Public utilities license	Occupation and Business License, NEC	Other licenses
United States	27,782,391	2,663,267	1,326,412	14,678,552	1,444,381
Alabama	220,483	33,425	14,146	75,914	1
Alaska	36,258	0	10,671	65,553	4,113
Arizona	230,095	29,922	20	173,274	1,633
Arkansas	164,617	22,631	8,346	149,452	1,849
California	4,635,040	281,045	752,340	4,535,825	27,002
Colorado	597,097	41,794	13,742	56,774	79
Connecticut	238,351	42,816	0	95,770	3,602
Delaware	58,969	5,838	134	117,494	8,242
Florida	1,449,604	165,332	24,424	171,749	9,683
Georgia	395,140	114,915	0	81,296	28,942
Hawaii	191,757	306	15,001	53,544	12,509
Idaho	195,431	10,341	58,067	47,431	4,539
Illinois	1,618,750	116,118	15,016	552,696	32,558
Indiana	321,055	252,033	0	51,828	77,603
Iowa	664,178	21,833	9,865	146,470	2,597
Kansas	222,978	31,881	5,857	98,132	2,774
Kentucky	211,646	16,795	0	112,292	5,540
Louisiana	79,284	15,477	7,577	106,475	4,206
Maine	112,557	10,816	0	113,492	9,844
Maryland	501,417	27,929	0	179,997	1,802
Massachusetts	444,827	101,432	0	301,510	256,143
Michigan	1,337,873	58,345	35,745	212,035	195,778
Minnesota	800,981	45,796	785	484,398	64,680
Mississippi	158,283	14,362	6,583	81,682	63,046
Missouri	296,849	17,596	19,628	142,822	77,874
Montana	168,827	7,883	17	110,183	16,312
Nebraska	113,733	11,538	0	36,475	1,060
Nevada	198,263	28,099	0	256,769	4,543
New Hampshire	82,270	8,508	23,555	216,120	7,600
New Jersey	657,956	57,214	21,812	485,902	1,940
New Mexico	200,727	5,004	1,529	44,871	0
New York	1,411,790	93,205	28,196	125,822	1,231
North Carolina	853,879	121,032	19,114	349,449	36,606
North Dakota	118,080	5,049	3	74,562	0
Ohio	787,276	80,227	34,222	875,280	47,593
Oklahoma	736,979	31,733	5	727	779
Oregon	539,474	39,758	14,577	381,707	6,651
Pennsylvania	1,183,964	72,896	56,798	1,038,215	21,094
Rhode Island	29,352	4,865	2,070	61,959	5,505
South Carolina	274,093	4,486	10,670	126,871	18,088
South Dakota	83,369	5,676	0	135,433	25,169
Tennessee	357,692	59,648	6,039	372,981	8,459
Texas	2,358,248	141,892	22,456	609,900	143,730
Utah	224,833	16,772	0	56,433	7,263
Vermont	72,957	11,972	0	25,674	4,329
Virginia	492,825	41,288	0	231,791	4,654
Washington	1,129,671	135,270	21,148	357,370	176,649
West Virginia	4,498	160,076	449	31,582	2,220
Wisconsin	518,115	40,398	65,805	464,571	6,267
Wyoming	91,663	4,158	0	40,309	0

Source: U.S. Census Bureau, 2018 Annual Survey of State Government Tax Collections

Notes:

1. Data users who create their own estimates using these data should cite only the U.S. Census Bureau as the source of the original data. Data in this table are based on information from public records and contain no confidential data. Although the data in this table come from a census of governmental units and are not subject to sampling error, the census results may contain nonsampling error. Additional information on nonsampling error, response rates, and definitions may be found within the survey methodology *https://www.census. gov/programs-surveys/state/technical-documentation/methodology. html.*

2. Detail may not add to total due to rounding.

TABLE 7.24
Summary of Financial Aggregates, By State: 2018 (In millions of dollars)

State	Total	Revenues General revenue	Utilities revenue	Liquor stores revenue	Insurance trust revenue (a)
United States	$2,630,991,358	$2,097,939,270	$14,018,753	$8,498,997	$510,534,338
Alabama	34,406,835	28,250,965	0	350,913	5,804,957
Alaska	9,919,282	8,152,092	21,482	0	1,745,708
Arizona	45,167,570	38,133,225	34,811	0	6,999,534
Arkansas	25,425,732	21,402,327	0	0	4,023,405
California	412,385,628	320,249,459	1,006,148	0	91,130,021
Colorado	42,389,685	30,878,620	0	0	11,511,065
Connecticut	35,139,473	30,490,255	43,872	0	4,605,346
Delaware	10,484,729	9,275,531	20,430	0	1,188,768
Florida	110,235,411	91,783,197	24,966	0	18,427,248
Georgia	55,479,427	45,135,668	10,478	0	10,333,281
Hawaii	16,150,841	14,078,337	0	0	2,072,504
Idaho	11,958,060	9,155,174	0	172,845	2,630,041
Illinois	92,717,937	72,948,065	0	0	19,769,872
Indiana	45,089,558	40,546,768	0	0	4,542,790
Iowa	28,867,827	24,072,068	0	320,530	4,475,229
Kansas	21,877,508	19,078,088	0	0	2,799,420
Kentucky	34,510,574	29,299,781	0	0	5,210,793
Louisiana	37,294,923	29,227,226	11,608	0	8,056,089
Maine	10,657,988	8,814,837	11,624	33	1,831,494
Maryland	48,040,253	42,101,136	148,014	0	5,791,103
Massachusetts	68,541,549	58,094,512	934,282	0	9,512,755
Michigan	81,630,737	66,231,312	0	1,123,653	14,275,772
Minnesota	56,306,765	44,475,950	103,017	0	11,727,798
Mississippi	23,421,200	19,137,029	0	360,281	3,923,890
Missouri	39,804,179	30,919,843	0	0	8,884,336
Montana	9,239,440	7,021,451	0	99,100	2,118,889
Nebraska	12,347,188	10,470,221	0	0	1,876,967
Nevada	21,771,811	16,087,532	45,363	0	5,638,916
New Hampshire	9,734,653	7,566,526	0	693,160	1,474,967
New Jersey	80,619,851	66,129,779	1,099,208	0	13,390,864
New Mexico	20,973,043	17,627,371	0	0	3,345,672
New York	223,525,982	175,700,469	8,089,496	0	39,736,017
North Carolina	67,302,674	56,343,509	512	0	10,958,653
North Dakota	8,880,056	7,746,544	0	0	1,133,512
Ohio	101,023,062	68,842,609	0	1,186,823	30,993,630
Oklahoma	26,986,320	22,075,260	641,586	0	4,269,474
Oregon	43,875,212	32,138,083	519	625,794	11,110,816
Pennsylvania	108,605,542	87,715,628	0	2,066,562	18,823,352
Rhode Island	9,904,803	8,406,086	23,249	0	1,475,468
South Carolina	35,446,262	28,177,916	1,740,867	0	5,527,479
South Dakota	5,614,951	4,409,773	4,338	0	1,200,840
Tennessee	35,851,416	30,234,945	0	0	5,616,471
Texas	171,756,387	137,622,906	0	0	34,133,481
Utah	24,322,339	18,687,798	0	403,667	5,230,874
Vermont	6,976,132	6,346,252	0	67,064	562,816
Virginia	62,586,631	50,882,334	0	812,979	10,891,318
Washington	68,160,975	50,923,984	0	0	17,236,991
West Virginia	15,551,414	12,970,565	2,167	97,399	2,481,283
Wisconsin	54,526,374	36,278,147	0	0	18,248,227
Wyoming	7,505,169	5,602,117	716	118,194	1,784,142

See footnotes at end of table

TABLE 7.24
Summary of Financial Aggregates, By State: 2018 (In millions of dollars) (continued)

State	Total expenditure	General expenditure	Utility expenditure	Liquor stores expenditure	Insurance trust expenditure (a)	Debt at end of fiscal year	Cash and security holdings at end of fiscal year
United States	$2,410,705,639	$2,067,954,884	$42,271,520	$7,066,707	$304,533,195	$1,173,606,967	$3,442,074,701
Alabama	33,899,390	29,951,784	135	340,566	3,606,905	9,856,082	39,602,773
Alaska	11,979,183	10,446,105	125,374	0	1,407,704	5,889,417	88,950,277
Arizona	41,145,292	36,650,241	35,359	0	4,460,692	13,703,759	57,921,027
Arkansas	22,520,209	20,438,295	5,672	0	2,081,914	6,832,598	27,870,451
California	375,092,304	319,549,260	1,662,973	0	53,930,038	148,027,188	492,984,712
Colorado	37,449,374	31,696,427	13,477	0	5,739,700	17,853,552	56,740,818
Connecticut	28,070,663	22,583,290	588,964	0	4,900,605	40,287,423	44,891,736
Delaware	9,991,686	9,104,556	157,209	0	730,430	5,127,188	12,105,695
Florida	96,821,778	86,782,792	403,808	0	9,748,062	27,593,512	162,461,982
Georgia	51,558,184	44,593,220	38,084	0	6,926,880	13,305,788	66,058,597
Hawaii	13,654,476	12,068,515	0	0	1,585,961	9,870,931	22,037,073
Idaho	10,431,120	9,113,460	2,955	134,897	1,182,763	3,439,046	19,655,832
Illinois	92,468,099	76,875,407	1,312,067	0	15,584,455	67,495,522	111,000,043
Indiana	41,636,298	38,771,326	81,177	0	2,864,972	22,026,355	39,281,758
Iowa	23,877,036	20,952,954	46,946	222,840	2,701,242	6,270,052	25,793,525
Kansas	19,572,429	17,632,190	0	0	1,940,239	6,136,579	16,091,719
Kentucky	35,312,518	30,635,111	56,455	4,661	4,649,330	14,617,245	30,088,192
Louisiana	35,118,216	30,403,826	6,531	0	4,707,859	18,155,260	49,492,144
Maine	9,236,942	8,154,539	28,486	0	1,053,917	4,759,978	21,292,213
Maryland	46,183,945	40,435,641	1,867,763	0	4,496,987	27,998,569	52,360,669
Massachusetts	67,366,110	56,700,849	3,765,986	0	6,967,133	78,620,996	46,872,609
Michigan	76,289,557	67,189,291	309,314	903,029	8,197,236	33,563,347	77,197,608
Minnesota	49,584,827	43,337,146	663,690	0	5,679,060	16,600,028	59,746,002
Mississippi	21,832,564	18,660,117	0	296,423	2,876,024	7,252,112	25,099,617
Missouri	34,992,860	30,079,041	52,693	0	4,907,655	17,854,734	56,309,750
Montana	7,805,481	6,595,193	18,572	85,974	1,108,873	2,739,404	20,499,545
Nebraska	11,123,881	10,317,689	0	0	806,192	2,056,773	22,192,904
Nevada	17,414,692	14,610,813	52,779	0	2,755,209	3,435,955	26,353,048
New Hampshire	8,907,923	7,521,532	12,634	550,093	823,664	7,739,271	12,122,865
New Jersey	78,906,750	62,187,390	2,870,443	0	13,848,917	65,574,574	71,631,817
New Mexico	21,468,456	18,973,297	14,342	0	2,494,069	7,268,214	43,067,956
New York	213,163,460	173,766,965	21,766,739	0	23,458,636	147,960,540	311,605,279
North Carolina	60,929,395	54,506,230	203,229	0	6,344,451	15,354,553	78,805,101
North Dakota	7,216,315	6,539,038	184,393	0	631,076	3,040,855	36,832,455
Ohio	89,026,066	70,721,000	40,851	937,686	17,367,367	31,622,762	150,593,257
Oklahoma	25,314,521	21,147,798	1,508,376	0	2,682,398	8,910,608	33,822,240
Oregon	39,369,778	32,946,999	69,852	469,412	5,928,802	14,285,969	76,735,488
Pennsylvania	102,651,514	87,902,698	1,514,990	1,937,382	12,811,434	49,064,189	105,234,020
Rhode Island	9,471,982	8,070,396	116,975	0	1,284,611	9,093,878	13,029,290
South Carolina	35,002,566	28,984,861	1,780,691	0	4,237,014	14,571,479	31,178,307
South Dakota	5,243,258	4,645,544	0	0	597,714	3,739,690	18,216,081
Tennessee	33,738,083	30,963,512	179	0	2,774,392	6,289,301	46,294,165
Texas	150,890,074	132,368,456	117,305	0	18,463,615	51,529,919	289,878,150
Utah	21,887,604	19,663,786	0	286,824	1,936,994	7,355,005	30,446,227
Vermont	7,021,342	6,546,073	30,645	64,164	411,082	3,580,807	8,664,425
Virginia	56,366,947	50,395,859	500,230	653,778	5,204,214	29,074,498	112,061,636
Washington	57,994,626	50,357,945	143,898	0	7,563,671	33,926,356	85,772,168
West Virginia	15,359,180	13,703,084	18,843	76,949	1,568,700	8,610,296	14,081,565
Wisconsin	42,177,837	36,483,821	40,766	0	5,665,042	22,812,370	71,701,733
Wyoming	6,168,848	5,229,522	39,670	102,029	837,295	832,440	29,348,157

See footnotes at end of table

TABLE 7.24
Summary of Financial Aggregates, By State: 2018 (In millions of dollars) (continued)

Source: U.S. Census Bureau, 2018 Annual Survey of State Government Finances.

Notes:

1. Data users who create their own estimates using these data should cite only the U.S. Census Bureau as the source of the original data. Data in this table are based on information from public records and contain no confidential data. Although the data in this table come from a census of governmental units and are not subject to sampling error, the census results may contain nonsampling error. Additional information on nonsampling error, response rates, and definitions may be found within the survey methodology *https://www.census.gov/programs-surveys/state/technical-documentation/methodology.html.*

2. Detail may not add to total due to rounding.

Key:

(a) Within insurance trust revenue, net earnings of state-administered pension systems is a calculated statistic (the item code in the data file is X08), and thus can be positive or negative. Net earnings is the sum of earnings on investments plus gains on investments minus losses on investments. The change made in 2002 for asset valuation from book to market value in accordance with Statement 34 of the Governmental Accounting Standards Board is reflected in the calculated statistics.

TABLE 7.25
National Totals of State Government Finances for Selected Years: 2009-2018
(In thousands of dollars)

Item	2018	2017	2016	2015	2014
Revenue total	$2,630,991,367	$2,531,287,976	$2,136,310,326	$2,203,229,979	$2,365,153,505
General revenue	2,097,939,270	1,975,972,558	1,908,997,159	1,853,494,640	1,742,915,609
Taxes	1,022,783,253	946,076,690	922,855,175	911,697,759	870,437,041
Intergovernmental revenue	688,138,024	658,791,527	637,256,254	604,627,441	550,721,503
From Federal Government	670,548,803	641,714,983	621,597,499	590,480,568	535,736,745
Public Welfare	454,338,760	427,047,756	417,307,189	389,191,243	332,492,959
Education	85,022,930	83,576,477	83,018,756	82,495,588	82,981,871
Highways	43,175,723	44,535,792	44,931,663	41,748,566	43,287,751
Employment security administration	3,827,853	3,829,699	3,745,803	4,200,959	4,307,823
Other	84,183,537	82,725,259	72,594,088	72,844,212	72,666,341
From local government	17,589,221	17,076,544	15,658,755	14,146,873	14,984,758
Charges and miscellaneous revenue	387,017,993	371,104,341	348,885,730	337,169,440	321,757,065
Liquor stores revenue	8,498,997	8,158,551	8,088,520	7,732,037	7,179,065
Utility revenue	14,018,753	13,607,538	13,823,602	14,714,935	14,310,794
Insurance trust revenue (a)	510,534,347	533,549,329	205,401,045	327,288,367	600,748,037
Employee retirement	447,968,712	468,477,581	135,165,729	251,702,166	515,792,141
Unemployment compensation	38,641,501	40,369,857	46,333,152	52,281,509	62,127,840
Worker compensation	14,956,426	16,533,351	16,146,248	15,712,648	15,169,230
Other	8,967,708	8,168,540	7,755,916	7,592,044	7,658,826
Expenditure total	2,410,705,638	2,315,996,558	2,238,572,373	2,192,506,489	2,048,937,368
General expenditure	2,067,954,884	1,985,929,177	1,919,478,613	1,840,867,694	1,738,757,437
Education	705,090,151	686,935,989	677,231,512	637,315,733	613,747,859
Intergovernmental expenditure	382,855,837	373,639,270	360,117,773	345,859,861	330,140,870
State institutions of higher education	258,430,143	253,093,494	258,132,773	232,811,232	227,411,126
Other education	59,804,573	56,094,227	55,931,789	54,436,132	51,740,480
Public welfare	716,794,523	680,404,169	638,897,229	612,553,893	544,711,480
Intergovernmental expenditure	58,184,136	59,895,676	57,049,413	52,704,375	54,781,687
Cash assistance, other	13,749,987	13,602,819	12,275,724	11,785,784	12,863,087
Other public welfare	679,017,050	641,365,524	600,825,436	576,817,660	507,740,883
Highways	134,774,210	132,496,590	126,682,211	122,472,455	119,270,200
Intergovernmental expenditure	20,512,463	20,217,035	19,675,932	20,420,805	20,992,876
Regular state highway facilities	121,742,978	119,687,509	114,763,236	111,591,023	109,242,610
State toll highways/facilities	13,031,232	12,809,081	11,918,975	10,881,432	10,027,590
Health and hospitals	155,481,645	149,120,384	144,626,375	136,661,426	135,918,963
Hospitals	90,476,187	85,700,081	80,924,025	73,917,087	71,711,969
Health	65,005,458	63,420,303	63,702,350	62,744,339	64,206,994
Natural resources	24,335,551	23,656,195	24,667,924	22,479,104	21,391,208
Corrections	53,379,501	51,476,590	51,871,719	51,725,417	50,218,902
Financial administration	27,324,399	26,678,519	24,959,910	24,050,951	23,304,855
Employment security administration	3,823,018	3,880,843	3,986,729	4,107,385	4,398,411
Police protection	17,342,880	16,621,322	16,480,160	16,108,379	15,668,996
Interest on general debt	45,900,748	43,751,987	44,623,911	44,835,071	45,479,391
Utility expenditure	31,150,853	28,349,937	27,246,160	28,826,069	26,284,373
Insurance trust expenditure	304,533,194	294,844,901	285,400,474	316,628,497	278,190,448
Employee retirement	260,162,813	248,606,815	236,985,953	267,071,846	213,328,101
Unemployment compensation	28,838,808	30,925,241	32,418,562	33,219,048	48,023,325
Other	15,531,573	15,312,845	15,995,959	16,337,603	16,839,022
Total expenditure by character and object	2,410,705,638	2,315,996,558	2,238,572,373	2,192,506,489	2,048,937,368
Direct expenditure	1,848,117,781	1,762,476,159	1,705,907,083	1,677,460,581	1,550,227,219
Current operation	1,307,732,632	1,240,597,095	1,198,124,432	1,144,425,741	1,063,609,670
Capital outlay	135,313,220	131,634,848	128,546,396	123,904,718	116,582,628
Assistance and subsidies	52,020,828	49,172,046	46,710,250	45,175,756	43,933,607
Interest on debt	48,517,907	46,227,269	47,125,531	47,325,869	47,910,866
Insurance benefits and repayments	304,533,194	294,844,901	285,400,474	316,628,497	278,190,448
Intergovernmental expenditure	562,587,857	553,520,399	532,665,290	515,045,908	498,710,149
Cash and security holdings at end of fiscal year	5,124,736,422	4,764,489,085	4,345,944,854	4,976,604,515	4,293,957,889

See footnotes at end of table

TABLE 7.25
National Totals of State Government Finances for Selected Years: 2009-2018
(In thousands of dollars) (continued)

Item	2013	2012	2011	2010	2009
Revenue total	$2,216,076,231	$1,905,807,119	$2,266,850,424	$2,039,926,569	$1,133,446,448
General revenue	1,709,786,388	1,629,267,996	1,658,377,770	1,567,206,839	1,493,989,614
Taxes	847,077,345	798,586,949	762,378,532	705,929,253	713,474,529
Intergovernmental revenue	551,464,163	533,655,081	595,028,792	575,371,668	494,782,446
From Federal Government	513,478,951	514,139,109	575,788,668	555,592,308	475,661,252
Public Welfare	307,610,126	296,964,692	332,256,781	315,808,952	280,281,988
Education	84,408,057	90,264,309	104,711,082	105,511,630	82,447,792
Highways	41,431,014	43,199,512	44,245,077	42,969,373	36,518,798
Employment security administration	4,647,159	4,771,326	5,174,051	4,888,356	4,455,882
Other	70,770,258	74,371,641	84,933,214	82,442,778	68,492,747
From local government	37,985,212	19,515,972	19,240,124	19,779,360	19,121,194
Charges and miscellaneous revenue	311,244,880	297,025,966	300,970,446	285,905,918	285,732,639
Liquor stores revenue	7,480,124	7,114,248	6,739,028	6,494,993	6,376,562
Utility revenue	13,574,604	13,626,445	14,991,180	15,121,578	16,471,341
Insurance trust revenue (a)	485,235,115	255,798,430	586,742,446	451,103,159	(383,391,069)
Employee retirement	388,424,920	152,590,817	476,654,285	353,373,854	(449,271,197)
Unemployment compensation	74,232,787	80,109,746	87,410,032	75,037,579	41,976,470
Worker compensation	15,295,670	15,526,364	15,032,589	15,311,140	16,618,791
Other	7,281,738	7,571,503	7,645,540	7,380,586	7,284,867
Expenditure total	2,005,911,667	1,981,197,761	2,005,947,956	1,943,522,632	1,832,596,801
General expenditure	1,683,170,060	1,648,195,648	1,654,428,735	1,593,693,957	1,560,046,263
Education	599,151,748	588,340,483	592,863,150	571,147,157	567,674,062
Intergovernmental expenditure	324,995,548	317,839,562	330,482,270	317,389,500	324,374,036
State institutions of higher education	232,678,490	230,296,706	222,760,979	214,010,622	207,010,341
Other education	366,473,258	358,043,777	370,102,171	357,136,535	360,663,721
Public welfare	519,178,293	489,162,351	494,828,803	462,430,908	438,744,629
Intergovernmental expenditure	55,565,254	55,913,067	56,678,841	58,858,443	58,741,316
Cash assistance, other	6,508,047	6,401,260	6,582,490	6,164,123	6,290,097
Other public welfare	484,584,008	453,538,093	460,117,393	426,985,892	404,409,141
Highways	112,174,050	115,296,570	109,397,936	111,169,808	107,286,437
Intergovernmental expenditure	18,158,521	17,787,581	17,243,590	18,043,061	16,492,780
Regular state highway facilities	104,088,029	105,496,969	101,913,730	102,742,620	98,889,122
State toll highways/facilities	8,086,021	9,799,601	7,484,206	8,427,188	8,397,315
Health and hospitals	130,680,311	130,621,569	126,020,387	122,754,039	120,594,797
Hospitals	67,433,480	69,265,569	65,985,505	64,509,024	58,041,020
Health	63,246,831	61,356,000	60,034,882	58,245,015	62,553,777
Natural resources	21,345,804	22,051,093	21,989,895	21,514,767	22,605,445
Corrections	48,407,786	48,439,991	49,166,999	48,549,551	50,382,439
Financial administration	23,136,739	21,771,566	22,334,533	22,610,662	22,978,925
Employment security administration	4,846,304	5,065,317	5,214,711	5,108,615	4,520,197
Police protection	15,106,964	14,275,634	14,248,537	13,828,055	13,676,971
Interest on general debt	46,138,932	47,273,956	46,653,282	45,259,591	45,281,069
Utility expenditure	24,661,698	23,724,473	25,548,643	23,864,159	26,295,576
Insurance trust expenditure	292,447,534	303,669,929	320,563,723	320,720,833	241,080,311
Employee retirement	203,454,835	190,622,956	180,712,886	166,956,051	156,708,757
Unemployment compensation	71,181,425	95,317,830	121,384,316	134,908,383	65,974,092
Other	17,811,274	17,729,143	18,466,521	18,856,399	18,397,462
Total expenditure by character and object	2,005,911,667	1,981,197,761	2,005,947,956	1,943,522,632	1,832,596,801
Direct expenditure	1,517,128,804	1,499,314,531	1,509,115,520	1,457,965,445	1,341,709,410
Current operation	1,020,376,950	986,062,966	984,180,683	934,321,563	901,310,643
Capital outlay	114,980,312	119,668,339	115,570,769	118,010,630	116,989,763
Assistance and subsidies	40,795,280	40,078,288	39,762,087	37,561,512	35,005,215
Interest on debt	48,528,728	49,835,009	49,038,258	47,350,907	47,323,478
Insurance benefits and repayments	292,447,534	303,669,929	320,563,723	320,720,833	241,080,311
Intergovernmental expenditure	488,782,863	481,883,230	496,832,436	485,557,187	490,887,391
Cash and security holdings at end of fiscal year	3,837,746,513	3,667,671,249	3,672,783,154	3,323,047,498	3,082,511,650

See footnotes at end of table

TABLE 7.25

National Totals of State Government Finances for Selected Years: 2009–2018

(in thousands of dollars) (continued)

Source: U.S. Census Bureau, Census of Governments: Finance (years ending in '2' and '7'), and Annual Survey of State Government Finances (remaining years).

Notes:

1. Data users who create their own estimates using these data should cite only the U.S. Census Bureau as the source of the original data. Data in this table are based on information from public records and contain no confidential data. Although the data in this table come from a census of governmental units and are not subject to sampling error, the census results may contain nonsampling error. Additional information on nonsampling error, response rates, and definitions may be found within the survey methodology *https://www.census.gov/programs-surveys/state/technical-documentation/methodology.html.*

2. Detail may not add to total due to rounding.

Key:

(a) Within insurance trust revenue, net earnings of state-administered pension systems is a calculated statistic (the item code in the data file is X08), and thus can be positive or negative. Net earnings is the sum of earnings on investments plus gains on investments minus losses on investments. The change made in 2002 for asset valuation from book to market value in accordance with Statement 34 of the Governmental Accounting Standards Board is reflected in the calculated statistics.

TABLE 7.26
State General Revenue, By Source and By State: 2018 (In thousands of dollars)

State	Total general revenue (a)	Total (b)	Taxes	Sales and gross receipts	
			Total (b)	General	Motor fuels
United States	$2,097,939,270	$1,022,783,253	$484,307,927	$319,702,418	$48,324,660
Alabama	28,250,965	11,055,577	5,534,807	2,786,833	648,639
Alaska	8,152,092	1,641,733	252,970	0	47,149
Arizona	38,133,225	16,212,105	9,708,694	7,687,992	869,183
Arkansas	21,402,327	9,843,173	4,834,983	3,498,073	492,945
California	320,249,459	175,016,884	57,345,108	39,682,734	6,351,756
Colorado	30,878,620	14,802,263	5,712,243	3,211,909	675,962
Connecticut	30,490,255	19,082,263	7,596,995	4,400,808	487,327
Delaware	9,275,531	4,219,572	585,645	0	131,864
Florida	91,783,197	45,961,204	38,456,615	29,562,900	2,799,610
Georgia	45,135,668	23,428,056	9,132,965	5,938,448	1,801,798
Hawaii	14,078,337	7,714,451	4,732,032	3,529,065	88,377
Idaho	9,155,174	4,845,431	2,396,117	1,790,830	362,234
Illinois	72,948,065	39,857,069	18,699,777	11,336,866	1,367,939
Indiana	40,546,768	19,397,879	12,119,558	7,795,091	1,420,135
Iowa	24,072,068	10,088,480	4,687,073	3,279,789	671,937
Kansas	19,078,088	9,546,790	4,494,809	3,304,091	461,075
Kentucky	29,299,781	12,059,970	5,714,427	3,600,598	702,651
Louisiana	29,227,226	11,357,686	6,864,723	4,252,693	631,641
Maine	8,814,837	4,410,632	2,250,293	1,529,113	250,468
Maryland	42,101,136	22,427,037	9,567,244	4,716,179	1,084,195
Massachusetts	58,094,512	29,654,803	9,022,362	6,490,305	769,144
Michigan	66,231,312	30,508,361	14,398,369	9,595,949	1,473,002
Minnesota	44,475,950	26,697,469	10,614,808	5,830,256	936,893
Mississippi	19,137,029	7,890,571	5,030,854	3,557,752	436,245
Missouri	30,919,843	13,027,504	5,539,227	3,686,274	717,894
Montana	7,021,451	2,944,827	655,034	0	258,958
Nebraska	10,470,221	5,393,093	2,502,020	1,900,037	373,889
Nevada	16,087,532	9,157,036	7,329,456	5,095,689	343,386
New Hampshire	7,566,526	2,920,888	1,025,902	.	183,366
New Jersey	66,129,779	35,365,046	15,424,507	10,459,419	458,892
New Mexico	17,627,371	5,671,904	2,874,807	2,073,118	230,303
New York	175,700,469	88,541,099	26,399,319	14,820,163	1,636,749
North Carolina	56,343,509	27,855,070	12,213,458	8,009,850	1,974,782
North Dakota	7,746,544	4,205,184	1,395,503	912,532	196,649
Ohio	68,842,609	29,130,040	18,056,988	12,148,485	1,912,191
Oklahoma	22,075,260	9,563,830	4,194,272	2,855,176	485,276
Oregon	32,138,083	12,644,869	1,654,829	0	533,976
Pennsylvania	87,715,628	40,709,545	21,034,252	10,920,832	3,375,429
Rhode Island	8,406,086	3,483,100	1,682,021	1,048,957	79,858
South Carolina	28,177,916	10,550,096	4,948,178	3,303,220	646,581
South Dakota	4,409,773	1,917,548	1,585,089	1,103,624	187,424
Tennessee	30,234,945	14,269,061	10,343,084	7,469,547	1,086,693
Texas	137,622,906	60,328,843	51,462,209	36,129,876	3,710,307
Utah	18,687,798	8,038,690	3,901,286	2,784,489	557,490
Vermont	6,346,252	3,284,231	1,095,321	397,691	82,953
Virginia	50,882,334	23,489,398	7,082,742	4,076,636	1,031,034
Washington	50,923,984	26,574,889	20,327,520	15,643,017	1,713,782
West Virginia	12,970,565	5,417,673	2,731,739	1,311,930	419,528
Wisconsin	36,278,147	18,742,929	8,232,896	5,484,375	1,051,479
Wyoming	5,602,117	1,837,401	862,797	689,207	113,622

See footnotes at end of table

TABLE 7.26

State General Revenue, By Source and By State: 2018 (In thousands of dollars) (continued)

State	Taxes (con't.)			Corporation net income	Intergovernmental revenue	Charges and miscellaneous general revenue
	Licenses					
	Total (b)	Motor vehicle	Individual income			
United States	$57,158,841	$27,874,054	$390,002,949	$47,647,798	$688,138,024	$387,017,993
Alabama	521,990	220,483	3,912,800	577,516	10,303,451	6,891,937
Alaska	153,636	36,258	0	196,321	3,457,365	3,052,994
Arizona	495,034	230,095	4,545,242	373,076	16,011,205	5,909,915
Arkansas	409,856	164,617	2,866,175	390,756	7,877,352	3,681,802
California	10,504,521	4,635,040	95,152,230	12,488,304	103,018,851	42,213,724
Colorado	816,832	597,097	7,510,366	660,100	9,402,733	6,673,624
Connecticut	431,196	238,351	9,733,258	778,232	7,440,296	3,967,696
Delaware	1,574,576	58,969	1,652,335	254,802	2,619,277	2,436,682
Florida	2,123,462	1,449,604	0	2,426,900	28,298,587	17,523,406
Georgia	719,422	395,140	11,643,781	1,004,298	15,295,883	6,411,729
Hawaii	275,600	191,757	2,430,032	146,831	3,013,717	3,350,169
Idaho	367,178	195,431	1,835,864	240,809	2,819,674	1,490,069
Illinois	2,751,479	1,618,750	15,296,693	2,587,141	22,429,882	10,661,114
Indiana	749,114	321,055	5,816,072	698,725	15,075,489	6,073,400
Iowa	954,503	664,178	3,897,236	443,187	6,075,843	7,907,745
Kansas	433,229	222,978	3,413,677	437,967	4,072,601	5,458,697
Kentucky	499,502	211,646	4,499,086	511,353	11,970,566	5,269,245
Louisiana	393,129	79,284	3,246,226	358,208	13,648,190	4,221,350
Maine	281,155	112,557	1,605,096	185,737	3,012,515	1,391,690
Maryland	850,913	501,417	9,507,776	1,033,175	13,023,465	6,650,634
Massachusetts	1,154,719	444,827	16,280,331	2,408,947	17,101,109	11,338,600
Michigan	1,945,619	1,337,873	10,238,864	1,095,023	21,365,685	14,357,266
Minnesota	1,476,228	800,981	11,882,330	1,357,004	11,742,550	6,035,931
Mississippi	492,415	158,283	1,852,937	437,407	8,271,815	2,974,643
Missouri	596,167	296,849	6,510,224	333,724	11,947,706	5,944,633
Montana	379,198	168,827	1,300,809	176,132	3,124,693	951,931
Nebraska	196,215	113,733	2,360,596	313,690	3,264,232	1,812,896
Nevada	661,240	198,263	0	0	5,454,068	1,476,428
New Hampshire	435,544	82,270	105,759	790,011	2,799,206	1,846,432
New Jersey	1,542,213	657,956	15,037,845	2,235,653	18,014,349	12,750,384
New Mexico	322,473	200,727	1,252,651	91,488	7,534,520	4,420,947
New York	1,771,629	1,411,790	52,738,515	3,617,910	64,587,716	22,571,654
North Carolina	2,197,653	853,879	12,609,608	742,512	18,704,775	9,783,664
North Dakota	214,463	118,080	367,635	107,277	1,742,138	1,799,222
Ohio	2,237,002	787,276	8,698,901	9,046	24,388,743	15,323,826
Oklahoma	1,018,657	736,979	3,495,264	234,868	7,100,962	5,410,468
Oregon	1,087,449	539,474	8,879,552	804,453	10,470,949	9,022,265
Pennsylvania	2,721,979	1,183,964	12,800,890	2,486,379	29,418,893	17,587,190
Rhode Island	110,799	29,352	1,329,152	118,118	2,868,687	2,054,299
South Carolina	582,294	274,093	4,432,104	424,048	9,916,827	7,710,993
South Dakota	291,896	83,369	0	32,376	1,499,310	992,915
Tennessee	1,763,747	357,692	246,508	1,644,159	11,826,420	4,139,464
Texas	3,635,024	2,358,248	0	0	47,201,933	30,092,130
Utah	347,888	224,833	3,991,400	400,885	4,724,208	5,924,900
Vermont	126,404	72,957	819,330	110,819	2,091,212	970,809
Virginia	878,751	492,825	14,105,766	861,897	10,957,750	16,435,186
Washington	2,070,931	1,129,671	0	0	14,446,364	9,902,731
West Virginia	219,003	4,498	1,950,571	110,068	4,846,089	2,706,803
Wisconsin	1,187,392	518,115	8,151,462	910,466	9,494,180	8,041,038
Wyoming	187,522	91,663	0	0	2,363,993	1,400,723

See footnotes at end of table

TABLE 7.26
State General Revenue, By Source and By State: 2018 (In thousands of dollars) (continued)

Source: U.S. Census Bureau, 2018 Annual Survey of State Government Finances.

Notes:

1. Data users who create their own estimates using these data should cite only the U.S. Census Bureau as the source of the original data. Data in this table are based on information from public records and contain no confidential data. Although the data in this table come from a census of governmental units and are not subject to sampling error, the census results may contain nonsampling error. Additional information on nonsampling error, response rates, and definitions may be found within the survey methodology *https://www.census.gov/programs-surveys/state/technical-documentation/methodology.html.*

2. Detail may not add to total due to rounding.

Key:

(a) Total general revenue equals total taxes plus intergovernmental revenue plus charges and miscellaneous revenue.

(b) Total includes other taxes not shown separately in this table.

(c) Source: U.S. Census Bureau, 2018 Annual Survey of State Government Tax Collections

TABLE 7.27
State Expenditure, By Character and Object and By State: 2018 (In thousands of dollars)

State	Intergovernmental expenditures	Direct expenditures Total	Current operation	Total	Capital outlay Construction	Other
United States	$562,587,857	$1,848,117,782	$1,307,732,632	$135,313,220	$114,419,655	$20,893,565
Alabama	7,006,778	26,892,612	18,465,571	2,397,764	1,866,960	530,804
Alaska	648,930	11,330,253	8,414,113	1,142,969	925,567	217,402
Arizona	10,268,171	30,877,121	23,083,588	1,747,664	1,411,687	335,977
Arkansas	5,489,804	17,030,405	12,951,596	1,364,490	1,248,030	116,460
California	108,218,508	266,873,796	190,565,162	9,438,084	8,298,926	1,139,158
Colorado	7,518,654	29,930,720	20,829,453	1,711,872	1,254,278	457,594
Connecticut	5,908,441	22,162,222	13,306,482	1,841,642	1,500,411	341,231
Delaware	1,611,413	8,380,273	6,373,474	713,138	591,920	121,218
Florida	18,958,978	77,862,800	57,473,878	7,427,393	6,921,210	506,183
Georgia	12,889,900	38,668,284	26,566,012	3,231,415	2,717,120	514,295
Hawaii	355,739	13,298,737	10,136,706	1,358,477	302,474	1,056,003
Idaho	2,570,844	7,860,276	5,628,078	735,909	613,879	122,030
Illinois	21,109,911	71,358,188	45,757,167	4,005,783	3,619,535	386,248
Indiana	10,328,805	31,307,493	23,687,675	2,355,800	1,910,900	444,900
Iowa	5,373,071	18,503,965	13,134,266	1,830,005	1,661,633	168,372
Kansas	5,030,280	14,542,149	11,206,738	1,016,388	862,730	153,658
Kentucky	4,890,345	30,422,173	21,918,436	2,038,511	1,807,481	231,030
Louisiana	6,380,598	28,737,618	20,478,025	2,031,489	1,595,354	436,135
Maine	1,347,094	7,889,848	6,157,472	350,777	313,933	36,844
Maryland	9,874,995	36,308,950	25,516,499	3,503,748	2,745,694	758,054
Massachusetts	9,434,585	57,931,525	42,170,593	4,856,630	4,254,933	601,697
Michigan	22,754,958	53,534,599	39,346,253	2,715,123	2,250,543	464,580
Minnesota	14,174,246	35,410,581	26,273,079	1,642,656	1,226,159	416,497
Mississippi	4,861,117	16,971,447	12,346,712	1,049,450	910,957	138,493
Missouri	6,336,401	28,656,459	21,010,758	1,346,219	1,133,341	212,878
Montana	1,113,197	6,692,284	4,982,167	404,754	364,693	40,061
Nebraska	2,668,741	8,455,140	6,628,165	737,197	640,356	96,841
Nevada	5,180,050	12,234,642	7,802,811	962,791	865,103	97,688
New Hampshire	1,764,616	7,143,307	5,363,400	403,614	323,612	80,002
New Jersey	15,250,952	63,655,798	41,022,722	4,881,770	3,533,380	1,348,390
New Mexico	5,176,572	16,291,884	12,750,523	389,427	335,975	53,452
New York	63,492,253	149,671,207	105,263,964	12,931,334	11,420,074	1,511,260
North Carolina	14,706,189	46,223,206	32,743,106	5,062,722	4,263,287	799,435
North Dakota	1,995,041	5,221,274	3,853,916	534,189	489,237	44,952
Ohio	18,933,185	70,092,881	45,118,929	4,621,346	4,200,064	421,282
Oklahoma	4,470,670	20,843,851	14,292,023	2,840,809	2,533,550	307,259
Oregon	6,320,421	33,049,357	24,709,888	1,471,019	1,271,619	199,400
Pennsylvania	22,327,616	80,323,898	53,989,427	8,870,696	7,803,287	1,067,409
Rhode Island	1,307,710	8,164,272	5,815,655	444,220	398,445	45,775
South Carolina	6,768,154	28,234,412	19,841,367	2,322,633	2,037,907	284,726
South Dakota	871,682	4,371,576	2,898,694	613,501	562,079	51,422
Tennessee	7,619,932	26,118,151	19,873,507	1,767,907	1,393,083	374,824
Texas	31,520,535	119,369,539	83,871,515	11,764,854	9,664,505	2,100,349
Utah	4,166,842	17,720,762	12,732,903	2,015,974	1,594,419	421,555
Vermont	1,839,019	5,182,323	4,148,629	330,332	283,540	46,792
Virginia	12,257,922	44,109,025	32,667,604	3,848,602	3,168,759	679,843
Washington	14,338,188	43,656,438	30,352,601	2,597,102	2,079,920	517,182
West Virginia	2,693,408	12,665,772	9,070,100	779,625	676,453	103,172
Wisconsin	11,108,614	31,069,223	21,740,427	2,350,081	2,078,415	271,666
Wyoming	1,353,782	4,815,066	3,400,803	513,325	492,238	21,087

See footnotes at end of table

TABLE 7.27
State Expenditure, By Character and Object and By State: 2018 (In thousands of dollars) (continued)

State	Direct expenditures (con't)		Insurance benefits and repayments	Exhibit: Total salaries and wages
	Assistance and subsidies	Interest on debt		
United States	$52,020,828	$48,517,907	$304,533,195	$279,060,869
Alabama	2,026,561	395,811	3,606,905	5,006,399
Alaska	156,646	208,821	1,407,704	1,693,777
Arizona	1,044,970	540,207	4,460,692	4,131,082
Arkansas	479,449	152,956	2,081,914	3,045,148
California	5,768,639	7,171,873	53,930,038	36,861,691
Colorado	863,014	786,681	5,739,700	5,694,648
Connecticut	506,209	1,607,284	4,900,605	4,535,820
Delaware	351,317	211,914	730,430	1,427,539
Florida	2,348,488	864,979	9,748,062	9,593,177
Georgia	1,349,426	594,551	6,926,880	6,861,976
Hawaii	117,347	100,246	1,585,961	3,250,714
Idaho	170,912	142,614	1,182,763	1,533,577
Illinois	1,619,236	4,391,547	15,584,455	8,044,553
Indiana	1,420,605	978,441	2,864,972	4,792,238
Iowa	623,092	215,360	2,701,242	3,527,619
Kansas	213,140	165,644	1,940,239	2,959,691
Kentucky	1,150,992	664,904	4,649,330	4,425,025
Louisiana	709,562	810,683	4,707,859	4,127,020
Maine	169,069	158,613	1,053,917	1,090,102
Maryland	1,552,242	1,239,474	4,496,987	5,373,400
Massachusetts	1,040,193	2,896,976	6,967,133	7,589,998
Michigan	1,570,238	1,705,749	8,197,236	10,233,587
Minnesota	1,243,256	572,530	5,679,060	5,767,789
Mississippi	403,554	295,707	2,876,024	2,546,158
Missouri	621,873	769,954	4,907,655	3,954,740
Montana	87,500	108,990	1,108,873	1,094,046
Nebraska	224,730	58,856	806,192	1,624,038
Nevada	574,416	139,415	2,755,209	1,838,635
New Hampshire	237,485	315,144	823,664	1,162,054
New Jersey	1,674,419	2,227,970	13,848,917	10,392,904
New Mexico	240,051	417,814	2,494,069	2,501,757
New York	2,026,985	5,990,288	23,458,636	18,772,845
North Carolina	1,429,827	643,100	6,344,451	8,348,468
North Dakota	129,454	72,639	631,076	1,049,222
Ohio	1,797,777	1,187,462	17,367,367	8,378,398
Oklahoma	622,361	406,260	2,682,398	3,364,146
Oregon	524,840	414,808	5,928,802	4,984,970
Pennsylvania	3,065,350	1,586,991	12,811,434	10,561,499
Rhode Island	175,387	444,399	1,284,611	1,344,672
South Carolina	1,288,726	544,672	4,237,014	4,025,773
South Dakota	138,315	123,352	597,714	764,981
Tennessee	1,391,419	310,926	2,774,392	4,221,590
Texas	3,588,207	1,681,348	18,463,615	18,769,065
Utah	811,121	223,770	1,936,994	3,719,162
Vermont	189,366	102,914	411,082	969,252
Virginia	1,226,394	1,162,211	5,204,214	7,708,152
Washington	1,621,721	1,521,343	7,563,671	8,567,327
West Virginia	658,436	588,911	1,568,700	1,874,275
Wisconsin	736,561	577,112	5,665,042	4,297,663
Wyoming	39,950	23,693	837,295	658,507

See footnotes at end of table

TABLE 7.27

State Expenditure, By Character and Object and By State: 2018 (In thousands of dollars) (continued)

Source: U.S. Census Bureau, 2018 Annual Survey of State Government Finances.

Notes:

1. Data users who create their own estimates using these data should cite only the U.S. Census Bureau as the source of the original data. Data in this table are based on information from public records and contain no confidential data. Although the data in this table come from a census of governmental units and are not subject to sampling error, the census results may contain nonsampling error. Additional information on nonsampling error, response rates, and definitions may be found within the survey methodology *https://www.census.gov/programs-surveys/state/technical-documentation/methodology.html.*

2. Detail may not add to total due to rounding.

TABLE 7.28

State General Expenditure, By Function and By State: 2018 (In thousands of dollars)

State	Total general expenditures (a)	Education	Public welfare	Highways	Hospitals
United States	$2,067,954,884	$705,090,151	$716,794,523	$134,774,210	$90,476,187
Alabama	29,951,784	12,051,715	8,612,680	2,078,347	3,009,374
Alaska	10,446,105	1,372,847	2,829,723	1,325,870	33,660
Arizona	36,650,241	12,377,309	15,233,186	2,372,631	251
Arkansas	20,438,295	8,086,351	6,805,974	1,783,776	1,182,854
California	319,549,260	102,372,367	141,298,829	11,133,335	13,661,880
Colorado	31,696,427	12,635,707	9,804,228	2,177,923	1,166,904
Connecticut	22,583,290	7,354,661	4,883,237	1,671,813	1,468,717
Delaware	9,104,556	3,267,523	2,708,613	578,469	80,689
Florida	86,782,792	28,660,079	27,812,728	8,456,153	1,448,208
Georgia	44,593,220	20,031,380	13,103,954	2,832,890	1,446,620
Hawaii	12,068,515	3,658,576	2,908,075	594,409	554,863
Idaho	9,113,460	3,382,019	2,715,286	882,023	54,726
Illinois	76,875,407	19,254,876	25,365,980	5,289,208	954,931
Indiana	38,771,326	16,263,389	13,971,440	2,762,006	140,266
Iowa	20,952,954	7,371,352	6,260,575	2,380,210	2,220,166
Kansas	17,632,190	7,482,546	4,187,002	1,008,522	2,682,388
Kentucky	30,635,111	10,274,643	11,926,347	1,803,079	1,959,379
Louisiana	30,403,826	9,276,658	12,158,245	1,444,825	360,569
Maine	8,154,539	2,176,832	3,325,199	775,769	104,638
Maryland	40,435,641	12,984,499	13,047,335	2,837,118	546,427
Massachusetts	56,700,849	13,317,694	23,880,903	2,630,888	699,023
Michigan	67,189,291	27,269,300	19,324,550	3,402,666	4,639,200
Minnesota	43,337,146	16,405,597	16,076,178	2,812,506	330,829
Mississippi	18,660,117	5,751,698	6,579,317	1,172,098	1,492,885
Missouri	30,079,041	9,820,813	9,685,146	1,533,420	2,436,367
Montana	6,595,193	1,893,109	2,220,855	648,130	63,105
Nebraska	10,317,689	3,869,733	2,843,906	870,351	183,303
Nevada	14,610,813	5,653,496	3,956,409	1,076,888	284,633
New Hampshire	7,521,532	2,304,692	2,597,379	553,746	63,389
New Jersey	62,187,390	22,648,321	18,814,173	5,016,444	2,119,311
New Mexico	18,973,297	6,022,626	6,238,404	709,107	1,165,291
New York	173,766,965	46,901,379	71,580,845	7,467,266	5,891,120
North Carolina	54,506,230	21,894,866	15,124,072	5,343,092	2,412,935
North Dakota	6,539,038	2,336,423	1,555,797	768,683	49,411
Ohio	70,721,000	23,297,437	28,265,068	4,344,194	3,485,303
Oklahoma	21,147,798	8,068,280	6,810,139	2,234,254	232,768
Oregon	32,946,999	10,549,695	11,235,890	1,153,745	2,580,178
Pennsylvania	87,902,698	26,638,852	29,548,636	9,530,078	5,441,838
Rhode Island	8,070,396	2,165,079	3,261,230	425,934	56,365
South Carolina	28,984,861	10,411,541	8,053,479	1,895,113	1,984,218
South Dakota	4,645,544	1,608,584	1,172,574	658,346	22,971
Tennessee	30,963,512	10,686,746	12,480,175	1,791,384	354,881
Texas	132,368,456	56,461,040	39,408,074	9,526,653	7,596,330
Utah	19,663,786	9,029,569	3,898,102	1,437,674	2,168,114
Vermont	6,546,073	2,883,613	1,789,827	451,526	22,769
Virginia	50,395,859	17,421,907	11,684,097	5,477,966	5,516,050
Washington	50,357,945	20,831,462	12,790,963	2,955,838	3,652,849
West Virginia	13,703,084	4,396,317	4,944,067	1,227,811	158,504
Wisconsin	36,483,821	12,317,405	11,162,054	2,958,776	2,291,169
Wyoming	5,229,522	1,897,548	853,578	511,257	3,568

See footnotes at end of table

TABLE 7.28

State General Expenditure, By Function and By State: 2018 (In thousands of dollars) (continued)

State	Natural resources	Health	Corrections	Financial administration	Employment security administration	Police
United States	$24,335,551	$65,005,458	$53,379,501	$27,324,399	$3,823,018	$17,342,880
Alabama	270,436	528,982	595,676	404,690	97,214	178,415
Alaska	564,528	273,110	435,826	260,824	33,984	185,933
Arizona	314,216	593,159	1,093,410	325,585	0	282,873
Arkansas	282,203	174,956	338,273	443,790	90,015	106,628
California	5,627,729	7,264,570	9,104,578	3,487,630	317,600	1,931,457
Colorado	425,244	491,923	1,093,736	446,711	64,892	221,140
Connecticut	209,028	1,015,650	616,242	315,227	20,880	248,298
Delaware	79,663	481,144	340,098	220,548	16,553	146,507
Florida	1,614,036	4,023,674	2,768,672	593,557	305,267	633,426
Georgia	582,562	1,362,561	1,355,774	634,959	30,598	459,715
Hawaii	154,917	546,530	228,068	231,537	6,883	44,930
Idaho	256,214	144,359	288,137	253,983	6,774	67,156
Illinois	259,199	1,163,348	1,958,336	1,139,162	45,692	509,105
Indiana	373,597	589,823	726,759	338,099	79,295	263,847
Iowa	306,130	244,446	282,045	250,131	51,428	106,324
Kansas	224,604	426,940	350,498	172,811	30,524	109,890
Kentucky	429,366	446,213	609,697	332,899	115,992	215,850
Louisiana	847,952	444,667	704,416	443,390	111,426	366,451
Maine	138,344	195,530	159,658	246,688	62,353	91,828
Maryland	516,597	2,201,263	1,447,811	718,272	48,243	666,408
Massachusetts	281,180	1,593,860	1,504,408	664,934	185,436	599,597
Michigan	413,764	2,139,562	1,914,217	945,438	177,082	521,117
Minnesota	656,288	537,345	655,076	488,380	42,146	485,123
Mississippi	312,207	417,704	325,624	234,503	72,732	142,346
Missouri	375,964	2,006,652	783,787	440,451	41,509	258,835
Montana	311,697	175,282	218,878	145,676	43,270	54,835
Nebraska	218,809	295,322	371,531	155,945	44,487	90,507
Nevada	148,965	303,777	339,980	245,776	64,571	98,896
New Hampshire	60,669	144,369	135,173	97,192	30,183	66,713
New Jersey	582,909	2,948,275	1,421,635	1,091,684	194,343	849,427
New Mexico	201,119	386,056	483,190	161,090	10,669	148,651
New York	572,127	10,046,952	3,199,404	2,530,068	206,807	1,064,365
North Carolina	520,176	1,665,329	1,412,095	690,189	56,704	604,212
North Dakota	150,952	127,917	104,432	75,904	15,328	29,140
Ohio	396,531	1,964,946	1,805,807	1,330,244	119,447	498,391
Oklahoma	175,197	867,839	611,411	312,475	75,662	177,128
Oregon	473,168	1,001,355	945,814	657,944	51,799	232,066
Pennsylvania	784,111	3,728,441	2,182,586	1,374,643	102,763	1,151,450
Rhode Island	78,868	225,931	219,705	142,142	40,881	90,313
South Carolina	208,474	1,216,517	513,277	318,642	98,474	173,934
South Dakota	166,839	160,503	125,620	95,658	24,653	49,317
Tennessee	387,474	753,484	955,135	572,678	59,451	240,927
Texas	799,779	3,165,266	4,052,989	1,100,572	91,145	1,279,130
Utah	241,862	341,573	379,926	455,449	12,455	159,512
Vermont	117,306	376,219	144,869	88,502	1,734	86,944
Virginia	302,288	1,573,641	1,586,514	588,033	78,214	713,547
Washington	856,296	2,938,904	1,039,580	463,590	192,278	470,737
West Virginia	267,618	291,850	306,006	190,030	21,546	77,494
Wisconsin	562,898	613,949	1,006,021	267,407	94,727	52,438
Wyoming	233,451	383,790	137,101	138,667	36,909	39,607

See footnotes at end of table

TABLE 7.28
State General Expenditure, By Function and By State: 2017 (In thousands of dollars) (continued)

Source: U.S. Census Bureau, 2018 Annual Survey of State Government Finances.

Notes:

1. Data users who create their own estimates using these data should cite only the U.S. Census Bureau as the source of the original data. Data in this table are based on information from public records and contain no confidentialdata. Although the data in this table come from a census of governmental units and are not subject to sampling error, the census results may contain nonsampling error.

Additional information on nonsampling error, response rates, and definitions may be found within the survey methodology <https://www.census.gov/programs-surveys/state/technical-documentation/methodology.html>.

2. Detail may not add to total due to rounding.

Key:

(a) Total includes other expenditures not shown separately in this table.

TABLE 7.29
State Debt Outstanding at End of Fiscal Year, by State: 2018 (In thousands of dollars)

State	Total	Long-term total	Short-term total	Net long-term total (a)
United States	$1,173,606,967	$1,165,350,673	$8,256,294	$701,872,827
Alabama	9,856,082	9,806,657	49,425	8,489,389
Alaska	5,889,417	5,836,148	53,269	1,987,469
Arizona	13,703,759	13,627,491	76,268	8,035,248
Arkansas	6,832,598	6,808,411	24,187	5,172,511
California	148,027,188	148,027,188	0	118,128,158
Colorado	17,853,552	17,765,295	88,257	6,295,739
Connecticut	40,287,423	40,287,423	0	24,730,849
Delaware	5,127,188	5,127,188	0	3,612,473
Florida	27,593,512	27,538,764	54,748	22,256,898
Georgia	13,305,788	13,194,560	111,228	9,817,549
Hawaii	9,870,931	9,870,931	0	9,105,035
Idaho	3,439,046	3,433,664	5,382	624,399
Illinois	67,495,522	67,495,522	0	37,837,997
Indiana	22,026,355	21,890,097	136,258	2,693,426
Iowa	6,270,052	6,270,052	0	1,655,881
Kansas	6,136,579	6,136,579	0	3,184,793
Kentucky	14,617,245	14,582,347	34,898	8,440,226
Louisiana	18,155,260	18,150,256	5,004	10,455,247
Maine	4,759,978	4,759,978	0	1,141,496
Maryland	27,998,569	27,998,569	0	15,466,494
Massachusetts	78,620,996	78,516,607	104,389	52,910,013
Michigan	33,563,347	33,093,830	469,517	16,491,908
Minnesota	16,600,028	16,600,028	0	9,921,256
Mississippi	7,252,112	7,230,924	21,188	5,576,023
Missouri	17,854,734	17,811,485	43,249	4,676,746
Montana	2,739,404	2,738,814	590	119,656
Nebraska	2,056,773	2,055,332	1,441	538,191
Nevada	3,435,955	3,435,955	0	2,470,524
New Hampshire	7,739,271	7,739,271	0	2,931,142
New Jersey	65,574,574	65,164,039	410,535	46,870,207
New Mexico	7,268,214	7,236,443	31,771	4,210,739
New York	147,960,540	147,109,807	850,733	83,824,747
North Carolina	15,354,553	15,260,118	94,435	6,705,612
North Dakota	3,040,855	3,040,436	419	1,318,159
Ohio	31,622,762	30,911,916	710,846	10,483,212
Oklahoma	8,910,608	8,898,017	12,591	6,048,877
Oregon	14,285,969	13,707,544	578,425	8,548,146
Pennsylvania	49,064,189	48,824,084	240,105	32,173,424
Rhode Island	9,093,878	9,024,676	69,202	2,483,058
South Carolina	14,571,479	14,426,995	144,484	11,650,341
South Dakota	3,739,690	3,734,340	5,350	986,023
Tennessee	6,289,301	6,019,882	269,419	1,544,803
Texas	51,529,919	48,463,432	3,066,487	34,044,941
Utah	7,355,005	7,272,605	82,400	4,601,351
Vermont	3,580,807	3,344,643	236,164	1,115,746
Virginia	29,074,498	28,900,868	173,630	15,725,322
Washington	33,926,356	33,926,356	0	22,478,682
West Virginia	8,610,296	8,610,296	0	3,992,767
Wisconsin	22,812,370	22,812,370	0	8,200,074
Wyoming	832,440	832,440	0	99,860

Source: U.S. Census Bureau, 2018 Annual Survey of State Government Finances.

Notes:

1. Data users who create their own estimates using these data should cite only the U.S. Census Bureau as the source of the original data. Data in this table are based on information from public records and contain no confidential data. Although the data in this table come from a census of governmental units and are not subject to sampling error, the census results may contain nonsampling error. Additional information on nonsampling error, response rates, and definitions may be found within the survey methodology *https://www.census.gov/programs-surveys/state/technical-documentation/methodology.html.*

2. Detail may not add to total due to rounding.

Key:

(a) Long-term debt outstanding minus long-term debt offsets.

TABLE 7.30
Membership of State Public-Employee Pension Systems By State: Fiscal Year 2018

State	Membership Total	Membership Active members	Membership Inactive members	Total beneficiaries receiving periodic benefit payments
United States	19,006,463	12,928,649	6,077,814	9,424,493
Alabama (a)	255,052	225,351	29,701	144,409
Alaska	32,780	22,488	10,292	49,743
Arizona	487,375	243,705	243,670	173,561
Arkansas	170,536	136,180	34,356	99,888
California	2,212,741	1,456,951	755,790	1,143,806
Colorado	490,300	231,710	258,590	128,259
Connecticut	125,450	110,901	14,549	94,996
Delaware	48,925	44,641	4,284	29,498
Florida	625,818	518,545	107,273	414,699
Georgia	593,855	369,537	224,318	219,655
Hawaii	75,520	66,271	9,249	48,563
Idaho	84,297	71,163	13,134	52,271
Illinois	695,450	461,104	234,346	391,834
Indiana	261,356	220,206	41,150	154,826
Iowa	245,584	175,116	70,468	125,913
Kansas	209,549	151,687	57,862	101,911
Kentucky	393,781	205,917	187,864	173,344
Louisiana	354,057	187,512	166,545	177,090
Maine	61,936	51,522	10,414	45,287
Maryland	247,918	195,085	52,833	162,282
Massachusetts	297,827	213,864	83,963	153,350
Michigan (a)	284,968	253,671	31,297	323,097
Minnesota	554,089	310,469	243,620	225,169
Mississippi	220,827	151,376	69,451	107,599
Missouri	362,358	247,623	114,735	189,523
Montana	94,019	54,147	39,872	42,794
Nebraska	96,127	62,437	33,690	27,532
Nevada	124,303	107,649	16,654	67,163
New Hampshire	62,053	48,179	13,874	41,526
New Jersey	461,069	456,096	4,973	329,318
New Mexico	183,091	117,216	65,875	90,097
New York	916,620	789,345	127,275	645,382
North Carolina	706,876	484,938	221,938	303,346
North Dakota	49,348	34,525	14,823	20,627
Ohio	1,415,590	693,724	721,866	475,093
Oklahoma	178,203	143,538	34,665	121,341
Oregon	322,090	276,097	45,993	147,595
Pennsylvania	543,022	368,332	174,690	368,288
Rhode Island	53,287	39,493	13,794	28,520
South Carolina	411,383	219,295	192,088	163,082
South Dakota	59,919	41,186	18,733	28,403
Tennessee	385,582	217,434	168,148	157,487
Texas (a)	1,836,171	1,266,358	569,813	656,639
Utah	152,723	97,522	55,201	65,428
Vermont	33,341	25,874	7,467	19,432
Virginia	499,273	343,005	156,268	206,776
Washington	398,385	329,154	69,231	188,566
West Virginia	103,819	71,462	32,357	66,069
Wisconsin	425,409	257,413	167,996	203,202
Wyoming	102,411	61,635	40,776	30,214

See footnotes at end of table

TABLE 7.30

Membership of State Public-Employee Pension Systems By State: Fiscal Year 2018 (continued)

Source: U.S. Census Bureau, 2018 Annual Survey of Public Pensions: State- and Locally-Administered Defined Benefit Data.

Notes:

1. Data users who create their own estimates using these data should cite the U.S. Census Bureau as the source of the original data only. The data in this table are based on information from public records and contain no confidential data. The data in this table come from a sample of governmental units and are thus subject to both sampling and nonsampling error. Additional information on nonsampling error, response rates, and definitions may be found within the survey methodology *https://www2.census.gov/programs-surveys/aspp/technical-documentation/methodology/2018/2018surveymethodology.pdf.*

2. Effective with the 2012 survey cycle, the Annual Survey of Public Pensions: State-Administered Defined Benefit Data revised the survey form to implement changes in asset classification. These changes apply to the categories designated as corporate stocks, corporate bonds, federal government securities, state and local government securities, and other securities. Federally-sponsored agency securities are classified under federal government securities instead of corporate bonds. Private equity, venture capital, and leverage buyouts are classified under corporate stocks instead

of other securities. Due to these changes in asset classification, there are shifts in the distribution of assets from corporate bonds to federal government securities and from other securities to corporate stocks. However, since investment decisions guide the distribution of assets, we cannot calculate the exact impact that the changes in classification had on the asset distribution for 2012. As such, for the above mentioned asset categories, any data comparisons between data from 2012 to the present, and data prior to 2012 should be exercised with caution.

3. Pension obligations and Covered payroll for defined benefit pension systems are only collected at the state level.

4. Detail may not add to total due to rounding.

Key:

(a) There are exceptions to the fiscal year rule for the state pension systems in Alabama, Michigan, and Texas. For systems in these states, the fiscal year moves beyond the June 30 cutoff. The data for the survey year 2018 covers the fiscal year ending August 31, 2018 for Texas and September 30, 2018 for Alabama and Michigan. These exceptions are made to better align the data with the Survey of State Government Finances.

Table 7.30 | Membership of State Public-Employee Pension Systems

Membership of State Public-Employee Pension Systems By State:
(Fiscal Year 2018)

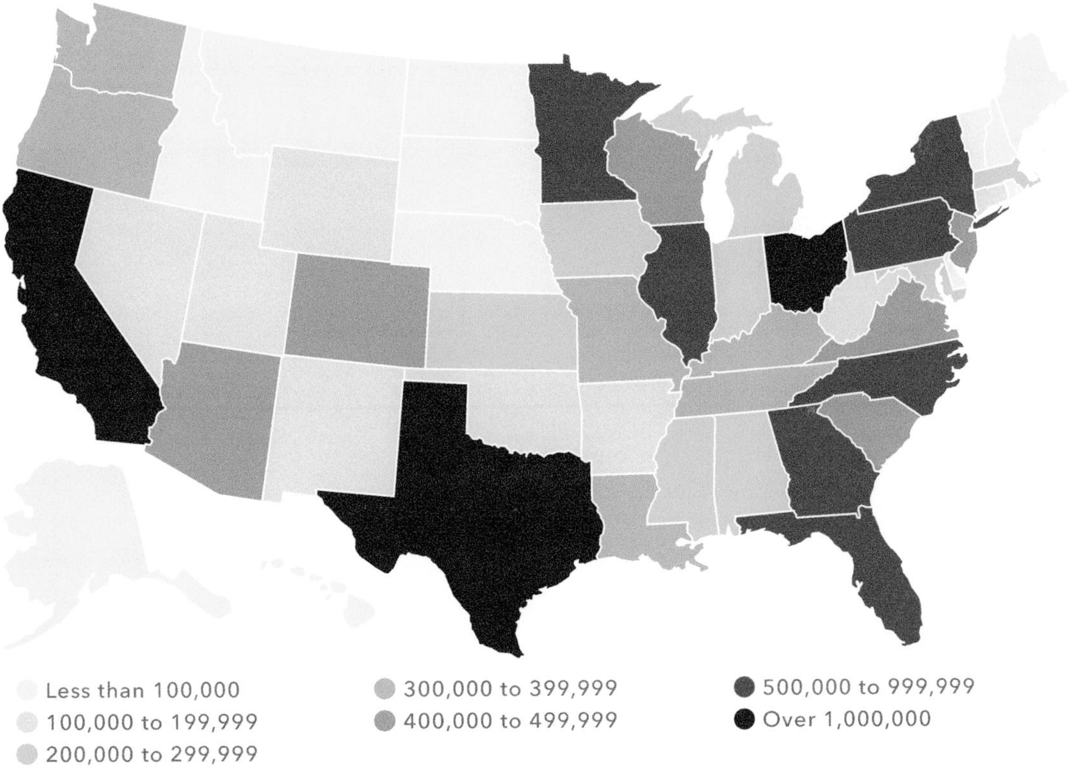

- Less than 100,000
- 100,000 to 199,999
- 200,000 to 299,999
- 300,000 to 399,999
- 400,000 to 499,999
- 500,000 to 999,999
- Over 1,000,000

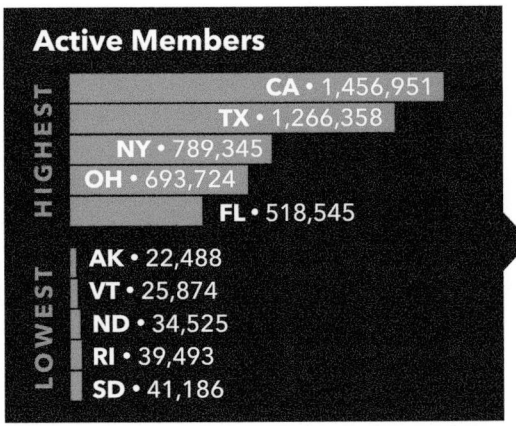

Active Members

HIGHEST
- CA • 1,456,951
- TX • 1,266,358
- NY • 789,345
- OH • 693,724
- FL • 518,545

LOWEST
- AK • 22,488
- VT • 25,874
- ND • 34,525
- RI • 39,493
- SD • 41,186

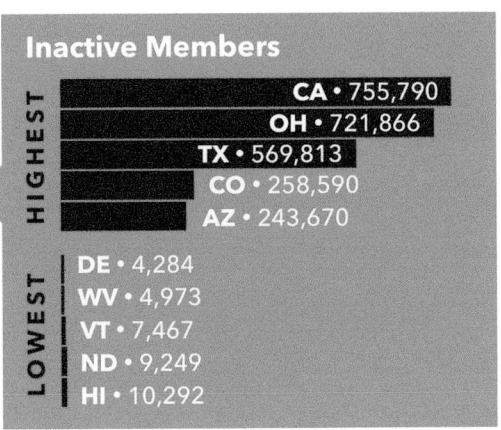

Inactive Members

HIGHEST
- CA • 755,790
- OH • 721,866
- TX • 569,813
- CO • 258,590
- AZ • 243,670

LOWEST
- DE • 4,284
- WV • 4,973
- VT • 7,467
- ND • 9,249
- HI • 10,292

TABLE 7.31
Finances of State-Administered Public-Employee Pension Systems, by State: Fiscal Year 2018*
(In thousands of dollars)

State and level of government	Total receipts	Employee contributions	Receipts during fiscal year Government contributions Total	From state government	From local government	Earnings on investments (b)	Payments during fiscal year Total payments	Benefits	Withdrawals	Other payments
United States	$519,232,163	$47,449,885	$124,789,613	$71,263,451	$53,526,162	$346,992,665	$274,139,250	$253,879,359	$6,283,454	$13,976,437
Alabama (a)	5,780,815	727,477	1,247,213	217,132	1,030,081	3,806,125	3,500,114	3,347,835	101,601	50,678
Alaska	1,961,185	130,476	538,946	370,601	168,345	1,291,762	1,311,508	1,278,129	15,708	17,671
Arizona	7,413,749	1,287,488	1,834,306	940,705	893,601	4,291,955	4,505,170	3,946,187	277,195	281,787
Arkansas	4,536,149	237,262	853,970	754,797	99,173	3,444,917	2,025,616	1,911,293	29,914	84,408
California	92,797,177	8,891,615	30,365,411	17,276,816	13,088,596	53,540,151	43,805,492	40,772,573	544,246	2,488,673
Colorado	10,951,819	886,653	1,633,571	745,295	888,275	8,431,596	5,194,829	4,766,534	162,326	265,970
Connecticut	6,550,385	530,861	2,924,390	2,745,015	179,375	3,095,134	4,192,278	4,144,931	44,448	2,899
Delaware	1,301,547	76,520	237,701	225,391	12,310	987,326	687,088	652,425	6,072	28,591
Florida	18,192,766	746,370	2,849,920	663,381	2,186,539	14,596,476	9,947,912	9,306,634	19,325	621,953
Georgia	12,287,909	808,145	3,246,698	2,749,803	496,895	8,232,736	6,675,221	6,480,959	93,586	100,676
Hawaii	2,524,205	252,686	851,041	639,128	211,912	1,420,478	1,489,496	1,395,676	20,847	72,974
Idaho	2,331,532	246,105	391,371	107,182	284,188	1,694,056	1,000,178	905,032	38,259	56,888
Illinois	25,480,892	1,872,594	8,832,855	7,788,725	1,044,129	14,775,443	14,346,234	13,472,978	262,505	610,751
Indiana	5,115,152	202,493	1,940,819	1,112,164	828,654	2,971,841	2,834,023	2,567,067	34,549	232,406
Iowa	4,137,040	521,251	816,396	137,656	678,739	2,799,393	2,425,318	2,258,361	60,987	105,970
Kansas	3,089,601	420,285	887,735	588,153	299,582	1,781,581	1,891,871	1,712,451	64,967	114,453
Kentucky	6,226,243	671,181	2,323,707	1,717,431	606,276	3,231,355	4,360,210	4,097,134	67,863	195,213
Louisiana	8,694,856	864,444	2,692,709	1,100,972	1,591,737	5,137,703	4,807,035	4,338,968	128,418	339,649
Maine	2,038,300	189,721	398,926	341,852	57,074	1,449,652	1,082,981	946,934	22,589	113,458
Maryland	7,148,774	795,898	2,036,015	2,036,015	0	4,316,861	4,189,930	3,781,335	69,408	339,186
Massachusetts	8,974,673	1,684,955	1,831,170	1,625,923	205,247	5,458,548	5,778,204	5,280,668	142,667	354,869
Michigan (a)	13,886,646	1,042,931	4,144,043	975,060	3,168,983	8,699,672	7,729,371	7,306,411	108,719	314,241
Minnesota	11,141,277	1,150,804	1,378,871	288,625	1,090,246	8,611,602	4,922,329	4,752,182	80,362	89,784
Mississippi	4,203,618	573,310	1,052,134	409,466	642,668	2,578,174	2,974,606	2,676,744	124,427	173,435
Missouri	9,081,393	1,009,156	1,779,507	722,249	1,057,257	6,292,731	5,310,974	4,449,667	73,200	788,107
Montana	1,980,966	295,266	317,974	198,624	119,350	1,367,727	934,058	840,184	25,157	68,717
Nebraska	1,877,741	239,041	308,163	91,025	217,137	1,330,537	784,521	641,143	91,861	51,517
Nevada	5,209,543	147,129	1,718,876	254,597	1,464,279	3,343,538	2,521,786	2,426,131	31,799	63,857
New Hampshire	1,402,134	218,317	429,005	6,845	422,160	754,812	809,217	748,354	24,010	36,853
New Jersey	14,727,756	2,093,554	4,422,551	4,421,746	805	8,211,651	11,155,380	10,911,471	189,105	54,804
New Mexico	3,474,671	566,202	737,277	323,750	413,527	2,171,192	2,499,874	2,237,114	92,436	170,324
New York	39,180,805	471,545	6,429,724	3,121,013	3,308,711	32,279,535	20,801,799	19,219,362	387,752	1,194,685
North Carolina	11,860,440	1,352,014	2,147,626	1,636,501	511,125	8,360,800	6,732,672	5,970,557	188,373	573,742
North Dakota	832,858	127,748	200,658	83,638	117,019	504,452	412,757	383,065	19,241	10,451
Ohio	30,065,256	3,462,889	4,259,627	2,220,463	2,039,164	22,342,740	16,364,431	15,428,383	595,001	341,048
Oklahoma	4,607,389	492,001	1,189,561	609,351	580,210	2,925,827	2,522,787	2,389,856	62,229	70,702
Oregon	9,719,671	634,836	1,370,441	409,164	961,276	7,714,395	5,894,984	5,160,716	13,876	720,391
Pennsylvania	17,452,434	1,457,484	6,199,849	1,922,917	4,276,933	9,795,101	11,461,042	10,017,775	751,369	691,898
Rhode Island	1,447,564	192,065	469,185	421,122	48,062	786,314	1,028,782	936,193	6,435	86,154
South Carolina	5,805,833	952,676	1,542,322	728,783	813,539	3,310,835	4,382,878	3,853,745	139,061	390,072
South Dakota	1,209,712	124,262	124,734	44,639	80,096	960,715	573,459	546,633	21,841	4,985
Tennessee	5,781,562	344,034	1,558,062	465,608	1,092,454	3,879,466	2,644,632	2,520,271	41,160	83,201
Texas (a)	32,890,791	4,958,761	5,952,439	2,710,576	3,241,863	21,979,591	16,201,525	15,077,864	696,286	427,376
Utah	5,619,329	70,049	1,115,698	938,692	177,006	4,433,582	1,597,160	1,575,533	9,626	12,001
Vermont	593,589	97,478	192,438	174,918	17,520	303,673	361,037	337,982	7,446	15,609
Virginia	11,111,413	938,128	2,527,786	703,032	1,824,754	7,645,499	4,922,214	4,752,889	122,968	46,357
Washington	14,417,470	1,088,902	2,601,212	2,532,645	68,566	10,727,356	4,832,654	4,267,553	82,872	482,229
West Virginia	2,637,769	168,634	664,195	476,868	187,327	1,804,940	1,331,971	1,292,143	26,581	13,247
Wisconsin	17,877,999	965,453	1,017,559	322,430	695,129	15,894,987	5,763,142	5,211,267	38,358	513,517
Wyoming	1,599,764	170,404	203,232	164,966	38,265	1,226,128	616,500	584,067	24,424	8,009

See footnotes at end of table

TABLE 7.31

Finances of State-Administered Public-Employee Pension Systems, by State: Fiscal Year 2018*
(In thousands of dollars) (continued)

Source: 2018 Annual Survey of Public Pensions: State- and Locally-Administered Defined Benefit Data.

Notes:

1. Data users who create their own estimates using these data should cite the U.S. Census Bureau as the source of the original data only. The data in this table are based on information from public records and contain no confidential data. The data in this table come from a sample of governmental units and are thus subject to both sampling and nonsampling error. Additional information on nonsampling error, response rates, and definitions may be found within the survey methodology <https://www2.census.gov/programs-surveys/aspp/technical-documentation/methodology/2018/2018surveymethodology.pdf?#>

2. *Effective with the 2012 survey cycle, the Annual Survey of Public Pensions: State-Administered Defined Benefit Data revised the survey form to implement changes in asset classification. These changes apply to the categories designated as corporate stocks, corporate bonds, federal government securities, state and local government securities, and other securities. Federally-sponsored agency securities are classified under federal government securities instead of corporate bonds. Private equity, venture capital, and leverage buyouts are classified under corporate stocks instead of other securities. Due to these changes in asset classification, there are shifts in the distribution of assets from corporate bonds to federal government securities and from other securities to corporate stocks. However, since investment decisions guide the distribution of assets, we cannot calculate the exact impact that the changes in classification had on the asset distribution for 2012. As such, for the above mentioned asset categories, any data comparisons between data from 2012 to the present, and data prior to 2012 should be exercised with caution.

3. Pension obligations and Covered payroll for defined benefit pension systems are only collected at the state level.

4. Detail may not add to total due to rounding.

Key:

(a) There are exceptions to the fiscal year rule for the state pension systems in Alabama, Michigan, and Texas. For systems in these states, the fiscal year moves beyond the June 30 cutoff. The data for the survey year 2018 covers the fiscal year ending August 31, 2018 for Texas and September 30, 2018 for Alabama and Michigan. These exceptions are made to better align the data with the Survey of State Government Finances.

(b) The total of "net earnings" is a calculated statistic and thus can be positive or negative. Net earnings is the sum of earnings on investments plus gains on investments minus losses on investments. The change made in 2002 for asset valuation from book to market value in accordance with Statement 34 of the Governmental Accounting Standards Board is reflected in the calculated statistics.

TABLE 7.32
National Summary of State-Administered Defined Benefit Pension System Finances: Fiscal Years, 2016-2018*

	Amount (in thousands of dollars)			Percentage distribution		
	2018	2017	2016	2018	2017	2016
Total contributions	$172,239,498	$157,386,474	$149,657,642	100.0	100.0	100.0
Employee contributions	47,449,885	46,944,545	43,150,277	27.5	29.8	28.8
Government contributions	124,789,613	110,441,928	106,507,365	72.5	70.2	71.2
State government contributions	71,263,451	64,089,546	59,594,514	41.4	40.7	39.8
Local government contributions	53,526,162	46,352,382	46,912,851	31.1	29.5	31.3
Earnings on investments (b)	346,992,665	375,445,862	45,411,198	100.0	100.0	100.0
Total Payments	274,139,250	261,585,890	248,284,997	100.0	100.0	100.0
Benefits	253,879,359	242,520,732	232,052,855	92.6	92.7	93.5
Withdrawals	6,283,454	6,226,056	5,080,298	2.3	2.4	2.0
Other payments	13,976,437	12,839,103	11,151,844	5.1	4.9	4.5
Total cash and investment holdings	3,528,147,973	3,299,651,933	3,051,596,871	100.0	100.0	100.0
Cash and short-term investments	118,855,375	121,753,990	114,828,590	3.4	3.7	3.8
Total securities	2,831,225,549	2,678,609,021	2,522,973,332	80.2	81.2	82.7
Government securities	349,968,780	293,175,593	234,301,397	9.9	8.9	7.7
Federal government	347,263,431	292,007,007	232,524,339	9.8	8.8	7.6
United States Treasury	256,759,464	216,693,813	149,766,700	7.3	6.6	4.9
Federal agency	90,503,967	75,313,194	82,757,639	2.6	2.3	2.7
State and local government	2,705,349	1,168,586	1,777,058	0.1	0.0	0.1
Nongovernmental securities	2,481,256,769	2,385,433,427	2,288,671,935	70.3	72.3	75.0
Corporate bonds	248,950,169	305,387,955	383,681,199	7.1	9.3	12.6
Corporate stocks	1,140,649,169	1,061,869,639	1,107,538,222	32.3	32.2	36.3
Mortgages	7,914,659	7,815,572	8,204,825	0.2	0.2	0.3
Funds held in trust	92,238,189	95,038,374	32,390,689	2.6	2.9	1.1
Foreign and international	758,034,370	708,881,545	570,655,405	21.5	21.5	18.7
Other nongovernmental securities	233,470,212	206,440,342	186,201,595	6.6	6.3	6.1
Other investments	578,067,049	499,288,922	413,794,949	16.4	15.1	13.6
Real property	55,606,123	75,978,186	118,527,861	1.6	2.3	3.9
Miscellaneous investments	522,460,927	423,310,736	295,267,088	14.8	12.8	9.7

Source: The 2016-2018 Annual Surveys of Public Pensions: State- and Locally-Defined Benefits Data.

Notes:

1. Data users who create their own estimates using data from this report should cite the U.S. Census Bureau as the source of the original data only. The data in this table are based on information from public records and contain no confidential data. The data in this table for the years ending in '2' and '7' come from a census of pension systems and are subject to nonsampling error. Data for the remaining years are from a sample of pension systems, and are thus subject to both sampling and nonsampling error. Additional information on nonsampling error, and response rates may be found at *https://www.census.gov/programs-surveys/aspp/technical-documentation/methodology/how-the-data-are-collected.html*

2.* Effective with the 2012 survey cycle, the Annual Survey of Public Pensions: State-Administered Defined Benefit Data revised the survey form to implement changes in asset classification. These changes apply to the categories designated as corporate stocks, corporate bonds, federal government securities, state and local government securities, and other securities. Federally-sponsored agency securities are classified under federal government securities instead of corporate bonds. Private equity, venture capital, and leverage buyouts are classified under corporate stocks instead of other securities. Due to these changes in asset classification, there are shifts in the distribution of assets from corporate bonds

to federal government securities and from other securities to corporate stocks. However, since investment decisions guide the distribution of assets, we cannot calculate the exact impact that the changes in classification had on the asset distribution for 2012. As such, for the above mentioned asset categories, any data comparisons between data from 2012 to the present, and data prior to 2012 should be exercised with caution.

3. Detail may not add to total due to rounding;

4. Total Receipts are the sum of earnings on investments and total contributions.

Key:

(a) There are exceptions to the fiscal year rule for the state pension systems in Alabama, Michigan, and Texas. For systems in these states, the fiscal year moves beyond the June 30 cutoff. The data for the survey year 2017 covers the fiscal year ending August 31, 2017 for Texas and September 30, 2017 for Alabama and Michigan. These exceptions are made to better align the data with the Survey of State Government Finances.

(b) The total of "net earnings" is a calculated statistic (the item code in the data file is X08), and thus can be positive or negative. Net earnings is the sum of earnings on investments plus gains on investments minus losses on investments. The change made in 2002 for asset valuation from book to market value in accordance with Statement 34 of the Governmental Accounting Standards Board is reflected in the calculated statistics.

CHAPTER EIGHT
STATE MANAGEMENT, ADMINISTRATION AND DEMOGRAPHICS

TABLE 8.1
Summary of State Government Employment: 1960-2018

Year (October)	Employment (in thousands)						Monthly payrolls (in millions of dollars)			Average monthly earnings of full-time employees		
	Total, full-time and part-time			Full-time equivalent								
	All	Education	Other	All	Education	Other	All	Education	Other	All	Education	Other
1960	1,527	474	1,053	1,353	332	1,021	524	168	356	386	439	365
1961	1,625	518	1,107	1,435	367	1,068	586	192	394	409	482	383
1962	1,680	555	1,126	1,478	389	1,088	635	202	433	429	518	397
1963	1,775	602	1,173	1,558	422	1,136	696	230	466	447	545	410
1964	1,873	656	1,217	1,639	460	1,179	761	258	504	464	560	427
1965	2,028	739	1,289	1,751	508	1,243	849	290	559	484	571	450
1966	2,211	866	1,344	1,864	575	1,289	975	353	622	522	614	483
1967	2,335	940	1,395	1,946	620	1,326	1,106	406	699	567	666	526
1968	2,495	1,037	1,458	2,085	694	1,391	1,257	477	780	602	687	544
1969	2,614	1,112	1,501	2,179	746	1,433	1,431	555	876	655	743	597
1970	2,755	1,182	1,573	2,302	803	1,499	1,612	630	982	700	797	605
1971	2,832	1,223	1,609	2,384	841	1,544	1,742	682	1,060	731	826	686
1972	2,957	1,267	1,690	2,487	867	1,619	1,937	747	1,190	778	871	734
1973	3,013	1,280	1,733	2,547	887	1,660	2,158	822	1,336	843	952	805
1974	3,155	1,357	1,798	2,653	929	1,725	2,410	933	1,477	906	1,023	855
1975	3,271	1,400	1,870	2,744	952	1,792	2,653	1,022	1,631	964	1,080	909
1976	3,343	1,434	1,910	2,799	973	1,827	2,894	1,112	1,782	1,031	1,163	975
1977	3,491	1,484	2,007	2,903	1,005	1,898	3,195	1,234	1,960	1,096	1,237	1,031
1978	3,539	1,508	2,032	2,966	1,016	1,950	3,483	1,333	2,150	1,167	1,311	1,102
1979	3,699	1,577	2,122	3,072	1,046	2,026	3,869	1,451	2,418	1,257	1,399	1,193
1980	3,753	1,599	2,154	3,106	1,063	2,044	4,285	1,608	2,677	1,373	1,523	1,305
1981	3,726	1,603	2,123	3,087	1,063	2,024	4,668	1,768	2,900	1,507	1,671	1,432
1982	3,747	1,616	2,131	3,083	1,051	2,032	5,028	1,874	3,154	1,625	1,789	1,551
1983	3,816	1,666	2,150	3,116	1,072	2,044	5,346	1,989	3,357	1,711	1,850	1,640
1984	3,898	1,708	2,190	3,177	1,091	2,086	5,815	2,178	3,637	1,825	1,991	1,740
1985	3,984	1,764	2,220	2,990	945	2,046	6,329	2,434	3,885	1,935	2,155	1,834
1986	4,068	1,800	2,267	3,437	1,256	2,181	6,801	2,583	4,227	2,052	2,263	1,956
1987	4,115	1,804	2,310	3,491	1,264	2,227	7,298	2,758	4,540	2,161	2,396	2,056
1988	4,236	1,854	2,381	3,606	1,309	2,297	7,842	2,929	4,914	2,260	2,490	2,158
1989	4,365	1,925	2,440	3,709	1,360	2,349	8,443	3,175	5,268	2,372	2,627	2,259
1990	4,503	1,984	2,519	3,840	1,418	2,432	9,083	3,426	5,657	2,472	2,732	2,359
1991	4,521	1,999	2,522	3,829	1,375	2,454	9,437	3,550	5,887	2,479	2,530	2,433
1992	4,595	2,050	2,545	3,856	1,384	2,472	9,828	3,774	6,054	2,562	2,607	2,521
1993	4,673	2,112	2,562	3,891	1,436	2,455	10,288	3,999	6,289	2,722	3,034	2,578
1994	4,694	2,115	2,579	3,917	1,442	2,475	10,666	4,177	6,489	2,776	3,073	2,640
1995	4,719	2,120	2,598	3,971	1,469	2,502	10,927	4,173	6,753	2,854	3,138	2,725
1996						(a)						
1997 (March)	4,733	2,114	2,619	3,987	1,484	2,503	11,413	4,372	7,041	2,968	3,251	2,838
1998 (March)	4,758	2,173	2,585	3,985	1,511	2,474	11,845	4,632	7,213	3,088	3,382	2,947
1999 (March)	4,818	2,229	2,588	4,034	1,541	2,493	12,564	4,957	7,608	3,236	3,544	3,087
2000 (March)	4,877	2,259	2,618	4,083	1,563	2,520	13,279	5,255	8,024	3,374	3,692	3,219
2001 (March)	4,985	2,329	2,656	4,173	1,615	2,559	14,136	5,621	8,516	3,521	3,842	3,362
2002 (March)	5,072	2,414	2,658	4,223	1,659	2,564	14,838	5,997	8,841	3,657	4,007	3,479
2003 (March)	5,043	2,413	2,630	4,191	1,656	2,534	15,116	6,154	8,962	3,751	4,115	3,566
2004 (March)	5,041	2,432	2,609	4,188	1,673	2,515	15,478	6,412	9,066	3,845	4,256	3,631
2005 (March)	5,078	2,459	2,620	4,209	1,684	2,525	16,062	6,669	9,393	3,966	4,390	3,745
2006 (March)	5,128	2,493	2,635	4,251	1,708	2,542	16,769	6,961	9,809	4,098	4,505	3,883
2007 (March)	5,200	2,538	2,663	4,307	1,740	2,566	17,789	7,419	10,370	4,276	4,670	4,063
2008 (March)	5,270	2,593	2,677	4,363	1,780	2,582	18,726	7,883	10,843	4,445	4,853	4,222
2009 (March)	5,346	2,649	2,697	4,408	1,814	2,594	19,425	8,279	11,146	4,565	5,007	4,320
2010 (March)	5,326	2,669	2,656	4,378	1,824	2,554	19,579	8,516	11,063	4,620	5,111	4,342
2011 (March)	5,314	2,704	2,609	4,359	1,847	2,512	19,972	8,813	11,159	4,735	5,233	4,446
2012 (March)	5,285	2,728	2,557	4,315	1,854	2,461	20,169	9,042	11,127	4,840	5,377	4,522
2013 (March)	5,304	2,749	2,554	4,315	1,867	2,449	20,473	9,242	11,231	4,917	5,463	4,589
2014 (March)	5,336	2,779	2,557	4,330	1,880	2,450	21,118	9,564	11,555	5,051	5,599	4,718
2015 (March)	5,353	2,794	2,559	4,342	1,890	2,452	21,591	9,766	11,826	5,159	5,708	4,824
2016 (March)	5,368	2,826	2,542	4,361	1,917	2,443	22,149	10,142	12,007	5,274	5,868	4,907
2017 (March)	5,418	2,851	2,567	4,400	1,934	2,466	23,024	10,570	12,453	5,426	6,042	5,044
2018 (March)	5,408	2,845	2,563	4,386	1,924	2,462	23,701	10,909	12,792	5,593	6,249	5,184

See footnotes at end of table

TABLE 8.1
Summary of State Government Employment: 1960-2018 (continued)

Source: U.S. Census Bureau, Census of Governments: Employment (for the years ending in '2' and '7') and the Annual Survey of Public Employment & Payroll for remaining years.

Note: Data users who create their own estimates using these data should cite the U.S. Census Bureau as the source of the original data only. The data in this table are based on information from public records and contain no confidential data. The data in this table for the years ending in '2' and '7' come from a census of governmental units and are subject to nonsampling error. Data for the remaining years are from a sample of governmental units, and are thus subject to both sampling and nonsampling error. Additional information on nonsampling error, response and definitions may be found within the survey technical documentation *https://www.census.gov/programs-surveys/apes/technical-documentation.html.*

Key:

(a) Due to a change in the reference period, from October to March, the October 1996 Annual Survey of Government Employment & Payroll was not conducted. This change in collection period was effective beginning with the March 1997 survey.

TABLE 8.2
Employment and Payrolls of State and Local Governments by Function: March 2018

Functions	All employees, full-time and part-time (in thousands of dollars)			March payrolls (in thousands of dollars)			Average March earnings of full-time employees
	Total	State government	Local government	Total	State government	Local government	
All functions	19,600,048	5,408,289	14,191,759	$82,677,997,413	$23,701,059,639	$58,976,937,774	$5,158
Education:							
Education - Elementary and Secondary Total	7,802,158	59,475	7,742,683	29,776,850,563	250,053,648	29,526,796,915	4,553
Education - Elementary and Secondary Instructional	5,319,924	44,034	5,275,890	23,292,786,473	200,734,401	23,092,052,072	5,058
Education - Higher Education Total	3,264,805	2,696,268	568,537	12,066,188,603	10,252,752,806	1,813,435,797	6,263
Education - Higher Education Instructional	1,130,541	857,689	272,852	5,484,157,181	4,540,928,792	943,228,389	8,422
Education - Other	89,738	89,738	0	406,541,194	406,541,194	0	5,013
Libraries	186,184	783	185,401	490,942,570	2,389,939	488,552,631	4,249
Selected functions:							
Financial Administration	439,765	174,748	265,017	2,117,656,307	895,370,437	1,222,285,870	5,242
Other Government Administration	413,478	55,445	358,033	1,379,195,215	261,171,073	1,118,024,142	5,187
Judicial and Legal	440,348	181,483	258,865	2,361,595,222	1,052,517,152	1,309,078,070	5,725
Police Protection Total	997,419	107,300	890,119	5,747,720,468	678,299,705	5,069,420,763	6,235
Police Protection - Persons with Power of Arrest	739,787	68,560	671,227	4,720,104,823	501,663,113	4,218,441,710	6,641
Fire Protection Total	437,282	0	437,282	2,397,347,288	0	2,397,347,288	6,832
Fire Protection - Firefighters	391,836	0	391,836	2,185,228,537	0	2,185,228,537	6,917
Corrections	712,797	441,471	271,326	3,436,105,959	2,121,771,519	1,314,334,440	4,912
Highways	509,205	215,264	293,941	2,400,459,075	1,094,017,987	1,306,441,088	4,951
Public Welfare	540,946	247,922	293,024	2,285,957,224	1,030,205,456	1,255,751,768	4,455
Hospitals	1,125,041	433,343	691,698	5,820,754,982	2,208,465,160	3,612,289,822	5,610
Social Insurance Administration	69,068	68,446	622	333,665,372	329,848,634	3,816,738	4,913
Natural Resources	192,081	145,798	46,283	833,694,204	643,556,643	190,137,561	4,967
State liquor stores	13,535	13,535	0	33,703,439	33,703,439	0	3,643
Utilities	449,204	44,780	404,424	33,703,439	33,703,439	0	3,643
Other and unallocable	1,472,705	432,490	1,040,215	6,530,788,820	2,106,899,765	4,423,889,055	5,196

Source: U.S. Census Bureau, 2018 Annual Survey of Public Employment & Payroll

Note: Data users who create their own estimates using these data should cite the U.S. Census Bureau as the source of the original data only. The data in this table are based on information from public records and contain no confidential data. The data in this table come from a census of governmental units and are subject to nonsampling error. Additional information on nonsampling error, response rates, and definitions may be found within the survey technical documentation *https://www.census.gov/programs-surveys/apes/technical-documentation.html.*

Note: Detail may not add to total due to rounding.

TABLE 8.3
State and Local Government Employment, By State: March 2018

State or other jurisdiction	All employees (full-time and part-time)			Full-time equivalent employment		
	Total	State	Local	Total	State	Local
United States	19,600,048	5,408,289	14,191,759	16,650,724	4,386,219	12,264,505
Alabama	322,383	112,868	209,515	283,939	91,993	191,946
Alaska	60,665	27,851	32,814	51,876	24,464	27,412
Arizona	330,000	93,739	236,261	278,779	72,829	205,950
Arkansas	193,816	72,928	120,888	169,448	62,434	107,014
California	2,280,252	540,350	1,739,902	1,872,571	427,272	1,445,299
Colorado	360,531	111,660	248,871	299,636	88,669	210,967
Connecticut	221,342	76,985	144,357	184,556	58,988	125,568
Delaware	56,356	30,097	26,259	49,350	25,416	23,934
Florida	1,018,359	211,746	806,613	899,621	181,059	718,562
Georgia	590,627	167,272	423,355	522,795	131,756	391,039
Hawaii	89,547	70,620	18,927	74,946	58,058	16,888
Idaho	109,214	32,007	77,207	85,544	24,907	60,637
Illinois	758,967	151,684	607,283	616,092	121,646	494,446
Indiana	402,970	125,586	277,384	331,556	96,586	234,970
Iowa	242,241	70,135	172,106	186,348	50,939	135,409
Kansas	247,509	66,797	180,712	202,356	53,667	148,689
Kentucky	276,730	98,513	178,217	244,093	85,167	158,926
Louisiana	291,223	88,370	202,853	258,038	74,116	183,922
Maine	87,639	26,454	61,185	69,649	19,881	49,768
Maryland	341,117	89,386	251,731	303,874	84,443	219,431
Massachusetts	404,520	128,191	276,329	341,164	104,092	237,072
Michigan	548,835	193,688	355,147	436,726	147,886	288,840
Minnesota	380,329	104,207	276,122	302,615	84,274	218,341
Mississippi	205,916	61,906	144,010	187,102	54,637	132,465
Missouri	377,038	103,698	273,340	318,635	84,877	233,758
Montana	71,443	26,420	45,023	57,186	19,887	37,299
Nebraska	146,449	36,957	109,492	121,858	31,969	89,889
Nevada	135,030	36,892	98,138	116,221	29,819	86,402
New Hampshire	85,834	25,874	59,960	69,929	19,104	50,825
New Jersey	546,720	156,995	389,725	473,729	139,102	334,627
New Mexico	142,817	54,416	88,401	124,467	45,332	79,135
New York	1,345,936	277,958	1,067,978	1,205,241	247,537	957,704
North Carolina	667,348	168,570	498,778	570,987	140,019	430,968
North Dakota	65,350	24,442	40,908	47,052	18,010	29,042
Ohio	705,280	183,835	521,445	589,389	135,359	454,030
Oklahoma	241,572	80,379	161,193	208,665	63,040	145,625
Oregon	261,472	89,386	172,086	206,777	72,657	134,120
Pennsylvania	657,320	201,901	455,419	559,999	160,402	399,597
Rhode Island	56,889	23,944	32,945	47,904	18,368	29,536
South Carolina	299,173	92,893	206,280	270,541	79,601	190,940
South Dakota	64,323	18,830	45,493	48,043	14,174	33,869
Tennessee	380,164	98,618	281,546	335,643	80,266	255,377
Texas	1,678,915	361,356	1,317,559	1,510,225	308,058	1,202,167
Utah	207,844	82,228	125,616	155,376	62,104	93,272
Vermont	50,237	17,281	32,956	39,642	14,296	25,346
Virginia	536,890	166,869	370,021	452,707	125,819	326,888
Washington	450,919	158,258	292,661	380,179	127,864	252,315
West Virginia	118,403	47,841	70,562	102,192	39,757	62,435
Wisconsin	373,762	104,683	269,079	284,159	71,254	212,905
Wyoming	60,102	14,725	45,377	50,162	12,365	37,797
Dist. of Columbia	51,730	N.A.	51,730	51,142	N.A.	51,142

Source: U.S. Census Bureau, 2018 Annual Survey of Public Employment & Payroll

Note: Data users who create their own estimates using these data should cite the U.S. Census Bureau as the source of the original data only. The data in this table are based on information from public records and contain no confidential data. The data in this table come from a census of governmental units and are subject to nonsampling error. Additional information on nonsampling error, response rates, and definitions may be found within the survey technical documentation *https://www.census.gov/programs-surveys/apes/technical-documentation.html.*

Note: Detail may not add to total due to rounding.

Key:

N.A. – Not applicable

Table 8.3 | State & Local Government Employment

Full- and Part-time Employees

TOTAL–HIGHEST AND LOWEST

CA · 2,280,252
TX · 1,678,915
NY · 1,345,936
FL · 1,018,359
IL · 758,967
AK · 60,665
WY · 60,102
RI · 56,889
DE · 56,356
VT · 50,237

STATE–HIGHEST AND LOWEST

CA · 540,350
TX · 361,356
NY · 277,958
FL · 211,746
PA · 201,901
ND · 24,442
RI · 23,944
SD · 18,830
VT · 17,281
WY · 14,725

LOCAL–HIGHEST AND LOWEST

CA · 1,739,902
TX · 1,317,559
NY · 1,067,978
FL · 806,613
IL · 607,283
VT · 32,956
RI · 32,945
AK · 32,814
DE · 26,259
HI · 18,927

Full-time Equivalent Employment

TOTAL–HIGHEST AND LOWEST

CA · 1,872,571
TX · 1,510,225
NY · 1,205,241
FL · 899,621
IL · 616,092
DE · 49,350
SD · 48,043
RI · 47,904
ND · 47,052
VT · 39,642

STATE–HIGHEST AND LOWEST

CA · 427,272
TX · 308,058
NY · 247,537
FL · 181,059
PA · 160,402
RI · 18,368
ND · 18,010
VT · 14,296
SD · 14,174
WY · 12,365

LOCAL–HIGHEST AND LOWEST

CA · 1,445,299
TX · 1,202,167
NY · 957,704
FL · 718,562
IL · 494,446
ND · 29,042
AK · 27,412
VT · 25,346
DE · 23,934
HI · 16,888

TABLE 8.4
State and Local Government Payrolls and Average Earnings of Full-Time Employees, By State: March 2018

State or other jurisdiction	Amount of Payroll			Percentage of March payroll		Average earnings of full-time state and local government employees (dollars)		
	Total	State government	Local government	State government	Local government	All	State government	Local government
United States	$82,677,997,413	$23,701,059,639	$58,976,937,774	29%	71%	$5,158	$5,593	$5,008
Alabama	1,151,729,746	425,201,110	726,528,636	37%	63%	4,169	4,851	3,864
Alaska	295,737,557	143,855,464	151,882,093	49%	51%	5,891	6,081	5,721
Arizona	1,297,209,898	350,858,908	946,350,990	27%	73%	4,856	5,169	4,752
Arkansas	613,289,568	258,628,573	354,660,995	42%	58%	3,708	4,297	3,379
California	12,369,106,850	3,130,719,390	9,238,387,460	25%	75%	7,047	7,559	6,895
Colorado	1,497,145,360	483,655,146	1,013,490,214	32%	68%	5,293	6,047	5,034
Connecticut	1,085,871,792	385,234,485	700,637,307	35%	65%	6,144	6,809	5,845
Delaware	236,967,134	121,243,321	115,723,813	51%	49%	5,008	4,902	5,119
Florida	3,884,004,657	814,762,681	3,069,241,976	21%	79%	4,429	4,623	4,383
Georgia	2,147,694,682	582,798,290	1,564,896,392	27%	73%	4,225	4,619	4,101
Hawaii	370,563,705	276,087,848	94,475,857	75%	25%	5,152	4,991	5,652
Idaho	354,102,519	130,249,237	223,853,282	37%	63%	4,316	5,584	3,818
Illinois	3,227,725,909	683,235,749	2,544,490,160	21%	79%	5,526	5,857	5,448
Indiana	1,309,137,282	407,011,992	902,125,290	31%	69%	4,154	4,526	4,004
Iowa	887,867,139	299,606,472	588,260,667	34%	66%	5,166	6,709	4,617
Kansas	810,428,448	251,371,009	559,057,439	31%	69%	4,125	4,819	3,874
Kentucky	952,156,170	375,824,091	576,332,079	39%	61%	4,055	4,715	3,727
Louisiana	1,009,505,841	350,514,492	658,991,349	35%	65%	4,023	4,903	3,679
Maine	289,479,604	92,583,702	196,895,902	32%	68%	4,278	4,728	4,096
Maryland	1,680,765,127	456,371,426	1,224,393,701	27%	73%	5,769	5,458	5,892
Massachusetts	1,936,859,136	644,629,678	1,292,229,458	33%	67%	5,869	6,311	5,674
Michigan	2,151,351,857	869,154,452	1,282,197,405	40%	60%	5,225	6,150	4,768
Minnesota	1,550,273,339	489,867,109	1,060,406,230	32%	68%	5,467	6,200	5,184
Mississippi	657,822,273	216,249,462	441,572,811	33%	67%	3,560	4,050	3,364
Missouri	1,219,633,322	335,881,694	883,751,628	28%	72%	3,945	4,079	3,897
Montana	241,039,183	92,918,528	148,120,655	39%	61%	4,406	4,865	4,165
Nebraska	541,287,951	137,932,057	403,355,894	25%	75%	4,698	4,715	4,692
Nevada	606,102,574	156,157,653	449,944,921	26%	74%	5,507	5,410	5,542
New Hampshire	317,562,547	98,694,605	218,867,942	31%	69%	4,951	5,572	4,723
New Jersey	2,881,877,249	882,685,160	1,999,192,089	31%	69%	6,378	6,567	6,298
New Mexico	510,374,338	212,477,545	297,896,793	42%	58%	4,194	4,791	3,864
New York	7,393,235,441	1,594,406,354	5,798,829,087	22%	78%	6,340	6,554	6,284
North Carolina	2,512,138,433	709,048,365	1,803,090,068	28%	72%	4,498	5,105	4,300
North Dakota	214,611,964	89,112,231	125,499,733	42%	58%	4,768	5,144	4,533
Ohio	2,703,314,031	711,589,726	1,991,724,305	26%	74%	4,809	5,678	4,576
Oklahoma	797,518,756	285,721,770	511,796,986	36%	64%	3,873	4,570	3,581
Oregon	1,105,092,586	423,381,473	681,711,113	38%	62%	5,532	5,882	5,335
Pennsylvania	2,859,354,182	897,003,786	1,962,350,396	31%	69%	5,290	5,513	5,200
Rhode Island	277,615,356	114,205,001	163,410,355	41%	59%	5,974	6,283	5,780
South Carolina	1,082,180,962	341,914,704	740,266,258	32%	68%	4,101	4,426	3,969
South Dakota	187,428,763	64,970,698	122,458,065	35%	65%	4,047	4,791	3,739
Tennessee	1,324,356,981	358,546,070	965,810,911	27%	73%	4,071	4,644	3,896
Texas	6,587,852,000	1,594,084,807	4,993,767,193	24%	76%	4,462	5,348	4,249
Utah	702,774,394	315,873,973	386,900,421	45%	55%	4,848	5,352	4,498
Vermont	191,321,175	82,319,679	109,001,496	43%	57%	4,982	5,738	4,531
Virginia	2,082,294,466	654,664,531	1,427,629,935	31%	69%	4,757	5,412	4,522
Washington	2,280,721,437	727,636,146	1,553,085,291	32%	68%	6,379	5,874	6,638
West Virginia	370,742,324	159,184,708	211,557,616	43%	57%	3,683	4,107	3,417
Wisconsin	1,326,681,937	365,006,673	961,675,264	28%	72%	4,951	5,487	4,779
Wyoming	226,330,252	55,927,615	170,402,637	25%	75%	4,730	4,689	4,744
Dist. of Columbia	367,759,216	N.A.	367,759,216	N.A.	100%	7,404	N.A.	7,404

Source: U.S. Census Bureau, 2018 Annual Survey of Public Employment & Payroll

Note: Data users who create their own estimates using these data should cite the U.S. Census Bureau as the source of the original data only. The data in this table are based on information from public records and contain no confidential data. The data in this table come from a census of governmental units and are subject to nonsampling error. Additional information on nonsampling error, response rates, and definitions may be found within the survey technical documentation <https://www.census.gov/programs-surveys/apes/technical-documentation.html>.

Note: Detail may not add to total due to rounding.

Key:

N.A. – Not applicable

TABLE 8.5
State Government Employment (Full-Time Equivalent) for Selected Functions, By State: March 2018

State	All functions	Education		Selected Functions							
		Higher education (a)	Other education	Highways	Public welfare	Hospitals	Corrections	Police protection	Natural resources	Financial admin.	Judicial and legal admin.
United States	4,386,219	1,793,782	82,067	209,972	243,844	401,985	437,958	105,624	132,374	171,266	176,811
Alabama	91,993	42,679	2,848	4,266	4,295	13,169	4,263	1,269	1,918	2,231	3,261
Alaska	24,464	4,860	227	2,894	1,723	214	2,161	691	1,942	1,151	1,326
Arizona	72,829	35,076	2,660	2,466	6,145	641	9,296	1,976	1,531	2,172	2,393
Arkansas	62,434	26,210	1,345	3,591	4,386	6,596	5,762	1,249	1,896	2,241	1,625
California	427,272	172,937	4,282	19,398	4,232	47,324	60,485	11,348	15,936	26,957	6,480
Colorado	88,669	50,950	1,698	3,067	2,278	6,681	7,413	1,451	1,115	2,130	5,121
Connecticut	58,988	18,257	3,034	3,064	5,473	6,285	5,520	1,834	642	1,603	5,261
Delaware	25,416	7,773	325	1,528	1,643	1,209	2,787	1,097	446	759	1,831
Florida	181,059	68,194	2,826	6,155	9,488	4,081	23,690	4,257	8,121	6,411	19,675
Georgia	131,756	65,966	2,795	4,039	7,072	8,079	15,862	2,872	5,008	3,035	3,627
Hawaii	58,058	12,230	127	787	389	2,921	2,360	0	807	695	2,888
Idaho	24,907	9,518	396	1,363	1,813	584	2,364	524	2,002	1,333	583
Illinois	121,646	55,122	2,051	6,339	9,320	10,492	12,973	3,107	2,611	4,597	2,668
Indiana	96,586	63,613	956	3,601	5,953	1,574	6,120	1,837	2,375	3,244	1,417
Iowa	50,939	24,206	1,024	2,068	2,363	8,843	2,564	842	1,427	1,276	2,109
Kansas	53,667	23,773	492	2,547	2,495	11,291	3,140	1,093	769	1,649	2,091
Kentucky	85,167	39,304	2,179	4,157	7,298	7,333	4,045	2,089	2,371	2,172	5,555
Louisiana	74,116	24,822	3,154	4,333	5,369	10,002	5,736	1,841	3,852	2,860	1,906
Maine	19,881	6,714	271	2,036	2,118	515	1,225	547	1,123	1,269	833
Maryland	84,443	28,450	1,968	4,400	6,176	3,382	10,620	2,219	2,017	3,148	5,323
Massachusetts	104,092	32,225	1,117	2,757	8,047	5,718	12,104	2,950	1,139	3,491	9,302
Michigan	147,886	77,132	613	2,685	11,380	18,603	11,776	2,897	3,425	4,241	1,474
Minnesota	84,274	36,621	3,625	4,809	3,139	5,277	4,411	974	3,163	5,094	4,046
Mississippi	54,637	19,504	1,330	3,143	4,225	10,638	2,322	1,214	2,815	1,575	453
Missouri	84,877	29,229	1,591	5,254	6,501	10,687	11,524	2,459	2,176	2,865	4,121
Montana	19,887	6,914	335	2,022	1,710	725	1,244	493	1,567	972	772
Nebraska	31,969	12,695	551	1,948	2,557	3,771	2,794	748	2,105	787	781
Nevada	29,819	10,868	170	1,742	2,487	1,308	3,656	823	922	1,591	695
New Hampshire	19,104	7,229	306	1,600	1,999	565	1,025	556	366	770	854
New Jersey	139,102	35,814	2,422	5,930	8,926	12,942	8,688	4,088	1,906	5,367	13,003
New Mexico	45,332	17,355	981	2,133	1,660	8,014	3,789	646	981	1,068	3,161
New York	247,537	57,594	3,760	10,687	4,629	40,455	33,025	6,182	2,966	16,170	19,430
North Carolina	140,019	56,920	2,964	8,792	1,102	22,835	16,877	5,566	3,975	4,017	6,659
North Dakota	18,010	7,973	296	931	717	794	945	197	1,036	654	618
Ohio	135,359	72,986	2,087	6,140	2,771	14,006	13,443	2,655	2,493	6,121	2,834
Oklahoma	63,040	27,389	1,552	2,858	6,740	1,033	4,852	1,929	1,713	2,349	2,470
Oregon	72,657	26,028	873	3,746	8,562	9,241	5,247	1,470	2,870	4,077	3,305
Pennsylvania	160,402	57,453	5,421	13,075	12,528	7,943	16,814	6,661	6,228	6,300	2,978
Rhode Island	18,368	5,334	473	726	1,395	717	1,414	321	355	951	1,162
South Carolina	79,601	31,507	3,234	4,390	5,442	6,666	7,671	2,090	2,122	3,520	954
South Dakota	14,174	5,479	415	1,018	1,639	315	727	361	965	405	666
Tennessee	80,266	35,414	2,176	3,886	7,514	2,944	5,924	1,750	3,622	4,086	2,610
Texas	308,058	141,099	2,344	12,338	23,660	23,062	38,874	7,482	10,946	7,779	5,697
Utah	62,104	29,827	1,647	1,583	2,855	10,744	3,297	913	1,333	2,457	1,572
Vermont	14,296	4,742	365	1,048	1,591	245	1,026	619	649	624	690
Virginia	125,819	57,016	1,937	7,817	3,107	11,394	13,334	3,145	2,688	4,725	3,864
Washington	127,864	54,996	2,265	6,689	10,696	14,453	8,948	2,229	5,043	3,212	2,124
West Virginia	39,757	14,392	1,262	4,984	3,362	1,451	3,473	1,000	1,747	1,777	1,630
Wisconsin	71,254	37,576	1,087	1,402	2,371	3,653	9,284	801	2,357	2,597	2,377
Wyoming	12,365	3,817	210	1,740	503	570	1,064	262	792	691	536

Source: U.S. Census Bureau, 2018 Annual Survey of Public Employment & Payroll

Note: Data users who create their own estimates using these data should cite the U.S. Census Bureau as the source of the original data only. The data in this table are based on information from public records and contain no confidential data. The data in this table come from a census of governmental units and are subject to nonsampling error. Additional information on nonsampling error, response rates, and definitions may be found within the survey technical documentation <https://www.census.gov/programs-surveys/apes/technical-documentation.html>.

Note: Detail may not add to total due to rounding.

Key:

(a) Includes instructional and other personnel.

TABLE 8.6
State Government Payrolls for Selected Functions, By State: March 2018 (In thousands of dollars)

| State | All functions | Education | | Selected functions | | |
		Higher education (a)	Other education	Highways	Public welfare	Hospitals
United States	$22,920,048,649	$10,252,752,806	$406,541,194	$1,094,017,987	$1,030,205,456	$2,208,465,160
Alabama	410,209,467	215,885,407	11,738,680	16,316,464	14,800,483	62,138,414
Alaska	142,151,749	30,130,417	1,357,496	17,832,378	8,043,704	1,194,878
Arizona	340,878,839	193,595,580	9,955,276	11,564,063	22,293,159	2,730,958
Arkansas	251,779,689	123,575,119	5,386,031	13,561,535	14,956,849	26,658,331
California	2,977,464,716	1,217,219,238	24,022,980	168,858,570	23,076,189	438,428,111
Colorado	459,118,172	287,618,663	8,802,171	15,214,890	11,078,012	33,485,201
Connecticut	377,948,174	121,343,104	19,349,225	20,081,924	34,296,965	39,599,466
Delaware	118,745,601	44,419,061	1,962,016	5,699,519	5,545,444	4,403,789
Florida	776,622,194	395,018,573	10,505,162	29,309,638	29,647,530	14,019,159
Georgia	556,701,241	326,655,924	13,877,636	14,964,241	23,547,586	33,130,418
Hawaii	279,420,700	58,171,248	572,970	4,190,876	1,842,678	17,386,559
Idaho	122,570,808	44,504,833	2,681,115	6,048,314	7,737,268	2,181,926
Illinois	683,283,763	297,554,153	10,745,284	39,786,304	51,198,396	52,921,930
Indiana	381,582,094	272,300,017	3,988,328	15,364,397	21,778,933	5,523,815
Iowa	297,791,595	148,336,774	6,149,856	11,548,346	12,736,570	50,206,528
Kansas	245,981,485	120,234,084	2,267,207	9,442,175	8,518,235	56,842,083
Kentucky	364,475,018	196,275,160	9,102,048	15,730,472	23,377,538	36,710,487
Louisiana	337,494,528	129,618,552	14,230,572	18,432,179	20,397,548	42,610,156
Maine	89,097,105	30,644,935	1,212,172	9,776,896	8,499,342	2,452,706
Maryland	457,950,608	165,833,673	10,345,758	23,644,028	27,573,408	16,918,478
Massachusetts	590,350,494	191,734,996	7,557,388	17,708,681	46,341,712	29,023,700
Michigan	825,054,944	475,890,208	3,917,052	15,369,020	56,548,542	108,640,563
Minnesota	473,259,378	218,907,522	21,116,709	26,586,430	14,211,810	25,988,423
Mississippi	216,596,303	94,419,016	4,632,428	9,834,089	12,636,261	38,203,206
Missouri	335,587,588	142,927,332	5,555,496	18,425,666	18,499,366	40,226,450
Montana	95,817,742	32,804,543	1,638,474	9,989,998	7,074,590	2,598,305
Nebraska	131,604,464	56,042,348	2,636,830	8,242,980	8,824,068	15,623,624
Nevada	144,755,390	62,020,371	891,412	8,728,701	9,956,171	6,601,381
New Hampshire	96,360,487	40,702,652	1,499,668	8,360,997	8,981,448	2,634,150
New Jersey	848,436,856	261,077,492	14,580,492	36,664,417	50,641,505	66,723,505
New Mexico	210,683,741	91,025,793	4,224,425	8,071,532	6,133,782	37,844,282
New York	1,535,953,566	359,396,362	22,878,767	62,474,196	25,039,569	235,727,755
North Carolina	681,756,491	329,740,637	14,550,040	37,929,160	4,498,828	112,032,228
North Dakota	91,480,042	40,136,436	1,337,078	5,567,259	3,127,041	3,286,717
Ohio	691,794,167	365,119,464	11,826,957	31,956,147	16,277,897	76,875,146
Oklahoma	275,076,106	142,390,206	6,324,844	10,920,421	22,959,785	3,569,256
Oregon	406,900,558	160,257,559	4,963,616	21,751,167	40,341,455	55,878,828
Pennsylvania	874,173,693	393,399,746	24,362,249	60,551,282	49,670,153	29,405,809
Rhode Island	110,456,856	29,951,630	3,073,912	4,956,214	8,672,821	4,355,759
South Carolina	335,979,627	157,653,902	13,137,988	16,038,944	17,142,754	24,014,032
South Dakota	65,712,945	25,560,607	1,827,762	4,879,973	6,933,353	1,149,547
Tennessee	341,670,507	166,918,989	9,203,764	15,574,114	28,632,628	12,114,241
Texas	1,582,232,617	855,353,814	12,860,200	58,112,997	87,176,375	111,746,875
Utah	296,707,807	167,550,422	7,242,608	7,663,164	10,803,409	52,328,732
Vermont	79,941,610	28,341,484	2,007,197	6,085,842	8,467,559	1,329,384
Virginia	645,958,864	329,358,967	9,950,907	41,459,784	15,124,901	58,351,794
Washington	691,839,114	330,811,846	11,884,168	38,751,094	52,419,850	89,553,494
West Virginia	151,375,663	69,977,666	6,032,753	18,826,832	9,221,183	4,593,804
Wisconsin	362,632,547	197,341,880	5,385,342	7,920,542	10,865,017	16,392,603
Wyoming	58,630,936	17,004,401	1,188,685	7,249,131	2,035,786	2,108,174

See footnotes at end of table

TABLE 8.6

State Government Payrolls for Selected Functions, By State: March 2018 (In thousands of dollars) (continued)

State	Corrections	Police protection	Natural resources	Financial admin.	Judicial and legal admin.
			Selected functions, cont.		
United States	$2,121,771,519	$678,299,705	$643,556,643	$895,370,437	$1,052,517,152
Alabama	17,397,912	5,801,418	7,269,361	10,128,526	13,888,359
Alaska	12,646,112	5,175,726	11,490,628	7,379,338	8,809,220
Arizona	34,693,132	10,390,201	6,824,010	9,978,566	11,944,769
Arkansas	15,688,204	5,051,820	6,961,360	9,137,670	6,929,998
California	475,871,392	100,975,475	107,786,802	150,575,052	48,991,618
Colorado	32,156,483	10,102,755	5,951,472	11,571,615	29,816,262
Connecticut	33,368,261	15,330,733	3,676,804	10,885,942	36,165,183
Delaware	13,424,488	7,647,658	2,160,335	2,490,479	8,717,085
Florida	75,510,925	17,634,410	29,116,378	25,459,038	85,039,905
Georgia	49,969,336	13,123,429	19,009,742	14,005,326	18,923,566
Hawaii	13,363,562	0	4,158,420	3,266,806	14,259,388
Idaho	14,006,998	2,848,741	11,119,535	7,629,211	5,847,110
Illinois	73,225,152	22,223,330	12,922,569	23,276,531	24,991,607
Indiana	21,257,821	8,164,899	8,658,204	13,039,262	11,350,391
Iowa	13,793,778	5,969,721	7,777,940	7,388,272	12,658,036
Kansas	10,884,465	5,458,397	3,388,555	6,667,635	9,329,585
Kentucky	13,786,515	8,494,222	8,895,510	8,776,550	19,520,603
Louisiana	23,903,004	12,906,511	17,478,879	14,329,398	8,817,526
Maine	5,610,107	3,179,144	5,440,763	5,644,240	4,461,097
Maryland	56,739,464	15,121,910	11,024,821	15,265,622	28,326,300
Massachusetts	71,825,911	29,941,139	7,933,445	22,108,276	60,647,195
Michigan	63,994,566	16,491,453	18,043,477	26,195,507	11,093,720
Minnesota	25,972,763	5,569,608	17,817,575	34,996,857	25,157,833
Mississippi	6,559,807	4,956,610	9,809,242	6,256,074	2,508,183
Missouri	31,916,504	11,128,752	7,622,762	11,103,816	17,231,284
Montana	5,066,540	2,402,404	7,211,955	4,393,135	4,011,489
Nebraska	12,728,387	3,896,859	8,183,781	3,298,293	4,528,828
Nevada	17,179,188	6,332,455	4,604,125	6,876,061	5,029,037
New Hampshire	5,766,820	2,928,502	1,874,810	4,009,793	4,366,372
New Jersey	49,187,523	30,199,498	11,259,170	27,866,527	79,963,459
New Mexico	14,227,649	3,222,687	4,490,732	4,942,368	15,194,126
New York	187,008,286	58,418,632	17,510,235	99,188,529	152,262,621
North Carolina	64,850,401	24,670,747	15,742,007	22,105,792	34,893,214
North Dakota	4,136,033	1,208,544	4,712,562	3,200,136	3,675,647
Ohio	65,368,480	15,360,954	12,309,996	37,402,621	21,543,446
Oklahoma	15,414,860	10,250,604	7,161,054	10,337,908	12,000,436
Oregon	28,707,772	9,417,008	14,645,771	23,182,174	20,276,918
Pennsylvania	88,192,447	42,740,203	29,864,185	29,277,538	31,074,409
Rhode Island	11,621,552	2,825,763	2,168,773	5,539,776	7,280,770
South Carolina	24,809,480	8,489,516	7,848,110	13,512,883	5,095,046
South Dakota	2,986,234	1,737,534	3,876,927	2,295,553	3,460,060
Tennessee	20,521,766	8,518,922	15,928,377	20,286,783	16,079,788
Texas	129,877,370	52,100,810	51,730,634	40,977,745	33,337,218
Utah	13,313,061	4,321,462	5,594,740	12,675,517	8,666,515
Vermont	5,457,428	4,242,959	3,675,551	3,438,435	3,963,064
Virginia	47,887,638	17,514,002	14,323,609	21,231,391	20,489,416
Washington	42,957,086	13,722,084	25,203,170	18,828,128	13,988,734
West Virginia	10,008,412	4,058,566	6,594,801	5,879,414	7,693,839
Wisconsin	42,872,170	4,633,713	10,734,392	13,382,167	15,393,496
Wyoming	4,058,274	1,397,215	3,968,587	3,686,161	2,823,381

Source: U.S. Census Bureau, 2018 Annual Survey of Public Employment & Payroll

Notes:

1. Data users who create their own estimates using these data should cite the U.S. Census Bureau as the source of the original data only. The data in this table are based on information from public records and contain no confidential data. The data in this table come from a census of governmental units and are subject to nonsampling error. Additional information on nonsampling error, response rates, and definitions may be found within the survey technical documentation *https://www.census.gov/programs-surveys/apes/technical-documentation.html*.

2. Detail may not add to total due to rounding.

Key:

(a) Includes instructional and other personnel.

TABLE 8.7
State Employees: Paid Holidays**

State or other jurisdiction	Major holidays (a)	Martin Luther King's Birthday (b)	Lincoln's Birthday	President's Day (c)	Washington's Birthday (c)	Good Friday	Memorial Day (d)
Alabama	★	★(h)	…	…	★(i)	…	★
Alaska	★	★	…	★	…	…	★
Arizona	★	★	…	★	…	…	★
Arkansas	★	★	…	…	★(i)	…	★
California	★	★	…	★	…	…	★
Colorado	★	★	…	★	…	…	★
Connecticut	★	★	★	…	★	★	★
Delaware	★	★	…	…	…	★	★
Florida	★	★	…	…	…	…	★
Georgia	★	★	…	…	(l)	…	★
Hawaii	★	★	…	★	…	★	★
Idaho	★	★(h)	…	★	…	…	★
Illinois	★	★	★	…	★	…	★
Indiana	★	★	(m)	…	(m)	★	★
Iowa	★	★	…	…	…	…	★
Kansas	★	★	…	…	…	…	★
Kentucky	★	★	…	…	…	★(n)	★
Louisiana	★	★	…	…	…	★	★
Maine	★	★	…	★	…	…	★
Maryland	★	★	…	★	…	…	★
Massachusetts	★	★	…	…	★	…	★
Michigan	★	★	…	★	…	…	★
Minnesota	★	★	…	★	…	…	★
Mississippi	★	★(h)	…	…	★	…	★(v)
Missouri	★	★	★	…	★	…	★
Montana	★	★	…	★	…	…	★
Nebraska	★	★	…	★	…	…	★
Nevada	★	★	…	★	…	…	★
New Hampshire	★	★(h)	…	★	…	…	★
New Jersey	★	★	…	★	…	★	★
New Mexico	★	★	…	(o)	…	…	★
New York	★	★	(j)	…	★	…	★
North Carolina	★	★	…	…	…	★	★
North Dakota	★	★	…	★	…	★	★
Ohio	★	★	…	★	…	…	★
Oklahoma	★	★	…	★	…	…	★
Oregon	★	★	…	★	…	…	★
Pennsylvania	★	★	…	★	…	…	★
Rhode Island	★	★	…	…	…	…	★
South Carolina	★	★	…	★	…	…	★
South Dakota	★	★	…	★	…	…	★
Tennessee	★	★	…	★	…	★	★
Texas	★	★	…	★	…	(r)	★
Utah	★	★	…	★	…	…	★
Vermont	★	★	…	★	…	…	★
Virginia	★	★	…	…	★	…	★
Washington	★	★	…	★	…	…	★
West Virginia	★	★	…	★	…	…	★
Wisconsin	★	★	…	…	…	…	★
Wyoming	★	★	…	★	…	…	★
Dist. of Columbia	★	★	…	…	★	…	★
American Samoa	★	★	…	★	…	★	★
Guam	★	★	…	…	…	…	★
CNMI*	★	★	…	★	…	★	★
Puerto Rico	★	★	…	★	…	★	★
U.S. Virgin Islands	★	★	…	★	…	★	★

See footnotes at end of table

TABLE 8.7
State Employees: Paid Holidays** (continued)

State or other jurisdiction	Columbus Day (e)	Veteran's Day	Day after Thanksgiving	Day before or after Christmas	Day before or after New Year's	Election Day (f)	Other (g)
Alabama	★	★	(k)	(k)	...	...	★
Alaska	(kk)	★	...	...	...	...	★
Arizona	★	★	...	...	...	...	...
Arkansas	...	★	(k)	Before	...	...	★
California	...	★	★	...	...	...	★
Colorado	★	★	...	...	...	...	★
Connecticut	★	★	...	...	...	...	...
Delaware	...	★	★	...	...	★	★
Florida	...	★	★	...	...	...	★
Georgia	★	★	(l)	(l)	...	...	★
Hawaii	...	★	...	...	...	★	★
Idaho	★	★	...	...	...	...	...
Illinois	★	★	★	...	...	★	...
Indiana	★	★	(m)	(m)	...	★	...
Iowa	...	★	★	...	...	...	★
Kansas	...	★	★	★	...	...	★
Kentucky	...	★	★	★	★	★(t)	...
Louisiana	...	★	...	...	...	★(u)	★
Maine	(ii)	★	★	...	...	...	★
Maryland	★	★	★(aa)	...	...	★	...
Massachusetts	★	★	...	...	...	...	★
Michigan	...	★	★	Before	Before	★(z)	...
Minnesota	...	★	★	...	...	...	★
Mississippi	...	★	(k)	(k)	...	...	★
Missouri	★	★	...	...	...	...	★
Montana	★	★	...	...	...	★	...
Nebraska	★	★	★	...	...	...	★
Nevada	...	★	★(cc)	...	...	...	★
New Hampshire	...	★	★	...	...	...	★
New Jersey	★	★	...	...	...	★	...
New Mexico	(hh)	★	(o)	...	...	(w)	...
New York	★	★	...	...	...	★	...
North Carolina	...	★	★	(x)	...	...	...
North Dakota	...	★	...	(p)	...	...	...
Ohio	★	★	...	...	...	...	...
Oklahoma	...	★	★	Before	...	...	...
Oregon	...	★	★	...	...	...	...
Pennsylvania	★	★	★	...	...	...	...
Rhode Island	★	★	...	...	...	★	★
South Carolina	...	★	★	Both	...	...	★
South Dakota	(y)	★	...	...	...	...	★
Tennessee	(q)	★	(q)	...	...	...	...
Texas	...	★	★	Both	...	...	★
Utah	★	★	...	...	...	...	★
Vermont	(jj)	★	(dd)	...	...	...	★
Virginia	★	★	★	(ee)	...	★	★
Washington	...	★	★(aa)	...	...	...	★
West Virginia	★	★	★	(s)	(s)	★	★
Wisconsin	...	...	...	Before	Before	...	...
Wyoming	...	★	...	...	...	...	...
Dist. of Columbia	(kk)	★	...	...	...	...	★
American Samoa	★	★	...	...	...	...	★
Guam	...	★	...	...	...	...	★
CNMI*	(ff)	★	...	...	...	...	★
Puerto Rico	★	★	...	Before	...	...	★
U.S. Virgin Islands	(gg)	★	...	(bb)	...	...	★

See footnotes at end of table

TABLE 8.7
State Employees: Paid Holidays** (continued)

**Holidays in addition to any other authorized paid personal leave granted state employees.

Source: The Council of State Governments' survey of state personnel office websites, October 2019.

Note: In some states, the governor may proclaim additional holidays or select from a number of holidays for observance by state employees. In some states, the list of paid holidays is determined by the personnel department at the beginning of each year; as a result, the number of holidays may change from year to year. Number of paid holidays may also vary across some employee classifications. If a holiday falls on a weekend, generally employees get the day preceding or following.

* Commonwealth of Northern Mariana Islands

Key:

★ –Paid holiday granted.

… –Paid holiday not granted.

(a) New Year's Day, Independence Day, Labor Day, Thanksgiving Day and Christmas Day.

(b) Third Monday in January.

(c) Generally, third Monday in February; Washington's Birthday or President's Day. In some states the holiday is called President's Day or Washington-Lincoln Day. Most frequently, this day recognizes George Washington and Abraham Lincoln.

(d) Last Monday in May in all states indicated. Generally, states follow the federal government's observance (last Monday in May) rather than the traditional Memorial Day (May 30).

(e) Second Monday in October.

(f) General election day only, unless otherwise indicated. In Indiana, primary and general election days.

(g) Additional holidays:

Alabama–Mardi Gras Day (Baldwin and Mobile counties only)(day before Ash Wednesday), Robert E. Lee's Birthday clebrated with MLK day, Confederate Memorial Day (fourth Monday in April), Jefferson Davis' Birthday (first Monday in June). Columbus Day is also celebrated as Fraternal Day and American Indian Heritage Day.

Alaska–Seward's Day (last Monday in March), Alaska Day (October 18).

Arkansas–Employee is granted one holiday to observe his or her birthday.

California–César Chávez Day (March 31), one personal holiday (employees become eligible for a personal holiday once they have completed six months of state employment).

Colorado–State employees may have César Chávez Day (March 31) off in lieu of any other legal holiday that occurs on a weekday in the same fiscal year.

Delaware–Eligible employees are granted two floating holidays per calendar year, Return Day after 12:00 noon (second day after a general election) in Sussex County only.

Florida–Full-time employees are entitled to one personal holiday each year. Personal holidays are credited to eligible employees on July 1, and must be taken by the employee by June 30 of each year.

Georgia–State Holiday days will be observed on Friday, April 10 and Friday, November 27.

Hawaii–Prince Jonah Kuhio Kalanianaole Day (March 26), King Kamehameha I Day (June 11), Statehood Day (third Friday in August).

Iowa–State employees are granted two days of paid leave each year

to be added to the vacation allowance and accrued under certain provisions.

Kansas–One discretionary holiday that can be used any time during the calendar year.

Louisiana–Mardi Gras Day (Tuesday before Ash Wednesday), Inauguration Day (every four years, in Baton Rouge only).

Maine–Patriot's Day (third Monday in April). Indigenous People's Day is now celebrated instead of Columbus Day.

Massachusetts–Patriot's Day (third Monday in April), Evacuation Day (March 17–Suffolk County only), Bunker Hill Day (June 17–Suffolk County only).

Minnesota–Regular and temporary employees with at least six months of employment shall receive two floating holidays each payroll year.

Mississippi–Confederate Memorial Day (last Monday in April).

Missouri–Harry Truman's Birthday (May 8).

Nebraska–Arbor Day (last Friday in April).

Nevada–Nevada Day (last Friday in October).

New Hampshire–Employees who are employed on a full-time basis are eligible for two floating holildays.

Rhode Island–Victory Day (second Monday in August).

South Carolina–Confederate Memorial Day (May 10).

Texas–The following are partial staffing holidays: Confederate Heroes Day (January 19), Texas Independence Day (March 2), San Jacinto Day (April 21), Emancipation Day in Texas (June 19) and Lyndon Baines Johnson Day (August 27). Staff offices are scheduled to be open on partial staffing holidays and optional holidays. An employee may observe optional holidays in lieu of any partial staffing holiday on which state offices are required to be open to conduct public business. Optional holidays include Cesar Chavez Day (March 31), Good Friday, Rosh Hashanah and Yom Kippur.

Utah–Pioneer Day (July 24).

Vermont–Town Meeting Day (first Tuesday in March), Bennington Battle Day (August 16).

Virginia–Lee-Jackson Day is no longer a state holiday. On April 12, 2020, Election Day became a state holiday.

Washington–One additional paid holiday per calendar year.

West Virginia–West Virginia Day (June 20).

District of Columbia–Presidential Inauguration Day (January 20) and District of Columbia Emancipation Day (April 16).

American Samoa–American Samoa Flag Day (April 17), Manu'a Cession Day (July 16).

Guam–Guam History & Chamorro Heritage Day (March 6), Liberation Day (July 21), All Souls' Day (November 2) and Our Lady of Camarin Day (December 8).

Commonwealth of Northern Mariana Islands–Commonwealth Covenant Day (March 25), Citizenship Day (November 4) and Constitution Day (December 8).

Puerto Rico–Three Kings Day (January 6), Birthday of Eugenio Maria de Hostos (second Monday in January), Birthday of Luis Muñoz Marin (February 18), Emancipation Day (March 22), Birthday of Jose de Diego (third Monday in April), Birthday of Don Luis Munoz Rivera (third Monday in July), Constitution or Puerto Rico Day (July 25), Birthday of Dr. José Celso Barbosa (July 27), Discovery of Puerto Rico (November 19).

TABLE 8.7
State Employees: Paid Holidays** (continued)

U.S. Virgin Islands–Three Kings Day (January 6), Holy Thursday (Thursday before Good Friday), Transfer Day (March 31), Easter Monday (Monday after Easter), Emancipation Day (July 3), Liberty Day (November 1).

(h) In Alabama and Mississippi also celebrate the day as Robert E. Lee's Birthday. In Idaho, also celebrated as Idaho Human Rights Day. In New Hampshire, also celebrated as Civil Rights Day.

(i) In Alabama, celebrated as George Washington's and Thomas Jefferson's Birthday. In Arkansas, celebrated as George Washington's Birthday and Daisy Gatson Bates Day.

(j) The state has designated Lincoln's birthday as a floating holiday in 2020 for state employees in certain bargaining units.

(k) At the discretion of the governor.

(l) In Georgia, Washington's Birthday is observed the day before Christmas and State Holiday is observed the day after Thanksgiving.

(m) In Indiana, Lincoln's Birthday is observed on the day after Thanksgiving, and Washington's Birthday is observed the day before Christmas.

(n) In Kentucky, half day.

(o) In New Mexico, President's Day is observed on the day after Thanksgiving.

(p) In North Dakota, state offices close at noon on Christmas Eve when it falls on Monday through Thursday.

(q) Pursuant to Tennessee Code Annotated, Section 4-4-105(a)(3), the Governor has designated that the Friday after Thanksgiving shall be substituted for the Columbus Day holiday

(r) In Texas, Good Friday is an optional holiday. An employee is entitled to observe optional holidays in lieu of any partial staffing holiday in which state offices are required to be open to conduct public business.

(s) Half day on Christmas Eve and New Year's Eve (closes at noon).

(t) Tuesday after first Monday in November of presidential election years

(u) General Election Day is a state holiday the first Tuesday after the first Monday in November in even-numbered years.

(v) Also celebrated as Jefferson Davis' Birthday.

(w) Employees are allowed up to two hours paid administrative leave to vote.

(x) Three days when Christmas Day falls on Tuesday, Wednesday or Thursday; two days when Christmas Day falls on Friday or Monday.

(y) Celebrated as Native Americans' Day since 1990.

(z) First Tuesday in November, even numbered years.

(aa) Observed as American Indian Heritage Day in Maryland and Native American Heritage Day in Washington.

(bb) Observed as Boxing Day.

(cc) Observed as Family Day.

(dd) Most state offices will be closed the day after Thanksgiving.

(ee) At the discretion of the governor. A paid holiday will be granted on the day before Christmas for 2020.

(ff) Celebrated as Commonwealth Cultural Day.

(gg) Also celebrated as V.I./P.R. Friendship Day.

(hh) In 2019 New Mexico celebrated Indigenous Peoples' Day for the first time.

(ii) In 2019 Maine celebrated Indigenous Peoples' Day for the first time.

(jj) In 2019 Vermont celebrated Indigenous Peoples' Day for the first time.

(kk) Celebrated as Indigenous Peoples' Day in Alaska. The Washington D.C. Council voted in Oct. 2019 to rename Columbus Day as Indigenous Peoples' Day, pending Congressional approval.

TABLE 8.8
Women Governors Throughout History

Name (Party-State)	Dates served	Special circumstances
Nellie Tayloe Ross (D-WY)	1925–1927	Won special election to replace deceased husband
Miriam "Ma" Ferguson (D-TX)	1925–1927, 1933–1935	Inaugurated 15 days after Ross; elected as surrogate for husband who could not succeed himself
Lurleen Wallace (D-AL)	1967–1968	Elected as surrogate for husband who could not succeed himself
Ella Grasso (D-CT)	1975–1980	First woman elected governor in her own right; resigned for health reasons
Dixy Lee Ray (D-WA)	1977–1981	
Vesta Roy (R-NH)	1982–1983	Elected to state senate and chosen as senate president; served as governor for seven days when incumbent died
Martha Layne Collins (D-KY)	1984–1987	
Madeleine Kunin (D-VT)	1985–1991	First woman to serve three terms as governor
Kay Orr (R-NE)	1987–1991	First Republican woman governor and first woman to defeat another woman in a gubernatorial race
Rose Mofford (D-AZ)	1988–1991	Elected as secretary of state, succeeded governor who was impeached and convicted
Joan Finney (D-KS)	1991–1995	First woman to defeat an incumbent governor
Ann Richards (D-TX)	1991–1995	
Barbara Roberts (D-OR)	1991–1995	
Christine Todd Whitman (R-NJ)	1994–2001	Resigned to take presidential appointment as commissioner of the Environmental Protection Agency
Jeanne Shaheen (D-NH)	1997–2003	
Jane Dee Hull (R-AZ)	1997–2003	Elected as secretary of state, succeeded governor who resigned; later elected to a full term
Nancy Hollister (R-OH)	1998–1999	Elected lieutenant governor; served as governor for 11 days when predecessor took U.S. Senate seat and successor had not yet been sworn in
Jane Swift (R-MA)	2001–2003	Elected as lieutenant governor, succeeded governor who resigned for an ambassadorial appointment
Judy Martz (R-MT)	2001–2005	
Olene Walker (R-UT)	2003–2005	Elected as lieutenant governor, succeeded governor who resigned to take a federal appointment
Ruth Ann Minner (D-DE)	2001–2009	
Jennifer M. Granholm (D-MI)	2003–2011	
Linda Lingle (R-HI)	2003–2011	
Janet Napolitano (D-AZ)	2003–2009	First woman to succeed another woman as governor; resigned to become U. S. Secretary of Homeland Security
Kathleen Sebelius (D-KS)	2003–2009	Father was governor of Ohio; resigned to become U.S. Secretary of Health and Human Services
Kathleen Blanco (D-LA)	2004–2008	
M. Jodi Rell (R-CT)	2004–2011	Elected as lieutenant governor, succeeded governor who resigned
Christine Gregoire (D-WA)	2005–2013	
Sarah Palin (R-AK)	2007–2009	Resigned
Beverly Perdue (D-NC)	2009–2013	
Jan Brewer (R-AZ)	2009–2015	Elected as secretary of state, succeeded governor who resigned
Nikki Haley (R-SC)	2011–2017	First Asian (Indian) American woman to be elected governor; resigned to become U.S. Ambassador to the United Nations
Maggie Hassan (D-NH)	2013–2017	
Mary Fallin (R-OK)	2011–present	
Susana Martinez (R-NM)	2011–present	First Latina to be elected governor
Gina Raimando (D-RI)	2015–present	
Kate Brown (D-OR)	2015–present	Elected as secretary of state, succeeded governor who resigned
Kay Ivey (R-AL)	2017–present	Elected as lieutenant governor, succeeded governor who resigned
Kim Reynolds (R-IA)	2017–present	Elected as lieutenant governor, succeeded governor who resigned
Laura Kelly (D-KS)	2019–present	
Michelle Lujan Grisham (D-NM)	2019–present	
Janet Mills (D-ME)	2019–present	
Kristi Noem (R-SD)	2019–present	
Gretchen Whitmer (D-MI)	2019–present	

Source: Center for American Women and Politics, Eagleton Institute
of Politics, Rutgers University. May 2020.

TABLE 8.9
Women in State Legislatures: 2020

State	Senate			House			Legislature (both houses)	
	Democrats	Republicans	% Women	Democrats	Republicans	% Women	% Women	State rank (a)
Alabama	4	0	11.4	11	7	17.1	15.7	47
Alaska	1	5	30.0	6	10	40.0	36.7	10
Arizona	7	6	43.3	14	8	36.7	38.9	7
Arkansas	3	4	20.0	10	17	27.0	25.2	36
California	11	3	35.0	21	3	30.0	31.7	17
Colorado	11	1	34.3	26	6	49.2	44.0	2
Connecticut	8	1	25.0	29	22	33.8	32.1	15
Delaware	4	1	23.8	9	1	24.4	24.2	40
Florida	6	6	30.0	22	13	29.2	29.4	24
Georgia	13	2	26.8	42	15	31.7	30.5	23
Hawaii	7	0	28.0	14	3	33.3	31.6	18
Idaho	4	5	25.7	8	16	34.3	31.4	20
Illinois	19	2	35.6	35	8	36.4	36.2	13
Indiana	2	8	20.0	17	11	28.0	25.3	35
Iowa	6	5	22.0	23	10	33.3	29.3	25
Kansas	6	7	32.5	18	15	26.4	27.9	29
Kentucky	2	2	10.5	19	10	29.0	23.9	41
Louisiana	3	3	15.4	8	12	19.0	18.1	44
Maine	8	4	34.3	47	11	38.4	37.6	8
Maryland	13	2	31.9	53	7	42.6	39.9	6
Massachusetts	11	0	27.5	38	6	28.1(b)	28.0	28
Michigan	8	3	28.9	26	17	39.1	36.5	12
Minnesota	10	6	23.9	35	13	35.8	31.8	16
Mississippi	4	8	23.1	10	6	13.1	16.1	46
Missouri	5	3	23.5	20	20	24.5	24.4	38
Montana	11	2	26.0	22	11	33.0	30.7	22
Nebraska (c)	—————Nonpartisan—————		28.6	————————Unicameral————————			28.6	27
Nevada	9	1	47.6	18	5	54.8	52.4	1
New Hampshire	7	3	41.7	109	25	33.5	34.0	14
New Jersey	9	1	25.0	20	7	33.8	30.8	21
New Mexico	7	2	21.4	25	7	45.7	36.6	11
New York	14	5	30.2	44	4	32.0	31.5	19
North Carolina	7	4	22.0	23	10	27.5	25.9	34
North Dakota	4	7	23.4	8	12	21.3	22.0	42
Ohio	4	4	24.2	19	9	28.3	27.3	30
Oklahoma	5	4	18.8	11	12	22.8	21.5	43
Oregon	7	2	30.0	22	7	48.3	42.2	3
Pennsylvania	7	6	26.0	31	24	27.1	26.9	32
Rhode Island	14	2	42.1	25	1	34.7	37.2	9
South Carolina	2	2	8.7	12	12	19.4	16.5	45
South Dakota	2	5	20.0	4	15	27.1	24.8	37
Tennessee	4	4	27.3	4	8	12.1	15.2	49
Texas	3	6	29.0	29	6	23.3	24.3	39
Utah	4	2	20.7	12	9	28.0	26.0	33
Vermont	10	0	33.3	42	14	42.0(d)	40.6	4
Virginia	7	4	27.5	24	6	30.0	29.3	25
Washington	12	7	38.8	30	10	40.8	40.1	5
West Virginia	0	3	8.8	8	7	15.0	13.4	50
Wisconsin	6	2	24.2	18	10	28.3	27.3	30
Wyoming	1	5	20.0	4	4	13.3	15.6	48

Source: Center for American Women and Politics, Eagleton Institute of Politics, Rutgers University. Figures are as of May 2020.
Key:
(a) States share the same rank if their proportions of women legislators are exactly equal or round off to be equal (Iowa, Ohio, Virginia, Wisconsin).

(b) Massachusetts percentage includes one Independent.
(c) Nebraska has a unicameral legislature with nonpartisan elections.
(d) Vermont percentage includes three Independents and four Progressives.

Table 8.9 | Proportion of Women among State Legislators

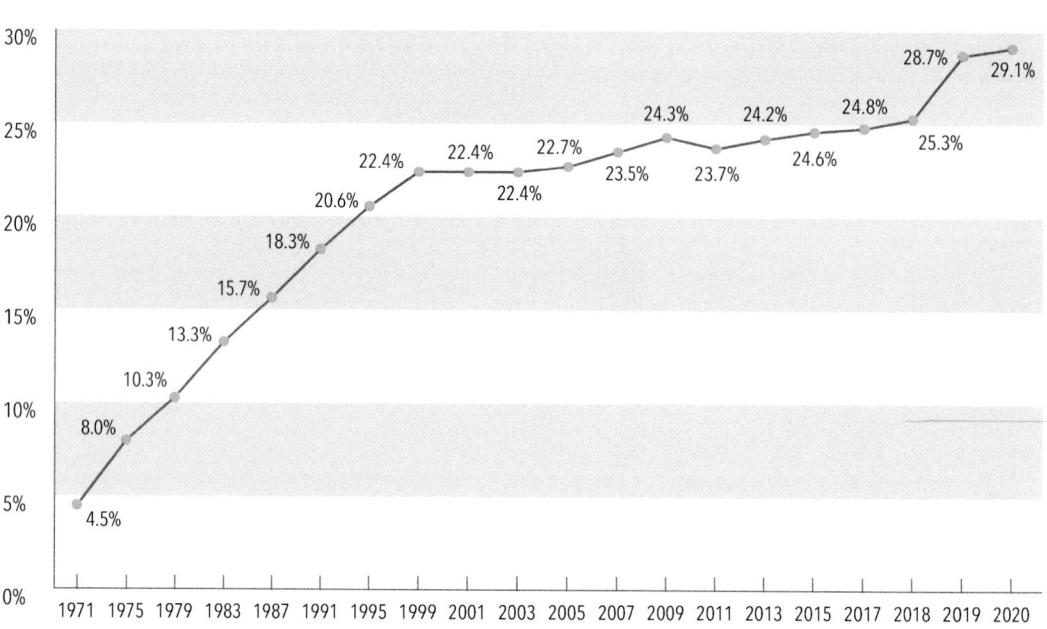

Source: Center for American Women and Politics, Eagleton Institue of Politics, Rutgers University.

TABLE 8.10
Women Statewide Elected Officials: 2020

State	Governor	Lieutenant Governor	Attorney General	Secretary of State	Treasurer
Alabama	W	★	★	★	★
Alaska	★	★	★	N.A.	N.A.
Arizona	★	N.A.	★	W	W
Arkansas	★	★	W	★	★
California	★	W	★	★	W
Colorado	★	W	★	W	★
Connecticut	★	W	★	W	★
Delaware	★	W	W	N.A.	W
Florida	★	W	W	N.A.	★
Georgia	★	★	★	★	N.A.
Hawaii	★	★	N.A.	N.A.	N.A.
Idaho	★	W	★	★	W
Illinois	★	W	★	★	★
Indiana	★	W	★	W	W
Iowa	W	★	★	★	★
Kansas	W	★	★	★	★
Kentucky	★	W	★	★	W
Louisiana	★	★	★	★	★
Maine	W	N.A.	N.A.	N.A.	N.A.
Maryland	★	★	★	N.A.	N.A.
Massachusetts	★	W	W	★	W
Michigan	W	★	W	W	N.A.
Minnesota	★	W	★	★	N.A.
Mississippi	★	★	W	★	★
Missouri	★	★	★	★	★
Montana	★	★	★	★	N.A.
Nebraska	★	★	★	★	N.A.
Nevada	★	W	★	W	★
New Hampshire	★	N.A.	N.A.	N.A.	N.A.
New Jersey	★	W	N.A.	N.A.	N.A.
New Mexico	W	★	★	W	★
New York	★	W	W	N.A.	N.A.
North Carolina	★	★	★	W	★
North Dakota	★	★	★	★	W
Ohio	★	★	★	★	★
Oklahoma	W	★	★	N.A.	★
Oregon	W	N.A.	W	W	★
Pennsylvania	★	★	★	N.A.	★
Rhode Island	W	★	★	W	★
South Carolina	★	W	★	★	★
South Dakota	W	★	★	★	★
Tennessee	★	N.A.	N.A.	N.A.	N.A.
Texas	★	★	★	N.A.	N.A.
Utah	★	★	★	N.A.	★
Vermont	★	★	★	★	W
Virginia	★	★	★	N.A.	N.A.
Washington	★	★	★	W	★
West Virginia	★	N.A.	★	★	★
Wisconsin	★	★	★	★	W
Wyoming	★	N.A.	N.A.	★	★

Source: Data for elected officials are current as of May 2020 and have been provided by the Center for American Women and Politics, Eagleton Institute of Politics, Rutgers University.

Key:
★–Denotes that this position is filled through a statewide election.
W–Denotes that this position is filled through a statewide election and is held by a woman.
N.A.–Not applicable

Table 8.10 | Proportion of Women among Statewide Elected Officials

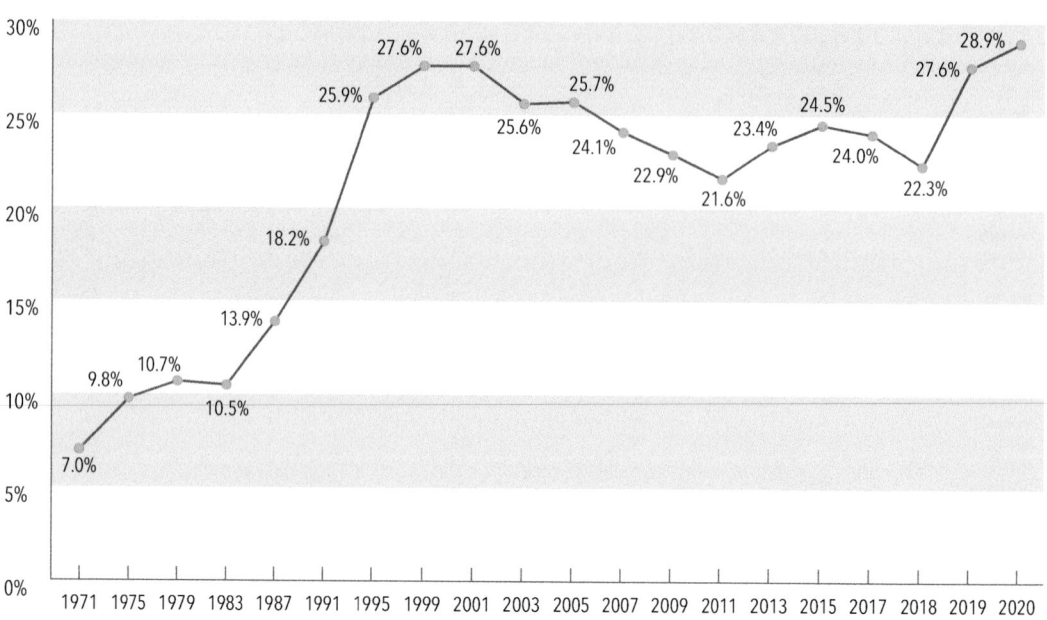

Source: Center for American Women and Politics, Eagleton Institue of Politics, Rutgers University.

CHAPTER NINE

SELECTED STATE POLICIES AND PROGRAMS

TABLE 9.1

Enrollment in Public Elementary And Secondary Schools, by Level, Grade, and State or Jurisdiction: Fall 2017

State or jurisdiction	Total, all grades	Elementary											Elementary ungraded
		Total	Prekinder-garten	Kinder-garten	Grade 1	Grade 2	Grade 3	Grade 4	Grade 5	Grade 6	Grade 7	Grade 8	
United States	50,685,567	35,496,055	1,471,216	3,684,238	3,667,166	3,684,091	3,787,970	3,859,475	3,877,267	3,827,023	3,776,565	3,772,276	88,768
Alabama	742,444	523,057	15,520	54,985	56,414	55,606	57,526	58,541	57,928	55,711	55,600	55,226	0
Alaska	132,872	94,618	3,586	10,196	10,243	10,331	10,409	10,398	10,229	10,007	9,741	9,478	0
Arizona	1,110,851	777,744	14,124	79,520	80,377	81,200	84,933	88,092	88,849	87,512	86,544	86,287	306
Arkansas	496,085	352,513	16,827	36,942	36,820	36,915	37,797	38,800	38,844	36,305	36,431	36,631	201
California	6,304,266	4,357,267	8,385 (b)	531,725	456,175	455,523	447,253	466,660	472,202	486,261	477,308	474,828	5,479
Colorado	910,280	639,875	33,048	63,574	64,967	65,616	67,991	69,784	69,821	69,321	67,899	67,854	0
Connecticut	531,288	365,546	18,579	36,225	36,783	36,848	38,020	38,873	40,145	39,621	40,142	40,310	0
Delaware	136,293	95,390	1,802	9,943	10,048	10,327	10,602	10,838	10,754	10,498	10,362	10,216	0
Florida	2,832,424	1,980,941	61,241	200,185	207,590	207,609	226,346	220,504	215,793	219,942	210,658	211,073	0
Georgia	1,768,642	1,246,608	47,726	126,400	128,192	130,015	135,911	138,249	139,160	135,448	132,993	132,514	0
Hawaii	180,837	130,255	1,582	14,316	14,755	14,981	11,986	15,443	15,308	14,425	13,996	13,226	237
Idaho	301,186	210,927	2,845	21,111	22,148	22,376	23,146	24,003	24,147	23,732	24,005	23,414	0
Illinois	2,005,153	1,388,977	83,664	132,075	137,580	139,991	145,553	148,792	151,331	149,568	149,227	151,180	16
Indiana	1,054,187	728,666	19,198	77,944	76,301	76,468	78,722	80,111	80,201	79,338	78,616	80,163	1,604
Iowa	511,850	363,718	30,454	38,293	34,934	36,056	36,683	37,980	38,071	37,618	37,138	36,491	0
Kansas	497,088	353,430	21,281	35,661	35,554	36,462	36,888	37,687	37,715	36,808	36,210	36,269	2,895
Kentucky	680,978	481,962	29,493	44,058	50,518	49,479	51,350	52,328	52,669	51,102	50,249	50,293	423
Louisiana	715,135	514,159	27,491	53,070	54,585	53,478	55,396	55,835	55,456	53,698	52,928	52,222	0
Maine	180,473	124,937	5,617	12,586	12,569	12,688	13,246	13,343	13,727	13,513	13,852	13,796	0
Maryland	893,684	633,791	30,422	64,045	66,082	66,879	68,516	70,330	69,515	67,059	65,571	65,372	0
Massachusetts	964,791	668,415	30,684	66,122	68,195	68,491	70,416	72,620	73,012	71,892	71,705	72,860	2,418
Michigan	1,516,398	1,037,784	44,258	116,636	105,819	103,930	105,399	107,959	112,263	112,397	111,842	114,521	2,760
Minnesota	884,944	614,476	22,692	64,111	63,518	64,385	65,710	67,226	67,694	66,560	66,152	66,428	0
Mississippi	478,321	341,927	5,732	35,988	36,391	36,409	37,952	38,880	38,842	35,783	35,864	35,613	4,473
Missouri	915,472	648,697	33,054	66,010	66,399	67,231	69,041	70,749	71,042	69,214	68,224	67,733	0
Montana	149,474	106,075	2,321	11,702	11,407	11,144	11,559	11,971	11,721	11,804	11,239	11,207	0
Nebraska	323,766	228,831	17,513	23,232	22,892	23,559	24,173	24,169	22,553	23,661	23,357	23,722	0
Nevada	485,785	343,807	8,908	35,083	36,354	36,375	36,959	38,624	39,062	38,004	37,216	36,389	833
New Hampshire	179,433	122,657	3,907	11,419	12,745	12,514	13,003	13,456	13,694	13,801	13,895	14,223	0
New Jersey	1,408,102	987,988	64,351	91,077	94,920	95,253	98,425	99,443	100,606	99,986	99,191	100,919	43,817
New Mexico	334,345	235,839	9,689	23,709	24,166	24,309	25,880	26,363	26,248	25,343	25,304	24,828	0
New York	2,724,663	1,880,208	65,558	193,045	197,155	198,490	200,783	202,149	203,385	199,743	197,715	198,879	23,306
North Carolina	1,553,513	1,080,861	18,734	115,064	115,584	117,037	121,228	122,866	122,997	119,927	117,127	110,297	0
North Dakota	111,920	81,031	2,778	9,273	8,739	8,713	8,876	8,781	8,746	8,575	8,307	8,243	0
Ohio	1,704,399	1,187,254	38,310	123,036	123,188	123,921	131,207	128,118	130,839	129,831	128,323	130,481	0
Oklahoma	695,092	503,796	41,727	51,920	52,328	51,834	53,565	52,385	52,257	50,368	47,950	49,462	0
Oregon	608,014	427,690	27,330 (b)	41,884	43,156	43,504	44,827	46,543	46,542	45,378	44,151	44,375	0
Pennsylvania	1,726,809	1,182,944	8,498	121,043	126,361	126,616	129,812	134,060	134,805	133,628	133,276	134,845	0
Rhode Island	142,949	98,737	2,477	10,006	10,297	10,434	10,583	11,003	11,119	10,913	10,853	11,052	0
South Carolina	777,507	553,414	27,006	55,598	57,183	57,012	60,334	60,890	61,389	59,112	57,857	57,033	0
South Dakota	137,823	99,878	3,393	11,720	10,432	10,494	10,655	10,966	10,921	10,677	10,516	10,104	0
Tennessee	1,001,967	710,398	28,379	75,482	74,633	74,144	74,844	78,085	78,681	76,941	75,058	74,150	0
Texas	5,401,341	3,852,952	256,022	371,638	388,650	394,381	409,998	413,843	414,412	402,634	402,512	398,662	0
Utah	668,274	475,107	15,904	47,591	49,791	50,429	51,635	52,970	53,368	51,951	50,841	50,627	0
Vermont	88,028	63,052	8,818	5,789	5,814	5,871	5,848	6,236	6,265	6,040	6,240	6,131	0
Virginia	1,291,462	900,027	33,617	91,002	94,312	94,166	96,946	99,305	99,548	97,617	96,633	96,881	0
Washington	1,110,367	769,992	15,754	80,917	82,843	83,077	85,583	87,366	86,667	83,947	82,040	81,798	0
West Virginia	272,266	193,961	16,665	19,521	19,402	19,150	19,659	20,069	20,218	19,539	19,780	19,958	0
Wisconsin	860,753	598,837	55,186	56,832	57,517	58,370	60,783	61,913	62,743	61,551	61,583	62,359	0
Wyoming	94,258	66,897	671	7,469	7,118	7,179	7,411	7,537	7,604	7,449	7,373	7,086	0
Dist. of Columbia	87,315	68,142	12,727	7,465	7,222	6,820	6,602	6,339	6,159	5,270	4,971	4,567	0
Bureau of Indian Education	46,330	35,064	N/A	4,601	4,064	3,899	3,931	3,962	3,774	3,756	3,614	3,463	0
DoDEA (c)	N/A	N/A	N/A	N/A	N/A	N/A	N/A	N/A	N/A	N/A	N/A	N/A	N/A
American Samoa	12,620	8,877	1,128	729	800	817	850	845	855	873	1,010	970	0
Guam	30,112	20,227	602	1,953	2,153	2,164	2,181	2,327	2,315	2,139	2,159	2,234	0
CNMI*	N/A	N/A	N/A	N/A	N/A	N/A	N/A	N/A	N/A	N/A	N/A	N/A	N/A
Puerto Rico	346,096	238,807	2,536	22,189	25,701	24,247	25,082	25,360	25,827	25,754	27,494	26,186	8,431
U.S. Virgin Islands	10,868	7,427	N/A	732	745	780	898	865	833	848	955	771	0

See footnotes at end of table

TABLE 9.1

**Enrollment in Public Elementary And Secondary Schools, by Level, Grade,
and State or Jurisdiction: Fall 2017** (continued)

State or other jurisdiction			Secondary			
	Total	Grade 9	Grade 10	Grade 11	Grade 12	Secondary ungraded (a)
United States	15,189,512	3,995,574	3,833,718	3,676,753	3,631,450	52,017
Alabama	219,387	57,301	55,318	53,920	52,848	0
Alaska	38,254	9,584	9,285	9,503	9,882	0
Arizona	333,107	86,236	83,999	78,514	84,330	28
Arkansas	143,572	37,758	37,245	35,387	33,097	85
California	1,946,999	495,277	483,745	475,696	489,221	3,060
Colorado	270,405	70,017	67,140	65,136	68,112	0
Connecticut	165,742	43,232	41,092	40,616	40,802	0
Delaware	40,903	11,806	10,476	9,521	9,100	0
Florida	851,483	219,313	216,578	212,640	202,952	0
Georgia	522,034	147,677	135,406	123,273	115,678	0
Hawaii	50,582	14,408	13,143	11,766	11,068	197
Idaho	90,259	23,599	22,935	22,210	21,512	3
Illinois	616,176	159,550	155,612	150,969	150,045	0
Indiana	325,521	80,535	80,799	83,712	80,475	0
Iowa	148,132	37,728	37,111	36,238	37,055	0
Kansas	143,658	37,510	35,904	34,718	34,437	1,089
Kentucky	199,016	53,687	50,822	48,739	45,593	175
Louisiana	200,976	56,596	51,715	47,551	45,114	0
Maine	55,536	13,814	13,846	13,946	13,930	0
Maryland	259,893	71,633	67,738	60,336	60,186	0
Massachusetts	296,376	77,572	74,170	72,950	71,684	0
Michigan	478,614	123,324	121,134	115,646	117,197	1,313
Minnesota	270,468	67,007	65,975	66,653	70,833	0
Mississippi	136,394	35,716	34,365	32,230	30,933	3,150
Missouri	266,775	69,398	67,397	65,697	64,283	0
Montana	43,399	11,556	11,245	10,667	9,931	0
Nebraska	94,935	23,832	23,747	23,007	24,349	0
Nevada	141,978	36,452	36,510	35,532	33,456	28
New Hampshire	56,776	14,992	14,567	13,779	13,435	3
New Jersey	420,114	103,655	100,781	99,613	98,845	17,220
New Mexico	98,506	28,522	25,597	22,814	21,573	0
New York	844,455	218,826	212,490	195,169	194,079	23,891
North Carolina	472,652	129,965	120,884	114,820	105,208	1,775
North Dakota	30,889	8,199	7,760	7,561	7,369	0
Ohio	517,145	141,280	133,705	120,359	121,801	0
Oklahoma	191,296	52,268	49,055	46,439	43,534	0
Oregon	180,324	44,819	44,257	44,003	47,245	0
Pennsylvania	543,865	141,407	136,286	133,081	133,091	0
Rhode Island	44,212	11,580	11,470	10,867	10,295	0
South Carolina	224,093	63,516	57,755	52,722	50,100	0
South Dakota	37,945	10,600	9,649	8,913	8,783	0
Tennessee	291,569	75,784	74,234	72,053	69,498	0
Texas	1,548,389	433,521	397,573	372,052	345,243	0
Utah	193,167	50,184	48,968	47,499	46,516	0
Vermont	24,976	6,447	6,430	6,192	5,907	0
Virginia	391,435	103,925	99,531	94,858	93,121	0
Washington	340,375	83,131	82,138	83,214	91,892	0
West Virginia	78,305	21,317	20,164	18,547	18,277	0
Wisconsin	261,916	65,980	64,354	64,556	67,026	0
Wyoming	27,361	7,453	6,893	6,610	6,405	0
Dist. of Columbia	19,173	6,085	4,725	4,259	4,104	0
Bureau of Indian Education	11,266	3,315	2,990	2,470	2,491	0
DoDEA (c)	N/A	N/A	N/A	N/A	N/A	N/A
American Samoa	3,743	1,007	946	982	808	0
Guam	9,885	2,888	2,834	2,350	1,813	0
CNMI*	N/A	N/A	N/A	N/A	N/A	N/A
Puerto Rico	107,289	25,865	26,222	25,627	25,064	4,511
U.S. Virgin Islands	3,441	1,196	875	676	694	0

See footnotes at end of table

TABLE 9.1

Enrollment in Public Elementary And Secondary Schools, by Level, Grade, and State or Jurisdiction: Fall 2017 (continued)

Source: U.S. Department of Education, National Center for Education Statistics, Common Core of Data (CCD), "State Nonfiscal Survey of Public Elementary/Secondary Education," 2017-18. (This table was prepared August 2019.)

* Commonwealth of Northern Mariana Islands

Note: The total ungraded counts of students were prorated to the elementary and secondary levels based on prior state reports of the percentage of elementary and of secondary ungraded students.

Key:

N/A – Not available

(a) Includes students reported as being enrolled in grade 13.

(b) Imputed by the National Center for Education Statistics.

(c) DoDEA = Department of Defense Education Activity. Includes both domestic and overseas schools.

TABLE 9.2
Number and Percentage Distribution of Teachers in Traditional Public and Public Charter Elementary and Secondary Schools, by Instructional Level and Selected Teacher and School Characteristics: 2017-18

Selected teacher or school characteristic	Number of teachers (in thousands)							Percentage distribution of teachers						
		Total		Elementary		Secondary		Total			Elementary		Secondary	
	Total	Traditional public	Public charter	Traditional public	Public charter	Traditional public	Public charter	Total	Traditional public	Public charter	Traditional public	Public charter	Traditional public	Public charter
Total	3,545	3,340	206	1,678	101	1,662	104	100.0	100.0	100.0	100.0	100.0	100.0	100.0
Sex														
Male	834	785	48	190	11	595	38	23.5	23.5	23.5	11.3	10.6	35.8	36.2
Female	2,712	2,555	157	1,487	91	1,067	66	76.5	76.5	76.5	88.7	89.4	64.2	63.8
Race/ethnicity														
White	2,811	2,671	140	1,332	70	1,339	70	79.3	80.0	68.0	79.4	69.1	80.6	66.9
Black	239	217	21	107	11	110	11	6.7	6.5	10.4	6.4	10.6	6.6	10.1
Hispanic	331	299	32	166	16	133	16	9.3	9.0	15.6	9.9	15.5	8.0	15.7
Asian	75	69	6	34	2	35	4	2.1	2.1	3.0	2.1	2.4	2.1	3.5
Pacific Islander	8	8	‡	4	‡	4	‡	0.2	0.2	0.4	0.2	‡	0.2	0.6
American Indian/ Alaska Native	18	18	‡	10	‡	8	‡	0.5	0.5	0.4	0.6	‡	0.5	0.4
Two or more races	63	58	5	25	2	33	3	1.8	1.7	2.3	1.5	1.8	2.0	2.8
Age														
Under 30	531	482	49	254	26	228	23	15.0	14.4	23.9	15.1	25.8	13.7	22.1
30 to 39	991	926	65	471	31	455	34	27.9	27.7	31.4	28.1	30.1	27.4	32.7
40 to 49	1,028	979	49	499	25	480	24	29.0	29.3	23.9	29.7	25.1	28.9	22.6
50 to 59	732	702	31	341	15	360	16	20.7	21.0	14.9	20.3	14.3	21.7	15.5
60 and over	263	251	12	113	5	139	7	7.4	7.5	5.9	6.7	4.7	8.3	7.0
Highest degree earned														
Less than bachelor's	97	90	7	33	3	57	3	2.7	2.7	3.2	2.0	3.4	3.4	3.1
Bachelor's	1,393	1,290	103	702	55	587	49	39.3	38.6	50.3	41.9	54.0	35.3	46.8
Postbaccalaureate	2,056	1,960	95	942	43	1,018	52	58.0	58.7	46.4	56.2	42.7	61.3	50.1
Master's	1,744	1,665	79	801	36	863	43	49.2	49.8	38.6	47.8	35.6	51.9	41.6
Education specialist (a)	271	258	13	129	6	129	6	7.6	7.7	6.3	7.7	6.3	7.8	6.2
Doctor's	41	38	3	12	‡	26	2	1.2	1.1	1.6	0.7	0.8	1.5	2.3
Years of full-time and part-time teaching experience														
Less than 3	318	285	34	150	17	135	17	9.0	8.5	16.3	8.9	16.4	8.1	16.2
3 to 9	1,003	917	87	474	45	442	41	28.3	27.4	42.1	28.3	44.5	26.6	39.7
10 to 20	1,416	1,353	63	665	29	688	34	39.9	40.5	30.5	39.6	28.7	41.4	32.4
Over 20	808	785	23	389	11	397	12	22.8	23.5	11.1	23.2	10.4	23.9	11.7
Certification type (b)														
Regular	3,205	3,048	157	1,545	80	1,503	78	90.4	91.3	76.5	92.1	78.4	90.5	74.6
Probationary	108	98	9	46	5	52	5	3.0	2.9	4.5	2.8	4.6	3.1	4.3
Provisional or temporary	137	121	16	54	8	67	9	3.9	3.6	7.9	3.2	7.5	4.0	8.3
Waiver or emergency	35	31	4	11	2	20	2	1.0	0.9	1.8	0.6	1.8	1.2	1.8
No certification	61	41	19	22	8	19	11	1.7	1.2	9.4	1.3	7.7	1.2	11.0
School locale														
City	1,032	932	100	496	49	436	52	29.1	27.9	48.7	29.6	47.9	26.2	49.4
Suburban	1,374	1,305	69	636	33	669	36	38.7	39.1	33.3	37.9	32.3	40.3	34.4
Town	413	398	15	199	7	199	8	11.6	11.9	7.1	11.9	6.6	12.0	7.7
Rural	727	705	22	347	13	358	9	20.5	21.1	10.8	20.7	13.2	21.6	8.5
Percent of students eligible for free or reduced-price lunch														
0 to 25	665	642	24	300	12	342	12	18.8	19.2	11.4	17.9	11.4	20.6	11.5
26 to 50	947	907	40	384	17	523	22	26.7	27.2	19.3	22.9	17.1	31.5	21.5
51 to 75	817	779	38	390	21	389	17	23.0	23.3	18.5	23.3	20.9	23.4	16.2
76 to 100	1,029	952	77	583	39	370	38	29.0	28.5	37.4	34.7	38.0	22.3	36.8
School does not participate	87	60	27	21	13	39	15	2.5	1.8	13.3	1.3	12.7	2.3	14.0

See footnotes at end of table

TABLE 9.2

Number and Percentage Distribution of Teachers in Traditional Public and Public Charter Elementary and Secondary Schools, by Instructional Level and Selected Teacher and School Characteristics: 2017–18 (continued)

Source: U.S. Department of Education, National Center for Education Statistics, National Teacher and Principal Survey (NTPS), "Public School Teacher Data File," 2017–18. (This table was prepared November 2019.)

Note: Excludes teachers who teach only prekindergarten. Data are based on a head count of full-time and part-time teachers rather than on the number of full-time-equivalent teachers reported in other tables. Teachers were classified as elementary or secondary on the basis of the grades they taught, rather than on the level of the school in which they taught. In general, elementary teachers include those teaching prekindergarten through grade 6 and those teaching multiple grades, with a preponderance of grades taught being kindergarten through grade 6. In general, secondary teachers include those teaching any of grades 7 through 12 and those teaching multiple grades, with a preponderance of grades taught being grades 7 through 12 and usually with no grade taught being lower than grade 5. Detail may not sum to totals because of rounding and cell suppression. Race categories exclude persons of Hispanic ethnicity. Standard errors appear in the original online report. See source cited above.

Key:

‡ – Reporting standards not met. Either there are too few cases for a reliable estimate or the coefficient of variation (CV) is 50 percent or greater.

(a) Education specialist degrees or certificates are generally awarded for 1 year's work beyond the master's level. Includes certificate of advanced graduate studies.

(b) Refers to certification of teachers to teach in the state where they are currently teaching. A teaching certificate is probationary if all requirements have been satisfied except completion of a probationary period. It is provisional or temporary if additional coursework, student teaching, or passage of a test is required to obtain regular certification. It is a waiver or emergency certificate if a certification program must be completed to continue teaching.

TABLE 9.3
Public Elementary and Secondary Teachers, by Level and State or Jurisdiction: Selected years, Fall 2016-Fall 2017 (In full-time equivalents)

State or jurisdiction	Fall 2016				Fall 2017			
	Total	Elementary	Secondary	Ungraded	Total	Elementary	Secondary	Ungraded
United States	3,169,499 (a)	1,759,610 (a)	1,232,805 (a)	177,803(a)	3,169,750 (a)	1,746,538 (a)	1,233,360 (a)	189,851 (a)
Alabama	42,533	22,476	20,057	0	41,802	22,301	19,501	0
Alaska	7,825	4,070	3,754	0	7,743	4,070	3,673	0
Arizona	48,220	33,135	15,085	0	47,868	33,299	14,569	0
Arkansas	35,730	18,317	14,768	2,645	35,800	18,177	14,862	2,760
California	271,287 (b)	182,600 (b)	86,140 (b)	2,547 (b)	271,523 (b)	181,402 (b)	85,849 (b)	4,272
Colorado	52,014	29,401	22,613	0	52,373	29,341	23,033	0
Connecticut	42,343	26,744	15,373	226	45,081	29,414	15,428	239
Delaware	9,208	4,678	4,530	0	9,399	4,788	4,611	0
Florida	186,339	76,301	67,849	42,190	186,128	75,746	67,474	42,908
Georgia	114,763	52,918	44,721	17,124	116,022	53,116	45,502	17,403
Hawaii	11,782	6,397	5,315	70	12,033	6,518	5,450	66
Idaho	16,204	7,648	8,556	0	16,592	7,764	8,828	0
Illinois	128,893	90,125	38,506	263	128,204	89,854	38,018	332
Indiana	60,162	31,163	28,999	0	61,018	31,621	29,398	0
Iowa	35,808	25,205	10,603	0	35,553	25,007	10,546	0
Kansas	36,193	18,496	17,697	0	36,387	18,729	17,658	0
Kentucky	42,029	24,772	10,058	7,199	42,064	24,701	10,092	7,270
Louisiana	48,408	32,806	15,602	0	40,281	27,409	12,872	0
Maine	14,750	10,284	4,467	0	14,760	10,329	4,431	0
Maryland	59,703	36,442	23,261	0	60,175	36,657	23,518	0
Massachusetts	72,413	47,382	25,031	0	73,381	47,733	25,648	0
Michigan	83,597	34,756	32,785	16,057	84,473	35,276	32,978	16,219
Minnesota	56,715	30,555	24,270	1,889	57,260	30,816	24,497	1,947
Mississippi	31,924	14,907	13,196	3,822	31,625	14,795	13,117	3,713
Missouri	67,926	35,235	32,691	0	68,496	35,725	32,771	0
Montana	10,555	7,391	3,127	36	10,515	7,383	3,097	35
Nebraska	23,611	15,221	8,390	0	23,771	15,321	8,450	0
Nevada	23,705	11,422	8,486	3,797	23,709	11,348	8,453	3,908
New Hampshire	14,760	9,761	4,999	0	14,589	9,859	4,730	0
New Jersey	115,729	61,286	37,911	16,532	115,496	61,197	37,635	16,664
New Mexico	21,331	9,454	8,123	3,754	21,092	9,387	7,960	3,745
New York	209,151	105,341	93,792	10,018	213,159	108,893	95,744	8,522
North Carolina	100,220	69,663	29,741	816	100,401	70,004	29,641	756
North Dakota	9,265	6,122	3,143	0	9,284	6,163	3,121	0
Ohio	102,600	57,122	41,128	4,350	98,912	43,987	41,543	13,382
Oklahoma	41,090	23,119	17,970	0	41,597	23,643	17,954	0
Oregon	29,756	21,089	8,667	0	29,909	21,158	8,752	0
Pennsylvania	122,552	58,732	52,965	10,855	121,918	58,334	52,638	10,946
Rhode Island	10,689	5,965	4,724	0	10,687	5,939	4,748	0
South Carolina	50,789	35,712	15,078	0	52,467	36,969	15,498	0
South Dakota	9,777	6,364	2,499	914	9,833	6,250	2,495	1,087
Tennessee	64,270	45,296	18,975	0	64,019	45,462	18,558	0
Texas	352,809	175,290	153,142	24,377	356,877	176,132	155,342	25,403
Utah	28,841 (c)	14,050 (c)	11,882 (c)	2,909 (c)	29,212 (c)	14,230 (c)	12,035 (c)	2,946 (c)
Vermont	8,187	3,326	2,736	2,124	8,313	3,176	2,745	2,392
Virginia	91,628	42,155	49,473	0	85,936	37,097	48,840	0
Washington	58,815	32,242	24,507	2,067	60,183	33,057	24,810	2,316
West Virginia	19,356	9,168	10,167	21	19,239	9,951	9,083	205
Wisconsin	59,011	29,429	29,125	457	58,598	28,986	29,198	414
Wyoming	7,506	4,089	3,417	0	7,335	3,948	3,387	0
Dist. of Columbia	6,727	3,990	2,713	24	6,659	4,078	2,581	0
Bureau of Indian Education	N/A	N/A	N/A	N/A	N/A	N/A	N/A	N/A
DoDEA (d)	N/A	N/A	N/A	N/A	N/A	N/A	N/A	N/A
American Samoa	N/A	N/A	N/A	N/A	N/A	N/A	N/A	N/A
Guam	2,289	1,154	1,135	0	2,202	1,068	1,134	0
CNMI*	N/A	N/A	N/A	N/A	N/A	N/A	N/A	N/A
Puerto Rico	28,899	13,097	10,140	5,661	28,039	16,617	6,275	5,147
U.S. Virgin Islands	1,154	546	593	15	1,066	500	553	13

See footnotes at end of table

TABLE 9.3

Public Elementary and Secondary Teachers, by Level and State or Jurisdiction: Selected years, Fall 2016–Fall 2017 (In full-time equivalents) (continued)

Source: U.S. Department of Education, National Center for Education Statistics, Common Core of Data (CCD), "State Nonfiscal Survey of Public Elementary/Secondary Education," 2000-01 through 2017-18. (This table was prepared August 2019.)
Note: Distribution of elementary and secondary teachers determined by reporting units.
* Commonwealth of Northern Mariana Islands

Key:
N/A – Not available
(a) Includes imputed values for states.
(b) Includes imputations to correct for underreporting of prekindergarten teachers.
(c) Imputed.
(d) Department of Defense Education Activity. Includes both domestic and overseas schools.

TABLE 9.4

Average Base Salary for Full-Time Public Elementary and Secondary School Teachers with a Master's Degree as Their Highest Degree, by Years of Teaching Experience and State: 2017-18

State	Total	Current dollars 2017-18			
		Years of full- and part-time teaching experience (a)			
		5 or fewer years	6 to 10 years	11 to 20 years	Over 20 years
United States	$63,120	$51,050	$56,140	$65,700	$73,430
Alabama	51,090	45,790	49,240	50,740	58,200
Alaska	74,580	62,310	67,350	79,390	84,390
Arizona	46,510	40,500	44,220	47,430	52,790
Arkansas	50,720	44,610	49,330	52,520	55,790
California	79,680	61,740	71,030	83,340	91,090
Colorado	56,140	49,540	48,810	60,740	63,580
Connecticut	74,220	56,850	64,690	78,840	90,150
Delaware	63,580	52,040	57,700	68,340	76,030
Florida	49,710	42,730	44,220	48,630	59,050
Georgia	55,110	46,840	51,580	56,860	63,660
Hawaii	57,800	53,100	55,630	59,350	64,870
Idaho	52,000	‡	44,770	53,930	60,380
Illinois	71,640	55,400	60,080	72,330	87,860
Indiana	56,490	41,400	47,380	54,410	66,130
Iowa	57,190	49,050	51,150	59,410	63,700
Kansas	52,520	46,000	46,980	53,210	59,040
Kentucky	52,250	46,290	47,340	54,230	62,570
Louisiana	48,380	44,950	44,760	49,910	‡
Maine	55,730	‡	‡	56,060	60,790
Maryland	‡	‡	‡	‡	‡
Massachusetts	73,510	58,980	68,620	79,560	82,740
Michigan	64,350	46,550	51,550	67,080	70,540
Minnesota	68,990	50,560	58,690	68,980	78,310
Mississippi	46,970	41,570	44,280	45,430	54,040
Missouri	52,240	45,220	46,180	53,960	59,410
Montana	54,640	‡	46,920	56,900	64,140
Nebraska	49,130	43,030	47,290	49,830	52,470
Nevada	56,860	46,710	51,310	58,760	67,700
New Hampshire	59,210	45,420	52,610	62,350	68,350
New Jersey	73,800	59,480	63,830	75,460	87,110
New Mexico	50,220	39,740	48,190	52,520	53,990
New York	80,030	62,230	72,410	82,230	95,660
North Carolina	47,320	42,050	43,710	48,580	56,040
North Dakota	55,810	‡	52,480	58,830	62,480
Ohio	62,410	46,340	55,380	64,400	71,300
Oklahoma	40,310	‡	‡	39,630	45,440
Oregon	58,770	46,280	52,460	65,840	69,300
Pennsylvania	68,830	52,210	58,030	72,550	79,070
Rhode Island	73,850	‡	66,520	75,790	78,840
South Carolina	49,100	42,890	45,020	50,490	56,530
South Dakota	49,390	‡	47,660	49,760	55,200
Tennessee	50,910	44,890	46,790	53,090	58,760
Texas	54,080	51,150	52,840	54,260	60,170
Utah	54,870	43,820	49,180	59,300	61,890
Vermont	62,210	50,800	53,010	63,470	70,550
Virginia	59,130	50,000	54,000	62,020	69,650
Washington	60,910	50,040	53,370	65,240	68,980
West Virginia	45,790	40,390	40,930	45,860	54,050
Wisconsin	58,040	45,470	52,090	58,070	65,120
Wyoming	59,340	51,690	55,910	59,990	65,780
Dist. of Columbia	‡	‡	‡	‡	‡

See footnotes at end of table

TABLE 9.4

Average Base Salary for Full-Time Public Elementary and Secondary School Teachers with a Master's Degree as Their Highest Degree, by Years of Teaching Experience and State: 2017-18 (continued)

Source: U.S. Department of Education, National Center for Education Statistics, Schools and Staffing Survey (SASS), "Public School Teacher Data File," 1993-94, 1999-2000, 2003-04, 2007-08, and 2011-12; SASS, "Public Charter School Teacher Data File," 1999-2000; and National Teacher and Principal Survey (NTPS), "Public School Teacher Data File," 2017-18. (This table was prepared November 2019.)

Note: This table includes regular full-time teachers only; it excludes other staff even when they have full-time teaching duties (regular part-time teachers, itinerant teachers, long-term substitutes, administrators, library media specialists, other professional staff, and support staff). Teachers' base salary does not include any supplemental contracts for additional work at a school during the school year (e.g., coaching) or during the summer (e.g., teaching summer sessions). Also does not include any income from non-school sources. Some data have been revised from previously published figures.

Key:
‡–Reporting standards not met. Data may be suppressed because the response rate is under 50 percent, there are too few cases for a reliable estimate, or the coefficient of variation (CV) is 50 percent or greater.

(a) Teachers were asked how many school years they had worked as a teacher. They were also asked how many of their teaching years were full time and how many were part time. Throughout this table, all school years are counted, regardless of whether teachers taught full time or part time.

TABLE 9.5
Estimated Average Annual Salary of Teachers in Public Elementary and Secondary Schools, by State: Selected Years: 1969-70 Through 2018-19

State	Current dollars							Percent change, 1999-2000 to 2018-19
	1969-70	1979-80	1989-90	1999-2000	2009-10	2017-18	2018-19	
United States	$8,626	$15,970	$31,367	$41,807	$55,370	$60,477	$61,730	(1.3)
Alabama	6,818	13,060	24,828	36,689	47,571	50,568	50,810	(7.4)
Alaska	10,560	27,210	43,153	46,462	59,672	69,682	70,277	1.1
Arizona	8,711	15,054	29,402	36,902	46,952	48,723	49,892	(9.6)
Arkansas	6,307	12,299	22,352	33,386	46,700	50,544	51,019	2.1
California	10,315	18,020	37,998	47,680	68,203	80,680	82,282	15.4
Colorado	7,761	16,205	30,758	38,163	49,202	52,701	53,301	(6.6)
Connecticut	9,262	16,229	40,461	51,780	64,350	74,517	76,465	(1.3)
Delaware	9,015	16,148	33,377	44,435	57,080	61,795	62,308	(6.3)
Florida	8,412	14,149	28,803	36,722	46,708	48,168	48,395	(11.9)
Georgia	7,276	13,853	28,006	41,023	53,112	56,329	57,137	(6.9)
Hawaii	9,453	19,920	32,047	40,578	55,063	57,866	59,757	(1.6)
Idaho	6,890	13,611	23,861	35,547	46,283	49,225	50,757	(4.6)
Illinois	9,569	17,601	32,794	46,486	62,077	65,721	66,600	(4.2)
Indiana	8,833	15,599	30,902	41,850	49,986	50,614	50,937	(18.6)
Iowa	8,355	15,203	26,747	35,678	49,626	57,018	58,140	8.9
Kansas	7,612	13,690	28,744	34,981	46,657	49,754	49,800	(4.8)
Kentucky	6,953	14,520	26,292	36,380	49,543	52,952	53,434	(1.8)
Louisiana	7,028	13,760	24,300	33,109	48,903	50,359	50,923	2.8
Maine	7,572	13,071	26,881	35,561	46,106	53,815	54,974	3.3
Maryland	9,383	17,558	36,319	44,048	63,971	69,627	70,463	6.9
Massachusetts	8,764	17,253	34,712	46,580	69,273	80,357	82,042	17.7
Michigan	9,826	19,663	37,072	49,044	57,958	61,911	61,825	(15.7)
Minnesota	8,658	15,912	32,190	39,802	52,431	57,782	58,221	(2.2)
Mississippi	5,798	11,850	24,292	31,857	45,644	44,926	45,574	(4.4)
Missouri	7,799	13,682	27,094	35,656	45,317	49,304	50,064	(6.1)
Montana	7,606	14,537	25,081	32,121	45,759	52,776	54,034	12.4
Nebraska	7,375	13,516	25,522	33,237	46,227	54,213	54,506	9.6
Nevada	9,215	16,295	30,590	39,390	51,524	54,280	54,280	(7.9)
New Hampshire	7,771	13,017	28,986	37,734	51,443	57,833	58,146	3.0
New Jersey	9,130	17,161	35,676	52,015	65,130	69,917	70,212	(9.8)
New Mexico	7,796	14,887	24,756	32,554	46,258	47,152	47,826	(1.8)
New York	10,336	19,812	38,925	51,020	71,633	84,227	85,889	12.5
North Carolina	7,494	14,117	27,883	39,404	46,850	51,231	53,975	(8.4)
North Dakota	6,696	13,263	23,016	29,863	42,964	52,850	53,434	19.6
Ohio	8,300	15,269	31,218	41,436	55,958	58,000	57,799	(6.8)
Oklahoma	6,882	13,107	23,070	31,298	47,691	46,300	52,412	11.9
Oregon	8,818	16,266	30,840	42,336	55,224	63,061	64,385	1.7
Pennsylvania	8,858	16,515	33,338	48,321	59,156	67,535	68,141	(5.7)
Rhode Island	8,776	18,002	36,057	47,041	59,686	66,758	67,040	(4.7)
South Carolina	6,927	13,063	27,217	36,081	47,508	50,182	50,395	(6.6)
South Dakota	6,403	12,348	21,300	29,071	38,837	47,631	48,786	12.2
Tennessee	7,050	13,972	27,052	36,328	46,290	50,900	51,714	(4.8)
Texas	7,255	14,132	27,496	37,567	48,261	53,334	54,155	(3.6)
Utah	7,644	14,909	23,686	34,946	45,885	49,655	50,342	(3.7)
Vermont	7,968	12,484	29,012	37,758	49,084	60,556	61,027	8.0
Virginia	8,070	14,060	30,938	38,744	50,015	51,994	52,466	(9.5)
Washington	9,225	18,820	30,457	41,043	53,003	55,693	72,965	18.8
West Virginia	7,650	13,710	22,842	35,009	45,959	45,642	47,681	(9.0)
Wisconsin	8,963	16,006	31,921	41,153	51,264	51,469	51,453	(16.4)
Wyoming	8,232	16,012	28,141	34,127	55,861	58,352	58,618	14.8
Dist. of Columbia	10,285	22,190	38,402	47,076	64,548	76,486	78,477	11.4

See footnotes at end of table

Source: National Education Association, Estimates of School Statistics, selected years, 1970 through 2019. (This table was prepared September 2019.)

Notes: Some data have been revised from previously published figures. Standard errors are not available for these estimates, which are based on state reports.

TABLE 9.6

Percentage of High School Dropouts Among Persons 16 Through 24 Years Old (Status Dropout Rate), By Race/Ethnicity and State: 2018

State or other jurisdiction	Total	White	Black	Hispanic	Asian	Pacific Islander	American Indian/ Alaska Native	Two or more races
United States	5.3	4.2	6.4	8.0	1.9	8.1	9.5	5.2
Alabama	5.4	4.5	5.7	10.7	‡	‡	‡	7.9
Alaska	4.4	2.7	‡	‡	‡	‡	9.0	‡
Arizona	7.7	6.0	8.1	9.6	1.4	‡	9.6	6.9
Arkansas	5.6	4.8	4.4	10.1	‡	‡	‡	10.0
California	4.3	2.3	6.1	6.0	1.5	4.8	5.6	2.7
Colorado	4.7	3.3	3.8	8.6	2.3	‡	‡	‡
Connecticut	3.9	2.4	2.5	10.0	‡	‡	‡	‡
Delaware	5.0	6.0	4.5	5.0	‡	‡	‡	‡
Florida	6.5	5.5	7.8	7.9	‡	‡	21.9	6.4
Georgia	6.2	6.2	4.8	11.9	2.1	‡	‡	5.5
Hawaii	5.5	‡	‡	5.2	7.4	9.7	‡	4.6
Idaho	7.4	6.2	‡	10.5	‡	‡	12.3	14.9
Illinois	4.6	3.6	7.1	6.2	1.6	‡	‡	4.6
Indiana	7.4	7.5	8.3	6.6	3.2	‡	‡	9.0
Iowa	4.7	3.9	12.7	10.5	‡	‡	‡	‡
Kansas	5.2	4.2	5.5	11.0	‡	‡	‡	‡
Kentucky	5.6	5.1	6.9	13.4	‡	‡	‡	5.5
Louisiana	7.8	4.9	10.9	11.6	‡	‡	‡	11.4
Maine	4.3	4.3	‡	‡	‡	‡	‡	‡
Maryland	3.9	2.9	4.7	7.6	‡	‡	‡	4.6
Massachusetts	3.8	2.7	6.7	8.7	1.0	‡	‡	2.6
Michigan	5.3	4.8	8.1	5.3	3.7	‡	4.1	3.7
Minnesota	4.2	3.1	5.4	7.3	4.3	‡	31.8	7.6
Mississippi	6.2	5.6	5.5	29.7	‡	‡	‡	‡
Missouri	6.0	5.8	7.0	8.4	5.9	‡	‡	3.7
Montana	6.5	6.1	‡	‡	‡	‡	9.0	‡
Nebraska	4.3	3.3	‡	11.2	‡	‡	‡	‡
Nevada	7.9	6.1	9.6	9.6	5.7	‡	‡	7.2
New Hampshire	4.1	3.8	‡	‡	‡	‡	‡	12.8
New Jersey	3.6	1.8	5.5	7.0	1.2	‡	‡	3.3
New Mexico	10.3	8.5	‡	12.2	‡	‡	8.3	‡
New York	4.8	3.2	5.3	8.8	1.6	‡	‡	7.0
North Carolina	5.7	4.3	6.5	9.1	6.6	‡	7.6	8.0
North Dakota	2.7	2.2	‡	‡	‡	‡	12.9	‡
Ohio	5.2	4.4	7.5	10.7	‡	‡	‡	6.2
Oklahoma	7.2	6.1	8.2	10.4	‡	‡	9.7	7.5
Oregon	6.1	4.9	‡	12.6	‡	‡	15.8	3.4
Pennsylvania	5.4	5.1	5.6	8.9	2.8	‡	‡	3.7
Rhode Island	4.0	5.3	‡	2.0	‡	‡	‡	‡
South Carolina	6.4	4.9	8.6	9.7	‡	‡	‡	7.0
South Dakota	8.1	5.9	‡	‡	‡	‡	20.7	‡
Tennessee	5.4	4.2	7.9	10.9	‡	‡	‡	3.0
Texas	6.0	3.8	4.5	8.3	2.0	‡	‡	6.0
Utah	3.9	3.1	‡	7.0	‡	‡	‡	‡
Vermont	4.1	4.4	‡	‡	‡	‡	‡	‡
Virginia	3.4	2.3	3.6	9.2	‡	‡	‡	3.4
Washington	6.0	5.1	4.6	11.6	1.2	15.5	11.5	3.9
West Virginia	6.4	6.2	10.1	‡	‡	‡	‡	‡
Wisconsin	4.4	2.7	15.5	9.6	2.7	‡	‡	6.1
Wyoming	2.8	3.0	‡	‡	‡	‡	‡	‡
Dist. of Columbia	4.5	‡	7.3	‡	‡	‡	‡	‡

See footnotes at end of table

TABLE 9.6

Percentage of High School Dropouts Among Persons 16 Through 24 Years Old (Status Dropout Rate), By Race/Ethnicity and State: 2018 (continued)

Source: U.S Department of Commerce, Census Bureau, American Community Survey (ACS), 2018. (This table was prepared December 2019.)

Note: Status dropouts are 16- to 24-year-olds who are not enrolled in school and who have not completed a high school program, regardless of when they left school. People who have received equivalency credentials, such as the GED, are counted as high school completers. Data are based on sample surveys of the entire population residing within the United States, including both non-institutionalized persons (e.g., those living in households, college housing, or military housing located within the United States) and institutionalized persons (e.g., those living in prisons, nursing facilities, or other healthcare facilities). Totals include other racial/ethnic groups not separately shown. Race categories exclude persons of Hispanic ethnicity.

Key:

‡–Reporting standards not met. Either there are too few cases for a reliable estimate or the coefficient of variation (CV) is 50 percent or greater.

TABLE 9.7
Rates of High School Completion and Bachelor's Degree Attainment Among Persons Age 25 and Over, by Race/Ethnicity and State: 2017

State	Percent with high school completion or higher (a)					
	Total (b)	White	Black	Hispanic	Asian	Two or more races
United States	88.0	92.9	86.1	68.8	87.0	91.9
Alabama	86.0	88.4	82.6	60.5	83.6	87.1
Alaska	91.6	95.1	96.2	89.5	77.6	96.7
Arizona	87.1	94.6	91.1	68.8	88.7	93.4
Arkansas	86.7	89.6	83.6	57.0	80.2	88.8
California	83.4	95.0	89.8	65.1	87.7	93.3
Colorado	91.7	96.3	92.6	73.3	83.8	93.8
Connecticut	90.5	94.4	87.6	71.8	89.1	91.3
Delaware	90.7	93.1	91.6	65.6	92.3	90.7
Florida	88.4	92.9	83.7	80.2	87.0	90.8
Georgia	87.0	90.9	86.1	60.9	87.5	89.8
Hawaii	91.7	97.1	97.3	87.7	89.4	94.1
Idaho	91.2	93.6	‡	69.8	87.9	94.0
Illinois	89.0	94.2	87.2	66.2	90.6	91.1
Indiana	88.8	90.7	86.4	64.4	82.2	91.7
Iowa	92.0	94.1	81.5	60.4	77.0	94.0
Kansas	91.0	94.4	84.4	65.1	89.9	89.1
Kentucky	86.5	86.7	88.6	76.4	81.4	86.7
Louisiana	85.0	89.0	79.2	70.4	77.6	90.9
Maine	92.7	93.0	90.5	91.2	80.2	90.5
Maryland	89.9	93.6	90.0	64.6	90.5	94.3
Massachusetts	90.8	94.0	86.5	72.2	86.1	91.3
Michigan	90.9	92.6	85.9	73.4	90.4	90.5
Minnesota	93.0	95.7	82.4	65.1	82.2	92.3
Mississippi	84.6	87.7	80.2	68.7	82.2	86.6
Missouri	89.6	90.8	84.4	74.2	91.5	91.0
Montana	92.6	93.6	‡	73.9	79.3	94.9
Nebraska	91.4	95.5	84.1	57.6	79.9	89.7
Nevada	86.8	94.1	88.8	66.3	91.1	96.1
New Hampshire	93.2	93.7	88.6	86.4	87.2	88.8
New Jersey	90.2	94.6	88.3	76.0	92.4	93.2
New Mexico	85.9	94.9	91.7	77.0	91.4	96.4
New York	86.6	93.4	84.4	69.7	78.2	89.7
North Carolina	88.0	91.6	86.1	60.5	86.5	89.5
North Dakota	93.1	94.1	88.5	82.1	83.5	88.2
Ohio	90.3	91.5	85.4	77.6	89.4	90.8
Oklahoma	88.1	90.9	89.6	64.5	79.8	90.1
Oregon	90.9	94.0	88.6	68.0	87.0	89.6
Pennsylvania	90.5	92.4	87.8	74.1	83.1	89.6
Rhode Island	88.2	90.4	86.0	76.0	85.2	93.4
South Carolina	87.6	90.9	82.1	68.2	84.7	92.0
South Dakota	91.8	94.0	94.3	71.6	95.2	94.0
Tennessee	87.7	88.9	87.3	63.6	89.2	90.2
Texas	83.7	94.0	89.9	66.2	88.5	92.9
Utah	92.1	95.5	86.7	69.9	90.7	92.3
Vermont	92.4	93.0	‡	83.2	62.9	95.2
Virginia	89.6	92.7	85.8	70.9	91.2	92.2
Washington	91.3	94.9	89.9	66.3	88.3	93.2
West Virginia	87.0	86.9	91.1	84.3	91.7	86.2
Wisconsin	92.5	94.7	81.3	69.7	86.3	94.0
Wyoming	93.1	94.8	‡	73.6	95.1	96.0
Dist. of Columbia	90.6	99.2	87.3	67.9	95.5	95.2

See footnotes at end of table

TABLE 9.7
Rates of High School Completion and Bachelor's Degree Attainment Among Persons Age 25 and Over, by Race/Ethnicity and State: 2017

State	Percent with bachelor's or higher degree					
	Total (b)	White	Black	Hispanic	Asian	Two or more races
United States	32.0	35.8	21.6	16.0	54.1	34.9
Alabama	25.6	28.8	17.0	15.9	45.8	29.0
Alaska	29.0	34.4	28.7	21.3	24.1	31.6
Arizona	29.2	35.6	23.5	12.6	58.7	34.1
Arkansas	23.5	25.4	15.6	11.3	48.2	21.2
California	33.7	43.8	25.7	13.1	52.6	41.0
Colorado	41.2	47.5	28.7	16.1	52.5	43.7
Connecticut	38.4	43.5	20.1	15.9	64.5	29.5
Delaware	31.9	34.9	22.9	10.0	69.5	22.9
Florida	29.6	33.2	18.8	23.9	52.1	35.7
Georgia	30.9	35.0	23.1	16.8	55.4	37.2
Hawaii	32.8	47.4	40.1	20.4	33.5	22.9
Idaho	26.8	28.3	‡	10.9	50.5	31.8
Illinois	34.4	38.8	21.1	14.1	64.4	41.3
Indiana	26.9	27.6	20.8	13.7	58.1	27.4
Iowa	29.2	30.0	20.0	10.6	41.4	29.0
Kansas	33.9	36.9	21.9	13.0	46.3	28.2
Kentucky	23.9	23.9	19.0	21.6	48.8	26.7
Louisiana	23.9	28.1	15.0	16.0	45.0	28.3
Maine	32.9	32.6	37.2	44.5	46.0	30.5
Maryland	40.0	45.5	29.2	22.1	62.8	46.0
Massachusetts	43.6	46.7	27.7	18.3	63.1	45.3
Michigan	29.0	30.3	16.8	17.5	64.0	32.7
Minnesota	35.7	37.1	24.4	17.1	45.1	29.6
Mississippi	21.7	25.3	15.2	15.5	37.4	38.1
Missouri	29.0	30.0	17.6	19.4	61.0	33.0
Montana	31.4	32.9	‡	20.7	39.4	19.5
Nebraska	31.2	33.4	14.9	12.1	52.4	29.9
Nevada	25.2	30.4	18.3	10.4	39.9	26.5
New Hampshire	37.1	36.8	29.6	26.7	61.0	31.1
New Jersey	39.7	43.6	25.1	20.2	70.2	39.9
New Mexico	27.3	40.4	22.2	16.3	61.0	43.3
New York	36.2	42.8	24.6	18.5	44.9	41.4
North Carolina	31.4	35.1	21.4	15.4	58.8	33.1
North Dakota	30.6	31.4	26.4	6.3	74.0	27.5
Ohio	28.0	29.0	17.3	18.6	62.7	27.3
Oklahoma	25.5	28.2	21.0	10.5	38.8	22.8
Oregon	33.7	35.4	27.6	16.0	52.7	27.2
Pennsylvania	31.7	33.1	20.0	16.4	56.8	32.7
Rhode Island	33.8	36.5	25.6	14.2	57.4	31.5
South Carolina	28.0	33.3	15.0	15.3	47.4	28.6
South Dakota	27.7	29.5	17.7	18.5	48.7	20.9
Tennessee	27.4	28.7	20.4	15.6	58.1	29.2
Texas	29.6	38.6	24.7	14.3	59.8	36.8
Utah	34.3	36.8	31.1	14.8	53.8	35.5
Vermont	37.2	37.3	‡	39.7	35.0	39.9
Virginia	38.8	42.1	24.6	25.3	60.9	42.1
Washington	35.6	37.0	25.9	16.8	51.7	33.5
West Virginia	20.2	20.0	18.0	20.2	53.9	28.4
Wisconsin	30.5	31.8	12.8	15.2	53.4	34.3
Wyoming	27.6	28.8	‡	15.5	46.5	26.5
Dist. of Columbia	57.2	90.5	26.6	43.3	82.1	83.3

See footnotes at end of table

TABLE 9.7
Rates of High School Completion and Bachelor's Degree Attainment Among Persons Age 25 and Over, by Race/Ethnicity and State: 2017 (continued)

Source: U.S. Department of Commerce, Census Bureau, 2017 American Community Survey (ACS) 1-Year Public Use Microdata Sample (PUMS) data. (This table was prepared February 2019.)

Note: Data are based on sample surveys of the entire population in the given age range residing within the United States, including both noninstitutionalized persons (e.g., those living in households, college housing, or military housing located within the United States) and institutionalized persons (e.g., those living in prisons, nursing facilities, or other healthcare facilities). Race categories exclude persons of Hispanic ethnicity.

Key:

‡–Reporting standards not met. Either there are too few cases for a reliable estimate or the coefficient of variation (CV) is 50 percent or greater.

(a) Includes completion of high school through equivalency programs, such as a GED program.

(b) Total includes racial/ethnic groups not shown separately.

TABLE 9.8
Revenues for Public Elementary and Secondary Schools, by Source of Funds and State or Jurisdiction: 2016-17

State or jurisdiction	Total (in thousands)	Federal			State	
		Amount (in thousands)	Per pupil	Percent of total	Amount (in thousands)	Percent of total
United States	$705,267,398	$57,310,693	$1,135	8.1	$331,322,010	47.0
Alabama	7,889,120	863,637	1,159	10.9	4,350,890	55.2
Alaska	2,508,281	354,045	2,667	14.1	1,600,510	63.8
Arizona	10,259,496	1,326,469	1,191	12.9	4,778,454	46.6
Arkansas	5,619,332	625,993	1,269	11.1	2,950,895	52.5
California	88,108,864	7,455,046	1,182	8.5	50,841,072	57.7
Colorado	10,600,561	706,162	780	6.7	4,602,299	43.4
Connecticut	11,583,918	503,812	941	4.3	4,494,453	38.8
Delaware	2,729,986	188,717	1,385	6.9	1,323,678	48.5
Florida	28,808,723	3,288,570	1,167	11.4	11,346,675	39.4
Georgia	20,443,717	1,925,205	1,091	9.4	9,439,804	46.2
Hawaii	2,844,167	252,145	1,389	8.9	2,534,177	89.1
Idaho	2,575,178	252,533	850	9.8	1,706,894	66.3
Illinois	35,480,443	2,312,325	1,141	6.5	13,710,764	38.6
Indiana	11,952,546	974,150	928	8.2	7,087,311	59.3
Iowa	6,904,458	497,385	976	7.2	3,732,324	54.1
Kansas	6,344,151	537,797	1,088	8.5	4,031,070	63.5
Kentucky	7,782,860	912,224	1,334	11.7	4,229,780	54.3
Louisiana	8,949,726	1,168,690	1,632	13.1	3,903,101	43.6
Maine	2,820,246	195,168	1,081	6.9	1,093,382	38.8
Maryland	15,045,717	851,860	961	5.7	6,625,703	44.0
Massachusetts	18,423,533	929,798	964	5.0	6,999,777	38.0
Michigan	20,163,387	1,734,557	1,135	8.6	12,224,090	60.6
Minnesota	13,242,082	743,953	850	5.6	8,762,296	66.2
Mississippi	4,753,225	672,881	1,393	14.2	2,415,769	50.8
Missouri	11,485,402	1,003,289	1,096	8.7	3,749,129	32.6
Montana	1,841,286	225,892	1,543	12.3	867,286	47.1
Nebraska	4,470,153	349,144	1,094	7.8	1,450,774	32.5
Nevada	4,919,401	444,730	939	9.0	1,780,380	36.2
New Hampshire	3,132,306	173,816	961	5.5	1,007,310	32.2
New Jersey	30,368,383	1,269,661	900	4.2	12,920,845	42.5
New Mexico	4,023,795	589,017	1,752	14.6	2,726,305	67.8
New York	69,228,226	3,657,578	1,373	5.3	28,253,045	40.8
North Carolina	14,481,275	1,641,260	1,059	11.3	9,057,842	62.5
North Dakota	1,757,100	163,446	1,490	9.3	1,014,779	57.8
Ohio	24,762,785	1,949,822	1,140	7.9	10,538,278	42.6
Oklahoma	6,361,194	726,159	1,046	11.4	3,007,742	47.3
Oregon	7,689,411	550,627	951	7.2	4,018,900	52.3
Pennsylvania	31,353,132	2,152,130	1,246	6.9	12,104,094	38.6
Rhode Island	2,561,477	192,929	1,357	7.5	1,087,361	42.5
South Carolina	9,992,973	913,225	1,184	9.1	4,867,687	48.7
South Dakota	1,580,004	205,299	1,506	13.0	540,408	34.2
Tennessee	10,077,253	1,161,636	1,160	11.5	4,629,304	45.9
Texas	60,006,975	6,298,581	1,175	10.5	23,339,969	38.9
Utah	5,757,609	459,308	696	8.0	3,183,265	55.3
Vermont	1,742,206	113,778	1,287	6.5	1,560,743	89.6
Virginia	16,611,639	1,131,683	879	6.8	6,565,661	39.5
Washington	15,654,623	1,071,035	972	6.8	9,846,364	62.9
West Virginia	3,526,416	404,295	1,476	11.5	1,917,056	54.4
Wisconsin	11,591,278	832,985	964	7.2	5,360,746	46.2
Wyoming	1,931,277	118,429	1,258	6.1	1,141,567	59.1
Dist. of Columbia	2,526,099	237,820	2,770	9.4	N.A.	N.A.
American Samoa	73,876	62,906	N/A	85.2	10,738	14.5
Guam	332,552	60,166	1,956	18.1	0	0.0
CNMI*	87,683	39,503	N/A	45.1	47,227	53.9
Puerto Rico	2,819,791	935,887	2,563	33.2	1,883,850	66.8
U.S. Virgin Islands	193,314	26,259	1,990	13.6	0	0.0

See footnotes at end of table

TABLE 9.8
Revenues for Public Elementary and Secondary Schools, by Source of Funds and State or Jurisdiction: 2016-17 (continued)

| | | | Local (including intermediate sources below the state level) | | | |
| | | | Property taxes | | Private (b) | |
State or jurisdiction	Amount (in thousands) (a)	Percent of total	Amount (in thousands)	Percent of total	Amount (in thousands)	Percent of total
United States	$316,634,696	44.9	$258,159,622	36.6	$11,665,181	1.7
Alabama	2,674,593	33.9	1,223,602	15.5	325,777	4.1
Alaska	553,726	22.1	319,889	12.8	18,951	0.8
Arizona	4,154,572	40.5	3,182,393	31.0	248,513	2.4
Arkansas	2,042,443	36.3	1,782,061	31.7	158,048	2.8
California	29,812,746	33.8	24,101,208	27.4	394,460	0.4
Colorado	5,292,101	49.9	4,287,369	40.4	393,355	3.7
Connecticut	6,585,653	56.9	6,431,528	55.5	92,242	0.8
Delaware	1,217,591	44.6	646,622	23.7	17,771	0.7
Florida	14,173,479	49.2	11,738,747	40.7	935,775	3.2
Georgia	9,078,707	44.4	6,020,224	29.4	474,428	2.3
Hawaii	57,844	2.0	0	0.0	28,852	1.0
Idaho	615,751	23.9	517,769	20.1	35,395	1.4
Illinois	19,457,354	54.8	17,082,907	48.1	480,875	1.4
Indiana	3,891,085	32.6	3,005,433	25.1	342,023	2.9
Iowa	2,674,750	38.7	2,187,985	31.7	145,240	2.1
Kansas	1,775,284	28.0	1,103,725	17.4	152,835	2.4
Kentucky	2,640,856	33.9	1,975,137	25.4	85,541	1.1
Louisiana	3,877,936	43.3	1,689,558	18.9	50,474	0.6
Maine	1,531,696	54.3	1,457,658	51.7	36,636	1.3
Maryland	7,568,154	50.3	3,703,439	24.6	115,109	0.8
Massachusetts	10,493,958	57.0	9,766,156	53.0	273,640	1.5
Michigan	6,204,741	30.8	5,289,166	26.2	273,047	1.4
Minnesota	3,735,833	28.2	2,449,514	18.5	350,318	2.6
Mississippi	1,664,576	35.0	1,393,467	29.3	110,153	2.3
Missouri	6,732,984	58.6	5,286,304	46.0	349,579	3.0
Montana	748,107	40.6	476,318	25.9	62,801	3.4
Nebraska	2,670,235	59.7	2,369,879	53.0	161,587	3.6
Nevada	2,694,292	54.8	1,201,302	24.4	28,596	0.6
New Hampshire	1,951,180	62.3	1,859,886	59.4	46,040	1.5
New Jersey	16,177,878	53.3	15,304,628	50.4	581,364	1.9
New Mexico	708,473	17.6	572,792	14.2	54,087	1.3
New York	37,317,603	53.9	34,657,273	50.1	305,467	0.4
North Carolina	3,782,173	26.1	3,290,986	22.7	166,817	1.2
North Dakota	578,875	32.9	423,505	24.1	69,564	4.0
Ohio	12,274,685	49.6	10,070,121	40.7	642,876	2.6
Oklahoma	2,627,292	41.3	2,007,824	31.6	281,400	4.4
Oregon	3,119,884	40.6	2,524,905	32.8	137,680	1.8
Pennsylvania	17,096,908	54.5	13,601,256	43.4	385,862	1.2
Rhode Island	1,281,187	50.0	1,242,366	48.5	25,406	1.0
South Carolina	4,212,060	42.2	3,195,782	32.0	245,374	2.5
South Dakota	834,297	52.8	716,885	45.4	44,816	2.8
Tennessee	4,286,312	42.5	2,008,470	19.9	438,170	4.3
Texas	30,368,425	50.6	27,675,817	46.1	1,022,545	1.7
Utah	2,115,036	36.7	1,598,326	27.8	241,408	4.2
Vermont	67,685	3.9	2,385	0.1	21,859	1.3
Virginia	8,914,296	53.7	5,399,824	32.5	241,647	1.5
Washington	4,737,224	30.3	4,056,493	25.9	299,337	1.9
West Virginia	1,205,066	34.2	1,115,409	31.6	19,618	0.6
Wisconsin	5,397,548	46.6	4,891,353	42.2	224,031	1.9
Wyoming	671,281	34.8	486,856	25.2	16,436	0.9
Dist. of Columbia	2,288,279	90.6	767,117	30.4	11,358	0.4
American Samoa	232	0.3	0	0.0	14	#
Guam	272,386	81.9	0	0.0	147	#
CNMI*	953	1.1	0	0.0	711	0.8
Puerto Rico	55	#	0	0.0	55	#
U.S. Virgin Islands	167,056	86.4	0	0.0	5	#

See footnotes at end of table

TABLE 9.8

Revenues for Public Elementary and Secondary Schools, by Source of Funds and State or Jurisdiction: 2016-17 (continued)

Source: U.S. Department of Education, National Center for Education Statistics, Common Core of Data (CCD), "National Public Education Financial Survey," 2016-17. (This table was prepared August 2019.)

Note: Excludes revenues for state education agencies. Detail may not sum to totals because of rounding.

* Commonwealth of Northern Mariana Islands

Key:
N.A. – Not applicable
N/A – Not available
– Rounds to zero.
(a) Includes other categories of revenue not separately shown.
(b) Includes revenues from gifts, and tuition and fees from patrons.

TABLE 9.9

Current Expenditures for Public Elementary and Secondary Education, by State or Jurisdiction: Selected Years, 2007-08 Through 2016-17 (In thousands of current dollars)

State or jurisdiction	2007–08	2008–09	2009–10	2010–11	2011–12	2012–13	2013–14	2014–15	2015–16	2016–17
United States	$506,884,219	$518,922,842	$524,715,242	$527,291,339	$527,207,246	$535,795,823	$553,501,209	$575,331,825	$596,201,554	$619,164,572
Alabama	6,832,439	6,683,843	6,670,517	6,592,925	6,386,517	6,532,358	6,742,829	6,806,467	6,885,677	7,097,472
Alaska	1,918,375	2,007,319	2,084,019	2,201,270	2,292,205	2,395,354	2,418,000	2,648,552	2,319,662	2,367,707
Arizona	8,403,221	8,726,755	8,482,552	8,340,211	7,976,089	8,164,529	8,187,607	8,370,884	8,551,673	8,966,684
Arkansas	4,156,368	4,240,839	4,459,910	4,578,136	4,606,995	4,637,169	4,778,074	4,813,321	4,872,214	4,936,465
California	61,570,555	60,080,929	58,248,662	57,526,835	57,975,189	58,323,458	61,050,894	65,953,946	72,003,129	76,663,731
Colorado	7,338,766	7,187,267	7,429,302	7,409,462	7,341,585	7,506,978	7,924,319	8,260,461	8,648,369	8,913,931
Connecticut	8,336,789	8,708,294	8,853,337	9,094,036	9,344,999	9,543,010	10,050,439	10,321,511	10,551,327	10,664,567
Delaware	1,489,594	1,518,786	1,549,812	1,613,304	1,751,143	1,761,559	1,816,383	1,860,732	1,941,408	2,029,229
Florida	24,224,114	23,328,028	23,349,314	23,870,090	22,732,752	23,214,634	24,363,817	25,123,548	25,621,239	26,404,135
Georgia	16,030,039	15,976,945	15,730,409	15,527,907	15,623,633	15,536,733	15,921,673	16,530,506	17,283,295	18,126,272
Hawaii	2,122,779	2,225,438	2,136,144	2,141,561	2,187,480	2,178,284	2,316,586	2,344,496	2,502,117	2,600,074
Idaho	1,891,505	1,957,740	1,961,857	1,881,746	1,854,556	1,925,676	1,949,963	2,015,654	2,107,693	2,245,167
Illinois	21,874,484	23,495,271	24,695,773	24,554,467	25,012,915	25,783,911	27,289,963	28,545,089	29,253,457	31,449,028
Indiana	9,281,709	9,680,895	9,921,243	9,687,949	9,978,491	9,811,166	9,841,337	9,970,350	10,140,639	10,309,827
Iowa	4,499,236	4,731,463	4,794,308	4,855,871	4,971,944	5,143,771	5,354,843	5,526,877	5,663,444	5,840,808
Kansas	4,633,517	4,806,603	4,731,676	4,741,372	4,871,381	4,895,863	5,083,374	5,136,532	5,065,968	5,154,894
Kentucky	5,822,550	5,886,890	6,091,814	6,211,453	6,360,799	6,354,306	6,375,119	6,583,287	6,750,052	6,897,155
Louisiana	6,814,455	7,276,651	7,393,452	7,522,098	7,544,782	7,492,539	7,721,469	7,960,448	8,027,058	8,150,463
Maine	2,308,071	2,350,447	2,370,085	2,377,878	2,330,842	2,357,739	2,441,064	2,538,313	2,579,299	2,641,420
Maryland	11,211,176	11,591,965	11,883,677	11,885,333	11,850,634	12,108,546	12,314,446	12,620,036	12,774,063	13,233,589
Massachusetts	13,182,912	13,937,097	13,356,373	13,962,366	14,151,659	14,627,898	15,183,018	15,723,617	16,374,676	17,089,142
Michigan	17,053,521	17,217,584	17,227,515	16,786,444	16,485,178	16,354,807	16,493,575	16,849,135	16,977,163	17,206,122
Minnesota	8,426,264	9,182,281	8,927,288	8,944,867	9,053,021	9,354,376	9,723,759	10,222,017	10,687,048	11,056,128
Mississippi	3,898,401	3,967,232	3,990,876	3,887,981	3,972,787	4,006,798	4,071,006	4,145,632	4,234,977	4,229,767
Missouri	8,526,641	8,827,224	8,923,448	8,691,880	8,719,925	8,905,756	9,125,949	9,390,061	9,545,816	9,776,478
Montana	1,392,449	1,436,062	1,498,252	1,518,818	1,504,531	1,523,696	1,576,937	1,601,097	1,652,848	1,688,944
Nebraska	2,970,323	3,053,575	3,213,646	3,345,530	3,462,575	3,563,939	3,654,376	3,805,871	3,911,805	4,041,479
Nevada	3,515,004	3,606,035	3,592,994	3,676,997	3,574,233	3,577,346	3,738,777	3,880,472	4,092,457	4,320,504
New Hampshire	2,399,330	2,490,623	2,576,956	2,637,911	2,643,256	2,655,077	2,720,225	2,764,233	2,833,893	2,886,649
New Jersey	24,357,079	23,446,911	24,261,392	23,639,281	24,391,278	25,417,320	25,733,921	25,993,208	26,825,114	27,622,861
New Mexico	3,057,061	3,186,252	3,217,328	3,127,463	3,039,461	3,099,308	3,189,842	3,309,622	3,343,152	3,345,338
New York	46,443,426	48,635,363	50,251,461	51,574,134	52,460,494	52,938,586	55,080,662	56,862,010	59,161,439	60,905,055
North Carolina	11,482,912	12,598,382	12,200,362	12,322,555	12,303,426	12,666,607	12,685,461	13,210,839	13,466,942	13,943,070
North Dakota	886,317	928,528	1,000,095	1,049,772	1,098,090	1,174,364	1,287,133	1,373,266	1,451,309	1,510,292
Ohio	18,892,374	19,387,318	19,801,670	19,988,921	19,701,810	19,506,123	19,714,149	20,231,423	20,484,182	21,494,254
Oklahoma	4,932,913	5,082,062	5,192,124	5,036,031	5,170,978	5,329,897	5,451,048	5,560,047	5,606,044	5,496,402
Oregon	5,409,630	5,529,831	5,401,667	5,430,888	5,389,273	5,395,742	5,647,470	5,969,321	6,238,574	6,514,334
Pennsylvania	21,157,430	21,831,816	22,733,518	23,485,203	23,190,198	23,712,931	24,264,551	25,109,991	26,045,127	27,263,106
Rhode Island	2,134,609	2,139,317	2,136,582	2,149,366	2,167,450	2,121,403	2,182,976	2,242,486	2,283,927	2,362,463
South Carolina	6,453,817	6,626,763	6,566,165	6,465,486	6,619,072	6,950,410	7,163,995	7,437,182	7,727,135	8,035,426
South Dakota	1,037,875	1,080,054	1,115,861	1,126,503	1,100,100	1,125,929	1,182,721	1,211,080	1,253,268	1,379,026
Tennessee	7,540,306	7,768,063	7,894,661	8,225,374	8,345,584	8,531,675	8,606,624	8,736,367	8,886,994	9,260,615
Texas	39,033,235	40,688,181	42,621,886	42,864,291	41,067,619	42,066,035	44,330,579	47,527,971	49,577,688	51,033,537
Utah	3,444,936	3,638,775	3,635,085	3,704,133	3,779,760	3,944,736	4,094,074	4,290,876	4,539,291	4,754,714
Vermont	1,356,165	1,413,329	1,432,683	1,424,507	1,497,093	1,549,228	1,602,256	1,638,720	1,671,433	1,722,621
Virginia	13,125,666	13,505,290	13,193,633	12,968,457	13,403,576	13,868,587	13,955,249	14,384,705	14,677,698	15,296,646
Washington	9,331,539	9,940,325	9,832,913	10,040,312	10,040,607	10,216,676	10,911,929	11,470,245	12,483,668	13,188,097
West Virginia	2,841,962	2,998,621	3,328,177	3,388,294	3,275,246	3,188,181	3,194,770	3,226,918	3,169,684	3,216,323
Wisconsin	9,366,134	9,696,228	9,966,244	10,333,016	9,704,932	9,758,650	9,920,370	10,054,346	10,122,041	10,340,697
Wyoming	1,191,736	1,268,407	1,334,655	1,398,444	1,432,216	1,439,041	1,466,579	1,509,532	1,556,321	1,555,016
Dist. of Columbia	1,282,437	1,352,905	1,451,870	1,482,202	1,466,888	1,557,117	1,605,030	1,668,528	1,778,057	1,936,852
American Samoa	63,105	65,436	70,305	75,355	80,105	65,039	71,709	63,693	58,675	65,490
Guam	229,243	235,711	235,639	266,952	290,575	279,077	286,844	293,713	298,708	298,340
CNMI*	229,243	235,711	235,639	266,952	290,575	279,077	286,844	293,713	298,708	298,340
Puerto Rico	3,433,229	3,502,757	3,464,044	3,519,547	3,351,423	3,676,880	3,510,706	3,247,136	2,970,386	2,789,459
U.S. Virgin Islands.	196,533	201,326	220,234	204,932	183,333	161,955	175,022	158,652	160,559	171,521

See footnotes at end of table

TABLE 9.9

Current Expenditures for Public Elementary and Secondary Education, by State or Jurisdiction: Selected Years, 2007-08 Through 2016-17 (In thousands of current dollars) (continued)

Source: U.S. Department of Education, National Center for Education Statistics, Statistics of State School Systems, 1969-70; Revenues and Expenditures for Public Elementary and Secondary Education, 1979-80; and Common Core of Data (CCD), "National Public Education Financial Survey," 1989-90 through 2016-17. (This table was prepared August 2019.)

Note: Current expenditures include instruction, support services, food services, and enterprise operations. Beginning in 1989-90, expenditures for state administration are excluded. Data are not adjusted for changes in the purchasing power of the dollar due to inflation. Detail may not sum to totals because of rounding. Some data have been revised from previously published figures.
* Commonwealth of Northern Mariana Islands

TABLE 9.10
Expenditures for Instruction in Public Elementary and Secondary Schools, by Subfunction and State or Jurisdiction: 2016-17 (In thousands of current dollars)

State or other jurisdiction	Total	Salaries	Employee benefits	Purchased services(a)	Supplies	Tuition and other
				2016-17		
United States	$376,069,486	$236,792,085	$98,321,490	$18,476,414	$14,900,908	$7,578,589
Alabama	4,049,192	2,582,189	996,372	177,983	270,097	22,552
Alaska	1,266,042	721,744	414,054	61,383	57,179	11,682
Arizona	4,828,965	3,260,105	972,152	338,868	221,550	36,290
Arkansas	2,769,224	1,876,614	530,842	124,196	201,653	35,919
California	45,442,062	28,385,595	11,385,176	2,364,304	2,359,697	947,290
Colorado	4,989,814	3,421,045	1,004,243	135,159	298,385	130,982
Connecticut	6,722,928	3,963,987	1,899,984	217,458	103,922	537,577
Delaware	1,269,553	758,279	419,882	17,908	51,864	21,620
Florida	16,305,281	9,375,840	2,907,840	3,366,298	529,449	125,854
Georgia	11,061,068	7,297,731	2,824,024	258,060	620,321	60,934
Hawaii	1,520,054	955,344	420,171	53,923	80,064	10,552
Idaho	1,323,118	902,280	316,921	50,903	51,567	1,448
Illinois	19,603,947	10,142,329	7,673,293	1,007,196	423,696	357,434
Indiana	5,939,926	3,687,499	1,911,384	113,159	218,550	9,334
Iowa	3,524,206	2,487,050	812,850	81,752	106,932	35,622
Kansas	3,074,527	2,173,096	633,067	94,200	147,246	26,919
Kentucky	3,954,611	2,678,619	1,061,769	63,738	136,607	13,878
Louisiana	4,551,129	2,786,077	1,331,231	152,312	215,036	66,472
Maine	1,545,474	993,471	386,470	42,733	35,655	87,145
Maryland	8,432,187	5,256,375	2,387,876	299,548	198,799	289,589
Massachusetts	10,912,548	6,823,131	2,863,534	99,994	273,503	852,386
Michigan	9,875,810	5,203,188	3,414,023	976,162	261,915	20,522
Minnesota	7,153,109	4,835,058	1,613,811	378,176	224,881	101,184
Mississippi	2,400,216	1,658,005	549,816	70,947	100,228	21,220
Missouri	5,767,922	3,973,411	1,213,296	185,357	365,050	30,808
Montana	991,332	660,424	201,945	59,733	63,835	5,395
Nebraska	2,616,805	1,679,453	660,061	134,212	119,991	23,089
Nevada	2,554,828	1,648,455	669,525	48,597	182,143	6,108
New Hampshire	1,839,343	1,085,209	510,293	50,275	35,204	158,362
New Jersey	16,589,382	9,803,635	4,888,507	660,988	443,100	793,153
New Mexico	1,914,568	1,282,898	450,510	74,019	106,860	280
New York	42,389,679	25,538,666	13,445,451	1,947,701	752,814	705,047
North Carolina	8,718,633	5,972,552	2,014,735	295,971	435,369	6
North Dakota	906,313	616,846	231,438	22,323	29,926	5,780
Ohio	12,703,608	7,852,213	2,868,220	934,872	475,638	572,665
Oklahoma	3,072,797	2,124,218	695,511	58,739	182,005	12,324
Oregon	3,807,508	2,239,094	1,186,291	139,382	202,781	39,959
Pennsylvania	16,871,795	9,396,615	5,724,229	833,924	541,482	375,546
Rhode Island	1,428,107	892,529	433,087	14,093	23,157	65,241
South Carolina	4,455,636	2,922,021	1,075,491	192,972	240,425	24,728
South Dakota	816,490	552,513	162,846	32,537	54,046	14,549
Tennessee	5,652,110	3,791,470	1,258,410	126,009	461,240	14,980
Texas	29,431,662	22,537,224	3,794,495	1,058,061	1,687,197	354,685
Utah	3,019,473	1,831,170	846,311	105,540	217,834	18,617
Vermont	1,107,391	613,350	317,302	58,196	20,116	98,428
Virginia	9,313,749	6,256,908	2,499,818	206,591	342,165	8,266
Washington	7,646,339	5,000,463	1,826,380	471,563	283,814	64,118
West Virginia	1,842,144	1,104,748	558,286	38,753	132,865	7,492
Wisconsin	6,136,689	3,898,231	1,631,245	100,318	248,504	258,391
Wyoming	920,260	583,957	259,585	31,325	42,383	3,010
Dist. of Columbia	1,039,933	709,164	167,435	48,003	22,171	93,159
American Samoa	31,446	22,500	4,691	1,230	1,193	1,831
Guam	142,210	104,755	36,469	479	507	0
CNMI*	41,483	24,861	6,288	3,828	4,502	2,004
Puerto Rico	1,128,669	836,793	225,101	53,047	13,402	326
U.S. Virgin Islands	100,419	66,997	28,139	2,249	3,034	0

See footnotes at end of table

TABLE 9.10

Expenditures for Instruction in Public Elementary and Secondary Schools, by Subfunction and State or Jurisdiction: 2016-17 (In thousands of current dollars) (continued)

Source: U.S. Department of Education, National Center for Education Statistics, Common Core of Data (CCD), "National Public Education Financial Survey," 2015-16 and 2016-17. (This table was prepared November 2019.)

Note: Excludes expenditures for state education agencies. Detail may not sum to totals because of rounding. Some data have been revised from previously published figures.

*Commonwealth of Northern Mariana Islands

Key:

(a) Includes purchased professional services of teachers or others who provide instruction for students.

TABLE 9.11
Total and Current Expenditures Per Pupil in Fall Enrollment in Public Elementary and Secondary Schools, by Function and State or Jurisdiction: 2016-17

State or jurisdiction	Total (a)	Total	Instruction	Total	Student support (b)	Instructional staff (c)	General administration	School administration	Operation and maintenance	Student transportation	Other support services	Food services	Enterprise operations (d)	Capital outlay (e)	Interest on school debt
United States	$13,834	$12,258	$7,445	$4,311	$712	$577	$244	$684	$1,137	$502	$455	$477	$25	$1,213	$363
Alabama	10,615	9,528	5,436	3,441	599	401	245	594	886	492	224	651	0	856	232
Alaska	19,396	17,838	9,538	7,638	1,383	1,481	255	1,091	2,138	608	683	579	83	1,277	281
Arizona	9,374	8,053	4,337	3,295	618	390	156	452	986	334	360	420	1	1,095	226
Arkansas	11,332	10,004	5,612	3,847	541	841	253	525	1,014	368	306	533	11	1,072	256
California	13,796	12,151	7,203	4,463	729	774	119	806	1,200	266	569	456	30	1,184	461
Colorado	11,662	9,849	5,513	3,945	555	567	160	751	900	293	720	338	53	1,306	506
Connecticut	21,354	19,929	12,563	6,755	1,280	627	447	1,166	1,711	1,004	520	438	172	1,197	227
Delaware	16,096	14,892	9,317	5,078	665	273	234	944	1,590	738	633	497	0	1,042	162
Florida	10,405	9,374	3,118	3,118	412	590	86	522	905	361	242	467	0	813	218
Georgia	11,512	10,274	6,269	3,421	534	534	131	648	772	480	321	554	30	1,111	127
Hawaii	15,210	14,322	8,373	5,228	1,348	483	72	1,029	1,593	348	355	721	0	889	0
Idaho	8,599	7,554	4,452	2,731	422	439	190	434	714	330	202	368	4	847	197
Illinois	16,985	15,517	9,673	5,461	1,093	560	583	808	1,204	659	554	383	0	995	473
Indiana	11,145	9,823	5,660	3,690	512	395	203	640	1,107	594	238	474	0	1,042	280
Iowa	13,282	11,456	6,912	4,023	669	716	292	648	950	402	346	508	13	1,595	231
Kansas	12,694	10,428	6,219	3,715	664	431	280	606	1,019	424	292	494	0	1,775	491
Kentucky	11,404	10,083	5,781	3,614	492	562	227	587	898	575	272	660	27	1,054	267
Louisiana	12,502	11,379	6,354	4,425	692	567	295	731	1,149	650	341	600	0	964	160
Maine	15,568	14,633	8,562	5,482	1,003	827	498	772	1,472	719	192	588	2	682	253
Maryland	16,508	14,933	9,515	4,992	672	689	145	1,008	1,260	781	438	425	0	1,396	179
Massachusetts	18,490	17,718	11,314	5,908	1,317	818	286	759	1,490	805	433	496	0	526	246
Michigan	12,639	11,256	6,460	4,380	890	570	253	628	988	471	579	415	0	910	473
Minnesota	15,554	12,635	8,175	3,872	370	646	474	508	853	714	306	534	54	2,465	454
Mississippi	9,611	8,755	4,968	3,250	464	407	294	533	898	418	235	536	0	746	111
Missouri	11,943	10,684	6,303	3,882	482	489	396	627	1,068	553	267	499	0	917	341
Montana	12,964	11,538	6,773	4,234	791	409	366	643	1,159	542	325	514	18	1,265	160
Nebraska	15,169	12,662	8,198	3,606	484	407	371	599	1,081	374	289	527	330	2,206	301
Nevada	10,475	9,120	5,393	3,372	500	504	148	669	844	357	349	355	0	1,009	346
New Hampshire	17,006	15,958	10,168	5,406	1,228	525	575	890	1,279	704	206	384	0	796	252
New Jersey	20,980	19,585	11,762	7,190	2,026	613	399	971	1,905	808	467	438	196	923	472
New Mexico	11,596	9,949	5,694	3,774	1,005	272	237	590	1,039	309	323	475	7	1,647	0
New York	24,377	22,861	15,911	6,495	732	589	370	876	2,102	1,154	673	455	0	967	550
North Carolina	9,886	8,995	5,625	2,895	489	309	156	533	740	367	301	475	0	877	14
North Dakota	16,526	13,767	8,261	4,484	554	473	594	712	1,181	548	422	640	381	2,462	298
Ohio	14,028	12,569	7,428	4,727	851	501	394	695	1,076	597	613	413	1	1,097	362
Oklahoma	8,935	7,921	4,576	2,888	539	320	237	441	831	250	271	524	80	918	96
Oregon	13,298	11,252	6,577	4,282	854	454	157	718	892	495	711	388	5	1,429	617
Pennsylvania	17,479	15,782	9,767	5,433	891	565	476	703	1,445	751	602	515	67	1,152	545
Rhode Island	17,345	16,620	10,046	6,118	1,750	637	249	794	1,290	720	679	452	4	449	277
South Carolina	12,525	10,419	5,777	4,080	803	646	101	675	1,023	394	438	534	27	1,668	438
South Dakota	11,478	10,117	5,990	3,552	563	359	339	492	1,053	360	385	524	51	1,118	243
Tennessee	10,318	9,246	5,643	3,087	416	546	192	560	767	347	260	516	0	847	225
Texas	11,985	9,520	5,490	3,499	469	489	140	546	1,003	277	574	531	0	1,833	632
Utah	8,794	7,206	4,576	2,252	281	289	81	474	656	213	259	362	16	1,408	180
Vermont	20,207	19,480	12,523	6,447	1,506	807	410	1,228	1,455	642	398	489	22	623	104
Virginia	12,992	11,885	7,237	4,188	602	787	193	697	1,061	612	236	458	3	1,032	75
Washington	14,483	11,971	6,940	4,555	879	776	205	726	1,016	448	505	364	111	2,114	399
West Virginia	12,566	11,745	6,727	4,261	610	464	201	630	1,267	872	218	756	0	768	53
Wisconsin	13,315	11,962	7,099	4,424	598	631	346	603	1,109	507	631	439	0	1,167	185
Wyoming	20,264	16,513	9,772	6,249	995	914	348	881	1,599	828	684	485	7	3,727	25
Dist. of Columbia	30,115	22,561	12,113	9,629	1,002	1,133	1,649	1,572	2,222	1,366	687	809	9	5,934	1,621
American Samoa	N/A	N/A	N/A	N/A	N/A	N/A	N/A	N/A	N/A	N/A	N/A	N/A	N/A	N/A	N/A
Guam	11,753	9,700	4,624	4,424	911	538	156	593	1,252	258	717	652	0	1,652	402
CNMI*	N/A	N/A	N/A	N/A	N/A	N/A	N/A	N/A	N/A	N/A	N/A	N/A	N/A	N/A	N/A
Puerto Rico	7,731	7,639	3,091	3,456	870	456	217	332	1,116	255	212	1,092	0	93	0
U.S. Virgin Islands	13,009	13,000	7,611	4,525	1,125	320	621	717	519	571	651	852	12	9	0

See footnotes at end of table

TABLE 9.11

Total and Current Expenditures Per Pupil in Fall Enrollment in Public Elementary and Secondary Schools, by Function and State or Jurisdiction: 2016-17 (continued)

Source: U.S. Department of Education, National Center for Education Statistics, Common Core of Data (CCD), "National Public Education Financial Survey," 2016-17. (This table was prepared August 2019.)

Note: Excludes expenditures for state education agencies. "0" indicates none or less than $0.50. Detail may not sum to totals because of rounding.

* Commonwealth of Northern Mariana Islands

Key:

N/A – Not available

(a) Excludes "Other current expenditures," such as community services, private school programs, adult education, and other programs not allocable to expenditures per pupil in public schools.

(b) Includes expenditures for guidance, health, attendance, and speech pathology services.

(c) Includes expenditures for curriculum development, staff training, libraries, and media and computer centers.

(d) Includes expenditures for operations funded by sales of products or services (e.g., school bookstore or computer time).

(e) Includes expenditures for property and for buildings and alterations completed by school district staff or contractors.

TABLE 9.12

Average Undergraduate Tuition and Fees and Room and Board Rates Charged for Full-Time Students in Degree-Granting Postsecondary Institutions, By Control and Level Of Institution and State or Jurisdiction: 2016-17 and 2017-18 (In current dollars)

State or other jurisdiction	Public 4-year						Out-of-state tuition and required fees, 2017–18
	In-state, 2016–17		In-state, 2017–18				
	Total	Tuition and required fees	Total	Tuition and required fees	Room	Board	
United States	$19,488	$8,804	$20,050	$9,037	$6,227	$4,786	$25,657
Alabama	19,052	9,466	19,673	9,827	5,534	4,311	24,939
Alaska	17,370	7,210	18,373	7,221	6,209	4,943	21,284
Arizona	21,491	10,057	22,629	10,557	7,081	4,992	26,067
Arkansas	16,871	7,924	17,479	8,187	5,139	4,153	20,061
California	21,356	7,896	22,081	8,020	7,896	6,166	29,173
Colorado	20,943	9,352	21,514	9,540	5,858	6,116	29,846
Connecticut	24,174	11,726	25,182	12,355	7,032	5,795	33,741
Delaware	21,698	9,578	22,371	9,999	7,382	4,990	29,356
Florida	14,806	4,435	14,896	4,455	5,856	4,585	18,241
Georgia	17,353	7,010	17,705	7,206	6,255	4,244	21,957
Hawaii	21,016	9,712	21,201	9,709	5,767	5,725	31,019
Idaho	14,457	7,005	15,455	7,247	3,911	4,297	22,601
Illinois	24,541	13,636	25,089	13,971	6,035	5,084	28,618
Indiana	19,001	8,876	19,297	9,038	5,476	4,783	28,805
Iowa	17,604	8,361	18,426	8,766	5,394	4,266	26,214
Kansas	17,560	8,489	17,963	8,737	4,813	4,414	22,615
Kentucky	19,673	10,014	20,745	10,365	5,889	4,490	24,632
Louisiana	18,319	8,813	18,835	9,165	5,664	4,007	21,632
Maine	19,073	9,219	19,500	9,664	5,028	4,808	26,939
Maryland	20,670	9,094	21,177	9,289	6,821	5,067	24,353
Massachusetts	24,473	12,331	25,229	12,778	7,771	4,680	29,774
Michigan	21,832	11,890	22,665	12,435	5,127	5,103	37,600
Minnesota	19,727	10,883	20,420	11,226	4,983	4,210	20,736
Mississippi	16,843	7,472	17,718	7,980	5,688	4,051	19,691
Missouri	17,639	8,176	18,106	8,387	6,016	3,703	19,519
Montana	15,241	6,503	15,800	6,783	4,184	4,834	23,678
Nebraska	17,379	7,732	18,449	8,188	5,517	4,744	20,555
Nevada	17,145	5,520	16,810	5,920	5,757	5,133	21,176
New Hampshire	26,968	15,491	27,570	15,949	7,047	4,574	28,130
New Jersey	26,070	13,297	26,542	13,633	7,966	4,943	28,649
New Mexico	15,528	6,825	15,803	6,718	4,567	4,518	17,533
New York	21,750	7,709	22,343	7,938	9,260	5,145	21,662
North Carolina	16,635	7,218	17,343	7,354	5,633	4,355	24,274
North Dakota	15,388	7,376	15,998	7,687	3,479	4,832	19,021
Ohio	20,961	9,827	21,674	10,026	6,632	5,017	24,098
Oklahoma	15,755	7,219	16,263	7,623	4,589	4,052	20,200
Oregon	21,324	9,739	22,710	10,363	7,262	5,085	30,487
Pennsylvania	25,331	14,068	25,795	14,534	6,743	4,518	27,129
Rhode Island	23,135	11,386	24,280	12,239	7,538	4,502	29,013
South Carolina	21,508	12,153	22,132	12,579	5,888	3,665	30,919
South Dakota	16,054	8,301	16,421	8,540	3,801	4,080	12,060
Tennessee	18,340	9,287	18,951	9,574	4,988	4,388	25,378
Texas	17,800	8,376	18,271	8,645	5,175	4,451	24,937
Utah	13,709	6,334	14,174	6,557	3,435	4,182	20,168
Vermont	26,786	15,537	27,782	16,103	7,381	4,297	38,968
Virginia	22,567	12,126	23,427	12,637	6,089	4,701	33,428
Washington	18,053	6,903	18,323	6,830	6,146	5,347	28,263
West Virginia	17,096	7,241	17,803	7,619	5,465	4,718	21,032
Wisconsin	16,246	8,419	16,544	8,475	4,864	3,205	23,500
Wyoming	14,354	4,311	14,486	4,443	4,493	5,550	13,731
Dist. of Columbia	N.A	5,612	N.A	5,756	N.A	N.A	12,092

See footnotes at end of table

TABLE 9.12

Average Undergraduate Tuition and Fees and Room and Board Rates Charged for Full-Time Students in Degree-Granting Postsecondary Institutions, By Control and Level Of Institution and State or Jurisdiction: 2016-17 and 2017-18 (In current dollars) (continued)

State or other jurisdiction	Private 4-year						Public 2-year, tuition and required fees		
	2016–17		2017–18				In-state, 2016-17	In-state, 2017-18	Out-of-state, 2017-18
	Total	Tuition and required fees	Total	Tuition and required fees	Room	Board			
United States	$41,465	$29,476	$43,139	$30,731	$6,967	$5,441	$3,156	$3,243	$7,971
Alabama	24,710	15,422	26,164	16,321	4,818	5,025	4,362	4,403	9,133
Alaska	26,297	19,052	26,887	19,360	3,598	3,929	3,820	N.A.	N.A.
Arizona	22,559	13,140	22,939	13,487	5,125	4,327	2,129	2,152	8,067
Arkansas	29,804	21,710	30,828	22,610	4,175	4,043	3,195	3,291	4,762
California	44,710	31,484	47,410	33,483	7,813	6,113	1,262	1,268	7,504
Colorado	34,337	22,627	35,152	22,873	7,188	5,092	3,565	3,638	10,354
Connecticut	53,198	38,975	54,819	40,410	8,227	6,182	4,189	4,312	12,879
Delaware	25,996	14,383	26,928	15,096	5,911	5,920	N.A.	N.A.	N.A.
Florida	35,876	24,360	37,336	25,531	6,720	5,084	2,552	2,506	9,111
Georgia	39,110	27,213	40,414	27,813	6,869	5,731	2,895	2,901	8,090
Hawaii	28,370	15,937	28,858	16,447	5,693	6,718	3,080	3,080	8,216
Idaho	13,010	5,925	13,488	5,833	3,275	4,380	3,227	3,282	7,732
Illinois	43,382	31,298	45,046	32,491	7,264	5,290	3,749	3,891	10,989
Indiana	41,852	30,928	43,764	32,338	6,029	5,397	4,175	4,255	8,211
Iowa	35,780	26,742	37,380	27,991	4,584	4,805	4,791	4,923	6,581
Kansas	28,653	20,198	30,240	21,316	4,319	4,604	3,221	3,382	4,611
Kentucky	34,895	25,846	35,948	26,719	4,673	4,556	3,962	4,106	13,825
Louisiana	47,557	35,190	49,452	36,715	7,031	5,706	4,031	4,093	7,057
Maine	48,107	35,547	49,994	37,043	6,533	6,418	3,673	3,698	6,498
Maryland	53,775	40,209	55,685	41,859	8,036	5,790	3,983	4,090	9,467
Massachusetts	57,363	42,655	59,559	44,384	8,835	6,340	4,785	4,991	10,006
Michigan	33,498	24,058	36,664	26,964	4,949	4,751	3,423	3,469	6,552
Minnesota	40,939	30,925	42,716	32,416	5,377	4,923	5,310	5,381	6,113
Mississippi	24,698	16,949	25,774	17,625	4,255	3,895	2,831	3,182	5,626
Missouri	33,433	23,702	34,623	24,615	5,700	4,308	3,028	3,273	6,157
Montana	32,375	23,657	33,739	24,953	4,161	4,625	3,381	3,631	8,482
Nebraska	32,201	23,110	34,598	23,659	4,716	6,223	2,991	3,212	4,101
Nevada	35,053	21,423	36,163	23,261	6,345	6,557	2,910	3,075	9,853
New Hampshire	46,533	33,235	47,030	33,322	8,620	5,089	7,002	7,337	15,907
New Jersey	48,439	35,224	50,321	36,589	8,064	5,668	4,366	4,536	8,049
New Mexico	32,373	22,535	33,620	23,865	5,655	4,100	1,590	1,666	5,318
New York	51,791	37,581	53,659	39,007	8,865	5,788	5,122	5,229	9,151
North Carolina	42,312	30,701	44,050	32,140	6,162	5,747	2,471	2,499	8,496
North Dakota	20,964	14,290	22,511	15,256	3,077	4,178	4,562	4,700	9,429
Ohio	40,975	30,291	42,254	31,242	5,742	5,270	3,654	3,672	7,456
Oklahoma	33,883	24,776	35,542	26,240	4,596	4,706	3,627	3,876	9,059
Oregon	48,658	37,053	50,617	38,674	6,266	5,677	4,262	4,487	8,503
Pennsylvania	52,134	39,187	53,239	40,068	7,271	5,900	5,048	5,173	13,679
Rhode Island	52,874	38,855	54,877	40,361	8,776	5,740	4,266	4,564	12,156
South Carolina	33,748	24,523	34,421	24,931	4,804	4,686	4,418	4,502	9,480
South Dakota	30,924	23,146	32,157	24,219	3,943	3,995	5,803	6,026	5,853
Tennessee	35,928	25,984	37,162	26,939	5,772	4,451	4,048	4,148	16,140
Texas	41,980	31,010	43,866	32,482	6,368	5,016	2,100	2,209	6,418
Utah	15,208	7,441	15,389	7,548	3,946	3,894	3,690	3,781	12,020
Vermont	54,015	41,068	56,172	42,637	7,431	6,105	6,222	6,414	12,678
Virginia	32,614	22,284	33,658	23,014	5,664	4,980	4,962	5,118	11,275
Washington	46,667	35,213	48,518	36,807	6,208	5,503	3,848	4,078	5,976
West Virginia	20,898	12,206	21,300	12,341	4,316	4,643	4,009	4,077	9,410
Wisconsin	41,503	31,662	43,332	33,156	5,869	4,307	4,292	4,337	6,257
Wyoming	N.A.	18,021	N.A.	N.A.	N.A.	N.A.	2,987	3,142	7,678
Dist. of Columbia	55,669	40,618	57,611	41,775	10,288	5,547	N.A.	N.A.	N.A.

See footnotes at end of table

TABLE 9.12

Average Undergraduate Tuition and Fees and Room and Board Rates Charged for Full-Time Students in Degree-Granting Postsecondary Institutions, By Control and Level Of Institution and State or Jurisdiction: 2016-17 and 2017-18 (In current dollars) (continued)

Source: U.S. Department of Education, National Center for Education Statistics, Integrated Postsecondary Education Data System (IPEDS), Fall 2016 and Fall 2017, Institutional Characteristics component; and Spring 2017 and Spring 2018, Fall Enrollment component. (This table was prepared November 2018.)

Note: Data are for the entire academic year and are average charges for full-time students. In-state tuition and fees were weighted by the number of full-time-equivalent undergraduates, but were not adjusted to reflect the number of students who were state residents. Out-of-state tuition and fees were weighted by the number of first-time freshmen attending the institution in fall 2016 from out of state. Institutional room and board rates are weighted by the number of full-time students. Degree-granting institutions grant associate's or higher degrees and participate in Title IV federal financial aid programs. Some data have been revised from previously published figures. Detail may not sum to totals because of rounding.

Key:
N.A. – Not applicable

TABLE 9.13

Degree-Granting Postsecondary Institutions, By Control and Classification of Institution and State or Jurisdiction: 2017-18

State or other jurisdiction	Total all degree granting institutions	All public institutions	All public institutions							
			Public 4-year institutions							Public 2-year
			Total	Research university, very high (a)	Research university, high (b)	Doctoral/ research university (c)	Master's (d)	Baccalaureate (e)	Special focus (f)	
United States	4,313	1,626	750	81	74	38	271	234	52	876
Alabama	72	40	14	1	4	0	8	1	0	26
Alaska	8	4	4	0	1	0	2	0	1	0
Arizona	78	30	10	2	1	2	2	1	2	20
Arkansas	53	33	11	1	0	1	6	2	1	22
California	441	151	49	8	2	3	18	16	2	102
Colorado	79	28	17	2	3	0	6	6	0	11
Connecticut	43	22	10	1	0	0	4	5	0	12
Delaware	8	3	3	1	0	0	1	1	0	0
Florida	201	43	42	5	2	1	4	30	0	1
Georgia	123	52	29	3	1	4	9	11	1	23
Hawaii	20	10	4	1	0	0	1	2	0	6
Idaho	17	8	4	0	1	2	0	1	0	4
Illinois	171	60	12	2	3	0	7	0	0	48
Indiana	80	15	14	2	2	1	7	2	0	1
Iowa	62	19	3	2	0	0	1	0	0	16
Kansas	69	33	8	2	1	0	4	0	1	25
Kentucky	67	24	8	2	0	0	5	1	0	16
Louisiana	60	32	17	1	2	2	8	1	3	15
Maine	31	15	8	0	1	0	1	6	0	7
Maryland	56	29	13	1	1	2	7	1	1	16
Massachusetts	116	31	15	1	3	0	7	1	3	16
Michigan	94	46	21	3	3	2	6	7	0	25
Minnesota	95	43	12	1	0	0	8	2	1	31
Mississippi	38	23	8	1	3	0	4	0	0	15
Missouri	115	27	13	1	3	0	6	3	0	14
Montana	23	17	7	0	2	0	1	3	1	10
Nebraska	41	16	7	1	0	1	4	0	1	9
Nevada	24	7	6	0	2	0	0	4	0	1
New Hampshire	25	13	6	0	1	0	2	2	1	7
New Jersey	75	32	13	1	2	2	8	0	0	19
New Mexico	42	28	9	1	1	0	4	1	2	19
New York	301	79	43	4	1	1	23	10	4	36
North Carolina	144	75	16	2	4	0	8	1	1	59
North Dakota	20	14	9	0	2	0	1	4	2	5
Ohio	185	60	35	2	7	1	1	21	3	25
Oklahoma	59	30	17	1	1	0	8	5	2	13
Oregon	57	26	9	2	1	0	4	1	1	17
Pennsylvania	239	62	45	3	0	1	16	23	2	17
Rhode Island	13	3	2	0	1	0	1	0	0	1
South Carolina	73	33	13	2	0	0	6	4	1	20
South Dakota	23	12	7	0	2	0	3	0	2	5
Tennessee	100	23	10	1	1	4	3	0	1	13
Texas	261	108	47	7	4	8	16	4	8	61
Utah	32	8	7	1	1	0	3	2	0	1
Vermont	23	6	5	0	1	0	1	3	0	1
Virginia	122	40	16	4	2	0	7	2	1	24
Washington	80	43	35	2	0	0	6	26	1	8
West Virginia	44	22	13	1	0	0	3	8	1	9
Wisconsin	76	33	16	2	0	0	9	5	0	17
Wyoming	10	8	1	0	1	0	0	0	0	7
Dist. of Columbia	19	2	2	0	0	0	1	0	1	0
U.S. Service Academies	5	5	5	0	0	0	0	5	0	0
Other jurisdictions total	89	17	9	0	0	0	3	4	2	8
American Samoa	1	1	1	0	0	0	0	1	0	0
Fed. States of Micronesia	1	1	0	0	0	0	0	0	0	1
Guam	3	2	1	0	0	0	1	0	0	1
Marshall Islands	1	1	0	0	0	0	0	0	0	1
CNMI*	1	1	1	0	0	0	0	1	0	0
Palau	1	1	0	0	0	0	0	0	0	1
Puerto Rico	80	9	5	0	0	0	1	2	2	4
U.S. Virgin Islands	1	1	1	0	0	0	1	0	0	0

See footnotes at end of table

TABLE 9.13
Degree-Granting Postsecondary Institutions, By Control and Classification of Institution and State or Jurisdiction: 2017–18 (continued)

State or other jurisdiction	All nonprofit institutions	All nonprofit institutions								For-profit institutions		
		Nonprofit 4-year institutions							Non-profit 2-year	For-profit institutions		
	All nonprofit institutions	Total (4-year)	Research university, very high (a)	Research university, high (b)	Doctoral/ research university (c)	Master's (d)	Baccalaureate (e)	Special focus (f)	Non-profit 2-year	Total for-profit	4-year	2-year
United States	1,689	1,590	34	30	54	413	462	597	99	998	488	510
Alabama	21	21	0	0	0	4	12	5	0	11	7	4
Alaska	3	2	0	0	0	1	0	1	1	1	0	1
Arizona	11	11	0	0	0	2	2	7	0	37	21	16
Arkansas	17	13	0	0	0	2	9	2	4	3	2	1
California	149	143	3	1	9	31	23	76	6	141	77	64
Colorado	15	12	0	1	0	3	3	5	3	36	19	17
Connecticut	18	18	1	0	1	8	4	4	0	3	3	0
Delaware	4	3	0	0	1	0	1	1	1	1	1	0
Florida	70	62	1	2	1	14	21	23	8	88	37	51
Georgia	40	36	1	1	1	5	19	9	4	31	12	19
Hawaii	6	6	0	0	0	2	3	1	0	4	3	1
Idaho	6	6	0	0	0	1	3	2	0	3	2	1
Illinois	83	80	2	2	4	19	16	37	3	28	16	12
Indiana	41	40	1	0	1	11	16	11	1	24	13	11
Iowa	34	34	0	0	0	9	15	10	0	9	7	2
Kansas	24	24	0	0	0	6	13	5	0	12	7	5
Kentucky	25	25	0	0	2	7	9	7	0	18	10	8
Louisiana	14	12	1	0	0	3	4	4	2	14	1	13
Maine	13	11	0	0	0	4	6	1	2	3	2	1
Maryland	19	19	1	0	0	6	4	8	0	8	3	5
Massachusetts	79	77	7	1	4	18	18	29	2	6	3	3
Michigan	40	40	0	0	1	10	13	16	0	8	4	4
Minnesota	36	35	0	0	2	8	11	14	1	16	14	2
Mississippi	9	9	0	0	0	3	4	2	0	6	1	5
Missouri	53	51	1	1	2	13	10	24	2	35	16	19
Montana	5	4	0	0	0	0	3	1	1	1	0	1
Nebraska	19	17	0	0	0	6	6	5	2	6	4	2
Nevada	5	4	0	0	0	1	0	3	1	12	5	7
New Hampshire	12	11	0	1	0	5	4	1	1	0	0	0
New Jersey	31	31	1	1	1	10	2	16	0	12	9	3
New Mexico	3	3	0	0	0	2	1	0	0	11	8	3
New York	186	173	5	5	7	37	26	93	13	36	22	14
North Carolina	50	49	1	1	1	10	24	12	1	19	10	9
North Dakota	5	5	0	0	0	1	1	3	0	1	1	0
Ohio	74	69	1	1	2	20	22	23	5	51	16	35
Oklahoma	14	13	0	1	0	6	3	3	1	15	6	9
Oregon	25	24	0	0	0	7	5	12	1	6	4	2
Pennsylvania	118	105	2	3	4	33	33	30	13	59	9	50
Rhode Island	10	10	1	0	0	5	1	3	0	0	0	0
South Carolina	22	21	0	0	0	7	13	1	1	18	8	10
South Dakota	7	7	0	0	0	2	2	3	0	4	4	0
Tennessee	47	44	1	0	3	13	11	16	3	30	12	18
Texas	71	64	1	3	1	18	18	23	7	82	33	49
Utah	11	10	0	1	0	3	3	3	1	13	12	1
Vermont	16	16	0	0	0	6	8	2	0	1	1	0
Virginia	45	42	0	0	3	6	16	17	3	37	20	17
Washington	25	21	0	0	1	10	4	6	4	12	9	3
West Virginia	10	10	0	0	0	3	4	3	0	12	3	9
Wisconsin	34	34	0	1	2	10	12	9	0	9	7	2
Wyoming	2	1	0	0	0	0	1	0	1	0	0	0
Dist. of Columbia	12	12	2	3	0	2	0	5	0	5	4	1
U.S. Service Academies	N.A.	N.A.	N.A.	N.A.	N.A.	N.A.	N.A.	N.A.	N.A.	N.A.	N.A.	N.A.
Other jurisdictions total	51	46	0	0	3	13	12	18	5	21	11	10
American Samoa	0	0	0	0	0	0	0	0	0	0	0	0
Fed. States of Micronesia	0	0	0	0	0	0	0	0	0	0	0	0
Guam	1	1	0	0	0	0	0	1	0	0	0	0
Marshall Islands	0	0	0	0	0	0	0	0	0	0	0	0
CNMI*	0	0	0	0	0	0	0	0	0	0	0	0
Palau	0	0	0	0	0	0	0	0	0	0	0	0
Puerto Rico	50	45	0	0	3	13	12	17	5	21	11	10
U.S. Virgin Islands	0	0	0	0	0	0	0	0	0	0	0	0

See footnotes at end of table

TABLE 9.13

Degree-Granting Postsecondary Institutions, By Control and Classification of Institution and State or Jurisdiction: 2017-18 (continued)

Source: U.S. Department of Education, National Center for Education Statistics, Integrated Postsecondary Education Data System (IPEDS), Fall 2017, Institutional Characteristics component. (This table was prepared October 2018.)

* Commonwealth of Northern Mariana Islands

Note: Branch campuses are counted as separate institutions. Relative levels of research activity for research universities were determined by an analysis of research and development expenditures, science and engineering research staffing, and doctoral degrees conferred, by field. Further information on the research index ranking may be obtained from *http://carnegieclassifications. iu.edu/*. Degree-granting institutions grant associate's or higher degrees and participate in Title IV federal financial aid programs.

Key:

N.A. – Not applicable

(a) Research universities with a very high level of research activity.

(b) Research universities with a high level of research activity.

(c) Institutions that award at least 20 research/scholarship doctor's degrees per year, but did not have a high level of research activity.

(d) Institutions that award at least 50 master's degrees and fewer than 20 doctor's degrees per year.

(e) Institutions that primarily emphasize undergraduate education. In addition to institutions that primarily award bachelor's degrees, also includes institutions classified as 4-year in the IPEDS system, but classified as 2-year baccalaureate/associate's colleges in the Carnegie Classification system because they primarily award associate's degrees.

(f) Four-year institutions that award degrees primarily in single fields of study, such as medicine, business, fine arts, theology, and engineering.

TABLE 9.14
Average Salary of Full-Time Instructional Faculty on 9-Month Contracts in 4-Year Degree-Granting Postsecondary, Institutions, By Control and Classification of Institution, Academic Rank of Faculty, and State or Jurisdiction: 2017–18 (In current dollars)

State or jurisdiction	Public doctoral (a) Professor	Public doctoral (a) Associate professor	Public doctoral (a) Assistant professor	Public master's (b) Professor	Public master's (b) Associate professor	Public master's (b) Assistant professor	Nonprofit doctoral (a) Professor	Nonprofit doctoral (a) Associate professor	Nonprofit doctoral (a) Assistant professor	Nonprofit master's (b) Professor	Nonprofit master's (b) Associate professor	Nonprofit master's (b) Assistant professor
United States	$131,773	$91,724	$79,860	$96,084	$78,316	$67,291	$160,220	$99,182	$84,079	$92,541	$74,409	$63,318
Alabama	127,963	90,856	75,108	82,673	68,604	61,421	100,337	72,443	40,898	63,483	56,626	49,023
Alaska	106,345	88,890	73,501	104,446	87,974	69,597	N.A.	N.A.	N.A.	64,878	49,771	46,676
Arizona	130,847	94,930	81,729	131,474	97,006	71,886	N.A.	N.A.	N.A.	102,855	70,699	68,672
Arkansas	107,859	80,126	70,406	72,821	63,958	55,849	80,637	67,795	61,052	71,905	60,683	57,892
California	157,398	107,063	91,776	106,717	90,993	81,007	171,805	108,564	92,503	102,760	81,946	71,902
Colorado	115,388	89,432	76,717	81,100	66,664	57,438	132,631	94,973	83,105	114,440	86,141	66,741
Connecticut	151,296	102,494	83,685	104,568	87,063	69,382	181,457	97,588	86,608	138,079	99,941	82,461
Delaware	147,967	103,107	89,469	N.A.	N.A.	N.A.	N.A.	N.A.	N.A.	100,360	81,706	74,641
Florida	131,375	92,378	82,227	109,385	85,990	68,717	134,981	94,032	78,552	97,164	79,770	67,048
Georgia	119,699	85,441	74,284	78,536	66,423	59,495	145,659	95,690	85,360	78,808	62,834	54,896
Hawaii	128,644	97,622	85,128	N.A.	N.A.	N.A.	N.A.	N.A.	N.A.	88,534	80,218	72,564
Idaho	94,465	77,181	69,354	N.A.	N.A.	N.A.	N.A.	N.A.	N.A.	65,028	53,955	50,839
Illinois	125,265	88,026	83,950	96,061	77,937	67,823	179,415	102,779	88,936	85,279	71,370	61,549
Indiana	133,168	91,958	82,484	89,351	72,386	64,648	142,812	90,094	73,813	82,727	66,339	56,538
Iowa	135,139	96,032	83,677	92,063	74,385	65,659	90,865	73,290	61,825	69,674	59,679	53,855
Kansas	115,684	82,458	72,060	75,885	65,820	59,130	65,640	53,748	50,240	65,025	59,224	52,881
Kentucky	110,730	79,024	70,024	78,394	66,073	56,327	80,053	64,439	55,239	62,905	55,209	49,231
Louisiana	110,756	77,970	72,734	75,294	62,221	56,855	130,762	83,586	83,056	58,577	58,435	55,342
Maine	107,197	82,956	65,380	77,668	63,024	52,310	94,402	76,102	63,547	67,458	57,908	49,334
Maryland	134,805	96,312	80,993	94,669	76,275	69,760	139,776	100,333	100,010	89,574	72,223	62,298
Massachusetts	147,087	108,171	89,875	101,968	81,056	69,212	187,894	112,953	99,508	125,028	91,110	75,986
Michigan	138,423	96,272	83,290	97,251	83,582	72,314	110,994	88,732	77,298	80,136	68,350	61,349
Minnesota	145,639	97,959	88,853	93,801	78,599	67,629	98,667	78,709	65,050	81,113	67,740	61,630
Mississippi	100,816	76,706	67,330	69,918	61,569	52,390	82,978	67,743	60,965	75,074	60,668	57,678
Missouri	110,036	77,445	69,587	79,598	64,923	56,816	147,955	91,239	78,982	83,260	66,082	57,684
Montana	95,841	74,738	69,213	76,954	68,105	57,828	N.A.	N.A.	N.A.	63,367	52,573	48,494
Nebraska	120,381	87,614	84,981	81,613	67,494	57,686	117,998	84,867	70,194	66,278	57,492	52,192
Nevada	130,632	95,142	74,618	N.A.	N.A.	N.A.	N.A.	N.A.	‡	‡	‡	‡
New Hampshire	133,295	103,394	83,522	96,382	79,452	66,440	190,058	120,522	96,399	91,889	74,796	65,767
New Jersey	160,011	110,435	88,365	126,826	100,460	82,485	194,639	104,405	95,071	102,656	90,177	69,710
New Mexico	104,166	75,615	70,507	77,832	70,460	62,013	N.A.	N.A.	N.A.	‡	‡	38,486
New York	136,296	97,611	83,120	110,336	85,039	72,010	168,067	106,382	88,621	100,633	80,507	69,956
North Carolina	126,889	86,784	78,502	94,385	75,736	68,976	162,917	98,133	75,308	72,081	62,291	56,331
North Dakota	106,453	83,595	71,641	80,945	63,356	55,741	71,134	64,383	55,754	N.A.	N.A.	N.A.
Ohio	123,955	89,065	78,875	77,729	65,037	61,901	111,762	79,992	72,858	80,057	66,151	57,953
Oklahoma	109,542	80,060	73,369	81,130	65,528	57,161	105,174	79,730	76,703	70,498	61,836	54,522
Oregon	125,660	92,971	80,833	79,862	67,892	54,421	102,534	79,796	65,343	64,651	58,340	51,981
Pennsylvania	144,186	100,818	82,896	111,553	90,748	72,485	159,612	100,108	87,310	94,625	77,057	65,536
Rhode Island	124,230	90,450	84,447	82,779	73,051	62,218	181,167	120,354	98,358	118,595	89,048	75,400
South Carolina	133,119	93,900	87,330	89,755	72,439	63,724	69,828	66,204	58,204	81,361	65,849	57,267
South Dakota	95,456	78,771	69,939	91,645	70,306	66,612	N.A.	N.A.	N.A.	68,849	61,866	54,836
Tennessee	109,870	80,751	70,847	83,192	67,464	58,894	148,018	92,959	77,979	81,797	66,043	58,151
Texas	133,214	92,012	78,114	93,992	76,894	67,683	146,520	97,766	86,205	89,628	73,246	62,593
Utah	124,297	87,970	79,559	89,441	72,923	65,367	151,842	108,014	75,936	86,851	76,225	53,748
Vermont	119,777	90,970	76,024	73,468	56,466	49,459	N.A.	N.A.	N.A.	104,727	78,247	71,211
Virginia	134,731	93,926	78,577	91,869	75,410	65,869	116,475	85,452	67,866	72,986	60,238	54,085
Washington	132,222	99,693	91,672	106,057	90,523	78,855	115,080	86,756	71,398	80,141	67,044	62,885
West Virginia	97,879	75,870	67,924	65,943	58,848	50,837	66,654	56,344	49,806	59,998	57,205	47,373
Wisconsin	120,857	82,647	78,930	74,621	63,929	62,503	105,740	82,221	71,965	75,641	63,648	56,714
Wyoming	118,002	82,290	79,942	N.A.	N.A.	N.A.	N.A.	N.A.	N.A.	N.A.	N.A.	N.A.
Dist. of Columbia	155,545	104,516	97,513	104,665	75,418	62,592	173,091	111,491	91,435	87,320	69,942	68,769
U.S. Service Academies	N.A.	N.A.	N.A.	N.A.	N.A.	N.A.	N.A.	N.A.	N.A.	N.A.	N.A.	N.A.
Other jurisdictions total	N.A.	N.A.	N.A.	84,828	72,306	60,962	N.A.	N.A.	49,789	N.A.	N.A.	48,321
American Samoa	N.A.	N.A.	N.A.	N.A.	N.A.	N.A.	N.A.	N.A.	N.A.	N.A.	N.A.	N.A.
Fed. States of Micronesia	N.A.	N.A.	N.A.	N.A.	N.A.	N.A.	N.A.	N.A.	N.A.	N.A.	N.A.	N.A.
Guam	N.A.	N.A.	N.A.	94,653	74,108	57,834	N.A.	N.A.	N.A.	N.A.	N.A.	N.A.
Marshall Islands	N.A.	N.A.	N.A.	N.A.	N.A.	N.A.	N.A.	N.A.	N.A.	N.A.	N.A.	N.A.
CNMI*	N.A.	N.A.	N.A.	N.A.	N.A.	N.A.	N.A.	N.A.	N.A.	N.A.	N.A.	N.A.
Palau	N.A.	N.A.	N.A.	N.A.	N.A.	N.A.	N.A.	N.A.	N.A.	N.A.	N.A.	N.A.
Puerto Rico	N.A.	N.A.	N.A.	83,765	72,036	63,110	N.A.	N.A.	49,789	N.A.	N.A.	48,321
U.S. Virgin Islands	N.A.	N.A.	N.A.	87,266	69,755	59,146	N.A.	N.A.	N.A.	N.A.	N.A.	N.A.

See footnotes at end of table

TABLE 9.14

Average Salary of Full-Time Instructional Faculty on 9-Month Contracts in 4-Year Degree-Granting Postsecondary, Institutions, By Control and Classification of Institution, Academic Rank of Faculty, and State or Jurisdiction: 2017–18 (In current dollars) (continued)

Source: U.S. Department of Education, National Center for Education Statistics, Integrated Postsecondary Education Data System (IPEDS), Spring 2018, Human Resources component, Salaries section. (This table was prepared November 2018.)

* Commonwealth of Northern Mariana Islands

Note: Data exclude instructional faculty at medical schools. Degree-granting institutions grant associate's or higher degrees and participate in Title IV federal financial aid programs. Data include imputations for nonrespondent institutions.

Key:

N.A.–Not applicable

‡–Reporting standards not met (too few cases).

(a) Institutions that awarded 20 or more doctor's degrees during the previous academic year.

(b) Institutions that awarded 20 or more master's degrees, but less than 20 doctor's degrees, during the previous academic year.

TABLE 9.15
Total Expenditures of Public Degree-Granting Postsecondary Institutions, by Level of Institution, Purpose of Expenditure, and State or Jurisdiction: 2016-17

State or other jurisdiction	2016-17					
	All institutions		4-year institutions		2-year institutions	
	Total (a)	Instruction	Total (a)	Instruction	Total (a)	Instruction
Unites States	$371,647,743	$111,991,558	$317,538,661	$89,514,596	$54,109,083	$22,476,963
Alabama	7,785,726	1,923,520	7,028,015	1,604,931	757,711	318,589
Alaska	839,381	255,595	839,381	255,595	0	0
Arizona	6,507,273	2,074,702	5,130,163	1,545,990	1,377,110	528,712
Arkansas	4,106,519	932,632	3,647,177	751,511	459,342	181,121
California	58,144,991	15,971,067	45,842,517	11,526,790	12,302,474	4,444,277
Colorado	7,781,063	2,301,843	7,265,477	2,085,437	515,585	216,406
Connecticut	3,798,052	1,165,155	3,277,990	955,315	520,062	209,840
Delaware	1,264,208	562,040	1,264,208	562,040	0	0
Florida	12,415,119	4,188,647	12,232,102	4,121,108	183,017	67,538
Georgia	8,496,265	2,579,557	7,570,386	2,174,679	925,880	404,878
Hawaii	1,847,752	601,583	1,575,966	458,619	271,786	142,964
Idaho	1,306,760	471,599	1,092,965	386,010	213,794	85,589
Illinois	12,961,076	4,452,819	9,604,390	3,142,088	3,356,686	1,310,731
Indiana	6,805,880	2,804,268	6,263,480	2,564,925	542,399	239,343
Iowa	5,789,532	1,255,477	4,842,637	840,859	946,894	414,618
Kansas	3,498,812	1,251,225	2,748,778	965,265	750,035	285,960
Kentucky	6,113,027	1,380,733	5,541,058	1,148,243	571,969	232,491
Louisiana	4,108,399	1,373,504	3,624,253	1,177,457	484,147	196,047
Maine	869,566	279,479	738,682	216,058	130,885	63,421
Maryland	6,725,079	2,074,529	5,287,563	1,470,866	1,437,516	603,663
Massachusetts	5,246,452	1,775,928	4,334,984	1,397,202	911,468	378,727
Michigan	16,259,165	4,377,216	14,803,153	3,725,153	1,456,011	652,063
Minnesota	5,927,210	1,745,469	4,738,233	1,233,452	1,188,977	512,017
Mississippi	4,623,103	1,166,969	3,675,243	790,117	947,861	376,852
Missouri	5,175,185	1,565,895	4,420,785	1,233,316	754,400	332,578
Montana	1,101,301	328,862	987,966	287,111	113,334	41,750
Nebraska	2,574,085	858,240	2,146,023	666,148	428,062	192,092
Nevada	1,701,829	724,989	1,633,648	696,477	68,181	28,512
New Hampshire	989,727	332,062	842,941	282,053	146,786	50,009
New Jersey	7,979,452	2,641,775	6,680,061	2,123,485	1,299,391	518,289
New Mexico	3,786,755	787,624	3,176,827	536,456	609,928	251,168
New York	18,075,297	6,707,552	14,594,521	4,987,013	3,480,775	1,720,540
North Carolina	11,144,591	3,724,035	8,942,833	2,757,537	2,201,758	966,498
North Dakota	1,194,445	477,978	1,090,829	435,270	103,616	42,708
Ohio	14,314,104	4,162,418	12,875,624	3,530,941	1,438,480	631,477
Oklahoma	4,364,905	1,397,292	3,884,702	1,205,208	480,203	192,084
Oregon	6,949,056	1,639,944	5,723,589	1,149,606	1,225,467	490,338
Pennsylvania	14,340,017	3,937,336	13,147,338	3,423,120	1,192,679	514,216
Rhode Island	792,218	267,875	667,893	204,799	124,325	63,076
South Carolina	4,658,792	1,759,817	3,839,914	1,383,878	818,877	375,940
South Dakota	841,747	298,998	754,648	256,928	87,099	42,070
Tennessee	4,503,298	1,841,308	3,836,474	1,544,052	666,824	297,256
Texas	35,450,170	10,298,201	30,299,084	8,128,711	5,151,087	2,169,490
Utah	6,189,020	1,104,524	5,971,621	1,003,765	217,399	100,759
Vermont	896,401	277,382	862,132	266,738	34,270	10,644
Virginia	10,253,120	3,165,805	9,125,778	2,615,792	1,127,342	550,013
Washington	9,892,889	3,025,334	9,472,192	2,857,194	420,697	168,140
West Virginia	1,889,691	612,504	1,752,931	557,667	136,760	54,837
Wisconsin	6,594,678	2,238,402	5,362,831	1,531,830	1,231,846	706,573
Wyoming	877,311	270,211	579,425	170,152	297,886	100,060
Dist. of Columbia	141,861	41,290	141,861	41,290	0	0
U.S. Service Academies	1,755,387	538,347	1,755,387	538,347	0	0
Other jurisdiction totals	981,678	256,366	885,289	225,040	96,389	31,326
American Samoa	14,337	4,548	14,337	4,548	0	0
Fed. States of Micronesia	20,331	7,089	0	0	20,331	7,089
Guam	127,294	30,927	88,902	19,391	38,392	11,536
Marshall Islands	15,022	2,439	0	0	15,022	2,439
CNMI*	17,443	2,776	17,443	2,776	0	0
Palau	9,621	3,663	0	0	9,621	3,663
Puerto Rico	701,403	189,732	688,381	183,132	13,022	6,600
U.S. Virgin Islands	76,227	15,193	76,227	15,193	0	0

See footnotes at end of table

TABLE 9.15

Total Expenditures of Public Degree-Granting Postsecondary Institutions, by Level of Institution, Purpose of Expenditure, and State or Jurisdiction: 2016-17 (continued)

Source: U.S. Department of Education, National Center for Education Statistics, Integrated Postsecondary Education Data System (IPEDS), Table 334.20, Spring 2018, Finance component. (This table was prepared December 2018.)

* Commonwealth of Northern Mariana Islands

Note: Degree-granting institutions grant associate's or higher degrees and participate in Title IV federal financial aid programs. Includes data for public institutions reporting data according to either the Governmental Accounting Standards Board (GASB) or the Financial Accounting Standards Board (FASB) questionnaire. Data in this table pertain to institutions' fiscal years that end in the academic year noted. Some data have been revised from previously published figures. Detail may not sum to totals because of rounding.

Key:

(a) Includes other categories not separately shown.

TABLE 9.16
Number and Percent of Children under 19 by Health Insurance Coverage and State: 2018 (In thousands)

State or other jurisdiction	Total	Children under 19			
		Insured (any coverage)		Uninsured	
		Number	Percent	Number	Percent
Alabama	1,163	1,122	96.5	41	3.5
Alaska	193	174	90.6	18	9.4
Arizona	1,746	1,599	91.6	146	8.4
Arkansas	747	713	95.5	34	4.5
California	9,514	9,216	96.9	299	3.1
Colorado	1,345	1,283	95.4	62	4.6
Connecticut	789	769	97.4	20	2.6
Delaware	215	207	96.4	8	3.6
Florida	4,488	4,149	92.4	339	7.6
Georgia	2,671	2,453	91.9	217	8.1
Hawaii	319	311	97.4	8	2.6
Idaho	471	442	93.9	29	6.1
Illinois	3,028	2,925	96.6	102	3.4
Indiana	1,660	1,551	93.4	109	6.6
Iowa	781	760	97.3	21	2.7
Kansas	747	709	94.9	38	5.1
Kentucky	1,066	1,026	96.2	40	3.8
Louisiana	1,160	1,121	96.6	39	3.4
Maine	264	250	94.5	15	5.5
Maryland	1,420	1,373	96.7	47	3.3
Massachusetts	1,471	1,453	98.8	18	1.2
Michigan	2,295	2,217	96.6	78	3.4
Minnesota	1,376	1,331	96.7	45	3.3
Mississippi	756	721	95.3	35	4.7
Missouri	1,453	1,371	94.3	83	5.7
Montana	244	229	93.9	15	6.1
Nebraska	501	475	94.8	26	5.2
Nevada	722	664	92	58	8
New Hampshire	280	273	97.4	7	2.6
New Jersey	2,059	1,979	96.1	80	3.9
New Mexico	511	484	94.7	27	5.3
New York	4,306	4,199	97.5	107	2.5
North Carolina	2,446	2,316	94.7	130	5.3
North Dakota	186	175	94	11	6
Ohio	2,748	2,616	95.2	133	4.8
Oklahoma	1,011	928	91.8	83	8.2
Oregon	924	891	96.4	33	3.6
Pennsylvania	2,821	2,697	95.6	124	4.4
Rhode Island	219	215	97.8	5	2.2
South Carolina	1,177	1,122	95.3	56	4.7
South Dakota	225	212	94.1	13	5.9
Tennessee	1,599	1,516	94.8	83	5.2
Texas	7,825	6,953	88.8	873	11.2
Utah	983	911	92.6	72	7.4
Vermont	125	122	98	2	2
Virginia	1,993	1,891	94.9	102	5.1
Washington	1,755	1,708	97.3	47	2.7
West Virginia	388	375	96.6	13	3.4
Wisconsin	1,350	1,299	96.2	51	3.8
Wyoming	142	132	92.9	10	7.1
Dist. of Columbia	137	135	98.2	2	1.8

Sources: U.S. Census Bureau, Health Insurance Coverage in the
United States: 2018, Issued November 2019. U.S. Census Bureau,
1-Year American Community Survey.

TABLE 9.17
Number and Percent of Persons Under 65, by Health Insurance Coverage and State: 2018 (In thousands)

State or other jurisdiction	Total	Insured		Uninsured		Medicaid expansion	Difference in Uninsured: 2018 less 2014	
		Number	Percent	Number	Percent		Number	Percentage pts.
Alabama	3,998	3,519	88	479	12	no	(96)	(2.2)
Alaska	627	537	85.7	89	14.3	9/1/2015	(32)	(4.5)
Arizona	5,818	5,077	87.3	740	12.7	1/1/14	(150)	(3.3)
Arkansas	2,470	2,229	90.2	241	9.8	1/1/14	(101)	(4.1)
California	33,490	30,723	91.7	2,767	9.3	1/1/14	(1,924)	(5.7)
Colorado	4,810	4,395	91.4	415	8.6	1/1/14	(121)	(3.0)
Connecticut	2,932	2,749	93.8	183	6.2	1/1/14	(58)	(1.8)
Delaware	775	722	93.2	53	6.8	1/1/14	(18)	(2.4)
Florida	16,705	14,027	84	2,678	16	no	(513)	(4.1)
Georgia	8,909	7,510	84.3	1,399	15.7	no	(158)	(2.2)
Hawaii	1,111	1,057	95.1	55	4.9	1/1/14	(15)	(1.2)
Idaho	1,459	1,267	86.8	192	13.2	1/1/2020	(25)	(2.5)
Illinois	10,638	9,781	91.9	857	8.1	1/1/14	(362)	(3.0)
Indiana	5,577	5,038	90.3	539	9.7	2/1/2015	(233)	(4.1)
Iowa	2,597	2,451	94.4	146	5.6	1/1/14	(42)	(1.6)
Kansas	2,411	2,163	89.7	248	10.3	no	(41)	(1.5)
Kentucky	3,679	3,433	93.3	245	6.7	1/1/14	(119)	(3.1)
Louisiana	3,857	3,498	90.7	359	9.3	7/1/2016	(308)	(7.7)
Maine*	1,056	950	90	106	10	1/10/2019*	(27)	(2.3)
Maryland	5,035	4,686	93.1	349	6.9	1/1/14	(105)	(2.0)
Massachusetts	5,727	5,542	96.8	185	3.2	1/1/14	(30)	(0.5)
Michigan	8,208	7,679	93.6	529	6.4	4/1/2014	(303)	(3.6)
Minnesota	4,695	4,454	94.9	242	5.1	1/1/14	(72)	(1.7)
Mississippi	2,459	2,106	85.6	353	14.4	no	(69)	(2.4)
Missouri	5,017	4,455	88.8	561	11.2	no	(130)	(2.5)
Montana	852	766	90	85	10	1/1/2016	(58)	(6.9)
Nebraska	1,608	1,451	90.3	157	9.7	10/1/2020**	(22)	(1.5)
Nevada	2,528	2,198	87	330	13	1/1/14	(90)	(4.4)
New Hampshire	1,103	1,026	93.1	76	6.9	8/15/2014	(44)	(3.9)
New Jersey	7,403	6,763	91.3	641	8.7	1/1/14	(308)	(3.9)
New Mexico	1,697	1,505	88.6	193	11.4	1/1/14	(99)	(5.4)
New York	16,186	15,168	93.7	1,018	6.3	1/1/14	(651)	(3.7)
North Carolina	8,535	7,452	87.3	1,083	12.7	no	(184)	(2.5)
North Dakota	634	580	91.6	53	8.4	1/1/14	(4)	(0.6)
Ohio	9,588	8,854	92.3	735	7.7	1/1/14	(210)	(2.1)
Oklahoma	3,261	2,717	83.3	544	16.7	no	(37)	(1.1)
Oregon	2,423	3,134	91.6	289	8.4	1/1/14	(91)	(3.1)
Pennsylvania	10,350	9,659	93.3	691	6.7	1/1/2015	(364)	(3.3)
Rhode Island	866	824	95.2	42	4.8	1/1/14	(34)	(3.9)
South Carolina	4,109	3,588	87.3	520	12.7	no	(118)	(3.3)
South Dakota	725	541	88.4	84	11.6	no	3	0.2
Tennessee	5,591	4,921	88	670	12	no	(102)	(2.1)
Texas	24,729	19,794	80	4,935	20	no	(54)	(1.3)
Utah	2,789	2,497	89.5	292	10.5	no	(72)	(3.3)
Vermont	500	475	95.1	24	4.9	1/1/14	(7)	(1.0)
Virginia	7,009	6,291	89.8	717	10.2	1/1/2019	(154)	(2.3)
Washington	6,284	5,813	92.5	471	7.5	1/1/14	(164)	(3.1)
West Virginia	1,425	1,312	92.1	113	7.9	1/1/14	(43)	(2.5)
Wisconsin	4,779	4,469	93.5	311	6.5	no	(104)	(2.1)
Wyoming	473	414	87.5	59	12.5	no	(9)	(1.2)
Dist. of Columbia	609	588	96.5	21	3.5	1/1/14	(12)	(2.3)

Sources: U.S. Census Bureau, Health Insurance Coverage in the United States: 2018, Issued November 2019. U.S. Census Bureau, 1-Year American Community Survey.

*Gov. Mills signed an executive order on Jan. 3, 2019 directing the Department of Health & Human Services to begin expansion implementation and provide coverage to those eligible retroactive to July 2, 2018. CMS approved the state's plan on April 3, 2019.

**Voters approved a Medicaid expansion ballot measure in Nov. 2018. Due to delays in approval from CMS, the Nebraska Department of Health & Human Services won't be able to implement expansion until Oct. 1, 2020.

Key:
( ) – Parentheses denote a negative number.

Table 9.17 | Adult Health Insurance Coverage, 2018

Highest Rates of Insured Adults, 18–64

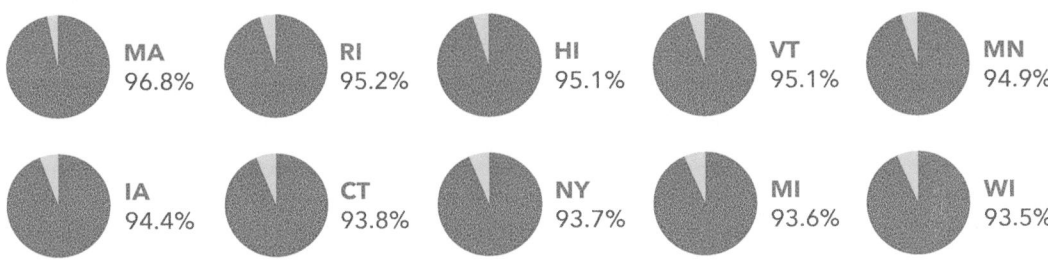

MA 96.8%	RI 95.2%	HI 95.1%	VT 95.1%	MN 94.9%
IA 94.4%	CT 93.8%	NY 93.7%	MI 93.6%	WI 93.5%

Highest Rates of Uninsured Adults, 18–64

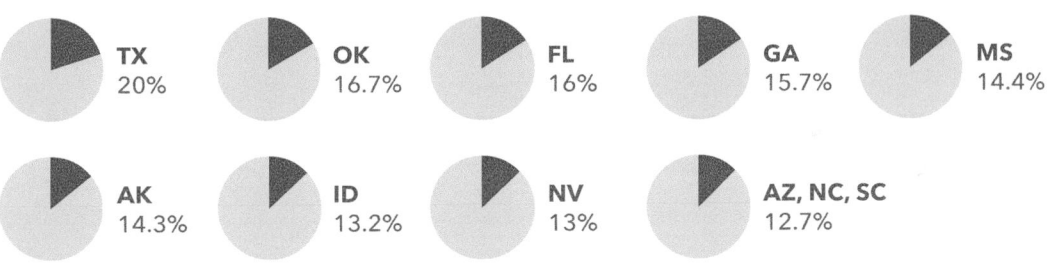

TX 20%	OK 16.7%	FL 16%	GA 15.7%	MS 14.4%
AK 14.3%	ID 13.2%	NV 13%	AZ, NC, SC 12.7%	

Highest Percent Change from 2014–2018

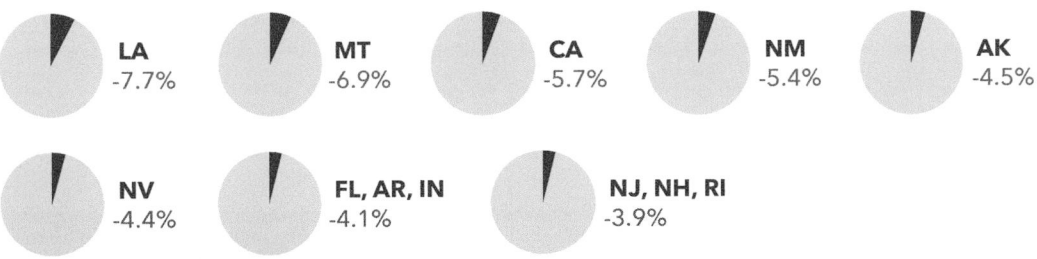

LA -7.7%	MT -6.9%	CA -5.7%	NM -5.4%	AK -4.5%
NV -4.4%	FL, AR, IN -4.1%	NJ, NH, RI -3.9%		

In the 13 states that had not expanded Medicaid as of January 2020, **2.3 MILLION POOR ADULTS FALL INTO A "COVERAGE GAP."**

These adults have incomes above Medicaid eligibility limits in their state but below the lower limit for marketplace premium tax credits, which begin at 100% of poverty. In non-expansion states, the median income eligibility level for parents is 40% of poverty and 0% for childless adults. **People in the coverage gap are concentrated in Southern states, with the largest number of people in the coverage gap in Texas (759,000 people, or 31%) followed by Florida (445,000, or 17%), Georgia (267,000, or 11%), and North Carolina (215,000, or 8%).**

TABLE 9.18
Revenues Used by States for State-Administered Highways: 2018* (In thousands of dollars)

State or other jurisdiction	Beginning balance total (a)	Highway-user revenues (b)				Appropriations from general funds (c)	Other state imposts (d)	Miscellaneous
		Motor-fuel taxes	Motor-vehicle and motor-carrier taxes	Road and crossing tolls	Total			
Total	$117,567,900	$35,739,157	$28,101,396	$14,562,091	$78,402,644	$8,079,823	$12,675,407	$12,882,618
Alabama	360,940	576,560	161,258	0	737,818	74,233	0	404,316
Alaska	0	30,876	35,217	48,397	114,490	283,435	0	195,610
Arizona	1,287,434	590,489	290,363	0	880,852	11,695	837,010	183,986
Arkansas	1,000,857	434,727	179,878	0	614,605	92,106	295,356	163,934
California	51,211,523	5,083,182	6,201,927	379,902	11,665,011	0	731,385	378,439
Colorado	2,150,394	604,043	1,127,747	14,778	1,746,568	582,012	0	53,581
Connecticut	1,234,419	290,223	129,230	222	419,675	39,684	413,365	63,478
Delaware	3,206,134	113,374	165,984	328,780	608,138	99,778	0	652,325
Florida	3,128,365	1,996,332	1,466,221	1,714,332	5,176,885	0	449,461	1,794,044
Georgia	3,674,320	1,529,504	82,122	13,571	1,625,197	474,032	38,797	242,360
Hawaii	350,537	76,562	169,628	0	246,190	0	0	2,454
Idaho	385,232	303,035	206,418	0	509,453	0	43,911	27,750
Illinois	3,524,755	888,307	931,106	1,421,780	3,241,193	791,298	179	137,304
Indiana	0	1,328,812	302,635	0	1,631,447	97,951	22,383	186,260
Iowa	270,685	612,730	1,015,569	0	1,628,299	61,423	15,432	7,937
Kansas	839,891	154,285	72,341	118,620	345,246	0	555,852	22,663
Kentucky	679,648	656,401	649,529	0	1,305,930	15,909	0	256,833
Louisiana	354,066	532,057	136,500	23,789	692,346	0	2,846	37,374
Maine	151,444	199,275	88,849	169,459	457,583	0	0	79,153
Maryland	1,442,734	351,731	432,874	1,232,886	2,017,491	347,054	181,382	29,220
Massachusetts (e)	372,282	171,024	133,350	893,312	1,197,686	0	287,403	124,079
Michigan	1,247,842	1,297,190	1,202,990	40,106	2,540,286	283,084	42,457	178,368
Minnesota	1,817,657	152,584	139,200	0	291,784	538,091	15,725	61,670
Mississippi	268,846	368,562	163,866	0	532,428	0	51,729	6,688
Missouri	797,119	696,623	314,468	0	1,011,091	4,168	421,528	19,448
Montana	(20,828	124,491	122,978	0	247,469	0	11,944	49,811
Nebraska	13,637	360,714	110,230	0	470,944	51,183	357,407	9,540
Nevada	643,183	303,432	251,160	811	555,403	0	76,728	86,095
New Hampshire	248,948	159,996	74,165	129,448	363,609	30,000	0	27,451
New Jersey	5,899,449	337,027	776,986	1,713,268	2,827,281	0	1,166,989	326,995
New Mexico	279,231	219,753	280,389	0	500,142	49,827	15,294	46,806
New York	(1,561,351	1,008,453	1,081,201	2,607,797	4,697,451	1,250,429	477,876	1,931,878
North Carolina	2,547,846	1,799,801	877,771	17,766	2,695,338	0	826,648	212,787
North Dakota	249,134	174,533	102,175	0	276,708	10,066	0	1,397
Ohio	1,660,042	1,744,508	521,239	259,894	2,525,641	468,101	0	216,221
Oklahoma	1,561,420	142,129	228,584	325,903	696,616	0	966,416	92,491
Oregon	3,925,228	476,974	498,401	0	975,375	61,867	12,769	38,348
Pennsylvania	4,471,557	2,624,367	730,505	1,108,495	4,463,367	1,000,771	19,131	376,757
Rhode Island	116,721	79,546	49,119	20,548	149,213	54,101	0	59,475
South Carolina	885,507	601,472	521,479	15,413	1,138,364	50,057	2,889	99,647
South Dakota	119,136	157,708	3,346	0	161,054	0	117,842	41,561
Tennessee	1,647,396	869,921	364,314	43	1,234,278	0	32,589	37,409
Texas	8,701,114	1,260,045	2,436,431	1,189,048	4,885,524	642,476	1,716,177	2,075,064
Utah	816,376	476,316	218,745	2,304	697,365	37,399	591,082	31,853
Vermont	12,957	73,661	129,839	0	203,500	52,914	1,844	23,266
Virginia	2,602,424	682,499	1,011,036	67,867	1,761,402	207,023	1,778,257	786,006
Washington	1,696,638	1,599,299	812,780	608,440	3,020,519	0	884	868,394
West Virginia	114,411	418,170	383,341	95,112	896,623	19,868	2,704	42,028
Wisconsin	1,075,687	913,791	610,278	0	1,524,069	124,702	89,136	66,806
Wyoming	46,303	81,185	63,353	0	144,538	49,382	4,600	25,241
Dist. of Columbia	58,610	10,878	42,281	0	53,159	123,704	0	17

See footnotes at end of table

TABLE 9.18
Revenues Used by States for State-Administered Highways: 2018* (In thousands of dollars) (continued)

State or other jurisdiction	Issue of bonds		Payments from other governments			
			Federal funds			
	For capital outlay	For debt service including refunding	Federal Hwy. Administration	Other agencies	From local government	Total receipts
Total	$14,649,732	$9,188,954	$40,418,236	$1,567,440	$4,729,903	$182,594,757
Alabama	0	0	896,439	13,658	55,189	2,181,653
Alaska	0	0	525,056	3,448	0	1,122,039
Arizona	75,306	0	737,806	18,983	0	2,745,638
Arkansas	0	0	730,830	39,869	12,002	1,948,702
California	428,628	273,011	3,701,418	195,593	720,993	18,094,478
Colorado	193,920	0	695,886	14,089	0	3,286,056
Connecticut	574,887	0	501,344	28,067	6,446	2,046,946
Delaware	330,568	0	174,203	5,256	0	1,870,268
Florida	695,897	706,068	2,360,805	34,912	231,765	11,449,837
Georgia	188,410	376,949	1,480,182	96,623	25,691	4,548,241
Hawaii	0	0	132,486	6,193	0	387,323
Idaho	7,876	101,145	319,612	14,722	3,778	1,028,247
Illinois	349,535	341,342	1,208,323	26,290	1,522	6,096,986
Indiana	212,514	210,650	956,042	12,585	75,930	3,405,762
Iowa	0	0	446,148	95,803	0	2,255,042
Kansas	200,888	0	394,581	9,247	22,379	1,550,856
Kentucky	23,983	151,365	730,798	8,311	0	2,493,129
Louisiana	376,309	377,225	717,440	11,400	34,951	2,249,891
Maine	172,546	0	210,572	6,192	393,365	1,319,411
Maryland	648,965	0	520,621	9,605	0	3,754,338
Massachusetts (e)	1,359,830	803,739	569,767	58,646	0	4,401,150
Michigan	0	0	737,822	16,137	15,510	3,813,664
Minnesota	125,985	102,665	598,563	16,875	1,059,187	2,810,545
Mississippi	0	0	509,734	12,161	56,969	1,169,709
Missouri	0	0	943,244	19,134	27,141	2,445,754
Montana	0	0	418,024	7,334	1,364	735,946
Nebraska	0	0	298,241	10,617	608,306	1,806,238
Nevada	135,730	0	360,434	5,410	22,761	1,242,561
New Hampshire	13,012	0	175,368	35,032	3,802	648,274
New Jersey	76,439	0	877,225	76,388	0	5,351,317
New Mexico	69,325	420,000	379,495	10,609	0	1,491,498
New York	1,946,010	0	1,561,925	46,800	23,460	11,935,829
North Carolina	35,385	374,855	1,125,014	69,420	19,093	5,358,540
North Dakota	0	0	238,714	4,494	30,051	561,430
Ohio	1,259,293	142,950	1,360,476	18,427	81,595	6,072,704
Oklahoma	415,838	0	641,229	13,260	33,377	2,859,227
Oregon	441,601	361,485	486,715	11,912	453,342	2,843,414
Pennsylvania	890,205	2,563,222	1,809,918	52,870	25,458	11,201,699
Rhode Island	1,000	0	199,639	8,232	0	471,660
South Carolina	0	0	943,781	37,192	26,849	2,298,779
South Dakota	0	0	248,994	5,674	6,375	581,500
Tennessee	0	0	842,171	36,635	36,873	2,219,955
Texas	25,777	24,090	3,627,092	124,178	171,494	13,291,872
Utah	341,692	109,500	384,492	60,235	13,999	2,267,617
Vermont	0	0	246,406	13,516	1,632	543,078
Virginia	1,452,088	975,255	1,013,659	20,429	279,593	8,273,712
Washington	285,409	32,090	763,524	28,217	16,056	5,015,093
West Virginia	975,120	44,865	391,299	5,838	1,403	2,379,748
Wisconsin	170,514	696,483	730,541	55,394	130,202	3,587,847
Wyoming	0	0	253,850	31,326	0	508,937
Dist. of Columbia	149,247	0	240,288	4,202	0	570,617

See footnotes at end of table

TABLE 9.18

Revenues Used by States for State-Administered Highways: 2018* (In thousands of dollars) (continued)

Source: U.S. Department of Transportation, Federal Highway Administration, Highway Statistics, 2018, Table SF-1 (January 2020).
Note: This table is compiled from reports of state authorities.
Key:
(a) Any differences between beginning balances and the closing balances on last year's table are the result of accounting adjustments, inclusion of funds not previously reported, etc.
(b) Amounts shown represent only those highway-user revenues that were expended on State or local roads.

(c) Amounts shown represent gross general fund appropriations for highways reduced by the amount of highway-user revenues placed in the State General Fund.
(d) Amounts shown represent data reported for 2017.

TABLE 9.19
State Disbursements for Highways: 2018* (In thousands of dollars)

State or other jurisdiction	Capital outlay			Maintenance and service total			Administration, research and planning	Highway law enforcement and safety
	State administered highways (a)	Local roads and streets	Total	State administered highways (a)	Local roads and streets	Total		
Total	$71,556,904	$6,504,700	$78,061,604	$24,320,544	$996,647	$25,317,191	$9,565,495	$10,103,854
Alabama	792,071	71,389	863,460	15,040	169,452	184,492	222,386	232,987
Alaska	899,986	0	899,986	221,032	0	221,032	100,529	44,633
Arizona	996,308	92,333	1,088,641	155,632	0	155,632	239,668	157,887
Arkansas	1,225,591	0	1,225,591	207,277	92,362	299,639	174,448	114,359
California	1,865,537	136,685	2,002,222	1,511,149	128,392	1,639,541	658,407	2,177,007
Colorado	959,208	150,580	1,109,788	427,225	0	427,225	173,377	10,463
Connecticut	938,453	0	938,453	235,590	0	235,590	84,961	30,410
Delaware	508,042	0	508,042	467,828	0	467,828	307,948	103,950
Florida	5,677,789	179,115	5,856,904	1,156,733	0	1,156,733	358,307	401,934
Georgia	1,629,104	205,914	1,835,018	592,434	9,187	601,621	768,008	294,257
Hawaii	293,475	0	293,475	65,024	0	65,024	18,784	8,160
Idaho	307,131	44,997	352,128	125,471	0	125,471	32,306	38,849
Illinois	3,544,877	96,400	3,641,277	794,463	11,940	806,403	254,738	108,945
Indiana	1,304,272	0	1,304,272	734,500	73,940	808,440	107,030	23,809
Iowa	1,034,361	0	1,034,361	213,488	0	213,488	58,935	127,942
Kansas	448,251	106,257	554,508	137,327	0	137,327	41,127	95,532
Kentucky	1,370,672	270,014	1,640,686	406,144	56,280	462,424	35,539	98,052
Louisiana	1,151,091	5,259	1,156,350	417,038	4,041	421,079	48,351	22,235
Maine	509,858	16,989	526,847	255,905	213,589	469,494	68,040	33,992
Maryland	1,451,730	85,298	1,537,028	405,612	0	405,612	113,189	535,607
Massachusetts (b)	1,756,843	219,660	1,976,503	325,635	1,056	326,691	281,549	172,361
Michigan	1,235,729	1,347,738	2,583,467	328,873	0	328,873	146,389	336,698
Minnesota	1,056,937	0	1,056,937	484,409	0	484,409	146,065	165,986
Mississippi	860,884	127,081	987,965	80,804	0	80,804	63,310	37,290
Missouri	758,828	147,789	906,617	494,387	0	494,387	73,815	257,624
Montana	401,266	0	401,266	123,349	0	123,349	59,945	70,138
Nebraska	545,976	312,458	858,434	199,848	134,384	334,232	111,138	78,778
Nevada	732,140	0	732,140	150,277	0	150,277	182,989	104,675
New Hampshire	260,665	0	260,665	164,293	0	164,293	63,021	12,214
New Jersey	2,301,582	7,092	2,308,674	736,431	0	736,431	180,258	416,631
New Mexico	381,462	0	381,462	99,036	0	99,036	274,027	15,765
New York	4,018,762	806,913	4,825,675	1,623,208	0	1,623,208	492,213	515,001
North Carolina	3,069,561	0	3,069,561	1,113,309	0	1,113,309	315,593	179,924
North Dakota	613,462	33,702	647,164	28,805	0	28,805	25,736	27,158
Ohio	2,406,441	393,060	2,799,501	464,757	0	464,757	94,689	352,648
Oklahoma	1,593,750	163,319	1,757,069	520,937	0	520,937	269,888	208,060
Oregon	924,356	97,812	1,022,168	291,763	13,609	305,372	161,290	77,880
Pennsylvania	3,356,765	214,739	3,571,504	1,730,214	0	1,730,214	551,539	812,385
Rhode Island	187,377	5,741	193,118	114,471	0	114,471	61,498	40,436
South Carolina	1,071,722	0	1,071,722	305,668	77,782	383,450	132,998	7,023
South Dakota	263,593	94,815	358,408	79,204	0	79,204	64,837	38,689
Tennessee	989,681	81,390	1,071,071	284,867	0	284,867	249,090	40,343
Texas	8,716,364	280,484	8,996,848	2,080,156	0	2,080,156	435,356	696,322
Utah	563,953	0	563,953	476,509	0	476,509	85,631	87,873
Vermont	180,091	73,272	253,363	116,821	77	116,898	74,526	74,168
Virginia	1,887,760	0	1,887,760	1,691,858	0	1,691,858	438,033	214,226
Washington	2,095,538	172,585	2,268,123	946,354	0	946,354	302,445	240,879
West Virginia	817,454	0	817,454	320,752	0	320,752	70,028	46,189
Wisconsin	1,279,547	124,784	1,404,331	261,666	0	261,666	219,234	73,729
Wyoming	320,608	0	320,608	99,851	0	99,851	43,955	41,751
Dist. of Columbia	0	339,036	339,036	37,120	10,556	47,676	28,332	0

See footnotes at end of table

TABLE 9.19
State Disbursements for Highways: 2018* (In thousands of dollars) (continued)

State or other jurisdiction	Interest	Bond retirement		Grants-in-aid to local governments	Total disbursements	Balances end of year		
		Current revenues or sinking funds	Refunding bonds			Reserves for current highway work	Reserves for debt service	Total
Total	$8,716,268	$8,745,104	$11,606,835	$16,549,324	$168,665,675	$118,373,123	$858,275	$119,231,398
Alabama	6,370	53,198	171,438	229,038	1,963,369	360,940	0	360,940
Alaska	4,769	5,346	0	778	1,277,073	0	0	0
Arizona	183,843	154,120	425,095	752,707	3,157,593	1,183,994	0	1,183,994
Arkansas	41,380	45,730	0	0	1,901,147	1,005,456	0	1,005,456
California	457,342	65,258	0	4,001,215	11,000,992	50,589,895	0	50,589,895
Colorado	28,741	4,741	0	327,003	2,081,338	1,870,781	0	1,870,781
Connecticut	244,753	270,550	75,565	95,076	1,975,358	1,036,899	0	1,036,899
Delaware	96,208	151,564	81,518	0	1,717,058	3,126,004	80,130	3,206,134
Florida	568,886	575,523	1,037,328	434,190	10,389,805	2,930,664	199,831	3,130,495
Georgia	130,349	601,773	324,875	240,346	4,796,247	3,450,989	145,355	3,596,344
Hawaii	111,590	54,085	111,590	39,167	701,875	410,893	0	410,893
Idaho	27,659	30,320	0	183,180	789,913	384,839	0	384,839
Illinois	311,652	379,363	355,541	492,172	6,350,091	3,083,616	314,147	3,397,763
Indiana	45,644	61,675	589,660	419,584	3,360,114	30,821	0	30,821
Iowa	0	0	0	906,157	2,340,883	270,685	0	270,685
Kansas	132,186	84,585	0	154,501	1,199,766	814,166	25,725	839,891
Kentucky	156,606	131,675	0	0	2,524,982	679,648	0	679,648
Louisiana	140,587	114,478	200,000	74,152	2,177,232	331,655	0	331,655
Maine	19,841	40,845	0	0	1,159,059	142,939	0	142,939
Maryland	231,422	421,545	253,040	175,102	3,672,545	1,497,523	5,769	1,503,292
Massachusetts (b)	266,701	193,733	803,739	342,985	4,364,262	409,170	0	409,170
Michigan	81,672	148,525	0	33,000	3,658,624	1,247,842	0	1,247,842
Minnesota	108,061	167,207	0	942,399	3,071,064	1,815,786	0	1,815,786
Mississippi	47,494	44,657	0	103,201	1,364,721	268,846	0	268,846
Missouri	103,928	308,595	0	277,104	2,422,070	760,672	0	760,672
Montana	3,016	12,400	0	27,680	697,794	4,112	0	4,112
Nebraska	0	0	0	338,764	1,721,346	70,723	554	71,277
Nevada	31,349	48,595	0	0	1,250,025	617,790	0	617,790
New Hampshire	31,257	48,000	2,564	59,802	641,816	240,914	0	240,914
New Jersey	1,466,708	768,430	2,525,615	142,116	8,544,863	5,465,593	0	5,465,593
New Mexico	64,898	93,655	0	26,682	955,525	259,821	0	259,821
New York	804,453	1,033,247	0	441,582	9,735,379	1,447,893	0	1,447,893
North Carolina	136,374	131,351	240,600	147,181	5,333,893	2,547,846	0	2,547,846
North Dakota	942	4,375	0	103,694	837,874	249,134	0	249,134
Ohio	105,617	241,940	137,208	1,146,398	5,342,758	1,557,047	0	1,557,047
Oklahoma	70,300	191,815	0	0	3,018,069	1,561,420	0	1,561,420
Oregon	107,845	77,840	361,485	457,206	2,571,086	4,197,556	0	4,197,556
Pennsylvania	628,442	216,651	2,173,214	406,824	10,090,773	4,384,793	86,764	4,471,557
Rhode Island	20,251	21,559	19,685	1,504	472,522	116,721	0	116,721
South Carolina	11,034	49,800	0	53,425	1,709,452	885,507	0	885,507
South Dakota	0	0	0	0	541,138	119,136	0	119,136
Tennessee	0	0	0	313,537	1,958,908	1,647,396	0	1,647,396
Texas	1,241,771	463,468	984,005	473,996	15,371,922	8,671,165	0	8,671,165
Utah	69,313	256,150	0	32,013	1,571,442	824,750	0	824,750
Vermont	2,501	3,096	0	27,453	552,005	(12,913	0	(12,913
Virginia	176,757	263,895	54,915	963,946	5,691,390	2,602,424	0	2,602,424
Washington	510	386,248	323,405	691,000	5,158,964	1,912,282	0	1,912,282
West Virginia	9,911	24,611	0	6,394	1,295,339	116,690	0	116,690
Wisconsin	185,335	259,823	202,305	465,070	3,071,493	1,075,687	0	1,075,687
Wyoming	0	0	0	0	506,165	46,303	0	46,303
Dist. of Columbia	0	39,064	152,445	0	606,553	58,610	0	58,610

Source: U.S. Department of Transportation, Federal Highway Administration, Highway Statistics, 2018, Table SF-2 (January 2020).

Notes: This table is compiled from reports of State authorities.

Key:
(a) Includes expenditures for local roads and streets under State control. Most local roads are under State control in Delaware, North Carolina, Virginia, and West Virginia.
(b) Amounts shown represent data reported for 2017.

TABLE 9.20
Public Road Length Miles by Ownership: 2018

State or other jurisdiction	State highway agency	County	Rural Town, township, municipal (a)	Other jurisdiction (b)	Federal agency (c)	Total
Grand Total	612,315	1,551,117	564,085	68,524	158,631	2,954,672
U.S. Total	611,531	1,551,117	561,695	68,524	158,614	2,951,481
Alabama	8,328	55,249	7,441	150	755	71,923
Alaska	4,949	3,504	1,373	2,347	1,563	13,735
Arizona	5,529	13,577	2,453	4,067	14,775	40,400
Arkansas	14,113	50,465	5,406	12,342	3,040	85,367
California	10,259	52,264	999	783	6,971	71,275
Colorado	7,532	51,215	2,181	837	6,394	68,160
Connecticut	1,170	0	4,234	266	21	5,691
Delaware	2,671	0	51	41	72	2,835
Florida	5,647	26,383	2,733	81	1,736	36,580
Georgia	12,620	58,163	4,198	87	1,081	76,149
Hawaii	483	1,002	0	47	113	1,645
Idaho	4,582	18,970	1,507	12,464	12,435	49,959
Illinois	10,418	13,841	71,321	423	216	96,219
Indiana	8,758	54,230	2,837	298	513	66,636
Iowa	7,836	88,122	5,506	441	113	102,018
Kansas	9,480	112,027	5,233	173	903	127,815
Kentucky	24,544	37,303	1,885	487	807	65,027
Louisiana	12,961	27,967	2,209	15	649	43,801
Maine	7,332	376	11,510	224	156	19,599
Maryland	2,664	9,641	393	107	755	13,561
Massachusetts	567	0	5,353	250	21	6,190
Michigan	6,853	72,800	2,842	2	1,672	84,169
Minnesota	10,173	43,413	59,867	1,884	1,929	117,266
Mississippi	9,521	50,832	3,189	79	792	64,413
Missouri	30,753	69,970	5,569	119	1,186	107,598
Montana	10,508	42,500	1,181	4,244	10,890	69,322
Nebraska	9,457	60,423	17,077	123	160	87,239
Nevada	4,650	23,969	315	220	9,017	38,170
New Hampshire	3,186	0	7,753	18	148	11,105
New Jersey	357	1,592	3,066	255	176	5,447
New Mexico	10,959	24,846	7,553	7,406	15,663	66,428
New York	9,630	15,535	37,706	638	378	63,886
North Carolina	59,464	0	2,379	1,071	2,958	65,872
North Dakota	7,151	15,467	60,873	70	1,590	85,152
Ohio	13,571	25,060	35,734	989	166	75,519
Oklahoma	10,844	77,341	7,872	1,045	141	97,243
Oregon	6,386	28,984	1,283	1,416	25,986	64,055
Pennsylvania	28,137	28	41,981	1,434	741	72,320
Rhode Island	374	0	939	17	28	1,359
South Carolina	29,770	22,976	711	82	1,589	55,129
South Dakota	7,494	34,782	32,821	1,523	2,469	79,089
Tennessee	10,043	49,041	3,617	411	1,185	64,298
Texas	64,843	127,977	10,772	14	2,063	205,668
Utah	4,698	23,239	2,213	394	6,998	37,543
Vermont	2,370	0	10,225	0	156	12,751
Virginia	46,121	62	446	20	2,105	48,754
Washington	5,512	32,827	1,401	8,387	8,268	56,394
West Virginia	30,426	0	606	240	919	32,191
Wisconsin	9,587	19,082	62,184	0	848	91,701
Wyoming	6,252	14,074	694	491	5,303	26,814
Dist. of Columbia	0	0	0	0	0	0
Puerto Rico (d)	784	0	2,391	0	17	3,191

See footnotes at end of table

TABLE 9.20
Public Road Length Miles by Ownership: 2018 (continued)

State or other jurisdiction	State highway agency	County	Urban Town, township, municipal (a)	Other jurisdiction (b)	Federal agency (c)	Total	Total rural and urban
Grand Total	172,678	250,586	801,152	8,348	7,837	1,240,601	4,195,274
U.S. Total	170,055	250,586	788,614	8,348	7,830	1,225,433	4,176,915
Alabama	2,607	4,723	21,165	1	543	29,039	100,962
Alaska	684	1,725	346	473	87	3,315	17,050
Arizona	1,255	4,318	20,166	381	260	26,381	66,782
Arkansas	2,354	2,896	10,902	995	108	17,255	102,622
California	4,833	19,387	79,163	122	810	104,315	175,589
Colorado	1,502	4,768	14,473	20	53	20,815	88,975
Connecticut	2,549	0	13,185	74	57	15,865	21,556
Delaware	2,759	0	780	37	50	3,626	6,461
Florida	6,457	43,989	35,606	8	460	86,519	123,099
Georgia	5,326	28,192	16,960	27	1,743	52,248	128,397
Hawaii	463	2,328	0	22	17	2,831	4,475
Idaho	400	368	4,939	663	18	6,388	56,347
Illinois	5,482	2,635	41,195	416	28	49,756	145,976
Indiana	2,377	10,848	16,958	74	70	30,326	96,962
Iowa	1,056	1,601	9,857	186	26	12,727	114,745
Kansas	808	2,197	11,311	65	3	14,385	142,200
Kentucky	3,127	2,881	8,898	87	160	15,153	80,180
Louisiana	3,721	4,753	9,124	10	7	17,615	61,416
Maine	1,018	0	2,130	65	4	3,216	22,815
Maryland	2,500	11,941	3,974	183	110	18,708	32,269
Massachusetts	2,439	0	27,649	403	82	30,573	36,763
Michigan	2,823	16,797	18,360	16	0	37,996	122,164
Minnesota	1,560	2,904	17,814	45	2	22,325	139,591
Mississippi	1,401	2,804	8,786	14	60	13,064	77,477
Missouri	3,085	3,580	17,737	34	59	24,496	132,094
Montana	515	0	3,736	0	0	4,251	73,573
Nebraska	487	818	6,638	8	71	8,022	95,262
Nevada	755	4,745	4,694	39	54	10,288	48,458
New Hampshire	717	0	4,259	89	0	5,065	16,171
New Jersey	1,977	5,114	25,688	560	134	33,473	38,919
New Mexico	995	1,670	7,904	577	32	11,177	77,605
New York	5,450	4,645	38,427	817	308	49,646	113,533
North Carolina	20,548	0	20,730	22	177	41,477	107,348
North Dakota	242	82	2,574	0	0	2,898	88,050
Ohio	5,679	4,054	37,530	147	86	47,495	123,014
Oklahoma	1,405	2,875	14,424	118	0	18,822	116,065
Oregon	1,222	3,843	10,011	102	33	15,211	79,266
Pennsylvania	11,593	381	35,731	489	75	48,270	120,590
Rhode Island	727	0	3,781	83	63	4,654	6,013
South Carolina	11,526	7,315	4,020	0	3	22,863	77,992
South Dakota	259	275	2,621	248	11	3,413	82,501
Tennessee	3,877	8,503	19,397	21	21	31,818	96,116
Texas	15,613	19,840	72,535	392	599	108,979	314,648
Utah	1,186	445	9,713	0	26	11,370	48,913
Vermont	259	0	1,237	0	7	1,502	14,253
Virginia	12,899	1,684	11,306	28	697	26,614	75,369
Washington	1,539	6,406	15,779	101	433	24,258	80,653
West Virginia	3,982	0	2,635	42	0	6,659	38,850
Wisconsin	2,155	1,684	19,990	0	78	23,907	115,609
Wyoming	493	573	1,775	5	5	2,851	29,666
Dist. of Columbia	1,374	0	0	38	102	1,514	1,514
Puerto Rico (d)	2,623	0	12,537	0	7	15,168	18,359

Source: U.S. Department of Transportation, Federal Highway Administration, Highway Statistics, 2018, Table HM-10 (August 30, 2019).

Note: Detail may not add to totals due to rounding. This table was compiled from reports of state authorities.

(a) Prior to 1999, municipal was included with other jurisdictions.

(b) Includes State park, State toll, other State agency, other local agency and other roadways not identified by ownership.

(c) Roadways in Federal parks, forests, and reservations that are not part of the State and local highway systems.

(d) Excludes 788 miles of Federal agency owned roads.

TABLE 9.21
Federal-Aid Highway Travel: 2018* Annual Vehicle Miles (In millions of miles)

| State or other jurisdiction | National highway system | | | | | | | | |
| | Interstate | | | Other | | | Total | | |
	Rural	Urban	Total	Rural	Urban	Total	Rural	Urban	Total
Grand Total	257,690	576,113	833,803	230,865	714,007	944,873	488,555	1,290,121	1,778,676
U.S. Total	257,240	571,415	828,655	230,669	710,045	940,714	487,909	1,281,460	1,769,369
Alabama	6,556	9,278	15,835	5,539	9,755	15,294	12,095	19,034	31,129
Alaska	827	753	1,580	350	982	1,332	1,177	1,735	2,912
Arizona	6,751	7,888	14,638	3,644	14,460	18,103	10,395	22,347	32,742
Arkansas	4,265	5,521	9,786	4,027	4,286	8,314	8,293	9,807	18,100
California	16,224	75,786	92,010	15,317	116,003	131,320	31,542	191,788	223,330
Colorado	4,846	9,812	14,658	4,644	15,041	19,685	9,489	24,854	34,343
Connecticut	487	9,902	10,390	739	8,014	8,753	1,226	17,916	19,142
Delaware	·	1,490	1,490	1,059	3,103	4,161	1,059	4,592	5,651
Florida	10,981	30,592	41,573	10,673	60,391	71,064	21,654	90,983	112,637
Georgia	7,734	24,292	32,025	7,063	21,199	28,262	14,797	45,491	60,287
Hawaii	·	2,080	2,080	351	2,595	2,946	351	4,675	5,026
Idaho	2,774	1,705	4,480	2,455	2,108	4,563	5,229	3,813	9,043
Illinois	9,504	25,199	34,703	4,027	21,838	25,865	13,531	47,037	60,568
Indiana	7,839	10,941	18,779	5,462	5,164	10,626	13,301	16,105	29,405
Iowa	5,167	3,150	8,318	6,211	4,103	10,314	11,379	7,253	18,632
Kansas	3,761	4,189	7,950	4,528	3,250	7,777	8,289	7,439	15,727
Kentucky	8,409	6,788	15,198	5,057	5,553	10,609	13,466	12,341	25,807
Louisiana	6,436	10,148	16,584	3,406	8,975	12,381	9,842	19,123	28,965
Maine	2,143	1,258	3,401	1,879	899	2,778	4,022	2,157	6,179
Maryland	2,190	15,738	17,928	2,481	17,320	19,801	4,671	33,058	37,729
Massachusetts (a)	864	17,402	18,266	865	20,259	21,124	1,729	37,661	39,390
Michigan	5,765	17,885	23,650	7,038	24,501	31,538	12,802	42,386	55,188
Minnesota	4,029	9,120	13,149	7,283	9,077	16,360	11,312	18,197	29,509
Mississippi	4,638	4,227	8,864	5,379	5,681	11,060	10,017	9,908	19,925
Missouri	7,059	14,342	21,402	8,269	11,043	19,312	15,328	25,386	40,714
Montana	2,629	635	3,264	2,590	1,112	3,702	5,219	1,748	6,966
Nebraska	2,978	1,673	4,651	3,418	3,312	6,731	6,396	4,985	11,381
Nevada	2,457	4,662	7,119	1,718	5,152	6,870	4,175	9,814	13,990
New Hampshire	1,087	2,025	3,112	1,426	2,855	4,281	2,513	4,881	7,393
New Jersey	1,225	15,444	16,669	1,160	29,485	30,645	2,385	44,929	47,314
New Mexico	4,566	2,793	7,359	3,107	2,327	5,434	7,673	5,120	12,793
New York	6,109	21,425	27,533	4,724	37,433	42,158	10,833	58,858	69,691
North Carolina	6,845	20,295	27,140	9,646	20,180	29,827	16,492	40,475	56,967
North Dakota	1,674	558	2,231	2,170	890	3,060	3,844	1,447	5,291
Ohio (a)	8,996	25,497	34,492	6,553	15,987	22,541	15,549	41,484	57,033
Oklahoma	5,443	5,734	11,177	5,508	5,513	11,021	10,951	11,247	22,199
Oregon	4,069	5,774	9,843	4,274	7,083	11,357	8,343	12,857	21,199
Pennsylvania	10,929	16,140	27,070	6,093	23,895	29,988	17,023	40,035	57,058
Rhode Island	319	1,914	2,233	289	3,132	3,422	608	5,047	5,655
South Carolina	8,367	7,797	16,164	4,759	9,425	14,185	13,127	17,222	30,349
South Dakota	2,094	777	2,872	1,973	587	2,560	4,067	1,364	5,432
Tennessee	8,436	15,578	24,013	4,797	15,906	20,702	13,233	31,483	44,716
Texas	19,407	51,843	71,251	22,606	73,484	96,091	42,014	125,328	167,341
Utah	3,437	8,286	11,723	2,046	5,999	8,046	5,483	14,285	19,769
Vermont	1,246	579	1,825	705	405	1,110	1,951	984	2,935
Virginia	9,347	17,110	26,457	7,074	18,249	25,323	16,421	35,359	51,781
Washington	4,974	12,453	17,427	4,267	15,951	20,218	9,241	28,404	37,645
West Virginia	2,496	3,591	6,087	2,207	2,372	4,579	4,703	5,963	10,666
Wisconsin	6,223	8,296	14,519	8,198	11,609	19,807	14,421	19,905	34,326
Wyoming	2,637	546	3,183	1,613	669	2,282	4,250	1,215	5,465
Dist. of Columbia	0	502	502	0	1,432	1,432	0	1,934	1,934
Puerto Rico	450	4,698	5,148	197	3,962	4,159	647	8,660	9,307

See footnotes at end of table

TABLE 9.21
Federal-Aid Highway Travel: 2018* Annual Vehicle Miles (In millions of miles) (continued)

State or other jurisdiction	Other federal-aid highways			All federal-aid highways			All non-federal highways			
	Rural	Urban	Total	Rural	Urban	Total	Rural	Urban	Total	Total
Grand Total	313,857	679,228	993,085	802,412	1,969,349	2,771,761	177,466	306,119	483,586	3,255,347
U.S. Totals	313,427	673,959	987,386	801,336	1,955,420	2,756,755	177,466	306,105	483,571	3,240,327
Alabama	8,966	12,122	21,089	21,062	31,156	52,218	7,727	11,223	18,949	71,167
Alaska	394	838	1,232	1,571	2,573	4,144	705	638	1,343	5,487
Arizona	4,035	20,931	24,966	14,430	43,278	57,708	1,913	6,523	8,437	66,145
Arkansas	6,528	6,991	13,519	14,820	16,798	31,618	2,967	2,090	5,057	36,675
California	18,087	75,402	93,489	49,628	267,190	316,819	8,804	23,173	31,977	348,796
Colorado	4,021	9,400	13,421	13,510	34,254	47,764	2,384	3,805	6,190	53,954
Connecticut	1,229	8,007	9,236	2,455	25,924	28,378	704	2,513	3,217	31,596
Delaware	817	2,080	2,896	1,875	6,672	8,548	594	1,038	1,632	10,179
Florida	7,927	54,608	62,536	29,581	145,591	175,172	7,161	39,482	46,643	221,816
Georgia	13,095	29,046	42,141	27,892	74,536	102,428	4,957	24,071	29,027	131,456
Hawaii	719	2,141	2,859	1,069	6,816	7,885	776	2,226	3,001	10,887
Idaho	2,545	2,747	5,293	7,774	6,561	14,335	2,406	968	3,374	17,709
Illinois	8,322	23,735	32,057	21,853	70,771	92,624	3,799	11,531	15,330	107,954
Indiana	9,189	21,112	30,302	22,490	37,217	59,707	7,201	14,620	21,821	81,529
Iowa	6,096	4,439	10,536	17,475	11,693	29,168	2,242	1,873	4,114	33,282
Kansas	5,005	6,834	11,839	13,294	14,273	27,566	2,051	2,573	4,624	32,190
Kentucky	7,798	8,157	15,955	21,264	20,497	41,762	5,351	2,431	7,782	49,544
Louisiana	6,388	9,778	16,166	16,230	28,901	45,131	3,304	1,610	4,914	50,045
Maine	3,918	1,989	5,907	7,940	4,146	12,086	2,239	459	2,698	14,784
Maryland	3,406	12,848	16,254	8,077	45,906	53,983	2,571	3,221	5,792	59,775
Massachusetts	679	17,985	18,664	2,408	55,646	58,054	661	8,057	8,718	66,772
Michigan	15,227	21,209	36,436	28,030	63,595	91,624	3,174	7,599	10,773	102,398
Minnesota	9,270	12,906	22,176	20,582	31,103	51,685	4,090	4,663	8,753	60,438
Mississippi	7,474	4,332	11,806	17,491	14,240	31,730	6,342	2,658	9,000	40,730
Missouri	8,817	10,272	19,089	24,145	35,658	59,803	9,021	7,771	16,792	76,595
Montana	1,955	1,245	3,200	7,174	2,993	10,166	1,581	953	2,533	12,700
Nebraska	3,791	3,103	6,894	10,187	8,088	18,276	1,429	1,270	2,699	20,975
Nevada	802	7,146	7,948	4,977	16,961	21,938	724	5,657	6,381	28,319
New Hampshire	2,073	2,584	4,657	4,585	7,464	12,050	899	828	1,727	13,776
New Jersey	1,473	16,235	17,708	3,858	61,164	65,022	1,010	11,507	12,517	77,539
New Mexico	3,627	5,049	8,677	11,301	10,170	21,470	4,879	939	5,818	27,288
New York	7,244	24,638	31,882	18,077	83,496	101,573	7,226	14,711	21,937	123,510
North Carolina	12,753	24,060	36,813	29,245	64,535	93,780	11,921	15,427	27,348	121,127
North Dakota	1,911	994	2,905	5,755	2,441	8,196	1,127	532	1,659	9,856
Ohio	12,064	28,255	40,319	27,613	69,739	97,352	7,024	10,098	17,123	114,474
Oklahoma	8,535	9,973	18,508	19,486	21,221	40,707	2,610	2,116	4,726	45,433
Oregon	3,725	7,434	11,160	12,068	20,291	32,359	2,521	1,968	4,489	36,848
Pennsylvania	10,150	19,961	30,111	27,173	59,996	87,169	7,145	7,795	14,940	102,109
Rhode Island	259	1,660	1,919	867	6,707	7,574	47	388	435	8,009
South Carolina	9,203	11,453	20,656	22,330	28,675	51,005	3,266	2,530	5,795	56,801
South Dakota	2,110	1,287	3,396	6,177	2,651	8,828	609	283	892	9,719
Tennessee	7,356	14,210	21,566	20,589	45,693	66,282	5,303	9,736	15,040	81,321
Texas	27,674	66,721	94,395	69,688	192,049	261,737	7,059	13,242	20,301	282,037
Utah	1,864	5,175	7,039	7,347	19,460	26,807	1,569	3,693	5,262	32,069
Vermont	2,138	844	2,982	4,089	1,828	5,918	1,128	301	1,429	7,346
Virginia	8,949	15,724	24,672	25,370	51,083	76,453	3,639	5,244	8,883	85,336
Washington	5,880	11,596	17,477	15,121	40,000	55,121	2,305	4,940	7,245	62,367
West Virginia	3,867	2,899	6,765	8,570	8,862	17,432	1,298	717	2,015	19,447
Wisconsin	12,844	9,633	22,477	27,265	29,538	56,803	6,092	2,990	9,083	65,885
Wyoming	1,227	1,188	2,415	5,477	2,403	7,879	1,910	649	2,559	10,438
Dist. of Col.	0	982	982	0	2,916	2,916	0	774	774	3,691
Puerto Rico	430	5,269	5,699	1,077	13,929	15,006	0	14	14	15,020

Source: U.S. Department of Transportation, Federal Highway Administration, Highway Statistics, 2018, Table VM-3 (August 2019).

Notes: Travel for the rural minor collector and rural/urban local functional systems is estimated by the States based on a model or other means and provided to the FHWA on a summary basis. Travel for all other systems are estimated from State-provided data in the Highway Performance Monitoring System.

Key:
(a) The State updated their travel procedures in 2018.

TABLE 9.22
Licensed Drivers, By State, 2010-2018*

State or other jurisdiction	2010	2011	2012	2013	2014
U.S. Totals	209,729,999	211,479,207	211,413,837	211,754,173	213,672,576
Alabama	3,805,751	3,798,552	3,827,522	3,859,403	3,881,542
Alaska	515,239	521,280	526,371	528,873	531,744
Arizona	4,443,647	4,592,398	4,697,579	4,791,450	4,881,801
Arkansas	2,077,806	1,956,091	2,199,164	2,097,201	2,111,873
California	23,753,441	23,856,600	24,200,997	24,390,236	24,813,346
Colorado	3,779,273	3,669,816	3,807,673	3,837,488	3,883,362
Connecticut	2,934,576	2,986,267	2,485,708	2,534,090	2,542,588
Delaware	695,036	716,109	720,290	723,657	732,349
Florida	13,949,726	13,882,423	13,896,581	13,670,441	13,898,347
Georgia	6,507,888	6,505,690	6,581,534	6,607,016	6,650,434
Hawaii	909,407	911,660	915,033	915,033	902,639
Idaho	1,069,542	1,083,992	1,092,977	1,111,485	1,128,497
Illinois	8,373,969	8,373,969	8,235,745	8,261,582	8,373,565
Indiana	5,550,469	6,569,665	5,375,973	4,500,403	4,448,099
Iowa	2,166,759	2,191,715	2,217,304	2,143,665	2,227,950
Kansas	2,033,092	2,025,581	2,018,029	2,017,759	2,021,271
Kentucky	2,950,191	2,959,881	2,985,234	3,019,283	3,004,919
Louisiana	3,133,631	3,186,227	2,923,744	3,278,143	3,312,630
Maine	1,019,738	1,014,826	1,008,190	1,011,385	1,018,918
Maryland	3,918,305	3,856,604	4,102,154	4,140,105	4,142,997
Massachusetts	4,592,500	4,683,323	4,733,936	4,765,586	4,765,586
Michigan	7,083,107	7,059,509	7,018,713	6,986,587	7,046,433
Minnesota	3,281,463	3,306,139	3,321,760	3,330,725	3,357,468
Mississippi	1,928,487	1,926,603	1,957,980	1,968,907	1,977,679
Missouri	4,246,249	4,277,037	4,288,488	4,280,438	4,295,224
Montana	743,611	752,483	757,812	766,716	768,703
Nebraska	1,351,516	1,356,377	1,363,596	1,374,529	1,383,693
Nevada	1,691,318	1,700,629	1,728,060	1,756,095	1,796,443
New Hampshire	1,037,083	1,056,889	1,064,604	1,061,433	1,071,963
New Jersey	5,952,583	5,977,458	6,039,623	6,081,386	6,152,634
New Mexico	1,405,926	1,418,641	1,430,475	1,456,500	1,444,857
New York	11,285,830	11,210,783	11,248,617	11,210,783	11,318,198
North Carolina	6,536,601	6,569,341	6,677,693	6,822,902	7,025,333
North Dakota	483,097	490,146	502,807	513,838	527,541
Ohio	7,963,372	7,982,149	8,006,183	8,030,421	7,915,907
Oklahoma	2,348,718	2,370,643	2,400,358	2,418,307	2,451,972
Oregon	2,769,734	2,773,956	2,769,757	2,773,373	2,785,446
Pennsylvania	8,737,162	8,796,774	8,842,587	8,896,590	8,915,641
Rhode Island	747,875	749,706	749,706	749,232	748,337
South Carolina	3,337,247	3,408,318	3,455,931	3,536,404	3,617,535
South Dakota	602,275	603,258	606,779	603,643	609,908
Tennessee	4,418,210	4,543,759	4,573,871	4,605,100	4,613,166
Texas	15,157,650	15,122,518	15,252,192	15,447,273	15,648,733
Utah	1,659,835	1,747,487	1,788,822	1,661,219	1,425,703
Vermont	513,481	521,666	529,501	543,057	545,312
Virginia	5,402,347	5,467,045	5,538,480	5,602,765	5,769,063
Washington	5,106,367	5,178,789	5,227,889	5,301,630	5,401,139
West Virginia	1,206,026	1,198,837	1,241,586	1,177,136	1,171,907
Wisconsin	4,133,377	4,147,470	4,056,649	4,171,427	4,188,194
Wyoming	419,466	421,928	421,580	421,473	423,987
Dist. of Col.	384,940	395,442	400,993	405,555	419,896

See footnotes at end of table

TABLE 9.22
Licensed Drivers, By State, 2010-2018* (continued)

State or other jurisdiction	2015	2016	2017	2018
U.S. Totals	217,628,863	221,222,087	224,825,201	227,021,164
Alabama	3,907,038	3,943,082	3,954,378	3,999,057
Alaska	533,227	534,585	534,585	536,033
Arizona	4,978,762	5,082,305	5,164,966	5,284,970
Arkansas	2,119,578	2,391,103	2,417,464	2,145,334
California	25,532,920	26,199,436	26,777,132	27,039,400
Colorado	3,974,521	4,066,580	4,156,138	4,244,713
Connecticut	2,566,673	2,611,007	2,586,994	2,605,612
Delaware	742,524	756,328	770,512	786,504
Florida	14,262,715	14,675,160	15,076,358	15,368,695
Georgia	6,906,191	6,975,900	7,060,344	7,168,733
Hawaii	909,797	931,703	951,008	948,417
Idaho	1,135,009	1,160,922	1,190,367	1,252,535
Illinois	8,462,193	8,514,644	8,529,404	8,714,788
Indiana	4,467,848	4,553,259	4,553,584	4,589,405
Iowa	2,224,130	2,245,640	2,246,829	2,260,271
Kansas	2,028,657	2,030,025	2,029,869	2,149,430
Kentucky	3,021,266	3,031,447	3,019,008	3,032,530
Louisiana	3,357,091	3,395,095	3,425,656	3,425,435
Maine	1,019,879	1,021,332	1,032,703	1,040,582
Maryland	4,185,752	4,264,875	4,329,503	4,407,973
Massachusetts	5,040,662	5,040,662	4,935,176	4,935,176
Michigan	7,104,484	7,074,674	7,095,778	7,153,645
Minnesota	3,351,430	3,377,910	3,394,815	3,391,057
Mississippi	1,988,396	2,018,862	2,053,924	2,058,036
Missouri	4,213,302	4,249,579	4,274,784	4,272,960
Montana	781,427	797,145	807,259	806,204
Nebraska	1,394,301	1,404,479	1,404,479	1,420,317
Nevada	1,835,511	1,872,376	1,918,305	1,983,453
New Hampshire	1,074,766	1,096,234	1,103,624	1,161,665
New Jersey	6,179,318	6,238,436	6,301,363	6,342,876
New Mexico	1,467,782	1,521,785	1,473,262	1,458,433
New York	11,689,839	11,947,568	12,185,313	12,194,360
North Carolina	7,160,621	7,267,042	7,389,467	7,509,231
North Dakota	545,027	555,935	561,667	561,333
Ohio	7,923,439	7,974,951	8,011,705	8,032,665
Oklahoma	2,621,733	2,498,178	2,505,989	2,504,253
Oregon	2,808,548	2,855,746	2,910,592	2,930,702
Pennsylvania	8,942,967	8,996,815	8,964,855	8,991,370
Rhode Island	745,470	753,143	753,202	756,966
South Carolina	3,683,824	3,746,681	3,810,962	3,846,069
South Dakota	655,707	622,663	628,506	638,428
Tennessee	4,621,401	5,197,904	5,377,653	5,422,429
Texas	15,879,876	15,879,876	17,099,340	17,370,383
Utah	1,913,564	1,960,366	1,995,377	2,030,644
Vermont	548,799	553,670	560,247	564,892
Virginia	5,820,209	5,912,048	5,926,430	5,929,031
Washington	5,516,134	5,635,715	5,768,281	5,909,967
West Virginia	1,167,346	1,159,348	1,148,786	1,136,775
Wisconsin	4,194,759	4,206,770	4,234,793	4,288,171
Wyoming	422,450	421,098	422,465	419,256
Dist. of Col.	455,602	489,831	521,056	527,731

Source: Highway Statistics, various years.
Note: The data in this table were obtained chiefly from State
  authorities. Where data are not available, estimates were made
  by the Federal Highway Administration. Total licensed drivers
  represents the total of male and female drivers.

TABLE 9.23
Motor-Fuel Use: 2018* (In thousands of gallons)

	Combined gasoline and gasohol										
	Highway use					Non-highway use					
			Public use								
State	Private and commercial	Federal civilian	State, county and municipal	Total	Total	Private and commercial	State, county and municipal	Total	Total use	Losses allowed for evaporation, handling, etc. (a)	Total consumption
Total	130,411,325	221,686	2,131,361	2,353,047	135,246,145	9,880,357	108,670	9,989,027	145,235,172	43,613	145,278,785
% of total use	69.5	0.1	1.1	1.3	72.1	5.3	0.1	5.3	77.4		77.5
Alabama	2,481,773	3,132	55,997	59,129	2,540,902	193,981	2,973	196,954	2,737,856	(a)	2,737,856
Alaska (b)	231,455	1,668	11,266	12,934	244,389	41,154	586	41,740	286,129	(a)	286,129
Arizona	2,744,653	7,212	31,352	38,564	2,783,217	230,006	1,636	231,642	3,014,859	(a)	3,014,859
Arkansas	1,358,775	1,717	18,923	20,640	1,379,415	126,407	993	127,400	1,506,815	(a)	1,506,815
California	14,179,346	26,329	330,426	356,755	14,536,101	974,780	17,245	992,025	15,528,126	(a)	15,528,126
Colorado (b)	2,173,455	4,741	32,781	37,522	2,210,977	178,521	1,721	180,242	2,391,219	(a)	2,391,219
Connecticut	1,440,184	1,948	557	2,505	1,442,689	78,030	29	78,059	1,520,748	8,704	1,529,452
Delaware	483,008	532	2,334	2,866	485,874	35,743	102	35,845	521,719	435	522,154
Florida	8,366,541	11,919	160,929	172,848	8,539,389	840,429	7,643	848,072	9,387,461	(a)	9,387,461
Georgia	4,704,939	6,581	87,110	93,691	4,798,630	264,091	4,545	268,636	5,067,266	(a)	5,067,266
Hawaii	416,669	2,371	12,069	14,440	431,109	33,432	632	34,064	465,173	(a)	465,173
Idaho	681,852	2,154	4,301	6,455	688,307	126,844	225	127,069	815,376	(a)	815,376
Illinois (b)	4,514,075	6,668	43,834	50,502	4,564,577	301,351	2,288	303,639	4,868,216	2,542	4,870,758
Indiana	2,954,965	3,201	13,363	16,564	2,971,529	194,108	700	194,808	3,166,337	(a)	3,166,337
Iowa	1,460,855	1,574	20,623	22,197	1,483,052	200,297	1,081	201,378	1,684,430	(a)	1,684,430
Kansas	1,196,993	1,868	6,797	8,665	1,205,658	102,675	357	103,032	1,308,690	23	1,308,713
Kentucky	2,079,461	2,747	48,228	50,975	2,130,436	120,316	2,518	122,834	2,253,270	(a)	2,253,270
Louisiana	1,985,402	3,197	48,651	51,848	2,037,250	161,898	2,756	164,654	2,201,904	(a)	2,201,904
Maine	584,683	823	7,747	8,570	593,253	64,799	405	65,204	658,457	(a)	658,457
Maryland	2,541,824	6,029	39,270	45,299	2,587,123	141,803	2,048	143,851	2,730,974	15,018	2,745,992
Massachusetts (c)	2,677,907	3,662	3,650	7,312	2,685,219	135,346	191	135,537	2,820,756	(a)	2,820,756
Michigan	4,366,878	5,136	40,106	45,242	4,412,120	453,638	2,090	455,728	4,867,848	(a)	4,867,848
Minnesota	2,372,208	2,883	26,754	29,637	2,401,845	274,101	1,401	275,502	2,677,347	(a)	2,677,347
Mississippi	1,585,909	2,210	7,203	9,413	1,595,322	86,311	378	86,689	1,682,011	(a)	1,682,011
Missouri	2,973,587	4,078	23,298	27,376	3,000,963	210,932	1,222	212,154	3,213,117	2,675	3,215,792
Montana	478,140	2,163	466	2,629	480,769	70,063	24	70,087	550,856	(a)	550,856
Nebraska	831,237	1,332	19,934	21,266	852,503	69,390	1,041	70,431	922,934	(a)	922,934
Nevada	1,141,596	2,615	11,384	13,999	1,155,595	93,776	594	94,370	1,249,965	(a)	1,249,965
New Hampshire	664,649	761	6,266	7,027	671,676	62,861	327	63,188	734,864	8	734,872
New Jersey	3,729,061	5,082	28,439	33,521	3,762,582	203,382	1,484	204,866	3,967,448	(a)	3,967,448
New Mexico	938,561	4,693	8,548	13,241	951,802	70,326	446	70,772	1,022,574	(a)	1,022,574
New York	5,407,771	9,810	26,695	36,505	5,444,276	398,795	1,393	400,188	5,844,464	(3,788)	5,840,676
North Carolina	4,405,417	5,221	81,491	86,712	4,492,129	375,965	3,491	379,456	4,871,585	(a)	4,871,585
North Dakota	394,719	1,201	8,131	9,332	404,051	41,844	425	42,269	446,320	(a)	446,320
Ohio	4,741,276	5,742	57,241	62,983	4,804,259	352,502	3,001	355,503	5,159,762	(a)	5,159,762
Oklahoma	1,809,539	2,806	9,550	12,356	1,821,895	168,237	499	168,736	1,990,631	8	1,990,639
Oregon	1,483,588	3,378	41,696	45,074	1,528,662	118,197	2,181	120,378	1,649,040	(a)	1,649,040
Pennsylvania	4,553,211	6,641	59,771	66,412	4,619,623	290,103	2,901	293,004	4,912,627	(a)	4,912,627
Rhode Island	360,917	765	8,452	9,217	370,134	22,229	413	22,642	392,776	16,265	409,041
South Carolina	2,524,801	3,046	119,100	122,146	2,646,947	202,454	6,407	208,861	2,855,808	(a)	2,855,808
South Dakota	433,084	1,066	11,663	12,729	445,813	37,649	614	38,263	484,076	(a)	484,076
Tennessee	3,115,964	4,460	90,296	94,756	3,210,705	205,990	4,445	210,435	3,421,140	(a)	3,421,140
Texas	13,864,341	17,265	163,539	180,804	14,045,145	654,542	8,547	663,089	14,708,234	(a)	14,708,234
Utah	1,123,352	2,689	15,607	18,296	1,141,648	76,105	818	76,923	1,218,571	961	1,219,532
Vermont	260,593	432	6,994	7,426	268,019	20,780	366	21,146	289,165	108	289,273
Virginia	3,834,187	9,740	75,513	85,253	3,919,440	213,616	3,939	217,555	4,136,995	(a)	4,136,995
Washington	2,646,023	6,524	113,311	119,835	2,765,858	183,521	4,976	188,497	2,954,355	(a)	2,954,355
West Virginia	769,547	1,535	20,590	22,125	791,672	54,952	1,075	56,027	847,699	(a)	847,699
Wisconsin	2,442,052	2,605	46,577	49,182	2,491,234	243,630	2,442	246,072	2,737,306	(a)	2,737,306
Wyoming	287,338	1,247	6,146	7,393	294,731	73,599	326	73,925	368,656	(a)	368,656
Dist. of Columbia	94,752	4,487	16,392	20,879	115,631	4,856	730	5,586	121,217	654	121,871

Source: U.S. Department of Transportation, Federal Highway Administration, Highway Statistics, 2018, Table MF-21 (December 2019).
Note: This table is one of a series giving an analysis of motor-fuel consumption, based on reports from State motor-fuel tax agencies. Gasohol is included with gasoline. In order to make the data uniform and complete, public use and nonhighway use were estimated by the Federal Highway Administration.

TABLE 9.23
Motor-Fuel Use: 2018* (In thousands of gallons) (continued)

State	Special Fuel — Private and commercial highway use	Summary of total use — Highway Amount	Summary of total use — Highway % change from prior year	Non-highway (gasoline only)	Total
Total	42,884,194	178,130,339	0.1	9,989,027	187,521,458
% of total use	22.9	95.0		5.0	100.0
Alabama	859,500	3,400,402	(1)	196,954	3,597,356
Alaska (b)	93,604	337,993	(11.5)	41,740	379,733
Arizona	894,569	3,677,786	2.2	231,642	3,909,428
Arkansas	681,891	2,061,306	(0.6)	127,400	2,188,706
California	3,282,512	17,818,613	(0.5)	992,025	18,810,638
Colorado (b)	672,871	2,883,848	0.8	180,242	3,064,090
Connecticut	284,610	1,727,299	1.1	78,059	1,805,358
Delaware	80,315	566,189	4.1	35,845	602,034
Florida	1,781,546	10,320,935	2.3	848,072	11,169,007
Georgia	1,322,853	6,121,483	(3.7)	268,636	6,390,119
Hawaii	51,074	482,183	(2.1)	34,064	516,247
Idaho	314,805	1,003,112	(3.5)	127,069	1,130,181
Illinois (b)	1,589,933	6,154,510	(1.1)	303,639	6,458,149
Indiana	1,239,956	4,211,485	(2.1)	194,808	4,406,293
Iowa	710,927	2,193,979	(0.2)	201,378	2,395,357
Kansas	479,360	1,685,018	1.8	103,032	1,788,050
Kentucky	825,713	2,956,149	0.8	122,834	3,078,983
Louisiana	668,177	2,705,427	(1.2)	164,654	2,870,081
Maine	180,116	773,369	(7.5)	65,204	838,573
Maryland	522,623	3,109,746	(0.7)	143,851	3,253,597
Massachusetts (c)	438,727	3,123,946	0.6	135,537	3,259,483
Michigan	1,037,517	5,449,637	2.3	455,728	5,905,365
Minnesota	848,394	3,250,239	(0.5)	275,502	3,525,741
Mississippi	707,874	2,303,196	(1.1)	86,689	2,389,885
Missouri	1,066,093	4,067,056	(0.5)	212,154	4,279,210
Montana	272,327	753,096	(1.1)	70,087	823,183
Nebraska	466,843	1,319,346	0.3	70,431	1,389,777
Nevada	353,072	1,508,667	0.1	94,370	1,603,037
New Hampshire	104,819	776,495	1.2	63,188	839,683
New Jersey	810,218	4,572,800	(2.1)	204,866	4,777,666
New Mexico	579,381	1,531,183	(0.4)	70,772	1,601,955
New York	1,325,256	6,769,532	(2.6)	400,188	7,169,720
North Carolina	1,173,039	5,665,168	0.5	379,456	6,044,624
North Dakota	324,171	728,222	1.8	42,269	770,491
Ohio	1,681,933	6,486,192	(0.4)	355,503	6,841,695
Oklahoma	945,059	2,766,954	0.5	168,736	2,935,690
Oregon	597,908	2,126,570	0.7	120,378	1,649,040
Pennsylvania	1,500,326	6,119,949	(2.9)	293,004	6,412,953
Rhode Island	64,881	435,015	4.4	22,642	457,657
South Carolina	837,517	3,484,464	(1.8)	208,861	3,693,325
South Dakota	237,857	683,670	(0.4)	38,263	721,933
Tennessee	1,032,616	4,243,321	(0.6)	210,435	4,453,756
Texas	5,854,781	19,899,926	2.6	663,089	20,563,015
Utah	491,761	1,633,409	(0.7)	76,923	1,710,332
Vermont	72,796	340,815	(6.4)	21,146	361,961
Virginia	1,043,447	4,962,887	(0.1)	217,555	5,180,442
Washington	739,029	3,504,887	3.6	188,497	3,693,384
West Virginia	508,187	1,299,859	12.5	56,027	1,355,886
Wisconsin	868,636	3,359,870	5.2	246,072	3,605,942
Wyoming	355,785	650,516	1.3	73,925	724,441
Dist. of Columbia	6,989	122,620	12.4	5,586	128,206

These estimates may not be comparable to data for prior years due to revised estimation procedures. For some States, data are not comparable to prior years due to changes in data analysis and/or improvements in reporting procedures. All data are subject to review and revision.

Key:
(a) Some States make a flat percentage allowance for losses in storage and handling, and others allow for actual losses not to exceed a specified percentage. Still others permit distributors to claim stock losses in reconciliations of inventories, thus exempting the lost volume from taxation. Losses by destruction, where reported separately, are also included in this column. The maximum allowance used in the analysis to cover losses in storage and handling was one percent. Because of accounting methods, losses can be reported as a net gain.

TABLE 9.24
Prisoners Under Jurisdiction of State or Federal Correctional Authorities, by Jurisdiction and Sex, 2017 and 2018

State or other jurisdiction	December 31, 2017 popluation			December 31, 2018 population			Percent change, 2017-2018		
	Total	Male	Female	Total	Male	Female	Total	Male	Female
U.S. total (a)(b)	1,489,189	1,377,815	111,374	1,465,158	1,354,313	110,845	(1.6)	(1.7)	(0.5)
Federal (a)	183,058	170,525	12,533	179,898	167,372	12,526	(1.7)	(1.8)	(0.1)
State (b)	1,306,131	1,207,290	98,841	1,285,260	1,186,941	98,319	(1.6)	(1.7)	(0.5)
Alabama	27,608	25,135	2,473	26,841	24,439	2,402	(2.8)	(2.8)	(2.9)
Alaska (c)	4,399	4,011	388	4,380	4,001	379	(0.4)	(0.2)	(2.3)
Arizona	42,030	37,971	4,059	42,005	37,820	4,185	(0.1)	(0.4)	3.1
Arkansas	18,070	16,651	1,419	17,799	16,396	1,403	(1.5)	(1.5)	(1.1)
California	131,039	125,180	5,859	128,625	122,847	5,778	(1.8)	(1.9)	(1.4)
Colorado	19,946	18,044	1,902	20,372	18,347	2,025	2.1	1.7	6.5
Connecticut (c)	14,040	13,069	971	13,681	12,679	1,002	(2.6)	(3.0)	3.2
Delaware (c)	6,443	5,931	512	6,067	5,646	421	(5.8)	(4.8)	(17.8)
Florida	98,504	91,779	6,725	97,538	90,812	6,726	(1.0)	(1.1)	0.0
Georgia	53,667	49,839	3,828	53,647	49,708	3,939	0.0	(0.3)	2.9
Hawaii (c)	5,630	5,006	624	5,375	4,716	659	(4.5)	(5.8)	5.6
Idaho	8,579	7,534	1,045	8,664	7,524	1,140	1.0	(0.1)	9.1
Illinois	41,427	39,148	2,279	39,965	37,627	2,338	(3.5)	(3.9)	2.6
Indiana	26,024	23,608	2,416	26,877	24,310	2,567	3.3	3.0	6.3
Iowa	9,024	8,218	806	9,419	8,582	837	4.4	4.4	3.8
Kansas (d)	10,015	9,112	903	10,218	9,289	929	2.0	1.9	2.9
Kentucky	23,543	20,522	3,021	23,431	20,380	3,051	(0.5)	(0.7)	1.0
Louisiana	33,739	31,782	1,957	32,397	30,649	1,748	(4.0)	(3.6)	(10.7)
Maine	2,404	2,177	227	2,425	2,188	237	0.9	0.5	4.4
Maryland	19,367	18,519	848	18,856	18,033	823	(2.6)	(2.6)	(2.9)
Massachusetts	9,133	8,602	531	8,692	8,168	524	(4.8)	(5.0)	(1.3)
Michigan	39,666	37,515	2,151	38,761	36,680	2,081	(2.3)	(2.2)	(3.3)
Minnesota	10,708	9,974	734	10,101	9,402	699	(5.7)	(5.7)	(4.8)
Mississippi	19,103	17,688	1,415	19,275	17,886	1,389	0.9	1.1	(1.8)
Missouri	32,601	29,205	3,396	30,369	27,255	3,114	(6.8)	(6.7)	(8.3)
Montana (e)	3,698	3,282	416	3,765	3,318	447	N.C.	N.C.	N.C.
Nebraska	5,313	4,884	429	5,491	5,061	430	3.4	3.6	0.2
Nevada (d)	13,721	12,441	1,280	13,641	12,349	1,292	(0.6)	(0.7)	0.9
New Hampshire (f)	2,750	2,524	226	2,745	2,519	226	N.C.	N.C.	N.C.
New Jersey	19,585	18,811	774	19,362	18,592	770	(1.1)	(1.2)	(0.5)
New Mexico (g)	7,276	6,492	784	7,030	6,256	774	N.C.	N.C.	N.C.
New York	49,461	47,184	2,277	46,636	44,544	2,092	(5.7)	(5.6)	(8.1)
North Carolina	36,394	33,553	2,841	34,899	32,171	2,728	(4.1)	(4.1)	(4.0)
North Dakota (g)	1,723	1,524	199	1,695	1,499	196	N.C.	N.C.	N.C.
Ohio	51,478	47,052	4,426	50,431	46,153	4,278	(2.0)	(1.9)	(3.3)
Oklahoma (h)	28,143	24,952	3,191	27,709	24,553	3,156	(1.5)	(1.6)	(1.1)
Oregon (f)	15,218	13,891	1,327	15,268	14,022	1,246	N.C.	N.C.	N.C.
Pennsylvania	48,333	45,482	2,851	47,239	44,305	2,934	(2.3)	(2.6)	2.9
Rhode Island (c)	2,861	2,690	171	2,767	2,613	154	(3.3)	(2.9)	(9.9)
South Carolina	19,906	18,514	1,392	19,033	17,706	1,327	(4.4)	(4.4)	(4.7)
South Dakota	3,970	3,430	540	3,948	3,377	571	(0.6)	(1.5)	5.7
Tennessee	28,980	25,969	3,011	26,321	23,642	2,679	(9.2)	(9.0)	(11.0)
Texas	162,523	148,565	13,958	163,628	149,193	14,435	0.7	0.4	3.4
Utah (d)(i)	6,219	5,726	493	6,648	6,073	575	N.C.	N.C.	N.C.
Vermont (c)	1,546	1,406	140	1,659	1,519	140	7.3	8.0	0.0
Virginia	37,158	34,004	3,154	36,660	33,620	3,040	(1.3)	(1.1)	(3.6)
Washington	19,656	17,914	1,742	19,523	17,803	1,720	(0.7)	(0.6)	(1.3)
West Virginia	7,092	6,274	818	6,775	5,989	786	(4.5)	(4.5)	(3.9)
Wisconsin	23,945	22,325	1,620	24,064	22,473	1,591	0.5	0.7	(1.8)
Wyoming	2,473	2,181	292	2,543	2,207	336	2.8	1.2	15.1

See footnotes at end of table

TABLE 9.24

Prisoners Under Jurisdiction of State or Federal Correctional Authorities, by Jurisdiction and Sex, 2017 and 2018 (continued)

Source: Bureau of Justice Statistics, National Prisoner Statistics, 2017 and 2018; Prisoners in 2018 NCJ 253516; Date of version: 4/30/2020.

Note: Jurisdiction refers to the legal authority of state or federal correctional officials over a prisoner, regardless of where the prisoner is held. For jurisdiction-level information, see Jurisdiction notes on the BJS website. Counts are for December 31 of each year. As of December 31, 2001, sentenced felons from the District of Columbia were the responsibility of the Federal Bureau of Prisons.

Key:

N.C. – Not calculated. Counts and rates for 2017 and 2018 are not comparable.

(a) Includes adult prisoners held in non-secure community-corrections facilities and adults and persons age 17 or younger held in privately operated facilities.

(b) Total and state estimates for 2018 include imputed counts for New Hampshire and Oregon, which did not submit 2018 National Prisoner Statistics (NPS) data. See Methodology. Total and state estimates for 2017 include imputed data for New Mexico and North Dakota, which did not submit 2017 NPS data. See Methodology in Prisoners in 2017 (NCJ 252156, BJS, April 2019).

(c) Prisons and jails form one integrated system. Data include total jail and prison populations. Data for these states are not reported in BJS's annual Jail Inmates bulletins.

(d) State submitted updated 2017 population counts.

(e) State converted offender data to a new system in 2018. Data from 2018 are not comparable to data for previous years.

(f) State did not submit 2018 NPS data. Counts were imputed for 2018 and should not be compared to 2017 counts.

(g) State did not submit 2017 NPS data. Counts were imputed for 2017 and should not be compared to 2018 counts.

(h) Includes persons who were waiting in county jails to be moved to state prison.

(i) Data for 2018 are not comparable to data for previous years. Total counts of the prisoner population from 2018 include an undetermined number of offenders excluded from counts in 2017 due to a change in legal-status requirements for a program for parole violators that was instituted in 2018.

TABLE 9.25
Prisoners Under Jurisdiction of State or Federal Correctional Authorities, by Jurisdiction and Race or Ethnicity, December 31, 2018

Jurisdiction	Total	White (a)	Black (a)	Hispanic	Asian (a)
Federal (b)(c)	179,898	50,946	66,714	56,056	2,416
Alabama	26,841	12,566	14,080	N.R.	2
Alaska	4,380	1,877	447	125	139
Arizona	42,005	16,379	6,119	16,274	210
Arkansas	17,799	9,802	7,277	569	69
California	128,625	26,921	36,491	56,731	1,423
Colorado	20,372	9,339	3,517	6,411	255
Connecticut	13,681	4,153	5,770	3,649	65
Delaware	6,067	2,144	3,618	293	6
Florida	97,538	39,167	45,735	12,239	20
Georgia	53,647	19,123	32,133	2,120	184
Hawaii	5,375	1,294	240	247	979
Idaho	8,664	6,318	237	1,326	48
Illinois	39,965	12,367	22,085	5,147	145
Indiana	26,877	16,670	8,850	1,075	66
Iowa	9,419	6,164	2,398	601	82
Kansas	10,218	5,851	2,773	1,266	97
Kentucky	23,431	17,844	4,929	320	37
Louisiana	32,397	10,547	21,700	34	38
Maine	2,425	1,911	234	126	14
Maryland (d)	18,856	4,587	13,215	700	48
Massachusetts	8,692	3,766	2,377	2,291	120
Michigan (d)	38,761	17,061	20,718	373	101
Minnesota	10,101	4,654	3,620	601	277
Mississippi	19,275	7,012	12,008	177	37
Missouri	30,369	19,442	10,125	551	72
Montana	3,765	2,772	97	74	N.A.
Nebraska	5,491	2,877	1,523	767	44
Nevada	13,641	5,873	4,234	2,845	402
New Hampshire (e)	2,745	2,300	179	173	11
New Jersey	19,362	4,125	11,847	3,031	124
New Mexico	7,030	1,786	496	4,193	17
New York	46,636	11,248	22,513	11,322	282
North Carolina	34,899	13,801	18,009	1,894	110
North Dakota	1,695	1,054	188	104	5
Ohio	50,431	25,887	22,662	1,420	66
Oklahoma	27,709	14,537	6,981	2,064	97
Oregon (e)	15,268	11,329	1,393	1,871	228
Pennsylvania	47,239	20,389	21,882	4,574	127
Rhode Island (c)	2,767	1,195	803	663	43
South Carolina	19,033	7,057	11,335	455	20
South Dakota	3,948	2,128	305	146	16
Tennessee	26,321	14,514	11,125	559	84
Texas	163,628	54,983	53,424	54,325	573
Utah	6,648	4,217	448	1,327	74
Vermont	1,659	1,418	174	4	7
Virginia/c	36,660	15,121	20,326	1,006	159
Washington	19,523	11,547	3,440	2,542	771
West Virginia	6,775	5,827	861	26	5
Wisconsin	24,064	10,899	10,065	1,887	271
Wyoming	2,543	1,917	127	327	11

See footnotes at end of table

TABLE 9.25
Prisoners Under Jurisdiction of State or Federal Correctional Authorities, by Jurisdiction and Race or Ethnicity, December 31, 2018 (continued)

Jurisdiction	Native Hawaiian/Other Pacific Islander (a)	American Indian/Alaska Native	Two or more races (a)	Other (a)	Unknown	Did not report
Federal (b)(c)	N.R.	3,765	N.A.	0	0	0
Alabama	0	1	N.R.	0	192	0
Alaska	85	1,679	N.A.	0	28	0
Arizona	0	2,249	0	679	27	68
Arkansas	6	53	0	17	6	0
California	381	1,463	0	5,215	0	0
Colorado	N.R.	729	N.R.	N.R.	3	118
Connecticut	0	42	0	0	2	0
Delaware	0	2	0	N.A.	4	0
Florida	10	87	N.R.	275	5	0
Georgia	1	21	N.R.	52	13	0
Hawaii	2,365	22	197	N.A.	31	0
Idaho	1	310	N.A.	N.A.	424	0
Illinois	0	66	62	N.A.	43	50
Indiana	11	50	98	0	57	0
Iowa	0	174	0	0	0	0
Kansas	0	230	0	1	0	0
Kentucky	0	16	266	N.A.	15	4
Louisiana	53	24	0	1	N.A.	0
Maine	2	71	27	0	40	0
Maryland (d)	15	98	N.R.	165	28	0
Massachusetts	0	46	0	92	0	0
Michigan (d)	5	360	0	0	143	0
Minnesota	N.R.	944	N.R.	N.R.	5	0
Mississippi	0	30	0	0	11	0
Missouri	N.R.	110	N.R.	N.R.	69	0
Montana	N.A.	805	N.A.	17	0	0
Nebraska	6	225	N.R.	45	4	0
Nevada	0	235	N.A.	0	52	0
New Hampshire (e)	N.A.	11	N.A.	33	38	0
New Jersey	N.A.	13	N.R.	N.R.	222	0
New Mexico	21	474	0	0	43	0
New York	N.R.	394	N.R.	613	264	0
North Carolina	21	929	N.R.	N.A.	135	0
North Dakota	3	336	5	N.A.	N.A.	0
Ohio	N.R.	86	N.R.	310	N.R.	0
Oklahoma	27	3,175	N.A.	75	N.A.	753
Oregon (e)	7	434	N.A.	N.A.	6	0
Pennsylvania	N.A.	42	0	0	225	0
Rhode Island (c)	N.R.	25	N.R.	38	0	0
South Carolina	1	33	N.R.	132	0	0
South Dakota	1	1,345	N.A.	7	0	0
Tennessee	N.R.	39	N.R.	N.R.	0	0
Texas	0	94	0	229	0	0
Utah	135	330	0	0	117	0
Vermont	0	15	N.R.	0	41	0
Virginia/c	0	27	0	0	21	0
Washington	N.R.	998	N.R.	87	138	0
West Virginia	1	6	0	49	0	0
Wisconsin	N.A.	928	N.R.	N.R.	14	0
Wyoming	9	148	0	3	1	0

See footnotes at end of table

TABLE 9.25
Prisoners Under Jurisdiction of State or Federal Correctional Authorities, by Jurisdiction and Race or Ethnicity, December 31, 2018 (continued)

Source: Bureau of Justice Statistics, Federal Justice Statistics Program, 2018 (preliminary); and National Prisoner Statistics, 2018; Prisoners in 2018 NCJ 253516; Date 4/30/2020.

Note: Jurisdiction refers to the legal authority of state or federal correctional officials over a prisoner, regardless of where the prisoner is held. For jurisdiction-level information, see Jurisdiction notes on the BJS website. Estimates were provided by state and federal departments of corrections' administrative record systems and may not reflect prisoners' self-identification of race or ethnicity. State, federal, and national totals by race or ethnicity differ from other tables in this report due to adjustments that BJS made in other tables to correct for differences between administrative records and prisoner self-reported data on race or ethnicity. As of December 31, 2001, sentenced felons from the District of Columbia were the responsibility of the Federal Bureau of Prisons (BOP).

Key:

N.A.–Not applicable. State does not track this race or ethnicity.

N.R.–Not reported.

(a) Excludes persons of Hispanic origin (e.g., "white" refers to non-Hispanic whites and "black" refers to non-Hispanic blacks).

(b) The BOP does not separate persons of Hispanic origin from the individual race categories when reporting to the National Prisoner Statistics (NPS). To do so, BJS used data from the 2018 Federal Justice Statistics Program (preliminary).

(c) Asians, Native Hawaiians, and Other Pacific Islanders were combined into a single category and reported as Asian.

(d) Persons of Hispanic origin may be undercounted due to ongoing changes in information systems.

(e) State did not submit 2018 NPS data on race or ethnicity. Counts were imputed.

TABLE 9.26
Prisoners Under Jurisdiction of State or Federal Correctional Authorities and Held in the Custody of Private Prisons or Local Jails, by Jurisdiction, 2017 and 2018

Jurisdicition	Prisoners held in private prisons (a)				Prisoners held in local jails			
	2017	2018	Percent change, 2017-2018	Percent of total jurisdiction population, 2018	2017	2018	Percent change, 2017-2018	Percent of total jurisdiction population, 2018
U.S. total	121,044	118,444	(2.1)	8.1	80,762	80,513	(0.3)	5.5
Federal (b)	27,569	27,747	0.6	15.4	869	649	(25.3)	0.4
State total	93,475	90,697	(3.0)	7.1	79,893	79,864	0.0	6.2
Alabama	264	369	39.8	1.4	2,021	2,061	2.0	7.7
Alaska (c)	248	209	(15.7)	4.8	39	35	(10.3)	0.8
Arizona	8,283	8,231	(0.6)	19.6	0	0	N.C	0.0
Arkansas	0	0	N.C	0.0	1,837	1,866	1.6	10.5
California	6,359	3,952	(37.9)	3.1	1,762	1,667	(5.4)	1.3
Colorado	3,760	3,909	4.0	19.2	164	259	57.9	1.3
Connecticut (c)	515	507	(1.6)	3.7	0	0	N.C	0.0
Delaware	N.A.	N.A.	N.C	0.0	0	0	N.C	0.0
Florida	11,676	10,524	(9.9)	10.8	1,119	1,123	0.4	1.2
Georgia	7,880	7,801	(1.0)	14.5	4,752	4,689	(1.3)	8.7
Hawaii (c)	1,602	1,483	(7.4)	27.6	0	0	N.C	0.0
Idaho (d)	432	1,126	160.6	13.0	680	595	(12.5)	6.9
Illinois	362	523	44.5	1.3	0	0	N.C	0.0
Indiana (e)	4,061	4,034	(0.7)	15.0	251	315	25.5	1.2
Iowa	0	0	N.C	0.0	0	0	N.C	0.0
Kansas	0	0	N.C	0.0	97	91	(6.2)	0.9
Kentucky	N.A.	839	N.C	3.6	11,531	11,137	(3.4)	47.5
Louisiana	0	0	N.C	0.0	18,587	17,517	(5.8)	54.1
Maine	0	0	N.C	0.0	17	15	(11.8)	0.6
Maryland	32	29	(9.4)	0.2	58	107	84.5	0.6
Massachusetts	N.A.	N.A.	N.C	0.0	261	226	(13.4)	2.6
Michigan	0	0	N.C	0.0	0	0	N.C	0.0
Minnesota	0	0	N.C	0.0	1,007	804	(20.2)	8.0
Mississippi	3,121	3,217	3.1	16.7	5,133	5,545	8.0	28.8
Missouri	0	0	N.C	0.0	0	0	N.C	0.0
Montana (f)	1,409	2,011	N.C	53.4	503	33	(93.4)	0.9
Nebraska	0	0	N.C	0.0	151	146	(3.3)	2.7
Nevada (g)	199	200	0.5	1.5	19	15	(21.1)	0.1
New Hampshire (h)	N.R.	N.R.	N.C	0.0	N.R.	N.R.	N.C	0.0
New Jersey	2,659	2,652	(0.3)	13.7	87	211	142.5	1.1
New Mexico (h)(i)	N.R.	2,051	N.C	29.2	0	0	N.C	0.0
New York	0	0	N.C	N.C	2	2	0.0	0.0
North Carolina	30	30	0.0	0.1	0	0	N.C	0.0
North Dakota (h)	N.R.	337	N.C	19.9	0	0	N.C	0.0
Ohio	7,224	6,567	(9.1)	13.0	0	0	N.C	0.0
Oklahoma	7,353	7,277	(1.0)	26.3	13	13	0.0	0.0
Oregon (h)	N.R.	N.R.	N.C	N.C	N.R.	N.R.	N.C	N.C
Pennsylvania	407	431	5.9	0.9	382	359	(6.0)	0.8
Rhode Island (c)	N.A.	N.A.	N.C	0.0	0	0	N.C	0.0
South Carolina (d)	24	73	204.2	0.4	341	314	(7.9)	1.6
South Dakota	34	38	11.8	1.0	0	0	N.C	0.0
Tennessee	7,608	7,615	0.1	28.9	7,038	6,828	(3.0)	25.9
Texas	12,728	12,491	(1.9)	7.6	11,549	13,504	16.9	8.3
Utah (f)	0	0	N.C	0.0	1,404	1,383	(1.5)	20.8
Vermont (c)(e)	0	221	N.C	13.3	0	0	N.C	0.0
Virginia	1,553	1,559	0.4	4.3	7,370	7,206	(2.2)	19.7
Washington	0	0	N.C	0.0	42	194	361.9	1.0
West Virginia	0	0	N.C	0.0	1,170	946	(19.1)	14.0
Wisconsin	N.A.	N.A.	N.C	0.0	412	507	23.1	2.1
Wyoming	237	391	65.0	15.4	21	87	314.3	3.4

See footnotes at end of table

TABLE 9.26

Prisoners Under Jurisdiction of State or Federal Correctional Authorities and Held in the Custody of Private Prisons or Local Jails, by Jurisdiction, 2017 and 2018 (continued)

Source: Bureau of Justice Statistics, National Prisoner Statistics, 2017 and 2018; Prisoners in 2018; NCJ 253516; Date 4/30/2020

Note: For jurisdiction-level information, see Jurisdiction notes on the BJS website. Counts are for December 31 of each year. As of December 31, 2001, sentenced felons from the District of Columbia were the responsibility of the Federal Bureau of Prisons.

Key:

N.A.–Not applicable.

N.C–Not calculated. Counts and rates for 2017 and 2018 are not comparable.

N.R.–Not reported.

(a) Includes prisoners held in private facilities in the jurisdiction of another state.

(b) Includes federal prisoners held in facilities that are non-secure and privately operated (9,597) and prisoners on home confinement (1,832). Excludes persons held in immigration-detention facilities pending adjudication.

(c) Prisons and jails form one integrated system. Data include total jail and prison populations.

(d) Prisoners held in private prisons outside the state account for the increases in private prison populations in Idaho and South Carolina.

(e) Includes prisoners in facilities owned by the state but staffed by employees of a private correctional company.

(f) Due to changes in reporting methods, 2017 and 2018 counts are not comparable.

(g) State submitted updated 2017 population counts for private prisons and local jails.

(h) Totals for 2017 include imputed counts for New Mexico and North Dakota, which did not submit 2017 National Prisoner Statistics (NPS) data. Totals for 2018 include imputed counts for New Hampshire and Oregon, which did not submit 2018 NPS data. BJS estimated counts of prisoners held in local jails and private facilities and included these estimates in the state and U.S. totals. See Methodology in this report and in Prisoners in 2017 (NCJ 252156, BJS, April 2019).

(i) In 2018, New Mexico moved all female prisoners who had been housed in private facilities to state-run correctional facilities.

TABLE 9.27
Prisoners Age 17 or Younger in the Custody of Publicly or Privately Operated Federal or State Prisons, by Jurisdiction and Sex, December 31, 2018

Jurisdiction	Total	Male	Female
U.S. total	735	708	27
Federal (a)	36	33	3
State total	699	675	24
Alabama	9	9	0
Alaska (b)	2	2	0
Arizona	51	48	3
Arkansas	8	8	0
California	N.R.	N.R.	N.R.
Colorado	9	9	0
Connecticut (b)	46	44	2
Delaware (b)	11	11	0
Florida	91	90	1
Georgia	33	30	3
Hawaii (b)	0	0	0
Idaho	0	0	0
Illinois	0	0	0
Indiana	28	28	0
Iowa	3	3	0
Kansas	0	0	0
Kentucky	0	0	0
Louisiana	14	14	0
Maine	0	0	0
Maryland	16	16	0
Massachusetts	0	0	0
Michigan	35	34	1
Minnesota	5	5	0
Mississippi	14	14	0
Missouri	3	3	0
Montana	0	0	0
Nebraska	3	2	1
Nevada	21	20	1
New Hampshire (c)	N.R.	N.R.	N.R.
New Jersey	0	0	0
New Mexico	0	0	0
New York	64	64	0
North Carolina	60	55	5
North Dakota	0	0	0
Ohio	40	40	0
Oklahoma	14	14	0
Oregon (c)	N.R.	N.R.	N.R.
Pennsylvania	14	13	1
Rhode Island	1	1	0
South Carolina	26	25	1
South Dakota	0	0	0
Tennessee	13	13	0
Texas	22	18	4
Utah	1	1	0
Vermont (b)	0	0	0
Virginia	11	11	0
Washington	10	10	0
West Virginia	0	0	0
Wisconsin	21	20	1
Wyoming	0	0	0

See footnotes at end of table

TABLE 9.27
Prisoners Age 17 or Younger in the Custody of Publicly or Privately Operated Federal or State Prisons, by Jurisdiction and Sex, December 31, 2018 (continued)

Source: Bureau of Justice Statistics, National Prisoner Statistics, 2018; Prisoners in 2018   NCJ 253516; Date 4/30/2020.

Note: In 2017, BJS began requesting that National Prisoner Statistics (NPS) respondents include all persons age 17 or younger held in the physical custody of state and federal correctional authorities and in private prisons, excluding prisoners held in local jails and in the custody of other jurisdictions. For jurisdiction-level information, see Jurisdiction notes on the BJS website. Data collected after 2016 should not be compared to data for previous years. See Methodology. As of December 31, 2001, sentenced felons from the District of Columbia were the responsibility of the Federal Bureau of Prisons (BOP).

Key:
N.R.–Not reported
(a) The BOP holds prisoners age 17 or younger in privately operated facilities.
(b) Prisons and jails form one integrated system. Data include total jail and prison populations.
(c) State did not provide any 2018 NPS data. Counts of prisoners age 17 or younger were imputed based on data for previous years and included in the state and U.S. totals.

TABLE 9.28
Admissions and Releases of Sentenced Prisoners Under Jurisdiction of State or Federal Correctional Authorities: 2017 and 2018

State or other jurisdiction	Admissions (a)					Releases (b)				
	2017 Total	2018 Total	Percent change, 2017-2018	2018 New court commitments	2018 Conditional supervision violations (c)	2017 Total	2018 Total	Percent change, 2017-2018	2018 Unconditional (d)	2018 Conditional (e)
U.S. total (g)	606,596	596,389	(1.7)	410,867	169,663	623,069	614,844	(1.3)	157,000	443,342
Federal (i)(f)	44,708	44,514	0.0	39,943	4,571	49,461	47,208	(5.0)	46,440	270
State (g)	561,888	551,875	(2.0)	370,924	165,092	573,608	567,636	(1.0)	110,560	443,072
Alabama	12,170	13,160	8.1	8,141	1,839	13,624	14,015	2.9	2,973	9,192
Alaska (h)	1,580	1,765	11.7	1,561	204	1,941	1,735	(10.6)	312	1,418
Arizona	13,423	13,753	2.5	11,339	2,340	14,075	13,683	(2.8)	2,132	11,422
Arkansas	8,971	9,572	6.7	5,209	4,363	8,443	9,805	16.1	792	8,933
California	37,091	35,330	(4.7)	30,957	4,373	36,894	34,461	(6.6)	57	33,854
Colorado	9,638	10,155	5.4	6,349	3,806	9,669	9,774	1.1	1,106	8,512
Connecticut (h)	4,401	4,162	(5.4)	3,441	577	5,169	4,843	(6.3)	2,263	2,559
Delaware (h)(i)	2,897	2,505	(13.5)	1,832	655	2,736	2,504	(8.5)	248	2,112
Florida (j)	28,189	28,495	1.1	27,687	77	30,467	30,132	(1.1)	18,423	11,245
Georgia	16,699	17,736	6.2	15,574	2,155	15,210	16,348	7.5	7,649	8,520
Hawaii (h)	1,528	1,784	16.8	1,081	703	1,834	1,816	(1.0)	345	713
Idaho	5,747	5,003	(12.9)	1,746	3,257	5,395	5,444	0.9	445	4,977
Illinois	24,468	22,835	(6.7)	14,459	8,373	26,850	24,415	(9.1)	4,129	20,197
Indiana	12,249	12,005	(2.0)	9,250	2,640	11,708	11,075	(5.4)	1,001	10,007
Iowa	5,619	5,342	(4.9)	3,685	1,635	5,632	5,434	(3.5)	1,151	4,232
Kansas	6,453	6,506	0.8	3,934	1,390	6,406	6,411	0.1	1,587	4,791
Kentucky	21,239	20,152	(5.1)	12,379	7,605	20,555	20,014	(2.6)	4,600	15,032
Louisiana	16,337	15,646	(4.2)	10,345	5,301	17,868	16,759	(6.2)	1,482	15,145
Maine (k)	960	892	N.C.	466	426	684	757	N.C.	362	395
Maryland (l)	8,243	7,661	(7.1)	5,727	1,925	8,850	8,141	(8.0)	2,512	5,561
Massachusetts	2,141	1,983	(7.4)	1,775	205	2,309	2,316	0.3	1,663	613
Michigan	12,013	11,307	(5.9)	6,608	2,581	13,470	12,212	(9.3)	510	9,699
Minnesota	8,195	7,317	(10.7)	4,345	2,972	8,092	7,838	(3.1)	810	6,997
Mississippi	7,553	7,439	(1.5)	5,267	2,172	7,748	7,502	(3.2)	450	6,712
Missouri	18,551	17,299	(6.7)	9,078	8,219	18,431	19,493	5.8	1,366	17,997
Montana	2,644	2,772	4.8	1,870	902	2,770	2,841	2.6	567	2,259
Nebraska	2,436	2,385	(2.1)	1,924	440	2,387	2,239	(6.2)	471	1,756
Nevada (m)	5,873	6,334	7.8	4,829	1,094	6,549	6,434	(1.8)	2,049	4,339
New Hampshire (n)	1,338	1,309	N.C.	626	683	1,409	1,335	N.C.	128	1,207
New Jersey	8,611	7,808	(9.3)	5,595	2,213	8,959	8,159	(8.9)	4,681	3,284
New Mexico (o)(p)	3,848	3,585	N.C.	2,133	1,207	3,631	3,598	N.C.	938	2,397
New York	20,421	18,954	(7.2)	11,429	7,452	21,667	21,691	0.1	2,072	19,270
North Carolina	18,242	17,251	(5.4)	12,614	4,636	17,244	18,111	5.0	2,556	15,442
North Dakota (q)	1,570	1,527	N.C.	N.R.	N.R.	1,627	1,555	N.C.	N.R.	N.R.
Ohio (p)	21,602	20,727	(4.1)	15,456	4,701	22,299	21,774	(2.4)	8,221	13,398
Oklahoma	10,228	9,318	(8.9)	7,176	2,092	9,682	9,111	(5.9)	2,137	6,862
Oregon (n)	5,566	5,580	N.C.	3,716	1,722	5,428	5,529	N.C.	34	5,285
Pennsylvania	19,297	17,954	(7.0)	8,526	8,551	19,673	18,550	(5.7)	3,159	15,199
Rhode Island (h)	572	613	7.2	486	127	875	768	(12.2)	512	252
South Carolina	6,017	5,769	(4.1)	4,662	1,099	6,847	6,598	(3.6)	1,780	4,714
South Dakota	3,896	4,116	5.6	1,481	631	3,859	4,298	11.4	286	2,787
Tennessee	11,541	12,726	10.3	7,775	4,951	13,307	13,718	3.1	5,249	8,348
Texas	76,877	78,741	2.4	48,695	26,640	77,196	77,714	0.7	10,008	65,069
Utah	4,047	3,733	(7.8)	1,777	1,956	3,781	3,514	(7.1)	614	2,882
Vermont (h)(r)	1,737	2,469	42.1	876	1,593	1,795	2,476	37.9	396	2,070
Virginia (s)	12,163	11,657	(4.2)	11,616	41	12,698	12,862	1.3	1,070	11,669
Washington (p)	25,483	24,829	(2.6)	6,224	18,602	25,658	26,861	4.7	2,335	24,480
West Virginia	3,590	3,831	6.7	2,316	1,281	3,652	4,148	13.6	910	2,977
Wisconsin	6,865	7,021	2.3	4,555	2,428	5,592	5,836	4.4	270	5,502
Wyoming	1,069	1,062	(0.7)	805	257	963	989	2.7	194	789

See footnotes at end of table

TABLE 9.28

Admissions and Releases of Sentenced Prisoners Under Jurisdiction of State or Federal Correctional Authorities: 2017 and 2018 (continued)

Source: Bureau of Justice Statistics, National Prisoner Statistics, 2017 and 2018; Prisoners in 2018 NCJ 253516; Date: 4/30/2020

Note: Jurisdiction refers to the legal authority of state or federal correctional officials over a prisoner, regardless of where the prisoner is held. For jurisdiction-level information, see Jurisdiction notes on the BJS website. Counts cover January 1 through December 31 for each year and are based on prisoners admitted to or released from state or federal correctional authorities with a sentence of more than one year. As of December 31, 2001, sentenced felons from the District of Columbia were the responsibility of the Federal Bureau of Prisons.

Key:

N.C. – Not calculated. Counts and rates for 2017 and 2018 are not comparable.

N.R. – Not reported

(a) Excludes transfers, escapes, and absences without leave. Includes other conditional-release violators, returns from appeal or bond, and other admissions. In 2018, 15,859 (2.7%) of total admissions were due to other conditional-release violations, returns from appeal or bond, and other types of admissions not included among new court commitments or conditional-supervision violations. See Methodology.

(b) Excludes transfers, escapes, and absences without leave. Includes deaths, releases to appeal or bond, and other releases. In 2018, 14,502 (2.4%) of total releases were due to death, releases to appeal or bond, releases to treatment facilities, and other types of releases not included among unconditional or conditional releases. See Methodology.

(c) Includes all conditional-release violators returned to prison from post-custody community supervision, including parole and probation, either for violations of conditions of release or for new crimes.

(d) Includes expirations of sentence, commutations, and other unconditional releases.

(e) Includes releases to probation, supervised mandatory releases, and other unspecified conditional releases.

(f) Includes adult prisoners held in non-secure community-corrections facilities and adults and persons age 17 or younger held in privately operated facilities. The 270 conditional releases from federal correctional facilities are persons who were sentenced before the 1984 Sentencing Reform Act, which eliminated federal parole.

(g) U.S. total and state estimates for 2017 include imputed counts for New Mexico, North Dakota, and Vermont, which did not submit 2017 National Prisoner Statistics (NPS) data on admissions and releases. U.S. total and state estimates for 2018 include imputed counts for New Hampshire, Oregon, and Vermont, which did not submit 2018 NPS data on admissions or releases. See Methodology in this report and in Prisoners in 2017 (NCJ 252156, BJS, April 2019).

(h) Prisons and jails form one integrated system. Data include total jail and prison populations.

(i) Releases include offenders who received a combined sentence of prison and probation of more than one year.

(j) Florida does not report prison admissions for technical violations. All admissions represent new sentences. The 77 admissions due to supervision violations represent persons who committed new crimes while on post-custody community supervision.

(k) Due to errors in an undetermined number of admission and release records, Maine's counts of admissions and releases for 2018 should be regarded as preliminary.

(l) Due to implementation concerns with a new information system, Maryland's counts of admissions and releases for 2017 and 2018 are estimates.

(m) Admissions include local jail inmates admitted to the Nevada Department of Corrections due to medical, behavioral, protective, or local staffing issues and persons ordered by judges to serve 6 months or less in prison prior to actual sentencing for felonies.

(n) State did not submit 2018 NPS data on admissions or releases. Total and detailed types of admissions and releases were imputed. Estimates of admissions and releases in 2018 are not comparable to data for previous years. See Methodology and Jurisdiction notes on the BJS website.

(o) State did not submit 2017 NPS data on admissions and releases. Total and detailed types of admissions and releases were imputed and included in U.S. and state totals. See Methodology and Jurisdiction notes on the BJS website.

(p) Includes all admissions and releases from state prison, regardless of sentence length. See Jurisdiction notes on the BJS website.

(q) State did not report 2017 NPS data on admissions or releases and reported only the total number of admissions and releases in 2018 without detail.

(r) State did not submit 2017 or 2018 NPS data on admissions or releases. Total and detailed types of admissions and releases were imputed and included in U.S. and state totals. See Methodology in this report and in Prisoners in 2017 (NCJ 252156, BJS, April 2019), as well as 2017 and 2018 Jurisdiction notes on the BJS website.

(s) Admission and release data are based on fiscal year and are preliminary.

TABLE 9.29
Prison Facility Capacity, Custody Population, and Percent of Capacity: December 31, 2018

State or other jurisdiction	Type of capacity measure				Custody population as a percent of:	
	Rated capacity	Operational capacity	Design capacity	Custody population	Lowest capacity	Highest capacity
Federal (a)	135,424	N.R.	N.R.	151,865	112.1	112.1
Alabama (b)	N/A	22,176	12,412	20,875	168.2	94.1
Alaska (c)	4,838	N.R.	4,664	4,235	90.8	87.5
Arizona (d)	39,714	41,447	39,714	41,937	105.6	101.2
Arkansas	16,081	16,120	15,297	15,578	101.8	96.6
California	N.R.	122,302	89,763	117,937	131.4	96.4
Colorado	N/A	14,738	13,115	16,086	122.7	109.1
Connecticut	N.R.	N.R.	N.R.	13,228	N.R.	N.R.
Delaware (b)	5,514	5,566	4,092	5,582	136.4	100.3
Florida	N/A	87,103	N/A	85,169	97.8	97.8
Georgia (d)	59,935	54,358	N.R.	53,268	98	88.9
Hawaii	N/A	3,527	3,527	3,527	100	100
Idaho (d)	N/A	7,288	N/A	8,069	110.7	110.7
Illinois (e)	51,329	51,329	N/A	39,392	76.7	76.7
Indiana (f)	N/A	29,140	N/A	26,562	91.2	91.2
Iowa	6,934	6,934	6,934	8,559	123.4	123.4
Kansas	9,974	9,916	9,164	9,938	108.4	99.6
Kentucky	12,784	12,784	12,764	12,290	96.3	96.1
Louisiana	17,956	16,344	16,764	14,880	91	82.9
Maine	2,365	2,591	3,481	2,384	100.8	68.5
Maryland (g)	N.R.	21,072	N.R.	19,180	91	91
Massachusetts	N/A	10,208	7,492	8,454	112.8	82.8
Michigan	40,454	39,702	N/A	38,761	97.6	95.8
Minnesota	N/A	9,504	N/A	9,314	98	98
Mississippi	N.R.	11,839	N.R.	10,061	85	85
Missouri (b)	N/A	31,320	N.R.	30,335	96.9	96.9
Montana	1,236	1,818	1,916	1,837	148.6	95.9
Nebraska (b)	N.R.	4,094	3,375	5,340	158.2	130.4
Nevada	13,803	12,328	9,567	13,182	137.8	95.5
New Hampshire (h)	2,760	2,760	1,810	2,561	141.5	92.8
New Jersey	16,424	17,753	23,072	16,393	99.8	71.1
New Mexico	N.R.	3,986	3,986	4,572	114.7	114.7
New York	50,955	51,149	50,417	46,778	92.8	91.5
North Carolina	N/A	35,138	40,237	35,157	100.1	87.4
North Dakota	1,403	1,403	1,403	1,336	95.2	95.2
Ohio	N.R.	N.R.	N.R.	43,870	N.R.	N.R.
Oklahoma	17,549	19,614	17,549	19,968	113.8	101.8
Oregon (h)	14,712	15,612	14,712	14,707	100	94.2
Pennsylvania	54,531	48,961	N/A	45,941	93.8	84.2
Rhode Island	3,989	3,774	3,975	2,580	68.4	64.7
South Carolina	N/A	21,312	N/A	18,559	87.1	87.1
South Dakota (b)(d)	N/A	4,406	N/A	3,847	87.3	87.3
Tennessee	16,009	15,585	N.R.	11,937	76.6	74.6
Texas (b)	157,375	151,284	157,375	137,286	90.7	87.2
Utah	N.R.	6,771	7,127	5,202	76.8	73
Vermont	1,461	1,561	1,561	1,492	102.1	95.6
Virginia	N/A	29,197	N/A	29,577	101.3	101.3
Washington	N.R.	16,775	N.R.	17,415	103.8	103.8
West Virginia	5,829	6,108	5,829	5,829	100	95.4
Wisconsin	N/A	23,386	17,031	23,576	138.4	100.8
Wyoming	2,427	2,116	2,437	2,053	97	84.2

See footnotes at end of table

TABLE 9.29

Prison Facility Capacity, Custody Population, and Percent of Capacity: December 31, 2018 (continued)

Source: Bureau of Justice Statistics, National Prisoner Statistics, 2018; Prisoners in 2018 NCJ 253516; Date 4/30/2020

Note: Excludes prisoners held in local jails, other states, or private facilities, unless otherwise noted. Rated capacity is the number of prisoners or beds that a facility can hold as set by a rating official. Operational capacity is the number of prisoners that a facility can hold based on staffing and services. Design capacity is the number of prisoners that a facility can hold as set by the architect or planner. Lowest capacity represents the minimum estimate of capacity submitted by the jurisdiction, while highest capacity represents the maximum estimate of capacity. When a jurisdiction could provide only a single estimate of capacity, it was used as both the lowest and highest capacity. For jurisdiction-level information, see Jurisdiction notes on the BJS website. As of December 31, 2001, sentenced felons from the District of Columbia were the responsibility of the Federal Bureau of Prisons.

Key:

 N/A – Not available. State does not measure this type of capacity.

N.R. – Not reported.

(a) Due to differences in the dates when data were extracted, the federal custody count reported for the calculation of capacity differs slightly from the year-end custody count reported in the National Prisoner Statistics (NPS). The count includes all federal prisoners, regardless of conviction status or sentence length.

(b) State defines capacity differently than BJS does. See Jurisdiction notes on the BJS website.

(c) Alaska's capacity excludes non-traditional confinement such as halfway houses and electronic monitoring.

(d) Private facilities are included in capacity and custody counts.

(e) Illinois' rated capacity is under revision, and these numbers are the ceiling operational capacity. Numbers are not comparable to prior reports.

(f) Indiana's capacity includes state-owned facilities that are staffed with employees of a private correctional company.

(g) Maryland's operational capacity may include some pre-trial detainee beds excluded from the custody count.

(h) Assumed to have not changed from the most recent year the state submitted NPS data.

TABLE 9.30
Adults on Probation, 2016

State or other jurisdiction	Probation population				Change during 2016		Number on probation per 100,000 adult residents, 12/31/2016 (a)
	1/1/2016 (a)	2016					
		Entries	Exits	12/31/2016 (a)	Number	Percent	
U.S. total	3,725,638	1,574,587	1,928,687	3,673,120	(52,518)	(1.4)	1,466
Federal	18,320	8,240	9,155	17,284	(1,036)	(5.7)	7
State	3,707,318	1,566,347	1,919,532	3,655,836	(51,482)	(1.4)	1,459
Alabama	51,694	14,477	13,994	52,177	483	0.9	1,382
Alaska	6,513	6,942	6,834	6,621	108	1.7	1,193
Arizona	76,005	24,136	22,768	77,373	1,368	1.8	1,447
Arkansas	29,003	11,328	9,450	30,881	1,878	6.5	1,347
California (b)	238,911	138,876	136,166	239,735	824	1.0	791
Colorado	78,810	55,501	53,701	80,740	1,930	2.4	1,870
Connecticut	42,064	21,483	20,920	41,311	(753)	(1.8)	1,461
Delaware	15,646	12,463	12,714	15,395	(251)	(1.6)	2,049
Florida	221,446	128,167	136,484	214,066	(7,380)	(3.3)	1,288
Georgia (c)	410,964	NK	NK	NK	NK	NK	NK
Hawaii	20,912	4,400	4,796	20,516	(396)	(1.9)	1,828
Idaho	32,898	12,480	12,969	32,409	(489)	(1.5)	2,578
Illinois	122,125	42,970	51,106	113,989	(8,136)	(6.7)	1,154
Indiana	111,709	77,640	81,047	108,302	(3,407)	(3.0)	2,135
Iowa	29,819	15,502	16,067	29,254	(565)	(1.9)	1,213
Kansas	16,588	21,493	21,427	16,654	66	0.4	758
Kentucky	52,266	17,125	17,834	48,457	(3,809)	(7.3)	1,411
Louisiana	40,959	12,875	13,660	40,174	(785)	(1.9)	1,124
Maine	6,702	3,290	3,307	6,817	115	1.7	632
Maryland	76,505	33,494	37,470	72,529	(3,976)	(5.2)	1,550
Massachusetts	64,934	65,772	68,917	61,789	(3,145)	(4.8)	1,133
Michigan	175,189	NK	NK	NK	NK	NK	NK
Minnesota	98,165	47,266	48,579	96,852	(1,313)	(1.3)	2,280
Mississippi	36,333	9,753	17,019	29,067	(7,266)	(20.0)	1,280
Missouri	44,762	25,127	26,090	43,799	(963)	(2.2)	928
Montana	8,818	4,444	4,143	9,132	314	3.6	1,115
Nebraska	12,626	9,951	12,425	13,489	863	6.8	937
Nevada	13,724	5,724	5,414	13,724	0	≤	601
New Hampshire	3,861	2,508	2,430	3,939	78	2.0	366
New Jersey	136,137	32,456	28,004	140,589	4,452	3.3	2,015
New Mexico	13,778	6,288	13,615	12,714	(1,064)	(7.7)	798
New York	101,789	26,494	30,355	97,928	(3,861)	(3.8)	628
North Carolina	85,634	48,995	52,163	82,466	(3,168)	(3.7)	1,044
North Dakota	6,343	4,591	4,593	6,341	(2)	≤	1,090
Ohio	236,375	122,295	123,450	236,754	379	0.2	2,624
Oklahoma	31,281	13,004	10,723	33,562	2,281	7.3	1,129
Oregon	35,938	28,028	27,308	36,658	720	2.0	1,127
Pennsylvania	183,868	94,091	97,467	180,492	(3,376)	(1.8)	1,783
Rhode Island	23,920	NK	NK	22,781	(1,139)	(4.8)	2,680
South Carolina	33,652	13,483	14,501	32,634	(1,018)	(3.0)	839
South Dakota	6,959	3,311	3,660	6,610	(349)	(5.0)	1,009
Tennessee	62,829	23,703	23,431	62,609	(220)	(0.4)	1,209
Texas	378,514	144,055	148,284	374,285	(4,229)	(1.1)	1,805
Utah	12,164	5,616	5,551	12,229	65	0.5	568
Vermont	5,164	NK	NK	4,904	(260)	(5.0)	969
Virginia	55,472	33,897	37,532	60,821	5,349	9.6	927
Washington	93,953	37,969	37,108	89,317	(4,636)	(4.9)	1,565
West Virginia	7,008	NK	1,539	6,523	(485)	(6.9)	448
Wisconsin (d)	46,183	NK	6,351	44,489	(1,694)	(3.7)	988
Wyoming	5,113	2,564	2,758	4,666	(194)	(4.0)	1,046
Dist. of Columbia	5,546	4,576	4,284	5,838	292	5.3	1,034

See footnotes at end of table

TABLE 9.30
Adults on Probation, 2016 (continued)

Source: Bureau of Justice Statistics, Annual Probation Survey and Annual Parole Survey, 2016.

Note: Data quality may vary across jurisdictions for counts of entries and exits; therefore, the population on December, 31, 2016, does not equal the population on January 1, 2016, plus entries, minus exits. Counts may not be actual as reporting agencies may provide estimates on some or all detailed data. January 1, 2015, plus entries, minus exits. Counts may not be actual as reporting agencies may provide estimates on some or all detailed data.

Key:
≤ – Less than 0.05%
NK – Not known
(a) Rates were computed using the estimated U.S. adult resident population in each jurisdiction on January 1, 2017.
(b) January 1, 2016, reflects a reporting change resulting in a decrease of 24,650 from the population reported for December 31, 2015.
(c) January 1, 2016, reflects a reporting change resulting in a decrease of 21,271 from the population reported for December 31, 2015.

TABLE 9.31
Adults on Parole, 2016

State or other jurisdiction	Parole population				Change during 2016		Number on parole on 12/31/16 per100,000 adult residents (a)
	1/1/2016	2016 Entries (a)	2016 Exits (a)	12/31/2016	Number	Percent	
U.S. total	870,657	422,975	428,022	874,777	4,120	0.5	349
Federal	114,746	45,469	48,108	114,385	(361)	(0.3)	46
State	755,911	377,506	379,914	760,392	4,481	0.6	303
Alabama	8,150	2,515	2,103	8,562	412	5.1	227
Alaska	2,100	717	1,005	1,812	(288)	(13.7)	326
Arizona	7,379	11,481	11,360	7,500	121	1.6	140
Arkansas	22,910	10,868	9,902	23,792	882	3.8	1,038
California (b)	86,053	26,007	23,212	93,598	7,545	8.8	309
Colorado	9,953	7,657	7,424	10,186	233	2.3	236
Connecticut	2,939	2,591	2,151	3,379	440	15	119
Delaware	425	129	167	387	(38)	(8.9)	52
Florida	4,611	6,110	6,155	4,566	(45)	(1)	27
Georgia	24,413	9,434	11,461	22,386	(2,027)	(8.3)	285
Hawaii	1,479	629	822	1,367	(112)	(7.6)	122
Idaho	4,875	3,055	2,876	5,054	179	3.7	402
Illinois	29,629	23,889	25,083	29,428	(201)	(0.7)	298
Indiana	9,420	7,056	8,091	8,385	(1,035)	(11)	165
Iowa	5,901	3,810	3,660	6,051	150	2.5	251
Kansas	4,331	4,465	3,966	4,830	499	11.5	220
Kentucky	16,536	10,757	11,910	15,383	(1,153)	(7)	448
Louisiana	31,187	15,888	16,168	30,907	(280)	(0.9)	864
Maine	21	1	1	21	0	..	2
Maryland	10,887	4,295	4,877	10,305	(582)	(5.3)	220
Massachusetts	1,995	2,111	2,255	1,851	(144)	(7.2)	34
Michigan	..	..	..	..	..	..	216
Minnesota	6,810	7,129	6,864	7,075	265	3.9	167
Mississippi	8,424	6,597	6,376	8,645	221	2.6	381
Missouri	17,657	13,255	13,120	17,792	135	0.8	377
Montana	1,092	533	551	1,074	(18)	(1.6)	131
Nebraska	1,050	1,537	1,499	1,088	38	3.6	76
Nevada	5,507	3,635	3,881	5,261	(246)	(4.5)	230
New Hampshire	2,451	1,461	1,476	2,436	(15)	(0.6)	226
New Jersey	15,180	5,539	5,591	15,128	(52)	(0.3)	217
New Mexico	2,763	2,384	2,367	2,780	17	0.6	175
New York	44,562	20,443	20,579	44,426	(136)	(0.3)	285
North Carolina	11,744	13,647	12,388	12,726	982	8.4	161
North Dakota	634	1,545	1,375	804	170	26.8	138
Ohio	18,284	8,085	6,735	19,634	1,350	7.4	218
Oklahoma	2,116	383	604	1,895	(221)	(10.4)	64
Oregon	24,077	9,561	8,927	24,711	634	2.6	760
Pennsylvania	112,351	61,179	62,443	111,087	(1,264)	(1.1)	1,097
Rhode Island	441	239	220	460	19	4.3	54
South Carolina	4,963	2,460	3,076	4,347	(616)	(12.4)	112
South Dakota	2,673	1,788	1,774	2,687	14	0.5	410
Tennessee	13,063	3,353	4,324	12,092	(971)	(7.4)	234
Texas	111,892	35,398	36,003	111,287	(605)	(0.5)	537
Utah	3,502	2,640	2,435	3,707	205	5.9	172
Vermont	1,083	..	..	935	(148)	(13.7)	185
Virginia	1,576	711	601	1,650	74	4.7	25
Washington	11,131	5,782	5,591	11,322	191	1.7	198
West Virginia	3,123	2,113	1,686	3,550	427	13.7	244
Wisconsin (c)	20,241	..	1,450	20,401	160	0.8	453
Wyoming	783	691	632	842	59	7.5	189
Dist. of Columbia	4,548	1,330	1,853	4,025	(523)	(11.5)	713

See footnotes at end of table

TABLE 9.31
Adults on Parole, 2016 (continued)

Source: Bureau of Justice Statistics, Annual Parole Survey, 2016. Probation and Parole in the United States, 2016 NCJ 250230, December 2016.

Note: Data quality may vary across jurisdictions for counts of entries and exits; therefore, the population on December, 31, 2016, does not equal the population on January 1, 2016, plus entries, minus exits. Counts may not be actual as reporting agencies may provide estimates on some or all detailed data.

Key:
-- Less than 0.05%.
.. Not known.

(a) Rates were computed using the estimated U.S. adult resident population in each jurisdiction on January 1, 2017.
(b) Includes Post-Release Community Supervision and Mandatory Supervision parolees: 44,687 parolees on January 1, 2016; and 27,093 entries, 22,343 exits, and 49,437 parolees on December 31, 2016.
(c) Exits reported were deaths and absconders.

TABLE 9.32
Adults Under Community Supervision, 2016

State or jurisdiction	Community supervision population, January 1, 2015 (a)	Entries	Exits	Community supervision population, 12/31/2015/(a)	Change, 2015		Number under community supervision per 100,000 adult residents, December 31, 2015 (b)
					Number	Percent	
U.S. total	4,723,100	2,244,000	2,307,800	4,650,900	(72,200)	(1.5)	1,868
Federal	128,400	58,600	55,600	132,800	4,400	3.4	53
State	4,594,700	2,185,400	2,252,300	4,518,100	(76,600)	(1.7)	1,814
Alabama	60,900	20,500	16,900	64,600	3,700	6	1,714
Alaska	..	..	..	..	..	..	..
Arizona	80,700	38,100	35,500	83,300	2,600	3.2	1,589
Arkansas	49,200	20,800	18,800	51,500	2,200	4.5	2,256
California	372,800	182,500	192,700	349,600	(23,200)	(6.2)	1,158
Colorado	89,100	62,000	62,900	89,200	100	0.1	2,102
Connecticut	45,600	25,000	23,700	45,300	(400)	(0.8)	1,598
Delaware	16,300	12,800	13,100	16,100	(300)	(1.7)	2,155
Florida	232,100	155,100	161,600	225,400	(6,700)	(2.9)	1,381
Georgia	502,200	267,700	324,100	451,800	(50,300)	(10)	5,823
Hawaii	22,500	5,700	6,000	22,500	0	(0.1)	1,996
Idaho	37,700	15,600	15,500	37,800	100	0.2	3,071
Illinois	151,800	..	..	151,300	(600)	(0.4)	1,526
Indiana	126,100	83,600	87,200	122,500	(3,600)	(2.8)	2,423
Iowa	35,400	18,000	17,700	35,600	200	0.7	1,481
Kansas	20,400	25,200	24,700	20,900	500	2.6	951
Kentucky	70,700	37,800	37,800	70,600	0	(0.1)	2,063
Louisiana	70,600	29,800	28,400	71,900	1,300	1.8	2,014
Maine	6,600	3,300	3,200	6,700	100	2.2	626
Maryland	91,100	42,900	46,600	87,400	(3,700)	(4)	1,870
Massachusetts	70,200	68,800	72,100	66,900	(3,300)	(4.7)	1,232
Michigan	192,700	104,500	104,600	193,900	1,200	0.6	2,507
Minnesota	103,700	55,200	53,800	105,100	1,400	1.3	2,489
Mississippi	44,300	17,800	17,300	44,800	500	1.1	1,972
Missouri	65,600	37,800	40,800	62,600	(3,000)	(4.6)	1,329
Montana	9,800	4,400	4,600	9,700	(100)	(0.6)	1,198
Nebraska	13,700	10,500	10,500	13,700	0	(0.1	955
Nevada	18,000	9,700	8,400	19,200	1,300	7.1	858
New Hampshire	6,300	4,100	4,100	6,300	0	0.1	590
New Jersey	152,000	33,200	33,900	151,300	(700)	(0.5)	2,167
New Mexico	17,600	8,200	7,900	16,800	(900)	(4.9)	1,054
New York	150,300	45,800	50,600	145,600	(4,800)	(3.2)	931
North Carolina	99,300	63,700	64,400	97,400	(1,900)	(1.9)	1,249
North Dakota	6,200	5,600	4,900	6,900	700	11.8	1,179
Ohio	258,400	131,200	129,700	262,000	3,600	1.4	2,908
Oklahoma	31,100	13,000	10,700	33,400	2,300	7.3	1,126
Oregon	..	..	..	..	..	..	..
Pennsylvania	281,400	177,700	162,800	296,200	14,900	5.3	2,923
Rhode Island	24,000	300	200	24,400	400	1.6	2,873
South Carolina	39,600	16,100	17,200	38,500	(1,000)	(2.6)	1,006
South Dakota	9,300	5,200	4,700	9,800	500	5.6	1,505
Tennessee	77,800	26,400	28,800	75,400	(2,400)	(3.1)	1,470
Texas	496,900	182,600	191,300	488,800	(8,000)	(1.6)	2,390
Utah	15,100	7,900	7,300	15,700	600	3.8	746
Vermont	6,300	..	..	6,300	0	..	1,236
Virginia	56,700	29,900	29,600	57,000	400	0.6	873
Washington	105,000	44,900	38,900	104,700	(300)	(0.2)	1,870
West Virginia	9,900	2,000	2,600	10,100	200	2.1	692
Wisconsin (c)	65,900	..	200	65,600	(300)	(0.5)	1,462
Wyoming	5,700	3,000	2,800	5,900	200	4	1,323
Dist. of Columbia	11,100	5,700	7,100	9,900	(1,100)	(10.3)	1,776

See footnotes at end of table

TABLE 9.32
Adults Under Community Supervision, 2016 (continued)

Source: Bureau of Justice Statistics, Annual Probation Survey and Annual Parole Survey, 2016.

Note: Counts are rounded to the nearest 100. Detail may not sum to total due to rounding. Data quality may vary across jurisdictions for counts of entries and exits; therefore, the population on December 31, 2016, does not equal the population on January 1, 2016, plus entries, minus exits.

Key:

-- Less than 0.05%.

.. Not known.

(a) The January 1, 2016, population excludes 9,375 offenders and the December 31, 2016, population excludes 10,822 offenders under community supervision who were on both probation and parole.

(b) Rates were computed using the estimated U.S. adult resident population in each jurisdiction on January 1, 2017.

(c) Exits reported were deaths and absconders.

TABLE 9.33
Capital Punishment

State or other jurisdiction	Capital offenses by state	Prisoners under sentence of death	Capital punishment abolished	Method of execution
Alabama	Intentional murder (Ala. Stat. Ann. 13A-5-40(a)(1)-(18)) with 10 aggravating factors (Ala. Stat. Ann. 13A-5-49).	175		Lethal injection, electrocution, lethal gas (u)
Alaska	…	…	1957	…
Arizona	First-degree murder, including pre-meditated murder and felony murder, accompanied by at least 1 of 14 aggravating factors (A.R.S. § 13-703(F)).	119		Lethal gas or lethal injection (a)
Arkansas	Capital murder (Ark. Code Ann. § 5-10-101) with a finding of at least 1 of 10 aggravating circumstances; treason (Ark. Code Ann. § 5-51-201) .	31		Lethal injection or electrocution (b)
California	First-degree murder with special circumstances; military sabotage; death in the course of train wrecking; treason; perjury causing execution of an innocent person; fatal assault by a prisoner serving a life sentence.	725		Lethal injection or lethal gas
Colorado	First-degree murder with at least 1 of 17 aggravating factors; first-degree kidnapping resulting in death; treason.	3		Lethal injection
Connecticut	… (c)	…	2012	…
Delaware	…(d)	(d)	2016	…
Florida (e)	First-degree murder with aggravating factors; felony murder.	347		Lethal injection or electrocution (v)
Georgia	Murder with aggravating circumstances; rape, armed robbery, or kidnapping with bodily injury or ransom when the victim dies; aircraft hijacking; treason (O.C.G.A. § 17-10-30).	48		Lethal injection
Hawaii	…	…	1957	…
Idaho	First-degree murder with aggravating factors; first-degree kidnapping; perjury resulting in the execution of an innocent person.	8		Lethal injection
Illinois	… (f)	…	2011	…
Indiana	Murder with 18 aggravating circumstances (IC 35-50-2-9).	8		Lethal injection
Iowa	…	…	1965	…
Kansas	Intentional and premeditated killing of a person in one or more of seven different circumstances (K.S.A. 21-5401).	10		Lethal injection
Kentucky	Capital murder with presence of at least one statutory aggravating circumstance; capital kidnapping (KRS 532.025).	28		Electrocution or lethal injection (g)
Louisiana (e)	First-degree murder with aggravating circumstances (La. R. S. 14:30); treason (La. R.S. 14:113).	69		Lethal injection
Maine	…	…	1887	…
Maryland	… (h)	…	2013	(h)
Massachusetts	…	…	1984	…
Michigan	…	…	1846	…
Minnesota	…	…	1911	…
Mississippi	Capital murder with aggravating circumstances (Miss Code Ann. § 97-3-19(2)); aircraft piracy (Miss Code Ann. § 97-25-55(1)).	43		Lethal injection, lethal gas, electrocution (w)
Missouri	First-degree murder with at least 1 statutory aggravating circumstances (565.020 RSMO 2000).	23		Lethal injection or lethal gas
Montana (e)	Capital murder with 1 of 9 aggravating circumstances (Mont. Code Ann. § 46-18-303); aggravated kidnapping; felony murder; capital sexual intercourse without consent (Mont. Code Ann. § 45-5-503).	2		Lethal injection
Nebraska (s)	First-degree murder with a finding of one or more statutory aggravating circumstances	12		Lethal injection
Nevada	First-degree murder with at least 1 of 15 aggravating circumstances (NRS 200.030, 200.033, 200.035).	74		Lethal injection
New Hampshire	… (i)	1	2019	(i)
New Jersey	… (j)	…	2007	…
New Mexico	… (k)	0	2009	(k)
New York	First-degree murder with 1 of 13 aggravating factors (NY Penal Law §125.27). (l)	0	2007	(l)
North Carolina	First-degree murder (NCGS §14-17) with the finding of at least 1 of 11 statutory aggravating circumstances.(N.C.G.S. §15A-2000).	145		Lethal injection
North Dakota	…	…	1973	…
Ohio	Aggravated murder with at least 1 of 10 aggravating circumstances (O.R.C. secs. 2903.01, 2929.02, and 2929.04).	141		Lethal injection
Oklahoma (e)	First-degree murder in conjunction with a finding of at least 1 of 8 statutorily-defined aggravating circumstances.	46		Electrocution, lethal injection or firing squad (m)
Oregon	(n) Aggravated murder (ORS 163.095).	31		Lethal injection
Pennsylvania	First-degree murder with 18 aggravating circumstances.	147		Lethal injection
Rhode Island	…	…	1984	…
South Carolina (e)	Murder with 1 of 12 aggravating circumstances (§ 16-3-20(C)(a)).	40		Electrocution or lethal injection
South Dakota	First-degree murder with 1 of 10 aggravating circumstances (S.D.C.L. 23A-27A-1).	1		Lethal injection
Tennessee	First-degree murder (Tenn. Code Ann. § 39-13-202) with 1 of 15 aggravating circumstances (Tenn. Code Ann. § 39-13-204).	52		Lethal injection or electrocution (o)
Texas (e)	Criminal homicide with 1 of 9 aggravating circumstances (TX Penal Code § 19.03).	218		Lethal injection

See footnotes at end of table

TABLE 9.33
Capital Punishment (continued)

State or other jurisdiction	Capital offenses by state	Prisoners under sentence of death	Capital punishment abolished	Method of execution
Utah	Aggravated murder (Utah Code Ann. § 76-5-202).	7		Lethal injection or firing squad (p)
Vermont	...	...	1964	
Virginia	Pre-meditated murder with 1 of 15 aggravating circumstances (VA Code § 18.2-31 (1-15)).	3		Electrocution or lethal injection
Washington	(t)	...	2018	(t)
West Virginia	...	...	1965	...
Wisconsin	...	...	1853	...
Wyoming	First-degree murder; murder during the commission of sexual assault, sexual abuse of a minor, arson, robbery, burglary, escape, resisting arrest, kidnapping, or abuse of a minor under 16 (W.S.A. § 6-2-101 (a)).	1		Lethal injection or lethal gas (q)
Dist. of Columbia	...	...	1981	...
American Samoa	First-degree murder (ASC §46.3513). (p)	0		Hanging (r)
Guam	...	...		...
CNMI*	...	...		...
Puerto Rico	...	...		...
U.S. Virgin Islands	...	...		...

Sources: The U.S. Department of Justice, Office of Justice Programs, Bureau of Justice Statistics, Capital Punishment, 2016 - Statistical Tables, April 2018; The Death Penalty Information Center, 2020.
* Commonwealth of Northern Mariana Islands
Notes:
1. The United States Supreme Court ruling in Roper v. Simmons, 543 U.S. 551 (2005) declared unconstitutional the imposition of the death penalty on persons under the age of 18.
2. The United States Supreme Court ruling in Atkins v. Virginia, 536 U.S. 304 (2002) declared unconstitutional the imposition of the death penalty on mentally handicapped persons.
3. The method of execution of Federal prisoners is lethal injection, pursuant to 28 CFR, Part 26. For offenses under the Violent Crime Control and Law Enforcement Act of 1994, the execution method is that of the State in which the conviction took place (18 U.S.C. 3596).
Key:
... – No capital punishment statute.
(a) Arizona authorizes lethal injection for persons sentenced after November 15, 1992; inmates sentenced before that date may select lethal injection or gas.
(b) Lethal injection is the method unless it is "invalidated by a finald and unappealable court order" and then the execution shall be electrocution."
(c) On April 25, 2012, Connecticut Governor Dannel Malloy signed into law a bill (SB 280) repealing the state's death penalty. The repeal law did not affect the status of the 11 prisoners then on death row. The Connecticut Supreme Court subsequently ruled in August 2015 that the death penalty violated the state constitution. The Court reaffirmed that holding in May 2016 and reiterated that the state's remaining death row prisoners must be resentenced to life without possibility of parole.
(d) The Delaware Supreme Court declared the state's death-penalty statute unconstutitional in 2016. The state's 13 former death-row prisoners have been resentenced to life without parole.
(e) The United States Supreme Court struck a portion of the Louisiana capital statute on June 25, 2008 (Kennedy v. Louisiana, U.S. 128 S.Ct. 2641). The statute (La. Rev. Stat. Ann. § 14:42(D)(2))

allowing execution as a punishment for the rape of a minor when no murder had been committed had been ruled constitutionally permissible by the Louisiana Supreme Court. The U.S. Supreme Court found that since no national consensus existed for application of the death penalty in cases of rape where no murder had been committed, such laws constitute cruel and unusual punishment under the Eighth and Fourteenth Amendments. The ruling affects laws passed in Florida, Oklahoma, South Carolina, Texas, and Montana.
(f) Governor Pat Quinn signed a bill (SB 3539) on March 9, 2011 that abolishes the death penalty effective July 1, 2011. He commuted all death sentences to life without parole.
(g) Kentucky authorizes lethal injection for persons sentenced on or after March 31, 1998; inmates sentenced before that date may select lethal injection or electrocution.
(h) On May 2, 2013, Governor Martin O'Malley signed into law a bill (SB 276) that abolishes the death penalty for future crimes. Gov. O'Malley announced on December 31, 2014, that he would commute the sentences of the four remaining death-row inmates to life in prison without the possibility of parole.
(i) The N.H. Legislature abolished the death penalty when they voted to override Gov. Sununu's veto of the legislation on May 30, 2019. The state has only one person on death row and last carried out an execution in 1939. The abolishment of the death penalty does not apply to the one person on death row.
(j) New Jersey repealed its death penalty statute in 2007.
(k) Gov. Bill Richardson signed a bill in March of 2009 abolishing the death penalty. The law is not retroactive and leaves two inmates on death row.
(l) The New York Court of Appeals has held that a portion of New York's death penalty sentencing statute (C.P.L. 400.27) was unconstitutional (People v. Taylor, 9 N.Y.3d 129 (2007)). No legislative action has been taken to amend the statute. As a result, capital cases are no longer pursued in New York.
(m) Oklahoma authorizes electrocution if lethal injection is held to be unconstitutional, and firing squad if both lethal injection and electrocution are held to be unconstitutional.

TABLE 9.33
Capital Punishment (continued)

(n) In November 2011, Governor John Kitzhaber placed a moratorium on all executions in Oregon. An amended bill to narrow the circumstances in which the death penalty may be imposed in Oregon has passed the state senate. On May 21, 2019 the Oregon Senate passed SB 1013, which would limit the state's use of capital punishment to three aggravating circumstances. The bill would allow prosecutors to pursue the death penalty for only three crimes: acts of terrorism in which at least two people are killed, the murder of a child younger than age 14, and murder committed in prison by a person already incarcerated for a previous murder conviction. Under Oregon's current law, 12 aggravating factors can make a murder death-eligible.

(o) Tennessee authorizes lethal injection for those whose capital offense occurred after December 31, 1998; those who committed the offense before that date may select electrocution by written waiver.

(p) Authorizes firing squad if lethal injection is held unconstitutional. Inmates who selected execution by firing squad prior to May 3, 2004, may still be entitled to execution by that method.

(q) Wyoming authorizes lethal gas if lethal injection is ever held to be unconstitutional.

(r) The last execution was in the 1920s.

(s) In a referendum on the November 8, 2016 ballot 60 percent of Nebraska voters elect to keep the death penalty and lethal injection as state law after it had been repealed by the legislature. On January 26, 2017 Gov. Ricketts signed a flexible execution protocol, allowing acquisition of necessary drugs to resume.

(t) On October 11, 2018, the Washington Supreme Court declared the state's death penalty statute unconstitutional, saying that it was applied in an arbitrary and racially discriminatory manner.

(u) Effective July 1, 2018, lethal injection will be administered unless the prisoner affirmatively chooses lethal gas or electrocution "in writing and delivered to the warden within 30 days after the certficate of judgement."

(v) Lethal injection will be administered unless the prisoner affiramtely chooses electrocution.

(w) Authorizes the use of lethal gas if either lethal injection is held unconstitutional or "otherwise unavailable;" then authorizes electrocution if both of those are held unconstitutionl or "otherwise unavailable."

TABLE 9.34
State Emergency Management Agency Structures and Staffing

State or other jurisdiction	Position appointed	Appointed/ selected by	Organizational structure	Agency operating budget for FY 2019 (excluding federal funds)	FTEs
Alabama	★	G	Governor's Office	$5,212,341	94
Alaska	★	G	Adjutant General/Military Affairs	2,491,000	61 (a)
Arizona	★	ADJ	Adjutant General/Military Affairs	2,969,789	50
Arkansas	★	G	Public Safety	9,457,514	108 (a)
California	★	G	Combined Emergency Management/Homeland Security	278,882,000	1251 (a)
Colorado	★	GHSA	Public Safety	37,859,887	139 (a)
Connecticut	...	PSS	Combined Emergency Management/Homeland Security	6,160,819	57 (a)
Delaware	★	G	Public Safety	2,242,899	39
Florida	★	G	Governor's Office	62,379,027	175
Georgia	★	G	Governor's Office	3,779,786	140 (a)
Hawaii	★	G	Adjutant General/Military Affairs	2,584,000	101
Idaho	★	ADJ	Adjutant General/Military Affairs	2,129,900	34
Illinois	★	G	Governor's Office	38,000,000	163 (a)
Indiana	★	G	Combined Emergency Management/Homeland Security	33,028,314	247 (a)
Iowa	★	G	Combined Emergency Management/Homeland Security	3,796,470	61 (a)
Kansas	★	G	Adjutant General/Military Affairs	1,080,190	49
Kentucky	★	G	Adjutant General/Military Affairs	6,276,815	93
Louisiana	★	G	Governor's Office	4,120,341	56 (a)
Maine	★	G	Adjutant General/Military Affairs	1,941,123	29 (a)
Maryland	★	G	Adjutant General/Military Affairs	2,323,471	67
Massachusetts	★	G	Public Safety	1,030,226	80
Michigan	★	G	State Police	6,549,700	79 (a)
Minnesota	★	PSS	Public Safety	8,348,061	65 (a)
Mississippi	★	G	Public Safety	4,298,000	152
Missouri	★	G	Public Safety	5,771,441	94
Montana	...	ADJ	Adjutant General/Military Affairs	1,167,940	23 (a)
Nebraska	★	ADJ	Adjutant General/Military Affairs	1,763,658	41 (a)
Nevada	★	PSS	Public Safety	636,000	34 (a)
New Hampshire	★	G	Combined Emergency Management/Homeland Security	3,723,258	43 (a)
New Jersey	★	G	State Police	1,800,000	250
New Mexico	★	G	Combined Emergency Management/Homeland Security	2,555,000	65 (a)
New York	★	G	Combined Emergency Management/Homeland Security	9,900,000	574 (a)
North Carolina	★	G	Public Safety	12,190,214	197 (a)
North Dakota	★	ADJ	Adjutant General/Military Affairs	4,083,617	41 (a)
Ohio	★	PSS	Public Safety	6,924,000	94
Oklahoma	★	G	Governor's Office	496,122	41
Oregon	★	ADJ	Adjutant General/Military Affairs	4,269,519	48 (a)
Pennsylvania	★	G	Governor's Office	19,004,000	173
Rhode Island	★	G	Governor's Office	3,023,309	32
South Carolina	★	ADJ	Adjutant General/Military Affairs	3,023,807	67
South Dakota	★	PSS	Public Safety	768,293	20
Tennessee	★	G	Adjutant General/Military Affairs	7,806,400	110
Texas	★	G	Governor's Office/TX A&M University System	5,210,826	330
Utah	★	PSS	Public Safety	1,447,700	58 (a)
Vermont	★	PSS	Public Safety	421,265	24
Virginia	★	G	Combined Emergency Management/Homeland Security	11,591,218	160 (a)
Washington	...	ADJ	Adjutant General/Military Affairs	4,142,000	113 (a)
West Virginia	★	G	Combined Emergency Management/Homeland Security	3,642,326	84 (a)
Wisconsin	★	G	Adjutant General/Military Affairs	3,446,996	65 (a)
Wyoming	★	G	Governor's Office	1,639,108	22 (a)
District of Columbia	★	M	Combined Emergency Management/Homeland Security	5,135,000	141 (a)

Source: National Emergency Management Association, June 2020.
Key:
★ Yes
... - No
G-Governor
ADJ-Adjutant General

GHSA-Governor's Homeland Security Advisor
M-Mayor
PSS-Public Safety Secretary/Commissioner
(a) Combined EM/HS staff.

TABLE 9.35
State Homeland Security Structures and Staffing

State or other jurisdiction	State homeland security advisor	Homeland security organizations	
	Designated homeland security advisor	Day-to-Day operations under	Full-time employee positions
Alabama	Public Safety Secretary/Commissioner	Public Safety	5
Alaska	Adjutant General	Combined Emerg. Mgt./Homeland Security Office	61 (a)
Arizona	Homeland Security Director	Homeland Security (stand-alone office)	15
Arkansas	Dual Title-Emerg. Mgt./Homeland Security Director	Combined Emerg. Mgt./Homeland Security Office	108 (a)
California	Dual Title-Emerg. Mgt./Homeland Security Director	Combined Emerg. Mgt./Homeland Security Office	1251 (a)
Colorado	Dual Title-Emerg. Mgt./Homeland Security Director	Public Safety	139 (a)
Connecticut	Public Safety Secretary/Commissioner	Combined Emerg. Mgt./Homeland Security Office	57 (a)
Delaware	Dual Title-Emerg. Mgt./Homeland Security Director	Public Safety	1
Florida	Public Safety Secretary/Commissioner	Public Safety	27
Georgia	Dual Title-Emerg. Mgt./Homeland Security Director	Combined Emerg. Mgt./Homeland Security Office	140 (a)
Hawaii	Adjutant General	Adjutant General/Military Affairs	9
Idaho	Dual Title-Emerg. Mgt./Homeland Security Director	Adjutant General/Military Affairs	5
Illinois	Dual Title-Emerg. Mgt./Homeland Security Director	Combined Emerg. Mgt./Homeland Security Office	163 (a)
Indiana	Dual Title-Emerg. Mgt./Homeland Security Director	Combined Emerg. Mgt./Homeland Security Office	247 (a)
Iowa	Dual Title-Emerg. Mgt./Homeland Security Director	Combined Emerg. Mgt./Homeland Security Office	61 (a)
Kansas	Adjutant General	Adjutant General/Military Affairs	5
Kentucky	Homeland Security Director	Governor's Office	16
Louisiana	Dual Title-Emerg. Mgt./Homeland Security Director	Combined Emerg. Mgt./Homeland Security Office	56 (a)
Maine	Adjutant General	Adjutant General/Military Affairs	29 (a)
Maryland	Homeland Security Director	Governor's Office	1
Massachusetts	Homeland Security Director	Public Safety	12
Michigan	State Police Superintendent/Director/Commissioner	State Police	79 (a)
Minnesota	Public Safety Secretary/Commissioner	Combined Emerg. Mgt./Homeland Security Office	65 (a)
Mississippi	Homeland Security Director	Governor's Office	18
Missouri	Public Safety Secretary/Commissioner	Public Safety	7
Montana	Adjutant General	Adjutant General/Military Affairs	23 (a)
Nebraska	Lieutenant Governor	Combined Emerg. Mgt./Homeland Security Office	41 (a)
Nevada	Public Safety Secretary/Commissioner	Public Safety	34 (a)
New Hampshire	Dual Title-Emerg. Mgt./Homeland Security Director	Public Safety	43 (a)
New Jersey	Homeland Security Director	Homeland Security (stand-alone office)	130
New Mexico	Dual Title-Emerg. Mgt./Homeland Security Director	Homeland Security (stand-alone office)	65 (a)
New York	Homeland Security Director	Combined Emerg. Mgt./Homeland Security Office	574 (a)
North Carolina	Public Safety Secretary/Commissioner	Public Safety	197 (a)
North Dakota	Homeland Security Director	Adjutant General/Military Affairs	41 (a)
Ohio	Public Safety Secretary/Commissioner	Public Safety	43
Oklahoma	Homeland Security Director	Homeland Security (stand-alone office)	17
Oregon	Adjutant General	Adjutant General/Military Affairs	48 (a)
Pennsylvania	Homeland Security Director	Governor's Office	8
Rhode Island	Adjutant General	Adjutant General/Military Affairs	3
South Carolina	State Police Superintendent/Director/Commissioner	State Police	15
South Dakota	Homeland Security Director	Public Safety	3
Tennessee	Public Safety Secretary/Commissioner	Public Safety	25
Texas	State Police Superintendent/Director/Commissioner	Public Safety	5
Utah	Public Safety Secretary/Commissioner	Public Safety	58 (a)
Vermont	Public Safety Secretary/Commissioner	State Police	4
Virginia	Public Safety Secretary/Commissioner	Combined Emerg. Mgt./Homeland Security Office	160 (a)
Washington	Adjutant General	Adjutant General/Military Affairs	113 (a)
West Virginia	Dual Title-Emerg. Mgt/Homeland Security Director	Combined Emerg. Mgt./Homeland Security Office	84 (a)
Wisconsin	Adjutant General	Adjutant General/Military Affairs	65 (a)
Wyoming	Dual Title-Emerg. Mgt./Homeland Security Director	Governor's Office	22 (a)
Dist. of Columbia	Dual Title-Emerg. Mgt./Homeland Security Director	Combined Emerg. Mgt./Homeland Security Office	141 (a)

Source: National Emergency Management Association's *2020 NEMA Biennial Survey.*

Key:

(a) Includes homeland security and emergency management positions.

TABLE 9.36
Statewide Mutual Aid Agreements and Authorities

State	Opt in	Opt out	Legisalation	Policy	MOA	Executive order
Alabama	...	...	...	...	★	...
Alaska	...	★	★	★	★	...
Arizona	★	...	★	...	★	...
Arkansas	...	...	★	...	...	...
California	...	★	★	★	★	...
Colorado						
Connecticut	...	★	★	...	...	...
Delaware	...	...	★	...	...	...
Florida	...	...	...	...	★	...
Georgia						
Hawaii						
Idaho	...	...	...	...	★	...
Illinois	★	...	★	...	★	...
Indiana	...	★	★	...	...	...
Iowa	...	★	★	...	...	...
Kansas	...	★	★	...	...	...
Kentucky	...	...	★	...	...	...
Louisiana	★	...	★	...	★	...
Maine	...	★	★	...	★	...
Maryland	...	...	★	...	★	...
Massachusetts	★	...	★	...	★	...
Michigan	★	...	★	★	...	...
Minnesota	★	...	★	★	★	★
Mississippi	★	...	★	★	★	★
Missouri	...	...	...	...	★	...
Montana	...	★	★	...	...	...
Nebraska						
Nevada	...	★	★	...	...	...
New Hampshire	...	...	...	...	★	...
New Jersey						
New Mexico						
New York	...	★	★	★	★	...
North Carolina	...	...	...	...	★	...
Ohio	...	...	...	...	★	...
Oklahoma	★	...	★	...	...	...
Oregon	...	★	★	...	...	...
Pennsylvania	...	★	★	...	...	...
Rhode Island						
South Carolina	...	...	...	...	★	...
South Dakota	...	...	★	...	...	...
Tennessee	...	★	★	...	★	...
Texas	...	...	★	...	...	...
Utah	...	★	★	★	★	...
Vermont						
Virginia	★	...	★	...	...	...
Washington	...	★	★	...	...	...
West Virginia	...	...	...	...	★	...
Wisconsin	★	...	★	...	★	...
Wyoming	...	...	...	...	★	...

Source: National Emergency Management Association, June 2020.
Key:
★ – Yes
... – No

CHAPTER TEN
STATE PAGES

TABLE 10.1
Official Names of States and Jurisdictions, Capitals, Zip Codes and Central Switchboards

State or other jurisdiction	Name of state capitol (a)	Capital	Zip code	Area code	Central switchboard (b)
Alabama, State of	State House	Montgomery	36130	334	242-7100
Alaska, State of	State Capitol	Juneau	99801	907	465-2111
Arizona, State of	State Capitol	Phoenix	85007	602	542-4331
Arkansas, State of	State Capitol	Little Rock	72201	501	682-2345
California, State of	State Capitol	Sacramento	95814	916	445-2841
Colorado, State of	State Capitol	Denver	80203	303	866-2471
Connecticut, State of	State Capitol	Hartford	06106	860	566-4840
Delaware, State of	Legislative Hall	Dover	19901	302	744-4101
Florida, State of	The Capitol	Tallahassee	32399	850	717-9337
Georgia, State of	State Capitol	Atlanta	30334	404	656-1776
Hawaii, State of	State Capitol	Honolulu	96813	808	586-2211
Idaho, State of	State Capitol	Boise	83720	208	334-2100
Illinois, State of	State House	Springfield	62706	217	782-0244
Indiana, State of	Statehouse	Indianapolis	46204	317	232-4567
Iowa, State of	State Capitol	Des Moines	50319	515	281-5211
Kansas, State of	The Capitol	Topeka	66612	785	296-3232
Kentucky, Commonwealth of	State Capitol	Frankfort	40601	502	564-2611
Louisiana, State of	State Capitol	Baton Rouge	70804	225	342-7015
Maine, State of	State House	Augusta	04333	207	287-3531
Maryland, State of	State House	Annapolis	21401	410	974-3901
Massachusetts, Commonwealth of	State House	Boston	02133	617	725-4005
Michigan, State of	State Capitol	Lansing	48909	517	373-3400
Minnesota, State of	State Capitol	St. Paul	55155	651	201-3400
Mississippi, State of	State Capitol	Jackson	39215	601	359-3150
Missouri, State of	State Capitol	Jefferson City	65101	573	751-0290
Montana, State of	State Capitol	Helena	59620	406	444-3111
Nebraska, State of	State Capitol	Lincoln	68509	402	471-2244
Nevada, State of	State Capitol	Carson City	89701	775	684-5670
New Hampshire, State of	State House	Concord	03301	603	271-2121
New Jersey, State of	State House	Trenton	08625	609	292-6000
New Mexico, State of	State Capitol	Santa Fe	87501	505	476-2200
New York, State of	State Capitol	Albany	12224	518	474-8390
North Carolina, State of	State Capitol	Raleigh	27601	919	733-5811
North Dakota, State of	State Capitol	Bismarck	58505	701	328-2200
Ohio, State of	Statehouse	Columbus	43215	614	466-3555
Oklahoma, State of	State Capitol	Oklahoma City	73105	405	521-2342
Oregon, State of	State Capitol	Salem	97301	503	378-4582
Pennsylvania, Commonwealth of	The Capitol	Harrisburg	17120	717	787-2500
Rhode Island and Providence Plantations, State of	State House	Providence	02903	401	222-2080
South Carolina, State of	State House	Columbia	29201	803	734-2100
South Dakota, State of	State Capitol	Pierre	57501	605	773-3212
Tennessee, State of	State Capitol	Nashville	37243	615	741-2001
Texas, State of	State Capitol	Austin	78711	512	463-2000
Utah, State of	State Capitol	Salt Lake City	84114	801	538-1000
Vermont, State of	State House	Montpelier	05609	802	828-3333
Virginia, Commonwealth of	State Capitol	Richmond	23219	804	786-2211
Washington, State of	Legislative Building	Olympia	98504	360	902-4111
West Virginia, State of	State Capitol	Charleston	25305	304	558-2000
Wisconsin, State of	State Capitol	Madison	53702	608	266-1212
Wyoming, State of	State Capitol	Cheyenne	82002	307	777-7434
District of Columbia	John A. Wilson Building	...	20004	202	727-6300
American Samoa, Territory of	Maota Fono Complex	Pago Pago	96799	684	633-4116
Guam, Territory of	Congress Building	Hagatna	96910	671	472-8931
No. Mariana Islands, Commonwealth of	Capital Hill	Saipan	96950	670	664-2280
Puerto Rico, Commonwealth of	The Capitol	San Juan	00902	787	721-7000
U.S. Virgin Islands, Territory of	Legislature Building	Charlotte Amalie, St. Thomas	00802	340	774-0001

Key:
(a) In some instances the name is not official.
(b) Numbers generally come from an executive branch office, such
   as the office of the governor.

TABLE 10.2
Historical Data on the States and Territories

State or other jurisdiction	Source of state or territorial lands	Date organized as territory	Date admitted to Union	Chronological order of admission to Union
Alabama	Mississippi Territory, 1798 (a)	March 3, 1817	Dec. 14, 1819	22
Alaska	Purchased from Russia, 1867	Aug. 24, 1912	Jan. 3, 1959	49
Arizona	Ceded by Mexico, 1848 (b)	Feb. 24, 1863	Feb. 14, 1912	48
Arkansas	Louisiana Purchase, 1803	March 2, 1819	June 15, 1836	25
California	Ceded by Mexico, 1848	(c)	Sept. 9, 1850	31
Colorado	Louisiana Purchase, 1803 (d)	Feb. 28, 1861	Aug. 1, 1876	38
Connecticut	Fundamental Orders, Jan. 14, 1638; Royal charter, April 23, 1662	(e)	Jan. 9, 1788 (f)	5
Delaware	Swedish charter, 1638; English charter, 1638	(e)	Dec. 7, 1787 (f)	1
Florida	Ceded by Spain, 1819	March 30, 1822	March 3, 1845	27
Georgia	Charter, 1732, from George II to Trustees for Establishing the Colony of Georgia	(e)	Jan. 2, 1788 (f)	4
Hawaii	Annexed, 1898	June 14, 1900	Aug. 21, 1959	50
Idaho	Treaty with Britain, 1846	March 4, 1863	July 3, 1890	43
Illinois	Northwest Territory, 1787	Feb. 3, 1809	Dec. 3, 1818	21
Indiana	Northwest Territory, 1787	May 7, 1800	Dec. 11, 1816	19
Iowa	Louisiana Purchase, 1803	June 12, 1838	Dec. 28, 1846	29
Kansas	Louisiana Purchase, 1803 (d)	May 30, 1854	Jan. 29, 1861	34
Kentucky	Part of Virginia until admitted as state	(c)	June 1, 1792	15
Louisiana	Louisiana Purchase, 1803 (g)	March 26, 1804	April 30, 1812	18
Maine	Part of Massachusetts until admitted as state	(c)	March 15, 1820	23
Maryland	Charter, 1632, from Charles I to Calvert	(e)	April 28, 1788 (f)	7
Massachusetts	Charter to Massachusetts Bay Company, 1629	(e)	Feb. 6, 1788 (f)	6
Michigan	Northwest Territory, 1787	Jan. 11, 1805	Jan. 26, 1837	26
Minnesota	Northwest Territory, 1787 (h)	March 3, 1849	May 11, 1858	32
Mississippi	Mississippi Territory (i)	April 7, 1798	Dec. 10, 1817	20
Missouri	Louisiana Purchase, 1803	June 4, 1812	Aug. 10, 1821	24
Montana	Louisiana Purchase, 1803 (j)	May 26, 1864	Nov. 8, 1889	41
Nebraska	Louisiana Purchase, 1803	May 30, 1854	March 1, 1867	37
Nevada	Ceded by Mexico, 1848	March 2, 1861	Oct. 31, 1864	36
New Hampshire	Grants from Council for New England, 1622 and 1629; made Royal province, 1679	(e)	June 21, 1788 (f)	9
New Jersey	Dutch settlement, 1618; English charter, 1664	(e)	Dec. 18, 1787 (f)	3
New Mexico	Ceded by Mexico, 1848 (b)	Sept. 9, 1850	Jan. 6, 1912	47
New York	Dutch settlement, 1623; English control, 1664	(e)	July 26, 1788 (f)	11
North Carolina	Charter, 1663, from Charles II	(e)	Nov. 21, 1789 (f)	12
North Dakota	Louisiana Purchase, 1803 (k)	March 2, 1861	Nov. 2, 1889	39
Ohio	Northwest Territory, 1787	May 7, 1800	March 1, 1803	17
Oklahoma	Louisiana Purchase, 1803	May 2, 1890	Nov. 16, 1907	46
Oregon	Settlement and treaty with Britain, 1846	Aug. 14, 1848	Feb. 14, 1859	33
Pennsylvania	Grant from Charles II to William Penn, 1681	(e)	Dec. 12, 1787 (f)	2
Rhode Island	Charter, 1663, from Charles II	(e)	May 29, 1790 (f)	13
South Carolina	Charter, 1663, from Charles II	(e)	May 23, 1788 (f)	8
South Dakota	Louisiana Purchase, 1803	March 2, 1861	Nov. 2, 1889	40
Tennessee	Part of North Carolina until land ceded to U.S. in 1789	June 8, 1790 (l)	June 1, 1796	16
Texas	Republic of Texas, 1845	(c)	Dec. 29, 1845	28
Utah	Ceded by Mexico, 1848	Sept. 9, 1850	Jan. 4, 1896	45
Vermont	From lands of New Hampshire and New York	(c)	March 4, 1791	14
Virginia	Charter, 1609, from James I to London Company	(e)	June 25, 1788 (f)	10
Washington	Oregon Territory, 1848	March 2, 1853	Nov. 11, 1889	42
West Virginia	Part of Virginia until admitted as state	(c)	June 20, 1863	35
Wisconsin	Northwest Territory, 1787	April 20, 1836	May 29, 1848	30
Wyoming	Louisiana Purchase, 1803 (d)(j)	July 25, 1868	July 10, 1890	44
Dist. of Columbia	Maryland (m)	…	…	…
American Samoa	-- Became a territory, 1900 --			
Guam	Ceded by Spain, 1898	Aug. 1, 1950	…	…
CNMI*	(o)	March 24, 1976	…	…
Puerto Rico	Ceded by Spain, 1898	…	July 25, 1952 (n)	…
U.S. Virgin Islands	-- Purchased from Denmark, March 31, 1917 --			

See footnotes at end of table

TABLE 10.2
Historical Data on the States and Territories (continued)

Source: The Council of State Governments
Key:
* Commonwealth of Northern Mariana Islands
(a) By the Treaty of Paris, 1783, England gave up claim to the 13 original Colonies, and to all land within an area extending along the present Canadian to the Lake of the Woods, down the Mississippi River to the 31st parallel, east to the Chattahoochee, down that river to the mouth of the Flint, border east to the source of the St. Mary's down that river to the ocean. The major part of Alabama was acquired by the Treaty of Paris, and the lower portion from Spain in 1813.
(b) Portion of land obtained by Gadsden Purchase, 1853.
(c) No territorial status before admission to Union.
(d) Portion of land ceded by Mexico, 1848.
(e) One of the original 13 Colonies.
(f) Date of ratification of U.S. Constitution.
(g) West Feliciana District (Baton Rouge) acquired from Spain, 1810; added to Louisiana, 1812.

(h) Portion of land obtained by Louisiana Purchase, 1803.
(i) See footnote (a). The lower portion of Mississippi also was acquired from Spain in 1813.
(j) Portion of land obtained from Oregon Territory, 1848.
(k) The northern portion of the Red River Valley was acquired by treaty with Great Britain in 1818.
(l) Date Southwest Territory (identical boundary as Tennessee's) was created.
(m) Area was originally 100 square miles, taken from Virginia and Maryland. Virginia's portion south of the Potomac was given back to that state in 1846. Site chosen in 1790, city incorporated 1802.
(n) On this date, Puerto Rico became a self-governing commonwealth by compact approved by the U.S. Congress and the voters of Puerto Rico as provided in U.S. Public Law 600 of 1950.
(o) The Commonwealth of the Northern Mariana Islands (CNMI) emerged from the Trust Territory of the Pacific Islands (TTPI) which the United States administered on behalf of the United Nations from 1947 until 1994.

TABLE 10.3
State Statistics

State or other jurisdiction	Land area		Population (a)		Percentage change 2018 to 2019	Density per square mile	Rank in nation
	In square miles (2010)	Rank in nation	Size	Rank in nation			
Alabama	50,645	28	4,903,185	24	0.3	96.8	27
Alaska	570,641	1	731,545	48	(0.5)	1.3	50
Arizona	113,594	6	7,278,717	14	1.7	64.1	32
Arkansas	52,035	27	3,017,804	33	0.3	58.0	34
California	155,779	3	39,512,223	1	0.1	253.6	11
Colorado	103,642	8	5,758,736	21	1.2	55.6	37
Connecticut	4,842	48	3,565,287	29	(0.2)	736.3	4
Delaware	1,949	49	973,764	45	0.9	499.7	6
Florida	53,625	26	21,477,737	3	1.1	400.5	8
Georgia	57,513	21	10,617,423	8	1.0	184.6	17
Hawaii	6,423	47	1,415,872	40	(0.3)	220.5	13
Idaho	82,643	11	1,787,065	39	2.1	21.6	44
Illinois	55,519	24	12,671,821	6	(0.4)	228.2	12
Indiana	35,826	38	6,732,219	17	0.5	187.9	16
Iowa	55,857	23	3,155,070	31	0.2	56.5	36
Kansas	81,759	13	2,913,314	35	0.1	35.6	41
Kentucky	39,486	37	4,467,673	26	0.1	113.1	23
Louisiana	43,204	33	4,648,794	25	(0.2)	107.6	25
Maine	30,843	39	1,344,212	42	0.4	43.6	39
Maryland	9,707	42	6,045,680	19	0.2	622.8	5
Massachusetts	7,800	45	6,892,503	15	0.1	883.6	3
Michigan	56,539	22	9,986,857	10	0.0	176.6	18
Minnesota	79,627	14	5,639,632	22	0.6	70.8	30
Mississippi	46,923	31	2,976,149	34	(0.2)	63.4	33
Missouri	68,742	18	6,137,428	18	0.3	89.3	28
Montana	145,546	4	1,068,778	43	0.8	7.3	48
Nebraska	76,824	15	1,934,408	37	0.5	25.2	43
Nevada	109,781	7	3,080,156	32	1.7	28.1	42
New Hampshire	8,953	44	1,359,711	41	0.5	151.9	21
New Jersey	7,354	46	8,882,190	11	0.0	1,207.8	1
New Mexico	121,298	5	2,096,829	36	0.2	17.3	45
New York	47,126	30	19,453,561	4	(0.4)	412.8	7
North Carolina	48,618	29	10,488,084	9	1.0	215.7	15
North Dakota	69,001	17	762,062	47	0.5	11.0	47
Ohio	40,861	35	11,689,100	7	0.1	286.1	10
Oklahoma	68,595	19	3,956,971	28	0.4	57.7	35
Oregon	95,988	10	4,217,737	27	0.9	43.9	38
Pennsylvania	44,743	32	12,801,989	5	0.0	286.1	9
Rhode Island	1,034	50	1,059,361	44	0.1	1,024.7	2
South Carolina	30,061	40	5,148,714	23	1.3	171.3	19
South Dakota	75,811	16	884,659	46	0.7	11.7	46
Tennessee	41,235	34	6,829,174	16	0.8	165.6	20
Texas	261,232	2	28,995,881	2	1.3	111.0	24
Utah	82,170	12	3,205,958	30	1.7	39.0	40
Vermont	9,217	43	623,989	49	(0.1)	67.7	31
Virginia	39,490	36	8,535,519	12	0.4	216.1	14
Washington	66,456	20	7,614,893	13	1.2	114.6	22
West Virginia	24,038	41	1,792,147	38	(0.7)	74.6	29
Wisconsin	54,158	25	5,822,434	20	0.3	107.5	26
Wyoming	97,093	9	578,759	50	0.2	6.0	49
Dist. of Columbia	61	N.A.	705,749	N.A.	0.6	11,569.7	N.A.
American Samoa (b)	76	N.A.	55,519	N.A.	(3.1)(c)	730.5	N.A.
Guam (b)	210	N.A.	159,358	N.A.	2.9 (c)	758.8	N.A.
CNMI*(b)	182	N.A.	53,833	N.A.	(22.2)(c)	295.8	N.A.
Puerto Rico	3,424	N.A.	3,193,694	N.A.	0.0	932.7	N.A.
U.S. Virgin Islands (b)	134	N.A.	106,405	N.A.	(2.0)(c)	794.1	N.A.

See footnotes at end of table

TABLE 10.3
State Statistics (continued)

State or other jurisdiction	Number of Representatives in Congress	Capital	Population (j)	Rank in state	Largest city	Population (j)
Alabama	7	Montgomery	198,218	2	Birmingham	209,880
Alaska	1	Juneau	32,113	2	Anchorage	291,538
Arizona	9	Phoenix	1,660,272	1	Phoenix	1,660,272
Arkansas	4	Little Rock	197,881	1	Little Rock	197,881
California	53	Sacramento	508,529	6	Los Angeles	3,990,456
Colorado	7	Denver	716,492	1	Denver	716,492
Connecticut	5	Hartford	122,587	4	Bridgeport	144,900
Delaware	1	Dover	38,079	2	Wilmington	70,635
Florida	27	Tallahassee	193,551	8	Jacksonville	903,889
Georgia	14	Atlanta	498,044	1	Atlanta	498,044
Hawaii	2	Honolulu	347,397	1	Honolulu	347,397
Idaho	2	Boise	228,790	1	Boise	228,790
Illinois	18	Springfield	114,694	6	Chicago	2,705,994
Indiana	9	Indianapolis	867,125	1	Indianapolis	867,125
Iowa	4	Des Moines	216,853	1	Des Moines	216,853
Kansas	4	Topeka	125,904	5	Wichita	389,255
Kentucky	6	Frankfort	27,679	15	Louisville (e)	620,118
Louisiana	6	Baton Rouge	221,599	2	New Orleans	391,006
Maine	2	Augusta	18,681	10	Portland	66,417
Maryland	8	Annapolis	39,174	7	Baltimore	602,495
Massachusetts	9	Boston	694,853	1	Boston	694,583
Michigan	14	Lansing	118,427	6	Detroit	672,662
Minnesota	8	St. Paul	307,695	2	Minneapolis	425,403
Mississippi	4	Jackson	164,422	1	Jackson	164,422
Missouri	8	Jefferson City	42,838	15	Kansas City	491,918
Montana	1	Helena	32,315	6	Billings	109,550
Nebraska	3	Lincoln	287,401	2	Omaha	468,262
Nevada	4	Carson City	55,414	6	Las Vegas	644,644
New Hampshire	2	Concord	43,412	3	Manchester	112,525
New Jersey	12	Trenton	83,974	6	Newark	282,090
New Mexico	3	Santa Fe	84,612	4	Albuquerque	560,218
New York	27	Albany	97,279	6	New York City	8,398,748
North Carolina	13	Raleigh	469,298	2	Charlotte	872,498
North Dakota	1	Bismarck	73,112	2	Fargo	124,844
Ohio	16	Columbus	892,533	1	Columbus	892,533
Oklahoma	5	Oklahoma City	649,021	1	Oklahoma City	649,021
Oregon	5	Salem	173,442	2	Portland	653,115
Pennsylvania	18	Harrisburg	49,229	9	Philadelphia (f)	1,584,138
Rhode Island	2	Providence	179,335	1	Providence	179,335
South Carolina	7	Columbia	133,451	2	Charleston	136,208
South Dakota	1	Pierre	13,980	8	Sioux Falls	181,883
Tennessee	9	Nashville (g)	669,053	1	Nashville (g)	669,053
Texas	36	Austin	964,254	4	Houston	2,325,502
Utah	4	Salt Lake City	200,591	1	Salt Lake City	200,591
Vermont	1	Montpelier	7,436	6	Burlington	42,899
Virginia	11	Richmond	228,783	4	Virginia Beach	450,189
Washington	10	Olympia	52,555	23	Seattle	744,955
West Virginia	3	Charleston	47,215	1	Charleston	47,215
Wisconsin	8	Madison	258,054	2	Milwaukee	592,025
Wyoming	1	Cheyenne	63,957	1	Cheyenne	63,957
Dist. of Columbia	1 (h)	N.A.	N.A.	N.A.	N.A.	N.A.
American Samoa (b)	1 (h)	Pago Pago	3,656 (b)	3	Tafuna	9,756 (b)
Guam (b)	1 (h)	Hagatna (d)	1,051 (b)	13	Dededo (d)	44943 (b)
CNMI*(b)	1 (h)	Saipan (d)	48,220 (b)	1	Saipan (d)	48,220 (b)
Puerto Rico	1 (i)	San Juan	337,288	1	San Juan	337,288
U.S. Virgin Islands (b)	1 (h)	Charlotte Amalie, St. Thomas	18,481 (b)	1	Charlotte Amalie, St. Thomas	18,481 (b)

See footnotes at end of table

TABLE 10.3
State Statistics (continued)

Source: U.S. Census Bureau, information available as of April 2020.
  *Commonwealth of Northern Mariana Islands
Key:
N.A.–Not applicable
(a) July 1, 2019 Census Bureau estimates.
(b) 2010 Census Bureau counts.
(c) Population change calculations are from 2000-2010.
(d) Municipality.
(e) This city is part of a consolidated city-county government and is coextensive with Jefferson County.

(f) Philadelphia County and Philadelphia city are coextensive.
(g) This city is part of a consolidated city-county government and is coextensive with Davidson County.
(h) Represented by one non-voting House Delegate.
(i) Represented by one non-voting House Resident Commissioner.
(j) July 1, 2018 Census Bureau estimates (released May 2019).

TABLE 10.4
Personal Income, Population, and Per Capita Personal Income, by State, 2018-2019

State or other jurisdiction	Personal income (millions of dollars)		Percent change 2018-19	Rank of percent change 2018-19	Population (thousands of persons) 2019 (a)	Per capita personal income (dollars)		
	2018	2019 (p)				2019 (p)	Rank in U.S. 2019 (p)	Percent of U.S. 2019 (p)
United States	17,813,035	18,599,062	4.4	N.A	328,240	56,663	N.A	100
Alabama	206,455	215,149	4.2	25	4,903	43,880	48	77
Alaska	43,818	45,430	3.7	40	732	62,102	10	110
Arizona	317,913	336,514	5.9	4	7,279	46,233	42	82
Arkansas	130,297	135,334	3.9	32	3,018	44,845	45	79
California	2,514,129	2,633,925	4.8	14	39,512	66,661	5	118
Colorado	332,943	353,287	6.1	1	5,759	61,348	11	108
Connecticut	273,152	281,967	3.2	48	3,565	79,087	1	140
Delaware	50,783	52,840	4.1	27	974	54,264	21	96
Florida	1,066,447	1,116,597	4.7	15	21,478	51,989	28	92
Georgia	488,964	511,745	4.7	17	10,617	48,199	38	85
Hawaii	78,721	81,343	3.3	45	1,416	57,450	17	101
Idaho	77,012	81,565	5.9	3	1,787	45,642	43	81
Illinois	724,189	746,820	3.1	49	12,672	58,935	14	104
Indiana	315,516	327,570	3.8	35	6,732	48,657	36	86
Iowa	158,197	166,070	5.0	11	3,155	52,636	26	93
Kansas	149,859	155,724	3.9	31	2,913	53,453	24	94
Kentucky	189,717	196,656	3.7	41	4,468	44,017	46	78
Louisiana	215,489	223,179	3.6	42	4,649	48,008	39	85
Maine	65,454	68,487	4.6	18	1,344	50,950	29	90
Maryland	382,829	397,100	3.7	36	6,046	65,683	6	116
Massachusetts	494,765	516,714	4.4	21	6,893	74,967	2	132
Michigan	484,030	502,540	3.8	34	9,987	50,320	32	89
Minnesota	322,728	336,590	4.3	22	5,640	59,683	13	105
Mississippi	112,992	117,165	3.7	39	2,976	39,368	50	69
Missouri	292,513	304,347	4.0	28	6,137	49,589	33	88
Montana	50,500	52,449	3.9	33	1,069	49,074	34	87
Nebraska	102,759	106,143	3.3	46	1,934	54,871	20	97
Nevada	149,219	156,727	5.0	9	3,080	50,883	30	90
New Hampshire	83,143	86,859	4.5	20	1,360	63,880	8	113
New Jersey	607,884	630,449	3.7	37	8,882	70,979	4	125
New Mexico	87,189	92,227	5.8	5	2,097	43,984	47	78
New York	1,341,932	1,389,760	3.6	43	19,454	71,440	3	126
North Carolina	478,862	501,362	4.7	16	10,488	47,803	41	84
North Dakota	42,148	43,819	4.0	30	762	57,501	16	101
Ohio	569,727	590,838	3.7	38	11,689	50,546	31	89
Oklahoma	182,302	189,740	4.1	26	3,957	47,951	40	85
Oregon	213,070	223,276	4.8	13	4,218	52,937	25	93
Pennsylvania	720,073	752,431	4.5	19	12,802	58,775	15	104
Rhode Island	57,994	59,899	3.3	47	1,059	56,542	19	100
South Carolina	222,189	233,308	5.0	10	5,149	45,314	44	80
South Dakota	46,066	47,705	3.6	44	885	53,925	22	95
Tennessee	317,515	332,999	4.9	12	6,829	48,761	35	86
Texas	1,445,270	1,522,411	5.3	7	28,996	52,504	27	93
Utah	146,423	155,153	6.0	2	3,206	48,395	37	85
Vermont	33,929	35,374	4.3	23	624	56,691	18	100
Virginia	492,313	513,121	4.2	24	8,536	60,116	12	106
Washington	467,399	494,189	5.7	6	7,615	64,898	7	115
West Virginia	73,809	75,873	2.8	50	1,792	42,336	49	75
Wisconsin	299,933	311,984	4.0	29	5,822	53,583	23	95
Wyoming	34,873	36,645	5.1	8	579	63,316	9	112
Dist. of Columbia	57,605	59,663	3.6	N.A.	706	84,538	N.A.	149

Source: U.S. Bureau of Economic Analysis, data released March 2020.
Key:
N.A.–Not applicable
(p)–Preliminary
(a) Census Bureau midyear population estimates available as of December 2019.

Table 10.4 | Personal Income

2019 Personal Income Per Capita by State

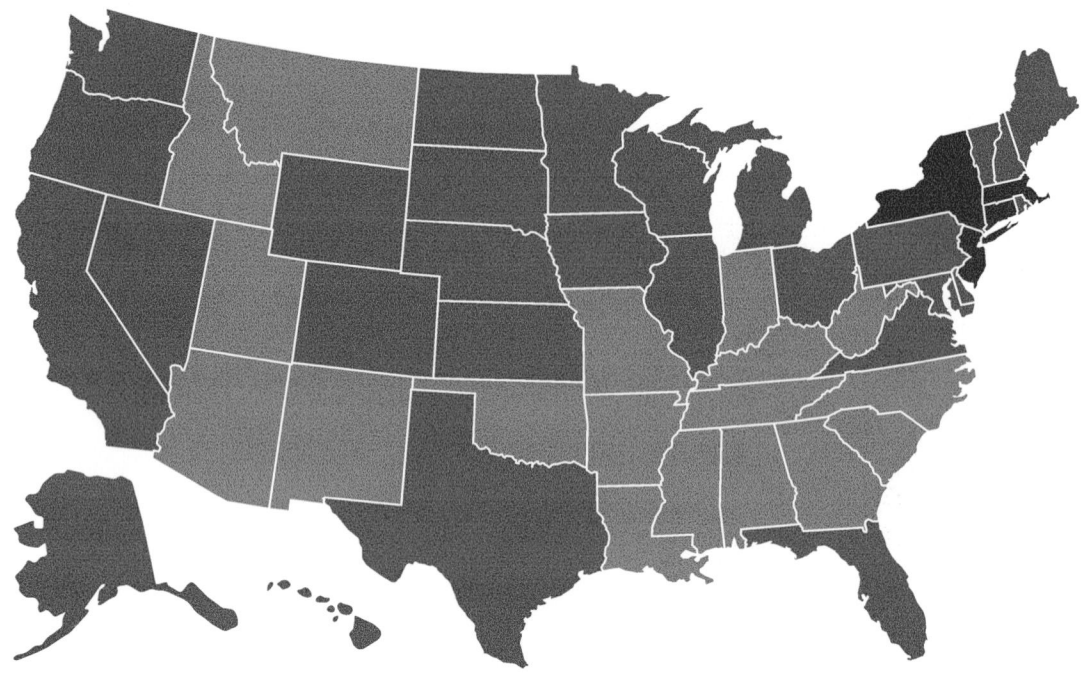

● $30,000 – $49,999   ● $50,000 – $69,999   ● $70,000 – $90,000

Rank of Percent Change

1. COLORADO	18. MAINE	35. INDIANA
2. UTAH	19. PENNSYLVANIA	36. MARYLAND
3. IDAHO	20. NEW HAMPSHIRE	37. NEW JERSEY
4. ARIZONA	21. MASSACHUSETTS	38. OHIO
5. NEW MEXICO	22. MINNESOTA	39. MISSISSIPPI
6. WASHINGTON	23. VERMONT	40. ALASKA
7. TEXAS	24. VIRGINIA	41. KENTUCKY
8. WYOMING	25. ALABAMA	42. LOUISIANA
9. NEVADA	26. OKLAHOMA	43. NEW YORK
10. SOUTH CAROLINA	27. DELAWARE	44. SOUTH DAKOTA
11. IOWA	28. MISSOURI	45. HAWAII
12. TENNESSEE	29. WISCONSIN	46. NEBRASKA
13. OREGON	30. NORTH DAKOTA	47. RHODE ISLAND
14. CALIFORNIA	31. KANSAS	48. CONNECTICUT
15. FLORIDA	32. ARKANSAS	49. ILLINOIS
16. NORTH CAROLINA	33. MONTANA	50. WEST VIRGINIA
17. GEORGIA	34. MICHIGAN	

Percentage Change

HIGHEST

#1 Colorado
#2 Utah
#3 Idaho
#4 Arizona
#5 New Mexico

LOWEST

#1 West Virginia
#2 Illinois
#3 Connecticut
#4 Rhode Island
#5 Nebraska

TABLE 10.5
Personal Income by State, 2018: Q3-2019:Q4

	Personal income (millions of dollars, seasonally adjusted at annual rate)					
	2018		2019			
	3rd Quarter	4th quarter	1rst Quarter(r)	2nd Quarter(r)	3rd Quarter(r)	4th Quarter (p)
United States	17,918,889	18,077,710	18,351,263	18,550,204	18,677,189	18,817,591
Alabama	207,199	209,434	212,367	214,201	216,246	217,784
Alaska	44,155	44,416	44,895	45,319	45,639	45,868
Arizona	320,206	323,426	330,002	334,659	339,324	342,069
Arkansas	130,648	132,567	133,107	135,088	136,122	137,020
California	2,528,020	2,558,708	2,597,167	2,639,073	2,639,790	2,659,672
Colorado	335,702	339,473	347,156	351,539	356,589	357,864
Connecticut	275,620	276,573	280,872	282,032	281,865	283,097
Delaware	51,109	51,313	52,169	52,666	53,009	53,516
Florida	1,074,087	1,083,427	1,101,149	1,114,323	1,121,145	1,129,771
Georgia	493,469	496,476	504,015	510,057	514,437	518,473
Hawaii	79,044	79,702	80,692	81,015	81,479	82,184
Idaho	77,240	78,609	79,773	81,182	82,386	82,920
Illinois	727,933	732,729	739,840	741,776	749,778	755,885
Indiana	316,541	320,078	323,347	325,924	329,524	331,486
Iowa	158,249	162,261	163,452	164,063	167,832	168,934
Kansas	150,316	152,286	153,411	154,552	156,902	158,032
Kentucky	190,293	191,855	194,288	195,630	197,348	199,356
Louisiana	216,206	219,063	221,805	222,491	223,549	224,871
Maine	65,919	66,193	67,605	68,251	68,780	69,314
Maryland	385,096	387,297	392,402	396,407	398,105	401,485
Massachusetts	497,289	501,330	512,810	516,775	516,641	520,627
Michigan	486,479	489,637	495,036	500,458	504,433	510,232
Minnesota	324,796	328,791	331,023	334,296	339,365	341,675
Mississippi	113,203	114,577	115,931	116,334	117,847	118,549
Missouri	293,277	296,564	300,257	302,536	306,126	308,467
Montana	50,632	51,406	51,536	51,961	52,945	53,354
Nebraska	102,474	104,737	104,351	105,027	107,214	107,981
Nevada	150,069	152,543	154,285	156,084	157,466	159,071
New Hampshire	83,698	83,899	86,448	86,688	86,834	87,464
New Jersey	612,041	614,546	624,111	629,276	632,803	635,608
New Mexico	87,924	88,736	90,408	91,659	93,047	93,795
New York	1,350,653	1,347,977	1,373,084	1,391,782	1,393,416	1,400,760
North Carolina	480,916	487,483	493,938	500,011	503,806	507,694
North Dakota	42,245	43,355	43,152	43,233	44,384	44,508
Ohio	573,252	577,736	584,705	588,203	592,950	597,491
Oklahoma	183,035	185,150	188,698	188,946	190,253	191,061
Oregon	214,599	217,004	220,279	222,662	224,148	226,015
Pennsylvania	725,567	731,921	743,171	751,865	754,614	760,073
Rhode Island	57,847	58,792	59,607	60,134	59,663	60,191
South Carolina	223,358	226,042	230,255	232,103	234,507	236,368
South Dakota	45,932	47,567	46,852	46,921	48,391	48,656
Tennessee	320,445	322,221	328,144	331,805	334,361	337,687
Texas	1,454,680	1,468,007	1,496,949	1,513,993	1,532,110	1,546,590
Utah	147,288	148,963	152,173	154,175	156,309	157,956
Vermont	34,108	34,390	35,127	35,241	35,448	35,681
Virginia	495,352	499,671	506,099	511,161	515,517	519,709
Washington	471,677	475,449	484,708	492,676	497,247	502,124
West Virginia	74,712	75,136	75,426	75,796	75,959	76,311
Wisconsin	301,100	304,379	308,010	312,250	312,744	314,931
Wyoming	35,123	35,520	36,217	36,464	36,879	37,018
Dist. of Columbia	58,068	58,297	58,957	59,441	59,910	60,342

See footnotes at end of table

TABLE 10.5
Personal Income by State, 2018: Q3-2019:Q4 (continued)

	Personal income (seasonally adjusted at annual rate)					
	Percent change from preceding quarter (a)					Rank
	2018 4th quarter	2019 1rst quarter	2019 2nd quarter	2019 3rd quarter	2019 4th quarter	2019:Q3-2019:Q4
United States	3.6	6.2	4.4	2.8	3.0	N.A
Alabama	4.4	5.7	3.5	3.9	2.9	31
Alaska	2.4	4.4	3.8	2.8	2.0	43
Arizona	4.1	8.4	5.8	5.7	3.3	15
Arkansas	6.0	1.6	6.1	3.1	2.7	34
California	4.9	6.1	6.6	0.1	3.0	26
Colorado	4.6	9.4	5.1	5.9	1.4	49
Connecticut	1.4	6.4	1.7	-0.2	1.8	46
Delaware	1.6	6.8	3.9	2.6	3.9	7
Florida	3.5	6.7	4.9	2.5	3.1	23
Georgia	2.5	6.2	4.9	3.5	3.2	18
Hawaii	3.4	5.1	1.6	2.3	3.5	10
Idaho	7.3	6.1	7.3	6.1	2.6	37
Illinois	2.7	3.9	1.1	4.4	3.3	13
Indiana	4.5	4.1	3.2	4.5	2.4	38
Iowa	10.5	3.0	1.5	9.5	2.7	36
Kansas	5.3	3.0	3.0	6.2	2.9	29
Kentucky	3.3	5.2	2.8	3.6	4.1	4
Louisiana	5.4	5.1	1.2	1.9	2.4	40
Maine	1.7	8.8	3.9	3.1	3.1	19
Maryland	2.3	5.4	4.1	1.7	3.4	11
Massachusetts	3.3	9.5	3.1	-0.1	3.1	22
Michigan	2.6	4.5	4.5	3.2	4.7	1
Minnesota	5.0	2.7	4.0	6.2	2.8	33
Mississippi	4.9	4.8	1.4	5.3	2.4	39
Missouri	4.6	5.1	3.1	4.8	3.1	25
Montana	6.3	1.0	3.3	7.8	3.1	20
Nebraska	9.1	-1.5	2.6	8.6	2.9	30
Nevada	6.8	4.6	4.7	3.6	4.1	3
New Hampshire	1.0	12.7	1.1	0.7	2.9	27
New Jersey	1.6	6.4	3.4	2.3	1.8	45
New Mexico	3.7	7.8	5.6	6.2	3.3	16
New York	-0.8	7.7	5.6	0.5	2.1	42
North Carolina	5.6	5.4	5.0	3.1	3.1	21
North Dakota	10.9	-1.9	0.8	11.1	1.1	50
Ohio	3.2	4.9	2.4	3.3	3.1	24
Oklahoma	4.7	7.9	0.5	2.8	1.7	47
Oregon	4.6	6.2	4.4	2.7	3.4	12
Pennsylvania	3.5	6.3	4.8	1.5	2.9	28
Rhode Island	6.7	5.7	3.6	-3.1	3.6	9
South Carolina	4.9	7.7	3.2	4.2	3.2	17
South Dakota	15.0	-5.9	0.6	13.1	2.2	41
Tennessee	2.2	7.6	4.5	3.1	4.0	5
Texas	3.7	8.1	4.6	4.9	3.8	8
Utah	4.6	8.9	5.4	5.7	4.3	2
Vermont	3.3	8.9	1.3	2.4	2.7	35
Virginia	3.5	5.2	4.1	3.5	3.3	14
Washington	3.2	8.0	6.7	3.8	4.0	6
West Virginia	2.3	1.5	2.0	0.9	1.9	44
Wisconsin	4.4	4.9	5.6	0.6	2.8	32
Wyoming	4.6	8.1	2.8	4.6	1.5	48
Dist. of Columbia	1.6	4.6	3.3	3.2	2.9	N.A

Source: U.S. Bureau of Economic Analysis, data released
  March 2020.
Note: Estimates may not add to totals because of rounding.
Key:
N.A.–Not applicable
(r)–Revised
(p)–Preliminary
(a) Percent changes are expressed at annual rates.

TABLE 10.6
Earnings Growth by Industry and State, 2018-2019 (In millions of dollars)

State or other jurisdiction	Total earnings	Farm	Forestry, fishing, and related activities	Mining, quarrying, and oil and gas extraction	Utilities	Construction	Manufacturing Durable goods	Nondurable goods
United States	564,755	11,549	2,066	7,776	1,620	34,877	22,228	13,354
Alabama	5,600	(439)	56	24	98	572	435	204
Alaska	1,152	(1)	52	159	5	67	4	55
Arizona	13,489	461	22	36	14	1,485	800	152
Arkansas	2,677	(444)	37	10	20	182	161	175
California	90,365	2,628	677	113	(56)	5,574	385	1,315
Colorado	16,512	483	45	752	89	947	696	245
Connecticut	4,865	(7)	7	7	42	341	503	343
Delaware	1,507	(119)	(D)	(D)	12	135	51	66
Florida	31,486	491	19	(1)	(133)	2,204	1,314	599
Georgia	16,852	(210)	59	39	182	1,136	342	(1,171)
Hawaii	1,823	45	12	4	(15)	115	5	(17)
Idaho	3,117	378	11	23	0	363	(77)	108
Illinois	16,987	(437)	25	92	134	436	622	548
Indiana	7,207	(243)	82	36	51	653	(91)	456
Iowa	4,996	1,782	44	9	(4)	182	254	329
Kansas	4,036	72	57	63	(11)	383	208	(22)
Kentucky	4,695	(11)	54	5	17	330	676	177
Louisiana	4,198	85	30	402	21	(907)	262	281
Maine	1,920	30	50	0	(7)	84	97	92
Maryland	9,261	(96)	20	6	47	613	248	139
Massachusetts	17,874	6	61	8	264	713	587	(227)
Michigan	9,638	297	36	16	142	424	875	285
Minnesota	9,470	1,453	31	6	40	950	485	212
Mississippi	2,200	292	39	24	(20)	6	163	118
Missouri	8,258	584	45	15	87	712	756	353
Montana	1,286	(72)	12	52	13	118	33	35
Nebraska	2,247	(288)	21	1	45	208	49	99
Nevada	4,971	49	(2)	68	10	919	337	82
New Hampshire	2,384	0	13	2	(18)	179	265	10
New Jersey	13,236	16	23	54	(104)	441	208	1,175
New Mexico	3,528	344	4	327	8	391	111	78
New York	42,662	324	25	135	71	1,300	495	191
North Carolina	16,190	65	23	22	(5)	1,457	629	372
North Dakota	1,219	(243)	18	143	(18)	339	49	32
Ohio	14,017	(171)	61	65	(9)	408	1,015	1,107
Oklahoma	5,172	253	(32)	(378)	179	362	248	171
Oregon	6,796	101	10	(3)	38	607	179	171
Pennsylvania	20,565	135	60	324	(191)	777	967	951
Rhode Island	1,065	2	(D)	(D)	(2)	89	39	9
South Carolina	7,067	(12)	16	49	54	580	747	411
South Dakota	1,012	(100)	13	5	4	77	41	68
Tennessee	11,348	291	18	18	21	895	639	314
Texas	63,521	2,094	38	4,843	485	5,116	3,811	1,780
Utah	7,148	125	3	51	54	615	360	137
Vermont	867	61	7	2	(13)	19	71	17
Virginia	14,156	(38)	2	18	(35)	1,007	476	239
Washington	21,077	337	69	4	63	1,428	1,095	277
West Virginia	566	(13)	18	47	19	(655)	25	34
Wisconsin	7,528	1,033	65	(34)	(33)	211	541	769
Wyoming	1,355	174	6	108	(1)	338	41	14
Dist. of Columbia	3,589	0	0	3	(30)	(51)	(5)	(3)

See footnotes at end of table

TABLE 10.6
Earnings Growth by Industry and State, 2018-2019 (In millions of dollars) (continued)

State or other jurisdiction	Wholesale trade	Retail trade	Transportation and warehousing	Information	Finance and insurance	Real estate and rental and leasing	Professional, scientific, and technical services	Management of companies and enterprises	Administrative and waste management services
United States	20,940	20,200	30,594	22,704	38,520	16,018	77,373	17,308	28,299
Alabama	196	307	294	97	192	131	596	117	355
Alaska	31	46	114	0	24	33	76	21	33
Arizona	376	514	474	237	1,685	391	1,144	398	812
Arkansas	161	93	182	82	217	62	153	395	73
California	3,070	2,396	8,349	5,324	4,144	3,300	16,285	350	4,499
Colorado	714	486	792	1,046	809	372	3,138	724	617
Connecticut	23	108	284	319	16	131	806	166	161
Delaware	48	40	92	11	147	42	216	43	67
Florida	1,468	815	2,501	1,075	2,344	962	4,233	1,665	1,234
Georgia	1,147	620	(912)	1,006	903	464	1,930	3,662	1,054
Hawaii	94	63	119	(68)	128	88	99	65	(307)
Idaho	188	117	105	36	151	61	373	98	87
Illinois	1,163	737	1,027	748	2,371	607	1,848	(745)	1,193
Indiana	280	332	425	38	589	430	616	156	314
Iowa	114	53	137	3	384	55	168	219	80
Kansas	71	49	341	111	227	173	247	391	45
Kentucky	254	181	475	61	160	139	350	104	184
Louisiana	192	136	351	44	(49)	148	495	8	176
Maine	30	128	42	2	116	25	198	123	8
Maryland	290	205	185	342	226	386	2,312	196	425
Massachusetts	550	891	418	608	1,396	401	4,763	401	1,031
Michigan	380	436	770	153	974	341	694	336	130
Minnesota	(10)	183	416	41	708	183	345	1,301	384
Mississippi	91	72	214	(12)	52	40	72	(1)	55
Missouri	126	196	309	87	655	261	892	(46)	229
Montana	52	82	58	10	116	40	147	8	33
Nebraska	155	97	156	13	268	59	219	18	149
Nevada	65	285	342	88	325	105	466	(231)	286
New Hampshire	107	143	60	68	162	56	282	60	104
New Jersey	552	815	914	(90)	483	368	1,622	761	790
New Mexico	114	5	78	24	118	55	400	21	180
New York	864	1,658	1,275	1,992	5,581	1,123	6,930	1,052	4,432
North Carolina	1,030	865	672	(230)	1,913	346	1,646	524	987
North Dakota	98	20	133	(1)	67	46	91	(115)	(12)
Ohio	740	514	821	58	699	366	1,601	1,060	731
Oklahoma	113	180	565	55	188	84	414	331	165
Oregon	336	253	299	109	266	285	669	284	293
Pennsylvania	673	630	1,278	1,586	1,240	336	3,166	350	958
Rhode Island	64	61	34	7	77	37	131	(255)	53
South Carolina	358	351	314	73	265	170	494	428	195
South Dakota	59	36	33	14	83	33	89	31	38
Tennessee	542	258	790	128	707	355	1,200	708	740
Texas	2,899	2,172	3,233	1,371	4,632	1,614	8,063	968	2,715
Utah	260	349	309	396	455	205	1,020	104	347
Vermont	7	28	27	21	38	12	123	41	45
Virginia	405	449	519	554	690	333	2,941	828	840
Washington	291	1,515	765	4,567	804	485	1,588	213	833
West Virginia	35	25	39	(8)	36	21	(10)	24	80
Wisconsin	(74)	157	274	274	597	146	788	(98)	229
Wyoming	34	27	110	1	61	28	102	(6)	23
Dist. of Columbia	114	19	(13)	230	81	82	1,146	54	126

See footnotes at end of table

TABLE 10.6
Earnings Growth by Industry and State, 2018-2019 (In millions of dollars) (continued)

State or other jurisdiction	Educational services	Health care and social assistance	Arts, entertainment, and recreation	Accommodation and food services	Other services (except government and government enterprises)	Federal, civilian	Military	State and local
						Government		
United States	8,722	69,452	8,079	24,287	22,084	13,734	5,303	47,670
Alabama	55	732	50	235	250	252	85	705
Alaska	11	159	7	60	26	61	14	94
Arizona	87	1,799	181	437	474	324	149	1,038
Arkansas	31	448	21	156	141	79	38	203
California	1,369	10,449	1,859	5,021	3,170	1,144	304	8,696
Colorado	149	1,048	242	645	507	238	215	1,513
Connecticut	227	762	52	137	191	63	28	156
Delaware	9	258	25	82	63	18	23	180
Florida	476	3,724	664	1,610	1,475	731	246	1,769
Georgia	304	2,543	251	653	774	632	394	1,052
Hawaii	36	335	51	339	111	152	183	187
Idaho	64	445	46	116	96	43	24	261
Illinois	355	1,863	239	916	720	268	96	2,158
Indiana	148	1,341	82	291	383	218	48	572
Iowa	13	391	29	84	251	65	25	328
Kansas	29	511	14	122	245	122	91	499
Kentucky	44	635	53	249	196	61	132	167
Louisiana	95	1,397	51	139	249	148	60	385
Maine	41	379	19	102	53	103	15	189
Maryland	61	1,090	(107)	442	359	816	158	900
Massachusetts	541	2,138	233	855	582	210	44	1,401
Michigan	88	1,100	38	384	423	211	27	1,080
Minnesota	78	952	113	284	420	134	38	724
Mississippi	19	328	7	84	114	110	87	246
Missouri	81	1,285	65	317	328	339	120	465
Montana	7	238	9	77	62	43	18	95
Nebraska	44	413	30	79	127	88	29	167
Nevada	21	488	131	421	131	115	75	396
New Hampshire	70	365	43	96	133	56	(13)	141
New Jersey	236	2,211	300	147	632	176	59	1,447
New Mexico	29	291	39	129	81	151	54	493
New York	719	6,941	911	1,773	1,180	569	109	3,010
North Carolina	390	1,748	184	722	882	393	111	1,446
North Dakota	12	336	5	38	47	(3)	24	111
Ohio	272	1,959	147	532	549	297	89	1,105
Oklahoma	56	533	7	166	170	198	135	1,010
Oregon	82	959	70	333	308	131	13	1,002
Pennsylvania	457	3,502	381	548	779	606	65	988
Rhode Island	64	293	55	71	64	18	14	132
South Carolina	48	564	81	392	340	221	178	751
South Dakota	(7)	282	6	39	63	11	20	73
Tennessee	257	1,299	236	517	453	287	34	641
Texas	830	5,116	756	2,506	2,410	1,060	747	4,261
Utah	193	485	79	266	320	291	63	659
Vermont	9	144	1	46	34	44	4	79
Virginia	136	1,340	134	442	296	845	478	1,258
Washington	163	1,979	105	646	752	415	225	2,457
West Virginia	21	304	12	44	61	151	8	248
Wisconsin	114	1,287	61	242	317	94	37	532
Wyoming	8	60	3	46	27	34	13	104
Dist. of Columbia	80	207	8	211	267	900	71	95

Source: U.S. Bureau of Economic Analysis, data released March 2020.
Key:
N.A.–Not applicable.
(D) Data are suppressed to avoid disclosure of confidential information.

INDEX

—A—

—B—

—C—

–D–

–E–

–F–

–M–

–N–

–O–

–P–

—T—

–W–

–X-Y-Z–